A CONCORDANCE TO THE
COMPLETE WORKS OF ANNE BRADSTREET

STUDIES IN PURITAN AMERICAN SPIRITUALITY

ISSN 1048-8553   Special Volume VII   ISBN 0-7734-7814-0

A CONCORDANCE TO THE COMPLETE WORKS OF ANNE BRADSTREET

A SPECIAL EDITION OF STUDIES IN PURITAN AMERICAN SPIRITUALITY

Volume 2

Raymond A. Craig

The Edwin Mellen Press
Lewiston•Queenston•Lampeter

Library of Congress Cataloging-in-Publication Data

Craig, Raymond A.
A concordance to the complete works of Anne Bradstreet / Raymond A. Craig.
    p.   cm.
"Special edition of studies in Puritan American spirituality."
Includes indexes.
ISBN 0-7734-7812-4 (v. 1) -- ISBN 0-7734-7814-0 (v. 2)
1. Bradstreet, Anne, 1612?-1672--Concordances. 2. Christian poetry,
American--Puritan authors--Concordances. I. Bradstreet, Anne, 1612?-1672. II. Title.

PS712.A2 C73 2000
811'.1--dc21

                                              99-462312

A CIP catalog record for this book is available from the British Library.

The Edwin Mellen Press
Box 450
Lewiston, New York
USA 14092-0450

The Edwin Mellen Press
Box 67
Queenston, Ontario
CANADA L0S 1L0

The Edwin Mellen Press, Ltd.
Lampeter, Ceredigion, Wales
UNITED KINGDOM SA48 8LT

Printed in the United States of America

Contents

Volume One

Volume Two

Key to Reference Codes

Title Code, Title, Page in McElrath-Robb (MR), Page in Hensley (H)
Codes are listed in alphanumeric order

Code	Title	MR	H
1HUSB	To my Dear and loving Husband	180	225
1LETTER	A Letter to her Husband	181	226
1SIMON	On . . . Simon Bradstreet	188	237
2LETTER	Another	181	227
2SIMON	For my deare Sonne Simon Bradstreet	195	271
2HUSB	Vpon my dear & loving husband	232	265
3LETTER	Another	182	229
11MAYA	May 11, 1657	226	256
11MAYB	May 11, 1661	228	259
13MAY	May 13, 1657	227	257
28AUG	August 28, 1656	225	254
30SEPT	September 30, 1657	227	257
ACK	In thankfull acknowledgmt	235	269
AGES	The Four Ages of Man	35	51
ANNEB	In memory of . . . Anne Bradstreet	187	236
AUTHOR	The Author to Her Book	177	221
BIRTH	Before the Birth of One of Her Children	179	224
BYNIGHT	By Night When Others Soundly Slept	220	247
CHILDRN	In reference to her Children	184	232
CONTEM	CONTEMPLATIONS	167	204
DAVID	Davids Lamentation for Saul and Jonathan	158	199
DDUDLEY	An EPITAPH on . . . Mrs. Dorothy Dudley	167	204
DIALOG	A Dialogue between Old England and New	141	179
DISTEMP	Vpon some distemper of body	179	223
DUBART	In honour of Du Bartas	152	192
ELEMEN	The Foure Elements	8	18
ELIZB	In memory of . . . Elizabeth Bradstreet	186	235
FAINTING	Deliverc from a fitt of Fainting	222	249
FATHER	To her most Honoured Father	5	13
FEVER	For Deliverc from a feaver	220	249
FLESH	The Flesh and the Spirit	175	215
HANNA	Vpon my Daughter Hanna Wiggin	230	263
HOURS	In my Solitary Houres	235	269

A CONCORDANCE TO THE
COMPLETE WORKS OF ANNE BRADSTREET

VOLUME 2

N

NABONASSER (1)
MASSYR62:1   H346   *Salmanasser,* or *Nabonasser.*

NAILES (1) [nails]
MEDDM201:25 Hp281 The words of the wise (sath Solom) are as nailes, and as

NAKED (3)
MASSYR65:22 H487 Thus {Then} cast him out, like to a naked Asse,
CONTEM170:1   H75   That turn'd his Sovereign to a naked thral.
13MAY226:27   H3   And leaues the naked Trees doe dresse

NAKEDNESSE (1)
MGREC108:34 H2250 Whose {Their} nakednesse could not endure their might;

NAM'D (4) [named]
MPERS85:36   H1312 Two sons she bore, the youngest *Cyrus* nam'd,
MGRÆC117:40 H2647 His base born Brother, *Aridæus* nam'd,
MGREC~~133:17~~ H3305 And his againe, also {was nam'd} *Demetrius.*
MGREC133:30 H3320 *Antiochus Soter* his son was nam'd,

NAME (51)
ELEMEN9:17   H51   Your spits, pots, jacks, what else I need not name,
ELEMEN11:40   H160 Yet let me name my *Grecia,* 'tis my heart
ELEMEN12:12   H172 That heaven it selfe was oft call'd by that name;
ELEMEN12:24   H184 But here, or there, I list now none to name;
ELEMEN15:30   H312 With thousands moe, which now I list not name,
ELEMEN~~16:10~~   H333 If I should shew,{name} more Seas, then thou hast Coasts.
HUMOUR23:21 H131 Nor is't my pleasure, thus to blur thy name:
HUMOUR26:6   H236 Which natural, vital, animal we name.
HUMOUR27:11 H282 But by what right, nor do'st, nor canst thou name;
HUMOUR28:40 H352 I've us'd no bitternesse, nor taxt your name,
HUMOUR29:18 H369 What mov'd thee thus to villifie my name?
HUMOUR31:5   ~~H438~~ Thou do'st assume my name, wel be it just;
HUMOUR32:27 H501 (Although my name do suffer detriment)
SEASONS50:1   H135 This month from *Julius Cæsar* took the {its} name,
SEASONS50:15 H149 *August,* of great *Augustus* took its name,
MASSYR~~55:32~~   H98   That undeserv'd, they blur'd her name and fame
MASSYR60:38 H303 In sacred Writ, he's known by name of *Pul,*
MPERS87:19   H1373 Their Captain hearing, but of *Cyrus* name.
MPERS87:21   ~~H1374~~ *Abrocomes,* was this base cowards name,
MGREC100:23 H1907 Men but in shape, and name, of valour none,
MGREC108:37 H2253 Which *Alexandria* he doth also {likewise} name,
MGREC~~110:38~~ H2342 Two Cities built, his fame {name} might there abide;
MGREC111:14 H2359 A City here he built, cal'd by his name,
MGREC114:36 H2506 Yea, and he kild *Calisthines* by name; {of fame.}
MGREC116:33 H2599 Still fearing that his Name might hap to die,
MGREC118:28 H2677 Under his name begins {began} to rule each thing.

NATIONS (6) [pl.]
ELEMEN15:19	H301	That she can spare, when Nations round are poore.
MPERS78:3	H984	His Army of all Nations, was compounded,
MGREC~~109:4~~	H2261	His warrs with sundry nations I'le omit,
MGREC111:13	H2358	These {Those} obscure Nations yeelded as before;
MROMAN138:32	H3522	And Nations twelve, of *Tuscany* subdues:
DIALOG148:25	H290	Then fulness of the Nations in shall flow,

NATIVE (6)
HUMOUR20:14	H6	The native qualities, that from each {them} flow,
MASSYR67:11	H557	And native *Canaan,* never see again,
MPERS~~84:32~~	H1268	And to his Country-men {native land} could bear no hate.
MPERS90:19	H1486	In peace they saw their Native soyl again.
SIDNEY151:31	~~H75~~	As *Vulcan* is, of *Venus* native hue.
TDUDLEY165:21	H23	Both in his native, and in foreign coast,

NATIVITY (3)
SEASONS52:23	H238	Now's held, a Guest, {(but ghest)} (but blest) Nativity.
MGREC93:20	H1617	The very day of his nativity,
SON231:14	H26	To th' Land of his Nativity.

NATURAL (5)
HUMOUR26:6	H236	Which natural, vital, animal we name.
HUMOUR26:11	H241	For th' natural, thou dost not much contest,
HUMOUR26:22	H252	I am as sure, the natural from me;
SEASONS48:6	H59	A natural Artificer compleate.
MASSYR66:31	H537	Which from no natural causes did proceed,

NATURALL (2) [natural]
DUBART153:34	H38	Thy Art, in Naturall Philosophy:
MEDDM209:22	Hp291	let his parts naturall and acquired spirituall and morall,

NATURALLY (1) See also NATUREALLY
SEASONS53:3	H259	*The first fell in so naturally,*

NATURE (33) See also NAURE
PROLOG7:5	H20	'Cause Nature made it so irreparable.
ELEMEN9:32	H66	And of the selfe same nature is with mine,
ELEMEN13:30	H23▪	Then dearth prevailes, that Nature to suffice,
ELEMEN18:31	H435	My moist hot nature, is so purely thinne,
ELEMEN18:38	H442	And in a trice, my own nature resume.
HUMOUR23:13	H123	Of that black region, Nature made thee Queen;
HUMOUR29:24	H375	Nature doth teach, to sheild the head from harm,
HUMOUR31:13	H448	Til filth and thee, nature exhonorates.
AGES35:29	H15	Upon his head a Garland Nature set:
SEASONS47:41	H53	Among the verduous Grasse hath Nature set,
MPERS87:23	H1375	This place was {so} made, by nature, and by art;
MGREC93:16	H1613	Great were the guifts of nature, which he had;
MGREC6:18	H1615	By Art, and Nature both, he was made fit,
MGREC111:20	H2365	But well observing th' nature of the tide,
MGREC116:29	H2595	Cruell by nature, and by custome too,
DUBART153:5	H9	Where Art, and more then Art in Nature shines;
DUBART153:40	H44	Sure liberall Nature, did with Art not small,
DUBART155:4	H89	*Art and Nature joyn'd, by heavens high decree,*
DUBART155:8	H93	*But Nature vanquish'd Art, so* Bartas *dy'd,*
CONTEM168:29	H36	And in the darksome womb of fruitful nature dive.
CONTEM169:15	H56	That nature had, thus decked liberally:

CONTEM171:27 H129   Yet seems by nature and by custome curs'd,
CONTEM172:35 H168   So nature taught, and yet you know not why,
SICKNES178:19 H2   Since nature gave me breath,
DISTEMP179:18 H6   Till nature had exhausted all her store,
BIRTH180:6   H16   What nature would, God grant to yours and you;
ELIZB187:5   H13   By nature Trees do rot when they are grown.
ELIZB187:11   H19   Is by his hand alone that guides nature and fate.
MERCY189:7   H28   E're nature would, it hither did arrive,
MEDDM196:31 Hp274   fit their nurture according to their Nature.
MEDDM206:21 Hp287   rather, then to beg forgiuenes for their sinnes, nature lookes
MEDDM208:31 Hp290   reversed the order of nature, quenched the violence of the fire,

NATURE'S (2) [nature is]
ELEMEN18:11   H415   So loath he is to go, though nature's spent,
HUMOUR31:34 H467   Flegm's patient, because her nature's tame:

NATUREALLY (1) [naturally]
2SIMON195:4   Hp271   their imitation Children do natureally, rather follow the failings

NATURES (3) [pl.]
FATHER6:1   H35   How divers natures, make one unity.
HUMOUR27:28 H299   Your hot, dry, moyst, cold, natures are {but} foure,
MEDDM196:28 Hp273   Diuerse children, haue their different natures, some are like

NATURES (7) [poss.]
MPERS92:14   ~~H1572~~   Then Natures debt he paid, quite Issue-lesse.
MGREC94:5   H1639   This done, against all {both} right, and natures laws,
MGREC117:33 H2640   By Natures right, these had enough to claime,
MGREC120:37 H2774   Two years and more since, Natures debt he paid,
MGREC125:34 H2984   Digg'd up his brother dead, 'gainst natures right,
DUBART155:6   H91   *And Natures Law; had it been revocable,*
1LETTER181:26 H24   Till natures sad decree shall call thee hence;

NAUGHT (3)
HUMOUR25:31 H220   That naught but blood, {death} the same may expiate.
MPERS83:3   H1191   His brothers recompence was naught but jears:
VANITY160:29 H39   Who drinks thereof, the world doth naught account.

NAURE (1) [nature]
AGES35:20   H6   Unstable, supple, moist, and cold's his Naure.

NAVIE (1) [navy]
MGREC98:15   H1817   Besides, {Moreover} he had a Navie at command,

NAVY (2)
MGREC~~132:20~~   H3258   A mighty Navy rig'd, an Army stout,
MGREC135:1   H3371   At *Actium* slain, {where} his Navy {Navy's} put to flight.

NAVY'S (1) [navy is]
MGREC~~135:1~~   H3371   At *Actium* slain, {where} his Navy {Navy's} put to flight.

NAY (17)
ELEMEN10:13   H88   Nay more then these, Rivers 'mongst stars are found,
ELEMEN14:11   ~~H253~~   With divers moe, nay, into plants it creeps;
ELEMEN~~14:11~~   H253   Nay into herbs and plants it sometimes creeps,
ELEMEN17:4   H368   Nay many times, my Ocean breaks his bounds:
ELEMEN18:13   H417   Nay, what are words, which doe reveale the mind?
HUMOUR21:31 H59   Nay milk-sops, at such brunts you look but blew,
HUMOUR24:1   H150   Nay, th' stomach, magazeen to all the rest,
HUMOUR25:28 H217   Nay should I tel, thou wouldst count me no blab,
HUMOUR25:35 H224   Nay; {No,} know 'tis pride, most diabolical.

HUMOUR27:36	H307	Nay, could I be from all your tangs but pure,
HUMOUR32:36	H510	Nay, I could tel you (what's more true then meet)
MPERS79:3	~~H1025~~	Nay, more then monstrous barb'rous cruelty!
QELIZ157:34	H102	Nay Masculines, you have thus tax'd us long,
CONTEM172:2	H139	Nay, they shall darken, perish, fade and dye,
1LETTER181:3	H1	My head, my heart, mine Eyes, my life, nay more,
MEDDM208:32	Hp290	become firme footing, for peter to walk on, nay more then all
MED223:9	Hp250	thy maker is thy husband. Nay more, I am a member of his

NE (1)

MGREC136:8	H3421	*Ne sutor ultra crepidum,* may write.

NEAR (13) See also NEARE, NEER

FATHER5:5	H6	Of fairer Dames, the sun near saw the face, /of the
ELEMEN18:3	H407	I aske the man condemn'd, that's near his death:
AGES41:36	H251	But if none, then for kindred near ally'd.
MGREC93:22	H1619	An Omen, to their near approaching woe;
MGREC104:1	H2053	But hearing, *Alexander* was so near;
MGREC~~118:24~~	H2673	That for a while they durst not come so near:
MGREC127:40	H3070	Sends forth his declaration from a {declarations near and}
MGREC131:11	H3203	Near *Ephesus,* each bringing all their {his} might,
TDUDLEY165:10	H12	Nor is't Relation near my hand shall tye;
TDUDLEY166:17	H59	He did exult his end was drawing near,
CONTEM170:28	H99	Though none on Earth but kindred near then could he find.
CHILDRN186:9	H76	But sing, my time so near is spent.
HANNA230:14	H7	And life was ended near.

NEARE (8) [near] See also NEER

ELEMEN12:36	H196	That with lesse cost, neare home, supplyes {supply} your
MGREC107:30	H2205	For Boats here's none, nor neare it any wood,
MGREC111:24	H2369	Whose inlets neare unto, he winter spent,
MGREC111:31	H2376	{And} So he at length drew neare to *Persia*;
MGREC112:2	H2388	That by this match he might be yet more neare.
MGREC117:32	H2639	Was neare her time to be delivered;
DIALOG143:20	H89	And for the Pestilence, who knowes how neare;
SIDNEY150:29	H56	Oh, who was neare thee, but did sore repine;

NEAR'ST (2)

MGREC121:3	H2781	Near'st unto him, and farthest from the rest.
CONTEM174:3	H204	Troubles from foes, from friends, from dearest, near'st

NEAT (1)

SEASONS48:5	H58	The outside strong, the inside warme and neat.

NEATLY (1)

MGREC123:11	H2873	How neatly {finely} *Eumenes* did here excell,

NEATNESSE (1)

MPERS78:25	H1006	Whose Gallies all the rest in neatnesse passe,

NEBOPOLASSAR (1)

MASSYR63:29	H416	*Nebuchadnezar, or Nebopolassar.*

NEBUCHADNEZAR (2)

MASSYR63:29	H416	*Nebuchadnezar, or Nebopolassar.*
MASSYR65:34	H499	The ninth, came *Nebuchadnezar* with power,

NEBULASSAR (2)

MASSYR63:22	H407	*Nebulassar.*
MASSYR63:23	H408	Brave *Nebulassar* to this King was Sonne,

NECESSARY (1)
MEDDM209:3   Hp291   thus potent but it is so necessary, that wthout faith there is no

NECESSITY (2)
HUMOUR20:36   H28   At present yeelded, to necessity.
MGREC115:14   H2523   Or of necessity, he must imply,

NECHO (2)
MASSYR64:20   H444   Quite vanquish'd *Pharaoh Necho,* and {with} his Band;
MASSYR64:23   H447   Then into *Ægypt, Necho* did retire,

NECK (5)
MASSYR63:26   H411   Now yeelds her neck unto captivity: [12 *years.*
MGREC108:2   H2218   (A coller of the same his neck containes)
MGREC125:27   H2977   At length yeelds to the Halter, her faire neck;
DIALOG148:14   H279   And tear his flesh, and set your feet on's neck,
1LETTER181:8   H6   If but a neck, soon should we be together:

NECKS (3) [pl.]
MASSYR58:37   H220   Makes {With} promises, their necks for {now} to un-yoak,
MGREC~~109:5~~   H2264   How to submit their necks at last they're glad.
MGREC120:1   H2732   But under servitude, their necks remain'd,

NEECE (1) [niece]
MROMAN136:27   H3441   Thus he deceiv'd his Neece, she might not know

NEECES (1) [nieces]
MPERS74:23   H846   Two of his Neeces takes to nuptiall bed;

NEED (27)
FATHER6:8   H42   I shall not need my {mine} innocence to clear,
ELEMEN9:17   H51   Your spits, pots, jacks, what else I need not name,
ELEMEN15:1   H283   When I am gone, their fiercenesse none need {needs} doubt;
ELEMEN17:14   H378   I need not say much of my Haile and Snow,
HUMOUR27:29   H300   I moderately am all, what need I more:
HUMOUR29:3   H356   Had need be armed wel, and active too,
HUMOUR32:18   H492   Patient I am, patient i'd need to be,
AGES42:9   H267   And gently lead the lambes, as they had need,
MASSYR61:3   H308   That those two made but one, we need not doubt:
MASSYR64:32   H456   None but the true *Ezekiel* need to tell:
MPERS~~70:7~~   H678   That all the world they neither {need not} feare, nor doubt;
MPERS81:20   H1128   If now in {their} need, they should thus fail {forsake} their
MPERS~~84:12~~   H1243   With gold and silver, and what ere they need:
MPERS91:8   H1516   To defend, more then offend, he had {there was} need.
MGREC96:16   H1736   Least he should need them, in his chariots stead.
MGREC119:19   H2709   come and {For succours} to release {relieve} him in his need,
MGREC~~124:3~~   H2908   For this *Antigonus* needed {did need} no spurs,
MGREC125:11   H2959   and succour {To save the King} her, in this great {their} need;
MROMAN138:19   H3509   Of Boats, and Oares, no more they need the aide;
DIALOG143:9   H78   No need of *Tudor,* Roses to unite,
DIALOG145:37   H186   This was deny'd, I need not say wherefore.
FLESH177:17   H98   Nor Sun, nor Moon, they have no need,
MEDDM198:11   Hp276   need ponder all his steps.
MEDDM204:7   Hp284   in need of him, to day as well as yesterday, and so shall for
MEDDM208:29   Hp290   possible to be done, it can remoue mountaines (if need were)
MEDDM209:23   Hp291   so large, yet he stands in need of something wch another man
HOUSE237:25   H55   . Ther's wealth enovgh I need no more,

NEEDED (1)
MGREC124:3   H2908 For this *Antigonus* needed {did need} no spurs,
NEEDETH (1)
HUMOUR31:3   H436   So plain a slander needeth no reply.
NEEDLE (1)
PROLOG7:15   H28   Who sayes, my hand a needle better fits,
NEEDS (18)
ELEMEN9:33   H67   Good {Cold} sister Earth, no witnesse needs but thine;
ELEMEN15:1   H283   When I am gone, their fiercenesse none need {needs} doubt;
HUMOUR27:14   H285   The help she needs, the loving Liver lends,
AGES36:22   H46   A {An} Harvest of the best, what needs he more.
MASSYR68:1   H587   Which horrid sight, he fears, must needs portend,
MPERS76:12   H910   The King will needs interpret their intent;
MGREC100:9   H1893 He Diabolicall must needs remaine,
MGREC102:28   H1998 But needs no force, 'tis rendred to his hands;
MGREC122:29   H2848 He wearied out, at last, would needs be gone,
MGREC125:21   H2971 And needs will have their lives as well as State:
MGREC130:20   H3175 The world must needs believe what he doth tell:
MGREC132:20   H3257 And with his son in law, will needs go fight:
MGREC132:35   H3282 Must needs goe try their fortune, and their might,
SIDNEY152:4   H76   That those that name his fame, he needs must spare,
TDUDLEY165:23 H25   So needs no Testimonial from his own;
MEDDM195:36   Hp272 vanity and lyes must needs lye down in the Bed of sorrow.
MEDDM202:27   Hp282 quite gone out of sight then must we needs walk in darknesse
MEDDM203:27   Hp284 and that he must needs perish if he haue no remedy, will
NEED'ST (1) [needest]
FLESH176:26   H66   How I do live, thou need'st not scoff,
NEER (1) [never] See also N'ER, NE'R, NE'RE, NER', NERE, NEUER
HUMOUR25:40   H229   Be dangers neer so high, and courage great,
NEER (2) [near] See also NEARE
SON230:29   H12   Of pyrates who were neer at hand
HOUSE236:14   H6   For sorrow neer I did not look,
NEGLECT (3)
ELEMEN14:28   H270   This your neglect, shewes your ingratitude;
ELEMEN16:13   H336   To speake of kinds of Waters I'le {I} neglect,
MYCHILD215:28 Hp241 vnto God. I was also troubled at yᵉ neglect of private Dutyes
NEGLECTED (3)
MPERS88:13   H1406 And all good discipline to be neglected.
MGREC118:15   H2662 Untouch, uncovered, slighted, and neglected,
MYCHILD216:35 Hp242 neglected wᶜʰ he would haue performed, and by his help I
NEGLIGENT (1)
MEDDM195:34   Hp272 a negligent youth is vsually attended by an ignorant middle
NEHEMIAH (1)
MPERS84:12   H1245 And *Nehemiah* in his twentieth year,
NEHEMIE (1)
MPERS91:32   H1546 He was the Master of good *Nehemie*
NEIGH (1)
MPERS74:5   H830   And he whose Horse before the rest should neigh,
NEIGHBOR (1)
DDUDLEY167:12 H9   *A friendly Neighbor, pitiful to poor,*

NEIGHBOURING (1)
ELEMEN11:5   H125   With neighbouring Townes I did consume to dust,
NEIGHBOURS (4) [pl.]
AGES38:7   H110   I had no Suits at law, neighbours to vex.
MASSYR54:28   H55   This Tyrant did his neighbours all oppresse,
MASSYR57:26   ~~H172~~   Which to her neighbours, when it was made known,
MROMAN137:9   H3460   They to their neighbours sue, for a supply;
NEIGHBOURS (1) [poss.]
DIALOG144:34   H142   Nor took I warning by my neighbours falls,
NEIGHED (1)
MPERS74:10   H835   *Darius* lusty stallion neighed full loud;
NEITHER (18)
ELEMEN19:23   H468   Which neither ships nor houses could withstand.
ELEMEN19:34   H475   Where neither houses, trees, nor plants, I spare;
HUMOUR22:2   H71   She'l neither say, she wil, nor wil she doe:
AGES36:16   H40   But neither us'd (as yet) for he was wise.
AGES42:23   H281   As neither sow, nor reape, nor plant, nor build.
AGES~~45:11~~   H393   But neither favour, riches, title, State,
MASSYR63:31   H418   Did neither *Homer, Hesiode, Virgil* sing;
MPERS70:7   H678   That all the world they neither {need not} feare, nor doubt;
MPERS87:15   ~~H1370~~   And yet with these, had neither heart, nor grace;
MGREC96:18   H1738   think {Suppos'd} he neither thought {meant} to fight nor fly,
MGREC105:12   H2105   Yea, {But} above all, that neither eare, nor eye,
MGREC~~132:16~~   H3253   In neither finds content if he sits still:
QELIZ158:12   H121   *On neither tree did grow such Rose before,*
CONTEM171:8   H113   Who neither guilt, nor yet the punishment could fly.
CONTEM173:19   H185   That neither toyles nor hoards up in thy barn,
CONTEM174:26   H224   Here's neither honour, wealth, or safety;
3LETTER183:25   H27   Who neither joyes in pasture, house nor streams,
MEDDM202:33   Hp282   obiects enter, yet is not that spacious roome filled neither
NEPHEW (4)
MPERS72:15   H763   Who would have born a Nephew, and a Son.
MPERS~~92:8~~   H1566   And scarce a Nephew left that now might reign:
MGREC125:4   H2952   And her young Nephew {grand-child} in his stead {State} t'
MROMAN138:15   H3505   Nephew unto *Pomphilius* dead, and gone;
NEPHEWES (1) nephews
AGES43:11   ~~H305~~   Nor Brothers, Nephewes, Sons, nor Sires I've spar'd.
NEPHEWS (1) [pl.]
AGES46:3   H434   Sons, Nephews, leave, my death {farewell} for to deplore;
NEPHEWS (1) [pl.; poss.]
CONTEM171:3   H108   Their long descent, how nephews sons they saw,
NEPTUN'S (1) [poss.]
CONTEM173:4   H172   Eftsoon to *Neptun's* glassie Hall repair
N'ER (1) [never] See also NEER, NE'R, NE'RE, NER', NERE, NEUER
ELEMEN~~16:11~~   H334   And be thy mountains n'er so high and steep,
NE'R (7) [never] See also NEER, N'ER, NE'RE, NER', NERE, NEUER
ELEMEN16:18   H341   Which wondring *Aristotles* wit, ne'r knowes.
ELEMEN17:25   H389   That in two hundred year, it ne'r prov'd good.
AGES37:31   H93   A Baron or a Duke, ne'r made my mark.
MGREC132:28   H3273   Did ne'r regain one foot in *Asia.*
QELIZ156:15   H42   Since first the Sun did run, his ne'r runn'd race,

TDUDLEY166:12	H54	Nor wonder 'twas, low things ne'r much did move
MYSOUL225:11	H15	Thy Sinns shall ne'r bee sumon'd vp

NE'RE (19) [never] See also NEER, N'RE, NE'R, NER', NERE, NEUER

ELEMEN17:6	H370	And swallowes Countryes up, ne're seen againe:
HUMOUR34:10	H565	Yet some may wish, oh, {O} had mine eyes ne're seene.
HUMOUR34:28	H583	Ne're did {Nor will} I heare {yield} that Choler was the witt'est;
MASSYR58:2	H187	Ne're shew'd his face, but revell'd with his Whores,
MASSYR62:21	H366	And pleasant *Canaan* ne're see again:
MASSYR62:25	H370	Or wild *Tartarians,* as yet ne're blest,
MASSYR66:6	H512	Yet as was told, ne're saw it with his eyes;
MPERS77:30	H971	And *Greece* such wondrous triumphs ne're had made.
MPERS89:31	H1465	But Kings ne're want such as can serve their will,
MGREC113:20	H2447	As he would ne're confesse, nor could {yet} reward,
MGREC114:31	H2501	Which vertues fame can ne're redeem by farre,
MGREC115:33	H2552	And for his Counsell, ne're the King to live.
MROMAN139:23	H3551	And people sweare, ne're to accept of King.
DAVID159:4	H19	As if his head ne're felt the sacred Oyle:
DAVID159:6	H21	The bow of *Jonathan* ne're turn'd in vaine,
VANITY~~160:36~~	H46	It brings to honour, which shall not {ne're} decay,
CONTEM173:22	H188	Thy cloaths ne're wear, thy meat is every where,
FLESH175:29	H29	Which wearing time shall ne're deject.
ANNEB187:30	H20	Farewel dear child, thou ne're shall come to me,

NER' (2) [never] See also NEER, N'RE, NE'R, NE'RE, NERE, NEUER

PILGRIM210:29	H29	W^th cares and fears ner' cumbred be
PILGRIM211:1	H42	as eare ner' heard nor tongue ere told

NERE (1) [never] See also NEER, N'ER, NE'R, NE'RE, NER', NEUER

SON231:6	H18	From such as 'fore nere saw his face.

NERVE (1)

HUMOUR34:1	H556	The optick nerve, coats, humours, all are mine,

NERVES (3) [pl.]

HUMOUR22:32	H101	The nerves should I not warm, soon would they freeze.
HUMOUR23:38	H148	Its not your muscles, nerves, nor this nor that:
HUMOUR34:14	H569	All nerves (except seven paire) to it retain;

NEST (6)

TDUDLEY165:36	H38	Upon the earth he did not build his nest,
CHILDRN184:14	H3	I had eight birds hatcht in one nest,
CHILDRN184:24	H13	Leave not thy nest, thy Dam and Sire,
CHILDRN185:13	H39	My other three, still with me nest,
CHILDRN186:16	H83	When each of you shall in your nest
PILGRIM210:2	H2	Hugs wth delight his silent nest

NET (2)

HUMOUR33:24	H538	Its ventricles, membranes, and wond'rous net,
CHILDRN185:26	H52	The net be spread, and caught, alas.

NEUER (8) [never] See also NEER, N'ER, NE'R, NE'RE, NER', NERE

MEDDM199:15	Hp278	Ambitious men are like hops that neuer rest climbing soe long
MEDDM200:30	Hp279	this transcends the spring, that their leafe shall neuer faile nor
MEDDM203:21	Hp283	He that neuer felt, what it was to be sick or wounded, doth not
MEDDM203:24	Hp283	he slighted before, so he that neuer felt the sicknes of sin, nor
MEDDM209:21	Hp291	Covntrys so it is with men, there was neuer yet any one man
MEDDM209:23	Hp291	be neuer so large, yet he stands in need of something w^ch
MYCHILD219:1	Hp244-5	neuer prevail against it, I know whom I haue trvsted, and

JULY223:30	Hp251	O Lord let me neuer forgett thy Goodnes, nor question thy

NEVER (52) See also NEER, N'ER, NE'R, NE'RE, NER', NERE, NEUER

ELEMEN16:12	H̶3̶3̶5̶	Then Seas are deep, Mountains are never high.
ELEMEN17:30	H394	That after times, shall never feel like woe:
HUMOUR22:34	H103	She thinks I never shot so farre amisse;
HUMOUR26:1	H231	But such thou never art, when al alone;
HUMOUR26:29	H259	Then never boast of what thou do'st receive,
HUMOUR32:12	H486	And things that never were, nor shal I see.
AGES41:10	H230	Clapt in that prison, never thence to start.
AGES42:36	H292	To greater things, I never did aspire,
SEASONS47:34	H̶4̶7̶	Yet never minute stil was known to stand,
SEASONS49:22	H̶1̶1̶3̶	'Mongst all ye shepheards, never but one man,
MASSYR56:35	H141	Who in her Country never more was seen.
MASSYR67:11	H557	And native *Canaan,* never see again,
MPERS79:25	H1051	Of so long time, his thoughts had never been.
MPERS80:36	H1103	Much, {fearing} that which never was intended!
MGREC103:19	H2030	But on their faithfullnesse, he never staid:
MGREC110:30	H2334	As never Horse his Provender could eye;
MGREC117:24	H2631	Did harm himself, but never reacht his foes:
MGREC118:12	H2659	For second offers {offer} there were {was} never made;
MGREC119:40	H2730	After this {which} time, the *Greeks* did never more
MGREC122:16	H2841	To warm the {his} seat, was never her intent,
MGREC127:23	H3053	Because he never would let go {forgoe} his trust:
MGREC1̶3̶3̶:̶2̶5̶	H3315	Such riches too As Rome did never see:
SIDNEY149:23	H22	To shew the world, they never saw before,
SIDNEY150:2	H27	Found *Cupids* Dame, had never such a Gin;
SIDNEY151:4	H̶6̶9̶	But thou art gone, such Meteors never last,
DUBART154:21	H66	Who in thy tryumphs (never won by wrongs)
DUBART154:32	H77	All ages wondring at, shall never clime.
QELIZ155:26	H17	Thou never didst, nor canst thou now disdaine,
QELIZ156:37	H64	Such Souldiers, and such Captaines never seen,
DAVID158:32	H12	O! *Gilbo* Mounts, let never pearled dew,
TDUDLEY165:24	H26	But now or never I must pay my Sum;
TDUDLEY166:28	H70	Forgotten never be his memory,
TDUDLEY166:33	H75	And parted more by death shal never be.
CONTEM171:36	H137	Shall I wish there, or never to had birth,
CONTEM173:32	H197	Where winter's never felt by that sweet airy legion.
CONTEM174:1	H202	From some of these he never finds cessation,
CONTEM174:22	H220	Feeding on sweets, that never bit of th' sowre,
FLESH176:14	H54	And never had more cause of woe
1LETTER181:22	H20	I wish my Sun may never set, but burn
CHILDRN185:36	H62	My throbs such now, as 'fore were never:
MEDDM201:8	Hp280	never sayd, I haue seen an end of all Sinning, what he did say,
MEDDM208:2	Hp289	shall fly away, and the day of eternity shall never end, seeing
MYCHILD216:21	Hp241	observed this yᵗ he hath never suffered me long to sitt loose
MYCHILD216:33	Hp242	way everlasting: and seldome or never but I haue fovnd either
MYCHILD217:22	Hp243	shall never pʳvail: yet haue I many Times sinkings &
MYCHILD217:34	Hp243	God, I never saw any miracles to confirm me, and those wᶜʰ I
JULY223:24	Hp251	but my God who never failed me, was not absent but helped
JULY223:33	Hp251	upon me. O never let Satan pʳvail against me, but strenghten
WHAT224:3	H3	O never let me from thee swerue

28AUG226:7	Hp254	and bee in continuall xpectat[n] of my change, and let me never
SON231:27	H39	O Lord gravnt that I may never forgett thy Loving kindness in
2HUSB232:30	H31	Thy Goodnes never failes.

NEW (40)

ELEMEN8:16	H14	All looked like a Chaos, or new birth;
ELEMEN9:29	H63	Our Sages new, another tale have told:
ELEMEN11:1	H121	That *Phaenix* from her Bed, is risen New.
AGES35:34	H20	And in his hand an hour-glasse new begun,
AGES40:22	H203	Some young {new} *Adonis* I do strive to be,
MASSYR60:16	H281	*Belosus* setled, in his new, old seat,
MASSYR60:30	H295	He thus inricht, by this new tryed gold,
MASSYR60:31	H296	Raises a Phœnix new, from grave o'th old;
MASSYR61:7	H312	He left his new got Kingdoms to his Son.
MPERS73:32	H817	The old, or new, which best, in what respect,
MPERS79:17	H1043	Was marching o're this interrupting Bay; {new devised way.}
MPERS84:40	H1276	Again dispersed, his new levyed hoast.
MPERS87:11	H1367	And others to be warm'd by this new sun,
MPERS88:34	H1427	After this trance, revenge, new spirits blew,
MPERS92:27	H1585	But from some daughter this new king was sprung
MGREC102:27	H1997	He then to *Sushan* goes, with his fresh {new} bands,
MGREC107:4	H2179	And for the rest new wars, and travels findes,
MGREC123:26	H2890	This new Protector's of another minde,
MGREC124:4	H2909	Hoping still {yet} more to gaine by these new stirs;
MGREC136:10	H3424	*To finish what {what's} begun, new thoughts impart*
MROMAN137:7	H3458	And this new gentle Government abide:
MROMAN138:16	H3506	*Rome* he inlarg'd, new built againe the wall,
MROMAN139:22	H3550	The Government they change, a new one bring,
DIALOG141:2	H2	*England* and New, concerning
DIALOG141:5	H4	*New England.*
DIALOG141:10	H9	What deluge of new woes thus over-whelme
DIALOG141:29	H28	*New England.*
DIALOG145:6	H155	*New England.*
DIALOG145:26	H175	Old customes, new Prerogatives stood on,
DIALOG146:27	H213	*New England.*
QELIZ156:16	H43	And earth had twice {once} a yeare, a new old face:
QELIZ158:5	H114	If then new things, their old form must {forms shall} retain,
CONTEM170:7	H80	And in her lap, her bloody *Cain* new born,
ELIZB187:9	H17	But plants new set to be eradicate,
ELIZB187:10	H18	And buds new blown, to have so short a date,
MEDDM198:21	Hp276	There is no new thing vnder y[e] Sun there is nothing that can
MYCHILD216:8	Hp241	this Covntry, where I fovnd a new World and new manners at
MYCHILD218:28	Hp244	But some new Troubles I haue had since y[e] world has been
THEART229:9	H11	And new Exper[c] I haue gain'd

NEW-BORN (1)

SEASONS52:15	H230	In Swadling clouts, like new-born infancy,

NEW-BOUGHT (1)

AGES40:21	H202	curling {to curle}, frisling up {and pounce my new-bought} hair;

NEW-ENGLAND (1)

TDUDLEY165:26	H28	One of thy Founders, him *New-England* know,

NEWES (8) [news]

MPERS72:38	H784	Toucht with this newes, to *Persia* he makes,

newly

MPERS86:37	H1353	But least {lest} some worser newes should fly to Court,
MGREC94:25	H1663	When newes of *Alexander,* came to th' Court,
MGREC95:18	H1697	Now newes, of *Memnons* death (the Kings Vice-roy)
MGREC100:37	H1921	When this sad newes (at first) *Darius* heares,
MGREC102:40	H2010	Which newes doth still augment *Darius* woes;
MGREC121:26	H2808	Now comes the newes of a great victory,
MGREC125:39	H2989	Where hearing of this newes he speeds away,

NEWLY (2)

MGREC128:5	H3078	*Thessalonica* he had newly wed,
MGREC132:4	H3237	(Whose daughter unto wife, he'd newly {not long before} ta'n)

NEW-MILCH-COW (1)

AGES42:34	H290	Oxe {thriving Cattle}, and my exuberous {new-milch-} Cow,

NEWS (1) [pl.] See also NEWES

MGREC116:10	H2571	When this sad news came to *Darius* Mother,

NEXT (60)

ELEMEN11:21	H141	The next in place, Earth judg'd to be her due,
ELEMEN19:4	H449	Next, of my Fowles such multitudes there are;
HUMOUR33:8	H522	Next difference {that} betwixt us twain doth lye,
AGES36:1	H25	Next, youth came up, in gorgeous attire;
AGES36:13	H37	The next came up, in a more {much} graver sort,
AGES38:16	H119	As he can tell, that next comes on the stage.
SEASONS48:9	H62	My next, and last, is pleasant fruitfull *May,*
SEASONS49:38	H131	*July* my next, the hot'st in all the year,
SEASONS50:11	H145	My next, and last, is *August,* fiery hot,
SEASONS51:20	H196	*October* is my next, we heare in this,
SEASONS52:24	H239	Cold frozen *January* next comes in,
MASSYR53:36	H26	Great *Nimrod* dead, *Bellus* the next, his Son,
MASSYR57:37	H182	T' *Sardanapalus* next we wil make haste.
MASSYR61:10	H315	Next treads the {those} steps, by which his Father won.
MASSYR62:2	H347	*Tiglath* deceas'd, *Salmanasser* is next,
MASSYR64:19	H443	The next year he, with unresisted hand,
MASSYR64:25	H449	A mighty Army next, he doth prepare,
MASSYR67:21	H567	Unworthy *Belshazzar* next weares the Crown,
MASSYR68:7	H593	And highest dignity, next to the King,
MPERS70:4	H675	Next war, the restlesse *Cyrus* thought upon,
MPERS71:20	H734	He next to *Cyprus* sends his bloudy Hoast,
MPERS78:15	H996	These {Such} his Land Forces were, then next, a Fleet
MPERS79:10	H1032	Next, o're the *Hellispont* a bridge he made,
MPERS83:27	H1215	Amongst the Monarchs next, this Prince had place
MPERS85:6	H1282	But he, with his next {second} brother {him} fell at strife,
MPERS86:15	H1331	His interest, in the Kingdome, now next heir,
MPERS86:33	H1349	Then next, the *Lacedemons* {*Spartans*} he takes to {into} pay;
MGREC94:14	H1648	His course to *Asia,* next Spring he steers.
MGREC95:12	H1691	Next *Alexander* marcht, t'wards the black sea;
MGREC96:15	H1735	A number of spare horses next were led,
MGREC97:38	H1799	Now {Next} *Alexander* unto *Tyre* doth goe,
MGREC101:34	H1959	And careless in his bed, next morne he lyes,
MGREC104:13	H2065	Next day this treason, to *Darius* known,
MGREC109:12	H2271	To th' river *Indus* next, his course he bends,
MGREC110:39	H2343	The first *Nicea,* the next *Bucephalon,*
MGREC113:38	H2465	The next that {who} in untimely death had part,

630

MGREC113:40　H2467　*Clitus,* belov'd next to *Ephestion,*
MGREC114:13　H2483　Next day, he tore his face, for what he'd done,
MGREC114:17　H2487　The next of worth, that suffered after these,
MGREC115:18　H2537　That he might next now act upon the Stage,
MGREC118:38　H2687　And *Ptolomy,* next sure of *Egypt* makes.
MGREC121:14　H2792　*Pithon,* next *Perdicas,* a Captaine high,
MGREC121:20　H2802　Next day into the Camp comes {came} *Ptolomy,*
MGREC123:20　H2884　And *Ptolomy,* now {next} to encroach begins,
MGREC132:29　H3276　Now {Next} dyed the brave and noble *Ptolomy,*
MGREC134:1　H3332　A third *Seleuchus* next sits on the seat,
MGREC134:3　H3336　{Fourth} *Seleuchus* next *Antiochus* succeeds,
MGREC134:4　H3337　And then {next} *Epiphanes,* whose wicked deeds,
MGREC134:9　H3340　*Antiochus Eupator* was the next,
MGREC134:18　H3349　In *Egypt* now {next,} a little time we'l spend.
MGREC134:20　H3351　Cal'd *Philadelphus,* next sat on {did possess} the throne,
MGREC134:30　H3361　And next to {after} him, did false *Lathurus* reigne,
MGREC134:32　H3363　Next *Auletes,* who cut off *Pompey's* head:
MGREC134:35　H3366　Fair *Cleopatra* next, last of that race,
MGREC135:21　H3393　Next, armes and breast, of silver to behold;
MROMAN137:1　H3452　A forme of Government he next begun;
MROMAN137:25　H3476　*Nvma Pompilius,* is next chosen {chose they} King,
MROMAN138:14　H3504　Next, *Ancus Martius* sits upon the Throne,
MROMAN138:38　H3528　Next, *Servius Tullius* sits upon {gets into} the Throne,
DIALOG145:36　H185　Next the *Militia* they urged sore,

NEXTLY (1)
HUMOUR26:5　H235　Nextly, the spirits thou do'st wholly claime,

NICEA (1)
MGREC110:39　H2343　The first *Nicea,* the next *Bucephalon,*

NICK-NAMES (1)
DIALOG143:39　H108　What false reports, which nick-names did they take,

NIECE See NEECE
NIECES See NEECES
NIGH (8)
ELEMEN15:36　H318　Or hast thou any colour can come nigh;
SEASONS51:32　H208　But when the Son of Righteousnesse drawes nigh,
MPERS88:1　H1394　arme, the King {with all his host} is now approaching nigh;
MPERS88:9　H1402　And black and blacker grew, as they drew nigh.
MGREC125:31　H2981　Till {'Gainst} all that lov'd *Cassander* was nigh spent; {she was
MGREC134:12　H3343　The Royall blood was quite {nigh} extinguished.
DIALOG148:22　H287　For sure the day of your redemption's nigh;
MERCY188:25　H11　I stood so nigh, it crusht me down withal;

NIGHT (23) See also NIGHT'S
AGES37:5　H67　But night and darkenesse, must with shame conceal.
AGES42:28　H285　For restlesse day and night, I'm rob'd of sleep,
SEASONS47:4　H18　Crosses the Line, and equals night and day,
SEASONS49:32　H121　Viewing the Sun by day, the Moon by night,
SEASONS50:39　H173　Now day and night are equal in each clime;
MASSYR59:5　H229　And set upon their Princes Camp that night;
MASSYR68:27　H613　That night victorious *Cyrus* took the town,
MPERS70:10　H681　That night *Belshazzar* feasted all his rout,
MGREC93:36　H1633　Restlesse both day and night, his heart now {then} was,

MGREC101:28	H1953	*Parmenio, Alexander* wisht, that night,
MGREC~~101:30~~	H1955	For tumult in the dark {night} doth cause most dread,
MGREC~~116:10~~	H2576	Till death inwrapt her in perpetual night.
DUBART153:25	H29	At night turnes to his Mothers cot againe,
CONTEM168:5	H15	More Heaven then Earth was here, no winter & no night.
CONTEM168:35	H41	Thy presence makes it day, thy absence night,
CONTEM171:15	H119	So unawares comes on perpetual night,
CONTEM174:2	H203	But day or night, within, without, vexation,
FLESH177:20	H101	For there shall be no darksome night.
MEDDM196:14	Hp273	that labours all the day comforts himself, that when night
MEDDM208:2	Hp289	long night shall fly away, and the day of eternity shall never
MYCHILD217:37	Hp243	of yᵉ Heaven + yᵉ Earth, the order of all things night and day,
BYNIGHT220:2	H3	By night when others soundly slept,
HOUSE236:13	H5	In silent night when rest I took

NIGHTENGALE See NITINGALE

NIGHTINGALES (2) [pl.]

ELEMEN18:20	H424	And so's the notes which Nightingales do frame.
CHILDRN185:8	H34	That nightingales he might excell.

NIGHTLY (1)

MEDDM207:32	Hp289	But the soundest of men, haue likewise their nightly monitor,

NIGHT'S (1) [night is]

2LETTER181:32	H2	The silent night's the fittest time for moan;

NIGHTS (4) [pl.]

AGES40:14	H195	Dayes, {Whole} nights, with Ruffins, Roarers, Fidlers spend,
SEASONS50:25	H159	His sweat, his toyl, his careful, wakeful nights,
MPERS79:16	H1042	Seven dayes and nights, his Hoast without least stay,
MPERS79:38	H1064	Two dayes and nights a fight they there maintain,

NIL (1)

HUMOUR20:34	H26	Or wil they nil they, Choler wil be cheife;

NILE (1)

ELEMEN15:18	H300	Which by my fatting Nile, doth yeeld such store;

NIMBLE (1)

AGES45:37	H427	My comely legs, as nimble as the Roe,

NIMROD (2)

MASSYR53:13	H3	beginning under *Nimrod,* 131. yeares
MASSYR53:36	H26	Great *Nimrod* dead, *Bellus* the next, his Son,

NINE (5)

PROLOG7:22	H34	Else of our Sex, why feigned they those nine,
HUMOUR33:3	H517	Sixty nine Princes, all stout *Hero* Knights,
AGES37:7	H69	Her nine months weary burden not declare.
MPERS87:14	H1370	And counts nine hundred thousand foot and horses:
QELIZ156:2	H29	The nine {'leven} *Olimp'ades* of her happy reigne;

NINE-FOLD (1)

SIDNEY149:22	H21	As if your nine-fold wit had been compacted;

NINESCORE (1)

MPERS83:38	H1226	Where ninescore days, are spent in banquetting,

NINETEEN (2)

MASSYR55:2	H68	The world then was two thousand nineteen old.
MPERS86:6	H1322	{this} *Nothus* reign'd {'bout} nineteen years, which run,

NINETY (2)

MGREC110:4	H2304	And ninety Elephants for war did bring;

MGREC~~111:3~~	H2348	one hundred {Whether} Embassadours, {ninety} or more,

NINIAS (3)

MASSYR57:1	H148	*Ninias* or *Zamies.*
MASSYR57:2	H149	His Mother dead, *Ninias* obtains his right,
MASSYR57:30	H175	For *Ninias,* and all his Race are left,

NINIVEH (1)

MASSYR63:24	H409	The ancient {famous} *Niniveh* by him was won;

NINIVIE (7)

MASSYR53:27	H17	And mighty *Ninivie,* he there begun,
MASSYR54:18	H45	And mighty *Ninivie* more mighty made,
MASSYR59:11	H235	And speeds himself to *Ninivie* amain;
MASSYR60:22	H287	Then did rebuild destroyed *Ninivie,*
MASSYR60:33	H298	As fair a Town, as the first *Ninivie.*
MASSYR62:39	H384	With shame then turn'd to *Ninivie* again,
MASSYR63:13	H398	All yeelds to him, but *Ninivie* kept free,

NINIVITES (1)

MASSYR60:4	H269	Of *Ninivites,* he caused none to dye,

NINTH (1)

MASSYR65:34	H499	The ninth, came *Nebuchadnezar* with power,

NINUS (7)

MASSYR54:15	H42	*Ninus.*
MASSYR54:16	H43	His father dead, *Ninus* begins his reign,
MASSYR54:25	H52	This stately seat of warlike *Ninus* stood.
MASSYR54:26	H53	This *Ninus* for a god, his father canoniz'd,
MASSYR55:4	H70	This great oppressing *Ninus* dead, and gone,
MASSYR55:23	H89	That *Ninus* of her, amorous soon did grow;
MASSYR55:26	H92	She flourishing with *Ninus,* long did reigne;

NINUS (2) [poss.]

ELEMEN10:39	H114	Where's *Ninus* great wal'd Town, and *Troy* of old?
MASSYR59:32	H256	This the last Monarch was, of {great} *Ninus* race,

NIPPING (1)

SEASONS47:16	H32	The croaking Frogs, whom nipping Winter kild,

NISA (1)

MGREC109:6	H2265	He t' *Nisa* goes, by *Bacchus* built long since,

NITINGALE (1) [nightengale]

SEASONS47:18	H34	The Nitingale, the Black-bird, and the Thrush,

NO (331)

FATHER5:32	H33	How Aire, and Earth, no correspondence hold,
FATHER6:5	H39	My goods are true (though poor) I love no stealth,
PROLOG6:32	H15	From School-boyes tongue, no Rhethorick we expect,
PROLOG7:4	H19	And this to mend, alas, no Art is able,
PROLOG7:12	H26	A weake or wounded braine admits no cure.
PROLOG7:38	H48	Give wholsome {Thyme or} Parsley wreath, I aske no Bayes:
ELEMEN9:33	H67	Good {Cold} sister Earth, no witnesse needs but thine;
ELEMEN11:17	H137	And then, because no matter more for fire:
ELEMEN~~12:16~~	H176	Nor will I stay, no not in *Tempe* Vale,
ELEMEN12:25	H185	No, though the fawning dog did urge me sore
ELEMEN13:15	H216	My cold, thy (fruitfull) heat, doth crave no lesse:
ELEMEN13:32	H233	The Husband knowes no Wife, nor father sons;
ELEMEN13:35	H236	But to such auditours 'twere of no use.
ELEMEN14:19	H261	Ile say no more, yet {but} this thing adde I must,

ELEMEN14:35	H277	Thou bear'st no {nor} grasse, nor {or} plant, nor tree, nor
ELEMEN15:2	H284	The Camell hath no strength, thy Bull no force;
ELEMEN15:2	H284	The Camell hath no strength, thy Bull no force;
ELEMEN15:39	H321	For it, to search my waves, they thought no scorne.
ELEMEN16:25	H348	Alas; thy ships and oares could do no good
ELEMEN16:40	H363	By adding cold to cold, no fruit proves sound;
ELEMEN17:21	H385	Till Sun release, their ships can saile no more.
ELEMEN18:7	H411	No world {earth}, thy witching trash, were all but vain.
ELEMEN18:32	H436	No place so subtilly made, but I get in.
ELEMEN18:40	H444	Me for no Element, longer to hold.
ELEMEN19:31	H472	Some overwelm'd with waves, and seen no more.
HUMOUR22:41	H110	No, no, {Alas,} thou hast no spirits, thy company
HUMOUR24:8	H157	I love no boasting, that's but childrens trade:
HUMOUR24:14	H163	Your selves may plead, your wrongs are no whit lesse,
HUMOUR24:28	H177	There is no Souldier, but thy selfe thou say'st,
HUMOUR24:29	H178	No valour upon earth, but what thou hast.
HUMOUR24:32	H181	No pattern, nor no Patron will I bring,
HUMOUR25:7	H196	Ile go no further then thy nose for test.
HUMOUR25:9	H198	Shal vanish as of no validity.
HUMOUR25:28	H217	Nay should I tel, thou wouldst count me no blab,
HUMOUR25:35	H224	Nay; {No,} know 'tis pride, most diabolical.
HUMOUR25:36	H225	If murthers be thy glory, tis no lesse.
HUMOUR26:7	H237	To play Philosopher, I have no list;
HUMOUR27:18	H289	Your slanders thus refuted, takes no place,
HUMOUR28:8	H320	As if she'd leave no flesh to turn to clay,
HUMOUR28:38	H350	No braggs i've us'd, t' your selves {to you} I dare appeale,
HUMOUR28:40	H352	I've us'd no bitternesse, nor taxt your name,
HUMOUR29:7	H360	The tongue's no weapon to assault a foe,
HUMOUR29:32	H383	It's no lesse glory to defend a town,
HUMOUR31:3	H436	So plain a slander needeth no reply.
HUMOUR31:18	H451	No further time ile spend, in confutations, {confutation}
HUMOUR31:20	H453	I now speake unto al, no more to one;
HUMOUR32:30	H504	Valour {Valours} I want, no Souldier am, 'tis true,
HUMOUR32:32	H506	I love no thundering Drums {guns}, nor bloody Wars,
HUMOUR33:12	H526	Thou speakest truth, and I can speak {say} no lesse,
HUMOUR33:17	H531	No debtor I, because 'tis {it's} paid else where;
HUMOUR34:5	H560	He was no foole, who thought the Soul lay here {there},
HUMOUR34:37	H592	To Melancholly i'le make no reply,
AGES36:9	H33	No wooden horse, but one of mettal try'd:
AGES36:36	H60	Both good and bad, but yet no more then's true.
AGES37:34	H96	No office coveted, wherein I might
AGES37:36	H98	No malice bare, to this, or that great Peer,
AGES37:38	H100	I gave no hand, nor vote, for death, or life:
AGES37:40	H102	No Statist I: nor Marti'list i' th' field;
AGES38:3	H106	My stroks did cause no death {blood}, nor wounds, nor {or}
AGES38:5	H108	My duel was no challenge, nor did seek.
AGES38:7	H110	I had no Suits at law, neighbours to vex.
AGES38:9	H112	I fear'd no stormes, nor al the windes that blows,
AGES38:10	H113	I had no ships at Sea, no fraughts to loose.
AGES38:11	H114	I fear'd no drought, nor wet, I had no crop,
AGES40:3	H184	I know no Law, nor reason, but my wil;

AGES40:13	H194	For he that loveth Wine, wanteth no woes;
AGES40:29	H210	I want a {have no} heart {at} all this for to deplore.
AGES42:37	H293	My dunghil thoughts, or hopes, could reach no higher.
AGES43:16	H311	The bottom nought, and so no longer stood.
AGES45:22	H411	What are my thoughts, this is no time to say.
AGES45:23	H413	These are no old wives tales, but this is truth;
AGES45:31	H421	No more rejoyce, at musickes pleasant {pleasing} noyse,
AGES46:2	H433	I then shal go, whence I shal come no more,
AGES46:5	H436	That earth can give no consolation sound.
AGES46:19	H450	There, {Where} I shal rest, til heavens shal be no more;
SEASONS48:34	H85	In this harsh strain, I find no melody,
SEASONS51:41	H217	No Sun, to lighten their obscurity;
MASSYR55:16	H82	But all agree, that from no lawfull bed;
MASSYR55:28	H94	That having no compeer, she might rule all,
MASSYR55:32	H98	And that her worth, deserved no such blame,
MASSYR57:11	H158	He sought no rule, til she was gone, and dead;
MASSYR57:12	H159	What then he did, of worth, can no man tel,
MASSYR57:24	H171	Again, the Country was left bare (there is no doubt)
MASSYR58:40	H223	To want no priviledge, Subjects should have,
MASSYR62:22	H367	Where now those ten Tribes are, can no man tel,
MASSYR62:36	H381	'Twixt them and *Israels* he knew no odds. [7 *years.*
MASSYR65:38	H503	The cursed King, by flight could no wise flee {fly}
MASSYR66:14	H520	No, nor {not} when *Moab, Edom* he had got.
MASSYR66:31	H537	Which from no natural causes did proceed,
MASSYR66:33	H539	The time expir'd, remains a Beast no more,
MASSYR67:7	H553	In seven and thirty years, had seen no jot,
MPERS69:12	H634	Adopts her Son for his, having no other:
MPERS69:28	H650	Who had no might to save himself from wrong;
MPERS70:3	H674	And with the *Lidians,* had no more to doe.
MPERS70:40	H711	Where that proud Conquerour could doe no lesse,
MPERS71:6	H722	*Cambyses,* no wayes like, his noble Sire,
MPERS71:10	H726	That Kings with Sisters match, no Law they finde,
MPERS71:40	H753	And though no gods, if he esteem them some,
MPERS72:6	H755	Who for no wrong, poore innocent must dye,
MPERS72:30	H774	'T would be no pleasant {pleasure}, but a tedious thing,
MPERS73:28	H813	But so or no, sure tis, they won the day.
MPERS74:13	H836	His happy wishes now doth no man spare,
MPERS74:21	H844	His title to make strong omits no thing;
MPERS74:35	H858	But strength {men} against those walls was {were} of no use;
MPERS74:39	H860	His manly face dis-figures, spares no bloud,
MPERS75:12	H873	To loose a nose, to win a Town's no shame,
MPERS80:27	H1094	Twice beaten thus by {at} Sea, he warr'd no more:
MPERS80:29	H1096	They no way able to withstand his force,
MPERS81:5	H1113	{Fearing} his best {bridge}, no longer for to {there would} stay;
MPERS81:29	H1137	No lesse then Grand-sire to great *Alexander.*
MPERS82:5	H1152	No longer dar'd, but fiercely {bravely} on-set gave,
MPERS83:9	H1197	Of life, no man had least security.
MPERS84:32	H1268	And to his Country-men {native land} could bear no hate.
MPERS85:35	H1311	No match was high enough, but their own blood,)
MPERS85:38	H1314	His father would no notice of that take;
MPERS86:32	H1348	For what was done, seemed no whit offended.

MPERS87:37	H1389	*Cyrus* finding his campe, and no man there;
MPERS89:16	H1450	That so *Europians* might no more molest;
MPERS89:20	H1454	Asking no favour, where they fear'd no bands.
MPERS90:4	H1478	The Country burnt, they no relief might take.
MPERS90:35	H1502	That *Tyssapherne* must be Vice-roy no more;
MPERS91:14	H1522	'Mongst these *Epimanondas* wants no fame;
MPERS91:35	H1549	Of whom no Record's extant of his deeds;
MPERS91:38	H1552	Or dealing with the *Persian,* now no more
MPERS92:6	H1564	I can no reason give, cause none I read;
MPERS92:7	H1565	It may be thought, surely he had no Son,
MPERS92:18	H1576	And was no sooner setled in his reign,
MPERS92:20	H1578	And the same sauce had served him no doubt,
MPERS92:32	H1590	And this 'mongst all's no controverted thing,
MGREC93:29	H1626	To save him from his might, no man was found.
MGREC94:6	H1640	kinsmen puts {put} to death without least {who gave no} cause;
MGREC94:7	H1641	That no combustion {rebellion in} in his absence be,
MGREC94:28	H1666	Stiles him disloyall servant, and no better;
MGREC95:19	H1698	To *Alexanders* heart's no little joy.
MGREC95:27	H1706	No stroake for it he struck, their hearts so quakes.
MGREC95:34	H1713	The rest attendants, which made up no lesse;
MGREC96:2	H1722	For since the world, was no such Pageant seen.
MGREC97:19	H1780	Commands, no man should doe them injury,
MGREC97:24	H1785	No sooner had this Captaine {Victor} won the field,
MGREC99:5	H1848	And the distressed King no way {whit} respects;
MGREC99:35	H1878	But in no hostile way (as I suppose)
MGREC99:41	H1884	No future dangers he did ever dread.
MGREC100:3	H1887	To see how fast he gain'd, is {was} no small wonder,
MGREC100:16	H1900	For no man to resist {man's there} his valour showes {Army to
MGREC101:16	H1941	To this, stout *Alexander,* gives no eare,
MGREC101:17	H1942	No, though *Parmenio* plead, he {yet} will not heare;
MGREC102:15	H1985	And to possesse, he counts no little blisse,
MGREC102:28	H1998	But needs no force, 'tis rendred to his hands;
MGREC106:28	H2162	No ways becomming such a mighty King;
MGREC107:1	H2176	But yet no notice takes, of what he hears;
MGREC107:9	H2184	And no man with his burden, burdened be,
MGREC109:4	H2261	To age, nor sex, no pitty doth expresse,
MGREC109:25	H2284	He glory sought, no silver, nor yet {no} gold;
MGREC109:25	H2284	He glory sought, no silver, nor yet {no} gold;
MGREC110:22	H2326	But so to doe, his Souldiers had no will;
MGREC110:24	H2328	Could by no means be further {farther} drawn, or led:
MGREC112:36	H2422	Which no merit could obliterate, or time:
MGREC113:1	H2428	The King would give no eare, but went from thence;
MGREC113:27	H2454	Thinking {Fearing} no harme, because he none did owe {doe},
MGREC114:11	H2479	*Alexander* now no longer could containe,
MGREC114:23	H2493	For this alone, and for no other cause,
MGREC115:24	H2543	His doing so, no whit displeas'd the King,
MGREC115:27	H2546	He might well dye, though he had done no wrong;
MGREC116:36	H2602	There was {were} no worlds, more, to be conquered:
MGREC116:41	H2607	His thoughts are perish'd he aspires no more,
MGREC117:5	H2612	To his posterity remain'd no jot,
MGREC117:20	H2627	His matchlesse force no Creature could abide;

MGREC118:25	H2674	On which, no signe of poyson could be {in his intrails} found,
MGREC119:2	H2692	*Perdicas* took no Province, like the rest,
MGREC119:23	H2713	His Lady take i'th' way, and no man know.
MGREC122:20	H2845	She daughter to his son, who had no other;
MGREC122:34	H2855	And this no man durst question, or resist;
MGREC124:3	H2908	For this *Antigonus* needed {did need} no spurs,
MGREC~~124:10~~	H2917	That no supply by these here might be lent,
MGREC124:26	H2933	More then he bidden was, could act no thing;
MGREC126:16	H3007	will not heare {Her foe would give no Ear}, such is his hate.
MGREC126:23	H3014	No sooner had he got her in his hands {hand},
MGREC126:32	H3023	But Royalty no good conditions brings;
MGREC126:40	H3029	How for no cause, but her inverterate hate;
MGREC~~127:17~~	H3047	Such as nor {no} threats, nor favour could acquire;
MGREC129:12	H3126	No sooner was great *Alexander* dead,
MGREC130:16	H3171	They for their great reward no better speed,
MGREC131:32	H3224	Who did no sooner understand the same,
MGREC132:37	H3284	'Twas no small joy, unto *Seleuchus* breast,
MGREC135:32	H3404	And when he had no appetite to eate,
MROMAN138:19	H3509	Of Boats, and Oares, no more they need the aide;
MROMAN140:6	H3569	No more I'le do, sith I have suffer'd wrack,
DIALOG143:1	H70	Nor Nobles siding, to make *John* no King
DIALOG143:3	H72	No *Edward, Richard,* to lose rule, and life,
DIALOG143:4	H73	Nor no *Lancastrians,* to renew old strife;
DIALOG143:5	~~H73~~	No Crook-backt Tyrant, now usurps the Seat,
DIALOG143:7	H74	No Duke of *York,* nor Earle of *March,* to soyle
DIALOG~~143:8~~	H76	No crafty Tyrant now usurps the Seat,
DIALOG143:9	H78	No need of *Tudor,* Roses to unite,
DIALOG143:15	H84	My Sister *Scotland* hurts me now no more,
DIALOG143:32	H101	The Gospel is trod {troden} down, and hath no right;
DIALOG145:19	H168	One saith its he, the other no such thing.
DIALOG145:33	H182	No prelate should his Bishoprick retain;
DIALOG146:7	H195	I that no warres, so many yeares have known,
DIALOG146:19	H205	The seed time's come, but Ploughman hath no hope,
DIALOG147:28	H252	If now you weep so much, that then no more,
DIALOG148:29	H294	No Canaanite shall then be found ith' land,
DIALOG148:31	H296	If this make way thereto, then sigh no more,
SIDNEY149:9	H8	No lesse {As well} an Honour to our *British* Land,
SIDNEY151:3	~~H69~~	I wish no more such Blazers we may see;
SIDNEY~~152:4~~	H76	The Muses aid I crav'd, they had no will
SIDNEY152:5	He	promis'd much, but th' muses had no will,
SIDNEY152:7	H78	With high disdain, they said they gave no more,
SIDNEY~~152:14~~	H84	Then wonder not if I no better sped,
DUBART153:29	H33	The silly Pratler speakes no word of sence;
QELIZ155:20	H11	That men account it no impiety,
QELIZ155:30	H21	Which makes me deeme, my rudenesse is no wrong,
QELIZ155:33	H24	No *Phoenix,* Pen, nor *Spencers* Poetry,
QELIZ155:34	H25	No *Speeds,* nor *Chamdens* learned History;
QELIZ156:1	H28	No memories, nor volumes can containe,
QELIZ157:25	H93	Yet for our Queen is no fit parallel:
QELIZ158:3	H112	No more shall rise or set such {so} glorious Sun,
DAVID159:10	H25	And in their deaths {death} was found no parting strife;

VANITY159:35	H7	No, they like beasts, and sonnes of men shall die,
VANITY160:1	H11	No, that's but labour anxious, care and pain.
VANITY160:8	H18	What is't in beauty? no, that's but a snare,
VANITY160:26	H36	There is a path, no vultures eye hath seen.
TDUDLEY165:19	H21	Such as in life, no man could justly deem.
TDUDLEY165:23	H25	So needs no Testimonial from his own;
TDUDLEY165:38	H40	High thoughts he gave no harbour in his heart,
TDUDLEY166:6	H48	No ostentation seen in all his wayes,
CONTEM168:5	H15	More Heaven then Earth was here, no winter & no night.
CONTEM168:5	H15	More Heaven then Earth was here, no winter & no night.
CONTEM168:20	H28	No wonder, some made thee a Deity:
CONTEM169:2	H44	Art thou so full of glory, that no Eye
CONTEM169:5	H47	As to approach it, can no earthly mould.
CONTEM169:24	H64	Whilst I as mute, can warble forth no higher layes.
CONTEM170:17	H89	But no such sign on false *Cain's* offering;
CONTEM170:22	H93	There *Abel* keeps his sheep, no ill he thinks,
CONTEM171:28	H130	No sooner born, but grief and care makes fall
CONTEM173:18	H184	O merry Bird (said I) that fears no snares,
CONTEM173:20	H186	Feels no sad thoughts, nor cruciating cares
FLESH175:39	H39	Disturb no more my setled heart,
FLESH176:11	H51	Thy flatt'ring shews Ile trust no more.
FLESH176:19	H59	Thy riches are to me no bait,
FLESH177:12	H93	Such as no Eye did e're behold,
FLESH177:17	H98	Nor Sun, nor Moon, they have no need,
FLESH177:19	H100	No Candle there, nor yet Torch light,
FLESH177:20	H101	For there shall be no darksome night.
SICKNES178:29	H12	no life is like to this.
SICKNES178:36	H19	No sooner blown, but dead and gone,
BIRTH179:29	H5	No tyes so strong, no friends so clear and sweet,
BIRTH179:29	H5	No tyes so strong, no friends so clear and sweet,
BIRTH180:11	H21	And when thou feel'st no grief, as I no harms,
BIRTH180:11	H21	And when thou feel'st no grief, as I no harms,
1HUSB180:31	H10	Thy love is such I can no way repay,
1HUSB180:34	H13	That when we live no more, we may live ever.
2LETTER182:19	H25	But for one moneth I see no day (poor soul)
3LETTER183:20	H22	I have a loving phere, yet seem no wife:
CHILDRN184:32	H21	A prettier bird was no where seen,
CHILDRN184:35	H24	On whom I plac'd no small delight;
CHILDRN186:7	H74	But former toyes (no joyes) adieu.
CHILDRN186:14	H81	No seasons cold, nor storms they see;
1SIMON188:4	H5	No sooner come, but gone, and fal'n asleep,
MERCY189:8	H29	No wonder it no longer did survive.
MERCY189:8	H29	No wonder it no longer did survive.
2SIMON195:7	Hp271	look vpon when you should see me no more, I could think of
MEDDM195:24	Hp272	There is no obiect that we see. no action that we doe, no good
MEDDM195:25	Hp272	no evill that we feele, or fear, but we may make some spiritull
MEDDM196:2	Hp272	A ship that beares much saile & little or no ballast, is easily
MEDDM196:3	Hp272	whose head hath great abilities and his heart little or no grace
MEDDM197:11	Hp274	If we had no winter the spring would not be so pleasant, if we
MEDDM197:19	Hp275	it, and that heart wch is not continually purifieing it self is no fit
MEDDM197:29	Hp275	'tis no wonder if he faint by the way.

MEDDM198:21	Hp276	There is no new thing vnder ye Sun there is nothing that can
MEDDM202:13	Hp282	among the dead, and no other reason can be giuen of all this
MEDDM202:17	Hp282	haue no kernell in them, and they that feed vpon them, may
MEDDM202:28	Hp282	and se no light, yet then must we trust in the lord and stay
MEDDM203:11	Hp283	be all convenient and comfortable for him yet he hath no
MEDDM203:27	Hp284	and that he must needs perish if he haue no remedy, will
MEDDM205:14	Hp286	and Judg, whom no bribes can pervert, nor flattery cause to
MEDDM205:16	Hp286	is this Court of Judicature, that there is no appeale from it, no
MEDDM205:16	Hp286	Court of Judicature, that there is no appeale from it, no not to
MEDDM207:9	Hp288	are lords we will come no more at thee If outward blessings,
MEDDM207:24	Hp289	and till the expiratnon of that time, no dangers no sicknes
MEDDM207:24	Hp289	and till the expiratnon of that time, no dangers no sicknes
MEDDM207:25	Hp289	no paines nor troubles, shall put a period to our dayes, the
MEDDM208:7	Hp289	you vse no other meanes to extinguish them so distance of
MEDDM208:8	Hp290	wth length of time (if there be no inter course) will coole the
MEDDM208:9	Hp290	friends, though there should be no displeasence betweene
MEDDM209:3	Hp291	but it is so necessary, that w^thout faith there is no salvation
MEDDM209:18	Hp291	hath by his prouidence so ordered, that no one Covntry hath all
PILGRIM210:7	H7	The burning sun no more shall heat
PILGRIM210:9	H9	The bryars and thornes no more shall scrat
PILGRIM210:11	H11	He erring pathes no more shall tread
PILGRIM210:14	H14	for thirst no more shall parch his tongue
PILGRIM210:15	H15	No rugged stones his feet shall gaule
PILGRIM210:26	H26	Mine eyes no more shall ever weep
PILGRIM210:27	H27	No fainting fits shall me assaile
MYCHILD215:15	Hp240	bequeath to yov, that when I am no more wth yov, yet I may
MYCHILD216:23	Hp242	So vsually thvs it hath been wth me that I haue no sooner
MYCHILD217:3	Hp242	by it: It hath been no small support to me in times of Darknes
MYCHILD217:7	Hp242	child, that no longer then the rod has been on my back
MYCHILD217:24	Hp243	in darknes and seen no light, yet haue I desired to stay my self
MYCHILD218:9	Hp244	mvst bee it or none. Haue I not fovnd y^t operation by it that no
MYCHILD218:10	Hp244	Invention can work vpon ye Soul, hath no Judgments befallen
FEVER220:24	H4	When in my flesh no part was fovnd
FEVER221:10	H25	My heart no more might quail.
SOREFIT222:3	H22	Thou know'st no life I did require
FAINTING222:18	H8	And liueing man no more shall see
FAINTING222:26	H16	O Lord, no longer bee my Dayes
MED223:18	Hp250	and let me bee no more afraid of Death, but even desire to
MYSOUL225:19	H23	No gain I find in ovght below
28AUG225:31	Hp254	men, he hath no benefitt by my adversity, nor is he ye better
28AUG226:9	Hp254	& bequeath my Soul to thee and Death seem'd no terrible
30SEPT227:22	Hp257	I haue fovnd by Exper^c. I can no more liue w^thout correction
SAMUEL228:10	H11	No freind I haue like Thee to trust
11MAYB228:24	Hp259	that I haue had no great fitt of sicknes, but this year from y^e
HOURS234:11	H25	I in this world no comfort haue,
HOURS234:16	H30	They are no Joy, but woe.
HOUSE236:18	H10	Let no man know is my Desire.
HOUSE236:25	H17	And when I could no longer look
HOUSE237:2	H32	And them behold no more shall I.
HOUSE237:3	H33	Vnder thy roof no gvest shall sitt,
HOUSE237:5	H35	No pleasant tale shall 'ere be told

HOUSE237:7	H37	No Candle 'ere shall shine in Thee
HOUSE237:25	H55	Ther's wealth enovgh I need no more,
HOUSE237:27	H57	The world no longer let me Love

NOBELS (1) [nobles]

AGES45:4	H384	And Land & Nobels sav'd with their anointed.

NOBILITY (4)

AGES41:38	H255	If not, yet wealth, {riches} Nobility can gain.
AGES43:7	H302	My thirst was higher, then Nobility.
MPERS74:31	H854	Much gain'd the hearts of his nobility.
MGREC106:34	H2168	Charging the same on his Nobility;

NOBLE (26)

HUMOUR21:11	H39	Our noble selves, in a lesse noble Gender.
HUMOUR21:11	H39	Our noble selves, in a lesse noble Gender.
HUMOUR31:30	H463	With me is noble patience also found,
HUMOUR33:38	H552	The five most noble Sences, here do dwel,
AGES41:37	H254	If Noble, then mine honour to {o} maintaine.
AGES43:16	H310	Though cemented with more the noble bloud,
AGES46:7	H438	To mean, to noble, fearful, or to bold:
SEASONS49:23	H114	Was like that noble, brave *Archadian.*
MASSYR67:26	H572	The Noble *Persians,* {Persian} to invade his rights.
MPERS71:6	H722	*Cambyses,* no wayes like, his noble Sire,
MPERS73:19	H806	And first these noble *Magi* 'gree upon,
MPERS77:12	H951	Thirty six years this royall {noble} Prince did reign,
MPERS78:29	H1010	O noble Queen, thy valour I commend,
MPERS80:7	H1074	O noble *Greeks,* how now, degenerate?
MPERS84:26	H1262	The {This} noble *Greek,* now fit for generall.
MPERS84:39	H1275	The King this noble Captaine having lost,
MPERS91:15	H1523	Who had (as noble *Raleigh* doth evince)
MGREC128:33	H3106	Curtious, as noble *Ptolomy,* or more,
MGREC132:29	H3276	Now {Next} dyed the brave and noble *Ptolomy,*
MGREC133:19	H3307	Between those Kings, and noble *Pyrrus* stout,
DIALOG146:38	H224	Blest be the Nobles of thy Noble Land,
SIDNEY149:8	H7	Her noble *Sidney* wore the Crown of Bayes;
SIDNEY150:36	H63	Of this our noble *Scipio* some good word?
SIDNEY150:37	H64	Noble {Great} *Bartas,* this to thy praise adds more,
QELIZ156:31	H58	Her Nobles sacrific'd their noble blood,
CONTEM171:26	H128	By birth more noble then those creatures all,

NOBLENESSE (1)

HUMOUR28:23	H335	I might here shew, the noblenesse of minde,

NOBLER (1)

HUMOUR26:23	H253	But thine the nobler, which I grant, yet mine

NOBLES (13) [pl.] See also NOBELS

AGES45:4	H382	A plot to blow up Nobles, and their King;
MASSYR62:10	H355	And did the people, nobles, and their King
MASSYR65:41	H506	With Children, Wives, and Nobles, all they bring,
MPERS74:11	H836	The Nobles all alight, {bow to} their King to greet,
MPERS83:39	H1227	His Princes, Nobles, and his Captaines calls,
MGREC111:40	H2385	A Wedding Feast to's Nobles then he makes,
MGREC122:35	H2856	For all the Princes {nobles} of great {King} *Alexander*
DIALOG142:20	H49	Must *Richmonds* ayd, the Nobles now implore,
DIALOG143:1	H70	Nor Nobles siding, to make *John* no King

DIALOG144:36	H144	I saw her people famish'd, Nobles slain,
DIALOG146:38	H224	Blest be the Nobles of thy Noble Land,
DIALOG147:24	H248	And yee brave Nobles, chase away all fear,
QELIZ156:31	H58	Her Nobles sacrific'd their noble blood,

NOBLEST (3)

ELEMEN8:6	H4	Which was the strongest, noblest, & the best,
ELEMEN8:28	H26	Being the most impatient Element.
HUMOUR33:22	H536	The Brain's the noblest member all allow,

NOBLY (1)

MPERS83:33	H1221	Which had they kept, *Greece* had more nobly done,

NOD (1)

CONTEM170:35	H105	A Vagabond to Land of *Nod* he goes,

NOE (1)

ELEMEN17:27	H391	But these are trifles to the Flood of *Noe.*

NOIS (1) [noise] See also NOYSE

HOUSE236:15	H7	I waken'd was wth thundring nois

NONE (64) See also NONE'S

ELEMEN10:28	H103	There's none more strange then *Ætna's* sulphery mount
ELEMEN11:26	H146	Which none ere gave, nor {or} you could claime of right,
ELEMEN12:9	H169	And *Hemus,* whose steep sides, none foote upon,
ELEMEN12:24	H184	But here, or there, I list now none to name;
ELEMEN15:1	H283	When I am gone, their fiercenesse none need {needs} doubt;
HUMOUR21:30	H58	But valour, when comes that? from none of you;
HUMOUR26:12	H242	For there are {is} none, thou say'st, if some, not best.
HUMOUR26:34	H264	But the materials none of thine, that's cleare,
HUMOUR27:4	H275	Can be imputed unto none, but Fire;
HUMOUR30:19	H411	You'l say, here none shal ere disturbe my right;
HUMOUR35:10	H606	Nor jars, nor scoffs, let none hereafter see,
AGES41:36	H251	But if none, then for kindred near ally'd.
AGES45:17	H399	Plotted and acted, so that none can tell,
SEASONS48:30	H83	But none in all that hath preheminence.
MASSYR55:34	H100	But were her vertues, more, or lesse, or none;
MASSYR55:37	H103	Admir'd of all, but equaliz'd of none.
MASSYR59:23	H247	For few, or none, did there {it seems} resistance make;
MASSYR60:4	H269	Of *Ninivites,* he caused none to dye,
MASSYR60:23	H288	A costly work, which none could doe but he,
MASSYR61:35	H340	Through *Syria* now he marcht, none stopt his way,
MASSYR62:33	H378	His Wars none better then himself can boast,
MASSYR63:20	H405	But by conjecture this, and none but he,
MASSYR64:32	H456	None but the true *Ezekiel* need to tell:
MASSYR65:23	H488	For this was {is} he, for whom none said, Alas!
MASSYR68:11	H597	None answers the affrighted Kings intent.
MPERS72:32	H776	Fear'd of all, but lov'd of few, or none,
MPERS73:37	H822	But others thought (none of the dullest braine,)
MPERS77:22	H963	None write by whom, nor how, 'twas over-past;
MPERS79:23	H1049	That none of these should {those could} live a {an} hundred
MPERS80:5	H1072	None cryes for quarter, nor yet seeks to run,
MPERS81:41	H1145	rest had} Weapons, they had none would {do little} harme;
MPERS84:4	H1232	To drink more then he list, none bidden was:
MPERS92:6	H1564	I can no reason give, cause none I read;
MGREC96:34	H1754	The *Greekes* would all adore, and {but} would none fight.

MGREC99:6	H1849	Tels him, these proffers great (in truth were none)
MGREC100:23	H1907	Men but in shape, and name, of valour none,
MGREC103:5	H2016	None like to this in riches did abound.
MGREC105:33	H2126	Which made their long restraint, seeme to be none;
MGREC107:30	H2205	For Boats here's none, nor neare it any wood,
MGREC113:27	H2454	Thinking {Fearing} no harme, because he none did owe {doe},
MGREC117:7	H2614	None of his Kindred, or {nor} his Race, long stood;
MGREC117:26	H2633	A King they'l have, but who, none can agree:
MGREC117:28	H2635	Yet {But} none so hardy found as so durst say.
MGREC117:29	H2636	Great *Alexander* has left {did leave} issue none,
MGREC119:7	H2697	That none might know, to frustrate his intent;
MGREC119:33	H2723	For personage, none was like {to} this Commander:
MGREC125:19	H2967	Nor Darts, nor Arrowes now, none shoots, nor flings;
MGREC128:8	H3081	Which none e're did but those of royall fame;
MGREC130:40	H3185	For to their Crowns, there's none can title make.
MROMAN140:5	H3568	Which none had cause to wail, nor I to boast.
DIALOG142:22	H51	If none of these, deare Mother, what's your woe?
DIALOG143:10	H79	None knowes which is the Red, or which the White:
SIDNEY149:33	~~H23~~	Let then, none dis-allow of these my straines,
SIDNEY~~150:12~~	H42	Then let none disallow of these my straines
QELIZ157:24	H92	(Whom none but great *Aurelius* could quell)
QELIZ157:32	H100	Now say, have women worth, or have they none?
CONTEM169:10	H51	Silent alone, where none or saw, or heard,
CONTEM170:28	H99	Though none on Earth but kindred near then could he find.
FLESH177:6	H87	There's none on Earth can parallel;
AUTHOR178:13	H23	If for thy Father askt, say, thou hadst none:
BIRTH180:4	H14	I may seem thine, who in effect am none.
VERSES184:10	H14	Such is my bond, none can discharge but I,
MEDDM206:27	Hp288	works and doings of god are wonderfull, but none more awfull
MYCHILD218:9	Hp244	this mvst bee it or none. Haue I not fovnd y^t operation by it

NONE'S (1) [none is]

HUMOUR34:31	H586	Again, none's fit for Kingly place but thou,

NOOK (1)

3LETTER183:1	H3	Perplext, in every bush & nook doth pry,

NOON (2)

HUMOUR33:7	H521	As at noon day to tel, the Sun doth shine.
AGES44:38	H371	And then, me thought, the world {day} at noon grew dark,

NOR (285) See also NOR's

FATHER5:9	H10	To climbe their Climes, I have nor strength, nor skill,
PROLOG7:1	H16	Nor yet a sweet Consort, from broken strings,
PROLOG7:2	H17	Nor perfect beauty, where's a maine defect,
PROLOG7:7	H21	Nor can I, like that fluent sweet tongu'd *Greek*
ELEMEN11:26	H146	Which none ere gave, nor {or} you could claime of right,
ELEMEN12:16	~~H176~~	Nor yet expatiate, in Temple vale;
ELEMEN~~12:16~~	H176	Nor will I stay, no not in *Tempe* Vale,
ELEMEN12:40	H200	Which guides, when Sun, nor Moon, nor Stars do shine.
ELEMEN13:32	H233	The Husband knowes no Wife, nor father sons;
ELEMEN~~14:35~~	H277	Thou bear'st no {nor} grasse, nor {or} plant, nor tree, nor
ELEMEN15:3	H285	Nor mettl's found in the couragious Horse:
ELEMEN16:19	H342	Nor will I speake of waters made by Art,
ELEMEN16:21	H344	Nor fruitfull dewes, nor drops {distil'd} from weeping eyes;

ELEMEN16:23	H346	Nor yet of Salt, and Sugar, sweet and smart,
ELEMEN19:23	H468	Which neither ships nor houses could withstand.
ELEMEN19:34	H475	Where neither houses, trees, nor plants, I spare;
HUMOUR22:2	H71	She'l neither say, she wil, nor wil she doe:
HUMOUR22:18	H87	Nor hath she wit, or heat, to blush at this.
HUMOUR22:25	H94	Nor sister Sanguine, from thy moderate heat,
HUMOUR23:10	H120	Thou canst not claime, the Liver, Head nor Heart;
HUMOUR23:21	H131	Nor is't my pleasure, thus to blur thy name:
HUMOUR23:38	H148	Its not your muscles, nerves, nor this nor that:
HUMOUR24:32	H181	No pattern, nor no Patron will I bring,
HUMOUR25:25	H214	Nor sparing Sex, nor age, nor fire, nor son.
HUMOUR25:37	H226	Ile not envy thy feats, nor happinesse.
HUMOUR26:8	H238	Nor yet Phisitian, nor Anatomist.
HUMOUR26:9	H239	For acting these, I have nor wil, nor art,
HUMOUR26:37	H267	But i'le not force retorts, nor do thee wrong,
HUMOUR27:11	H282	But by what right, nor do'st, nor canst thou name;
HUMOUR27:19	H290	Nor what you've said, doth argue my disgrace,
HUMOUR28:40	H352	I've us'd no bitternesse, nor taxt your name,
HUMOUR31:32	H465	What Sanguine is, she doth not heed, nor care.
HUMOUR32:1	H475	Nor are ye free, from this inormity,
HUMOUR32:6	H480	Nor cold, nor hot, Ague, nor Plurisie;
HUMOUR32:7	H481	Nor Cough, nor Quinsie, nor the burning Feavor.
HUMOUR32:12	H486	And things that never were, nor shal I see.
HUMOUR32:14	H488	Nor multitude of words, argues our strength;
HUMOUR32:23	H497	Nor how her Gaul on me she causeless brake;
HUMOUR32:24	H498	Nor wonder 'twas, for hatred there's not smal,
HUMOUR32:32	H506	I love no thundering Drums {guns}, nor bloody Wars,
HUMOUR34:28	H583	Ne're did {Nor will} I heare {yield} that Choler was the witt'est;
HUMOUR35:10	H606	Nor jars, nor scoffs, let none hereafter see,
HUMOUR35:12	H608	Nor be discern'd, here's water, earth, aire, fire,
AGES37:25	H87	That its own worth, it did not know, nor mind.
AGES37:32	H94	Nor studious was, Kings favours how to buy,
AGES37:37	H99	Nor unto buzzing whisperors, gave ear.
AGES37:38	H100	I gave no hand, nor vote, for death, or life:
AGES37:40	H102	No Statist I: nor Marti'list i' th' field;
AGES38:3	H106	stroks did cause no death {blood}, nor wounds, nor {or} skars.
AGES38:5	H108	My duel was no challenge, nor did seek.
AGES38:8	H111	Nor evidence for land, {lands} did me perplex.
AGES38:9	H112	I fear'd no stormes, nor al the windes that blows,
AGES38:11	H114	I fear'd no drought, nor wet, I had no crop,
AGES38:12	H115	Nor yet on future things did place {set} my hope.
AGES39:15	H158	Nor ignorant {And so likewise} what they in Country do;
AGES39:21	H164	Nor wait til good advice {success} our hopes do crown;
AGES40:3	H184	I know no Law, nor reason, but my wil;
AGES40:33	H212	Nor yet that heavy reckoning for {soon} to come;
AGES42:23	H281	As neither sow, nor reape, nor plant, nor build.
AGES43:11	H305	Nor Brothers, Nephewes, Sons, nor Sires I've spar'd.
AGES44:12	H345	It's not my valour, honour, nor my gold,
AGES44:16	H349	It's not my goodly house {state}, nor bed of down,
AGES44:18	H351	Nor from alliance now can I have hope,
AGES45:11	H393	But not their Princes love, nor state so high;

AGES45:34	H424	Nor sapors find, in what I drink or eat.
AGES45:36	H426	I cannot labour, nor {much less} I cannot {can} fight:
SEASONS46:35	H12	Nor hot nor cold, she spake, but with a breath,
SEASONS49:30	H119	*Orthobulus,* nor yet *Sebastia* great,
SEASONS51:18	H192	Which shewes, nor Summer, Winter, nor the Spring,
SEASONS51:19	H194	Nor could that temp'rate Clime such difference make,
MASSYR57:9	H156	This fraud, in war, nor peace, at all appears;
MASSYR57:20	H167	Nor can those Reasons which wise *Raleigh* finds,
MASSYR62:15	H360	On whom, nor threats, nor mercies could do good;
MASSYR63:32	H419	Nor of his acts {Wars} have we the certainty,
MASSYR63:35	H422	Nor his restoring from old legends took;
MASSYR64:39	H463	But the *Chaldeans* had nor ships, nor skill,
MASSYR66:14	H520	No, nor {not} when *Moab, Edom* he had got.
MASSYR68:18	H604	Who doth not flatter, nor once cloake the thing.
MPERS70:7	H678	That all the world they neither {need not} feare, nor doubt;
MPERS72:25	H773	He spar'd nor foe, nor friend, nor favorite.
MPERS75:16	H877	Nor can *Darius* in his Monarchy,
MPERS77:22	H963	None write by whom, nor how, 'twas over-past;
MPERS80:5	H1072	None cryes for quarter, nor yet seeks to run,
MPERS81:26	H1134	Nor could the brave Ambassador be {he} sent,
MPERS82:6	H1153	The other not a hand, nor sword will {would} wave,
MPERS82:26	H1173	Yet words {Nor prayers}, nor guifts, could win him least
MPERS82:27	H1174	Nor matching of her daughter, to his son:
MPERS83:4	H1192	The grieved Prince finding nor right, nor love,
MPERS84:28	H1264	His Country, nor his Kindred {Friends} would {much} esteem,
MPERS84:33	H1269	Nor yet disloyall to his Prince would prove,
MPERS86:25	H1341	He hop'd, if fraud, nor force the Crown could {would} gaine;
MPERS87:15	H1370	And yet with these, had neither heart, nor grace;
MPERS88:33	H1426	Nor *Gorgons* {head} like to this, transform'd to stones.
MPERS89:5	H1439	Nor lackt they any of their number small,
MPERS89:6	H1440	Nor wound receiv'd, but one among them all:
MPERS90:8	H1481	Nor rivers course, nor *Persians* force could stay,
MPERS91:32	H1546	A King nor good, nor valiant, wise nor just
MGREC94:8	H1642	In seeking after {Nor making Title unto} Soveraignity:
MGREC94:11	H1645	Nor wonder is't, if he in blood begin,
MGREC96:18	H1738	think {Suppos'd} he neither thought {meant} to fight nor fly,
MGREC101:7	H1932	(Nor was such match, in all the world beside)
MGREC101:19	H1944	Nor infamy had wak'd, when he had slept;
MGREC101:25	H1950	Nor yet two Monarchs in one World reside;
MGREC105:12	H2105	Yea, {But} above all, that neither eare, nor eye,
MGREC105:13	H2106	Should heare, nor see, his groans, and {dying} misery:
MGREC106:18	H2152	Such country there, nor yet such people finde.
MGREC107:30	H2205	For Boats here's none, nor neare it any wood,
MGREC107:40	H2215	But coward, durst not fight, nor could he fly,
MGREC108:15	H2231	Nor sex, nor age, nor one, nor other spar'd,
MGREC108:17	H2233	Nor could he reason give, for this great wrong,
MGREC109:4	H2261	To age, nor sex, no pitty doth expresse,
MGREC109:8	H2267	Nor had that drunken god, one that {who} would take
MGREC109:25	H2284	He glory sought, no silver, nor yet {no} gold;
MGREC110:17	H2317	Nor was't dishonour, at the length to yeeld;
MGREC112:20	H2406	*Philotas* was not least, nor yet the last;

MGREC113:20	H2447	As he would ne're confesse, nor could {yet} reward,
MGREC113:21	H2448	Nor could his Captaines bear so great regard;
MGREC114:22	H2492	Nor would adore him for a Deity:
MGREC114:32	H2502	Nor all felicity, of his in war;
MGREC115:37	H2556	Nor by his baits could be ensnared so:
MGREC116:10	H2573	Nor meat, nor drink, nor comfort would she take,
MGREC117:1	H2608	Nor can he kill, or save as heretofore,
MGREC117:7	H2614	None of his Kindred, or {nor} his Race, long stood;
MGREC120:2	H2733	Nor former liberty, or glory gain'd;
MGREC121:38	H2820	Nor could *Craterus* (whom he much did love)
MGREC124:21	H2928	Nor could Mother, nor Sons of *Alexander,*
MGREC124:35	H2942	Nor counts {thought} he that indignity but {was} small,
MGREC125:19	H2967	Nor Darts, nor Arrowes now, none shoots, nor flings;
MGREC127:17	H3047	Such as nor {no} threats, nor favour could acquire;
MGREC131:16	H3208	Nor to his son did there {e're} one foot remain,
MGREC135:4	H3376	For 'twas not death, nor danger, she did dread,
MROMAN140:5	H3568	Which none had cause to wail, nor I to boast.
MROMAN140:8	H3571	Nor matter is't this last, the world now sees,
DIALOG142:31	H60	Though Armes, nor Purse she hath, for your releif:
DIALOG142:37	H66	But forraigne Foe, nor fained friend I feare,
DIALOG142:39	H68	Nor is it *Alcies* Son, and {nor} *Henries* Daughter,
DIALOG142:39	H68	Nor is it *Alcies* Son, and {nor} *Henries* Daughter,
DIALOG143:1	H70	Nor Nobles siding, to make *John* no King
DIALOG143:4	H73	Nor no *Lancastrians,* to renew old strife;
DIALOG143:7	H74	No Duke of *York,* nor Earle of *March,* to soyle
DIALOG143:40	H109	Nor for their owne, but for their Masters sake;
DIALOG144:34	H142	Nor took I warning by my neighbours falls,
DIALOG145:4	H153	Nor sip I of that cup, and just 't may be,
DIALOG147:19	H245	Not false to King, nor Countrey in thy heart, {to the better part;}
QELIZ155:26	H17	Thou never didst, nor canst thou now disdaine,
QELIZ155:33	H24	No *Phoenix,* Pen, nor *Spencers* Poetry,
QELIZ155:34	H25	No *Speeds,* nor *Chamdens* learned History;
QELIZ156:1	H28	No memories, nor volumes can containe,
QELIZ156:5	H32	Nor say I more then duly is her due,
QELIZ156:9	H36	*Spaines* Monarch sa's not so; nor yet his Hoast,
QELIZ156:32	H59	Nor men, nor coyne she spar'd, to doe them good;
DAVID158:29	H9	Nor published in streets of *Askelon,*
DAVID158:33	H13	Nor fruitfull showers your barren tops bestrew,
DAVID158:34	H14	Nor fields of offerings e're on you grow,
DAVID158:35	H15	Nor any pleasant thing e're may you show;
DAVID159:7	H22	Nor from the fat, and spoyles, of mighty men,
VANITY160:19	H29	Nor laugh, nor weep, let things go ill or well:
VANITY160:22	H32	If not in honour, beauty, age, nor treasure,
VANITY160:23	H33	Nor yet in learning, wisdome, youth nor pleasure,
VANITY160:27	H37	Where lions fierce, nor lions whelps hath {have} been,
VANITY160:40	H50	Nor strength nor wisdome, nor fresh youth shall fade,
VANITY160:41	H51	Nor death shall see, but are immortal made,
VANITY161:3	H54	Nor change of state, nor cares shall ever see,
TDUDLEY165:10	H12	Nor is't Relation near my hand shall tye;
TDUDLEY165:16	H18	Nor was his name, or life lead so obscure
TDUDLEY165:39	H41	Nor honours pufft him up, when he had part:

TDUDLEY166:12	H54	Nor wonder 'twas, low things ne'r much did move
TDUDLEY166:21	H63	Where storms, nor showrs, nor ought can damnifie.
CONTEM170:32	H102	Nor Male-factor ever felt like warr,
CONTEM171:8	H113	Who neither guilt, nor yet the punishment could fly.
CONTEM171:21	H124	Nor age nor wrinkle on their front are seen;
CONTEM171:30	H132	Nor youth, nor strength, nor wisdom spring again
CONTEM171:31	H133	Nor habitations long their names retain,
CONTEM172:16	H151	I markt, nor crooks, nor rubs that there did lye
CONTEM172:20	H155	Nor is it rocks or shoals that can obstruct thy pace.
CONTEM172:22	H156	Nor is't enough, that thou alone may'st slide,
CONTEM173:19	H185	That neither toyles nor hoards up in thy barn,
CONTEM173:20	H186	Feels no sad thoughts, nor cruciating cares
CONTEM173:24	H190	Reminds not what is past, nor whats to come dost fear.
CONTEM174:9	H209	Nor all his losses, crosses and vexation,
CONTEM174:34	H231	Nor wit nor gold, nor buildings scape times rust;
FLESH176:20	H60	Thine honours doe, nor will I love;
FLESH176:32	H72	Nor are they shadows which I catch,
FLESH176:33	H73	Nor fancies vain at which I snatch,
FLESH176:40	H80	My garments are not silk nor gold,
FLESH176:41	H81	Nor such like trash which Earth doth hold,
FLESH177:17	H98	Nor Sun, nor Moon, they have no need,
FLESH177:19	H100	No Candle there, nor yet Torch light,
FLESH177:23	H104	Nor withering age shall e're come there,
1HUSB180:30	H9	Nor ought but love from thee, give recompence.
1LETTER181:11	H9	Whom whilst I 'joy'd, nor storms, nor frosts I felt,
3LETTER183:16	H18	Her fellow lost, nor joy nor life do wish,
3LETTER183:25	H27	Who neither joyes in pasture, house nor streams,
CHILDRN184:17	H6	Nor cost, nor labour did I spare,
CHILDRN186:14	H81	No seasons cold, nor storms they see;
2SIMON195:8	Hp271	fit for you nor of more ease to my self then these short
MEDDM200:30	Hp279	this transcends the spring, that their leafe shall neuer faile nor
MEDDM203:24	Hp283	he slighted before, so he that neuer felt the sicknes of sin, nor
MEDDM205:14	Hp286	whom no bribes can pervert, nor flattery cause to favour but
MEDDM206:31	Hp288	Souerainty of god, who will not be tyed to time nor place, nor
MEDDM207:25	Hp289	no paines nor troubles, shall put a period to our dayes, the
PILGRIM210:8	H8	Nor stormy raines, on him shall beat
PILGRIM210:10	H10	nor hungry wolues at him shall catch
PILGRIM210:12	H12	Nor wild fruits eate, in stead of bread
PILGRIM210:16	H16	nor stumps nor rocks cause him to fall
PILGRIM210:28	H28	nor grinding paines, my body fraile.
PILGRIM210:30	H30	Nor losses know, nor sorrowes see.
PILGRIM211:1	H42	as eare ner' heard nor tongue ere told
FEVER220:32	H12	Nor could I read my Evidence
SOREFIT222:5	H24	Nor ovght on Earth worthy Desire,
JULY223:30	Hp251	let me neuer forgett thy Goodnes, nor question thy faithfullnes
WHAT224:18	H18	Nor son of man to 'vnsay
MYSOUL225:12	H16	Nor come in memory.
28AUG225:30	Hp254	doth not afflict willingly, nor take delight in greiving ye children
28AUG225:31	Hp254	he hath no benefitt by my adversity, nor is he ye better for my
11MAYB228:31	Hp259	loving kindnes, nor take ye cup of salvation wth Thanksgiving
RESTOR230:7	H22	Nor turnd his ear away from me

2HUSB232:12	H13	Nor novght could keep him back
ACK235:10	H10	Nor payd me after my desert
HOUSE237:4	H34	Nor at thy Table eat a bitt.
HOUSE237:6	H36	Nor things recovnted done of old.
HOUSE237:8	H38	Nor bridegroom's voice ere heard shall bee.

NORMAN (1)

DIALOG142:10	H39	Or is't a *Norman,* whose victorious hand

NOR'S (1) [nor his]

MASSYR63:34	H421	Nor's Metamorphosis from *Ovids* Book,

NORTH (3)

ELEMEN16:28	H351	Transfers his goods, from North and South and East;
SEASONS49:6	H97	His progresse to the North; now's fully done,
MGREC133:39	H3329	And calls them there, the Kings of South, and North;

NORTHERN (4)

SEASONS47:2	H17	And now makes glad those blinded Northern wights,
SEASONS47:5	H20	And now makes glad the darkned northern wights
SEASONS51:21	H197	The Northern Winter blasts begin to hisse;
SEASONS51:39	H215	The Northern Pole beholdeth not one ray.

NORTH-WARD (2) [northward]

SEASONS52:27	H242	And North-ward his unwearied race {Course} doth run;
SEASONS52:35	H250	And North-ward stil approaches to the Line;

NORTHWARD (1) See also NORTH-WARD, NORWARD

1LETTER181:21	H19	But when thou *Northward* to me shalt return,

NORTH-WEST (1) [northwest] See also NOR-WEST

SEASONS47:27	H43	The pinching Nor-west {North-west} cold, {wind} of fierce

NORWARD (1) [northward] See also NORTH-WARD

CHILDRN184:31	H20	They *Norward* steer'd with filled sayles.

NOR-WEST (1) [northwest] See also NORTH-WEST

SEASONS47:27	H43	The pinching Nor-west {North-west} cold, {wind} of fierce

NOSE (7)

HUMOUR22:38	H107	Out at her nose, or melteth at her eyes;
HUMOUR25:7	H196	Ile go no further then thy nose for test.
HUMOUR30:40	H432	Then is thy torrid nose, or brasen brow.
MPERS74:40	H861	With his own hands cuts off his eares, and nose,
MPERS75:7	H868	For they beleev'd his nose, more then his tongue;
MPERS75:12	H873	To loose a nose, to win a Town's no shame,
MPERS82:31	H1178	Cut off her lilly breasts, her nose, and ears;

NOSES (1) [pl.]

SEASONS52:31	H246	And Travellers sometimes their noses leese.

NOT (436)

FATHER6:4	H38	I honour him, but dare not wear his wealth,
FATHER6:6	H40	But if I did, I durst not send them you;
FATHER6:8	H42	I shall not need my {mine} innocence to clear,
PROLOG6:23	H8	My obscure Verse,{Lines} shal not so dim their worth.
PROLOG6:27	H11	Foole, I doe grudge, the Muses did not part
ELEMEN9:6	H40	The adverse wall's not shak'd, the Mine's not blowne,
ELEMEN9:6	H40	The adverse wall's not shak'd, the Mine's not blowne,
ELEMEN9:17	H51	Your spits, pots, jacks, what else I need not name,
ELEMEN10:41	H116	Which when they could not be o're come by foes
ELEMEN11:13	H133	Not sparing life when I can take the same;
ELEMEN11:16	H136	Not before then, shal cease my raging ire,

ELEMEN11:22	H142	Sister, in worth {quoth shee} I come not short of you;
ELEMEN11:27	H147	Among my praises this I count not least,
ELEMEN11:36	H156	Soone would they passe, not hundreds, but legions,
ELEMEN11:39	H159	I have not time to thinke of every part,
ELEMEN12:15	H175	But ile skip {leap} o're these Hills, not touch a Dale,
ELEMEN12:16	H176	Nor will I stay, no not in *Tempe* Vale,
ELEMEN13:6	H207	Will not my goodly face, your rage suffice?
ELEMEN13:26	H227	My sap, to plants and trees, I must not grant,
ELEMEN14:30	H272	Not one of us, all knowes, that's like to thee,
ELEMEN15:11	H293	He knowes such sweets, lyes not in earths dry roots,
ELEMEN15:15	H297	If not, soon ends his life, as did his voyce.
ELEMEN15:16	H298	That this is true, earth thou canst not deny;
ELEMEN15:20	H302	When I run low, and not o'reflow her brinks;
ELEMEN15:27	H309	Such wealth, but not such like, Earth thou mayst show.
ELEMEN15:30	H312	With thousands moe, which now I list not name,
ELEMEN15:33	H315	Not thou, but shell-fish yeelds, as *Pliny* clears.
ELEMEN16:3	H326	Earth, thou hast not more Countrys, Vales and Mounds,
ELEMEN17:14	H378	I need not say much of my Haile and Snow,
ELEMEN17:23	H387	Wherein not men, but mountaines seem'd to wade
ELEMEN17:36	H400	Though {Yet am} not through ignorance, {ignorant} first was my
ELEMEN17:39	H403	Mortalls, what one of you, that loves not me,
ELEMEN18:8	H412	If my pure Aire, thy sonnes did not sustain.
ELEMEN19:19	H464	That birds have not scap'd death, as they have flown,
ELEMEN20:8	H490	But dare not go, beyond my Element.
HUMOUR20:28	H20	The second, third, or last could not digest;
HUMOUR20:30	H22	Her wisedome spake not much, but thought the more.
HUMOUR20:31	H23	Cold {Mild} flegme, did not contest for highest {chiefest} place,
HUMOUR21:28	H56	Have ye not heard of Worthies, Demi-gods?
HUMOUR21:37	H65	A Chamber wel, in field she dares not come;
HUMOUR22:9	H78	But be she beaten, she'l not run away,
HUMOUR22:10	H79	She'l first advise, if't be not best to stay.
HUMOUR22:17	H86	She dare, {dares} not challenge if I speake amisse;
HUMOUR22:24	H93	{But tis} Not from our dul slow Sisters motions:
HUMOUR22:32	H101	The nerves should I not warm, soon would they freeze.
HUMOUR23:3	H113	Thou wast not made for Souldier, or for Schollar;
HUMOUR23:10	H120	Thou canst not claime, the Liver, Head nor Heart;
HUMOUR23:38	H148	Its not your muscles, nerves, nor this nor that:
HUMOUR24:22	H171	To pay with railings, is not mine intent,
HUMOUR25:8	H197	Thy other scoffes not worthy of reply:
HUMOUR25:37	H226	Ile not envy thy feats, nor happinesse.
HUMOUR26:11	H241	For th' natural, thou dost not much contest,
HUMOUR26:12	H242	For there are {is} none, thou say'st, if some, not best.
HUMOUR26:14	H244	Of greatest use, if reason do not erre:
HUMOUR26:18	H248	Thine without mine, is not, 'tis evident:
HUMOUR26:37	H267	But i'le not force retorts, nor do thee wrong,
HUMOUR26:39	H269	Challenge not all, 'cause part we do allow,
HUMOUR27:12	H283	It is her own heat, not thy faculty,
HUMOUR27:38	H309	But here's {here} one thrusts her heat, where'ts not requir'd
HUMOUR28:9	H321	Her languishing diseases, though not quick,
HUMOUR28:35	H347	Yet could not be more breif, without much wrong.
HUMOUR28:39	H351	If modesty my worth do not conceale.

HUMOUR29:6	H359	Though Choler rage, and raile, i'le not do so,
HUMOUR29:17	~~H368~~	If not as yet, by me, thou shalt be quell'd:
HUMOUR29:19	H370	Not past all reason, but in truth all shame:
HUMOUR29:30	H381	This warinesse count not for cowardise,
HUMOUR29:31	H382	He is not truly valiant that's not wise;
HUMOUR29:31	H382	He is not truly valiant that's not wise;
HUMOUR29:33	H384	Then by assault to gain one, not our own.
HUMOUR29:36	H387	And if thy haste, my slownesse should not temper,
HUMOUR29:41	H392	But's not thy {thine} ignorance shal thus deceive me.
HUMOUR30:14	H406	If I have not more part, then al ye three:
HUMOUR30:27	H419	Likewise the useful spleen, though not the best,
HUMOUR31:6	~~H439~~	This transmutation is, but not excretion,
HUMOUR31:31	H464	Impatient Choler loveth not the sound.
HUMOUR31:32	H465	What Sanguine is, she doth not heed, nor care.
HUMOUR32:5	H479	Unto diseases not inclin'd as ye:
HUMOUR32:13	H487	Talke I love not, reason lyes not in length.
HUMOUR32:13	H487	Talke I love not, reason lyes not in length.
HUMOUR32:22	H496	I've not forgot how bitter Choler spake,
HUMOUR32:24	H498	Nor wonder 'twas, for hatred there's not smal,
HUMOUR32:33	H507	My polish'd skin was not ordain'd for skars,
HUMOUR33:40	H554	This point for {now} to discusse longs not to me,
HUMOUR34:27	H582	Then, my head {brain} for learning is not the fittest,
HUMOUR34:30	H585	For memory, the sand is not more brittle.
AGES35:33	H19	His hobby striding, did not ride, but run,
AGES36:10	H34	He seems to flye, or swim, and not to ride.
AGES37:7	H69	Her nine months weary burden not declare.
AGES37:25	H87	That its own worth, it did not know, nor mind.
AGES37:30	H92	How to be rich, or great, I did not carke;
AGES38:1	H104	My quarrells, not for Diadems did rise;
AGES38:26	H129	Then nought can please, and yet I know not why.
AGES38:38	H141	Strangely preserv'd, yet mind it not at all.
AGES39:9	H152	Then let not him, which {that} hath most craft dissemble;
AGES39:40	H182	Martial deeds I love not, 'cause they're vertuous,
AGES40:7	H188	Of all at once, who not so wise, as fair,
AGES40:32	H211	Remembring not the dreadful day of Doom,
AGES41:7	H227	That yet my bed in darknesse is not made,
AGES41:32	H249	My family to keep, but not for gaines.
AGES41:38	H255	If not, yet wealth, {riches} Nobility can gain.
AGES41:40	H257	I wanted not my ready allegation.
AGES41:41	H258	Yet all my powers, for self-ends are not spent,
AGES43:22	H317	I hate {not} for to be had, {held} in small {high'st} account.
AGES43:37	H332	And to conclude, I may not tedious be,
AGES44:12	H345	It's not my valour, honour, nor my gold,
AGES44:14	H347	It's not my Learning, Rhetorick, wit so large,
AGES44:16	H349	It's not my goodly house {state}, nor bed of down,
AGES45:11	~~H393~~	But not their Princes love, nor state so high;
SEASONS49:29	H118	Oh! happy Shepheard, which had not to lose,
SEASONS50:12	H146	For yet {For much,} the South-ward Sun abateth not;
SEASONS50:22	H156	Although their Bread have not so white a face.
SEASONS51:14	H188	For then in *Eden* was not only seen
SEASONS51:37	H213	So farre remote, his glances warm not us;

SEASONS51:39	H215	The Northern Pole beholdeth not one ray.
SEASONS52:29	H244	The cold not lessened, but augmented more.
SEASONS52:33	H248	I care not how the Winter time doth haste;
SEASONS53:4	H260	*I could {knew} not tell how to passe't by:*
SEASONS53:5	H261	*The last, though bad, I could not mend,*
MASSYR53:16	H6	Man did not {proudly} strive for Soveraignty,
MASSYR53:28	H18	Not finished, til he his race had run;
MASSYR54:1	H28	Whose acts, and power, is not for certainty,
MASSYR56:41	H147	But by what means, we are not certifi'd.
MASSYR57:34	H179	And such as care not, what befals their fames,
MASSYR59:28	H252	*Sardanapalus* did not seek to fly,
MASSYR59:38	H262	He did repent, therefore it {the threatning} was not done,
MASSYR60:6	H271	Yet would not {granting} let them {now} to inhabite there;
MASSYR60:12	H277	Not pertinent to what we have in hand;
MASSYR60:17	H282	Not so content, but aiming to be great,
MASSYR60:27	H292	The fire, those Mettals could not damnifie;
MASSYR60:40	H305	That he, and *Belochus,* one could not be,
MASSYR61:3	H308	That those two made but one, we need not doubt:
MASSYR64:28	H452	As might not him, but all the world out-face;
MASSYR64:29	H453	That in her pride, she knew not which to boast,
MASSYR65:5	H470	Requited not the cost {loss}, the toyle, and pain.
MASSYR66:13	H519	With all these Conquests, *Babels* King rests not,
MASSYR66:14	H520	No, nor {not} when *Moab, Edom* he had got.
MASSYR66:25	H531	His Image, *Iudahs* Captives worship not,
MASSYR68:18	H604	Who doth not flatter, nor once cloake the thing.
MPERS70:7	H678	That all the world they neither {need not} feare, nor doubt;
MPERS70:13	H684	Not finding a defendant thereupon;
MPERS71:24	H738	The Temples {Their Temple} he destroyes not, for his zeal,
MPERS73:39	H824	What arguments they us'd, I know not well,
MPERS75:6	H867	This told, for enterance he stood not long,
MPERS75:21	H880	Thy falshood, not thy {craft more then} valour did prevaile;
MPERS76:4	H902	Sharp wants, not swords, his vallour did oppose;
MPERS76:8	H906	He warr'd defensive, not offensive, more;
MPERS76:14	H912	But wise *Gobrias* reads not half so farre:
MPERS77:17	H958	The {His} Father not so full of lenity,
MPERS79:29	H1055	Which was not vaine, as it {after} soon appeared:
MPERS80:16	H1083	{The Harbours} to receive, {contain} the Harbour was not able;
MPERS82:6	H1153	The other not a hand, nor sword will {would} wave,
MPERS82:22	H1169	Yet ceases not to act his villany:
MPERS83:21	H1209	For which he dyed, and not he alone.
MPERS83:31	H1219	Although to *Xerxes,* they not long before,
MPERS84:19	H1255	The King not little joyfull of this chance,
MPERS84:27	H1263	Who for his wrong, he could not chuse but deem,
MPERS86:10	H1326	Yet doubts, {fears} all he injoyes, is not his own.
MPERS86:20	H1336	To win by force, what right could not obtain.
MPERS87:22	H1374	Not worthy to be known, but for his shame:
MPERS87:29	H1381	Had not a Captain; {his Captains} sore against his will;
MPERS87:35	H1387	Yet for his brothers comming, durst not stay,
MPERS87:38	H1390	Rejoyced {Was} not a little {jocund} at his feare.
MPERS88:14	H1407	But long under their fears, they did not stay,
MPERS88:19	H1412	Had not his too much valour put him by.

MPERS88:28	H1421	His Host in chase, knowes not of his {this} disaster,
MPERS89:29	H1463	The King's {King} perplext, there dares not let them stay,
MPERS90:17	~~H1484~~	For these incursions he durst not abide;
MPERS~~91:25~~	H1539	But long in ease and pleasure did not lye,
MPERS91:37	~~H1551~~	Made Writers work at home, they sought not far?
MPERS91:39	~~H1553~~	Their Acts recorded not, as heretofore
MPERS92:8	~~H1566~~	So fell to him, which else it had not done:
MPERS92:9	H1567	What Acts he did, time hath not now left pend,
MPERS92:17	~~H1575~~	By favour, force, or fraud, is not set down:
MPERS92:18	~~H1576~~	If not (as is before) of *Cyrus* race,
MPERS92:21	~~H1579~~	And that great *Cyrus* line, yet was not run,
MPERS92:26	~~H1584~~	Thus learned *Pemble,* whom we may not slight,
MPERS~~92:26~~	H1584	Some write great *Cyrus* line was not yet run,
MPERS~~92:28~~	H1586	If so, or not, we cannot tell, but find
MGREC93:34	H1631	(For as worlds Monarch, now we speak not on,
MGREC95:22	H1701	stead} *Arsemes* {*Arses*} was plac'd, yet {but} durst not stay;
MGREC96:10	H1730	An object not so much of fear, as laughter.
MGREC96:30	H1750	Had not been spoile, and booty rich enough,
MGREC97:23	H1784	By too much heat, not wounds (as Authors write.)
MGREC97:32	H1793	But down his haughty stomach could not bring,
MGREC97:36	H1797	A King he was, and that not only so,
MGREC98:5	H1807	But they accept not this, in any wise,
MGREC98:12	H1814	He leaves not, till he makes {made} the sea firme shoar;
MGREC99:10	H1853	*Darius* offers I would not reject,
MGREC99:33	H1876	Why didst not heap up honour, and reward?
MGREC100:10	H1894	That his humanity will not retaine;
MGREC~~100:36~~	H1920	The more because not set at liberty;
MGREC101:17	H1942	No, though *Parmenio* plead, he {yet} will not heare;
MGREC~~101:34~~	H1963	But long they stood not e're they're forc'd to run,
MGREC101:37	H1966	But 'tis not known what slaughters here they {was} made.
MGREC103:7	H2018	Yet to compare with this, they might not do.
MGREC104:6	H2058	Perswades him not to fight, with *Alexander.*
MGREC105:20	H2113	Who not a little chear'd, to have some eye,
MGREC105:24	H2117	And not to pardon such disloyalty,
MGREC105:26	H2119	If not, because *Darius* thus did pray,
MGREC105:29	H2122	And not by Traitors hands untimely dye.
MGREC106:24	H2158	And not beseeming such a dignity;
MGREC107:40	H2215	But coward, durst not fight, nor could he fly,
MGREC108:9	H2225	These not a little joy'd, this day to see,
MGREC108:34	H2250	Whose {Their} nakednesse could not endure their might;
MGREC108:38	H2254	And furlongs sixty could not {but} round the same.
MGREC109:3	H2260	Those that {Such as} doe not, both they, {them} and theirs, are
MGREC109:29	H2288	But *Porus* stout, who will not yeeld as yet;
MGREC110:6	H2306	On *Tygris* side, here now he had not been;
MGREC~~110:18~~	H2320	In looks or gesture not abased ought,
MGREC111:15	H2360	Which could not sound too oft, with too much fame;
MGREC111:21	H2366	Upon those Flats they did not long abide;
MGREC112:20	H2406	*Philotas* was not least, nor yet the last;
MGREC112:21	H2407	Accus'd, because he did not certifie
MGREC112:30	H2416	Must suffer, not for what he did, but thought:
MGREC113:16	H2443	They knew not; wherefore, best now to be done,

MGREC114:21	H2491	In his esteem, a God he could not be,
MGREC114:28	H2498	This censure passe, and not unwisely, say,
MGREC114:30	H2500	Which shall not be obliterate by time,
MGREC114:39	H2509	All this he did, who knows not to be true,
MGREC115:15	H2531	What e're he did, or thought not so content,
MGREC115:21	H2540	(Not suffering her to meddle in {with} the State)
MGREC115:29	H2548	Or if remembred, yet regarded not;
MGREC116:34	H2600	And fame not last unto Eternity:
MGREC117:38	H2645	Claim'd not, perhaps her Sex might hindrance be.
MGREC118:19	H2666	And yet not so content, unlesse that he
MGREC118:24	H2673	That for a while they durst not come so near:
MGREC119:27	H2717	He joyn not with *Antipater,* that {their} foe.
MGREC120:13	H2748	Yet to regain them, how he did not know,
MGREC120:14	H2749	For's Souldiers 'gainst those Captains would not goe;
MGREC120:20	H2755	If not in word {stile}, in deed a Soveraigne.
MGREC120:38	H2775	And yet till now, at quiet was not laid.
MGREC121:15	H2794	Who could not book so great indignity,
MGREC122:13	H2838	Perceives {Sees} *Aridæus* must not king it long,
MGREC123:28	H2892	*Cassander* could not (like his father) see
MGREC125:30	H2980	This done, the cruell Queen rests not content,
MGREC126:16	H3007	Cassander will not heare {Her foe would give no Ear}, such is
MGREC129:21	H3135	But from {by} their hands, who thought not once of this.
MGREC129:40	H3154	*Antigonus* for all this doth not mourn,
MGREC130:4	H3159	And vile {lewd} *Cassander* too, sticks not for shame;
MGREC130:14	H3169	So hinders him of her, he could not gain.
MGREC130:22	H3177	Except *Cassanders* wife, who yet not dead,
MGREC130:33	H3181	If *Alexander* was not poysoned,
MGREC131:3	H3193	Not like a King, but like some God they fain'd;
MGREC131:23	H3215	Tries foes, since friends will not compassionate,
MGREC131:29	H3221	Yet dares {durst} not say, he loves {lov'd} his fathers wife;
MGREC132:4	H3237	(Whose daughter unto wife, he'd newly {not long before} ta'n)
MGREC135:4	H3376	For 'twas not death, nor danger, she did dread,
MGREC135:41	H3413	This taske befits not women, like to men:
MGREC136:18	H3432	*As faults proceeding from my head, not heart.*
MROMAN136:25	H3439	His Father was not *Mars,* as some devis'd,
MROMAN136:27	H3441	Thus he deceiv'd his Neece, she might not know
MROMAN139:1	H3529	Ascends not up, by merits of his owne,
MROMAN139:37	H3563	And for the same, I hours not few did spend,
DIALOG141:19	H18	And thou a childe, a Limbe, and dost not feele
DIALOG141:27	H26	Then weigh our case, if't be not justly sad,
DIALOG142:1	H30	In generall terms, but will not say wherefore:
DIALOG142:3	H32	If th' wound's {wound} so dangerous I may not know?
DIALOG142:23	H52	Pray, doe not {you} feare *Spaines* bragging Armado?
DIALOG143:18	H87	But trust not much unto his Excellence;
DIALOG143:25	H94	But yet, I answer not what you demand,
DIALOG144:4	H114	From crying bloods, yet cleansed am not I,
DIALOG144:25	H134	I then believ'd not, now I feel and see,
DIALOG145:3	H152	My {Mine} heart obdurate, stood not yet agast.
DIALOG145:12	H161	Not what you feel, but what you do expect.
DIALOG145:27	H176	Had they not held law fast, all had been gone,
DIALOG145:35	H184	This must be done by Gospel, not by law.

DIALOG145:37	H186	This was deny'd, I need not say wherefore.
DIALOG146:20	H206	Because he knows not, who shall inn his crop:
DIALOG147:6	H232	And shall I not on those {them} with *Mero's* curse,
DIALOG147:7	H233	That help thee not with prayers, arms, and purse,
DIALOG147:19	H245	Not false to King, nor Countrey in thy heart, {to the better part;}
DIALOG147:40	H264	Then bribes shall cease, and suits shall not stick long,
DIALOG148:32	H297	But if at all, thou didst not see't before.
SIDNEY149:21	H20	Are not his Tragick Comedies so acted,
SIDNEY149:25	H23	I praise thee not for this, it is unfit,
SIDNEY150:9	H34	That sees not learning, valour, and morality,
SIDNEY150:12	H37	Such were prejudicate, and did not look:
SIDNEY150:30	H57	He rescued not with life, that life of thine,
SIDNEY151:22	H72	With endlesse turnes, the way I find not out,
SIDNEY152:14	H84	Then wonder not if I no better sped,
SIDNEY152:15	H85	Not because, sweet *Sydney's* fame was not dear,
DUBART153:40	H44	Sure liberall Nature, did with Art not small,
DUBART154:33	H78	Thy sacred works are not for imitation,
DUBART154:40	H85	Good will, not skill, did cause me bring my mite.
QELIZ156:9	H36	*Spaines* Monarch sa's not so; nor yet his Hoast,
QELIZ156:11	H38	The *Salique* Law had not in force now been,
QELIZ157:27	H95	Her ashes not reviv'd more Phoenix she;
QELIZ157:30	H98	Which I may not, my pride doth but aspire,
QELIZ157:41	H109	Then wonder not, *Eliza* moves not here.
QELIZ157:41	H109	Then wonder not, *Eliza* moves not here.
DAVID158:28	H8	In *Gath,* let not this thing {things} be spoken on,
DAVID159:20	H35	In mid'st of strength not succoured at all:
VANITY160:17	H27	He knows not all, that here is to be known,
VANITY160:22	H32	If not in honour, beauty, age, nor treasure,
VANITY160:30	H40	The depth, and sea, hath {have} said its not in me,
VANITY160:31	H41	With pearl and gold it shall not valued be:
VANITY160:36	H46	It brings to honour, which shall not {ne're} decay,
TDUDLEY165:4	H6	By duty bound, and not by custome led
TDUDLEY165:25	H27	While others tell his worth, I'le not be dumb:
TDUDLEY165:36	H38	Upon the earth he did not build his nest,
CONTEM167:33	H9	I wist not what to wish, yet sure thought I,
CONTEM168:21	H29	Had I not better known, (alas) the same had I.
CONTEM170:30	H100	Who fancyes not his looks now at the Barr,
CONTEM171:2	H107	Who thinks not oft upon the Fathers ages.
CONTEM172:35	H168	So nature taught, and yet you know not why,
CONTEM172:36	H169	You watry folk that know not your felicity.
CONTEM173:24	H190	Reminds not what is past, nor whats to come dost fear.
CONTEM174:8	H208	Joyes not in hope of an eternal morrow;
CONTEM174:31	H228	Their sumptuous monuments, men know them not,
FLESH175:21	H21	To catch at shadowes which are not?
FLESH175:36	H36	Then let not goe, what thou maist find,
FLESH176:6	H46	For from one father are we not,
FLESH176:26	H66	How I do live, thou need'st not scoff,
FLESH176:27	H67	For I have meat thou know'st not off;
FLESH176:40	H80	My garments are not silk nor gold,
FLESH177:3	H84	My Crown not Diamonds, Pearls, and gold,
FLESH177:25	H106	This City pure is not for thee,

FLESH177:26	H107	For things unclean there shall not be:
AUTHOR177:35	H7	Where errors were not lessened (all may judg).
AUTHOR177:36	H8	At thy return my blushing was not small,
AUTHOR178:11	H21	In Criticks hands, beware thou dost not come;
AUTHOR178:12	H22	And take thy way where yet thou art not known,
SICKNES178:18	H1	Twice ten years old, not fully told
BIRTH180:5	H15	And if I see not half my dayes that's due,
1LETTER181:25	H23	Where ever, ever stay, and go not thence,
2LETTER182:17	H23	And when thou canst not treat by loving mouth,
2LETTER182:34	H40	By all our loves conjure him not to stay.
VERSES184:4	H8	My stock's so small, I know not how to pay,
VERSES184:8	H12	Such is my debt, I may not say forgive,
VERSES184:11	H15	Yet paying is not payd until I dye.
CHILDRN184:24	H13	Leave not thy nest, thy Dam and Sire,
CHILDRN186:8	H75	My age I will not once lament,
1SIMON188:9	H10	Such was his will, but why, let's not dispute,
MERCY189:1	H22	Thou being gone, she longer could not be,
MEDDM196:33	Hp274	wch thousands of enemys wthout hath not been able to take
MEDDM197:1	Hp274	temptations of Sathan without could not hurt, hath, been foild
MEDDM197:11	Hp274	If we had no winter the spring would not be so pleasant, if we
MEDDM197:11	Hp274	had no winter the spring would not be so pleasant, if we did not
MEDDM197:12	Hp274	times tast of adversity, prosperity would not be so welcome
MEDDM197:18	Hp275	That house wch is not often swept makes the cleanly inhabitant
MEDDM197:19	Hp275	it, and that heart wch is not continually purifieing it self is no
MEDDM197:22	Hp275	Few men are so humble, as not to be proud of their abilitys,
MEDDM197:27	Hp275	will finde it a wearysome if not an impossible task so he that
MEDDM197:32	Hp275	is not fit for bread, god so deales wth his servants, he grindes
MEDDM198:32	Hp277	pleasant thing to behold the light, but sore eyes are not able to
MEDDM199:6	Hp277	do not often fall till after threat'ning.
MEDDM200:3	Hp278	sin, is it not a little one? will ere long say of a greater Tush god
MEDDM200:4	Hp278	it not
MEDDM200:15	Hp279	A prudent mother will not cloth her little childe wth a long and
MEDDM200:33	Hp280	A wise father will not lay a burden on a child of seven yeares
MEDDM201:4	Hp280	go vpright vnder them, but it matters not whether the load be
MEDDM201:9	Hp280	by many, but what he did not say, cannot (truly) be vttered
MEDDM201:12	Hp280	Fire hath its force abated by water not by wind, and anger
MEDDM201:13	Hp280	alayed, by cold words and not by blustering threats.
MEDDM201:19	Hp280	often se stones hang wth drops not from any innate moisture,
MEDDM201:21	Hp281	seem full of contrition, but it is not from any dew of grace
MEDDM201:28	Hp281	not only to bid them hold fast the form of sound Doctrin, but
MEDDM202:33	Hp282	obiects enter, yet is not that spacious roome filled neither
MEDDM203:2	Hp283	Had not the wisest of men, taught vs this lesson, that all is
MEDDM203:21	Hp283	neuer felt, what it was to be sick or wounded, doth not much
MEDDM203:25	Hp283	of a guilty Conscience, cares not how far he keeps from him
MEDDM204:23	Hp285	fixe his eye on the command, and not on his own ends, lest he
MEDDM204:26	Hp285	would be content, wth a mean condition, must not cast his eye
MEDDM204:29	Hp285	comfortably it will help to quiet him, but if that will not do
MEDDM205:16	Hp286	Court of Judicature, that there is no appeale from it, no not to
MEDDM205:27	Hp286	or else we should not so often faile in our whole Course of
MEDDM205:29	Hp286	will not sinne against him.
MEDDM205:37	Hp287	and ther are some (and they sincere ones too) who haue not

MEDDM206:22	Hp287	at a Compensation then at a pardon, but he that will not Come
MEDDM206:31	Hp288	of god, who will not be tyed to time nor place, nor yet
MEDDM206:36	Hp288	they abide not in vnbeleif, god is able to grafte them in, the
MEDDM207:4	Hp288	that god, bestows on the sons of men, are not only abused
MEDDM207:9	Hp288	lords we will come no more at thee If outward blessings, be not
MEDDM207:29	Hp289	may be sure of an euer lasting habitation that fades not away.
MEDDM207:34	Hp289	not only their death, but their graue, is liuely represented
MEDDM208:13	Hp290	to haue a good repute among good men, yet it is not that, w^{ch}
MEDDM209:2	Hp291	will not let thee go replys Jacob till thou blesse me, faith is not
MEDDM209:8	Hp291	by the Canaanites, not destroy them, but put them vnder
MEDDM209:13	Hp291	Command of god, and endeavour not to the vtmost to driue
MEDDM209:24	Hp291	(perhaps meaner then himself) wch shews us perfection is not
PILGRIM210:13	H13	for waters cold he doth not long
MYCHILD215:15	Hp240	not) and bequeath to yov, that when I am no more wth yov, yet
MYCHILD215:18	Hp240	haue not studyed in this yov read to shew my skill, but to
MYCHILD215:19	Hp240	Truth, not to sett forth my self, but ye Glory of God. If I had
MYCHILD215:27	Hp240	a great Trouble, & I could not be at rest 'till by prayer I had
MYCHILD216:6	Hp241	me. But I rendered not to him according to ye benefitt rec.
MYCHILD216:13	Hp241	try me & doe me Good: and it was not altogether ineffectuall. It
MYCHILD217:15	Hp243	I haue often been p^{r}plexed y^t I haue not fovnd that constant
MYCHILD217:17	Hp243	haue, although he hath not left me altogether wthout a
MYCHILD217:20	Hp243	world knowes not, & haue sett vp my Ebenez^r. and haue
MYCHILD217:23	Hp243	not enjoyed that felicity that somt. I haue done, But when I
MYCHILD218:9	Hp244	mvst bee it or none. Haue I not fovnd y^t operation by it that no
MYCHILD218:11	Hp244	who haue scornd + contemd it, hath it not been p^{r}served thro:
MYCHILD218:14	Hp244	+ how ye world came to bee as wee see, Do wee not know y^e
MYCHILD218:15	Hp244	prophecyes in it fullfilled wch could not haue been so long
MYCHILD218:19	Hp244	word, yet why may not ye popish Relign. bee ye right, They
MYCHILD218:24	Hp244	of the Saints, wch admitt were y^y as they terme y^m yet not
MYCHILD218:31	Hp244	there Faith vpon ye Earth? & I haue not known what to think,
BYNIGHT220:10	H10	In vain I did not seek or cry.
FEVER220:29	H9	So faint I could not speak.
FEVER220:34	H14	Hide not thy face from me I cry'd
FAINTING222:13	H3	But ah! it's not in me
MED223:2	Hp250	Consolations wch the world knowes not.
MED223:5	Hp250	master I thy servant, But hence arises not my comfort, Thou
MED223:8	Hp250	vnto my God and your God—But least this should not bee
MED223:10	Hp250	he my head. Such priviledges had not ye word of Truth made
JULY223:21	Hp251	fitt of fainting wch lasted 2 or 3 dayes, but not in y^t xtremity
JULY223:24	Hp251	God who never failed me, was not absent but helped me, and
JULY223:25	Hp251	manifested his Love to me, wch I dare not passe by without
JULY223:31	Hp251	for thov art my God, Thou hast said and shall not I beleiue it?
WHAT224:13	H13	My God he is not like to y^{rs}
WHAT224:17	H17	He is not man y^t he should lye.
28AUG225:30	Hp254	doth not afflict willingly, nor take delight in greiving ye children
28AUG226:1	Hp254	me a vessell fitt for his vse why should I not bare it not only
28AUG226:2	Hp254	but joyfully? The Lord knowes I dare not desire that health
28AUG226:10	Hp254	O let me ever see Thee that Art invisible, and I shall not bee
11MAYA226:24	Hp255	a little while and he that shall come will come and will not tarry.
30SEPT227:19	Hp257	but not in y^t sore manner somt. he hath. I desire not only
30SEPT227:19	Hp257	not in y^t sore manner somt. he hath. I desire not only willingly

30SEPT227:24	Hp257	then thy stroakes shall bee welcome, I haue not been refined
30SEPT227:32	Hp257	yov out of distresse forget not to giue him thankes, but to walk
11MAYB228:33	Hp259	testefye my thankfullnes not only in word, but in Deed, that my
THEART229:14	H16	My praise lyes not in Talk.
RESTOR230:5	H20	Praises to him who hath not left
2HUSB232:14	H15	O help and bee not slack.
2HUSB232:18	H19	Hide not thy face Away.
2HUSB232:24	H25	Impute thov not to me
2HUSB233:5	H38	Let not thine own Inheritance
HOURS234:7	H21	And when I know not what to doe
HOURS234:15	H29	Yet if I see Thee not thro: them
HOUSE236:14	H6	For sorrow neer I did not look,
HOUSE236:22	H14	And not to leaue me succourlesse.
HOUSE236:29	H21	It was his own it was not mine

NOTE (1)

ELEMEN16:11	~~H334~~	But note this maxime in Philosophy:

NOTES (3) [pl.]

ELEMEN18:20	H424	And so's the notes which Nightingales do frame.
SEASONS51:26	H202	Which notes, when youth, and strength, have past their prime,
CONTEM173:27	H192	Sets hundred notes unto thy feathered crew,

NOTHING (28)

ELEMEN11:32	H152	Would so passe time, I could say nothing else;
HUMOUR28:31	H343	And nothing wanting but solidity.
HUMOUR30:35	H427	Of al the rest, thou'st nothing there to do;
HUMOUR31:27	H460	Constant in nothing, but inconstancy {unconstancy},
HUMOUR32:29	H503	And when i've nothing left to say, be mute;
AGES37:3	H65	A nothing, here to day, but {and} gone to morrow.
MASSYR62:38	H383	Which made his Army into nothing melt;
MASSYR66:4	H510	Was nothing, but such gastly meditation;
MGREC105:41	H2134	I've nothing left, at this my dying hour;
MGREC112:24	H2410	Nothing was found {prov'd}, wherein he had offended;
MGREC114:3	H2471	Nothing more pleasing to mad *Clitus* tongue,
MGREC114:5	H2473	Nothing toucht *Alexander* to the quick
MGREC119:1	H2691	But nothing lesse: each one himself intends.
MGREC126:20	H3011	Expecting nothing, but of death to taste;
MGREC130:23	H3178	And by their means, who thought of nothing lesse
FLESH175:11	H11	Nothing but Meditation?
SICKNES179:5	H25	Bestow much cost there's nothing lost,
2SIMON195:7	Hp271	you should see me no more, I could think of nothing more
2SIMON195:11	Hp271	conceptions because I would leaue you nothing but myne
MEDDM195:35	Hp272	and both by an empty old age, he that hath nothing to feed on
MEDDM196:29	Hp273	nothing but salt will keep from putrefaction, some again like
MEDDM197:23	Hp275	nothing will abase them more, then this What hast thou, but
MEDDM198:21	Hp276	is no new thing vnder ye Sun there is nothing that can be sayd
MEDDM199:21	Hp278	of both, and findes nothing but vanity and vexation of spirit
MEDDM202:2	Hp281	There is nothing admits of more admiration, then gods various
MEDDM205:33	Hp286	and some haue nothing to shew but leaues only, and some
MEDDM206:2	Hp287	there are others that haue nothing to commend them, but only
MEDDM208:20	Hp290	But perform nothing, and so leaue those in the lurch that most

NOTHING'S (1) [nothing is]

VERSES184:7	H11	Where nothing's to be had Kings loose their right

NOTHUS (3)

MPERS85:3	H1279	*Daryus Nothus.*
MPERS85:8	H1284	Then the surviver is by *Nothus* slaine;
MPERS86:6	H1322	{this} *Nothus* reign'd {'bout} nineteen years, which run,

NOTICE (2)

MPERS85:38	H1314	His father would no notice of that take;
MGREC107:1	H2176	But yet no notice takes, of what he hears;

NOTION (2)

ELEMEN17:12	H376	Some say I swallowed up (sure 'tis a notion)
FLESH175:15	H15	Notion without Reality?

NOTIONS (1) [pl.]

HUMOUR22:23	H92	{From} Whence flow fine spirits, and witty notions?

NOTORIOUS (1)

MASSYR68:20	H606	And of his own notorious sins, withall;

NOTW^{TH}STANDING (1) [notwithstanding]

MEDDM207:14	Hp288	that notw^{th}standing we take great delight, for a season in

NOTWITHSTANDING (1)

MPERS74:32	H855	Yet notwithstanding he did all so well,

NOUGHT (18) See also NOVGHT

PROLOG7:26	H38	The *Greeks* did nought, but play the foole and lye.
ELEMEN9:38	H72	And though nought but *Sal'manders* live in fire;
ELEMEN16:8	H331	*Asphaltis* Lake, where nought remains alive.
ELEMEN19:25	H470	If nought was {were} known, but that before *Algire.*
AGES37:39	H101	I'd nought to do, 'twixt Prince, {King} and peoples strife.
AGES38:26	H129	Then nought can please, and yet I know not why.
AGES43:16	H311	The bottom nought, and so no longer stood.
MASSYR62:7	H352	To *Ægypts* King, which did avail him nought;
MPERS69:38	H664	And viewing all, at all nought mov'd was he:
MPERS85:7	H1283	That nought appeas'd him, but his brothers life.
MPERS91:13	H1521	Whose courage nought but death could ever tame,
MGREC114:12	H2480	Nought but his life for this could satisfie;
MGREC116:31	H2597	Ambitious so, that nought could satisfie.
DIALOG144:7	H117	For nought, but title to a fading Crown?
DUBART153:24	H28	But seeing empty wishes nought obtaine,
CONTEM168:13	H22	If so, all these as nought, Eternity doth scorn.
AUTHOR178:9	H19	But nought save home-spun Cloth, i' th' house I find.
2LETTER182:29	H35	Nought but the fervor of his ardent beams

NOUGHT'S (1) [nought is]

SEASONS51:4	H178	For nought's so good, but it may be abused,

NOURISH (2)

SEASONS47:39	H51	growes long, the tender Lambs {hungry beast} to nourish;
DIALOG148:4	H269	When truth and righteousnesse they thus shall nourish.

NOURISHED (1)

MASSYR55:18	H84	For which, she was obscurely nourished.

NOURISHMENT (3)

HUMOUR26:17	H247	If thou giv'st life, I give thee nourishment,
MPERS69:17	H639	His nourishment afforded by a Bitch,
MPERS90:5	H1478	So to deprive them of all nourishment;

NOURISHT (1)

AGES42:7	H265	The lyars curb'd but nourisht verity.

NOVEM (1) [november]

SAMUEL228:1   H1-2   Vpon my Son Samuel his goeing for England Novem. 6. 1657.

NOVEMB (1) [november]

1SIMON188:2   H2-3   *Who dyed on* 16. Novemb. 1669. *being but*

NOVEMBER (1)

SEASONS51:34   H210   *November* is my last, for time doth haste,

NOVGHT (4) [nought]

FEVER221:4   H19   Tho: flesh consume to novght,

SOREFIT221:17   H3   When novght on Earth could comfort giue

2HUSB232:12   H13   Nor novght could keep him back

2HUSB233:6   H39   Bee sold away for Novght.

NOW (369)

FATHER5:13   H14   I bring my four times {and} four, now meanly clad,

ELEMEN8:8   H6   In placide terms they thought now to discourse,

ELEMEN8:26   H24   All stormes now laid, and they in perfect peace,

ELEMEN11:18   H138   Now Sisters, pray proceed, each in her {your} course,

ELEMEN11:38   H158   Whose numbers now are growne innumerous;

ELEMEN12:24   H184   But here, or there, I list now none to name;

ELEMEN13:22   H223   Now might {must} I shew my {mine} adverse quality,

ELEMEN15:30   H312   With thousands moe, which now I list not name,

ELEMEN16:32   H355   I now must shew what force {ill} there in me lyes.

ELEMEN17:33   H397   And now give place unto our sister Aire.

ELEMEN19:10   H455   With thousands moe, which now I may omit;

HUMOUR20:11   H3   The former foure, now ending their Discourse,

HUMOUR21:9   H37   Now Feminines (a while) for love we owe

HUMOUR22:11   H80   But {Now} let's give, cold, white, Sister Flegme her right.

HUMOUR22:19   H88   Here's three of you, all sees {see} now what you are,

HUMOUR22:33   H102   But Flegme her self, is now provok'd at this,

HUMOUR24:9   H158   To what you now shal say, I wil attend,

HUMOUR25:11   H200   But now Ile shew, what Souldier thou art.

HUMOUR26:16   H246   His life now animal, from vegative?

HUMOUR27:20   H291   Now through your leaves, some little time i'le spend;

HUMOUR29:15   H368   And in contentions lists, now justly enter.

HUMOUR31:8   H441   Now {But} by your leave, Ile let your greatnesse see;

HUMOUR31:20   H453   I now speake unto al, no more to one;

HUMOUR31:33   H466   Now up, now down, transported like the Aire.

HUMOUR31:33   H466   Now up, now down, transported like the Aire.

HUMOUR31:38   H471   Now could I stain my ruddy sisters face,

HUMOUR32:3   H477   My prudence, judgement, now I might reveale,

HUMOUR32:21   H495   Enough of both, my wrongs for {now} to expresse;

HUMOUR33:18   H532   With all your flourishes, now Sisters three,

HUMOUR33:40   H554   This point for {now} to discusse longs not to me,

HUMOUR34:41   H596   Let's now be freinds, 'tis {its} time our spight was {were} spent,

AGES35:17   H3   Loe now! four other acts {act} upon the stage,

AGES36:37   H61   With heed now stood, three ages of fraile man;

AGES38:40   H143   That wonder tis, my glasse till now doth hold.

AGES40:23   H204   *Sardana Pallas,* now survives in me:

AGES41:8   H228   And I in black oblivions den long {now} laid;

AGES41:16   H235   And now am grown more staid, that {who} have been green,

AGES41:19   H238   Now age is more, more good ye do {may} expect;

AGES43:26   H321   Now in a word, what my diseases be.

AGES44:9	H342	But now, *Bis pueri senes,* is too true;
AGES44:11	H344	An end of all perfection now I see.
AGES44:13	H346	My ruin'd house, now falling can uphold;
AGES44:15	H348	Now hath the power, Deaths Warfare, to discharge;
AGES44:18	H351	Nor from alliance now can I have hope,
AGES45:27	H417	My {Mine} Almond-tree (gray haires) doth flourish now,
AGES45:29	H419	My grinders now are few, my sight doth faile
AGES45:38	H428	Now stiffe and numb, can hardly creep or go.
AGES45:40	H430	Now trembling, and {is all} fearful, sad, and cold;
AGES46:15	H446	And my last period now e'n almost run;
SEASONS47:2	~~H17~~	And now makes glad those blinded Northern wights,
SEASONS~~47:5~~	H20	And now makes glad the darkned northern wights
SEASONS47:6	H22	Now goes the Plow-man to his merry toyl,
SEASONS47:8	H24	The Seeds-man now {too} doth lavish out his Grain,
SEASONS47:10	H26	The Gardner, now superfluous branches lops,
SEASONS47:12	H28	Now digs, then sows, his hearbs, his flowers, and roots,
SEASONS47:14	H30	The Pleiades, their influence now give,
SEASONS47:17	H33	Like Birds, now chirp, and hop about the field;
SEASONS47:19	H35	Now tune their layes, on sprays of every bush;
SEASONS47:21	H37	Now {Do} jump, and play, before their feeding Dams,
SEASONS47:30	~~H45~~	The Sun now keeps his posting residence
SEASONS47:38	H50	The Pear, the Plumbe, and Apple-tree now flourish,
SEASONS48:3	H56	The fearful Bird, his little house now builds,
SEASONS48:7	H60	clocking hen, her chipping brood now {chirping chickins} leads,
SEASONS48:11	H64	The sun now enters, loving *Geminie,*
SEASONS48:15	H68	All flowers before the {with his} sun-beames now discloses,
SEASONS48:17	H70	Now swarmes the busie buzzing {witty,} hony Bee.
SEASONS49:7	H98	And {Then} retrograde, now is {must be} my burning Sun.
SEASONS49:16	H107	Now go those frolick swaines, the shepheard lad,
SEASONS49:36	H129	The Cherry, Goos-berry, is {are} now i'th prime,
SEASONS49:39	H132	The Sun in {thro} Leo now hath {takes} his carrear,
SEASONS50:3	H137	Now go the Mowers to their slashing toyl,
SEASONS50:17	H151	With Sickles now, the painful {bending} Reapers go,
SEASONS50:39	H173	Now day and night are equal in each clime;
SEASONS51:2	H176	The Vintage now is ripe, the Grapes are prest,
SEASONS51:6	H180	The Raisins now in clusters dryed be,
SEASONS51:9	H183	And Apples now their yellow sides do show;
SEASONS51:11	H185	The season's now at hand, of all, and each;
SEASONS51:22	H198	In *Scorpio* resideth now the Sun,
SEASONS51:24	H200	The fruitful trees, all withered now do stand,
SEASONS51:35	H211	We now of Winters sharpness 'gin to taste;
SEASONS51:40	H216	Now *Green-land, Groen-land, Lap-land, Fin-land,* see
SEASONS52:5	H220	Beef, Brawn, and Pork, are now in great'st {great} request,
SEASONS52:12	H227	What Winter hath to tel, now let him say.
SEASONS52:14	H229	Cold, moist, young, flegmy Winter now doth lye
SEASONS52:18	H233	*December* is the {my} first, and now the Sun
SEASONS52:26	H241	In *Aquarias,* now keeps the loved {long wisht} Sun,
SEASONS52:30	H245	Now toes, and eares, and fingers often freeze,
SEASONS52:34	H249	In *Pisces* now the golden Sun doth shine,
SEASONS52:36	H251	The Rivers now do {'gin to} ope, and {the} Snows do {to} melt,
MASSYR57:21	~~H168~~	Would now advantage take, their own to gain;

MASSYR~~58:37~~	H220	Makes {With} promises, their necks for {now} to un-yoak,
MASSYR~~59:8~~	H232	But all {And now} surpris'd, by this unlookt for fright,
MASSYR59:24	H248	And now they saw fulfill'd a Prophesie;
MASSYR59:39	H263	But was accomplished now, in his {wicked} Son.
MASSYR~~60:6~~	H271	Yet would not {granting} let them {now} to inhabite there;
MASSYR61:35	H340	Through *Syria* now he marcht, none stopt his way,
MASSYR62:13	H358	Did Justice now, by him, eradicate: [10 *years.*
MASSYR62:22	H367	Where now those ten Tribes are, can no man tel,
MASSYR63:9	H394	So he's now stil'd, the King of *Babylon;*
MASSYR63:26	H411	Now yeelds her neck unto captivity: [12 *years.*
MASSYR65:14	H479	But he (alas) whose fortunes {all were} now i'th ebbe,
MASSYR65:31	H496	*Iudah* {They} lost more {now} (then e're they lost) by him;
MASSYR65:37	H502	The wals so strong, that stood so long, now fall;
MASSYR66:5	H511	In mid'st of *Babel* now, til death he lyes,
MASSYR66:10	H516	Now *Zim,* and *Iim, {Jim}* lift up their shriking {scrieching}
MASSYR66:11	H517	All now of worth, are captive led with tears,
MASSYR66:20	H526	To *Babylons* proud King, now yeelds the day.
MASSYR67:2	H548	*Babels* great Monarch, now laid in the dust,
MASSYR67:9	H555	Is *Judah's* King, now lifted up on high.
MASSYR67:30	H576	To banquetting, and revelling now falls,
MASSYR68:16	H602	Was held in more request, {account} then now he was,
MASSYR68:30	H616	And now the *Persian* Monarchy began.
MPERS69:40	H670	Now up, now {and} down, as fortune turnes her hand,
MPERS69:40	H670	Now up, now {and} down, as fortune turnes her hand,
MPERS70:6	H677	Now trebble wall'd, and moated so about,
MPERS70:22	H693	*Cyrus* doth now the *Jewish* captives free,
MPERS~~71:4~~	H718	Now quiet lyes under one marble stone.
MPERS72:7	~~H756~~	*Praraspes* now must act this tragedy;
MPERS73:5	H792	The Male line, of great *Cyrus* now did {had} end.
MPERS73:24	~~H809~~	And now with his accomplyces lye slaine.
MPERS73:31	H816	What forme of Government now to erect,
MPERS74:13	~~H836~~	His happy wishes now doth no man spare,
MPERS74:16	H839	Let tyranny now with {dead} *Cambyses* dye.
MPERS74:22	H845	He two of *Cyrus* Daughters now {then} doth wed,
MPERS74:26	H849	And now a King, by marriage, choyce, and bloud,
MPERS74:37	~~H858~~	And fear'd, he now with scorn must march away:
MPERS75:28	H885	He like a King, now grants a Charter large,
MPERS76:27	H925	But as before, so now with ill successe,
MPERS76:29	H927	*Athens* perceiving now their desperate state,
MPERS77:16	H955	Grand-childe to *Cyrus,* now sits on the throne;
MPERS78:24	H1005	In person {present} there, now for his help {aid} was seen;
MPERS79:27	H1053	How of this enterprise his thoughts now stands;
MPERS80:7	H1074	O noble *Greeks,* how now, degenerate?
MPERS~~81:16~~	H1124	And leave them out, the {this} shock {now} for to sustaine,
MPERS81:20	H1128	If now in {their} need, they should thus fail {forsake} their
MPERS82:10	H1157	And troublesome *Mardonius* now must dye:
MPERS83:36	H1224	And payes them now, {both} according as he owes,
MPERS84:20	H1256	Thinking his *Grecian* wars now to advance.
MPERS84:26	H1262	The {This} noble *Greek,* now fit for generall.
MPERS84:29	H1265	Provisions, {then} and season now being fit,
MPERS85:9	H1285	Who now sole Monarch, doth of all remaine,

MPERS86:9	H1325	*Mnemon* now sits {set} upon his fathers Throne,
MPERS86:15	H1331	His interest, in the Kingdome, now next heir,
MPERS86:21	H1337	And thought it best, now in his mothers time,
MPERS86:31	H1347	The King finding, revenues now amended;
MPERS87:10	H1366	Seven hundred *Greeks* now further {repair for} his intents:
MPERS87:27	H1379	The mazed King, was now {then} about to fly;
MPERS88:1	H1394	arme, the King {with all his host} is now approaching nigh;
MPERS88:35	H1428	And now more eagerly their foes pursue,
MPERS89:4	H1438	Being Victors oft, now to their Camp they came;
MPERS90:20	H1487	The *Greeks* now (as the *Persian* King suspects)
MPERS90:24	H1491	And now {how} their Nation with facility,
MPERS90:36	H1503	*Tythraustes* now {then} is placed in his stead,
MPERS91:2	H1510	height, {*Spartan* State} which now apace doth {so fast did} rise;
MPERS91:9	H1517	They now {Their winnings} lost all, and were a peace {their
MPERS91:19	H1527	The King from forraign foes, and all {parts now well} at ease,
MPERS91:36	~~H1550~~	Was it because the *Grecians* now at war,
MPERS91:38	~~H1552~~	Or dealing with the *Persian,* now no more
MPERS~~92:5~~	H1559	*Arsames* plac'd now in his fathers stead,
MPERS~~92:8~~	H1566	And scarce a Nephew left that now might reign:
MPERS92:9	H1567	What Acts he did, time hath not now left pend,
MPERS~~92:24~~	H1582	This *Codomanus* now upon the stage
MGREC93:33	H1630	Which honour to his son, now did befall.
MGREC6:34	H1631	(For as worlds Monarch, now we speak not on,
MGREC6:36	H1633	Restlesse both day and night, his heart now {then} was,
MGREC94:10	H1644	Now taste of death, (least they deserv't {deserv'd} in time)
MGREC94:12	H1646	For cruelty now, was his parentall sin.
MGREC94:13	H1647	Thus eased now, of troubles, and of fears;
MGREC94:41	H1679	Those banks so steep, the *Greeks,* now {yet} scramble up
MGREC95:18	H1697	Now newes, of *Memnons* death (the Kings Vice-roy)
MGREC95:26	H1705	Now {Then} *Alexander* all *Cilicia* takes:
MGREC~~95:30~~	H1709	And on {Then o're} he goes *Darius* {now} so to meet;
MGREC96:6	H1726	As if they were, {if address} now all to run at {a} tilt:
MGREC96:29	H1749	Now least this Gold, and all this goodly stuffe,
MGREC97:5	H1766	Now finds both leggs, and Horse, to run away;
MGREC97:10	H1771	The Regall ornaments now {were} lost, the treasure
MGREC97:17	H1778	Conquer'd himself (now he had conquered)
MGREC97:28	H1789	*Darius* now, more humble {less lofty} then before,
MGREC97:38	H1799	Now {Next} *Alexander* unto *Tyre* doth goe,
MGREC98:8	H1810	In the old town (which now {then} lay like a wood)
MGREC98:11	H1813	And now, as *Babels* King did once before,
MGREC98:14	H1816	The former ruines, help to him now lend; {forwarded his end:}
MGREC98:18	H1820	Whose glory, now {then} a second time's brought down;
MGREC98:20	H1822	Eight thousand by the sword now also dy'd,
MGREC98:31	H1833	*Ephestion* now, hath the {having chief} command o' th' Fleet,
MGREC~~98:32~~	H1834	And {now} must at *Gaza, Alexander* meet;
MGREC98:34	H1836	By his Embassadours now sues for peace:
MGREC99:7	H1850	For all he offered {offers} now, was but his owne:
MGREC99:14	H1857	He now to *Gaza* goes, and there doth meet
MGREC100:11	H1895	Now {Thence} back to *Ægypt* goes, and in few dayes,
MGREC100:17	H1901	Had *Betis* now been there, but with his Band,
MGREC100:20	H1904	And now of valour both were {are} destitute;

MGREC100:33	H1917	Now bids the world adieu, her time {with pain} being spent,
MGREC101:4	H1929	And now for peace he sues, as once before,
MGREC101:41	H1970	And now {Together} with it, the town also obtain'd.
MGREC102:5	H1975	This Conquerour now {then} goes to *Babylon,*
MGREC102:21	H1991	Where four and thirty dayes he now doth stay,
MGREC102:38	H2008	Now falls {fall} into the *Macedonians* hands.
MGREC103:23	H2034	Now makes this King, his vertues all to drown.
MGREC103:24	H2035	He walloweth now, {That wallowing} in all licenciousnesse,
MGREC103:36	H2047	Now {The} to *Darius,* he directs his way,
MGREC103:39	H2050	Had now his fourth, and last Army compounded,
MGREC104:2	H2054	Thought now this once, to try his fortunes here,
MGREC104:20	H2072	And of {by} his Guard, and Servitors now left.
MGREC104:35	H2087	Whose Army now, was almost within sight,
MGREC105:32	H2125	To's Mother, Children deare, and Wife now gone,
MGREC106:4	H2138	And though a Monarch once {late}, now lyes like clay;
MGREC106:7	H2141	Now to the East great *Alexander* goes,
MGREC106:15	H2149	*Thalestris,* Queen of th' *Amazons,* now brought
MGREC106:29	H2163	His greatnesse now he takes, to represent,
MGREC106:32	H2166	Are strictly now commanded to adore;
MGREC106:35	H2169	His manners, habit, gestures, now doth {all did} fashion,
MGREC107:8	H2183	Now that his Hoast from luggage might be free,
MGREC107:20	H2195	Now with his Army, doth he hast {post} away,
MGREC108:1	H2217	Is by his owne, now bound in Iron chaines,
MGREC108:11	H2227	And now reviv'd with hopes, held up their head,
MGREC108:25	H2241	And now the *Bactrians* 'gainst him {now} rebel,
MGREC~~108:25~~	H2241	And now the *Bactrians* 'gainst him {now} rebel,
MGREC108:39	H2255	His {A} third supply, *Antipater* now sent,
MGREC109:1	H2258	He enters now {then} the *Indian* Kings among;
MGREC109:15	H2274	Had to his mind, made all things now {to} accord:
MGREC109:40	H2299	Is now resolv'd to passe *Hidaspes* floud,
MGREC110:6	H2306	On *Tygris* side, here now he had not been;
MGREC110:21	H2325	East-ward, now *Alexander* would goe still,
MGREC111:32	H2377	Now through these goodly countries as he past,
MGREC111:35	H2380	Who now obscure at *Passagardis* lay;
MGREC112:15	H2401	Now, *Alexanders* conquests, all are done,
MGREC112:33	H2419	Enveighs against his Father, now absent,
MGREC113:10	H2437	Are {Were} now inflicted on *Parmenio's* Son,
MGREC113:16	H2443	They knew not; wherefore, best now to be done,
MGREC114:11	~~H2479~~	*Alexander* now no longer could ~~containe,~~
MGREC115:4	H2515	Now *Alexander* goes to *Media,*
MGREC~~115:15~~	H2527	Of stately *Ecbatane* who now must shew,
MGREC115:18	H2537	That he might next now act upon the Stage,
MGREC115:26	H2545	But now, *Antipater* had liv'd thus {so} long,
MGREC115:39	H2558	His age, and journey long, he now {then} pretends;
MGREC117:3	H2610	Now like a mortall helplesse man he lies;
MGREC117:10	H2617	Four of his Captains, all doe now divide,
MGREC117:25	H2632	Now Court, and Camp, all in confusion be,
MGREC118:21	H2668	Now lay a spectacle, to testifie
MGREC118:36	~~H2685~~	Thought timely for themselves, now to provide.
MGREC~~118:36~~	H2685	For their security did now provide
MGREC118:41	H2690	These now to govern for the King pretends,

MGREC119:13	H2703	Their ancient liberty, afresh now seeks,
MGREC119:22	H2712	For to *Antipater* he now might go,
MGREC119:34	H2724	Now to *Antipater, Craterus* goes,
MGREC120:3	H2734	Now dy'd (about the end of th' *Lamian* warre)
MGREC120:5	H2740	*Craterus,* and *Antipater* now joyn
MGREC120:24	H2761	The Acts of his Vice-royes, {Vice-Roy} now grown so high:
MGREC120:29	H2766	He, and *Craterus,* both with him now {do} joyn,
MGREC120:31	H2768	Brave *Ptolomy,* to make a fourth now {then} sent,
MGREC120:38	H2775	And yet till now, at quiet was not laid.
MGREC120:41	H2778	*Perdicas* hears, his foes are now {all} combin'd,
MGREC121:24	H2806	With what he held, he now was well {more} content,
MGREC121:26	H2808	Now comes the newes of a great victory,
MGREC121:35	H2817	But he alone now {most} faithfull did abide:
MGREC121:40	H2822	Two battells now he fought, and had {of both} the best,
MGREC122:11	H2836	*Python* now chose protector of the State,
MGREC122:26	H2845	Which made her now begin to play her part;
MGREC123:14	H2878	Now {When} great *Antipater,* the world doth {must} leave
MGREC123:20	H2884	And *Ptolomy,* now {next} to encroach begins,
MGREC123:22	H2886	Now {Then} *Polisperchon* 'gins to act in's place,
MGREC123:31	H2895	And to be great {chief} himselfe now bends his aymes;
MGREC123:34	H2898	Are now at the devotion of the Son,
MGREC124:6	H2911	*Cassander* for return all speed now made:
MGREC124:23	H2930	The great ones now begin to shew their minde,
MGREC125:2	H2950	She now with *Polisperchon* doth combine,
MGREC125:14	H2962	*Olimpias* now {soon} enters *Macedon,*
MGREC125:19	H2967	Nor Darts, nor Arrowes now, none shoots, nor flings;
MGREC126:15	H3006	Faine would she come now to {this wretched Queen}
MGREC127:2	H3032	Now in her age she's forc't to taste that Cup,
MGREC127:4	H3034	Now many Townes in *Macedon* supprest,
MGREC127:13	H3043	And {now} for a while, let's into *Asia* turn,
MGREC127:28	H3058	*Antigonus,* all *Persia* now gains {doth gain},
MGREC127:32	H3062	The Princes all begin now to envie
MGREC128:3	H3076	And how he aymes {aiming now} to make himselfe a King,
MGREC128:15	H3088	Now {Then} *Ptolomy* would gaine the *Greeks* likewise,
MGREC128:40	H3113	That each shall {should} hold what he doth {did} now possesse,
MGREC129:4	H3118	He sees the *Greeks* now favour their young Prince,
MGREC129:5	H3119	Whom he in durance held, now and long since,
MGREC129:25	H3139	And now they are, {were} free Lords, of what they had,
MGREC130:1	H3156	But that some title he might now pretend,
MGREC130:5	H3160	She now {then} in *Lydia* at *Sardis* lay,
MGREC130:19	H3174	And now he thinks {hopes}, he's ordered all so well,
MGREC130:25	H3180	Now blood was paid with blood, for what was done
MGREC130:32	H3181	And *Cleopatra's* blood, now likewise spill'd,
MGREC130:39	H3184	These Captains now, the stile of Kings do take,
MGREC131:6	H3196	These Kings fall now afresh to {their} warres again,
MGREC131:10	H3202	*Antigonus* and *Seleuchus,* now {then his} fight
MGREC131:12	H3204	And he that conquerour shall now remain,
MGREC131:21	H3213	Now shut their gates in his adversity,
MGREC131:34	H3226	*Cassander* now must die, his race is run,
MGREC132:6	H3239	Who took away his now pretended right:
MGREC132:16	H3251	And now as King, in *Macedon* he reigns;

MGREC132:29	H3276	Now {Next} dyed the brave and noble *Ptolomy,*
MGREC132:33	H3280	Of the old Heroes, now but two remaine,
MGREC132:38	H3285	That now he had out-lived all the rest:
MGREC133:7	H3295	A little now, how the Succession run:
MGREC134:18	H3349	In *Egypt* now {next,} a little time we'l spend.
MGREC135:10	H3382	Now up, now down, now chief, and then brought under;
MGREC135:10	H3382	Now up, now down, now chief, and then brought under;
MGREC135:10	H3382	Now up, now down, now chief, and then brought under;
MGREC135:36	H3408	With these three Monarchies, now have I done,
MGREC136:7	H3420	This my presumption (some now) to requite,
MGREC136:12	H3426	*This fourth to th' other three, now might be brought.*
MROMAN137:18	H3469	The *Romans* now more potent 'gin to grow,
MROMAN138:10	H3500	But now demolished, to make *Rome* great.
MROMAN140:8	H3571	Nor matter is't this last, the world now sees,
DIALOG141:20	H19	My weakned fainting body now to reele?
DIALOG142:20	H49	Must *Richmonds* ayd, the Nobles now implore,
DIALOG143:5	H73	No Crook-backt Tyrant, now usurps the Seat,
DIALOG143:8	H76	No crafty Tyrant now usurps the Seat,
DIALOG143:15	H84	My Sister *Scotland* hurts me now no more,
DIALOG144:25	H134	I then believ'd not, now I feel and see,
DIALOG146:3	H191	But now I come to speak of my disaster,
DIALOG146:8	H196	Am now destroy'd, and slaughter'd by mine own,
DIALOG146:14	H200	Pray now dear child, for sacred *Zion's* sake,
DIALOG146:25	H211	For my relief now use thy utmost skill {do what there lyes in
DIALOG146:29	H215	Shake off your dust, chear up, and now arise,
DIALOG146:34	H221	Though now beclouded all with tears and blood:
DIALOG146:37	H223	But now the Sun in's brightnesse shall appear,
DIALOG147:28	H252	If now you weep so much, that then no more,
DIALOG148:24	H289	And him you shall adore, who now despise,
SIDNEY151:21	H71	But now into such Lab'rinths am I led
SIDNEY151:26	H74	And {Which} makes me now with *Sylvester* confesse,
DUBART155:5	H90	*Now shew'd what once they ought, Humanity,*
QELIZ155:14	H5	Although great Queen, thou now in silence lye,
QELIZ155:26	H17	Thou never didst, nor canst thou now disdaine,
QELIZ156:11	H38	The *Salique* Law had not in force now been,
QELIZ156:13	H40	But can you Doctors now this point dispute,
QELIZ156:28	H55	The States united now her fame doe sing;
QELIZ157:32	H100	Now say, have women worth, or have they none?
QELIZ157:37	H105	Know 'tis a slander now, but once was treason.
VANITY159:37	H9	He's now a slave {captive}, that was a Prince {King} of late.
TDUDLEY165:24	H26	But now or never I must pay my Sum;
TDUDLEY166:18	H60	Now fully ripe, as shock of wheat that's grown,
TDUDLEY166:25	H67	Who after all his toyle, is now at rest:
CONTEM167:25	H2	Sometime now past in the Autumnal Tide,
CONTEM170:30	H100	Who fancyes not his looks now at the Barr,
CONTEM171:11	H115	Who to the tenth of theirs doth now arrive?
CONTEM172:11	H147	Now thought the rivers did the trees excel,
CONTEM172:32	H165	Now salt, now fresh where you think best to glide
CONTEM172:32	H165	Now salt, now fresh where you think best to glide
CONTEM174:16	H215	And now becomes great Master of the seas;
1LETTER181:13	H11	My chilled limbs now nummed lye forlorn;

1LETTER181:19	H17	O strange effect! now thou art *Southward* gone,
2LETTER182:33	H39	Now post with double speed, mark what I say,
3LETTER183:3	H5	So doth my anxious soul, which now doth miss,
3LETTER183:12	H14	Bewail my turtle true, who now is gone,
CHILDRN185:2	H28	She now hath percht, to spend her years;
CHILDRN185:36	H62	My throbs such now, as 'fore were never:
MERCY188:24	H10	I saw the branches lopt the Tree now fall,
MERCY189:9	H30	So with her Chidren four, she's now at rest,
PILGRIM210:1	H1	As weary pilgrim, now at rest
PILGRIM210:3	H3	His wasted limbes, now lye full soft
PILGRIM210:18	H18	and meanes in safity now to dwell.
MYCHILD215:17	Hp240	now doe) by y^t yov may gain some spirit: Advantage by my
MYCHILD216:16	Hp241	after him gave me many more, of whom I now take ye care, y^t
MYCHILD216:18	Hp241	+ feares brovght yov to this, I now travail in birth again of yov
MYCHILD217:9	Hp242	I was afflicted I went astray, but now I keep thy statutes.
MYCHILD218:34	Hp244	told yov before. That hath stayed my heart, and I can now
MYCHILD219:3	Hp245	Now to ye King Imortall, Eternall invisible, the only wise God,
JULY223:28	Hp251	possesse that I now hope for, y^t so they may bee encourag^d to
WHAT224:22	H22	That dy'd but now doth liue,
28AUG226:5	Hp254	Now I can wait, looking every day when my Sav^r shall call for
11MAYA226:18	Hp255	of Baca many pools of water, That wch now I cheifly labour
13MAY227:2	H11	And former clowdes seem now all fled
SON230:20	H3	All praise to him who hath now turn'd
HOUSE236:27	H19	That layd my goods now in ye dvst

NOW'S (8) [now is]

HUMOUR34:35	H590	Wel, to be breif, Choler I hope now's laid,
SEASONS48:19	H72	The cleanly huswives Dary, now's ith' prime,
SEASONS49:6	H97	His progresse to the North; now's fully done,
SEASONS50:27	H161	Now's ripe the Pear, Pear-plumbe, and Apricock,
SEASONS52:23	H238	Now's held, a Guest, {(but ghest)} (but blest) Nativity.
MPERS92:12	H1570	But now's divolved, to another Stem.
MGREC98:26	H1828	For now's the time, Captains like Kings may live;
MGREC115:28	H2547	His service great now's suddenly forgot,

NOYSE (2) [noise]

AGES45:31	H421	No more rejoyce, at musickes pleasant {pleasing} noyse,
MASSYR66:9	H515	Where late, of Harp, and Lute, was {were} heard the noyse,

NULLIFIE (1) [nullify]

MGREC120:23	H2760	And by his presence there, to nullifie

NUMA (1) See also NVMA

MROMAN137:24	H3475	*Numa Pompilius.*

NUMB (1)

AGES45:38	H428	Now stiffe and numb, can hardly creep or go.

NUMBED See NUMMED

NUMBER (8) See also NVMBER

MASSYR56:28	H134	Her Camells, Chariots, Gallyes in such number,
MPERS80:24	H1091	If that smal number his great force could bide;
MPERS89:5	H1439	Nor lackt they any of their number small,
MGREC96:15	H1735	A number of spare horses next were led,
2LETTER182:12	H18	Or in a corn-field number every grain,
2LETTER182:14	H20	May count my sighs, and number all my drops:
MEDDM206:13	Hp287	a lesse degree, & others (and they indeed the most in number)

MEDDM207:27   Hp289   should make vs so to number our dayes as to apply our hearts

NUMBERLESSE (5) [numberless] See also NVMBERLES

ELEMEN15:24   H306   Fishes so numberlesse I there do hold;

ELEMEN19:20   H465   Of murrain, Cattle numberlesse did fall.

MPERS78:7   H988   His Camels, beasts, for carriage numberlesse,

MGREC95:35   H1714   (Both sexes there) was almost numberlesse.

MGREC103:12   H2023   Statues of {some} gold, and silver numberlesse,

NUMBERS (6) [pl.]

ELEMEN11:38   H158   Whose numbers now are growne innumerous;

ELEMEN12:22   H182   Out of huge {great} numbers, I might pick my choyce,

MPERS81:31   H1139   To adde unto his numbers, layes about,

MPERS87:12   H1368   In numbers from his brother daily run.

MPERS88:6   H1399   Of whose great numbers, their intelligence,

MGREC100:30   H1914   His numbers might the victory obtaine.

NUMEDIA (1)

ELEMEN12:17   H177   Ile here let goe, my Lions of *Numedia,*

NUMEROUS (1)

CONTEM172:34   H167   In Lakes and ponds, you leave your numerous fry,

NUMMED (2) [numbed]

SEASONS46:35   H13   Fit to revive, the nummed earth from death.

1LETTER181:13   H11   My chilled limbs now nummed lye forlorn;

NUN (1)

MASSYR55:10   H76   Others report, she was a vestal Nun,

NUPTIALL (1)

MPERS74:23   H846   Two of his Neeces takes to nuptiall bed;

NURSE (2)

FATHER5:20   H21   These are of all, the life, the nurse, the grave,

DIALOG146:30   H216   You are my mother, nurse, {and} I once your flesh,

NURSING (1)

DIALOG147:37   H261   That nursing Kings, shall come and lick thy dust:

NURST (2)

CHILDRN184:16   H5   I nurst them up with pain and care,

CHILDRN186:21   H88   And nurst you up till you were strong,

NURTRITIVE (1) [nutritive]

HUMOUR27:22   H293   This hot, moist, nurtritive humour of mine,

NURTURE (3)

AGES39:12   H155   With nurture trained up in vertues Schools,

MEDDM196:31   Hp274   fit their nurture according to their Nature.

MEDDM205:5   Hp285   nurture they are brought into a fit capacity, let the seed of good

NVMA (1) [numa]

MROMAN137:25   H3476   *Nvma Pompilius,* is next chosen {chose they} King,

NVMBER (1) [number]

REMB236:6   H21   In nvmber nvmberles,

NVMBERLES (1) [numberless] See also NUMBERLESSE

REMB236:6   H21   In nvmber nvmberles,

O

O (81) [exclamation]

ELEMEN9:1	H35	O {Ye} Martialist! what weapon {weapons} for your fight?
ELEMEN14:3	H245	O dreadfull Sepulcher! that this is true,
HUMOUR34:3	H558	O! mixture strange, oh {O} colour, colourlesse,
HUMOUR34:3	H558	O! mixture strange, oh {O} colour, colourlesse,
HUMOUR34:7	H562	O! good, O bad, O true, O traiterous eyes!
HUMOUR34:10	H565	Yet some may wish, oh, {O} had mine eyes ne're seene.
MPERS72:16	H764	O hellish Husband, Brother, Vnckle, Sire,
MPERS78:29	H1010	O noble Queen, thy valour I commend,
MPERS79:2	H1024	O most inhumain incivility!
MPERS80:7	H1074	O noble *Greeks,* how now, degenerate?
DIALOG144:10	H120	O *Jane,* why didst thou dye in flowring prime,
DIALOG147:5	H231	O cry: the sword of God, and *Gideon:*
DIALOG147:26	H250	O mother, can you weep, and have such Peeres.
SIDNEY149:2	H23	This was thy shame, O miracle of wit:
SIDNEY150:8	H33	(O brave Refiner of our *Brittish* Tongue;)
SIDNEY150:19	H44	O brave *Achilles,* I wish some *Homer* would
SIDNEY150:23	H50	O *Zutphon, Zutphon,* that most fatall City,
SIDNEY151:8	H69	O Princely *Philip,* rather *Alexander,*
DUBART154:11	H56	O *France,* in him thou didst more glory gain,
QELIZ157:39	H107	O {Yea} happy, happy, had those dayes still been,
DAVID158:32	H12	O! *Gilbo* Mounts, let never pearled dew,
DAVID159:13	H28	O *Israels* Dames, o're-flow your beauteous eyes,
DAVID159:19	H34	O! how in battell did the mighty fall,
DAVID159:21	H36	O! lovely *Jonathan,* how wert {wast} thou slaine,
VANITY159:31	H3	O vanity, O vain all under skie,
CONTEM172:18	H153	O happy Flood, quoth I, that holds thy race
CONTEM172:27	H161	O could I lead my Rivolets to rest,
CONTEM173:18	H184	O merry Bird (said I) that fears no snares,
CONTEM174:29	H226	O Time the fatal wrack of mortal things,
SICKNES178:34	H17	O Bubble blast, how long can'st last?
SICKNES179:1	H21	O whil'st I live, this grace me give,
SICKNES179:7	H27	O great's the gain, though got with pain,
BIRTH180:16	H26	These O protect from step Dames injury.
1LETTER181:19	H17	O strange effect! now thou art *Southward* gone,
2LETTER182:22	H28	O how they joy when thou dost light the skyes.
2LETTER182:23	H29	O *Phoebus,* hadst thou but thus long from thine
3LETTER183:26	H28	The substance gone, O me, these are but dreams.
CHILDRN185:29	H55	O would my young, ye saw my breast,
CHILDRN185:41	H67	O to your safety have an eye,

MYCHILD218:35	Hp244	Return o my Soul to thy Rest, vpon this Rock Xt Jesus will I
FEVER221:3	H18	O heal my Soul thov know'st I said,
FEVER221:11	H26	O praises to my mighty God
SOREFIT221:33	H19	O make it frvitfull faithfull Lord
SOREFIT222:8	H27	O Lord for aye is my request
SOREFIT222:9	H28	O gravnt I doe it in this state,
FAINTING222:12	H2	Worthy art Thou o Ld of praise,
FAINTING222:26	H16	O Lord, no longer bee my Dayes
JULY223:30	Hp251	O Lord let me neuer forgett thy Goodnes, nor question thy
JULY223:33	Hp251	upon me. O never let Satan p^rvail against me, but strenghten
WHAT224:3	H3	O never let me from thee swerue
WHAT224:7	H7	On High my heart O doe thou raise
MYSOUL225:23	H27	O let me covnt each hour a Day
28AUG226:10	Hp254	O let me ever see Thee that Art invisible, and I shall not bee
13MAY227:9	H18	O hast thou made my pilgrimage
SAMUEL228:8	H9	He's mine, but more O Lord thine own
SAMUEL228:12	H13	P^rserve O Lord from stormes & wrack
THEART229:11	H13	An hvble, faithfull life O Lord
THEART229:15	H17	Accept O Lord my simple mite
SON231:19	H31	O help me pay my Vowes O Lord
SON231:27	H39	O Lord gravnt that I may never forgett thy Loving kindness in
2HUSB232:3	H4	O thov most high who rulest All
2HUSB232:5	H6	O hearken Lord vnto my suit
2HUSB232:11	H12	At thy comand O Lord he went
2HUSB232:14	H15	O help and bee not slack.
2HUSB232:15	H16	Vphold my heart in Thee O God
2HUSB232:22	H23	O Lord accept of it.
2HUSB232:25	H26	O Lord thov know'st my weak desires
HOURS233:20	H3	O Lord thou hear'st my dayly moan
HOURS234:5	H19	O stay my heart on thee my God
HOURS234:17	H31	O shine vpon me blessed Lord
HOURS234:21	H35	O hear me Lord in this Reqvest
ACK235:5	H5	O Thou that hear'st ye prayers of Thine
REMB235:26	H7	O Lord thov know'st I'm weak.
REMB235:31	H12	O thou y^t hearest prayers Lord
REMB236:9	H24	O help thy Saints y^t sovght thy Face

OAK (1)

CONTEM168:7	H16	Then on a stately Oak I cast mine Eye,

OAKEN (1)

DUBART154:19	H64	The Oaken garland ought to deck their browes,

OARE (2) [oar]

MASSYR64:38	H462	And Mariners, to handle sayle, and oare;
MGREC111:19	H2364	Depriv'd at once, the use of Saile, and Oare;

OARES (3) [oars]

ELEMEN12:38	H198	And Oares to row, when both my sisters failes?
ELEMEN16:25	H348	Alas; thy ships and oares could do no good
MROMAN138:19	H3509	Of Boats, and Oares, no more they need the aide;

OATES (1) [oats]

AGES41:23	H240	When my Wilde Oates, were sown, and ripe, & mown,

OATH (2)

MASSYR65:11	H476	*Jehoiakim* his Oath had clean forgot;

MPERS84:25   H1261   For punishment, their breach of oath did call,

OATHES (2) [oaths]

MPERS89:35   H1469   And with all {the} Oathes, and deepest flattery,

DIALOG143:35   H104   For Oathes, and Blasphemies did ever eare

OATHS (1)

AGES40:24   H205   Cards, Dice, and Oaths, concomitant, I love;

OBDURATE (1)

DIALOG145:3   H152   My {Mine} heart obdurate, stood not yet agast.

OBED^C (3) [obedience]

THEART229:13 H15   Let my obed^c testefye

RESTOR229:31 H14   Let thy obed^c testefye

2HUSB232:19   H20   I in obed^c to thy Will

OBEDIENCE (4)

MASSYR57:4   H151   Or else was his obedience very great,

MASSYR61:14 H319   And *Syria* t' obedience did subdue;

MASSYR63:28 H413   By whom in firm obedience she's kept.

MPERS~~72:37~~   H783   Obedience yielded as to *Cyrus* son.

OBEDIENT (1)

DDUDLEY167:11 H8   *A loving Mother and obedient wife,*

OBEISANCE See OBEYSANCE

OBEY (4)

ELEMEN13:19   H220   And how I force the grey head to obey.

ELEMEN16:36   H359   Yet {And} *Luna* for my Regent I obey.

AGES42:12   H270   If a Souldier {I}, with speed I did obey,

MPERS75:9   H870   If he command, obey the greatest must:

OBEYSANCE (1) [obeisance]

HUMOUR20:19 H11   All having made obeysance to each Mother,

OBIECT (1) n. [object]

MEDDM195:24 Hp272 There is no obiect that we see. no action that we doe, no good

OBIECTS (1)

MEDDM202:33 Hp282 innumerable obiects enter, yet is not that spacious roome filled

OBJECT (1) n. See also OBIECT

MGREC96:10   H1730 An object not so much of fear, as laughter.

OBJECT (1) v.

MASSYR57:16 ~~H163~~ Some may object, his Parents ruling all,

OBJECTS (1) [pl.]

HUMOUR23:23 H133 As objects best appear, by contraries.

OBLATION (1)

MGREC131:5   H3195 Who incense burnt, and offered oblation.

OBLIG'D (1) [obliged]

MPERS84:34   H1270 To {By} whom oblig'd, by favour {bounty}, and by love;

OBLIQUE (2)

SEASONS47:33 ~~H47~~ Twelve houses of the oblique Zodiack,

CONTEM168:32 H38   Thy daily streight, and yearly oblique path,

OBLITERATE (3)

MGREC112:36 H2422 Which no merit could obliterate, or time:

MGREC114:30 H2500 Which shall not be obliterate by time,

CONTEM171:29 H131 That state obliterate he had at first:

OBLIVION (2)

MASSYR57:31 H176   In deep oblivion, of acts bereft,

CONTEM171:32 H134 But in oblivion to the final day remain.

OBLIVIONS (2) [poss.]
AGES41:8   H228   And I in black oblivions den long {now} laid;
CONTEM174:30 H227   That draws oblivions curtains over kings,
OBLIVIOUS (1)
BIRTH180:8   H18   Let be interr'd in my oblivious grave;
OBLOQUIE (1) [obliquy]
HUMOUR32:2   H476   Although she beare the greatest obloquie.
OBNOXIOUS (1)
PROLOG7:14   H27   I am obnoxious to each carping tongue,
OBSCENITY (1)
AGES40:15   H196   To all obscenity, my {mine} eares I bend. {lend;}
OBSCURE (7)
PROLOG6:23   H8   My obscure Verse,{Lines} shal not so dim their worth.
MASSYR57:5   H152   To sit, thus long (obscure) wrong'd {rob'd} of his seat;
MGREC111:13   H2358   These {Those} obscure Nations yeelded as before;
MGREC111:35   H2380   Who now obscure at *Passagardis* lay;
QELIZ157:4   H72   *Semiramis* to her is but obscure,
TDUDLEY165:16 H18   Nor was his name, or life lead so obscure
MEDDM206:14   Hp287   but small and obscure, yet all receiue their luster (be it more or
OBSCURELY (1)
MASSYR55:18   H84   For which, she was obscurely nourished.
OBSCURITY (1)
SEASONS51:41 H217   No Sun, to lighten their obscurity;
OBSEQUIES (2) [pl.]
MGREC115:7   H2518   He celebrates his mournfull obsequies;
MGREC~~132:28~~ H3275   Whose obsequies with wondrous pomp was done.
OBSERV'D (1) [observed]
TDUDLEY165:12 H14   Who heard or saw, observ'd or knew him better?
OBSERVATIONS (1) [pl.]
CONTEM171:4   H109   The starry observations of those Sages,
OBSERVE (2)
MGREC107:19   H2194   For {Here} to observe the rashnesse of the King.
MYCHILD215:22 Hp240   The method I will observe shall bee thisI will begin wth Gods
OBSERVED (1) See also OBSERV'D
MYCHILD216:21 Hp241   constantly observed this y^t he hath never suffered me long to
OBSERVING (1)
MGREC111:20   H2365   But well observing th' nature of the tide,
OBSTACLES (1) [pl.]
DIALOG145:24 H173   So many obstacles comes {came} in their way,
OBSTRUCT (1)
CONTEM172:20 H155   Nor is it rocks or shoals that can obstruct thy pace.
OBSTRUCTION (1)
HUMOUR~~23:14~~ H124   paine and sore obstructions, {obstruction} thou dost work;
OBSTRUCTIONS (1) [pl.]
HUMOUR23:14   H124   paine and sore obstructions, {obstruction} thou dost work;
OBTAIN (7) See also OBTAINE
MPERS~~84:12~~   H1242   Did for the Jews commission large obtain,
MPERS86:20   H1336   To win by force, what right could not obtain.
MPERS86:26   H1342   Her prevailence, a pardon might obtain.
MPERS92:19   ~~H1577~~ By one of these, he must obtain the place.
VANITY~~159:38~~ H10   What is't in wealth, great treasures for to gain {obtain}?

MEDDM201:29	Hp281	run that they might obtain
MEDDM209:4	Hp291	all our seekings and gettings, let vs aboue all seek to obtain

OBTAIN'D (2) [obtained]

MASSYR59:7	H231	For victory obtain'd the other day;
MGREC101:41	H1970	And now {Together} with it, the town also obtain'd.

OBTAIND (1) [obtained]

MYCHILD216:15	Hp241	to me, and cost me many prayers + tears before I obtaind one,

OBTAINE (3) [obtain]

MGREC100:30	H1914	His numbers might the victory obtaine.
DUBART153:24	H28	But seeing empty wishes nought obtaine,
MEDDM203:4	Hp283	for what do we obtaine of all these things, but it is wth labour

OBTAINES (1) [obtains]

MROMAN139:3	H3531	Of *Tanaquil,* late Queen, obtaines the place;

OBTAINS (1)

MASSYR57:2	H149	His Mother dead, *Ninias* obtains his right,

OCCASION (3)

ELEMEN14:13	H255	Thus I occasion death to man and beast,
MGREC118:11	H2658	He hold of {on} this occasion should have laid,
JULY223:26	Hp251	y^t it may bee a support to me when I shall haue occasion

OCCASIONED (1)

MASSYR61:15	H320	*Iuda's* bad King occasioned this War,

OCCASIONS (1) [pl.]

MGREC126:21	H̶3̶0̶1̶2̶	But he unwilling longer there to stay,

OCEAN (9)

FATHER6:13	H47	Then waters, {water} in the boundlesse Ocean flowes.
ELEMEN15:23	H305	But what's the wealth that my rich Ocean brings?
ELEMEN16:26	H349	Did they but want my Ocean, and my Flood.
ELEMEN17:4	H368	Nay many times, my Ocean breaks his bounds:
ELEMEN17:13	H377	A mighty Country ith' *Atlanticke* Ocean.
MGREC114:38	H2508	From *Hellispont,* to th' furthest {farthest} Ocean;
DIALOG147:29	H253	The briny Ocean will o'rflow your shore,
CONTEM172:15	H150	Which to the long'd for Ocean held its course,
2LETTER182:9	H15	He that can tell the starrs or Ocean sand,

OCEAN'S (1) [ocean is]

ELEMEN18:26	H430	And when I smile, your Ocean's like a Poole.

OCHUS (5)

MPERS91:33	H1547	*Darius Ochus.*
MPERS91:34	H̶1̶5̶4̶8̶	Great *Artaxerxes* dead, *Ochus* succeeds,
MPERS9̶1̶:̶3̶4̶	H1548	*Ochus* a wicked and Rebellious son
MPERS92:22	H̶1̶5̶8̶0̶	That *Ochus* unto *Arsames* was father,
MGREC101:15	H1940	*Ochus* his Son a hostage shall {should} endure.

OCHUS (1) [poss.]

MPERS9̶2̶:̶5̶	H1561	Some write that *Arsames* was *Ochus* brother,

OCRAZAPES (1)

MASSYR57:39	H184	*Sardanapalus,* (Son t' *Ocrazapes*)

OCTOBER (1)

SEASONS51:20	H196	*October* is my next, we heare in this,

ODDS (2) [pl.] See also ODS

HUMOUR21:29	H57	'Twixt them and others, what ist makes the odds
MASSYR62:36	H381	'Twixt them and *Israels* he knew no odds. [7 *years.*

ODIOUS (2)

MGREC127:39	H3069	To make *Cassander* odious to them, seeks,
MGREC129:24	H3138	That he was {is} odious to the world, they'r glad,

ODS (1) [odds]

MGREC127:30	H3060	Then with *Seleuchus* straight at ods doth fall,

OFF (23)

HUMOUR24:13	H162	To vent my griefe, and wipe off my disgrace.
HUMOUR28:36	H348	I've scarce wip'd off the spots, proud Choler cast,
SEASONS49:2	H93	Wiping her {the} sweat from off {of} her brow, that ran,
MPERS73:10	H797	Cut off in's wickednesse, in's strength, and prime.
MPERS74:40	H861	With his own hands cuts off his eares, and nose,
MPERS76:39	H937	Which soon cut off, {inrag'd,} he with the {his} left
MPERS77:1	H940	Off flyes his head, down showres his frolick bloud.
MPERS82:31	H1178	Cut off her lilly breasts, her nose, and ears;
MGREC94:40	H1678	And think {strive} to keep his men from off the land,
MGREC104:15	H2067	Grinding his teeth, and plucking off his haire,
MGREC~~115:15~~	H2526	The battlements from off the walls are torne.
MGREC118:29	H2678	His chief opponents who kept off the Crown, {Control'd his
MGREC119:14	H2704	{And gladly would} Shakes {shake} off the yoke, sometimes
MGREC127:19	H3049	*Antigonus* came off still honourlesse,
MGREC134:32	H3363	Next *Auletes,* who cut off *Pompey's* head:
DIALOG146:29	H215	Shake off your dust, chear up, and now arise,
QELIZ156:7	H34	She hath wip'd off th' aspersion of her Sex,
QELIZ157:9	H77	Had put her Harnesse off, had she but seen
FLESH176:27	H67	For I have meat thou know'st not off;
AUTHOR178:5	H15	And rubbing off a spot, still made a flaw.
CHILDRN185:34	H60	And with my wings kept off all harm,
MEDDM200:7	Hp279	mustard, they wil either wipe it off, or else suck down sweet
FAINTING222:16	H6	My life as Spiders webb's cutt off

OFFENCE (3)

MASSYR65:19	H484	Whom he chastised {thus} for his proud offence;
MGREC112:26	H2412	He death deserv'd, for this so high offence;
MGREC136:5	H3418	To frame Apologie for some offence,

OFFEND (2)

MPERS91:8	H1516	To defend, more then offend, he had {there was} need.
DIALOG142:12	H41	Or is't intestine Wars that thus offend?

OFFENDED (2)

MPERS86:32	H1348	For what was done, seemed no whit offended.
MGREC112:24	H2410	Nothing was found {prov'd}, wherein he had offended;

OFFENDER (1)

HUMOUR~~29:12~~	H365	But when the first offenders {offender} I have laid,

OFFENDERS (1) [pl.]

HUMOUR29:12	H365	But when the first offenders {offender} I have laid,

OFFENSIVE (1)

MPERS76:8	H906	He warr'd defensive, not offensive, more;

OFFER (3)

MGREC98:2	H1804	Desires to offer unto *Hercules,*
MGREC~~118:12~~	H2659	For second offers {offer} there were {was} never made;
MGREC~~121:18~~	H2800	And offers {offer} him his Honours, and his place,

OFFER'D (1) [offered] See also OFF'RED

MGREC94:23	H1661	He offer'd, and for good successe did pray

OFFERED (4) See also OFFER'D, OFF'RED
MASSYR54:10   H37   So oft profanely offered sacred rites;
MGREC99:7   H1850   For all he offered {offers} now, was but his owne:
MGREC100:38   H1922   Some injury was offered, he feares;
MGREC131:5   H3195   Who incense burnt, and offered oblation.

OFFERING (1)
CONTEM170:17   H89   But no such sign on false *Cain's* offering;

OFFERINGS (1) [pl.] See also OFF'RINGS
DAVID158:34   H14   Nor fields of offerings e're on you grow,

OFFERS (2) [pl.]
MGREC99:1   H1844   And a most Princely Dowry with her proffers; {offers.}
MGREC118:12   H2659   For second offers {offer} there were {was} never made;

OFFERS (6) v.
MGREC97:31   H1792   For whom he offers him a ransome high;
MGREC98:41   H1843   His eldest Daughter, (him) {he} in marriage offers,
MGREC99:7   H1850   For all he offered {offers} now, was but his owne:
MGREC99:10   H1853   *Darius* offers I would not reject,
MGREC101:5   H1930   And offers all he did, and Kingdoms more;
MGREC121:18   H2800   And offers {offer} him his Honours, and his place,

OFFICE (2)
AGES37:34   H96   No office coveted, wherein I might
MGREC124:27   H2934   *Polisperchon* hoping for's office long,

OFFICER (1)
HUMOUR31:9   H442   What officer thou art to al us three.

OFFICERS (1) [pl.]
MPERS72:34   H778   At last, two of his Officers he hears,

OFFICES (1) [pl.]
DIALOG143:33   H102   Church Offices are {were} sold, and bought, for gaine,

OFF'RED (1) [offered]
DUBART153:15   H19   And prostrate off'red at great *Bartas* Herse.

OFF'RINGS (1) [offerings]
QELIZ155:22   H13   Thousands bring off'rings, (though out of date)

OFFSPRING (2)
HUMOUR33:26   H540   That divine Essence, {Offspring} the immortal Soul,
AUTHOR177:30   H2   Thou ill-form'd offspring of my feeble brain,

OFT (52)
FATHER5:25   H26   Sweet harmony they keep, yet jar oft times,
ELEMEN11:12   H132   The rich I oft make poore, the strong I maime,
ELEMEN12:12   H172   That heaven it selfe was oft call'd by that name;
ELEMEN13:23   H224   And how I oft work mans mortality.
ELEMEN14:2   H244   Your Cities and your selves I oft intombe.
ELEMEN16:22   H345   Which pitty moves, and oft deceives the wise.
ELEMEN16:37   H360   As I with showers oft time {times} refresh the earth;
ELEMEN16:38   H361   So oft in my excesse, I cause a dearth:
HUMOUR25:27   H216   Thou oft hast broke bounds of humanity.
AGES38:25   H128   Oft stubborn, peevish, sullen, pout, and cry:
AGES40:35   H214   And gastly death oft threats me with her {his} power,
AGES41:4   H224   That oft for it, in *Bedlam* I remain.
AGES43:8   H303   And {I} oft long'd sore, to taste on Royalty.
AGES43:29   H324   The windy Cholick oft my bowels rend,
AGES43:33   H328   The Quinsie, and the Feavours, oft distaste me,

AGES44:23 H356 In this short Pilgrimage I oft have had;
AGES44:28 H361 Such private changes oft mine eyes have seen,
SEASONS51:3 H177 Whose lively liquor oft is curst, and blest;
MASSYR54:8 H35 Whose Preists, in Stories, oft are mentioned;
MASSYR54:10 H37 So oft profanely offered sacred rites;
MASSYR56:17 H123 From whence, Astrologers, oft view'd the skies.
MPERS89:4 H1438 Being Victors oft, now to their Camp they came;
MGREC111:15 H2360 Which could not sound too oft, with too much fame;
MGREC116:30 H2596 As oft his Acts throughout his reigne did {doth} shew:
MGREC116:35 H2601 This conquerour did oft lament ('tis sed)
MGREC~~122:27~~ H2846 *Pithons* commands, {as oft} She ever countermands
MGREC126:34 ~~H2845~~ She oft forgot bounds of Humanity.
MGREC127:20 H3050 When victor oft had {he'd} been, and so might still,
MGREC133:35 H3325 Which we oft wish were {was} extant as before.
MROMAN139:34 H3560 Though oft perswaded, I as oft deny'd,
MROMAN139:34 H3560 Though oft perswaded, I as oft deny'd,
DIALOG~~143:12~~ H81 *France* knowes, how of {oft} my fury she hath drunk;
DIALOG~~147:41~~ H265 Patience, and purse of Clients for {oft} to wrong:
DUBART154:23 H68 Oft have I wondred at the hand of heaven,
VANITY159:36 H8 And whilst they live, how oft doth turn their State? {fate,}
TDUDLEY166:4 H46 And oft and oft, with speeches mild and wise,
TDUDLEY166:4 H46 And oft and oft, with speeches mild and wise,
TDUDLEY166:16 H58 Oft spake of death, and with a smiling chear,
DDUDLEY167:13 H10 *Whom oft she fed, and clothed with her store;*
CONTEM170:8 H81 The weeping Imp oft looks her in the face,
CONTEM171:2 H107 Who thinks not oft upon the Fathers ages.
FLESH176:12 H52 How oft thy slave, hast thou me made,
CHILDRN185:39 H65 Oft times in grass, on trees, in flight,
CHILDRN186:18 H85 In chirping languages, oft them tell,
ANNEB187:18 H8 How oft with disappointment have I met,
PILGRIM210:4 H4 That myrie steps, haue troden oft
MYCHILD217:18 Hp243 his holy spirit who hath oft given me his word & sett to his Seal
MYCHILD217:27 Hp243 me to powder it would bee but Light to me, yea oft haue I
FEVER220:33 H13 Wᶜʰ oft I read before.
ACK235:12 H12 For whom I thee so oft besovght
HOUSE236:33 H25 When by the Ruines oft I past
HOUSE236:36 H28 Where oft I sate and long did lye,

OFTEN (19)

HUMOUR25:29 H218 How often for the lye, thou'st giv'n the stab.
HUMOUR30:37 H429 Again, you often touch my swarthy hew,
SEASONS52:30 H245 Now toes, and eares, and fingers often freeze,
MPERS74:25 H848 That by such steps to Kingdoms often climbs {clime}.
MPERS90:13 ~~H1484~~ Into *Bithynia* often in-rodes made;
MPERS92:28 ~~H1586~~ And he that story reads, shall often find;
MGREC127:3 H3033 Which she had often made others to sup:
CONTEM170:25 H96 But since that time she often hath been cloy'd;
MEDDM197:18 Hp275 That house wᶜʰ is not often swept makes the cleanly inhabitant
MEDDM199:6 Hp277 do not often fall till after threat'ning.
MEDDM199:20 Hp278 at profit by the one & content in the other, but often misses
MEDDM201:19 Hp280 We often se stones hang wᵗʰ drops not from any innate
MEDDM203:7 Hp283 he haue good cause often to repeat that sentence, vanity of

MEDDM205:3	Hp285	of discipline goe often ouer them, before they bee fit soile, to
MEDDM205:27	Hp286	vs, or else we should not so often faile in our whole Course of
MEDDM207:33	Hp289	of death, wch is their sleep (for so is death often calld) and
MYCHILD215:29	Hp241	too often tardy y^t way. I also fovnd much comfort in reading y^e
MYCHILD215:32	Hp241	a long fitt of sicknes wch I had on my bed I often comvned w^th
MYCHILD217:15	Hp243	I haue often been p^rplexed y^t I haue not fovnd that constant

OH (21)

PROLOG7:35	H45	And oh, ye high flown quils, that soare the skies,
ELEMEN19:41	H482	That earth appeares in heaven, oh wonder great!
HUMOUR22:39	H108	Oh, who would misse this influence of thine,
HUMOUR34:3	H558	O! mixture strange, oh {O} colour, colourlesse,
HUMOUR34:10	H565	Yet some may wish, oh, {O} had mine eyes ne're seene.
AGES38:13	H116	This was mine innocence, but oh {ah!} the seeds,
AGES45:21	H403	Oh may you live, and so you will I trust
SEASONS49:29	H118	Oh! happy Shepheard, which had not to lose,
MGREC96:3	H1723	Oh {Sure} 'twas a goodly sight, there to behold;
MGREC113:5	H2432	Oh, *Alexander,* thy free clemency,
DIALOG144:9	H119	Oh, *Edwards* Babes {youths}, and *Clarence* haplesse Son,
DIALOG146:15	H201	Oh pity me, in this sad perturbation,
DIALOG148:21	H286	Oh *Abrahams* seed lift up your heads on high.
SIDNEY149:28	H23	What doe thy vertues then? Oh, honours crown!
SIDNEY150:29	H56	Oh, who was neare thee, but did sore repine;
DUBART154:30	H75	Oh pregnant brain, Oh comprehension vast:
DUBART154:30	H75	Oh pregnant brain, Oh comprehension vast:
BIRTH179:32	H8	A common thing, yet oh inevitable;
3LETTER183:27	H29	Together at one Tree, oh let us brouze,
MERCY188:32	H18	Oh how I simpathize with thy sad heart,
PILGRIM210:23	H23	Oh how I long to be at rest

OIL See OYLE

OILY See OYLY

OINTMENT See OYNTMENT

OLD (64)

ELEMEN9:28	H62	The Sun, an Orbe of Fire was held of old,
ELEMEN10:25	H100	Of old, when Sacrifices were divine,
ELEMEN10:39	H114	Where's *Ninus* great wal'd Town, and *Troy* of old?
ELEMEN11:2	H122	Old sacred *Zion,* I demolish'd thee;
ELEMEN11:24	H144	And Mother Earth, of old, men did me call,
AGES36:20	H44	Leaning upon his staffe, comes {came} up old age.
AGES36:32	H56	That he was young, before he grew so old.
AGES44:1	H334	*Old Age.*
AGES45:23	H413	These are no old wives tales, but this is truth;
AGES45:24	H414	We old men love to tell, what's done in youth.
AGES46:6	H437	To great, to rich, to poore, to young, or old,
SEASONS50:31	H165	Like good Old Age, whose younger juycie roots,
SEASONS51:30	H206	So doth Old Age stil tend unto his Grave,
SEASONS51:33	H209	His dead old stock, again shall mount on high.
SEASONS52:9	H224	Old cold, dry age, and earth, Autumne resembles,
MASSYR55:2	H68	The world then was two thousand nineteen old.
MASSYR60:16	H281	*Belosus* setled, in his new, old seat,
MASSYR60:31	H296	Raises a Phœnix new, from grave o'th old;
MASSYR63:35	H422	Nor his restoring from old legends took;

MASSYR64:41	H465	Fetch {Fetcht} rubbish from the opposite old town,
MPERS73:32	H817	The old, or new, which best, in what respect,
MPERS84:23	H1259	His Grand-sires old disgrace, did vex him sore,
MPERS87:3	H1359	The young Queen, and old, at bitter jars:
MPERS~~90:39~~	H1506	Whom the old Queen did bear a mortal hate.
MPERS~~91:22~~	H1531	But the old Queen implacable in strife,
MGREC94:3	H1637	*Thebes,* and old {stiff} *Athens,* both 'gainst him rebell,
MGREC94:21	H1659	Then on he march'd, in's way he veiw'd old *Troy;*
MGREC95:13	H1692	And easily takes old *Gordium* in his way;
MGREC95:38	H1717	His mother old, {his} beautious wife, {Queen} and daughters,
MGREC98:8	H1810	In the old town (which now {then} lay like a wood)
MGREC102:18	H1988	Yet old foundations shew'd, and somewhat more;
MGREC103:18	H2029	On their old Governours, titles he laid;
MGREC~~120:20~~	H2757	Acknowledged for Chief that old Commander)
MGREC122:36	~~H2857~~	Acknowledged for chief, this old Commander:
MGREC~~125:21~~	H2970	But the old Queen pursues them with her hate,
MGREC127:10	H3040	Old *Thebes* he then re-built (so much of fame)
MGREC131:24	H3216	His peace he then with old *Seleuchus* makes,
MGREC132:33	H3280	Of the old Heroes, now but two remaine,
MGREC~~133:31~~	H3321	To whom Ancient {the old} *Berosus* (so much fam'd)
MROMAN138:8	H3498	And from old *Alba* fetch the wealth away;
DIALOG141:1	H1	A Dialogue between Old
DIALOG141:14	H13	**Old England.**
DIALOG142:34	H63	**Old England.**
DIALOG143:4	H73	Nor no *Lancastrians,* to renew old strife;
DIALOG145:15	H164	**Old England.**
DIALOG145:26	H175	Old customes, new Prerogatives stood on,
QELIZ156:16	H43	And earth had twice {once} a yeare, a new old face:
QELIZ158:5	H114	If then new things, their old form must {forms shall} retain,
CONTEM171:19	H122	And then the earth (though old) stil clad in green,
CONTEM171:24	H127	But Man grows old, lies down, remains where once he's laid.
CONTEM173:29	H194	And warbling out the old, begin anew,
FLESH176:7	H47	Thou by old Adam wast begot, .
SICKNES178:18	H1	Twice ten years old, not fully told
CHILDRN186:12	H79	Where old ones, instantly grow young,
ELIZB186:33	H4-5	*being a year and half old.*
ANNEB187:15	H5	*seven Moneths old.*
1SIMON188:3	H4	*a moneth, and one day old.*
MEDDM195:33	Hp272	is the time of getting middle age of improuing, and old age of
MEDDM195:35	Hp272	age, and both by an empty old age, he that hath nothing to
MEDDM199:23	Hp278	Dimne eyes, are the concomitants of old age, and short
MEDDM199:31	Hp278	Sore labourers haue hard hands and old sinners haue brawnie
MEDDM200:33	Hp280	father will not lay a burden on a child of seven yeares old, w^{ch}
30SEPT227:18	Hp257	It pleased god to viset me wth my old Distemper of weaknes
HOUSE237:6	H36	Nor things recovnted done of old.

OLD-AGE (2)

AGES35:18	H4	Childhood, and Youth, the Manly, and Old-age.
AGES36:29	H53	But wise Old-age, did with all gravity,

OLIMP'ADES (1) [olympiads]

QELIZ156:2	H29	The nine {'leven} *Olimp'ades* of her happy reigne;

OLIMPIAD (1) [olympiad]
MGREC93:9   H1606   in the 112 *Olimpiad.*
OLIMPIAS (8) [olympias]
MGREC93:12   H1609   The cruell, proud, *Olimpias,* was his mother,
MGREC115:20   H2539   The Queen *Olimpias,* bears him deadly hate,
MGREC123:23   H2887   Recals *Olimpias,* the Court to grace;
MGREC124:39   H2946   *Olimpias, Aridæus* deadly hates,
MGREC125:14   H2962   *Olimpias* now {soon} enters *Macedon,*
MGREC125:29   H2979   On which *Olimpias* of the like might taste.
MGREC126:5   H2996   And with the rest *Olimpias* pursues,
MGREC126:19   H3010   *Olimpias* wills to keep it, {means to hold out} to the last,
OLIMPUS (1) [olympus]
ELEMEN12:11   H171   And wonderous high *Olimpus,* of such fame,
OLINTHIANS (1) [pl.]
MGREC128:10   H3083   Th' hatefull *Olinthians* to *Greece* re-brings;
OLIVE (1)
ELEMEN13:27   H228   The Vine, the Olive, and the Figtree want:
OLYMPIAD See OLIMPIAD
OLYMPIADS See OLIMP'ADES
OLYMPIAS (3)
MGREC129:29   H3143   (But, *Olympias,* thought to {would} preferre th' other:)
MGREC130:29   H3181   *Philip* and *Olympias* both were slain,
MGREC130:31   H3181   Two other children by *Olympias* kill'd,
OLYMPUS See OLIMPUS
OMEN (2)
MGREC93:22   H1619   An Omen, to their near approaching woe;
SIDNEY151:7   H69   That such an omen once was in our land,
OMINOUS (1)
ELEMEN17:16   H380   Whereof the first, so ominous I rain'd,
OMIT (2)
ELEMEN19:10   H455   With thousands moe, which now I may omit;
MGREC109:4   H2261   His warrs with sundry nations I'le omit,
OMITS (1)
MPERS74:21   H844   His title to make strong omits no thing;
OMNIPOTENT (1)
MEDDM208:33   Hp290   it hath ouer come the omnipotent himself, as when Moses
OMPHALA (1)
SIDNEY151:14   H69   But *Omphala,* set *Hercules* to spin,
OMPHIS (1)
MGREC109:17   H2276   And *Omphis,* King of that part of the land:
ONCE (57)
ELEMEN13:41   H242   If {When} once you feele me, your foundation, quake,
ELEMEN17:7   H371   And that an Island makes, which once was maine.
ELEMEN18:21   H425   Ye forging Smiths, if Bellowes once were gone;
HUMOUR21:8   H36   We both once Masculines, the world doth know,
HUMOUR21:18   H46   Where if your rule once grow {prove} predominant,
HUMOUR23:16   H126   If once thou'rt great, what followes thereupon?
AGES40:7   H188   Of all at once, who not so wise, as fair,
AGES45:12   H394   Could once reverse, their shamefull destiny.
AGES45:12   H394   Could length their dayes or once reverse their fate
AGES45:28   H418   And back, once straight, begins apace to bow.

ONE (137)

ELEMEN14:30	H272	Not one of us, all knowes, that's like to thee,
ELEMEN17:10	H374	And but one land was *Affrica* and *Spayne,*
ELEMEN17:39	H403	Mortalls, what one of you, that loves not me,
ELEMEN19:1	H446	For all Philosophers make one of me.
HUMOUR20:20	H12	Had leave to speake, succeeding one the other;
HUMOUR21:6	H34	My self, and Mother, one as you shal see,
HUMOUR21:17	H45	One of your selves are my compeers, in place:
HUMOUR23:30	H140	But one of you would make a worthy King:
HUMOUR24:5	H154	And one thing more to close with {up} my narration.
HUMOUR26:2	H232	Yet such, when we al four are joyn'd in one.
HUMOUR27:35	H306	One touch thereof so beautifies the skin;
HUMOUR27:38	H309	But here's {here} one thrusts her heat, where'ts not requir'd
HUMOUR29:33	H384	Then by assault to gain one, not our own.
HUMOUR30:32	H424	These two in one cannot have residence.
HUMOUR31:20	H453	I now speake unto al, no more to one;
HUMOUR31:29	H462	Unstable is the one, so is {and} the other.
HUMOUR33:5	H519	Rather then loose, one beateous *Hellena;*
HUMOUR34:24	H579	But a mad one, say I, where 'tis too great,
HUMOUR34:25	H580	Phrensie's worse, then folly, one would more glad,
AGES36:9	H33	No wooden horse, but one of mettal try'd:
AGES36:14	H38	As one that cared, for a good report.
AGES36:33	H57	To do as he, the rest {each one} ful soon assents,
AGES41:28	H245	Thus out of one extreame, into another.
AGES45:4	H386	A royal one by gifts from strangers hands
AGES45:8	H390	A Royall one, by almes from Subjects hands,
AGES45:13	H395	I've seen one stab'd, another {and some to} loose his head
SEASONS48:22	H75	One hangs his head, the other stands upright:
SEASONS49:22	H113	'Mongst all ye shepheards, never but one man,
SEASONS51:39	H215	The Northern Pole beholdeth not one ray.
MASSYR53:17	H7	But each one thought his petty rule was high,
MASSYR53:34	H24	One hundred fourteen years, he after dyed.
MASSYR54:22	H49	The walls one hundred sixty foot upright,
MASSYR60:40	H305	That he, and *Belochus,* one could not be,
MASSYR61:3	H308	That those two made but one, we need not doubt:
MASSYR68:13	H599	As thus amort {dead, alive} he sits, as all {one} undone:
MASSYR68:25	H611	And did one thing worthy a King (though late)
MPERS70:31	H702	And at one blow, worlds head, she headlesse makes;
MPERS71:4	H718	Now quiet lyes under one marble stone.
MPERS72:18	H766	This strange severity, one time {sometimes} he us'd,
MPERS72:25	H773	Having one son, in whom he did delight,
MPERS73:14	H801	The Princes meet to chuse one in his stead,
MPERS73:38	H823	But {That} better one, then many Tyrants reigne.
MPERS78:38	H1019	One of his five Sons there, might be releast;
MPERS79:21	H1047	One King, so many Subjects should possesse;
MPERS80:9	H1076	When as one thousand, could some Millions {a million} daunt;
MPERS81:12	H1120	And that with *Xerxes* they would be at one,
MPERS81:35	H1143	{In all} One hundred thousand, and ten thousand make.
MPERS81:39	H1143	For one maine Battell shortly, both provide;
MPERS82:2	H1148	Then for one battel shortly all provide,
MPERS82:18	H1165	Scarce one was left, to carry home the fame;
MPERS84:7	H1235	And a {one} more worthy, placed in her roome,

MPERS86:34	H1350	(One *Greeke* could make ten *Persians* run away)
MPERS87:4	H1360	The one {last} accus'd the other, {first} for these {sad} wars:
MPERS89:6	H1440	Nor wound receiv'd, but one among them all:
MPERS89:13	H1447	may come, and {in short time might} place one in his Throne,
MPERS~~91:22~~	H1532	By poyson caus'd, the young one to lose her life.
MPERS92:19	~~H1577~~	By one of these, he must obtain the place.
MPERS92:25	~~H1583~~	By one *Bagoas,* an Eunuch (as is sed.)
MPERS92:39	H1597	One deluge came, and swept them all away;
MGREC95:23	H1702	But sets {Yet set} one in his roome, and ran away.
MGREC98:29	H1831	He scorns to have one worse then had the other,
MGREC101:25	H1950	Nor yet two Monarchs in one World reside;
MGREC107:14	H2189	And thus unwisely, in one raging {mading} fume,
MGREC108:15	H2231	Nor sex, nor age, nor one, nor other spar'd,
MGREC~~108:41~~	H2257	And being an {one} hundred twenty thousand strong,
MGREC109:8	H2267	Nor had that drunken god, one that {who} would take
MGREC111:3	H2348	Where one hundred {Whether} Embassadours, {ninety} or
MGREC113:39	H2466	Was one of more esteem, but lesse desart;
MGREC~~114:12~~	H2481	From one stood by he snacht a partizan,
MGREC117:30	H2637	Except by *Artabasus* daughter one;
MGREC119:1	H2691	But nothing lesse: each one himself intends.
MGREC129:8	H3122	Resolves to quit his fears by one deed done,
MGREC129:11	H3125	But for one act she did, just was her end,
MGREC131:16	H3208	Nor to his son did there {e're} one foot remain,
MGREC132:8	H3243	And so falls out to be extinct in one,
MGREC132:28	H3273	Did ne'r regain one foot in *Asia.*
MGREC136:15	H3429	*Yet in this Chaos, one shall easily spy,*
MROMAN137:17	H3468	And *Sabins,* as one people, dwelt in *Rome.*
MROMAN139:22	H3550	The Government they change, a new one bring,
DIALOG145:19	H168	One saith its he, the other no such thing.
DIALOG146:10	H198	One battell, two or three I might abide,
DIALOG148:26	H291	And Jew and Gentile, to one worship go,
SIDNEY149:11	H10	*Mars* and *Minerva* did in one agree,
SIDNEY149:24	H23	That this one Volumne should exhaust your store.
SIDNEY151:13	~~H69~~	To be within the bounds of one world kept,
SIDNEY152:10	~~H79~~	In being done by one of their own sex;
SIDNEY152:25	H94	Philip *and* Alexander *both in one.*
DUBART154:24	H69	In giving one, what would have served seven.
QELIZ158:20	H129	*In every one, be her great glory famed.*
TDUDLEY165:26	H28	One of thy Founders, him *New-England* know,
CONTEM167:26	H3	When *Phœbus* wanted but one hour to bed,
CONTEM169:20	H60	They kept one tune, and plaid on the same string,
CONTEM173:28	H193	So each one tunes his pretty instrument,
FLESH175:6	H6	One flesh was call'd, who had her eye
FLESH176:6	H46	For from one father are we not,
AUTHOR177:38	H10	I cast thee by as one unfit for light,
BIRTH179:26	H1-2	*Before the Birth of one of her Children.*
BIRTH180:3	H13	That when that knot's unty'd that made us one,
1HUSB180:23	H2	If ever two were one, then surely we.
1LETTER181:5	H3	If two be one, as surely thou and I,
1LETTER181:28	H26	I here, thou there, yet both but one.
2LETTER182:19	H25	But for one moneth I see no day (poor soul)

3LETTER183:27	H29	Together at one Tree, oh let us brouze,
3LETTER183:28	H30	And like two Turtles roost within one house,
3LETTER183:29	H31	And like the Mullets in one River glide,
3LETTER183:30	H32	Let's still remain but one, till death divide.
CHILDRN184:14	H3	I had eight birds hatcht in one nest,
CHILDRN185:3	H29	One to the Academy flew
1SIMON188:3	H4	*a moneth, and one day old.*
MERCY189:3	H24	One week she only past in pain and woe,
MERCY189:11	H32	She one hath left, a joy to thee and me,
MEDDM196:34	Hp274	hath been deliuered vp by one traytor w^th^in, and that man w^ch^
MEDDM197:1	Hp274	of Sathan without could not hurt, hath, been foild by one
MEDDM199:20	Hp278	man aimes at profit by the one & content in the other, but often
MEDDM200:3	Hp278	sin, is it not a little one? will ere long say of a greater Tush god
MEDDM200:34	Hp280	he knows is enough for one of twice his strength, much lesse
MEDDM201:26	Hp281	for Contrary ends, the one holds fast, the other puts forward,
MEDDM202:5	Hp281	or sprung out of the loynes of one Adam, some set in y^e^
MEDDM203:31	Hp284	of ten lepers that were Cleansed, but of one that returned
MEDDM204:17	Hp285	doth many times, both reward and punish for one and ye same
MEDDM204:27	Hp285	vpon one that is in a far better estate then himself, but let him
MEDDM204:28	Hp285	that is lower then he is and if he se, that such a one beares
MEDDM206:6	Hp287	We se in the firmament there is but one Sun, among a
MEDDM206:7	Hp287	and those starres also, to differ much one from the other, in
MEDDM206:9	Hp287	one Sun, so is it in the Church both militant and triumphant,
MEDDM206:10	Hp287	but one Christ, who is the Sun of righteousnes, in the midest of
MEDDM209:18	Hp291	hath by his prouidence so ordered, that no one Covntry hath all
MEDDM209:21	Hp291	so it is with men, there was neuer yet any one man that had
MEDDM209:25	Hp291	below, as also that god will haue vs beholden one to another
MYCHILD216:15	Hp241	to me, and cost me many prayers + tears before I obtaind one,
MYCHILD216:22	Hp241	but by one afflict^n^ or other hath made me look home, and
MYCHILD218:20	Hp244	the same Christ, ye same word, They only enterprett it one
HOURS234:3	H17	I haue a more beloued one
HOURS234:27	H41	And talk to my Beloued one

ONELY (2) [only]

HUMOUR23:22	H132	Onely to raise my honours to the Skyes,
MGREC132:24	H3269	Onely restrained of his liberty;

ONES (12) [pl.]

ELEMEN11:7	H127	Which Kings, and mighty ones; amaz'd with wonder,
AGES45:10	H392	And worthy {better} ones, put to {suffer} extremity:
MPERS91:30	H~~1544~~	As all the mighty ones, have done, and must:
MGREC124:23	H2930	The great ones now begin to shew their minde,
DIALOG144:8	H118	'Mongst all the cruelties which I have {by great ones} done,
DAVID159:1	H16	For the mighty ones did soone decay,
TDUDLEY166:7	H49	As in the mean ones, of our foolish dayes,
CONTEM173:5	H173	To see what trade they great ones there do drive,
CHILDRN186:12	H79	Where old ones, instantly grow young,
CHILDRN186:17	H84	Among your young ones take your rest,
MEDDM205:37	Hp287	and ther are some (and they sincere ones too) who haue not
SON231:9	H21	When royall ones y^t^ Time did dye,

ONIX (1) [onyx]

VANITY160:32	H42	For *Saphyre, Onix, Topas,* who will {would} change,

ONLY (35) See also ONELY

HUMOUR20:32	H24	Only she crav'd, to have a vacant space.
HUMOUR21:41	H69	She loves her sword, only because its gilt;
HUMOUR24:4	H153	What differences the Sex, but only heat?
HUMOUR24:20	H169	Ile only shew the wrongs, thou'st done to me.
HUMOUR27:3	H274	Besides the vehement heat, only there known,
HUMOUR30:10	H402	As of that only part I was {were} the Queen:
AGES37:20	H82	My sillinesse did only take delight,
AGES43:17	H312	Sometimes vaine-glory is the only bait,
SEASONS47:35	H47	But only once at *Joshua's* strange command;
SEASONS51:14	H188	For then in *Eden* was not only seen
MASSYR58:41	H224	Only intreats them, {to} joyn their force with his,
MPERS70:38	H709	But in this {his} Tombe was only to be found
MPERS72:28	H773	And only for his fathers faithfullnesse,
MPERS82:12	H1159	Three thousand scapes, for to {only can} run home agen;
MGREC94:18	H1656	Reply'd, enough, sith only hope he kept.
MGREC97:36	H1797	A King he was, and that not only so,
MGREC132:40	H3287	And so himselfe the only Monarch make;
MGREC133:11	H3299	So three Successors only did remaine;
CONTEM174:27	H225	Only above is found all with security.
FLESH175:37	H37	For things unknown, only in mind.
3LETTER183:23	H25	Return my Dear, my joy, my only Love,
MERCY189:3	H24	One week she only past in pain and woe,
MEDDM201:28	Hp281	not only to bid them hold fast the form of sound Doctrin, but
MEDDM202:21	Hp282	Sometimes the sun is only shadowed by a cloud, that wee
MEDDM205:33	Hp286	and some haue nothing to shew but leaues only, and some
MEDDM206:2	Hp287	are others that haue nothing to commend them, but only a gay
MEDDM207:4	Hp288	that god, bestows on the sons of men, are not only abused
MEDDM207:34	Hp289	not only their death, but their graue, is liuely represented
MEDDM209:2	Hp291	not let thee go replys Jacob till thou blesse me, faith is not only
MYCHILD218:20	Hp244	the same Christ, yᵉ same word, They only enterprett it one
MYCHILD219:3	Hp245	Now to yᵉ King Imortall, Eternall invisible, the only wise God,
JULY223:29	Hp251	him who is the only portion of his Servants.
28AUG226:1	Hp254	me a vessell fitt for his vse why should I not bare it not only
30SEPT227:19	Hp257	not in yᵗ sore manner somt. he hath. I desire not only willingly
11MAYB228:33	Hp259	testefye my thankfullnes not only in word, but in Deed, that my

ON-SET (1)

MPERS82:5	H1152	No longer dar'd, but fiercely {bravely} on-set gave,

ONYX See ONIX

OPE (4)

ELEMEN9:9	H43	Set ope those gates, that 'fore so strong was {were} barr'd.
ELEMEN13:37	H238	To ope those veines of Mine, audacious bold:
SEASONS52:36	H251	The Rivers now do {'gin to} ope, and {the} Snows do {to} melt,
MROMAN137:28	H3479	Kept shut in peace, but {set} ope when bloud was spilt;

OPEN (4)

MASSYR61:36	H341	And *Ahaz* open, at his mercy lay,
MGREC103:2	H2013	With open Gates, the wealthy town did stand,
MEDDM196:22	Hp273	open a prosperous state makes a secure christian, but
BYNIGHT220:4	H5	My waking eyes were open kept

OPENLY (1)

MGREC106:39	H2173	The ruder sort, did openly deride

OPERATION (1)
MYCHILD218:9 Hp244 mvst bee it or none. Haue I not fovnd y^t operation by it that no
OPPONENT (2)
MGREC~~124:8~~ H2913 His proud opponent hopes soon to withstand.
MGREC124:14 H2921 And his opponent still got {*Cassanders* forces had the} upper
OPPONENTS (1) [pl.]
MGREC118:29 H2678 His chief opponents who kept off the Crown, {Control'd his
OPPORTUNITY (3)
MASSYR63:6 H391 Of opportunity advantage takes,
MPERS75:10 H871 When opportunity he saw was fit,
MGREC124:24 H2931 And act, as opportunity they finde:
OPPORTVNITY (1) [opportunity]
MYCHILD215:13 Hp240 opportvnity to speak to any of yov much lesse to All, thovght it
OPPOSE (7)
AGES43:6 H301 That did oppose me, to my longed bay:
MPERS76:4 H902 Sharp wants, not swords, his vallour did oppose;
MGREC100:16 H1900 to resist {man's there} his valour showes {Army to oppose};
MGREC106:8 H2142 To see if any dare his might oppose;
MGREC108:28 H2244 Where *Scithians* rude, his valour {army} doth oppose,
MGREC121:7 H2785 Brave *Ptolomy* to th' utmost to oppose.
MGREC124:12 H2919 Whom *Polisperchon* labours to oppose,
OPPOSED (1)
MYCHILD218:13 Hp244 opposed it? Is there any story but that wch showes the
OPPOSITE (1)
MASSYR64:41 H465 Fetch {Fetcht} rubbish from the opposite old town,
OPPOSITES (1) [pl.]
MPERS84:~~12~~ H1248 And o're his opposites still got the day,
OPPOSITION (1)
HUMOUR32:25 H499 Where opposition is diametrical:
OPPRESS'D (1) [oppressed]
AGES42:19 H277 Did toile, did broile, oppress'd, did steal and lye.
OPPRESSE (2) [oppress]
MASSYR54:28 H55 This Tyrant did his neighbours all oppresse,
MEDDM199:19 Hp278 wearys the body, and many thoughts oppresse the minde
OPPRESSED (2) See also OPPRESS'D
AGES42:6 H264 The proud I crush'd, th' oppressed I set free,
2LETTER182:32 H38 Oppressed minds, abruptest tales do tell.
OPPRESSING (1)
MASSYR55:4 H70 This great oppressing *Ninus* dead, and gone,
OPPRESSION (1)
DIALOG144:14 H124 With Usury, Extortion, and Oppression,
OPPREST (1)
AGES43:5 H300 Opprest, and sunke, and sact, {stav'd} all in my way;
OPPROBRIOUS (1)
HUMOUR25:12 H201 And though thou'st us'd me, with opprobrious spight, {right:}
OPTICK (1)
HUMOUR34:1 H556 The optick nerve, coats, humours, all are mine,
ORACLE (3)
MPERS69:23 H645 And the ambiguous Oracle did trust,
MPERS82:2 H1147 Was Victory, by Oracle fore-told:
MGREC112:37 H2423 He did the Oracle of *Iupiter* {*Jove*} deride,

ORACLES (1) [pl.]
HUMOUR23:27 H137 They're held for Oracles, they are so wise.
ORANGE (1)
SEASONS51:7 H181 The Orange, Lemon, Dangle on the tree;
ORATOUR (1)
MGREC120:4 H2735 *Demosthenes,* that sweet tongu'd oratour.
ORBE (1) [orb]
ELEMEN9:28 H62 The Sun, an Orbe of Fire was held of old,
ORCHARD (2)
DUBART153:13 H17 Flowers, fruits, in garden, orchard, or in field;
MEDDM205:34 Hp286 them are dry stocks so is it in the church wch is gods orchard,
ORCHARDS (2) [pl.]
ELEMEN11:30 H150 In vine-yards, orchards, gardens, and corne fields,
MEDDM205:31 Hp286 We see in orchards, some trees soe fruitfull, that the waight of
ORDAIN'D (5) [ordained]
HUMOUR32:33 H507 My polish'd skin was not ordain'd for skars,
AGES42:24 H282 If to Agricolture, I was ordain'd:
MPERS85:20 H1296 *Amerges,* whom their {for} Vice-roy he ordain'd
DIALOG143:23 H92 They're for my punishments ordain'd on high,
CHILDRN185:16 H42 As is ordain'd, so shall they light.
ORDER (5)
ELEMEN8:9 H7 And {That} in due order each her turne should speake,
MPERS88:10 H1403 But when their order, and {their} silence they saw;
MEDDM208:31 Hp290 reversed the order of nature, quenched the violence of the fire,
MYCHILD216:24 Hp242 felt my heart out of order, but I haue expected correct^n for it,
MYCHILD217:37 Hp243 + ye Earth, the order of all things night and day, Summer
ORDER'D (1) [ordered]
MGREC122:40 H2861 All to be order'd there as he thought best:
ORDERED (4)
MPERS83:18 H1206 And by his craft, ordered the matter so,
MGREC130:19 H3174 And now he thinks {hopes}, he's ordered all so well,
DDUDLEY167:17 H14 *The which she ordered with dexterity.*
MEDDM209:18 Hp291 god hath by his prouidence so ordered, that no one Covntry
ORDERETH (1)
MEDDM203:34 Hp284 great ingratitude after their successes, but he that ordereth his
ORDERS (1)
MPERS76:25 H923 Which husht, he straight so orders his affaires;
ORDER'ST (1)
SON231:1 H13 And order'st so the adverse wind
ORE See URE
O'RE-CHARG'D (1) [overcharged]
MGREC112:39 H2425 *Philotas* thus o're-charg'd, with wrong, and greif,
O'RE COME (1) [overcome]
ELEMEN 10:41 H116 Which when they could not be o're come by foes
O'RE-FLOW (1) [overflow] See also O'REFLOW, O'RFLOW
DAVID159:13 H28 O *Israels* Dames, o're-flow your beauteous eyes,
O'REFLOW (1) [overflow] See also O'RE-FLOW, O'RFLOW
ELEMEN15:20 H302 When I run low, and not o'reflow her brinks;
O'RE-FLOWN (1) [overflown] See also O'REFLOWN
MPERS82:38 H1185 O're-flown with torrent of her ruby {guiltless} blood.

O'REFLOWN (1) [overflown] See also O'RE-FLOWN
  MASSYR59:20 H244   For by the rain, was *Tygris* so o'reflown,
O'REWHELM'D (1) [overwhelmed] See also O'R-WHELMED
  MGREC104:16 H2068 Sate down o'rewhelm'd, with sorrow, and despair,
O'RFLOW (1) [overflow] See also O'RE-FLOW, O'REFLOW
  DIALOG147:29 H253   The briny Ocean will o'rflow your shore,
ORGANS (1) [pl.]
  ELEMEN18:15 H419   Your Drums, your Trumpets, and your Organs sound,
ORIENT (1)
  MGREC115:1 H2512 Unto the furthest {farthest} bounds of th' orient;
ORIGINAL (2)
  ELEMEN19:37 H478   Imprisoned I, am the original.
  MASSYR53:31 H21   Of *Saturn,* he was the original,
ORIGINALL (1) [original]
  ELEMEN11:28 H148   I am th' originall of man and beast,
ORION (1)
  ELEMEN10:3 H78   With {There's} *Orion* arm'd, attended by his dog,
ORNAMENTS (5) [pl.]
  MASSYR64:17 H441   The temple of rich ornaments defac'd,
  MGREC96:21 H1741 Their golden Ornaments so {how} to set forth,
  MGREC97:10 H1771 The Regall ornaments now {were} lost, the treasure
  MGREC102:3 H1973 At *Arbela* left, his ornaments, and treasure,
  DAVID159:17 H32   On your array put ornaments of gold,
ORPHAN (1)
  MGREC129:31 H3145 This {Orphan} Prince began for to compassionate.
ORTHOBULUS (1)
  SEASONS49:30 H119 *Orthobulus,* nor yet *Sebastia* great,
ORTHOS (1)
  MPERS79:9   H1031 A Sea passage cuts, behind *Orthos* {*Athos*} Mount.
O'R-WHELM'D (1) [overwhelmed] See also O'REWHELM'D
  MPERS71:29   H743   The stormed dust o'r-whelm'd his daring bands;
OSTENTATION (2)
  HUMOUR33:14 H528   Yet without ostentation I may say,
  TDUDLEY166:6 H48   No ostentation seen in all his wayes,
OSTIA (1)
  MROMAN138:20 H3510 Faire *Ostia* he built, this Town, it stood,
OSTRACISME (1)
  MPERS84:14   H1250 When under Ostracisme he did lye.
OSTRICH (2)
  ELEMEN15:7 H289   The Peacock, and the Ostrich, share in woe:
  ELEMEN19:6 H451   The Ostrich with her plumes, th'Eagle with her eyne;
OTHER (68)
  FATHER5:29 H30   My other foures, do intermixed tell
  ELEMEN14:31 H273   Ever in craving, from the other three:
  HUMOUR20:13 H5   Loe! other foure step up, crave leave to shew
  HUMOUR20:20 H12   Had leave to speake, succeeding one the other;
  HUMOUR20:24 H16   Who had precedency of all the other.
  HUMOUR21:32 H60   Here's Sister Ruddy, worth the other two,
  HUMOUR25:8 H197   Thy other scoffes not worthy of reply:
  HUMOUR31:29 H462   Unstable is the one, so is {and} the other.
  HUMOUR34:17 H572   Some other parts there issue from the Brain,

HUMOUR35:7	H603	Her dry, dry Cholers other hand shal grasp;
AGES35:17	H3	Loe now! four other acts {act} upon the stage,
AGES36:23	H47	In's other hand a glasse, ev'n almost run,
AGES46:12	H443	Though reading other Works, doth much refresh,
SEASONS48:22	H75	One hangs his head, the other stands upright:
MASSYR59:7	H231	For victory obtain'd the other day;
MPERS69:12	H634	Adopts her Son for his, having no other:
MPERS77:35	H976	Flattering *Mardonius* on th' other side,
MPERS78:40	H1021	The other four he freely gave away:
MPERS80:20	H1087	In this Streight, as the other, firmly stand.
MPERS81:34	H1142	The other *Greeks,* which were confederate,
MPERS81:41	H1145	For other {The rest had} Weapons, they had none would {do
MPERS82:3	H1150	Ten dayes these Armies did each other face,
MPERS82:6	H1153	The other not a hand, nor sword will {would} wave,
MPERS86:13	H1329	*Cyrus* o'th' other side, weighs in his mind,
MPERS87:4	H1360	The one {last} accus'd the other, {first} for these {sad} wars:
MPERS89:28	H1462	They quak'd, to heare them, to each other call.
MPERS90:16	H̶1̶4̶8̶4̶	Straight to transport them to the other side,
MPERS92:1	H̶1̶5̶5̶5̶	In after wars were burnt, 'mongst other things?
MPERS9̶2̶:̶5̶	H1562	Inthron'd by *Bogoas* in the room of th' other:
MGREC96:28	H1748	And as much good she did, as any other.
MGREC98:16	H1818	The other by his men fetcht all by Land;
MGREC98:29	H1831	He scorns to have one worse then had the other,
MGREC101:38	H1967	Some write, th' other had a million, some more,
MGREC107:5	H2180	That other matters may {might} take up their minds.
MGREC107:29	H2204	How to passe {the River} over, and gaine {to} the other Land;
MGREC107:37	H2212	They all passe over, to the other place;
MGREC108:15	H2231	Nor sex, nor age, nor one, nor other spar'd,
MGREC110:10	H2310	With *Ptolomy,* sends part o' th' other side.
MGREC114:23	H2493	For this alone, and for no other cause,
MGREC115:15	H2524	The other was the greatest Deity.
MGREC1̶1̶6̶:̶1̶0̶	H2572	She laid it more to heart, then any other,
MGREC121:5	H2783	From the invasions of the other three;
MGREC121:13	H2791	And from the other, {side} daily some did gaine.
MGREC121:27	H2809	That *Eumenes* got of the other three,
MGREC122:20	H2845	She daughter to his son, who had no other;
MGREC122:32	H2851	Who vext the Queen more then the other farre;
MGREC123:12	H2874	That {And} by the selfe-same traps the other laid,
MGREC127:12	H3042	But leave him building, other in their urn,
MGREC129:27	H3141	*Polisperchon* brings up the other son,
MGREC129:29	H3143	(But, *Olympias,* thought to {would} preferre th' other:)
MGREC130:31	H̶3̶1̶8̶1̶	Two other children by *Olympias* kill'd,
MGREC136:12	H3426	*This fourth to th' other three, now might be brought.*
MROMAN1̶3̶8̶:̶5̶	H3495	The *Romans* Conquereth, others {other} yeeld the day,
DIALOG145:19	H168	One saith its he, the other no such thing.
DUBART153:33	H37	Thy profound Learning; viewing other while
FLESH175:8	H8	The other Spirit, who did rear
CHILDRN185:13	H39	My other three, still with me nest,
MEDDM199:20	Hp278	at profit by the one & content in the other, but often misses
MEDDM201:26	Hp281	Contrary ends, the one holds fast, the other puts forward, such
MEDDM201:33	Hp281	is (of all other) most Comfortable

MEDDM202:13	Hp282	among the dead, and no other reason can be giuen of all this
MEDDM202:25	Hp282	some other time, yet he affords so much light as may direct
MEDDM204:34	Hp285	land askes much more paines, then some other doth to be
MEDDM206:7	Hp287	and those starres also, to differ much one from the other, in
MEDDM207:15	Hp288	shadow very comfortable, yet there is some worm or other,
MEDDM208:7	Hp289	you vse no other meanes to extinguish them so distance of
MYCHILD216:22	Hp242	but by one afflict^n or other hath made me look home, and
SON230:27	H10	The other sank low in the Deep.

OTHERS (23) [pl.]

HUMOUR21:29	H57	'Twixt them and others, what ist makes the odds
AGES39:11	H154	As might my self, and others, profit much:
AGES43:16	~~H308~~	Which others scatter, like the dew in *May.*
AGES44:32	H365	And like a Cedar, others so surmount,
AGES45:14	H396	And others fly their Country, through their {struck both with gilt
MASSYR55:10	H76	Others report, she was a vestal Nun,
MPERS73:37	H822	But others thought (none of the dullest braine,)
MPERS87:11	H1367	And others to be warm'd by this new sun,
MGREC116:7	H2567	By others thought, and that more generally,
MGREC117:9	H2616	So the same cup to his, did others fill.
MGREC121:36	H2818	The others all, had kingdomes in their eye,
MGREC127:1	H3031	Some slew, some fry'd, of others, stopt the breath;
MGREC127:3	H3033	Which she had often made others to sup:
MROMAN137:22	H3473	Others, the seven and thirtyeth of his reigne
MROMAN138:5	H3495	The *Romans* Conquereth, others {other} yeeld the day,
DIALOG144:5	H115	Martyrs, and others, dying causelesly:
QELIZ157:31	H99	To read what others write, and then {so} admire.
TDUDLEY165:25	H27	While others tell his worth, I'le not be dumb:
CHILDRN185:18	H44	Let others know what are my fears
MEDDM206:2	Hp287	there are others that haue nothing to commend them, but only
MEDDM206:13	Hp287	a lesse degree, & others (and they indeed the most in number)
BYNIGHT220:2	H3	By night when others soundly slept,
JULY223:27	Hp251	read this hereafter, and to others that shall read it when I shall

OTHERS (5) [pl.; poss.]

ELEMEN8:25	H23	The others enmity: {difference,} being lesse, did cease
AGES40:10	H191	Sometimes I sit carousing others health,
AGES~~45:4~~	H385	I've Princes seen to live on others lands;
AGES45:7	~~H390~~	I've seen a Prince, to live on others lands,
2SIMON195:11	Hp271	vpon others conceptions because I would leaue you nothing

OTHERS (4) [poss.]

FATHER5:30	H31	Each others faults, and where themselves excell:
MPERS90:37	H1504	And {Commission} hath command, to take the others head,
MGREC~~128:16~~	H3089	For {And} he declares against his {the others} injuries;
TDUDLEY166:32	H74	Where we with joy each others face shall see,

OTHERWISE (1)

SAMUEL228:18	H19	If otherwise I goe to Rest

OUERCAME (1) [overcame] See also OVER-CAME

MEDDM209:11	Hp291	thornes in their sides, and at last ouercame them, and kept

OUGHT (10) n. See also OVGHT

ELEMEN13:3	H204	That you ambition laid, ought but my bones?
ELEMEN13:10	H211	If ought you have to use, to wear, to eate?
HUMOUR23:39	H149	Without my lively heat, do's ought thats flat.

MGREC~~110:18~~	H2320	In looks or gesture not abased ought,
TDUDLEY165:31	H33	Who is't can tax thee ought, but for thy zeal?
TDUDLEY166:21	H63	Where storms, nor showrs, nor ought can damnifie.
CONTEM172:17	H152	Could hinder ought, but still augment its force:
1HUSB180:30	H9	Nor ought but love from thee, give recompence.
VERSES183:36	H3	If worth in me, or ought I do appear,
11MAYB228:32	Hp259	ought to doe. Lord Thou y^t knowest All things know'st that I

OUGHT (7) v. See also OVGHT

MASSYR61:30	H335	To whom, he ought all loyalty of heart.
SIDNEY149:32	H41	The love thy {his} Country ought thee {him}, was as much.
DUBART154:19	H64	The Oaken garland ought to deck their browes,
DUBART155:5	H90	*Now shew'd what once they ought, Humanity,*
TDUDLEY165:9	H11	To whom I ought whatever I could doe:
MEDDM208:3	Hp289	these things must be what manner of persons ought we to be,
REMB236:11	H26	And walk before thee as they ought,

OUT-BID (1)

HUMOUR21:35	H63	And there she wil out-bid us all, I think;

OUT-BRAV'D (1) [out-braved]

MPERS71:30	H744	But scorning thus by *Jove* to be out-brav'd,

OUT-CRIES (1)

MGREC108:29	H2245	And with their out-cries, in a {an} hideous sort,

OUT-FACE (1)

MASSYR64:28	H452	As might not him, but all the world out-face;

OUT-LIVED (1)

MGREC132:38	H3285	That now he had out-lived all the rest:

OUT-LIVING (1)

DUBART155:9	H94	*But Fame, out-living both, he is reviv'd.*

OUT-MATCH (1)

MPERS80:17	H1084	Yet thinking to out-match his foes at Sea,

OUT-RAGES (1) [outrages]

MGREC126:39	H3028	Her out-rages too tedious to relate,

OUTRAGES (2) [pl.]

ELEMEN13:33	H234	But to all outrages their hunger runnes.
MGREC~~127:41~~	H3072	*Cassanders* outrages at large doth tell,

OUTRIGHT (1)

ELEMEN~~14:10~~	H252	Some kill outright, and some do stupifye:

OUTSIDE (1)

SEASONS48:5	H58	The outside strong, the inside warme and neat.

OUTWARD (4)

AGES~~41:2~~	H222	With ugly {outward} marks of his eternal {inward loathsome}
MEDDM207:9	Hp288	are lords we will come no more at thee If outward blessings,
MYSOUL225:1	H5	What tho: thy outward Man decay,
11MAYA226:22	Hp255	while my body decayes, and ye weaknes of this outward

OVEN (1)

SEASONS49:12	H103	Like as an oven, that long time hath been heat.

OVER-CAME (4) [overcame] See also OUERCAME

MGREC97:21	H1782	Then that the *Persian* King he over-came;
MGREC113:34	H2461	This that *Parmenio,* who still over-came,
MGREC114:35	H2505	The mighty *Persian* King he over-came,
SIDNEY150:34	H61	Thus being over-come, he over-came.

OVERCAME (2) See also OUERCAME, OVER-CAME
MGREC95:9   H1688 *Miletus,* and *Pamphilia* overcame,
MGREC116:15   H2581 But with the world his vertues overcame,
OVERCHARGED See O'RE-CHARG'D
OVER-COME (2) [overcome] See also O'RE COME
MPERS69:30   H652 With pressing grief, and sorrow, over-come,
SIDNEY150:34 H61 Thus being over-come, he over-came.
OVER-CURIOUS (2)
ELEMEN10:30   H105 The over-curious second *Pliny* slew:
MPERS69:21   H643 Who over-curious of wars event,
OVERFLOW See O'RE-FLOW, O'REFLOW, O'RFLOW
OVERFLOWN See O'RE-FLOWN, O'REFLOWN
OVER-FLUENT (1)
PROLOG6:28   H12 'Twixt him and me, that over-fluent store;
OVER-GLAD (1)
DUBART153:26 H30 And tells her tales; (his full heart over-glad)
OVER-GOE (1)
MPERS90:31   H1498 {Their King} *Agesilus* himself doth over-goe {goe};
OVER-GONE (1)
MGREC112:16   H2402 And his long travells past, and over-gone;
OVER-PAST (1)
MPERS77:22   H963 None write by whom, nor how, 'twas over-past;
OVER-PLUS (1)
MASSYR60:2   H267 With over-plus of all treasures {the wealth} therein,
OVER-RUN (1) [overrun]
MPERS83:34   H1222 Then when the world, they after over-run:
OVERTAKEN (1)
MYCHILD215:26 Hp240 et^c. I avoided it. If at any time I was overtaken wth ye evills, it
OVER-THROW (7) [overthrow]
MPERS80:26   H1093 Received there, a shameful over-throw.
MPERS82:14   H1161 To certifie this finall over-throw.
MPERS90:34   H1501 Which over-throw incens'd the King so sore,
MGREC96:38   H1758 Which made {To make} his over-throw more fierce, and sure.
MGREC97:12   H1773 Yet all this grief, this losse, this over-throw,
MGREC99:39   H1882 How he should over-throw this Monarchy;
MROMAN137:19 H3470 And *Fedinates* they wholly over-throw:
OVERTHROW (2)
MPERS80:22   H1089 That their split sides, witness'd his overthrow;
DIALOG146:12 H200 Who knows, the worst, the best {this} may {be my} overthrow;
OVER-THROWES (1) [overthrows]
MPERS70:27   H698 And *Tomris* Son, an Army over-throwes;
OVER-THROWN (3) [overthrown]
MASSYR61:25   H330 When *Rezin's* slain, his Army over-thrown,
MPERS69:7   H629 When *Sardanapalus* was over-thrown,
MPERS69:24   H646 So over-thrown of *Cyrus,* as was just;
OVERTHROWN (3)
ELEMEN14:17   H259 whole Armies {*Cambyses* Armie} I have {was} overthrown;
MASSYR59:21   H245 of the {that stately} wal it level caus'd to lye; {was overthrown.}
MPERS85:30   H1306 {strength} by their {*Grecians*} helpe were {was} overthrown,
OVERTHROWS (1) See also OVERTHROWES
MPERS83:35   H1223 *Greeks* and *Egyptians* both, he overthrows,

OVER-TOPS (1)
MGREC123:4   H2866   Who in few years the rest so over-tops,
OVER-TURNINGS (1) [overturnings]
MGREC135:9   H3381   Their standings, over-turnings, bounds and fates;
OVERWELM'D (1) [overwhelmed]
ELEMEN19:31   H472   Some overwelm'd with waves, and seen no more.
OVERWHELM (1)
CONTEM172:8   H144   Where gliding streams the Rocks did overwhelm;
OVER-WHELME (1) [overwhelm]
DIALOG141:10   H9   What deluge of new woes thus over-whelme
OVERWHELMED See O'REWHELM'D, O'R-WHELMED, OVERWELM'D
OVGHT (2) n. [ought] See also OUGHT
SOREFIT222:5   H24   Nor ovght on Earth worthy Desire,
MYSOUL225:19 H23   No gain I find in ovght below
OVGHT (2) v. See also OUGHT
MED223:17   Hp250   him as I ovght. Lord haueing this hope let me purefye my self
MYSOUL225:15 H19   And praise thee shall ev'n as I ovght
OVIDS (1) [poss.]
MASSYR63:34   H421   Nor's Metamorphosis from *Ovids* Book,
OW (1) [owe]
REMB235:27   H8   I ow so mvch so little can
OWE (7)
HUMOUR21:9   H37   Now Feminines (a while) for love we owe
MPERS84:16   H1252   This valiant Knight, whom they so much did owe;
MGREC113:27 H2454   Thinking {Fearing} no harme, because he none did owe {doe},
QELIZ156:30   H57   Unto our dread Virago, what they owe:
11MAYA226:15 Hp255   a respite, & some ability to p^rform ye Dutyes I owe to him, and
HOURS234:35   H49   To pay the vowes wch I doe owe
HOURS235:2   H54   Return Thee what I owe.
OWES (3)
FATHER6:12   H46   From her, that to your selfe more duty owes,
HUMOUR30:29 H421   The Liver, Stomach, owes it {their} thanks of right:
MPERS83:36   H1224   And payes them now, {both} according as he owes,
OWLES (1) [owls]
MPERS70:19   H690   For Owles, and Satyres, makes {made} a residence;
OWN (38) See also OWNE
ELEMEN18:38   H442   And in a trice, my own nature resume.
HUMOUR27:12 H283   It is her own heat, not thy faculty,
HUMOUR29:33 H384   Then by assault to gain one, not our own.
AGES37:25   H87   That its own worth, it did not know, nor mind.
AGES40:5   H186   Or stab the man, in's own defence, that's worse.
AGES40:11   H192   Until mine own be gone, my wit, and wealth;
AGES45:2   H380   Wailing his fate. & our own destinies.
MASSYR57:21   H168   Would now advantage take, their own to gain;
MASSYR57:27   H172   Did then incite, them to regain their own.
MASSYR61:26   H331   *Syria* he makes a Province of his own.
MASSYR67:27   H573   Who with his own, and Uncles power anon;
MASSYR68:20   H606   And of his own notorious sins, withall;
MPERS69:8   H630   And from that time, had held it as his own;
MPERS71:23   H737   To hold his own, of his free courtesie;
MPERS74:40   H861   With his own hands cuts off his eares, and nose,

MPERS78:33	H1014	Feasts all this multitude, of his own charge,
MPERS81:33	H1141	He fifty thousand joynes unto his own;
MPERS85:29	H1305	Re-gaines his own, and then {doth} the Rebell breaks: {break,}
MPERS85:35	H1311	No match was high enough, but their own blood,)
MPERS86:10	H1326	Yet doubts, {fears} all he injoyes, is not his own.
MPERS89:11	H1445	If *Greeks* unto their Country-men {own Country should}
MGREC103:16	H2027	Here of his own, he sets a Garrison,
MGREC108:10	H2226	Wherein their own had {got the} soveraignity.
MGREC109:27	H2286	And of his own, a thousand Tallents more.
DIALOG146:8	H196	Am now destroy'd, and slaughter'd by mine own,
SIDNEY152:10	H79	In being done by one of their own sex;
TDUDLEY165:23	H25	So needs no Testimonial from his own;
AUTHOR178:2	H12	Yet being mine own, at length affection would
ANNEB187:29	H19	As if mine own, when thus impermanent.
MERCY188:35	H21	Who lov'd thee more (it seem'd) then her own life.
MEDDM204:23	Hp285	fixe his eye on the command, and not on his own ends, lest he
MYCHILD216:25	Hp242	comonly hath been vpon my own person, in sicknesse
MYCHILD218:27	Hp244	me to my own Relig^n again.
13MAY227:15	H24	All I can giue is but thine own
SAMUEL228:8	H9	He's mine, but more O Lord thine own
2HUSB233:5	H38	Let not thine own Inheritance
HOUSE236:29	H21	It was his own it was not mine
HOUSE237:24	H54	Yet by his Gift is made thine own.

OWN'D (2) [owned]

HUMOUR20:17	H9	Choler was own'd by Fire, and Blood by Aire,
MASSYR60:24	H289	Who own'd the treasures of proud *Babylon,*

OWNE (22) [own]

PROLOG7:23	H35	And poesy made, *Calliope's* owne childe,
ELEMEN9:7	H41	And in despight the City keeps her owne,
HUMOUR27:2	H273	Which without all dispute, is Cholers owne;
HUMOUR28:13	H325	Of all the perverse humours from mine owne.
AGES41:24	H241	I then receiv'd a {an} harvest of mine owne.
AGES42:3	H261	With mine owne fleece, and with my houshold bread.
SEASONS48:29	H82	Each man his owne peculiar excellence,
MPERS72:13	H761	That by her Husbands charge, she caught her owne;
MPERS75:29	H886	Out of his owne revenues beares the charge;
MPERS85:31	H1307	And so each man again possest his owne.
MPERS91:26	H1540	Who sooths him up, his owne desires are Lawes:
MGREC99:7	H1850	For all he offered {offers} now, was but his owne:
MGREC108:1	H2217	Is by his owne, now bound in Iron chaines,
MGREC112:41	H2427	Faine would have spoke, and made his owne defence,
MGREC118:16	H2663	So much these Princes their owne ends respected.
MGREC121:12	H2790	Did make his owne firme to his cause remaine,
MROMAN139:1	H3529	Ascends not up, by merits of his owne,
DIALOG143:40	H109	Nor for their owne, but for their Masters sake;
2SIMON195:12	Hp271	owne, though in value they fall short of all in this kinde yet I
MEDDM203:3	Hp283	of spirit, yet our owne experience would soon haue speld it out,
MEDDM204:12	Hp284	call him to reckoning, he may receiue his owne wth advantage
MEDDM204:30	Hp285	let him look on his owne vnworthynes and that will make him

OXE (1) [ox]

AGES42:34	H290	My fatted Oxe {thriving Cattle}, and my exuberous {new-milch-

OXUS (1) [poss.]
MGREC107:24 H2199 At length, they came to th' River *Oxus* brink,
OYLE (2) [oil]
MPERS75:30 H887 Gives sacrifices, wheat, wine, oyle, and salt,
DAVID159:4 H19 As if his head ne're felt the sacred Oyle:
OYLY (1) [oily]
ELEMEN15:26 H308 There lives the oyly Whale, whom all men know,
OYNTMENT (1) [ointment]
MEDDM208:12 Hp290 A good name, is as a precious oyntment, and it is a great

P

PACE (3)
HUMOUR22:7 H76 To march her pace, to some is greater pain,
MPERS87:8 H1364 Which *Cyrus* heares, and so fore-slowes his pace:
CONTEM172:20 H155 Nor is it rocks or shoals that can obstruct thy pace.
PACES (1) [pl.]
MASSYR56:2 H108 Each Square, was fifteen thousand paces long,
PACK (1)
DIALOG147:22 H247 Let Gaoles be fill'd with th' remnant of that pack,
PAGAN (1)
MGREC100:7 H1891 The Pagan Priest through hire, or else mistake,
PAGE (2)
SEASONS48:18 H71 Whose praise deserves a page, from more then me.
MPERS92:25 H1583 Was to his Predecessors Chamber page.
PAGEANT (1)
MGREC96:2 H1722 For since the world, was no such Pageant seen.
PAID (7) See also PAYD
HUMOUR33:17 H531 No debtor I, because 'tis {it's} paid else where;
MPERS92:14 H1572 Then Natures debt he paid, quite Issue-lesse.
MGREC98:22 H1824 And thus the *Tyrians* for mistrust were paid,
MGREC101:12 H1937 With thirty thousand Tallents, to be paid
MGREC120:37 H2774 Two years and more since, Natures debt he paid,
MGREC130:25 H3180 Now blood was paid with blood, for what was done
HOUSE237:21 H51 'Its purchasèd + paid for too
PAIN (22)
HUMOUR22:7 H76 To march her pace, to some is greater pain,
HUMOUR28:6 H318 With cold distempers, to pain every part;
AGES38:31 H134 What gripes of wind, mine infancy did pain?
SEASONS50:24 H158 He plow'd with pain, but reaping doth rejoyce;
MASSYR64:34 H458 Can *Babels* tired Souldiers tell with pain;
MASSYR65:5 H470 Requited not the cost {loss}, the toyle, and pain.
MPERS90:18 H1485 So after all {Thus finishing} their travell, danger, pain,
MGREC100:33 H1917 Now bids the world adieu, her time {with pain} being spent,

MGREC~~107:39~~	H2214	With little pain there might have kept them still:
VANITY160:1	H11	No, that's but labour anxious, care and pain.
VANITY160:21	H31	While man is man, he shall have ease or pain.
CONTEM170:3	H77	To get his bread with pain, and sweat of face:
CONTEM173:36	H200	Subject to sorrows, losses, sickness, pain,
CONTEM174:7	H207	This weather-beaten vessel wrackt with pain,
SICKNES179:7	H27	O great's the gain, though got with pain,
DISTEMP179:24	H12	He eas'd my Soul of woe, my flesh of pain,
CHILDRN184:16	H5	I nurst them up with pain and care,
CHILDRN185:31	H57	Great was my pain when I you bred,
MERCY189:3	H24	One week she only past in pain and woe,
MEDDM197:33	Hp275	greif and pain till they turn to dust, and then are they fine
MYCHILD217:25	Hp243	Lord, and when I haue been in sicknes + pain, I haue thought
THEART229:2	H4	From sicknes, death, + pain.

PAIN'D (1) [pained]

MASSYR64:6	H430	Kild, sav'd, pull'd down, set up, or pain'd, or eas'd;

PAINE (6)

PROLOG7:10	H24	A full requitall of his striving paine:
ELEMEN9:13	H47	That so in time it might require your paine;
ELEMEN13:24	H225	He sometimes findes, maugre his toyling paine,
HUMOUR23:14	H124	Where paine and sore obstructions, {obstruction} thou dost
AGES37:9	H71	To tel that paine, which cann't be told by tongue;
AGES45:19	~~H401~~	I've seen a land unmoulded with great paine.

PAINED See **PAIN'D**

PAINEFULL (1) [painful]

AGES42:27	H285	My wakefull thoughts, up to my painefull gaine.

PAINES (9) [pains]

AGES41:31	H248	Be my condition mean, I then take paines;
AGES43:28	H323	{The Strangury} Torments me with intollerable {sore} paines;
MEDDM204:34	Hp285	and some land askes much more paines, then some other doth
MEDDM207:25	Hp289	no paines nor troubles, shall put a period to our dayes, the
PILGRIM210:21	H21	By age and paines brought to decay
PILGRIM210:28	H28	nor grinding paines, my body fraile.
MYCHILD216:17	Hp241	yov into ye world, and wth great paines, weaknes, cares
MYCHILD216:25	Hp242	hath been vpon my own person, in sicknesse weaknes, paines,
FEVER220:23	H3	And paines within & out

PAINFUL (2) See also **PAINEFULL**

AGES40:40	H219	Sometimes the Cough, Stitch, {the Quinsey} painful Plurisie,
SEASONS50:17	H151	With Sickles now, the painful {bending} Reapers go,

PAINFULL (1) [painful]

MEDDM196:15	Hp273	he shall both take his rest and receiue his reward, the painfull

PAINS (3) [pl.] See also **PAINES**

AGES~~37:8~~	H70	To shew her bearing pangs {pains}, I should do wrong,
MROMAN140:4	H3567	And thus my pains (with better things) I lost,
DISTEMP179:15	H3	And wasting pains, which best my body knows,

PAINTED (1)

CONTEM167:29	H6	Their leaves & fruits seem'd painted, but was true

PAINTS (1)

HUMOUR32:38	H512	When sister Sanguine paints my Ivory face,

PAIRE (1) [pair]

HUMOUR34:14	H569	All nerves (except seven paire) to it retain;

PALACE (2)
MASSYR60:26　H291　But {For} though his Palace, did in ashes lye,
MGREC102:33　H2003　The sumptuous Palace of Queen *Hester* {*Esther*} here,
PALACES (1) [pl.]
MASSYR66:8　H514　The Towers, and Palaces, brought to decay;
PALASSER (1)
MASSYR61:8　H313　*Tiglath Palasser.*
PALATE See PALLAT
PALATINATE (1)
AGES45:6　H390　And poor *Palatinate* for ever lost;
PALE (3)
AGES45:30　H420　My skin is wrinkled, and my cheeks are pale.
SEASONS47:40　H52　The Primrose pale, and azure Violet,
MASSYR68:23　H609　The guilty King, with colour pale, and dead,
PALESTINE (1)
DIALOG148:8　H273　As did thine Ancestours in *Palestine,*
PALLAS (2)
AGES40:23　H204　*Sardana Pallas,* now survives in me:
QELIZ156:38　H65　As were the subjects of our *(Pallas)* Queen:
PALLAT (1) [palate]
MGREC109:11　H2270　And with delicious meats, his Pallat choak'd,
PALLED (1)
HUMOUR23:4　H114　Of greasie paunch, and palled {bloated} cheeks, go vaunt,
PALLIARDIZING (1)
MASSYR58:1　H186　That palliardizing sot, that out of doores
PALSIE (1) [palsy]
HUMOUR23:2　H112　The Palsie, Gout, or Cramp, or some such dolor,
PALSY (1)
AGES43:33　H328　The Astma, Megrim, Palsy, Lethargie,
PAMPHILIA (1)
MGREC95:9　H1688　*Miletus,* and *Pamphilia* overcame,
PAMPHILIANS (1) [pl.]
MPERS78:17　H998　Mann'd by {with} *Phenisians,* and *Pamphilians,*
PANCH (1) [paunch]
SEASONS52:8　H223　Our pinched flesh, and empty panch {hungry mawes} requires:
PANGS (1) [pl.]
AGES37:8　H70　To shew her bearing pangs {pains}, I should do wrong,
PANT (1)
DUBART154:5　H50　My full astonish'd heart doth pant to break,
PANTHERS (1) [pl.]
ELEMEN12:18　H178　My Panthers, and my Leopards of *Libia,*
PAPER (1)
BIRTH180:19　H29　And kiss this paper for thy loves dear sake,
PAPERS (1) [pl.]
MROMAN140:3　H3566　My papers fell a prey to th' raging fire.
PARACELSIANS (1) [pl.]
ELEMEN9:20　H54　Ye Paracelsians too, in vaine's your skil
PARADICE (1)
SEASONS51:19　H193　Great *Adam* {Our Grand-Sire} was of Paradice made King.
PARADISE (2)
MGREC112:11　H2397　If an Ideall Paradise, a man should {would} frame,

CONTEM170:10 H83 His Mother sighs, to think of Paradise,
PARALELLS (1) [parallels]
FATHER5:8 H9 Their paralells to find I scarcely know,
PARALIZE (1) [paralyze]
DIALOG144:13 H123 Where is the Nation, I cann't paralize;
PARALLEL (2)
QELIZ157:25 H93 Yet for our Queen is no fit parallel:
FLESH177:6 H87 There's none on Earth can parallel;
PARALLEL'D (1) [paralleled]
MGREC~~126:30~~ H3021 Whose fury yet unparalleld {scarcely parallel'd} hath been;
PARALLELS See PARALELLS
PARAMOUR (1)
MGREC134:39 H3368 She with her Paramour *Mark Antony,*
PARCH (2)
MGREC107:23 H2198 drought, and heat, their bodies much doth {sore did} parch;
PILGRIM210:14 H14 for thirst no more shall parch his tongue
PARCHED (1)
SEASONS50:14 H148 The dryed earth is parched by {with} his face.
PARCHING (2)
SEASONS49:9 H100 Yet doth his parching heat the {but} more augment,
MEDDM201:31 Hp281 A shadow in the parching sun, & a shelter in a blustering
PARDON (8)
SEASONS53:8 H264 *Shall at your feet for pardon cry.*
MPERS86:26 H1342 Her prevailence, a pardon might obtain.
MGREC105:24 H2117 And not to pardon such disloyalty,
MGREC112:28 H2414 His Royall pardon gave, for this same thing;
MGREC115:40 H2559 And pardon craves, for his unwilling stay,
MGREC136:3 H3416 Pardon to crave, for errours, is but vaine,
DUBART154:10 H55 Pardon, if I adore, when I admire.
MEDDM206:22 Hp287 more at a Compensation then at a pardon, but he that will not
PARENTALL (1) [parental]
MGREC94:12 H1646 For cruelty now, was his parentall sin.
PARENTS (9) [pl.]
MASSYR57:16 ~~H163~~ Some may object, his Parents ruling all,
2SIMON195:3 Hp271 Parents perpetuate their liues in their posterity, and their
MEDDM196:30 Hp274 are best preserued wᵗʰ sugar, those parents are wise that can
MEDDM206:29 Hp288 how many good parents haue had bad children, and againe
MEDDM206:30 Hp288 bad parents haue had pious children, it should make vs adore
MEDDM206:33 Hp288 alsoe teach the children of godly parents to walk wᵗʰ feare
MEDDM206:35 Hp288 may also be a support to such as haue or had wicked parents,
MYCHILD215:10 Hp240 by experᶜ. yᵗ yᵉ exhortatˢ. of parents take most effect wn yᵉ
MYCHILD215:25 Hp240 wayes, & what I knew was sinfull as lying, disobedᶜ. to parents.
PARENTS (1) [pl.; poss.]
AGES39:37 H180 My woful Parents longing hopes all {are} crost,
PARLE (1)
HUMOUR20:33 H25 Wel, thus they parle, and chide, but to be briefe,
PARLIAMENT (3)
AGES45:2 ~~H375~~ And silenc'd we, by Act of Parliament.
DIALOG145:20 H169 {'Tis said,} My better part in Court of Parliament,
DIALOG148:33 H298 Farewell dear mother, Parliament, {rightest cause} prevail,

PARMENIO (14)

MGREC95:8	H1687	And by *Parmenio* (of renowned fame)
MGREC97:27	H1788	Unto *Parmenio*, of all, most fit;
MGREC98:24	H1826	Who was the son of that *Parmenio* brave;
MGREC99:8	H1851	But, quoth *Parmenio*, (that brave Commander)
MGREC99:13	H1856	And so if I *Parmenio* were, would I.
MGREC101:17	H1942	No, though *Parmenio* plead, he {yet} will not heare;
MGREC101:28	H1953	*Parmenio, Alexander* wisht, that night,
MGREC103:30	H2041	*Parmenio* wise, intreats him to desist,
MGREC113:15	H2442	Look on *Parmenio*, after this disaster,
MGREC113:23	H2450	It was decreed *Parmenio* should dye:
MGREC113:30	H2457	This is *Parmenio*, which {who} so much had done,
MGREC113:34	H2461	This that *Parmenio*, who still over-came,
MGREC114:16	H2486	Then all the wrong to brave *Parmenio* done.
MGREC115:5	H2516	Findes there the want of wise *Parmenio*,

PARMENIO'S (4) [poss.]

MGREC113:10	H2437	Are {Were} now inflicted on *Parmenio's* Son,
MGREC113:24	H2451	*Polidamus*, who seem'd *Parmenio's* friend,
MGREC114:10	H2478	That of *Parmenio's* death him plainly told.
MGREC115:35	H2554	*Parmenio's* death's too fresh before his eyes;

PARNASSUS (3)

ELEMEN12:13	H173	Sweet *Parnassus*, I dote too much on thee,
MPERS80:41	H1108	Two mighty Rocks, brake from *Parnassus* Hil,
SIDNEY152:14	H83	And drave me from *Parnassus* in a rage,

PARNASSUS (1) [poss.]

DUBART155:2	H87	*Here lyes the pearle of* France, Parnassus *glory,*

PARSLEY (1)

PROLOG7:38	H48	Give wholsome {Thyme or} Parsley wreath, I aske no Bayes:

PART (42)

PROLOG6:27	H11	Foole, I doe grudge, the Muses did not part
ELEMEN11:39	H159	I have not time to thinke of every part,
HUMOUR23:11	H121	Yet hast thy {the} seat assign'd, a goodly part,
HUMOUR23:36	H146	Again, ye know, how I act every part:
HUMOUR25:10	H199	Of thy black calumnies, this is but part:
HUMOUR26:10	H240	Yet shal with equity give thee thy part,
HUMOUR26:39	H269	Challenge not all, 'cause part we do allow,
HUMOUR28:6	H318	With cold distempers, to pain every part;
HUMOUR29:29	H380	For {There} to defend my self, thy better part;
HUMOUR30:10	H402	As of that only part I was {were} the Queen:
HUMOUR30:14	H406	If I have not more part, then al ye three:
HUMOUR30:24	H416	But whilst he lives, Ile shew what part I have.
HUMOUR33:27	H541	Though it in all, and every part be whole:
MASSYR59:21	H245	Part of the {that stately} wal it level caus'd to lye; {was
MASSYR65:16	H481	For this great King, with-drawes part of his force,
MASSYR66:38	H544	This King among the righteous had a part:
MPERS73:33	H818	The greater part, declin'd a Monarchy.
MPERS80:1	H1068	How part, {some} might o're the Mountains goe about,
MPERS80:38	H1105	Part of his Hoast to *Delphos* sent from thence,
MGREC95:41	H1720	To shew, how great *Darius* plaid his part:
MGREC109:17	H2276	And *Omphis*, King of that part of the land:
MGREC110:10	H2310	With *Ptolomy*, sends part o' th' other side.

MGREC113:38	H2465	The next that {who} in untimely death had part,
MGREC122:26	~~H2845~~	Which made her now begin to play her part;
MGREC123:19	H2883	On most part of *Assyria* doth seize,
MGREC126:3	H2994	His Army he divides, sends part away,
MGREC131:40	H3232	The eld'st enrag'd did play the vipers part,
MGREC~~133:22~~	H3311	(Part of whose Kingdomes *Titus Quintius* won)
MGREC136:17	H3431	*What e're is found amisse, take in best {good} part,*
DIALOG145:9	H158	My guilty hands (in part) hold up with you,
DIALOG145:20	H169	{'Tis said,} My better part in Court of Parliament,
DIALOG147:19	H245	Not false to King, nor Countrey in thy heart, {to the better part;}
DUBART153:23	H27	Some part, at least, of that brave wealth was his;
DUBART154:29	H74	Thou hast {hadst} thy part of all, but of the last,
TDUDLEY165:39	H41	Nor honours pufft him up, when he had part:
CONTEM169:19	H59	The black clad Cricket, bear a second part,
FLESH175:38	H38	*Spir.* Be still thou unregenerate part,
VERSES184:6	H10	Yet for part payment take this simple mite,
MERCY188:33	H19	And in thy griefs still bear a second part:
MEDDM195:30	Hp272	then the practique part, but he is a true Christian that is a
MEDDM207:16	Hp288	or feare, or greife that lyes at the root wch in great part
FEVER220:24	H4	When in my flesh no part was fovnd

PARTAKE (1)

HUMOUR27:26	H297	Of all your qualities, I do partake,

PARTAKERS (1) [pl.]

MPERS83:40	H1228	To be partakers in {of} these festivalls.

PARTED (1)

TDUDLEY166:33	H75	And parted more by death shal never be.

PARTIAL (1)

HUMOUR30:5	H397	If I be partial judg'd, or thought to erre,

PARTICULAR (2)

MASSYR56:18	H124	This to discribe, {deseribe} in each particular,
SON231:28	H39	Particular, and how gratiovsly thov hast answered my Desires.

PARTING (3)

DAVID159:10	H25	And in their deaths {death} was found no parting strife;
BIRTH179:30	H6	But with deaths parting blow is sure to meet.
1SIMON188:5	H6	Acquaintance short, yet parting caus'd us weep,

PARTIZAN (1) [partisan]

MGREC~~114:12~~	H2481	From one stood by he snacht a partizan,

PARTNER (3)

HUMOUR27:8	H279	And let me by thy Partner, which is due.
MGREC105:4	H2097	*(Bessus,* his Partner in this Tragedy,
MGREC129:15	H3129	*Perdicas* was her partner in this plot:

PARTRICH (1) [partridge]

ELEMEN19:8	H453	The Stork, the Crane, the Partrich, and the Phesant;

PARTS (12) [pl.]

FATHER5:4	H5	Of your four sisters, deckt {cloth'd} in black & white /four parts
ELEMEN10:32	H107	*Apulia's* jacent parts were covered;
HUMOUR22:22	H91	Who rarifies the intellectuall parts?
HUMOUR33:32	H546	The conjugations {Conjugation} of the parts toth' brain
HUMOUR34:17	H572	Some other parts there issue from the Brain,
AGES43:19	H314	Be I of worth {wit}, of learning, or {and} of parts;
MPERS79:2	H1024	O most inhumain incivility!

MPERS87:28	H1380	To th' utmost parts of *Bactr'a,* and {for a time} there lye.
MPERS~~91:19~~	H1527	The King from forraign foes, and all {parts now well} at ease,
VANITY160:13	H23	Sure if on earth, it must be in those parts;
CONTEM174:33	H230	Their parts, their ports, their pomp's all laid in th' dust
MEDDM209:22	Hp291	all excellences, let his parts naturall and acquired spirituall and

PARTY (1)

| MGREC96:14 | H1734 | Support a party coloured canopy. |

PASARGADA (1)

| MPERS70:36 | H707 | And in his Town of *Pasargada* {Pasargades} lyes, |

PASARGADES (1)

| MPERS~~70:36~~ | H707 | And in his Town of *Pasargada* {Pasargades} lyes, |

PASS (1) See also PASSE

| CONTEM173:30 | H195 | And thus they pass their youth in summer season, |

PASSAGARDIS (1)

| MGREC111:35 | H2380 | Who now obscure at *Passagardis* lay; |

PASSAGE (4)

HUMOUR31:15	H446	Show them thy passage to th' *Duodenum.*
MPERS79:9	H1031	A Sea passage cuts, behind *Orthos* {Athos} Mount.
MPERS87:25	H1377	*Cyrus* dispair'd, a passage there to gain;
MGREC126:2	H2993	Sea passage gets, and lands in *Thessaly;*

PASSE (15) [pass]

ELEMEN10:19	H94	Ile here let passe, my Choler cause of warres,
ELEMEN11:32	H152	Would so passe time, I could say nothing else;
ELEMEN11:36	H156	Soone would they passe, not hundreds, but legions,
HUMOUR34:36	H591	And I passe by what sister Sanguine said;
MPERS78:25	H1006	Whose Gallies all the rest in neatnesse passe,
MPERS84:3	H1231	The royall wine, in golden cups doth {did} passe,
MGREC93:37	H1634	His high resolves which way to bring to passe:
MGREC107:17	H2192	The Souldiers should let passe this injury;
MGREC107:29	H2204	How to passe {the River} over, and gaine {to} the other Land;
MGREC107:37	H2212	They all passe over, to the other place;
MGREC109:40	H2299	Is now resolv'd to passe *Hidaspes* floud,
MGREC114:28	H2498	This censure passe, and not unwisely, say,
MGREC133:18	H3306	I must let passe those many battels fought,
MEDDM207:24	Hp289	cannot passe, and till the expiratnon of that time, no dangers
JULY223:25	Hp251	manifested his Love to me, wch I dare not passe by without

PASSE'T (1) [pass it]

| SEASONS53:4 | H260 | *I could {knew} not tell how to passe't by:* |

PASSED (2) See also PAST

| DIALOG145:32 | H181 | This done, an Act they would have passed fain, |
| 30SEPT227:29 | Hp257 | that I haue passed thro: to ye End y^t if you meet wth the like |

PASSENGERS (1) [pl.]

| MEDDM205:11 | Hp286 | his slight and flitting thoughts are like passengers, that trauell |

PASSES (3)

MASSYR66:23	H529	His sumptuous buildings passes all conceit,
MEDDM198:10	Hp276	sets his foot And he that passes through the wildernes of this
MEDDM208:15	Hp290	Judgment we must be tryed and as he passes the sentence, so

PASSING (2)

| MGREC111:22 | H2367 | Passing faire *Indus* mouth, his course he stear'd, |
| DAVID159:24 | H39 | Thy love was wonderfull, passing {surpassing} a man; |

PASSION (1)
MGREC104:14   H2066   Transported sore, with griefe and passion;
PASSIONS (1) [pl.]
HUMOUR34:6   H561   Whence her affections, passions, speak so clear;
PAST (32) [passed]
HUMOUR29:19   H370   Not past all reason, but in truth all shame:
AGES35:38   H24   Then may he live, til {out} threescore years or past.
AGES37:18   H80   When Infancy was past, my Childishnesse,
AGES44:6   H339   Sicknesse, dangers, and anxieties have past,
SEASONS51:26   H202   Which notes, when youth, and strength, have past their prime,
MASSYR57:36   H181   It is enough {may suffice}, if all be true that's past,
MASSYR65:3   H468   The Sea firm Land, whereon the Army past,
MPERS69:29   H651   But as he past, his Son, who was born dumbe,
MPERS~~72:33~~   H777   {wisht} his short reign long, till {past before} it was done.
MGREC106:25   H2159   His past sobriety doth also hate,
MGREC111:32   H2377   Now through these goodly countries as he past,
MGREC112:16   H2402   And his long travells past, and over-gone;
MGREC123:40   H2904   By all the Bonds 'twixt him and's father past,
MGREC129:26   H3140   When this foul tragedy was past, and done,
MGREC136:1   H3414   For what is past I blush, excuse to make,
MROMAN139:35   H3561   At length resolv'd, when many years had past,
DIALOG145:2   H151   Such cruelty as all reports have past.
CONTEM167:25   H2   Sometime now past in the Autumnal Tide,
CONTEM168:11   H20   Hath hundred winters past since thou wast born?
CONTEM169:26   H65   When present times look back to Ages past,
CONTEM173:24   H190   Reminds not what is past, nor whats to come dost fear.
FLESH175:5   H5   Things that are past, and things to come;
BIRTH179:31   H7   The sentence past is most irrevocable,
CHILDRN186:5   H72   And things that past, to mind I'le bring.
MERCY189:3   H24   One week she only past in pain and woe,
MEDDM197:31   Hp275   Corne till it haue past through the Mill and been ground to
MEDDM207:1   Hp288   say how vnsearchable are his wayes and his footsteps past
PILGRIM210:6   H6   his dangers past, and travailes done
13MAY227:1   H10   My winters past my stormes are gone
2HUSB232:23   H24   Vnthankfullnes for mercyes past
HOURS234:28   H42   Of all thy Goodnes past.
HOUSE236:33   H25   When by the Ruines oft I past
PASTOR (1)
AGES42:8   H266   Was I a pastor, I my flock did feed:
PASTURE (1)
3LETTER183:25   H27   Who neither joyes in pasture, house nor streams,
PASTURES (1) [pl.]
MEDDM198:4   Hp276   makes them lye down in green pastures and leades them
PATCH (1)
SIDNEY151:40   ~~H75~~   *Apollo* laught to patch up what's begun,
PATH (3)
SIDNEY151:20   H70   I shew, how thou {he} fame's path didst {paths did} tread,
VANITY160:26   H36   There is a path, no vultures eye hath seen.
CONTEM168:32   H38   Thy daily streight, and yearly oblique path,
PATHES (1) [paths]
PILGRIM210:11   H11   He erring pathes no more shall tread

PATHLESS (1)
  CONTEM169:11 H52   In pathless paths I lead my wandring feet,
PATHS (2) See also PATHES
  SIDNEY~~151:20~~ H70   I shew, how thou {he} fame's path didst {paths did} tread,
  CONTEM169:11 H52   In pathless paths I lead my wandring feet,
PATIENCE (3)
  HUMOUR24:15 H164   Your patience more then mine, I must confesse.
  HUMOUR31:30 H463   With me is noble patience also found,
  DIALOG147:41 H265   Patience, and purse of Clients for {oft} to wrong:
PATIENT (4)
  HUMOUR31:34 H467   Flegm's patient, because her nature's tame:
  HUMOUR32:18 H492   Patient I am, patient i'd need to be,
  HUMOUR32:18 H492   Patient I am, patient i'd need to be,
  MGREC122:10 H2835 He was both valiant, faithfull, patient, wise.
PATIENTLY (1)
  MEDDM197:16 Hp274 more patiently then he that excells him, both in gifts & graces
PATIENTS (1) [pl.]
  ELEMEN12:34 H194   Doe cure your patients, fill your purse with pence;
PATRES (1)
  MROMAN137:3 H3454 And with the stile of *Patres* honour'd those;
PATRIOT (2)
  TDUDLEY165:30 H32   True Patriot of this little Commonweal,
  TDUDLEY166:35 H77   *Within this Tomb a Patriot lyes*
PATRON (1)
  HUMOUR24:32 H181   No pattern, nor no Patron will I bring,
PATTERN (2)
  HUMOUR24:32 H181   No pattern, nor no Patron will I bring,
  QELIZ158:15   H124   *Here lies the pride of Queens, pattern of Kings,*
PATTERNE (1) [pattern]
  SIDNEY149:12 H11   Of Armes, and Arts, thou {he} should'st a patterne be.
PAUL (1)
  MEDDM204:5   Hp284 and he that hath deliuered mee saith paul, will deliuer me, god
PAULS (1) [poss.]
  SIDNEY152:22 H91   His bones do lie interr'd in stately *Pauls.*
PAUNCH (1) See also PANCH
  HUMOUR23:4   H114   Of greasie paunch, and palled {bloated} cheeks, go vaunt,
PAUSANIAS (1)
  MGREC93:14   H1611 This Prince (his father by *Pausanias* slain)
PAW (2)
  MEDDM204:3   Hp284 he that deliuered me, sath Dauid, from the paw of the Lion
  MEDDM204:4   Hp284 the paw of the Beare will deliuer mee from this vncircumscised
PAY (13)
  HUMOUR24:22 H171   To pay with railings, is not mine intent,
  AGES42:15   H273   As chearfully as ere I took my pay.
  MASSYR56:11 H117   Bestow'd their labour, and receiv'd their pay,
  MPERS86:33   H1349 Then next, the *Lacedemons* {*Spartans*} he takes to {into} pay;
  MGREC132:12 H3247 Yet must his children pay for fathers ill.
  DIALOG146:21 H207   The poore they want their pay, their children bread,
  DIALOG148:2   H267   And Pursevants and Catchpoles want their pay,
  DIALOG148:9   H274   And let her spoils, full pay, with int'rest be,
  TDUDLEY165:24 H26   But now or never I must pay my Sum;

VERSES184:4	H8	My stock's so small, I know not how to pay,
VERSES184:9	H13	But as I can, I'le pay it while I live:
SON231:19	H31	O help me pay my Vowes O Lord
HOURS234:35	H49	To pay the vowes wch I doe owe

PAYD (2) [paid]

VERSES184:11	H15	Yet paying is not payd until I dye.
ACK235:10	H10	Nor payd me after my desert

PAYES (2) [pays]

ELEMEN12:32	H192	My rich commodities payes double rent.
MPERS83:36	H1224	And payes them now, {both} according as he owes,

PAYING (2)

MGREC129:16	H3130	The Heavens seem'd slow in paying her the same,
VERSES184:11	H15	Yet paying is not payd until I dye.

PAYMENT (1)

VERSES184:6	H10	Yet for part payment take this simple mite,

PAYS See PAYES

PEACE (24)

ELEMEN8:26	H24	All stormes now laid, and they in perfect peace,
AGES44:36	H369	I saw all peace at home, terror to foes,
MASSYR57:9	H156	This fraud, in war, nor peace, at all appears;
MASSYR60:34	H299	When this was built, and all matters in peace,
MPERS70:35	H706	In honour, peace, and wealth, with a grey head,
MPERS73:29	H814	All things in peace, and Rebells throughly quel'd,
MPERS81:10	H1118	He instantly to *Athens* sends for peace,
MPERS81:22	H1130	But the *Athenians,* this peace detest,
MPERS85:1	H1277	'Rest of his time in peace he did remain;
MPERS85:24	H1300	The King was glad, with *Sparta* to make peace,
MPERS89:22	H1456	And sues for peace, that they his friends remain;
MPERS90:19	H1486	In peace they saw their Native soyl again.
MPERS91:9	H1517	winnings} lost all, and were a peace {their glad} to make,
MGREC98:34	H1836	By his Embassadours now sues for peace:
MGREC101:4	H1929	And now for peace he sues, as once before,
MGREC128:38	H3111	Sought for a peace, and laid aside their jarres:
MGREC131:24	H3216	His peace he then with old *Seleuchus* makes,
MROMAN137:16	H3467	But in the end, to finall peace they come,
MROMAN137:28	H3479	Kept shut in peace, but {set} ope when bloud was spilt;
DIALOG141:7	H6	With honour, wealth, and peace, happy and blest;
DIALOG147:33	H257	At that thy setled Peace, thy wealth and splendour,
DIALOG148:5	H270	When thus in Peace: thine Armies brave send out,
DUBART153:39	H43	Valour in War, in Peace good Husbandry.
TDUDLEY166:23	H65	And to his Fathers gathered is in peace.

PEACEFUL (1)

SEASONS50:16	H150	*Romes* second Emperour of peaceful {lasting} fame;

PEACEFULL (1) [peaceful]

DIALOG142:9	H38	The regall, peacefull Scepter from thee tane?

PEACH (1)

SEASONS51:10	H184	of Warden, {Almonds, Quinces, Wardens} and of Peach,

PEA COCK (1) [peacock]

MEDDM196:6	Hp272	It is reported of the pea cock that prideing himself in his gay

PEACOCK (1)

ELEMEN15:7	H289	The Peacock, and the Ostrich, share in woe:

PEAR (2)

SEASONS47:38	H50	The Pear, the Plumbe, and Apple-tree now flourish,
SEASONS50:27	H161	Now's ripe the Pear, Pear-plumbe, and Apricock,

PEARL (3)

VANITY160:31	H41	With pearl and gold it shall not valued be:
VANITY161:1	H52	This pearl of price, this tree of life, this spring,
FLESH177:9	H90	The Gates of Pearl, both rich and clear,

PEARLE (2) [pearl]

DUBART155:2	H87	*Here lyes the pearle of* France, Parnassus *glory,*
MEDDM209:5	Hp291	this pearle of prise

PEARLED (1)

DAVID158:32	H12	O! *Gilbo* Mounts, let never pearled dew,

PEARLES (1) [pearls]

ELEMEN15:32	H314	My pearles that dangle at thy darlings ears;

PEARLS (3) [pl.]

MGREC96:36	H1756	That valour was more worth than Pearls, or gold,
FLESH175:32	H32	Earth hath more silver, pearls and gold,
FLESH177:3	H84	My Crown not Diamonds, Pearls, and gold,

PEAR-PLUMBE (1)

SEASONS50:27	H161	Now's ripe the Pear, Pear-plumbe, and Apricock,

PEAS See PEASE

PEASANT (1)

ELEMEN19:9	H454	Pye {Thrush}, the Jay {wren}, the Larke, a prey to th' Peasant.

PEASANTS (1) [pl.]

MROMAN136:30	H3444	Where Swaines, and rustick Peasants made {kept} their Holds.

PEASE (2) [peas]

SEASONS48:26	H79	The hasty Pease, and wholesome red {cool} Strawberry,
SEASONS49:37	H130	And for all sorts of Pease this is the time.

PECKING (1)

CHILDRN185:21	H47	Whilst pecking corn, and void of care

PECULIAR (2)

SEASONS48:29	H82	Each man his owne peculiar excellence,
MPERS91:16	H1524	All the peculiar vertues of a Prince:

PEDESTALL (1) [pedestal]

FATHER5:6	H7	(though made a pedestall for *Adams* Race) /world

PEDIGREE (3)

HUMOUR21:2	H30	To shew my great {high} descent, and pedigree,
AGES35:21	H7	The second, frolick, claimes his pedigree,
MPERS69:13	H635	This is of *Cyrus* the true pedigree,

PEECE (1) [piece]

MPERS77:2	H941	Go *Persians,* carry home that angry peece,

PEECES (1) [pieces]

MGREC114:25	H2495	He on the wrack, his limbs in peeces rent,

PEELED (1)

MASSYR65:9	H474	With peeled shoulders, and with balded heads,

PEER (2)

AGES37:36	H98	No malice bare, to this, or that great Peer,
MGREC95:20	H1699	For in that Peer, more valour did abide;

PEERES (2) [peers]

DIALOG145:17	H166	'Twixt King and Peeres a question of state,
DIALOG147:26	H250	O mother, can you weep, and have such Peeres.

PEERS (2) [pl.]
MPERS73:26   H811   And two of these great Peers, in place {Field} lay dead:
MPERS74:6   H831   Of all the Peers should have precedency.
PEEVISH (2)
HUMOUR22:3   H72   But peevish, Male-content, musing she sits,
AGES38:25   H128   Oft stubborn, peevish, sullen, pout, and cry:
PEIRCE (1) [pierce]
MEDDM208:24   Hp290   like the reeds of Egipt that peirce insteed of supporting like
PEIRCED (1) [pierced]
MGREC105:19   H2112   Findes poore *Darius,* peirced to the heart;
PEIRCING (1) [piercing]
DUBART153:36 H40   Thy peircing skill in high Astronomy,
PEKAH (1)
MASSYR61:22   H327   From *Rezin,* and from *Pekah* set me free:
PELF (1)
HOUSE237:26   H56   Farewell my pelf, farewell my Store.
PELLAS (1)
MGREC127:5   H3035   And *Pellas* faine to yeeld amongst the rest;
PELLOPONESUS (1)
MGREC125:38   H2988   In *Pelloponesus* then *Cassander* lay,
PELOPONESUS (1)
MGREC129:36   H3150   {And} Gives *Peloponesus* unto him for {his} hire,
PEMBLE (1)
MPERS92:26   H̶1̶5̶8̶4̶   Thus learned *Pemble,* whom we may not slight,
PEN (14)
FATHER5:12   H13   My lowly pen, might wait upon those four,
PROLOG6:20   H5   For my mean Pen, are too superiour things,
PROLOG7:16   H29   A Poets Pen, all scorne, I should thus wrong;
MASSYR67:22   H568   Whose prophane acts, a sacred pen sets down.
MGREC94:35   H1673   Ah! fond vaine man, whose pen was taught ere while,
MGREC135:40   H3412   My tired braine, leaves to a {some} better pen,
SIDNEY151:32 H̶7̶5̶   Goodwill, did make my head-long pen to run,
SIDNEY152:11 H80   They took from me, the scribling pen I had,
SIDNEY152:18 H87   *Errata,* through their leave threw me my pen,
SIDNEY152:28 H97   *His praise is much, this shall suffice my pen,*
DUBART154:8   H53   Had I an Angels voice, or *Barta's* pen,
QELIZ155:33   H24   No *Phoenix,* Pen, nor *Spencers* Poetry,
QELIZ157:29   H97   Must dip his Pen i'th' Heliconian Well;
RESTOR229:29 H12   My thankfull heart wth pen record
PENALTY (1)
CONTEM170:4   H78   A penalty impos'd on his backsliding Race.
PENCE (1)
ELEMEN12:34   H194   Doe cure your patients, fill your purse with pence;
PENCESTAS (1)
MGREC127:21   H3051   *Pencestas* did betray him by a wile,
PEN'D (2) [penned] See also PEND, PENN'D
FATHER5:17   H18   But by my humble hand thus rudely pen'd
MROMAN140:1   H3564   And weary lines (though lanke) I many pen'd:
PEND (2) [penned] See also PEN'D, PENN'D
AGES43:30   H325   To break the darksome prison, where it's pend;
MPERS92:9   H1567   What Acts he did, time hath not now left pend,

PEN-MEN (1)
MASSYR63:36   H423   But by the Prophets, Pen-men most Divine,
PENN'D (2) [penned] See also PEN'D, PEND
SEASONS53:6   H262   *Accept therefore of what is penn'd,*
SIDNEY149:20   H19   (Witnesse *Arcadia,* penn'd in his youth)
PENSIVE (2)
SIDNEY152:17   H86   I pensive for my fault, sat down, and then,
3LETTER183:7   H9   Or as the pensive Dove doth all alone
PENT (1)
DIALOG144:28   H136   Some lost their livings, some in prison pent,
PENVEL (1) [penuel]
MEDDM209:1   Hp291   wrestled wth god face to face in penvel Let me go, sath that
PEOPLE (16)
MASSYR54:4   H31   He taught the people first to Idolize;
MASSYR54:27   H54   To whom the sottish people sacrific'd;
MASSYR57:7   H154   Which made the people think they serv'd her Son;
MASSYR62:10   H355   And did the people, nobles, and their King
MPERS72:37   H782   The people ignorant of what was done,
MPERS73:35   H820   And thought the people, would more happy be,
MPERS85:21   H1297   Revolts, having treasure, and people gain'd:
MGREC106:18   H2152   Such country there, nor yet such people finde.
MROMAN137:17   H3468   And *Sabins,* as one people, dwelt in *Rome.*
MROMAN137:34   H3485   So to delude the people he was bold:
MROMAN139:4   H3532   He ranks the people, into each degree,
MROMAN139:23   H3551   And people sweare, ne're to accept of King.
DIALOG144:36   H144   I saw her people famish'd, Nobles slain,
DIALOG147:20   H246   But those that hurt his people and his Crown,
QELIZ156:19   H46   Was ever people better rul'd then hers?
MEDDM208:34   Hp290   intercedes for the people, god sath to him Let me alone, that I
PEOPLES (3) [pl.; poss.]
AGES37:39   H101   I'd nought to do, 'twixt Prince, {King} and peoples strife.
MASSYR58:5   H190   Knowing his basenesse, and the peoples hate,
MPERS74:28   H851   Yet more the peoples hearts firmly to binde,
PERCEIUE (2) [perceive]
MEDDM203:22   Hp283   the company of the phisitian or chirurgian, but if he perceiue a
MEDDM207:18   Hp289   that we perceiue a decay, in their greennes for were earthly
PERCEIUES (2) [perceives]
MEDDM196:17   Hp273   drought of the day, when he perceiues his sun apace to decline
MEDDM198:18   Hp276   of men, wch they all catch gre¯dily at but few perceiues
PERCEIVES (1)
MGREC122:13   H2838   Perceives {Sees} *Aridæus* must not king it long,
PERCEIVING (1)
MPERS76:29   H927   *Athens* perceiving now their desperate state,
PERCH (1)
CHILDRN185:12   H38   On higher boughs he'l perch at length.
PERCHT (2)
CONTEM173:12   H179   The sweet-tongu'd Philomel percht ore my head,
CHILDRN185:2   H28   She now hath percht, to spend her years;
PERDICA'S (2) [poss.]
MGREC118:35   H2684   The Princes seeing *Perdica's* power and Pride,
MGREC121:16   H2795   Some of the Souldiers enters *Perdica's* tent,

PERDICAS (11) See also PERDICCAS

MGREC118:3	H2650	This choyse *Perdicas,* vehemently disclaim'd,
MGREC118:27	H2676	*Perdicas,* seeing *Aridæus* must be King,
MGREC119:2	H2692	*Perdicas* took no Province, like the rest,
MGREC120:11	H2746	*Perdicas* griev'd, to see the Princes bold,
MGREC120:30	H2767	And 'gainst *Perdicas,* all their strength combine.
MGREC120:41	H2778	*Perdicas* hears, his foes are now {all} combin'd,
MGREC121:14	~~H2792~~	*Pithon,* next *Perdicas,* a Captaine high,
MGREC121:32	H2814	Whilst *Perdicas* thus staid {encamp'd} in *Africa,*
MGREC122:19	H2844	Who was *Perdicas, Philips* elder {eldest} brother,
MGREC129:15	H3129	*Perdicas* was her partner in this plot:
MGREC129:20	H3134	*Perdicas* had before, for his amisse,

PERDICAS (2) [poss.]

MGREC121:8	H2786	*Perdicas* surly carriage, and his pride,
MGREC121:28	H2810	Had it but in *Perdicas* life arriv'd,

PERDICCAS (2) [perdicas]

MGREC~~121:14~~	H2792	*Perdiccas* in his pride did ill intreat
MGREC~~121:16~~	H2796	The souldiers 'gainst *Perdiccas* they incense,

PERFECT (7)

PROLOG7:2	H17	Nor perfect beauty, where's a maine defect,
ELEMEN8:26	H24	All stormes now laid, and they in perfect peace,
HUMOUR26:33	H263	The spirits through thy heat, are made perfect there,
HUMOUR34:4	H559	Thy perfect temperament, who can expresse?
HUMOUR35:11	H607	But all admire our perfect amity;
ANNEB187:23	H13	Or perfect bliss without mixture of woe.
MEDDM202:14	Hp282	it pleased him, whose will is the perfect rule of righteousnesse,

PERFECTION (4)

AGES44:11	H344	An end of all perfection now I see.
MEDDM201:7	Hp280	I haue seen an end of all perfection (sayd the royall prophet)
MEDDM206:1	Hp287	to that fruitfullnes, altho they aime at perfection And again
MEDDM209:24	Hp291	(perhaps meaner then himself) wch shews us perfection is not

PERFECTIONS (1) [pl.]

QELIZ157:28	H96	Her personall perfections, who would tell,

P^{R}FECTLY (1) [perfectly]

MED223:16	Hp250	p^{r}fectly what he hath done for me, and then shall I bee able to

P^{R}FORM (2) [perform]

MYCHILD216:36	Hp242	and Bonds vpon my Soul to p^{r}form his righteovs comands.
11MAYA226:15	Hp255	& some ability to p^{r}form ye Dutyes I owe to him, and the work

PERFORM (1)

MEDDM208:20	Hp290	But perform nothing, and so leaue those in the lurch that most

PERFORM'D (2) [performed]

MASSYR68:26	H612	Perform'd his word, to him, that told his fate;
MGREC101:14	H1939	And till all this be wel perform'd, and sure,

PERFORMANCES (1)

MEDDM199:9	Hp277	dry and sapless performances are simptoms of little spiritull

PERFORMED (1) See also PERFORM'D

MYCHILD216:35	Hp242	neglected wch he would haue performed, and by his help I

PERFUME (2)

QELIZ158:10	H119	*Whose sweet perfume fills the all-filling aire,*
PILGRIM210:32	H32	it is the bed Christ did perfume

PERFUMING (1)
ELEMEN15:40   H322   Thy gallant rich perfuming Amber-greece:

PERHAPS (10)
AGES38:36   H139   And some perhaps, I carry to my grave.
MPERS91:40   ~~H1554~~   Or else, perhaps the deeds of *Persian* Kings
MGREC95:32   H1711   Though some there be, and that {(perhaps)} more likely, write;
MGREC101:18   H1943   Which had he done (perhaps) his fame had {he'd} kept,
MGREC117:38   H2645   Claim'd not, perhaps her Sex might hindrance be.
DIALOG142:4   H33   But you perhaps would have me guesse it out,
ANNEB187:25   H15   That's here to day, perhaps gone in an hour;
MEDDM200:17   Hp279   but falls and bruises, or perhaps somewhat worse, much more
MEDDM209:24   Hp291   hath (perhaps meaner then himself) wch shews us perfection is
MYCHILD215:20   Hp240   ye former it had been perhaps better pleasing to yov, but seing

PERILS (1) [pl.]
CHILDRN185:38 H64   Of perils you are ignorant,

PERIOD (3)
AGES46:15   H446   And my last period now e'n almost run;
MGREC127:26   H3056   But as that to a period did haste,
MEDDM207:25   Hp289   no paines nor troubles, shall put a period to our dayes, the

PERISH (4)
CONTEM172:2   H139   Nay, they shall darken, perish, fade and dye,
MEDDM203:27   Hp284   and that he must needs perish if he haue no remedy, will
MYCHILD218:36   Hp244   my faith, + if I perish, I perish, But I know all ye powers of Hell

PERISH'D (2) [perished]
ELEMEN17:28   H392   Then wholly perish'd, earths ignoble race;
MGREC116:41   H2607   His thoughts are perish'd he aspires no more,

PERISHED (2)
MGREC133:34   H3324   But this is perished with many more,
DAVID159:28   H43   And war-like weapons perished away.

PERJUR'D (3) [perjured]
MASSYR65:30   H495   But he, as perjur'd as *Iehoiakim,*
MPERS83:30   H1218   To whom the perjur'd *Grecians* lent their aide,
MPERS90:38   H1505   Of that false perjur'd wretch, this was the last {fate},

PERMANENT (2)
MEDDM207:19   Hp289   permanent who would look for heauenly?
HOUSE237:20   H50   Stands permanent tho: this bee fled.

PERNICIOUS (1)
HUMOUR29:23   H374   Know, in a General its most pernicious.

PERPETRATE (1)
DIALOG144:19   H129   That with high hand I still did perpetrate;

PERPETUAL (3)
MASSYR62:11   H356   Into perpetual thraldome that time bring;
MGREC~~116:10~~   H2576   Till death inwrapt her in perpetual night.
CONTEM171:15   H119   So unawares comes on perpetual night,

PERPETUALL (2) [perpetual]
MROMAN139:21 H3549   In banishment perpetuall, to dwell;
MEDDM209:15   Hp291   last fall in to perpetuall bondage vnder them vnlesse the great

PERPETUALLY (1)
CONTEM169:28 H67   It makes things gone perpetually to last,

PERPETUATE (1)
2SIMON195:3   Hp271   Parents perpetuate their liues in their posterity, and their

PERPLEX (2)

AGES38:8   H111   Nor evidence for land, {lands} did me perplex.

SIDNEY152:9   H̶7̶9̶   That this contempt it did the more perplex,

PᴿPLEXED (1) [perplexed]

MYCHILD217:15   Hp243   I haue often been pʳplexed yᵗ I haue not fovnd that constant

PERPLEXED (1)

AGES44:5   H338   And in perplexed Middle-age have bin,

PERPLEXT (3)

MPERS89:29   H1463   The King's {King} perplext, there dares not let them stay,

3LETTER183:1   H3   Perplext, in every bush & nook doth pry,

PILGRIM210:19   H19   A pilgrim I, on earth, perplext

PERSAPOLIS (1)

MGREC102:39   H2009   From *Sushan,* to *Persapolis* he goes,

PᴿSECUTIONS (1) [persecutions]

MYCHILD218:24   Hp244   pʳsecutions of the Saints, wch admitt were yʸ as they terme yᵐ

PERSEUS (3)

ELEMEN10:5   H80   The Valiant *Perseus* who *Medusa* slew,

MGREC133:23   H̶3̶3̶1̶2̶   He *Perseus,* from him the kingdom's won,

MGREC1̶3̶3̶:̶2̶3̶   H3312   *Philip* had *Perseus,* who was made a Thrale

PERSEVER (1)

1HUSB180:33   H12   Then while we live, in love lets so persever,

PERSEVER'D (1) [persevered]

MPERS79:13   H̶1̶0̶3̶5̶   Yet *Xerxes* in his enterprise persever'd;

PERSIA (9)

MPERS6̶9̶:̶1̶   H623   *Cyrus Cambyses,* Son of *Persia's* {Persia} King,

MPERS69:6   H628   Who had in *Persia* the Lieutenants place.

MPERS7̶2̶:̶7̶   H756   *Praxaspes* into *Persia* then is sent,

MPERS72:8   H̶7̶5̶6̶   Who into *Persia* with Commission sent,

MPERS72:38   H784   Toucht with this newes, to *Persia* he makes,

MPERS83:23   H1211   Such Justice then, in *Persia* {Persian court} did remain, {reign.}

MPERS91:18   H1526   And turne to *Persia,* as is pertinent;

MGREC111:31   H2376   {And} So he at length drew neare to *Persia*;

MGREC127:28   H3058   *Antigonus,* all *Persia* now gains {doth gain},

PERSIA'S (1) [poss.]

MPERS69:1   H623   *Cyrus Cambyses,* Son of *Persia's* {Persia} King,

PERSIAN (27)

MASSYR6̶7̶:̶2̶6̶   H572   The Noble *Persians,* {Persian} to invade his rights.

MASSYR68:30   H616   And now the *Persian* Monarchy began.

MPERS68:33   H619   being the *Persian,* begun {began} under

MPERS71:11   H727   But that the *Persian* King, may act his minde;

MPERS73:1   H788   Which ends before begun, the *Persian* {his home-bred} Warre,

MPERS74:12   H̶8̶3̶6̶   And after *Persian* manner, kisse his feet.

MPERS78:4   H985   That the large {vast} *Persian* government surrounded;

MPERS78:10   H991   To Princes of the *Persian* bloud descended,

MPERS83:23   H1211   Such Justice then, in *Persia* {Persian court} did remain, {reign.}

MPERS85:34   H1310   (For *Persian* Kings, did deem {then deem'd} themselves so

MPERS90:20   H1487   The *Greeks* now (as the *Persian* King suspects)

MPERS91:38   H̶1̶5̶5̶2̶   Or dealing with the *Persian,* now no more

MPERS91:40   H̶1̶5̶5̶4̶   Or else, perhaps the deeds of *Persian* Kings

MPERS92:33   H1591   That this *Darius* was last *Persian* King,

MPERS93:5   H1602   *The end of the* Persian *Monarchy.*

MGREC93:27	H1624	Who {That} ran in fury, {Choler} on the *Persian* Ram,
MGREC97:21	H1782	Then that the *Persian* King he over-came;
MGREC99:19	H1862	Then in the *Persian* Monarchy beside;
MGREC102:30	H2000	For 'twas the seat of *Persian* Kings renown'd;
MGREC103:9	H2020	Which {That} did pertain unto the *Persian* Kings.
MGREC106:33	H2167	With *Persian* Robes, himselfe doth dignifie,
MGREC107:27	H2202	Then did {all} their wars, against the *Persian* King.
MGREC112:3	H2389	He fourscore *Persian* Ladies also gave;
MGREC113:33	H2460	By him was set upon the *Persian* Throne:
MGREC114:35	H2505	The mighty *Persian* King he over-came,
MGREC135:13	H3385	But yet the *Persian* got the upper hand;
MGREC135:16	H3388	The *Grecian* longer then the *Persian* stood,

PERSIANS (20) [pl.]

MASSYR58:17	H202	The last, the *Medes* and *Persians* doth invite.
MASSYR60:10	H275	Of {To} *Medes,* and *Persians,* {when he crav'd} their assisting
MASSYR67:26	H572	The Noble *Persians,* {Persian} to invade his rights.
MPERS76:35	H933	The *Persians* to their Gallies post with speed,
MPERS77:2	H941	Go *Persians,* carry home that angry peece,
MPERS79:39	H1065	Till twenty thousand *Persians* falls down slain;
MPERS81:25	H1133	Against the *Persians* they would use {bend} their force.
MPERS82:9	H1156	Which found, like *Greeks* they fight, the *Persians* fly,
MPERS85:17	H1293	For sixty years maugre the *Persians* might.
MPERS86:34	H1350	(One *Greeke* could make ten *Persians* run away)
MPERS88:15	H1408	For at first charge the *Persians* ran away.
MPERS89:12	H1446	What dastards in the field the *Persians* are;
MPERS89:27	H1461	Such terrour on the *Persians* then did fall,
MPERS90:23	H1490	The many thousand *Persians* they had slain;
MGREC94:39	H1677	The *Persians* for encounter ready stand,
MGREC95:1	H1680	And beat the coward *Persians* from the top,
MGREC96:4	H1724	The *Persians* clad in silk, and glitt'ring {glistering} gold;
MGREC96:8	H1728	(For Sun and Fire the *Persians* worship most)
MGREC100:22	H1906	Of *Persians, Scithians, Indians,* in a cluster;
MGREC101:34	~~H1959~~	Both Armies meet, *Greeks* fight, the *Persians* run,

PERSIANS (4) [pl.; poss.]

MPERS90:8	H1481	Nor rivers course, nor *Persians* force could stay,
MGREC96:40	H1760	Let fly their Arrowes, in the *Persians* face;
MGREC~~101:34~~	H1961	The Armyes joyn'd a while, the Persians fight,
MGREC103:33	H2044	And just procuring of the *Persians* hate.

PERSIST (2)

MGREC103:31	H2042	And layes before his eyes, if he persist
SIDNEY151:23	H73	For {How} to persist, my muse is more in doubt:

PERSON (6)

MASSYR68:2	H588	Destruction to his Crown, to's Person end.
MPERS78:24	H1005	In person {present} there, now for his help {aid} was seen;
DIALOG~~147:39~~	H263	Without respect of persons {person}, or of case,
3LETTER183:6	H8	His voice to hear, or person to discry.
MEDDM200:19	Hp279	and strength of the person he bestowes them on, larg
MYCHILD216:25	Hp242	comonly hath been vpon my own person, in sicknesse

PERSONAGE (1)

MGREC119:33	H2723	For personage, none was like {to} this Commander:

PERSONALL (1) [personal]
QELIZ157:28   H96   Her personall perfections, who would tell,
PERSONS (5) [pl.]
DIALOG147:39   H263   Without respect of persons {person}, or of case,
CONTEM169:32   H71   While of their persons & their acts his mind doth treat.
MEDDM196:21   Hp273   Downny beds make drosey persons but hard lodging, keeps
MEDDM206:32   Hp288   persons, but takes and chuses, when and where and whom he
MEDDM208:3   Hp289   these things must be what manner of persons ought we to be,
PERSWADE (1) [persuade]
SAMUEL228:20   H21   Perswade my heart I shall him see
PERSWADED (2) [persuaded]
MROMAN139:34   H3560   Though oft perswaded, I as oft deny'd,
2SIMON195:5   Hp271   their predecessors, but I am perswaded better things of yᵒ you
PERSWADES (1) [persuades]
MGREC104:6   H2058   Perswades him not to fight, with *Alexander.*
PERSWASION (1) [persuasion]
MGREC109:18   H2277   Through his perswasion *Alexander* meets;
PERSWASIONS (1) [persuasions]
HUMOUR22:5   H74   If great perswasions, cause her meet her foe;
PERTAIN (1)
MGREC103:9   H2020   Which {That} did pertain unto the *Persian* Kings.
PERTINENT (3)
HUMOUR27:17   H288   Th' rest to our Sisters, is more pertinent.
MASSYR60:12   H277   Not pertinent to what we have in hand;
MPERS91:18   H1526   And turne to *Persia,* as is pertinent;
PERTURBATION (1)
DIALOG146:15   H201   Oh pity me, in this sad perturbation,
PERVERSE (2)
HUMOUR28:13   H325   Of all the perverse humours from mine owne,
AGES38:21   H124   A perverse will, a love to what's forbid:
PERVERT (1)
MEDDM205:14   Hp286   Judg, whom no bribes can pervert, nor flattery cause to favour
PESTILENCE (4)
ELEMEN19:14   H459   Then Feavours, Purples, Pox, and Pestilence;
DIALOG142:28   H57   Is't Drought, is't Famine, or is't Pestilence?
DIALOG143:20   H89   And for the Pestilence, who knowes how neare;
MEDDM199:27   Hp278   the arrow of pestilence, and the arrow of a slanderous tongue,
PETARD (1)
ELEMEN9:8   H42   But I with one Granado, or Petard,
PETER (1)
MEDDM208:32   Hp290   the water become firme footing, for peter to walk on, nay more
PETITION (1)
2HUSB232:6   H7   And my petition signe.
PETTY (3)
MASSYR53:17   H7   But each one thought his petty rule was high,
MASSYR57:19   H166   With petty Kings to joyne Confederate.
MGREC113:32   H2459   Who from a petty King of *Macedon,*
PHÆNIX (1) [phœnix]
ELEMEN11:1   H121   That *Phænix* from her Bed, is risen New.
PHAETON (3)
ELEMEN10:14   H89   *Eridanus,* where *Phaeton* was drown'd,

SIDNEY151:33 ~~H75~~ Like unwise *Phaeton* his ill guided sonne,
SIDNEY151:36 ~~H75~~ So proudly foolish I, with *Phaeton* strive,

PHANE (2) [fane]
MGREC95:7 H1686 Where stood of late *Diana's,* wondrous Phane,
MGREC100:5 H1889 Then to the Phane of *Jupiter,* he went,

PHANTASIE (2)
HUMOUR28:29 H341 {With} An ingenius working phantasie,
HUMOUR32:11 H485 Strange Chymera's are in my phantasie,

PHARAOH (1) [pharoah]
MASSYR64:20 H444 Quite vanquish'd *Pharaoh Necho,* and {with} his Band;

PHARMUS (1)
MASSYR54:33 H60 *Pharmus, {Thermus}* their King, he caused to be slain;

PHARAOH See PHARAOH

PHAROES (1) [pharoahs]
MASSYR66:18 H524 All rule, he from the ancient *Pharoes* takes;

PHENICIA (2) [phoenicia]
MGREC97:25 H1786 But all *Phenicia* to his pleasures {pleasure} yeeld;
MGREC123:21 H2885 All *Syria,* and, *Phenicia* he wins;

PHENISIAN (1) [phoenician]
MGREC101:9 H1934 *Phenisian* Sea, and great *Euphrates* high,

PHENISIANS (1) [phoenicians]
MPERS78:17 H998 Mann'd by {with} *Phenisians,* and *Pamphilians,*

PHERE (1) [fere]
3LETTER183:20 H22 I have a loving phere, yet seem no wife:

PHESANT (1) [pheasant]
ELEMEN19:8 H453 The Stork, the Crane, the Partrich, and the Phesant;

PHILA (1)
MGREC120:7 H2742 *Craterus* doth his daughter *Phisa {Phila}* wed,

PHILADELPHUS (2)
MGREC132:32 H3279 To *Philadelphus,* his more worthy Son.
MGREC134:20 H3351 Cal'd *Philadelphus,* next sat on {did possess} the throne,

PHILIP (11) See also PHILLIP
AGES44:35 H368 And *Philip,* and *Albertus,* half undone;
MGREC113:31 H2458 For *Philip* dead, and his surviving Son,
MGREC116:4 H2564 By *Philip,* and *Cassander,* to him brought,
MGREC119:15 H2705 {Sometimes} By warlike *Philip,* and his conquering son.
MGREC130:29 ~~H3181~~ *Philip* and *Olympias* both were slain,
MGREC133:22 H3310 *Demetrius* had *Philip* to his son,
MGREC~~133:23~~ H3312 *Philip* had *Perseus,* who was made a Thrale
SIDNEY149:3 H3 Sir *Philip Sidney,* who was untimely
SIDNEY151:8 ~~H69~~ O Princely *Philip,* rather *Alexander,*
SIDNEY151:16 ~~H69~~ Then wonder lesse, if warlike *Philip* yield,
SIDNEY152:25 ~~H94~~ Philip *and* Alexander *both in one.*

PHILIPS (6) [poss.] See also PHILLIPS
MGREC122:19 H2844 Who was *Perdicas, Philips* elder {eldest} brother,
MGREC130:21 H3176 Thus *Philips* house was quite extinguished,
MGREC131:36 H3228 Two sons he left, born of King *Philips* daughter,
MGREC132:1 H3234 (Rather then *Philips* child must {race should} longer live
MGREC132:7 H3242 Thus *Philips,* and *Cassander's* race is {both} gone,
SIDNEY151:6 ~~H69~~ But that it is record by *Philips* hand,

PHILISTIN (1) [philistine]
MEDDM204:5   Hp284   philistin and he that hath deliuered mee saith paul, will deliuer
PHILISTINS (1) [philistines]
DAVID158:30   H10   Lest Daughters of the *Philistins* rejoyce,
PHILISTRIUS (1)
MASSYR55:8   H74   Her birth-place was *Philistrius Ascalon,*
PHILLIP (2) See also PHILIP
MGREC93:30   H1627   *Phillip,* on this great conquest had an eye;
MGREC128:6   H3079   Daughter to *Phillip,* their renowned head;
PHILLIPS (1) [poss.] See also PHILIPS
MGREC93:10   H1607   Great *Alexander,* was wise *Phillips* son,
PHILOMEL (1)
CONTEM173:12 H179   The sweet-tongu'd Philomel percht ore my head,
PHILOMETER (1)
MGREC134:29 H3360   *Philometer:* then *Evergetes* again.
PHILOPATER (1)
MGREC134:27 H3358   *Philopater* was *Evergete's* son,
PHILOSOPHER (1)
HUMOUR26:7   H237   To play Philosopher, I have no list;
PHILOSOPHERS (2) [pl.]
ELEMEN9:22   H56   And you Philosophers, if ere you made
ELEMEN19:1   H446   For all Philosophers make one of me.
PHILOSOPHY (3)
ELEMEN16:11   H334   But note this maxime in Philosophy:
HUMOUR31:7   H440   Thou wants Philosophy, and yet discretion.
DUBART153:34 H38   Thy Art, in Naturall Philosophy:
PHILOTAS (6)
MGREC98:23   H1825   The rule of this he to *Philotas* gave,
MGREC112:20   H2406   *Philotas* was not least, nor yet the last;
MGREC112:29   H2415   Yet is *Philotas* unto Judgement brought,
MGREC112:35   H2421   But *Philotas,* his unpardonable crime,
MGREC112:39   H2425   *Philotas* thus o're-charg'd, with wrong, and greif,
MGREC113:4   H2431   *Philotas* after him sends out this cry,
PHISA (1)
MGREC120:7   H2742   *Craterus* doth his daughter *Phisa {Phila}* wed,
PHISICK (1) [physic]
DUBART153:38 H42   Thy Phisick, Musick, and State policy,
PHISICK-PURGING-POTION (1) [physic-purging-potion]
DIALOG141:21 H20   This Phisick-purging-potion I have taken,
PHISITIAN (3) [physician] See also PHYSITIAN
HUMOUR26:8   H238   Nor yet Phisitian, nor Anatomist.
MGREC115:10 H2519 Hangs his Phisitian, the reason why,
MEDDM203:22 Hp283   care for the company of the phisitian or chirurgian, but if he
PHLEGM See FLEGME
PHLEGM'S See FLEGM'S
PHLEGMY See FLEGMY
PHOCIANS (1) [phocæans]
MPERS80:28   H1095   But {the} *Phocians* Land, {Country} he then wasted sore:
PHŒBUS (4)
SIDNEY151:35 He   left that charge by *Phœbus* to be man'd:
CONTEM167:26 H3   When *Phœbus* wanted but one hour to bed,

2LETTER181:31 H1   *Phœbus* make haste, the day's too long, be gone,

2LETTER182:23 H29   O *Phœbus,* hadst thou but thus long from thine

PHOENICIA (1) See also PHENICIA

MGREC100:14   H1898 In *Syria, Ægypt,* and *Phoenicia;*

PHOENICIAN See PHENICIAN

PHOENICIANS See PHENICIANS

PHŒNIX (7) See also PHÆNIX

ELEMEN19:7   H452   The Phœnix too (if any be) are mine;

MASSYR60:31   H296   Raises a Phœnix new, from grave o'th old;

SIDNEY~~150:38~~ H66   And *Phœnix Spencer* doth unto his life,

QELIZ155:33   H24   No *Phœnix,* Pen, nor *Spencers* Poetry,

QELIZ156:18   H45   Come shew me such a Phœnix if you can;

QELIZ157:26   H94   She was a Phœnix Queen, so shall she be,

QELIZ157:27   H95   Her ashes not reviv'd more Phœnix she;

PHRENSIE (1) [frenzy]

AGES41:3   H223   Sometimes the Phrensie, strangely madds my Brain,

PHRENSIE'S (1) [frensy is]

HUMOUR34:25   H580   Phrensie's worse, then folly, one would more glad,

PHRIGIA (1)

MGREC94:38   H1676 Which twixt *Phrigia,* and *Propontis* lyes.

PHRIGIAN (1)

MGREC122:23 ~~H2845~~ *Ceria* the *Phrigian* Queen for to withstand,

PHYSIC See PHISICK, PHISICK-PURGING-POTION

PHYSICIAN (1) See also PHISITIAN, PHYSITIAN

MGREC131:30   H3222 When his disease the skilfull Physician found,

PHYSITIAN (1) [physician]

SON231:8   H20   His help & his physitian wer't

PICK (2)

ELEMEN12:22   H182   Out of huge {great} numbers, I might pick my choyce,

MYCHILD219:7 Hp245 & imperfectly done, but if yov can pick any Benefitt out of it, It

PICTURE (1)

QELIZ156:34   H61   And {the proud} *Tiron* bound, before her picture fell.

PICTURES (1) [pl.]

1LETTER181:18 H16   True living Pictures of their Fathers face.

PIDNA (1)

MGREC126:7   H2998 She with the flow'r {chief} o'th Court to *Pidna* flyes,

PIE See PYE

PIECE See PEICE

PIECES See PEICES

PIERCE (2) See also [PEIRCE]

MGREC131:41   H3233 his Sword did pierce his mothers {run her through the} heart,

FLESH176:38   H78   Mine Eye doth pierce the heavens, and see

PIERCED See PEIRCED

PIERCING See PEIRCING

PIETY (2)

MROMAN137:26 H3477 Held for his Piety, some sacred thing;

MEDDM198:13 Hp276 Want of prudence as well as piety hath brought men into great

PIKE (3)

ELEMEN9:3   ~~H37~~   My force? your sword, your Pike, your flint and steele,

AGES39:19   H162   glistring {glitt'ring} Sword, {the Pistol} and wel advanced Pike;

MPERS69:35   H657   Then on a Pike being {wood-pile} set, where all might eye,

PILGRIM (3)
TDUDLEY165:37 H39   But as a Pilgrim what he had, possest.
PILGRIM210:1   H1   As weary pilgrim, now at rest
PILGRIM210:19 H19   A pilgrim I, on earth, perplext
PILGRIMAGE (4)
AGES44:23   H356   In this short Pilgrimage I oft have had;
MYCHILD217:16 Hp243 pilgrimage and refreshing wch I supposed most of the servants
11MAYA226:17 Hp255 Many refreshments haue I fovnd in this my weary pilgrimage,
13MAY227:9   H18   O hast thou made my pilgrimage
PILGRIMS (1) [pl.]
MEDDM203:17 Hp283 sees land we must therfore be heer as strangers and pilgrims,
PILLOW (2)
MGREC116:24 H2590 And under's pillow laid them when he slept.
MEDDM198:25 Hp276 An akeing head requires a soft pillow, and a drooping heart a
PILOTT (2) [pilot]
2HUSB232:27   H28   Lord bee thov pilott to ye ship
ACK235:13   H13   Thou wast the pilott to the ship
PINCH'D (1) [pinched]
MPERS76:7   H905   By these alone his Hoast was pinch'd so sore,
PINCHED (2)
SEASONS52:8   H223   Our pinched flesh, and empty panch {hungry mawes} requires:
MGREC126:17 H3008 The Souldiers pinched with this scarcity,
PINCHING (1)
SEASONS47:27 H43   The pinching Nor-west {North-west} cold, {wind} of fierce
PIN D (1) [pinned]
MGREC~~116:10~~ H2574 But pin d in grief till life did her forsake:
PINE (1)
ELEMEN15:8   H290   The Pine, the Cedars, yea and *Daph'nes* tree;
PINKS (2) [pl.]
AGES36:5   H29   Garland of Roses, Pinks, and Gilliflowers,
SEASONS48:16 H69   Except the double Pinks, and matchlesse Roses.
PINNED See **PIN D**
PIOUS (5)
MPERS~~71:36~~ H750   If all his {this} heat, had been for a good {pious} end,
TDUDLEY166:30 H72 His pious Footsteps followed by his race,
TDUDLEY166:36 H78 *That was both pious, just and wise,*
MEDDM195:27 Hp272 pious.
MEDDM202:9 Hp281 beasts then men, some pious saints, some incarnate Deuils,
MEDDM206:30 Hp288 bad parents haue had pious children, it should make vs adore
PIPE (2)
AGES40:12   H193   From pipe to pot, from pot to words, and blows,
SEASONS49:26 H115 Carelesse of worldly wealth, you sit {sing} and pipe,
PIPES (1)
SEASONS49:17 H108 To wash their {the} thick cloath'd flocks, with pipes ful glad.
PIPPIN (1)
DUBART154:12 H57   Then in thy *Pippin, Martell, Charlemain.*
PIRATES See **PYRATES**
PISCES (1)
SEASONS52:34 H249 In *Pisces* now the golden Sun doth shine,
PISIDIA (2)
MPERS86:36   H1352 The Rovers in *Pisidia,* should drive out.

MGREC95:10   H1689 *Hallicarnassus* and *Pisidia*

PISSIRUS (1)
MPERS79:32   H1058 And for his Cattell, all *Pissirus* Lake

PISTOL (1)
AGES~~39:19~~   H162   The glistring {glitt'ring} Sword, {the Pistol} and wel advanced

PISTOLS (1) [pl.]
AGES43:9   ~~H305~~   Whence poyson, Pistols, and dread instruments,

PIT (1) See also **PITT**
MPERS91:28   ~~H1542~~ He must leave all, and in the pit remain;

PITCHED (1)
HUMOUR32:34 H508   And {But} though the pitched field i've ever fled,

PITCHERS (1) [pl.]
MEDDM208:26 Hp290 them, return with their empty pitchers ashamed,

PITCHT (1)
ELEMEN19:39 H480   As battells pitcht ith' Aire (as Countries know;)

PITEOVS (1) [piteous]
HOUSE236:16 H8   And piteovs shreiks of dreadfull voice.

PITHON (3)
MGREC121:14 ~~H2792~~ *Pithon,* next *Perdicas,* a Captaine high,
MGREC121:23 H2805 Confers {Yields} them {to} *Pithon* on, for's courtesie;
MGREC121:31 H2813 And *Pithon* turn'd to *Asia* againe.

PITHONS (1) [poss.]
MGREC122:27 H2846 *Pithons* commands, {as oft} She ever countermands

PITHYUS (1)
MPERS78:32   H1013 Whither rich *Pithyus* comes, *Xerxes* to greet;

PITIFUL (1)
DDUDLEY167:12H9   *A friendly Neighbor, pitiful to poor,*

PITT (1) [pit]
FEVER221:13 H28   Who hath redeem'd my Soul from pitt,

PITTANCE (1)
SEASONS48:33 H84   Melodious {Sweet fragrant} Spring, with thy short pittance flye,

PITTY (9) [pity]
ELEMEN16:22 H345   Which pitty moves, and oft deceives the wise.
MPERS69:39   H669   With pitty *Cyrus* mov'd, knowing Kings stand,
MPERS78:30   H1011 But pitty 'twas, thine ayde that {thou} here did'st lend,
MPERS82:13   H1160 For pitty, let those few to *Xerxes* go,
MGREC106:1   H2135 Thy pitty, and compassion to reward,
MGREC109:4   ~~H2261~~ To age, nor sex, no pitty doth expresse,
SIDNEY150:24 H51   Made famous by thy fall {death}, much more's {more} the pitty;
TDUDLEY165:17H19   That pitty might some Trumpeters procure.
SOREFIT221:31H17   Where pitty most of all I see.

PITY (3)
DIALOG146:15 H201   Oh pity me, in this sad perturbation,
DIALOG146:23 H209   If any pity in thy heart remain,
DIALOG146:32 H218   Your griefs I pity much, but should do wrong {hope to see},

PLAC'D (12) [placed]
PROLOG7:24   H36   So 'mongst the rest, they plac'd the Arts divine:
MASSYR56:14 H120   Which is the midst, of this brave Town was plac'd,
MASSYR62:18 H363   {He} Plac'd *Israel* in's Land {there}, where he thought best,
MASSYR64:18 H442   And in his Idols house the Vassal's {vessels} plac'd.
MPERS72:21   H769   Over his Seat, then plac'd his Son therein;

MPERS92:5	H1559	*Arsames* plac'd now in his fathers stead,
MGREC95:22	H1701	There {In's stead} *Arsemes* {*Arses*} was plac'd, yet {but} durst
MGREC120:35	H2772	At *Alexandria,* in *Ægypt* Land, {his tomb he plac'd}
MGREC122:33	H2854	He plac'd, displac'd, controld, rul'd, as he list,
MGREC134:38	H3367	For *Pompey's* life, then plac'd her in his stead,
QELIZ157:6	H74	She plac'd {built} her glory but on *Babels* walls,
CHILDRN184:35	H24	On whom I plac'd no small delight;

PLACE (56)

ELEMEN11:21	H141	The next in place, Earth judg'd to be her due,
ELEMEN17:33	H397	And now give place unto our sister Aire.
ELEMEN18:32	H436	No place so subtilly made, but I get in.
HUMOUR20:31	H23	Cold {Mild} flegme, did not contest for highest {chiefest} place,
HUMOUR21:17	H45	One of your selves are my compeers, in place:
HUMOUR22:16	H85	And 'fore she be assaulted, quits the place,
HUMOUR24:12	H161	Good sisters give me leave (as is my place)
HUMOUR25:38	H227	But if in fitting time, and place, on foes; {'gainst foe}
HUMOUR27:18	H289	Your slanders thus refuted, takes no place,
HUMOUR27:24	H295	Shal firstly {chiefly} take her {the} place, as is her {my} due,
HUMOUR29:27	H378	I then command, proud Choler stand thy place,
HUMOUR33:28	H542	Within this stately place of eminence,
HUMOUR34:31	H586	Again, none's fit for Kingly place but thou,
AGES38:12	H115	Nor yet on future things did place {set} my hope.
AGES39:31	H174	Makes {Make} all to place their future hopes on me.
AGES41:39	H256	For time, for place, likewise for each relation,
AGES42:4	H262	Yea justice I have done, was I in place;
AGES44:27	H360	Sometime an abject, then again in place,
SEASONS50:21	H155	The Barley, and the Rye, should first had place,
MASSYR59:33	H257	Which {That} for twelve hundred years had held that place;
MASSYR63:2	H387	His Son, weak *Essarhadon* reign'd in's place,
MASSYR64:27	H451	Such was the scituation of this place,
MASSYR65:28	H493	His Unckle, he established in's place.
MPERS69:6	H628	Who had in *Persia* the Lieutenants place.
MPERS73:26	H811	And two of these great Peers, in place {Field} lay dead:
MPERS77:16	H956	(His eldest brother put beside the place,
MPERS83:27	H1215	Amongst the Monarchs next, this Prince had place
MPERS87:23	H1375	This place was {so} made, by nature, and by art;
MPERS89:13	H1447	may come, and {in short time might} place one in his Throne,
MPERS92:19	H1577	By one of these, he must obtain the place.
MGREC103:20	H2031	Their charge, {place} gave to his Captains (as most {was} just}
MGREC107:37	H2212	They all passe over, to the other place;
MGREC121:18	H2800	And offers {offer} him his Honours, and his place,
MGREC122:30	H2849	Resign'd his place, and so let all alone;
MGREC123:15	H2879	To *Polisperchon,* then his place he gave, {did bequeath}
MGREC123:22	H2886	Now {Then} *Polisperchon* 'gins to act in's place,
MGREC123:32	H2896	Such as his father had advanc'd to place,
MGREC129:33	H3147	And place their hopes o'th heire of *Alexander,*
MGREC134:8	H3339	I'th' holy place, which caused desolation;
MGREC134:36	H3367	Whom *Julius Cæsar* set in Royall place,
MROMAN138:23	H3513	Then unto death unwillingly gives place.
MROMAN139:3	H3531	Of *Tanaquil,* late Queen, obtaines the place;
DIALOG147:38	H262	Then Justice shall in all thy Courts take place,

TDUDLEY166:31	H73	At last will bring us to that happy place
CONTEM170:2	H76	Who like a miscreant's driven from that place,
CONTEM170:6	H79	Here sits our Grandame in retired place,
CONTEM172:9	H145	A lonely place, with pleasures dignifi'd.
CONTEM172:19	H154	Till thou arrive at thy beloved place,
FLESH175:2	H2	In secret place where once I stood
SICKNES178:27	H10	in place of highest bliss,
MEDDM203:12	Hp283	desire to make y^t his place of residence, but longs to put in at
MEDDM203:15	Hp283	must beware of desireing to make this the place of his abode,
MEDDM206:31	Hp288	Souerainty of god, who will not be tyed to time nor place, nor
MEDDM208:7	Hp290	other meanes to extinguish them so distance of place together
SON231:4	H16	And freinds rais'd him in every place
HOUSE236:24	H16	The flame consvme my dwelling place,

PLACED (2) See also PLAC'D

MPERS84:7	H1235	And a {one} more worthy, placed in her roome,
MPERS90:36	H1503	*Tythraustes* now {then} is placed in his stead,

PLACES (5) [pl.]

DAVID158:26	H6	Upon thy places, mountain'ous and high,
DAVID159:22	H37	In places high, full low thou dost {didst} remaine;
MYCHILD215:30	Hp241	those places I thought most concerned my Condition, and
HOURS233:30	H13	In secrett places, Thee I find
HOUSE236:35	H27	And here and there ye places spye

PLACIDE (1) [placid]

ELEMEN8:8	H6	In placide terms they thought now to discourse,

PLAGUE (2)

DIALOG143:21	H90	Famine, and Plague, two sisters of the Sword,
DIALOG144:26	H135	The plague of stubborn incredulity.

PLAGUES (1) [pl.]

ELEMEN20:2	H484	Portentious signes, of Famines, Plagues and Wars.

PLAID (2) [played]

MGREC95:41	H1720	To shew, how great *Darius* plaid his part:
CONTEM169:20	H60	They kept one tune, and plaid on the same string,

PLAIN (6)

HUMOUR22:37	H106	My absence proves, it plain, her wit then flyes
HUMOUR31:3	H436	So plain a slander needeth no reply.
MASSYR54:17	H44	Transfers his Seat, to the *Assyrian* plain,
MASSYR56:22	H128	On {In} *Shinar* plain, by the *Euphratan* flood,
MGREC100:29	H1913	Yet had some hope, that on that even {the spacious} plain,
DIALOG145:13	H162	Pray in plain termes, what is your present grief,

PLAINE (1) [plain]

PROLOG7:8	H22	lisp'd at first, speake afterwards more {in future times} plaine

PLAINES (1) [plains] See also PLANES

MPERS79:18	H1044	And {Then} in *Abidus* Plaines, mustring his Forces,

PLAINLY (2)

MGREC114:10	H2478	That of *Parmenio's* death him plainly told.
MEDDM203:18	Hp283	that we may plainly declare that we seek a citty aboue and

PLAINS See PLAINES, PLANES

PLAINTS (1) [complaints]

SOREFIT221:21	H7	My plaints & Groanes were heard of Thee

'PLIANTS (1) [complaints]

REMB235:34	H15	My 'plaints haue had accesse.

PLAISTER (1) [plaster]
  MEDDM203:28 Hp284 welcome, that brings a plaister for his sore, or a cordiall for his
PLANES (1) [plains]
  ELEMEN12:23 H183 Thousands in woods, and planes, both wild, and tame,
PLANETS (1) [pl.]
  ELEMEN10:1 H76 My Planets, of both Sexes, whose degree
PLANT (2)
  ELEMEN14:35 H277 Thou bear'st no {nor} grasse, nor {or} plant, nor tree, nor
  AGES42:23 H281 As neither sow, nor reape, nor plant, nor build.
PLANTS (8) [pl.]
  ELEMEN12:35 H195 Besides the use you have {of roots}, of Hearbs and Plants,
  ELEMEN13:26 H227 My sap, to plants and trees, I must not grant,
  ELEMEN14:11 H253 With divers moe, nay, into plants it creeps;
  ELEMEN14:11 H253 Nay into herbs and plants it sometimes creeps,
  ELEMEN19:34 H475 Where neither houses, trees, nor plants, I spare;
  HUMOUR26:20 H250 As plants, trees, and small Embryon know'th,
  SEASONS47:37 H49 All Plants, and Flowers, {set and sown} for all delights, and
  ELIZB187:9 H17 But plants new set to be eradicate,
PLASTER See PLAISTER
PLATE (3)
  MGREC96:32 H1752 Loaden with gold, with jewels and with Plate,
  MGREC103:11 H2022 And taken mony, plate, and golden treasure;
  DUBART153:20 H24 The glittering Plate, and Jewels, he admires,
PLAY (13)
  PROLOG7:26 H38 The *Greeks* did nought, but play the foole and lye.
  HUMOUR21:15 H43 Where Monarch-like I play, and sway alone.
  HUMOUR26:7 H237 To play Philosopher, I have no list;
  HUMOUR29:21 H372 To play such furious pranks I am too wise;
  SEASONS47:21 H37 Now {Do} jump, and play, before their feeding Dams,
  MASSYR58:26 H209 *Sardanapalus* leaves his Apish play.
  MGREC102:22 H1992 And gives {gave} himself to banqueting, and play:
  MGREC122:26 H2845 Which made her now begin to play her part;
  MGREC126:4 H2995 *Polisperchon* to hold a while in play,
  MGREC131:40 H3232 The eld'st enrag'd did play the vipers part,
  MROMAN138:6 H3496 Yet for {in} their compact, after false they play:
  DIALOG142:25 H54 Or, doth {do} the *Scots* play false behind your back?
  QELIZ156:8 H35 That women wisdome lack to play the Rex;
PLAY'D (1) [played] See also PLAID
  MASSYR55:6 H72 She like a brave Virago, play'd the rex,
PLAYED See PLAID, PLAY'D
PLAYES (1) [plays]
  AGES40:25 H206 To Masques, to Playes, to Taverns stil I move;
PLEA (1)
  MGREC117:35 H2642 Alleadg'd by those, which {who} by their subtill plea
PLEAD (3)
  HUMOUR24:14 H163 Your selves may plead, your wrongs are no whit lesse,
  MGREC101:17 H1942 No, though *Parmenio* plead, he {yet} will not heare;
  MGREC126:25 H3016 And plead the blood of their deare Kindred {friends and
PLEADING (1)
  HUMOUR20:26 H18 Pleading her selfe, was most of all desir'd;

PLEAS'D (6) [pleased]

HUMOUR35:14	H610	This loving counsel pleas'd them all so wel,
MASSYR64:5	H429	This was that King of Kings, did what he pleas'd,
MPERS74:29	H852	Made wholsome gentle Laws, which pleas'd each mind.
MGREC113:18	H2445	This sound advice, at heart, pleas'd *Alexander,*
MGREC116:28	H2594	For those that {such as} pleas'd him: had both wealth and
MGREC129:23	H3137	But 'twas in shew, in heart it pleas'd them best.

PLEASANT (23)

ELEMEN15:10	H292	Man wants his bread, and wine, and pleasant fruits;
ELEMEN18:19	H423	Your songs and pleasant tunes, they are the same,
HUMOUR28:25	H337	They're liberal, pleasant, kinde, and courteous,
AGES45:31	H421	No more rejoyce, at musickes pleasant {pleasing} noyse,
AGES45:33	H423	I cannot scent, savours of pleasant meat,
SEASONS47:5	H19	Stil adds to th' last, til after pleasant *May;*
SEASONS48:9	H62	My next, and last, is pleasant fruitfull *May,*
SEASONS49:22	H113	Blest rustick Swains, your pleasant quiet life,
MASSYR54:24	H51	Upon the pleasant banks of *Tigris* flood,
MASSYR62:21	H366	And pleasant *Canaan* ne're see again:
MPERS72:30	H774	'T would be no pleasant {pleasure}, but a tedious thing,
MPERS79:37	H1063	That pleasant *Thessaly,* from *Greece* divide;
MGREC110:37	H2341	He on the faire *Hidaspis* pleasant side,
DAVID158:35	H15	Nor any pleasant thing e're may you show;
DAVID159:9	H24	Pleasant and lovely were they both in life,
DAVID159:26	H41	So pleasant hast thou been, deare brother mine:
TDUDLEY167:1	H83	*In manners pleasant and severe*
CHILDRN186:6	H73	Once young and pleasant, as are you,
MEDDM197:11	Hp274	If we had no winter the spring would not be so pleasant, if we
MEDDM198:32	Hp277	It is a pleasant thing to behold the light, but sore eyes are not
13MAY227:10	H19	Thvs pleasant fair and good,
HOUSE237:1	H31	My pleasant things in ashes lye
HOUSE237:5	H35	No pleasant tale shall 'ere be told

PLEASANT'ST (1) [pleasantest]

AGES46:10	H441	Yea knowing much, the pleasant'st {pleasants} life of all,

PLEASANTS (1) [pl.]

AGES46:10	H441	Yea knowing much, the pleasant'st {pleasants} life of all,

PLEASE (4)

AGES38:26	H129	Then nought can please, and yet I know not why.
MASSYR57:18	H165	This answer may suffice, whom it wil please,
MPERS73:16	H803	(Who like to Kings, rul'd Kingdomes as they please,)
VANITY160:6	H16	The sensuall senses for a time they please,

PLEASED (6) See also PLEAS'D

MEDDM202:14	Hp282	but so it pleased him, whose will is the perfect rule of
MYCHILD216:14	Hp241	pleased God to keep me a long time wthout a child wch was a
28AUG225:27	Hp254	times my faith weak likewise, the Lord was pleased to vphold
30SEPT227:18	Hp257	It pleased god to viset me wth my old Distemper of weaknes
11MAYB228:23	Hp259	It hath pleased God to giue me a long Time of respite for these
11MAYB228:28	Hp259	it ye more tedious, but it pleased ye Lord to support my heart

PLEASES (3)

MEDDM199:13	Hp277	on his anuile into what frame he pleases
MEDDM206:32	Hp288	but takes and chuses, when and where and whom he pleases,
MEDDM207:23	Hp289	pleases our great landlord to let: All haue their bounds set ouer

PLEASING (6)

AGES38:22	H125	A serpents sting in pleasing face lay hid.
AGES45:31	H421	No more rejoyce, at musickes pleasant {pleasing} noyse,
MGREC114:3	H2471	Nothing more pleasing to mad *Clitus* tongue,
CONTEM168:33	H39	Thy pleasing fervor, and thy scorching force,
MYCHILD215:20	Hp240	ye former it had been perhaps better pleasing to yov, but seing
MYCHILD215:21	Hp240	last is the best, let it be best pleasing to yov.

PLEASURE (17)

HUMOUR23:21	H131	Nor is't my pleasure, thus to blur thy name:
MPERS72:30	H774	'T would be no pleasant {pleasure}, but a tedious thing,
MPERS73:23	H809	Who little pleasure had, in his short reigne,
MPERS91:25	H1539	But long in ease and pleasure did not lye,
MGREC97:11	H1772	Divided at the *Macedonians* pleasure.
MGREC97:25	H1786	But all *Phenicia* to his pleasures {pleasure} yeeld;
MGREC102:4	H1974	Which *Alexander* deals, as suits his pleasure.
MGREC103:10	H2021	For when the Souldiers, had rifled their pleasure,
MGREC109:31	H2290	His pleasure is, that forthwith he repaire
MGREC122:37	H2858	When to his pleasure all things they had done,
VANITY160:23	H33	Nor yet in learning, wisdome, youth nor pleasure,
CONTEM174:21	H219	So he that saileth in this world of pleasure,
FLESH175:34	H34	Affect's thou pleasure? take thy fill,
FLESH176:31	H71	Then can thy hours in pleasure spent.
ELIZB186:35	H7	Farewel sweet babe, the pleasure of mine eye,
MEDDM207:17	Hp288	withers the pleasure wch else we should take in them, and well
11MAYA226:21	Hp255	pleasure espec: seing it is for my spirit^l. advantage, For I hope

PLEASURES (14) [pl.]

AGES46:4	H435	In pleasures, and in labours, I have found,
MASSYR57:10	H157	It is more like, being {his lust} with pleasures fed,
MPERS69:38	H663	His Treasures, pleasures, pomp and power dfd see,
MPERS92:38	H1596	Whose honours, treasures, pleasures, had short stay;
MGREC97:25	H1786	But all *Phenicia* to his pleasures {pleasure} yeeld;
MGREC102:19	H1989	With all pleasures that on earth was {are} found,
MGREC103:22	H2033	The pleasures and the riches of this town,
MGREC132:22	H3267	Within an Isle that was with pleasures fed,
VANITY160:4	H14	What then? content in pleasures canst thou find?
VANITY160:38	H48	It yeeldeth pleasures, farre beyond conceit,
CONTEM171:16	H120	And puts all pleasures vain unto eternal flight.
CONTEM172:9	H145	A lonely place, with pleasures dignifi'd.
FLESH176:18	H58	Thy sinfull pleasures I doe hate,
MEDDM208:21	Hp290	so is it wth the wealth honours and pleasures of this world

PLEDGE (2)

MERCY189:6	H27	The fifth and last pledge of her dying love,
JULY223:32	Hp251	Thou hast given me a pledge of y^t Inheritc thou hast promised

PLEDGES (2) [pl.]

MASSYR64:13	H437	His Vassal is, gives pledges for his truth,
MED223:4	Hp250	pledges of thy Loue. First thov art my Creator, I thy creature,

PLEIADES (1)

SEASONS47:14	H30	The Pleiades, their influence now give,

PLENTIFULL (1) [plentiful]

MEDDM205:7	Hp285	plentifull crop may be expected in the haruest of their yeares.

PLENTY (2)
ELEMEN17:18   H382   And of my chilling colds, such plenty be;
AGES44:24   H357   Sometimes the Heavens with plenty smil'd on me,

PLIGHTED (1)
WHAT224:19   H19   His word he plighted hath on high

PLINY (2)
ELEMEN10:30   H105   The over-curious second *Pliny* slew:
ELEMEN15:33   H315   Not thou, but shell-fish yeelds, as *Pliny* clears.

PLOT (2)
AGES45:4   H382   A plot to blow up Nobles, and their King;
MGREC129:15   H3129   *Perdicas* was her partner in this plot:

PLOTTED (1)
AGES45:17   H399   Plotted and acted, so that none can tell,

PLOUGH (1)
MEDDM205:1   Hp285   land) are of so tough and morose a dispotion that the plough

PLOUGHED (1) See also PLOW'D
MEDDM204:35   Hp285   brought into tilth yet all must be ploughed and harrowed Some

PLOUGHMAN (1)
DIALOG146:19   H205   The seed time's come, but Ploughman hath no hope,

PLOW'D (1) [plowed] See also PLOUGHED
SEASONS50:24   H158   He plow'd with pain, but reaping doth rejoyce;

PLOW-MAN (1)
SEASONS47:6   H22   Now goes the Plow-man to his merry toyl,

PLOWMAN (1)
ELEMEN16:41   H364   The Farmer, and the Plowman both {Grasier do} complain

PLUCK'D (1) [plucked]
MASSYR65:25   H490   Then from his throne, he pull'd {pluck'd} him down again:

PLUCKING (1)
MGREC104:15   H2067   Grinding his teeth, and plucking off his haire,

PLUCKT (1)
SIDNEY150:25   H52   Ah, in his blooming prime, death pluckt this Rose,

PLUMBE (2) [plum]
AGES38:2   H105   But for an Apple, Plumbe, or some such prize,
SEASONS47:38   H50   The Pear, the Plumbe, and Apple-tree now flourish,

PLUMBS (2) [plums]
SEASONS50:28   H162   The Prince of Plumbs, whose stone is {as} hard as Rock.
ELIZB187:6   H14   And Plumbs and Apples throughly ripe do fall,

PLUMES (3) [pl.]
ELEMEN19:6   H451   The Ostrich with her plumes, th'Eagle with her eyne;
DUBART153:21   H25   The Hats, and Fans, the Plumes, and Ladies tires,
MEDDM196:7   Hp273   them vp, but spying his black feet, he soon lets fall his plumes,

PLUNDER'D (1) [plundered]
AGES45:22   H409   I've seen it plunder'd, taxt and soak'd in bloud,

PLUNDERED (1)
DIALOG146:16   H202   My plundered Townes, my houses devastation,

PLUNDERS (1)
MPERS85:22   H1298   Invades {Plunders} the Country, and much trouble {mischief}

PLURISIE (2) [pleurisy]
HUMOUR32:6   H480   Nor cold, nor hot, Ague, nor Plurisie;
AGES40:40   H219   Sometimes the Cough, Stitch, {the Quinsey} painful Plurisie,

PLUS (1)
HUMOUR28:18 H330 The over plus I send unto the reines;
PLUTARCH (1)
MPERS~~91:30~~ H1544 His life may read in *Plutarch* to be seen.
PLUTARCHS (1) [poss.]
MGREC~~122:8~~ H2833 In *Plutarchs Lives* his history many find.
POEM (2)
SIDNEY152:19 H88 For to conclude my poem two lines they daigne,
QELIZ155:32 H23 *The Poem.*
POESIE (1)
SIDNEY149:14 H13 Of Poesie, and of Musick thou wert {he was} King;
POESY (1)
PROLOG7:23 H35 And poesy made, *Calliope's* owne childe,
POETRY (1)
QELIZ155:33 H24 No *Phoenix,* Pen, nor *Spencers* Poetry,
POETS (2) [pl.]
PROLOG6:22 H7 Let Poets, and Historians set these forth,
MASSYR56:36 H142 The Poets feign her turn'd into a Dove,
POETS (1) [poss.]
PROLOG7:16 H29 A Poets Pen, all scorne, I should thus wrong;
POINT (3)
HUMOUR33:40 H554 This point for {now} to discusse longs not to me,
AGES43:1 ~~H297~~ If honour was the point, to which I steer'd;
QELIZ156:13 H40 But can you Doctors now this point dispute,
POINTS (1) [pl.]
HUMOUR25:21 H210 A Souldier most compleat in al points makest.
POISING See POYZING
POISON (1) See also POYSON
MGREC~~120:4~~ H2738 To end his dayes by poison, rather chose
POISONED See POYSONED
POISONOUS See POYSONOUS
POISONS See POYSONS
POLE (3)
AGES39:29 H172 {elevate} my {high} thoughts above {beyond} the Pole.
SEASONS51:39 H215 The Northern Pole beholdeth not one ray.
2LETTER182:20 H26 Like those far scituate under the pole,
POLES (1) [pl.]
SEASONS47:11 H27 And Poles erects, for his green {young} clambering Hops;
POLICIE (1) [policy]
HUMOUR29:40 H391 Of Learning, and of Policie, thou would'st bereave me,
POLICIES (2) [pl.]
HUMOUR23:26 H136 Whose Serene {profound} heads, I line with policies,
MGREC122:7 H2830 His policies, how he did extricate
POLICY (2)
MGREC123:8 H2870 But vaine it was to use his policy,
DUBART153:38 H42 Thy Phisick, Musick, and State policy,
POLIDAMUS (1)
MGREC113:24 H2451 *Polidamus,* who seem'd *Parmenio's* friend,
POLIMNIA (1)
SIDNEY149:15 H14 Thy {His} Rhethorick it struck *Polimnia* dead,

POLISH (1)
MEDDM197:5   Hp274   bruise, then polish
POLISH'D (1) [polished]
HUMOUR32:33   H507   My polish'd skin was not ordain'd for skars,
POLISPERCHON (11)
MGREC123:15   H2879   To *Polisperchon,* then his place he gave, {did bequeath}
MGREC123:22   H2886   Now {Then} *Polisperchon* 'gins to act in's place,
MGREC124:2   H2907   To take down *Polisperchon* grown so high;
MGREC124:7   H2912   *Polisperchon,* knowing he did relye
MGREC124:9   H2914   But in his absence *Polisperchon* takes
MGREC124:12   H2919   Whom *Polisperchon* labours to oppose,
MGREC124:27   H2934   *Polisperchon* hoping for's office long,
MGREC125:2   H2950   She now with *Polisperchon* doth combine,
MGREC126:4   H2995   *Polisperchon* to hold a while in play,
MGREC129:27   H3141   *Polisperchon* brings up the other son,
MGREC129:35   H3149   So *Polisperchon* to his Counsell drew,
POLISPERCHONS (1) [poss.]
MGREC123:29   H2893   This *Polisperchons* great ability,
POLISTRATUS (1)
MGREC105:14   H2107   And thus he lay, *Polistratus* a *Greeke*
POLITICKE (1) [politic]
MPERS73:40   H825   Too politicke (tis {its} like) for me to tell,
POLITITIAN (1)
HUMOUR30:1   H393   What greater Clerke, or polititian lives?
POLL'D (1) [polled]
DIALOG148:10 H275   Of what unjustly once she poll'd from thee,
POMGRANET (1) [pomegranate]
SEASONS51:8   H182   The Figge is {are} ripe, the Pomgranet also,
POMP (2) See also POMP'S [pomp is]
MPERS69:38   H663   His Treasures, pleasures, pomp and power dfd see,
MGREC132:28   H3275   Whose obsequies with wondrous pomp was done.
POMPE (1)
MGREC96:1   H1721   The splendor, and the pompe, he marched in,
POMPEY'S (2) [poss.]
MGREC134:32   H3363   Next *Auletes,* who cut off *Pompey's* head:
MGREC134:38   H3367   For *Pompey's* life, then plac'd her in his stead,
POMPHILIUS (1)
MROMAN138:15 H3505   Nephew unto *Pomphilius* dead, and gone;
POMPILIUS (2)
MROMAN137:24 H3475   *Numa Pompilius.*
MROMAN137:25 H3476   *Nvma Pompilius,* is next chosen {chose they} King,
POMPOUS (1)
MGREC102:6   H1976   Is entertain'd with joy, and pompous train {showes},
POMP'S (1) [pomp is]
CONTEM174:33 H230   Their parts, their ports, their pomp's all laid in th' dust
PONDER (1)
MEDDM198:11   Hp276   need ponder all his steps.
PONDS (2) [pl.]
ELEMEN16:4   H327   Then I have Fountaines, Rivers, Lakes and Ponds:
CONTEM172:34 H167   In Lakes and ponds, you leave your numerous fry,

PONTICKE (1)
ELEMEN16:7   H330   The *Ponticke, {Aegean} Caspian,* Golden Rivers fine. {five,}

POOLE (1) [pool]
ELEMEN18:26   H430   And when I smile, your Ocean's like a Poole.

POOLS (1) [pl.]
11MAYA226:18   Hp255   this valley of Baca many pools of water, That wch now I cheifly

POOR (20)
FATHER6:5   H39   My goods are true (though poor) I love no stealth,
ELEMEN10:2   H77   Poor Heathen judg'd worthy a Diety:
HUMOUR22:26   H95   Poor spirits the Liver breeds, which is thy seat,
HUMOUR30:18   H410   When you poor bankrupts prove, then have I most.
AGES41:34   ~~H249~~   To bear me out i'th' world, and feed the poor,
AGES~~41:36~~   H253   To bear a port i'th' world, and feed the poor.
AGES42:20   H278   Was I as poor, as poverty could be,
AGES45:6   H390   And poor *Palatinate* for ever lost;
SEASONS52:1   H218   Poor wretches, that in total darknesse lye,
MASSYR55:25   H91   Which was the cause, poor *Menon* lost his life,
MASSYR60:35   H300   Molests poor *Israel,* his wealth t' encrease.
MASSYR62:23   H368   Or how they fare, rich, poor, or ill, or wel;
MASSYR64:11   H435   *Iudah's* poor King besieg'd, who {and} succourlesse,
MASSYR67:6   H552   Poor forlorn Prince, that {who} had all state forgot,
MPERS83:19   H1207   That the poor {Prince} innocent, to death must {did} go.
DDUDLEY167:12   H9   *A friendly Neighbor, pitiful to poor,*
FLESH175:19   H19   That all in th' world thou count'st but poor?
AUTHOR178:14   H24   And for thy Mother, she alas is poor,
2LETTER182:19   H25   But for one moneth I see no day (poor soul)
SOREFIT221:26   H12   Yea when I was most low and poor,

POORE (11) [poor]
ELEMEN11:12   H132   The rich I oft make poore, the strong I maime,
ELEMEN11:33   H153   The rich and {the} poore, wise, foole, and every sort,
ELEMEN15:19   H301   That she can spare, when Nations round are poore.
AGES46:6   H437   To great, to rich, to poore, to young, or old,
MPERS72:6   ~~H755~~   Who for no wrong, poore innocent must dye,
MGREC100:21   H1905   Yet he (poore Prince) another Hoast doth muster,
MGREC105:19   H2112   Findes poore *Darius,* peirced to the heart;
DIALOG143:41   H110   And thou, poore soule, wast {wert} jeer'd among the rest,
DIALOG145:1   H150   I saw poore *Ireland* bleeding out her last,
DIALOG146:21   H207   The poore they want their pay, their children bread,
QELIZ155:29   H20   The acclamations of the poore, as rich;

POPE (1)
DIALOG143:34   H103   That Pope, had hope, to find *Rome* here againe;

POPELINGS (1) [pl.]
DIALOG~~147:11~~   H237   To root out Prelates, {Popelings} head, tail, branch, and rush.

POPERY (1)
DIALOG146:36   H222   After dark Popery the day did clear,

POPISH (2)
AGES~~45:20~~   H402   By bloudy Popish, hellish miscreants:
MYCHILD218:19   Hp244   yet why may not ye popish Relign. bee ye right, They haue the

POPULOUS (1)
ELEMEN11:37   H157   My cities famous, rich, and populous,

PORK (1)
SEASONS52:5　H220　Beef, Brawn, and Pork, are now in great'st {great} request,

PORT (6)
ELEMEN16:30　H353　The wealthy fraught, unto his wished Port.
ELEMEN18:24　H428　And speed you to your Port, with wished gales.
AGES41:36　H253　To bear a port i'th' world, and feed the poor.
CONTEM174:18 H217　And makes him long for a more quiet port,
MEDDM203:12　Hp283　make y^t his place of residence, but longs to put in at that port
SON230:26　H9　Did'st that ship bring to quiet port,

PORTEND (2)
MASSYR68:1　H587　Which horrid sight, he fears, must needs portend,
SIDNEY150:41　H69　I feare thou wert a Commet, did portend

PORTENTIOUS (1)
ELEMEN20:2　H484　Portentious signes, of Famines, Plagues and Wars.

PORTERS (1) [pl.]
FLESH177:10　H91　And Angels are for Porters there;

PORTION (3)
HUMOUR30:23　H415　Thus he is ours, his portion is the grave.
DUBART154:26　H71　Thy double portion would have served many.
JULY223:29　Hp251　him who is the only portion of his Servants.

PORTS (1) [pl.]
CONTEM174:33 H230　Their parts, their ports, their pomp's all laid in th' dust

PORUS (5)
MGREC109:29　H2288　But *Porus* stout, who will not yeeld as yet;
MGREC109:34　H2293　But Kingly *Porus* this brave answer sent,
MGREC110:1　H2301　But on the banks doth {stout} *Porus* ready stand,
MGREC110:11　H2311　*Porus* encounters them, thinking {and thinks} all's there,
MGREC110:16　H2316　For to the last, stout *Porus* kept his ground.

POSEY (1)
HUMOUR35:9　H605　A golden Ring, the Posey, *Unity:*

POSSESS (2)
AGES43:8　H305　I might possess that throne which was their right;
MGREC134:20　H3351　Cal'd *Philadelphus,* next sat on {did possess} the throne,

POSSESSE (5) [possess]
HUMOUR33:9　H523　Who doth possesse the Brain, or thou, or I;
MPERS79:21　H1047　One King, so many Subjects should possesse;
MGREC102:15　H1985　And to possesse, he counts no little blisse,
MGREC128:40　H3113　That each shall {should} hold what he doth {did} now possesse,
JULY223:28　Hp251　possesse that I now hope for, y^t so they may bee encourag^d to

POSSESSED (1)
VANITY161:2　H53　Who is possessed of, shall reign a King.

POSSESSES (1)
MASSYR67:3　H549　His son possesses wealth, and rule, as just;

POSSESSION (2)
MPERS76:13　H911　Possession of water, earth, and aire,
MGREC132:39　H3286　Possession he of *Europe* thinks to take,

POSSEST (3)
MPERS85:31　H1307　And so each man again possest his owne.
MGREC118:18　H2665　That he, who late, possest all earthly things,
TDUDLEY165:37 H39　But as a Pilgrim what he had, possest.

POSSIBLE (2)
MEDDM208:29 Hp290 (almost) possible to be done, it can remoue mountaines (if
MYCHILD218:33 Hp244 it were possible yᵉ very elect should bee deceived. Behold
POST (3)
MPERS76:35 H933 The *Persians* to their Gallies post with speed,
MGREC~~107:20~~ H2195 Now with his Army, doth he hast {post} away,
2LETTER182:33 H39 Now post with double speed, mark what I say,
POSTERITY (7)
MGREC110:25 H2329 Yet that his fame might to posterity,
MGREC117:5 H2612 To his posterity remain'd no jot,
MGREC132:27 H3272 For his posterity unto this day,
MGREC133:15 H3303 And his posterity, the same retaines,
MGREC133:29 H3319 In *Syria* by his posterity,
TDUDLEY166:29 H71 His blessing rest on his posterity:
2SIMON195:3 Hp271 Parents perpetuate their liues in their posterity, and their
POSTING (3)
SEASONS47:30 ~~H45~~ The Sun now keeps his posting residence
MPERS86:40 H1356 With posting speed {on} towards the King he goes;
DIALOG146:1 H189 The writing, printing, posting to and fro,
POSTS (2)
MPERS77:39 H980 And by this choyce, unwarily posts on,
MGREC104:31 H2083 Who doubling of his march, posts on amain,
POT (3)
AGES40:12 H193 From pipe to pot, from pot to words, and blows,
AGES40:12 H193 From pipe to pot, from pot to words, and blows,
MGREC114:15 H2485 This pot companion he did more bemoan,
POTENCY (1)
MASSYR55:35 H101 She for her potency, must go alone.
POTENT (6)
MASSYR57:23 ~~H170~~ Until that potent Empire did decay.
MPERS71:3 ~~H715~~ Some thirty years this potent Prince did reign,
MGREC110:3 H2303 A potent Army with him, like a King,
MROMAN137:18 H3469 The *Romans* now more potent 'gin to grow,
QELIZ157:22 H90 *Zenobia,* potent Empresse of the East,
MEDDM209:3 Hp291 thus potent but it is so necessary, that wᵗʰout faith there is no
POTS (1) [pl.]
ELEMEN9:17 H51 Your spits, pots, jacks, what else I need not name,
POUERTY (1) [poverty]
MEDDM204:29 Hp285 pouerty comfortably it will help to quiet him, but if that will not
POUNCE (1)
AGES40:21 H202 curling {to curle}, frisling up {and pounce my new-bought} hair;
POUR (1)
DIALOG148:12 H277 Execute toth' full {And on her pour} the vengeance threatned.
POURE (1)
MPERS79:7 H1029 I Rhethorick want, to poure out execration:
POURES (1)
MPERS75:34 H891 And on all Kings he poures out execrations,
POURS (1)
MGREC122:1 H2824 For this great {sad} strife, he pours out his complaints,
POUT (1)
AGES38:25 H128 Oft stubborn, peevish, sullen, pout, and cry:

POVERTY (3) See also POVERTY

AGES42:18	H276	In meannesse, greatnesse, riches, poverty;
AGES42:20	H278	Was I as poor, as poverty could be,
DIALOG142:32	H61	Such is her poverty, yet shall be found

POWDER (3)

ELEMEN9:4	H38	Your Cannon's bootlesse, and your powder too
MEDDM197:31	Hp275	till it haue past through the Mill and been ground to powder,
MYCHILD217:27	Hp243	grovnd me to powder it would bee but Light to me, yea oft

POWER (20) See also POW'R

ELEMEN19:17	H462	The living, scarce had power, to bury dead.
HUMOUR33:33	H547	Doth shew, hence flowes {flow} the power {pow'rs} which they
AGES40:35	H214	And gastly death oft threats me with her {his} power,
AGES44:15	H348	Now hath the power, Deaths Warfare, to discharge;
SEASONS47:24	H40	For though the Frost hath lost his binding power,
MASSYR54:1	H28	Whose acts, and power, is not for certainty,
MASSYR65:34	H499	The ninth, came *Nebuchadnezar* with power,
MASSYR67:27	H573	Who with his own, and Uncles power anon;
MPERS69:38	H663	His Treasures, pleasures, pomp and power dfd see,
MPERS70:28	H699	Which to revenge, she hires a mighty power,
MPERS74:8	H833	Praying to Fortune, for a Kingly power;
MGREC105:40	H2133	Of all good things (quoth he) once in my power,
MGREC118:31	H2680	Him {And} by a wile he got within his power,
MGREC118:35	H2684	The Princes seeing *Perdica's* power and Pride,
MGREC120:12	H2747	So many Kingdoms in their power to hold,
MROMAN138:12	H3502	Leaves {Left} *Rome*, in wealth and power, still growing high.
CONTEM168:2	H12	Whose power and beauty by his works we know.
2LETTER182:30	H36	Hath power to dry the torrent of these streams.
MEDDM208:28	Hp290	It is admirable to Consider the power of faith, by wch all things
PILGRIM210:38	H38	in power 'tis rais'd by Christ alone

POWERFULL (1) [powerful]

MGREC135:35	H3407	All trembling stand, before that powerfull Lambe.

POWERS (3) [pl.] See also POW'RS

AGES41:41	H258	Yet all my powers, for self-ends are not spent,
QELIZ157:17	H85	How vanisheth her glory, wealth, and powers;
MYCHILD218:36	Hp244	+ if I perish, I perish, But I know all ye powers of Hell shall

POW'R (1) [power]

WHAT224:15	H15	I find his Love, I know his pow'r.

POW'RS (1) [powers]

HUMOUR33:33	H547	shew, hence flowes {flow} the power {pow'rs} which they retain;

POX (3)

ELEMEN19:14	H459	Then Feavours, Purples, Pox, and Pestilence;
AGES41:1	H221	Sometimes the loathsome {two fold} Pox, my face {me sore}
MYCHILD216:4	Hp241	small pox, When I was in my afflict^n. I besovght the Lord, and

POYSON (8) [poison]

ELEMEN14:9	H251	Again, what veines of poyson in me lye;
AGES43:9	H305	Whence poyson, Pistols, and dread instruments,
MPERS84:38	H1274	Strong poyson took, and {so} put an end to's dayes.
MPERS91:22	H1532	By poyson caus'd, the young one to lose her life.
MGREC116:3	H2563	Poyson had put an end to's dayes 'twas thought,
MGREC118:25	H2674	On which, no signe of poyson could be {in his intrails} found,
MGREC124:41	H2948	She gave him poyson formerly ('tis thought)

MGREC125:24　H2974　A Halter, cup of Poyson, and a Sword,
POYSONED (1) [poisoned]
　MGREC130:33　H3181　If *Alexander* was not poysoned,
POYSONOUS (1) [poisonous]
　MGREC135:2　H3374　Then poysonous {His brave *Virago*} Aspes she sets unto {to}
POYSONS (1) [poisons]
　ELEMEN12:20　H180　Poysons sure antidote lyes in his horne.
POYZING (1) [poising]
　SEASONS51:1　H175　And doth in poyzing *Libra* this month shine.
PRACTICES (1) [pl.] See also PRACTISES
　MPERS92:19　H1577　But *Bogoas* falls to's practices again,
PRACTIQUE (1)
　MEDDM195:30　Hp272　Theory, then the practique part, but he is a true Christian that
PRACTISES (1) [pl.] See also PRACTICES
　MGREC127:44　H3073　Shews his ambitious practises as well.
PRAISE (35)
　PROLOG7:36　H46　And ever with your prey, still catch your praise,
　HUMOUR25:41　H230　Ile praise that fury, {prowess} valour, choler, heat.
　AGES41:18　H237　As was their praise, or shame, so mine must be.
　SEASONS48:18　H71　Whose praise deserves a page, from more then me.
　MASSYR67:35　H581　Did praise his gods of mettall, wood, and stone,
　MROMAN137:35　H3486　Forty three yeares he rul'd with generall praise;
　SIDNEY149:25　H23　I praise thee not for this, it is unfit,
　SIDNEY150:14　H49　Thy fame, and praise, is farre beyond my straine;
　SIDNEY150:37　H64　Noble {Great} *Bartas,* this to thy praise adds more,
　SIDNEY152:28　H97　*His praise is much, this shall suffice my pen,*
　DUBART154:39　H84　Ile leave thy praise, to those shall doe thee right,
　QELIZ155:35　H26　*Eliza's* works, wars, praise, can e're compact,
　TDUDLEY165:15　H17　He was my Father, and Ile praise him still.
　TDUDLEY166:27　H69　As joy in heaven, on earth let praise resound.
　CONTEM169:23　H63　And in their kind resound their makers praise:
　CONTEM171:34　H135　Shall I then praise the heavens, the trees, the earth
　FEVER221:12　H27　Praise to my Lord I say,
　SOREFIT221:27　H13　I said I shall praise thee at lenght.
　SOREFIT222:2　H21　To praise in thought, in Deed, in Word.
　SOREFIT222:4　H23　Longer then still thy Name to praise,
　SOREFIT222:7　H26　Thy Name & praise to celebrate
　FAINTING222:12　H2　Worthy art Thou o Ld of praise,
　FAINTING222:24　H14　Why should I liue but to thy praise
　MED223:16　Hp250　what he hath done for me, and then shall I bee able to praise
　WHAT224:5　H5　My thankfull mouth shall speak thy praise
　MYSOUL225:15　H19　And praise thee shall ev'n as I ovght
　SAMUEL228:16　H17　Then shall I celebrate thy praise
　THEART229:14　H16　My praise lyes not in Talk.
　HANNA230:16　H9　And celebrate thy praise
　SON230:20　H3　All praise to him who hath now turn'd
　2HUSB232:26　H27　Was to sing praise to Thee.
　2HUSB233:13　H46　That wee together may sing praise
　HOURS234:25　H39　So shall I celebrate thy praise.
　ACK235:19　H19　For All these mercyes I thee praise
　REMB236:10　H25　T' Return vnto thee praise

PRAISED (1)
ELEMEN14:26   H268   Among your boastings to have praised me;

PRAISES (12) [pl.]
ELEMEN11:27   H147   Among my praises this I count not least,
SIDNEY150:17   H49   Then let such Crowes as I, thy praises sing,
DUBART154:7   H52   Vollies of praises could I eccho then,
QELIZ155:31   H22   Though I resound thy greatnesse {praises} 'mongst the throng.
TDUDLEY165:5   H7   To celebrate the praises of the dead,
FEVER221:11   H26   O praises to my mighty God
FEVER221:14   H29   Praises to him for Aye.
13MAY226:32   H8   My heart exvlts & praises sings
RESTOR230:5   H20   Praises to him who hath not left
2HUSB233:18   H51   All praises vnto Thee.
HOURS234:30   H44   W^th praises shall recovnt
REMB235:24   H5   Or how thy praises speak

PRANKS (1) [pl.]
HUMOUR29:21   H372   To play such furious pranks I am too wise;

PRARASPES (2)
MPERS72:7   H756   *Praraspes* now must act this tragedy;
MPERS72:24   H772   *Praraspes,* to *Cambyses* favourite,

PRATLER (1)
DUBART153:29   H33   The silly Pratler speakes no word of sence;

PRAUNCING (1) [prancing]
AGES36:11   H35   Then prauncing on the Stage, about he wheels;

PRAXASPES (1)
MPERS72:7   H756   *Praxaspes* into *Persia* then is sent,

PRAY (11)
ELEMEN11:18   H138   Now Sisters, pray proceed, each in her {your} course,
HUMOUR31:21   H454   Pray hear, admire, and learn instruction.
HUMOUR32:15   H489   I've done, pray Sister Flegme proceed in course,
MGREC94:23   H1661   He offer'd, and for good successe did pray
MGREC105:26   H2119   If not, because *Darius* thus did pray,
MGREC130:6   H3161   Where, by Embassage, all these Princes pray,
DIALOG142:23   H52   Pray, doe not {you} feare *Spaines* bragging Armado?
DIALOG145:13   H162   Pray in plain termes, what is your present grief,
DIALOG146:14   H200   Pray now dear child, for sacred *Zion's* sake,
1HUSB180:32   H11   The heavens reward thee manifold I pray.
FAINTING222:14   H4   My sinking heart I pray thee raise

PRAY'D (2) [prayed]
DIALOG146:33   H219   To weep for that we both have pray'd for long,
TDUDLEY166:14   H56   For which he sigh'd and pray'd & long'd full sore

PRAYED (1)
MYCHILD217:11   Hp242   Answers to me, either in granting ye Thing I prayed for, or else

PRAYER (2)
2SIMON195:16   Hp271   wh^ch is the continuall prayer, of
MYCHILD215:27   Hp240   Trouble, & I could not be at rest 'till by prayer I had confest

PRAYERS (9) [pl.]
MPERS82:26   H1173   Yet words {Nor prayers}, nor guifts, could win him least
DIALOG147:7   H233   That help thee not with prayers, arms, and purse,
MYCHILD216:15   Hp241   to me, and cost me many prayers + tears before I obtaind one,
MYCHILD217:10   Hp242   I haue had great xper^c of Gods hearing my prayers, and

SAMUEL228:4	H5	The Son of prayers, of vowes, of teares
11MAYB228:29	Hp259	in his goodnes, and to hear my prayers, and to deliuer me out
2HUSB232:4	H5	And hear'st the prayers of Thine
ACK235:5	H5	O Thou that hear'st yᵉ prayers of Thine
REMB235:31	H12	O thou yᵗ hearest prayers Lord

PRAYES (2) [prays]

MGREC100:41	H1925	He prayes the immortall gods, for to {they would} reward
MGREC105:22	H2115	Prayes him, to *Alexander* to commend,

PRAYING (3)

MPERS74:8	H833	Praying to Fortune, for a Kingly power;
MGREC105:34	H2127	Praying the immortall gods, that Sea, and Land,
MGREC125:28	H2978	Praying, that fatall day might quickly haste,

PRAYS See PRAYES

PREACHERS (2)

DIALOG144:21	H131	I mock'd the Preachers, put it farre away;
DIALOG147:4	H230	Blest be thy Preachers, who do chear thee on,

PRECEDE See PRECEED

PRECEDENCY (5)

FATHER5:16	H17	Might seem of yours to claime precedency;
PROLOG7:29	H40	Men have precedency, and still excell,
HUMOUR20:24	H16	Who had precedency of all the other.
AGES36:30	H54	To childish childhood, give precedency.
MPERS74:6	H831	Of all the Peers should have precedency.

PRECEED (1) [precede]

MEDDM199:5	Hp277	Lightening doth vsually preceed thunder, and stormes raine,

PRECEPTS (2) [pl.]

CONTEM171:5	H110	And how their precepts to their sons were law,
MEDDM201:27	Hp281	should be the precepts of the wise masters of assemblys to

PRECINCTS (1) [pl.]

HUMOUR30:11	H403	Let me wel make thy precincts, the gal;

PRECIOUS (7) See also PRETIOUS

ELEMEN12:28	H188	But time's too short, and precious so to spend.
HUMOUR29:22	H373	If in a Souldier rashnesse be so precious,
SEASONS51:5	H179	But its a precious juyce, when wel it's used.
MGREC103:8	H2019	Here lay the bulk, of all those precious things;
MGREC111:5	H2350	Bringing their Presents, rare, and precious things:
FLESH175:31	H31	Behold enough of precious store.
MEDDM208:12	Hp290	A good name, is as a precious oyntment, and it is a great

PREDECESSORS (2)

MPERS~~92:25~~	H1583	Was to his Predecessors Chamber page.
2SIMON195:5	Hp271	vertues of their predecessors, but I am perswaded better

PREDOMINANCE (1)

HUMOUR20:22	H14	Which of the foure should have predominance;

PREDOMINANT (1)

HUMOUR21:18	H46	Where if your rule once grow {prove} predominant,

PREFERRE (1) [prefer]

MGREC129:29	H3143	(But, *Olympias,* thought to {would} preferre th' other:)

PREFERRS (1) [prefers]

MPERS71:38	H752	But he that 'fore the gods, himself preferrs,

PREFERS (1)

MPERS85:39	H1315	Prefers his brother, for his birth-rights sake.

PREGNANT (1)
DUBART154:30 H75   Oh pregnant brain, Oh comprehension vast:
PREHEMINENCE (4)
PROLOG7:32   H43   Preheminence in each, and all is yours,
HUMOUR22:20   H89   Then yeeld to me, preheminence in War.
SEASONS48:30 H83   But none in all that hath preheminence.
SIDNEY151:18 ~~H69~~   Yet this preheminence thou hast above,
PREISTS (1) [priests]
MASSYR54:8   H35   Whose Preists, in Stories, oft are mentioned;
PREJUDICATE (1)
SIDNEY150:12 H37   Such were prejudicate, and did not look:
PRELATE (1)
DIALOG145:33 H182   No prelate should his Bishoprick retain;
PRELATES (1) [pl.]
DIALOG147:11 H237   To root out Prelates, {Popelings} head, tail, branch, and rush.
PREMISES (1) [pl.]
HUMOUR35:2   H598   Such premises wil force a sad conclusion,
PREPAR'D (1) [prepared]
TDUDLEY166:13 H55   For he a Mansion had, prepar'd above,
PREPARATION (2)
MPERS77:23   H964   But for the last he made such preparation,
MPERS84:21   H1257 And for that end, great preparation made,
PREPARE (2)
MASSYR64:25   H449   A mighty Army next, he doth prepare,
MGREC109:13   H2272 Boats to prepare, *Ephestion* first he sends,
PREPARED See PREPAR'D
PREPARES (4)
MPERS76:26   H924   For *Attica* an Army he prepares;
MPERS~~86:38~~   H1354 He meant {Prepares} himselfe to carry the report.
MGREC101:27   H1952 Prepares against tomorrow for the war;
MGREC104:36   H2088 His hopes being dasht, prepares himself for flight:
PREPARING (1)
DDUDLEY167:21 H18   *Preparing still for death, till end of dayes:*
PREROGATIVES (1) [pl.]
DIALOG145:26 H175   Old customes, new Prerogatives stood on,
PRESAGES (1) [pl.]
SIDNEY151:2   ~~H69~~   If such Stars as these, sad presages be,
P^RSENCE (1) [presence]
ACK235:18   H18   Whose p^rsence I so much doe lack.
PRESENCE (6)
MGREC120:23   H2760 And by his presence there, to nullifie
CONTEM168:35 H41   Thy presence makes it day, thy absence night,
3LETTER183:13 H15   His presence and his safe return, still wooes,
MEDDM198:35   Hp277 behold the presence of the lamb
MEDDM205:24   Hp286 himself alway in the awefull presence of god, the consideration
MYCHILD217:31 Hp243 absence and presence of God y^t makes Heaven or Hell.
PRESENCE (1) [presents]
AGES~~37:33~~   H95   With costly presents, {presence} or base flattery.
PRESENT (2) n.
MASSYR61:20   H325   And to *Assyria's* King a Present sends.
MGREC98:1   H1803 Their present he receives with thankfullnesse,

PRESENT (13) v.

HUMOUR20:36	H28	At present yeelded, to necessity.
AGES39:6	H149	But what is best i'le first present to view,
SEASONS46:33	H9	At present claim'd, and had priority,
MASSYR64:12	H436	Yeelds to his mercy, and the present stresse;
MPERS77:40	H981	To present losse, future subversion;
MPERS~~78:24~~	H1005	In person {present} there, now for his help {aid} was seen;
DIALOG141:3	H3	their present troubles.
DIALOG141:24	H23	Which present help may ease this {my} malady.
DIALOG142:36	H65	My beauteous Body at this present maime;
DIALOG145:13	H162	Pray in plain termes, what is your present grief,
SIDNEY~~150:39~~	H67	His death present in sable to his wife.
CONTEM169:26	H65	When present times look back to Ages past,
MEDDM204:2	Hp284	of former deliuerances, is a great support in present

PRESENTED (1)

FATHER5:2	H2-3	*Thomas Dudley* Esq; *these humbly presented.*

PRESENTS (4) [pl.] See also PRESENCE n.

AGES37:33	H95	With costly presents, {presence} or base flattery.
MGREC109:26	H2285	His Presents all, with thanks he doth {did} restore;
MGREC111:5	H2350	Bringing their Presents, rare, and precious things:
MGREC125:23	H2973	And to the Queen, these presents she doth {did} send;

PRESENTS (2) v.

MGREC109:22	H2281	Presents himselfe, {first} there with a golden Crowne,
TDUDLEY165:7	H9	Presents my Lamentations at his Herse,

PRESERUED (1) [preserved] See also PRESERV'D, P^{R}SERVED

MEDDM196:30	Hp273	fruits that are best preserued wth sugar, those parents are wise

PRESERV'D (2) [preserved] See also P^{R}SERVED, PRESERUED

AGES38:38	H141	Strangely preserv'd, yet mind it not at all.
MGREC97:18	H1779	Preserv'd their honour, us'd them courteously {bounteously},

PRESERVATION (1)

MPERS69:16	H638	His preservation in his misery;

P^{R}SERVE (5) [preserve]

30SEPT227:26	Hp257	wth sugar then brine, yet will he p^{r}serve me to his heavenly
SAMUEL228:12	H13	P^{r}serve O Lord from stormes & wrack
SON230:24	H7	Thou di'st p^{r}serve him as he went,
2HUSB232:9	H10	Thy servant Lord. Keep & p^{r}serve
2HUSB232:29	H30	In stormes and sicknes Lord p^{r}serve.

PRESERVE (1)

HUMOUR25:33	H222	So spils {shed'st} that life {blood}, thou'rt bounden to preserve.

P^{R}SERVED (2) [preserved] See also PRESERUED, PRESERV'D

MYCHILD218:11	Hp244	who haue scornd + contemd it, hath it not been p^{r}served thro:
30SEPT227:26	Hp257	p^{r}served wth sugar then brine, yet will he p^{r}serve me to his

PRESERVES (1)

ELEMEN19:12	H457	As my fresh Aire preserves, all things in life;

P^{R}SERVING (1) [preserving]

MYCHILD218:2	Hp243	hovshold vpon ye Earth, ye p^{r}serving + directing of All to its

PRESS (1) n.

AUTHOR177:34	H6	Made thee in raggs, halting to th' press to trudge,

PRESS (1) v.

CONTEM172:28	H162	So may we press to that vast mansion, ever blest.

PRESSING (1)
MPERS69:30   H652   With pressing grief, and sorrow, over-come,
PREST (5) [presst]
SEASONS51:2   H176   The Vintage now is ripe, the Grapes are prest,
MASSYR58:34   H217   Prest for this service, by the Kings command;
MASSYR64:16   H440   By the victorious King to *Babel's* prest;
MGREC123:35   H2899   Prest to accomplish what he would have done;
TDUDLEY165:6   H8   My mournfull mind, sore prest, in trembling verse
PRESUM'D (1) [presumed] See also P^RSUMED
MGREC~~131:1~~   H3187   {by his Example all} the rest full soon presumes, {presum'd}
PRESUME (3)
HUMOUR25:18   H207   But let her leave the rest, and {then} I presume,
SIDNEY151:28   ~~H75~~   Too late my errour see, that durst presume
2SIMON195:12   Hp271   though in value they fall short of all in this kinde yet I presume
P^RSUMED (1) [presumed] See also PRESUM'D
MED223:12   Hp250   p^rsumed to haue thought it? So wonderfull are these thoughts
PRESUMES (1)
MGREC131:1   H3187   {by his Example all} the rest full soon presumes, {presum'd}
PRESUMPTION (1)
MGREC136:7   H3420   This my presumption (some now) to requite,
PRETENCE (1)
MPERS86:35   H1351   Great care was his pretence, those Souldiers stout,
PRETEND (1)
MGREC130:1   H3156   But that some title he might now pretend,
PRETENDED (3)
HUMOUR29:4   H357   Especially when freindship is pretended:
MGREC104:11   H2063   This counsell, for his safety, he pretended,
MGREC132:6   ~~H3239~~   Who took away his now pretended right:
PRETENDING (1)
MPERS86:29   H1345   Pretending still, the profit of the King,
PRETENDS (3)
MPERS89:26   H1460   And courtesie to th' utmost he pretends;
MGREC115:39   H2558   His age, and journey long, he now {then} pretends;
MGREC118:41   H2690   These now to govern for the King pretends,
PRETIOUS (1) [precious]
FLESH177:8   H89   Are made of pretious *Jasper* stone;
PRETTIER (1)
CHILDRN184:32 H21   A prettier bird was no where seen,
PRETTY (2)
CONTEM173:28 H193   So each one tunes his pretty instrument,
1SIMON188:14 H15   Go pretty babe, go rest with Sisters twain
P^RVAIL (2) [prevail]
MYCHILD217:22 Hp243   shall never p^rvail: yet haue I many Times sinkings &
JULY223:33   Hp251   upon me. O never let Satan p^rvail against me, but strenghten
PREVAIL (2)
DIALOG148:33 H298   Farewell dear mother, Parliament, {rightest cause} prevail,
MYCHILD219:1 Hp245   neuer prevail against it, I know whom I haue trvsted, and
PREVAIL'D (1) [prevailed]
MGREC110:14 H2314   The last set on his back, and so prevail'd:
PREVAILE (1)
MPERS75:21   H880   Thy falshood, not thy {craft more then} valour did prevaile;

PREVAILENCE (1) [prevalence]
MPERS86:26   H1342   Her prevailence, a pardon might obtain.
PREVAILES (1) [prevails]
ELEMEN13:30   H231   Then dearth prevailes, that Nature to suffice,
PREVALENCE See PREVAILENCE
PREVARICATION (1)
HUMOUR24:25   H174   So ful of boasting, and prevarication.
PREVENT (3)
HUMOUR28:11   H323   All to prevent, this curious care I take;
DIALOG143:24   H93   Unlesse thy {our} teares prevent it speedily.
CONTEM173:26 H191   The dawning morn with songs thou dost prevent,
PREY (5)
PROLOG7:36   H46   And ever with your prey, still catch your praise,
ELEMEN19:9   H454   Pye {Thrush}, the Jay {wren}, the Larke, a prey to th' Peasant.
MROMAN140:3 H3566 My papers fell a prey to th' raging fire.
DAVID159:12   H27   Stronger then Lions, ramping for their prey.
CONTEM173:7   H175   And take the trembling prey before it yield,
PREYS (1)
MPERS70:15   H686   Upon earths richest spoyles his Souldiers preys;
PRICE (3) See also PRISE
VANITY161:1   H52   This pearl of price, this tree of life, this spring,
ANNEB187:21   H11   To value things according to their price:
MEDDM206:23 Hp287 for mercy wthout mony & wthout price but bring his filthy raggs
PRICKES (1) [pricks]
MEDDM209:10 Hp291 was y^c Issue, they became a snare vnto them, prickes in their
PRICKING (1)
DIALOG142:19 H48   That from the red, white pricking Roses sprung?
PRICKS See PRICKES
PRIDE (24)
HUMOUR25:26 H215   To satisfie thy pride, and cruelty
HUMOUR25:35 H224   Nay; {No,} know 'tis pride, most diabolical.
AGES36:4   H28   In's countenance, his pride quickly was seen.
SEASONS49:33 H125   If pride within your lowly Cells ere haunt,
MASSYR64:29 H453   That in her pride, she knew not which to boast,
MASSYR66:32 H538   But for his pride so had the heavens decreed.
MASSYR67:38 H584   And with a hand, soon dashed all his pride.
MASSYR68:22 H608   His pride, and sottish grosse Idolatry.
MPERS71:26   H740   Yea, in his pride, he ventured so farre,
MPERS77:18   H959   As is {was} the Son, of pride, and cruelty;
MPERS77:36   H977   With certainty {conquest} of {all} *Europe* feeds his pride;
MPERS85:33   H1309 More by {To which} his pride, {more} then {his} lust, thereunto
MGREC103:25 H2036 In pride, and cruelty, to th' highest {high} excesse.
MGREC106:40 H2174 His fained Deity, and foolish pride:
MGREC116:38 H2604 For had he had but wisdome to his pride,
MGREC118:35 H2684 The Princes seeing *Perdica's* power and Pride,
MGREC121:8   H2786 *Perdicas* surly carriage, and his pride,
MGREC121:14 H2792 *Perdiccas* in his pride did ill intreat
MGREC126:33 H3023 So boundlesse was her pride, and cruelty,
QELIZ157:30 H98   Which I may not, my pride doth but aspire,
QELIZ158:15 H124   *Here lies the pride of Queens, pattern of Kings,*
CONTEM167:27 H4   The trees all richly clad, yet void of pride,

MEDDM206:25   Hp287   empty beareing the reproch of his pride and folly.
MYCHILD216:5   Hp241   my pride and Vanity and he was entreated of me, and again

PRIDEING (1) [priding]

MEDDM196:6   Hp272   of the pea cock that prideing himself in his gay feathers

PRIEST (2)

MGREC99:38   H1881   The Priest shews him good *Daniels Prophesie,*
MGREC100:7   H1891   The Pagan Priest through hire, or else mistake,

PRIESTLY (1)

MGREC99:36   H1879   Him in his Priestly Robes, high *Jaddus* meets,

PRIESTS (2) See also PREISTS

MGREC96:9   H1729   The Priests in their strange habit follow after;
MROMAN137:30 H3481   And Priests, and Flamines likewise he deputed;

PRIME (10)

AGES40:31   H̶2̶1̶0̶   My youth, my best, my strength, my bud, and prime:
AGES45̶:̶2̶   H378   In prime of youth seiz'd by heavens angry hand,
SEASONS48:19 H72   The cleanly huswives Dary, now's ith' prime,
SEASONS49:36 H129   The Cherry, Goos-berry, is {are} now i'th prime,
SEASONS50:38 H172   Of Autumne months, *September* is the prime,
SEASONS51:26 H202   Which notes, when youth, and strength, have past their prime,
MPERS73:10   H797   Cut off in's wickednesse, in's strength, and prime.
DIALOG144:10   H120   O *Jane,* why didst thou dye in flowring prime,
SIDNEY150:25   H52   Ah, in his blooming prime, death pluckt this Rose,
CONTEM171:18   H121   When I behold the heavens as in their prime,

PRIMROSE (2)

AGES35:30   H16   Of Dazy, Primrose, and {or} the Violet.
SEASONS47:40   H52   The Primrose pale, and azure Violet,

PRINCE (46)

HUMOUR23:34   H144   Take choler from a Prince, what is he more,
AGES37:39   H101   I'd nought to do, 'twixt Prince, {King} and peoples strife.
AGES45̶:̶2̶   H377   I've seen a Prince, the glory of our land
AGES45:7   H̶3̶9̶0̶   I've seen a Prince, to live on others lands,
AGES45:18   H400   Who gave the counsel, but the Prince of hell.
SEASONS50:28 H162   The Prince of Plumbs, whose stone is {as} hard as Rock.
MASSYR57:3   H150   A Prince wedded to ease, and to delight,
MASSYR57:20   H̶1̶6̶7̶   Each wronged Prince, or childe that did remain,
MASSYR58:22   H207   The rule from their unworthy Prince to take.
MASSYR63:37   H424   This Prince in's magnitude doth ever shine;
MASSYR64:9   H433   This Prince, the last year of his Fathers reign,
MASSYR65:18   H483   And unexpected findes the feeble Prince,
MASSYR65:33   H498   But in the eighth, against his Prince rebels;
MASSYR67:6   H552   Poor forlorn Prince, that {who} had all state forgot,
MASSYR67:34   H580   Carous'd they in; and sacrilegious Prince,
MPERS69:41   H671   Weighing the age, and greatnesse of the Prince,
MPERS71:3   H̶7̶1̶5̶   Some thirty years this potent Prince did reign,
MPERS7̶1̶:̶3̶   H715   Thirty two years in all this Prince
MPERS74:33   H856   The *Babylonians* 'gainst their Prince rebell;
MPERS75:4   H865   Desiring of the Prince to raise the siege,
MPERS77:12   H951   Thirty six years this royall {noble} Prince did reign,
MPERS79:5   H1027   Is this to doe like *Xerxes,* or a Prince?
MPERS83:4   H1192   The grieved Prince finding nor right, nor love,
MPERS8̶3̶:̶1̶9̶   H1207   That the poor {Prince} innocent, to death must {did} go.

MPERS83:27	H1215	Amongst the Monarchs next, this Prince had place
MPERS84:12	H1240	The might o'th' Prince, the tribute on {of} the Isles.
MPERS84:17	H1253	entertainment {royal bounty} with this {his} Prince he found,
MPERS84:33	H1269	Nor yet disloyall to his Prince would prove,
MPERS85:37	H1313	A hopefull Prince, whose worth {by *Xenophon*} is ever fam'd.
MPERS91:16	H1524	All the peculiar vertues of a Prince:
MGREC93:14	H1611	This Prince (his father by *Pausanias* slain)
MGREC6:23	H1620	Whose glory to the Earth, this Prince {king} did throw,
MGREC100:21	H1905	Yet he (poore Prince) another Hoast doth muster,
MGREC103:21	H2032	For such revolters false, what Prince will {King can} trust:
MGREC104:26	H2078	In more dispight, the thrawled Prince to hold.
MGREC109:7	H2266	Whose feasts are celebrated by this Prince;
MGREC~~110:18~~	H2321	But him a Prince of an undaunted mind
MGREC124:28	H2935	Thinks to enthrone the Prince when riper grown;
MGREC129:4	H3118	He sees the *Greeks* now favour their young Prince,
MGREC129:31	H3145	This {Orphan} Prince began for to compassionate.
MGREC129:37	H3151	Who slew the prince according to desire:
MGREC134:25	H3356	His son was *Evergetes* the last Prince
SIDNEY151:1	~~H69~~	Such prince as he, his race should shortly end:
QELIZ156:35	H62	Had ever Prince such Counsellors as she?
QELIZ158:17	H126	Here lies the envy'd, yet unparralell'd Prince,
VANITY159:37	H9	He's now a slave {captive}, that was a Prince {King} of late.

PRINCE-DOME (1)

AGES~~45:4~~	H388	Who lost a Prince-dome and a Monarchy.

PRINCELY (6)

HUMOUR23:25	H135	The Princely quality, {qualities} befitting Kings.
MGREC99:1	H1844	And a most Princely Dowry with her proffers; {offers.}
MGREC101:6	H1931	His eldest Daughter, for his Princely Bride,
MGREC116:13	H2579	His princely qualities, had he retain'd
DIALOG144:6	H116	How many Princely heads on blocks laid down,
SIDNEY151:8	~~H69~~	O Princely *Philip,* rather *Alexander,*

PRINCES (18) [pl.]

HUMOUR33:1	H515	Princes hath slav'd, and Captains captived:
HUMOUR33:3	H517	Sixty nine Princes, all stout *Hero* Knights,
AGES~~45:4~~	H385	I've Princes seen to live on others lands;
MPERS73:14	H801	The Princes meet to chuse one in his stead,
MPERS78:10	H991	To Princes of the *Persian* bloud descended,
MPERS83:39	H1227	His Princes, Nobles, and his Captaines calls,
MGREC118:16	H2663	So much these Princes their owne ends respected.
MGREC118:35	H2684	The Princes seeing *Perdica's* power and Pride,
MGREC~~119:32~~	H2722	'Mongst all the Captains {princes} of great *Alexander,*
MGREC120:11	H2746	*Perdicas* griev'd, to see the Princes bold,
MGREC~~120:20~~	H2756	(For all the princes of great *Alexander*
MGREC122:35	H2856	For all the Princes {nobles} of great {King} *Alexander*
MGREC127:32	H3062	The Princes all begin now to envie
MGREC~~128:23~~	H3096	*Antigonus* {These princes} at {the} Sea soone had a fight,
MGREC128:37	H3110	At last these Princes tired out with warres,
MGREC129:22	H3136	*Cassander's* dead, the Princes {do} all detest,
MGREC130:6	H3161	Where, by Embassage, all these Princes pray,
MGREC134:11	H3342	So many Princes still were murthered,

PRINCES (4) [poss.]
AGES45:11   ~~H393~~   But not their Princes love, nor state so high;
MASSYR59:5   H229   And set upon their Princes Camp that night;
MPERS72:5   ~~H755~~   Complots the Princes death, in his green years,
MPERS73:34   H819   So late crusht by their Princes Tyranny;

PRINCESS (1)
QELIZ155:11 H2   Princess, Queen ELIZABETH, of

PRINCESSE (2) [princess]
MGREC130:13 H3168 Resolves at last the Princesse should be slain,
QELIZ157:12 H80   Within that Princesse to have residence,

PRINCIPLE (1)
VERSES184:2 H6   The principle might yield a greater sum,

PRINCIPLES (2) [pl.]
HUMOUR30:13 H405   Reduce the man to's principles, then see
MGREC116:19 H2585 The principles of what he then had learn'd

PRINT (1)
AUTHOR177:37 H9   My rambling brat (in print) should mother call,

PRINTING (1)
DIALOG146:1 H189   The writing, printing, posting to and fro,

PRIORITY (2)
HUMOUR26:24 H254   Shal justly claime priority of thine;
SEASONS46:33 H9   At present claim'd, and had priority,

PRIS'D (1) [prized]
2SIMON195:13 Hp271 they will be better pris'd by you, for the Authors sake. the lord

PRISCUS (3)
MROMAN138:24 H3514 *Tarquinius Priscus.*
MROMAN138:34 H3524 Much {Some} state, and glory, {splendor} did this *Priscus* adde:
MROMAN139:9 H3537 And then by *Tarquin, Priscus* Son, was slaine.

PRISE (1) [price]
MEDDM209:5   Hp291 this pearle of prise

PRISE (2) [prize]
SEASONS50:9 H143   The groaning Carts to bear away this prise,
HOUSE237:23 H53   A prise so vast as is vnknown

PRISON (7)
HUMOUR30:12 H404   To {So} prison thee within that bladder smal.
AGES41:10   H230   Clapt in that prison, never thence to start.
AGES43:30   H325   To break the darksome prison, where it's pend;
MASSYR65:27 H492   And more then {seven and} thirty years in prison fed;
MGREC~~124:10~~ H2916 By death by prison, or by banishment,
MGREC128:2   H3075 His Wife, and Son, in prison close had shut;
DIALOG144:28 H136   Some lost their livings, some in prison pent,

PRISONER (1)
MPERS70:30   H701   There routs his Hoast, himself she prisoner takes,

PRISONERS (3) [pl.]
MASSYR62:16 H361   Laden with honour, prisoners, and with spoyl,
MGREC97:7   H1768 And forty thousand Prisoners also tane;
MGREC128:31 H3104 But bravely sends the Prisoners back againe,

PRISONMENT (1)
MGREC119:39 H2729 *Antipater* releas'd from's prisonment,

PRIVACY (1)
MPERS89:36   H1470 Gets them to treat with him in privacy,

PRIVATE (2)
AGES44:28   H361   Such private changes oft mine eyes have seen,
MYCHILD215:28 Hp241   God. I was also troubled at yᵉ neglect of private Dutyes tho:

PRIVATELY (1)
MPERS83:12   H1200 Which wretch, {Who} him privately smother'd in's bed,

PRIVILEDGE (2)
SEASONS48:35 H86   Yet above all, this priviledge is thine,
MASSYR58:40   H223   To want no priviledge, Subjects should have,

PRIVILEDGES (2) [pl.]
MROMAN137:5 H3456 Great priviledges then, to all he grants,
MED223:10   Hp250 he my head. Such priviledges had not yᵉ word of Truth made

PRIZE (4) n. [booty]
HUMOUR29:20 H371   Thy fiery spirit shal bear away this prize,
MPERS70:37   ~~H708~~ Where *Alexander* fought, in hope of prize,
MPERS~~70:37~~ H708   Where some long after fought in vain for prize
MGREC117:27 H2634 Each Captain wisht this prize to beare away,

PRIZE (5) n. [reward] See also PRISE
ELEMEN12:29 H189   But hark, ye worthy Merchants who for prize
ELEMEN~~14:4~~   H248   Bur'ing himself alive for honours prize.
AGES38:2   H105   But for an Apple, Plumbe, or some such prize,
QELIZ156:4   H31   From all the Kings on earth she won the prize;
TDUDLEY166:5 H47   Gave his in charge, that Jewel rich to prize.

PRIZE (3) v. [value]
AGES39:16   H159   The brave attempts of valiant Knights I prize,
MPERS~~91:22~~ H1535 But shortly calls her home, her counsells prize,
1HUSB180:27 H6   I prize thy love more then whole Mines of gold,

PRIZED See PRIS'D

PRIZER (1)
TDUDLEY166:40 H82   *A Prizer of good Company*

PROBABILITIES (1) [pl.]
MPERS92:23   ~~H1581~~ Which by some probabilities (seems rather;)

PROCEED (5)
ELEMEN11:18 H138   Now Sisters, pray proceed, each in her {your} course,
HUMOUR32:15 H489   I've done, pray Sister Flegme proceed in course,
MASSYR66:31 H537   Which from no natural causes did proceed,
FLESH177:14 H95   Which doth proceed from the Lambs Throne:
FLESH177:18 H99   For glory doth from God proceed:

PROCEEDING (1)
MGREC136:18 H3432 *As faults proceeding from my head, not heart.*

PROCEEDS (1)
MPERS85:19   H1295 Which from remissenesse, in {Less} Asia proceeds {breeds.}

PROCLAIM'D (2) [proclaimed]
MGREC117:39 H2646 After much tumult, they at last proclaim'd
MGREC118:4   H2651 And th' unborn babe of *Roxan* be proclaim'd;

PROCLAIME (1) [proclaim]
QELIZ155:16 H7   Thy wondrous worth proclaime, in every clime,

PROCLAIMED See PROCLAIM'D

PROCURE (3)
MGREC125:13 H2961 Some Forces did procure, with her to joyne.
QELIZ157:5   H73   More infamie than fame she did procure;
TDUDLEY165:17 H19   That pitty might some Trumpeters procure.

PROCURING (1)
MGREC103:33　H2044　And just procuring of the *Persians* hate.
PRODIGIOUS (1)
ELEMEN19:38　H479　Then what prodigious sights, sometimes I show:
PRODUCE (2)
ELEMEN13:34　H235　Dreadfull examples, soon I might produce,
MEDDM200:16　Hp279　garment, she easily foresees what euents it is like to produce,
PRODUCED (3)
MPERS77:26　H967　Produced but derision, and laughter;
MPERS79:22　H1048　But yet this goodly sight {from him} produced teares,
MEDDM204:33　Hp285　Corne is produced wth much labour (as the husbandman well
PRODUCES (2)
SEASONS47:36　H48　This is the month whose fruitfull showers produces
MEDDM201:22　Hp281　some black Clouds that impends them, wch produces these
PROEM (1)
QELIZ155:13　H4　*The Proem.*
PROFANE See PROPHANE
PROFANENESS See PROPHAINNESSE, PROPHANNESS
PROFANELY (1)
MASSYR54:10　H37　So oft profanely offered sacred rites;
PROFESSION (2)
SICKNES179:8　H28　comes by profession pure.
MEDDM206:3　Hp287　profession, and these are but leavie Christians, wch are in as
PROFEST (1)
MPERS71:25　H739　But {For} he would be profest god of their Weal;
PROFFERS (3) [pl.]
MGREC99:1　H1844　And a most Princely Dowry with her proffers; {offers.}
MGREC99:6　H1849　Tels him, these proffers great (in truth were none)
MGREC121:22　H2804　Their proffers he refus'd, with modesty
PROFICIENT (1)
MEDDM195:31　Hp272　proficient in both.
PROFIT (7)
AGES39:11　H154　As might my self, and others, profit much:
MPERS85:28　H1304　The King much profit reapeth, by these leagues {this league},
MPERS86:29　H1345　Pretending still, the profit of the King,
MGREC104:8　H2060　The little hope, of profit like to rise.
MGREC129:41　H3155　He knows to's profit, all i'th end {this at last} will turn,
MEDDM199:20　Hp278　man aimes at profit by the one & content in the other, but often
MEDDM209:9　Hp291　could do (as they thought) wth lesse hazard and more profit,
PROFOUND (2)
HUMOUR23:26　H136　Whose Serene {profound} heads, I line with policies,
DUBART153:33　H37　Thy profound Learning; viewing other while
PROFUSE (1)
QELIZ157:18　H86　Proud profuse *Cleopatra,* whose wrong name,
PROFUSELY (1)
MGREC116:27　H2593　Profusely bountifull, without desert,
PROGENY (2)
MASSYR60:13　H278　But *Belochus* in's progeny pursue,
CONTEM171:6　H111　How Adam sigh'd to see his Progeny,
PROGRESS (1)
MROMAN139:33　H3559　All thoughts of further progress laid aside,

738

PROGRESSE (3) [progress]
SEASONS47:32 ~~H47~~ For though in's running progresse he doth take
SEASONS49:6 H97 His progresse to the North; now's fully done,
MASSYR56:34 H140 This was last progresse of this mighty Queen,
PROJECT (1)
MGREC119:4 H2694 And had a higher project in his head,
PROLIXITY (1)
HUMOUR21:3 H31 Your selves would judge, but vain prolixity.
PROLOGUE (1)
PROLOG6:16 H2 *Prologue.*
PROMIS (2)
MYCHILD217:21 Hp243 my self y^t agst svch a promis, svch tasts of sweetnes ye Gates
2HUSB232:13 H14 Then let thy promis joy his heart
PROMIS'D (1) [promised]
SIDNEY152:5 He promis'd much, but th' muses had no will,
PROMISE (5)
MASSYR60:9 H274 Thus {Such} was the {his} promise bound, since first {which} he
MGREC126:22 H3013 Gives promise for her life, and {so} wins the day:
MGREC~~131:1~~ H3189 Doth promise liberty to *Athens* State;
MEDDM206:34 Hp288 trembling, lest they through vnbeleif fall short of a promise, it
MEDDM208:19 Hp290 to deceitfull friends who speak faire and promise much
PROMISED (2) See also PROMIS'D
MASSYR58:15 H200 *Belosus,* promised *Arbaces* aide,
JULY223:32 Hp251 Thou hast given me a pledge of y^t Inheritc thou hast promised
PROMISES (2) [pl.]
MASSYR58:37 H220 Makes {With} promises, their necks for {now} to un-yoak,
MGREC125:12 H2960 Then by intreaties, promises, and coyne,
PRONE (1)
VANITY160:11 H21 The first is prone to vice, the last to rage.
PROP (2)
AGES44:19 H352 But what I have done wel, that is my prop;
MGREC~~127:27~~ H3057 So *Eumenes* {(the prop)} of destiny {death} must taste.
PROPAGATION (1)
HUMOUR24:6 H155 Of all that lives, I cause the propagation.
PROPER (2)
HUMOUR21:13 H41 Yet man for Choler, is the proper seat.
MYCHILD218:2 Hp243 vpon ye Earth, ye prserving + directing of All to its proper
PROPERTY (3)
HUMOUR27:13 ~~H284~~ Thou do'st unjustly claime, her property,
HUMOUR~~27:13~~ H284 And so thou challengest her property.
HUMOUR32:31 H505 I'le leave that manly property to you;
PROPHAINNESSE (1) [profaneness] See also PROPHANNESSE
MASSYR68:21 H607 His drunkennesse, and his prophainnesse high,
PROPHANE (2) [profane]
MASSYR67:22 H568 Whose prophane acts, a sacred pen sets down.
MPERS71:39 H753 Is more prophane, then grosse Idolaters;
PROPHANNESSE (1) [profaneness] See also PROPHAINNESSE
DIALOG144:3 H113 Did ever Land prophannesse more expresse?
PROPHECYES (1) [prophecies]
MYCHILD218:15 Hp244 prophecyes in it fullfilled wch could not haue been so long

PROPHESIE (3) [prophecy]

MASSYR58:23   H207   By prophesie, *Belosus* strength's their hands,

MASSYR59:24   H248   And now they saw fulfill'd a Prophesie;

MGREC99:38   H1881   The Priest shews him good *Daniels* Prophesie,

PROPHESIED (1)

MGREC117:11   H2618   As *Daniel,* before had Prophesied;

PROPHET (1)

MEDDM201:7   Hp280   seen an end of all perfection (sayd the royall prophet) but he

PROPHETICK (1) [prophetic]

MGREC95:16   H1695   There {where} the Prophetick knot, he cuts in twain;

PROPHETS (1) [pl.]

MASSYR63:36   H423   But by the Prophets, Pen-men most Divine,

PROPHETS (1) [poss.]

DIALOG144:24   H133   These Prophets mouthes (alas the while) was stopt,

PROPONTIS (1)

MGREC94:38   H1676   Which twixt *Phrigia,* and *Propontis* lyes.

PROPORTION (2)

MEDDM200:18   Hp279   will the alwise god proportion his dispensations according to

MEDDM201:1   Hp280   strength he will proportion the load, as god hath his little

PROPOSE (1)

MGREC104:28   H2080   Great recompence, in's thoughts, he did propose;

PROPS (1) [pl.]

MEDDM199:16   Hp278   any thing to stay vpon, but take away their props and they are

PROSECUTE (1)

MROMAN139:36 H3562   To prosecute my story to the last;

PROSPER'D (1) [prospered]

MPERS75:37   H894   Built on, and prosper'd, till their walls did {house they} close;

PROSPERITY (5)

MGREC101:20   H1945   For his unlimited prosperity,

MGREC131:20   H3212   But they adoring in prosperity,

MEDDM197:12   Hp274   times tast of adversity, prosperity would not be so welcome

28AUG225:32   Hp254   prosperity, but he doth it for my Advantage, and y^t I may bee a

30SEPT227:21   Hp257   Love to my straying Soul wch in prosperity is too much in Love

PROSPEROUS (3)

AGES45:2   H376   We joy'd in many blest and prosperous dayes.

MEDDM196:22   Hp273   open a prosperous state makes a secure christian, but

2HUSB232:28   H29   And send them prosperous gailes

PROSTRATE (2)

DUBART153:15   H19   And prostrate off'red at great *Bartas* Herse.

QELIZ157:13   H81   And prostrate yeelded to her Excellence:

PROTECT (2)

BIRTH180:16   H26   These O protect from step Dames injury.

SAMUEL228:13   H14   Protect him there & bring him back.

PROTECTOR (3)

MGREC98:3   H1805   Protector of their Town; by whom defended,

MGREC121:19   H2801   With stile of the Protector, would him {to} grace;

MGREC122:11   H2836   *Python* now chose protector of the State,

PROTECTOR'S (1) [protector is]

MGREC123:26   H2890   This new Protector's of another minde,

PROTECTORS (1) [pl.]

MASSYR67:36   H582   Protectors of his {this} Crown, and *Babylon,*

PROTECTRIX (1)

| QELIZ156:29 | H56 | She their Protectrix was, they well doe know, |

PROUD (35)

ELEMEN11:8	H128	Which made a *Cæsar,* (Romes) the worlds proud head,
ELEMEN~~17:11~~	H375	Untill straight {proud} *Gibralter,* did make them twaine,
HUMOUR20:27	H19	Proud Melancholy, more envious then the rest,
HUMOUR24:24	H173	I will annalise, {this} thy so proud relation;
HUMOUR28:36	H348	I've scarce wip'd off the spots, proud Choler cast,
HUMOUR29:27	H378	I then command, proud Choler stand thy place,
AGES42:6	H264	The proud I crush'd, th' oppressed I set free,
MASSYR53:23	H13	The strong foundation of proud *Babel* laid,
MASSYR60:24	H289	Who own'd the treasures of proud *Babylon,*
MASSYR65:19	H484	Whom he chastised {thus} for his proud offence;
MASSYR66:20	H526	To *Babylons* proud King, now yeelds the day.
MASSYR67:28	H574	Layes siedge to's regall seat, proud *Babylon,*
MPERS70:40	~~H711~~	Where that proud Conquerour could doe no lesse,
MPERS74:9	H834	Then mounting on their snorting coursers proud,
MPERS75:2	H863	Tels them, how harshly the proud King had dealt,
MPERS81:30	H1138	*Mardonius* proud, hearing this answer stout,
MPERS89:19	H1453	The *Greeks* with scorn reject his proud commands;
MPERS~~92:3~~	H1557	Was by his *Eunuch* the proud *Bagoas* slain.
MGREC93:12	H1609	The cruell, proud, *Olimpias,* was his mother,
MGREC~~6:25~~	H1622	universe, scarce bounds {bound} his large {proud} vast minde;
MGREC94:29	H1667	Reproves him, for his proud audacity;
MGREC~~99:12~~	H1855	To which, brave {proud} *Alexander* did {made} reply,
MGREC102:16	H1986	The Towers, and Bowers, of proud *Semiramis:*
MGREC~~103:28~~	H2039	He at a bold, base {proud} Strumpets, lewd desire;
MGREC~~124:8~~	H2913	His proud opponent hopes soon to withstand.
MGREC124:32	H2939	Was to this proud, vindicative *Cassander,*
MGREC129:32	H3146	Begin to mutter much 'gainst proud *Cassander,*
MROMAN139:12	H3540	*Tarquin* the proud, from manners called so,
DIALOG142:40	H69	Whose proud contention cause this slaughter;
DIALOG145:22	H171	To crush the proud, and right to each man deal.
DIALOG148:6	H271	To sack proud *Rome,* and all her vassalls rout:
QELIZ~~156:34~~	H61	And {the proud} *Tiron* bound, before her picture fell.
QELIZ157:14	H82	*Dido* first Foundresse of proud *Carthage* walls,
QELIZ157:18	H86	Proud profuse *Cleopatra,* whose wrong name,
MEDDM197:22	Hp275	Few men are so humble, as not to be proud of their abilitys,

PROUDLY (2)

| MASSYR~~53:16~~ | H6 | Man did not {proudly} strive for Soveraignty, |
| SIDNEY151:36 | ~~H75~~ | So proudly foolish I, with *Phaeton* strive, |

PROUE (2) [prove]

| MEDDM207:10 | Hp288 | to help vs mount vpwards, they will Certainly proue Clogs |
| MEDDM208:24 | Hp290 | proue like the reeds of Egipt that peirce insteed of supporting |

PROUIDENCE (1) [providence]

| MEDDM209:18 | Hp291 | god hath by his prouidence so ordered, that no one Covntry |

PROUISION (1) [provision]

| MEDDM203:11 | Hp283 | prouision, be all convenient and comfortable for him yet he |

PROV'D (7) [proved]

| ELEMEN17:25 | H389 | That in two hundred year, it ne'r prov'd good. |
| MASSYR59:19 | H243 | But in the third, the River prov'd his friend, |

MASSYR59:25   H249   That when the River prov'd their enemy,
MPERS76:34   H932   Where *Grecians* prov'd themselves right Souldiers, stout;
MGREC112:24   H2410   Nothing was found {prov'd}, wherein he had offended;
MROMAN136:36 H3450   And bloudy hath it prov'd, since first it stood:
QELIZ157:19   H87   Instead of glory prov'd her Countries shame:

PROVE (7)
PROLOG7:18   H31   If what I doe prove well, it wo'nt advance,
ELEMEN12:14   H174   Unlesse thou prove a better friend to me;
HUMOUR21:18   H46   Where if your rule once grow {prove} predominant,
HUMOUR30:18   H410   When you poor bankrupts prove, then have I most.
HUMOUR33:6   H520   But 'twere as vain, to prove the {this} truth of mine,
MASSYR61:1   H306   But circumstance, doth prove the verity;
MPERS84:33   H1269   Nor yet disloyall to his Prince would prove,

PROVED See PROV'D
PROVENDER (1)
MGREC110:30   H2334   As never Horse his Provender could eye;

PROVES (8)
ELEMEN16:40   H363   By adding cold to cold, no fruit proves sound;
HUMOUR21:19   H47   The man proves boyish, sottish, ignorant,
HUMOUR22:37   H106   My absence proves, it plain, her wit then flyes
HUMOUR27:33   H304   My sweet complexion, proves the verity,
SEASONS48:32   H83   Sometime a theame that's large, proves barren fields.
MASSYR61:32   H337   Proves unto *Ahaz* but a feigned friend;
MASSYR64:24   H448   Which in few years proves the *Assyrians* hire;
MGREC126:14   H3005   So succours, and endeavours proves but vaine:

PROVIDE (7)
AGES41:35   H250   If a father {I}, then for children must provide:
MPERS81:39   H1143   For one maine Battell shortly, both provide;
MPERS82:2   H1148   Then for one battel shortly all provide,
MGREC118:36   H2685   Thought timely for themselves, now to provide.
MGREC118:36   H2685   For their security did now provide
MROMAN138:4   H3494   And *Curiatii,* three *Albans* provide;
SON231:3   H15   In covntry strange thou did'st provide

PROVIDED (2)
MASSYR59:16   H240   There with all store he was so wel provided,
MGREC109:36   H2295   And come as well provided as he could,

PROVIDED'T (1) [provided it]
HUMOUR21:39   H67   And break a staffe, provided't be in jest,

PROVIDENCE See PROUIDENCE
PROVIDES (1)
AGES44:21   H354   Provides a staffe for {then} to support his age.

PROVIDING (1)
MYCHILD218:1   Hp243   Winter, Spring and Autvmne, the dayly providing for this great

PROVINCE (4)
MASSYR57:22   H169   So Province, after Province, rent away,
MASSYR61:26   H331   *Syria* he makes a Province of his own.
MGREC119:2   H2692   *Perdicas* took no Province, like the rest,

PROVINCES (2) [pl.]
MGREC114:37   H2507   All Kingdoms, Countries, Provinces, he won, {wan}
MGREC115:32   H2551   Of larger Provinces, the rule to give,

PROVISION (5) See also PROUISION
MPERS70:16   H687   Here twenty yeares provision {good} he found,
MPERS89:25   H1459   The King great store of all provision sends,
MGREC~~97:41~~   H1802   Therefore a Crown, and great provisions {Provision} send;
MGREC111:28   H2373   Thus Winter, Souldiers, and provision {provisions} spent,
MGREC~~131:1~~   H3190   With Arms and with provision stores them well,

PROVISIONS (4) [pl.]
MPERS78:2   H983   In great provisions, for this great intent;
MPERS84:29   H1265   Provisions, {then} and season now being fit,
MGREC97:41   H1802   Therefore a Crown, and great provisions {Provision} send;
MGREC~~111:28~~   H2373   Thus Winter, Souldiers, and provision {provisions} spent,

PROVOCATIONS (1) [pl.]
HUMOUR24:30   H179   Thy foolish {silly} provocations, I despise.

PROVOK'D (3) [provoked]
HUMOUR22:33   H102   But Flegme her self, is now provok'd at this,
MPERS86:2   H1318   The King provok'd, sends for him to the Court,
SICKNES178:25 H8   when he so high provok'd.

PROVOKED (1)
ELEMEN8:18   H16   Both by their darings; Water so provoked,

PROWESS (1)
HUMOUR~~25:44~~   H230   Ile praise that fury, {prowess} valour, choler, heat.

PRUDENCE (5)
HUMOUR32:3   H477   My prudence, judgement, now I might reveale,
MASSYR67:13   H559   Prudence, and magnanimity, did lack
MGREC113:36   H2463   Who for his prudence, valour, care, and trust,
DIALOG145:28   H177   Which by their prudence stood them in such stead,
MEDDM198:13   Hp276   Want of prudence as well as piety hath brought men into great

PRUDENT (2)
MEDDM200:15   Hp279   A prudent mother will not cloth her little childe wth a long and
MEDDM205:4   Hp285   of morality, much lesse of grace in them But when by prudent

PRY (1)
3LETTER183:1   H3   Perplext, in every bush & nook doth pry,

PTOLEMY (1)
MGREC~~121:2~~   H2780   But first 'gainst *Ptolemy* he judg'd was

PTOLOMY (27)
MGREC110:10   H2310   With *Ptolomy*, sends part o' th' other side.
MGREC118:38   H2687   And *Ptolomy*, next sure of *Egypt* makes.
MGREC120:31   H2768   Brave *Ptolomy*, to make a fourth now {then} sent,
MGREC120:39   H2776   Great love did *Ptolomy* by this act gain.
MGREC121:2   ~~H2780~~   With *Ptolomy* for to begin was best,
MGREC121:7   H2785   Brave *Ptolomy* to th' utmost to oppose.
MGREC121:10   H2788   But *Ptolomy* by affability,
MGREC121:17   H2799   Knocks out his braines, to *Ptolomy* then went,
MGREC121:20   H2802   Next day into the Camp comes {came} *Ptolomy*,
MGREC121:30   H2812   Thus *Ptolomy* rich *Ægypt* did retaine,
MGREC123:20   H2884   And *Ptolomy*, now {next} to encroach begins,
MGREC127:31   H3061   But {And} he for aid to *Ptolomy* doth call.
MGREC127:36   H3066   *Seleuchus, Ptolomy, Cassander* joynes,
MGREC128:15   H3088   Now {Then} *Ptolomy* would gaine the *Greeks* likewise,
MGREC128:24   H3097   Where {great Antigonus} *Ptolomy*, and the rest {was} put him
MGREC128:26   H3099   So *Syria* to *Ptolomy* did yeeld;

MGREC128:29	H3102	*Demetrius* againe with *Ptolomy* did fight,
MGREC128:33	H3106	Curtious, as noble *Ptolomy,* or more,
MGREC130:3	H3158	*Lysimachus* and *Ptolomy,* the same,
MGREC130:7	H3162	Choise above all, of *Ptolomy* she makes
MGREC131:7	H3197	*Demetrius* of *Ptolomy* doth gain;
MGREC132:29	H3276	Now {Next} dyed the brave and noble *Ptolomy,*
MGREC133:1	H3289	He was by *Ptolomy Cerannus* slaine.
MGREC133:2	H3290	The second Son of the first *Ptolomy,*
MGREC133:9	H3297	With *Ptolomy,* reign'd after *Alexander;*
MGREC134:19	H3350	First *Ptolomy* being dead, his famous son,
MGREC134:33	H3364	To all these names we *Ptolomy* must adde,

PUBLICK (3) [public]

DDUDLEY167:18	H15	*The publick meetings ever did frequent,*
AUTHOR177:33	H5	Who thee abroad, expos'd to publick view,
1LETTER181:2	H0	*Publick employment.*

PUBLISH'D (1) [published]

MPERS75:25	H882	An Edict for the *Jews* publish'd again,

PUBLISHED (1)

DAVID158:29	H9	Nor published in streets of *Askelon,*

PUERI (1)

AGES44:9	H342	But now, *Bis pueri senes,* is too true;

PUFFING (2)

ELEMEN8:21	H19	The rumbling, hissing, puffing was so great,
SEASONS49:3	H94	With haire all wet, she puffing thus began.

PUFFT (1)

TDUDLEY165:39	H41	Nor honours pufft him up, when he had part:

PUL (1)

MASSYR60:38	H303	In sacred Writ, he's known by name of *Pul,*

PULL (1)

MEDDM207:11	Hp288	and waights that will pull us lower downward

PULL'D (2) [pulled]

MASSYR64:6	H430	Kild, sav'd, pull'd down, set up, or pain'd, or eas'd;
MASSYR65:25	H490	Then from his throne, he pull'd {pluck'd} him down again:

PUNISH (2)

MGREC115:13	H2522	To punish, where himself deserved blame:
MEDDM204:17	Hp285	doth many times, both reward and punish for one and ye same

PUNISHED (1)

MEDDM204:21	Hp285	Jehu, he was rewarded for the matter, and yet punished for the

PUNISHMENT (5)

MPERS75:31	H888	Threats punishment to him, that through default
MPERS84:25	H1261	For punishment, their breach of oath did call,
MPERS92:22	H1580	And so this wretch (a punishment too small)
CONTEM171:8	H113	Who neither guilt, nor yet the punishment could fly.
MEDDM204:24	Hp285	wth Jehu's reward, wch will end in punishment

PUNISHMENT'S (1) [punishment is]

DIALOG145:10	H159	A sharer in your punishment's my due,

PUNISHMENTS (1) [pl.]

DIALOG143:23	H92	They're for my punishments ordain'd on high,

PURCHASE (2)

ELEMEN18:4	H408	How gladly should his gold purchase his breath,
SIDNEY149:27	H23	Yet doth thy shame (with all) purchase renown,

PURCHASÈD (1)

HOUSE237:21   H51   'Its purchasèd + paid for too

PURE (12)

ELEMEN18:8   H412   If my pure Aire, thy sonnes did not sustain.

ELEMEN18:33   H437   I grow more pure and pure, as I mount higher,

ELEMEN18:33   H437   I grow more pure and pure, as I mount higher,

HUMOUR25:14   H203   Thy Choler is but rage, when tis most pure.

HUMOUR27:23   H294   When 'tis untaint, pure, and most genuine

HUMOUR27:36   H307   Nay, could I be from all your tangs but pure,

FLESH177:16   H97   Which shall remain for ever pure,

FLESH177:25   H106   This City pure is not for thee,

SICKNES179:8   H28   comes by profession pure.

MEDDM198:33   Hp277   look vpon it, the pure in heart shall se god, but the defiled in

MEDDM205:23   Hp286   He that would keep a pure heart and lead a blamlesse life,

MED223:18   Hp250   art pure, and let me bee no more afraid of Death, but even

PUREFYE (1) [purify]

MED223:17   Hp250   I ovght. Lord haueing this hope let me purefye my self as thou

PURELY (2)

ELEMEN18:31   H435   My moist hot nature, is so purely thinne,

SEASONS49:20   H111   Whose fleece when purely {finely} spun, and deeply dy'd,

PUREST (3)

ELEMEN16:1   H324   With rowling graines of purest massy gold:

MPERS78:35   H1016   Three thousand Tallents of the purest gold;

MEDDM196:11   Hp273   finest bread hath the least bran the purest hony the least wax

PURIFIEING (1) [purifying]

MEDDM197:19   Hp275   it, and that heart wch is not continually purifieing it self is no fit

PURIFY See **PUREFYE**

PURLING (1)

SEASONS~~49:33~~   H124   By purling Brooks looking how fishes swims.

PURPLE (5)

ELEMEN15:37   H319   The *Roman* Purple, double *Tirian* dye.

HUMOUR31:39   H472   With purple dye {deeper red}, to shew but {you} her disgrace.

MPERS84:1   H1229   His hangings, white, and green, and purple dye;

MGREC102:35   H2005   Those purple hangings, mixt with green, and white,

MGREC105:17   H2110   Whose wounds had made their skins of purple dye;

PURPLES (1) [pl.]

ELEMEN19:14   H459   Then Feavours, Purples, Pox, and Pestilence;

PURPOSELY (1)

MGREC122:28   H2847   What he appoints, She purposely withstands.

PURSE (6)

ELEMEN12:34   H194   Doe cure your patients, fill your purse with pence;

AGES36:18   H42   His golden god in's purse, which was his charm.

AGES40:4   H185   Sometimes lay wait to take a wealthy purse,

DIALOG142:31   H60   Though Armes, nor Purse she hath, for your releif:

DIALOG147:7   H233   That help thee not with prayers, arms, and purse,

DIALOG147:41   H265   Patience, and purse of Clients for {oft} to wrong:

PURSEVANTS (1) [pursuivants]

DIALOG148:2   H267   And Pursevants and Catchpoles want their pay,

PURSU'D (1) [pursued]

MASSYR59:13   H237   The King pursu'd unto the City wals;

PURSUE (5)

MASSYR60:13	H278	But *Belochus* in's progeny pursue,
MPERS88:35	H1428	And now more eagerly their foes pursue,
MPERS89:3	H1437	But they too faint, still to pursue their game,
MGREC~~132:20~~	H3264	Disaster on disaster him pursue,
FLESH176:1	H41	Thee as a foe, still to pursue.

PURSUED See PURSU'D

PURSUERS (1) [pl.]

MASSYR59:14	H238	But he once in, pursuers came too late,

PURSUES (4)

MPERS69:25	H647	Who him pursues to *Sardis,* takes the town,
MPERS76:37	H935	Pursues his flying-foes, and {then} on the strand;
MGREC~~125:21~~	H2970	But the old Queen pursues them with her hate,
MGREC126:5	H2996	And with the rest *Olimpias* pursues,

PUT (35) See also PUTT, PVTT

AGES~~43:8~~	H304	Then Kings must be depos'd or put to flight,
AGES45:10	H392	And worthy {better} ones, put to {suffer} extremity:
MASSYR57:6	H153	Some write, his Mother put his habite on,
MASSYR66:1	H507	Where to the sword, all but himself was {were} put,
MASSYR66:21	H527	Then *Put,* and *Lud,* doe at his mercy stand,
MPERS~~77:16~~	H956	(His eldest brother put beside the place,
MPERS~~79:13~~	H1038	The work-men put to death the bridge that made,
MPERS84:38	H1274	Strong poyson took, and {so} put an end to's dayes.
MPERS86:5	H1321	His fathers death, did {so} put an end to's fear.
MPERS88:19	H1412	Had not his too much valour put him by.
MGREC~~94:6~~	H1640	His kinsmen puts {put} to death without least {who gave no}
MGREC101:29	H1954	To force his Camp, so put {vanquish} them all to {by} flight;
MGREC116:3	H2563	Poyson had put an end to's dayes 'twas thought,
MGREC124:22	H2929	Put trust in any, but in this Commander;
MGREC126:12	H3003	To raise the Seige, and put her foes to flight;
MGREC126:28	H3019	For Justice sake she being put to th' sword.
MGREC128:1	H3074	The Mother of their King to death he'd put,
MGREC128:24	H3097	{great Antigonus} *Ptolomy,* and the rest {was} put him to flight;
MGREC128:30	H3103	And comming unawares put him to flight;
MGREC129:9	H3123	And put {So puts} to death, the mother and her son,
MGREC130:17	H3172	For straight way by command they'r put to death,
MGREC131:37	H3229	Who had an end put to their dayes by slaughter.
MGREC135:1	H3371	At *Actium* slain, {where} his Navy {Navy's} put to flight.
DIALOG144:21	H131	I mock'd the Preachers, put it farre away;
SIDNEY149:30	~~H23~~	Put with an Epithet of dignity;
SIDNEY~~150:12~~	H39	Put with an Epithite of dignity,
QELIZ157:9	H77	Had put her Harnesse off, had she but seen
DAVID159:17	H32	On your array put ornaments of gold,
1SIMON188:10	H11	With humble hearts and mouths put in the dust,
MEDDM202:3	Hp281	his gifts among the sons of men, betwixt whom he hath put so
MEDDM203:12	Hp283	make y^t his place of residence, but longs to put in at that port
MEDDM207:25	Hp289	no paines nor troubles, shall put a period to our dayes, the
MEDDM207:28	Hp289	that when wee are put out of these houses of Clay, we
MEDDM208:22	Hp290	miserably delude men and make them put great Confidence in
MEDDM209:8	Hp291	Canaanites, not destroy them, but put them vnder tribute, for

PUTREFACTION (1)
MEDDM196:29   Hp273   nothing but salt will keep from putrefaction, some again like

PUTS (8)
AGES35:31   H17   flowers (as these) blossome {the spring puts forth} betime,
MPERS89:38   H1472   And Villaine-like, there puts them {all} to the sword.
MGREC94:6   H1640   His kinsmen puts {put} to death without least {who gave no}
MGREC108:13   H2229   But *Alexander* puts them to the sword,
MGREC~~129:9~~   H3123   And put {So puts} to death, the mother and her son,
DIALOG145:25   H174   As puts me to a stand what I should say,
CONTEM171:16   H120   And puts all pleasures vain unto eternal flight.
MEDDM201:26   Hp281   Contrary ends, the one holds fast, the other puts forward, such

PUTT (2) [put]
BYNIGHT220:13 H12   He in his Bottle putt my teares,
SON231:21   H33   And may putt him in mind of what

PUZZELLS (1) [puzzles]
MASSYR56:29   H135   As puzzells best hystorians to remember:

PVTT (1) [put]
MYCHILD218:17 Hp244   I haue gott over this Block y^n have I another pvtt in my way, &

PYE (1) [pie]
ELEMEN19:9   H454   The Pye {Thrush}, the Jay {wren}, the Larke, a prey to th'

PYRATES (1) [pirates]
SON230:29   H12   Of pyrates who were neer at hand

PYRAUSTA (1)
ELEMEN9:39   H73   The Flye *Pyrausta* cal'd, all else expire.

PYRENIAN (1)
ELEMEN12:4   H164   Whether Pyrenian, or the Alpes; both lyes

PYRRUS (1)
MGREC133:19   H3307   Between those Kings, and noble *Pyrrus* stout,

PYTHON (2)
MGREC~~121:15~~   H2793   *Python* of haughty mind, and courage great.
MGREC122:11   H2836   *Python* now chose protector of the State,

Q

QUADRANGLE (1)
MASSYR56:1   H107   Quadrangle was the forme, it stood upon:

QUAIL (2)
FEVER221:10   H25   My heart no more might quail.
RESTOR229:23 H6   When heart did faint & Spirits quail

QUAK'D (1) [quaked]
MPERS89:28   H1462   They quak'd, to heare them, to each other call.

QUAKE (2)
ELEMEN13:41   H242   If {When} once you feele me, your foundation, quake,
MPERS90:29   H1496   Which rumor makes great *Artaxerxes* quake;

QUAKED See QUAK'D
QUAKES (1)
  MGREC95:27 H1706 No stroake for it he struck, their hearts so quakes.
QUAKING (3)
  ELEMEN8:13 H11 The quaking Earth did groan, the skie look't black,
  MASSYR68:3 H589 With quaking knees, and heart appall'd, he crys,
  DIALOG141:22 H21 Will bring Consumption, or an Ague quaking,
QUALITIES (4) [pl.]
  HUMOUR20:14 H6 The native qualities, that from each {them} flow,
  HUMOUR23:25 H135 The Princely quality, {qualities} befitting Kings.
  HUMOUR27:26 H297 Of all your qualities, I do partake,
  MGREC116:13 H2579 His princely qualities, had he retain'd
QUALITY (5)
  FATHER5:15 H16 Who for their age, their worth, and quality,
  ELEMEN13:22 H223 Now might {must} I shew my {mine} adverse quality,
  HUMOUR23:25 H135 The Princely quality, {qualities} befitting Kings.
  HUMOUR31:12 H444 Thy bittering quality, stil irretates,
  HUMOUR31:15 H447 Thy biting quality still irritates,
QUARELSOME (1) [quarrelsome]
  AGES35:24 H10 Vindicative, and quarelsome dispos'd.
QUARREL (1)
  MPERS81:18 H1126 That *Xerxes* quarrel was 'gainst *Athens* State,
QUARREL'S (1) [quarrel is]
  AGES39:39 H182 My valour, in some beastly quarrel's spent;
QUARRELLS (1) [quarrels]
  AGES38:1 H104 My quarrells, not for Diadems did rise;
QUARRELS (1) [pl.]
  MPERS91:6 H1514 With broyls, and quarrels, sets all *Greece* on fire.
QUARRELSOME See QUARELSOME
QUARTAN (1)
  AGES43:34 H329 The quartan Ague, dropsy, Lunacy:
QUARTER (1)
  MPERS80:5 H1072 None cryes for quarter, nor yet seeks to run,
QUATERNAL (1)
  CONTEM168:36 H42 Quaternal Seasons caused by thy might:
QUATERNIAN (1)
  SEASONS46:29 H5 Of four times four, the last quaternian;
QUEEN (53)
  HUMOUR23:13 H123 Of that black region, Nature made thee Queen;
  HUMOUR30:10 H402 As of that only part I was {were} the Queen:
  HUMOUR34:9 H564 Of all the Sences, Sight shal be the Queen;
  AGES45:2 H375 We chang'd our queen for king under whose rayes
  SEASONS46:35 H11 She gently thus began, like some fair Queen;
  MASSYR56:34 H140 This was last progresse of this mighty Queen,
  MASSYR68:14 H600 In comes the Queen, to chear her heartlesse son.
  MPERS70:20 H691 Yet wondrous Monuments this stately Queen,
  MPERS77:6 H945 His Queen *Attossa*, caused all {author of} this stir,
  MPERS78:29 H1010 O noble Queen, thy valour I commend,
  MPERS82:29 H1176 When jealous Queen *Amestris*, of this knew,
  MPERS84:5 H1233 Queen *Vashty* also feasts, but 'fore tis ended,
  MPERS85:11 H1287 To be by *Hester,* {fair Queen Ester} to her husband brought.

MPERS87:3	H1359	The young Queen, and old, at bitter jars:
MPERS90:39	H1506	Whom the old Queen did bear a mortal hate.
MPERS91:22	H1531	But the old Queen implacable in strife,
MPERS91:29	H1543	His match incestuous, cruelties of th' Queen,
MGREC95:38	H1717	His mother old, {his} beautious wife, {Queen} and daughters,
MGREC100:31	H1915	About this time, *Darius* beauteous Queen,
MGREC100:36	H1920	For this lost Queen (though in captivity).
MGREC102:33	H2003	The sumptuous Palace of Queen *Hester* {*Esther*} here,
MGREC106:15	H2149	*Thalestris,* Queen of th' *Amazons,* now brought
MGREC115:20	H2539	The Queen *Olimpias,* bears him deadly hate,
MGREC122:12	H2837	His rule Queen *Euridice* begins to hate,
MGREC122:23	H2845	*Ceria* the *Phrigian* Queen for to withstand,
MGREC122:32	H2851	Who vext the Queen more then the other farre;
MGREC122:38	H2859	The King, and Queen, along with him he takes. {to *Macedon*}
MGREC124:37	H2944	These, with his love, unto the amorous Queen
MGREC125:15	H2963	The Queen to meet her, bravely marched {marches} on;
MGREC125:16	H2964	But when her Souldiers saw their ancient Queen,
MGREC125:20	H2968	Then {The} King, and Queen, to *Amphipolis* doe fly, {seeing
MGREC125:21	H2970	But the old Queen pursues them with her hate,
MGREC125:23	H2973	And to the Queen, these presents she doth {did} send;
MGREC125:26	H2976	The Queen with many a curse, and bitter check,
MGREC125:30	H2980	This done, the cruell Queen rests not content,
MGREC125:41	H2991	So goes to finde this {cruel} Queen in *Macedon;*
MGREC126:15	H3006	Faine would she come now to {this wretched Queen}
MGREC126:29	H3020	This was the end of this most cruell Queen,
MGREC127:7	H3037	Of *Aridæus,* and his Queen, with state;
MGREC130:30	H3181	*Aridaeus* and his Queen by slaughters ta'ne;
MROMAN139:3	H3531	Of *Tanaquil,* late Queen, obtaines the place;
DIALOG141:6	H5	Alas, deare Mother, fairest Queen, and best,
QELIZ155:11	H2	Princess, Queen ELIZABETH, of
QELIZ155:14	H5	Although great Queen, thou now in silence lye,
QELIZ156:12	H39	If *France* had ever hop'd for such a Queen;
QELIZ156:38	H65	As were the subjects of our *(Pallas)* Queen:
QELIZ157:8	H76	Feirce *Tomris* (*Cirus* Heads-man, *Sythians* Queen)
QELIZ157:21	H89	But that she was a rich *Ægyptian* Queen;
QELIZ157:25	H93	Yet for our Queen is no fit parallel:
QELIZ157:26	H94	She was a Phoenix Queen, so shall she be,
QELIZ157:33	H101	Or had they some, but with our Queen ist gone?
QELIZ157:38	H106	But happy *England,* which had such a Queen,
QELIZ158:8	H117	*Here sleeps THE Queen, this is the royall bed.*

QUEENE (1) [queen]

MPERS78:23	H1004	*Artemesia, Halicarna's* Queene,

QUEEN-MOTHER (1)

MGREC101:13	H1938	For his {the} Queen-Mother, and the royall Maid;

QUEENS (3) [pl.]

MPERS91:21	H1529	The two Queens, by his means, 'gin {seem} to abate
MGREC97:8	H1769	Besides, the Queens, and Ladies of the Court,
QELIZ158:15	H124	*Here lies the pride of Queens, pattern of Kings,*

QUEENS (1) [poss.]

MGREC123:36	H2900	Besides, he was the young Queens favourite,

QUEL (1) [quell]
MGREC108:26 H2242 But he their stubbornnesse full soone {in time} doth quel;
QUEL'D (1) [quelled]
MPERS73:29   H814   All things in peace, and Rebells throughly quel'd,
QUELL (4) See also QUEL
MPERS92:35 H1593 In *Alexanders* reign who did him quell,
MGREC94:4   H1638 But he their mutinies, {by valour} full soon doth {he} quell.
QELIZ156:33   H60   The rude untamed *Irish* she did quell,
QELIZ157:24   H92   (Whom none but great *Aurelius* could quell)
QUELL'D (1) [quelled] See also QUEL'D
HUMOUR29:17 ~~H368~~ If not as yet, by me, thou shalt be quell'd:
QUENCH (3)
MPERS79:31 H1057 His Hoast, who {all} *Lissus* drinks to quench their thirst,
MGREC105:39 H2132 To quench his thirst, and to allay his heat;
1HUSB180:29 H8   My love is such that Rivers cannot quench,
QUENCHED (1)
MEDDM208:31 Hp290 reversed the order of nature, quenched the violence of the fire,
QUESTION (3)
MGREC122:34 H2855 And this no man durst question, or resist;
DIALOG145:17 H166 'Twixt King and Peeres a question of state,
JULY223:30 Hp251 let me neuer forgett thy Goodnes, nor question thy faithfullnes
QUICK (7)
HUMOUR22:8 H77 Then by a quick encounter, to be slaine;
HUMOUR28:9 H321 Her languishing diseases, though not quick,
MPERS76:17 H915 Or fly like birds, in unknown wayes full quick;
MPERS87:1 H1357 But fame more quick, arrives ere he came {comes} there,
MGREC114:5 H2473 Nothing toucht *Alexander* to the quick
MGREC~~124:6~~ H2911 And so he quick returns thus well appaid,
MEDDM201:16 Hp280 so a quick reception, and a deliberate cogitation argues a
QUICKEN (1)
MEDDM205:26 Hp286 quicken on to good dutys, we certainly dream of some
QUICKLY (3) See also QVICKLY
AGES36:4 H28 In's countenance, his pride quickly was seen.
MGREC125:28 H2978 Praying, that fatall day might quickly haste,
JULY223:36 Hp251 Come Lord Jesus, come quickly.
QUICKS (1)
HUMOUR30:30 H422 The first it draines, o'th' last quicks appetite,
QUIET (6)
SEASONS~~49:22~~ H113 Blest rustick Swains, your pleasant quiet life,
MPERS~~71:4~~ H718 Now quiet lyes under one marble stone.
MGREC120:38 H2775 And yet till now, at quiet was not laid.
CONTEM174:18 H217 And makes him long for a more quiet port,
MEDDM204:29 Hp285 pouerty comfortably it will help to quiet him, but if that will not
SON230:26 H9 Did'st that ship bring to quiet port,
QUIETNESSE (1) [quietness]
MPERS85:23 H1299 Before to quietnesse things could be brought,
QUILL (2)
FATHER5:10 H11 To mount so high, requires an Eagles quill:
SIDNEY152:6 H77 To give to their detractor any quill.
QUILS (1) [quills]
PROLOG7:35 H45 And oh, ye high flown quils, that soare the skies,

QUINCE (1)
SEASONS51:10 H184 Of Medlar, Quince, of Warden, {Almonds, Quinces, Wardens}
QUINCES (1) [pl.]
SEASONS51:10 H184 Of Medlar, Quince, of Warden, {Almonds, Quinces, Wardens}
QUINSEY (1) [quinsy]
AGES40:40 H219 Sometimes the Cough, Stitch, {the Quinsey} painful Plurisie,
QUINSIE (2) [quinsy]
HUMOUR32:7 H481 Nor Cough, nor Quinsie, nor the burning Feavor.
AGES43:33 H328 The Quinsie, and the Feavours, oft distaste me,
QUINTESSENCE (2)
SIDNEY152:29 H98 *That* Sidney *dy'd the quintessence {most renown'd} of men.*
DUBART154:18 H63 Thine the quintessence of an Heroick brain.
QUINTIUS (1)
MGREC133:22 H3311 (Part of whose Kingdomes *Titus Quintius* won)
QUINTUS (1)
MGREC101:39 H1968 But *Quintus Curtius,* as was said before.
QUIRE (1) [choir]
CHILDRN184:25 H14 Fly back and sing amidst this Quire.
QUIT (5)
MPERS90:41 H1508 And hopes by craft to quit his Masters harmes;
MGREC129:8 H3122 Resolves to quit his fears by one deed done,
MGREC135:3 H3375 To take her life, and quit her from all harmes;
MROMAN139:18 H3546 Her Husband sore incens'd, to quit this wrong,
DIALOG142:26 H55 Doth *Holland* quit you ill, for all your love?
QUITE (13)
HUMOUR27:40 H311 And of the sweet, calme temper, quite bereft,
MASSYR64:20 H444 Quite vanquish'd *Pharaoh Necho,* and {with} his Band;
MPERS87:20 H1374 Ran back, and quite abandoned the same,
MPERS92:14 H1572 Then Natures debt he paid, quite Issue-lesse.
MGREC103:27 H2038 (Filled with madnesse, and quite void of reason)
MGREC104:19 H2071 Who was of hopes, and comfort quite bereft;
MGREC112:17 H2403 His vertues dead, buried, and all {quite} forgot,
MGREC130:21 H3176 Thus *Philips* house was quite extinguished,
MGREC131:27 H3219 Is for this fresh young Lady half {quite} undone,
MGREC134:12 H3343 The Royall blood was quite {nigh} extinguished.
CHILDRN184:21 H10 To Regions far, and left me quite:
MEDDM200:20 Hp279 wealth, or a helthfull body, would quite ouer throw, some weak
MEDDM202:27 Hp282 set and be quite gone out of sight then must we needs walk in
QUITS (1)
HUMOUR22:16 H85 And 'fore she be assaulted, quits the place,
QUOTH (12)
ELEMEN11:22 H142 Sister, in worth {quoth shee} I come not short of you;
ELEMEN14:25 H267 Sister (quoth she) it had full well behov'd
ELEMEN17:35 H399 Content (quoth Aire) to speake the last of you,
HUMOUR34:23 H578 A foolish Brain (saith {quoth} Choler) wanting heat,
SEASONS46:36 H14 Three months {(quoth she)} there are allotted to my share,
MASSYR61:21 H326 I am thy Servant, and thy Son (quoth he)
MPERS69:38 H667 (Quoth he) that man for happy we commend,
MPERS76:15 H913 Quoth he, like Frogs, in water we must dive;
MGREC99:8 H1851 But, quoth *Parmenio,* (that brave Commander)
MGREC105:40 H2133 Of all good things (quoth he) once in my power,

751

CONTEM172:18 H153   O happy Flood, quoth I, that holds thy race
FLESH175:10 H10   Sister, quoth Flesh, what liv'st thou on

QVICKLY (1) [quickly]
MYSOUL225:21 H25   Come Jesvs qvickly, Blessed Lord

R

RAC'D (1) [raced]
MGREC~~102:17~~ H1987 Though worn by time, and raz'd {rac'd} by foes full sore,

RACE (12) n. [course]
SEASONS52:19 H234 To th' Southward tropick his swift race hath {doth} run;
SEASONS52:27 H242 And North-ward his unwearied race {Course} doth run;
MASSYR53:28 H18   Not finished, til he his race had run;
MASSYR61:6   H311 Forty eight years he reign'd, his race then run,
MGREC131:34 H3226 *Cassander* now must die, his race is run,
MROMAN138:22 H3512 Twenty foure yeare, {years} th' time of his royall race,
SIDNEY151:1 ~~H69~~   Such prince as he, his race should shortly end:
QELIZ156:15 H42   Since first the Sun did run, his ne'r runn'd race,
CONTEM168:24 H31   And as a strong man, joyes to run a race,
CONTEM172:18 H153 O happy Flood, quoth I, that holds thy race
SICKNES178:20 H3   My race is run, my thread is spun,
SICKNES179:9 H29   The race is run, the field is won,

RACE (21) n. [lineage]
FATHER5:6   H7   (though made a pedestall for *Adams* Race) /world
ELEMEN17:28 H392 Then wholly perish'd, earths ignoble race;
MASSYR57:30 H175 For *Ninias,* and all his Race are left,
MASSYR59:32 H256 This the last Monarch was, of {great} *Ninus* race,
MASSYR60:11 H276 A while he, and his race, aside must stand,
MASSYR63:3   H388 The fifth, and last, of great *Belosus* race;
MASSYR65:29 H494 Who was last King of holy *Davids* race;
MASSYR68:29 H615 With him did end the race of *Baladan,*
MPERS69:5   H627 *Cambyses* was of *Achemenes* race,
MPERS~~77:16~~ H957 Because this was, first born of *Cyrus* race.)
MPERS83:28 H1216 The best that ever sprang {sprung} of *Cyrus* race.
MPERS92:11 H1569 Whose race long time had worn the Diadem,
MPERS92:18 ~~H1576~~ If not (as is before) of *Cyrus* race,
MGREC117:7   H2614 None of his Kindred, or {nor} his Race, long stood;
MGREC129:38 H3152 Thus was the race, and house of *Alexander*
MGREC~~132:1~~ H3234 (Rather then *Philips* child must {race should} longer live
MGREC132:7   H3242 Thus *Philips,* and *Cassander's* race is {both} gone,
MGREC134:35 H3366 Fair *Cleopatra* next, last of that race,
TDUDLEY166:3 H45   He left it to his race for Legacy:
TDUDLEY166:30 H72 His pious Footsteps followed by his race,
CONTEM170:4 H78   A penalty impos'd on his backsliding Race.

RACK (1)
HUMOUR34:12   H567   Which runs through all the spondles of the rack,

RACT (1) [wracked] See also WRACK'D
QELIZ156:24   H51   She ract, she sackt, she sunk his Armadoe;

RADIANT (1)
AGES44:39   H372   When it had lost that radiant Sun-like spark,

RAFTS (1) [pl.]
MGREC107:31   H2206   To make them rafts, to waft them or'e the floud;

RAGE (12)
FATHER5:28   H29   My first do shew, their good, and then their rage,
ELEMEN8:7   H5   Who the most good could shew, & who most rage
ELEMEN13:6   H207   Will not my goodly face, your rage suffice?
HUMOUR25:14   H203   Thy Choler is but rage, when tis most pure.
HUMOUR29:6   H359   Though Choler rage, and raile, i'le not do so,
MGREC114:2   H2470   *Alexander,* to rage, to kill, and sweare,
MGREC114:12   H2482   And in a rage him through the body ran,
MGREC121:16   H2798   And in a rage they rush into his tent,
MGREC125:40   H2990   With rage, and with revenge, he's hurried on,
SIDNEY152:14   H83   And drave me from *Parnassus* in a rage,
VANITY160:7   H17   Mean while the conscience rage, who shall appease?
VANITY160:11   H21   The first is prone to vice, the last to rage.

RAGGED (1)
FATHER6:9   H43   These ragged lines, will do't, when they appear.

RAGGS (2) [rags]
AUTHOR177:34 H6   Made thee in raggs, halting to th' press to trudge,
MEDDM206:23   Hp287   for mercy w^{th}out mony & w^{th}out price but bring his filthy raggs

RAGING (7)
ELEMEN11:1   H119   My raging flame did make a mournful story,
ELEMEN11:16   H136   Not before then, shal cease my raging ire,
MGREC103:35   H2046   Those stately streets with raging flames doth {flame did} fil.
MGREC107:14   H2189   And thus unwisely, in one raging {mading} fume,
MGREC135:17   H3389   Then came the *Romane,* like a raging flood,
MROMAN140:3   H3566   My papers fell a prey to th' raging fire.
SON230:25   H8   In raging stormes did'st safely keep

RAGS See RAGGS

RAIGN (1) [reign] See also REIGNE
MPERS92:2   H1556   And in the twenty third of's cruel raign

RAILE (1)
HUMOUR29:6   H359   Though Choler rage, and raile, i'le not do so,

RAILEIH (1) [raleigh]
MASSYR57:20   H167   Nor can those Reasons which wise *Raleigh* finds,

RAILINGS (1) [pl.]
HUMOUR24:22   H171   To pay with railings, is not mine intent,

RAIMENT See RAYMENT

RAIN (3) See also RAINE
MASSYR59:20   H244   Which through much rain, then swelling up so high,
MASSYR59:20   H244   For by the rain, was *Tygris* so o'reflown,
2LETTER182:11 H17   The leaves in th' woods, the hail or drops of rain,

RAIN'D (2) [rained]
ELEMEN17:16   H380   Whereof the first, so ominous I rain'd,
AGES44:25   H358   Sometimes {Sometime} again, rain'd all adversity;

753

RAINE (1) [rain]
MEDDM199:5   Hp277 Lightening doth vsually preceed thunder, and stormes raine,

RAINED See RAIN'D

RAINES (2) [rains]
ELEMEN8:12   H10 Whence issu'd raines, and winds, lightning and thunder;
PILGRIM210:8   H8 Nor stormy raines, on him shall beat

RAIS'D (6) [raised]
MPERS74:34   H857 An Hoast he rais'd, the City to reduce,
MGREC124:8   H2913 Upon those friends, his father rais'd on high,
MGREC127:11   H3041 And rais'd *Cassandria* after his name,
PILGRIM210:38 H38 in power 'tis rais'd by Christ alone
SON231:4   H16 And freinds rais'd him in every place
ACK235:14   H14 And rais'd him vp when he was sick.

RAISE (15)
HUMOUR23:22 H132 Onely to raise my honours to the Skyes,
AGES39:27   H170 And by my mirth can raise the heart deprest;
MPERS73:21   H808 Their {Then} Forces instantly they raise, and rout,
MPERS75:4   H865 Desiring of the Prince to raise the siege,
MPERS87:7   H1363 The King dismay'd, a mighty Hoast doth raise;
MGREC95:29   H1708 To raise more force, for what he yet {to further his} intends.
MGREC100:12 H1896 Faire *Alexandria* from the ground doth raise;
MGREC108:36 H2252 A goodly City doth compleatly raise;
MGREC123:3   H2865 On which *Antigonus* his height doth raise:
MGREC126:12 H3003 To raise the Seige, and put her foes to flight;
CONTEM169:22 H62 Shall Creatures abject, thus their voices raise?
CONTEM170:20 H92 Upon whose blood his future good he hopes to raise.
FAINTING222:14 H4 My sinking heart I pray thee raise
WHAT224:7   H7 On High my heart O doe thou raise
HOUSE237:15 H45 Raise vp thy thovghts above the skye

RAISED (1) See also RAIS'D
MEDDM208:30 Hp290 it hath stayd the Course of the Sun raised the dead, cast out

RAISES (2)
MASSYR60:31   H296 Raises a Phœnix new, from grave o'th old;
MPERS91:40   H1554 Then raises forces, conquers *Egypt* land,

RAISINS (1) [pl.]
SEASONS51:6   H180 The Raisins now in clusters dryed be,

RAIS'ST (1)
RESTOR229:25 H8 Thou rais'st him vp I feard to loose

RAKED (1)
AGES38:14   H117 Lay raked up; of all the cursed weeds,

RAKES (1) n.
SEASONS50:7   H141 The Forks, and Rakes do follow them amain,

RAKES (1) v.
MASSYR60:28   H293 From rubbish these, with diligence he rakes,

RALEIGH (2) See also RAILEIH
MPERS91:15   H1523 Who had (as noble *Raleigh* doth evince)
MPERS92:27   H1585 But as before doth (well read) *Raleigh* write,

RAM (3)
ELEMEN10:9   H84 The Ram, the Bull, the Lyon, and the Beagle;
MGREC93:27   H1624 Who {That} ran in fury, {Choler} on the *Persian* Ram,
MGREC135:34 H3406 But yet this Lion, Bear, this Leopard, Ram,

RAMBLING (1)

AUTHOR177:37 H9 My rambling brat (in print) should mother call,

RAMPING (1)

DAVID159:12 H27 Stronger then Lions, ramping for their prey.

RAN (8)

SEASONS49:2 H93 Wiping her {the} sweat from off {of} her brow, that ran,

MPERS87:20 H1374 Ran back, and quite abandoned the same,

MPERS88:15 H1408 For at first charge the *Persians* ran away.

MPERS88:25 H1418 And with a full career, at him he ran.

MGREC93:27 H1624 Who {That} ran in fury, {Choler} on the *Persian* Ram,

MGREC95:23 H1702 But sets {Yet set} one in his roome, and ran away.

MGREC97:1 H1762 Most basely run {ran}, and left their King at large,

MGREC114:12 H2482 And in a rage him through the body ran,

RANGED (1)

MPERS88:4 H1397 And ranged stood, by great *Euphrates* side,

RANKS (1)

MROMAN139:4 H3532 He ranks the people, into each degree,

RANSOME (1)

MGREC97:31 H1792 For whom he offers him a ransome high;

RAPID (1)

MGREC135:18 H3390 And with the torrent of his rapid course,

RAPS (2)

AGES39:28 H171 Sweet Musick rapteth {raps} my {brave} harmonious Soul,

QELIZ155:19 H10 The sound thereof raps every humane sence;

RAPT (2)

CONTEM167:31 H8 Rapt were my sences at this delectable view.

CONTEM173:14 H181 Which rapt me so with wonder and delight,

RAPTED (1)

DUBART154:31 H76 Thy haughty stile, and rapted wit sublime,

RAPTETH (1)

AGES39:28 H171 Sweet Musick rapteth {raps} my {brave} harmonious Soul,

RARE (5)

ELEMEN12:19 H179 The Behemoth, and rare found Unicorne,

HUMOUR31:23 H456 The first, my constancy, that jewel rare.

MASSYR56:19 H125 A structure rare, I should but rudely marre,

MASSYR62:26 H371 Or else those *Chinoes* rare, whose wealth, and Arts,

MGREC111:5 H2350 Bringing their Presents, rare, and precious things:

RARELY (1)

HUMOUR32:8 H482 I rarely feel to act his fierce indeavour.

RARIFI'D (1) [rarified]

ELEMEN18:34 H438 And when I'm throughly rarifi'd, turn fire.

RARIFIES (1)

HUMOUR22:22 H91 Who rarifies the intellectuall parts?

RASH (2)

HUMOUR31:24 H457 Choler's too rash, this golden gift to hold.

MGREC123:17 H2881 Too young {rash} to beare that charge, if on him lay'd;

RASHNESSE (3)

HUMOUR29:22 H373 If in a Souldier rashnesse be so precious,

HUMOUR35:1 H597 Lest we too late, this rashnesse do repent,

MGREC107:19 H2194 For {Here} to observe the rashnesse of the King.

RATE (1)
HUMOUR25:30 H219 To take the wal's a sin, of such {so} high rate,
RATHER (13)
HUMOUR31:40 H473 But I rather with silence, vaile her shame;
HUMOUR33:5 H519 Rather then loose, one beateous *Hellena;*
MPERS92:23 ~~H1581~~ Which by some probabilities (seems rather;)
MGREC104:3 H2055 Chusing {And} rather {chose} an honorable death:
MGREC108:3 H2219 And in this sort, they rather drag, then bring,
MGREC~~120:4~~ H2738 To end his dayes by poison, rather chose
MGREC132:1 H3234 (Rather then *Philips* child must {race should} longer live
SIDNEY151:8 ~~H69~~ O Princely *Philip,* rather *Alexander,*
SIDNEY151:12 ~~H69~~ I rather judg'd thee of his mind that wept,
2SIMON195:4 Hp271 imitation Children do natureally, rather follow the failings then
MEDDM198:34 Hp277 shall rather choose to be buried vnder rocks and mountains
MEDDM206:21 Hp287 their wayes rather, then to beg forgiuenes for their sinnes,
30SEPT227:25 Hp257 furnace of affliction as some haue been, but haue rather been
RATTLES (1) [pl.]
AGES37:22 H84 In Rattles, Bables, and such toyish stuffe.
RAVEN (1)
ELEMEN10:10 H85 The Bear, the Goate, the Raven, and the Eagle,
RAVISHT (2)
DIALOG146:17 H203 My ravisht {weeping} virgins, and my young men slain,
DUBART152:35 H4 My ravisht eyes, and heart, with faltering tongue,
RAW (1)
SEASONS51:15 H189 Boughs full of leaves, or fruits, but raw, and {unripe or} green,
RAY (1)
SEASONS51:39 H215 The Northern Pole beholdeth not one ray.
RAYES (5) [rays]
AGES~~45:2~~ H375 We chang'd our queen for king under whose rayes
DUBART153:8 H12 Which Rayes, darting upon some richer ground,
QELIZ158:2 H111 She set, she set, like *Titan* in his rayes,
CONTEM169:3 H45 Hath strength, thy shining Rayes once to behold?
2LETTER182:18 H24 Thy rayes afar, salute her from the south.
RAYMENT (1) [raiment]
SEASONS48:13 H66 Our Winter {thicker} rayment, makes us lay aside,
RAYS See RAYES
RAZ'D (1) [razed]
MGREC102:17 H1987 Though worn by time, and raz'd {rac'd} by foes full sore,
RAZE (1)
MPERS75:35 H892 That shall, but {once} dare {to} raze those firme foundations;
REACH (3)
AGES42:37 H293 My dunghil thoughts, or hopes, could reach no higher.
MGREC125:33 H2983 That were {fell} within her reach, came to their ends;
FLESH176:34 H74 But reach at things that are so high,
REACHING (1)
ELEMEN12:3 H163 I'le here skip o're my mountaines, reaching skies,
REACHT (1)
MGREC117:24 H2631 Did harm himself, but never reacht his foes:
READ (16)
PROLOG6:26 H10 Great *Bartas* sugar'd lines doe but read o're;
MASSYR68:5 H591 This language strange, to read, and to unfold;

MASSYR68:24	H610	There hears his *Mene,* and his *Tekel* read;
MPERS91:30	H1544	His life may read in *Plutarch* to be seen.
MPERS92:6	H1564	I can no reason give, cause none I read;
MPERS92:27	H1585	But as before doth (well read) *Raleigh* write,
MGREC134:6	H3339	Against {Amongst} the Jewes, we read in *Macchabees,*
QELIZ157:31	H99	To read what others write, and then {so} admire.
MEDDM199:26	Hp278	We read in Scripture of three sorts of Arrows the arrow of an
MEDDM203:31	Hp284	We read of ten lepers that were Cleansed, but of one that
MYCHILD215:18	Hp240	haue not studyed in this yov read to shew my skill, but to
MYCHILD217:34	Hp243	I never saw any miracles to confirm me, and those wch I read
FEVER220:32	H12	Nor could I read my Evidence
FEVER220:33	H13	W^ch oft I read before.
JULY223:27	Hp251	to read this hereafter, and to others that shall read it when I
JULY223:27	Hp251	read this hereafter, and to others that shall read it when I shall

READERS (1) [pl.]

MGREC107:18	H2193	Nor wonder lesse, to Readers may it bring,

READILY (1)

AGES42:13	H271	As readily as could my Leader say:

READING (4)

AGES46:12	H443	Though reading other Works, doth much refresh,
MGREC106:17	H2151	Though some {most} of reading best, and soundest minde,
DUBART153:32	H36	Thus weake brain'd I, reading the lofty stile,
MYCHILD215:29	Hp241	too often tardy y^t way. I also fovnd much comfort in reading y^e

READINGS (1) [pl.]

AGES46:14	H445	My studies, labours, readings, all are done,

READS (2)

MPERS76:14	H912	But wise *Gobrias* reads not half so farre:
MPERS92:28	H1586	And he that story reads, shall often find;

READY (9)

AGES41:40	H257	I wanted not my ready allegation.
MPERS88:23	H1416	They {ready} were about to leave their King and fly,
MGREC94:39	H1677	The *Persians* for encounter ready stand,
MGREC96:31	H1751	A thousand Mules, and Camells ready wait.
MGREC109:16	H2275	The Vessells ready were, at his command;
MGREC110:1	H2301	But on the banks doth {stout} *Porus* ready stand,
MEDDM203:32	Hp284	thanks, we are more ready to receiue mercys then we are to
MEDDM207:8	Hp288	driuen them the further from him, that they are ready to say,
PILGRIM211:2	H43	Lord make me ready for that day

REAL (1)

HUMOUR25:5	H194	And real complements, base flattery.

REALITY (1)

FLESH175:15	H15	Notion without Reality?

REALME (1)

DIALOG141:11	H10	The glories of thy ever famous Realme?

REAP (1)

MYCHILD217:2	Hp242	mercyes, For if yee bee his yee shall reap the greatest

REAPE (1)

AGES42:23	H281	As neither sow, nor reape, nor plant, nor build.

REAPERS (1) [pl.]

SEASONS50:17	H151	With Sickles now, the painful {bending} Reapers go,

REAPETH (1)
MPERS85:28 H1304 The King much profit reapeth, by these leagues {this league},

REAPING (1)
SEASONS50:24 H158 He plow'd with pain, but reaping doth rejoyce;

REAR (2) v.
MGREC135:29 H3401 The third a Leopard, which four wings did rear;
FLESH175:8 H8 The other Spirit, who did rear

REAR'D (3) [reared]
AGES39:17 H160 climbe Battlements, {scale walls and forts} rear'd to the skies;
MASSYR56:13 H119 The wondrous Temple was, she rear'd to *Bell;*
CONTEM169:12 H53 My humble Eyes to lofty Skyes I rear'd

REARE (1) n. [rear]
MGREC96:23 H1743 Great *Sisigambis,* she brought up the Reare;

REARED See REAR'D

REARS (1)
MGREC110:33 H2337 Twelve Altars, he for Monuments then rears,

REASON (24)
ELEMEN18:10 H414 His moveing reason is, give least I dye.
HUMOUR26:14 H244 More useful then the rest, don't reason erre;
HUMOUR26:14 H244 Of greatest use, if reason do not erre:
HUMOUR29:19 H370 Not past all reason, but in truth all shame:
HUMOUR32:13 H487 Talke I love not, reason lyes not in length.
HUMOUR33:35 H549 The Reason, Fancy, and the Memory;
AGES36:31 H55 And to the rest, his reason mildly told;
AGES40:3 H184 I know no Law, nor reason, but my wil;
AGES41:25 H242 My reason, then bad judge, how little hope,
SEASONS49:10 H101 The reason why {Though he decline}, because his flames so
MASSYR66:30 H536 Which for seven years his reason took away;
MPERS69:37 H659 The Reason of those words *Cyrus* demands,
MPERS87:30 H1382 By reason, and by force, detain'd him still.
MPERS92:6 H1564 I can no reason give, cause none I read;
MGREC103:27 H2038 (Filled with madnesse, and quite void of reason)
MGREC103:34 H2045 But deafe to reason, (bent to have his will;)
MGREC108:17 H2233 Nor could he reason give, for this great wrong,
MGREC115:10 H2519 Hangs his Phisitian, the reason why,
QELIZ157:36 H104 Let such, as say our sex is void of reason,
FLESH175:4 H4 I heard two sisters reason on
MERCY188:23 H9 Who might in reason yet have lived long,
MEDDM197:7 Hp274 The reason why christians are so loth to exchang this world for
MEDDM202:13 Hp282 among the dead, and no other reason can be giuen of all this
MYCHILD217:35 Hp243 know but they were feigned. That there is a God my Reason

REASONS (1) [pl.]
MASSYR57:20 H167 Nor can those Reasons which wise *Raleigh* finds,

REBEL (2)
MGREC108:25 H2241 And now the *Bactrians* 'gainst him {now} rebel,
MGREC131:1 H3191 The better 'gainst *Cassander* to rebel.

REBELL (3) [rebel]
MPERS74:33 H856 The *Babylonians* 'gainst their Prince rebell;
MPERS85:29 H1305 Re-gaines his own, and then {doth} the Rebell breaks: {break,}
MGREC94:3 H1637 *Thebes,* and old {stiff} *Athens,* both 'gainst him rebell,

REBELLION (3)
MPERS92:1   H1555   Which in rebellion sixty years did stand:
MGREC94:7   H1641   That no combustion {rebellion in} in his absence be,
MGREC133:3   H3291   Who for rebellion unto him did fly,

REBELLIOUS (2)
MPERS91:34   H1548   *Ochus* a wicked and Rebellious son
MGREC128:11   H3084   Rebellious *Thebs* he had re-edified,

REBELLS (2) [pl.]
MPERS73:29   H814   All things in peace, and Rebells throughly quel'd,
MGREC134:10   H3341   By Rebells and imposters daily vext;

REBELLS (1) v.
MPERS85:14   H1290   Disquiet {Revolting} Egypt, 'gainst this King rebells,

REBELS (1) v.
MASSYR65:33   H498   But in the eighth, against his Prince rebels;

REBOUND (1)
ELEMEN18:16   H420   What is't? but forced Aire which must {doth} rebound,

RE-BRINGS (1)
MGREC128:10   H3083   Th' hatefull *Olinthians* to *Greece* re-brings;

RE-BUILD (1)
MPERS75:26   H883   The temple to re-build, for that did rest

REBUILD (1)
MASSYR60:22   H287   Then did rebuild destroyed *Ninivie,*

RE-BUILT (1)
MGREC127:10   H3040   Old *Thebes* he then re-built (so much of fame)

REBUILT (1)
MPERS84:12   H1247   Rebuilt those walls which long in rubbish lay,

RECALS (1) [recalls]
MGREC123:23   H2887   Recals *Olimpias,* the Court to grace;

RECEIPT See RECEIT

RECEIPTS (1) [pl.]
MEDDM204:9   Hp284   great receipts, call for great returnes, the more that any man is

RECEIT (1) [receipt]
MGREC103:1   H2012   For his receit with joy, they all accord;

RECEIUE (5) [receive]
MEDDM196:15   Hp273   comes he shall both take his rest and receiue his reward, the
MEDDM203:32   Hp284   thanks, we are more ready to receiue mercys then we are to
MEDDM204:12   Hp284   call him to reckoning, he may receiue his owne wth advantage
MEDDM206:8   Hp287   of bignes and brightnes, yet all receiue their light from that
MEDDM206:14   Hp287   and obscure, yet all receiue their luster (be it more or lesse)

RECEIUED (1) [received] See also RECEIV'D, RECEIVD, REC., REC'D
MEDDM197:24   Hp275   receiued? Come giue an account of thy stewardship.

RECEIUS (1) [receives]
MEDDM202:35   Hp282   giue, & wch is most strang, the more it receius the more empty

RECEIV'D (5) [received] See also RECEIUED, REC., REC'D, RECEIVD
AGES41:24   H241   I then receiv'd a {an} harvest of mine owne.
MASSYR56:11   H117   Bestow'd their labour, and receiv'd their pay,
MPERS89:6   H1440   Nor wound receiv'd, but one among them all:
MPERS90:11   H1484   These {Who} after all, receiv'd them joyfully:
MGREC121:29   H2811   With greater joy it would have been receiv'd;

RECEIVD (1) See also RECEIUE, RECEIV'D, REC., REC'D
SON231:25   H37   That all thy favours great receivd

RECEIVE (5) See also RECEIUE

HUMOUR26:29	H259	Then never boast of what thou do'st receive,
MPERS77:19	H960	He with his Crown, receive a double warre,
MPERS80:16	H1083	Them {The Harbours} to receive, {contain} the Harbour was
MGREC95:3	H1682	Who in their backs did all their wounds receive.
MGREC110:2	H2302	For to receive {To give} him, {welcome} when he comes to

REC. (1) [received] See also REC'D.

MYCHILD216:6	Hp241	me. But I rendered not to him according to yᵉ benefitt rec.

REC'D. (1) [received] See also REC.

ACK235:3	H1-3	In thankfull acknowledgmt for yᵉ lrs rec'd. from my

RECEIVED (2) See also RECEIUED, RECEIV'D, RECEIVD, REC., REC'D

MPERS80:26	H1093	Received there, a shameful over-throw.
MGREC121:21	H2803	And is of all received {most} joyfully;

RECEIVES (1) See also RECEIUS

MGREC98:1	H1803	Their present he receives with thankfullnesse,

RECEIVING (1)

MPERS91:5	H1513	They to their discontent, receiving hire,

RECEPTION (1)

MEDDM201:16	Hp280	body, so a quick reception, and a deliberate cogitation argues

RECITE (1)

AGES41:5	H225	Too many's {many} my Diseases to recite,

RECKONING (2)

AGES40:33	H212	Nor yet that heavy reckoning for {soon} to come;
MEDDM204:12	Hp284	shall call him to reckoning, he may receiue his owne wᵗʰ

RE-COLLECTS (1)

MPERS89:9	H1443	After a while his {hurri'd} thoughts he re-collects,

RECOMMEND (1)

BIRTH180:2	H12	These farewell lines to recommend to thee,

RECOMPENCE (10)

MPERS72:23	H771	Like fault must look, for the like recompence.
MPERS75:18	H878	But yet thou has sufficient recompence,
MPERS79:4	H1026	For his great love, is this thy recompence?
MPERS83:3	H1191	His brothers recompence was naught but jears:
MGREC104:28	H2080	Great recompence, in's thoughts, he did propose;
MGREC107:13	H2188	The recompence of travels, wars, and toyls;
MGREC121:16	H2797	Who vow to make this captain recompence,
DIALOG146:26	H212	And recompence me {that} good, for all my ill {I've done to
FLESH175:23	H23	Industry hath its recompence.
1HUSB180:30	H9	Nor ought but love from thee, give recompence.

RECORD (4)

DIALOG144:22	H132	The Sermons yet upon record doe stand,
SIDNEY151:6	H69	But that it is record by *Philips* hand,
CONTEM174:32	H229	Their names without a Record are forgot,
RESTOR229:29	H12	My thankfull heart wᵗʰ pen record

RECORD'S (1) [record is]

MPERS91:35	H1549	Of whom no Record's extant of his deeds;

RECORDED (1)

MPERS91:39	H1553	Their Acts recorded not, as heretofore

RECORDS (2)

SIDNEY149:29	H23	In all records, thy Name I ever see,
SIDNEY150:12	H38	In all Records his name I ever see

RECOUERY (1) [recovery]

HANNA230:9   H1-2   Vpon my Daughter Hannah Wiggin her recouery from a

RECOUNT (3) See also RECOVNT

ELEMEN10:15   H90   Their magnitude and height should I recount,

ELEMEN10:27   H102   'Mong all my wonders which I might recount;

MPERS79:8   H1030   First thing, *Xerxes* {he} did worthy {of} recount,

RECOUNTED See RECOVNTED

RECOURSE (1)

30SEPT227:30   Hp257   haue recourse to yᵉ same God who hath heard + deliuered

RECOVER (2)

MGREC132:19   H3256   These to recover, musters all his might,

MROMAN137:15   H3466   For {Then} to recover them, a Feild was fought;

RECOVERS (1)

MGREC128:27   H3100   And *Seleuchus* recovers *Babylon,*

RECOVERY See RECOUERY

RECOVNT (2) [recount]

HOURS234:30   H44   Wᵗʰ praises shall recovnt

REMB236:7   H22   Impossible for to recovnt

RECOVNTED (1) [recounted]

HOUSE237:6   H36   Nor things recovnted done of old.

RECUR'D (1) [recurred]

THEART229:1   H3   Who hath restor'd, redeem'd, recur'd

RED (11)

ELEMEN18:22   H426   Your red hot work, more coldly would go on.

ELEMEN20:1   H483   Sometimes strange {red} flaming swords, and blazing stars,

HUMOUR31:39   H472   With purple dye {deeper red}, to shew but {you} her disgrace.

HUMOUR32:40   H514   My Lilly white, when joyned with her red,

AGES36:8   H32   When blushing first, she 'gins to red {light} the Aire.

SEASONS48:26   H79   The hasty Pease, and wholesome red {cool} Strawberry,

DIALOG142:19   H48   That from the red, white pricking Roses sprung?

DIALOG143:10   H79   None knowes which is the Red, or which the White:

SIDNEY149:16   H15   Thine {His} Eloquence made *Mercury* wax red;

QELIZ158:9   H118   *O'th' Damask Rose, sprung from the white and red,*

CONTEM167:30   H7   Of green, of red, of yellow, mixed hew,

REDEEM (2)

MGREC107:3   H2178   So heaps up gifts, his credit to redeem;

MGREC114:31   H2501   Which vertues fame can ne're redeem by farre,

REDEEM'D (2) [redeemed]

FEVER221:13   H28   Who hath redeem'd my Soul from pitt,

THEART229:1   H3   Who hath restor'd, redeem'd, recur'd

REDEEMER (1)

AGES46:23   H454   My strong Redeemer, comming in the skies;

REDEMPTION'S (1) [redemption is]

DIALOG148:22   H287   For sure the day of your redemption's nigh;

REDUCE (3)

HUMOUR30:13   H405   Reduce the man to's principles, then see

MPERS74:34   H857   An Hoast he rais'd, the City to reduce,

MPERS77:20   H961   Th' *Ægyptians* to reduce, and *Greece* to marre;

REE (1)

AGES45:5   H389   I've seen designes at {for} *Ree,* and *Cades* {*Rochel*} crost,

REED (1)
MPERS84:9   H1237   What *Hester* {*Esther*} was, and did, her story reed,
RE-EDIFIED (1)
MGREC128:11   H3084   Rebellious *Thebs* he had re-edified,
REEDS (1) [pl.]
MEDDM208:24   Hp290   proue like the reeds of Egipt that peirce insteed of supporting
REEK (1)
AGES38:6   H109   My foe should weltering, with {in} his bowels reek.
REELE (1) [reel]
DIALOG141:20   H19   My weakned fainting body now to reele?
REFERENCE (1)
CHILDRN184:13   H1-2   *In reference to her Children, 23. June, 1659.*
REFINE (1)
ELEMEN9:24   H58   Ye Silver-smiths, your ure I do refine,
REFINED (1)
30SEPT227:24   Hp257   then thy stroakes shall bee welcome, I haue not been refined
REFINER (1)
SIDNEY150:8   H33   (O brave Refiner of our *Brittish* Tongue;)
REFINES (1)
HUMOUR22:27   H96   What comes from thence, my heat refines the same,
REFLECT (1)
ELEMEN9:31   H65   A burning fiery heat we find reflect;
REFLECTION (1)
DUBART153:6   H10   Reflection from their beaming altitude,
REFLECTS (1)
CONTEM168:26   H33   The Earth reflects her glances in thy face.
REFORM (1)
MEDDM206:20   Hp287   of turning to god, the first thing wch they eye, is how to reform
REFORMED (1)
MYCHILD216:34   Hp242   some sin I lay vnder wch God would haue reformed, or some
REFRAIN (1)
HUMOUR34:18   H573   Whose use and worth to tel, I must refrain;
REFRESH (6)
ELEMEN9:34   H68   How doth his warmth refresh thy frozen backs, {back}
ELEMEN16:37   H360   As I with showers oft time {times} refresh the earth;
AGES44:17   H350   That can refresh, or ease, if Conscience frown;
AGES46:12   H443   Though reading other Works, doth much refresh,
DIALOG146:31   H217   Your sunken bowels gladly would refresh:
MEDDM196:25   Hp273   Sweet words are like hony, a little may refresh, but too much
REFRESHED (1)
MED223:1   Hp250   Meditations when my Soul hath been refreshed wth the
REFRESHING (2)
MEDDM196:19   Hp273   ioy, knowing his refreshing is at hand
MYCHILD217:16   Hp243   pilgrimage and refreshing wch I supposed most of the servants
REFRESHMENT (1)
MYCHILD217:5   Hp242   abundance of Sweetnes and refreshment after affliction and
REFRESHMENTS (1) [pl.]
11MAYA226:17   Hp255   Many refreshments haue I fovnd in this my weary pilgrimage,
REFUS'D (2) [refused]
MGREC118:9   H2656   But he refus'd, with fained modesty,
MGREC121:22   H2804   Their proffers he refus'd, with modesty

REFUSES (2)
MPERS82:24   H1171   The chaste, and beautious Dame, refuses still.
MGREC104:39   H2091   This {The} wofull King, his courtesie refuses,
REFUTED (1)
HUMOUR27:18   H289   Your slanders thus refuted, takes no place,
REGAIN (3)
MASSYR57:27   ~~H172~~   Did then incite, them to regain their own.
MGREC120:13   H2748   Yet to regain them, how he did not know,
MGREC132:28   H3273   Did ne'r regain one foot in *Asia.*
RE-GAINES (1) [regains]
MPERS85:29   H1305   Re-gaines his own, and then {doth} the Rebell breaks: {break,}
REGAL (3)
HUMOUR21:14   H42   I in his heart erect my regal throne,
MASSYR54:14   H41   At twenty five, ended his regal date.
MASSYR62:9   H354   Besieg'd his regal town, and spoyl'd his Coast,
REGALL (4) [regal]
MASSYR67:28   H574   Layes siedge to's regall seat, proud *Babylon,*
MGREC95:14   H1693   (Of Asse-eard) *Midas,* once the regall seat,
MGREC97:10   H1771   The Regall ornaments now {were} lost, the treasure
DIALOG142:9   H38   The regall, peacefull Scepter from thee tane?
REGARD (7)
MGREC99:32   H1875   If of thy future fame thou hadst regard,
MGREC101:1   H1926   Great *Alexander,* for this good regard;
MGREC106:2   ~~H2136~~   Wherefore the gods requite thy kinde regard.
MGREC~~106:2~~   H2136   But *Alexander* will, for this regard
MGREC113:21   H2448   Nor could his Captaines bear so great regard;
SIDNEY152:2   ~~H75~~   For dear regard he had of *Sydney's* state,
MEDDM206:8   Hp287   regard of bignes and brightnes, yet all receiue their light from
REGARDED (3)
MGREC115:29   H2548   Or if remembred, yet regarded not;
MGREC116:21   H2587   Learning, and learned men, he much regarded,
ACK235:6   H6   And 'mongst y^m hast regarded Mine,
REGARD'EST (1)
SOREFIT221:23 H9   Thov help'st and thov regard'est me.
REGARDLESLY (1)
FLESH175:13   H13   Regardlesly to let earth goe?
REGARDS (1)
MEDDM200:3   Hp278   not a little one? will ere long say of a greater Tush god regards
REGAU'ST (1) [regavest]
RESTOR229:26 H9   Regau'st me him again
REGENT (1)
ELEMEN16:36   H359   Yet {And} *Luna* for my Regent I obey.
REGION (3)
HUMOUR23:13   H123   Of that black region, Nature made thee Queen;
CONTEM172:30 H163   Ye Fish which in this liquid Region 'bide,
CONTEM173:31 H196   Then follow thee into a better Region,
REGIONS (2) [pl.]
ELEMEN11:35   H155   To tell you of my Countries, and my regions
CHILDRN184:21 H10   To Regions far, and left me quite:
REHEARSE (1)
MGREC122:4   H2827   And much eclipse his {great Acts and} glory to rehearse

REHOBOTH (1)
MASSYR53:29	H19	*Resen, Caleb,* and *Rehoboth* likewise,

REIGN (22) See also RAIGN, REIGNE
MASSYR54:13	H40	His reign was short, for as I calculate,
MASSYR54:16	H43	His father dead, *Ninus* begins his reign,
MASSYR64:9	H433	This Prince, the last year of his Fathers reign,
MASSYR65:24	H489	His Son three months he suffered to reign,
MPERS71:3	H715	Some thirty years this potent Prince did reign,
MPERS71:8	H724	His reign with Bloud, and Incest, first begins,
MPERS71:14	H728	He wages warre, the fifth year of his reign,
MPERS72:33	H777	All thought {wisht} his short reign long, till {past before} it was
MPERS75:24	H881	*Darius* in the second of his reign,
MPERS75:38	H895	And in the sixth yeare of his friendly reign
MPERS77:12	H951	Thirty six years this royall {noble} Prince did reign,
MPERS83:23	H1211	Such Justice then, in *Persia* {Persian court} did remain, {reign.}
MPERS84:12	H1241	Good *Ezra* in the seventh year of his reign,
MPERS85:2	H1278	And dy'd the two and fortieth of his reign.
MPERS91:27	H1541	But yet for all his greatnesse, and long reign,
MPERS91:27	H1541	Such as would know at large his warrs and reign,
MPERS92:8	H1566	And scarce a Nephew left that now might reign:
MPERS92:18	H1576	And was no sooner setled in his reign,
MPERS92:35	H1593	In *Alexanders* reign who did him quell,
MGREC93:15	H1612	The twenty first of's age, began to reign.
MGREC118:1	H2648	That so under his feeble wit, and reign,
VANITY161:2	H53	Who is possessed of, shall reign a King.

REIGN'D (13) [reigned]
MASSYR55:1	H67	Fifty two years he reign'd (as we are told)
MASSYR56:40	H146	Forty two years she reign'd, and then she dy'd,
MASSYR59:34	H258	Twenty he reign'd, same time, as Stories tel,
MASSYR61:6	H311	Forty eight years he reign'd, his race then run,
MASSYR61:39	H344	Thus *Tiglath* reign'd, and warr'd, twenty seven years,
MASSYR63:2	H387	His Son, weak *Essarhadon* reign'd in's place,
MASSYR66:39	H545	Forty four years he reign'd, which being run,
MPERS73:9	H796	Eight years he reign'd, a short, yet too long time,
MPERS86:6	H1322	{this} *Nothus* reign'd {'bout} nineteen years, which run,
MPERS92:2	H1556	That three and twenty years he reign'd, I finde,
MPERS92:13	H1571	Three years he reign'd, as Chronicles expresse, {then drank
MGREC133:9	H3297	With *Ptolomy,* reign'd after *Alexander;*
MGREC133:41	H3331	*Seleuchus* reign'd, when he had lost his life,

REIGNE (11) [reigne] See also RAIGN
MASSYR55:26	H92	She flourishing with *Ninus,* long did reigne;
MPERS73:23	H809	Who little pleasure had, in his short reigne,
MPERS73:38	H823	But {That} better one, then many Tyrants reigne.
MPERS93:1	H1598	And in the sixt year of his haplesse reigne,
MGREC116:30	H2596	As oft his Acts throughout his reigne did {doth} shew:
MGREC134:30	H3361	And next to {after} him, did false *Lathurus* reigne,
MROMAN137:22	H3473	Others, the seven and thirtyeth of his reigne
MROMAN138:11	H3501	Thirty two years doth *Tullus* reigne, then dye,
MROMAN138:35	H3525	Thirty eight yeares (this Stranger borne) did reigne,
MROMAN139:8	H3536	Forty foure yeares did *Servius Tullius* reigne,
QELIZ156:2	H29	The nine {'leven} *Olimp'ades* of her happy reigne;

REIGNED See REIGN'D
REIGNING (1)
MPERS68:35 H621 and his Father in Law) reigning
REIGNS (1)
MGREC132:16 H3251 And now as King, in *Macedon* he reigns;
REINES (2) [reins]
HUMOUR28:18 H330 The over plus I send unto the reines;
AGES43:27 H322 The vexing Stone, in bladder and in reines,
REIOYCEING (1) [rejoicing]
2SIMON195:15 Hp271 wth reioyceing at that great day of appearing, wch is the
REJECT (2)
MPERS89:19 H1453 The *Greeks* with scorn reject his proud commands;
MGREC99:10 H1853 *Darius* offers I would not reject,
REJECTS (1)
MGREC99:4 H1847 But he with scorn, his courtesie rejects,
REJOICE (3) See also REJOYCE
MYSOUL224:25 H1 My Soul rejoice thou in thy God
13MAY226:31 H7 My Soul and Body doth rejoice,
2HUSB233:10 H43 Rejoice wth heavenly chear—
REJOICED See REJOYC'D, REJOYCED
REJOICING See REIOYCING
REJOYC'D (2) [rejoiced]
DUBART155:3 H88 *The world rejoyc'd at's birth, at's death was sorry;*
TDUDLEY167:4 H86 *If some rejoyc'd, more did lament.*
REJOYCE (7) [rejoice]
ELEMEN9:36 H70 Both man and beast, rejoyce at his approach,
ELEMEN15:14 H296 If I supply, his heart and veines rejoyce;
AGES45:31 H421 No more rejoyce, at musickes pleasant {pleasing} noyse,
SEASONS48:23 H76 But both rejoyce, at th'heavens clear smiling face,
SEASONS50:24 H158 He plow'd with pain, but reaping doth rejoyce;
MGREC128:35 H3108 *Antigonus* did much rejoyce his son,
DAVID158:30 H10 Lest Daughters of the *Philistins* rejoyce,
REJOYCED (1) [rejoiced] See also REJOYC'D
MPERS87:38 H1390 Rejoyced {Was} not a little {jocund} at his feare.
RELATE (6)
HUMOUR31:41 H474 Then cause her blush, while I dilate {relate} the same.
AGES38:17 H120 But yet let me relate, before I go,
MGREC112:9 H2395 Spectators here, could scarce relate the story,
MGREC126:39 H3028 Her out-rages too tedious to relate,
MGREC131:8 H3198 'Twould be an endlesse story to relate
DIALOG144:18 H128 Of more then thou canst heare, or I relate,
RELATION (5)
HUMOUR24:24 H173 I will annalise, {this} thy so proud relation;
AGES41:39 H256 For time, for place, likewise for each relation,
MPERS78:22 H1003 {Which to} Three thousand (or more) {came} by best relation,
TDUDLEY165:10 H12 Nor is't Relation near my hand shall tye;
CONTEM174:3 H204 from foes, from friends, from dearest, near'st Relation.
RELATIONS (1) [pl.]
MERCY188:20 H6 And live I still to see Relations gone,
RELEAS'D (2) [released]
MASSYR61:40 H345 Then by his death, releas'd, was *Israels* fears.

MGREC119:39   H2729   *Antipater* releas'd from's prisonment,

RELEASE (2)

ELEMEN17:21   H385   Till Sun release, their ships can saile no more.

MGREC119:19   H2709   come and {For succours} to release {relieve} him in his need,

RELEASED See RELEAS'D

RELEAST (1) [released]

MPERS78:38   H1019   One of his five Sons there, might be releast;

RELEIF (2) [relief]

MGREC112:40   H2426   Sunk in despair, without hope of releif;

DIALOG142:31   H60   Though Armes, nor Purse she hath, for your releif:

RELEIV'D (1) [relieved]

ACK235:9   H9   Thou hast releiv'd my fainting heart

RELIED See RELYED

RELIEF (3) See also RELEIF

MPERS~~90~~:4   H1478   The Country burnt, they no relief might take.

DIALOG145:14   H163   Then let's join heads, and hands {& hearts} for your relief.

DIALOG146:25   H211   For my relief now use thy utmost skill {do what there lyes in

RELIEVE (1)

MGREC~~119:19~~   H2709   come and {For succours} to release {relieve} him in his need,

RELIG^N (1)

MYCHILD218:27   Hp244   me to my own Relig^n again.

RELIGN. (2)

MYCHILD218:19   Hp244   word, yet why may not ye popish Relign. bee ye right, They

MYCHILD218:23   Hp244   that are in their Relign: together wth their lying miracles, and

RELIGION (2)

DIALOG146:13   ~~H200~~   Religion, Gospell, here lies at the stake,

TDUDLEY165:34   H36   Thy love to true Religion e're shall shine,

RELIGIOUS (2)

MROMAN137:29   H3480   Religious Rites, and Customs instituted,

DDUDLEY167:20   H17   *Religious in all her words and wayes,*

RELY (1)

MYCHILD218:5   Hp243   a God as I worship in Trinity, + such a Sav^r as I rely upon, tho:

RELYE (1) [rely]

MGREC124:7   ~~H2912~~   *Polisperchon,* knowing he did relye

RELYED (1) [relied]

MEDDM208:20   Hp290   nothing, and so leaue those in the lurch that most relyed

REMAIN (27) See also REMAINE

AGES41:4   H224   That oft for it, in *Bedlam* I remain.

MASSYR57:20   ~~H167~~   Each wronged Prince, or childe that did remain,

MASSYR62:20   H365   Thus *Iacobs* Sons, in exile must remain,

MASSYR67:10   H556   But yet in *Babell,* he must still remain:

MASSYR67:19   H565   His Kingdome to *Belshazzar* did remain.

MPERS71:4   ~~H716~~   Unto *Cambyses* then, all did remain.

MPERS77:13   H952   Unto {Then to} his eldest {second} Son, all did remain.

MPERS83:23   H1211   Such Justice then, in *Persia* {*Persian* court} did remain, {reign.}

MPERS85:1   H1277   'Rest of his time in peace he did remain;

MPERS89:22   H1456   And sues for peace, that they his friends remain;

MPERS91:28   ~~H1542~~   He must leave all, and in the pit remain;

MPERS~~91:38~~   H1552   And being king commands those that remain,

MGREC95:17   H1696   Which who so did {doth}, must Lord of all remain,

MGREC119:30   H2720   For fighting still, whilst there did hope remain,

MGREC120:19 H2754 But this again dislikes, and {he} would remain,
MGREC120:40 H2777 And made the Souldiers on his side remain;
MGREC~~127:29~~ H3059 And Master of the treasure he remains; {sole remain:}
MGREC128:20 H3093 And Lord o'th' City {royal} *Susha* did remain.
MGREC131:12 H3204 And he that conquerour shall now remain,
MGREC131:16 H3208 Nor to his son did there {e're} one foot remain,
DIALOG144:37 H145 Her fruitfull land, a barren heath remain.
DIALOG146:23 H209 If any pity in thy heart remain,
CONTEM171:32 H134 But in oblivion to the final day remain.
FLESH177:16 H97 Which shall remain for ever pure,
AUTHOR177:31 H3 Who after birth did'st by my side remain,
3LETTER183:30 H32 Let's still remain but one, till death divide.
1SIMON188:15 H16 Among the blest in endless joyes remain.

REMAIN'D (3) [remained]
MGREC116:14 H2580 Unparalel'd, for ever had remain'd;
MGREC117:5 H2612 To his posterity remain'd no jot,
MGREC120:1 H2732 But under servitude, their necks remain'd,

REMAINDER (2)
MPERS82:15 H1162 Same day, the small remainder of his Fleet,
2HUSB233:15 H48 And the Remainder of o^r Dayes

REMAINE (10) [remain]
MPERS85:9 H1285 Who now sole Monarch, doth of all remaine,
MGREC100:9 H1893 He Diabolicall must needs remaine,
MGREC111:27 H2372 That of them all, the fourth did scarce remaine.
MGREC121:12 H2790 Did make his owne firme to his cause remaine,
MGREC124:17 H2924 Whilst hot in wars these two in *Greece* remaine,
MGREC126:13 H3004 *Cassander* is resolv'd, there to remaine,
MGREC132:33 H3280 Of the old Heroes, now but two remaine,
MGREC132:41 H3288 Whilst with these hopes, in *Greece* he did remaine,
MGREC133:11 H3299 So three Successors only did remaine;
DAVID159:22 H37 In places high, full low thou dost {didst} remaine;

REMAINED See REMAIN'D

REMAINES (1) [remains]
MGREC112:18 H2404 But vice remaines, to his eternall blot.

REMAINS (2) [pl.]
MGREC119:37 H2727 And the remains of *Leonatus* takes;
BIRTH180:14 H24 Look to my little babes my dear remains.

REMAINS (5) v.
ELEMEN16:8 H331 *Asphaltis* Lake, where nought remains alive.
MASSYR66:33 H539 The time expir'd, remains a Beast no more,
MGREC127:29 H3059 And Master of the treasure he remains; {sole remain:}
CONTEM171:24 H127 But Man grows old, lies down, remains where once he's laid.
VERSES184:5 H9 My Bond remains in force unto this day;

REMB^{RC} (1) [remembrance] See also REMBRANCE, REME BRANCE, REMEMBERANCE
REMB235:21 H1-3 In thankfull Remb^{rc} for my dear husbands safe Arrivall.

REMBER (2) [remember]
HANNA230:15 H8 Gravnt shee rember w^t thov'st done
2HUSB233:3 H36 Rember Lord thy folk whom thou

REMBRANCE (1) [remembrance] See also REMB^{RC}, REME BRANCE, REMEMBERANCE
MYCHILD215:16 Hp240 bee dayly in y^r rembrance, (Altho: y^t is the least in my aim in

REME⁻BRANCE (1) [remembrance] See also REMEMBERANCE, REMB^RC, REME⁻BRANCE
  JULY223:26   Hp251 Reme⁻brance, y^t it may bee a support to me when I shall haue
REME⁻BRED (1) [remembered]
  MYCHILD218:32 Hp244 I haue r m bred the words of Christ that so it must bee, and
REMED'LESS (1) [remediless]
  ELEMEN~~14:6~~   H250   What she hath lost by these my dreadfull {remed'less} woes.
REMEDY (1)
  MEDDM203:27 Hp284 and that he must needs perish if he haue no remedy, will
REMEMBER (3) See also REMBER
  ELEMEN14:20   H262   Remember sonnes, your mould is of my dust,
  SEASONS47:26 H42   Doth darken *Sols* bright face, makes us remember
  MASSYR56:29 H135   As puzzells best hystorians to remember:
REMEMBERANCE (1) [rememberance]
  MPERS72:22   H770   To whom he gave this in rememberance,
REMEMBERED See REME⁻BRED, REMEMBRED
REMEMBERING See REMEMBRING
REMEMBRANCE (1) See also REMB^RC, REME⁻BRANCE, REMBERANCE
  MEDDM204:2   Hp284 The remembrance of former deliuerances, is a great support in
REMEMBRED (1) [remembred] See also REME⁻BRED
  MGREC115:29 H2548 Or if remembred, yet regarded not;
REMEMBRING (2)
  AGES40:32   H211   Remembring not the dreadful day of Doom,
  MGREC125:17 H2965 Remembring {Calling to mind} what sometime she had been,
RE-MINDS (1) [reminds]
  MASSYR68:19 H605   Re-minds him of his Grand-sires height, and fall,
REMINDS (1)
  CONTEM173:24 H190   Reminds not what is past, nor whats to come dost fear.
REMISSENESSE (2) [remissness]
  MASSYR67:14 H560   Faire *Ægypt* is, by his remissenesse lost;
  MPERS85:19   H1295 Which from remissenesse, in *{Less}* Asia proceeds {breeds.}
REMNANT (1)
  DIALOG147:22 ~~H247~~ Let Gaoles be fill'd with th' remnant of that pack,
REMOTE (2)
  SEASONS51:37 H213   So farre remote, his glances warm not us;
  MGREC105:7   H2100 To hide themselves, remote, in *Bactria;*
REMOTNES (1) [remoteness]
  MEDDM205:26 Hp286 to good dutys, we certainly dream of some remotnes betwixt
REMOUE (1) [remove]
  MEDDM208:29 Hp290 possible to be done, it can remoue mountaines (if need were)
REMOVE (3)
  SEASONS49:14 H105   That if you do, remove {withdtaw} her burning store,
  MPERS83:5   H1193 To *Bactria* his houshold did remove.
  FEVER221:7   H22   Thou hear'dst, thy rod thou didst remove
REMUS (1)
  MROMAN136:33 H3447 His Brother *Remus* there, by him was slaine,
REND (1)
  AGES43:29   H324   The windy Cholick oft my bowels rend,
RENDER (5)
  HUMOUR~~21:10~~ H38   Unto your Sister-hood, which makes us tender {render}
  MGREC129:7   H3121 To render up such kingdomes as he had
  SOREFIT221:28 H14   What shall I render to my God

11MAYB228:30 Hp259 But alas! I cannot render vnto yᵉ Lord according to all his
REMB235:23 H4 What shall I render to thy Name
RENDERED (1)
MYCHILD216:6 Hp241 me. But I rendered not to him according to yᵉ benefitt rec.
RENDRED (1)
MGREC102:28 H1998 But needs no force, 'tis rendred to his hands;
RENEW (1)
DIALOG143:4 H73 Nor no *Lancastrians,* to renew old strife;
RENEWES (1) [renews]
MROMAN138:31 H3521 Warres with the *Latins* he againe renewes,
RENEWS (1)
MPERS76:40 H938 Renews his hold; but {and} when of that bereft,
RENOWN (1)
SIDNEY149:27 H23 Yet doth thy shame (with all) purchase renown,
RENOWN'D (5) [renowned]
MGREC99:30 H1873 Sith valour, with Heroyicks is renown'd,
MGREC102:14 H1984 Whose fame throughout the world, was so renown'd;
MGREC102:30 H2000 For 'twas the seat of *Persian* Kings renown'd;
MGREC132:30 H3277 Renown'd for bounty, valour, clemency,
SIDNEY152:29 H98 *That* Sidney *dy'd the quintessence {most renown'd} of men.*
RENOWNED (5)
MASSYR55:17 H83 This great renowned Empresse, issued.
MGREC95:8 H1687 And by *Parmenio* (of renowned fame)
MGREC113:29 H2456 (The most renowned Captaine of his time)
MGREC128:6 H3079 Daughter to *Phillip,* their renowned head;
SIDNEY149:2 H2 and renowned Knight,
RENT (1) n.
ELEMEN12:32 H192 My rich commodities payes double rent.
RENT (5) v.
AGES45:21 H403 I've seen it shaken, rent, and soak'd in blood,
AGES45:22 H407 I've seen a state unmoulded, rent in twain,
MASSYR57:22 H169 So Province, after Province, rent away,
MGREC114:25 H2495 He on the wrack, his limbs in peeces rent,
MGREC130:36 H3181 And's kingdomes rent away by each Commander:
RENTS (1) [pl.]
MPERS86:30 H1346 Whose rents and customes, duly he sent in.
REPAID (4)
HUMOUR29:13 H366 Thy soothing girds shal fully be repaid;
MASSYR58:16 H201 *Arbaces* him, fully to be repaid.
MGREC123:13 H2875 He to his cost was righteously repaid.
BIRTH180:13 H23 And when thy loss shall be repaid with gains
REPAIR (2)
MPERS87:10 H1366 Seven hundred *Greeks* now further {repair for} his intents:
CONTEM173:4 H172 Eftsoon to *Neptun's* glassie Hall repair
REPAIRE (2) [repair]
MASSYR64:26 H450 And unto wealthy *Tyre* with {in} hast repaire.
MGREC109:31 H2290 His pleasure is, that forthwith he repaire
REPAIRS (1)
MGREC105:18 H2111 To them he goes, and {repairs then} looking in the Cart,
REPAY (4)
HUMOUR23:41 H149 They coole my heat, and so repay my good.

MGREC130:38	H3183	That hand is righteous still which doth repay:
DIALOG144:32	H140	And will repay it sevenfold in my lap,
1HUSB180:31	H10	Thy love is such I can no way repay,

REPEAT (1)

MEDDM203:7	Hp283	he haue good cause often to repeat that sentence, vanity of

REPEL (1)

HUMOUR32:28	H502	What's slanderous, repel; doubtful, dispute;

REPELL (1) [repel]

THEART229:10	H12	My future Doubts repell.

REPELL'D (2) [repelled]

HUMOUR29:16	H368	Thy boasted valour stoutly's been repell'd,
SEASONS52:4	H219	When cold, the sap to th' roots hath low'st repell'd;

REPELLING (1)

MGREC108:23	H2239	Repeling these two marks of honour got,

REPENT (3)

HUMOUR35:1	H597	Lest we too late, this rashnesse do repent,
MASSYR59:38	H262	He did repent, therefore it {the threatning} was not done,
MPERS76:20	H918	His {This} fruitlesse war, began late to repent;

REPINE (3)

SIDNEY150:29	H56	Oh, who was neare thee, but did sore repine;
11MAYA226:20	Hp255	of God it should bee thus. Who am I y^t I should repine at his
HOUSE236:30	H22	Far be it y^t I should repine,

REPLEAT (1) [REPLETE]

DISTEMP179:14	H2	In anguish of my heart repleat with woes,

REPLENISH (1)

MROMAN137:4	H3455	His City to replenish, men he wants,

REPLENISHED (1)

SEASONS51:17	H191	But trees with goodly fruits replenished;

REPLETE See REPLEAT

REPLIED See REPLY'D

REPLIES See REPLYS

REPLY (8)

HUMOUR25:8	H197	Thy other scoffes not worthy of reply:
HUMOUR31:3	H436	So plain a slander needeth no reply.
HUMOUR34:37	H592	To Melancholly i'le make no reply,
MPERS89:23	H1457	The smiling *Greeks* reply, they first must bait,
MGREC97:35	H1796	And in short termes, sends this reply againe;
MGREC98:9	H1811	With this reply, he was so sore {deep} enrag'd,
MGREC99:12	H1855	To which, brave {proud} *Alexander* did {made} reply,
MGREC109:38	H2297	Great *Alexander* vext at this reply,

REPLY'D (3) [replied]

HUMOUR23:33	H143	Forsooth you are to blame, he grave reply'd.
MPERS81:23	H1131	And thus reply'd unto *Mardon's* request;
MGREC94:18	H1656	Reply'd, enough, sith only hope he kept.

REPLYS (1) [replies]

MEDDM209:2	Hp291	will not let thee go replys Jacob till thou blesse me, faith is not

REPORT (8)

ELEMEN11:34	H154	Of these so common things, can make report:
ELEMEN18:17	H421	And such are Ecchoes, and report o'th gun
AGES36:14	H38	As one that cared, for a good report.
MASSYR55:10	H76	Others report, she was a vestal Nun,

MPERS69:38   H661   Then to the King he makes this true report,
MPERS86:24   H1340   She to the King, would make a fair report:
MPERS86:38   H1354   He meant {Prepares} himselfe to carry the report.
MGREC97:9   H1770   If *Curtius* be true, in his report.

REPORTED (1)
MEDDM196:6   Hp272   It is reported of the pea cock that prideing himself in his gay

REPORTS (3) [pl.]
ELEMEN13:9   H210   My bounty calls you forth to make reports,
DIALOG143:39   H108   What false reports, which nick-names did they take,
DIALOG145:2   H151   Such cruelty as all reports have past.

REPORTS (1) v.
MPERS70:34   H705   But *Zenophon* reports, he dy'd in's bed,

REPOSE (1)
SEASONS49:25   H114   Though you repose on grasse under the skye.

REPRESENT (1)
MGREC106:29   H2163   His greatnesse now he takes, to represent,

REPRESENTED (1)
MEDDM207:34   Hp289   their death, but their graue, is liuely represented before their

REPROACH See **REPROCH**

REPROBATION (1)
MEDDM206:28   Hp288   then his great worke of election and Reprobation, when we

REPROCH (1) [reproach]
MEDDM206:25   Hp287   empty beareing the reproch of his pride and folly.

REPROOF (1)
MGREC136:2   H3415   But humbly stand, some grave reproof to take:

REPROVES (1)
MGREC94:29   H1667   Reproves him, for his proud audacity;

REPUBLIQUE (1)
MEDDM199:24   Hp278   those that are eyes of a Republique, foretels a declineing

REPULSE (1)
MGREC99:18   H1861   For more repulse, the *Grecians* here abide,

REPUTE (2)
MGREC128:36   H3109   His lost repute with victorie had won;
MEDDM208:13   Hp290   to haue a good repute among good men, yet it is not that, w^ch

REQUEST (5) See also REQVEST
SEASONS52:5   H220   Beef, Brawn, and Pork, are now in great'st {great} request,
MASSYR68:16   H602   Was held in more request, {account} then now he was,
MPERS78:37   H1018   He humbly to the King then makes request,
MPERS81:23   H1131   And thus reply'd unto *Mardon's* request;
SOREFIT222:8   H27   O Lord for aye is my request

REQUESTS (1)
MGREC128:24   H3094   So therefore craves {requests} their help to take him down,

REQUIR'D (2) [required]
HUMOUR20:25   H17   But Sanguine did disdaine, what she requir'd,
HUMOUR27:38   H309   But here's {here} one thrusts her heat, where'ts not requir'd

REQUIRE (4)
SEASONS48:27   H80   More solid fruits, require a longer time.
MASSYR58:19   H204   *Belosus* the *Chaldeans* doth require,
SOREFIT222:3   H22   Thou know'st no life I did require
REMB236:4   H19   I hu¯bly this Require.

REQUIRED See REQUIR'D
REQUIRES (5)
FATHER5:10 H11 To mount so high, requires an Eagles quill:
SEASONS52:8 H223 Our pinched flesh, and empty panch {hungry mawes} requires:
MGREC119:20 H2710 The like of *Leonatus,* he requires,
MGREC128:13 H3086 Requires them therefore to take up their Armes,
MEDDM198:25 Hp276 An akeing head requires a soft pillow, and a drooping heart a
REQUISITE (1)
HUMOUR34:33 H588 But if love be, as requisite as feare,
REQUITALL (1) [requital]
PROLOG7:10 H24 A full requitall of his striving paine:
REQUITE (5)
ELEMEN9:13 H47 That so in time it might requite your paine;
MGREC106:2 H2136 Wherefore the gods requite thy kinde regard.
MGREC115:23 H2542 This great indignity for to {he should} requite.
MGREC128:14 H3087 And to requite this Traytor for those {these} harmes:
MGREC136:7 H3420 This my presumption (some now) to requite,
REQUITED (1)
MASSYR65:5 H470 Requited not the cost {loss}, the toyle, and pain.
REQUITES (1)
SEASONS50:26 H160 His fruitful crop, abundantly requites.
REQVEST (2) [request]
SON231:17 H29 And thvs hath granvnted my Reqvest
HOURS234:21 H35 O hear me Lord in this Reqvest
RESCUE (2)
DUBART155:7 H92 *To rescue him from death, Art had been able:*
MEDDM209:16 Hp291 Christ Jesus come to their rescue.
RESCUED (1)
SIDNEY150:30 H57 He rescued not with life, that life of thine,
RESEMBLES (1)
SEASONS52:9 H224 Old cold, dry age, and earth, Autumne resembles,
RESEMBLING (1)
SEASONS48:40 H91 Resembling choler, fire and middle-age;
RESEN (1)
MASSYR53:29 H19 *Resen, Caleh,* and *Rehoboth* likewise,
RESERVED (1)
DIALOG145:5 H154 The bottome dregs reserved are for me.
RESIDE (2)
MGREC101:25 H1950 Nor yet two Monarchs in one World reside;
MROMAN137:6 H3457 That wil within these strong built walls reside,
RESIDENCE (7)
HUMOUR30:32 H424 These two in one cannot have residence.
HUMOUR33:29 H543 Doth doubtlesse keep its mighty residence;
SEASONS47:30 H45 The Sun now keeps his posting residence
SEASONS47:31 H46 The Sun in *Taurus* keeps his residence,
MPERS70:19 H690 For Owles, and Satyres, makes {made} a residence;
QELIZ157:12 H80 Within that Princesse to have residence,
MEDDM203:12 Hp283 desire to make y^t his place of residence, but longs to put in at
RESIDENT (1)
HUMOUR31:37 H470 But these with you, are seldome resident.

RESIDETH (1)
SEASONS51:22 H198 In *Scorpio* resideth now the Sun,
RESIDUE (1)
MGREC135:33 H3405 The residue he stamped under's feet:
RESIGN'D (2) [resigned]
MGREC122:30 H2849 Resign'd his place, and so let all alone;
MGREC131:33 H3225 But willingly resign'd the beauteous dame:
RESIGNE (2) [resign]
MGREC125:3 H2951 To make the King by force his seat resigne;
SAMUEL228:3 H4 I here resigne into thy hand,
RESIGNED See RESIGN'D
RESIN (1)
MASSYR61:13 H318 *Resin* their valiant King, he also slew,
RESINS (1) [poss.]
MASSYR61:16 H321 When *Resins* force his borders sore did mar.
RESIST (4)
MPERS69:26 H648 Where all that doe {dare} resist, are slaughter'd down;
MGREC100:16 H1900 For no man to resist {man's there} his valour showes {Army to
MGREC104:24 H2076 Who wanting means t' resist, these wrongs abides.
MGREC122:34 H2855 And this no man durst question, or resist;
RESISTANCE (3)
MASSYR59:23 H247 few, or none, did there {it seems} resistance make; {makes:}
MPERS90:28 H1495 Town after town, with small resistance take,
MGREC110:5 H2305 Had *Alexander* such resistance seen,
RESOLUED (1) [resolved] See also RESOLV'D
MEDDM205:10 Hp286 Commonwealth, his more fixed and resolued thoughts, are like
RESOLUTE (1)
MPERS79:30 H1056 But *Xerxes* resolute, to *Thrace* goes first,
RESOLUTION (1)
HUMOUR22:6 H75 In her dul resolution, she's {so} slow.
RESOLV'D (3) [resolved] See also RESOLUED
MGREC109:40 H2299 Is now resolv'd to passe *Hidaspes* floud,
MGREC126:13 H3004 *Cassander* is resolv'd, there to remaine,
MROMAN139:35 H3561 At length resolv'd, when many years had past,
RESOLVE (1)
MYCHILD218:4 Hp243 resolve me that there is an Eternall Being. But how should I
RESOLVED (2) See also RESOLUED, RESOLV'D
MGREC107:32 H2207 But he that was resolved in his minde,
MYCHILD217:20 Hp243 knowes not, & haue sett vp my Ebenez[r]. and haue resolved
RESOLVES (2) [pl.]
MGREC93:37 H1634 His high resolves which way to bring to passe:
MGREC136:11 H3425 *And maugre all resolves, my fancy wrought*
RESOLVES (2) v.
MGREC129:8 H3122 Resolves to quit his fears by one deed done,
MGREC130:13 H3168 Resolves at last the Princesse should be slain,
RESOUND (4)
QELIZ155:31 H22 Though I resound thy greatnesse {praises} 'mongst the throng.
QELIZ156:22 H49 Her Victories in forraigne Coasts resound?
TDUDLEY166:27 H69 As joy in heaven, on earth let praise resound.
CONTEM169:23 H63 And in their kind resound their makers praise:

RESPECT (4)

MPERS73:32	H817	The old, or new, which best, in what respect,
MPERS74:31	H854	Did win him loyalty, and all respect;
MROMAN136:32	H3446	The Mistris of the World, in each respect.
DIALOG147:39	H263	Without respect of persons {person}, or of case,

RESPECTED (1)

| MGREC118:16 | H2663 | So much these Princes their owne ends respected. |

RESPECTS (1)

| MGREC99:5 | H1848 | And the distressed King no way {whit} respects; |

RESPITE (2)

| 11MAYA226:15 | Hp255 | a respite, & some ability to p^rform ye Dutyes I owe to him, and |
| 11MAYB228:23 | Hp259 | God to giue me a long Time of respite for these 4 years |

'REST (1) [the rest]

| MPERS85:1 | H1277 | 'Rest of his time in peace he did remain; |

REST (48) [remain; remainder]

ELEMEN8:27	H25	That Fire should first begin, the rest consent,
AGES37:14	H76	With wayward cryes, I did disturbe her rest;
AGES42:30	H286	My weary beast, rest from his toile can find;
AGES42:31	H287	But if I rest, the more distrest my mind.
AGES46:19	H450	There, {Where} I shal rest, til heavens shal be no more;
MASSYR61:5	H310	To rest content we must, in ignorance.
MGREC136:9	H3423	*After some dayes of rest, my restlesse heart,*
DIALOG148:27	H292	Then follows dayes of happinesse and rest,
TDUDLEY166:25	H67	Who after all his toyle, is now at rest:
TDUDLEY166:29	H71	His blessing rest on his posterity.
CONTEM172:27	H161	O could I lead my Rivolets to rest,
CHILDRN185:30	H56	And knew what thoughts there sadly rest,
CHILDRN186:17	H84	Among your young ones take your rest,
1SIMON188:14	H15	Go pretty babe, go rest with Sisters twain
MERCY189:9	H30	So with her Chidren four, she's now at rest,
MEDDM196:15	Hp273	comes he shall both take his rest and receiue his reward, the
MEDDM199:15	Hp278	Ambitious men are like hops that neuer rest climbing soe long
PILGRIM210:1	H1	As weary pilgrim, now at rest
PILGRIM210:23	H23	Oh how I long to be at rest
MYCHILD215:27	Hp240	Trouble, & I could not be at rest 'till by prayer I had confest
MYCHILD218:35	Hp244	Return o my Soul to thy Rest, vpon this Rock Xt Jesus will I
BYNIGHT220:3	H4	And hath at once both ease and Rest,
SAMUEL228:18	H19	If otherwise I goe to Rest
HOUSE236:13	H5	In silent night when rest I took

REST (24) [repose]

PROLOG7:24	H36	So 'mongst the rest, they plac'd the Arts divine:
ELEMEN11:10	H130	Of Meteors, *Ignis Fatuus,* and the rest,
ELEMEN12:7	H167	And huge great *Taurus,* longer then the rest,
ELEMEN14:32	H274	But thou art bound to me, above the rest;
HUMOUR20:27	H19	Proud Melancholy, more envious then the rest,
HUMOUR24:1	H150	Nay, th' stomach, magazeen to all the rest,
HUMOUR25:18	H207	But let her leave the rest, and {then} I presume,
HUMOUR26:14	H244	More useful then the rest, don't reason erre;
HUMOUR27:17	H288	Th' rest to our Sisters, is more pertinent.
HUMOUR30:28	H420	Yet is a bowel cal'd wel as the rest.
HUMOUR30:35	H427	Of al the rest, thou'st nothing there to do;

AGES36:31	H55	And to the rest, his reason mildly told;
AGES36:33	H57	To do as he, the rest {each one} ful soon assents,
SEASONS46:37	H15	*March, April, May,* of all the rest most faire;
MASSYR56:33	H139	The rest *Staurobates* in fight did slay.
MASSYR64:15	H439	Wise *Daniel,* and his fellows 'mongst the rest,
MPERS74:5	H830	And he whose Horse before the rest should neigh,
MPERS75:26	H883	The temple to re-build, for that did rest
MPERS78:25	H1006	Whose Gallies all the rest in neatnesse passe,
MPERS78:27	H1008	{But} Hers she kept stil, seperate from the rest,
MPERS80:12	H1079	Amongst the rest, two brothers he lost there;
MPERS81:2	H1110	Which accident, the rest affrighted so,
MPERS81:41	H1145	For other {The rest had} Weapons, they had none would {do
MPERS92:3	~~H1557~~	The rest is but conjecture of my minde.
MGREC95:34	H1713	The rest attendants, which made up no lesse;
MGREC107:4	H2179	And for the rest new wars, and travels findes,
MGREC109:37	H2296	But for the rest, his sword advise him should.
MGREC110:12	H2312	Then {When} covertly, the rest gets {get} o're else-where;
MGREC114:19	H2489	Who lov'd his Master more then did the rest,
MGREC118:8	H2655	More then to th' rest, his favour testified:
MGREC119:2	H2692	*Perdicas* took no Province, like the rest,
MGREC120:18	H2753	That by his help, the rest might low be brought:
MGREC121:3	H2781	Near'st unto him, and farthest from the rest.
MGREC121:41	H2823	And brave *Craterus* slew, amongst the rest,
MGREC122:39	H2860	Two Sons of *Alexander,* and the rest,
MGREC123:4	H2866	Who in few years the rest so over-tops,
MGREC126:5	H2996	And with the rest *Olimpias* pursues,
MGREC127:5	H3035	And *Pellas* faine to yeeld amongst the rest;
MGREC128:24	H3097	{great Antigonus} *Ptolomy,* and the rest {was} put him to flight;
MGREC131:1	H3187	{by his Example all} the rest full soon presumes, {presum'd}
MGREC132:38	H3285	That now he had out-lived all the rest:
MGREC135:30	H3402	The last more strong, and dreadfull, then the rest,
DIALOG143:41	H110	And thou, poore soule, wast {wert} jeer'd among the rest,
SIDNEY149:36	~~H23~~	But leaves the rest, as most unprofitable:
VANITY~~161:6~~	H57	{And all} The rest's {rest} but vanity, and vain we find.
CHILDRN184:15	H4	Four Cocks there were, and Hens the rest,
CHILDRN185:6	H32	That he might chant above the rest,
CHILDRN185:14	H40	Untill they'r grown, then as the rest,

REST'S (1) [rest is]

VANITY161:6	H57	{And all} The rest's {rest} but vanity, and vain we find.

RESTING (1)

SEASONS~~49:33~~	H123	Upon the grass resting your healthy limbs,

RESTLESSE (6)

HUMOUR31:26	H459	Here, there, her restlesse thoughts do ever flye;
AGES42:28	~~H285~~	For restlesse day and night, I'm rob'd of sleep,
MPERS70:4	H675	Next war, the restlesse *Cyrus* thought upon,
MPERS77:5	H944	And for revenge his heart still restlesse burnes;
MGREC93:36	H1633	Restlesse both day and night, his heart now {then} was,
MGREC136:9	H3423	*After some dayes of rest, my restlesse heart,*

RESTOR'D (1) [restored]

THEART229:1	H3	Who hath restor'd, redeem'd, recur'd

RESTORATION (1)
RESTOR229:19 H1-2 For the restoration of my dear Husband from a burning
RESTORE (9)
ELEMEN16:20 H343 Which can to life, restore a fainting heart:
MPERS85:26 H1302 But they in *Asia,* must first restore
MGREC97:29 H1790 Writes unto {To} *Alexander,* to {he would} restore
MGREC106:11 H2145 Such as submits, he doth againe restore,
MGREC109:2 H2259 Those that submit, he doth restore {give them rule} again.
MGREC109:26 H2285 His Presents all, with thanks he doth {did} restore;
SOREFIT221:24 H10 My wasted flesh thou didst restore
THEART229:17 H19 What thou bestow'st I shall restore
HANNA230:11 H4 Bles't bee thy Name who did'st restore
RESTORED (1) See also RESTOR'D
MYCHILD216:5 Hp241 and Vanity and he was entreated of me, and again restored
RESTORES (1)
MGREC110:20 H2324 Restores him, and his bounds further {farther} extends;
RESTORING (1)
MASSYR63:35 H422 Nor his restoring from old legends took;
RESTRAIN (1)
MEDDM205:25 Hp286 allseeing eye will be a bridle to restrain from evill, and a spur,
RESTRAIN'D (1) [restrained]
2LETTER182:24 H30 Restrain'd the beams of thy beloved shine,
RESTRAINED (1)
MGREC132:24 H3269 Onely restrained of his liberty;
RESTRAINING (1)
AGES43:32 H327 And the restraining lame Sciatica;
RESTRAINT (1)
MGREC105:33 H2126 Which made their long restraint, seeme to be none;
RESTS (3)
SEASONS51:29 H205 There rests, untill the Sun give it a birth:
MASSYR66:13 H519 With all these Conquests, *Babels* King rests not,
MGREC125:30 H2980 This done, the cruell Queen rests not content,
RESUM'D (1) [resumed]
MPERS71:19 H733 Who grown a man, resum'd again his state)
RESUME (2)
ELEMEN18:38 H442 And in a trice, my own nature resume.
MEDDM200:26 Hp279 to resume their former vigor and beavty in a more ample
RESUMED See RESUM'D
RESUMES (1)
MASSYR66:34 H540 {But} Resumes his Government, as heretofore,
RESURRECTION (2)
MEDDM200:24 Hp279 The spring is a liuely emblem of the resurrection, after a long
MEDDM207:36 Hp289 resurrection, and the sun approaching, of the appearing of the
RETAIN (8) See also RETAINE
HUMOUR33:33 H547 shew, hence flowes {flow} the power {pow'rs} which they retain;
HUMOUR34:14 H569 All nerves (except seven paire) to it retain;
MPERS71:4 H716 But eight whilst *Babylon,* he did retain:
MGREC131:13 H3205 Of *Asia* the Lordship shall retain.
DIALOG145:33 H182 No prelate should his Bishoprick retain;
DIALOG146:24 H210 Or any child-like love thou dost retain,
QELIZ158:5 H114 If then new things, their old form must {forms shall} retain,

CONTEM171:31 H133   Nor habitations long their names retain,
RETAIN'D (1) [retained]
 MGREC116:13   H2579   His princely qualities, had he retain'd
RETAINE (3) [retain]
 MPERS93:2   H1599   Of all, did scarce his winding sheet retaine.
 MGREC100:10   H1894   That his humanity will not retaine;
 MGREC121:30   H2812   Thus *Ptolomy* rich *Ægypt* did retaine,
RETAINED See RETAIN'D
RETAINES (1) [retains]
 MGREC133:15   H3303   And his posterity, the same retaines,
RETAINING (1)
 MASSYR55:13   H79   Her beautious face (they feign) retaining still.
RETAINS See RETAINES
RETAKES (1)
 HUMOUR30:22   H414   His mother (mine) him to her wombe retakes,
RETHORICK (1) [rhetoric] See also RHETHORICK, RHETORICK
 SIDNEY149:38 H25   Who knowes the Spels that in thy {his} Rethorick lurks?
RETIR'D (1) [retired]
 MGREC103:37   H2048   Who was retir'd, and gone to {as far as} *Media*.
RETIRE (1)
 MASSYR64:23   H447   Then into *Ægypt, Necho* did retire,
RETIRED (1) See also RETIR'D
 CONTEM170:6   H79   Here sits our Grandame in retired place,
RETORTS (1) [pl.]
 HUMOUR26:37   H267   But i'le not force retorts, nor do thee wrong,
RETREAT (2)
 ELEMEN19:40   H481   Their joyning, fighting, forcing, and retreat;
 MPERS80:34   H1101   For his retreat, to have an eye thereto:
RETROGRADE (1)
 SEASONS49:7   H98   And {Then} retrograde, now is {must be} my burning Sun.
RETURN (21) See also RETURNE
 MASSYR62:29   H374   They shal return, and *Zion* see, with blisse.
 MPERS89:15   H1449   That their return be stopt, he judg'd was best,
 MPERS89:15   H1449   To hinder their return by craft or force,
 MGREC124:6   H2911   *Cassander* for return all speed now made:
 DIALOG145:39 H188   They humbly beg return, shew their intents,
 AUTHOR177:36 H8   At thy return my blushing was not small,
 1LETTER181:14 H12   Return, return sweet *Sol* from *Capricorn;*
 1LETTER181:14 H12   Return, return sweet *Sol* from *Capricorn;*
 1LETTER181:21 H19   But when thou *Northward* to me shalt return,
 2LETTER182:25 H31   At thy return, if so thou could'st or durst
 3LETTER183:13 H15   His presence and his safe return, still wooes,
 3LETTER183:23 H25   Return my Dear, my joy, my only Love,
 CHILDRN184:23 H12   Till he return, or I do end,
 1SIMON188:12 H13   He will return, and make up all our losses,
 MEDDM208:26   Hp290   them, return with their empty pitchers ashamed,
 MYCHILD218:35 Hp244   say, Return o my Soul to thy Rest, vpon this Rock Xt Jesus will
 SON230:19   H1-2   On my Sons Return out of England. July. 17. 1661.
 HOURS235:2   H54   Return Thee what I owe.
 ACK235:17   H17   And y^t thov wilt return him back
 REMB235:28   H9   Return vnto thy Name

REMB236:10 H25 T' Return vnto thee praise

RETURN'D (4) [returned]
ELEMEN14:22 H264 As earth at first, so into earth return'd.
MPERS76:21 H919 Return'd with little honour, and lesse gaine;
MPERS76:28 H926 Return'd with wondrous losse, and honour lesse:
13MAY226:30 H6 My Svns return'd wth healing wings

RETURN'T (1) [return it]
SIDNEY152:20 H89 Which writ, she bad return't to them again.

RETURNE (1) [return]
AGES45:25 H415 But I returne, from whence I stept awry,

RETURNED (1) See also RETURN'D
MEDDM203:31 Hp284 read of ten lepers that were Cleansed, but of one that returned

RETURNES (2) [returns]
MPERS77:4 H943 *Darius* light, he {yet} heavie, home returnes,
MEDDM204:9 Hp284 great receipts, call for great returnes, the more that any man is

RETURNING (1)
MYCHILD217:10 Hp242 had great xper^c of Gods hearing my prayers, and returning

RETURNS (3) See also RETURNES
MASSYR62:17 H362 Returns triumphant Victor to his soyl;
MGREC~~124:6~~ H2911 And so he quick returns thus well appaid,
CONTEM171:23 H126 A Spring returns, and they more youthfull made;

REVEAL (1)
HUMOUR34:19 H574 Some worthy {curious} learned *Crooke* may these reveal,

REVEALE (3) [reveal]
ELEMEN18:13 H417 Nay, what are words, which doe reveale the mind?
HUMOUR32:3 H477 My prudence, judgement, now I might reveale,
AGES37:4 H66 Whose mean beginning, blushing cann't reveale,

REVEALED (1)
MYCHILD218:8 Hp244 If ever this God hath revealed himself it mvst bee in his word,

REVELL'D (1) [revelled]
MASSYR58:2 H187 Ne're shew'd his face, but revell'd with his Whores,

REVELLING (3)
MASSYR59:6 H230 Who revelling in Cups, sung care away,
MASSYR67:30 H576 To banquetting, and revelling now falls,
MGREC102:25 H1995 Whilst revelling at *Babylon,* he lyes,

REVENGE (7)
MASSYR55:29 H95 Or else she sought, revenge for *Menons* fall:
MPERS70:28 H699 Which to revenge, she hires a mighty power,
MPERS77:5 H944 And for revenge his heart still restlesse burnes;
MPERS88:34 H1427 After this trance, revenge, new spirits blew,
MGREC105:23 H2116 The just revenge of this his wofull end;
MGREC125:40 H2990 With rage, and with revenge, he's hurried on,
SIDNEY152:13 H82 For {Then} to revenge his {this} wrong, themselves ingage,

REVENGETH (1)
MGREC117:6 H2613 For by that hand, which still revengeth bloud,

REVENUES (2) [pl.]
MPERS75:29 H886 Out of his owne revenues beares the charge;
MPERS86:31 H1347 The King finding, revenues now amended;

REVERENCE (2)
MGREC99:37 H1880 Whom with great reverence *Alexander* greets;
MGREC106:31 H2165 And such as shew'd but reverence before,

REVERENT (1)
DIALOG144:26 ~~H135~~ Their reverent cheeks, did beare the glorious markes
REVERSE (2)
AGES45:12 ~~H394~~ Could once reverse, their shamefull destiny.
AGES~~45:12~~ H394 Could length their dayes or once reverse their fate
REVERSED (1)
MEDDM208:31 Hp290 reversed the order of nature, quenched the violence of the fire,
REVIEW'D (1) [reviewed]
DUBART153:4 H8 My dazled sight of late, review'd thy lines,
REVIUE (1) [revive]
FAINTING222:20 H10 My feblee Spirit thou did's reviue
REVIV'D (3) [revived]
MGREC108:11 H2227 And now reviv'd with hopes, held up their head,
DUBART155:9 H94 *But Fame, out-living both, he is reviv'd.*
QELIZ157:27 H95 Her ashes not reviv'd more Phoenix she;
REVIVE (3) See also REVIUE
AGES44:40 H373 In midst of greifs, I saw some {our} hopes revive,
SEASONS~~46:35~~ H13 Fit to revive, the nummed earth from death.
CONTEM168:28 H35 Thy heat from death and dulness doth revive:
REVOAKE (1) [revoke]
MASSYR58:38 H221 And their Taxations sore, all to revoake,
REVOCABLE (1)
DUBART155:6 H91 *And Natures Law; had it been revocable,*
REVOK'D (1) [revoked]
SICKNES178:23 H6 this cannot be revok'd.
REVOKE See REVOAKE
REVOLTERS (1) [pl.]
MGREC103:21 H2032 For such revolters false, what Prince will {King can} trust:
REVOLTING (2)
MPERS83:29 H1217 He first, war with revolting *Ægypt* made.
MPERS~~85:14~~ H1290 Disquiet {Revolting} Egypt, 'gainst this King rebells,
REVOLTS (1)
MPERS85:21 H1297 Revolts, having treasure, and people gain'd:
REVOLUTION (1)
QELIZ158:4 H113 Untill the heavens great revolution:
REWARD (12)
FATHER6:7 H41 Who must reward a theife, but with his due.
MGREC99:33 H1876 Why didst not heap up honour, and reward?
MGREC100:41 H1925 He prayes the immortall gods, for to {they would} reward
MGREC106:1 H2135 Thy pitty, and compassion to reward,
MGREC113:20 H2447 As he would ne're confesse, nor could {yet} reward,
MGREC113:37 H2464 Had his reward most cruel, and unjust.
MGREC130:16 H3171 They for their great reward no better speed,
DDUDLEY167:15 H12 *And as they did, so they reward did find:*
1HUSB180:32 H11 The heavens reward thee manifold I pray.
MEDDM196:15 Hp273 comes he shall both take his rest and receiue his reward, the
MEDDM204:17 Hp285 doth many times, both reward and punish for one and ye same
MEDDM204:24 Hp285 wth Jehu's reward, wch will end in punishment
REWARDED (3)
MGREC116:22 H2588 And curious Artists evermore rewarded.
MEDDM204:18 Hp285 as we see in Jehu, he is rewarded wth a kingdome to the fourth

MEDDM204:21 Hp285 of Jehu, he was rewarded for the matter, and yet punished for

REWARDS (1) [pl.]
MGREC111:10 H2355 With rich rewards, he sent them home again,

REX (2)
MASSYR55:6 H72 She like a brave Virago, play'd the rex,
QELIZ156:8 H35 That women wisdome lack to play the Rex;

REZIN (1)
MASSYR61:22 H327 From *Rezin,* and from *Pekah* set me free:

REZIN'S (1) [rezin is]
MASSYR61:25 H330 When *Rezin's* slain, his Army over-thrown,

RHEA (1)
MROMAN136:24 H3438 Whom vestall *Rhea,* into {to} th' world did bring

RHETHORICK (3) [rhetoric] See also RETHORICK, RHETHORIC
PROLOG6:32 H15 From School-boyes tongue, no Rhethorick we expect,
MPERS79:7 H1029 I Rhethorick want, to poure out execration:
SIDNEY149:15 H14 Thy {His} Rhethorick it struck *Polimnia* dead,

RHETORICK (2) [rhetorick] See also RETHORICK, RHETHORICK
AGES44:14 H347 It's not my Learning, Rhetorick, wit so large,
MPERS81:27 H1135 With Rhetorick, t' gain better complement:

RHYMES See RIMES

RICH (33)
FATHER5:7 H8 Their worth so shines, in those rich lines you show.
ELEMEN11:12 H132 The rich I oft make poore, the strong I maime,
ELEMEN11:33 H153 The rich and {the} poore, wise, foole, and every sort,
ELEMEN11:37 H157 My cities famous, rich, and populous,
ELEMEN12:32 H192 My rich commodities payes double rent.
ELEMEN15:23 H305 But what's the wealth that my rich Ocean brings?
ELEMEN15:34 H316 Was ever gem so rich found in thy trunke?
ELEMEN15:40 H322 Thy gallant rich perfuming Amber-greece:
ELEMEN19:28 H472 How many rich fraught vessells, have I split?
AGES37:30 H92 How to be rich, or great, I did not carke;
AGES41:33 H249 If rich, I'm urged then to gather more.
AGES41:36 H252 If rich, I'm urged then to gather more,
AGES42:38 H294 If to be rich, or great, it was my fate;
AGES46:6 H437 To great, to rich, to poore, to young, or old,
SEASONS48:10 H63 Wherein the earth, is clad in rich aray:
MASSYR62:23 H368 Or how they fare, rich, poor, or ill, or wel;
MASSYR64:17 H441 The temple of rich ornaments defac'd,
MASSYR66:17 H523 A totall Conquest of rich *Ægypt* makes,
MASSYR67:17 H563 (Within which broiles, rich *Crœsus* was engaged,)
MPERS78:32 H1013 Whither rich *Pithyus* comes, *Xerxes* to greet;
MGREC93:13 H1610 Shee to the rich *Molossians* {*Epirus* warlike} King, was
MGREC96:30 H1750 Had not been spoile, and booty rich enough,
MGREC99:2 H1845 All those rich Kingdoms large, which {that} doe abide
MGREC101:10 H1935 With fertile *Ægypt,* and rich *Syria,*
MGREC103:6 H2017 Though *Babylon* was rich, and *Sushan* too;
MGREC111:10 H2355 With rich rewards, he sent them home again,
MGREC121:30 H2812 Thus *Ptolomy* rich *Ægypt* did retaine,
MGREC132:31 H3278 Rich *Ægypt* left, and what else he had won
QELIZ155:29 H20 The acclamations of the poore, as rich;
QELIZ157:21 H89 But that she was a rich *Ægyptian* Queen;

TDUDLEY166:5	H47	Gave his in charge, that Jewel rich to prize.
CONTEM167:28	H5	Were gilded o're by his rich golden head.
FLESH177:9	H90	The Gates of Pearl, both rich and clear,

RICHARD (2)

DIALOG142:17	H46	That second *Richard* must be clapt i'th' Tower?
DIALOG143:3	H72	No *Edward, Richard,* to lose rule, and life,

RICHER (1)

DUBART153:8	H12	Which Rayes, darting upon some richer ground,

RICHES (24) [pl.]

AGES39:5	H148	Declare some greater riches are within;
AGES41:38	H255	If not, yet wealth, {riches} Nobility can gain.
AGES42:18	H276	In meannesse, greatnesse, riches, poverty;
AGES43:15	H307	Then heapt up gold, and riches as the clay;
AGES45:11	H393	But neither favour, riches, title, State,
SEASONS50:4	H138	The Medows of their burden {riches} to dispoyl;
MGREC103:5	H2016	None like to this in riches did abound.
MGREC103:22	H2033	The pleasures and the riches of this town,
MGREC106:12	H2146	And {he} makes their riches, and their honours more;
MGREC115:31	H2550	His honours, and his riches, to augment
MGREC133:25	H3315	Such riches too As Rome did never see:
MGREC133:33	H3323	Tells of their warres, their names, their riches, fates;
MGREC135:19	H3391	Their Crownes, their Titles, riches beares by force.
DUBART153:17	H21	Who sees the riches of some famous Fayre;
DUBART154:27	H72	Unto each man his riches are {is} assign'd,
QELIZ158:1	H110	Full fraught with honour, riches, and with dayes:
VANITY160:2	H12	He heaps up riches, and he heaps up sorrow,
FLESH175:30	H30	For riches dost thou long full sore?
FLESH176:19	H59	Thy riches are to me no bait,
1HUSB180:28	H7	Or all the riches that the East doth hold.
MERCY188:29	H15	Was ignorant what riches thou hadst lost.
MEDDM197:28	Hp275	to mount to heaven clog'd wth the Cares and riches of this Life,
MEDDM208:18	Hp290	Well doth the Apostle call riches deceitfull riches, and they

RICHEST (4)

MASSYR64:2	H426	The richest, and the dreadfull'st to behold;
MPERS70:15	H686	Upon earths richest spoyles his Souldiers preys;
MGREC102:37	H2007	And furniture, the richest of {in} all Lands,
DAVID159:15	H30	Who cloathed you in cloath of richest dye,

RICHLY (3)

CONTEM167:27	H4	The trees all richly clad, yet void of pride,
CONTEM168:4	H14	That hath this under world so richly dight:
HOUSE237:19	H49	W^th glory richly furnished

RICHMONDS (1) [poss.]

DIALOG142:20	H49	Must *Richmonds* ayd, the Nobles now implore,

RID (5)

AGES43:13	H306	There set, I rid my selfe straight out of hand.
MASSYR60:37	H302	Who to be rid of such a guest, was glad;
MPERS72:4	H755	He strait to rid himself of causlesse fears,
FEVER220:25	H5	Then didst thou rid me out.
RESTOR229:22	H5	Then did'st thou rid me out,

RIDE (3)

HUMOUR21:38	H66	She'l ride a Horse as bravely, as the best,

AGES35:33	H19	His hobby striding, did not ride, but run,
AGES36:10	H34	He seems to flye, or swim, and not to ride.

RIFE (2)

ELEMEN19:13	H458	So when'ts corrupt, mortality is rife.
SEASONS49:27	H116	Whilst they're imbroyl'd in Wars, and troubles ripe; {rife:}

RIFLED (1)

MGREC103:10	H2021	For when the Souldiers, had rifled their pleasure,

RIG'D (1) [rigged]

MGREC132:20	H3258	A mighty Navy rig'd, an Army stout,

RIGHT (32)

ELEMEN11:26	H146	Which none ere gave, nor {or} you could claime of right,
HUMOUR20:23	H15	Choler {first} hotly claim'd, right by her mother,
HUMOUR22:11	H80	But {Now} let's give, cold, white, Sister Flegme her right.
HUMOUR24:21	H170	Then let my sisters, right their injury.
HUMOUR25:12	H201	And though thou'st us'd me, with opprobrious spight, {right:}
HUMOUR25:13	H202	My ingenuity must give thee right.
HUMOUR27:11	H282	But by what right, nor do'st, nor canst thou name;
HUMOUR30:19	H411	You'l say, here none shal ere disturbe my right;
HUMOUR30:29	H421	The Liver, Stomach, owes it {their} thanks of right:
AGES37:35	H97	Make strong my selfe, and turne aside weak right.
AGES43:8	H305	I might possess that throne which was their right;
MASSYR57:2	H149	His Mother dead, *Ninias* obtains his right,
MASSYR59:9	H233	Bereft of wits, were slaughtered down right.
MPERS76:34	H932	Where *Grecians* prov'd themselves right Souldiers, stout;
MPERS83:4	H1192	The grieved Prince finding nor right, nor love,
MPERS85:16	H1292	with the *Greeks,* and so maintains {maintain} their right,
MPERS86:20	H1336	To win by force, what right could not obtain.
MGREC94:5	H1639	This done, against all {both} right, and natures laws,
MGREC117:33	H2640	By Natures right, these had enough to claime,
MGREC125:34	H2984	Digg'd up his brother dead, 'gainst natures right,
MGREC132:6	H3239	Who took away his now pretended right:
DIALOG143:32	H101	The Gospel is trod {troden} down, and hath no right;
DIALOG145:22	H171	To crush the proud, and right to each man deal.
DIALOG146:35	H221	That Right may have its right, though't be with blood;
DUBART154:39	H84	Ile leave thy praise, to those shall doe thee right,
QELIZ156:26	H53	*Don Anthony* in's right for {there} to install;
TDUDLEY166:37	H79	*To Truth a shield, to right a Wall,*
VERSES183:37	H4	Who can of right better demand the same?
VERSES184:7	H11	Where nothing's to be had Kings loose their right
MEDDM205:21	Hp286	stands right there.
MYCHILD218:19	Hp244	yet why may not yᵉ popish Relign. bee yᵉ right, They haue

RIGHTEOUS (2) See also RIGHTEOVS

MASSYR66:38	H544	This King among the righteous had a part:
MGREC130:38	H3183	That hand is righteous still which doth repay:

RIGHTEOUSLY (2)

MGREC123:13	H2875	He to his cost was righteously repaid.
DIALOG144:31	H139	{saw} their cause, and wrongs {hath} judg'd righteously,

RIGHTEOUSNES (3) [righteousness]

MEDDM202:30	Hp282	of righteousnes will arise wᵗʰ healing in his wings.
MEDDM206:10	Hp287	but one Christ, who is the Sun of righteousnes, in the midest of
MEDDM208:1	Hp289	righteousnes, at whose comeing they shall all rise out of their

RIGHTEOUSNESS (1)
TDUDLEY166:26 H68   His hoary head in righteousness was found:
RIGHTEOUSNESSE (3) [righteousness]
SEASONS51:32 H208   But when the Son of Righteousnesse drawes nigh,
DIALOG148:4   H269   When truth and righteousnesse they thus shall nourish.
MEDDM202:14 Hp282 it pleased him, whose will is the perfect rule of righteousnesse,
RIGHTEOUSSNES (1) [righteousness]
MEDDM200:28 Hp279 when the Sun of righteoussnes shall appear those dry bones
RIGHTEOVS (1) [righteous]
MYCHILD216:36 Hp242 and Bonds vpon my Soul to pᵣform his righteovs comands.
RIGHTEST (1)
DIALOG~~148:33~~ H298   Farewell dear mother, Parliament, {rightest cause} prevail,
RIGHTS (1) [pl.]
MASSYR67:26 H572   The Noble *Persians,* {Persian} to invade his rights.
RILS (1) [pl.]
HUMOUR26:26 H256   Through th' warme, blew conduits of my veinal rils;
RIMES (1) [rhymes]
FATHER5:26   H27   Their discord may {doth} appear, by these harsh rimes.
RING (2) [circle]
HUMOUR35:9   H605   A golden Ring, the Posey, *Unity:*
MGREC118:6   H2653 Because his Master gave to him his Ring,
RING (1) [sound]
MPERS74:14   H837   {And joyfull} acclamations ecchoes in the aire; {shrill they ring,}
RIOTING See RYOTING
RIPE (9)
ELEMEN18:27   H431   I {help to} ripe the corne, I turne the grinding mill;
AGES41:23   H240   When my Wilde Oates, were sown, and ripe, & mown,
SEASONS49:27 H116   Whilst they're imbroyl'd in Wars, and troubles ripe; {rife:}
SEASONS50:27 H161   Now's ripe the Pear, Pear-plumbe, and Apricock,
SEASONS51:2   H176   The Vintage now is ripe, the Grapes are prest,
SEASONS51:8   H182   The Figge is {are} ripe, the Pomgranet also,
SIDNEY150:26   H53   E're he was ripe; his thred cut *Atropos.*
TDUDLEY166:18 H60   Now fully ripe, as shock of wheat that's grown,
ELIZB187:6   H14   And Plumbs and Apples throughly ripe do fall,
RIPENING (1)
ELEMEN10:23   H98   The Summer ripening season I do claime;
RIPER (2)
AGES37:21   H83   In that which riper age did scorn, and slight:
MGREC124:28 H2935 Thinks to enthrone the Prince when riper grown;
RISE (17)
ELEMEN12:30   H190   Send forth your well man'd ships, where sun doth rise.
ELEMEN14:16   H258   Which rise like mighty {tumbling} billowes on the lands: {Land}
AGES38:1   H104   My quarrells, not for Diadems did rise;
MASSYR53:30   H20   By him, to Cities eminent did rise;
MASSYR56:16   H122   Whose stately top, beyond {above} the clouds did rise;
MPERS82:8   H1155 The signall of their victory doth {did} rise;
MPERS84:11   H1239 Of *Hamans* fall, and *Mordica's* great rise;
MPERS91:2   H1510 height, {*Spartan* State} which now apace doth {so fast did} rise;
MGREC98:36   H1838 The dangers, difficulties, like to rise;
MGREC~~101:34~~ H1960 By Captains twice is call'd before hee'l rise,
MGREC104:8   H2060 The little hope, of profit like to rise.

MGREC117:12	H2619	The Leopard down, his {the} four wings 'gan to rise,
MGREC135:24	H3396	The Stone out of the Mountaine then did rise,
DIALOG142:14	H43	Doe Barons rise, and side against their King?
QELIZ158:3	H112	No more shall rise or set such {so} glorious Sun,
MEDDM208:1	Hp289	at whose comeing they shall all rise out of their beds, The
PILGRIM210:36	H36	a glorious body it shall rise

RISEN (1)

ELEMEN~~11:1~~	H121	That *Phaenix* from her Bed, is risen New.

RISETH (1)

SEASONS50:40	H174	The tenth {twelfth} of this, *Sol* riseth in the Line,

RISING (2)

MPERS74:4	H829	Upon a Green to meet, by rising Sun;
MGREC105:37	H2130	As men, the rising, setting Sun shall see.

RITES (2) [pl.]

MASSYR54:10	H37	So oft profanely offered sacred rites;
MROMAN137:29	H3480	Religious Rites, and Customs instituted,

RIVER (15)

ELEMEN15:12	H294	Then seeks me out, in River and in Well;
MASSYR56:9	H115	That like a river, long it did abide.
MASSYR56:32	H138	The River *Indus* swept them half away,
MASSYR59:19	H243	But in the third, the River prov'd his friend,
MASSYR59:25	H249	That when the River prov'd their enemy,
MPERS70:11	H682	He cuts those banks, and let the river out;
MGREC94:37	H1675	To th' river *Granicke, Alexander* hyes,
MGREC107:24	H2199	At length, they came to th' River *Oxus* brink,
MGREC~~107:29~~	H2204	How to passe {the River} over, and gaine {to} the other Land;
MGREC108:27	H2243	From hence he to *Jaxartis* river goes,
MGREC108:35	H2251	Upon this River banck in seventeen dayes,
MGREC109:12	H2271	To th' river *Indus* next, his course he bends,
MGREC110:7	H2307	Within this spacious river, deep, and wide,
FLESH177:13	H94	A Chrystal River there doth run,
3LETTER183:29	H31	And like the Mullets in one River glide,

RIVERS (8) [pl.]

ELEMEN10:13	H88	Nay more then these, Rivers 'mongst stars are found,
ELEMEN15:22	H304	But {And} such I am, in Rivers, showers and springs;
ELEMEN16:4	H327	Then I have Fountaines, Rivers, Lakes and Ponds:
ELEMEN16:7	H330	The *Ponticke, {Aegean} Caspian,* Golden Rivers fine. {five,}
ELEMEN17:20	H384	Mine Ice doth glaze *Europs* big'st Rivers o're,
SEASONS52:36	H251	The Rivers now do {'gin to} ope, and {the} Snows do {to} melt,
CONTEM172:11	H147	Now thought the rivers did the trees excel,
1HUSB180:29	H8	My love is such that Rivers cannot quench,

RIVERS (8) [poss.]

MPERS90:8	H1481	Nor rivers course, nor *Persians* force could stay,
CONTEM172:7	H143	Close sate I by a goodly Rivers side,

RIVOLETS (1) [pl.]

CONTEM172:27	H161	O could I lead my Rivolets to rest,

ROAM (1)

AUTHOR178:10	H20	In this array, 'mongst Vulgars mayst thou roam,

ROARERS (1) [pl.]

AGES40:14	H195	Dayes, {Whole} nights, with Ruffins, Roarers, Fidlers spend,

ROARING (3)
ELEMEN8:19	H17	That roaring in it came, and with its source
ELEMEN17:2	H366	And with my wasting floods, and roaring torrent;
QELIZ155:24	H15	'Mongst hundred Hecatombs of roaring Verse,

ROB (2)
MPERS80:39	H1106	To rob the wealthy Temple of *Apollo,*
MPERS89:14	H1448	And rob him both of Scepter, and of Crown;

ROB'D (2) [robbed]
AGES42:28	H285	For restlesse day and night, I'm rob'd of sleep,
MASSYR57:5	H152	To sit, thus long (obscure) wrong'd {rob'd} of his seat;

ROBE (2)
MASSYR68:6	H592	With guifts of Scarlet robe, and Chaines {Chain} of gold,
MGREC111:36	H2381	Upon his Monument his Robes {Robe} he spread,

ROBES (7) [pl.]
SEASONS49:21	H112	With robes thereof, Kings have been dignifi'd.
MASSYR61:19	H324	The temple robes, so to fulfill his ends,
MGREC96:12	H1732	With Robes and Crowne, most glorious to behold.
MGREC99:36	H1879	Him in his Priestly Robes, high *Jaddus* meets,
MGREC106:33	H2167	With *Persian* Robes, himselfe doth dignifie,
MGREC111:36	H2381	Upon his Monument his Robes {Robe} he spread,
FLESH177:1	H82	But Royal Robes I shall have on,

ROCHEL (2)
AGES45:5	H389	I've seen designes at {for} *Ree,* and *Cades* {*Rochel*} crost,
DIALOG144:40	H148	I saw strong *Rochel* yeelding to her foe,

ROCHETS (1) [pl.]
DIALOG147:14	H240	Copes, Rochets, Crossiers, and such {empty} trash,

ROCK (3)
SEASONS50:28	H162	The Prince of Plumbs, whose stone is {as} hard as Rock.
MEDDM198:6	Hp276	ouer their heads he then leads them to the Rock wch is higher
MYCHILD218:35	Hp244	o my Soul to thy Rest, vpon this Rock Xt Jesus will I build

ROCKS (8) [pl.]
ELEMEN19:29	H472	Some upon sands, some upon rocks have hit.
AGES43:4	H299	That over flats, and sands, and rocks I hurried,
MPERS80:41	H1108	Two mighty Rocks, brake from *Parnassus* Hil,
MPERS90:7	H1480	O're mountains, rocks, and hils, as Lions bold;
CONTEM172:8	H144	Where gliding streams the Rocks did overwhelm;
CONTEM172:20	H155	Nor is it rocks or shoals that can obstruct thy pace.
MEDDM198:34	Hp277	shall rather choose to be buried vnder rocks and mountains
PILGRIM210:16	H16	nor stumps nor rocks cause him to fall

ROD (5)
MYCHILD217:7	Hp242	child, that no longer then the rod has been on my back
FEVER221:7	H22	Thou hear'dst, thy rod thou didst remove
SOREFIT221:30	H16	Even for his mercyes in his rod,
MYSOUL224:27	H3	Walk in his Law, and kisse his Rod
RESTOR229:32	H15	He taught thee by his rod.

RODE (1)
ELEMEN14:8	H250	Who bravely rode into my yawning chinke.

RODS (2) [pl.]
MGREC94:33	H1671	To whip him well with rods, and then {so} to bring,
WHAT224:12	H12	And sanctefye their rods,

ROE (1)

  AGES45:37   H427   My comely legs, as nimble as the Roe,

ROLL (1) See also ROWL

  HOURS234:8   H22   I'le on thy mercyes roll!

ROLLING See ROWLING

ROLLS (1) [pl.]

  SIDNEY152:21   H90   So *Sydney's* fame, I leave to *England's* Rolls,

ROMAN (9)

  ELEMEN~~14:4~~   H247   So did that Roman, far more stout then wise,

  ELEMEN15:37   H319   The *Roman* Purple, double *Tirian* dye.

  MGREC133:24   H3313   {T'} *Emillius* the *Roman* Generall,

  MGREC133:27   H3317   kingdomes {Empire was} were subdu'd by {to} th' *Roman* state.

  MGREC~~134:2~~   H3335   By *Scipio* the Roman General;

  MROMAN136:19 H3433   The *Roman* Monarchy,

  MROMAN137:38 H3489   *Tullus Hostilius,* was third *Roman* King,

  MROMAN139:11 H3539   *Roman* King. {of the Romans}

  MROMAN139:24 ~~H3551~~   *The end of the* Roman *Monarchy,*

ROMANE (2) [roman]

  MGREC134:15   H3346   Him *Lucullus,* the *Romane* Generall

  MGREC135:17   H3389   Then came the *Romane,* like a raging flood,

ROMANS (7) [pl.]

  SEASONS50:2   H136   By *Romans* celebrated to his fame.

  MGREC135:7   H3379   Which by the *Romans* had its destiny.

  MROMAN137:14 H3465   Their Daughters by the *Romans* then were caught,

  MROMAN137:18 H3469   The *Romans* now more potent 'gin to grow,

  MROMAN138:5   H3495   The *Romans* Conquereth, others {other} yeeld the day,

  MROMAN138:7   H3497   The *Romans* sore incens'd, their Generall slay,

  MROMAN139:11 H3539   *Roman* King. {of the Romans}

ROMANS (1) [pl.; poss.]

  MROMAN138:3   H3493   Three call'd *Horatii,* on *Romans* side,

ROME (13)

  ELEMEN14:7   ~~H250~~   And *Rome,* her *Curtius,* can't forget I think;

  AGES45:3   H381   I've seen from *Rome,* an execrable thing,

  MGREC~~133:25~~   H3315   Such riches too As Rome did never see:

  MROMAN137:17 H3468   And *Sabins,* as one people, dwelt in *Rome.*

  MROMAN138:10 H3500   But now demolished, to make *Rome* great.

  MROMAN138:12 H3502   Leaves {Left} *Rome,* in wealth and power, still growing high.

  MROMAN138:16 H3506   *Rome* he inlarg'd, new built againe the wall,

  MROMAN138:27 H3517   Is entertain'd at *Rome,* and in short time,

  MROMAN138:33 H3523   To such rude triumphs, as young *Rome* then had,

  MROMAN139:20 H3548   The *Tarquins* they from *Rome* with speed {by force} expell,

  DIALOG143:34 H103   That Pope, had hope, to find *Rome* here againe;

  DIALOG148:6   H271   To sack proud *Rome,* and all her vassalls rout:

  DIALOG148:20   H285   And do to *Gog,* as thou hast done to *Rome.*

ROMES (5) [poss.]

  HUMOUR29:34   H385   And if *Marcellus* bold, be call'd *Romes* sword,

  SEASONS50:16   H150   *Romes* second Emperour of peaceful {lasting} fame;

  MROMAN136:23 H3437   Stout *Romulus, Romes* Founder, and first King,

  DIALOG147:17   H243   We hate *Romes* Whore, with all her trumperie.

ROMES (1) [rome is]

  ELEMEN11:8   H128   Which made a *Cæsar,* (Romes) the worlds proud head,

ROMISH (1)

DIALOG144:27 ~~H135~~ Of stinking, stigmatizing, Romish Clerkes;

ROMULUS (4)

MROMAN136:23 H3437 Stout *Romulus, Romes* Founder, and first King,

MROMAN136:31 H3445 A Citty faire did *Romulus* erect:

MROMAN137:11 H3462 So *Romulus* was forc'd this course to take.

MROMAN137:20 H3471 But *Romulus* then comes unto his end,

ROOF (1)

HOUSE237:3 H33 Vnder thy roof no gvest shall sitt,

ROOM (3)

AGES43:20 H315 I judge, I should have room, in all mens hearts.

MPERS~~92:5~~ H1562 Inthron'd by *Bogoas* in the room of th' other:

MGREC~~122:31~~ H2850 In's stead, {room} the Souldiers chose *Antipater,*

ROOME (4) [room]

MPERS74:17 H840 They then {all} attend him, to his royall roome,

MPERS84:7 H1235 And a {one} more worthy, placed in her roome,

MGREC95:23 H1702 But sets {Yet set} one in his roome, and ran away.

MEDDM202:33 Hp282 obiects enter, yet is not that spacious roome filled neither

ROOST (1)

3LETTER183:28 H30 And like two Turtles roost within one house,

ROOT (2) n.

MERCY188:26 H12 My bruised heart lies sobbing at the Root,

MEDDM207:16 Hp288 or feare, or greife that lyes at the root wch in great part

ROOT (1) v.

DIALOG147:11 H237 To root out Prelates, {Popelings} head, tail, branch, and rush.

ROOTS (6) [pl.]

ELEMEN~~12:35~~ H195 Besides the use you have {of roots}, of Hearbs and Plants,

ELEMEN15:11 H293 He knowes such sweets, lyes not in earths dry roots,

SEASONS47:12 H28 Now digs, then sows, his hearbs, his flowers, and roots,

SEASONS50:31 H165 Like good Old Age, whose younger juycie roots,

SEASONS52:4 ~~H219~~ When cold, the sap to th' roots hath low'st repell'd;

DIALOG144:16 H126 These be the bitter fountains, heads, and roots,

ROSE (5) n.

MPERS82:37 H1184 To see that face, where Rose and Lilly stood,

SIDNEY150:25 H52 Ah, in his blooming prime, death pluckt this Rose,

QELIZ158:9 H118 *O'th' Damask Rose, sprung from the white and red,*

QELIZ158:11 H120 *This Rose is withered, once so lovely faire,*

QELIZ158:12 H121 *On neither tree did grow such Rose before,*

ROSE (5) v.

ELEMEN11:1 H117 The Army through my helpe victorious rose;

MASSYR55:19 H85 Whence rose that fable, she by birds was fed.

MPERS88:7 H1400 Was gather'd by the dust that rose from thence:

MROMAN139:19 H3547 With *Junius Brutus* rose, and being strong,

MYCHILD216:9 Hp241 wch my heart rose, But after I was convinced it was ye way of

ROSES (5) [pl.]

AGES36:5 H29 Garland of Roses, Pinks, and Gilliflowers,

SEASONS48:16 H69 Except the double Pinks, and matchlesse Roses.

SEASONS49:34 H127 This Month the Roses are distill'd in Glasses,

DIALOG142:19 H48 That from the red, white pricking Roses sprung?

DIALOG143:9 H78 No need of *Tudor,* Roses to unite,

ROSIE (2)

HUMOUR24:35	H184	A rosie cheek'd {cheek} musitian, thou know'st wel.
HUMOUR29:10	H363	Faire rosie Sister, so might'st thou scape free,

ROT (2)

AGES46:20	H451	And when this flesh shal rot, and be consum'd,
ELIZB187:5	H13	By nature Trees do rot when they are grown.

ROTS (1)

HUMOUR28:7	H319	The Lungs, she rots, the body weares away,

ROTTEN (1)

ELEMEN17:1	H365	Of rotten sheep, lean kine, and mildew'd grain.

ROUGH See ROVGH

ROUND (7) See also ROVND

ELEMEN15:19	H301	That she can spare, when Nations round are poore.
SEASONS52:39	H255	And thus the year in circle runneth round:
MPERS70:17	H688	Forty five mile {miles} this City scarce could round;
MPERS70:39	H710	Two *Sythian* bowes, a sword, and target round;
MGREC102:13	H1983	With greedy eyes, he views this City round,
MGREC108:38	H2254	And furlongs sixty could not {but} round the same.
QELIZ156:39	H66	Her Sea-men through all straights the world did round,

ROUT (1) [crowd]

MPERS70:10	H681	That night *Belshazzar* feasted all his rout,

ROUT (2) [defeat]

MPERS73:21	H808	Their {Then} Forces instantly they raise, and rout,
DIALOG148:6	H271	To sack proud *Rome,* and all her vassalls rout:

ROUTED (1)

MASSYR67:18	H564	His Army routed, and himselfe there slain,

ROUTS (1)

MPERS70:30	H701	There routs his Hoast, himself she prisoner takes,

ROVERS (1)

MPERS86:36	H1352	The Rovers in *Pisidia,* should drive out.

ROVGH (1) [rough]

28AUG226:11	Hp254	vnwilling to come tho: by so rovgh a Messenger.

ROVND (1) [round]

FEVER220:22	H2	When Sorrowes had begyrt me rovnd,

ROW (1)

ELEMEN12:38	H198	And Oares to row, when both my sisters failes?

ROWL (1)

FEVER221:2	H17	I on thy Mercyes Rowl.

ROWLING (1)

ELEMEN16:1	H324	With rowling graines of purest massy gold:

ROXAN (2)

MGREC117:31	H2638	And *Roxan* faire, whom late he married,
MGREC118:4	H2651	And th' unborn babe of *Roxan* be proclaim'd;

ROXANE (1)

MGREC129:10	H3124	This *Roxane* for her beautie all commend,

ROYAL (11)

HUMOUR34:13	H568	It is the substitute o'th royal Brain,
AGES45:4	H386	A royal one by gifts from strangers hands
MASSYR64:14	H438	Children of Royal bloud, unblemish'd youth;
MPERS69:14	H636	Whose Ancestors, were royal in degree;
MPERS71:16	H730	And all of Royal bloud that came to hand,

MPERS~~76:6~~	H904	Which two then to assaile, his {royal} Camp was bold:
MPERS~~84:17~~	H1253	Such entertainment {royal bounty} with this {his} Prince he
MGRECY ~~110:19~~	H2323	His fortitude his Kingly {royal} foe commends;
MGREC~~128:20~~	H3093	And Lord o'th' City {royal} *Susha* did remain.
MGREC130:41	H3186	*Demetrius* is first, that so assumes, {the royal stile asum'd,}
FLESH177:1	H82	But Royal Robes I shall have on,

ROYALL (20) [royal]

AGES45:8	~~H390~~	A Royall one, by almes from Subjects hands,
MASSYR67:24	H570	A Royall State, rul'd by a bruitish mind.
MPERS74:17	H840	They then {all} attend him, to his royall roome,
MPERS77:12	H951	Thirty six years this royall {noble} Prince did reign,
MPERS84:3	H1231	The royall wine, in golden cups doth {did} passe,
MGREC97:14	H1775	The Royall Captives, brought to *Alexander,*
MGREC101:13	H1938	For his {the} Queen-Mother, and the royall Maid;
MGREC102:31	H2001	Here stood the Royall houses of delight,
MGREC105:35	H2128	Might be subjected to his royall hand;
MGREC111:39	H2384	He at the last to royall *Sushan* went;
MGREC112:28	H2414	His Royall pardon gave, for this same thing;
MGREC128:8	H3081	Which none e're did but those of royall fame;
MGREC134:12	H3343	The Royall blood was quite {nigh} extinguished.
MGREC134:36	H3367	Whom *Julius Cæsar* set in Royall place,
MROMAN138:22	H3512	Twenty foure yeare, {years} th' time of his royall race,
DIALOG144:11	H121	Because of Royall Stem, that was thy crime;
QELIZ155:25	H16	Mine bleating stands before thy royall Herse:
QELIZ158:8	H117	*Here sleeps THE Queen, this is the royall bed.*
MEDDM201:7	Hp280	seen an end of all perfection (sayd the royall prophet) but he
SON231:9	H21	When royall ones y^t Time did dye,

ROYALLY (1)

MGREC100:39	H1923	But when inform'd, how royally the King

ROYALTY (6)

AGES43:8	H303	And {I} oft long'd sore, to taste on Royalty.
MASSYR67:4	H550	And in the first year of his royalty,
MPERS~~84:6~~	H1234	Alas, she from her Royalty's {Royalty} suspended.
MGREC126:32	H3023	But Royalty no good conditions brings;
MGREC132:23	H3268	Injoy'd what so {ere} beseem'd his Royalty,
MGREC133:28	H3318	Longer *Seleuchus* held the Royalty

ROYALTY'S (1) [royalty is]

MPERS84:6	H1234	Alas, she from her Royalty's {Royalty} suspended.

RUB'D (1) [rubbed]

MEDDM200:6	Hp279	Some children are hardly weaned although the teat be rub'd

RUBBING (2)

SEASONS49:19	H110	Rubbing their dirty coates, till they look white.
AUTHOR178:5	H15	And rubbing off a spot, still made a flaw.

RUBBISH (4)

MASSYR60:28	H293	From rubbish these, with diligence he rakes,
MASSYR64:41	H465	Fetch {Fetcht} rubbish from the opposite old town,
MPERS~~84:12~~	H1247	Rebuilt those walls which long in rubbish lay,
SIDNEY150:6	H31	A world of treasure, in {wealth within} that rubbish lye;

RUBS (1) [pl.]

CONTEM172:16	H151	I markt, nor crooks, nor rubs that there did lye

RUBY (1)
MPERS82:38   H1185   O're-flown with torrent of her ruby {guiltless} blood.

RUDDY (3)
ELEMEN18:29   H433   The ruddy sweet sanguine, is like to Aire,
HUMOUR21:32   H60   Here's Sister Ruddy, worth the other two,
HUMOUR31:38   H471   Now could I stain my ruddy sisters face,

RUDE (3)
MGREC108:28   H2244   Where *Scithians* rude, his valour {army} doth oppose,
MROMAN138:33 H3523   To such rude triumphs, as young *Rome* then had,
QELIZ156:33   H60   The rude untamed *Irish* she did quell,

RUDELY (2)
FATHER5:17   H18   But by my humble hand thus rudely pen'd
MASSYR56:19   H125   A structure rare, I should but rudely marre,

RUDENESSE (2)
HUMOUR25:4   H193   Thy rudenesse counts, good manners vanity,
QELIZ155:30   H21   Which makes me deeme, my rudenesse is no wrong,

RUDER (1)
MGREC106:39   H2173   The ruder sort, did openly deride

RUEFUL (1)
MGREC115:15   H2528   A rueful face in this so general woe;

RUFFINS (1) [pl.]
AGES40:14   H195   Dayes, {Whole} nights, with Ruffins, Roarers, Fidlers spend,

RUFFLES (1)
MEDDM196:7   Hp272   he ruffles them vp, but spying his black feet, he soon lets fall

RUFFLING (1)
CONTEM168:8   H17   Whose ruffling top the Clouds seem'd to aspire;

RUGGED (1)
PILGRIM210:15 H15   No rugged stones his feet shall gaule

RUIN'D (2) [ruined]
AGES43:16   H309   But in a trice 'tis ruin'd by a blast,
AGES44:13   H346   My ruin'd house, now falling can uphold;

RUINES (2) [ruins]
MGREC98:14   H1816   The former ruines, help to him now lend; {forwarded his end:}
HOUSE236:33   H25   When by the Ruines oft I past

RUINS (1)
MASSYR63:7   H392   And on his Masters ruins, his house makes;

RUL'D (10) [ruled]
AGES44:31   H364   When it was rul'd by that Celestial she;
MASSYR58:13   H198   These two rul'd *Media* and *Babylon,*
MASSYR67:24   H570   A Royall State, rul'd by a bruitish mind.
MPERS73:16   H803   (Who like to Kings, rul'd Kingdomes as they please,)
MPERS91:31   H1545   Forty three years he rul'd, then turn'd to dust,
MGREC118:40   H2689   *Antipater,* had long rul'd *Macedon,*
MGREC122:33   H2854   He plac'd, displac'd, controld, rul'd, as he list,
MROMAN137:35 H3486   Forty three yeares he rul'd with generall praise;
DIALOG148:13   H278   Bring forth the beast that rul'd the world with's beck,
QELIZ156:19   H46   Was ever people better rul'd then hers?

RULE (25)
HUMOUR21:18   H46   Where if your rule once grow {prove} predominant,
MASSYR53:17   H7   But each one thought his petty rule was high,
MASSYR53:33   H23   When thus with rule he had been dignified,

MASSYR53:37	H27	Confirmes the rule his Father had begun,
MASSYR55:28	H94	That having no compeer, she might rule all,
MASSYR57:11	H158	He sought no rule, til she was gone, and dead;
MASSYR58:22	H207	The rule from their unworthy Prince to take.
MASSYR66:18	H524	All rule, he from the ancient *Pharoes* takes;
MASSYR67:3	H549	His son possesses wealth, and rule, as just;
MGREC93:24	H1621	His rule to *Greece,* he scorn'd should be confin'd:
MGREC98:23	H1825	The rule of this he to *Philotas* gave,
MGREC105:36	H2129	And that his rule as farre extended be,
MGREC109:2	H2259	Those that submit, he doth restore {give them rule} again.
MGREC115:32	H2551	Of larger Provinces, the rule to give,
MGREC118:28	H2677	Under his name begins {began} to rule each thing.
MGREC122:12	H2837	His rule Queen *Euridice* begins to hate,
MGREC125:5	H2953	That under him she might rule all alone.
MGREC131:15	H3207	For here *Antigonus* lost rule, and life,
MGREC~~132:20~~	H3261	In his long absence to rule *Macedon.*
MGREC133:25	~~H3315~~	Did take his rule, his sons, himself and all.
MGREC134:17	H3348	Of *Greece,* and *Syria* thus the rule did end,
MGREC135:11	H3383	The Heavens thus rule, to fill the earth {world} with wonder.
DIALOG143:3	H72	No *Edward, Richard,* to lose rule, and life,
QELIZ158:6	H115	*Eliza* shall rule *Albian* once again.
MEDDM202:14	Hp282	it pleased him, whose will is the perfect rule of righteousnesse,

RULED See RUL'D

RULES (1) [pl.]

AGES39:13	H156	Of Science, Arts, and Tongues, I know the rules,

RULES (1) v.

MPERS91:29	~~H1543~~	Forty three years he rules, then turns to dust,

RULEST (1)

2HUSB232:3	H4	O thov most high who rulest All

RULING (2)

MASSYR57:16	~~H163~~	Some may object, his Parents ruling all,
MPERS72:37	H781	Ruling as they thought good, {best} under his head.

RUMBLING (1)

ELEMEN8:21	H19	The rumbling, hissing, puffing was so great,

RUMOR (1)

MPERS90:29	H1496	Which rumor makes great *Artaxerxes* quake;

RUN (38) See also RVN

PROLOG6:21	H6	And {Or} how they all, or each, their dates have run:
ELEMEN15:20	H302	When I run low, and not o'reflow her brinks;
HUMOUR22:9	H78	But be she beaten, she'l not run away,
AGES35:33	H19	His hobby striding, did not ride, but run,
AGES35:37	H23	But if he hold, til it have run its last,
AGES36:23	H47	In's other hand a glasse, ev'n almost run,
AGES43:2	~~H297~~	To run my hull upon disgrace I fear'd,
AGES46:15	H446	And my last period now e'n almost run;
SEASONS52:19	H234	To th' Southward tropick his swift race hath {doth} run;
SEASONS52:27	H242	And North-ward his unwearied race {Course} doth run;
MASSYR53:28	H18	Not finished, til he his race had run;
MASSYR54:23	H50	So broad, three Chariots run abrest there might,
MASSYR61:6	H311	Forty eight years he reign'd, his race then run,
MASSYR66:39	H545	Forty four years he reign'd, which being run,

MPERS80:5	H1072	None cryes for quarter, nor yet seeks to run,
MPERS81:24	H1132	That whilst the Sun did run his endlesse course,
MPERS82:12	H1159	Three thousand scapes, for to {only can} run home agen;
MPERS86:6	H1322	{this} *Nothus* reign'd {'bout} nineteen years, which run,
MPERS86:34	H1350	(One *Greeke* could make ten *Persians* run away)
MPERS87:12	H1368	In numbers from his brother daily run.
MPERS92:21	H1579	And that great *Cyrus* line, yet was not run,
MPERS92:26	H1584	Some write great *Cyrus* line was not yet run,
MGREC96:6	H1726	As if they were, {if addrest} now all to run at {a} tilt:
MGREC97:1	H1762	Most basely run {ran}, and left their King at large,
MGREC97:5	H1766	Now finds both leggs, and Horse, to run away;
MGREC101:34	H1959	Both Armies meet, *Greeks* fight, the *Persians* run,
MGREC101:34	H1963	But long they stood not e're they're forc'd to run,
MGREC131:34	H3226	*Cassander* now must die, his race is run,
MGREC131:41	H3233	his Sword did pierce his mothers {run her through the} heart,
MGREC133:7	H3295	A little now, how the Succession run:
SIDNEY151:32	H75	Goodwill, did make my head-long pen to run,
QELIZ156:15	H42	Since first the Sun did run, his ne'r runn'd race,
CONTEM168:24	H31	And as a strong man, joyes to run a race,
FLESH177:13	H94	A Chrystal River there doth run,
SICKNES178:20	H3	My race is run, my thread is spun,
SICKNES179:9	H29	The race is run, the field is won,
MEDDM200:22	Hp279	a trim that they might run the wayes of his Commandment
MEDDM201:29	Hp281	run that they might obtain

RUN'ST (1) [runnest]

AUTHOR178:7	H17	Yet still thou run'st more hobling then is meet;

RUNN'D (1) [runned]

QELIZ156:15	H42	Since first the Sun did run, his ne'r runn'd race,

RUNNES (1) [runs]

ELEMEN13:33	H234	But to all outrages their hunger runnes.

RUNNETH (1)

SEASONS52:39	H255	And thus the year in circle runneth round:

RUNNING (1)

SEASONS47:32	H47	For though in's running progresse he doth take

RUNS (4) See also RUNNES

HUMOUR34:12	H567	Which runs through all the spondles of the rack,
MPERS89:2	H1436	The King upon the spur, runs back again;
MGREC95:25	H1704	Goes {Runs} after too {two}, and leaves all to disaster.
SIDNEY150:12	H43	Whilst English blood yet runs within my veins.

RUSH (1) n.

DIALOG147:11	H237	To root out Prelates, {Popelings} head, tail, branch, and rush.

RUSH (1) v.

MGREC121:16	H2798	And in a rage they rush into his tent,

RUSHES (1)

CONTEM168:23	H30	Thou as a Bridegroom from thy Chamber rushes,

RUSSLING (1)

SEASONS50:18	H152	The russling tresse of *terra* for {down} to moe,

RUST (1)

CONTEM174:34	H231	Nor wit nor gold, nor buildings scape times rust;

RUSTICK (2) [rustic]

SEASONS49:22	H113	Blest rustick Swains, your pleasant quiet life,

MROMAN136:30 H3444　Where Swaines, and rustick Peasants made {kept} their Holds.

RVN (1) [run]

13MAY227:4　　H13　I'le rvn where I was succoured.

RYE (1)

SEASONS50:21　H155　The Barley, and the Rye, should first had place,

RYOTING (1) [rioting]

MGREC111:33　H2378　Much time in feasts, and ryoting doth {did} wast;

S

SABBATH-BREAKING (1)

DIALOG144:2　　H112　For Sabbath-breaking, and for Drunkennesse,

SABINS (2) [pl.]

MROMAN137:13 H3464　To see these sports, the *Sabins* all are bent;

MROMAN137:17 H3468　And *Sabins,* as one people, dwelt in *Rome.*

SABLE (1)

SIDNEY150:39　H67　His death present in sable to his wife.

SACK (1)

DIALOG148:6　　H271　To sack proud *Rome,* and all her vassalls rout:

SACKT (1) See also SACT

QELIZ156:24　　H51　She ract, she sackt, she sunk his Armadoe;

SACRED (10)

ELEMEN11:2　　H122　Old sacred *Zion,* I demolish'd thee;

MASSYR54:10　H37　So oft profanely offered sacred rites;

MASSYR60:38　H303　In sacred Writ, he's known by name of *Pul,*

MASSYR67:22　H568　Whose prophane acts, a sacred pen sets down.

MROMAN137:26 H3477　Held for his Piety, some sacred thing;

DIALOG143:28　H97　Which are my Sins, the breach of sacred Lawes;

DIALOG146:14　H200　Pray now dear child, for sacred *Zion's* sake,

DIALOG148:19　H284　And lay her wast, for so's the sacred doom,

DUBART154:33　H78　Thy sacred works are not for imitation,

DAVID159:4　　H19　As if his head ne're felt the sacred Oyle:

SACRIFIC'D (2) [sacrificed]

MASSYR54:27　H54　To whom the sottish people sacrific'd;

QELIZ156:31　　H58　Her Nobles sacrific'd their noble blood,

SACRIFICE (3)

MPERS82:7　　H1154　Till in the entrails of their Sacrifice,

MGREC98:6　　H1808　Least he intend more fraud, then sacrifice;

CONTEM170:14 H86　Here *Cain* and *Abel* come to sacrifice,

SACRIFICED See SACRIFIC'D

SACRIFICES (3) [pl.]

ELEMEN10:25　H100　Of old, when Sacrifices were divine,

MPERS75:30　　H887　Gives sacrifices, wheat, wine, oyle, and salt,

MROMAN136:37 H3451　This City built, and Sacrifices done,

SACRILEDGE (1)

MPERS80:40 H1107 But mischief, Sacriledge doth ever follow;

SACRILEGIOUS (2)

MASSYR67:34 H580 Carous'd they in; and sacrilegious Prince,
MPERS71:33 H747 So left his sacrilegious bold intents:

SACT (1) See also SACKT

AGES43:5 H300 Opprest, and sunke, and sact, {stav'd} all in my way;

SAD (28)

HUMOUR22:1 H70 Then here's our sad black Sister, worse then you,
HUMOUR35:2 H598 Such premises wil force a sad conclusion,
AGES40:41 H220 With sad affrights of death, doth menace me;
AGES44:22 H355 Great mutations, some joyful, and some sad,
AGES45:40 H430 Now trembling, and {is all} fearful, sad, and cold;
MASSYR68:12 H598 Who still expects some fearfull sad event,
MPERS84:37 H1273 In this sad conflict, marching on his ways,
MPERS87:4 H1360 The one {last} accus'd the other, {first} for these {sad} wars:
MPERS93:3 H1600 And last; a sad catastrophe to end,
MGREC100:37 H1921 When this sad newes (at first) *Darius* heares,
MGREC116:10 H2571 When this sad news came to *Darius* Mother,
MGREC122:1 H2824 For this great {sad} strife, he pours out his complaints,
DIALOG141:9 H8 And sit i'th dust, to sigh these sad alarms?
DIALOG141:27 H26 Then weigh our case, if't be not justly sad,
DIALOG144:35 H143 I saw sad *Germanie's* dismantled walls.
DIALOG145:7 H156 To all you've said, sad mother, I assent
DIALOG146:15 H201 Oh pity me, in this sad perturbation,
SIDNEY150:38 H65 In sad, sweet verse, thou didst his death deplore;
SIDNEY150:41 H69 For the sad loss of her dear *Astrophel.*
SIDNEY151:2 H69 If such Stars as these, sad presages be,
CONTEM173:20 H186 Feels no sad thoughts, nor cruciating cares
CONTEM174:25 H223 But sad affliction comes & makes him see
BIRTH180:18 H28 With some sad sighs honour my absent Herse;
1LETTER181:26 H24 Till natures sad decree shall call thee hence;
3LETTER183:11 H13 Ev'n thus doe I, with many a deep sad groan
MERCY188:32 H18 Oh how I simpathize with thy sad heart,
MERCY189:15 H36 What though, thy strokes full sad & grievous be,
SON230:22 H5 My Teares to smiles, my sad to glad

SADLY (4)

ELEMEN14:5 H249 And since, faire *Italy* full sadly knowes
AGES43:31 H326 The knotty {Cramp and} Gout doth sadly torture me,
MGREC100:34 H1918 {Whose death} her wofull Lord for to {full sadly did} lament.
CHILDRN185:30 H56 And knew what thoughts there sadly rest,

SAFE (4)

MASSYR56:7 H113 With great facility, march safe upon't.
MASSYR65:32 H497 Seven years he keeps his faith, and safe he dwels,
3LETTER183:13 H15 His presence and his safe return, still wooes,
REMB235:21 H1-3 In thankfull Remb^rc for my dear husbands safe Arrivall.

SAFELY (2)

SON230:25 H8 In raging stormes did'st safely keep
ACK235:11 H11 Thou hast to shore him safely brovght

SAFEST (2)

MPERS87:36 H1388 He surest {safest} was, when furthest {farthest} out o'th' way.

MPERS~~89:16~~ H1450 He judg'd his wisest and his safest Course.

SAFETY (5) See also SAFITY

MGREC104:11 H2063 This counsell, for his safety, he pretended,
MGREC105:27 H2120 Yet that succeeding Kings in safety may
CONTEM174:26 H224 Here's neither honour, wealth, or safety;
DISTEMP179:23 H11 My Anchor cast i'th' vale with safety.
CHILDRN185:41 H67 O to your safety have an eye,

SAFFERNS (1) [saffrons]

HUMOUR31:17 H450 And so {thence} with jaundise, Safferns al the skin.

SAFITY (1) [safety]

PILGRIM210:18 H18 and meanes in safity now to dwell.

SAGE (4) ·

AGES44:20 H353 He that in youth is godly, wise, and sage,
MPERS77:27 H968 Sage *Artabanus* counsell, had he taken, ·
MGREC94:15 H1649 Leaves sage *Antipater* at home to sway,
MGREC104:7 H2059 With sage advice, he layes {sets} before his eyes,

SAGES (4) [pl.]

ELEMEN9:29 H63 Our Sages new, another tale have told:
ELEMEN18:30 H434 And youth, and spring, sages to me compare.
ELEMEN19:2 H447 And what those Sages, did, or {either} spake, or writ,
CONTEM171:4 H109 The starry observations of those Sages,

SAGITARIUS (1)

SEASONS51:36 H212 This month's {moneth} the Sun {Sun's} in *Sagitarius,*

SAID (32) See also SAYD, SED

ELEMEN20:5 H487 I have said lesse, then did my sisters three;
ELEMEN20:7 H489 To adde to all I've said, was my intent,
HUMOUR24:7 H156 I have been sparing, what I might have said, ·
HUMOUR~~27:19~~ H290 Nor what you've said, doth argue my disgrace,
HUMOUR34:36 H591 And I passe by what sister Sanguine said;
HUMOUR34:38 H593 The worst she said, was, instability,
AGES41:12 H231 Thus I have said, and what i've said {been,} you see,
AGES41:12 H231 Thus I have said, and what i've said {been,} you see,
MASSYR63:19 H404 Of whom is little said in any thing; [22 years.
MASSYR65:23 H488 For this was {is} he, for whom none said, Alas!
MPERS72:29 ~~H773~~ Who said but what, the King bad him expresse.
MPERS77:7 H946 For *Grecian* Maids ('tis said) to wait on her;
MPERS~~92:7~~ H1565 His brother, as tis said, long since was slain,
MGREC101:39 H1968 But *Quintus Curtius,* as was said before.
MGREC105:38 H2131 This said, the *Greek* for water doth intreat,
MGREC106:3 H2137 This said, his fainting breath did fleet away,
MGREC114:33 H2503 When e're 'tis said, he thousand thousands slew,
MGREC122:9 H2834 For all that should be said, let this suffice,
DIALOG145:7 H156 To all you've said, sad mother, I assent
DIALOG~~145:20~~ H169 {'Tis said,} My better part in Court of Parliament,
SIDNEY152:7 H78 With high disdain, they said they gave no more,
VANITY159:30 H2 As he said vanity, so vain say I,
VANITY160:30 H40 The depth, and sea, hath {have} said its not in me,
CONTEM168:18 H26 And softly said, what glory's like to thee?
CONTEM173:18 H184 O merry Bird (said I) that fears no snares,
FLESH176:13 H53 When I believ'd, what thou hast said,
MYCHILD216:31 Hp242 haue I gone to searching, and haue said wth David Lord search

MYCHILD218:30 Hp244   haue been carryed away wth them, that somt: I haue said, Is
FEVER221:3   H18   O heal my Soul thov know'st I said,
SOREFIT221:27 H13   I said I shall praise thee at lenght.
FAINTING222:17 H7   Thvs fainting haue I said
JULY223:31   Hp251   for thov art my God, Thou hast said and shall not I beleiue it?

SAID'ST (1)
SOREFIT221:19 H5   Then Lord thou said'st vnto me Liue.

SAITH See SATH

SAILE (4) [sail] See also SAYLE
ELEMEN17:21   H385   Till Sun release, their ships can saile no more.
MGREC111:19   H2364   Depriv'd at once, the use of Saile, and Oare;
MEDDM196:2   Hp272   A ship that beares much saile & little or no ballast, is easily
MEDDM203:10 Hp283   He that is to saile into a farre country, although the ship,

SAILES (3) [sails]
ELEMEN12:37   H197   But Marriners, where got you ships and sailes?
ELEMEN18:23   H427   Ye Mariners, tis I that fill your Sailes,
AGES43:3   H298   But {And} by ambitious sailes, I was so carryed;

SAILETH (1)
CONTEM174:21 H219   So he that saileth in this world of pleasure,

SAILING (2) See also SAYLING
MERCY188:28   H14   Thou then on Seas sailing to forreign Coast;
MEDDM203:13 Hp283   his bussines lyes, a christian is sailing through this world vnto

SAILS See SAILES, SAYLES

SAINT (1)
DUBART154:13 H58   Then in Saint *Lewis,* or thy last *Henry* great,

SAINT-LIKE (1)
DUBART153:35 H39   Thy Saint-like minde in grave Divinity,

SAINTES (1) [saints]
MEDDM206:11 Hp287   Company of Saints, and Angels those Saintes haue their

SAINTS (6) [pl.]
DIALOG143:37 H106   What scorning of the Saints of the most high,
TDUDLEY166:24 H66   Ah happy Soul, 'mongst Saints and Angels blest,
MEDDM202:9   Hp281   beasts then men, some pious saints, some incarnate Deuils,
MEDDM206:11 Hp287   innumerable Company of Saints, and Angels those Saintes
MYCHILD218:24 Hp244   p[r]secutions of the Saints, wch admitt were y[y] as they terme y[m]
REMB236:9   H24   O help thy Saints y[t] sovght thy Face

SAITH (5)
HUMOUR34:23 H578   A foolish Brain (saith {quoth} Choler) wanting heat,
DIALOG145:19 H168   One saith its he, the other no such thing.
MEDDM204:5   Hp284   and he that hath deliuered mee saith paul, will deliuer me, god
MYCHILD218:33 Hp244   possible y[e] very elect should bee deceived. Behold saith o[r]
MED223:6   Hp250   I thy child, yee shall be my Sons and Daughters saith y[e] Lord

SAKE (15)
MASSYR54:39 H66   Then drown himself, did *Menon,* for her sake;
MASSYR61:24 H329   And succours *Ahaz,* yet for *Tiglath's* sake,
MPERS73:8   H795   And built fair *Meroe,* for his sisters sake.
MPERS81:8   H1116   Who for his sake, he knew, would venture far,
MPERS85:39   H1315   Prefers his brother, for his birth-rights sake.
MGREC109:9   H2268   His liquors more devoutly in, for's sake.
MGREC124:16 H2923   Firm (for his Fathers sake) to him abide.
MGREC126:28 H3019   For Justice sake she being put to th' sword.

DIALOG143:40	H109	Nor for their owne, but for their Masters sake;
DIALOG146:14	~~H200~~	Pray now dear child, for sacred *Zion's* sake,
SICKNES178:24	H7	For Adams sake, this word God spake
BIRTH180:19	H29	And kiss this paper for thy loves dear sake,
2SIMON195:13	Hp271	they will be better pris'd by you, for the Authors sake. the lord
WHAT224:21	H21	And for his sake y^t faithfull is
HOURS234:18	H32	Ev'n for my Sav^rs sake

SAKES (1)

MPERS75:3	H864	That for their sakes, his cruelty he felt;

SAL'MANDERS (1) [salamanders]

ELEMEN9:38	H72	And though nought but *Sal'manders* live in fire;

SALAMIS (1)

MPERS80:23	H1090	Yet {Then} in the Streights of *Salamis* he try'd,

SALIQUE (1)

QELIZ156:11	H38	The *Salique* Law had not in force now been,

SALMANASSER (3)

MASSYR62:1	H346	*Salmanasser,* or *Nabonasser.*
MASSYR62:2	H347	*Tiglath* deceas'd, *Salmanasser* is next,
MASSYR62:8	H353	For *Salmanasser,* with a mighty Hoast,

SALMANESER (1)

MASSYR62:31	H376	*Senacherib Salmaneser* succeeds,

SALMENEUS (1)

MASSYR59:12	H236	But *Salmeneus* slaine, his {the} Army fals,

SALT (5)

ELEMEN16:23	H346	Nor yet of Salt, and Sugar, sweet and smart,
MPERS75:30	H887	Gives sacrifices, wheat, wine, oyle, and salt,
CONTEM172:32	H165	Now salt, now fresh where you think best to glide
BIRTH180:20	H30	Who with salt tears this last Farewel did take.
MEDDM196:29	Hp273	nothing but salt will keep from putrefaction, some again like

SALUTE (1)

2LETTER182:18	H24	Thy rayes afar, salute her from the south.

SALUTED (1)

SIDNEY150:16	~~H49~~	To be saluted by a silly Crow;

SALVAGES (1)

MPERS76:9	H907	The Salvages did laugh at his distresse,

SALVAT^N. (1)

JULY223:35	Hp251	Salvat^n. of my Soul.

SALVATION (3)

SICKNES179:6	H26	to make Salvation sure,
MEDDM209:3	Hp291	but it is so necessary, that w^thout faith there is no salvation
11MAYB228:31	Hp259	kindnes, nor take ye cup of salvation wth Thanksgiving as I

SAME (54)

FATHER5:19	H20	These same are they, of {from} whom we being have,
ELEMEN9:32	H66	And of the selfe same nature is with mine,
ELEMEN11:13	H133	Not sparing life when I can take the same;
ELEMEN15:31	H313	Thy silence of thy beasts, doth cause the same.
ELEMEN18:19	H423	Your songs and pleasant tunes, they are the same,
HUMOUR22:27	H96	What comes from thence, my heat refines the same,
HUMOUR23:31	H141	Like our sixt *Henry,* that same worthy {virtuous} thing.
HUMOUR25:31	H220	That naught but blood, {death} the same may expiate.
HUMOUR28:41	H353	As I to you, to me, do ye the same.

HUMOUR31:35	H468	But I by vertue, do acquire the same.
HUMOUR31:41	H474	Then cause her blush, while I dilate {relate} the same.
AGES41:17	H236	What they have done, the same was done by me,
AGES46:22	H453	And I shal see, with these same very eyes,
SEASONS49:24	H~~114~~	Yet hath your life, made Kings the same envy,
MASSYR55:33	H99	As {By} their aspersions, cast upon the same.
MASSYR59:34	H258	Twenty he reign'd, same time, as Stories tel,
MPERS~~70:40~~	H711	And *Alexander* coming to the same,
MPERS72:35	H779	Had set a *Smerdis* up, of the same years;
MPERS~~79:13~~	H1037	He fetters cast therein the same to chain.
MPERS~~79:13~~	H1039	Because they wanted skill the same to've staid.
MPERS82:15	H1162	Same day, the small remainder of his Fleet,
MPERS82:17	H1164	And there so utterly they wrack'd the same,
MPERS87:20	H~~1374~~	Ran back, and quite abandoned the same,
MPERS~~92:14~~	H1572	By the same Eunuch who first set him up.
MPERS~~92:20~~	H1578	And the same sauce had served him no doubt,
MGREC106:34	H2168	Charging the same on his Nobility;
MGREC108:2	H2218	(A coller of the same his neck containes)
MGREC108:22	H2238	And there most fiercely set upon the same;
MGREC108:38	H2254	And furlongs sixty could not {but} round the same.
MGREC112:4	H2390	At the {this} same time, unto his Captains brave;
MGREC112:12	H2398	He might this feast imagine by the same.
MGREC112:28	H2414	His Royall pardon gave, for this same thing;
MGREC117:9	H2616	So the same cup to his, did others fill.
MGREC117:34	H2641	But meannesse of their Mothers bard the same:
MGREC~~122:32~~	H2853	That he might settle matters in the same.
MGREC129:16	H3130	The Heavens seem'd slow in paying her the same,
MGREC130:3	H3158	*Lysimachus* and *Ptolomy,* the same,
MGREC130:24	H3179	Then vengeance just, against the same {them} t' expresse;
MGREC131:32	H3224	Who did no sooner understand the same,
MGREC133:15	H3303	And his posterity, the same retaines,
MROMAN139:37	H3563	And for the same, I hours not few did spend,
DIALOG143:14	H83	Her Lillies in mine Armes avouch the same.
CONTEM168:21	H29	Had I not better known, (alas) the same had I.
CONTEM169:20	H60	They kept one tune, and plaid on the same string,
FLESH175:26	H26	Dost honour like? acquire the same,
VERSES183:37	H4	Who can of right better demand the same?
MEDDM202:4	Hp281	disproportion that they scarcly seem made of the same lump,
MEDDM204:6	Hp284	is the same yesterday, to day and for euer, we are the same
MEDDM204:6	Hp284	yesterday, to day and for euer, we are the same that stand
MEDDM204:17	Hp285	doth many times, both reward and punish for one and ye same
MYCHILD218:20	Hp244	same God, the same Christ, ye same word, They only
30SEPT227:30	Hp257	recourse to ye same God who hath heard + deliuered me,

SAME'S (1) [same is]

ELEMEN~~20:6~~	H488	what's their worth, {wrath} or force, but more's {same's} in me.

SAM. (1) [samuel]

DAVID158:23	H2-3	and *Jonathan,* 2 Sam. I. 19.

SAMUEL (1)

SAMUEL228:1	H1-2	Vpon my Son Samuel his goeing for England Novem. 6. 1657.

SANCTEFYE (1) [sanctify]

WHAT224:12	H12	And sanctefye their rods,

SAND (4)
ELEMEN14:15	H257	Much might I say, of the *Arabian* sands; {hot *Libian* sand}
HUMOUR34:30	H585	For memory, the sand is not more brittle.
MGREC111:17	H2362	His Gallies stuck upon the sand, {flats} and mud;
2LETTER182:9	H15	He that can tell the starrs or Ocean sand,

SANDS (4) [pl.]
ELEMEN14:15	H257	Much might I say, of the *Arabian* sands; {hot *Libian* sand}
ELEMEN19:29	H472	Some upon sands, some upon rocks have hit.
AGES43:4	H299	That over flats, and sands, and rocks I hurried,
MPERS71:28	H742	But as they marched o're those desart sands,

SANGUINE (9)
ELEMEN18:29	H433	The ruddy sweet sanguine, is like to Aire,
HUMOUR20:25	H17	But Sanguine did disdaine, what she requir'd,
HUMOUR22:25	H94	Nor sister Sanguine, from thy moderate heat,
HUMOUR28:24	H336	Of such as to the Sanguine are inclin'd,
HUMOUR31:25	H458	And Sanguine is more fickle many fold. {manifold,}
HUMOUR31:32	H465	What Sanguine is, she doth not heed, nor care.
HUMOUR32:38	H512	When sister Sanguine paints my Ivory face,
HUMOUR34:36	H591	And I passe by what sister Sanguine said;
HUMOUR35:4	H600	Let Sanguine, Choler, with her hot hand hold,

SANK (1)
SON230:27	H10	The other sank low in the Deep.

SAP (7)
ELEMEN13:26	H227	My sap, to plants and trees, I must not grant,
ELEMEN14:33	H275	Which {Who} am thy drink, thy blood, thy sap, and best.
SEASONS50:35	H169	To feed his boughes, exhausted hath his sap,
SEASONS51:28	H204	The sap doth slily creep towards the earth,
SEASONS52:4	H219	When cold, the sap to th' roots hath low'st repell'd;
MEDDM199:8	Hp277	Yellow leaues argue want of sap and gray haires want of
MEDDM200:31	Hp279	their sap decline

SAPHYRE (1) [saphire]
VANITY160:32	H42	For *Saphyre, Onix, Topas,* who will {would} change,

SAPLESS (1)
MEDDM199:9	Hp277	dry and sapless performances are simptoms of little spiritull

SAPLESSE (1) [sapless]
SEASONS51:25	H201	Whose yellow saplesse leaves by winds are fann'd:

SAPORS (1) [pl.]
AGES45:34	H424	Nor sapors find, in what I drink or eat.

SARDANA (1)
AGES40:23	H204	*Sardana Pallas,* now survives in me:

SARDANAPAL'S (1) [sardanapal is]
MASSYR60:25	H290	And those which {that} seem'd with *Sardanapal's* gone;

SARDANAPALUS (6)
MASSYR57:37	H182	T' *Sardanapalus* next we wil make haste.
MASSYR57:38	H183	*Sardanapalus.*
MASSYR57:39	H184	*Sardanapalus,* (Son t' *Ocrazapes*)
MASSYR58:26	H209	*Sardanapalus* leaves his Apish play.
MASSYR59:28	H252	*Sardanapalus* did not seek to fly,
MPERS69:7	H629	When *Sardanapalus* was over-thrown,

SARDIS (4)
MPERS69:25	H647	Who him pursues to *Sardis,* takes the town,

MPERS78:31   H1012   At *Sardis,* in *Lidia,* these all doe meet,
MGREC95:6   H1685   *Sardis,* then he, and *Ephesus,* did gaine,
MGREC130:5   H3160   She now {then} in *Lydia* at *Sardis* lay,

SA'S (1) [says]
QELIZ156:9   H36   *Spaines* Monarch sa's not so; nor yet his Hoast,

SAT (5) See also SATE
MGREC96:11   H1731   The King sat in a chariot made of gold,
MGREC122:18   H2843   Grandchild to him, who once sat on that throne,
MGREC134:20   H3351   Cal'd *Philadelphus,* next sat on {did possess} the throne,
MGREC134:28   H3359   After *Epiphanes,* sat on the Throne
SIDNEY152:17   H86   I pensive for my fault, sat down, and then,

SATAN (3) See also SATHAN
MEDDM198:17   Hp276   hooke vnder all, Satan that great Angler hath his sundry baits
MYCHILD217:32   Hp243   Many times hath Satan troubled me concerning ye verity of y^e
JULY223:33   Hp251   upon me. O never let Satan p^rvail against me, but strenghten

SATE (4) [sat]
MGREC104:16   H2068   Sate down o'rewhelm'd, with sorrow, and despair,
MROMAN139:13   H3541   Sate on the Throne, when he had slaine his foe;
CONTEM172:7   H143   Close sate I by a goodly Rivers side,
HOUSE236:36   H28   Where oft I sate and long did lye,

SATH (5) [saith]
MEDDM201:25   Hp281   The words of the wise (sath Solom) are as nailes, and as
MEDDM204:3   Hp284   he that deliuered me, sath Dauid, from the paw of the Lion
MEDDM204:20   Hp285   while (sath god) and I will avenge the blood of Jezerel vpon
MEDDM208:34   Hp290   intercedes for the people, god sath to him Let me alone, that I
MEDDM209:1   Hp291   wth god face to face in penvel Let me go, sath that Angell, I

SATHAN (1) [satan]
MEDDM197:1   Hp274   temptations of Sathan without could not hurt, hath, been foild

SATIATES (1)
VANITY161:5   H56   This satiates the soul, this stayes the mind,

SATISFIE (6) [satisfy]
HUMOUR25:26   H215   To satisfie thy pride, and cruelty
MASSYR57:21   H168   Well satisfie the most considerate minds:
MGREC113:22   H2449   Wherefore at once all these to satisfie,
MGREC114:12   H2480   Nought but his life for this could satisfie;
MGREC116:31   H2597   Ambitious so, that nought could satisfie,
MGREC122:8   H2832   He that at large would satisfie his mind,

SATISFIED (1)
MEDDM202:19   Hp282   but cannot be satisfied wth them.

SATISFY (1) See also SATISFIE
FLESH175:14   H14   Can Speculation satisfy

SATISFYING (1)
MYCHILD217:12   Hp242   in satisfying my mind w^thout it, and I haue been confident it

SATRAPES (1) [pl.]
MPERS73:15   H802   Of which the cheife were {was} seven, call'd *Satrapes,*

SATURN (1)
MASSYR53:31   H21   Of *Saturn,* he was the original,

SATYRES (1) [pl.]
MPERS70:19   H690   For Owles, and Satyres, makes {made} a residence;

SAUCE (1)
MPERS92:20   H1578   And the same sauce had served him no doubt,

SAUL (5)

DAVID158:22	H1-2	*Davids* Lamentation for *Saul,*
DAVID158:25	H5	Illustrious *Saul,* whose beauty did excell
DAVID159:2	H17	The Shield of *Saul* was vilely cast away;
DAVID159:8	H23	Did *Saul* with bloodlesse Sword turne back agen:
DAVID159:14	H29	For valiant *Saul,* who on Mount *Gilbo* lyes;

SAV'D (3) [saved]

AGES44:34	H367	Then saw I *France,* and *Holland* sav'd, *Cales* won,
AGES45:4	H384	And Land & Nobels sav'd with their anointed.
MASSYR64:6	H430	Kild, sav'd, pull'd down, set up, or pain'd, or eas'd;

SAVAGE (1)

ELEMEN15:5	H287	The Woolves and savage Beasts, forsake their Dens.

SAVE (3) [except]

MASSYR57:33	H178	Save a few names anew, *Berosus* writ.
MGREC104:38	H2090	And bids him, save himself, by speedy course:
AUTHOR178:9	H19	But nought save home-spun Cloth, i' th' house I find.

SAVE (9) [preserve]

MPERS69:28	H650	Who had no might to save himself from wrong;
MPERS74:15	H838	A thousand times, God save {long live} the King, they cry,
MPERS78:26	H1007	Save the *Zidonians,* where *Xerxes* was.
MGREC93:29	H1626	To save him from his might, no man was found.
MGREC117:1	H2608	Nor can he kill, or save as heretofore,
MGREC120:32	H2769	To save himself from dangers eminent;
MGREC125:11	H2959	To come and succour {To save the King} her, in this great
MGREC125:21	H2969	To save their lives t' *Amphipolis* do fly;
CHILDRN186:25	H92	What would save life, and what would kill.

SAVED See SAV'D

SAV^R. (6) [saviour]

MYCHILD218:5	Hp243	a God as I worship in Trinity, + such a Sav^r as I rely upon, tho:
MYCHILD218:34	Hp244	Sav^r. I have told yov before. That hath stayed my heart, and I
BYNIGHT220:17	H15	What to my Sav^r. shall I giue?
WHAT224:2	H2	What Sav^r. like to mine?
28AUG226:5	Hp254	Now I can wait, looking every day when my Sav^r shall call for

SAVIOUR (1)

ANNEB187:33	H23	Thou with thy Saviour art in endless bliss.

SAV^RS (1) [saviour's]

HOURS234:18	H32	Ev'n for my Sav^rs sake

SAVOURS (1)

AGES45:33	H423	I cannot scent, savours of pleasant meat,

SAW (33)

FATHER5:5	H6	Of fairer Dames, the sun near saw the face, /of the
AGES44:34	H367	Then saw I *France,* and *Holland* sav'd, *Cales* won,
AGES44:36	H369	I saw all peace at home, terror to foes,
AGES44:37	H370	But ah, I saw at last those eyes to close:
AGES44:40	H373	In midst of greifs, I saw some {our} hopes revive,
AGES45:1	H374	I saw hopes dasht, our forwardnesse was shent,
AGES45:4	H383	But saw their horrid fact soon disappointed,
MASSYR56:21	H127	All eyes that saw, or ears that hears, {hear} admires.
MASSYR59:24	H248	And now they saw fulfill'd a Prophesie;
MASSYR66:6	H512	Yet as was told, ne're saw it with his eyes;
MPERS72:2	H754	He after this, saw in a Vision {upon suspition vain},

MPERS75:10	H871	When opportunity he saw was fit,
MPERS88:10	H1403	But when their order, and {their} silence they saw;
MPERS90:19	H1486	In peace they saw their Native soyl again.
MGREC96:17	H1737	But they that saw him in this state to lye;
MGREC125:16	H2964	But when her Souldiers saw their ancient Queen,
DIALOG144:31	H139	Who heard {saw} their cause, and wrongs {hath} judg'd
DIALOG144:35	H143	I saw sad *Germanie's* dismantled walls.
DIALOG144:36	H144	I saw her people famish'd, Nobles slain,
DIALOG144:38	H146	I saw (unmov'd) her Armies foil'd and fled,
DIALOG144:40	H148	I saw strong *Rochel* yeelding to her foe,
DIALOG145:1	H150	I saw poore *Ireland* bleeding out her last,
DIALOG145:34	H183	Here tugg'd they hard indeed, for all men saw,
SIDNEY149:23	H22	To shew the world, they never saw before,
TDUDLEY165:12	H14	Who heard or saw, observ'd or knew him better?
CONTEM169:10	H51	Silent alone, where none or saw, or heard,
CONTEM171:3	H108	Their long descent, how nephews sons they saw,
AUTHOR178:4	H14	I wash'd thy face, but more defects I saw,
CHILDRN185:29	H55	O would my young, ye saw my breast,
MERCY188:24	H10	I saw the branches lopt the Tree now fall,
MYCHILD216:12	Hp241	wth a lamenesse wch correction I saw the Lord sent to hu̅ble
MYCHILD217:34	Hp243	God, I never saw any miracles to confirm me, and those wch I
SON231:6	H18	From such as 'fore nere saw his face.

SAXON (1)

DIALOG142:5	H34	What, hath some *Hengist,* like that *Saxon* stout,

SAY (66)

PROLOG7:19	H32	They'l say its stolne, or else, it was by chance.
ELEMEN8:32	H30	But what I am, let learned *Grecians* say;
ELEMEN11:6	H126	What shal I say of Lightning, and of Thunder,
ELEMEN11:32	H152	Would so passe time, I could say nothing else;
ELEMEN14:15	H257	Much might I say, of the *Arabian* sands; {hot *Libian* sand}
ELEMEN14:19	H261	Ile say no more, yet {but} this thing adde I must,
ELEMEN17:12	H376	Some say I swallowed up (sure 'tis a notion)
ELEMEN17:14	H378	I need not say much of my Haile and Snow,
ELEMEN17:32	H396	Much might I say of wracks, but that Ile spare,
HUMOUR22:2	H71	She'l neither say, she wil, nor wil she doe:
HUMOUR24:9	H158	To what you now shal say, I wil attend,
HUMOUR26:41	H271	But thou wilt say, I deale unequally,
HUMOUR30:19	H411	You'l say, here none shal ere disturbe my right;
HUMOUR32:29	H503	And when i've nothing left to say, be mute;
HUMOUR33:10	H524	Shame forc'd thee say, the matter that was mine,
HUMOUR33:12	H526	Thou speakest truth, and I can speak {say} no lesse,
HUMOUR33:14	H528	But yet thou art as much, I truly say,
HUMOUR33:14	H528	Yet without ostentation I may say,
HUMOUR33:39	H553	Of three, its hard to say, which doth excel;
HUMOUR34:24	H579	But a mad one, say I, where 'tis too great,
HUMOUR34:40	H595	A warning good, hereafter i'le say lesse.
AGES36:26	H50	And al gave eare, to what he had to say.
AGES39:2	H145	For 'tis but little, that a childe can say.
AGES42:13	H271	As readily as could my Leader say:
AGES44:3	H336	And all you say, say I, and something {somewhat} more;
AGES45:22	H411	What are my thoughts, this is no time to say.

SEASONS52:12	H227	What Winter hath to tel, now let him say.
MASSYR56:6	H112	Most {Some} writers say, six chariots might a front,
MASSYR56:31	H137	(They say) but twenty, ere came back agen.
MASSYR~~57:22~~	H169	We may with learned *Vsher* better say,
MPERS92:20	H~~1578~~	Some writers say, that he was *Arses* son,
MGREC94:24	H1662	To him, his mothers Ancestor (men say.)
MGREC114:28	H2498	This censure passe, and not unwisely, say,
MGREC117:28	H2635	Yet {But} none so hardy found as so durst say.
MGREC130:37	H3182	Thus may we hear, and fear, and ever say,
MGREC131:29	H3221	Yet dares {durst} not say, he loves {lov'd} his fathers wife;
MROMAN137:21	H3472	Some faining say, to heav'n {to the Gods} he did ascend;
DIALOG142:1	H30	In generall terms, but will not say wherefore:
DIALOG145:11	H160	But all you say, amounts to this effect,
DIALOG145:25	H174	As puts me to a stand what I should say,
DIALOG145:37	H186	This was deny'd, I need not say wherefore.
SIDNEY149:19	H18	*Thalia,* and *Melpomene,* say th' truth,
SIDNEY150:13	H48	But to {The more I} say truth, {the more} thy worth I shall but
QELIZ155:21	H12	To say, thou wert a fleshly Deity:
QELIZ156:5	H32	Nor say I more then duly is her due,
QELIZ157:32	H100	Now say, have women worth, or have they none?
QELIZ157:36	H104	Let such, as say our sex is void of reason,
VANITY159:30	H2	As he said vanity, so vain say I,
VANITY159:32	H4	Where is the man can say, lo, I have found
AUTHOR178:13	H23	If for thy Father askt, say, thou hadst none:
2LETTER182:31	H37	Tell him I would say more, but cannot well,
2LETTER182:33	H39	Now post with double speed, mark what I say,
VERSES184:8	H12	Such is my debt, I may not say forgive,
1SIMON188:11	H12	Let's say he's merciful, as well as just,
MEDDM200:2	Hp278	comes to its height by degrees, He that dares say of a lesse
MEDDM200:3	Hp278	not a little one? will ere long say of a greater Tush god regards
MEDDM201:8	Hp280	I haue seen an end of all Sinning, what he did say, may be
MEDDM201:9	Hp280	sayd by many, but what he did not say, cannot (truly) be
MEDDM202:34	Hp282	doth it euer say it is enough, but like the daughters of the
MEDDM204:30	Hp285	look on his owne vnworthynes and that will make him say w^th
MEDDM207:1	Hp288	god and say how vnsearchable are his wayes and his footsteps
MEDDM207:8	Hp288	driuen them the further from him, that they are ready to say,
MYCHILD218:35	Hp244	say, Return o my Soul to thy Rest, vpon this Rock Xt Jesus will
FEVER221:12	H27	Praise to my Lord I say,
HANNA230:17	H10	And let her Conversation say

SAYD (7) [said]

MEDDM198:21	Hp276	is no new thing vnder ye Sun there is nothing that can be sayd
MEDDM198:23	Hp276	sayd before—
MEDDM201:7	Hp280	I haue seen an end of all perfection (sayd the royall prophet)
MEDDM201:8	Hp280	never sayd, I haue seen an end of all Sinning, what he did say,
MEDDM201:9	Hp280	easily sayd by many, but what he did not say, cannot (truly) be
MEDDM207:21	Hp289	All men are truly sayd to be tenants at will, and it may as truly
MEDDM207:22	Hp289	sayd that all haue a lease of their liues, some longer some

SAYES (1) [says]

PROLOG7:15	H28	Who sayes, my hand a needle better fits,

SAYLE (1) [sail] See also SAILE

MASSYR64:38	H462	And Mariners, to handle sayle, and oare;

SAYLES (1) [sails] See also SAILES
 CHILDRN184:31 H20 They *Norward* steer'd with filled sayles.
SAYLING (2) [sailing]
 MGREC111:12 H2357 Then sayling South, and comming to the {that} shore,
 MGREC111:16 H2361 Hence {Then} sayling down by th' mouth of *Indus* floud,
SAYS See SA's, SAYES
SAY'ST (2)
 HUMOUR24:28 H177 There is no Souldier, but thy selfe thou say'st,
 HUMOUR26:12 H242 For there are {is} none, thou say'st, if some, not best.
SAYST (3)
 HUMOUR23:7 H117 Thou sayst, thy wits are stai'd, subtle and fine:
 HUMOUR24:40 H189 Thou sayst I love my sword, because tis {it's} guilt. {gilt,}
 HUMOUR30:31 H423 Laughter (though thou sayst malice) flowes from hence,
SCALE (2)
 HUMOUR21:25 H53 To storme a Breach, or scale a City wal?
 AGES39:17 H160 climbe Battlements, {scale walls and forts} rear'd to the skies;
SCALES (2) [pl.]
 DIALOG148:23 H288 The scales shall fall from your long blinded eyes,
 CONTEM173:8 H176 Whose armour is their scales, their spreading fins their shield.
SCAN (1)
 MGREC123:9 H2871 'Gainst him, that all deceits could scan, and try:
SCANDALL (1)
 SON231:13 H25 That wthout scandall he might come
'SCAP'D (1) [scaped]
 MPERS73:27 H812 Some write that sorely hurt, they 'scap'd away;
SCAP'D (3) [scaped]
 ELEMEN19:19 H464 That birds have not scap'd death, as they have flown,
 MPERS71:18 H732 (But little *Marus,* {*Narus*} scap'd that cruel fate,
SCAPE (4)
 HUMOUR29:10 H363 Faire rosie Sister, so might'st thou scape free,
 MPERS69:27 H649 Disguised *Cressus,* hop'd to scape i'th throng,
 MGREC98:39 H1841 These he may scape, and if he so desire,
 CONTEM174:34 H231 Nor wit nor gold, nor buildings scape times rust;
SCAPED See 'SCAP'D, SCAP'D
SCAPES (1) [pl.]
 MPERS82:12 H1159 Three thousand scapes, for to {only can} run home agen;
SCARCE (15) See also SCARSE
 ELEMEN14:24 H266 Scarce Earth had done, but th' angry waters {water} mov'd;
 ELEMEN19:5 H450 Earths Beasts, and Waters Fish, scarce can compare.
 ELEMEN19:17 H462 The living, scarce had power, to bury dead.
 HUMOUR28:36 H348 I've scarce wip'd off the spots, proud Choler cast,
 MPERS70:17 H688 Forty five mile {miles} this City scarce could round;
 MPERS76:22 H920 His enemies scarce seen, then much lesse, slaine;
 MPERS79:33 H1059 Was scarce enough, for each a draught to take.
 MPERS82:18 H1165 Scarce one was left, to carry home the fame;
 MPERS92:8 H1566 And scarce a Nephew left that now might reign:
 MPERS93:2 H1599 Of all, did scarce his winding sheet retaine.
 MGREC93:25 H1622 The universe, scarce bounds {bound} his large {proud} vast
 MGREC106:9 H2143 (For scarce the world, or any bounds thereon,
 MGREC111:27 H2372 That of them all, the fourth did scarce remaine.
 MGREC112:9 H2395 Spectators here, could scarce relate the story,

CHILDRN185:9 H35 My fifth, whose down is yet scarce gone

SCARCELY (4) See also SCARCLY

FATHER5:8 H9 Their paralells to find I scarcely know,

MGREC~~120:36~~ H2773 Which eating time hath scarcely yet defac'd.

MGREC~~126:30~~H3021 Whose fury yet unparalleld {scarcely parallel'd} hath been;

1SIMON188:6 H7 Three flours, two scarcely blown, the last i'th' bud,

SCARCITY (1)

MGREC126:17 H3008 The Souldiers pinched with this scarcity,

SCARCLY (1) [scarcely]

MEDDM202:4 Hp281 disproportion that they scarcly seem made of the same lump,

SCARFE (1) [scarf]

AGES36:3 H27 His Suit of Crimson, and his Scarfe of Green:

SCARLET (2)

HUMOUR27:34 H305 This scarlet die's a badge of what's within,

MASSYR68:6 H592 With guifts of Scarlet robe, and Chaines {Chain} of gold,

SCARS (1)

AGES41:2 H222 ugly {outward} marks of his eternal {inward loathsome} scars;

SCARSE (1) [scarce]

MPERS75:17 H878 Scarse finde enough to thank thy loyalty;

SCARSITY (1) [scarcity]

MROMAN137:8 H3459 Of Wives there was so great a scarsity,

SCATTER (1)

AGES43:16 ~~H308~~ Which others scatter, like the dew in *May.*

SCENT (2)

AGES45:33 H423 I cannot scent, savours of pleasant meat,

SEASONS49:35 H128 Whose fragrant scent, {smel} all made-perfume surpasses;

SCEPTER (3)

MPERS89:14 H1448 And rob him both of Scepter, and of Crown;

DIALOG142:9 H38 The regall, peacefull Scepter from thee tane?

SIDNEY149:10 H9 Then {As} she that sway'd the Scepter with her hand:

SCEPTERS (1) [pl.]

HUMOUR32:37 H511 That Kings have laid their Scepters at my feet,

SCHOLAR See SCHOLLAR

SCHOLARS (1) [pl.]

MEDDM195:29 Hp272 speak well, but few can do well. We are better scholars in the

SCHOLLAR (1) [scholar]

HUMOUR23:3 H113 Thou wast not made for Souldier, or for Schollar;

SCHOOL-BOYES (1) [poss.]

PROLOG6:32 H15 From School-boyes tongue, no Rhethorick we expect,

SCHOOLS (1)

AGES39:12 H155 With nurture trained up in vertues Schools,

SCIATICA (1)

AGES43:32 H327 And the restraining lame Sciatica;

SCIENCE (2)

HUMOUR22:21 H90 Again, who sits, for learning, science, Arts?

AGES39:13 H156 Of Science, Arts, and Tongues, I know the rules,

SCIENCES (1) [pl.]

HUMOUR28:27 H339 For Arts, and Sciences, they are the fittest,

SCIPIO (2)

MGREC~~134:2~~ H3335 By *Scipio* the Roman General;

SIDNEY150:36 H63 Of this our noble *Scipio* some good word?

SCITED (1) [cited]
SEASONS~~51:19~~ H195   If scited as the most Judicious take.
SCITHIANS (2) [pl.]
MGREC100:22 H1906 Of *Persians, Scithians, Indians,* in a cluster;
MGREC108:28 H2244 Where *Scithians* rude, his valour {army} doth oppose,
SCITUATE (1) [situate]
2LETTER182:20 H26   Like those far scituate under the pole,
SCITUATION (2) [situation]
HUMOUR33:23 H537 The scituation, and {Its} form wil it avow,
MASSYR64:27 H451 Such was the scituation of this place,
SCOFF (1)
FLESH176:26 H66 How I do live, thou need'st not scoff,
SCOFFES (1) [scoffs]
HUMOUR25:8 H197 Thy other scoffes not worthy of reply:
SCOFFS (1) [pl.]
HUMOUR35:10 H606 Nor jars, nor scoffs, let none hereafter see,
SCORCHED (1)
ELEMEN8:17 H15 Fire broyled Earth, and scorched Earth it choaked,
SCORCHING (1)
CONTEM168:33 H39 Thy pleasing fervor, and thy scorching force,
SCORE (1)
MEDDM204:10 Hp284 the larger his accounts stands vpon gods score it therfore
SCORN (10) See also SCORNE
AGES37:21 H83 In that which riper age did scorn, and slight:
AGES39:22 H165 I scorn the heavy Corslet, Musket-proof,
MASSYR67:32 H578 To chear his friends, and scorn his foes the more.
MPERS71:35 H749 Laughing to scorn that calvish, sottish crew.
MPERS74:37 ~~H858~~ And fear'd, he now with scorn must march away:
MPERS89:19 H1453 The *Greeks* with scorn reject his proud commands;
MGREC94:26 H1664 To scorn at him, *Darius* had good sport:
MGREC99:4 H1847 But he with scorn, his courtesie rejects,
SIDNEY150:3 H28 Which makes severer eyes but scorn thy {slight that} Story,
CONTEM168:13 H22 If so, all these as nought, Eternity doth scorn.
SCORN'D (4) [scorned] See also SCORND
ELEMEN8:11 H9 All would be cheife, and all scorn'd to be under,
MPERS82:21 H1168 Scorn'd *Xerxes,* hated for his cruelty,
MGREC93:24 H1621 His rule to *Greece,* he scorn'd should be confin'd:
MGREC124:25 H2932 *Aridæus* the scorn'd, and simple King,
SCORND (1) [scorned] See also SCORN'D
MYCHILD218:11 Hp244 Diverse who haue scornd + contemd it, hath it not been
SCORNE (2) [scorn]
PROLOG7:16 H29 A Poets Pen, all scorne, I should thus wrong;
ELEMEN15:39 H321 For it, to search my waves, they thought no scorne.
SCORNES (2) [scorns]
HUMOUR22:12 H81 So loving unto all, she scornes to fight.
MPERS85:40 H1316 But *Cyrus* scornes, his brothers feeble wit;
SCORNFULLY (1)
MGREC121:15 ~~H2793~~ Being entreated by him scornfully,
SCORNING (2)
MPERS71:30 H744 But scorning thus by *Jove* to be out-brav'd,
DIALOG143:37 H106 What scorning of the Saints of the most high,

SCORNS (1) See also SCORNES

MGREC98:29　　H1831　He scorns to have one worse then had the other,

SCORN'ST (2) [scornest]

HUMOUR24:39　H188　　And scorn'st all Knightly sports, at turnament.

HUMOUR25:22　H211　　But when thou scorn'st to take the helpe we lend,

SCORPIO (1)

SEASONS51:22　H198　In *Scorpio* resideth now the Sun,

SCORPION (1)

ELEMEN10:7　　H82　　My Crabbe, my Scorpion, fishes, you may see,

SCOTLAND (1)

DIALOG143:15　H84　　My Sister *Scotland* hurts me now no more,

SCOTS (1) [pl.]

DIALOG142:25　H54　　Or, doth {do} the *Scots* play false behind your back?

SCOUTS (1) [pl.]

MPERS87:41　　H1393　When suddenly their Scouts come in and cry,

SCRAMBLE (1)

MGREC94:41　　H1679　Those banks so steep, the *Greeks,* now {yet} scramble up

SCRAT (1) [scratch]

PILGRIM210:9　H9　　The bryars and thornes no more shall scrat

SCREECHING See SCRIECHING

SCRIBLING (1)

SIDNEY152:11　H80　　They took from me, the scribling pen I had,

SCRIECHING (1)

MASSYR66:10　　H516　　Now *Zim,* and *Iim, {Jim}* lift up their shriking {scrieching}

SCRIPTURE (1)

MEDDM199:26　Hp278　We read in Scripture of three sorts of Arrows the arrow of an

SCRIPTURES (2) [pl.]

MYCHILD215:30 Hp241　Scriptures, espec: those places I thought most concerned my

MYCHILD217:33 Hp243　Scriptures, many times by Atheisme how I could know whether

SCUDS (1)

3LETTER182:37 H2　　Scuds through the woods and Fern with harkning ear,

SCUM (1)

AGES42:22　　H280　　Such scum, as Hedges, and High-wayes do yeeld,

SE (9) [see]

MEDDM197:8　　Hp274　they haue more sence then faith they se what they inioy,

MEDDM198:33　Hp277　it, the pure in heart shall se god, but the defiled in conscience

MEDDM200:25　Hp279　we se the leaulesse trees and dry stocks (at the approach of

MEDDM201:19　Hp280　We often se stones hang wth drops not from any innate

MEDDM201:20　Hp281　from a thick ayre about them so may we sometime se, marble

MEDDM202:21　Hp282　the sun is only shadowed by a cloud, that wee cannot se his

MEDDM202:28　Hp282　and se no light, yet then must we trust in the lord and stay

MEDDM204:28　Hp285　vpon him that is lower then he is and if he se, that such a one

MEDDM206:6　　Hp287　We se in the firmament there is but one Sun, among a

SEA (25)

ELEMEN8:15　　H13　　The sea did threat the heavens, the heavens the earth,

ELEMEN19:22　H467　　Then of my tempests, felt at Sea and Land,

AGES38:10　　H113　　I had no ships at Sea, no fraughts to loose.

MASSYR65:3　　H468　　The Sea firm Land, whereon the Army past,

MPERS79:9　　H1031　A Sea passage cuts, behind *Orthos {Athos}* Mount.

MPERS79:13　　H1035　To cross the sea such strength he found too weak,

MPERS79:13　　H1036　Then whips the sea, and with a mind most vain

MPERS79:28	H1054	His answer was, both Land and Sea he feared,
MPERS80:13	H1080	And as at Land, so he at Sea was crost,
MPERS80:17	H1084	Yet thinking to out-match his foes at Sea,
MPERS80:19	H1086	But they as valiant by {fortunate at} Sea, as Land,
MPERS80:27	H1094	Twice beaten thus by {at} Sea, he warr'd no more:
MGREC95:12	H1691	Next *Alexander* marcht, t'wards the black sea;
MGREC98:12	H1814	He leaves not, till he makes {made} the sea firme shoar;
MGREC101:9	H1934	*Phenisian* Sea, and great *Euphrates* high,
MGREC105:34	H2127	Praying the immortall gods, that Sea, and Land,
MGREC~~124:7~~	H2912	With ships at Sea, an Army for the Land,
MGREC124:13	H2920	But had the worst {beaten was} at Sea, as well as {and foil'd
MGREC126:2	H2993	Sea passage gets, and lands in *Thessaly;*
MGREC126:8	H2999	Well fortified, and on the Sea it lies;
MGREC128:23	H3096	*Antigonus* {These princes} at {the} Sea soone had a fight,
MGREC~~131:9~~	H3200	Their fights by Sea, their victories by land,
DUBART154:36	H81	And whilst there's aire, or fire, or sea or land.
VANITY160:30	H40	The depth, and sea, hath {have} said its not in me,
SAMUEL228:2	H3	Thou mighty God of Sea and Land

SEA-GREEN (1)

CONTEM173:6	H174	Who forrage o're the spacious sea-green field,

SEA-MEN (1)

QELIZ156:39	H66	Her Sea-men through all straights the world did round,

SEAL (1)

MYCHILD217:18	Hp243	spirit who hath oft given me his word & sett to his Seal that it

SEARCH (5)

ELEMEN15:39	H321	For it, to search my waves, they thought no scorne.
MPERS83:13	H1201	But yet by search, he was found murthered,
VANITY160:24	H34	Where shall I climbe, sound, seek, search or find,
MYCHILD216:22	Hp241-2	one afflict[n] or other hath made me look home, and search
MYCHILD216:31	Hp242	haue I gone to searching, and haue said wth David Lord search

SEARCHING (1)

MYCHILD216:31	Hp242	Then haue I gone to searching, and haue said wth David Lord

SEAS (6) [pl.]

ELEMEN16:5	H328	My sundry Seas, Black, White, and Adriatique
ELEMEN16:10	H333	If I should shew,{name} more Seas, then thou hast Coasts.
ELEMEN16:12	~~H335~~	Then Seas are deep, Mountains are never high.
ELEMEN~~16:12~~	H335	I soon can match them with my seas as deep.
CONTEM174:16	H215	And now becomes great Master of the seas;
MERCY188:28	H14	Thou then on Seas sailing to forreign Coast;

SEASES (1) [seizes]

REMB235:29	H10	Confusion seases on my Soul

SEASON (13)

ELEMEN10:23	H98	The Summer ripening season I do claime;
ELEMEN13:18	H219	How the Autumnal season I do sway;
SEASONS46:31	H7	In season all these Seasons I shal bring;
SEASONS48:25	H78	For fruits, my season yeelds, the early Cherry,
SEASONS48:28	H81	Each season, hath his fruit, so hath each clime.
MPERS84:29	H1265	Provisions, {then} and season now being fit,
MGREC103:26	H2037	Being inflam'd with wine upon a season,
MGREC117:15	H2622	We may hereafter shew, in season due.
CONTEM172:31	H164	That for each season, have your habitation,

CONTEM173:30	H195	And thus they pass their youth in summer season,
1LETTER181:9	H7	I like the earth this season, mourn in black,
ELIZB187:7	H15	And Corn and grass are in their season mown,
MEDDM207:14	Hp288	notwthstanding we take great delight, for a season in them,

SEASON'S (1) [season is]

SEASONS51:11	H185	The season's now at hand, of all, and each;

SEASONS (6) [pl.]

SEASONS46:26	H1-2	The four Seasons of the Yeare.
SEASONS46:31	H7	In season all these Seasons I shal bring;
CONTEM168:36	H42	Quaternal Seasons caused by thy might:
CHILDRN184:29	H18	And Seasons twain they there did spend:
CHILDRN186:14	H81	No seasons cold, nor storms they see;
MEDDM201:32	Hp281	all seasons the most welcom so a faithfull friend in time of

SEAT (21)

HUMOUR21:13	H41	Yet man for Choler, is the proper seat.
HUMOUR22:26	H95	Poor spirits the Liver breeds, which is thy seat,
HUMOUR22:35	H104	The Brain she challenges, the Head's her seat,
HUMOUR23:11	H121	Yet hast thy {the} seat assign'd, a goodly part,
MASSYR54:17	H44	Transfers his Seat, to the *Assyrian* plain,
MASSYR54:25	H52	This stately seat of warlike *Ninus* stood.
MASSYR57:5	H152	To sit, thus long (obscure) wrong'd {rob'd} of his seat;
MASSYR60:8	H273	And then to {unto} *Media* transfer'd his seat.
MASSYR60:16	H281	*Belosus* setled, in his new, old seat,
MASSYR61:11	H316	*Damascus,* ancient seat of famous Kings,
MASSYR64:35	H459	Within an Island had this City seat,
MASSYR67:28	H574	Layes siedge to's regall seat, proud *Babylon,*
MPERS72:21	H769	Over his Seat, then plac'd his Son therein;
MGREC95:14	H1693	(Of Asse-eard) *Midas,* once the regall seat,
MGREC102:30	H2000	For 'twas the seat of *Persian* Kings renown'd;
MGREC122:16	H2841	To warm the {his} seat, was never her intent,
MGREC125:3	H2951	To make the King by force his seat resigne;
MGREC134:1	H3332	A third *Seleuchus* next sits on the seat,
MROMAN138:9	H3499	Of *Latine* Kings this was long since the Seat,
DIALOG143:5	~~H73~~	No Crook-backt Tyrant, now usurps the Seat,
DIALOG~~143:8~~	H76	No crafty Tyrant now usurps the Seat,

SEATD (1) [seated]

11MAYB228:26	Hp259	this month I had a feaver seatd vpon me wch indeed was the

SEATS (2) [pl.]

ELEMEN10:37	H112	The stately seats of mighty Kings by me:
MPERS81:36	~~H1143~~	The *Beotian* Fields, of war, the seats,

SEAZ'D (1) [seized] See also SEIZ'D

MGREC~~132:6~~	H3241	Seaz'd upon that, and slew him traitrously.

SEBASTIA (1)

SEASONS49:30	H119	*Orthobulus,* nor yet *Sebastia* great,

SECOND (23)

ELEMEN10:30	H105	The over-curious second *Pliny* slew:
HUMOUR20:28	H20	The second, third, or last could not digest;
HUMOUR26:36	H266	The first my self, second my sister faire,
AGES35:21	H7	The second, frolick, claimes his pedigree,
SEASONS47:28	H44	My second month is *April,* green, and fair,
SEASONS50:16	H150	*Romes* second Emperour of peaceful {lasting} fame;

MPERS68:32	H618	The Second Monarchy,
MPERS71:31	H745	A second Army there {he} had almost grav'd;
MPERS75:24	H881	*Darius* in the second of his reign,
MPERS~~77:13~~	H952	Unto {Then to} his eldest {second} Son, all did remain.
MPERS83:25	H1213	The second was inthron'd, in's fathers stead.
MPERS~~85:6~~	H1282	But he, with his next {second} brother {him} fell at strife,
MPERS85:18	H1294	A second trouble, after this succeeds.
MPERS91:24	H1538	And weds his Daughter for a second wife;
MGREC98:18	H1820	Whose glory, now {then} a second time's brought down;
MGREC118:12	H2659	For second offers {offer} there were {was} never made;
MGREC133:2	H3290	The second Son of the first *Ptolomy*,
MGREC135:28	H3400	The first a Lion, second was a Beare,
DIALOG142:17	H46	That second *Richard* must be clapt i'th' Tower?
DIALOG143:11	H80	*Spaines* braving Fleet a second time is sunke,
CONTEM169:19	H59	The black clad Cricket, bear a second part,
CHILDRN184:26	H15	My second bird did take her flight,
MERCY188:33	H19	And in thy griefs still bear a second part:

SECRET (3) See also SECRETT

MPERS~~72:9~~	H757	To act in secret, this his lewd intent:
MPERS80:31	H1098	In secret manner word to *Xerxes* sends,
FLESH175:2	H2	In secret place where once I stood

SECRETLY (2)

MGREC~~119:5~~	H2695	Which was his Masters sister for {secretly} to wed:
MGREC119:6	H2696	So, to the Lady secretly he sent,

SECRETT (1) [secret]

HOURS233:30	H13	In secrett places, Thee I find

SECTARIES (1) [pl.]

MYCHILD218:29	Hp244	Blasphemy, and Sectaries, and some who hauest been acct[d].

SECTARYES (1) [sectaries]

TDUDLEY166:38	H80	*To Sectaryes a whip and Maul,*

SECURE (2)

CONTEM170:36	H106	A City builds, that wals might him secure from foes.
MEDDM196:22	Hp273	open a prosperous state makes a secure christian, but

SECURELY (2)

MPERS70:12	H683	And to the walls securely marches on,
MGREC108:20	H2236	And in his Camp strong, and securely lay,

SECURITY (4)

MPERS83:9	H1197	Of life, no man had least security.
MPERS87:32	H1384	For his security, against his foes.
MGREC~~118:36~~	H2685	For their security did now provide
CONTEM174:27	H225	Only above is found all with security.

SED (2) [said]

MPERS92:25	~~H1583~~	By one *Bagoas,* an Eunuch (as is sed.)
MGREC116:35	H2601	This conquerour did oft lament ('tis sed)

SEDITION (1)

MROMAN138:26	H3516	Who for sedition from his Country fled;

SEE (87) See also SEE'T

ELEMEN9:11	H45	Your shares, {Hooes} your mattocks, and what e're you see,
ELEMEN9:37	H71	And birds do sing, to see his glittering Coach.
ELEMEN10:7	H82	My Crabbe, my Scorpion, fishes, you may see,
ELEMEN10:38	H113	In confus'd heaps of ashes may ye see.

ELEMEN13:7	H208	But you will see what in my bowels lyes?
ELEMEN14:27	H269	Cause of your fruitfulnesse, as you shall see:
HUMOUR21:6	H34	My self, and Mother, one as you shal see,
HUMOUR~~22:19~~	H88	Here's three of you, all sees {see} now what you are,
HUMOUR27:32	H303	My vertues hid, i've let you dimly see;
HUMOUR28:33	H345	Thousand examples, you may daily see
HUMOUR30:13	H405	Reduce the man to's principles, then see
HUMOUR31:8	H441	Now {But} by your leave, Ile let your greatnesse see;
HUMOUR32:12	H486	And things that never were, nor shal I see.
HUMOUR35:10	H606	Nor jars, nor scoffs, let none hereafter see,
AGES39:35	H178	That who would see vain man, may look on me:
AGES41:12	H231	Thus I have said, and what i've said {been,} you see,
AGES43:25	H320	Thus good, and bad, and what I am, you see,
AGES44:11	H344	An end of all perfection now I see.
AGES45:22	~~H404~~	But out of troubles, ye may see much good,
AGES~~45:22~~	H404	To see them swill in blood untill they burst.
AGES~~45:22~~	H410	But out of evil you may see much good.
AGES46:22	H453	And I shal see, with these same very eyes,
SEASONS51:40	H216	Now *Green-land, Groen-land, Lap-land, Fin-land,* see
MASSYR60:32	H297	And from this heap did after Ages see,
MASSYR62:21	H366	And pleasant *Canaan* ne're see again:
MASSYR62:29	H374	They shal return, and *Zion* see, with blisse.
MASSYR67:11	H557	And native *Canaan,* never see again,
MPERS~~69:38~~	H663	His Treasures, pleasures, pomp and power dfd see,
MPERS82:37	H1184	To see that face, where Rose and Lilly stood,
MPERS82:39	H1186	To see those breasts, where chastity did dwel,
MPERS88:24	H1417	Whom *Cyrus* spi'd, cries out, I see the man,
MGREC95:36	H1715	For this wise King, had brought to see the sport;
MGREC95:39	H1718	It seemes to see the *Macedonians* {*Macedonian*} slaughters.
MGREC100:3	H1887	To see how fast he gain'd, is {was} no small wonder,
MGREC105:13	H2106	Should heare, nor see, his groans, and {dying} misery:
MGREC105:37	H2130	As men, the rising, setting Sun shall see.
MGREC106:8	H2142	To see if any dare his might oppose;
MGREC108:9	H2225	These not a little joy'd, this day to see,
MGREC120:11	H2746	*Perdicas* griev'd, to see the Princes bold,
MGREC123:28	H2892	*Cassander* could not (like his father) see
MGREC~~133:25~~	H3315	Such riches too As Rome did never see:
MROMAN137:13	H3464	To see these sports, the *Sabins* all are bent;
DIALOG~~144:25~~	H134	I then believ'd not, now I feel and see,
DIALOG146:32	H218	Your griefs I pity much, but should do wrong {hope to see},
DIALOG146:34	H220	To see these {those} latter dayes of hop'd for good,
DIALOG147:16	H242	Light Christendome, and all the world to see,
SIDNEY149:29	~~H23~~	In all records, thy Name I ever see,
SIDNEY~~150:12~~	H38	In all Records his name I ever see
SIDNEY150:28	H55	Brave *Hector* by the walls of *Troy,* we see:
SIDNEY151:3	~~H69~~	I wish no more such Blazers we may see;
SIDNEY151:28	~~H75~~	Too late my errour see, that durst presume
VANITY160:41	H51	Nor death shall see, but are immortal made,
VANITY161:3	H54	Nor change of state, nor cares shall ever see,
TDUDLEY166:32	H74	Where we with joy each others face shall see,
DDUDLEY167:22	H19	*Of all her Children, Children, liv'd to see,*

811

CONTEM171:6	H111	How Adam sigh'd to see his Progeny,
CONTEM173:5	H173	To see what trade they great ones there do drive,
CONTEM174:25	H223	But sad affliction comes & makes him see
FLESH175:24	H24	What canst desire, but thou maist see
FLESH175:33	H33	Then eyes can see, or hands can hold.
FLESH176:3	H43	Untill I see thee laid in th' dust.
FLESH176:36	H76	Eternal substance I do see,
FLESH176:38	H78	Mine Eye doth pierce the heavens, and see
SICKNES179:10	H30	the victory's mine I see,
DISTEMP179:22	H10	He chac'd away those clouds, and let me see
BIRTH180:5	H15	And if I see not half my dayes that's due,
2LETTER182:19	H25	But for one moneth I see no day (poor soul)
CHILDRN186:14	H81	No seasons cold, nor storms they see;
MERCY188:20	H6	And live I still to see Relations gone,
2SIMON195:7	Hp271	look vpon when you should see me no more, I could think of
MEDDM195:24	Hp272	There is no obiect that we see. no action that we doe, no good
MEDDM204:18	Hp285	action, as we see in Jehu, he is rewarded wth a kingdome to
MEDDM205:31	Hp286	We see in orchards, some trees soe fruitfull, that the waight of
PILGRIM210:30	H30	Nor losses know, nor sorrowes see.
MYCHILD216:32	Hp242	me and try me, see what wayes of wickednes are in me, and
MYCHILD217:36	Hp243	would soon tell me by the wondrovs workes that I see, the vast
MYCHILD218:8	Hp244	see, If ever this God hath revealed himself it mvst bee in his
MYCHILD218:14	Hp244	+ how ye world came to bee as wee see, Do wee not know y^e
SOREFIT221:31	H17	Where pitty most of all I see.
FAINTING222:18	H8	And liueing man no more shall see
MYSOUL225:16	H20	For wonders that I see.
MYSOUL225:22	H26	Thy face when shall I see
28AUG226:10	Hp254	Thing. O let me ever see Thee that Art invisible, and I shall not
SAMUEL228:15	H16	That I again may see his face,
SAMUEL228:20	H21	Perswade my heart I shall him see
2HUSB233:11	H44	Lord let my Eyes see once Again
HOURS234:15	H29	Yet if I see Thee not thro: them

SEED (6)

AGES41:26	H243	Such {My} empty seed should yeeld a better crop.
MGREC132:10	H3245	His seed to be extirpt, was destined,
DIALOG146:19	H205	The seed time's come, but Ploughman hath no hope,
DIALOG148:21	H286	Oh *Abrahams* seed lift up your heads on high.
MEDDM205:4	Hp285	seed of morality, much lesse of grace in them But when by
MEDDM205:5	Hp285	nurture they are brought into a fit capacity, let the seed of good

SEED'S (1) [seed is]

MGREC133:26	H3316	This of *Antigonus,* his seed's the fate,

SEEDS (1) [pl.]

AGES38:13	H116	This was mine innocence, but oh {ah!} the seeds,

SEEDS-MAN (1)

SEASONS47:8	H24	The Seeds-man now {too} doth lavish out his Grain,

SEEING (11) See also SEING

HUMOUR20:35	H27	They seeing her imperiosity, {impetuosity}
MPERS76:19	H917	The King, seeing his men, and victuall spent;
MPERS81:4	H1112	He seeing {finding} all thus tend unto {to his} decay,
MPERS89:39	H1473	The *Greeks,* having {seeing} their valiant Captaines slaine,
MGREC118:27	H2676	*Perdicas,* seeing *Aridæus* must be King,

MGREC118:35 H2684 The Princes seeing *Perdica's* power and Pride,
MGREC~~125:20~~ H2968 King, and Queen, to *Amphipolis* doe fly, {seeing their destiny,}
MGREC~~135:1~~ H3372 He seeing his honour lost, his Kingdome end,
DUBART153:24 H28 But seeing empty wishes nought obtaine,
DUBART153:30 H34 And {But} seeing utterance fayle his great desires,
MEDDM208:2 Hp289 shall fly away, and the day of eternity shall never end, seeing

SEEK (11)
ELEMEN14:14 H256 When they seek food, and harme mistrust the least.
AGES38:5 H108 My duel was no challenge, nor did seek.
AGES40:27 H208 Seek out a Brittish, bruitish Cavaleer;
MASSYR59:28 H252 *Sardanapalus* did not seek to fly,
MGREC105:15 H2108 Wearied with his long march, did water seek,
MGREC134:23 H3354 The seventy two interpreters did seek,
DIALOG142:2 H31 What Medicine shall I seek to cure this woe,
VANITY160:24 H34 Where shall I climbe, sound, seek, search or find,
MEDDM203:18 Hp283 may plainly declare that we seek a citty aboue and wait all the
MEDDM209:4 Hp291 all our seekings and gettings, let vs aboue all seek to obtain
BYNIGHT220:10 H10 In vain I did not seek or cry.

SEEKE (1) [seek]
PROLOG7:9 H23 By Art, he gladly found what he did seeke,

SEEKETH (1)
MPERS91:20 H1528 His home-bred troubles seeketh {sought how} to appease;

SEEKING (1)
MGREC94:8 H1642 In seeking after {Nor making Title unto} Soveraignity:

SEEKINGS (1) [pl.]
MEDDM209:4 Hp291 wth all our seekings and gettings, let vs aboue all seek to

SEEKS (6)
ELEMEN15:12 H294 Then seeks me out, in River and in Well;
MPERS80:5 H1072 None cryes for quarter, nor yet seeks to run,
MGREC119:13 H2703 Their ancient liberty, afresh now seeks,
MGREC~~119:26~~ H2716 Striving {And seeks} to stop *Leonatus,* that so
MGREC123:38 H2902 Unto these helps, in *Greece,* {at home} he seeks out more,
MGREC127:39 H3069 To make *Cassander* odious to them, seeks,

SEEM (12) See also SEEME
FATHER5:16 H17 Might seem of yours to claime precedency;
ELEMEN13:38 H239 While they thus in my {mine} intralls seem {love} to dive;
AGES40:1 H182 But doing so, might seem magnanimous.
MPERS~~91:21~~ H1529 The two Queens, by his means, 'gin {seem} to abate
MGREC94:2 H1636 Which makes each moment seem, more then a day:
TDUDLEY165:18 H20 Who after death might make him falsly seem
BIRTH180:4 H14 I may seem thine, who in effect am none.
3LETTER183:20 H22 I have a loving phere, yet seem no wife:
MEDDM201:21 Hp281 sinners, seem full of contrition, but it is not from any dew of
MEDDM202:4 Hp281 a disproportion that they scarcly seem made of the same
13MAY227:2 H11 And former clowdes seem now all fled
HANNA230:13 H6 When death did seem ev'n to approach

SEEM'D (11) [seemed]
ELEMEN17:23 H387 Wherein not men, but mountaines seem'd to wade
SEASONS47:15 H31 And all that seem'd as dead, afresh do live.
MASSYR60:25 H290 And those which {that} seem'd with *Sardanapal's* gone;
MGREC108:32 H2248 They flew so thick they seem'd to dark the aire:

MGREC113:24 H2451 *Polidamus,* who seem'd *Parmenio's* friend,
MGREC129:16 H3130 The Heavens seem'd slow in paying her the same,
CONTEM167:29 H6 Their leaves & fruits seem'd painted, but was true
CONTEM168:8 H17 Whose ruffling top the Clouds seem'd to aspire;
MERCY188:35 H21 Who lov'd thee more (it seem'd) then her own life.
SOREFIT221:22 H8 And how in sweat I seem'd to melt
28AUG226:9 Hp254 & bequeath my Soul to thee and Death seem'd no terrible

SEEME (4) [seem]
ELEMEN8:22 H20 The worlds confusion it did seeme to threat;
MGREC105:33 H2126 Which made their long restraint, seeme to be none;
MGREC128:4 H3077 And that some title he might seeme to bring,
MEDDM202:7 Hp281 earth some so wise and learned, that they seeme like Angells

SEEMED (2) See also SEEM'D
AGES36:6 H30 Seemed to grow on's head (bedew'd with showers:)
MPERS86:32 H1348 For what was done, seemed no whit offended.

SEEMES (2) [seems]
MGREC95:39 H1718 It seemes to see the *Macedonians* {*Macedonian*} slaughters.
MEDDM202:26 Hp282 go forwards to the Citty of habitation, but when he seemes to

SEEMING (1)
CONTEM169:21 H61 Seeming to glory in their little Art.

SEEMINGLY (1)
AGES41:29 H246 But yet laid hold, on vertue seemingly,

SEEMS (7) See also SEEMES
AGES36:10 H34 He seems to flye, or swim, and not to ride.
SEASONS50:29 H163 The Summer's {Summer seems but} short, the beauteous
MASSYR59:23 H247 For few, or none, did there {it seems} resistance make;
MPERS92:23 H1581 Which by some probabilities (seems rather;)
MGREC132:20 H3265 His story seems a Fable more then true.
CONTEM169:34 H72 Sometimes in *Eden* fair, he seems to be,
CONTEM171:27 H129 Yet seems by nature and by custome curs'd,

SEEM'ST (1)
THEART229:3 H5 I cry'd thov seem'st to make some stay

SEEN (44)
ELEMEN17:6 H370 And swallowes Countryes up, ne're seen againe:
ELEMEN19:31 H472 Some overwelm'd with waves, and seen no more.
AGES36:4 H28 In's countenance, his pride quickly was seen.
AGES41:15 H234 Childehood and youth, forgot, sometimes I've seen,
AGES44:4 H337 Babes innocence, Youths wildnes I have seen,
AGES44:28 H361 Such private changes oft mine eyes have seen,
AGES44:30 H363 I've seen a Kingdom flourish like a tree,
AGES45:2 H377 I've seen a Prince, the glory of our land
AGES45:3 H381 I've seen from *Rome,* an execrable thing,
AGES45:4 H385 I've Princes seen to live on others lands;
AGES45:5 H389 I've seen designes at {for} *Ree,* and *Cades* {*Rochel*} crost,
AGES45:7 H390 I've seen a Prince, to live on others lands,
AGES45:9 H391 I've seen base {unworthy} men, advanc'd to great degree
AGES45:13 H395 I've seen one stab'd, another {and some to} loose his head
AGES45:15 H397 I've seen, and so have ye, for 'tis but late,
AGES45:19 H401 I've seen a land unmoulded with great paine.
AGES45:21 H403 I've seen it shaken, rent, and soak'd in blood,
AGES45:22 H405 I've seen a King by force thrust from his throne,

AGES45:22	H407	I've seen a state unmoulded, rent in twain,
AGES45:22	H409	I've seen it plunder'd, taxt and soak'd in bloud,
SEASONS47:3	H17	Who for some months have seen but starry lights;
SEASONS51:14	H188	For then in *Eden* was not only seen
MASSYR56:35	H141	Who in her Country never more was seen.
MASSYR67:7	H553	In seven and thirty years, had seen no jot,
MPERS70:21	H692	Had after {A} thousand yeares faire to be seen.
MPERS76:22	H920	His enemies scarce seen, then much lesse, slaine;
MPERS78:24	H1005	In person {present} there, now for his help {aid} was seen;
MPERS91:30	H1544	His life may read in *Plutarch* to be seen.
MGREC96:2	H1722	For since the world, was no such Pageant seen.
MGREC100:32	H1916	Who had long {sore} travaile, and much sorrow seen,
MGREC110:5	H2305	Had *Alexander* such resistance seen,
MGREC124:38	H2945	Did make him vow her servant to be seen.
QELIZ156:37	H64	Such Souldiers, and such Captaines never seen,
QELIZ157:9	H77	Had put her Harnesse off, had she but seen
QELIZ157:20	H88	Of her what worth in Story's to be seen,
VANITY160:26	H36	There is a path, no vultures eye hath seen.
TDUDLEY166:6	H48	No ostentation seen in all his wayes,
CONTEM171:21	H124	Nor age nor wrinkle on their front are seen;
CHILDRN184:32	H21	A prettier bird was no where seen,
MEDDM201:7	Hp280	I haue seen an end of all perfection (sayd the royall prophet)
MEDDM201:8	Hp280	never sayd, I haue seen an end of all Sinning, what he did say,
MYCHILD217:24	Hp243	in darknes and seen no light, yet haue I desired to stay my self
30SEPT227:28	Hp257	Thus (dear children) haue yee seen ye many sicknesses and
ACK235:7	H7	Hast heard my cry's, + seen my Teares,

SEENE (1) [seen]

HUMOUR34:10	H565	Yet some may wish, oh, {O} had mine eyes ne're seene.

SEES (11)

HUMOUR22:19	H88	Here's three of you, all sees {see} now what you are,
MGREC122:13	H2838	Perceives {Sees} *Aridæus* must not king it long,
MGREC129:4	H3118	He sees the *Greeks* now favour their young Prince,
MROMAN140:8	H3571	Nor matter is't this last, the world now sees,
SIDNEY150:9	H34	That sees not learning, valour, and morality,
DUBART153:17	H21	Who sees the riches of some famous Fayre;
CONTEM169:35	H73	Sees glorious *Adam* there made Lord of all,
CONTEM170:27	H98	Thinks each he sees will serve him in his kind,
MEDDM199:11	Hp277	till it be throughly heat is vncapable to be wrought, so god sees
MEDDM202:36	Hp282	finds it self, and sees an impossibility, euer to be filled, but by
MEDDM203:17	Hp283	before he sees land we must therfore be heer as strangers and

SEE'ST (2)

2HUSB232:17	H18	Thou see'st how weak + frail I am,
HOURS233:21	H4	And see'st my dropping teares.

SEE'T (3) [see it]

AGES45:20	H402	But yet may live, to see't made up again:
AGES45:22	H408	But ye may live to see't made up again.
DIALOG148:32	H297	But if at all, thou didst not see't before.

SEGREGATION (1)

HUMOUR28:12	H324	Ith' last concoction, segregation make.

SEIGE (3) [siege] See also SIEDGE

MGREC125:10	H2958	To leave his Seige at *Tagra* {*Tegea*}, and with speed

MGREC126:12	H3003	To raise the Seige, and put her foes to flight;
SIDNEY149:4	H4	slaine at the Seige of *Zutphon,*

SEING (3) [seeing]

MYCHILD215:20	Hp240	former it had been perhaps better pleasing to yov, but seing y^e
11MAYA226:19	Hp255	contented thankfull h^t vnder my affliction & weaknes seing it is
11MAYA226:21	Hp255	pleasure espec: seing it is for my spiri^tl. advantage, For I hope

SEIZ'D (1) [seized] See also SEAZ'D

AGES45:2	H378	In prime of youth seiz'd by heavens angry hand,

SEIZE (3)

HUMOUR30:17	H409	When death doth seize the man, your stock is lost,
MASSYR61:17	H322	And divers Cities, by strong hand did seize,
MGREC123:19	H2883	On most part of *Assyria* doth seize,

SEIZED (1) See also SEAZ'D, SEIZ'D

MPERS71:17	H731	He seized first of life, and then of Land;

SEIZES (1) See also SEASES

HUMOUR28:1	H313	So Melancholly ceases {seizes} on a man;

SELDOM (2)

ELEMEN17:19	H383	That *Caucasus* high mounts, are seldom free.
MEDDM198:14	Hp276	but he that is well stored wth both, seldom is so insnared

SELDOME (2)

HUMOUR31:37	H470	But these with you, are seldome resident.
MYCHILD216:33	Hp242	way everlasting: and seldome or never but I haue fovnd either

SELEUCHUS (18)

MGREC118:39	H2688	*Seleuchus* afterward held *Babylon;*
MGREC127:30	H3060	Then with *Seleuchus* straight at ods doth fall,
MGREC127:36	H3066	*Seleuchus, Ptolomy, Cassander* joynes,
MGREC128:18	H3091	*Seleuchus* drove {driven} from government, and lands;
MGREC128:27	H3100	And *Seleuchus* recovers *Babylon,*
MGREC131:10	H3202	*Antigonus* and *Seleuchus,* now {then his} fight
MGREC131:24	H3216	His peace he then with old *Seleuchus* makes,
MGREC131:26	H3218	*Antiochus, Seleuchus* dear lov'd son,
MGREC132:17	H3254	*Seleuchus, Asia* holds, that grieves him sore,
MGREC132:34	H3281	*Seleuchus,* and *Lysimachus;* those {these} twaine
MGREC132:37	H3284	'Twas no small joy, unto *Seleuchus* breast,
MGREC133:4	H3292	*Seleuchus* was as {a} Father, and a friend,
MGREC133:8	H3296	*Antigonus, Seleuchus,* and *Cassander,*
MGREC133:13	H3301	Unto *Seleuchus,* author of that strife.
MGREC133:28	H3318	Longer *Seleuchus* held the Royalty
MGREC133:41	H3331	*Seleuchus* reign'd, when he had lost his life,
MGREC134:1	H3332	A third *Seleuchus* next sits on the seat,
MGREC134:3	H3336	{Fourth} *Seleuchus* next *Antiochus* succeeds,

SELEUCUS (1)

MGREC132:28	H3274	His body *Seleucus* sends to his Son,

SELF (22) See also SELFE, SELF'S

HUMOUR21:6	H34	My self, and Mother, one as you shal see,
HUMOUR22:33	H102	But Flegme her self, is now provok'd at this,
HUMOUR26:36	H266	The first my self, second my sister faire,
HUMOUR27:5	H276	Which is thy self, thy Mother, and thy Sire;
HUMOUR29:29	H380	For {There} to defend my self, thy better part;
AGES39:11	H154	As might my self, and others, profit much:
DIALOG147:8	H234	And for my self, let miseries abound,

DIALOG147:27　H251　When they are gone, then drown your self in teares.
BIRTH180:15　H25　And if thou love thy self, or loved'st me
VERSES184:1　H5　Then may your worthy self from whom it came.
2SIMON195:8　Hp271　you nor of more ease to my self then these short meditations
MEDDM196:12　Hp273　the sincerest christian the least self loue
MEDDM197:19　Hp275　it, and that heart wch is not continually purifieing it self is no fit
MEDDM202:36　Hp282　finds it self, and sees an impossibility, euer to be filled, but by
MEDDM209:19　Hp291　Commoditys w^thin it self, but what it wants, another shall
MYCHILD215:19　Hp240　Truth, not to sett forth my self, but ye Glory of God. If I had
MYCHILD217:8　Hp242　at least in sight) but I haue been apt to forgett him and my Self
MYCHILD217:21　Hp243　my self y^t agst svch a promis, svch tasts of sweetnes ye Gates
MYCHILD217:24　Hp243　and seen no light, yet haue I desired to stay my self upon
MYCHILD217:28　Hp243　thovght were it hell it self and could there find ye Love of God
MYCHILD218:7　Hp244　me over. I haue argved thvs wth my self, That there is a God I
MED223:17　Hp250　I ovght. Lord haueing this hope let me purefye my self as thou

SELFE (13) [self] See also SELF'S

FATHER6:12　H46　From her, that to your selfe more duty owes,
ELEMEN9:32　H66　And of the selfe same nature is with mine,
ELEMEN12:12　H172　That heaven it selfe was oft call'd by that name;
ELEMEN18:28　H432　And with my selfe, I every vacuum fill.
HUMOUR20:26　H18　Pleading her selfe, was most of all desir'd;
HUMOUR24:18　H167　Do'st know thy selfe so well, us so amisse?
HUMOUR24:28　H177　There is no Souldier, but thy selfe thou say'st,
HUMOUR31:4　H437　When by thy heat, thou'st bak'd thy selfe to crust,
AGES37:35　H97　Make strong my selfe, and turne aside weak right.
AGES43:13　H306　There set, I rid my selfe straight out of hand.
DIALOG141:17　H16　And must my selfe dissect my tatter'd state,
SIDNEY150:7　H32　And doth thy {his} selfe, thy {his} worke, and {his} honour
QELIZ156:36　H63　Her selfe *Minerva,* caus'd them so to be;

SELF-ENDS (1)

AGES41:41　H258　Yet all my powers, for self-ends are not spent,

SELFE-SAME (1) [self-same]

MGREC123:12　H2874　That {And} by the selfe-same traps the other laid,

SELF'S (1) [self is]

HUMOUR23:9　H119　Thy self's as dul, as is thy mother Earth.

SELF-SAME (1) See also SELFE-SAME

SIDNEY149:34　H23　Which have the self-same blood yet in my veines;

SELVES (8) [pl.]

ELEMEN14:2　H244　Your Cities and your selves I oft intombe.
HUMOUR21:3　H31　Your selves would judge, but vain prolixity.
HUMOUR21:11　H39　Our noble selves, in a lesse noble Gender.
HUMOUR21:17　H45　One of your selves are my compeers, in place:
HUMOUR24:14　H163　Your selves may plead, your wrongs are no whit lesse,
HUMOUR28:38　H350　No braggs i've us'd, t' your selves {to you} I dare appeale,
HUMOUR29:9　H362　To spare our selves, and beat the whistling winde.
WHAT224:14　H14　Your selves shall Judges bee;

SEMIRAMIS (6)

MASSYR54:38　H65　*Semiramis* from *Menon* he did take,
MASSYR55:3　H69　*Semiramis.*
MASSYR55:5　H71　His wife, *Semiramis,* usurp'd the throne,
MASSYR57:24　H171　And that *Semiramis* then flourished,

MGREC102:16	H1986	The Towers, and Bowers, of proud *Semiramis:*
QELIZ157:4	H72	*Semiramis* to her is but obscure,

SENACHERIB (2)

MASSYR62:30	H375	*Senacherib.*
MASSYR62:31	H376	*Senacherib Salmaneser* succeeds,

SENATE (1)

MROMAN137:23	H3474	Affirme, that by the Senate he was slaine.

SENATORS (1) [pl.]

MROMAN137:2	H3453	A hundred Senators he likewise chose,

SENATOURS (1) [senators]

MROMAN138:30	H3520	A hundred Senatours he more did adde;

SENCE (6) [sense]

MPERS75:19	~~H878~~	In that thy fame shall sound whilst men have sence;
DUBART153:29	H33	The silly Pratler speakes no word of sence;
QELIZ155:19	H10	The sound thereof raps every humane sence;
FLESH175:22	H22	Come, come, Ile shew unto thy sence,
MEDDM197:8	Hp274	they haue more sence then faith they se what they inioy,
ACK235:18	H18	Whose p'sence I so much doe lack.

SENCELESSE (2) [senseless]

MPERS88:32	H1425	Sencelesse and mute they stand, yet breath out groans,
DUBART154:3	H48	More sencelesse then the Stones to *Amphions* Lute,

SENCES (5) [senses, pl.]

HUMOUR33:38	H552	The five most noble Sences, here do dwel,
HUMOUR34:9	H564	Of all the Sences, Sight shal be the Queen;
MGREC112:6	H2392	Whose Sences all, were glutted with delights:
DUBART154:1	H46	A thousand thousand times my senslesse Sences,
CONTEM167:31	H8	Rapt were my sences at this delectable view.

SEND (17)

FATHER6:6	H40	But if I did, I durst not send them you;
ELEMEN12:30	H190	Send forth your well man'd ships, where sun doth rise.
HUMOUR23:37	H147	By th' influence I send still from the heart.
HUMOUR28:18	H330	The over plus I send unto the reines;
MASSYR61:18	H323	To *Tiglath* then doth *Ahaz* send for ease.
MASSYR65:20	H485	Fast bound, intends at {to} *Babel* he shal stay {him to send},
MPERS90:26	H1493	They then *Dercilladas,* send with an Hoast,
MPERS93:4	H1601	Him, to the grave, did Traytor *Bessus* send.
MGREC97:41	H1802	Therefore a Crown, and great provisions {Provision} send;
MGREC113:25	H2452	To doe this deed, they into *Media* send;
MGREC125:23	H2973	And to the Queen, these presents she doth {did} send;
MGREC130:2	H3157	For marriage to *Cleopatra,* doth send
MGREC~~135:1~~	H3373	Did by his Sword his life soon after send.
DIALOG148:5	H270	When thus in Peace: thine Armies brave send out,
AUTHOR178:15	H25	Which caus'd her thus to send thee out of door.
CHILDRN184:22	H11	My mournful chirps I after send,
2HUSB232:28	H29	And send them prosperous gailes

SENDETH (1)

DISTEMP179:21	H9	Who sendeth help to those in misery;

SENDS (29)

HUMOUR22:28	H97	And through the arteries sends {it} o're the frame,
MASSYR61:20	H325	And to *Assyria's* King a Present sends.
MPERS71:9	H725	Then sends to finde a Law for these his sins;

MPERS71:20	H734	He next to *Cyprus* sends his bloudy Hoast,
MPERS80:31	H1098	In secret manner word to *Xerxes* sends,
MPERS81:10	H1118	He instantly to *Athens* sends for peace,
MPERS86:2	H1318	The King provok'd, sends for him to the Court,
MPERS89:17	H1451	Forth-with {Then} he sends {that} to's Tent, they straight
MPERS89:21	H1455	The troubled King, his Herauld sends again,
MPERS89:25	H1459	The King great store of all provision sends,
MGREC94:27	H1665	Sends him a frothy, and contemptuous letter,
MGREC94:31	H1669	Then to his Lieutenant, {he} in *Asia* sends,
MGREC95:28	H1707	To *Greece* he thirty thousand talents sends;
MGREC97:35	H1796	And in short termes, sends this reply againe;
MGREC102:26	H1996	*Antipater,* from *Greece,* sends great {fresh} supplyes;
MGREC102:41	H2011	In his approach, the Governour sends word,
MGREC105:8	H2101	*Darius* bath'd in bloud, sends out his groanes,
MGREC105:30	H2123	He also sends his humble thankfulnesse,
MGREC109:13	H2272	Boats to prepare, *Ephestion* first he sends,
MGREC110:10	H2310	With *Ptolomy,* sends part o' th' other side.
MGREC112:13	H2399	To every Guest, a cup of gold he sends,
MGREC113:4	H2431	*Philotas* after him sends out this cry,
MGREC115:38	H2557	But his excuse with humble thanks he sends,
MGREC119:18	H2708	To brave *Craterus,* then, he sends with speed,
MGREC125:9	H2957	In hast {haste} unto her deare *Cassander* sends,
MGREC126:3	H2994	His Army he divides, sends part away,
MGREC127:40	H3070	Sends forth his declaration from a {declarations near and}
MGREC128:31	H3104	But bravely sends the Prisoners back againe,
MGREC~~132:28~~	H3274	His body *Seleucus* sends to his Son,

SENECA (1)
MGREC114:27	H2497	Of this unkingly deed, {act} doth *Seneca*

SENES (1)
AGES44:9	H342	But now, *Bis pueri senes,* is too true;

SENSATIVE (1) [sensitive]
HUMOUR33:30	H544	And surely the Souls {Soul} sensative here lives,

SENSE See SENCE

SENSES (1) [pl.] See also SENCES
VANITY160:6	H16	The sensuall senses for a time they please,

SENSITIVE See SENSATIVE

SENSLESSE (1) [senseless] See also SENCELESS
DUBART154:1	H46	A thousand thousand times my senslesse Sences,

SENSUALL (1) [sensual]
VANITY160:6	H16	The sensuall senses for a time they please,

SENT (25)
HUMOUR26:27	H257	What hath the heart, but what's sent from the liver?
AGES42:1	H259	For hundreds blesse me, for my bounty sent {lent}.
MASSYR62:19	H364	Then sent his Colonies, theirs to invest;
MASSYR63:15	H400	Embassadours to *Hezekiah* sent, [21 *years.*
MPERS~~72:7~~	H756	*Praxaspes* into *Persia* then is sent,
MPERS72:8	~~H756~~	Who into *Persia* with Commission sent,
MPERS76:11	H909	A Frog, a Mouse, a Bird, an Arrow sent,
MPERS80:38	H1105	Part of his Hoast to *Delphos* sent from thence,
MPERS81:26	H1134	Nor could the brave Ambassador be {he} sent,
MPERS83:6	H1194	His wicked brother, {soon} after sent {him} a crew,

MPERS86:30	H1346	Whose rents and customes, duly he sent in.
MPERS87:17	H1371	Three hundred thousand, yet {he} to *Syria* sent;
MPERS91:3	H1511	To these {them} he thirty thousand Tallents sent,
MGREC98:7	H1809	Sent word, that *Hercules* his Temple stood,
MGREC108:39	H2255	His {A} third supply, *Antipater* now sent,
MGREC109:34	H2293	But Kingly *Porus* this brave answer sent,
MGREC110:41	H2345	His fourth, and last supply, was hither sent,
MGREC111:10	H2355	With rich rewards, he sent them home again,
MGREC~~115:15~~	H2532	His messenger to *Jupiter* he sent,
MGREC115:17	H2536	To meet him there, t' *Antipater* had {he'd} sent,
MGREC119:6	H2696	So, to the Lady secretly he sent,
MGREC119:10	H2700	To whom she sent a message of her mind,
MGREC120:31	H2768	Brave *Ptolomy,* to make a fourth now {then} sent,
MERCY189:2	H23	Because her Soul she'd sent along with thee.
MYCHILD216:12	Hp241	wth a lamenesse wch correction I saw the Lord sent to hu¯ble

SENTENCE (3)

BIRTH179:31	H7	The sentence past is most irrevocable,
MEDDM203:7	Hp283	he haue good cause often to repeat that sentence, vanity of
MEDDM208:15	Hp290	Judgment we must be tryed and as he passes the sentence, so

SENT'ST (1) [sentest]

THEART229:6	H8	And sent'st me help from High.

SEPERATE (1)

MPERS78:27	H1008	{But} Hers she kept stil, seperate from the rest,

SEPHARUAIM'S (1) [poss.]

MASSYR62:35	H380	On *Hena's, {Hevahs* and on *Sepharuaim's* gods,

SEPT. (3) [september]

MERCY188:18	H2-4	*Mrs. Mercy Bradstreet, who deceased* Sept. 6.
30SEPT227:17	Hp257	Sept. 30. 1657.
REMB235:22	H3	Sept. 3. 1662.

SEPTEMBER (1)

SEASONS50:38	H172	Of Autumne months, *September* is the prime,

SEPULCHER (2)

ELEMEN14:3	H245	O dreadfull Sepulcher! that this is true,
MGREC111:34	H2379	Then visits *Cyrus* Sepulcher in's way,

SERAPHIMS (1) [pl.]

CHILDRN186:13	H80	And there with Seraphims set song:

SERENE (1)

HUMOUR23:26	H136	Whose Serene {profound} heads, I line with policies,

SERJEANT (1) [sergeant]

AGES41:11	~~H230~~	Ceas'd by the gripes of Serjeant Death's Arrests:

SERMONS (1) [pl.]

DIALOG144:22	H132	The Sermons yet upon record doe stand,

SERPENTS (1) [poss.]

AGES38:22	H125	A serpents sting in pleasing face lay hid.

SERUICE (1) [service]

MEDDM204:22	Hp285	wch should warn him, that doth any speciall seruice for god, to

SERV'D (4) [served]

MASSYR57:7	H154	Which made the people think they serv'd her Son;
MPERS76:1	H899	A bridge he made, which serv'd for boat, and barge,
MGREC96:37	H1757	And how {that} his wealth serv'd but for baits t'allure,
TDUDLEY166:22	H64	His Generation serv'd his labours cease;

SERVANT (7)

ELEMEN10:33	H108	And though I be a servant to each man;
MASSYR61:21	H326	I am thy Servant, and thy Son (quoth he)
MGREC94:28	H1666	Stiles him disloyall servant, and no better;
MGREC104:17	H2069	Bidding his {Then bids} servant *Artabassus* true;
MGREC124:38	H2945	Did make him vow her servant to be seen.
MED223:5	Hp250	master I thy servant, But hence arises not my comfort, Thou
2HUSB232:9	H10	Thy servant Lord. Keep & p^rserve

SERVANTS (6) [pl.]

MGREC105:1	H2094	Then slew his servants, that were faithfull found;
DDUDLEY167:14	H11	*To Servants wisely aweful, but yet kind,*
MEDDM197:32	Hp275	is not fit for bread, god so deales wth his servants, he grindes
MYCHILD217:16	Hp243	and refreshing wch I supposed most of the servants of God
JULY223:29	Hp251	him who is the only portion of his Servants.
2HUSB233:9	H42	That I and all thy servants may

SERVE (8)

MASSYR58:10	H195	Longer to serve this Metamorphos'd beast;
MPERS89:31	H1465	But Kings ne're want such as can serve their will,
MGREC122:15	H2840	But that her Husband serve for supplement,
CONTEM170:27	H98	Thinks each he sees will serve him in his kind,
CONTEM174:19	H218	Which 'gainst all adverse winds may serve for fort.
BYNIGHT220:19	H17	I'le serve him here whilst I shall liue
WHAT224:1	H1	What God is like to him I serve
HOURS234:31	H45	And serve thee better then before

SERVED (3) See also SERV'D

MPERS~~92:20~~	H1578	And the same sauce had served him no doubt,
DUBART154:24	H69	In giving one, what would have served seven.
DUBART154:26	H71	Thy double portion would have served many.

SERVICE (5) See also SERUICE

MASSYR58:34	H217	Prest for this service, by the Kings command;
MPERS72:26	~~H773~~	His cruell Master, for all service done,
MGREC115:28	H2547	His service great now's suddenly forgot,
DUBART153:1	H5	In humble wise have vow'd their service long;
28AUG226:6	Hp254	Lord gravnt y^t while I live I may doe y^t service I am able in this

SERVITORS (1)

MGREC104:20	H2072	And of {by} his Guard, and Servitors now left.

SERVITUDE (2)

MASSYR62:6	H351	But weary of his servitude, he sought,
MGREC120:1	H2732	But under servitude, their necks remain'd,

SERVIUS (3)

MROMAN138:37	H3527	*Servius Tullius.*
MROMAN138:38	H3528	Next, *Servius Tullius* sits upon {gets into} the Throne,
MROMAN139:8	H3536	Forty foure yeares did *Servius Tullius* reigne,

SET (1) n.

HUMOUR33:25	H539	*Galen, Hipocrates,* drives {drive} to a set.

SET (54) v. See also SETT

PROLOG6:22	H7	Let Poets, and Historians set these forth,
ELEMEN9:9	H43	Set ope those gates, that 'fore so strong was {were} barr'd.
AGES35:29	H15	Upon his head a Garland Nature set:
AGES~~38:12~~	H115	Nor yet on future things did place {set} my hope.
AGES42:6	H264	The proud I crush'd, th' oppressed I set free,

AGES42:41	H297	And greater stil, did {and thirst for honour,} set my heart on
AGES43:13	H306	There set, I rid my selfe straight out of hand.
SEASONS47:37	H49	All Plants, and Flowers, {set and sown} for all delights, and
SEASONS47:41	H53	Among the verduous Grasse hath Nature set,
SEASONS48:2	H55	These might as Lace, set out her Garments fine;
MASSYR59:5	H229	And set upon their Princes Camp that night;
MASSYR61:22	H327	From *Rezin,* and from *Pekah* set me free:
MASSYR64:6	H430	Kild, sav'd, pull'd down, set up, or pain'd, or eas'd;
MPERS69:35	H657	Then on a Pike being {wood-pile} set, where all might eye,
MPERS72:35	H779	Had set a *Smerdis* up, of the same years;
MPERS75:39	H896	Set up a Temple (though, a lesse) again.
MPERS86:9	H1325	*Mnemon* now sits {set} upon his fathers Throne,
MPERS88:20	H1413	He with six hundred, on a squadron set,
MPERS92:14	H1572	By the same Eunuch who first set him up.
MPERS92:16	H1574	*Darius* by this *Bogoas* set in throne,
MPERS92:17	H1575	By favour, force, or fraud, is not set down:
MGREC95:23	H1702	But sets {Yet set} one in his roome, and ran away.
MGREC96:21	H1741	Their golden Ornaments so {how} to set forth,
MGREC100:36	H1920	The more because not set at liberty;
MGREC101:26	H1951	The afflicted King, finding him set to jar,
MGREC103:29	H2040	Commands to set this goodly town on fire.
MGREC108:22	H2238	And there most fiercely set upon the same;
MGREC110:14	H2314	The last set on his back, and so prevail'd;
MGREC111:37	H2382	And set his Crown on his supposed head;
MGREC113:33	H2460	By him was set upon the *Persian* Throne:
MGREC123:37	H2901	On whom ('twas thought) she set her chief delight;
MGREC132:20	H3263	As Heaven and Earth against him had been set:
MGREC133:38	H3328	The affinities and warres *Daniel* set forth,
MGREC134:7	H3339	By him was set up the abomination
MGREC134:36	H3367	Whom *Julius Cæsar* set in Royall place,
MROMAN137:28	H3479	Kept shut in peace, but {set} ope when bloud was spilt;
DIALOG148:14	H279	And tear his flesh, and set your feet on's neck,
SIDNEY149:18	H17	More worth was thine, {his} then *Clio* could set down.
SIDNEY151:14	H69	But *Omphala,* set *Hercules* to spin,
QELIZ158:2	H111	She set, she set, like *Titan* in his rayes,
QELIZ158:2	H111	She set, she set, like *Titan* in his rayes,
QELIZ158:3	H112	No more shall rise or set such {so} glorious Sun,
VANITY159:34	H6	What is't in honour, to be set on high?
TDUDLEY166:8	H50	Which all they have, and more still set to view,
1LETTER181:22	H20	I wish my Sun may never set, but burn
CHILDRN186:13	H80	And there with Seraphims set song:
ELIZB187:9	H17	But plants new set to be eradicate,
ANNEB187:19	H9	When I on fading things my hopes have set?
MEDDM196:2	Hp272	that beares much saile & little or no ballast, is easily ouer set,
MEDDM202:5	Hp281	out of the loynes of one Adam, some set in yᵉ highest dignity,
MEDDM202:22	Hp282	although we may walk by his light, but when he is set, we are
MEDDM202:27	Hp282	set and be quite gone out of sight then must we needs walk in
MEDDM205:23	Hp286	would keep a pure heart and lead a blamlesse life, must set
MEDDM207:23	Hp289	our great landlord to let: All haue their bounds set ouer wᶜʰ

SETLED (6) [settled]

MASSYR60:16	H281	*Belosus* setled, in his new, old seat,

seven

MPERS90:10   H1483   There was of *Greeks,* setled a Colony,
MPERS~~92:18~~   H1576   And was no sooner setled in his reign,
DIALOG147:33   H257   At that thy setled Peace, thy wealth and splendour,
FLESH175:39   H39   Disturb no more my setled heart,
ELIZB187:3   H12   Sith thou art setled in an Everlasting state.

SETLING (1) [settling]
MGREC100:13   H1897   Then setling all things in lesse *Asia,*

SETS (13)
MASSYR59:31   H255   Then on himself, and them, a fire he sets;
MASSYR67:22   H568   Whose prophane acts, a sacred pen sets down.
MPERS70:24   H695   He with his Vnckle *Daniel* sets on high,
MPERS70:29   H700   And sets on *Cyrus,* in a fatall houre;
MPERS91:6   H1514   With broyls, and quarrels, sets all *Greece* on fire.
MGREC95:23   H1702   But sets {Yet set} one in his roome, and ran away.
MGREC103:16   H2027   Here of his own, he sets a Garrison,
MGREC~~104:7~~   H2059   With sage advice, he layes {sets} before his eyes,
MGREC107:12   H2187   Which done, sets fire upon those costly {goodly} spoyls
MGREC135:2   H3374   {His brave *Virago*} Aspes she sets unto {to} her Armes,
CONTEM173:27 H192   Sets hundred notes unto thy feathered crew,
MEDDM198:10   Hp276   sets his foot And he that passes through the wildernes of this
MEDDM205:28   Hp286   we doe, but he that wth David, sets the lord alway in his sight

SETT (6) v. [set]
MYCHILD215:19 Hp240   Truth, not to sett forth my self, but ye Glory of God. If I had
MYCHILD215:33 Hp241   made my Suplicat^n. to the most High who sett me free from
MYCHILD217:18 Hp243   spirit who hath oft given me his word & sett to his Seal that it
MYCHILD217:20 Hp243   world knowes not, & haue sett vp my Ebenez^r. and haue
28AUG226:4   Hp254   sett vpon the world.
SON231:12   H24   Without (all fraud) did'st sett him free

SETTING (1)
MGREC105:37   H2130   As men, the rising, setting Sun shall see.

SETTLE (1)
MGREC~~122:32~~   H2853   That he might settle matters in the same.

SETTLED See SETLED

SETTLING See SETLING

SEUERALL (1) [several]
MEDDM198:3   Hp275   their seuerall conditions, if he will make his face to shine vpon

SEVEN (19)
HUMOUR34:14   H569   All nerves (except seven paire) to it retain;
MASSYR61:39   H344   Thus *Tiglath* reign'd, and warr'd, twenty seven years,
MASSYR~~65:27~~   H492   And more then {seven and} thirty years in prison fed;
MASSYR65:32   H497   Seven years he keeps his faith, and safe he dwels,
MASSYR66:26   H532   Although the Furnace be seven times more hot;
MASSYR66:30   H536   Which for seven years his reason took away;
MASSYR67:7   H553   In seven and thirty years, had seen no jot,
MPERS73:15   H802   Of which the cheife were {was} seven, call'd *Satrapes,*
MPERS74:2   H827   That {Out} of the seven a Monarch chosen be;
MPERS79:14   H1040   Seven thousand Gallies chain'd, by *Tyrians* skil,
MPERS79:16   H1042   Seven dayes and nights, his Hoast without least stay,
MPERS87:10   H1366   Seven hundred *Greeks* now further {repair for} his intents:
MGREC98:17   H1819   In seven months space {time} he takes this lofty {took that
MGREC118:14   H2661   Seven dayes the Corps of their great Master lyes

MGREC134:22	H3353	{And} With seven hundred thousand volumes fill'd,
MROMAN137:22	H3473	Others, the seven and thirtyeth of his reigne
DUBART154:24	H69	In giving one, what would have served seven.
ANNEB187:15	H5	*seven Moneths old.*
MEDDM200:33	Hp280	wise father will not lay a burden on a child of seven yeares old,

SEVENFOLD (1)

DIALOG144:32	H140	And will repay it sevenfold in my lap,

SEVENTEEN (2)

MPERS78:5	H986	His Foot was seventeen hundred thousand strong,
MGREC108:35	H2251	Upon this River banck in seventeen dayes,

SEVENTH (2)

MPERS69:4	H626	He in descent the seventh from *Arbaces*.
MPERS84:~~12~~	H1241	Good *Ezra* in the seventh year of his reign,

SEVENTY (2)

MASSYR66:12	H518	There {And} sit bewailing *Zion* seventy years,
MGREC134:23	H3354	The seventy two interpreters did seek,

SEVER (1)

1LETTER181:7	H5	So many steps, head from the heart to sever

SEVERALL (7) [several]

MPERS92:29	H1587	That severall men, will have their severall mind;
MPERS92:29	H1587	That severall men, will have their severall mind;
MGREC96:25	H1745	Like severall houses moving upon wheeles:
MGREC131:9	H3199	Their severall battells, and their severall fate,
MGREC131:9	H3199	Their severall battells, and their severall fate,
MEDDM198:16	Hp276	The skillfull fisher hath his severall baits, for severall fish, but

SEVERALLY (1)

MPERS78:9	H990	The charge of all he severally commended,

SEVERE (1)

TDUDLEY167:1	H83	*In manners pleasant and severe*

SEVERED (1)

MEDDM208:6	Hp289	As the brands of a fire, if once severed, will of themselues goe

SEVERER (1)

SIDNEY150:3	H28	Which makes severer eyes but scorn thy {slight that} Story,

SEVERITY (1)

MPERS72:18	H766	This strange severity, one time {sometimes} he us'd,

SEX (10)

PROLOG7:22	H34	Else of our Sex, why feigned they those nine,
HUMOUR24:4	H153	What differences the Sex, but only heat?
HUMOUR25:25	H214	Nor sparing Sex, nor age, nor fire, nor son.
MASSYR55:7	H73	And was both shame, and glory of her sex;
MGREC108:15	H2231	Nor sex, nor age, nor one, nor other spar'd,
MGREC109:4	~~H2261~~	To age, nor sex, no pitty doth expresse,
MGREC117:38	H2645	Claim'd not, perhaps her Sex might hindrance be.
SIDNEY152:10	~~H79~~	In being done by one of their own sex;
QELIZ156:7	H34	She hath wip'd off th' aspersion of her Sex,
QELIZ157:36	H104	Let such, as say our sex is void of reason,

SEXES (2) [pl.]

ELEMEN10:1	H76	My Planets, of both Sexes, whose degree
MGREC95:35	H1714	(Both sexes there) was almost numberlesse.

SEXTUS (1)

MROMAN139:14	H3542	*Sextus* his Son, doth {did} (most unworthily)

SHADED (1)
  CONTEM168:16 H24   Whose beams was shaded by the leavie Tree,

SHADOW (7)
  MASSYR64:4   H428   Under whose shadow, birds, and beasts, had birth;
  MGREC112:8   H2394 To shadow forth these short felicities:
  CONTEM172:6 H142   Under the cooling shadow of a stately Elm
  ANNEB187:27 H17   Or like a shadow turning as it was.
  MEDDM201:31 Hp281 A shadow in the parching sun, & a shelter in a blustering
  MEDDM207:15 Hp288 find their shadow very comfortable, yet there is some worm or
  13MAY227:6   H15   A shadow from ye fainting heat

SHADOWED (1)
  MEDDM202:21 Hp282 Sometimes the sun is only shadowed by a cloud, that wee

SHADOWES (2) [shadows]
  FLESH175:21   H21   To catch at shadowes which are not?
  MEDDM196:18 Hp273 and the shadowes of his euening to be stretched out, lifts vp

SHADOWS (1) [pl.]
  FLESH176:32   H72   Nor are they shadows which I catch,

SHADY (2)
  CONTEM172:10 H146   I once that lov'd the shady woods so well,
  CHILDRN186:4 H71   In shady woods I'le sit and sing,

SHAK'D (1) [shaked]
  ELEMEN9:6   H40   The adverse wall's not shak'd, the Mine's not blowne,

SHAKE (5)
  ELEMEN13:40 H241   Ye affrighted wights, appall'd how do you shake
  SEASONS50:30 H164   To shake his fruit, of most delicious tastes;
  MGREC~~119:14~~ H2704 {And gladly would} Shakes {shake} off the yoke, sometimes
  DIALOG146:29 H215   Shake off your dust, chear up, and now arise,
  MEDDM200:12 Hp279 affliction on their loynes that so they might shake hands wth

SHAKED See SHAK'D

SHAKEN (4)
  AGES40:37   H216   Sometimes by {with} Agues all my body shaken;
  AGES45:21   ~~H403~~   I've seen it shaken, rent, and soak'd in blood,
  MASSYR59:27 H251   By this accomplishment, their hearts were shaken:
  MGREC99:23   H1866 (For 'twas decreed, that Empire should be shaken)

SHAKES (1)
  MGREC119:14 H2704 {And gladly would} Shakes {shake} off the yoke, sometimes

SHAL (39) [shall]
  PROLOG6:23   H8   My obscure Verse,{Lines} shal not so dim their worth.
  ELEMEN11:6   H126   What shal I say of Lightning, and of Thunder,
  ELEMEN11:14 H134   And in a word, the World I shal consume,
  ELEMEN11:16 H136   Not before then, shal cease my raging ire,
  HUMOUR21:5   H33   It shal suffice, to tel {shew} you what I am:
  HUMOUR21:6   H34   My self, and Mother, one as you shal see,
  HUMOUR24:9   H158   To what you now shal say, I wil attend,
  HUMOUR25:9   H198   Shal vanish as of no validity.
  HUMOUR26:10 H240   Yet shal with equity give thee thy part,
  HUMOUR26:24 H254   Shal justly claime priority of thine;
  HUMOUR26:30 H260   For of such glory I shal thee bereave;
  HUMOUR27:16 H287   To meddle further, I shal be but shent,
  HUMOUR27:24 H295   Shal firstly {chiefly} take her {the} place, as is her {my} due,
  HUMOUR29:13 H366   Thy soothing girds shal fully be repaid;

HUMOUR29:20	H371	Thy fiery spirit shal bear away this prize,
HUMOUR29:41	H392	But's not thy {thine} ignorance shal thus deceive me.
HUMOUR30:6	H398	The melancholy Snake shal it aver.
HUMOUR30:16	H408	Yet time and age, shal soon declare it mine.
HUMOUR30:19	H411	You'l say, here none shal ere disturbe my right;
HUMOUR32:12	H486	And things that never were, nor shal I see.
HUMOUR32:16	H490	We shal expect much sound, but little force.
HUMOUR34:9	H564	Of all the Sences, Sight shal be the Queen;
HUMOUR35:6	H602	My cold, cold Melanchollies {melancholy} hand shal clasp,
HUMOUR35:7	H603	Her dry, dry Cholers other hand shal grasp;
AGES41:21	H239	But what's of worth, your eyes shal first behold,
AGES46:1	H432	Shal both be broke, by wracking death so strong;
AGES46:2	H433	I then shal go, whence I shal come no more,
AGES46:2	H433	I then shal go, whence I shal come no more,
AGES46:8	H439	From King to begger, all degrees shal finde
AGES46:19	H450	There, {Where} I shal rest, til heavens shal be no more;
AGES46:19	H450	There, {Where} I shal rest, til heavens shal be no more;
AGES46:20	H451	And when this flesh shal rot, and be consum'd,
AGES46:21	H452	This body, by this soul, shal be assum'd;
AGES46:22	H453	And I shal see, with these same very eyes,
AGES46:24	H455	Triumph I shal, o're Sin, o're Death, o're Hel,
SEASONS46:31	H7	In season all these Seasons I shal bring;
MASSYR62:29	H374	They shal return, and *Zion* see, with blisse.
MASSYR65:20	H485	Fast bound, intends at {to} *Babel* he shal stay {him to send},
TDUDLEY166:33	H75	And parted more by death shal never be.

SHALL (193)

FATHER6:8	H42	I shall not need my {mine} innocence to clear,
ELEMEN14:27	H269	Cause of your fruitfulnesse, as you shall see:
ELEMEN17:30	H394	That after times, shall never feel like woe:
HUMOUR27:9	H280	So wil {shall} I give the dignity to you.
SEASONS51:33	H209	His dead old stock, again shall mount on high.
SEASONS53:7	H263	*And all the faults which {that} you shall spy,*
SEASONS53:8	H264	*Shall at your feet for pardon cry.*
MPERS75:19	H878	In that thy fame shall sound whilst men have sence;
MPERS75:32	H889	Shall let the work, or keep back any thing,
MPERS75:35	H892	That shall, but {once} dare {to} raze those firme foundations;
MPERS92:28	H1586	And he that story reads, shall often find;
MGREC101:15	H1940	*Ochus* his Son a hostage shall {should} endure.
MGREC105:37	H2130	As men, the rising, setting Sun shall see.
MGREC106:6	H2140	Though gods on earth, like Sons of men shall {they} dye.
MGREC114:30	H2500	Which shall not be obliterate by time,
MGREC116:11	H2577	Monarchs fame} must last, whilst world shall {doth} stand,
MGREC128:40	H3113	That each shall {should} hold what he doth {did} now possesse,
MGREC129:1	H3115	Who then shall {should} be installed in the throne:
MGREC131:12	H3204	And he that conquerour shall now remain,
MGREC131:13	H3205	Of *Asia* the Lordship shall retain.
MGREC132:2	H3235	He, whom she gave his life, her death must {shall} give
MGREC136:15	H3429	*Yet in this Chaos, one shall easily spy,*
DIALOG142:2	H31	What Medicine shall I seek to cure this woe,
DIALOG142:32	H61	Such is her poverty, yet shall be found
DIALOG146:20	H206	Because he knows not, who shall inn his crop:

DIALOG146:37	H223	But now the Sun in's brightnesse shall appear,
DIALOG147:6	H232	And shall I not on those {them} with *Mero's* curse,
DIALOG~~147:31~~	H255	Out of all mists, such glorious dayes will {shall} bring,
DIALOG147:32	H256	That dazzled eyes beholding much shall wonder
DIALOG147:35	H259	That all shall joy that thou display'dst thy banner,
DIALOG147:37	H261	That nursing Kings, shall come and lick thy dust:
DIALOG147:38	H262	Then Justice shall in all thy Courts take place,
DIALOG147:40	H264	Then bribes shall cease, and suits shall not stick long,
DIALOG147:40	H264	Then bribes shall cease, and suits shall not stick long,
DIALOG148:1	H266	Then High Commissions shall fall to decay,
DIALOG148:3	H268	So shall thy happy Nation ever flourish,
DIALOG148:4	H269	When truth and righteousnesse they thus shall nourish.
DIALOG148:23	H288	The scales shall fall from your long blinded eyes,
DIALOG148:24	H289	And him you shall adore, who now despise,
DIALOG148:25	H290	Then fulness of the Nations in shall flow,
DIALOG148:29	H294	No Canaanite shall then be found ith' land,
DIALOG148:30	H295	And holinesse, on horses bells shall stand,
SIDNEY150:13	H48	{The more I} say truth, {the more} thy worth I shall but staine,
SIDNEY152:28	H97	*His praise is much, this shall suffice my pen,*
DUBART153:14	H18	They shall be consecrated in my Verse,
DUBART154:32	H77	All ages wondring at, shall never clime.
DUBART154:35	H80	Thus *Bartas* fame shall last while starres do stand,
DUBART154:39	H84	Ile leave thy praise, to those shall doe thee right,
QELIZ157:26	H94	She was a Phoenix Queen, so shall she be,
QELIZ158:3	H112	No more shall rise or set such {so} glorious Sun,
QELIZ~~158:5~~	H114	If then new things, their old form must {forms shall} retain,
QELIZ158:6	H115	*Eliza* shall rule *Albian* once again.
VANITY159:35	H7	No, they like beasts, and sonnes of men shall die,
VANITY160:7	H17	Mean while the conscience rage, who shall appease?
VANITY160:21	H31	While man is man, he shall have ease or pain.
VANITY160:24	H34	Where shall I climbe, sound, seek, search or find,
VANITY160:31	H41	With pearl and gold it shall not valued be:
VANITY160:36	H46	It brings to honour, which shall not {ne're} decay,
VANITY160:40	H50	Nor strength nor wisdome, nor fresh youth shall fade,
VANITY160:41	H51	Nor death shall see, but are immortal made,
VANITY161:2	H53	Who is possessed of, shall reign a King.
VANITY161:3	H54	Nor change of state, nor cares shall ever see,
TDUDLEY165:10	H12	Nor is't Relation near my hand shall tye;
TDUDLEY165:34	H36	Thy love to true Religion e're shall shine,
TDUDLEY166:32	H74	Where we with joy each others face shall see,
CONTEM169:22	H62	Shall Creatures abject, thus their voices raise?
CONTEM171:34	H135	Shall I then praise the heavens, the trees, the earth
CONTEM171:36	H137	Shall I wish there, or never to had birth,
CONTEM172:2	H139	Nay, they shall darken, perish, fade and dye,
CONTEM172:3	H140	And when unmade, so ever shall they lye,
CONTEM174:36	H233	Shall last and shine when all of these are gone.
FLESH175:29	H29	Which wearing time shall ne're deject.
FLESH176:22	H62	My greatest honour it shall be
FLESH176:24	H64	And triumph shall, with laurel head,
FLESH177:1	H82	But Royal Robes I shall have on,
FLESH177:16	H97	Which shall remain for ever pure,

FLESH177:20	H101	For there shall be no darksome night.
FLESH177:22	H103	For evermore they shall be free,
FLESH177:23	H104	Nor withering age shall e're come there,
FLESH177:24	H105	But beauty shall be bright and clear;
FLESH177:26	H107	For things unclean there shall not be:
SICKNES178:26	H9	Yet live I shall, this life's but small,
SICKNES178:28	H11	Where I shall have all I can crave,
SICKNES179:3	H23	Then deaths arrest I shall count best,
BIRTH180:13	H23	And when thy loss shall be repaid with gains
BIRTH180:17	H27	And if chance to thine eyes shall bring this verse,
1LETTER181:26	H24	Till natures sad decree shall call thee hence;
CHILDRN185:16	H42	As is ordain'd, so shall they light.
CHILDRN186:3	H70	Till my weak layes with me shall end,
CHILDRN186:16	H83	When each of you shall in your nest
ANNEB187:30	H20	Farewel dear child, thou ne're shall come to me,
ANNEB187:31	H21	But yet a while, and I shall go to thee;
MEDDM196:15	Hp273	comes he shall both take his rest and receiue his reward, the
MEDDM198:33	Hp277	it, the pure in heart shall se god, but the defiled in conscience
MEDDM198:34	Hp277	shall rather choose to be buried vnder rocks and mountains
MEDDM200:27	Hp279	what they lost in the Autumn so shall it be at that great day
MEDDM200:28	Hp279	when the Sun of righteoussnes shall appear those dry bones
MEDDM200:29	Hp279	shall arise in far more glory, then that wch they lost at their
MEDDM200:30	Hp279	in this transcends the spring, that their leafe shall neuer faile
MEDDM203:19	Hp283	dayes of our appointed time till our chang shall come,
MEDDM204:7	Hp284	need of him, to day as well as yesterday, and so shall for euer,
MEDDM204:12	Hp284	shall call him to reckoning, he may receiue his owne wth
MEDDM206:17	Hp287	shall they be, when they are fixt in their heauenly spheres
MEDDM206:24	Hp287	barter for it, shall meet with miserable disapointment, going
MEDDM207:25	Hp289	no paines nor troubles, shall put a period to our dayes, the
MEDDM208:1	Hp289	at whose comeing they shall all rise out of their beds, The
MEDDM208:2	Hp289	night shall fly away, and the day of eternity shall never end,
MEDDM208:2	Hp289	shall fly away, and the day of eternity shall never end, seeing
MEDDM208:15	Hp290	we must be tryed and as he passes the sentence, so shall we
MEDDM209:14	Hp291	accursed inmates, but make a league with them, they shall at
MEDDM209:19	Hp291	w^{thin} it self, but what it wants, another shall supply, that
PILGRIM210:7	H7	The burning sun no more shall heat
PILGRIM210:8	H8	Nor stormy raines, on him shall beat
PILGRIM210:9	H9	The bryars and thornes no more shall scrat
PILGRIM210:10	H10	nor hungry wolues at him shall catch
PILGRIM210:11	H11	He erring pathes no more shall tread
PILGRIM210:14	H14	for thirst no more shall parch his tongue
PILGRIM210:15	H15	No rugged stones his feet shall gaule
PILGRIM210:25	H25	This body shall in silence sleep,
PILGRIM210:26	H26	Mine eyes no more shall ever weep
PILGRIM210:27	H27	No fainting fits shall me assaile
PILGRIM210:31	H31	What tho my flesh shall there consume
PILGRIM210:33	H33	And when a few yeares shall be gone
PILGRIM210:34	H34	this mortall shall be cloth'd vpon
PILGRIM210:36	H36	a glorious body it shall rise
PILGRIM210:39	H39	Then soule and body shall vnite
PILGRIM210:41	H41	Such lasting ioyes, shall there behold

TOCHILD215:7	H7	And God shall blesse yov from above.
MYCHILD215:12	Hp240	latest, + being ignorant whether on my death bed I shall haue
MYCHILD215:22	Hp240	The method I will observe shall bee this—I will begin wth Gods
MYCHILD217:2	Hp242	mercyes, For if yee bee his yee shall reap the greatest
MYCHILD217:19	Hp243	shall bee well with me. I haue somt. tasted of y^t hidden Manna
MYCHILD217:22	Hp243	shall never p^{r}vail: yet haue I many Times sinkings &
MYCHILD218:36	Hp244	+ if I perish, I perish, But I know all ye powers of Hell shall
BYNIGHT220:17	H15	What to my Sav^r. shall I giue?
BYNIGHT220:19	H17	I'le serve him here whilst I shall liue
FEVER221:5	H20	What tho: in dust it shall bee lay'd
FEVER221:6	H21	To Glory t' shall bee brovght.
SOREFIT221:27	H13	I said I shall praise thee at lenght.
SOREFIT221:28	H14	What shall I render to my God
SOREFIT222:1	H20	My life shall dedicated bee
FAINTING222:15	H5	So shall I giue it thee.
FAINTING222:18	H8	And liueing man no more shall see
MED223:6	Hp250	I thy child, yee shall be my Sons and Daughters saith ye Lord
MED223:15	Hp250	is my comfort, When I come into Heaven, I shall vnderstand
MED223:16	Hp250	what he hath done for me, and then shall I bee able to praise
JULY223:26	Hp251	y^t it may bee a support to me when I shall haue occasion
JULY223:27	Hp251	read this hereafter, and to others that shall read it when I shall
JULY223:31	Hp251	for thov art my God, Thou hast said and shall not I beleiue it?
JULY223:34	Hp251	my faith in Thee, 'till I shall attain ye End of my hopes, Even
WHAT224:5	H5	My thankfull mouth shall speak thy praise
WHAT224:6	H6	My Tongue shall talk of Thee
WHAT224:14	H14	Your selves shall Judges bee;
WHAT224:20	H20	And I shall liue for aye.
WHAT224:24	H24	Me lasting life shall giue.
MYSOUL225:2	H6	Thy inward shall waxe strong,
MYSOUL225:3	H7	Thy body vile it shall bee chang'd,
MYSOUL225:5	H9	Wth Angels-wings thy Soul shall movnt
MYSOUL225:9	H13	Thy teares shall All bee dryed vp
MYSOUL225:10	H14	Thy Sorrowes all shall flye.
MYSOUL225:11	H15	Thy Sinns shall ne'r bee sumon'd vp
MYSOUL225:13	H17	Then shall I know what thov hast done
MYSOUL225:15	H19	And praise thee shall ev'n as I ovght
MYSOUL225:22	H26	Thy face when shall I see
28AUG226:5	Hp254	I can wait, looking every day when my Sav^r shall call for me.
28AUG226:10	Hp254	O let me ever see Thee that Art invisible, and I shall not bee
11MAYA226:22	Hp255	shall flourish while my body decayes, and ye weaknes of this
11MAYA226:23	Hp255	man shall bee a meanes to strenghten my inner-man
11MAYA226:24	Hp255	Yet a little while and he that shall come will come and will not
13MAY227:13	H22	I studiovs am what I shall doe
30SEPT227:24	Hp257	amendment, and then thy stroakes shall bee welcome, I haue
30SEPT227:31	Hp257	ye like for yov if you trvst in him; And when he shall deliuer
SAMUEL228:16	H17	Then shall I celebrate thy praise
SAMUEL228:20	H21	Perswade my heart I shall him see
THEART228:36	H2	Shall celebrate thy Name.
THEART229:7	H9	Lord whilst my fleeting time shall last
THEART229:17	H19	What thou bestow'st I shall restore
2HUSB233:2	H35	He shall make his Addresse.

2HUSB233:16	H49	Shall consecrated bee
HOURS234:25	H39	So shall I celebrate thy praise.
HOURS234:26	H40	Ev'n while my Dayes shall last
HOURS234:30	H44	Wth praises shall recovnt
HOURS234:34	H48	Then better shall I bee,
HOURS235:1	H53	If thou assist me Lord I shall
REMB235:23	H4	What shall I render to thy Name
REMB235:25	H6	My thankes how shall I testefye?
REMB235:32	H13	To Thee shall come all Flesh,
HOUSE237:2	H32	And them behold no more shall I.
HOUSE237:3	H33	Vnder thy roof no gvest shall sitt,
HOUSE237:5	H35	No pleasant tale shall 'ere be told
HOUSE237:7	H37	No Candle 'ere shall shine in Thee
HOUSE237:8	H38	Nor bridegroom's voice ere heard shall bee.

SHALLOW (1)

SEASONS48:31	~~H83~~	Some subject, shallow braines, much matter yeelds,

SHALT (6)

HUMOUR29:17	H368	If not as yet, by me, thou shalt be quell'd:
DIALOG141:25	H24	If I decease, dost think thou shalt survive?
FLESH176:25	H65	When thou my Captive shalt be led,
1LETTER181:21	H19	But when thou *Northward* to me shalt return,
SAMUEL228:14	H15	And if thou shalt spare me a space
HOUSE237:9	H39	In silence ever shalt thou lye

SHAME (21)

HUMOUR23:20	H130	But I am weary to dilate thy shame;
HUMOUR29:19	H370	Not past all reason, but in truth all shame:
HUMOUR31:40	H473	But I rather with silence, vaile her shame;
HUMOUR33:10	H524	Shame forc'd thee say, the matter that was mine,
AGES37:5	H67	But night and darkenesse, must with shame conceal.
AGES41:18	H237	As was their praise, or shame, so mine must be.
MASSYR55:7	H73	And was both shame, and glory of her sex;
MASSYR62:39	H384	With shame then turn'd to *Ninivie* again,
MPERS75:12	H873	To loose a nose, to win a Town's no shame,
MPERS79:6	H1028	Thou shame of Kings, of men the detestation,
MPERS84:24	H1260	His father *Xerxes* losse, and shame, much more,
MPERS~~87:20~~	H1374	Forsook his charge to his eternal shame:
MPERS87:22	~~H1374~~	Not worthy to be known, but for his shame:
MGREC99:26	H1869	To imitate *Achilles* (in his shame)
MGREC102:2	H1972	Accompani'd with sorrow, fear, and shame;
MGREC130:4	H3159	And vile {lewd} *Cassander* too, sticks not for shame;
SIDNEY149:26	~~H23~~	This was thy shame, O miracle of wit:
SIDNEY149:27	~~H23~~	Yet doth thy shame (with all) purchase renown,
QELIZ157:19	H87	Instead of glory prov'd her Countries shame:
MEDDM204:14	Hp284	Sin and shame euer goe together He that would be freed from
REMB235:30	H11	And I am filld wth shame,

SHAMEFUL (1)

MPERS80:26	H1093	Received there, a shameful over-throw.

SHAMEFULL (2)

AGES45:12	~~H394~~	Could once reverse, their shamefull destiny.
MPERS80:11	H1078	This shamefull Victory cost *Xerxes* deare,

SHAPE (1)
MGREC100:23 H1907 Men but in shape, and name, of valour none,
SHAR'D (1) [shared]
MGREC108:16 H2232 But in his cruelty alike they shar'd;
SHARE (6)
ELEMEN15:7 H289 The Peacock, and the Ostrich, share in woe:
SEASONS46:36 H14 Three months {(quoth she)} there are allotted to my share,
MGREC103:14 H2025 The share of *Alexander* did amount,
MGREC118:37 H2686 *Antigonus,* for his share *Asia* takes,
SIDNEY152:3 H75 Who in his Deity, had so deep share,
TDUDLEY165:29 H31 That After-comers in them might have share.
SHARED See **SHAR'D**
SHARER (1)
DIALOG145:10 H159 A sharer in your punishment's my due,
SHARES (1) [pl.]
ELEMEN9:11 H45 Your shares, {Hooes} your mattocks, and what e're you see,
SHARP (3)
MPERS76:4 H902 Sharp wants, not swords, his vallour did oppose;
MGREC96:41 H1761 The cowards feeling this sharp stinging charge,
MEDDM201:15 Hp280 A sharp appetite and a through Concoction, is a signe of an
SHARPE (1) [sharp]
HUMOUR24:37 H186 And how to strike ful sweet, as wel as sharpe.
SHARPEST (1)
MPERS86:3 H1319 Meaning to chastise him, in sharpest sort,
SHARPNESS (1)
SEASONS51:35 H211 We now of Winters sharpness 'gin to taste;
SHE'D (1) [she would]
HUMOUR28:8 H320 As if she'd leave no flesh to turn to clay,
SHE'D (3) [she had]
MASSYR55:11 H77 Adjudged to be drown'd, for what {th' crime} she'd done;
MGREC96:26 H1746 As if she'd drawne, whole *Sushan* at her heeles.
MERCY189:2 H23 Because her Soul she'd sent along with thee.
SHE'L (6) [she will]
HUMOUR21:38 H66 She'l ride a Horse as bravely, as the best,
HUMOUR22:2 H71 She'l neither say, she wil, nor wil she doe:
HUMOUR22:9 H78 But be she beaten, she'l not run away,
HUMOUR22:10 H79 She'l first advise, if't be not best to stay.
HUMOUR22:13 H82 If any threaten her, she'l in a trice,
MGREC125:25 H2975 Bids chuse her death, such kindnesse she'l afford:
SHE'S (8) [she is]
HUMOUR22:6 H75 In her dul resolution, she's {so} slow.
SEASONS49:15 H106 She's {Tis} for a time as fervent as before.
MASSYR63:27 H412 A Vice-roy from her foe, she's glad t' accept,
MASSYR63:28 H413 By whom in firm obedience she's kept.
MGREC126:9 H3000 There by *Cassander* she's block'd up, so long,
MGREC127:2 H3032 Now in her age she's forc't to taste that Cup,
QELIZ156:14 H41 She's argument enough to make you mute;
MERCY189:9 H30 So with her Chidren four, she's now at rest,
SHEAFE (1) [sheaf]
AGES36:21 H45 Under his arme a Sheafe of wheat he bore,

SHEAVES (1) [pl.]
SEASONS50:19 H153 And bundles up in sheaves the weighty Wheat,
SHED (3)
ELEMEN10:31 H106 And with the ashes, that it sometimes shed
MPERS73:25 H810 But yet, 'fore this was done, much blood was shed,
MROMAN139:17 H3545 And shed her guiltlesse blood, with guilty knife,
SHED'ST (1)
HUMOUR25:33 H222 So spils {shed'st} that life {blood}, thou'rt bounden to preserve.
SHEEP (4)
ELEMEN17:1 H365 Of rotten sheep, lean kine, and mildew'd grain.
AGES42:35 H291 My fleeced Ewe {Sheep}, and ever {fruitful} farrowing Sow.
MROMAN136:29 H3443 Where Shepheards once had Coats, and Sheep their Folds,
CONTEM170:22 H93 There *Abel* keeps his sheep, no ill he thinks,
SHEET (1)
MPERS93:2 H1599 Of all, did scarce his winding sheet retaine.
SHEILD (1) v. [shield]
HUMOUR29:24 H375 Nature doth teach, to sheild the head from harm,
SHELL (1)
CONTEM168:12 H21 Or thousand since thou brakest thy shell of horn,
SHELL-FISH (1)
ELEMEN15:33 H315 Not thou, but shell-fish yeelds, as *Pliny* clears.
SHELTER (2)
MEDDM201:31 Hp281 in the parching sun, & a shelter in a blustering storme are
13MAY227:5 H14 I haue a shelter from yᵉ storm
SHELVES (1) [pl.]
SEASONS48:20 H73 Her shelves, and Firkins fill'd for winter time.
SHENT (2)
HUMOUR27:16 H287 To meddle further, I shal be but shent,
AGES45:1 H374 I saw hopes dasht, our forwardnesse was shent,
SHEPHEARD (2) [shepherd]
SEASONS49:16 H107 Now go those frolick swaines, the shepheard lad,
SEASONS49:29 H118 Oh! happy Shepheard, which had not to lose,
SHEPHEARDS (2) [shepherds]
SEASONS49:22 H113 'Mongst all ye shepheards, never but one man,
MROMAN136:29 H3443 Where Shepheards once had Coats, and Sheep their Folds,
SHEPHERD (1) See also SHEPHEARD
SEASONS49:33 H126 Of him that was Shepherd, then King go vaunt.
SHEPHERDS [pl.] See SHEPHEARDS
SHEW (41) [show]
FATHER5:28 H29 My first do shew, their good, and then their rage,
ELEMEN8:7 H5 Who the most good could shew, & who most rage
ELEMEN13:22 H223 Now might {must} I shew my {mine} adverse quality,
ELEMEN16:10 H333 If I should shew, {name} more Seas, then thou hast Coasts.
ELEMEN16:32 H355 I now must shew what force {ill} there in me lyes.
HUMOUR20:13 H5 Loe! other foure step up, crave leave to shew
HUMOUR21:2 H30 To shew my great {high} descent, and pedigree,
HUMOUR21:5 H33 It shal suffice, to tel {shew} you what I am:
HUMOUR24:20 H169 Ile only shew the wrongs, thou'st done to me.
HUMOUR25:11 H200 But now Ile shew, what Souldier thou art.
HUMOUR28:5 H317 And Flegme likewise can shew, her cruel art,
HUMOUR28:23 H335 I might here shew, the noblenesse of minde,

HUMOUR30:24	H416	But whilst he lives, Ile shew what part I have.
HUMOUR31:39	H472	With purple dye {deeper red}, to shew but {you} her disgrace.
HUMOUR33:33	H547	Doth shew, hence flowes {flow} the power {pow'rs} which they
AGES37:8	H70	To shew her bearing pangs {pains}, I should do wrong,
MASSYR67:31	H577	To shew his little dread, but greater store,
MPERS71:4	H720	To shew how little Land he then should take.
MGREC95:41	H1720	To shew, how great *Darius* plaid his part:
MGREC115:15	H2527	Of stately *Ecbatane* who now must shew,
MGREC116:30	H2596	As oft his Acts throughout his reigne did {doth} shew:
MGREC117:15	H2622	We may hereafter shew, in season due.
MGREC122:5	H2828	{To shew} The difficulties {dangers} *Eumenes* befell,
MGREC124:23	H2930	The great ones now begin to shew their minde,
MGREC125:35	H2985	And throwes {threw} his bones about, to shew her spight.
MGREC129:23	H3137	But 'twas in shew, in heart it pleas'd them best.
DIALOG142:30	H59	Your humble Childe intreats you, shew your grief,
DIALOG143:26	H95	To shew the grievance of my troubled Land;
DIALOG143:27	H96	Before I tell the effect, ile shew the cause,
DIALOG145:21	H170	To ease my groaning land shew {shew'd} their intent,
DIALOG145:39	H188	They humbly beg return, shew their intents,
DIALOG147:18	H244	on brave *Essex*, shew whose son thou art {with a loyal heart},
SIDNEY149:23	H22	To shew the world, they never saw before,
SIDNEY151:20	H70	Fain would I shew, how thou {he} fame's path didst {paths did}
QELIZ156:18	H45	Come shew me such a Phoenix if you can;
TDUDLEY166:9	H51	Their greatness may be judg'd by what they shew.
FLESH175:22	H22	Come, come, Ile shew unto thy sence,
2LETTER182:4	H10	Shew him the sorrows of his widdowed wife;
MEDDM203:34	Hp284	shew great ingratitude after their successes, but he that
MEDDM205:33	Hp286	and some haue nothing to shew but leaues only, and some
MYCHILD215:18	Hp240	haue not studyed in this yov read to shew my skill, but to

SHEW'D (13) [showed]

HUMOUR20:15	H7	But first they wisely shew'd their high descent,
AGES42:11	H269	And shew'd them how, in face of foes to stand.
MASSYR55:36	H102	Her wealth she shew'd, in building *Babylon;*
MASSYR58:2	H187	Ne're shew'd his face, but revell'd with his Whores,
MPERS76:36	H934	Where an *Athenian* shew'd a valiant deed,
MGREC102:18	H1988	Yet old foundations shew'd, and somewhat more;
MGREC106:31	H2165	And such as shew'd but reverence before,
MGREC111:9	H2354	To th' utmost shew'd, the glory of a King;
MGREC134:26	H3357	That valour shew'd, vertue or excellence.
DIALOG145:21	H170	To ease my groaning land shew {shew'd} their intent,
DUBART155:5	H90	*Now shew'd what once they ought, Humanity,*
CHILDRN186:23	H90	She shew'd you joy and misery;
SOREFIT221:29	H15	For all his Bovnty shew'd to me

SHEWED [showed] See SHEW'D

SHEWES (7) [shows] See also SHEWS, SHOWES

ELEMEN14:28	H270	This your neglect, shewes your ingratitude;
HUMOUR30:41	H433	But that which shewes how high thy spight is bent,
SEASONS51:18	H192	Which shewes, nor Summer, Winter, nor the Spring,
MGREC115:41	H2560	He shewes his grief, he's forc'd to disobey:
MGREC127:9	H3039	And shewes of lamentation for them made.
MROMAN137:12	H3463	Great shewes he makes at Tilt, and Turnament,

SIDNEY149:31 ~~H23~~   Which shewes, thy worth was great, thine honour such,

SHEWN (1) [shown] See also SHOWNE

MASSYR62:32 H377   Whose haughty heart is shewn in works, and deeds;

SHEWS (7) [shows] See also SHEWES, SHOWES

MGREC99:38 H1881   The Priest shews him good *Daniels* Prophesie,

MGREC127:41 H3071   And shews {clear} what cause they {he} had to take up {make

MGREC~~127:41~~ H3073   Shews his ambitious practises as well.

DIALOG146:2 H190   Shews all was done, I'll therefore let it go.

SIDNEY~~150:12~~ H40   Which shews his worth was great, his honour such,

FLESH176:11 H51   Thy flatt'ring shews Ile trust no more.

MEDDM209:24 Hp291   hath (perhaps meaner then himself) wch shews us perfection is

SHEW'ST (1)

FEVER221:9 H24   Thou shew'st to me thy tender Love,

SHIELD (3) n.

DAVID159:2 H17   The Shield of *Saul* was vilely cast away;

TDUDLEY166:37 H79   *To Truth a shield, to right a Wall,*

CONTEM173:8 H176   Whose armour is their scales, their spreading fins their shield.

SHIELD (1) v. See also SHEILD

AGES37:41 H103   Where e're I went, mine innocence was shield.

SHINAR (2)

MASSYR53:25 H15   These were his first, all stood in *Shinar* land,

MASSYR56:22 H128   On {In} *Shinar* plain, by the *Euphratan* flood,

SHINE (19)

PROLOG8:2 H50   Will make your glistering gold but more to shine.

ELEMEN9:25 H59   What mingled lay with earth, I cause to shine.

ELEMEN12:40 H200   Which guides, when Sun, nor Moon, nor Stars do shine.

HUMOUR33:7 H521   As at noon day to tel, the Sun doth shine.

AGES40:19 H200   For sure my suit more then my vertues shine;

SEASONS48:1 H54   That when the Sun (on's love) the earth doth shine,

SEASONS49:5 H96   Ith' first, *Sol* doth in crabed *Cancer* shine.

SEASONS51:1 H175   And doth in poyzing *Libra* this month shine.

SEASONS52:34 H249   In *Pisces* now the golden Sun doth shine,

MASSYR63:37 H424   This Prince in's magnitude doth ever shine;

DIALOG148:7 H272   There let thy name, thy fame, thy valour {glory} shine,

TDUDLEY165:34 H36   Thy love to true Religion e're shall shine,

CONTEM172:12 H148   And if the sun would ever shine, there would I dwell.

CONTEM174:36 H233   Shall last and shine when all of these are gone.

2LETTER182:24 H30   Restrain'd the beams of thy beloved shine,

MEDDM198:3 Hp275   conditions, if he will make his face to shine vpon them, he

MEDDM206:16 Hp287   shine so bright while they moue on earth, how transcendently

HOURS234:17 H31   O shine vpon me blessed Lord

HOUSE237:7 H37   No Candle 'ere shall shine in Thee

SHINES (2)

FATHER5:7 H8   Their worth so shines, in those rich lines you show.

DUBART153:5 H9   Where Art, and more then Art in Nature shines;

SHINING (1)

CONTEM169:3 H45   Hath strength, thy shining Rayes once to behold?

SHIP (5)

MEDDM196:2 Hp272   A ship that beares much saile & little or no ballast, is easily

MEDDM203:10 Hp283   that is to saile into a farre country, although the ship, cabbin

SON230:26 H9   Did'st that ship bring to quiet port,

2HUSB232:27	H28	Lord bee thov pilott to yᵉ ship
ACK235:13	H13	Thou wast the pilott to the ship

SHIPS (13) [pl.]

ELEMEN12:30	H190	Send forth your well man'd ships, where sun doth rise.
ELEMEN12:37	H197	But Marriners, where got you ships and sailes?
ELEMEN16:25	H348	Alas; thy ships and oares could do no good
ELEMEN17:21	H385	Till Sun release, their ships can saile no more.
ELEMEN19:23	H468	Which neither ships nor houses could withstand.
AGES38:10	H113	I had no ships at Sea, no fraughts to loose.
MASSYR64:37	H461	Of costly Ships, and Gallies, she had store,
MASSYR64:39	H463	But the *Chaldeans* had nor ships, nor skill,
MPERS80:14	H1081	Four hundred stately Ships by stormes was lost,
MGREC94:16	H1650	And through the *Hellispont,* his ships make {made} way.
MGREC120:27	H2764	This he avoyds, and ships himself, and's Son,
MGREC~~124:7~~	H2912	With ships at Sea, an Army for the Land,
QELIZ156:23	H50	Ships more invincible then *Spaines,* her foe

SHOALS (1)

CONTEM172:20	H155	Nor is it rocks or shoals that can obstruct thy pace.

SHOAR (2) [shore] See also SHOARE

MGREC94:17	H1651	Comming to land, his dart on shoar he throwes,
MGREC98:12	H1814	He leaves not, till he makes {made} the sea firme shoar;

SHOARE (1) [shore] See also SHOAR

ELEMEN19:30	~~H472~~	Some have I forc'd, to gaine an unknown shoare;

SHOCK (2)

MPERS81:16	H1124	And leave them out, the {this} shock {now} for to sustaine,
TDUDLEY166:18	H60	Now fully ripe, as shock of wheat that's grown,

SHOOTS (2)

MGREC125:19	H2967	Nor Darts, nor Arrowes now, none shoots, nor flings;
SIDNEY151:17	~~H69~~	When such a *Hero* shoots him out o'th' field,

SHORE (7) See also SHOAR, SHOARE

MGREC111:2	H2347	Some time he after spent upon that shore,
MGREC111:12	H2357	Then sayling South, and comming to the {that} shore,
DIALOG147:29	H253	The briny Ocean will o'rflow your shore,
DISTEMP179:25	H13	And brought me to the shore from troubled Main.
3LETTER183:17	H19	But lanches on that shore, there for to dye,
MEDDM203:16	Hp283	meet wᵗʰ such tossings that may cause him to long for shore,
ACK235:11	H11	Thou hast to shore him safely brovght

SHORNE (1) [shorn]

MGREC~~115:15~~	H2525	The Mules and Horses are for sorrow shorne,

SHORT (30) See also SHORT'S

ELEMEN11:22	H142	Sister, in worth {quoth shee} I come not short of you;
ELEMEN12:28	H188	But time's too short, and precious so to spend.
ELEMEN13:20	H221	I should here make a short, yet true narration,
AGES44:23	H356	In this short Pilgrimage I oft have had;
AGES45:26	H416	My memory is short {bad}, and braine is dry.
SEASONS48:33	H84	Melodious {Sweet fragrant} Spring, with thy short pittance flye,
SEASONS50:29	H163	The Summer's {Summer seems but} short, the beauteous
SEASONS52:11	H226	I must be short, and short's, the shortned day,
MASSYR54:13	H40	His reign was short, for as I calculate,
MPERS72:33	H777	All thought {wisht} his short reign long, till {past before} it was
MPERS73:9	H796	Eight years he reign'd, a short, yet too long time,

MPERS73:23	~~H809~~	Who little pleasure had, in his short reigne,
MPERS83:20	H1208	But in short time, this wickednesse was knowne,
MPERS86:23	H1339	If in his enterprize he should fall short,
MPERS89:13	H1447	may come, and {in short time might} place one in his Throne,
MPERS92:38	H1596	Whose honours, treasures, pleasures, had short stay;
MGREC97:35	H1796	And in short termes, sends this reply againe;
MGREC112:8	H2394	To shadow forth these short felicities:
MROMAN138:27	H3517	Is entertain'd at *Rome,* and in short time,
SIDNEY151:30	~~H75~~	Which are in worth, as far short of his due,
CONTEM171:12	H116	And though thus short, we shorten many wayes,
ELIZB187:10	H18	And buds new blown, to have so short a date,
1SIMON188:5	H6	Acquaintance short, yet parting caus'd us weep,
2SIMON195:8	Hp271	you nor of more ease to my self then these short meditations
2SIMON195:12	Hp271	though in value they fall short of all in this kinde yet I presume
MEDDM199:23	Hp278	eyes, are the concomitants of old age, and short sightednes in
MEDDM200:21	Hp279	Christian, therfore god cuts their garments short, to keep them
MEDDM206:34	Hp288	trembling, lest they through vnbeleif fall short of a promise,
MYCHILD215:14	Hp240	I was able to compose some short matters, (for wᵗ else to call
MYCHILD216:7	Hp241	After a short time I changed my Condition & was marryed, and

SHORTEN (1)

CONTEM171:12	H116	And though thus short, we shorten many wayes,

SHORTER (1)

MEDDM207:22	Hp289	that all haue a lease of their liues, some longer some shorter,

SHORTEST (1)

SEASONS51:38	H214	Almost at shortest is the shortned day,

SHORTLY (5)

MPERS80:32	H1099	That *Greeks* to break his bridge shortly intends;
MPERS81:39	~~H1143~~	For one maine Battell shortly, both provide;
MPERS82:2	H1148	Then for one battel shortly all provide,
MPERS91:22	H1535	But shortly calls her home, her counsells prize,
SIDNEY151:1	~~H69~~	Such prince as he, his race should shortly end:

SHORTNED (3)

SEASONS51:38	H214	Almost at shortest is the shortned day,
SEASONS52:11	H226	I must be short, and short's, the shortned day,
SEASONS52:21	H236	From thence he 'gins to length the shortned morn,

SHORTNESSE (1)

MGREC136:13	H3427	*Shortnesse of time, and inability,*

SHORT'S (1) [short is]

SEASONS52:11	H226	I must be short, and short's, the shortned day,

SHOT (3)

HUMOUR22:34	H103	She thinks I never shot so farre amisse;
MPERS72:27	~~H773~~	Shot through the heart of his beloved son:
MGREC108:24	H2240	Imprinted deep in's legg, by Arrowes shot;

SHOULD (103)

PROLOG7:16	H29	A Poets Pen, all scorne, I should thus wrong;
ELEMEN8:9	H7	And {That} in due order each her turne should speake,
ELEMEN8:27	H25	That Fire should first begin, the rest consent,
ELEMEN10:15	H90	Their magnitude and height should I recount,
ELEMEN13:20	H221	I should here make a short, yet true narration,
ELEMEN16:9	H332	But I should go beyond thee in thy {my} boasts,
ELEMEN16:10	H333	If I should shew, {name} more Seas, then thou hast Coasts.

ELEMEN18:4	H408	How gladly should his gold purchase his breath,
ELEMEN18:6	H410	How freely should it go, so he might live.
HUMOUR20:22	H14	Which of the foure should have predominance;
HUMOUR22:32	H101	The nerves should I not warm, soon would they freeze.
HUMOUR25:28	H217	Nay should I tel, thou wouldst count me no blab,
HUMOUR26:31	H261	But why the heart, should be usurpt by thee,
HUMOUR28:21	H333	That my intents should meet with interruption,
HUMOUR28:32	H344	But why, alas, thus tedious should I be?
HUMOUR29:36	H387	And if thy haste, my slownesse should not temper,
HUMOUR31:14	H445	If any doubt this {the} truth, whence this should come;
AGES36:35	H59	That each should tel, what of himselfe he knew;
AGES37:8	H70	To shew her bearing pangs {pains}, I should do wrong,
AGES38:6	H109	My foe should weltering, with {in} his bowels reek.
AGES41:26	H243	Such {My} empty seed should yeeld a better crop.
AGES43:20	H315	I judge, I should have room, in all mens hearts.
SEASONS50:21	H155	The Barley, and the Rye, should first had place,
SEASONS53:2	H258	*Or better Lines you should have had;*
MASSYR56:19	H125	A structure rare, I should but rudely marre,
MASSYR57:17	H164	How he thus suddenly should be thus small?
MASSYR57:18	H165	So suddenly should loose so great a state,
MASSYR58:40	H223	To want no priviledge, Subjects should have,
MASSYR59:26	H250	Their strong wall'd town should suddenly be taken;
MPERS71:4	H720	To shew how little Land he then should take.
MPERS74:5	H830	And he whose Horse before the rest should neigh,
MPERS74:6	H831	Of all the Peers should have precedency.
MPERS79:21	H1047	One King, so many Subjects should possesse;
MPERS79:23	H1049	That none of these should {those could} live a {an} hundred
MPERS81:13	H1121	So should all favour to their State be shown.
MPERS81:20	H1128	now in {their} need, they should thus fail {forsake} their friends,
MPERS86:23	H1339	If in his enterprize he should fall short,
MPERS86:36	H1352	The Rovers in *Pisidia,* should drive out.
MPERS86:37	H1353	But least {lest} some worser newes should fly to Court,
MPERS89:11	H1445	If *Greeks* unto their Country-men {own Country should}
MPERS92:5	H1559	Why *Arsames* his brother should succeed,
MGREC93:24	H1621	His rule to *Greece,* he scorn'd should be confin'd:
MGREC96:16	H1736	Least he should need them, in his chariots stead.
MGREC97:19	H1780	Commands, no man should doe them injury,
MGREC97:37	H1798	But of *Darius* King, as he should know.
MGREC99:23	H1866	(For 'twas decreed, that Empire should be shaken)
MGREC99:31	H1874	Though in an enemy it should be found;
MGREC99:39	H1882	How he should over-throw this Monarchy;
MGREC101:15	H1940	*Ochus* his Son a hostage shall {should} endure.
MGREC101:33	H1958	The Sun should witnesse of his valour be:
MGREC105:13	H2106	Should heare, nor see, his groans, and {dying} misery:
MGREC107:17	H2192	The Souldiers should let passe this injury;
MGREC109:37	H2296	But for the rest, his sword advise him should.
MGREC112:11	H2397	If an Ideall Paradise, a man should {would} frame,
MGREC113:14	H2441	But how these Captaines should, or yet their Master,
MGREC113:23	H2450	It was decreed *Parmenio* should dye:
MGREC115:12	H2521	This act (me thinks) his god-head should ashame;
MGREC115:23	H2542	This great indignity for to {he should} requite.

MGREC118:11	H2658	He hold of {on} this occasion should have laid,
MGREC119:11	H2701	That if he came, good welcome he should find:
MGREC122:3	H2826	I should but snip a story into verse, {bits}
MGREC122:9	H2834	For all that should be said, let this suffice,
MGREC~~128:40~~	H3113	That each shall {should} hold what he doth {did} now possesse,
MGREC~~129:1~~	H3115	Who then shall {should} be installed in the throne:
MGREC130:13	H3168	Resolves at last the Princesse should be slain,
MGREC131:38	H3230	Which should succeed, at variance they fell,
MGREC131:39	H3231	The mother would the youngest should {might} excell,
MGREC~~132:1~~	H3234	(Rather then *Philips* child must {race should} longer live
MGREC132:11	H3246	For blood which was decreed, that he should spill,
DIALOG145:25	H174	As puts me to a stand what I should say,
DIALOG145:33	H182	No prelate should doe his Bishoprick retain;
DIALOG146:32	H218	Your griefs I pity much, but should do wrong {hope to see},
SIDNEY149:24	H23	That this one Volumne should exhaust your store.
SIDNEY150:32	H59	Though *Sidney* dy'd, his valiant name should live;
SIDNEY151:1	~~H69~~	Such prince as he, his race should shortly end:
DUBART154:37	H82	But lest my {mine} ignorance should doe thee wrong,
AUTHOR177:37	H9	My rambling brat (in print) should mother call,
1LETTER181:8	H6	If but a neck, soon should we be together:
CHILDRN185:19	H45	Lest this my brood some harm should catch,
ELIZB187:1	H10	Blest babe why should I once bewail thy fate,
2SIMON195:7	Hp271	look vpon when you should see me no more, I could think of
MEDDM196:8	Hp273	so he that glorys in his gifts and adornings, should look vpon
MEDDM201:27	Hp281	should be the precepts of the wise masters of assemblys to
MEDDM204:22	Hp285	manner, wch should warn him, that doth any speciall seruice
MEDDM205:27	Hp286	vs, or else we should not so often faile in our whole Course of
MEDDM206:30	Hp288	parents haue had pious children, it should make vs adore the
MEDDM206:33	Hp288	it should alsoe teach the children of godly parents to walk wth
MEDDM206:37	Hp288	all should make vs wth the Apostle to admire the iustice and
MEDDM207:17	Hp289	withers the pleasure wch else we should take in them, and well
MEDDM207:27	Hp289	should make vs so to number our dayes as to apply our hearts
MEDDM208:9	Hp290	friends, though there should be no displeasence betweene
MYCHILD218:4	Hp243	me that there is an Eternall Being. But how should I know he is
MYCHILD218:33	Hp244	it were possible ye very elect should bee deceived. Behold
FAINTING222:24	H14	Why should I liue but to thy praise
MED223:3	Hp250	Lord why should I doubt any more w^n thov hast given me such
MED223:8	Hp250	father, vnto my God and your God—But least this should not
MED223:14	Hp250	who hath done so much for me, should haue so little from me,
WHAT224:17	H17	He is not man y^t he should lye.
28AUG226:1	Hp254	me a vessell fitt for his vse why should I not bare it not only
28AUG226:3	Hp254	y^t somt. I haue had, least my heart should bee drawn from
11MAYA226:20	Hp255	will of God it should bee thus. Who am I y^t I should repine at
HOUSE236:30	H22	Far be it y^t I should repine,

SHOULDERS (3) [pl.]

MASSYR64:40	H464	Their shoulders must their Masters minde fulfill;
MASSYR65:9	H474	With peeled shoulders, and with balded heads,
MEDDM201:3	Hp280	many times he imposes waighty burdens on their shoulders,

SHOULD'ST (1)

SIDNEY149:12	H11	Of Armes, and Arts, thou {he} should'st a patterne be.

SHOULDST (1)
ELEMEN15:25 H307   Shouldst thou but buy, it would exhaust thy gold.

SHOW (13) See also SHEW
FATHER5:7   H8   Their worth so shines, in those rich lines you show.
ELEMEN8:31   H29   Where {In} little is, {time} I can but little show,
ELEMEN15:27 H309   Such wealth, but not such like, Earth thou mayst show.
ELEMEN19:38 H479   Then what prodigious sights, sometimes I show:
HUMOUR24:26 H175   Thy childish {foolish} incongruities, Ile show:
HUMOUR31:15 H446   Show them thy passage to th' *Duodenum.*
AGES35:27   H13   Childhood was cloath'd in white, and given {green} to show,
SEASONS51:9 H183   And Apples now their yellow sides do show;
MASSYR55:22 H88   Taking a towne, such valour she did show,
MPERS84:15   H1251 For such ingratitude, did *Athens* show
DAVID158:35 H15   Nor any pleasant thing e're may you show;
13MAY227:14 H23   To show my Duty wth delight
HOURS234:38 H52   But still my frailty show?

SHOW'D (1) [showed] See also SHEW'D
MGREC106:14 H2148 For his fidelity to 's Master show'd;

SHOWERS (8) [pl.] See also SHOWRES, SHOWRS
ELEMEN14:37 H279   With springs below, and showers from above;
ELEMEN15:22 H304   But {And} such I am, in Rivers, showers and springs;
ELEMEN16:37 H360   As I with showers oft time {times} refresh the earth;
AGES36:6   H30   Seemed to grow on's head (bedew'd with showers:)
SEASONS47:36 H48   This is the month whose fruitfull showers produces
SEASONS48:24 H77   More at her showers, which water them a space.
MGREC102:7   H1977 With showers of Flowers, the streets along are strown,
DAVID158:33 H13   Nor fruitfull showers your barren tops bestrew,

SHOWERS v. See SHOWRES

SHOWES (3) [shows] See also SHEWES, SHEWS
MGREC100:16 H1900 to resist {man's there} his valour showes {Army to oppose};
MGREC102:6   H1976 Is entertain'd with joy, and pompous train {showes},
MYCHILD218:13 Hp244 it? Is there any story but that wch showes the beginnings of

SHOWN (3) See also SHEWN
MPERS81:13   H1121 So should all favour to their State be shown.
MGREC102:32 H2002 Where Kings have shown their glory, wealth, and might;
SAMUEL228:9 H10   For sure thy Grace on him is shown.

SHOWNE (1) [shown] See also SHEWN
DUBART152:33 H2   Amongst the happy wits this Age hath showne,

SHOWR'D (1) [showered]
DUBART154:25 H70   If e'r this golden gift was showr'd on any,

SHOWRE (1) [shower]
SEASONS47:25 H41   Yet many a fleece of Snow, and stormy showre,

SHOWRES (2) n. [showers] See also SHOWRS
MPERS83:2   H1190 But for his deep complaints; and showres of tears,

SHOWRES (1) v. [showers]
MPERS77:1   H940   Off flyes his head, down showres his frolick bloud.

SHOWRS (1) [showers] See also SHOWRES
TDUDLEY166:21 H63   Where storms, nor showrs, nor ought can damnifie.

SHOWS See SHEWES, SHEWS, SHOWES

SHREIKS (1) [pl.]
HOUSE236:16 H8   And piteovs shreiks of dreadfull voice.

SHRIKING (1)

MASSYR66:10 H516   Now *Zim,* and *lim, {Jim}* lift up their shriking {scrieching}

SHRILL (2)

AGES~~45:32~~ H422   {waking glad to hear} at the cocks clanging {shrill} voyce.

MPERS~~74:14~~ H837   {And joyfull} acclamations ecchoes in the aire; {shrill they ring,}

SHRINKING (2)

ELEMEN9:19 H53   Your shrinking limbs, which winters cold doth harme;

SEASONS52:25 H240   Chilling the blood, and shrinking up the skin.

SHRUBS (2) [pl.]

AGES44:33 H366   That but for shrubs they did themselves account;

CHILDRN185:10 H36   Is 'mongst the shrubs and bushes flown,

SHUN (2)

CONTEM173:21 H187   To gain more good, or shun what might thee harm

MEDDM204:15 Hp284 must be sure to shun the company of the first.

SHUNS (2)

HUMOUR21:40 H68   But shuns to look on wounds, and bloud that's spilt,

MGREC~~116:10~~ H2575 All friends she shuns, yea, banished the light,

SHUT (6)

MASSYR66:2 H508   And with that woful sight his eyes close shut.

MPERS70:9 H680   But till convenient time their heads kept shut;

MGREC119:17 H2707 To *Lamia,* where he shut up doth ly:

MGREC128:2 H3075 His Wife, and Son, in prison close had shut;

MGREC131:21 H3213 Now shut their gates in his adversity,

MROMAN137:28 H3479 Kept shut in peace, but {set} ope when bloud was spilt;

SICK (5)

MASSYR58:12 H197   Who sick of his disease, he soone did finde.

MGREC131:28 H3220 Falls so extreamly sick, all fear {fear'd} his life,

FLESH175:20 H20   Art fancy sick, or turn'd a Sot

MEDDM203:21 Hp283 He that neuer felt, what it was to be sick or wounded, doth not

ACK235:14 H14   And rais'd him vp when he was sick.

SICKLE (1)

TDUDLEY166:19 H61   Death as a Sickle hath him timely mown,

SICKLES (1) [pl.]

SEASONS50:17 H151   With Sickles now, the painful {bending} Reapers go,

SICKNES (14) [sickness]

AGES37:6 H68   My mothers breeding sicknes, I will spare;

MEDDM203:24 Hp283 he slighted before, so he that neuer felt the sicknes of sin, nor

MEDDM207:24 Hp289 and till the expiratnon of that time, no dangers no sicknes

MYCHILD215:32 Hp241 In a long fitt of sicknes wch I had on my bed I often comvned

MYCHILD216:11 Hp241 some time I fell into a lingering sicknes like a consvmption

MYCHILD216:27 Hp242 towards him. Somt. he hath smott a child wth sicknes, somt.

MYCHILD217:25 Hp243 Lord, and when I haue been in sicknes + pain, I haue thought if

28AUG225:26 Hp254 After mvch weaknes & sicknes when my spirits were worn out,

11MAYA226:13 Hp255 I had a sore sicknes and weaknes took hold of me wch hath by

11MAYB228:24 Hp259 that I haue had no great fitt of sicknes, but this year from y^e

THEART229:2 H4   From sicknes, death, + pain.

SON231:7 H19   In sicknes when he lay full sore

2HUSB232:29 H30   In stormes and sicknes Lord p^rserve.

HOURS233:26 H9   Tho: losse and sicknes me assail'd,

SICKNESS (3)

CONTEM173:36 H200   Subject to sorrows, losses, sickness, pain,

FLESH177:21	H102	From sickness and infirmity,
SICKNES178:16	H0	Upon a Fit of Sickness, *Anno,* 1632.

SICKNESSE (5) [sickness]

HUMOUR32:9	H483	My sicknesse cheifly in conceit doth lye,
AGES38:28	H131	For sin brings sorrow, sicknesse, death, and woe.
AGES44:6	H339	Sicknesse, dangers, and anxieties have past,
MYCHILD216:25	Hp242	hath been vpon my own person, in sicknesse weaknes, paines,
MYCHILD219:6	Hp245	This was written in mvch sicknesse and weaknes, and is very

SICKNESSES (1)

30SEPT227:28	Hp257	children) haue yee seen yᵉ many sicknesses and weaknesses

SIDE (24)

ELEMEN12:5	H165	On either side the country of the *Gaules,*
HUMOUR23:32	H142	That when a Varlet, struck him o're the side,
HUMOUR28:15	H327	I turn into his cel, close by my side,
AGES36:15	H39	His Sword by's side, and choler in his eyes;
MPERS77:35	H976	Flattering *Mardonius* on th' other side,
MPERS86:13	H1329	*Cyrus* o'th' other side, weighs in his mind,
MPERS88:4	H1397	And ranged stood, by great *Euphrates* side,
MPERS90:16	H1484	Straight to transport them to the other side,
MGREC98:38	H1840	And then at *Tigris,* and *Araxis* side:
MGREC99:3	H1846	Betwixt the *Hellespont,* and *Hallis* side;
MGREC110:6	H2306	On *Tygris* side, here now he had not been;
MGREC110:10	H2310	With *Ptolomy,* sends part o' th' other side.
MGREC110:37	H2341	He on the faire *Hidaspis* pleasant side,
MGREC120:40	H2777	And made the Souldiers on his side remain;
MGREC121:9	H2787	Did alienate the Souldiers from his side;
MGREC121:13	H2791	And from the other, {side} daily some did gaine.
MGREC121:34	H2816	And fain would draw *Eumenes* to their side,
MGREC124:19	H2926	Still labours *Eumenes* might {would} with him side,
MROMAN138:3	H3493	Three call'd *Horatii,* on *Romans* side,
DIALOG142:14	H43	Doe Barons rise, and side against their King?
CONTEM172:7	H143	Close sate I by a goodly Rivers side,
AUTHOR177:31	H3	Who after birth did'st by my side remain,
FEVER220:28	H8	From side to side for ease I toyle,
FEVER220:28	H8	From side to side for ease I toyle,

SIDES (9) [pl.]

ELEMEN12:9	H169	And *Hemus,* whose steep sides, none foote upon,
SEASONS51:9	H183	And Apples now their yellow sides do show;
MASSYR59:4	H228	Both sides their hearts, their hands, their {&} bands unite,
MPERS76:18	H916	Or *Sythian* arrows in our sides must stick.
MPERS79:2	H1024	Then laid his parts on both sides of the way,
MPERS80:22	H1089	That their split sides, witness'd his overthrow;
MPERS81:37	H1143	Where both sides exercis'd their manly feats;
TDUDLEY165:27	H29	Who staid thy feeble sides when thou wast low,
MEDDM209:11	Hp291	eyes and thornes in their sides, and at last ouercame them,

SIDING (1)

DIALOG143:1	H70	Nor Nobles siding, to make *John* no King

SIDNEY (4) See also SYDNEY

SIDNEY149:3	H3	Sir *Philip Sidney,* who was untimely
SIDNEY149:8	H7	Her noble *Sidney* wore the Crown of Bayes;
SIDNEY150:32	H59	Though *Sidney* dy'd, his valiant name should live;

SIDNEY152:29 H98   *That* Sidney *dy'd the quintessence {most renown'd} of men.*

SIEDGE (1) [siege]
MASSYR67:28 H574   Layes siedge to's regall seat, proud *Babylon,*

SIEGE (1) See also SEIGE, SIEDGE
MPERS75:4   H865   Desiring of the Prince to raise the siege,

SIGH (3)
DIALOG141:9 H8   And sit i'th dust, to sigh these sad alarms?
DIALOG148:31 H296   If this make way thereto, then sigh no more,
ELIZB187:2   H11   Or sigh thy dayes so soon were terminate;

SIGH'D (2) [sighed]
TDUDLEY166:14 H56   For which he sigh'd and pray'd & long'd full sore
CONTEM171:6 H111   How Adam sigh'd to see his Progeny,

SIGHES (1) [sighs, pl.]
SON230:21   H4   My feares to Joyes, my sighes to song

SIGHS (3) [pl.]
BIRTH180:18 H28   With some sad sighs honour my absent Herse;
2LETTER182:14 H20   May count my sighs, and number all my drops:
3LETTER183:14 H16   With thousand dolefull sighs & mournfull Cooes.

SIGHS (1) v.
CONTEM170:10 H83   His Mother sighs, to think of Paradise,

SIGHT (24)
FATHER5:3   H4   Deare Sir, of late delighted with the sight, /T D on the
HUMOUR33:41 H555   I'le touch the Sight, great'st wonder of the three;
HUMOUR34:9 H564   Of all the Sences, Sight shal be the Queen;
AGES45:29   H419   My grinders now are few, my sight doth faile
MASSYR58:27 H210   And though of wars, he did abhor the sight;
MASSYR66:2   H508   And with that woful sight his eyes close shut.
MASSYR68:1   H587   Which horrid sight, he fears, must needs portend,
MPERS79:22 H1048   But yet this goodly sight {from him} produced teares,
MPERS82:35 H1182   He dying to behold, that wounding sight;
MGREC96:3   H1723   Oh {Sure} 'twas a goodly sight, there to behold;
MGREC96:33 H1753   For sure *Darius* thought, at the first sight,
MGREC104:35 H2087   Whose Army now, was almost within sight,
MGREC117:21 H2628   But by *Ulysses,* having lost his sight,
MGREC~~123:13~~ H2877   To *Greece* and *Macedon* lets turn our sight.
MGREC135:22 H3394   The third, belly and thighs of brasse in sight,
DUBART153:4 H8   My dazled sight of late, review'd thy lines,
CONTEM173:15 H182   I judg'd my hearing better then my sight,
AUTHOR178:1 H11   Thy Visage was so irksome in my sight;
CHILDRN184:27 H16   And with her mate flew out of sight;
CHILDRN186:11 H78   Into a country beyond sight,
MEDDM202:27 Hp282   quite gone out of sight then must we needs walk in darknesse
MEDDM205:28 Hp286   we doe, but he that wth David, sets the lord alway in his sight
PILGRIM210:40 H40   and of their maker haue the sight
MYCHILD217:8 Hp242   (or at least in sight) but I haue been apt to forgett him and my

SIGHTEDNES (1) [sightedness]
MEDDM199:23 Hp278   eyes, are the concomitants of old age, and short sightednes in

SIGHTLESSE (1) [sightless]
DUBART154:4 H49   Mine eyes are sightlesse, and my tongue is mute;

SIGHTS (2) [pl.]
ELEMEN19:38 H479   Then what prodigious sights, sometimes I show:

DUBART153:27 H31 Of all the glorious sights his eyes have had:

SIGN (1) See also SIGNE
CONTEM170:17 H89 But no such sign on false *Cain's* offering;

SIGNALL (1) [signal]
MPERS82:8 H1155 The signall of their victory doth {did} rise;

SIGNE (5) [sign]
ELEMEN10:26 H101 I of acceptance was the holy signe.
SEASONS47:31 H46 In *Taurus* Signe, yet hasteth straight from thence;
MGREC118:25 H2674 On which, no signe of poyson could be {in his intrails} found,
MEDDM201:15 Hp280 appetite and a through Concoction, is a signe of an healthfull
2HUSB232:6 H7 And my petition signe.

SIGNES (1) [signs]
ELEMEN20:2 H484 Portentious signes, of Famines, Plagues and Wars.

SILENC'D (1) [silenced]
AGES45:2 H374 And silenc'd we, by Act of Parliament.

SILENCE (11)
ELEMEN15:31 H313 Thy silence of thy beasts, doth cause the same.
HUMOUR31:40 H473 But I rather with silence, vaile her shame;
MASSYR57:32 H177 And eleav'n {many} hundred of years in silence sit,
MPERS69:32 H654 Brake his long silence, cry'd, spare *Cressus* life:
MPERS88:10 H1403 But when their order, and {their} silence they saw;
MGREC112:25 H2411 His silence, guilt was, of such consequence,
DUBART153:31 H35 Sits down in silence, deeply he admires:
QELIZ155:14 H5 Although great Queen, thou now in silence lye,
PILGRIM210:25 H25 This body shall in silence sleep,
FAINTING222:19 H9 But bee in silence layd.
HOUSE237:9 H39 In silence ever shalt thou lye

SILENCED See SILENC'D

SILENCEST (1)
HUMOUR20:29 H21 She was the silencest {silentest} of all the foure,

SILENT (6)
ELEMEN18:41 H445 Let such suspend their thoughts, and silent be;
DIALOG144:30 H138 Their silent tongues to heaven did vengeance cry,
CONTEM169:10 H51 Silent alone, where none or saw, or heard,
2LETTER181:32 H2 The silent night's the fittest time for moan;
PILGRIM210:2 H2 Hugs wth delight his silent nest
HOUSE236:13 H5 In silent night when rest I took

SILENTEST (1)
HUMOUR20:29 H21 She was the silencest {silentest} of all the foure,

SILK (2)
MGREC96:4 H1724 The *Persians* clad in silk, and glitt'ring {glistering} gold;
FLESH176:40 H80 My garments are not silk nor gold,

SILLINESSE (1) [silliness]
AGES37:20 H82 My sillinesse did only take delight,

SILLY (3)
HUMOUR24:30 H179 Thy foolish {silly} provocations, I despise.
SIDNEY150:16 H49 To be saluted by a silly Crow;
DUBART153:29 H33 The silly Pratler speakes no word of sence;

SILVER (10)
ELEMEN13:5 H206 For gemmes, for silver, treasures which I hold:
AGES45:41 H431 My golden Bowl, and silver Cord, e're long,

MPERS84:2	H1230	With gold and silver beds, most gorgiously.
MPERS84:12	H1243	With gold and silver, and what ere they need:
MGREC102:8	H1978	And Insence burnt, the silver Altars on;
MGREC103:12	H2023	Statues of {some} gold, and silver numberlesse,
MGREC109:25	H2284	He glory sought, no silver, nor yet {no} gold;
MGREC135:21	H3393	Next, armes and breast, of silver to behold;
MGREC135:26	H3398	Then gold, silver, brasse, iron, and all that {the} store,
FLESH175:32	H32	Earth hath more silver, pearls and gold,

SILVER-SMITHS (1) [pl.]

ELEMEN9:24	H58	Ye Silver-smiths, your ure I do refine,

SIMON (2)

1SIMON188:1	H1-2	*On my dear Grand-child* Simon Bradstreet,
2SIMON195:2	Hp271	Simon Bradstreet

SIMPATHIZE (2) [sympathize]

DIALOG141:13	H12	Ah, tell thy Daughter, she may simpathize.
MERCY188:32	H18	Oh how I simpathize with thy sad heart,

SIMPLE (5)

PROLOG6:30	H14	But simple I, according to my skill.
MGREC124:25	H2932	*Aridæus* the scorn'd, and simple King,
VERSES184:6	H10	Yet for part payment take this simple mite,
13MAY227:16	H25	And at ye most a simple mite.
THEART229:15	H17	Accept O Lord my simple mite

SIMPTOMS (1) [symptoms]

MEDDM199:9	Hp277	and sapless performances are simptoms of little spiritull vigor

SIN (11) See also SINNE

HUMOUR25:30	H219	To take the wal's a sin, of such {so} high rate,
AGES37:2	H64	Ah me! conceiv'd in sin, and born in {with} sorrow,
AGES38:20	H123	From thence I 'gan to sin, as soon as act.
AGES38:28	H131	For sin brings sorrow, sicknesse, death, and woe.
AGES46:24	H455	Triumph I shal, o're Sin, o're Death, o're Hel,
MGREC94:12	H1646	For cruelty now, was his parentall sin.
CONTEM174:6	H206	This lump of wretchedness, of sin and sorrow,
MEDDM200:3	Hp278	sin, is it not a little one? will ere long say of a greater Tush god
MEDDM203:24	Hp283	he slighted before, so he that neuer felt the sicknes of sin, nor
MEDDM204:14	Hp284	Sin and shame euer goe together He that would be freed from
MYCHILD216:34	Hp242	some sin I lay vnder wch God would haue reformed, or some

SINCE (27) See also SITH

ELEMEN14:5	H249	And since, faire *Italy* full sadly knowes
MASSYR60:9	H274	promise bound, since first {which} he crav'd {firmly made},
MASSYR67:33	H579	The holy vessells, thither brought long since,
MPERS75:27	H884	Since *Cyrus* time, *Cambyses* did molest;
MPERS92:7	H1565	His brother, as tis said, long since was slain,
MGREC96:2	H1722	For since the world, was no such Pageant seen.
MGREC109:6	H2265	He t' *Nisa* goes, by *Bacchus* built long since,
MGREC118:7	H2654	And had to him, still since *Ephestion* dyed,
MGREC120:37	H2774	Two years and more since, Natures debt he paid,
MGREC129:5	H3119	Whom he in durance held, now and long since,
MGREC131:23	H3215	Tries foes, since friends will not compassionate,
MGREC134:34	H3365	For since the first, that title still they had,
MROMAN136:36	H3450	And bloudy hath it prov'd, since first it stood:
MROMAN138:9	H3499	Of *Latine* Kings this was long since the Seat,

SIDNEY152:8	H79	Since *Sydney* had exhausted all their store,
SIDNEY~~152:15~~	H85	Since I the Muses thus have injured.
QELIZ156:15	H42	Since first the Sun did run, his ne'r runn'd race,
QELIZ156:17	H44	Since time was time, and man unmanly man,
QELIZ158:18	H127	Whose living vertues speak (though dead long since)
CONTEM168:9	H18	How long since thou wast in thine Infancy?
CONTEM168:11	H20	Hath hundred winters past since thou wast born?
CONTEM168:12	H21	Or thousand since thou brakest thy shell of horn,
CONTEM169:29	H68	And calls back moneths and years that long since fled
CONTEM170:25	H96	But since that time she often hath been cloy'd;
SICKNES178:19	H2	Since nature gave me breath,
SICKNES178:31	H14	since first we came from womb,
MYCHILD218:28	Hp244	some new Troubles I haue had since yᵉ world has been filled

SINCERE (2)

MEDDM205:37	Hp287	and ther are some (and they sincere ones too) who haue not
MYCHILD218:29	Hp244	and Sectaries, and some who hauest been acctᵈ. sincere

SINCEREST (1)

MEDDM196:12	Hp273	the sincerest christian the least self loue

SINCERITY (1)

MYCHILD216:27	Hp242	Sincerity towards him. Somt. he hath smott a child wᵗʰ

SINFULL (5) [sinful]

AGES38:19	H122	From birth stayned, with Adams sinfull fact;
CONTEM171:7	H112	Cloath'd all in his black sinfull Livery,
CONTEM174:5	H205	And yet this sinfull creature, frail and vain,
FLESH176:18	H58	Thy sinfull pleasures I doe hate,
MYCHILD215:25	Hp240	wayes, & what I knew was sinfull as lying, disobedᶜ. to parents.

SING (18)

PROLOG6:18	H3	To sing of Wars, of Captaines, and of Kings,
ELEMEN9:37	H71	And birds do sing, to see his glittering Coach.
SEASONS49~~:26~~	H115	Carelesse of worldly wealth, you sit {sing} and pipe,
MASSYR63:31	H418	Did neither *Homer, Hesiode, Virgil* sing;
SIDNEY149:13	H12	*Calliope* with *Terpsechor* did sing,
SIDNEY150:17	H49	Then let such Crowes as I, thy praises sing,
SIDNEY151:27	H75	But *Sydney's* Muse, can sing his worthinesse.
QELIZ156:28	H55	The States united now her fame doe sing;
CONTEM169:13	H54	To sing some Song, my mazed Muse thought meet.
CONTEM169:18	H58	I heard the merry grashopper then sing,
CHILDRN184:19	H8	Mounted the Trees, and learn'd to sing;
CHILDRN184:25	H14	Fly back and sing amidst this Quire.
CHILDRN185:23	H49	Or whilst on trees they sit and sing,
CHILDRN186:4	H71	In shady woods I'le sit and sing,
CHILDRN186:9	H76	But sing, my time so near is spent.
2HUSB232:26	H27	Was to sing praise to Thee.
2HUSB233:13	H46	That wee together may sing praise
2HUSB233:17	H50	Wᵗʰ an Engaged heart to sing

SINGLE (1)

HUMOUR~~27:27~~	H298	And what you singly {single} are, the whole I make.

SINGLY (1)

HUMOUR27:27	H298	And what you singly {single} are, the whole I make.

SINGS (3)

PROLOG7:3	H18	My foolish, broken, blemish'd Muse so sings;

CONTEM174:14 H213		Sings merrily, and steers his Barque with ease,
13MAY226:32 H8		My heart exvlts & praises sings

SINK (1)

MYCHILD215:11 Hp240   leaue to speak, and those espec. sink deepest wch are spoke

SINKE (3) [sink]

FATHER5:22	H23	That sinke, that swim, that fill, that upwards flye,
HUMOUR23:12	H122	The sinke of all us three, the hatefull spleen;
HUMOUR30:34	H426	The Spleen for al you three, was made a sinke,

SINKING (2)

AGES40:39	H218	My heart lyes frying, and my {mine} eyes are sinking;
FAINTING222:14	H4	My sinking heart I pray thee raise

SINKINGS (1) [pl.]

MYCHILD217:22 Hp243   never pᴿvail: yet haue I many Times sinkings & droopings,

SINKS (1) [pl.]

HUMOUR31:10   H443   The Kitchin Drudge, the cleanser of the sinks,

SINNE (1) [sin]

MEDDM205:29 Hp286   will not sinne against him.

SINNERS (2) [pl.]

MEDDM199:31	Hp278	Sore labourers haue hard hands and old sinners haue brawnie
MEDDM201:21	Hp281	sinners, seem full of contrition, but it is not from any dew of

SINNES (2) [sins] See also SINNS

DIALOG145:8	H157	Your fearfull sinnes, great cause there's to lament,
MEDDM206:21	Hp287	their wayes rather, then to beg forgiuenes for their sinnes,

SINNING (1)

MEDDM201:8   Hp280   never sayd, I haue seen an end of all Sinning, what he did say,

SINNS (2) [sins] See also SINNES

PILGRIM210:20	H20	Wᵗʰ sinns wᵗʰ cares and sorrows vext
MYSOUL225:11	H15	Thy Sinns shall ne'r bee sumon'd vp

SINS (6) [poss.] See also SINNES, SINNS

AGES38:18	H121	The sins, and dangers I am subject to.
AGES38:27	H130	As many was {are} my sins, so dangers too:
MASSYR59:37	H261	When *Jonah* for their sins denounc'd such {those} woes;
MASSYR68:20	H606	And of his own notorious sins, withall;
MPERS71:9	H725	Then sends to finde a Law for these his sins;
DIALOG143:28	H97	Which are my Sins, the breach of sacred Lawes;

SIP (1)

DIALOG145:4   H153   Nor sip I of that cup, and just 't may be,

SIR (2)

FATHER5:3	H4	Deare Sir, of late delighted with the sight, /T D on the
SIDNEY149:3	H3	Sir *Philip Sidney,* who was untimely

SIRE (5)

HUMOUR27:5	H276	Which is thy self, thy Mother, and thy Sire;
MPERS71:6	H722	*Cambyses,* no wayes like, his noble Sire,
MPERS72:16	H764	O hellish Husband, Brother, Vnckle, Sire,
MPERS79:1	H1023	Cuts him in twain, for whom his Sire besought.
CHILDRN184:24	H13	Leave not thy nest, thy Dam and Sire,

SIRENS See SYRENS

SIRES (1) [pl.]

AGES43:11   ~~H305~~   Nor Brothers, Nephewes, Sons, nor Sires I've spar'd.

SISIGAMBIS (1)

MGREC96:23   H1743   Great *Sisigambis,* she brought up the Reare;

SISTER (26)

ELEMEN9:33	H67	Good {Cold} sister Earth, no witnesse needs but thine;
ELEMEN11:22	H142	Sister, in worth {quoth shee} I come not short of you;
ELEMEN13:12	H213	And cholerick sister, thou (for all thine ire)
ELEMEN14:18	H260	But windy sister, 'twas when you have blown.
ELEMEN14:25	H267	Sister (quoth she) it had full well behov'd
ELEMEN17:33	H397	And now give place unto our sister Aire.
HUMOUR21:32	H60	Here's Sister Ruddy, worth the other two,
HUMOUR22:1	H70	Then here's our sad black Sister, worse then you,
HUMOUR22:11	H80	But {Now} let's give, cold, white, Sister Flegme her right.
HUMOUR22:25	H94	Nor sister Sanguine, from thy moderate heat,
HUMOUR26:36	H266	The first my self, second my sister faire,
HUMOUR29:10	H363	Faire rosie Sister, so might'st thou scape free,
HUMOUR29:38	H389	Enough of that, by our Sister {sisters} heretofore,
HUMOUR32:15	H489	I've done, pray Sister Flegme proceed in course,
HUMOUR32:38	H512	When sister Sanguine paints my Ivory face,
HUMOUR34:36	H591	And I passe by what sister Sanguine said;
MPERS72:10	H758	His sister, whom incestuously he wed,
MPERS78:14	H995	Who married the sister of *Darius:*
MPERS85:32	H1308	The {This} King, his sister, like *Cambyses,* wed;
MGREC112:1	H2387	Her Sister gives to his *Ephestion* deare,
MGREC117:37	H2644	A Sister *Alexander* had, but she
MGREC119:5	H2695	Which was his Masters sister for {secretly} to wed:
MGREC122:21	H2845	Her mother *Cyna* sister to *Alexander,*
MGREC126:31	H3022	The Daughter, Sister, Mother, Wife to Kings,
DIALOG143:15	H84	My Sister *Scotland* hurts me now no more,
FLESH175:10	H10	Sister, quoth Flesh, what liv'st thou on

SISTER-HOOD (1)

HUMOUR21:10	H38	Unto your Sister-hood, which makes us tender {render}

SISTERS (17) [pl.]

FATHER5:4	H5	Of your four sisters, deckt {cloth'd} in black & white /four parts
ELEMEN11:18	H138	Now Sisters, pray proceed, each in her {your} course,
ELEMEN12:38	H198	And Oares to row, when both my sisters failes?
ELEMEN17:40	H404	Abundantly more then my sisters three?
ELEMEN20:5	H487	I have said lesse, then did my sisters three;
HUMOUR24:12	H161	Good sisters give me leave (as is my place)
HUMOUR24:21	H170	Then let my sisters, right their injury.
HUMOUR27:17	H288	Th' rest to our Sisters, is more pertinent.
HUMOUR29:38	H389	Enough of that, by our Sister {sisters} heretofore,
HUMOUR33:18	H532	With all your flourishes, now Sisters three,
AGES46:17	H448	Mother, and sisters both; the worms, that crawl,
MPERS71:10	H726	That Kings with Sisters match, no Law they finde,
MPERS73:8	H795	And built fair *Meroe,* for his sisters sake.
DIALOG143:21	H90	Famine, and Plague, two sisters of the Sword,
FLESH175:4	H4	I heard two sisters reason on
FLESH176:4	H44	Sisters we are, yea twins we be,
1SIMON188:14	H15	Go pretty babe, go rest with Sisters twain

SISTERS (2) [poss.]

HUMOUR22:24	H93	{But tis} Not from our dul slow Sisters motions:
HUMOUR31:38	H471	Now could I stain my ruddy sisters face,

SIT (9) See also SITT

AGES40:10	H191	Sometimes I sit carousing others health,
SEASONS49:26	H115	Carelesse of worldly wealth, you sit {sing} and pipe,
MASSYR57:5	H152	To sit, thus long (obscure) wrong'd {rob'd} of his seat;
MASSYR57:32	H177	And eleav'n {many} hundred of years in silence sit,
MASSYR66:12	H518	There {And} sit bewailing *Zion* seventy years,
MPERS72:3	~~H755~~	His brother *Smerdis* sit upon his throne;
DIALOG141:9	H8	And sit i'th dust, to sigh these sad alarms?
CHILDRN185:23	H49	Or whilst on trees they sit and sing,
CHILDRN186:4	H71	In shady woods I'le sit and sing,

SITH (5) [since]

HUMOUR29:8	H361	But sith we fight with words, we might be kind,
MGREC~~94:18~~	H1656	Reply'd, enough, sith only hope he kept.
MGREC99:30	H1873	Sith valour, with Heroyicks is renown'd,
MROMAN140:6	H3569	No more I'le do, sith I have suffer'd wrack,
ELIZB187:3	H12	Sith thou art setled in an Everlasting state.

SITS (12)

HUMOUR22:3	H72	But peevish, Male-content, musing she sits,
HUMOUR22:21	H90	Again, who sits, for learning, science, Arts?
MASSYR66:35	H541	In splender, and in Majesty, he sits,
MASSYR68:13	H599	As thus amort {dead, alive} he sits, as all {one} undone:
MPERS77:16	H955	Grand-childe to *Cyrus,* now sits on the throne;
MPERS86:9	H1325	*Mnemon* now sits {set} upon his fathers Throne,
MGREC~~132:16~~	H3253	In neither finds content if he sits still:
MGREC134:1	H3332	A third *Seleuchus* next sits on the seat,
MROMAN138:14	H3504	Next, *Ancus Martius* sits upon the Throne,
MROMAN138:38	H3528	Next, *Servius Tullius* sits upon {gets into} the Throne,
DUBART153:31	H35	Sits down in silence, deeply he admires:
CONTEM170:6	H79	Here sits our Grandame in retired place,

SITT (2) [sit]

MYCHILD216:21	Hp241	observed this y[t] he hath never suffered me long to sitt loose
HOUSE237:3	H33	Vnder thy roof no gvest shall sitt,

SITTING (1)

MYCHILD216:2	Hp241	& sitting loose from God, vanity & y[e] follyes of Youth take hold

SITUATE See SCITUATE

SITUATION See SCITUATION

SIX (10)

MASSYR56:6	H112	Most {Some} writers say, six chariots might a front,
MASSYR62:5	H350	And him six years his tributary made;
MPERS77:12	H951	Thirty six years this royall {noble} Prince did reign,
MPERS87:33	H1385	Six yards the {in} depth, and forty miles the length,
MPERS88:20	H1413	He with six hundred, on a squadron set,
MPERS88:21	H1414	Of six thousand, wherein the King was yet;
MGREC107:36	H2211	On these, together ty'd, in six dayes space,
MGREC109:20	H2279	Fifty six Elephants he brings to's hands: {hand,}
MGREC112:5	H2391	Six thousand Guests he to {unto} this feast invites,
MROMAN138:2	H3492	The strife to end, six Brothers doe ingage;

SIXT (2) [sixth]

HUMOUR23:31	H141	Like our sixt *Henry,* that same worthy {virtuous} thing.
MPERS93:1	H1598	And in the sixt year of his haplesse reigne,

SIXTEEN (1)
  MASSYR66:19 H525 Who had for sixteen hundred years born sway,
SIXTH (1) See also SIXT
  MPERS75:38 H895 And in the sixth yeare of his friendly reign
SIXTY (7)
  HUMOUR33:3 H517 Sixty nine Princes, all stout *Hero* Knights,
  MASSYR54:22 H49 The walls one hundred sixty foot upright,
  MASSYR56:4 H110 Three hundred sixty foot, the walls in heighth:
  MPERS85:17 H1293 For sixty years maugre the *Persians* might.
  MPERS87:34 H1386 Some fifty, or else sixty foote in breadth.
  MPERS92:1 H1555 Which in rebellion sixty years did stand:
  MGREC108:38 H2254 And furlongs sixty could not {but} round the same.
SKARRES (1) [scars] See also SKARS
  DUBART154:14 H59 Who tam'd his foes, in bloud, in skarres {warrs,} and sweat,
SKARS (2) [scars] See also SKARRES
  HUMOUR32:33 H507 My polish'd skin was not ordain'd for skars,
  AGES38:3 H106 stroks did cause no death {blood}, nor wounds, nor {or} skars.
SKIE (3) [sky] See also SKYE
  ELEMEN8:13 H11 The quaking Earth did groan, the skie look't black,
  MGREC116:31 H2597 More boundles in ambition then the skie,
  VANITY159:31 H3 O vanity, O vain all under skie,
SKIES (6) [pl.] See also SKYES
  PROLOG7:35 H45 And oh, ye high flown quils, that soare the skies,
  ELEMEN12:3 H163 I'le here skip o're my mountaines, reaching skies,
  AGES39:17 H160 climbe Battlements, {scale walls and forts} rear'd to the skies;
  AGES46:23 H454 My strong Redeemer, comming in the skies;
  MASSYR56:17 H123 From whence, Astrologers, oft view'd the skies.
  CONTEM170:16 H88 On *Abels* gift the fire descends from Skies,
SKIL (6) [skill]
  ELEMEN9:20 H54 Ye Paracelsians too, in vaine's your skil
  HUMOUR28:19 H331 But yet for all my toyl, my care, my skil,
  AGES42:10 H268 A Captain I, with skil I train'd my band;
  MASSYR55:39 H105 That after ages, skil, by them were {was} taught.
  MPERS79:14 H1040 Seven thousand Gallies chain'd, by *Tyrians* skil,
  MPERS81:32 H1140 And of those *Greeks,* which by his skil he'd won,
SKILFULL (1) [skillful]
  MGREC131:30 H3222 When his disease the skilfull Physician found,
SKILL (11) See also SKIL
  FATHER5:9 H10 To climbe their Climes, I have nor strength, nor skill,
  PROLOG6:30 H14 But simple I, according to my skill.
  ELEMEN9:14 H48 Though strong limb'd *Vulcan* forg'd it by his skill,
  MASSYR64:39 H463 But the *Chaldeans* had nor ships, nor skill,
  MPERS79:13 H1039 Because they wanted skill the same to've staid.
  MGREC127:14 H3044 True *Eumenes* endeavours by all skill,
  DIALOG146:25 H211 For my relief now use thy utmost skill {do what there lyes in
  DUBART153:36 H40 Thy peircing skill in high Astronomy,
  DUBART154:40 H85 Good will, not skill, did cause me bring my mite.
  MEDDM203:26 Hp283 that hath skill to cure it, but when he findes his diseases to
  MYCHILD215:18 Hp240 haue not studyed in this yov read to shew my skill, but to
SKILL'D (1) [skilled]
  ELEMEN8:33 H31 What I can doe, well skill'd Mechanicks may,

SKILLFULL (1) [skillful] See also SKILFULL

MEDDM198:16 Hp276 The skillfull fisher hath his severall baits, for severall fish, but

SKIN (8)

HUMOUR27:35 H306 One touch thereof so beautifies the skin;

HUMOUR31:17 H450 And so {thence} with jaundise, Safferns al the skin.

HUMOUR32:33 H507 My polish'd skin was not ordain'd for skars,

AGES39:4 H147 My goodly cloathing, and my beauteous skin,

AGES43:23 H318 If *Bias* like, I'm stript unto my skin,

AGES45:30 H420 My skin is wrinkled, and my cheeks are pale.

SEASONS52:25 H240 Chilling the blood, and shrinking up the skin.

MPERS72:20 H768 Flayd him alive, hung up his stuffed skin

SKINS (1) [pl.]

MGREC105:17 H2110 Whose wounds had made their skins of purple dye;

SKIP (2)

ELEMEN12:3 H163 I'le here skip o're my mountaines, reaching skies,

ELEMEN12:15 H175 But ile skip {leap} o're these Hills, not touch a Dale,

SKY (2) See also SKIE, SKYE

SEASONS52:2 H219 With minds more dark, then is the darkned sky;

QELIZ155:15 H6 Yet thy loud Herauld Fame, doth to the sky

SKYE (3) [sky] See also SKIE

SEASONS49:25 H̶1̶1̶4̶ Though you repose on grasse under the skye.

MPERS88:8 H1401 Which like a mighty cloud darkned the skye;

HOUSE237:15 H45 Raise vp thy thovghts above the skye

SKYES (3) [skies]

HUMOUR23:22 H132 Onely to raise my honours to the Skyes,

CONTEM169:12 H53 My humble Eyes to lofty Skyes I rear'd

2LETTER182:22 H28 O how they joy when thou dost light the skyes.

SLACK (1)

2HUSB232:14 H15 O help and bee not slack.

SLAIN (23)

MASSYR54:33 H60 *Pharmus, {Thermus}* their King, he caused to be slain;

MASSYR61:25 H330 When *Rezin's* slain, his Army over-thrown,

MASSYR62:40 H385 And by his Sons in's Idols house was slain.

MASSYR67:18 H564 His Army routed, and himselfe there slain,

MPERS71:15 H729 'Gainst *Ægypts* King, who there by him was slain,

MPERS7̶2̶:̶3̶ H755 Unjustly caus'd his brother to be slain.

MPERS79:39 H1065 Till twenty thousand *Persians* falls down slain;

MPERS83:22 H1210 But all his family was likewise slain,

MPERS90:23 H1490 The many thousand *Persians* they had slain;

MPERS9̶1̶:̶3̶9̶ H1553 Of brethren and of kindred to be slain.

MPERS9̶2̶:̶3̶ H1557 Was by his *Eunuch* the proud *Bagoas* slain.

MPERS9̶2̶:̶7̶ H1565 His brother, as tis said, long since was slain,

MGREC93:14 H1611 This Prince (his father by *Pausanias* slain)

MGREC109:3 H2260 that {Such as} doe not, both they, {them} and theirs, are slain;

MGREC119:31 H2721 The valiant Chief, amidst his foes was slain,

MGREC130:13 H3168 Resolves at last the Princesse should be slain,

MGREC130:29 H̶3̶1̶8̶1̶ *Philip* and *Olympias* both were slain,

MGREC130:35 H̶3̶1̶8̶1̶ His wife and sons then slain by this *Cassander,*

MGREC132:3 H3236 This by *Lysimachus* soon {was} after slain,

MGREC135:1 H3371 At *Actium* slain, {where} his Navy {Navy's} put to flight.

DIALOG144:36 H144 I saw her people famish'd, Nobles slain,

DIALOG146:17	H203	My ravisht {weeping} virgins, and my young men slain,
DUBART154:17	H62	Their trophies were but heaps of wounded slain,

SLAINE (27) [slain]

HUMOUR22:8	H77	Then by a quick encounter, to be slaine;
MASSYR55:27	H93	Till her ambition, caus'd him to be slaine:
MASSYR59:12	H236	But *Salmeneus* slaine, his {the} Army fals,
MPERS73:24	H809	And now with his accomplyces lye slaine.
MPERS76:22	H920	His enemies scarce seen, then much lesse, slaine;
MPERS85:8	H1284	Then the surviver is by *Nothus* slaine;
MPERS89:39	H1473	The *Greeks,* having {seeing} their valiant Captaines slaine,
MGREC95:5	H1684	With losse of thirty four, of his there slaine:
MGREC97:6	H1767	Two hundred thousand men that day were slaine,
MGREC99:20	H1863	And by these walls, so many men were slaine,
MGREC111:26	H2371	By hunger, and by cold, so many slaine,
MGREC113:28	H2455	Most wickedly was slaine, without least crime,
MGREC114:12	H2480	But instantly commands him to be slaine;
MGREC114:14	H2484	And would have slaine himself, for *Clitus* gone,
MGREC128:19	H3092	Had {The} valiant *Eumenes* unjustly slaine,
MGREC132:36	H3283	And so *Lysimachus* was slaine in fight.
MGREC133:1	H3289	He was by *Ptolomy Cerannus* slaine.
MGREC133:10	H3298	*Cassanders* Sons, soone after's death were slaine,
MROMAN136:33	H3447	His Brother *Remus* there, by him was slaine,
MROMAN137:23	H3474	Affirme, that by the Senate he was slaine.
MROMAN138:36	H3526	And after all, by *Ancus* Sons was slaine.
MROMAN139:9	H3537	And then by *Tarquin, Priscus* Son, was slaine.
MROMAN139:13	H3541	Sate on the Throne, when he had slaine his foe;
SIDNEY149:4	H4	slaine at the Seige of *Zutphon,*
DAVID158:24	H4	Alas, slaine is the head of *Israel,*
DAVID159:5	H20	Sometimes from crimson blood of gastly slaine,
DAVID159:21	H36	O! lovely *Jonathan,* how wert {wast} thou slaine,

SLANDER (3)

HUMOUR31:3	H436	So plain a slander needeth no reply.
MASSYR55:30	H96	Some think the *Greeks,* this slander on her cast,
QELIZ157:37	H105	Know 'tis a slander now, but once was treason.

SLANDEROUS (2) See also SLANDROUS

HUMOUR32:28	H502	What's slanderous, repel; doubtful, dispute;
MEDDM199:27	Hp278	of pestilence, and the arrow of a slanderous tongue, the two

SLANDERS (1) [pl.]

HUMOUR27:18	H289	Your slanders thus refuted, takes no place,

SLANDROUS (1) [slanderous]

HUMOUR31:19	H452	I trust I've clear'd your slandrous imputations {inputation}.

SLASHING (1)

SEASONS50:3	H137	Now go the Mowers to their slashing toyl,

SLAUERY (1) [slavery]

MEDDM209:12	Hp291	them vnder slauery, so it is most certain that those that are

SLAUGHTER (3)

MPERS77:25	H966	Yet all his men, and instruments of slaughter,
MGREC131:37	H3229	Who had an end put to their dayes by slaughter.
DIALOG142:40	H69	Whose proud contention cause this slaughter;

SLAUGHTER'D (2) [slaughtered]

MPERS69:26	H648	Where all that doe {dare} resist, are slaughter'd down;

DIALOG146:8	H196	Am now destroy'd, and slaughter'd by mine own,

SLAUGHTERED (2)

AGES45:19	H401	Three hundred thousand slaughtered innocents,
MASSYR59:9	H233	Bereft of wits, were slaughtered down right.

SLAUGHTERS (4) [pl.]

MPERS88:37	H1430	grew weake, through {by their} slaughters that they made.
MGREC95:39	H1718	It seemes to see the *Macedonians* {*Macedonian*} slaughters.
MGREC101:37	H1966	But 'tis not known what slaughters here they {was} made.
MGREC130:30	H3181	*Aridaeus* and his Queen by slaughters ta'ne;

SLAV'D (1) [slaved]

HUMOUR33:1	H515	Princes hath slav'd, and Captains captived:

SLAVE (2)

VANITY159:37	H9	He's now a slave {captive}, that was a Prince {King} of late.
FLESH176:12	H52	How oft thy slave, hast thou me made,

SLAVED See SLAV'D

SLAVERY See SLAUERY

SLAVES (1) [pl.]

MGREC98:21	H1823	And thirteen thousand Gally slaves he made,

SLAY (2)

MASSYR56:33	H139	The rest *Staurobates* in fight did slay.
MROMAN138:7	H3497	The *Romans* sore incens'd, their Generall slay,

SLAYES (2) [slays]

MPERS70:14	H685	Enters the town, the sottish King he slayes,
MPERS91:37	H1551	(To his great grief) most subtilly he slayes:

SLEEP (3)

AGES42:28	H285	For restlesse day and night, I'm rob'd of sleep,
MEDDM207:33	Hp289	of death, wch is their sleep (for so is death often calld) and
PILGRIM210:25	H25	This body shall in silence sleep,

SLEEPING (1)

CONTEM171:14	H118	In eating, drinking, sleeping, vain delight

SLEEPS (2) [pl.]

ELEMEN14:12	H254	In hot, and cold, and some benums with sleeps,
ELEMEN14:12	H254	In heats & colds & gripes & drowsy sleeps:

SLEEPS (1) v.

QELIZ158:8	H117	*Here sleeps THE Queen, this is the royall bed.*

SLEIGHTS (1)

MGREC123:7	H2869	And by his sleights to circumvent him sought;

SLEPT (3)

MGREC101:19	H1944	Nor infamy had wak'd, when he had slept;
MGREC116:24	H2590	And under's pillow laid them when he slept.
BYNIGHT220:2	H3	By night when others soundly slept,

SLEW (17)

ELEMEN10:5	H80	The Valiant *Perseus* who *Medusa* slew,
ELEMEN10:30	H105	The over-curious second *Pliny* slew:
MASSYR54:36	H63	*Zoroaster,* their King, he likewise slew,
MASSYR61:13	H318	*Resin* their valiant King, he also slew,
MASSYR65:21	H486	But chang'd his minde, and slew him by the way; {& caus'd his
MPERS71:34	H748	The Ægyptian *Apis* then he likewise slew,
MPERS83:7	H1195	Which {With} him, and his, most barbarously there slew,
MGREC105:1	H2094	Then slew his servants, that were faithfull found;
MGREC114:33	H2503	When e're 'tis said, he thousand thousands slew,

MGREC114:40	H2510	But yet withall, *Calisthines* he slew;
MGREC115:3	H2514	But yet withall, *Calisthines* he slew.
MGREC121:41	H2823	And brave *Craterus* slew, amongst the rest,
MGREC122:24	H2845	And in a Battell slew her hand to hand;
MGREC124:9	H2914	Those absent, banished, or else he slew
MGREC127:1	H3031	Some slew, some fry'd, of others, stopt the breath;
MGREC129:37	H3151	Who slew the prince according to desire:
MGREC132:6	H3241	Seaz'd upon that, and slew him traitrously.

SLIDE (2)

HUMOUR33:37	H551	The spirits animal, from whence doth {hence do} slide,
CONTEM172:22	H156	Nor is't enough, that thou alone may'st slide,

SLIGHT (4)

AGES37:21	H83	In that which riper age did scorn, and slight:
MPERS92:26	H1584	Thus learned *Pemble,* whom we may not slight,
SIDNEY150:3	H28	Which makes severer eyes but scorn thy {slight that} Story,
MEDDM205:11	Hp286	inhabitants his slight and flitting thoughts are like passengers,

SLIGHTED (2)

MGREC118:15	H2662	Untoucht, uncovered, slighted, and neglected,
MEDDM203:24	Hp283	whom he slighted before, so he that neuer felt the sicknes of

SLIGHTS (1) v.

MGREC123:30	H2894	Slights his commands, his actions he disclaimes,

SLILY (1) [slyly]

SEASONS51:28	H204	The sap doth slily creep towards the earth,

SLOW (4)

HUMOUR22:6	H75	In her dul resolution, she's {so} slow.
HUMOUR22:24	H93	{But tis} Not from our dul slow Sisters motions:
MPERS86:4	H1320	But in his slow approach, ere he came there;
MGREC129:16	H3130	The Heavens seem'd slow in paying her the same,

SLOWNESSE (1)

HUMOUR29:36	H387	And if thy haste, my slownesse should not temper,

SLUCES (1) [sluices]

MPERS70:8	H679	To drain this ditch, he many sluces cut,

SLUMBERS (1) [pl.]

DISTEMP179:16	H4	In tossing slumbers on my wakeful bed,

SLYLY See SLILY

SMAL (3) [small]

HUMOUR30:12	H404	To {So} prison thee within that bladder smal.
HUMOUR32:24	H498	Nor wonder 'twas, for hatred there's not smal,
MPERS80:24	H1091	If that smal number his great force could bide;

SMALL (26)

PROLOG7:33	H44	Yet grant some small acknowledgement of ours.
HUMOUR26:20	H250	As plants, trees, and small Embryon know'th,
AGES43:22	H317	I hate {not} for to be had, {held} in small {high'st} account.
MASSYR57:17	H164	How he thus suddenly should be thus small?
MPERS80:15	H1082	Of Vessels small almost innumerable,
MPERS82:15	H1162	Same day, the small remainder of his Fleet,
MPERS89:5	H1439	Nor lackt they any of their number small,
MPERS90:28	H1495	Town after town, with small resistance take,
MPERS92:22	H1580	And so this wretch (a punishment too small)
MGREC100:3	H1887	To see how fast he gain'd, is {was} no small wonder,
MGREC100:28	H1912	But on their fortitude he had small stay;

MGREC111:25	H2370	Unto his starved Souldiers small content;
MGREC124:35	H2942	Nor counts {thought} he that indignity but {was} small,
MGREC132:37	H3284	'Twas no small joy, unto *Seleuchus* breast,
MGREC~~134:2~~	H3334	Whose large Dominions after was made small,
MGREC135:38	H3410	And how from small beginnings it did grow,
DUBART153:2	H6	But knowing th' taske so great, and strength but small,
DUBART153:40	H44	Sure liberall Nature, did with Art not small,
AUTHOR177:36	H8	At thy return my blushing was not small,
SICKNES178:26	H9	Yet live I shall, this life's but small,
VERSES184:4	H8	My stock's so small, I know not how to pay,
CHILDRN184:35	H24	On whom I plac'd no small delight;
2SIMON195:9	Hp271	as they are I bequeath to you, Small legacys are accept[d] by
MEDDM206:14	Hp287	but small and obscure, yet all receiue their luster (be it more or
MYCHILD216:4	Hp241	small pox, When I was in my afflict[n]. I besovght the Lord, and
MYCHILD217:3	Hp242	by it: It hath been no small support to me in times of Darknes

SMART (3)

ELEMEN16:23	H346	Nor yet of Salt, and Sugar, sweet and smart,
DIALOG142:29	H58	Dost feele the smart, or feare the consequence?
MERCY189:14	H35	In him alone, that caused all this smart;

SMARTING (1)

BYNIGHT220:14	H13	My smarting wounds washt in his blood,

SMEL (1) [smell]

SEASONS~~49:35~~	H128	Whose fragrant scent, {smel} all made-perfume surpasses;

SMELS (1) [smells, pl.]

ELEMEN11:31	H151	Their kinds, their tasts, their colours, and their smels,

SMERDIS (4)

MPERS72:3	~~H755~~	His brother *Smerdis* sit upon his throne;
MPERS72:35	H779	Had set a *Smerdis* up, of the same years;
MPERS72:36	H780	And like in feature, to the *Smerdis* dead,
MPERS73:20	H807	To thrust th' Imposter *Smerdis* out of throne,

SMIL'D (1) [smiled]

AGES44:24	H357	Sometimes the Heavens with plenty smil'd on me,

SMILE (2)

ELEMEN18:26	H430	And when I smile, your Ocean's like a Poole.
1SIMON188:13	H14	And smile again, after our bitter crosses.

SMILED See SMIL'D

SMILES (2) [pl.]

CONTEM168:25	H32	The morn doth usher thee, with smiles & blushes,
SON230:22	H5	My Teares to smiles, my sad to glad

SMILING (4)

SEASONS46:34	H10	With smiling Sun-shine face, and garments {somewhat} green,
SEASONS48:23	H76	But both rejoyce, at th'heavens clear smiling face,
MPERS89:23	H1457	The smiling *Greeks* reply, they first must bait,
TDUDLEY166:16	H58	Oft spake of death, and with a smiling chear,

SMITHS (1) [pl.]

ELEMEN18:21	H425	Ye forging Smiths, if Bellowes once were gone;

SMOOTH (1)

CONTEM174:13	H212	The Mariner that on smooth waves doth glide,

SMOTE (1) See also SMOTT

MGREC135:25	H3397	And smote those feet, those legs, those arms and thighs;

SMOTHER (1)
HUMOUR28:3   H315   The body dryes, the minde sublime doth smother,

SMOTHER'D (1) [smothered]
MPERS83:12   H1200   Which wretch, {Who} him privately smother'd in's bed,

SMOTT (2) [smote]
MYCHILD216:3   Hp241   16. The Lord layd his hand sore vpon me & smott me wth y^e
MYCHILD216:27   Hp242   towards him. Somt. he hath smott a child wth sicknes, somt.

SNACHT (1) See also SNATCHT
MGREC~~114:12~~   H2481   From one stood by he snacht a partizan,

SNAKE (1)
HUMOUR30:6   H398   The melancholy Snake shal it aver.

SNARE (3)
VANITY160:8   H18   What is't in beauty? no, that's but a snare,
CHILDRN185:22   H48   They fall un'wares in Fowlers snare:
MEDDM209:10   Hp291   was y^c Issue, they became a snare vnto them, prickes in their

SNARES (1) [pl.]
CONTEM173:18   H184   O merry Bird (said I) that fears no snares,

SNATCH (1)
FLESH176:33   H73   Nor fancies vain at which I snatch,

SNATCHT (1) See also SNACHT
AUTHOR177:32   H4   Till snatcht from thence by friends, less wise then true

SNIP (1)
MGREC122:3   H2826   I should but snip a story into verse, {bits}

SNORTING (2)
AGES39:18   H161   The snorting Horse, the Trumpet, Drum I like,
MPERS74:9   H834   Then mounting on their snorting coursers proud,

SNOW (3)
ELEMEN17:14   H378   I need not say much of my Haile and Snow,
AGES35:28   H14   His spring was intermixed with some snow.
SEASONS47:25   H41   Yet many a fleece of Snow, and stormy showre,

SNOWIE (1) [snowy]
SEASONS52:32   H247   Moyst snowie *February* is my last,

SNOWS (2) [pl.]
SEASONS52:16   H231   Bound up with Frosts, and furr'd with Hails, and Snows,
SEASONS52:36   H251   The Rivers now do {'gin to} ope, and {the} Snows do {to} melt,

SNOWY See SNOWIE

SNUFFING (1)
AGES39:33   H176   To be as wilde as is the snuffing Asse,

SO (438) See also SOE, SO's
FATHER5:7   H8   Their worth so shines, in those rich lines you show.
FATHER5:10   H11   To mount so high, requires an Eagles quill:
PROLOG6:23   H8   My obscure Verse,{Lines} shal not so dim their worth.
PROLOG7:3   H18   My foolish, broken, blemish'd Muse so sings;
PROLOG7:5   H20   'Cause Nature made it so irreparable.
PROLOG7:24   H36   So 'mongst the rest, they plac'd the Arts divine:
ELEMEN8:18   H16   Both by their darings; Water so provoked,
ELEMEN8:21   H19   The rumbling, hissing, puffing was so great,
ELEMEN8:23   H21   But {Till gentle} Aire at length, contention so abated,
ELEMEN9:9   H43   Set ope those gates, that 'fore so strong was {were} barr'd.
ELEMEN9:13   H47   That so in time it might requite your paine;

HUMOUR33:20	H534	My excellencies are so great, so many,
HUMOUR33:20	H534	My excellencies are so great, so many,
HUMOUR34:6	H561	Whence her affections, passions, speak so clear;
HUMOUR35:13	H609	But here's a {so} compact body, whole, entire:
HUMOUR35:14	H610	This loving counsel pleas'd them all so wel,
AGES36:32	H56	That he was young, before he grew so old.
AGES37:24	H86	My high-borne soule, so straitly was confin'd:
AGES38:27	H130	As many was {are} my sins, so dangers too:
AGES39:15	H158	Nor ignorant {And so likewise} what they in Country do;
AGES39:25	H168	So affable that I do {can} suit each mind;
AGES40:1	H182	But doing so, might seem magnanimous.
AGES40:7	H188	Of all at once, who not so wise, as fair,
AGES41:18	H237	As was their praise, or shame, so mine must be.
AGES43:3	H298	But {And} by ambitious sailes, I was so carryed;
AGES43:16	H311	The bottom nought, and so no longer stood.
AGES44:14	H347	It's not my Learning, Rhetorick, wit so large,
AGES44:32	H365	And like a Cedar, others so surmount,
AGES45:11	H393	But not their Princes love, nor state so high;
AGES45:15	H397	I've seen, and so have ye, for 'tis but late,
AGES45:17	H399	Plotted and acted, so that none can tell,
AGES45:21	H403	Oh may you live, and so you will I trust
AGES46:1	H432	Shal both be broke, by wracking death so strong;
SEASONS48:28	H81	Each season, hath his fruit, so hath each clime.
SEASONS49:10	H101	reason why {Though he decline}, because his flames so faire,
SEASONS49:13	H104	Whose vehemency, at length doth grow so great,
SEASONS50:22	H156	Although their Bread have not so white a face.
SEASONS51:4	H178	For nought's so good, but it may be abused,
SEASONS51:30	H206	So doth Old Age stil tend unto his Grave,
SEASONS51:37	H213	So farre remote, his glances warm not us;
SEASONS53:3	H259	*The first fell in so naturally,*
MASSYR54:10	H37	So oft profanely offered sacred rites;
MASSYR54:23	H50	So broad, three Chariots run abrest there might,
MASSYR55:38	H104	The walls so strong, and curiously were {was} wrought;
MASSYR56:8	H114	About the wall, a ditch so deep and wide,
MASSYR57:18	H165	So suddenly should loose so great a state,
MASSYR57:22	H169	So Province, after Province, rent away,
MASSYR57:25	H172	When famous *Troy* was so beleaguered:
MASSYR58:30	H213	*Arbaces* courage he did sore {so} abate:
MASSYR59:16	H240	There with all store he was so wel provided,
MASSYR59:20	H244	Which through much rain, then swelling up so high,
MASSYR59:20	H244	For by the rain, was *Tygris* so o'reflown,
MASSYR60:17	H282	Not so content, but aiming to be great,
MASSYR60:39	H304	Which makes the world of differences {difference} so ful,
MASSYR61:2	H307	And times of both computed, so fall out,
MASSYR61:19	H324	The temple robes, so to fulfill his ends,
MASSYR61:38	H343	(This was that *Ahaz,* which so much {high} transgrest.)
MASSYR63:9	H394	So he's now stil'd, the King of *Babylon;*
MASSYR63:28,	H415	Then being Father to so great a Son.
MASSYR65:37	H502	The wals so strong, that stood so long, now fall;
MASSYR65:37	H502	The wals so strong, that stood so long, now fall;
MASSYR66:24	H530	Which wealth, and strong ambition made so great;

MASSYR66:32	H538	But for his pride so had the heavens decreed.
MASSYR67:25	H571	His life so base, and dissolute, invites
MPERS69:10	H632	And so unites two Kingdoms, without strife;
MPERS69:24	H646	So over-thrown of *Cyrus*, as was just;
MPERS70:6	H677	Now trebble wall'd, and moated so about,
MPERS71:26	H740	Yea, in his pride, he ventured so farre,
MPERS71:33	H747	So left his sacrilegious bold intents:
MPERS72:12	H760	His woful fate with tears did so bemoane,
MPERS73:2	H789	Yeelding {So yields} to death, that dreadfull Conquerer.
MPERS73:22	H809	This King, with {his} conspirators so stout,
MPERS73:28	H813	But so or no, sure tis, they won the day.
MPERS73:34	H819	So late crusht by their Princes Tyranny;
MPERS74:32	H855	Yet notwithstanding he did all so well,
MPERS76:7	H905	By these alone his Hoast was pinch'd so sore,
MPERS76:14	H912	But wise *Gobrias* reads not half so farre:
MPERS76:25	H923	Which husht, he straight so orders his affaires;
MPERS76:27	H925	But as before, so now with ill successe,
MPERS77:17	H958	The {His} Father not so full of lenity,
MPERS79:21	H1047	One King, so many Subjects should possesse;
MPERS79:25	H1051	Of so long time, his thoughts had never been.
MPERS80:13	H1080	And as at Land, so he at Sea was crost,
MPERS80:21	H1088	And *Xerxes* mighty Gallies batter'd so,
MPERS81:2	H1110	Which accident, the rest affrighted so,
MPERS81:13	H1121	So should all favour to their State be shown.
MPERS82:17	H1164	And there so utterly they wrack'd the same,
MPERS83:18	H1206	And by his craft, ordered the matter so,
MPERS84:8	H1236	By *Memucan's* advice, this {so} was the doome.
MPERS84:16	H1252	This valiant Knight, whom they so much did owe;
MPERS84:35	H1271	Either to wrong, did wound his heart so sore,
MPERS84:38	H1274	Strong poyson took, and {so} put an end to's dayes.
MPERS85:12	H1288	If {so} they were hers, the greater was her moan;
MPERS85:16	H1292	Joynes with the *Greeks,* and so maintains {maintain} their
MPERS85:25	H1301	So that he might, these tumults {those troubles} soon appease.
MPERS85:31	H1307	And so each man again possest his owne.
MPERS85:34	H1310	*Persian* Kings, did deem {then deem'd} themselves so good,
MPERS86:5	H1321	His fathers death, did {so} put an end to's fear.
MPERS87:8	H1364	Which *Cyrus* heares, and so fore-slowes his pace:
MPERS87:23	H1375	This place was {so} made, by nature, and by art;
MPERS87:26	H1378	So hir'd a fleet, to waft him ore the Maine,
MPERS88:18	H1411	So had he been, and got the victory,
MPERS88:22	H1415	And brought his Souldiers on so gallantly,
MPERS89:16	H1450	That so *Europians* might no more molest;
MPERS90:5	H1478	So to deprive them of all nourishment;
MPERS90:18	H1485	So after all {Thus finishing} their travell, danger, pain,
MPERS90:30	H1497	The *Greeks* by this successe, incourag'd so,
MPERS90:34	H1501	Which over-throw incens'd the King so sore,
MPERS91:2	H1510	height, {*Spartan* State} which now apace doth {so fast did} rise;
MPERS91:11	H1519	Dissention in *Greece* continued {so} long,
MPERS92:8	H1566	So fell to him, which else it had not done:
MPERS92:22	H1580	And so this wretch (a punishment too small)
MPERS92:28	H1586	If so, or not, we cannot tell, but find

MGREC93:31	H1628	But death did terminate, those thoughts so high.
MGREC94:33	H1671	To whip him well with rods, and then {so} to bring,
MGREC94:34	H1672	That boy so mallepart, before the King.
MGREC94:41	H1679	Those banks so steep, the *Greeks,* now {yet} scramble up
MGREC95:17	H1696	Which who so did {doth}, must Lord of all remain,
MGREC95:27	H1706	No stroake for it he struck, their hearts so quakes.
MGREC95:30	H1709	And on {Then o're} he goes *Darius* {now} so to meet;
MGREC96:10	H1730	An object not so much of fear, as laughter.
MGREC96:20	H1740	For so to fright the *Greekes* he judg'd was best,
MGREC96:21	H1741	Their golden Ornaments so {how} to set forth,
MGREC97:36	H1797	A King he was, and that not only so,
MGREC98:9	H1811	With this reply, he was so sore {deep} enrag'd,
MGREC98:30	H1832	And therefore {So} gives this {his little} Lord-ship to another.
MGREC98:39	H1841	These he may scape, and if he so desire,
MGREC99:13	H1856	And so if I *Parmenio* were, would I.
MGREC99:20	H1863	And by these walls, so many men were slaine,
MGREC99:40	H1883	By which he was so much incouraged,
MGREC101:29	H1954	To force his Camp, so put {vanquish} them all to {by} flight;
MGREC101:35	H1964	So make {made} an end, before they {as soon as} well begun;
MGREC102:14	H1984	Whose fame throughout the world, was so renown'd;
MGREC104:1	H2053	But hearing, *Alexander* was so near;
MGREC104:10	H2062	Then with so few, how likely to be crost.
MGREC105:16	H2109	So chanc'd these bloudy Horses to espy,
MGREC106:22	H2156	So daily of his vertues doth he lose;
MGREC107:3	H2178	So heaps up gifts, his credit to redeem;
MGREC107:25	H2200	Where most {so} immoderatly these thirsty drink;
MGREC107:34	H2209	So {Then} from his carriages the Hides he takes,
MGREC108:31	H2247	Of Darts, and Arrowes, made so little spare,
MGREC108:32	H2248	They flew so thick they seem'd to dark the aire:
MGREC110:14	H2314	The last set on his back, and so prevail'd:
MGREC110:22	H2326	But so to doe, his Souldiers had no will;
MGREC110:29	H2333	His Maungers he erected up so high,
MGREC110:32	H2336	Which might be found, and so for {great} wonders kept:
MGREC110:36	H2340	And so his memory might {would} fade away,
MGREC111:26	H2371	By hunger, and by cold, so many slaine,
MGREC111:31	H2376	{And} So he at length drew neare to *Persia*;
MGREC112:10	H2396	They were so wrapt with this externall glory.
MGREC112:14	H2400	So after many dayes this {the} Banquet ends.
MGREC112:26	H2412	He death deserv'd, for this so high offence;
MGREC113:12	H2439	At last he did: So they were justified,
MGREC113:19	H2446	Who was so much engag'd, to this Commander,
MGREC113:21	H2448	Nor could his Captaines bear so great regard;
MGREC113:30	H2457	This is *Parmenio,* which {who} so much had done,
MGREC114:9	H2477	From jeast, to earnest, and at last so bold,
MGREC114:11	H2479	Which *Alexanders* wrath incens'd so high,
MGREC115:15	H2528	A rueful face in this so general woe;
MGREC115:15	H2531	What e're he did, or thought not so content,
MGREC115:24	H2543	His doing so, no whit displeas'd the King,
MGREC115:26	H2545	But now, *Antipater* had liv'd thus {so} long,
MGREC115:34	H2553	So to be caught, *Antipater's* too wise,
MGREC115:37	H2556	Nor by his baits could be ensnared so:

MGREC116:16	H2582	And so with black, be-clouded all his fame.
MGREC116:18	H2584	Had so instructed him in morall truth.
MGREC~~116:31~~	H2597	Ambitious so, that nought could satisfie,
MGREC117:9	H2616	So the same cup to his, did others fill.
MGREC117:28	H2635	Yet {But} none so hardy found as so durst say.
MGREC117:28	H2635	Yet {But} none so hardy found as so durst say.
MGREC118:1	H2648	That so under his feeble wit, and reign,
MGREC118:16	H2663	So much these Princes their owne ends respected.
MGREC118:19	H2666	And yet not so content, unlesse that he
MGREC~~118:24~~	H2672	His countenance so lively did appear,
MGREC~~118:24~~	H2673	That for a while they durst not come so near:
MGREC~~118:32~~	H2681	And {So} took his life unworthily that houre:
MGREC119:6	H2696	So, to the Lady secretly he sent,
MGREC119:26	H2716	Striving {And seeks} to stop *Leonatus,* that so
MGREC120:12	H2747	So many Kingdoms in their power to hold,
MGREC120:24	H2761	The Acts of his Vice-royes, {Vice-Roy} now grown so high:
MGREC~~121:15~~	H2794	Who could not book so great indignity,
MGREC122:30	H2849	Resign'd his place, and so let all alone;
MGREC123:4	H2866	Who in few years the rest so over-tops,
MGREC124:2	H2907	To take down *Polisperchon* grown so high;
MGREC~~124:6~~	H2911	And so he quick returns thus well appaid,
MGREC125:41	H2991	So goes to finde this {cruel} Queen in *Macedon;*
MGREC126:9	H3000	There by *Cassander* she's block'd up, so long,
MGREC126:14	H3005	So succours, and endeavours proves but vaine:
MGREC~~126:22~~	H3013	Gives promise for her life, and {so} wins the day:
MGREC126:27	H3018	And so was he acquitted of his word,
MGREC126:33	~~H3023~~	So boundlesse was her pride, and cruelty,
MGREC126:36	H3025	The Authours death she did so much lament,
MGREC127:10	H3040	Old *Thebes* he then re-built (so much of fame)
MGREC127:20	H3050	When victor oft had {he'd} been, and so might still,
MGREC127:27	H3057	So *Eumenes* {(the prop)} of destiny {death} must taste.
MGREC127:33	H3063	*Antigonus,* his growing up so hye,
MGREC128:21	H3094	So therefore craves {requests} their help to take him down,
MGREC128:26	H3099	So *Syria* to *Ptolomy* did yeeld;
MGREC~~129:9~~	H3123	And put {So puts} to death, the mother and her son,
MGREC129:30	H3144	The *Greeks* touch'd with the murther done so {of} late,
MGREC129:35	H3149	So *Polisperchon* to his Counsell drew,
MGREC130:14	H3169	So hinders him of her, he could not gain.
MGREC130:19	H3174	And now he thinks {hopes}, he's ordered all so well,
MGREC130:41	H3186	*Demetrius* is first, that so assumes, {the royal stile asum'd,}
MGREC131:28	H3220	Falls so extreamly sick, all fear {fear'd} his life,
MGREC132:8	H3243	And so falls out to be extinct in one,
MGREC~~132:20~~	H3262	*Demetrius* with so many troubles met,
MGREC132:23	H3268	Injoy'd what so {ere} beseem'd his Royalty,
MGREC132:36	H3283	And so *Lysimachus* was slaine in fight.
MGREC132:40	H3287	And so himselfe the only Monarch make;
MGREC133:11	H3299	So three Successors only did remaine;
MGREC133:31	H3321	To whom Ancient {the old} *Berosus* (so much fam'd)
MGREC134:11	H3342	So many Princes still were murthered,
MROMAN137:8	H3459	Of Wives there was so great a scarsity,
MROMAN137:11	H3462	So *Romulus* was forc'd this course to take.

MROMAN137:34	H3485	So to delude the people he was bold:
MROMAN139:12	H3540	*Tarquin* the proud, from manners called so,
MROMAN139:16	H3544	She loathed so the fact, she loath'd her life,
DIALOG142:3	H32	If th' wound's {wound} so dangerous I may not know?
DIALOG145:24	H173	So many obstacles comes {came} in their way,
DIALOG146:5	H193	They worded it so long, they fell to blows,
DIALOG146:7	H195	I that no warres, so many yeares have known,
DIALOG147:28	H252	If now you weep so much, that then no more,
DIALOG147:36	H260	And discipline erected, so I trust,
DIALOG148:3	H268	So shall thy happy Nation ever flourish,
DIALOG148:15	H280	And make his filthy den so desolate,
SIDNEY149:21	H20	Are not his Tragick Comedies so acted,
SIDNEY151:5	H69	And as thy beauty, so thy name would wast,
SIDNEY151:10	H69	How could that *Stella,* so confine thy will?
SIDNEY151:25	H69	Enough for me to look, and so admire.
SIDNEY151:36	H69	So proudly foolish I, with *Phaeton* strive,
SIDNEY152:3	H75	Who in his Deity, had so deep share,
SIDNEY152:21	H90	So *Sydney's* fame, I leave to *England's* Rolls,
DUBART153:2	H6	But knowing th' taske so great, and strength but small,
DUBART155:8	H93	*But Nature vanquish'd Art, so* Bartas *dy'd,*
QELIZ155:17	H8	And so has {hath} vow'd, whilst there is world, or time;
QELIZ155:18	H9	So great's thy glory, and thine excellence,
QELIZ156:3	H30	Who was so good, so just, so learn'd, so wise,
QELIZ156:9	H36	*Spaines* Monarch sa's not so; nor yet his Hoast,
QELIZ156:21	H48	Did ever wealth in *England* so {more} abound?
QELIZ156:36	H63	Her selfe *Minerva,* caus'd them so to be;
QELIZ157:2	H70	But time would faile me, so my wit {tongue} would to,
QELIZ157:26	H94	She was a Phoenix Queen, so shall she be,
QELIZ157:31	H99	To read what others write, and then {so} admire.
QELIZ158:3	H112	No more shall rise or set such {so} glorious Sun,
QELIZ158:11	H120	*This Rose is withered, once so lovely faire,*
QELIZ158:16	H125	So blaze it fame, here's feathers for thy wings,
DAVID159:3	H18	There had his dignity so sore a soyle,
DAVID159:11	H26	Swifter then swiftest Eagles, so were they,
DAVID159:26	H41	So pleasant hast thou been, deare brother mine:
VANITY159:30	H2	As he said vanity, so vain say I,
TDUDLEY165:16	H18	Nor was his name, or life lead so obscure
TDUDLEY165:23	H25	So needs no Testimonial from his own;
TDUDLEY165:33	H35	Which caus'd Apostates to maligne so.
TDUDLEY166:2	H44	His humble mind so lov'd humility,
DDUDLEY167:15	H12	*And as they did, so they reward did find:*
CONTEM167:34	H10	If so much excellence abide below;
CONTEM168:4	H14	That hath this under world so richly dight:
CONTEM168:13	H22	If so, all these as nought, Eternity doth scorn.
CONTEM169:2	H44	Art thou so full of glory, that no Eye
CONTEM169:4	H46	And is thy splendid Throne erect so high?
CONTEM171:13	H117	Living so little while we are alive;
CONTEM171:15	H119	So unawares comes on perpetual night,
CONTEM172:3	H140	And when unmade, so ever shall they lye,
CONTEM172:10	H146	I once that lov'd the shady woods so well,
CONTEM172:24	H158	So hand in hand along with thee they glide

CONTEM172:28	H162	So may we press to that vast mansion, ever blest.
CONTEM172:35	H168	So nature taught, and yet you know not why,
CONTEM173:14	H181	Which rapt me so with wonder and delight,
CONTEM173:28	H193	So each one tunes his pretty instrument,
CONTEM174:21	H219	So he that saileth in this world of pleasure,
FLESH175:12	H12	Doth Contemplation feed thee so
FLESH175:40	H40	For I have vow'd (and so will doe)
FLESH176:34	H74	But reach at things that are so high,
AUTHOR178:1	H11	Thy Visage was so irksome in my sight;
AUTHOR178:3	H13	Thy blemishes amend, if so I could:
SICKNES178:22	H5	All men must dye, and so must I
SICKNES178:25	H8	when he so high provok'd.
BIRTH179:29	H5	No tyes so strong, no friends so clear and sweet,
BIRTH179:29	H5	No tyes so strong, no friends so clear and sweet,
1HUSB180:33	H12	Then while we live, in love lets so persever,
1LETTER181:7	H5	So many steps, head from the heart to sever
1LETTER181:10	H8	My sun is gone so far in's Zodiack,
1LETTER181:20	H18	I weary grow, the tedious day so long;
2LETTER182:25	H31	At thy return, if so thou could'st or durst
3LETTER183:3	H5	So doth my anxious soul, which now doth miss,
3LETTER183:10	H12	Whose loss hath made her so unfortunate:
VERSES184:4	H8	My stock's so small, I know not how to pay,
CHILDRN185:16	H42	As is ordain'd, so shall they light.
CHILDRN186:1	H68	So happy may you live and die:
CHILDRN186:9	H76	But sing, my time so near is spent.
ELIZB187:2	H11	Or sigh thy dayes so soon were terminate;
ELIZB187:10	H18	And buds new blown, to have so short a date,
MERCY188:25	H11	I stood so nigh, it crusht me down withal;
MERCY189:9	H30	So with her Chidren four, she's now at rest,
MERCY189:12	H33	The Heavens vouchsafe she may so ever be.
MEDDM196:8	Hp273	so he that glorys in his gifts and adornings, should look vpon
MEDDM197:7	Hp274	reason why christians are so loth to exchang this world for a
MEDDM197:11	Hp274	If we had no winter the spring would not be so pleasant, if we
MEDDM197:12	Hp274	times tast of adversity, prosperity would not be so welcome
MEDDM197:15	Hp274	so a man of weak faith and mean abilities, may vndergo a
MEDDM197:22	Hp275	Few men are so humble, as not to be proud of their abilitys,
MEDDM197:27	Hp275	will finde it a wearysome if not an impossible task so he that
MEDDM197:32	Hp275	is not fit for bread, god so deales wth his servants, he grindes
MEDDM198:14	Hp276	but he that is well stored wth both, seldom is so insnared
MEDDM198:29	Hp277	it, so an enemy w^thout may disturb a Commonwealth, but
MEDDM199:8	Hp277	leaues argue want of sap and gray haires want of moisture so
MEDDM199:11	Hp277	till it be throughly heat is vncapable to be wrought, so god sees
MEDDM200:8	Hp279	bitter together so is it wth some Christians, let god imbitter all
MEDDM200:9	Hp279	this life, that so they might feed vpon more substantiall food,
MEDDM200:10	Hp279	are so childishly sottish that they are still huging and sucking
MEDDM200:12	Hp279	or lay affliction on their loynes that so they might shake hands
MEDDM200:27	Hp279	what they lost in the Autumn so shall it be at that great day
MEDDM201:1	Hp280	he will proportion the load, as god hath his little Children so
MEDDM201:16	Hp280	so a quick reception, and a deliberate cogitation argues a
MEDDM201:20	Hp280	from a thick ayre about them so may we sometime se, marble
MEDDM201:28	Hp281	to bid them hold fast the form of sound Doctrin, but also, so to

MEDDM201:32	Hp281	the most welcom so a faithfull friend in time of adversity,
MEDDM202:3	Hp281	his gifts among the sons of men, betwixt whom he hath put so
MEDDM202:6	Hp281	is capable of, and some again so base that they are Viler
MEDDM202:7	Hp281	then ye earth some so wise and learned, that they seeme like
MEDDM202:8	Hp281	and some againe, so ignorant and sotish that they are more
MEDDM202:10	Hp281	beauty full, and some extreamly deformed some so strong
MEDDM202:12	Hp281	some againe so weak and feeble, that while they liue, they are
MEDDM202:14	Hp282	but so it pleased him, whose will is the perfect rule of
MEDDM202:23	Hp282	till he arise againe, so god doth somtime vaile his face but for
MEDDM202:25	Hp282	time, yet he affords so much light as may direct our way, that
MEDDM203:6	Hp283	then they are lesse then vanity & more then vexation, so that
MEDDM203:24	Hp283	he slighted before, so he that neuer felt the sicknes of sin, nor
MEDDM204:7	Hp284	need of him, to day as well as yesterday, and so shall for euer,
MEDDM204:11	Hp284	behoues euery man so to improue his talents, that when his
MEDDM205:1	Hp285	land) are of so tough and morose a dispotion that the plough
MEDDM205:9	Hp286	man is called the little world so his heart may be cal'd the little
MEDDM205:15	Hp286	so he absolues or condemnes, yea so Absolute
MEDDM205:15	Hp286	the evidence, so he absolues or condemnes, yea so Absolute
MEDDM205:27	Hp286	vs, or else we should not so often faile in our whole Course of
MEDDM205:34	Hp286	them are dry stocks so is it in the church wch is gods orchard,
MEDDM206:9	Hp287	one Sun, so is it in the Church both militant and triumphant,
MEDDM206:16	Hp287	shine so bright while they moue on earth, how transcendently
MEDDM207:6	Hp288	giuen for, as health wealth and honour, wch might be so many
MEDDM207:27	Hp289	should make vs so to number our dayes as to apply our hearts
MEDDM207:33	Hp289	of death, wch is their sleep (for so is death often calld)
MEDDM208:7	Hp289	other meanes to extinguish them so distance of place together
MEDDM208:15	Hp290	we must be tryed and as he passes the sentence, so shall we
MEDDM208:20	Hp290	nothing, and so leaue those in the lurch that most relyed
MEDDM208:21	Hp290	so is it wth the wealth honours and pleasures of this world
MEDDM209:3	Hp291	thus potent but it is so necessary, that w^{th}out faith there is no
MEDDM209:12	Hp291	slauery, so it is most certain that those that are disobedient
MEDDM209:18	Hp291	god hath by his prouidence so ordered, that no one Covntry
MEDDM209:20	Hp291	so there may be a mutuall commerce through ye world As it is
MEDDM209:21	Hp291	Covntrys so it is with men, there was neuer yet any one man
MEDDM209:23	Hp291	be neuer so large, yet he stands in need of something w^{ch}
MYCHILD215:31	Hp241	to haue more vnderstanding, so ye more solace I took in them.
MYCHILD216:23	Hp242	So vsually thvs it hath been wth me that I haue no sooner
MYCHILD218:15	Hp244	in it fullfilled wch could not haue been so long foretold by any
MYCHILD218:25	Hp244	so to bee dealt withall.
MYCHILD218:32	Hp244	I haue reme͞bred the words of Christ that so it must bee, and
BYNIGHT220:5	H6	And so to lye I fovnd it best.
FEVER220:29	H9	So faint I could not speak.
FAINTING222:15	H5	So shall I giue it thee.
MED223:12	Hp250	to haue thought it? So wonderfull are these thoughts that my
MED223:14	Hp250	that God who hath done so much for me, should haue so little
MED223:14	Hp250	who hath done so much for me, should haue so little from me,
JULY223:22	Hp251	first it took me, and so mvch the sorer it was to me because
JULY223:28	Hp251	that I now hope for, y^t so they may bee encourag^d to trust in
28AUG226:8	Hp254	forgett thy great Love to my soul so lately expressed,
28AUG226:11	Hp254	vnwilling to come tho: by so rovgh a Messenger.
13MAY227:8	H17	Who is a God so wondrous great.

SON231:1	H13	And order'st so the adverse wind
SON231:22	H34	Tho'st done for him, + so for me.
2HUSB232:21	H22	It was my Duty so to doe
HOURS234:2	H16	Whom I doe loue so well
HOURS234:25	H39	So shall I celebrate thy praise.
HOURS234:29	H43	So both of vs thy Kindnes Lord
ACK235:12	H12	For whom I thee so oft besovght
ACK235:18	H18	Whose prsence I so much doe lack.
ACK235:20	H20	And so desire Ev'n all my Dayes.
REMB235:27	H8	I ow so mvch so little can
REMB235:27	H8	I ow so mvch so little can
REMB236:5	H20	Thy mercyes Lord haue been so great
HOUSE236:28	H20	Yea so it was, and so 'twas jvst.
HOUSE236:28	H20	Yea so it was, and so 'twas jvst.
HOUSE237:23	H53	A prise so vast as is vnknown

SOAK'D (3) [soaked]

AGES45:21	~~H403~~	I've seen it shaken, rent, and soak'd in blood,
AGES~~45:22~~	H409	I've seen it plunder'd, taxt and soak'd in bloud,
MGREC109:10	H2269	When thus, ten dayes, his brain with wine he'd soak'd,

SOAR'D (2) [soared]

MASSYR56:37	H143	Leaving the world, to *Venus,* soar'd above,
MERCY189:5	H26	A Babe she left before, she soar'd above,

SOARE (3)

FATHER5:11	H12	Yet view thereof, did cause my thoughts to soare,
PROLOG7:35	H45	And oh, ye high flown quils, that soare the skies,
PILGRIM210:24	H24	And soare on high among the blest.

SOARED See SOAR'D

SOBBING (1)

MERCY188:26	H12	My bruised heart lies sobbing at the Root,

SOBER (2)

HUMOUR24:16	H165	Did ever sober tongue, such language speak?
MGREC116:20	H2586	Might to the last (when sober) be discern'd.

SOBRIETY (1)

MGREC106:25	H2159	His past sobriety doth also hate,

SOBS (1) [pl.]

2LETTER182:6	H12	My sobs, my longing hopes, my doubting fears,

SOCRATES (1)

MGREC98:25	H1827	*Cilcia* he to *Socrates* doth give,

SODOME (1) [sodom]

ELEMEN11:4	H124	And more then bruitish *Sodome* for her lust,

SODOMS (1) [poss.]

MASSYR57:14	H161	Who warr'd with *Sodoms,* and *Gomorahs* King,

SOE (3) [so]

MEDDM199:15	Hp278	men are like hops that neuer rest climbing soe long as they
MEDDM205:31	Hp286	We see in orchards, some trees soe fruitfull, that the waight of
MEDDM205:35	Hp287	some eminent Christians, that are soe frequent in good dutys,

SOER (1) [sore]

MPERS~~94:26~~	H1540	His sons soer vext him by disloyalty.

SOFT (4)

SEASONS47:20	H36	The wanton frisking Kids, and soft fleec'd Lambs,
CHILDRN185:33	H59	Long did I keep you soft and warm,

MEDDM198:25	Hp276	An akeing head requires a soft pillow, and a drooping heart a
PILGRIM210:3	H3	His wasted limbes, now lye full soft

SOFTLY (1)

CONTEM168:18	H26	And softly said, what glory's like to thee?

SOIL n. [earth] See SOILE, SOYL, SOYLE

SOIL n. [stain] See SOYLE

SOIL v. [stain] See SOYLE

SOILE (1) n. [soil; earth] See also SOYL, SOYLE

MEDDM205:3	Hp285	goe often ouer them, before they bee fit soile, to sow the

SOL (4)

SEASONS46:38	H16	The tenth o'th' first *Sol* into *Aries* enters,
SEASONS49:5	H96	Ith' first, *Sol* doth in crabed *Cancer* shine.
SEASONS50:40	H174	The tenth {twelfth} of this, *Sol* riseth in the Line,
1LETTER181:14	H12	Return, return sweet *Sol* from *Capricorn;*

SOLACE (1)

MYCHILD215:31	Hp241	to haue more vnderstanding, so yᵉ more solace I took in them.

SOLD (2)

DIALOG143:33	H102	Church Offices are {were} sold, and bought, for gaine,
2HUSB233:6	H39	Bee sold away for Novght.

SOLDIER See SOULDIER

SOLDIERS See SOULDIERS

SOLE (2)

MPERS85:9	H1285	Who now sole Monarch, doth of all remaine,
MGREC~~127:29~~	H3059	And Master of the treasure he remains; {sole remain:}

SOLICITS See SOLLICITES

SOLID (2)

AGES35:26	H12	Solid, hating all lightnesse, and al folly.
SEASONS48:27	H80	More solid fruits, require a longer time.

SOLIDITY (1)

HUMOUR28:31	H343	And nothing wanting but solidity.

SOLID'ST (1) [solidest]

SEASONS52:6	H221	And solid'st meats, our stomachs can digest;

SOLITARY (1)

HOURS233:19	H1-2	In my Solitary houres in my dear husband his Absence.

SOLLICITES (1) [solicits]

MPERS82:23	H1170	His brothers wife, sollicites to his will;

SOLOM (1)

MEDDM201:25	Hp281	The words of the wise (sath Solom) are as nailes, and as

SOLON (6)

MPERS69:36	H658	He *Solon, Solon, Solon,* thrice did cry.
MPERS69:36	H658	He *Solon, Solon, Solon,* thrice did cry.
MPERS69:36	H658	He *Solon, Solon, Solon,* thrice did cry.
MPERS69:38	~~H660~~	And told, how *Solon* in his hight had spoke.
MPERS~~69:38~~	H660	Who *Solon* was? to whom he lifts his hands;
MPERS~~69:38~~	H662	That *Solon* sometimes at his stately Court,

SOLS (1) [poss.]

SEASONS47:26	H42	Doth darken *Sols* bright face, makes us remember

SOME (181)

FATHER6:2	H36	Some thing {something} of all (though mean) I did intend,
PROLOG7:33	H44	Yet grant some small acknowledgement of ours.
ELEMEN~~14:10~~	H252	Some kill outright, and some do stupifye:

ELEMEN14:12	H254	In hot, and cold, and some benums with sleeps,
ELEMEN17:12	H376	Some say I swallowed up (sure 'tis a notion)
ELEMEN18:39	H443	Some for this cause (of late) have been so bold,
ELEMEN19:29	H472	Some upon sands, some upon rocks have hit.
ELEMEN19:30	H472	Some have I forc'd, to gaine an unknown shoare;
ELEMEN19:31	H472	Some overwelm'd with waves, and seen no more.
ELEMEN19:35	H476	But some fall down, and some flye up with aire.
HUMOUR22:7	H76	To march her pace, to some is greater pain,
HUMOUR23:2	H112	The Palsie, Gout, or Cramp, or some such dolor,
HUMOUR26:12	H242	For there are {is} none, thou say'st, if some, not best.
HUMOUR26:13	H243	That there are some, and best, I dare averre;
HUMOUR27:20	H291	Now through your leaves, some little time i'le spend;
HUMOUR28:17	H329	Likewise the Whey, some use I in the veines,
HUMOUR34:10	H565	Yet some may wish, oh, {O} had mine eyes ne're seene.
HUMOUR34:17	H572	Some other parts there issue from the Brain,
HUMOUR34:19	H574	Some worthy {curious} learned *Crooke* may these reveal,
AGES35:28	H14	His spring was intermixed with some snow.
AGES38:2	H105	But for an Apple, Plumbe, or some such prize,
AGES38:36	H139	And some perhaps, I carry to my grave.
AGES38:37	H140	Some times in fire, sometimes in waters {water} fall:
AGES39:5	H148	Declare some greater riches are within;
AGES39:39	H182	My valour, in some beastly quarrel's spent;
AGES40:22	H203	Some young {new} *Adonis* I do strive to be,
AGES43:36	H331	Though some more incident to age, or youth:
AGES44:22	H355	Great mutations, some joyful, and some sad,
AGES44:22	H355	Great mutations, some joyful, and some sad,
AGES44:40	H373	In midst of greifs, I saw some {our} hopes revive,
AGES45:13	H395	I've seen one stab'd, another {and some to} loose his head
AGES46:11	H442	Hath yet amongst that sweet, some bitter gall.
SEASONS46:35	H11	She gently thus began, like some fair Queen;
SEASONS47:3	H21	Who for some months have seen but starry lights;
SEASONS48:31	H83	Some subject, shallow braines, much matter yeelds,
SEASONS48:34	H85	Let some describe thee better then can I.
SEASONS52:37	H252	And some warm glances from the Sun {his face} are felt,
MASSYR55:30	H96	Some think the *Greeks,* this slander on her cast,
MASSYR56:6	H112	Most {Some} writers say, six chariots might a front,
MASSYR57:6	H153	Some write, his Mother put his habite on,
MASSYR57:16	H163	Some may object, his Parents ruling all,
MASSYR58:6	H191	Kept ever close, fearing some dismal {his well deserved} fate;
MASSYR63:33	H420	From some *Thucidides* grave History,
MASSYR68:12	H598	Who still expects some fearfull sad event,
MPERS70:37	H708	Where some long after fought in vain for prize
MPERS71:3	H715	Some thirty years this potent Prince did reign,
MPERS71:7	H723	But {Yet} to enlarge his state, had some desire;
MPERS71:40	H753	And though no gods, if he esteem them some,
MPERS73:27	H812	Some write that sorely hurt, they 'scap'd away;
MPERS80:1	H1068	How part, {some} might o're the Mountains goe about,
MPERS80:9	H1076	When as one thousand, could some Millions {a million} daunt;
MPERS82:25	H1172	Some years by him in this vain suit was spent,
MPERS86:28	H1344	Some Townes commodious in lesse *Asia,*
MPERS86:37	H1353	But least {lest} some worser newes should fly to Court,

MPERS87:34	H1386	Some fifty, or else sixty foote in breadth.
MPERS90:12	H1484	There for some time they were, but whilst they staid,
MPERS92:5	H1561	Some write that *Arsames* was *Ochus* brother,
MPERS92:20	H1578	Some writers say, that he was *Arses* son,
MPERS92:23	H1581	Which by some probabilities (seems rather;)
MPERS92:26	H1584	Some write great *Cyrus* line was not yet run,
MPERS92:27	H1585	But from some daughter this new king was sprung
MGREC95:32	H1711	Though some there be, and that {(perhaps)} more likely, write;
MGREC97:4	H1765	Of late, like some immovable he lay,
MGREC100:29	H1913	Yet had some hope, that on that even {the spacious} plain,
MGREC100:38	H1922	Some injury was offered, he feares;
MGREC101:34	H1962	And spilt the Greeks some bloud before their flight
MGREC101:38	H1967	Some write, th' other had a million, some more,
MGREC101:38	H1967	Some write, th' other had a million, some more,
MGREC103:12	H2023	Statues of {some} gold, and silver numberlesse,
MGREC104:29	H2081	But some detesting, this his wicked fact,
MGREC105:20	H2113	Who not a little chear'd, to have some eye,
MGREC106:17	H2151	Though some {most} of reading best, and soundest minde,
MGREC107:33	H2208	Would by {without} some means a transportation finde;
MGREC108:19	H2235	Whilst thus he spent some time in *Bactria,*
MGREC111:2	H2347	Some time he after spent upon that shore,
MGREC111:38	H2383	From hence to *Babylon,* some time there spent,
MGREC118:5	H2652	Some wished him, to take the stile of King,
MGREC118:23	H2670	After this {some} time, when stirs began to calme,
MGREC121:13	H2791	And from the other, {side} daily some did gaine.
MGREC121:16	H2795	Some of the Souldiers enters *Perdica's* tent,
MGREC124:1	H2906	By these, and all, to grant him some supply,
MGREC125:13	H2961	Some Forces did procure, with her to joyne.
MGREC127:1	H3031	Some slew, some fry'd, of others, stopt the breath;
MGREC128:4	H3077	And that some title he might seeme to bring,
MGREC130:1	H3156	But that some title he might now pretend,
MGREC131:3	H3193	Not like a King, but like some God they fain'd;
MGREC131:9	H3201	How some when down, straight got the upper hand
MGREC135:5	H3377	But some disgrace, in triumph to be led.
MGREC135:40	H3412	My tired braine, leaves to a {some} better pen,
MGREC136:2	H3415	But humbly stand, some grave reproof to take:
MGREC136:5	H3418	To frame Apologie for some offence,
MGREC136:7	H3420	This my presumption (some now) to requite,
MGREC136:9	H3423	*After some dayes of rest, my restlesse heart,*
MROMAN136:25	H3439	His Father was not *Mars,* as some devis'd,
MROMAN136:34	H3448	For leaping o're the Walls {wall} with some disdaine;
MROMAN137:21	H3472	Some faining say, to heav'n {to the Gods} he did ascend;
MROMAN137:26	H3477	Held for his Piety, some sacred thing;
MROMAN137:36	H3487	Accounted for some {a} god in after dayes.
MROMAN138:34	H3524	Much {Some} state, and glory, {splendor} did this *Priscus* adde:
DIALOG141:23	H22	Unlesse some Cordial thou fetch from high,
DIALOG142:5	H34	What, hath some *Hengist,* like that *Saxon* stout,
DIALOG142:35	H64	I must confesse, some of those Sores you name,
DIALOG143:17	H86	What *Holland* is, I am in some suspence,
DIALOG143:19	H88	For wants, sure some I feele, but more I feare,
DIALOG144:25	H134	Unworthily, some backs whipt, and eares cropt;

DIALOG144:28	H136	Some lost their livings, some in prison pent,
DIALOG144:29	H137	Some grossely fin'd, from {house &} friends to exile went:
SIDNEY150:1	H26	But some infatuate fooles soone caught therein,
SIDNEY150:19	H44	O brave *Achilles,* I wish some *Homer* would
SIDNEY150:36	H63	Of this our noble *Scipio* some good word?
DUBART153:8	H12	Which Rayes, darting upon some richer ground,
DUBART153:17	H21	Who sees the riches of some famous Fayre;
DUBART153:23	H27	Some part, at least, of that brave wealth was his;
QELIZ157:33	H101	Or had they some, but with our Queen ist gone?
TDUDLEY165:17	H19	That pitty might some Trumpeters procure.
TDUDLEY165:40	H42	Those titles loath'd, which some too much do love
TDUDLEY167:4	H86	*If some rejoyc'd, more did lament.*
CONTEM168:20	H28	No wonder, some made thee a Deity:
CONTEM169:13	H54	To sing some Song, my mazed Muse thought meet.
CONTEM174:1	H202	From some of these he never finds cessation,
FLESH175:27	H27	As some to their immortal fame:
DISTEMP179:13	H1	*Vpon some distemper of body.*
BIRTH180:18	H28	With some sad sighs honour my absent Herse;
VERSES183:34	H1	*To her Father with some verses.*
CHILDRN185:19	H45	Lest this my brood some harm should catch,
CHILDRN185:24	H50	Some untoward boy at them do fling.
CHILDRN185:28	H54	Or by some greedy hawks be spoyl'd.
2SIMON195:6	Hp271	once desired me to leaue some thing for you in writeing that
MEDDM195:25	Hp272	no evill that we feele, or fear, but we may make some spiritull
MEDDM196:28	Hp273	children, haue their different natures, some are like flesh w^ch
MEDDM196:29	Hp273	but salt will keep from putrefaction, some again like tender
MEDDM197:12	Hp274	some times tast of adversity, prosperity would not be so
MEDDM199:12	Hp277	good to cast some men into the furnace of affliction and then
MEDDM200:6	Hp279	Some children are hardly weaned although the teat be rub'd
MEDDM200:8	Hp279	bitter together so is it wth some Christians, let god imbitter all
MEDDM200:20	Hp279	or a helthfull body, would quite ouer throw, some weak
MEDDM201:22	Hp281	but from some black Clouds that impends them, wch produces
MEDDM202:5	Hp281	out of the loynes of one Adam, some set in ye highest dignity,
MEDDM202:6	Hp281	is capable of, and some again so base that they are Viler
MEDDM202:7	Hp281	then ye earth some so wise and learned, that they seeme like
MEDDM202:8	Hp281	men, and some againe, so ignorant and sotish that they are
MEDDM202:9	Hp281	beasts then men, some pious saints, some incarnate Deuils,
MEDDM202:9	Hp281	then men, some pious saints, some incarnate Deuils, some
MEDDM202:10	Hp281	beauty full, and some extreamly deformed some so strong
MEDDM202:12	Hp281	and some againe so weak and feeble, that while they liue, they
MEDDM202:25	Hp282	some other time, yet he affords so much light as may direct
MEDDM204:34	Hp285	and some land askes much more paines, then some other doth
MEDDM204:35	Hp285	into tilth yet all must be ploughed and harrowed Some children
MEDDM205:26	Hp286	to good dutys, we certainly dream of some remotnes betwixt
MEDDM205:31	Hp286	We see in orchards, some trees soe fruitfull, that the waight of
MEDDM205:32	Hp286	Burden, is the breaking of their limbes, some again, are but
MEDDM205:33	Hp286	and some haue nothing to shew but leaues only, and some
MEDDM205:35	Hp286	there are some eminent Christians, that are soe frequent in
MEDDM205:37	Hp287	and ther are some (and they sincere ones too) who haue not
MEDDM206:12	Hp287	euen in this life, some are Stars of the first magnitude,
MEDDM206:13	Hp287	some of a lesse degree, & others (and they indeed the most in

MEDDM206:15 Hp287 that glorious sun that inlightens all in all, and if some of them
MEDDM207:15 Hp288 shadow very comfortable, yet there is some worm or other,
MEDDM207:22 Hp289 that all haue a lease of their liues, some longer some shorter,
MEDDM209:7 Hp291 Some christians do by their lusts and corruptions as the Isralits
MYCHILD215:14 Hp240 I was able to compose some short matters, (for w^t else to call
MYCHILD215:17 Hp240 now doe) by y^t yov may gain some spirit: Advantage by my
MYCHILD216:11 Hp241 After some time I fell into a lingering sicknes like a
MYCHILD216:34 Hp242 some sin I lay vnder wch God would haue reformed, or some
MYCHILD216:34 Hp242 sin I lay vnder wch God would haue reformed, or some duty
MYCHILD218:28 Hp244 But some new Troubles I haue had since ye world has been
MYCHILD218:29 Hp244 Blasphemy, and Sectaries, and some who hauest been acct^d.
11MAYA226:15 Hp255 a respite, & some ability to p^rform ye Dutyes I owe to him, and
30SEPT227:25 Hp257 in ye furnace of affliction as some haue been, but haue rather
THEART229:3 H5 I cry'd thov seem'st to make some stay

SOMETHING (4)
FATHER6:2 H36 Some thing {something} of all (though mean) I did intend,
AGES44:3 H336 And all you say, say I, and something {somewhat} more;
MEDDM198:22 Hp276 done, but either that or something like it, hath been both done
MEDDM209:23 Hp291 so large, yet he stands in need of something wch another man

SOMETIME (7) See also SOMTIME
AGES44:25 H358 Sometimes {Sometime} again, rain'd all adversity;
AGES44:27 H360 Sometime an abject, then again in place,
SEASONS48:32 H83 Sometime a theame that's large, proves barren fields.
MPERS82:36 H1183 Where he had sometime gaz'd with great delight.
MGREC125:17 H2965 Remembring {Calling to mind} what sometime she had been,
CONTEM167:25 H2 Sometime now past in the Autumnal Tide,
MEDDM201:20 Hp280 from a thick ayre about them so may we sometime se, marble

SOMETIMES (34) See also SOMT.
ELEMEN10:31 H106 And with the ashes, that it sometimes shed
ELEMEN13:24 H225 He sometimes findes, maugre his toyling paine,
ELEMEN14:11 H253 Nay into herbs and plants it sometimes creeps,
ELEMEN19:38 H479 Then what prodigious sights, sometimes I show:
ELEMEN20:1 H483 Sometimes strange {red} flaming swords, and blazing stars,
AGES38:37 H140 Some times in fire, sometimes in waters {water} fall:
AGES40:4 H185 Sometimes lay wait to take a wealthy purse,
AGES40:6 H187 Sometimes I cheat (unkind) a female Heir,
AGES40:10 H191 Sometimes I sit carousing others health,
AGES40:36 H215 Sometimes by wounds in idle combates taken,
AGES40:37 H216 Sometimes by {with} Agues all my body shaken;
AGES40:38 H217 Sometimes by Feavers, all my moisture drinking,
AGES40:40 H219 Sometimes the Cough, Stitch, {the Quinsey} painful Plurisie,
AGES41:1 H221 Sometimes the loathsome {two fold} Pox, my face {me sore}
AGES41:3 H223 Sometimes the Phrensie, strangely madds my Brain,
AGES41:15 H234 Childehood and youth, forgot, sometimes I've seen,
AGES42:16 H274 Thus hath mine age (in all) sometimes done wel.
AGES42:17 H275 Sometimes {again,} mine age (in all) {mine Age} been worse
AGES43:17 H312 Sometimes vaine-glory is the only bait,
AGES44:24 H357 Sometimes the Heavens with plenty smil'd on me,
AGES44:25 H358 Sometimes {Sometime} again, rain'd all adversity;
AGES44:26 H359 Sometimes in honour, sometimes in disgrace,
AGES44:26 H359 Sometimes in honour, sometimes in disgrace,

AGES45:39 H429 My heart sometimes as fierce, as Lions bold,
SEASONS52:31 H246 And Travellers sometimes their noses leese.
MPERS69:38 H662 That *Solon* sometimes at his stately Court,
MPERS72:18 H766 This strange severity, one time {sometimes} he us'd,
MGREC119:14 H2704 would} Shakes {shake} off the yoke, sometimes before laid on
MGREC119:15 H2705 {Sometimes} By warlike *Philip,* and his conquering son.
MGREC120:17 H2752 With *Antipater* t' joyn, sometimes he thought,
MGREC131:17 H3209 Of those dominions {vast Kindgomes} he did sometimes gain,
DAVID159:5 H20 Sometimes from crimson blood of gastly slaine,
CONTEM169:34 H72 Sometimes in *Eden* fair, he seems to be,
MEDDM202:21 Hp282 Sometimes the sun is only shadowed by a cloud, that wee

SOMEWHAT (6)

HUMOUR26:32 H262 I must confesse, is somewhat strange to me,
HUMOUR29:39 H390 I'le come to that which wounds me somewhat more:
AGES44:3 H336 And all you say, say I, and something {somewhat} more;
SEASONS46:34 H10 With smiling Sun-shine face, and garments {somewhat} green,
MGREC102:18 H1988 Yet old foundations shew'd, and somewhat more;
MEDDM200:17 Hp279 but falls and bruises, or perhaps somewhat worse, much more

SOMT. (9) [sometimes]

MYCHILD216:26 Hp242 somt. on my soul in Doubts & feares of Gods displeasure, and
MYCHILD216:27 Hp242 towards him. Somt. he hath smott a child wth sicknes, somt.
MYCHILD217:19 Hp243 shall bee well with me. I haue somt. tasted of y^t hidden Manna
MYCHILD217:23 Hp243 not enjoyed that felicity that somt. I haue done, But when I
MYCHILD218:22 Hp244 This hath somt. stuck with me, and more it would, by ye vain
MYCHILD218:30 Hp244 Xtians haue been carryed away wth them, that somt: I haue
28AUG226:3 Hp254 y^t somt. I haue had, least my heart should bee drawn from
30SEPT227:19 Hp257 but not in y^t sore manner somt. he hath. I desire not only

SOMTIME (1) [sometime]

MEDDM202:23 Hp282 till he arise againe, so god doth somtime vaile his face but for

SON (94) See also SONNE

HUMOUR25:25 H214 Nor sparing Sex, nor age, nor fire, nor son.
AGES35:19 H5 The first: son unto Flegme, grand-child to water,
AGES43:14 H307 Of such as might my son, {Competitors} or his {as might in
SEASONS51:32 H208 But when the Son of Righteousnesse drawes nigh,
MASSYR53:36 H26 Great *Nimrod* dead, *Bellus* the next, his Son,
MASSYR57:7 H154 Which made the people think they serv'd her Son;
MASSYR57:16 H163 But this is farre unlike, he being Son
MASSYR57:39 H184 *Sardanapalus,* (Son t' *Ocrazapes*)
MASSYR59:39 H263 But was accomplished now, in his {wicked} Son.
MASSYR61:7 H312 He left his new got Kingdoms to his Son.
MASSYR61:9 H314 *Belosus* dead, *Tiglath* his warlike Son
MASSYR61:21 H326 I am thy Servant, and thy Son (quoth he)
MASSYR63:2 H387 His Son, weak *Essarhadon* reign'd in's place,
MASSYR63:4 H389 Brave *Merodach,* the Son of *Balladan,*
MASSYR63:28 H415 Then being Father to so great a Son.
MASSYR65:24 H489 His Son three months he suffered to reign,
MASSYR66:40 H546 He left his Wealth, and Conquest, to his Son.
MASSYR67:3 H549 His son possesses wealth, and rule, as just;
MASSYR68:14 H600 In comes the Queen, to chear her heartlesse son.
MPERS69:1 H623 *Cyrus Cambyses,* Son of *Persia's* {Persia} King,
MPERS69:12 H634 Adopts her Son for his, having no other:

MPERS69:29	H651	But as he past, his Son, who was born dumbe,
MPERS70:27	H698	And *Tomris* Son, an Army over-throwes;
MPERS72:15	H763	Who would have born a Nephew, and a Son.
MPERS72:21	H769	Over his Seat, then plac'd his Son therein;
MPERS72:25	H773	Having one son, in whom he did delight,
MPERS72:27	H773	Shot through the heart of his beloved son:
MPERS72:37	H783	Obedience yielded as to *Cyrus* son.
MPERS77:13	H952	Unto {Then to} his eldest {second} Son, all did remain.
MPERS77:15	H954	*Xerxes, Darius,* and *Attossa's* Son,
MPERS77:18	H959	As is {was} the Son, of pride, and cruelty;
MPERS78:13	H994	He was the Son of the fore-nam'd *Gobrias,*
MPERS80:6	H1073	But on their ground they dye, each Mothers Son.
MPERS82:27	H1174	Nor matching of her daughter, to his son:
MPERS83:16	H1204	Accus'd *Darius, Xerxes* eldest son,
MPERS83:24	H1212	The eldest son, thus immaturely dead,
MPERS86:7	H1323	His large Dominions left, to's eldest son.
MPERS91:34	H1548	*Ochus* a wicked and Rebellious son
MPERS92:5	H1563	But why brother 'fore his son succeeds
MPERS92:7	H1565	It may be thought, surely he had no Son,
MPERS92:20	H1578	Some writers say, that he was *Arses* son,
MPERS92:24	H1582	That son, and father, both were murthered
MGREC93:10	H1607	Great *Alexander,* was wise *Phillips* son,
MGREC6:33	H1630	Which honour to his son, now did befall.
MGREC98:24	H1826	Who was the son of that *Parmenio* brave;
MGREC100:8	H1892	The Son of *Jupiter* did straight him make:
MGREC101:15	H1940	*Ochus* his Son a hostage shall {should} endure.
MGREC106:5	H2139	Yea, {And} thus must every Son of *Adam* lye,
MGREC113:10	H2437	Are {Were} now inflicted on *Parmenio's* Son,
MGREC113:17	H2444	Was to dispatch the Father, as the Son.
MGREC113:31	H2458	For *Philip* dead, and his surviving Son,
MGREC115:22	H2541	And by her Letters did her Son incite,
MGREC119:15	H2705	{Sometimes} By warlike *Philip,* and his conquering son.
MGREC120:27	H2764	This he avoyds, and ships himself, and's Son,
MGREC122:20	H2845	She daughter to his son, who had no other;
MGREC123:16	H2880	Fearing his Son *Cassander* was unstay'd,
MGREC123:34	H2898	Are now at the devotion of the Son,
MGREC128:2	H3075	His Wife, and Son, in prison close had shut;
MGREC128:25	H3098	His Son at *Gaza* likewise lost the field,
MGREC128:35	H3108	*Antigonus* did much rejoyce his son,
MGREC129:3	H3117	Imprisoning both the mother, and her {the} son,
MGREC129:9	H3123	And put {So puts} to death, the mother and her son,
MGREC129:19	H3133	The life of her must go, and of her son.
MGREC129:27	H3141	*Polisperchon* brings up the other son,
MGREC130:26	H3181	By cruell father, mother, cruell son,
MGREC131:16	H3208	Nor to his son did there {e're} one foot remain,
MGREC131:26	H3218	*Antiochus, Seleuchus* dear lov'd son,
MGREC132:5	H3238	*Demetrius* is call'd in by th' youngest Son,
MGREC132:20	H3257	And with his son in law, will needs go fight:
MGREC132:20	H3260	Leaving *Antigonus* his eldest Son,
MGREC132:26	H3271	In *Greece,* unto *Antigonus,* his son,
MGREC132:28	H3274	His body *Seleucus* sends to his Son,

MGREC132:32	H3279	To *Philadelphus,* his more worthy Son.
MGREC133:2	H3290	The second Son of the first *Ptolomy,*
MGREC133:14	H3302	His Son *Demetrius,* all *Cassanders* gaines,
MGREC133:16	H3304	*Demetrius* Son was call'd *Antigonus,*
MGREC133:20	H3308	And his son *Alexander* of *Epire,*
MGREC133:22	H3310	*Demetrius* had *Philip* to his son,
MGREC133:30	H3320	*Antiochus Soter* his son was nam'd,
MGREC133:36	H3326	*Antiochus Theos* was *Soters* son,
MGREC134:19	H3350	First *Ptolomy* being dead, his famous son,
MGREC134:25	H3356	His son was *Evergetes* the last Prince
MGREC134:27	H3358	*Philopater* was *Evergete's* son,
MROMAN139:9	H3537	And then by *Tarquin, Priscus* Son, was slaine.
MROMAN139:14	H3542	*Sextus* his Son, doth {did} (most unworthily)
DIALOG142:39	H68	Nor is it *Alcies* Son, and {nor} *Henries* Daughter,
DIALOG144:9	H119	Oh, *Edwards* Babes {youths}, and *Clarence* haplesse Son,
DIALOG147:18	H244	on brave *Essex,* shew whose son thou art {with a loyal heart},
SIDNEY152:26	H95	*Heire to the Muses, the Son of* Mars *in truth,*
MERCY188:27	H13	That thou dear Son has lost both Tree and fruit:
MERCY189:13	H34	Chear up (dear Son) thy fainting bleeding heart,
WHAT224:18	H18	Nor son of man to 'vnsay
SAMUEL228:1	H1-2	Vpon my Son Samuel his goeing for England Novem. 6. 1657.
SAMUEL228:4	H5	The Son of prayers, of vowes, of teares

SONG (5)

DUBART154:38	H83	To celebrate thy merits in my Song,
CONTEM169:13	H54	To sing some Song, my mazed Muse thought meet.
CHILDRN186:13	H80	And there with Seraphims set song:
MERCY188:22	H8	Ah, woe is me, to write thy Funeral Song,
SON230:21	H4	My feares to Joyes, my sighes to song

SONGS (2) [pl.]

ELEMEN18:19	H423	Your songs and pleasant tunes, they are the same,
CONTEM173:26	H191	The dawning morn with songs thou dost prevent,

SONNE (4) [son]

MASSYR63:23	H408	Brave *Nebulassar* to this King was Sonne,
SIDNEY151:33	H75	Like unwise *Phaeton* his ill guided sonne,
2SIMON195:1	Hp271	For my deare sonne
HOURS234:24	H38	As thou didst once my Sonne.

SONNES (4) [sons]

ELEMEN14:20	H262	Remember sonnes, your mould is of my dust,
ELEMEN17:31	H395	Her confirm'd sonnes, behold my colour'd bow.
ELEMEN18:8	H412	If my pure Aire, thy sonnes did not sustain.
VANITY159:35	H7	No, they like beasts, and sonnes of men shall die,

SONS (28)

ELEMEN13:32	H233	The Husband knowes no Wife, nor father sons;
AGES43:11	H305	Nor Brothers, Nephewes, Sons, nor Sires I've spar'd.
AGES46:3	H434	Sons, Nephews, leave, my death {farewell} for to deplore;
MASSYR53:20	H10	The boysterous Sons of *Cush, {Chus,}* Grand-child to *Ham,*
MASSYR62:20	H365	Thus *Iacobs* Sons, in exile must remain,
MASSYR62:40	H385	And by his Sons in's Idols house was slain.
MPERS71:1	H713	Three Daughters, and two Sons, he left behind,
MPERS78:38	H1019	One of his five Sons there, might be releast;
MPERS85:4	H1280	Three sons great *Artaxerxes* left behind;

MPERS85:10	H1286	These two lewd {first} sons, are by hystorians thought,
MPERS85:36	H1312	Two sons she bore, the youngest *Cyrus* nam'd,
MPERS91:26	H1540	His sons soer vext him by disloyalty.
MGREC106:6	H2140	Though gods on earth, like Sons of men shall {they} dye.
MGREC116:5	H2565	Sons of *Antipater,* {and} bearers of his Cup,
MGREC122:39	H2860	Two Sons of *Alexander,* and the rest,
MGREC124:21	H2928	Nor could Mother, nor Sons of *Alexander,*
MGREC130:35	H3181	His wife and sons then slain by this *Cassander,*
MGREC131:36	H3228	Two sons he left, born of King *Philips* daughter,
MGREC133:10	H3298	*Cassanders* Sons, soone after's death were slaine,
MGREC133:24	H3314	Him with his Sons in Triumph lead did he,
MGREC133:25	H3315	Did take his rule, his sons, himself and all.
MROMAN138:36	H3526	And after all, by *Ancus* Sons was slaine.
CONTEM171:3	H108	Their long descent, how nephews sons they saw,
CONTEM171:5	H110	And how their precepts to their sons were law,
MEDDM202:3	Hp281	dispensation of his gifts among the sons of men, betwixt whom
MEDDM207:4	Hp288	The gifts that god, bestows on the sons of men, are not only
MED223:6	Hp250	I thy child, yee shall be my Sons and Daughters saith ye Lord
SON230:19	H1-2	On my Sons Return out of England. July. 17. 1661.

SOON (42) See also SOON'T

ELEMEN13:29	H230	And buds from fruitfull trees, before they'r {as soon as} blowne:
ELEMEN13:34	H235	Dreadfull examples, soon I might produce,
ELEMEN15:15	H297	If not, soon ends his life, as did his voyce.
ELEMEN16:12	H335	I soon can match them with my seas as deep.
HUMOUR22:32	H101	The nerves should I not warm, soon would they freeze.
HUMOUR27:41	H312	Which makes the mansion, by the soul soon left;
HUMOUR30:16	H408	Yet time and age, shal soon declare it mine.
AGES36:33	H57	To do as he, the rest {each one} ful soon assents,
AGES38:4	H107	My little wrath did cease {end} soon as my wars.
AGES38:20	H123	From thence I 'gan to sin, as soon as act.
AGES38:23	H126	A lying tongue as soon as it could speak,
AGES40:33	H212	Nor yet that heavy reckoning for {soon} to come;
AGES45:4	H383	But saw their horrid fact soon disappointed,
MASSYR55:23	H89	That *Ninus* of her, amorous soon did grow;
MASSYR67:38	H584	And with a hand, soon dashed all his pride.
MPERS71:21	H735	Who landed {landing} soon upon that fruitful coast,
MPERS76:39	H937	Which soon cut off, {inrag'd,} he with the {his} left
MPERS79:12	H1034	But winds, and waves, these couples soon dissever'd,
MPERS79:29	H1055	Which was not vaine, as it {after} soon appeared:
MPERS83:6	H1194	His wicked brother, {soon} after sent {him} a crew,
MPERS84:31	H1267	But he all injury, had soon forgate,
MPERS85:25	H1301	So that he might, these tumults {those troubles} soon appease.
MPERS90:33	H1500	Lieftenant to the King, but soon he fled
MGREC94:4	H1638	But he their mutinies, {by valour} full soon doth {he} quell.
MGREC101:35	H1964	So make {made} an end, before they {as soon as} well begun;
MGREC103:41	H2052	Was straight in *Bactria* these {soon} to augment,
MGREC105:6	H2099	This done, they with their Hoast, soon speed away,
MGREC124:8	H2913	His proud opponent hopes soon to withstand.
MGREC125:14	H2962	*Olimpias* now {soon} enters *Macedon,*
MGREC131:1	H3187	he, {by his Example all} the rest full soon presumes,
MGREC132:3	H3236	This by *Lysimachus* soon {was} after slain,

MGREC~~135:1~~	H3373	Did by his Sword his life soon after send.
FLESH175:17	H17	And dost thou hope to dwell there soon?
BIRTH179:33	H9	How soon, my Dear, death may my steps attend,
1LETTER181:8	H6	If but a neck, soon should we be together:
ELIZB187:2	H11	Or sigh thy dayes so soon were terminate;
MERCY188:30	H16	But ah too soon those heavy tydings fly,
MEDDM196:7	Hp273	them vp, but spying his black feet, he soon lets fall his plumes,
MEDDM202:17	Hp282	in them, and they that feed vpon them, may soon Stuffe
MEDDM203:3	Hp283	of spirit, yet our owne experience would soon haue speld it out,
MYCHILD217:36	Hp243	would soon tell me by the wondrovs workes that I see, the vast
MYCHILD218:26	Hp244	consideration of these things and many ye like would soon turn

SOONE (18) [soon] See also SOON'T

PROLOG7:25	H37	But this weake knot they will full soone untye,
ELEMEN8:20	H18	Soone made the combatants abate their force;
ELEMEN11:36	H156	Soone would they passe, not hundreds, but legions,
MASSYR58:12	H197	Who sick of his disease, he soone did finde.
MASSYR68:28	H614	Who soone did terminate his Life, and Crown:
MPERS89:13	H1447	They soone may come, and {in short time might} place one in
MGREC99:11	H1854	But th'Kingdoms, and the Ladies, {Lady} soone accept;
MGREC108:26	H2242	But he their stubbornnesse full soone {in time} doth quel;
MGREC108:33	H2249	But soone the *Grecians* {his souldiers} forc'd them to a flight,
MGREC125:21	~~H2969~~	But soone are brought into captivity;
MGREC128:23	H3096	*Antigonus* {These princes} at {the} Sea soone had a fight,
MGREC133:10	H3298	*Cassanders* Sons, soone after's death were slaine,
DIALOG143:22	H91	Destruction to a Land doth soone afford;
SIDNEY150:1	H26	But some infatuate fooles soone caught therein,
DUBART153:9	H13	Had caused flowers, and fruits, soone to abound;
DUBART153:28	H32	But findes too soone his want of Eloquence,
DAVID159:1	H16	For the mighty ones did soone decay,
MEDDM197:18	Hp275	wch is not often swept makes the cleanly inhabitant soone

SOONER (9)

MPERS~~92:18~~	H1576	And was no sooner setled in his reign,
MGREC97:24	H1785	No sooner had this Captaine {Victor} won the field,
MGREC126:23	H3014	No sooner had he got her in his hands {hand},
MGREC129:12	H3126	No sooner was great *Alexander* dead,
MGREC131:32	H3224	Who did no sooner understand the same,
CONTEM171:28	H130	No sooner born, but grief and care makes fall
SICKNES178:36	H19	No sooner blown, but dead and gone,
1SIMON188:4	H5	No sooner come, but gone, and fal'n asleep,
MYCHILD216:23	Hp242	So vsually thvs it hath been wth me that I haue no sooner

SOON'T (1) [soon it]

BIRTH179:34	H10	How soon't may be thy Lot to lose thy friend,

SOOTHING (1)

HUMOUR29:13	H366	Thy soothing girds shal fully be repaid;

SOOTHS (1)

MPERS91:26	~~H1540~~	Who sooths him up, his owne desires are Lawes:

SOOTHSAYERS (1) [pl.]

MASSYR68:4	H590	For the Soothsayers, and Magicians wise;

SORDID (1)

MGREC106:27	H2161	His temperance, is but a sordid thing,

SORDIDNESSE (1) [sordidness]
AGES42:32　　H288　　If happinesse my sordidnesse hath found,

SORE (46) See also SOER
ELEMEN12:25　H185　No, though the fawning dog did urge me sore
HUMOUR23:14　H124　Where paine and sore obstructions, {obstruction} thou dost
AGES44:1　　H221　the loathsome {two fold} Pox, my face {me sore} be-mars,
AGES43:8　　H303　And {I} oft long'd sore, to taste on Royalty.
AGES43:28　H323　{The Strangury} Torments me with intollerable {sore} paines;
MASSYR58:30　H213　*Arbaces* courage he did sore {so} abate:
MASSYR58:38　H221　And their Taxations sore, all to revoake,
MASSYR61:16　H321　When *Resins* force his borders sore did mar.
MPERS76:7　　H905　By these alone his Hoast was pinch'd so sore,
MPERS80:28　H1095　But {the} *Phocians* Land, {Country} he then wasted sore:
MPERS84:23　H1259　His Grand-sires old disgrace, did vex him sore,
MPERS84:35　H1271　Either to wrong, did wound his heart so sore,
MPERS87:29　H1381　Had not a Captain; {his Captains} sore against his will;
MPERS90:34　H1501　Which over-throw incens'd the King so sore,
MGREC98:9　　H1811　With this reply, he was so sore {deep} enrag'd,
MGREC100:32　H1916　Who had long {sore} travaile, and much sorrow seen,
MGREC102:17　H1987　Though worn by time, and raz'd {rac'd} by foes full sore,
MGREC104:14　H2066　Transported sore, with griefe and passion;
MGREC105:10　H2103　His lost felicity did greive him sore,
MGREC107:22　H2197　But sore {much} distrest for water, in their march,
MGREC107:23　H2198　The drought, and heat, their bodies much doth {sore did}
MGREC111:18　H2363　Which the stout *Macedonians* mazed sore
MGREC122:2　H2825　And his beloved foe, full sore laments.
MGREC129:2　H3116　This touch'd *Cassander* sore, for what he'd done,
MGREC132:17　H3254　*Seleuchus, Asia* holds, that grieves him sore,
MROMAN138:7　H3497　The *Romans* sore incens'd, their Generall slay,
MROMAN139:18 H3546　Her Husband sore incens'd, to quit this wrong,
DIALOG145:36　H185　Next the *Militia* they urged sore,
SIDNEY150:29　H56　Oh, who was neare thee, but did sore repine;
DAVID159:3　　H18　There had his dignity so sore a soyle,
TDUDLEY165:6　H8　My mournfull mind, sore prest, in trembling verse
TDUDLEY166:14 H56　For which he sigh'd and pray'd & long'd full sore
FLESH175:30　H30　For riches dost thou long full sore?
FLESH176:10　H50　Thou speak'st me fair, but hat'st me sore,
CHILDRN185:40 H66　Sore accidents on you may light.
MEDDM198:28　Hp277　A sore finger may disquiet the whole body, but an vlcer w[th]in
MEDDM198:32　Hp277　pleasant thing to behold the light, but sore eyes are not able to
MEDDM199:31　Hp278　Sore labourers haue hard hands and old sinners haue brawnie
MEDDM203:28　Hp284　him welcome, that brings a plaister for his sore, or a cordiall
MYCHILD216:3　Hp241　16. The Lord layd his hand sore vpon me & smott me wth y[e]
FEVER220:31　H11　Of thy Displeasure sore
SOREFIT221:15 H1　From another sore fitt. etc.
JULY223:21　　Hp251　I had a sore fitt of fainting w[ch] lasted 2 or 3 dayes, but not in y[t]
11MAYA226:13　Hp255　I had a sore sicknes and weaknes took hold of me w[ch] hath by
30SEPT227:19　Hp257　fainting, but not in y[t] sore manner somt. he hath. I desire not
SON231:7　　H19　In sicknes when he lay full sore

SORELY (2)
MPERS73:27　H812　Some write that sorely hurt, they 'scap'd away;

MGREC131:22	H3214	He sorely griev'd at this his desperate state,

SORER (1)

JULY223:22	Hp251	first it took me, and so mvch the sorer it was to me because

SORES (1) [pl.]

DIALOG142:35	H64	I must confesse, some of those Sores you name,

SOREST (1)

11MAYB228:27	Hp259	and sorest yt ever I had lasting 4 dayes, and ye weather being

SORROW (13)

AGES37:2	H64	Ah me! conceiv'd in sin, and born in {with} sorrow,
AGES38:28	H131	For sin brings sorrow, sicknesse, death, and woe.
MPERS69:30	H652	With pressing grief, and sorrow, over-come,
MPERS82:34	H1181	The sorrow of his heart, did close his eye:
MGREC100:32	H1916	Who had long {sore} travaile, and much sorrow seen,
MGREC102:2	H1972	Accompani'd with sorrow, fear, and shame;
MGREC104:16	H2068	Sate down o'rewhelm'd, with sorrow, and despair,
MGREC115:15	H2525	The Mules and Horses are for sorrow shorne,
VANITY160:2	H12	He heaps up riches, and he heaps up sorrow,
CONTEM174:6	H206	This lump of wretchedness, of sin and sorrow,
ANNEB187:17	H7	The Heavens have chang'd to sorrow my delight.
MEDDM195:36	Hp272	vanity and lyes must needs lye down in the Bed of sorrow.
HOUSE236:14	H6	For sorrow neer I did not look,

SORROWES (5) [sorrows]

PILGRIM210:30	H30	Nor losses know, nor sorrowes see.
FEVER220:22	H2	When Sorrowes had begyrt me rovnd,
SOREFIT221:20	H6	Thou knowest the sorrowes yt I felt
MYSOUL225:10	H14	Thy Sorrowes all shall flye.
RESTOR229:21	H4	When feares and sorrowes me besett

SORROWING (1)

HOUSE236:34	H26	My sorrowing eyes aside did cast

SORROWS (6) [pl.] See also SORROWES

AGES42:25	H283	Great labours, sorrows, crosses I sustain'd.
MGREC103:38	H2049	(And there with sorrows, fears, and cares surrounded)
CONTEM173:36	H200	Subject to sorrows, losses, sickness, pain,
2LETTER182:4	H10	Shew him the sorrows of his widdowed wife;
MERCY189:4	H25	And then her sorrows all at once did go;
PILGRIM210:20	H20	Wth sinns wth cares and sorrows vext

SORRY (1)

DUBART155:3	H88	*The world rejoyc'd at's birth, at's death was sorry;*

SORT (6)

ELEMEN11:33	H153	The rich and {the} poore, wise, foole, and every sort,
AGES36:13	H37	The next came up, in a more {much} graver sort,
MPERS86:3	H1319	Meaning to chastise him, in sharpest sort,
MGREC106:39	H2173	The ruder sort, did openly deride
MGREC108:3	H2219	And in this sort, they rather drag, then bring,
MGREC108:29	H2245	And with their out-cries, in a {an} hideous sort,

SORTS (5) [pl.]

ELEMEN8:35	H33	All sorts of Artists, here declare your mind,
ELEMEN13:8	H209	And ye Artificers, all trades and sorts;
SEASONS49:37	H130	And for all sorts of Pease this is the time.
MEDDM199:26	Hp278	We read in Scripture of three sorts of Arrows the arrow of an
SON231:5	H17	And courtesies of svndry sorts

SO'S (3) [so is]

ELEMEN18:20	H424	And so's the notes which Nightingales do frame.
MGREC100:19	H1903	But as the King is, so's the multitude,
DIALOG148:19	H284	And lay her wast, for so's the sacred doom,

SOT (2)

MASSYR58:1	H186	That palliardizing sot, that out of doores
FLESH175:20	H20	Art fancy sick, or turn'd a Sot

SOTER (1)

MGREC133:30	H3320	*Antiochus Soter* his son was nam'd,

SOTERS (1) [poss.]

MGREC133:36	H3326	*Antiochus Theos* was *Soters* son,

SOTISH (1)

MEDDM202:8	Hp281	and some againe, so ignorant and sotish that they are more

SOTTISH (6)

HUMOUR21:19	H47	The man proves boyish, sottish, ignorant,
MASSYR54:27	H54	To whom the sottish people sacrific'd;
MASSYR68:22	H608	His pride, and sottish grosse Idolatry.
MPERS70:14	H685	Enters the town, the sottish King he slayes,
MPERS71:35	H749	Laughing to scorn that calvish, sottish crew.
MEDDM200:10	Hp279	yet they are so childishly sottish that they are still huging and

SOUERAINTY (1) [sovereinty] See also SOVERAIGNITY, SOVERAIGNTY

MEDDM206:31	Hp288	Souerainty of god, who will not be tyed to time nor place, nor

SOUGHT (10)

AGES37:15	H77	Who sought stil to appease me, with her {the} brest,
MASSYR55:29	H95	Or else she sought, revenge for *Menons* fall:
MASSYR57:11	H158	He sought no rule, til she was gone, and dead;
MASSYR62:6	H351	But weary of his servitude, he sought,
MPERS90:3	H1477	He sought all sustinance from them to take;
MPERS91:20	H1528	His home-bred troubles seeketh {sought how} to appease;
MPERS91:37	H1551	Made Writers work at home, they sought not far?
MGREC109:25	H2284	He glory sought, no silver, nor yet {no} gold;
MGREC123:7	H2869	And by his sleights to circumvent him sought;
MGREC128:38	H3111	Sought for a peace, and laid aside their jarres:

SOUL (40) See also SOULE

ELEMEN17:38	H402	I am the breath of every living soul.
HUMOUR27:41	H312	Which makes the mansion, by the soul soon left;
HUMOUR33:26	H540	That divine Essence, {Offspring} the immortal Soul,
HUMOUR33:30	H544	And surely the Souls {Soul} sensative here lives,
HUMOUR34:5	H560	He was no foole, who thought the Soul lay here {there},
AGES39:28	H171	Sweet Musick rapteth {raps} my {brave} harmonious Soul,
AGES46:21	H452	This body, by this soul, shal be assum'd;
VANITY161:5	H56	This satiates the soul, this stayes the mind,
TDUDLEY166:24	H66	Ah happy Soul, 'mongst Saints and Angels blest,
CONTEM168:19	H27	Soul of this world, this Universes Eye,
DISTEMP179:24	H12	He eas'd my Soul of woe, my flesh of pain,
2LETTER182:19	H25	But for one moneth I see no day (poor soul)
3LETTER183:3	H5	So doth my anxious soul, which now doth miss,
MERCY189:2	H23	Because her Soul she'd sent along with thee.
MYCHILD216:26	Hp242	somt. on my soul in Doubts & feares of Gods displeasure, and
MYCHILD216:36	Hp242	and Bonds vpon my Soul to p'form his righteovs comands.
MYCHILD218:10	Hp244	humane Invention can work vpon ye Soul, hath no Judgments

MYCHILD218:35	Hp244	say, Return o my Soul to thy Rest, vpon this Rock Xt Jesus will
BYNIGHT220:7	H7	I sovght him whom my Soul did Love
BYNIGHT220:12	H11	My hungry Soul fill'd wth Good,
FEVER220:30	H10	Beclouded was my Soul wth fear
FEVER220:35	H15	From Burnings keep my Soul.
FEVER221:3	H18	O heal my Soul thov know'st I said,
FEVER221:13	H28	Who hath redeem'd my Soul from pitt,
SOREFIT221:18	H4	And when my Soul these things abhor'd
MED223:1	Hp250	Meditations when my Soul hath been refreshed wth the
JULY223:35	Hp251	Salvat^n. of my Soul.
MYSOUL224:25	H1	My Soul rejoice thou in thy God
MYSOUL225:5	H9	Wth Angels-wings thy Soul shall movnt
28AUG225:29	Hp254	stayes my Soul that this condition y^t I am in is ye best for me,
28AUG226:8	Hp254	forgett thy great Love to my soul so lately expressed, when I
28AUG226:9	Hp254	lye down & bequeath my Soul to thee and Death seem'd no
11MAYA226:21	Hp255	espec: seing it is for my spirit^l. advantage, For I hope my soul
13MAY226:31	H7	My Soul and Body doth rejoice,
30SEPT227:21	Hp257	Love to my straying Soul wch in prosperity is too much in Love
RESTOR230:6	H21	My Soul as destitute
HOURS233:25	H8	Thy help my soul hath fovnd
HOURS233:29	H12	Wth Thee my soul can talk
HOURS234:6	H20	Vphold my fainting soul
REMB235:29	H10	Confusion seases on my Soul

SOULDIER (8) [soldier]

HUMOUR21:22	H50	Be he a Souldier, I more fence his heart
HUMOUR23:3	H113	Thou wast not made for Souldier, or for Schollar;
HUMOUR24:28	H177	There is no Souldier, but thy selfe thou say'st,
HUMOUR25:11	H200	But now Ile shew, what Souldier thou art.
HUMOUR25:21	H210	A Souldier most compleat in al points makest.
HUMOUR29:22	H373	If in a Souldier rashnesse be so precious,
HUMOUR32:30	H504	Valour {Valours} I want, no Souldier am, 'tis true,
AGES42:12	H270	If a Souldier {I}, with speed I did obey,

SOULDIERS (26) [soldiers]

MASSYR64:34	H458	Can *Babels* tired Souldiers tell with pain;
MPERS70:15	H686	Upon earths richest spoyles his Souldiers preys;
MPERS76:34	H932	Where *Grecians* prov'd themselves right Souldiers, stout;
MPERS77:29	H970	His Souldiers, credit, wealth, at home had stay'd,
MPERS79:3	H1025	'Twixt which his souldiers marcht in good array.
MPERS86:35	H1351	Great care was his pretence, those Souldiers stout,
MPERS87:39	H1391	On this, he and his Souldiers carelesse grow,
MPERS88:22	H1415	And brought his Souldiers on so gallantly,
MGREC94:18	H1654	His little wealth among his Souldiers gave.
MGREC102:23	H1993	He, and his Souldiers, wax effeminate,
MGREC103:10	H2021	For when the Souldiers, had rifled their pleasure,
MGREC107:17	H2192	The Souldiers should let passe this injury;
MGREC108:33	H2249	But soone the *Grecians* {his souldiers} forc'd them to a flight,
MGREC110:22	H2326	But so to doe, his Souldiers had no will;
MGREC110:28	H2332	And for his Souldiers larger Cabins make;
MGREC111:25	H2370	Unto his starved Souldiers small content;
MGREC111:28	H2373	Thus Winter, Souldiers, and provision {provisions} spent,
MGREC120:14	H2749	For's Souldiers 'gainst those Captains would not goe;

MGREC120:40   H2777   And made the Souldiers on his side remain;
MGREC121:9   H2787   Did alienate the Souldiers from his side;
MGREC121:16   H2795   Some of the Souldiers enters *Perdica's* tent,
MGREC121:16   H2796   The souldiers 'gainst *Perdiccas* they incense,
MGREC122:31   H2850   In's stead, {room} the Souldiers chose *Antipater,*
MGREC125:16   H2964   But when her Souldiers saw their ancient Queen,
MGREC126:17   H3008   The Souldiers pinched with this scarcity,
QELIZ156:37   H64   Such Souldiers, and such Captaines never seen,

SOULE (5) [soul]
AGES37:24   H86   My high-borne soule, so straitly was confin'd:
AGES43:18   H313   Whereby my empty soule, is lur'd and caught.
DIALOG143:41   H110   And thou, poore soule, wast {wert} jeer'd among the rest,
MEDDM202:32   Hp282   The eyes and the eares are the inlets or doores of the soule,
PILGRIM210:39 H39   Then soule and body shall vnite

SOULES (1) [souls, pl.]
MROMAN139:7   H3535   To eighty thousand soules then did amount:

SOULS (1) [poss.]
HUMOUR33:30 H544   And surely the Souls {Soul} sensative here lives,

SOUND (7) adj. [healthy] See also SOVND
ELEMEN16:40   H363   By adding cold to cold, no fruit proves sound;
AGES46:5   H436   That earth can give no consolation sound.
MGREC113:18   H2445   This sound advice, at heart, pleas'd *Alexander,*
MGREC118:26   H2675   But all his bowels, coloured well, and sound.
VANITY159:33   H5   On brittle earth, a consolation sound?
MEDDM201:16   Hp280   a quick reception, and a deliberate cogitation argues a sound
MEDDM201:28   Hp281   not only to bid them hold fast the form of sound Doctrin, but

SOUND (9) [noise] See also SOVND
ELEMEN18:15   H419   Your Drums, your Trumpets, and your Organs sound,
HUMOUR31:31 H464   Impatient Choler loveth not the sound.
HUMOUR32:16 H490   We shal expect much sound, but little force.
MPERS75:19   H878   In that thy fame shall sound whilst men have sence;
MGREC111:15   H2360   Which could not sound too oft, with too much fame;
QELIZ155:19   H10   The sound thereof raps every humane sence;
QELIZ156:40   H67   *Terra incognitae* might know her {the} sound;
2LETTER181:36 H6   The woful accents of my doleful sound,
MERCY188:21   H7   And yet survive to sound this wailing tone;

SOUND (2) v. [fathom] See also SOVND
MGREC131:31   H3223   He wittily his fathers mind did sound,
VANITY160:24   H34   Where shall I climbe, sound, seek, search or find,

SOUNDEST (2)
MGREC106:17   H2151   Though some {most} of reading best, and soundest minde,
MEDDM207:32   Hp289   But the soundest of men, haue likewise their nightly monitor,

SOUNDLY (1)
BYNIGHT220:2   H3   By night when others soundly slept,

SOUR See SOWRE

SOURCE (2)
ELEMEN8:19   H17   That roaring in it came, and with its source
DIALOG144:17   H127   Whence flow'd the source, the sprigs, the boughs, and fruits;

SOUTH (4)
ELEMEN16:28   H351   Transfers his goods, from North and South and East;
MGREC111:12   H2357   Then sayling South, and comming to the {that} shore,

MGREC133:39 H3329 And calls them there, the Kings of South, and North;
2LETTER182:18 H24 Thy rayes afar, salute her from the south.

SOUTH-WARD (1)
SEASONS50:12 H146 For yet {For much,} the South-ward Sun abateth not;

SOUTHERN (1)
CHILDRN184:30 H19 Till after blown by *Southern* gales,

SOUTHWARD (4)
SEASONS49:8 H99 Who to his Southward tropick still is bent,
SEASONS52:19 H234 To th' Southward tropick his swift race hath {doth} run;
1LETTER181:19 H17 O strange effect! now thou art *Southward* gone,
CHILDRN184:28 H17 *Southward* they both their course did bend,

SOVERAIGN (1) [sovereign] See also SOVERAIGNE
MASSYR63:8 H393 And {As} *Belosus,* first, his {Soveraign} did unthrone,

SOVERAIGNE (4) [sovereign] See also SOVERAIGN
MGREC109:33 H2292 His Homage unto him {to himself} as Soveraigne doe.
MGREC111:11 H2356 Acknowledg'd for their Masters Soveraigne;
MGREC114:24 H2494 Against his Soveraigne, or against his Lawes,
MGREC120:20 H2755 If not in word {stile}, in deed a Soveraigne.

SOVERAIGNITY (2) [sovereignty] See also SOUERAINTY, SOVERAIGNTY
MGREC94:8 H1642 In seeking after {Nor making Title unto} Soveraignity:
MGREC108:10 H2226 Wherein their own had {got the} soveraignity.

SOVERAIGNTY (2) [sovereignty] See also SOUERAINTY, SOVERAIGNITY
MASSYR53:16 H6 Man did not {proudly} strive for Soveraignty,
MGREC109:41 H2300 And there {by force} his Soveraignty for to make good;

SOVEREIGN (2) See also SOVERAIGN, SOVERAIGNE
MGREC109:19 H2278 And as his Sovereign Lord, him humbly greets.
CONTEM170:1 H75 That turn'd his Sovereign to a naked thral.

SOVEREIGNTY See SOUERAINTY, SOVERAIGNITY, SOVERAIGNTY

SOVGHT (5) [sought]
BYNIGHT220:7 H7 I sovght him whom my Soul did Love
BYNIGHT220:8 H8 Wth tears I sovght him earnestly·
SOREFIT221:16 H2 In my distresse I sovght ye Lord
THEART229:4 H6 I sovght more earnestly
REMB236:9 H24 O help thy Saints y^t sovght thy Face

SOVND (1) [sound; noise]
HOUSE236:17 H9 That fearfull sovnd of fire and fire,

SOW (1) n.
AGES42:35 H291 My fleeced Ewe {Sheep}, and ever {fruitful} farrowing Sow.

SOW (2) v.
AGES42:23 H281 As neither sow, nor reape, nor plant, nor build.
MEDDM205:3 Hp285 goe often ouer them, before they bee fit soile, to sow the

SOWN (3)
AGES41:23 H240 When my Wilde Oates, were sown, and ripe, & mown,
SEASONS47:37 H49 All Plants, and Flowers, {set and sown} for all delights, and
MEDDM205:6 Hp285 instruction and exhortation be sown, in the spring of their

SOWNE (1) [sown]
PILGRIM210:37 H37 In weaknes and dishonour sowne

SOWRE (2) [sour]
CONTEM174:22 H220 Feeding on sweets, that never bit of th' sowre,
MEDDM205:1 Hp285 (like sowre land) are of so tough and morose a dispotion that

SOWS (1) v.
SEASONS47:12 H28   Now digs, then sows, his hearbs, his flowers, and roots,

SOYL (3) n. [soil; earth] See also SOYLE
SEASONS47:7 H23   For to {He might} unloose his Winter-locked soyl;
MASSYR62:17 H362   Returns triumphant Victor to his soyl;
MPERS90:19 H1486 In peace they saw their Native soyl again.

SOYLE (1) [soil; earth]
ELEMEN11:29 H149   To tell what sundry fruits my fat soyle yeelds,

SOYLE (1) [soil; stain]
DAVID159:3 H18   There had his dignity so sore a soyle,

SOYLE (1) v. [soil]
DIALOG143:7 H74   No Duke of *York,* nor Earle of *March,* to soyle

SPACE (9)
HUMOUR20:32 H24   Only she crav'd, to have a vacant space.
SEASONS48:24 H77   More at her showers, which water them a space.
SEASONS50:13 H147   This month he keeps with *Virgo* for a space,
MGREC98:17 H1819 In seven months space {time} he takes this lofty {took that
MGREC107:36 H2211 On these, together ty'd, in six dayes space,
1LETTER181:17 H15   Which sweet contentment yield me for a space,
ELIZB186:36 H8   Farewel fair flower that for a space was lent,
SAMUEL228:14 H15   And if thou shalt spare me a space
HOUSE236:23 H15   Then coming out beheld a space

SPACIOUS (5)
AGES37:26 H88   This little house of flesh, did spacious count:
MGREC~~100:29~~ H1913 Yet had some hope, that on that even {the spacious} plain,
MGREC110:7 H2307 Within this spacious river, deep, and wide,
CONTEM173:6 H174   Who forrage o're the spacious sea-green field,
MEDDM202:33 Hp282 obiects enter, yet is not that spacious roome filled neither

SPAIN See SPAYNE

SPAINES (5) [spain's]
ELEMEN16:2 H325   Which *Spaines Americans,* do gladly hold.
DIALOG142:23 H52   Pray, doe not {you} feare *Spaines* bragging Armado?
DIALOG143:11 H80   *Spaines* braving Fleet a second time is sunke,
QELIZ156:9 H36   *Spaines* Monarch sa's not so; nor yet his Hoast,
QELIZ156:23 H50   Ships more invincible then *Spaines,* her foe

SPAKE (6)
ELEMEN19:2 H447   And what those Sages, did, or {either} spake, or writ,
HUMOUR20:30 H22   Her wisedome spake not much, but thought the more.
HUMOUR32:22 H496   I've not forgot how bitter Choler spake,
SEASONS46:~~35~~ H12   Nor hot nor cold, she spake, but with a breath,
TDUDLEY166:16 H58   Oft spake of death, and with a smiling chear,
SICKNES178:24 H7   For Adams sake, this word God spake

SPANISH (2)
ELEMEN12:6 H166   Strong forts from *Spanish* and *Italian* braules,
QELIZ156:41 H68   Her *Drake* came laded home with *Spanish* gold,

SPAR'D (5) [spared]
AGES43:11 ~~H305~~   Nor Brothers, Nephewes, Sons, nor Sires I've spar'd.
MPERS~~72:25~~ H773   He spar'd nor foe, nor friend, nor favorite.
MGREC108:15 H2231 Nor sex, nor age, nor one, nor other spar'd,
QELIZ156:32 H59   Nor men, nor coyne she spar'd, to doe them good;
FEVER221:8 H23   And spar'd by Body frail,

SPARE (14)

ELEMEN15:19	H301	That she can spare, when Nations round are poore.
ELEMEN17:32	H396	Much might I say of wracks, but that Ile spare,
ELEMEN19:34	H475	Where neither houses, trees, nor plants, I spare;
HUMOUR29:9	H362	To spare our selves, and beat the whistling winde.
AGES37:6	H68	My mothers breeding sicknes, I will spare;
AGES40:20	H201	If any time from company {leud Companions} I {can} spare,
MPERS69:32	H654	Brake his long silence, cry'd, spare *Cressus* life:
MPERS74:13	H836	His happy wishes now doth no man spare,
MGREC96:15	H1735	A number of spare horses next were led,
MGREC106:19	H2153	Then tell her errand, we had better spare
MGREC108:31	H2247	Of Darts, and Arrowes, made so little spare,
SIDNEY152:4	H76	That those that name his fame, he needs must spare,
CHILDRN184:17	H6	Nor cost, nor labour did I spare,
SAMUEL228:14	H15	And if thou shalt spare me a space

SPARED See SPAR'D

SPARES (1)

MPERS74:39	H860	His manly face dis-figures, spares no bloud,

SPARING (3)

ELEMEN11:13	H133	Not sparing life when I can take the same;
HUMOUR24:7	H156	I have been sparing, what I might have said,
HUMOUR25:25	H214	Nor sparing Sex, nor age, nor fire, nor son.

SPARK (1)

AGES44:39	H372	When it had lost that radiant Sun-like spark,

SPARTA (1)

MPERS85:24	H1300	The King was glad, with *Sparta* to make peace,

SPARTAN (3)

MPERS79:35	H1061	The *Spartan* meets him, brave *Leonade,*
MPERS90:15	H1484	Unto the *Spartan* Admirall did sue,
MPERS91:2	H1510	The *Spartans* height, {*Spartan* State} which now apace doth

SPARTANS (3) [pl.]

MPERS81:14	H1122	The *Spartans,* fearing *Athens* would agree,
MPERS86:33	H1349	Then next, the *Lacedemons* {*Spartans*} he takes to {into} pay;
MPERS90:27	H1494	Who with his {the} *Spartans* on the *Asia* coast;

SPARTANS (1) [pl.; poss.]

MPERS91:2	H1510	The *Spartans* height, {*Spartan* State} which now apace doth

SPAYNE (1) [spain]

ELEMEN17:10	H374	And but one land was *Affrica* and *Spayne,*

SPEAK (23)

ELEMEN12:26	H186	In his behalfe to speak a word the more;
ELEMEN18:14	H418	Speak, who, or what they will, they are but wind.
HUMOUR24:16	H165	Did ever sober tongue, such language speak?
HUMOUR33:12	H526	Thou speakest truth, and I can speak {say} no lesse,
HUMOUR33:21	H535	I am confounded, 'fore I speak of any:
HUMOUR34:6	H561	Whence her affections, passions, speak so clear;
AGES36:28	H52	Intend to speak, according to their age:
AGES38:23	H126	A lying tongue as soon as it could speak,
AGES45:22	H412	Men may more freely speak another day.
MGREC93:34	H1631	(For as worlds Monarch, now we speak not on,
MROMAN139:32	H3558	With many moe discouragements did speak.
DIALOG146:3	H191	But now I come to speak of my disaster,

DUBART154:6	H51	Through grief it wants a faculty to speak,
QELIZ158:18	H127	Whose living vertues speak (though dead long since)
CHILDRN186:27	H94	And dead, yet speak, and counsel give:
MEDDM195:29	Hp272	Many can speak well, but few can do well. We are better
MEDDM208:19	Hp290	be compared to deceitfull friends who speak faire and promise
MYCHILD215:11	Hp240	speakers leaue to speak, and those espec. sink deepest wch
MYCHILD215:13	Hp240	opportvnity to speak to any of yov much lesse to All, thovght it
FEVER220:29	H9	So faint I could not speak.
WHAT224:5	H5	My thankfull mouth shall speak thy praise
11MAYB228:34	Hp259	Conversation may speak that thy vowes are vpon me.
REMB235:24	H5	Or how thy praises speak

SPEAKE (8) [speak]

PROLOG7:8	H22	Who lisp'd at first, speake afterwards more {in future times}
ELEMEN8:9	H7	And {That} in due order each her turne should speake,
ELEMEN16:13	H336	To speake of kinds of Waters I'le {I} neglect,
ELEMEN16:19	H342	Nor will I speake of waters made by Art,
ELEMEN17:35	H399	Content (quoth Aire) to speake the last of you,
HUMOUR20:20	H12	Had leave to speake, succeeding one the other;
HUMOUR22:17	H86	She dare, {dares} not challenge if I speake amisse;
HUMOUR31:20	H453	I now speake vnto al, no more to one;

SPEAKERS (1)

MYCHILD215:11	Hp240	speakers leaue to speak, and those espec. sink deepest wch

SPEAKES (1) [speaks]

DUBART153:29	H33	The silly Pratler speakes no word of sence;

SPEAKEST (1) See also SPEAK'ST

HUMOUR33:12	H526	Thou speakest truth, and I can speak {say} no lesse,

SPEAKING (1)

SICKNES178:37	H20	ev'n as a word that's speaking.

SPEAKS See SPEAKES

SPEAK'ST (1)

FLESH176:10	H50	Thou speak'st me fair, but hat'st me sore,

SPECIALL (2) [special]

MROMAN139:2	H3530	But by the favour, and the speciall grace
MEDDM204:22	Hp285	wch should warn him, that doth any speciall seruice for god, to

SPECTACLE (1)

MGREC118:21	H2668	Now lay a spectacle, to testifie

SPECTATORS (1) [pl.]

MGREC112:9	H2395	Spectators here, could scarce relate the story,

SPECULATION (1)

FLESH175:14	H14	Can Speculation satisfy

SPED (2)

DIALOG148:11	H276	Of all the woes thou canst let her be sped,
SIDNEY~~152:14~~	H84	Then wonder not if I no better sped,

SPEECH (2)

HUMOUR33:36	H550	The faculty of speech doth here abide,
MASSYR59:2	H226	Won by his loving looks, more loving {by his} speech,

SPEECHES (1)

TDUDLEY166:4	H46	And oft and oft, with speeches mild and wise,

SPEED (17)

ELEMEN18:24	H428	And speed you to your Port, with wished gales.
AGES42:12	H270	If a Souldier {I}, with speed I did obey,

AGES39:39	H182	My valour, in some beastly quarrel's spent;
AGES40:21	H202	'Tis spent in curling {to curle}, frisling up {and pounce my
AGES41:41	H258	Yet all my powers, for self-ends are not spent,
MASSYR65:6	H471	Full thirteen yeares in this strange work he spent,
MPERS76:19	H917	The King, seeing his men, and victuall spent;
MPERS78:1	H982	Although he hasted, yet foure yeares was spent,
MPERS82:25	H1172	Some years by him in this vain suit was spent,
MPERS83:38	H1226	Where ninescore days, are spent in banquetting,
MGREC100:33	H1917	Now bids the world adieu, her time {with pain} being spent,
MGREC108:19	H2235	Whilst thus he spent some time in *Bactria,*
MGREC111:2	H2347	Some time he after spent upon that shore,
MGREC111:24	H2369	Whose inlets neare unto, he winter spent,
MGREC111:28	H2373	Thus Winter, Souldiers, and provision {provisions} spent,
MGREC111:38	H2383	From hence to *Babylon,* some time there spent,
MGREC112:34	H2420	And's Brethren, whom {who} for him their lives had spent;
MGREC113:9	H2436	Or flesh, or {and} life, could bear, till both were spent
MGREC114:26	H2496	Thus was he tortur'd, till his life was spent.
MGREC115:9	~~H2518~~	Twelve thousand Tallents on it franckly spent;
MGREC125:31	H2981	Till {'Gainst} all that lov'd *Cassander* was nigh spent; {she was
TDUDLEY165:28	H30	Who spent his state, his strength, & years with care
TDUDLEY167:3	H85	*And when his time with years was spent*
DDUDLEY167:19	H16	*And in her Closet constant hours she spent;*
FLESH176:31	H71	Then can thy hours in pleasure spent.
CHILDRN186:9	H76	But sing, my time so near is spent.

SPHERE (2)

QELIZ157:40	H108	But happinesse, lies in a higher sphere,
FLESH175:9	H9	Her thoughts unto a higher sphere:

SPHERES (1) [pl.]

MEDDM206:17	Hp287	shall they be, when they are fixt in their heauenly spheres

SPI'D (1) [spied]

MPERS88:24	H1417	Whom *Cyrus* spi'd, cries out, I see the man,

SPIDERS (2) [poss.]

MASSYR65:15	H480	Had all his hopes like to a Spiders web;
FAINTING222:16	H6	My life as Spiders webb's cutt off

SPIED See **SPI'D**

SPIGHT (7) [spite]

HUMOUR25:12	H201	And though thou'st us'd me, with opprobrious spight, {right:}
HUMOUR30:41	H433	But that which shewes how high thy spight is bent,
HUMOUR34:41	H596	Let's now be freinds, 'tis {its} time our spight was {were} spent,
MPERS75:36	H893	They thus backt of {by} the King, in spight of foes,
MGREC113:3	H2430	To wreak their spight, and hate, on every limbe.
MGREC125:35	H2985	And throwes {threw} his bones about, to shew her spight.
SIDNEY150:33	H60	And live it doth, in spight of death, through fame,

SPILL (2)

MGREC117:8	H2615	And {But} as he took delight, much bloud to spill,
MGREC132:11	H3246	For blood which was decreed, that he should spill,

SPILL'D (1) [spilled]

MGREC130:32	~~H3181~~	And *Cleopatra's* blood, now likewise spill'd,

SPILS (1) [spills]

HUMOUR25:33	H222	So spils {shed'st} that life {blood}, thou'rt bounden to preserve.

SPILT (5) [spillt]

HUMOUR21:40	H68	But shuns to look on wounds, and bloud that's spilt,
MGREC101:34	H1962	And spilt the Greeks some bloud before their flight
MGREC126:25	H3016	the blood of their deare Kindred {friends and kindreds} spilt,
MGREC130:28	H3181	And wronging innocents whose blood they spilt,
MROMAN137:28	H3479	Kept shut in peace, but {set} ope when bloud was spilt;

SPIN (1)

SIDNEY151:14	H69	But *Omphala*, set *Hercules* to spin,

SPIRES (2) [pl.]

MASSYR56:20	H126	Her gardens, bridges, arches, mounts, and spires;
MGREC102:10	H1980	The firm foundations, {strong Foundation} and the lofty spires;

SPIR. (1) [spirit]

FLESH175:38	H38	*Spir.* Be still thou unregenerate part,

SPIRIT (10)

HUMOUR29:20	H371	Thy fiery spirit shal bear away this prize,
FLESH175:1	H1	*The Flesh and the Spirit.*
FLESH175:8	H8	The other Spirit, who did rear
MEDDM197:20	Hp275	temple for the spirit of god to dwell in
MEDDM199:21	Hp278	of both, and findes nothing but vanity and vexation of spirit
MEDDM203:3	Hp283	vexation of spirit, yet our owne experience would soon haue
MYCHILD215:17	Hp240	now doe) by y^t yov may gain some spirit: Advantage by my
MYCHILD217:18	Hp243	his holy spirit who hath oft given me his word & sett to his Seal
FAINTING222:20	H10	My feblee Spirit thou did's reviue
MED223:13	Hp250	spirit failes in me at y^e consideration $y^r$of, and I am

SPIRITS (11) [pl.]

HUMOUR22:23	H92	{From} Whence flow fine spirits, and witty notions?
HUMOUR22:26	H95	Poor spirits the Liver breeds, which is thy seat,
HUMOUR22:29	H98	The vitall spirits they're call'd, and wel they may,
HUMOUR22:41	H110	No, no, {Alas,} thou hast no spirits, thy company
HUMOUR26:5	H235	Nextly, the spirits thou do'st wholly claime,
HUMOUR26:21	H251	And if vital spirits do flow from thee,
HUMOUR26:33	H263	The spirits through thy heat, are made perfect there,
HUMOUR33:11	H525	But the spirits, by which it acts are thine;
MPERS88:34	H1427	After this trance, revenge, new spirits blew,
28AUG225:26	Hp254	After mvch weaknes & sicknes when my spirits were worn out,
RESTOR229:23	H6	When heart did faint & Spirits quail

SPIRITS (1) [poss.]

HUMOUR33:37	H551	The spirits animal, from whence doth {hence do} slide,

SPIRI^{TL} (1) [spiritual]

11MAYA226:21	Hp255	pleasure espec: seing it is for my spiri^{tl}. advantage, For I hope

SPIRITUALL (1) [spiritual]

MEDDM209:22	Hp291	let his parts naturall and acquired spirituall and morall,

SPIRITULL (2) [spiritual]

MEDDM195:25	Hp272	no evill that we feele, or fear, but we may make some spiritull
MEDDM199:9	Hp277	and sapless performances are simptoms of little spiritull vigor

SPITS (1) [pl.]

ELEMEN9:17	H51	Your spits, pots, jacks, what else I need not name,

SPLEEN (5)

HUMOUR23:12	H122	The sinke of all us three, the hatefull spleen;
HUMOUR28:16	H328	The Melancholly to the Spleen to 'bide;
HUMOUR30:9	H401	Thirdly, {Again} thou dost confine me to the spleen,

HUMOUR30:27 H419 Likewise the useful spleen, though not the best,
HUMOUR30:34 H426 The Spleen for al you three, was made a sinke,
SPLENDER (1)
MASSYR66:35 H541 In splender, and in Majesty, he sits,
SPLENDID (2)
CONTEM169:4 H46 And is thy splendid Throne erect so high?
MEDDM206:16 Hp287 bright while they moue on earth, how transcendently splendid
SPLENDOR (2)
MGREC96:1 H1721 The splendor, and the pompe, he marched in,
MROMAN~~138:34~~ H3524 Much {Some} state, and glory, {splendor} did this *Priscus* adde:
SPLENDOUR (1)
DIALOG147:33 H257 At that thy setled Peace, thy wealth and splendour,
SPLIT (2)
ELEMEN19:28 ~~H472~~ How many rich fraught vessells, have I split?
MPERS80:22 H1089 That their split sides, witness'd his overthrow;
SPOILE (2) [spoil] See also SPOYL, SPOYLE
MPERS84:10 H1238 And how her Country-men from spoile she freed.
MGREC96:30 H1750 Had not been spoile, and booty rich enough,
SPOILED See SPOYL'D
SPOILES (1) [spoils] See also SPOYLES, SPOYLS
CONTEM174:17 H216 But suddenly a storm spoiles all the sport,
SPOILS (1) See also SPOILES, SPOYLES, SPOYLS
DIALOG148:9 H274 And let her spoils, full pay, with int'rest be,
SPOKE (4)
MPERS69:38 ~~H660~~ And told, how *Solon* in his hight had spoke.
MGREC112:41 H2427 Faine would have spoke, and made his owne defence,
DIALOG145:30 H179 And to their *Laud* be't spoke, they held i'th' Tower,
MYCHILD215:11 Hp240 leaue to speak, and those espec. sink deepest wch are spoke
SPOKEN (1)
DAVID158:28 H8 In *Gath,* let not this thing {things} be spoken on,
SPONDLES (1) [pl.]
HUMOUR34:12 H567 Which runs through all the spondles of the rack,
SPONGY (1)
HUMOUR23:40 ~~H149~~ The spongy Lungs, I feed with frothy blood.
SPORT (3)
MGREC94:26 H1664 To scorn at him, *Darius* had good sport:
MGREC95:36 H1715 For this wise King, had brought to see the sport;
CONTEM174:17 H216 But suddenly a storm spoiles all the sport,
SPORTS (2) [pl.]
HUMOUR24:39 H188 And scorn'st all Knightly sports, at turnament.
MROMAN137:13 H3464 To see these sports, the *Sabins* all are bent;
SPOT (1)
AUTHOR178:5 H15 And rubbing off a spot, still made a flaw.
SPOTS (1) [pl.]
HUMOUR28:36 H348 I've scarce wip'd off the spots, proud Choler cast,
SPOUSE (1)
2LETTER182:16 H22 That once a day, thy Spouse thou mayst imbrace;
SPOYL (2) [spoil] See also SPOYLE
MASSYR62:16 H361 Laden with honour, prisoners, and with spoyl,
MPERS71:27 H741 To spoyl the Temple of great *Jupiter;*

SPOYL'D (2) [spoiled]
MASSYR62:9   H354   Besieg'd his regal town, and spoyl'd his Coast,
CHILDRN185:28 H54   Or by some greedy hawks be spoyl'd.

SPOYLE (1) [spoil] See also SPOYLE
MGREC128:32 H3105 And {With} all the spoyle and booty they {he} had tane;

SPOYLES (2) [spoils] See also SPOYLS
MPERS70:15   H686   Upon earths richest spoyles his Souldiers preys;
DAVID159:7   H22   Nor from the fat, and spoyles, of mighty men,

SPOYLS (2) [spoils] See also SPOYLES
MASSYR53:22   H12   Both Beasts and Men subjected to his spoyls.
MGREC107:12 H2187 Which done, sets fire upon those costly {goodly} spoyls

SPRANG (1)
MPERS83:28   H1216 The best that ever sprang {sprung} of *Cyrus* race.

SPRAYS (1) [pl.]
SEASONS47:19 H35   Now tune their layes, on sprays of every bush;

SPREAD (3)
MGREC111:36 H2381 Upon his Monument his Robes {Robe} he spread,
DUBART154:15 H60   Thy fame is spread as farre, I dare be bold,
CHILDRN185:26 H52   The net be spread, and caught, alas.

SPREADING (1)
CONTEM173:8   H176   Whose armour is their scales, their spreading fins their shield.

SPRIGS (1) [pl.]
DIALOG144:17 H127   Whence flow'd the source, the sprigs, the boughs, and fruits;

SPRING (23)
ELEMEN18:30   H434   And youth, and spring, sages to me compare.
AGES35:28   H14   His spring was intermixed with some snow.
AGES35:31   H17   flowers (as these) blossome {the spring puts forth} betime,
SEASONS46:27 H3   *Spring.*
SEASONS46:30 H6   The Winter, Summer, Autumne, and the Spring,
SEASONS46:32 H8   Sweet Spring, like man in his minority,
SEASONS48:33 H84   Melodious {Sweet fragrant} Spring, with thy short pittance flye,
SEASONS48:38 H89   When Spring had done, then {the} Summer must {did} begin,
SEASONS49:1   H92   As Spring did aire, blood, youth in's equipage.
SEASONS51:18 H192   Which shewes, nor Summer, Winter, nor the Spring,
MGREC94:14   H1648 His course to *Asia,* next Spring he steers.
DUBART153:11 H15   A homely flower in this my latter spring:
VANITY161:1   H52   This pearl of price, this tree of life, this spring,
CONTEM171:23 H126   A Spring returns, and they more youthfull made;
CONTEM171:30 H132   Nor youth, nor strength, nor wisdom spring again
CHILDRN186:15 H82   But spring lasts to eternity,
MEDDM197:11   Hp274 If we had no winter the spring would not be so pleasant, if we
MEDDM200:24   Hp279 The spring is a liuely emblem of the resurrection, after a long
MEDDM200:30   Hp279 and in this transcends the spring, that their leafe shall neuer
MEDDM205:6   Hp285 and exhortation be sown, in the spring of their youth,
MYCHILD218:1 Hp243 & Winter, Spring and Autvmne, the dayly providing for this
11MAYA226:14 Hp255 lasted all this spring till this 11. May, yet hath my God given
13MAY226:26   H2   As spring the winter doth succeed

SPRINGING (1)
13MAY227:12   H21   My Baca made a springing flood?

SPRINGS (2) [pl.]
ELEMEN14:37   H279   With springs below, and showers from above;

ELEMEN15:22	H304	But {And} such I am, in Rivers, showers and springs;

SPROUTED (1)

AGES38:15	H118	Which sprouted forth, in my {mine} insuing age,

SPRUNG (5)

MPERS~~83:28~~	H1216	The best that ever sprang {sprung} of *Cyrus* race.
MPERS~~92:27~~	H1585	But from some daughter this new king was sprung
DIALOG142:19	H48	That from the red, white pricking Roses sprung?
QELIZ158:9	H118	*O'th' Damask Rose, sprung from the white and red,*
MEDDM202:5	Hp281	or sprung out of the loynes of one Adam, some set in yᵉ

SPUN (3)

SEASONS49:20	H111	Whose fleece when purely {finely} spun, and deeply dy'd,
MGREC116:2	H2562	The thread of *Alexanders* life was spun;
SICKNES178:20	H3	My race is run, my thread is spun,

SPUR (2)

MPERS89:2	H1436	The King upon the spur, runs back again;
MEDDM205:25	Hp286	allseeing eye will be a bridle to restrain from evill, and a spur,

SPURS (1) [pl.]

MGREC124:3	H2908	For this *Antigonus* needed {did need} no spurs,

SPY (5)

SEASONS53:7	H263	*And all the faults which {that} you shall spy,*
MASSYR58:8	H193	His master like a Strumpet chanc'd to {clad did} spy,
MASSYR67:40	H586	The fingers of his {a} hand-writing did spy.
MPERS88:30	H1423	At {But when} last his head they spy upon a Launce,
MGREC136:15	H3429	*Yet in this Chaos, one shall easily spy,*

SPYE (2) [spy]

HOUSE236:19	H11	I starting vp yᵉ light did spye,
HOUSE236:35	H27	And here and there yᵉ places spye

SPYING (1)

MEDDM196:7	Hp272	he ruffles them vp, but spying his black feet, he soon lets fall

SQUADRON (1)

MPERS88:20	H1413	He with six hundred, on a squadron set,

SQUADRONS (1) [pl.]

MPERS79:19	H1045	He glories in his Squadrons, and his Horses;

SQUARE (1)

MASSYR56:2	H108	Each Square, was fifteen thousand paces long,

STAB (2)

HUMOUR25:29	H218	How often for the lye, thou'st giv'n the stab.
AGES40:5	H186	Or stab the man, in's own defence, that's worse.

STAB'D (1) [stabbed]

AGES45:13	H395	I've seen one stab'd, another {and some to} loose his head

STABLE (1)

ANNEB187:22	H12	Was ever stable joy yet found below?

STABLE-GROOME (1)

MPERS74:18	H841	Thanks for all this to's crafty Stable-groome.

STACKS (1) [pl.]

SEASONS50:10	H144	To Barns, and Stacks, where it for Fodder lyes.

STAFFE (4) [staff]

HUMOUR21:39	H67	And break a staffe, provided't be in jest,
AGES36:20	H44	Leaning upon his staffe, comes {came} up old age.
AGES44:21	H354	Provides a staffe for {then} to support his age.
RESTOR230:1	H16	And wᵗʰ his staffe did thee support

STAGE (8)

AGES35:17	H3	Loe now! four other acts {act} upon the stage,
AGES36:11	H35	Then prauncing on the Stage, about he wheels;
AGES36:19	H43	And last of al, to act upon this Stage;
AGES38:16	H119	As he can tell, that next comes on the stage.
AGES39:8	H151	For thus to do, we on this Stage assemble,
AGES44:7	H340	And on this Stage am come to act my last:
MPERS~~92:24~~	H1582	This *Codomanus* now upon the stage
MGREC115:18	H2537	That he might next now act upon the Stage,

STAI'D (1) [staid]

HUMOUR23:7	H117	Thou sayst, thy wits are stai'd, subtle and fine:

STAID (6)

AGES41:16	H235	And now am grown more staid, that {who} have been green,
MPERS~~79:13~~	H1039	Because they wanted skill the same to've staid.
MPERS90:12	~~H1484~~	There for some time they were, but whilst they staid,
MGREC103:19	H2030	But on their faithfullnesse, he never staid:
MGREC121:32	H2814	Whilst *Perdicas* thus staid {encamp'd} in *Africa,*
TDUDLEY165:27	H29	Who staid thy feeble sides when thou wast low,

STAIN (1)

HUMOUR31:38	H471	Now could I stain my ruddy sisters face,

STAINE (1) [stain]

SIDNEY150:13	H48	{The more I} say truth, {the more} thy worth I shall but staine,

STAINED See STAYNED

STAKE (2) [post]

DIALOG146:13	~~H200~~	Religion, Gospell, here lies at the stake,

STAKE (2) [wager]

MPERS75:13	H874	But who dare venture such a stake for th' game;

STALLION (2)

MPERS74:10	H835	*Darius* lusty stallion neighed full loud;
MGREC110:40	H2344	Where he entomb'd his stately stallion.

STAMPED (1)

MGREC135:33	H3405	The residue he stamped under's feet:

STAMPT (1)

MPERS89:8	H1442	With infamy upon each fore-head stampt;

STAND (31)

HUMOUR29:27	H378	I then command, proud Choler stand thy place,
AGES42:11	H269	And shew'd them how, in face of foes to stand.
SEASONS47:34	~~H47~~	Yet never minute stil was known to stand,
SEASONS51:24	H200	The fruitful trees, all withered now do stand,
MASSYR60:11	H276	A while he, and his race, aside must stand,
MASSYR66:21	H527	Then *Put,* and *Lud,* doe at his mercy stand,
MASSYR68:9	H595	But dumb the gazing Astrologers stand,
MPERS69:39	H669	With pitty *Cyrus* mov'd, knowing Kings stand,
MPERS80:20	H1087	In this Streight, as the other, firmly stand.
MPERS88:32	H1425	Sencelesse and mute they stand, yet breath out groans,
MPERS88:41	H1434	Hoping with {by} that to make the *Greeks* stand stil,
MPERS~~92:1~~	H1555	Which in rebellion sixty years did stand:
MGREC94:39	H1677	The *Persians* for encounter ready stand,
MGREC103:2	H2013	With open Gates, the wealthy town did stand,
MGREC107:28	H2203	Here *Alexander's* almost at a stand,
MGREC110:1	H2301	But on the banks doth {stout} *Porus* ready stand,

MGREC116:11	H2577	Monarchs fame} must last, whilst world shall {doth} stand,
MGREC120:36	H2773	His sumptuous monument long time did stand;
MGREC126:24	H3015	But made in Judgement her Accusers stand,
MGREC135:12	H3384	The *Assyrian* Monarchy long time did stand,
MGREC135:35	H3407	All trembling stand, before that powerfull Lambe.
MGREC136:2	H3415	But humbly stand, some grave reproof to take:
DIALOG144:22	H132	The Sermons yet upon record doe stand,
DIALOG145:25	H174	As puts me to a stand what I should say,
DIALOG146:39	H225	With (ventur'd lives) for truths defence that stand,
DIALOG148:30	H295	And holinesse, on horses bells shall stand,
DUBART154:2	H47	Movelesse, stand charm'd by thy sweet influences,
DUBART154:35	H80	Thus *Bartas* fame shall last while starres do stand,
2LETTER182:10	H16	Or all the grass that in the Meads do stand,
MEDDM204:6	Hp284	yesterday, to day and for euer, we are the same that stand
MEDDM208:16	Hp290	stand.

STANDINGS (1) [pl.]

MGREC135:9	H3381	Their standings, over-turnings, bounds and fates;

STANDS (9)

SEASONS48:22	H75	One hangs his head, the other stands upright:
MASSYR65:13	H478	While *Babels* King thus deep ingaged stands;
MPERS79:27	H1053	How of this enterprise his thoughts now stands;
DIALOG141:18	H17	Which 'mazed Christendome stands wondring at?
QELIZ155:25	H16	Mine bleating stands before thy royall Herse:
MEDDM204:10	Hp284	wthall, the larger his accounts stands vpon gods score it
MEDDM205:21	Hp286	stands right there.
MEDDM209:23	Hp291	be neuer so large, yet he stands in need of something w^{ch}
HOUSE237:20	H50	Stands permanent tho: this bee fled.

STAR (1)

SEASONS49:41	H134	Increased by the Star *Canicular;*

STARRES (4) [stars] See also STARRS

ELEMEN10:20	H95	And influence if divers of those starres,
DUBART154:35	H80	Thus *Bartas* fame shall last while starres do stand,
MEDDM206:7	Hp287	starres and those starres also, to differ much one from the

STARRS (1) [stars] See also STARRES

2LETTER182:9	H15	He that can tell the starrs or Ocean sand,

STARRY (3)

SEASONS47:3	H47	Who for some months have seen but starry lights;
SEASONS47:5	H21	Who for some months have been but starry lights.
CONTEM171:4	H109	The starry observations of those Sages,

STARS (5) [pl.] See also STARRS, STARRES

ELEMEN10:13	H88	Nay more then these, Rivers 'mongst stars are found,
ELEMEN12:40	H200	Which guides, when Sun, nor Moon, nor Stars do shine.
ELEMEN20:1	H483	Sometimes strange {red} flaming swords, and blazing stars,
SIDNEY151:2	H69	If such Stars as these, sad presages be,
MEDDM206:12	Hp287	euen in this life, some are Stars of the first magnitude, and

START (1)

AGES41:10	H230	Clapt in that prison, never thence to start.

STARTING (1)

HOUSE236:19	H11	I starting vp ye light did spye,

STARVED (2)

MGREC111:25	H2370	Unto his starved Souldiers small content;

DIALOG144:41	H149	Thousands of starved Christian there also.

STATE (50)

AGES43:16	H308	Then thought my state firm founded sure to last,
AGES44:16	H349	It's not my goodly house {state}, nor bed of down,
AGES44:29	H362	In various times of state i've also been.
AGES45:11	H393	But not their Princes love, nor state so high;
AGES45:11	H393	But neither favour, riches, title, State,
AGES45:16	H398	The desolation, of a goodly State.
AGES45:22	H407	I've seen a state unmoulded, rent in twain,
MASSYR57:18	H165	So suddenly should loose so great a state,
MASSYR67:6	H552	Poor forlorn Prince, that {who} had all state forgot,
MASSYR67:24	H570	A Royall State, rul'd by a bruitish mind.
MPERS71:7	H723	But {Yet} to enlarge his state, had some desire;
MPERS71:19	H733	Who grown a man, resum'd again his state)
MPERS76:29	H927	*Athens* perceiving now their desperate state,
MPERS80:8	H1075	Where is the valour, of your antient State?
MPERS81:13	H1121	So should all favour to their State be shown.
MPERS81:18	H1126	That *Xerxes* quarrel was 'gainst *Athens* State,
MPERS91:2	H1510	The *Spartans* height, {*Spartan* State} which now apace doth
MGREC96:17	H1737	But they that saw him in this state to lye;
MGREC103:32	H2043	His names {fames} dishonour, losse unto his State.
MGREC106:26	H2160	As most incompatible to his state;
MGREC111:6	H2351	These, all he feasts in state, on beds of gold,
MGREC115:21	H2540	(Not suffering her to meddle in {with} the State)
MGREC120:33	H2770	In midst of these, *Garboyles,* with wondrous state,
MGREC122:11	H2836	*Python* now chose protector of the State,
MGREC125:4	H2952	her young Nephew {grand-child} in his stead {State} t' inthrone,
MGREC125:21	H2971	And needs will have their lives as well as State:
MGREC127:7	H3037	Of *Aridæus,* and his Queen, with state;
MGREC127:34	H3064	Fearing their state {his force}, and what might hap ere long
MGREC131:1	H3189	Doth promise liberty to *Athens* State;
MGREC131:22	H3214	He sorely griev'd at this his desperate state,
MGREC133:27	H3317	kingdomes {Empire was} were subdu'd by {to} th' *Roman* state.
MROMAN138:34	H3524	Much {Some} state, and glory, {splendor} did this *Priscus* adde:
DIALOG141:17	H16	And must my selfe dissect my tatter'd state,
DIALOG141:26	H25	Or by my wasting state, dost think to thrive?
DIALOG141:30	H29	And thus, alas, your state you much deplore,
DIALOG145:17	H166	'Twixt King and Peeres a question of state,
DIALOG147:9	H235	If mindlesse of thy state I e'r be found.
DIALOG148:16	H281	To th' 'stonishment of all that knew his state,
SIDNEY152:2	H75	For dear regard he had of *Sydney's* state,
DUBART153:38	H42	Thy Phisick, Musick, and State policy,
DUBART154:28	H73	Of names {Name}, of state, of body, or {and} of mind,
VANITY159:36	H8	And whilst they live, how oft doth turn their State? {fate,}
VANITY161:3	H54	Nor change of state, nor cares shall ever see,
TDUDLEY165:28	H30	Who spent his state, his strength, & years with care
CONTEM171:29	H131	That state obliterate he had at first:
CONTEM173:37	H201	Each storm his state, his mind, his body break,
ELIZB187:3	H12	Sith thou art setled in an Everlasting state.
MEDDM196:22	Hp273	open a prosperous state makes a secure christian, but
MEDDM199:24	Hp278	that are eyes of a Republique, foretels a declineing State.

SOREFIT222:9	H28	O gravnt I doe it in this state,

STATELY (22)

ELEMEN10:37	H112	The stately seats of mighty Kings by me:
ELEMEN11:1	H118	And stately *London,* (our great *Britain's* glory)
HUMOUR30:26	H418	The strong foundation of the stately frame.
HUMOUR33:28	H542	Within this stately place of eminence,
MASSYR54:25	H52	This stately seat of warlike *Ninus* stood.
MASSYR56:16	H122	Whose stately top, beyond {above} the clouds did rise;
MASSYR59:21	H245	Part of the {that stately} wal it level caus'd to lye; {was
MPERS69:38	H662	That *Solon* sometimes at his stately Court,
MPERS70:5	H676	Was conquest of the stately *Babylon,*
MPERS70:20	H691	Yet wondrous Monuments this stately Queen,
MPERS80:14	H1081	Four hundred stately Ships by stormes was lost,
MGREC96:5	H1725	The stately Horses trapt, the launces guilt;
MGREC103:35	H2046	Those stately streets with raging flames doth {flame did} fil.
MGREC110:40	H2344	Where he entomb'd his stately stallion.
MGREC115:8	H2518	For him erects a stately Monument,
MGREC115:15	H2527	Of stately *Ecbatane* who now must shew,
MROMAN138:18	H3508	A stately Bridge he over *Tyber* made,
SIDNEY152:22	H91	His bones do lie interr'd in stately *Pauls.*
QELIZ156:25	H52	Her stately Troops advanc'd to *Lisbons* wall,
CONTEM168:7	H16	Then on a stately Oak I cast mine Eye,
CONTEM172:6	H142	Under the cooling shadow of a stately Elm
FLESH177:7	H88	The stately Walls both high and strong,

STATES (4) [pl.]

ELEMEN20:4	H486	By death, or great mutations {mutation} of their States.
MPERS73:30	H815	A Consultation by the {those} States was held.
DIALOG147:3	H229	With hearts, and states, to testifie their will.
QELIZ156:28	H55	The States united now her fame doe sing;

STATIRAH (1)

MGREC111:41	H2386	And *Statirah, Darius* daughter takes,

STATIST (1)

AGES37:40	H102	No Statist I: nor Marti'list i' th' field;

STATUE (1)

MPERS75:15	H876	Who doth deserve a Statue made of gold;

STATUES (1) [pl.]

MGREC103:12	H2023	Statues of {some} gold, and silver numberlesse,

STATURE (3)

CONTEM168:10	H19	Thy strength, and stature, more thy years admire,
MEDDM200:18	Hp279	god proportion his dispensations according to the stature
MEDDM201:2	Hp280	his strong men, such as are come to a full stature in Christ,

STATUTES (1)

MYCHILD217:9	Hp242	I was afflicted I went astray, but now I keep thy statutes.

STAUROBATES (2)

MASSYR56:25	H131	Great King *Staurobates,* for {his Country} to invade.
MASSYR56:33	H139	The rest *Staurobates* in fight did slay.

STAV'D (1) [staved]

AGES43:5	H300	Opprest, and sunke, and sact, {stav'd} all in my way;

STAY (25) [remain]

ELEMEN12:16	H176	Nor will I stay, no not in *Tempe* Vale,
HUMOUR22:10	H79	She'l first advise, if't be not best to stay.

MASSYR65:20	H485	Fast bound, intends at {to} *Babel* he shal stay {him to send},
MPERS79:16	H1042	Seven dayes and nights, his Hoast without least stay,
MPERS81:5	H1113	{Fearing} his best {bridge}, no longer for to {there would} stay;
MPERS87:35	H1387	Yet for his brothers comming, durst not stay,
MPERS88:14	H1407	But long under their fears, they did not stay,
MPERS89:29	H1463	The King's {King} perplext, there dares not let them stay,
MPERS90:8	H1481	Nor rivers course, nor *Persians* force could stay,
MPERS92:38	H1596	Whose honours, treasures, pleasures, had short stay;
MGREC94:1	H1635	Yet for a while, in *Greece* is forc'd to stay,
MGREC95:22	H1701	stead} *Arsemes* {*Arses*} was plac'd, yet {but} durst not stay;
MGREC102:21	H1991	Where four and thirty dayes he now doth stay,
MGREC107:39	~~H2214~~	He easily might have made them stay there stil;
MGREC115:40	H2559	And pardon craves, for his unwilling stay,
MGREC126:21	~~H3012~~	But he unwilling longer there to stay,
1LETTER181:25	H23	Where ever, ever stay, and go not thence,
2LETTER181:33	H3	But stay this once, unto my suit give ear,
2LETTER182:1	H7	If in thy swift Carrier thou canst make stay,
2LETTER182:34	H40	By all our loves conjure him not to stay.
MEDDM199:16	Hp278	haue any thing to stay vpon, but take away their props and
MEDDM202:28	Hp282	se no light, yet then must we trust in the lord and stay vpon our
MYCHILD217:24	Hp243	and seen no light, yet haue I desired to stay my self upon
THEART229:3	H5	I cry'd thov seem'st to make some stay
HOURS234:5	H19	O stay my heart on thee my God

STAY (5) [support]

MPERS78:39	H1020	To be to's age a comfort, and a stay,
MGREC100:28	H1912	But on their fortitude he had small stay;
DIALOG145:23	H172	To help the Church, and stay the Common-Weal,
VANITY160:25	H35	That *summum Bonum* which may stay my mind?
2HUSB232:16	H17	Thou art my strenght and stay;

STAY'D (3) [stayed]

MPERS76:24	H922	But troubles in lesse *Asia* him stay'd;
MPERS77:29	H970	His Souldiers, credit, wealth, at home had stay'd,
SAMUEL228:5	H6	The child I stay'd for many yeares.

STAYD (1) [stayed]

MEDDM208:30	Hp290	it hath stayd the Course of the Sun raised the dead, cast out

STAYED (1)

MYCHILD218:34	Hp244	I have told yov before. That hath stayed my heart, and I can

STAYES (2) [stays; remain]

MPERS76:38	H936	He stayes a landing {lanching} Gally with his hand;
MGREC130:9	H3164	*Antigonus'* Lieutenant stayes her still,

STAYES (2) [stays; support]

VANITY161:5	H56	This satiates the soul, this stayes the mind,
28AUG225:29	Hp254	stayes my Soul that this condition yᵗ I am in is yᵉ best for me,

STAYEST (1)

1LETTER181:6	H4	How stayest thou there, whilst I at *Ipswich* lye?

STAYNED (1) [stained]

AGES38:19	H122	From birth stayned, with Adams sinfull fact;

STAYS See STAYES

STEAD (12)

MPERS73:14	H801	The Princes meet to chuse one in his stead,
MPERS83:25	H1213	The second was inthron'd, in's fathers stead.

MPERS90:36	H1503	*Tythraustes* now {then} is placed in his stead,
MPERS~~92:5~~	H1559	*Arsames* plac'd now in his fathers stead,
MGREC~~95:22~~	H1701	There {In's stead} *Arsemes* {*Arses*} was plac'd, yet {but} durst
MGREC96:16	H1736	Least he should need them, in his chariots stead.
MGREC122:31	H2850	In's stead, {room} the Souldiers chose *Antipater,*
MGREC125:4	H2952	her young Nephew {grand-child} in his stead {State} t' inthrone,
MGREC134:31	H3362	*Alexander,* then *Lathurus* in's stead,
MGREC134:38	~~H3367~~	For *Pompey's* life, then plac'd her in his stead,
DIALOG145:28	H177	Which by their prudence stood them in such stead,
PILGRIM210:12	H12	Nor wild fruits eate, in stead of bread

STEAL (1)

AGES42:19	H277	Did toile, did broile, oppress'd, did steal and lye.

STEALE (1)

MGREC101:32	H1957	But he disdain'd to steale a victorie,

STEALING (1)

CONTEM172:14	H149	While on the stealing stream I fixt mine eye,

STEALTH (2)

FATHER6:5	H39	My goods are true (though poor) I love no stealth,
MGREC126:18	H3009	By stealth unto *Cassander* daily fly;

STEAR'D (1) [steered]

MGREC111:22	H2367	Passing faire *Indus* mouth, his course he stear'd,

STEEL (1)

ELEMEN~~9:3~~	H37	My force? your sword, & Gun, your lance of steel

STEELE (1)

ELEMEN9:3	~~H37~~	My force? your sword, your Pike, your flint and steele,

STEEP (4)

ELEMEN12:9	H169	And *Hemus,* whose steep sides, none foote upon,
ELEMEN~~16:11~~	H334	And be thy mountains n'er so high and steep,
MGREC94:41	H1679	Those banks so steep, the *Greeks,* now {yet} scramble up
MEDDM197:26	Hp275	He that will vntertake to climb vp a steep mountain wth a great

STEER (1)

3LETTER183:21	H23	But worst of all, to him can't steer my course,

STEER'D (2) [steered] See also STEAR'D

AGES43:1	~~H297~~	If honour was the point, to which I steer'd;
CHILDRN184:31	H20	They *Norward* steer'd with filled sayles.

STEERES (1) [steers]

VANITY160:37	H47	It steeres {stores} with wealth, which time cann't wear away.

STEERS (2)

MGREC94:14	H1648	His course to *Asia,* next Spring he steers.
CONTEM174:14	H213	Sings merrily, and steers his Barque with ease,

STELLA (3)

SIDNEY150:39	~~H67~~	Illustrious *Stella,* thou didst thine full well,
SIDNEY~~150:40~~	H68	*Stella* the fair, whose streams from Conduits fell
SIDNEY151:10	~~H69~~	How could that *Stella,* so confine thy will?

STEM (2)

MPERS92:12	H1570	But now's divolved, to another Stem.
DIALOG144:11	H121	Because of Royall Stem, that was thy crime;

STEP (2)

HUMOUR20:13	H5	Loe! other foure step up, crave leave to shew
BIRTH180:16	H26	These O protect from step Dames injury.

STEPHEN (1)
DIALOG142:13 H42 Doe *Maud,* and *Stephen* for the Crown contend?
STEPS (9) [pl.]
MASSYR61:10 H315 Next treads the {those} steps, by which his Father won.
MPERS74:25 H848 That by such steps to Kingdoms often climbs {clime}.
MPERS86:22 H1338 By lesser {lower} steps, towards the top to climbe;
BIRTH179:33 H9 How soon, my Dear, death may my steps attend,
1LETTER181:7 H5 So many steps, head from the heart to sever
2LETTER182:15 H21 Tell him, the countless steps that thou dost trace,
MEDDM198:11 Hp276 need ponder all his steps.
MEDDM207:7 Hp288 steps to draw men to god in consideration of his bounty
PILGRIM210:4 H4 That myrie steps, haue troden oft
STEPT (1)
AGES45:25 H415 But I returne, from whence I stept awry,
STEWARDSHIP (1)
MEDDM197:24 Hp275 receiued? Come giue an account of thy stewardship.
STIBIUM (1)
ELEMEN14:10 H252 As *Stibium* and unfixt *Mercury:*
STICK (3)
MPERS76:18 H916 Or *Sythian* arrows in our sides must stick.
DIALOG147:40 H264 Then bribes shall cease, and suits shall not stick long,
MEDDM198:5 Hp276 the still waters, if they stick in deepe mire and clay, and all his
STICKS (2)
MPERS76:41 H939 His whetted teeth he sticks {claps} in the firm wood,
MGREC130:4 H3159 And vile {lewd} *Cassander* too, sticks not for shame;
STIFF (1)
MGREC94:3 H1637 *Thebes,* and old {stiff} *Athens,* both 'gainst him rebell,
STIFFE (2)
AGES45:38 H428 Now stiffe and numb, can hardly creep or go.
MGREC118:30 H2679 Was stiffe *Meleager,* whom he would take down {away},
STIGMATIZING (1)
DIALOG144:27 H135 Of stinking, stigmatizing, Romish Clerkes;
STIL (26) [still]
ELEMEN9:21 H55 In chymestry, unlesse I help you Stil,
HUMOUR26:4 H234 The friendly coadjutors, stil to {of} thee.
HUMOUR27:7 H278 If stil thou take along my Aliment,
HUMOUR27:37 H308 Mans life to boundlesse time might stil endure;
HUMOUR28:28 H340 And maugre (Choler) stil they are the wittest,
HUMOUR31:12 H444 Thy bittering quality, stil irretates,
AGES37:11 H73 My mother stil did waste, as I did thrive:
AGES37:15 H77 Who sought stil to appease me, with her {the} brest,
AGES40:25 H206 To Masques, to Playes, to Taverns stil I move;
AGES42:41 H297 And greater stil, did {and thirst for honour,} set my heart on
SEASONS47:5 H19 Stil adds to th' last, til after pleasant *May;*
SEASONS47:34 H47 Yet never minute stil was known to stand,
SEASONS48:36 H87 Thy dayes stil lengthen, without least decline.
SEASONS50:32 H166 Hath stil ascended up in {to bear} goodly Fruits,
SEASONS51:30 H206 So doth Old Age stil tend unto his Grave,
SEASONS52:17 H232 And like an Infant, stil he {it} taller growes.
SEASONS52:35 H250 And North-ward stil approaches to the Line;
MASSYR60:18 H283 Incroached {Incroaching} stil upon the bord'ring Lands,

MASSYR61:37	H342	Who stil implor'd his love, but was distress'd,
MPERS71:12	~~H727~~	Which Law includes all Lawes, though lawlesse stil,
MPERS78:27	H1008	{But} Hers she kept stil, seperate from the rest,
MPERS82:28	H1175	But she was stil, as when it {he} first begun.
MPERS~~85:7~~	H1283	Stil making war, till first had lost his life:
MPERS88:41	H1434	Hoping with {by} that to make the *Greeks* stand stil,
MGREC107:39	~~H2214~~	He easily might have made them stay there stil;
CONTEM171:19	H122	And then the earth (though old) stil clad in green,

STIL'D (1) [stilled]

MASSYR63:9	H394	So he's now stil'd, the King of *Babylon;*

STILE (10) [style]

MGREC94:36	H1674	In lower termes to write {was taught} a higher stile,
MGREC97:33	H1794	To give his Conquerour, the stile of King;
MGREC118:5	H2652	Some wished him, to take the stile of King,
MGREC~~120:20~~	H2755	If not in word {stile}, in deed a Soveraigne.
MGREC121:19	H2801	With stile of the Protector, would him {to} grace;
MGREC130:39	H3184	These Captains now, the stile of Kings do take,
MGREC130:41	H3186	*Demetrius* is first, that so assumes, {the royal stile asum'd,}
MROMAN137:3	H3454	And with the stile of *Patres* honour'd those;
DUBART153:32	H36	Thus weake brain'd I, reading the lofty stile,
DUBART154:31	H76	Thy haughty stile, and rapted wit sublime,

STILES (1) v. [styles]

MGREC94:28	H1666	Stiles him disloyall servant, and no better;

STILL (80) See also STIL

PROLOG7:29	H40	Men have precedency, and still excell,
PROLOG7:36	H46	And ever with your prey, still catch your praise,
HUMOUR23:37	H147	By th' influence I send still from the heart.
HUMOUR~~24:3~~	H152	And yet to make, my greatnesse far {still} more great:
HUMOUR~~31:15~~	H447	Thy biting quality still irritates,
AGES38:30	H133	Yet griefs, in my fraile flesh, I still do find.
SEASONS49:8	H99	Who to his Southward tropick still is bent,
MASSYR55:13	H79	Her beautious face (they feign) retaining still.
MASSYR67:10	H556	But yet in *Babell,* he must still remain:
MASSYR68:12	H598	Who still expects some fearfull sad event,
MPERS~~70:3~~	H674	Did to him still his chief designs commend.
MPERS72:17	H765	Thy cruelty will {all} Ages still admire.
MPERS77:5	H944	And for revenge his heart still restlesse burnes;
MPERS82:24	H1171	The chaste, and beautious Dame, refuses still.
MPERS~~84:12~~	H1248	And o're his opposites still got the day,
MPERS86:11	H1327	Still on his brother, casts a jealous eye,
MPERS86:29	H1345	Pretending still, the profit of the King,
MPERS87:5	H1361	The wife, against the mother, still doth cry
MPERS87:9	H1365	But as he goes, his Forces still augments,
MPERS87:30	H1382	By reason, and by force, detain'd him still.
MPERS89:3	H1437	But they too faint, still to pursue their game,
MPERS90:2	H1477	But when through difficulties still {all} they brake,
MGREC98:33	H1835	*Darius* finding troubles still increase,
MGREC100:27	H1911	For in his multitudes his trust still lay,
MGREC102:40	H2010	Which newes doth still augment *Darius* woes;
MGREC104:4	H2056	Then still with infamy, to draw his breath.
MGREC107:2	H2177	With those of worth, he still desires esteem,

MGREC~~107:39~~	H2214	With little pain there might have kept them still:
MGREC110:21	H2325	East-ward, now *Alexander* would goe still,
MGREC113:34	H2461	This that *Parmenio,* who still over-came,
MGREC116:23	H2589	The Illiads of *Homer* he still kept,
MGREC116:33	H2599	Still fearing that his Name might hap to die,
MGREC117:6	H2613	For by that hand, which still revengeth bloud,
MGREC117:23	H2630	For ayming still amisse, his dreadfull blowes
MGREC118:2	H2649	Their ends they might the better still attain.
MGREC118:7	H2654	And had to him, still since *Ephestion* dyed,
MGREC119:30	H2720	For fighting still, whilst there did hope remain,
MGREC119:35	H2725	Blockt up in *Lamia,* still by his foes;
MGREC124:4	H2909	Hoping still {yet} more to gaine by these new stirs;
MGREC124:14	H2921	And his opponent still got {*Cassanders* forces had the} upper
MGREC124:19	H2926	Still labours *Eumenes* might {would} with him side,
MGREC124:33	H2940	He still kept fresh {lockt} within his memory,
MGREC125:37	H2987	Wisht in *Epire* she still had been confin'd;
MGREC127:15	H3045	To keep *Antigonus* from *Susha* still,
MGREC127:19	H3049	*Antigonus* came off still honourlesse,
MGREC127:20	H3050	When victor oft had {he'd} been, and so might still,
MGREC128:28	H3101	Still gaining Countries East-ward goes he on.
MGREC130:9	H3164	*Antigonus'* Lieutenant stayes her still,
MGREC130:11	H3166	To let her go, or hold her still, he fears,
MGREC130:38	H3183	That hand is righteous still which doth repay:
MGREC~~132:16~~	H3253	In neither finds content if he sits still:
MGREC134:11	H3342	So many Princes still were murthered,
MGREC134:34	H3365	For since the first, that title still they had,
MROMAN138:12	H3502	Leaves {Left} *Rome,* in wealth and power, still growing high.
MROMAN139:29	H3555	Essays I many made but still gave out,
DIALOG144:19	H129	That with high hand I still did perpetrate;
DIALOG147:2	H228	Blest be thy Counties which do {who did} aid thee still
QELIZ157:39	H107	O {Yea} happy, happy, had those dayes still been,
VANITY160:16	H26	And he that knows the most doth still bemoan,
TDUDLEY165:15	H17	He was my Father, and Ile praise him still.
TDUDLEY165:32	H34	Truths friend thou wert, to errors still a foe,
TDUDLEY166:8	H50	Which all they have, and more still set to view,
DDUDLEY167:21	H18	*Preparing still for death, till end of dayes:*
CONTEM172:17	H152	Could hinder ought, but still augment its force:
FLESH175:38	H38	*Spir.* Be still thou unregenerate part,
FLESH176:1	H41	Thee as a foe, still to pursue.
AUTHOR178:5	H15	And rubbing off a spot, still made a flaw.
AUTHOR178:7	H17	Yet still thou run'st more hobling then is meet;
BIRTH179:28	H4	Adversity doth still our joyes attend;
3LETTER183:5	H7	Still wait with doubts, & hopes, and failing eye,
3LETTER183:13	H15	His presence and his safe return, still wooes,
3LETTER183:30	H32	Let's still remain but one, till death divide.
CHILDRN185:5	H31	Ambition moves still in his breast
CHILDRN185:13	H39	My other three, still with me nest,
MERCY188:20	H6	And live I still to see Relations gone,
MERCY188:33	H19	And in thy griefs still bear a second part:
MEDDM198:5	Hp276	the still waters, if they stick in deepe mire and clay, and all his
MEDDM200:10	Hp279	are so childishly sottish that they are still huging and sucking

CONTEM174:35	H232	But he whose name is grav'd in the white stone
FLESH177:8	H89	Are made of pretious *Jasper* stone;

STONES (7) [pl.]

ELEMEN13:2	H203	Was {Were} those compiled heapes of massy stones?
MPERS88:33	H1426	Nor *Gorgons* {head} like to this, transform'd to stones.
MROMAN136:35	H3449	The Stones at first was cimented with bloud,
DUBART154:3	H48	More sencelesse then the Stones to *Amphions* Lute,
CONTEM171:20	H123	The stones and trees, insensible of time,
MEDDM201:19	Hp280	We often se stones hang wth drops not from any innate
PILGRIM210:15	H15	No rugged stones his feet shall gaule

'STONISHMENT (1) [astonishment]

DIALOG148:16	H281	To th' 'stonishment of all that knew his state,

STOOD (29)

ELEMEN17:24	H388	As when *Achaia,* all under water stood,
AGES36:37	H61	With heed now stood, three ages of fraile man;
AGES43:16	H311	The bottom nought, and so no longer stood.
MASSYR53:25	H15	These were his first, all stood in *Shinar* land,
MASSYR54:21	H48	On which stood fifteen hundred towers stout:
MASSYR54:25	H52	This stately seat of warlike *Ninus* stood.
MASSYR56:1	H107	Quadrangle was the forme, it stood upon:
MASSYR56:23	H129	This wonder of the world, this *Babell* stood.
MASSYR65:37	H502	The wals so strong, that stood so long, now fall;
MPERS73:18	H805	And kinsmen in account, to th'King they stood,
MPERS75:6	H867	This told, for enterance he stood not long,
MPERS82:37	H1184	To see that face, where Rose and Lilly stood,
MPERS88:4	H1397	And ranged stood, by great *Euphrates* side,
MGREC95:7	H1686	Where stood of late *Diana's,* wondrous Phane,
MGREC98:7	H1809	Sent word, that *Hercules* his Temple stood,
MGREC101:34	H1963	But long they stood not e're they're forc'd to run,
MGREC102:31	H2001	Here stood the Royall houses of delight,
MGREC114:12	H2481	From one stood by he snacht a partizan,
MGREC117:7	H2614	None of his Kindred, or {nor} his Race, long stood;
MGREC135:16	H3388	The *Grecian* longer then the *Persian* stood,
MROMAN136:36	H3450	And bloudy hath it prov'd, since first it stood:
MROMAN138:20	H3510	Faire *Ostia* he built, this Town, it stood,
DIALOG145:3	H152	My {Mine} heart obdurate, stood not yet agast.
DIALOG145:26	H175	Old customes, new Prerogatives stood on,
DIALOG145:28	H177	Which by their prudence stood them in such stead,
DIALOG147:1	H227	And thine {thy} infringed Lawes have boldly stood.
FLESH175:2	H2	In secret place where once I stood
MERCY188:25	H11	I stood so nigh, it crusht me down withal;
HOUSE236:37	H29	Here stood that Trunk, and there y^t chest

STOOP (1)

MEDDM197:15	Hp274	stoop, so a man of weak faith and mean abilities, may vndergo

STOP (3)

MPERS90:1	H1476	To {Did} stop the way in this their enterprise;
MGREC119:26	H2716	Striving {And seeks} to stop *Leonatus,* that so
FLESH176:16	H56	Ile stop mine ears at these thy charms,

STOPT (7)

HUMOUR31:16	H449	If there thou'rt stopt, to th' Liver thou turn'st in,
MASSYR61:35	H340	Through *Syria* now he marcht, none stopt his way,

MPERS89:15	H1449	That their return be stopt, he judg'd was best,
MGREC126:1	H2992	But being stopt, at Straight *Tharmipoley*
MGREC127:1	H3031	Some slew, some fry'd, of others, stopt the breath;
MGREC130:18	H3173	As vile conspiratours that took {stopt} her breath,
DIALOG144:24	H133	These Prophets mouthes (alas the while) was stopt,

STORE (19)

PROLOG6:28	H12	'Twixt him and me, that over-fluent store;
ELEMEN15:18	H300	Which by my fatting Nile, doth yeeld such store;
AGES46:18	H449	In my dark house, such kindred I have store,
SEASONS49:14	H105	That if you do, remove {withdtaw} her burning store,
MASSYR59:16	H240	There with all store he was so wel provided,
MASSYR64:37	H461	Of costly Ships, and Gallies, she had store,
MASSYR67:31	H577	To shew his little dread, but greater store,
MPERS77:9	H948	His men, his coyn, his honour, and his store;
MPERS89:25	H1459	The King great store of all provision sends,
MGREC135:26	H3398	Then gold, silver, brasse, iron, and all that {the} store,
SIDNEY149:24	H23	That this one Volumne should exhaust your store.
SIDNEY152:8	H79	Since *Sydney* had exhausted all their store,
DDUDLEY167:13	H10	*Whom oft she fed, and clothed with her store;*
FLESH175:18	H18	Hast treasures there laid up in store
FLESH175:31	H31	Behold enough of precious store.
DISTEMP179:18	H6	Till nature had exhausted all her store,
1LETTER181:4	H2	My joy, my Magazine of earthly store,
HOUSE236:38	H30	There lay that store I covnted best
HOUSE237:26	H56	Farewell my pelf, farewell my Store.

STORED (1)

MEDDM198:14	Hp276	but he that is well stored wth both, seldom is so insnared

STORES (2)

MGREC131:1	H3190	With Arms and with provision stores them well,
VANITY160:37	H47	It steeres {stores} with wealth, which time cann't wear away.

STORIES (5) [pl.] See also STORYES

ELEMEN10:40	H115	*Carthage,* and hundred moe, in stories told,
MASSYR54:8	H35	Whose Preists, in Stories, oft are mentioned;
MASSYR59:34	H258	Twenty he reign'd, same time, as Stories tel,
MPERS70:1	H672	(His Mothers Vnckle, stories doe evince:)
MGREC103:13	H2024	Yet after all, as stories do expresse,

STORK (1)

ELEMEN19:8	H453	The Stork, the Crane, the Partrich, and the Phesant;

STORKE (1) [stork]

ELEMEN15:6	H288	The lofty Eagle and the Storke flye low,

STORM (3)

CONTEM173:37	H201	Each storm his state, his mind, his body break,
CONTEM174:17	H216	But suddenly a storm spoiles all the sport,
13MAY227:5	H14	I haue a shelter from ye storm

STORME (3) [storm]

HUMOUR21:25	H53	To storme a Breach, or scale a City wal?
DIALOG142:27	H56	Whence is this {the} storme, from Earth, or Heaven above?
MEDDM201:31	Hp281	shadow in the parching sun, & a shelter in a blustering storme

STORMED (1)

MPERS71:29	H743	The stormed dust o'r-whelm'd his daring bands;

STORMES (8) [storms]

ELEMEN8:26	H24	All stormes now laid, and they in perfect peace,
AGES38:9	H112	I fear'd no stormes, nor al the windes that blows,
MPERS80:14	H1081	Four hundred stately Ships by stormes was lost,
MEDDM199:5	Hp277	Lightening doth vsually preceed thunder, and stormes raine,
13MAY227:1	H10	My winters past my stormes are gone
SAMUEL228:12	H13	Prserve O Lord from stormes & wrack
SON230:25	H8	In raging stormes did'st safely keep
2HUSB232:29	H30	In stormes and sicknes Lord prserve.

STORMS (4) [pl.]

ELEMEN~~19:32~~	H473	Again, what tempests,{furious storms} and what hericanoes
TDUDLEY166:21	H63	Where storms, nor showrs, nor ought can damnifie.
1LETTER181:11	H9	Whom whilst I 'joy'd, nor storms, nor frosts I felt,
CHILDRN186:14	H81	No seasons cold, nor storms they see;

STORMY (2)

SEASONS47:25	H41	Yet many a fleece of Snow, and stormy showre,
PILGRIM210:8	H8	Nor stormy raines, on him shall beat

STORY (11) See also STORY'S

ELEMEN10:16	H91	My story to a Volume would amount:
ELEMEN~~11:1~~	H119	My raging flame did make a mournful story,
MPERS84:9	H1237	What *Hester* {*Esther*} was, and did, her story reed,
MPERS92:28	~~H1586~~	And he that story reads, shall often find;
MGREC112:9	H2395	Spectators here, could scarce relate the story,
MGREC122:3	H2826	I should but snip a story into verse, {bits}
MGREC131:8	H3198	'Twould be an endlesse story to relate
MGREC~~132:20~~	H3265	His story seems a Fable more then true.
MROMAN139:36	H3562	To prosecute my story to the last;
SIDNEY150:3	H28	Which makes severer eyes but scorn thy {slight that} Story,
MYCHILD218:13	Hp244	it? Is there any story but that wch showes the beginnings of

STORYES (1) [stories]

MASSYR~~67:23~~	H569	His lust, and cruelty, {crueltyes} in books {storyes} we find,

STORY'S (1) [story is]

QELIZ157:20	H88	Of her what worth in Story's to be seen,

STOUT (20)

ELEMEN10:4	H79	The *Theban* stout *Alcides,* with his club:
ELEMEN~~14:4~~	H247	So did that Roman, far more stout then wise,
ELEMEN14:40	H282	Thy Bear, thy Tyger, and thy Lyon stout,
HUMOUR33:3	H517	Sixty nine Princes, all stout *Hero* Knights,
MASSYR54:21	H48	On which stood fifteen hundred towers stout:
MPERS73:22	H809	This King, with {his} conspirators so stout,
MPERS76:34	H932	Where *Grecians* prov'd themselves right Souldiers, stout;
MPERS80:2	H1069	And wound the backs of those bold {brave} Warriours stout.
MPERS81:30	H1138	*Mardonius* proud, hearing this answer stout,
MPERS86:35	H1351	Great care was his pretence, those Souldiers stout,
MGREC101:16	H1941	To this, stout *Alexander,* gives no eare,
MGREC109:29	H2288	But *Porus* stout, who will not yeeld as yet;
MGREC~~110:1~~	H2301	But on the banks doth {stout} *Porus* ready stand,
MGREC110:16	H2316	For to the last, stout *Porus* kept his ground.
MGREC111:18	H2363	Which the stout *Macedonians* mazed sore
MGREC~~132:20~~	H3258	A mighty Navy rig'd, an Army stout,
MGREC133:19	H3307	Between those Kings, and noble *Pyrrus* stout,

902

MROMAN136:23	H3437	Stout *Romulus, Romes* Founder, and first King,
DIALOG142:5	H34	What, hath some *Hengist,* like that *Saxon* stout,
DIALOG144:15	H125	These be the *Hydra's* of my stout transgression;

STOUTLY (1)

MGREC~~99:16~~	H1859	Where valiant *Betis,* doth defend {stoutly keeps} the town,

STOUTLY'S (1) [stoutly has]

HUMOUR29:16	H363	Thy boasted valour stoutly's been repell'd,

STRAFFORD (1)

DIALOG145:29	H178	They took high *Strafford* lower by the head,

STRAIGHT (17) See also STRAIT, STREIGHT

ELEMEN17:11	H375	Untill straight {proud} *Gibralter,* did make them twaine,
AGES43:13	H306	There set, I rid my selfe straight out of hand.
AGES45:28	H418	And back, once straight, begins apace to bow.
SEASONS47:31	~~H46~~	In *Taurus* Signe, yet hasteth straight from thence;
MPERS76:25	H923	Which husht, he straight so orders his affaires;
MPERS82:33	H1180	Straight comes her Lord, and finds his wife thus lie,
MPERS88:17	H1410	They straight adored *Cyrus* for their King,
MPERS89:17	H1451	{Then} he sends {that} to's Tent, they straight addresse,
MPERS90:16	~~H1484~~	Straight to transport them to the other side,
MGREC100:8	H1892	The Son of *Jupiter* did straight him make:
MGREC103:41	H2052	Was straight in *Bactria* these {soon} to augment,
MGREC104:21	H2073	Straight *Bessus* comes, and with his traiterous hands,
MGREC124:5	H2910	Straight furnisht him with a sufficient aide,
MGREC126:1	H2992	But being stopt, at Straight *Tharmipoley*
MGREC127:30	H3060	Then with *Seleuchus* straight at ods doth fall,
MGREC130:17	H3172	For straight way by command they'r put to death,
MGREC~~131:9~~	H3201	How some when down, straight got the upper hand

STRAIGHTS (1) [straits]

QELIZ156:39	H66	Her Sea-men through all straights the world did round,

STRAIN (2)

SEASONS48:34	~~H85~~	In this harsh strain, I find no melody,
CONTEM173:13	H180	And chanted forth a most melodious strain

STRAINE (2) [strain]

MGREC136:4	H3417	The Subject was too high, beyond my straine;
SIDNEY150:14	H49	Thy fame, and praise, is farre beyond my straine;

STRAINES (2) [strains]

SIDNEY149:33	~~H23~~	Let then, none dis-allow of these my straines,
SIDNEY~~150:12~~	H42	Then let none disallow of these my straines

STRAIT (1) [straight]

MPERS72:4	He	strait to rid himself of causlesse fears,

STRAITLY (1)

AGES37:24	H86	My high-borne soule, so straitly was confin'd:

STRAITS See STRAIGHTS

STRAND (1)

MPERS76:37	H935	Pursues his flying-foes, and {then} on the strand;

STRANG (1) [strange]

MEDDM202:35	Hp282	& wch is most strang, the more it receius the more empty it

STRANGE (17)

ELEMEN10:28	H103	There's none more strange then *Ætna's* sulphery mount
ELEMEN16:14	H337	My divers Fountaines and their strange effect;
ELEMEN20:1	H483	Sometimes strange {red} flaming swords, and blazing stars,

HUMOUR26:32	H262	I must confesse, is somewhat strange to me,
HUMOUR32:11	H485	Strange Chymera's are in my phantasie,
HUMOUR34:3	H558	O! mixture strange, oh {O} colour, colourlesse,
SEASONS47:35	H47	But only once at *Joshua's* strange command;
MASSYR62:14	H359	This was that strange degenerated brood,
MASSYR65:6	H471	Full thirteen yeares in this strange work he spent,
MASSYR66:29	H535	Strange melancholly humours on him lay,
MASSYR68:5	H591	This language strange, to read, and to unfold;
MPERS72:18	H766	This strange severity, one time {sometimes} he us'd,
MGREC96:9	H1729	The Priests in their strange habit follow after;
MROMAN137:31	H3482	Their Augurs strange, their habit, and attire,
VANITY160:33	H43	Its hid from eyes of men, they count it strange,
1LETTER181:19	H17	O strange effect! now thou art *Southward* gone,
SON231:3	H15	In covntry strange thou did'st provide

STRANGELY (2)

AGES38:38	H141	Strangely preserv'd, yet mind it not at all.
AGES41:3	H223	Sometimes the Phrensie, strangely madds my Brain,

STRANGER (1)

MROMAN138:35	H3525	Thirty eight yeares (this Stranger borne) did reigne,

STRANGERS (1) [pl.]

MEDDM203:17	Hp283	sees land we must therfore be heer as strangers and pilgrims,

STRANGERS (1) [poss.]

AGES45:4	H386	A royal one by gifts from strangers hands

STRANGURY (1)

AGES43:28	H323	{The Strangury} Torments me with intollerable {sore} paines;

STRATAGEMS (1) [pl.]

MGREC122:6	H2829	His stratagems, wherein he did excel,

STRATONICA (1)

MGREC131:25	H3217	Who his fair daughter *Stratonica* takes,

STRAW (1)

MGREC107:35	H2210	And stuffing them with straw, he bundles makes;

STRAWBERRY (1)

SEASONS48:26	H79	The hasty Pease, and wholesome red {cool} Strawberry,

STRAYING (1)

30SEPT227:21	Hp257	Love to my straying Soul wch in prosperity is too much in Love

STREAM (1)

CONTEM172:14	H149	While on the stealing stream I fixt mine eye,

STREAMES (1) [streams]

SEASONS49:18	H109	In the coole streames they labour with delight,

STREAMS (4) [pl.]

SIDNEY150:40	H68	*Stella* the fair, whose streams from Conduits fell
CONTEM172:8	H144	Where gliding streams the Rocks did overwhelm;
2LETTER182:30	H36	Hath power to dry the torrent of these streams.
3LETTER183:25	H27	Who neither joyes in pasture, house nor streams,

STREET (1)

MGREC99:25	H1868	And by command was drawn through every street,

STREETS (4) [pl.]

MGREC102:7	H1977	With showers of Flowers, the streets along are strown,
MGREC103:35	H2046	Those stately streets with raging flames doth {flame did} fil.
DAVID158:29	H9	Nor published in streets of *Askelon,*
FLESH177:11	H92	The Streets thereof transparent gold,

STREIGHT (4) adv.

MGREC~~117:22~~	H2629	Each man {All men} began for {streight} to contemn his might;
CONTEM168:32	H38	Thy daily streight, and yearly oblique path,
CONTEM173:3	H171	Then to the colder bottome streight they dive,
HOUSE237:11	H41	Then streight I 'gin my heart to chide,

STREIGHT (3) n. [strait]

MPERS79:34	H1060	Then marching {on} to the streight *Thermopyle,*
MPERS~~80:18~~	H1085	Inclos'd their Fleet i'th' streights {streight} of *Eubea;*
MPERS80:20	H1087	In this Streight, as the other, firmly stand.

STREIGHTS (3) [straits]

MPERS80:18	H1085	Inclos'd their Fleet i'th' streights {streight} of *Eubea;*
MPERS80:23	H1090	Yet {Then} in the Streights of *Salamis* he try'd,
MPERS87:18	H1372	To keep those streights, to hinder his intent.

STRENGHT (3) [strength] See also STRENGTH'S

SOREFIT221:25	H11	My feeble loines didst gird w'th strenght
RESTOR229:28	H11	W'th strenght didst him sustain.
2HUSB232:16	H17	Thou art my strenght and stay;

STRENGHTEN (3) [strengthen]

JULY223:33	Hp251	upon me. O never let Satan p'vail against me, but strenghten
11MAYA226:23	Hp255	man shall bee a meanes to strenghten my inner-man
HOUSE236:21	H13	To strenghten me in my Distresse

STRENGTH (31) See also STRENGHT, STRENGTH'S

FATHER5:9	H10	To climbe their Climes, I have nor strength, nor skill,
ELEMEN15:2	H284	The Camell hath no strength, thy Bull no force;
HUMOUR32:14	H488	Nor multitude of words, argues our strength;
AGES40:31	~~H210~~	My youth, my best, my strength, my bud, and prime:
SEASONS50:33	H167	Until his head be gray, and strength be gone,
SEASONS51:26	H202	Which notes, when youth, and strength, have past their prime,
MASSYR60:20	H285	And either by compound, or else by strength,
MASSYR64:30	H454	Whether her wealth, or yet her strength was most;
MASSYR64:33	H457	And for her strength, how hard she was to gain,
MASSYR67:29	H575	The coward King, whose strength lay in his walls,
MPERS73:10	H797	Cut off in's wickednesse, in's strength, and prime.
MPERS74:35	H858	But strength {men} against those walls was {were} of no use;
MPERS75:8	H869	With all the Cities strength they him betrust,
MPERS~~79:13~~	H1035	To cross the sea such strength he found too weak,
MPERS~~85:30~~	H1306	Whose forces {strength} by their {*Grecians*} helpe were {was}
MGREC109:21	H2280	And tenders him the strength of all his lands, {land;}
MGREC120:30	H2767	And 'gainst *Perdicas,* all their strength combine.
DUBART153:2	H6	But knowing th' taske so great, and strength but small,
DAVID159:20	H35	In mid'st of strength not succoured at all:
VANITY160:40	H50	Nor strength nor wisdome, nor fresh youth shall fade,
TDUDLEY165:28	H30	Who spent his state, his strength, & years with care
CONTEM168:10	H19	Thy strength, and stature, more thy years admire,
CONTEM169:3	H45	Hath strength, thy shining Rayes once to behold?
CONTEM171:30	H132	Nor youth, nor strength, nor wisdom spring again
CONTEM171:35	H136	Because their beauty and their strength last longer
CONTEM173:35	H199	In knowledg ignorant, in strength but weak,
SICKNES178:32	H15	Our strength doth waste, our time doth hast,
CHILDRN185:11	H37	And as his wings increase in strength,
MEDDM200:19	Hp279	and strength of the person he bestowes them on, larg

MEDDM200:34   Hp280   he knows is enough for one of twice his strength, much lesse
MEDDM201:1   Hp280   strength he will proportion the load, as god hath his little
STRENGTHENED (1) See also STRENGHTEN
MGREC120:8   H2743   Their friendship may {might} the more be strengthened:
STRENGTH'S (1) [strength is]
MASSYR58:23   ~~H207~~   By prophesie, *Belosus* strength's their hands,
STRESSE (1)
MASSYR64:12   H436   Yeelds to his mercy, and the present stresse;
STRETCH (1)
MGREC108:6   H2222   With wracks, and tortures, every limbe to stretch.
STRETCHED (1)
MEDDM196:18   Hp273   and the shadowes of his euening to be stretched out, lifts vp
STRETCHT (1)
AUTHOR178:6   H16   I stretcht thy joynts to make thee even feet,
STREWN See STROWN
STRICT (1)
REMB236:12   H27   In strict + vpright wayes.
STRICTLY (1)
MGREC106:32   H2166   Are strictly now commanded to adore;
STRIDING (1)
AGES35:33   H19   His hobby striding, did not ride, but run,
STRIFE (16)
AGES37:39   H101   I'd nought to do, 'twixt Prince, {King} and peoples strife.
SEASONS~~49:23~~   H114   Hath envy bred in Kings that were at strife,
MPERS69:10   H632   And so unites two Kingdoms, without strife;
MPERS69:31   H653   Amidst {Among} the tumult, bloud-shed, and the strife,
MPERS77:11   H950   ('Tis thought) through grief and his {this} succeslesse strife.
MPERS85:6   H1282   But he, with his next {second} brother {him} fell at strife,
MPERS~~91:22~~   H1531   But the old Queen implacable in strife,
MGREC~~120:4~~   H2737   For animating the *Athenian* strife:
MGREC122:1   H2824   For this great {sad} strife, he pours out his complaints,
MGREC131:14   H3206   This day twixt these two foes {Kings} ends all the strife,
MGREC133:13   H3301   Unto *Seleuchus,* author of that strife.
MROMAN138:2   H3492   The strife to end, six Brothers doe ingage;
DIALOG143:4   H73   Nor no *Lancastrians,* to renew old strife;
DIALOG~~146:9~~   H197   But could the field alone this cause {strife} decide,
DAVID159:10   H25   And in their deaths {death} was found no parting strife;
SICKNES178:30   H13   For what's this life, but care and strife?
STRIKE (2)
HUMOUR24:37   H186   And how to strike ful sweet, as wel as sharpe.
MERCY188:31   H17   To strike thee with amazing misery;
STRING (1)
CONTEM169:20   H60   They kept one tune, and plaid on the same string,
STRINGS (2) [pl.]
PROLOG7:1   H16   Nor yet a sweet Consort, from broken strings,
MPERS74:27   H850   Three strings to's bow, the least of which is good;
STRIPT (2)
AGES43:23   H318   If *Bias* like, I'm stript unto my skin,
MGREC102:1   H1971   *Darius* stript of all, to *Media* came,
STRIVE (4)
AGES40:22   H203   Some young {new} *Adonis* I do strive to be,

906

MASSYR53:16	H6	Man did not {proudly} strive for Soveraignty,
MGREC~~94:40~~	H1678	And think {strive} to keep his men from off the land,
SIDNEY151:36	~~H75~~	So proudly foolish I, with *Phaeton* strive,

STRIVES (1)

MGREC110:18	H2318	When *Alexander* strives to win the field,

STRIVING (4)

PROLOG7:10	H24	A full requitall of his striving paine:
MGREC119:26	H2716	Striving {And seeks} to stop *Leonatus,* that so
MGREC127:25	H3055	Striving t'uphold his Masters family,
CHILDRN185:7	H33	Striving for more then to do well,

STROAKE (1) [stroke]

MGREC95:27	H1706	No stroake for it he struck, their hearts so quakes.

STROAKES (1) [strokes]

30SEPT227:24	Hp257	and then thy stroakes shall bee welcome, I haue not been

STROAKS (2) [strokes]

SEASONS50:5	H139	With weary stroaks, they take all in their way,
MEDDM199:5	Hp277	doth vsually preceed thunder, and stormes raine, and stroaks

STROKES (1) [pl.]

MERCY189:15	H36	What though, thy strokes full sad & grievous be,

STROKS (1) [strokes]

AGES38:3	H106	My stroks did cause no death {blood}, nor wounds, nor {or}

STRONG (43)

ELEMEN9:9	H43	Set ope those gates, that 'fore so strong was {were} barr'd.
ELEMEN9:14	H48	Though strong limb'd *Vulcan* forg'd it by his skill,
ELEMEN11:12	H132	The rich I oft make poore, the strong I maime,
ELEMEN12:6	H166	Strong forts from *Spanish* and *Italian* braules,
HUMOUR30:26	H418	The strong foundation of the stately frame.
HUMOUR34:15	H570	And the strong ligaments, from hence arise,
AGES37:35	H97	Make strong my selfe, and turne aside weak right.
AGES44:8	H341	I have bin young, and strong, and wise as you,
AGES45:35	H425	My hands and armes, once strong, have lost their might,
AGES46:1	H432	Shal both be broke, by wracking death so strong;
AGES46:23	H454	My strong Redeemer, comming in the skies;
SEASONS48:5	H58	The outside strong, the inside warme and neat.
MASSYR53:21	H11	That mighty Hunter, who in his strong toyls,
MASSYR53:23	H13	The strong foundation of proud *Babel* laid,
MASSYR55:38	H104	The walls so strong, and curiously were {was} wrought;
MASSYR56:3	H109	An hundred gates, it had, of mettall strong.
MASSYR59:26	H250	Their strong wall'd town should suddenly be taken;
MASSYR61:17	H322	And divers Cities, by strong hand did seize,
MASSYR65:37	H502	The wals so strong, that stood so long, now fall;
MASSYR66:24	H530	Which wealth, and strong ambition made so great;
MPERS74:21	H844	His title to make strong omits no thing;
MPERS78:5	H986	His Foot was seventeen hundred thousand strong,
MPERS84:38	H1274	Strong poyson took, and {so} put an end to's dayes.
MPERS91:12	H1520	Til many a Captain fel, both wise, and strong,
MGREC~~102:10~~	H1980	The firm foundations, {strong Foundation} and the lofty spires;
MGREC108:20	H2236	And in his Camp strong, and securely lay,
MGREC108:41	H2257	And being an {one} hundred twenty thousand strong,
MGREC122:14	H2839	If once young *Alexander* grow more strong,
MGREC126:10	H3001	Untill the Famine growes exceeding strong.

MGREC127:35	H3065	Enter {Enters} into a combination strong:
MGREC135:30	H3402	The last more strong, and dreadfull, then the rest,
MROMAN137:6	H3457	That wil within these strong built walls reside,
MROMAN139:19	H3547	With *Junius Brutus* rose, and being strong,
DIALOG144:40	H148	I saw strong *Rochel* yeelding to her foe,
CONTEM168:24	H31	And as a strong man, joyes to run a race,
FLESH177:7	H88	The stately Walls both high and strong,
BIRTH179:29	H5	No tyes so strong, no friends so clear and sweet,
CHILDRN186:21	H88	And nurst you up till you were strong,
ELIZB187:8	H16	And time brings down what is both strong and tall.
MEDDM198:25	Hp276	head requires a soft pillow, and a drooping heart a strong
MEDDM201:2	Hp280	he hath his strong men, such as are come to a full stature in
MEDDM202:10	Hp281	beauty full, and some extreamly deformed some so strong
MYSOUL225:2	H6	Thy inward shall waxe strong,

STRONGER (3)

MROMAN138:17	H3507	Much stronger, and more beautifull withall;
DAVID159:12	H27	Stronger then Lions, ramping for their prey.
CONTEM172:1	H138	Because they're bigger, & their bodyes stronger?

STRONGEST (1)

ELEMEN8:6	H4	Which was the strongest, noblest, & the best,

STROWN (1) [strewn]

MGREC102:7	H1977	With showers of Flowers, the streets along are strown,

STRUCK (4)

HUMOUR23:32	H142	That when a Varlet, struck him o're the side,
AGES45:14	H396	fly their Country, through their {struck both with gilt and} dread.
MGREC95:27	H1706	No stroake for it he struck, their hearts so quakes.
SIDNEY149:15	H14	Thy {His} Rhethorick it struck *Polimnia* dead,

STRUCTURE (1)

MASSYR56:19	H125	A structure rare, I should but rudely marre,

STRUMPET (1)

MASSYR58:8	H193	His master like a Strumpet chanc'd to {clad did} spy,

STRUMPETS (1) [pl.]

MGREC103:28	H2039	He at a bold, base {proud} Strumpets, lewd desire;

STUBBORN (2)

AGES38:25	H128	Oft stubborn, peevish, sullen, pout, and cry:
DIALOG144:26	H135	The plague of stubborn incredulity.

STUBBORNNESSE (1)

MGREC108:26	H2242	But he their stubbornnesse full soone {in time} doth quel;

STUCK (2)

MGREC111:17	H2362	His Gallies stuck upon the sand, {flats} and mud;
MYCHILD218:22	Hp244	hath somt. stuck with me, and more it would, by ye vain

STUDIED See STUDYED

STUDIES (1)

AGES46:14	H445	My studies, labours, readings, all are done,

STUDIOUS (1)

AGES37:32	H94	Nor studious was, Kings favours how to buy,

STUDIOVS (1) [studious]

13MAY227:13	H22	I studiovs am what I shall doe

STUDYED (1) [studied]

MYCHILD215:18	Hp240	haue not studyed in this yov read to shew my skill, but to

STUDYING (1)
AGES46:13   H444   Yet studying much, brings wearinesse to th' flesh;
STUFFE (4) [stuff]
PROLOG8:1   H49   This meane and unrefined stuffe {ure} of mine,
AGES37:22   H84   In Rattles, Bables, and such toyish stuffe.
MGREC96:29   H1749   Now least this Gold, and all this goodly stuffe,
MEDDM202:17   Hp282   in them, and they that feed vpon them, may soon Stuffe
STUFFED (1)
MPERS72:20   H768   Flayd him alive, hung up his stuffed skin
STUFFING (1)
MGREC107:35   H2210   And stuffing them with straw, he bundles makes;
STUMP (1)
ELEMEN14:35   H277   bear'st no {nor} grasse, nor {or} plant, nor tree, nor stump.
STUMPS (1) [pl.]
PILGRIM210:16   H16   nor stumps nor rocks cause him to fall
STUPIFYE (1) [stupify]
ELEMEN~~14:10~~   H252   Some kill outright, and some do stupifye:
STURDY (1)
DIALOG147:23   ~~H247~~   And sturdy *Tyburn* loaded till it crack,
STYLE See STILE
STYLES See STILES
SUÆ (1)
SICKNES178:17   H0   *Ætatis suæ,* 19.
SUB-SERVIENT (1)
HUMOUR21:20   H48   But if ye yeeld sub-servient unto me,
SUBDU'D (1) [subdued]
MGREC133:27   H3317   kingdomes {Empire was} were subdu'd by {to} th' *Roman* state.
SUBDUE (4)
ELEMEN9:12   H46   Subdue the earth, and fit it for your graine,
MASSYR54:37   H64   And all the greater *Asia* did subdue;
MASSYR61:14   H319   And *Syria* t' obedience did subdue;
MGREC135:14   H3386   The *Grecian,* them did utterly subdue,
SUBDUED See SUBDU'D
SUBDUES (1)
MROMAN138:32   H3522   And Nations twelve, of *Tuscany* subdues:
SUBJECT (8)
HUMOUR23:29   H139   Their courage, {Courage it} friend, and foe, and subject awes,
AGES38:18   H121   The sins, and dangers I am subject to.
AGES43:35   H330   Subject to all Diseases, {distempers} that's the truth,
SEASONS48:31   ~~H83~~   Some subject, shallow braines, much matter yeelds,
MGREC99:17   H1860   (A loyall Subject to *Darius* Crown)
MGREC136:4   H3417   The Subject was too high, beyond my straine;
MROMAN139:31   H3557   The subject large my mind and body weak,
CONTEM173:36   H200   Subject to sorrows, losses, sickness, pain,
SUBJECTED (3)
MASSYR53:22   H12   Both Beasts and Men subjected to his spoyls.
MGREC105:35   H2128   Might be subjected to his royall hand;
MGREC135:15   H3387   And Millions were subjected unto few:
SUBJECTION (1)
MASSYR61:12   H317   Under subjection by his sword he brings;

SUBJECTS (4) [pl.]
MASSYR58:40 H223 To want no priviledge, Subjects should have,
MPERS79:21 H1047 One King, so many Subjects should possesse;
DIALOG146:4 H192 Contention's {Contention} grown 'twixt Subjects and their
QELIZ156:38 H65 As were the subjects of our *(Pallas)* Queen:
SUBJECTS (1) [pl.; poss.]
AGES45:8 ~~H390~~ A Royall one, by almes from Subjects hands,
SUBJECTS (1) [subject is]
SEASONS53:1 H257 *My Subjects bare, my Brains are {Brain is} bad,*
SUBLIME (3)
HUMOUR28:3 H315 The body dryes, the minde sublime doth smother,
DUBART154:31 H76 Thy haughty stile, and rapted wit sublime,
TDUDLEY166:10 H52 His thoughts were more sublime, his actions wise,
SUBMISSION (1)
MGREC111:4 H2349 Came with submission, from the *Indian* Kings
SUBMIT (3) See also SUBMITT
MGREC109:2 H2259 Those that submit, he doth restore {give them rule} again.
MGREC~~109:5~~ H2264 How to submit their necks at last they're glad.
MGREC109:28 H2287 Thus all the *Indian* Kings, to him submit;
SUBMITS (1)
MGREC106:11 H2145 Such as submits, he doth againe restore,
SUBMITT (2) [submit]
30SEPT227:20 Hp257 but thankfully to submitt him for I trvst it is out of his
2HUSB232:20 H21 Thov knowest did submitt
SUBMITTED (1)
MYCHILD216:10 Hp241 submitted to it & joined to yᵉ chh., at Boston.
SUBSTANCE (3)
FLESH175:25 H25 True substance in variety?
FLESH176:36 H76 Eternal substance I do see,
3LETTER183:26 H28 The substance gone, O me, these are but dreams.
SUBSTANTIALL (1) [substantial]
MEDDM200:9 Hp279 this life, that so they might feed vpon more substantiall food,
SUBSTITUTE (2)
HUMOUR34:13 H568 It is the substitute o'th royal Brain,
MGREC95:24 H1703 His substitute, as fearfull as his master,
SUBTILE (1) [subtle] See also SUBTILL
MGREC115:36 H2555 He was too subtile for his crafty foe,
SUBTILL (1) [subtle] See also SUBTILE
MGREC117:35 H2642 Alleadg'd by those, which {who} by their subtill plea
SUBTILLY (3) [subtly] See also SUBT'LY
ELEMEN18:32 H436 No place so subtilly made, but I get in.
HUMOUR30:7 H399 Those {Whose} cold dry heads, {head} more subtilly doth yeild,
MPERS~~91:37~~ H1551 (To his great grief) most subtilly he slayes:
SUBTILTY (1) [subtlety]
ELEMEN14:29 H271 And how your subtilty would men delude.
SUBTLE (1) See also SUBTILE, SUBTILL
HUMOUR23:7 H117 Thou sayst, thy wits are stai'd, subtle and fine:
SUBT'LY (1) [subtly] See also SUBTILLY
AGES~~45:22~~ H406 And an Usurper subt'ly mount thereon.
SUBVERSION (1)
MPERS77:40 H981 To present losse, future subversion;

SUCCEED (5)
MPERS85:5	H1281	The eldest to succeed, that was his mind.
MPERS92:5	~~H1559~~	Why *Arsames* his brother should succeed,
MGREC100:2	H1886	Where happily in's wars he did succeed;
MGREC131:38	H3230	Which should succeed, at variance they fell,
13MAY226:26	H2	As spring the winter doth succeed

SUCCEEDING (3)
HUMOUR20:20	H12	Had leave to speake, succeeding one the other;
MASSYR53:32	H22	Whom succeeding times a god did call:
MGREC105:27	H2120	Yet that succeeding Kings in safety may

SUCCEEDS (6)
MASSYR62:31	H376	*Senacherib Salmaneser* succeeds,
MPERS85:18	H1294	A second trouble, after this succeeds.
MPERS91:34	~~H1548~~	Great *Artaxerxes* dead, *Ochus* succeeds,
MPERS~~91:35~~	H1549	Succeeds in th' throne his father being gone.
MPERS~~92:5~~	H1563	But why brother 'fore his son succeeds
MGREC134:3	H3336	{Fourth} *Seleuchus* next *Antiochus* succeeds,

SUCCESLESSE (1) [successless]
MPERS77:11	H950	('Tis thought) through grief and his {this} succeslesse strife.

SUCCESS (1)
AGES~~39:21~~	H164	Nor wait til good advice {success} our hopes do crown;

SUCCESSE (8) [success]
MASSYR54:29	H56	Where e're he warr'd he had too good successe,
MPERS76:27	H925	But as before, so now with ill successe,
MPERS77:32	H973	His Fathers ill successe in's enterprise,
MPERS90:30	H1497	The *Greeks* by this successe, incourag'd so,
MGREC94:23	H1661	He offer'd, and for good successe did pray
MGREC127:18	H3048	In divers battels, he had good successe,
2HUSB232:32	H33	Lord gravnt thov good Successe
ACK235:15	H15	And hope thov'st given of good successe,

SUCCESSES (1) [pl.]
MEDDM203:34	Hp284	shew great ingratitude after their successes, but he that

SUCCESSION (1)
MGREC133:7	H3295	A little now, how the Succession run:

SUCCESSLESS See SUCCESLESSE

SUCCESSOR (1)
MASSYR63:18	H403	*Ben. Merodach,* Successor to this King,

SUCCESSORS (1) [pl.]
MGREC133:11	H3299	So three Successors only did remaine;

SUCCOUR (2)
MGREC125:11	H2959	To come and succour {To save the King} her, in this great
MGREC131:19	H3211	Hoping {Hopes} to find succour {succours} in {his} miseries.

SUCCOURED (3)
MASSYR58:32	H215	But with fresh hopes *Belosus* succoured.
DAVID159:20	H35	In mid'st of strength not succoured at all:
13MAY227:4	H13	I'le rvn where I was succoured.

SUCCOURER (1)
WHAT224:16	H16	A Succourer of mee.

SUCCOURLESSE (2) [succourless]
MASSYR64:11	H435	*Iudah's* poor King besieg'd, who {and} succourlesse,
HOUSE236:22	H14	And not to leaue me succourlesse.

SUCCOURS (4) [pl.]

MASSYR61:24	H329	And succours *Ahaz,* yet for *Tiglath's* sake,
MGREC~~119:19~~	H2709	To come and {For succours} to release {relieve} him in his
MGREC126:14	H3005	So succours, and endeavours proves but vaine:
MGREC~~131:19~~	H3211	Hoping {Hopes} to find succour {succours} in {his} miseries.

SUCCOUR'ST (1) [succourest]

THEART229:5	H7	And in due time thou succour'st me

SUCH (160) See also SVCH

PROLOG7:17	H30	For such despight they cast on female wits:
ELEMEN11:25	H145	Such was {is} my fruitfulnesse; and Epithite
ELEMEN12:11	H171	And wonderous high *Olimpus,* of such fame,
ELEMEN13:35	H236	But to such auditours 'twere of no use.
ELEMEN15:11	H293	He knowes such sweets, lyes not in earths dry roots,
ELEMEN15:18	H300	Which by my fatting Nile, doth yeeld such store;
ELEMEN15:22	H304	But {And} such I am, in Rivers, showers and springs;
ELEMEN15:27	H309	Such wealth, but not such like, Earth thou mayst show.
ELEMEN15:27	H309	Such wealth, but not such like, Earth thou mayst show.
ELEMEN17:18	H382	And of my chilling colds, such plenty be;
ELEMEN18:17	H421	And such are Ecchoes, and report o'th gun
ELEMEN18:41	H445	Let such suspend their thoughts, and silent be;
ELEMEN19:4	H449	Next, of my Fowles such multitudes there are;
ELEMEN19:16	H461	Whereof such multitudes have dy'd and fled,
HUMOUR21:31	H59	Nay milk-sops, at such brunts you look but blew,
HUMOUR23:2	H112	The Palsie, Gout, or Cramp, or some such dolor,
HUMOUR24:16	H165	Did ever sober tongue, such language speak?
HUMOUR24:17	H166	Or honestie such ties, unfriendly break?
HUMOUR25:2	H191	Yet do abhorre, such timerarious deeds,
HUMOUR25:30	H219	To take the wal's a sin, of such {so} high rate,
HUMOUR26:1	H231	But such thou never art, when al alone;
HUMOUR26:2	H232	Yet such, when we al four are joyn'd in one.
HUMOUR26:3	H233	And when such thou art, even such are we.
HUMOUR26:3	H233	And when such thou art, even such are we.
HUMOUR26:30	H260	For of such glory I shal thee bereave;
HUMOUR28:24	H336	Of such as to the Sanguine are inclin'd,
HUMOUR28:37	H349	Such venome lyes in words, though but a blast,
HUMOUR29:21	H372	To play such furious pranks I am too wise;
HUMOUR35:2	H598	Such premises wil force a sad conclusion,
AGES35:31	H17	Such cold mean flowers (as these) blossome {the spring puts
AGES37:22	H84	In Rattles, Bables, and such toyish stuffe.
AGES38:2	H105	But for an Apple, Plumbe, or some such prize,
AGES39:10	H153	Mine {My} education, and my learning's {learning} such,
AGES40:28	H209	Such wretch, such monster am I; but yet more,
AGES40:28	H209	Such wretch, such monster am I; but yet more,
AGES41:26	H243	Such {My} empty seed should yeeld a better crop.
AGES42:22	H280	Such scum, as Hedges, and High-wayes do yeeld,
AGES43:14	H307	Of such as might my son, {Competitors} or his {as might in
AGES44:2	H335	What you have been, ev'n such have I before,
AGES44:28	H361	Such private changes oft mine eyes have seen,
AGES46:18	H449	In my dark house, such kindred I have store,
SEASONS~~51:19~~	H194	Nor could that temp'rate Clime such difference make,
MASSYR55:22	H88	Taking a towne, such valour she did show,

MASSYR55:32	H98	And that her worth, deserved no such blame,
MASSYR56:28	H134	Her Camells, Chariots, Gallyes in such number,
MASSYR57:34	H179	And such as care not, what befals their fames,
MASSYR59:37	H261	When *Jonah* for their sins denounc'd such {those} woes;
MASSYR60:9	H274	Thus {Such} was the {his} promise bound, since first {which} he
MASSYR60:37	H302	Who to be rid of such a guest, was glad;
MASSYR64:27	H451	Such was the scituation of this place,
MASSYR66:4	H510	Was nothing, but such gastly meditation;
MPERS69:18	H640	Are fit for such, whose eares for fables itch;
MPERS70:33	H704	Using such taunting words as she thought good.
MPERS74:25	H848	That by such steps to Kingdoms often climbs {clime}.
MPERS75:13	H874	But who dare venture such a stake for th' game;
MPERS77:21	H962	The first begun, and finish'd in such hast,
MPERS77:23	H964	But for the last he made such preparation,
MPERS77:30	H971	And *Greece* such wondrous triumphs ne're had made.
MPERS78:15	H996	These {Such} his Land Forces were, then next, a Fleet
MPERS79:13	H1035	To cross the sea such strength he found too weak,
MPERS83:8	H1196	Unto such height did grow his cruelty,
MPERS83:23	H1211	Such Justice then, in *Persia* {*Persian* court} did remain, {reign.}
MPERS84:15	H1251	For such ingratitude, did *Athens* show
MPERS84:17	H1253	Such entertainment {royal bounty} with this {his} Prince he
MPERS85:13	H1289	That for such gracelesse wretches she did groan,
MPERS88:16	H1409	Which did such courage to the *Grecians* bring,
MPERS88:36	H1429	And heaps on heaps, such multitudes they laid,
MPERS89:27	H1461	Such terrour on the *Persians* then did fall,
MPERS89:31	H1465	But Kings ne're want such as can serve their will,
MPERS91:10	H1518	The Kings {on such} conditions they are forc't to take; {as King
MPERS91:27	H1541	Such as would know at large his warrs and reign,
MPERS92:30	H1588	Yet in these {such} differences, we may behold; {be bold,}
MGREC94:30	H1668	To lift his hand, 'gainst such a Monarchy.
MGREC96:2	H1722	For since the world, was no such Pageant seen.
MGREC96:24	H1744	Then such a world of Wagons did appear,
MGREC101:7	H1932	(Nor was such match, in all the world beside)
MGREC103:21	H2032	For such revolters false, what Prince will {King can} trust:
MGREC105:24	H2117	And not to pardon such disloyalty,
MGREC106:11	H2145	Such as submits, he doth againe restore,
MGREC106:18	H2152	Such country there, nor yet such people finde.
MGREC106:18	H2152	Such country there, nor yet such people finde.
MGREC106:24	H2158	And not beseeming such a dignity;
MGREC106:28	H2162	No ways becomming such a mighty King;
MGREC106:31	H2165	And such as shew'd but reverence before,
MGREC109:3	H2260	Those that {Such as} doe not, both they, {them} and theirs, are
MGREC110:5	H2305	Had *Alexander* such resistance seen,
MGREC112:25	H2411	His silence, guilt was, of such consequence,
MGREC113:8	H2435	Such torments great, as wit could first {worst} invent,
MGREC116:6	H2566	Least {Lest} of such like, their Father chance to sup:
MGREC116:28	H2594	For those that {such as} pleas'd him: had both wealth and
MGREC123:32	H2896	Such as his father had advanc'd to place,
MGREC124:10	H2915	All such as he suspected to him true.
MGREC124:10	H2915	Such friends away as for his Interest makes
MGREC125:25	H2975	Bids chuse her death, such kindnesse she'l afford:

MGREC126:16	H3007	will not heare {Her foe would give no Ear}, such is his hate.
MGREC127:17	H3047	Such as nor {no} threats, nor favour could acquire;
MGREC129:7	H3121	To render up such kingdomes as he had
MGREC~~133:25~~	H3315	Such riches too As Rome did never see:
MROMAN138:33	H3523	To such rude triumphs, as young *Rome* then had,
DIALOG142:32	H61	Such is her poverty, yet shall be found
DIALOG143:36	H105	From *Beelzebub* himself, such language heare?
DIALOG145:2	H151	Such cruelty as all reports have past.
DIALOG145:19	H168	One saith its he, the other no such thing.
DIALOG145:28	H177	Which by their prudence stood them in such stead,
DIALOG147:14	H240	Copes, Rochets, Crossiers, and such {empty} trash,
DIALOG147:26	H250	O mother, can you weep, and have such Peeres.
DIALOG147:31	H255	Out of all mists, such glorious dayes will {shall} bring,
DIALOG147:34	H258	Thy Church and Weal, establish'd in such manner,
SIDNEY149:31	~~H23~~	Which shewes, thy worth was great, thine honour such,
SIDNEY150:2	H27	Found *Cupids* Dame, had never such a Gin;
SIDNEY150:12	H37	Such were prejudicate, and did not look:
SIDNEY~~150:12~~	H40	Which shews his worth was great, his honour such,
SIDNEY150:17	~~H49~~	Then let such Crowes as I, thy praises sing,
SIDNEY151:1	~~H69~~	Such prince as he, his race should shortly end:
SIDNEY151:2	~~H69~~	If such Stars as these, sad presages be,
SIDNEY151:3	~~H69~~	I wish no more such Blazers we may see;
SIDNEY151:4	~~H69~~	But thou art gone, such Meteors never last,
SIDNEY151:7	~~H69~~	That such an omen once was in our land,
SIDNEY151:17	~~H69~~	When such a *Hero* shoots him out o'th' field,
SIDNEY151:21	H71	But now into such Lab'rinths am I led
SIDNEY152:12	H81	I to be eas'd of such a task was glad.
QELIZ156:12	H39	If *France* had ever hop'd for such a Queen;
QELIZ156:18	H45	Come shew me such a Phoenix if you can;
QELIZ156:35	H62	Had ever Prince such Counsellors as she?
QELIZ156:37	H64	Such Souldiers, and such Captaines never seen,
QELIZ156:37	H64	Such Souldiers, and such Captaines never seen,
QELIZ157:36	H104	Let such, as say our sex is void of reason,
QELIZ157:38	H106	But happy *England,* which had such a Queen,
QELIZ158:3	H112	No more shall rise or set such {so} glorious Sun,
QELIZ158:12	H121	*On neither tree did grow such Rose before,*
VANITY160:20	H30	Such stoicks are but stocks, such teaching vain:
VANITY160:20	H30	Such stoicks are but stocks, such teaching vain:
TDUDLEY165:19	H21	Such as in life, no man could justly deem.
TDUDLEY166:11	H53	Such vanityes he justly did despise.
CONTEM170:17	H89	But no such sign on false *Cain's* offering;
FLESH176:41	H81	Nor such like trash which Earth doth hold,
FLESH177:4	H85	But such as Angels heads infold.
FLESH177:12	H93	Such as no Eye did e're behold,
1HUSB180:29	H8	My love is such that Rivers cannot quench,
1HUSB180:31	H10	Thy love is such I can no way repay,
1LETTER181:12	H10	His warmth such frigid colds did cause to melt.
VERSES184:8	H12	Such is my debt, I may not say forgive,
VERSES184:10	H14	Such is my bond, none can discharge but I,
CHILDRN185:36	H62	My throbs such now, as 'fore were never:
1SIMON188:9	H10	Such was his will, but why, let's not dispute,

2SIMON195:9	Hp271	Such as they are I bequeath to you, Small legacys are accept^d
MEDDM195:26	Hp272	of all and he that makes such improvment is wise as well as
MEDDM200:21	Hp279	therfore god cuts their garments short, to keep them in such
MEDDM200:35	Hp280	father (who knowes our mould) lay such afflictions vpon his
MEDDM201:2	Hp280	his strong men, such as are come to a full stature in Christ,
MEDDM201:26	Hp281	Contrary ends, the one holds fast, the other puts forward, such
MEDDM203:16	Hp283	lest he meet wth such tossings that may cause him to long for
MEDDM204:28	Hp285	that is lower then he is and if he se, that such a one beares
MEDDM206:35	Hp288	may also be a support to such as haue or had wicked parents,
PILGRIM210:41	H41	Such lasting ioyes, shall there behold
MYCHILD218:5	Hp243	such a God as I worship in Trinity, + such a Sav^r as I rely
MED223:3	Hp250	should I doubt any more wⁿ thov hast given me such assured
MED223:10	Hp250	he my head. Such priviledges had not ye word of Truth made
SON231:6	H18	From such as 'fore nere saw his face.

SUCK (1)

MEDDM200:7	Hp279	they wil either wipe it off, or else suck down sweet and

SUCKING (1)

MEDDM200:10	Hp279	are so childishly sottish that they are still huging and sucking

SUDDEN (2)

MPERS73:13	H800	Childlesse *Cambyses,* on the sudden dead,
MPERS88:31	H1424	Who knowes the sudden change made by this chance;

SUDDENLY (7)

HUMOUR27:39	H310	So suddenly, the body all is fir'd:
MASSYR57:17	~~H164~~	How he thus suddenly should be thus small?
MASSYR~~57:18~~	H165	So suddenly should loose so great a state,
MASSYR59:26	H250	Their strong wall'd town should suddenly be taken;
MPERS87:41	H1393	When suddenly their Scouts come in and cry,
MGREC115:28	H2547	His service great now's suddenly forgot,
CONTEM174:17	H216	But suddenly a storm spoiles all the sport,

SUE (4)

HUMOUR32:39	H513	The Monarchs bend, and sue, but for my grace;
MASSYR66:16	H522	All Vassals, at his hands, for grace must sue;
MPERS90:15	~~H1484~~	Unto the *Spartan* Admirall did sue,
MROMAN137:9	H3460	They to their neighbours sue, for a supply;

SUES (3)

MPERS89:22	H1456	And sues for peace, that they his friends remain;
MGREC98:34	H1836	By his Embassadours now sues for peace:
MGREC101:4	H1929	And now for peace he sues, as once before,

SUFFER (5)

HUMOUR32:27	H501	(Although my name do suffer detriment)
AGES~~45:10~~	H392	And worthy {better} ones, put to {suffer} extremity:
MGREC112:30	H2416	Must suffer, not for what he did, but thought:
MGREC115:11	H2520	Because he let {He suffer, his friend} *Ephestion* to dye.
MGREC120:15	H2750	To suffer them goe on, as they begun,

SUFFER'D (1) [suffered]

MROMAN140:6	H3569	No more I'le do, sith I have suffer'd wrack,

SUFFERED (4)

MASSYR60:5	H270	But suffered, with {their} goods to go elsewhere,
MASSYR65:24	H489	His Son three months he suffered to reign,
MGREC114:17	H2487	The next of worth, that suffered after these,
MYCHILD216:21	Hp241	observed this y^t he hath never suffered me long to sitt loose

SUFFERING (1)

MGREC115:21   H2540   (Not suffering her to meddle in {with} the State)

SUFFERS (1)

MASSYR60:29   H294   *Arbaces* suffers all, and all he takes.

SUFFICE (8)

ELEMEN13:6   H207   Will not my goodly face, your rage suffice?

ELEMEN13:30   H231   Then dearth prevailes, that Nature to suffice,

ELEMEN16:31   H354   These be my benefits which may suffice:

HUMOUR21:5   H33   It shal suffice, to tel {shew} you what I am:

MASSYR57:18   ~~H165~~   This answer may suffice, whom it wil please,

MASSYR~~57:36~~   H181   It is enough {may suffice}, if all be true that's past,

MGREC122:9   H2834   For all that should be said, let this suffice,

SIDNEY152:28   H97   *His praise is much, this shall suffice my pen,*

SUFFICIENT (3)

MPERS75:18   ~~H878~~   But yet thou has sufficient recompence,

MGREC124:5   H2910   Straight furnisht him with a sufficient aide,

HOUSE236:32   H24   But yet sufficient for us left.

SUGAR (3)

ELEMEN16:23   H346   Nor yet of Salt, and Sugar, sweet and smart,

MEDDM196:30   Hp274   fruits that are best preserued wth sugar, those parents are wise

30SEPT227:26   Hp257   p^rserved wth sugar then brine, yet will he p^rserve me to his

SUGAR'D (1) [sugared]

PROLOG6:26   H10   Great *Bartas* sugar'd lines doe but read o're;

SUGGEST (1)

MASSYR57:29   H174   We may suggest our thoughts, but cannot tel;

SUGGESTED See SVGGESTED

SUIT (8)

AGES36:3   H27   His Suit of Crimson, and his Scarfe of Green:

AGES39:25   H168   So affable that I do {can} suit each mind;

AGES40:19   H200   For sure my suit more then my vertues shine;

MPERS82:25   H1172   Some years by him in this vain suit was spent,

MPERS91:4   H1512   With suit, their force, {Arms} against his {their} foes be bent;

2LETTER181:33   H3   But stay this once, unto my suit give ear,

RESTOR230:8   H23   But graunted hath my Suit.

2HUSB232:5   H6   O hearken Lord vnto my suit

SUITABLE See SUTABLE

SUITED (1)

MGREC119:21   H2711   (Which at this time well suited his desires)

SUITOUR (1)

MGREC119:8   H2698   But *Cleopatra,* this suitour did deny,

SUITS (2) [pl.]

AGES38:7   H110   I had no Suits at law, neighbours to vex.

DIALOG147:40   H264   Then bribes shall cease, and suits shall not stick long,

SUITS (1) v.

MGREC102:4   H1974   Which *Alexander* deals, as suits his pleasure.

SULLEN (2)

AGES38:25   H128   Oft stubborn, peevish, sullen, pout, and cry:

CONTEM170:18   H90   With sullen hateful looks he goes his wayes.

SULPHERY (1)

ELEMEN10:28   H103   There's none more strange then *Ætna's* sulphery mount

SUM (3)

MPERS78:36	H1017	Which mighty sum, all wondred to behold.
TDUDLEY165:24	H26	But now or never I must pay my Sum;
VERSES184:2	H6	The principle might yield a greater sum,

SUMMER (9)

ELEMEN10:23	H98	The Summer ripening season I do claime;
SEASONS46:30	H6	The Winter, Summer, Autumne, and the Spring,
SEASONS48:37	H88	*Summer.*
SEASONS48:38	H89	When Spring had done, then {the} Summer must {did} begin,
SEASONS50:29	H163	The Summer's {Summer seems but} short, the beauteous
SEASONS51:18	H192	Which shewes, nor Summer, Winter, nor the Spring,
DUBART153:12	H16	If Summer, or my Autumne age, doe yeeld
CONTEM173:30	H195	And thus they pass their youth in summer season,
MYCHILD217:37	Hp243	+ yᵉ Earth, the order of all things night and day, Summer

SUMMER'S (1) [summer is]

SEASONS50:29	H163	The Summer's {Summer seems but} short, the beauteous

SUMMON (1)

AGES42:26	H284	The early Cock, did summon but in vaine,

SUMMONED See SUMON'D

SUMMONS (1)

MGREC120:26	H2763	And summons him, to answer these {his} complaints;

SUMMUM (1)

VANITY160:25	H35	That *summum Bonum* which may stay my mind?

SUMON'D (1) [summoned]

MYSOUL225:11	H15	Thy Sinns shall ne'r bee sumon'd vp

SUMPTUOUS (7)

MASSYR66:23	H529	His sumptuous buildings passes all conceit,
MPERS83:37	H1225	Which done, a sumptuous feast; makes like a King
MGREC102:33	H2003	The sumptuous Palace of Queen *Hester* {*Esther*} here,
MGREC111:7	H2352	His furniture most sumptuous to behold;
MGREC115:15	H2530	Upon a sumptuous monument to spend:
MGREC120:36	H2773	His sumptuous monument long time did stand;
CONTEM174:31	H228	Their sumptuous monuments, men know them not,

SUN (55) See also SUN'S

FATHER5:5	H6	Of fairer Dames, the sun near saw the face, /of the
ELEMEN9:28	H62	The Sun, an Orbe of Fire was held of old,
ELEMEN10:21	H96	When in conjunction with the sun, yet {do} more,
ELEMEN12:30	H190	Send forth your well man'd ships, where sun doth rise.
ELEMEN12:40	H200	Which guides, when Sun, nor Moon, nor Stars do shine.
ELEMEN17:21	H385	Till Sun release, their ships can saile no more.
HUMOUR33:7	H521	As at noon day to tel, the Sun doth shine.
AGES35:32	H18	Before the Sun hath throughly warm'd {heat} the clime.
SEASONS47:30	H45	The Sun now keeps his posting residence
SEASONS47:31	H46	The Sun in *Taurus* keeps his residence,
SEASONS48:1	H54	That when the Sun (on's love) the earth doth shine,
SEASONS48:11	H64	The sun now enters, loving *Geminie,*
SEASONS49:7	H98	And {Then} retrograde, now is {must be} my burning Sun.
SEASONS49:32	H121	Viewing the Sun by day, the Moon by night,
SEASONS49:39	H132	The Sun in {thro} Leo now hath {takes} his carrear,
SEASONS50:12	H146	For yet {For much,} the South-ward Sun abateth not;
SEASONS51:22	H198	In *Scorpio* resideth now the Sun,

SEASONS51:29	H205	There rests, untill the Sun give it a birth:
SEASONS51:36	H212	This month's {moneth} the Sun {Sun's} in *Sagitarius,*
SEASONS51:41	H217	No Sun, to lighten their obscurity;
SEASONS52:18	H233	*December* is the {my} first, and now the Sun
SEASONS52:26	H241	In *Aquarias,* now keeps the loved {long wisht} Sun,
SEASONS52:34	H249	In *Pisces* now the golden Sun doth shine,
SEASONS52:37	H252	And some warm glances from the Sun {his face} are felt,
MPERS74:4	H829	Upon a Green to meet, by rising Sun;
MPERS81:24	H1132	That whilst the Sun did run his endlesse course,
MPERS87:11	H1367	And others to be warm'd by this new sun,
MGREC96:8	H1728	(For Sun and Fire the *Persians* worship most)
MGREC101:33	H1958	The Sun should witnesse of his valour be:
MGREC105:37	H2130	As men, the rising, setting Sun shall see.
DIALOG146:37	H223	But now the Sun in's brightnesse shall appear,
SIDNEY151:41	H75	He bad me drive, and he would hold the Sun;
QELIZ156:15	H42	Since first the Sun did run, his ne'r runn'd race,
QELIZ158:3	H112	No more shall rise or set such {so} glorious Sun,
CONTEM168:15	H23	Then higher on the glistering Sun I gaz'd,
CONTEM172:12	H148	And if the sun would ever shine, there would I dwell.
FLESH177:2	H83	More glorious then the glistring Sun;
FLESH177:17	H98	Nor Sun, nor Moon, they have no need,
1LETTER181:10	H8	My sun is gone so far in's Zodiack,
1LETTER181:22	H20	I wish my Sun may never set, but burn
MEDDM196:17	Hp273	drought of the day, when he perceiues his sun apace to decline
MEDDM198:21	Hp276	There is no new thing vnder ye Sun there is nothing that can
MEDDM200:25	Hp279	the leavlesse trees and dry stocks (at the approach of the Sun)
MEDDM200:28	Hp279	when the Sun of righteoussnes shall appear those dry bones
MEDDM201:31	Hp281	A shadow in the parching sun, & a shelter in a blustering
MEDDM202:21	Hp282	Sometimes the sun is only shadowed by a cloud, that wee
MEDDM202:29	Hp282	when ye morning (wch is the appointed time) is come the Sun
MEDDM206:6	Hp287	We se in the firmament there is but one Sun, among a
MEDDM206:9	Hp287	one Sun, so is it in the Church both militant and triumphant,
MEDDM206:10	Hp287	but one Christ, who is the Sun of righteousnes, in the midest of
MEDDM206:15	Hp287	from that glorious sun that inlightens all in all, and if some of
MEDDM207:36	Hp289	resurrection, and the sun approaching, of the appearing of the
MEDDM207:36	Hp289	and the sun approaching, of the appearing of the Sun of
MEDDM208:30	Hp290	it hath stayd the Course of the Sun raised the dead, cast out
PILGRIM210:7	H7	The burning sun no more shall heat

SUN-BEAMES (1) [pl.]

SEASONS48:15	H68	All flowers before the {with his} sun-beames now discloses,

SUN-BURNT (1)

ELEMEN14:38	H280	Or else thy sun-burnt face, and gaping chapps;

SUNDER (1)

ELEMEN8:14	H12	The Fire, the forced Aire, in sunder crack;

SUNDRY (5) See also SVNDRY

ELEMEN11:29	H149	To tell what sundry fruits my fat soyle yeelds,
ELEMEN16:5	H328	My sundry Seas, Black, White, and Adriatique
MGREC109:4	H2261	His warrs with sundry nations I'le omit,
MEDDM198:17	Hp276	vnder all, Satan that great Angler hath his sundry baits for
MEDDM198:18	Hp276	sundry tempers of men, wch they all catch gre͞dily at but few

SUNG (2)
| AGES37:16 | H78 | With weary armes, she danc'd, and *By, By,* sung, |
| MASSYR59:6 | H230 | Who revelling in Cups, sung care away, |

SUNK (2)
| MGREC112:40 | H2426 | Sunk in despair, without hope of releif; |
| QELIZ156:24 | H51 | She ract, she sackt, she sunk his Armadoe; |

SUNKE (2) [sunk]
| AGES43:5 | H300 | Opprest, and sunke, and sact, {stav'd} all in my way; |
| DIALOG143:11 | H80 | *Spaines* braving Fleet a second time is sunke, |

SUNKEN (1)
| DIALOG146:31 | H217 | Your sunken bowels gladly would refresh: |

SUN-LIKE (1)
| AGES44:39 | H372 | When it had lost that radiant Sun-like spark, |

SUN'S (1) [sun is]
| SEASONS51:36 | H212 | This month's {moneth} the Sun {Sun's} in *Sagitarius,* |

SUNS (1) [pl.] See also SVNS
| MGREC101:23 | H1948 | The Firmament two Suns cannot contain; |

SUN-SHINE (2) See also SVN-SHINE
| SEASONS46:34 | H10 | With smiling Sun-shine face, and garments {somewhat} green, |
| 2LETTER182:13 | H19 | Or every mote that in the sun-shine hops, |

SUP (2)
| MGREC116:6 | H2566 | Least {Lest} of such like, their Father chance to sup: |
| MGREC127:3 | H3033 | Which she had often made others to sup: |

SUPERBUS (1)
| MROMAN139:10 | H3538 | *Tarquinius Superbus,* the last |

SUPERFLUOUS (1)
| SEASONS47:10 | H26 | The Gardner, now superfluous branches lops, |

SUPERIOUR (1)
| PROLOG6:20 | H5 | For my mean Pen, are too superiour things, |

SUPERSTITIOUS (1)
| DIALOG143:30 | H99 | With foolish superstitious adoration; |

SUPLICAT^N. (1)
| MYCHILD215:33 | Hp241 | heart, and made my Suplicat^n. to the most High who sett me |

SUPPLANTER (1)
| DIALOG143:29 | H98 | Idolatry, supplanter of a Nation, |

SUPPLE (1)
| AGES35:20 | H6 | Unstable, supple, moist, and cold's his Naure. |

SUPPLEMENT (1)
| MGREC122:15 | H2840 | But that her Husband serve for supplement, |

SUPPLIANT See SUPPLYANT

SUPPLIES See SUPPLYES

SUPPLICATION See SUPLICAT^N.

SUPPLY (10)
ELEMEN12:36	H196	That with lesse cost, neare home, supplyes {supply} your
ELEMEN15:14	H296	If I supply, his heart and veines rejoyce;
ELEMEN18:9	H413	The famist, thirsty man, that craves supply:
MGREC99:21	H1864	That *Greece* must {was forc'd to} yeeld a fresh supply againe;
MGREC108:39	H2255	His {A} third supply, *Antipater* now sent,
MGREC110:41	H2345	His fourth, and last supply, was hither sent,
MGREC124:1	H2906	By these, and all, to grant him some supply,
MGREC124:10	H2917	That no supply by these here might be lent,

MROMAN137:9　H3460　They to their neighbours sue, for a supply;
MEDDM209:19　Hp291　wthin it self, but what it wants, another shall supply, that

SUPPLYANT (1) [suppliant]
DIALOG142:33　H62　A supplyant for your help, as she is bound.

SUPPLYES (2) [supplies]
ELEMEN12:36　H196　That with lesse cost, neare home, supplyes {supply} your
MGREC102:26　H1996　*Antipater,* from *Greece,* sends great {fresh} supplyes;

SUPPORT (9)
AGES44:21　H354　Provides a staffe for {then} to support his age.
MGREC96:14　H1734　Support a party coloured canopy.
MEDDM198:26　Hp276　support,
MEDDM204:2　Hp284　of former deliuerances, is a great support in present
MEDDM206:35　Hp288　may also be a support to such as haue or had wicked parents,
MYCHILD217:3　Hp242　by it: It hath been no small support to me in times of Darknes
JULY223:26　Hp251　y^t it may bee a support to me when I shall haue occasion
11MAYB228:28　Hp259　it ye more tedious, but it pleased ye Lord to support my heart
RESTOR230:1　H16　And wth his staffe did thee support

SUPPORTING (1)
MEDDM208:24　Hp290　like the reeds of Egipt that peirce insteed of supporting like

SUPPORTS (1)
MEDDM198:2　Hp275　hath sutable comforts and supports for his children according

SUPPOS'D (2) [supposed]
MASSYR57:13　H160　But is suppos'd to be that *Amraphel,*
MGREC96:18　H1738　Would think {Suppos'd} he neither thought {meant} to fight nor

SUPPOSE (4)
ELEMEN17:37　H401　I doe suppose, you'l yeeld without controle;
MASSYR59:36　H260　His Father was then King (as we suppose)
MPERS92:10　H1568　But as 'tis thought, {most suppose} in him had {did} *Cyrus* end:
MGREC99:35　H1878　But in no hostile way (as I suppose)

SUPPOSED (2) See also SUPPOS'D
MGREC111:37　H2382　And set his Crown on his supposed head;
MYCHILD217:16　Hp243　and refreshing wch I supposed most of the servants of God

SUPPREST (1)
MGREC127:4　H3034　Now many Townes in *Macedon* supprest,

SURE (30)
PROLOG7:11　H25　Art can doe much, but this maxime's most sure,
PROLOG7:21　H33　But sure the antick *Greeks* were far more milde,
ELEMEN12:20　H180　Poysons sure antidote lyes in his horne.
ELEMEN17:12　H376　Some say I swallowed up (sure 'tis a notion)
HUMOUR21:26　H54　In dangers to account himself more sure,
HUMOUR26:22　H252　I am as sure, the natural from me;
AGES40:19　H200　For sure my suit more then my vertues shine;
AGES43:16　H308　Then thought my state firm founded sure to last,
SEASONS51:12　H186　Sure at this time, Time first of all began,
MASSYR55:14　H80　Sure from this fiction, *Dagon* first began,
MPERS73:28　H813　But so or no, sure tis, they won the day.
MGREC95:40　H1719　Sure its {much} beyond my time, and little Art;
MGREC96:3　H1723　Oh {Sure} 'twas a goodly sight, there to behold;
MGREC96:33　H1753　For sure *Darius* thought, at the first sight,
MGREC96:38　H1758　Which made {To make} his over-throw more fierce, and sure.
MGREC101:14　H1939　And till all this be wel perform'd, and sure,

MGREC118:38	H2687	And *Ptolomy,* next sure of *Egypt* makes.
DIALOG143:19	H88	For wants, sure some I feele, but more I feare,
DIALOG148:22	H287	For sure the day of your redemption's nigh;
DUBART153:40	H44	Sure liberall Nature, did with Art not small,
VANITY160:13	H23	Sure if on earth, it must be in those parts;
CONTEM167:33	H9	I wist not what to wish, yet sure thought I,
CONTEM168:3	H13	Sure he is goodness, wisdome, glory, light,
FLESH177:15	H96	Of Life, there are the waters sure,
SICKNES179:6	H26	to make Salvation sure,
BIRTH179:30	H6	But with deaths parting blow is sure to meet.
MEDDM204:15	Hp284	must be sure to shun the company of the first.
MEDDM205:20	Hp286	must be sure to carry a certificate from the Court of
MEDDM207:29	Hp289	may be sure of an euer lasting habitation that fades not away.
SAMUEL228:9	H10	For sure thy Grace on him is shown.

SURELY (4)

HUMOUR33:30	H544	And surely the Souls {Soul} sensative here lives,
MPERS92:7	H1565	It may be thought, surely he had no Son,
1HUSB180:23	H2	If ever two were one, then surely we.
1LETTER181:5	H3	If two be one, as surely thou and I,

SUREST (1)

| MPERS87:36 | H1388 | He surest {safest} was, when furthest {farthest} out o'th' way. |

SURLY (1)

| MGREC121:8 | H2786 | *Perdicas* surly carriage, and his pride, |

SURMOUNT (3)

AGES37:27	H89	Through ignorance, all troubles did surmount.
AGES43:21	H316	And envy gnawes, if any do surmount.
AGES44:32	H365	And like a Cedar, others so surmount,

SURMOVNT (1) [surmount]

| HOURS234:32 | H46 | Whose Blessings thvs surmovnt. |

SURNAM'D (1) [surnamed]

| MGREC134:2 | H3333 | And then *Antiochus* surnam'd the great, |

SURPASSE (2) [surpass]

| ELEMEN11:23 | H143 | In wealth and use I doe surpasse you all, |
| HUMOUR31:22 | H455 | My vertues yours surpasse, without compare: |

SURPASSES (1)

| SEASONS49:35 | H128 | Whose fragrant scent, {smel} all made-perfume surpasses; |

SURPASSING (1)

| DAVID159:24 | H39 | Thy love was wonderfull, passing {surpassing} a man; |

SURPLICES (1) [pl.]

| DIALOG147:13 | H239 | Their Myters, Surplices, and all their tire, |

SURPRIS'D (1) [surprised]

| MASSYR59:8 | H232 | But all {And now} surpris'd, by this unlookt for fright, |

SURPRIZ'D (1) [surprised]

| CHILDRN185:20 | H46 | And be surpriz'd for want of watch, |

SURROUNDED (2)

| MPERS78:4 | H985 | That the large {vast} *Persian* government surrounded; |
| MGREC103:38 | H2049 | (And there with sorrows, fears, and cares surrounded) |

SURVIVE (3)

DIALOG141:25	H24	If I decease, dost think thou shalt survive?
MERCY188:21	H7	And yet survive to sound this wailing tone;
MERCY189:8	H29	No wonder it no longer did survive.

SURVIVER (1) [survivor]
MPERS85:8   H1284   Then the surviver is by *Nothus* slaine;
SURVIVES (1)
AGES40:23   H204   *Sardana Pallas,* now survives in me:
SURVIVING (1)
MGREC113:31   H2458   For *Philip* dead, and his surviving Son,
SURVIVOR See SURVIVER
SUSHA (2)
MGREC127:15   H3045   To keep *Antigonus* from *Susha* still,
MGREC128:20   H3093   And Lord o'th' City {royal} *Susha* did remain.
SUSHAN (6)
MGREC96:26   H1746   As if she'd drawne, whole *Sushan* at her heeles.
MGREC102:27   H1997   He then to *Sushan* goes, with his fresh {new} bands,
MGREC102:39   H2009   From *Sushan,* to *Persapolis* he goes,
MGREC103:6   H2017   Though *Babylon* was rich, and *Sushan* too;
MGREC103:17   H2028   (As first at *Sushan,* and at *Babylon*)
MGREC111:39   H2384   He at the last to royall *Sushan* went;
SUSPECTED (1)
MGREC124:10   H2915   All such as he suspected to him true.
SUSPECTS (2)
MPERS90:20   H1487   The *Greeks* now (as the *Persian* King suspects)
MGREC94:9   H1643   And many more, {all} whom he suspects {or fears} will climbe,
SUSPENCE (1) [suspense]
DIALOG143:17   H86   What *Holland* is, I am in some suspence,
SUSPEND (1)
ELEMEN18:41   H445   Let such suspend their thoughts, and silent be;
SUSPENDED (1)
MPERS84:6   H1234   Alas, she from her Royalty's {Royalty} suspended.
SUSPENSE See SUSPENCE
SUSPICION (1)
MGREC112:23   H2409   Upon suspicion being apprehended,
SUSPITION (2) [suspicion]
MPERS72:2   H754   He after this, saw in a Vision {upon suspition vain},
MPERS83:15   H1203   That from suspition he might be freed,
SUSTAIN (4) See also SUSTAINE
ELEMEN18:8   H412   If my pure Aire, thy sonnes did not sustain.
AGES38:32   H135   What tortures I, in breeding teeth sustain?
MPERS91:28   H1542   What troubles in his house he did sustain,
RESTOR229:28   H11   W^th strenght didst him sustain.
SUSTAIN'D (2) [sustained]
ELEMEN19:26   H471   Where famous *Charles* the fift, more losse sustain'd,
AGES42:25   H283   Great labours, sorrows, crosses I sustain'd.
SUSTAINE (2) [sustain]
MASSYR59:10   H234   The King his Brother leaves, all to sustaine,
MPERS81:16   H1124   And leave them out, the {this} shock {now} for to sustaine,
SUSTAINED See SUSTAIN'D
SUSTINANCE (1)
MPERS90:3   H1477   He sought all sustinance from them to take;
SUTABLE (1) [suitable]
MEDDM198:2   Hp275   God hath sutable comforts and supports for his children

SUTOR (1)
MGREC136:8   H3421   *Ne sutor ultra crepidum,* may write.

SVCH (2) [such]
MYCHILD217:21 Hp243 my self y^t agst svch a promis, svch tasts of sweetnes ye Gates

SVGGESTED (1) [suggested]
MYCHILD218:6 Hp243-4 this hath thovsands of Times been svggested to me, yet

SVN-SHINE (1) [sunshine]
13MAY226:29 H5   At Svn-shine each their joy expresse.

SVNDRY (1) [sundry]
SON231:5   H17   And courtesies of svndry sorts

SVNS (1) [suns]
13MAY226:30 H6   My Svns return'd wth healing wings

SWADLING (1) [swaddling]
SEASONS52:15 H230   In Swadling clouts, like new-born infancy,

SWAINES (2) [swains]
SEASONS49:16 H107   Now go those frolick swaines, the shepheard lad,
MROMAN136:30 H3444 Where Swaines, and rustick Peasants made {kept} their Holds.

SWAINS (1) [pl.]
SEASONS49:22 H113   Blest rustick Swains, your pleasant quiet life,

SWALLOWED (1)
ELEMEN17:12   H376   Some say I swallowed up (sure 'tis a notion)

SWALLOWES (1) [swallows]
ELEMEN17:6   H370   And swallowes Countryes up, ne're seen againe:

SWARMES (1) [swarms]
SEASONS48:17 H70   Now swarmes the busie buzzing {witty,} hony Bee.

SWARTH (2)
HUMOUR20:18 H10   Earth knew her black swarth childe, Water her faire;
HUMOUR28:2   H314   With her uncheerful visage, swarth and wan;

SWARTHY (1)
HUMOUR30:37 H429   Again, you often touch my swarthy hew,

SWAY (6)
ELEMEN13:18 H219   How the Autumnal season I do sway;
ELEMEN16:35 H358   O're childehood, and {ore} Winter, I bear the sway;
HUMOUR21:15 H43   Where Monarch-like I play, and sway alone.
MASSYR66:19 H525   Who had for sixteen hundred years born sway,
MGREC94:15   H1649 Leaves sage *Antipater* at home to sway,
MGREC118:29 H2678 chief opponents who kept off the Crown, {Control'd his sway,}

SWAY'D (1) [swayed]
SIDNEY149:10 H9   Then {As} she that sway'd the Scepter with her hand:

SWEARE (2) [swear]
MGREC114:2   H2470 *Alexander,* to rage, to kill, and sweare,
MROMAN139:23 H3551 And people sweare, ne're to accept of King.

SWEAT (7)
ELEMEN13:11 H212   But what I freely yeeld upon your sweat?
SEASONS49:2   H93   Wiping her {the} sweat from off {of} her brow, that ran,
SEASONS50:25 H159   His sweat, his toyl, his careful, wakeful nights,
DUBART154:14 H59   Who tam'd his foes, in bloud, in skarres {warrs,} and sweat,
CONTEM170:3   H77   To get his bread with pain, and sweat of face:
FEVER220:26   H6   My burning flesh in sweat did boyle
SOREFIT221:22 H8   And how in sweat I seem'd to melt

SWEATING (1)
MEDDM201:23   Hp281   produces these sweating effects,
SWEEP (1)
ELEMEN17:3   H367   Their Cattle, Hay, and Corne, I sweep down current,
SWEET (27)
FATHER5:25   H26   Sweet harmony they keep, yet jar oft times,
PROLOG7:1   H16   Nor yet a sweet Consort, from broken strings,
PROLOG7:7   H21   Nor can I, like that fluent sweet tongu'd *Greek*
ELEMEN12:13   H173   Sweet *Parnassus,* I dote too much on thee,
ELEMEN16:23   H346   Nor yet of Salt, and Sugar, sweet and smart,
ELEMEN18:29   H433   The ruddy sweet sanguine, is like to Aire,
HUMOUR24:37   H186   And how to strike ful sweet, as wel as sharpe.
HUMOUR27:33   H304   My sweet complexion, proves the verity,
HUMOUR27:40   H311   And of the sweet, calme temper, quite bereft,
AGES39:28   H171   Sweet Musick rapteth {raps} my {brave} harmonious Soul,
AGES46:11   H442   Hath yet amongst that sweet, some bitter gall.
SEASONS46:32   H8   Sweet Spring, like man in his minority,
SEASONS48:33   H84   Melodious {Sweet fragrant} Spring, with thy short pittance flye,
MGREC120:4   H2735   *Demosthenes,* that sweet tongu'd oratour.
MGREC121:11   H2789   His sweet demeanour, and his courtesie,
SIDNEY150:38   H65   In sad, sweet verse, thou didst his death deplore;
SIDNEY152:15   H85   Not because, sweet *Sydney's* fame was not dear,
DUBART152:34   H3   Great, deare, sweet *Bartas,* thou art matchlesse knowne;
DUBART154:2   H47   Movelesse, stand charm'd by thy sweet influences,
QELIZ158:10   H119   *Whose sweet perfume fills the all-filling aire,*
CONTEM173:32   H197   Where winter's never felt by that sweet airy legion.
BIRTH179:29   H5   No tyes so strong, no friends so clear and sweet,
1LETTER181:14   H12   Return, return sweet *Sol* from *Capricorn;*
1LETTER181:17   H15   Which sweet contentment yield me for a space,
ELIZB186:35   H7   Farewel sweet babe, the pleasure of mine eye,
MEDDM196:25   Hp273   Sweet words are like hony, a little may refresh, but too much
MEDDM200:7   Hp279   they wil either wipe it off, or else suck down sweet and
SWEET-TONGU'D (1) [sweet-tongued]
CONTEM173:12   H179   The sweet-tongu'd Philomel percht ore my head,
SWEETNES (2) [sweetness]
MYCHILD217:5   Hp242   abundance of Sweetnes and refreshment after affliction and
MYCHILD217:21   Hp243   y^t agst svch a promis, svch tasts of sweetnes ye Gates of Hell
SWEETNESS (1)
CONTEM168:37   H43   Hail Creature, full of sweetness, beauty & delight.
SWEETS (3)
ELEMEN15:11   H293   He knowes such sweets, lyes not in earths dry roots,
CONTEM174:22   H220   Feeding on sweets, that never bit of th' sowre,
MEDDM200:9   Hp279   sweets of this life, that so they might feed vpon more
SWELLING (1)
MASSYR59:20   H244   Which through much rain, then swelling up so high,
SWEPT (3)
MASSYR56:32   H138   The River *Indus* swept them half away,
MPERS92:39   H1597   One deluge came, and swept them all away;
MEDDM197:18   Hp275   That house wch is not often swept makes the cleanly inhabitant
SWERUE (1) [swerve]
WHAT224:3   H3   O never let me from thee swerue

SWIFT (3)

SEASONS52:19	H234	To th' Southward tropick his swift race hath {doth} run;
CONTEM168:31	H37	Thy swift Annual, and diurnal Course,
2LETTER182:1	H7	If in thy swift Carrier thou canst make stay,

SWIFTER (2)

MGREC97:3	H1764	And cast away his Crown, for swifter flight;
DAVID159:11	H26	Swifter then swiftest Eagles, so were they,

SWIFTEST (1)

DAVID159:11	H26	Swifter then swiftest Eagles, so were they,

SWILL (1)

AGES45:22	H404	To see them swill in blood untill they burst.

SWIM (2)

FATHER5:22	H23	That sinke, that swim, that fill, that upwards flye,
AGES36:10	H34	He seems to flye, or swim, and not to ride.

SWIMS (1)

SEASONS49:33	H124	By purling Brooks looking how fishes swims.

SWORD (28)

ELEMEN9:3	H37	My force? your sword, your Pike, your flint and steele,
ELEMEN9:3	H37	My force? your sword, & Gun, your lance of steel
HUMOUR21:23	H51	Then Iron Corslet, 'gainst a sword or dart;
HUMOUR21:41	H69	She loves her sword, only because its gilt;
HUMOUR24:36	H185	He knew {well} how, for to handle, Sword and Harpe,
HUMOUR24:40	H189	Thou sayst I love my sword, because tis {it's} guilt. {gilt,}
HUMOUR29:28	H379	To use thy sword, thy courage, and thy Art,
HUMOUR29:34	H385	And if *Marcellus* bold, be call'd *Romes* sword,
AGES36:15	H39	His Sword by's side, and choler in his eyes;
AGES39:19	H162	The glistring {glitt'ring} Sword, {the Pistol} and wel advanced
MASSYR61:12	H317	Under subjection by his sword he brings;
MASSYR66:1	H507	Where to the sword, all but himself was {were} put,
MPERS70:39	H710	Two *Sythian* bowes, a sword, and target round;
MPERS72:39	H785	But in the way, his sword just vengeance takes.
MPERS82:6	H1153	The other not a hand, nor sword will {would} wave,
MPERS89:38	H1472	And Villaine-like, there puts them {all} to the sword.
MGREC98:20	H1822	Eight thousand by the sword now also dy'd,
MGREC108:13	H2229	But *Alexander* puts them to the sword,
MGREC109:5	H2262	But all fall by his sword, most mercilesse.
MGREC109:37	H2296	But for the rest, his sword advise him should.
MGREC125:24	H2974	A Halter, cup of Poyson, and a Sword,
MGREC126:28	H3019	For Justice sake she being put to th' sword.
MGREC126:38	H3027	His sword unto *Apollo* consecrates:
MGREC131:41	H3233	And with his Sword did pierce his mothers {run her through
MGREC135:1	H3373	Did by his Sword his life soon after send.
DIALOG143:21	H90	Famine, and Plague, two sisters of the Sword,
DIALOG147:5	H231	O cry: the sword of God, and *Gideon:*
DAVID159:8	H23	Did *Saul* with bloodlesse Sword turne back agen:

SWORDS (4)

ELEMEN20:1	H483	Sometimes strange {red} flaming swords, and blazing stars,
MPERS76:4	H902	Sharp wants, not swords, his vallour did oppose;
MGREC100:24	H1908	Fit for to blunt the swords of *Macedon;*
DIALOG148:17	H282	This done, with brandish'd swords, to *Turky* go,

SWORE (1)
MPERS~~83:32~~   H1220   A league of amity, had sworn before. {firmly swore,}
SWORN (1)
MPERS83:32   H1220   A league of amity, had sworn before. {firmly swore,}
SYDNEY (1) See also SIDNEY
SIDNEY152:8   H79   Since *Sydney* had exhausted all their store,
SYDNEY'S (4) [poss.]
SIDNEY151:27   H75   But *Sydney's* Muse, can sing his worthinesse.
SIDNEY152:2   ~~H75~~   For dear regard he had of *Sydney's* state,
SIDNEY152:15   ~~H85~~   Not because, sweet *Sydney's* fame was not dear,
SIDNEY152:21   H90   So *Sydney's* fame, I leave to *England's* Rolls,
SYLVESTER (1)
SIDNEY151:26   H74   And {Which} makes me now with *Sylvester* confesse,
SYMPATHIZE See SIMPATHIZE
SYMPTOMS See SIMPTOMS
SYRENS (1)
ELEMEN16:16   H339   My water *Syrens,* with their guilefull lures:
SYRIA (11)
MASSYR61:14   H319   And *Syria* t' obedience did subdue;
MASSYR61:26   H331   *Syria* he makes a Province of his own.
MASSYR61:35   H340   Through *Syria* now he marcht, none stopt his way,
MASSYR64:22   H446   Which was the losse of *Syria* withall;
MPERS87:17   H1371   Three hundred thousand, yet {he} to *Syria* sent;
MGREC100:14   H1898   In *Syria, Ægypt,* and *Phoenicia;*
MGREC101:10   H1935   With fertile *Ægypt,* and rich *Syria,*
MGREC123:21   H2885   All *Syria,* and, *Phenicia* he wins;
MGREC128:26   H3099   So *Syria* to *Ptolomy* did yeeld;
MGREC133:29   H3319   In *Syria* by his posterity,
MGREC134:17   H3348   Of *Greece,* and *Syria* thus the rule did end,
SYTHIAN (2)
MPERS70:39   H710   Two *Sythian* bowes, a sword, and target round;
MPERS76:18   H916   Or *Sythian* arrows in our sides must stick.
SYTHIANS (4) [pl.]
MPERS70:26   H697   Long after this, he 'gainst the *Sythians* goes,
MPERS75:40   H897   *Darius* on the *Sythians* made a war,
MPERS77:33   H974   Against the *Sythians,* and *Grecians* too,
QELIZ157:8   H76   Feirce *Tomris* (*Cirus* Heads-man, *Sythians* Queen)

T

T (1) [T]
FATHER5:3   H4   Deare Sir, of late delighted with the sight, /T D on the
T' (1) [too]
FEVER221:6   H21   To Glory t' shall bee brovght.
TABLE (1)
HOUSE237:4   H34   Nor at thy Table eat a bitt.
T'ACCOMPLISH (1) [to accomplish]
MGREC93:19   H1616   T'accomplish that, which long before was writ.
TACKLING (1)
ELEMEN12:39   H199   Your Tackling, Anchor, Compasse too, is mine;
TA'EN (1) [taken] See also TA'N, TA'NE, TANE
ELIZB186:37   H9   Then ta'en away unto Eternity.
TAGRA (1)
MGREC125:10   H2958   To leave his Seige at *Tagra* {*Tegea*}, and with speed
TAIL (1)
DIALOG147:11   H237   To root out Prelates, {Popelings} head, tail, branch, and rush.
TAKE (76)
ELEMEN11:13   H133   Not sparing life when I can take the same;
HUMOUR23:34   H144   Take choler from a Prince, what is he more,
HUMOUR25:22   H211   But when thou scorn'st to take the helpe we lend,
HUMOUR25:30   H219   To take the wal's a sin, of such {so} high rate,
HUMOUR27:7   H278   If stil thou take along my Aliment,
HUMOUR27:24   H295   Shal firstly {chiefly} take her {the} place, as is her {my} due,
HUMOUR28:11   H323   All to prevent, this curious care I take;
HUMOUR30:20   H412   You high born (from that lump) then take your flight
HUMOUR35:5   H601   To take her moyst, my moistnesse {moisture} wil be bold;
AGES37:20   H82   My sillinesse did only take delight,
AGES40:4   H185   Sometimes lay wait to take a wealthy purse,
AGES40:18   H199   If any care I take, 'tis to be fine,
AGES41:31   H248   Be my condition mean, I then take paines;
SEASONS47:32   H47   For though in's running progresse he doth take
SEASONS50:5   H139   With weary stroaks, they take all in their way,
SEASONS51:19   H195   If scited as the most Judicious take.
MASSYR54:5   H32   Titles divine, he to himself did take,
MASSYR54:38   H65   *Semiramis* from *Menon* he did take,
MASSYR57:21   H168   Would now advantage take, their own to gain;
MASSYR58:22   H207   The rule from their unworthy Prince to take.
MASSYR59:22   H246   *Arbaces* marches in, the town did {he} take {takes},
MASSYR61:23   H328   Gladly doth *Tiglath* this advantage take,
MPERS71:4   H720   To shew how little Land he then should take.
MPERS79:33   H1059   Was scarce enough, for each a draught to take.

MPERS85:38	H1314	His father would no notice of that take;
MPERS90:3	~~H1477~~	He sought all sustinance from them to take;
MPERS~~90:4~~	H1478	The Country burnt, they no relief might take.
MPERS90:28	H1495	Town after town, with small resistance take,
MPERS90:37	H1504	And {Commission} hath command, to take the others head,
MPERS91:10	H1518	The Kings {on such} conditions they are forc't to take; {as King
MGREC107:5	H2180	That other matters may {might} take up their minds.
MGREC109:8	H2267	Nor had that drunken god, one that {who} would take
MGREC110:27	H2331	Doth for his Camp a greater circuit take,
MGREC~~116:10~~	H2573	Nor meat, nor drink, nor comfort would she take,
MGREC118:5	H2652	Some wished him, to take the stile of King,
MGREC118:30	H2679	Was stiffe *Meleager,* whom he would take down {away},
MGREC119:23	H2713	His Lady take i'th' way, and no man know.
MGREC~~120:4~~	H2736	Who fear'd *Antipater* would take his life
MGREC124:2	H2907	To take down *Polisperchon* grown so high;
MGREC127:41	H3071	{clear} what cause they {he} had to take up {make this} warre.
MGREC128:13	H3086	Requires them therefore to take up their Armes,
MGREC128:21	H3094	So therefore craves {requests} their help to take him down,
MGREC130:39	H3184	These Captains now, the stile of Kings do take,
MGREC132:39	H3286	Possession he of *Europe* thinks to take,
MGREC133:25	~~H3315~~	Did take his rule, his sons, himself and all.
MGREC134:14	H3345	To take the government was called in,
MGREC135:3	H3375	To take her life, and quit her from all harmes;
MGREC136:2	H3415	But humbly stand, some grave reproof to take:
MGREC136:17	H3431	*What e're is found amisse, take in best {good} part,*
MROMAN137:11	H3462	So *Romulus* was forc'd this course to take.
DIALOG143:39	H108	What false reports, which nick-names did they take,
DIALOG147:38	H262	Then Justice shall in all thy Courts take place,
CONTEM173:7	H175	And take the trembling prey before it yield,
CONTEM173:16	H183	And wisht me wings with her a while to take my flight.
FLESH175:34	H34	Affect's thou pleasure? take thy fill,
FLESH177:28	H109	Take thou the world, and all that will.
AUTHOR178:12	H22	And take thy way where yet thou art not known,
BIRTH180:20	H30	Who with salt tears this last Farewel did take.
VERSES184:6	H10	Yet for part payment take this simple mite,
CHILDRN184:26	H15	My second bird did take her flight,
CHILDRN185:15	H41	Or here or there, they'l take their flight,
CHILDRN186:10	H77	And from the top bough take my flight,
CHILDRN186:17	H84	Among your young ones take your rest,
MEDDM196:15	Hp273	comes he shall both take his rest and receiue his reward, the
MEDDM196:33	Hp274	wch thousands of enemys w^thout hath not been able to take
MEDDM199:16	Hp278	any thing to stay vpon, but take away their props and they are
MEDDM207:14	Hp288	that notw^thstanding we take great delight, for a season in
MEDDM207:17	Hp289	withers the pleasure wch else we should take in them, and well
MYCHILD215:10	Hp240	by exper^c. y^t ye exhortat^s. of parents take most effect wn y^e
MYCHILD215:24	Hp240	yovng years about 6. or 7. as I take it I began to make cons^c.
MYCHILD216:2	Hp241	loose from God, vanity & ye follyes of Youth take hold of me.
MYCHILD216:16	Hp241	after him gave me many more, of whom I now take ye care,
MYCHILD217:1	Hp242	at any time yov are chastened of God take it as Thankfully and
28AUG225:30	Hp254	doth not afflict willingly, nor take delight in greiving ye children
11MAYB228:31	Hp259	loving kindnes, nor take ye cup of salvation wth Thanksgiving

HOURS234:20 H34 And there content I'll take

TAKEING (1) [taking]

MEDDM204:19 Hp285 generation for takeing veangence on the house of Ahab and

TAKEN (7) See also TA'EN, TA'N, TA'NE, TANE

AGES40:36 H215 Sometimes by wounds in idle combates taken,

MASSYR59:26 H250 Their strong wall'd town should suddenly be taken;

MPERS77:27 H968 Sage *Artabanus* counsell, had he taken,

MGREC99:22 H1865 But yet, this well defended town is {was} taken,

MGREC103:11 H2022 And taken mony, plate, and golden treasure;

MGREC132:21 H3266 There was he {At last he's} taken and imprisoned

DIALOG141:21 H20 This Phisick-purging-potion I have taken,

TAKER (1)

HUMOUR26:28 H258 If thou'rt the taker, I must be the giver:

TAKES (33)

HUMOUR27:18 H289 Your slanders thus refuted, takes no place,

SEASONS49:39 H132 The Sun in {thro} Leo now hath {takes} his carrear,

MASSYR59:22 H246 *Arbaces* marches in, the town did {he} take {takes},

MASSYR60:29 H294 *Arbaces* suffers all, and all he takes.

MASSYR61:33 H338 All *Israels* Land, {lands} beyond *Iordan,* he takes.

MASSYR63:6 H391 Of opportunity advantage takes,

MASSYR66:18 H524 All rule, he from the ancient *Pharoes* takes;

MPERS69:25 H647 Who him pursues to *Sardis,* takes the town,

MPERS70:30 H701 There routs his Hoast, himself she prisoner takes,

MPERS72:39 H785 But in the way, his sword just vengeance takes.

MPERS74:23 H846 Two of his Neeces takes to nuptiall bed;

MPERS80:30 H1097 That brave *Thymistocles* takes this wise course,

MPERS86:1 H1317 And takes more on him, then was judged fit.

MPERS86:27 H1343 From the Lieutenant first, he takes away,

MPERS86:33 H1349 Then next, the *Lacedemons* {Spartans} he takes to {into} pay;

MGREC95:11 H1690 He for his master takes, with *Lycia,*

MGREC95:13 H1692 And easily takes old *Gordium* in his way;

MGREC95:26 H1705 Now {Then} *Alexander* all *Cilicia* takes:

MGREC98:17 H1819 space {time} he takes this lofty {took that wealthy} town,

MGREC106:29 H2163 His greatnesse now he takes, to represent,

MGREC107:1 H2176 But yet no notice takes, of what he hears;

MGREC107:34 H2209 So {Then} from his carriages the Hides he takes,

MGREC111:41 H2386 And *Statirah, Darius* daughter takes,

MGREC118:37 H2686 *Antigonus,* for his share *Asia* takes,

MGREC119:37 H2727 And the remains of *Leonatus* takes;

MGREC122:38 H2859 The King, and Queen, along with him he takes. {to *Macedon*}

MGREC124:9 H2914 But in his absence *Polisperchon* takes

MGREC127:22 H3052 *Antigonus,* then takes {who took} his life unjust,

MGREC130:8 H3163 With his Embassadour, her journey takes,

MGREC131:25 H3217 Who his fair daughter *Stratonica* takes,

MROMAN139:6 H3534 A generall Muster takes, which by account,

CONTEM174:24 H222 Fond fool, he takes this earth ev'n for heav'ns bower.

MEDDM206:32 Hp288 but takes and chuses, when and where and whom he pleases,

TAKEST (1)

HUMOUR25:20 H209 Whil'st us, for thine associates thou takest,

TAKING (2) See also TAKEING

MASSYR55:22 H88 Taking a towne, such valour she did show,

MPERS~~72:19~~ H767 Upon a Judge, for breach of Law {taking bribes} accus'd;

TALE (4)
ELEMEN9:29 H63 Our Sages new, another tale have told:
ELEMEN19:11 H456 Without impeachment, to my tale or wit.
DIALOG148:34 H299 And in a while you'l tell another tale.
HOUSE237:5 H35 No pleasant tale shall 'ere be told

TALENTS (3) [pl.] See also TALLENTS
MGREC95:28 H1707 To *Greece* he thirty thousand talents sends;
MGREC~~115:15~~ H2529 Twelve thousand Talents also did intend,
MEDDM204:11 Hp284 behoues euery man so to improue his talents, that when his

TALES (3) [pl.]
AGES45:23 H413 These are no old wives tales, but this is truth;
DUBART153:26 H30 And tells her tales; (his full heart over-glad)
2LETTER182:32 H38 Oppressed minds, abruptest tales do tell.

T'ALIGHT (1) [to alight]
MGREC97:2 H1763 Who from his golden Coach is glad t'alight,

TALK (6)
HUMOUR21:33 H61 That much wil talk, but little dares she do,
HUMOUR34:39 H594 And too much talk; both which, I do {here} confesse,
WHAT224:6 H6 My Tongue shall talk of Thee
THEART229:14 H16 My praise lyes not in Talk.
HOURS233:29 H12 W^th Thee my soul can talk
HOURS234:27 H41 And talk to my Beloued one

TALKE (1) [talk]
HUMOUR32:13 H487 Talke I love not, reason lyes not in length.

TALKT (1)
MGREC116:12 H2578 And Conquests be talkt of, whilst there is Land;

TALL (1)
ELIZB187:8 H16 And time brings down what is both strong and tall.

TALLENTS (8) [talents]
MASSYR60:36 H301 A thousand tallents of *Menahem* had,
MPERS78:35 H1016 Three thousand Tallents of the purest gold;
MPERS91:3 H1511 To these {them} he thirty thousand Tallents sent,
MGREC101:12 H1937 With thirty thousand Tallents, to be paid
MGREC103:15 H2026 To a {an} hundred thousand Tallents by account.
MGREC109:23 H2282 And {Then} eighty Tallents to his Captaines down.
MGREC109:27 H2286 And of his own, a thousand Tallents more.
MGREC115:9 ~~H2518~~ Twelve thousand Tallents on it franckly spent;

TALLER (2)
SEASONS52:17 H232 And like an Infant, stil he {it} taller growes.
MEDDM197:14 Hp274 man, can goe vpright, vnder that door, wher a taller is glad to

T'ALLURE (1) [to allure]
MGREC96:37 H1757 And how {that} his wealth serv'd but for baits t'allure,

TAM'D (1) [tamed]
DUBART154:14 H59 Who tam'd his foes, in bloud, in skarres {warrs,} and sweat,

TAME (4)
ELEMEN12:23 H183 Thousands in woods, and planes, both wild, and tame,
HUMOUR31:34 H467 Flegm's patient, because her nature's tame:
HUMOUR34:26 H581 With a tame foole converse, then with a mad.
MPERS91:13 H1521 Whose courage nought but death could ever tame,

TAMED See TAM'D

TANAQUIL (1)
MROMAN139:3   H3531   Of *Tanaquil,* late Queen, obtaines the place;
TA'N (2) [taken] See also TA'EN, TA'NE, TANE
MGREC132:4   H3237   (Whose daughter unto wife, he'd newly {not long before} ta'n)
SIDNEY151:15   ~~H69~~   And *Mars* himself was ta'n by *Venus* gin;
TA'NE (1) [taken] See also TA'EN, TA'N, TANE
MGREC130:30   ~~H3181~~   *Aridaeus* and his Queen by slaughters ta'ne;
TANE (5) [taken] See also TA'EN, TA'N, TA'NE
MGREC94:32   H1670   That he be tane alive, (for he intends)
MGREC97:7   H1768   And forty thousand Prisoners also tane;
MGREC99:24   H1867   The Captaine {Thus *Betis*} tane, had holes bor'd through his
MGREC128:32   H3105   And {With} all the spoyle and booty they {he} had tane;
DIALOG142:9   H38   The regall, peacefull Scepter from thee tane?
TANGS (1) [pl.]
HUMOUR27:36   H307   Nay, could I be from all your tangs but pure,
TARDY (1)
MYCHILD215:29   Hp241   too often tardy y^t way. I also fovnd much comfort in reading y^e
TARGET (1)
MPERS70:39   H710   Two *Sythian* bowes, a sword, and target round;
TARQUIN (3)
MROMAN138:25 H3515   *Tarquin,* a *Greek,* at *Corinth* borne, and bred,
MROMAN139:9   H3537   And then by *Tarquin, Priscus* Son, was slaine.
MROMAN139:12 H3540   *Tarquin* the proud, from manners called so,
TARQUINIUS (2)
MROMAN138:24 H3514   *Tarquinius Priscus.*
MROMAN139:10 H3538   *Tarquinius Superbus,* the last
TARQUINS (1) [pl.]
MROMAN139:20 H3548   The *Tarquins* they from *Rome* with speed {by force} expell,
TARRY (1)
11MAYA226:24   Hp255   a little while and he that shall come will come and will not tarry.
TARTARIANS (1) [pl.]
MASSYR62:25   H370   Or wild *Tartarians,* as yet ne're blest,
TASK (2)
SIDNEY152:12   H81   I to be eas'd of such a task was glad.
MEDDM197:27   Hp275   will finde it a wearysome if not an impossible task so he that
TASKE (2) [task]
MGREC135:41   H3413   This taske befits not women, like to men:
DUBART153:2   H6   But knowing th' taske so great, and strength but small,
TAST (3) [taste]
MPERS90:39   ~~H1506~~   Who of his cruelty made many tast,
CONTEM173:2   H170   Look how the wantons frisk to tast the air,
MEDDM197:12   Hp274   some times tast of adversity, prosperity would not be so
TASTE (8)
AGES43:8   H303   And {I} oft long'd sore, to taste on Royalty.
SEASONS51:35   H211   We now of Winters sharpness 'gin to taste;
MGREC94:10   H1644   Now taste of death, (least they deserv't {deserv'd} in time)
MGREC112:19   H2405   'Mongst those, that of his cruelty did taste,
MGREC125:29   H2979   On which *Olimpias* of the like might taste.
MGREC126:20   H3011   Expecting nothing, but of death to taste;
MGREC127:2   H3032   Now in her age she's forc't to taste that Cup,
MGREC127:27   H3057   So *Eumenes* {(the prop)} of destiny {death} must taste.

TASTED (1)
MYCHILD217:19 Hp243   bee well with me. I haue somt. tasted of y^t hidden Manna y^t y^e
TASTES (1) [pl.]
SEASONS50:30 H164   To shake his fruit, of most delicious tastes;
TASTS (2) [tastes]
ELEMEN11:31   H151   Their kinds, their tasts, their colours, and their smels,
MYCHILD217:21 Hp243 y^t agst svch a promis, svch tasts of sweetnes ye Gates of Hell
TATTER'D (1) [tattered]
DIALOG141:17   H16   And must my selfe dissect my tatter'd state,
TAUGHT (10)
MASSYR54:4   H31   He taught the people first to Idolize;
MASSYR55:39   H105   That after ages, skil, by them were {was} taught.
MGREC94:35   H1673   Ah! fond vaine man, whose pen was taught ere while,
MGREC94:36   H1674   In lower termes to write {was taught} a higher stile,
SIDNEY151:34   H75   Till taught to's cost, for his too hasty hand,
QELIZ156:10   H37   She taught them better manners to their cost.
CONTEM172:35 H168   So nature taught, and yet you know not why,
CHILDRN186:24 H91   Taught what was good, and what was ill,
MEDDM203:2   Hp283   not the wisest of men, taught vs this lesson, that all is vanity
RESTOR229:32 H15   He taught thee by his rod.
TAUNTING (1)
MPERS70:33   H704   Using such taunting words as she thought good.
TAUNTS (1) [pl.]
HUMOUR32:19   H493   To bear {with} the injurious taunts of three;
TAUNY (1) [tawny]
SEASONS48:39 H90   With melted tauny face, and garments thinne.
TAURUS (3)
ELEMEN12:7   H167   And huge great *Taurus,* longer then the rest,
SEASONS47:31 H46   In *Taurus* Signe, yet hasteth straight from thence;
SEASONS47:31 H46   The Sun in *Taurus* keeps his residence,
TAVERNS (1) [pl.]
AGES40:25   H206   To Masques, to Playes, to Taverns stil I move;
TAWNY See TAUNY
TAX (1)
TDUDLEY165:31 H33   Who is't can tax thee ought, but for thy zeal?
TAX'D (1) [taxed]
QELIZ157:34   H102   Nay Masculines, you have thus tax'd us long,
TAXATIONS (1)
MASSYR58:38   H221   And their Taxations sore, all to revoake,
TAXT (2)
HUMOUR28:40   H352   I've us'd no bitternesse, nor taxt your name,
AGES45:22   H409   I've seen it plunder'd, taxt and soak'd in bloud,
TEACH (2)
HUMOUR29:24   H375   Nature doth teach, to sheild the head from harm,
MEDDM206:33   Hp288   it should alsoe teach the children of godly parents to walk w^{th}
TEACHING (1)
VANITY160:20   H30   Such stoicks are but stocks, such teaching vain:
TEAR (1)
DIALOG148:14   H279   And tear his flesh, and set your feet on's neck,
TEARES (9) [tears]
MPERS79:22   H1048   But yet this goodly sight {from him} produced teares,

DIALOG143:24	H93	Unlesse thy {our} teares prevent it speedily.
DIALOG147:27	H251	When they are gone, then drown your self in teares.
BYNIGHT220:13	H12	He in his Bottle putt my teares,
MYSOUL225:9	H13	Thy teares shall All bee dryed vp
SAMUEL228:4	H5	The Son of prayers, of vowes, of teares
SON230:22	H5	My Teares to smiles, my sad to glad
HOURS233:21	H4	And see'st my dropping teares.
ACK235:7	H7	Hast heard my cry's, + seen my Teares,

TEARING (2)

DIALOG143:6	H73	Whose tearing tusks did wound, and kill, and threat:
DIALOG143:8	H77	Whose tearing tusks did wound, and kill, and threat:

TEARS (14) [pl.] See also TEARES

AGES37:10	H72	With tears into this {the} world I did arrive;
AGES45:2	H379	Which fil'd our hearts with fears, with tears our eyes,
MASSYR66:11	H517	All now of worth, are captive led with tears,
MPERS72:12	H760	His woful fate with tears did so bemoane,
MPERS82:32	H1179	And leaves her thus, besmear'd with {in} blood, and tears.
MPERS83:2	H1190	But for his deep complaints; and showres of tears,
DIALOG146:22	H208	Their wofull mother's tears unpitied.
DIALOG146:34	H221	Though now beclouded all with tears and blood:
DISTEMP179:17	H5	Bedrencht with tears that flow'd from mournful head.
BIRTH180:20	H30	Who with salt tears this last Farewel did take.
2LETTER182:5	H11	My dumpish thoughts, my groans, my brakish tears
CHILDRN185:17	H43	If birds could weep, then would my tears
MYCHILD216:15	Hp241	to me, and cost me many prayers + tears before I obtain one,
BYNIGHT220:8	H8	Wth tears I sovght him earnestly

TEAT (1)

MEDDM200:6	Hp279	Some children are hardly weaned although the teat be rub'd

TEDIOUS (7)

HUMOUR28:32	H344	But why, alas, thus tedious should I be?
AGES43:37	H332	And to conclude, I may not tedious be,
SEASONS47:1	H17	And bids defiance to all tedious Winters:
MPERS72:30	H774	'T would be no pleasant {pleasure}, but a tedious thing,
MGREC126:39	H3028	Her out-rages too tedious to relate,
1LETTER181:20	H18	I weary grow, the tedious day so long;
11MAYB228:28	Hp259	made it ye more tedious, but it pleased ye Lord to support my

TEETH (5)

HUMOUR22:15	H84	Her teeth wil chatter, dead and wan's her face,
AGES38:32	H135	What tortures I, in breeding teeth sustain?
MPERS76:41	H939	His whetted teeth he sticks {claps} in the firm wood,
MGREC104:15	H2067	Grinding his teeth, and plucking off his haire,
MGREC135:31	H3403	Whose Iron teeth devoured every beast;

TEGEA (1)

MGREC125:10	H2958	To leave his Seige at *Tagra* {*Tegea*}, and with speed

TEKEL (1)

MASSYR68:24	H610	There hears his *Mene,* and his *Tekel* read;

TEL (13) [tell]

HUMOUR21:5	H33	It shal suffice, to tel {shew} you what I am:
HUMOUR24:34	H183	Whose glorious deeds in armes, the world can tel,
HUMOUR25:28	H217	Nay should I tel, thou wouldst count me no blab,
HUMOUR32:36	H510	Nay, I could tel you (what's more true then meet)

HUMOUR33:7	H521	As at noon day to tel, the Sun doth shine.
HUMOUR34:18	H573	Whose use and worth to tel, I must refrain;
AGES36:35	H59	That each should tel, what of himselfe he knew;
AGES37:9	H71	To tel that paine, which cann't be told by tongue;
SEASONS52:12	H227	What Winter hath to tel, now let him say.
MASSYR57:12	H159	What then he did, of worth, can no man tel,
MASSYR57:29	H174	We may suggest our thoughts, but cannot tel;
MASSYR59:34	H258	Twenty he reign'd, same time, as Stories tel,
MASSYR62:22	H367	Where now those ten Tribes are, can no man tel,

TELL (34)

FATHER5:29	H30	My other foures, do intermixed tell
ELEMEN9:40	H74	Yet men and beasts, {beast} Astronomers can tell,
ELEMEN11:29	H149	To tell what sundry fruits my fat soyle yeelds,
ELEMEN11:35	H155	To tell you of my Countries, and my regions
AGES38:16	H119	As he can tell, that next comes on the stage.
AGES45:17	H399	Plotted and acted, so that none can tell,
AGES45:24	H414	We old men love to tell, what's done in youth.
SEASONS53:4	H260	*I could {knew} not tell how to passe't by:*
MASSYR64:32	H456	None but the true *Ezekiel* need to tell:
MASSYR64:34	H458	Can *Babels* tired Souldiers tell with pain;
MPERS72:31	H775	To tell the facts, of this most bloody King.
MPERS73:40	H825	Too politicke (tis {its} like) for me to tell,
MPERS92:28	H1586	If so, or not, we cannot tell, but find
MPERS92:34	H1592	Whose warres and losses we may better tell;
MGREC106:19	H2153	Then tell her errand, we had better spare
MGREC123:10	H2872	In this Epitomy, too long to tell
MGREC127:41	H3072	*Cassanders* outrages at large doth tell,
MGREC130:20	H3175	The world must needs believe what he doth tell:
DIALOG141:13	H12	Ah, tell thy Daughter, she may simpathize.
DIALOG143:27	H96	Before I tell the effect, ile shew the cause,
DIALOG148:34	H299	And in a while you'l tell another tale.
QELIZ157:3	H71	To tell of halfe she did, or she could doe;
QELIZ157:28	H96	Her personall perfections, who would tell,
VANITY160:18	H28	What is it then? to do as Stoicks tell,
TDUDLEY165:25	H27	While others tell his worth, I'le not be dumb:
2LETTER181:34	H4	And tell my griefs in either Hemisphere:
2LETTER182:9	H15	He that can tell the starrs or Ocean sand,
2LETTER182:15	H21	Tell him, the countless steps that thou dost trace,
2LETTER182:27	H33	Tell him here's worse then a confused matter,
2LETTER182:31	H37	Tell him I would say more, but cannot well,
2LETTER182:32	H38	Oppressed minds, abruptest tales do tell.
CHILDRN186:18	H85	In chirping languages, oft them tell,
MYCHILD217:36	Hp243	would soon tell me by the wondrovs workes that I see, the vast
THEART229:8	H10	Thy Goodnes let me Tell,

TELLS (5)

ELEMEN18:18	H422	Which {That} tells afar, th' exployt which he {it} hath done.
MASSYR68:15	H601	Of *Daniel* tells, who in his Grand-sires dayes,
MGREC104:30	H2082	To *Alexander* fly, {flyes} and told {tells} this act;
MGREC133:33	H3323	Tells of their warres, their names, their riches, fates;
DUBART153:26	H30	And tells her tales; (his full heart over-glad)

TELS (4) [tells]
MPERS75:2	H863	Tels them, how harshly the proud King had dealt,
MPERS83:1	H1189	Tels as he could, his unexpressed woes,
MGREC99:6	H1849	Tels him, these proffers great (in truth were none)
MGREC120:28	H2765	Goes to *Antipater,* and tels what's done;

TEMPE (1)
| ELEMEN~~12:16~~ | H176 | Nor will I stay, no not in *Tempe* Vale, |

TEMPER (3)
ELEMEN13:16	H217	But how my cold, dry temper, works upon
HUMOUR27:40	H311	And of the sweet, calme temper, quite bereft,
HUMOUR29:36	H387	And if thy haste, my slownesse should not temper,

TEMPERAMENT (1)
| HUMOUR34:4 | H559 | Thy perfect temperament, who can expresse? |

TEMPERANCE (2)
| HUMOUR31:36 | H469 | My temperance, chastity, is eminent, |
| MGREC106:27 | H2161 | His temperance, is but a sordid thing, |

TEMPERATE (1) See also TEMP'RATE
| SEASONS47:29 | H45 | Of longer dayes, and a more temperate air; |

TEMPERS (2) [pl.]
| FATHER5:33 | H34 | And yet in equall tempers, how they gree, |
| MEDDM198:18 | Hp276 | sundry tempers of men, wch they all catch gre⁻dily at but few |

TEMPESTS (2) [pl.]
| ELEMEN19:22 | H467 | Then of my tempests, felt at Sea and Land, |
| ELEMEN19:32 | H473 | Again, what tempests,{ furious storms} and what hericanoes |

TEMPESTUOUS (1)
| DIALOG142:7 | H36 | And {Or} by tempestuous Wars thy fields trod down? |

TEMPLE (16)
ELEMEN11:3	H123	So great *Diana's* Temple was by me.
ELEMEN12:16	~~H176~~	Nor yet expatiate, in Temple vale;
MASSYR56:13	H119	The wondrous Temple was, she rear'd to *Bell;*
MASSYR61:19	H324	The temple robes, so to fulfill his ends,
MASSYR64:17	H441	The temple of rich ornaments defac'd,
MASSYR65:35	H500	Besieg'd his City, Temple, *Zions* Tower;
MPERS70:23	H694	An Edict makes {made}, the Temple builded be,
MPERS~~71:24~~	H738	The Temples {Their Temple} he destroyes not, for his zeal,
MPERS71:27	H741	To spoyl the Temple of great *Jupiter;*
MPERS75:26	H883	The temple to re-build, for that did rest
MPERS75:39	H896	Set up a Temple (though, a lesse) again.
MPERS80:39	H1106	To rob the wealthy Temple of *Apollo,*
MGREC93:21	H1618	To th' ground was burnt, *Diana's* Temple high,
MGREC98:7	H1809	Sent word, that *Hercules* his Temple stood,
MROMAN137:27	H3478	To *Janus,* he that famous Temple built,
MEDDM197:20	Hp275	temple for the spirit of god to dwell in

TEMPLE'S (1) [temple is]
| MASSYR66:7 | H513 | The Temple's burnt, the Vessels had away, |

TEMPLES (1) [pl.]
| MPERS71:24 | H738 | The Temples {Their Temple} he destroyes not, for his zeal, |

TEMP'RATE (2) [temperate]
| SEASONS~~51:19~~ | H194 | Nor could that temp'rate Clime such difference make, |
| DUBART154:16 | H61 | In all the Zones, the temp'rate, hot and cold, |

TEMPTATIONS (1) [pl.]
MEDDM197:1   Hp274 temptations of Sathan without could not hurt, hath, been foild
TEN (9)
HUMOUR33:4   H518 Under *Troys* wals, ten years wil wast {wear} away,
MASSYR62:22 H367 Where now those ten Tribes are, can no man tel,
MPERS74:36   H858 For twice ten months before the town he lay,
MPERS81:35   H1143 {In all} One hundred thousand, and ten thousand make.
MPERS82:3   H1150 Ten dayes these Armies did each other face,
MPERS86:34   H1350 (One *Greeke* could make ten *Persians* run away)
MGREC109:10 H2269 When thus, ten dayes, his brain with wine he'd soak'd,
SICKNES178:18 H1   Twice ten years old, not fully told
MEDDM203:31 Hp284 We read of ten lepers that were Cleansed, but of one that
TENANTS (1) [pl.]
MEDDM207:21 Hp289 All men are truly sayd to be tenants at will, and it may as truly
TEND (2)
SEASONS51:30 H206 So doth Old Age stil tend unto his Grave,
MPERS81:4   H1112 He seeing {finding} all thus tend unto {to his} decay,
TENDER (6)
ELEMEN13:31 H232 The tender mother on her Infant flyes:
HUMOUR21:10 H38   Unto your Sister-hood, which makes us tender {render}
SEASONS47:22 H38   The tender tops of budding Grasse they crop,
SEASONS47:39 H51   growes long, the tender Lambs {hungry beast} to nourish;
MEDDM196:29 Hp273 but salt will keep from putrefaction, some again like tender
FEVER221:9   H24   Thou shew'st to me thy tender Love,
TENDERS (1)
MGREC109:21 H2280 And tenders him the strength of all his lands, {land;}
TENDS (1) [attends]
MPERS86:12   H1328 Judging all's {his} actions, tends to's injury.
TENDS (1) [inclines]
AGES40:16   H197 All counsel hate, which tends to make me wise,
TENT (3)
MPERS89:17   H1451 Forth-with {Then} he sends {that} to's Tent, they straight
MGREC121:16 H2795 Some of the Souldiers enters *Perdica's* tent,
MGREC121:16 H2798 And in a rage they rush into his tent,
TENTH (3)
SEASONS46:38 H16   The tenth o'th' first *Sol* into *Aries* enters,
SEASONS50:40 H174 The tenth {twelfth} of this, *Sol* riseth in the Line,
CONTEM171:11 H115 Who to the tenth of theirs doth now arrive?
TERME (1) [term]
MYCHILD218:24 Hp244 of the Saints, wch admitt were y^y as they terme y^m yet not
TERMES (3) [terms]
MGREC94:36   H1674 In lower termes to write {was taught} a higher stile,
MGREC97:35   H1796 And in short termes, sends this reply againe;
DIALOG145:13 H162 Pray in plain termes, what is your present grief,
TERMINATE (5)
MASSYR59:15 H239 The wals, and gates, their course {hast} did terminate;
MASSYR68:28 H614 Who soone did terminate his Life, and Crown:
MGREC93:31   H1628 But death did terminate, those thoughts so high.
MGREC113:7   H2434 Thy Kingly word can easily terminate;
ELIZB187:2   H11   Or sigh thy dayes so soon were terminate;

TERMS (4) [pl.] See also TERMES
ELEMEN8:8   H6   In placide terms they thought now to discourse,
MASSYR58:36   H219   And with all terms of amity, he greets, {them greet.}
MGREC128:39   H3112   The terms of their agreement thus expresse,
DIALOG142:1   H30   In generall terms, but will not say wherefore:

TERPSECHOR (1)
SIDNEY149:13   H12   *Calliope* with *Terpsechor* did sing,

TERRA (2)
SEASONS50:18   H152   The russling tresse of *terra* for {down} to moe,
QELIZ156:40   H67   *Terra incognitae* might know her {the} sound;

TERRIBLE (1)
28AUG226:9   Hp254   & bequeath my Soul to thee and Death seem'd no terrible

TERRIFI'D (1) [terrified]
SEASONS48:14   H67   Least by his fervor, we be terrifi'd,

TERROR (1)
AGES44:36   H369   I saw all peace at home, terror to foes,

TERROUR (2)
MPERS89:27   H1461   Such terrour on the *Persians* then did fall,
MGREC135:39   H3411   To fill the world with terrour, and with woe:

TERROUR-STRUCK (1)
SIDNEY151:38   H75   Till terrour-struck for my too weighty charge.

TEST (1)
HUMOUR25:7   H196   Ile go no further then thy nose for test.

TESTEFYE (4) [testify]
11MAYB228:33   Hp259   testefye my thankfullnes not only in word, but in Deed, that my
THEART229:13   H15   Let my obed^c testefye
RESTOR229:31   H14   Let thy obed^c testefye
REMB235:25   H6   My thankes how shall I testefye?

TESTIFIE (3) [testify]
MGREC118:21   H2668   Now lay a spectacle, to testifie
DIALOG147:3   H229   With hearts, and states, to testifie their will.
QELIZ156:6   H33   Millions will testifie that this is true;

TESTIFIED (1)
MGREC118:8   H2655   More then to th' rest, his favour testified:

TESTIFY See TESTEFYE, TESTIFIE

TESTIMONIAL (1)
TDUDLEY165:23 H25   So needs no Testimonial from his own;

T'EXCELL (1) [to excel]
ELEMEN18:2   H406   Yet Aire, beyond all these ye know t'excell.

THALESTRIS (1)
MGREC106:15   H2149   *Thalestris,* Queen of th' *Amazons,* now brought

THALIA (1)
SIDNEY149:19   H18   *Thalia,* and *Melpomene,* say th' truth,

THAN (2) See also THEN
MGREC96:36   H1756   That valour was more worth than Pearls, or gold,
QELIZ157:5   H73   More infamie than fame she did procure;

THANK (1)
MPERS75:17   H878   Scarse finde enough to thank thy loyalty;

THANKES (2) [thanks]
30SEPT227:32   Hp257   yov out of distresse forget not to giue him thankes, but to walk
REMB235:25   H6   My thankes how shall I testefye?

937

THANKFULL (7) [thankful]

WHAT224:5	H5	My thankfull mouth shall speak thy praise
11MAYA226:19	Hp255	for is a contented thankfull h^t vnder my affliction & weaknes
THEART228:35	H1	My thankfull heart wth glorying Tongve
RESTOR229:29	H12	My thankfull heart wth pen record
SON231:20	H32	That ever I may thankfull bee
ACK235:3	H1-3	In thankfull acknowledgmt for ye lrs rec'd. from my
REMB235:21	H1-3	In thankfull Remb^{rc} for my dear husbands safe Arrivall.

THANKFULLNES (4) [thankfulness] See also THANKFULLNESSE, THANKFULNESSE

MYCHILD217:14	Hp242	in Thankfullnes to him.
11MAYB228:33	Hp259	testefye my thankfullnes not only in word, but in Deed, that my
SON231:24	H36	Of Duty + of Thankfullnes,
REMB236:3	H18	But Thankfullnes even all my dayes

THANKFULLNESSE (1) [thankfulness] See also THANKFULLNES, THANKFULNESSE

MGREC98:1	H1803	Their present he receives with thankfullnesse,

THANKFULLY (2)

MYCHILD217:1	Hp242	If at any time yov are chastened of God take it as Thankfully
30SEPT227:20	Hp257	but thankfully to submitt to him for I trvst it is out of his

THANKFULNESSE (2) [thankfulness] See also THANKFULLNES, THANKFULLNESSE

MASSYR61:28	H333	His humble thankfulnesse (with {in} hast) to bring,
MGREC105:30	H2123	He also sends his humble thankfulnesse,

THANKS (6)

ELEMEN13:14	H215	As I ingenuously (with thanks) confesse
HUMOUR30:29	H421	The Liver, Stomach, owes it {their} thanks of right:
MPERS74:18	H841	Thanks for all this to's crafty Stable-groome.
MGREC109:26	H2285	His Presents all, with thanks he doth {did} restore;
MGREC115:38	H2557	But his excuse with humble thanks he sends,
MEDDM203:32	Hp284	thanks, we are more ready to receiue mercys then we are to

THANKSGIVING (1)

11MAYB228:31	Hp259	kindnes, nor take ye cup of salvation wth Thanksgiving as I

TH'ARM (1) [the arm]

HUMOUR29:25	H376	The blow that's aim'd thereat is latch'd by th'arm,

THARMIPOLEY (1)

MGREC126:1	H2992	But being stopt, at Straight *Tharmipoley*

THAT'S (23) [that is]

ELEMEN14:30	H272	Not one of us, all knowes, that's like to thee,
ELEMEN18:3	H407	I aske the man condemn'd, that's near his death:
HUMOUR21:40	H68	But shuns to look on wounds, and bloud that's spilt,
HUMOUR24:8	H157	I love no boasting, that's but childrens trade:
HUMOUR26:34	H264	But the materials none of thine, that's cleare,
HUMOUR29:25	H376	The blow that's aim'd thereat is latch'd by th'arm,
HUMOUR29:31	H382	He is not truly valiant that's not wise;
HUMOUR32:10	H484	What I imagine, that's my malady.
AGES39:23	H166	I fly to catch the Bullet that's {that} aloof;
AGES40:2	H183	My Lust doth hurry me, to all that's ill,
AGES40:5	H186	Or stab the man, in's own defence, that's worse.
AGES43:35	H330	Subject to all Diseases, {distempers} that's the truth,
SEASONS48:32	H83	Sometime a theame that's large, proves barren fields.
MASSYR57:36	H181	It is enough {may suffice}, if all be true that's past,
DAVID159:25	H40	Exceeding all the Love that's Feminine,
VANITY160:1	H11	No, that's but labour anxious, care and pain.

VANITY160:5	H15	More vain then all, that's but to grasp the wind.
VANITY160:8	H18	What is't in beauty? no, that's but a snare,
TDUDLEY166:18	H60	Now fully ripe, as shock of wheat that's grown,
CONTEM174:23	H221	That's full of friends, of honour and of treasure,
SICKNES178:37	H20	ev'n as a word that's speaking.
BIRTH180:5	H15	And if I see not half my dayes that's due,
ANNEB187:25	H15	That's here to day, perhaps gone in an hour;

THATS (1) [that is]

HUMOUR23:39	H149	Without my lively heat, do's ought thats flat.

THAW (1)

DUBART153:7	H11	Did thaw my frozen hearts ingratitude;

TH'EAGLE (1) [the eagle]

ELEMEN19:6	H451	The Ostrich with her plumes, th'Eagle with her eyne;

THEAM (1) [theme] See also THEAME

MGREC114:8	H2476	Upon this dangerous theam fond *Clitus* fell;

THEAME (1) [theme] See also THEAM

SEASONS48:32	H83	Sometime a theame that's large, proves barren fields.

THEATER (1)

QELIZ155:36	H27	The World's the Theater where she did act;

THEBAN (1)

ELEMEN10:4	H79	The *Theban* stout *Alcides,* with his club:

THEBES (3)

MPERS81:15	H1123	As had *Macedon, Thebes,* and *Thessalie,*
MGREC94:3	H1637	*Thebes,* and old {stiff} *Athens,* both 'gainst him rebell,
MGREC127:10	H3040	Old *Thebes* he then re-built (so much of fame)

THEBS (1)

MGREC128:11	H3084	Rebellious *Thebs* he had re-edified,

THEFTS (1) [pl.]

DIALOG144:12	H122	For Bribery, Adultery, for Thefts, and Lyes,

THEIFE (1) [thief]

FATHER6:7	H41	Who must reward a theife, but with his due.

THEME See THEAM, THEAME

THEMSELUES (2) [themselves]

MEDDM206:20	Hp287	themselues of turning to god, the first thing wch they eye, is
MEDDM208:6	Hp289	of a fire, if once severed, will of themselues goe out altho

THEMSELVES (11) [pl.]

FATHER5:30	H31	Each others faults, and where themselves excell:
ELEMEN8:8	H6	For to declare, themselves they all ingage;
HUMOUR20:21	H13	But 'mongst themselves they were at variance,
AGES44:33	H366	That but for shrubs they did themselves account;
MPERS76:34	H932	Where *Grecians* prov'd themselves right Souldiers, stout;
MPERS85:34	H1310	*Persian* Kings, did deem {then deem'd} themselves so good,
MPERS90:22	H1489	The many victories themselves did gain,
MGREC105:7	H2100	To hide themselves, remote, in *Bactria;*
MGREC117:36	H2643	Had hope themselves, to beare the Crown away;
MGREC118:36	H2685	Thought timely for themselves, now to provide.
SIDNEY152:13	H82	For {Then} to revenge his {this} wrong, themselves ingage,

THEN (147) [than]

ELEMEN10:13	H88	Nay more then these, Rivers 'mongst stars are found,
ELEMEN10:28	H103	There's none more strange then *Ætna's* sulphery mount
ELEMEN11:4	H124	And more then bruitish *Sodome* for her lust,

ELEMEN12:7	H167	And huge great *Taurus,* longer then the rest,
ELEMEN14:4	H247	So did that Roman, far more stout then wise,
ELEMEN16:10	H333	If I should shew,{name} more Seas, then thou hast Coasts.
ELEMEN17:40	H404	Aboundantly more then my sisters three?
ELEMEN19:3	H448	Is more authentick then their {our} moderne wit.
ELEMEN20:5	H487	I have said lesse, then did my sisters three;
HUMOUR20:27	H19	Proud Melancholy, more envious then the rest,
HUMOUR21:23	H51	Then Iron Corslet, 'gainst a sword or dart;
HUMOUR21:27	H55	Then timerous Hares, whom Castles doe immure?
HUMOUR21:36	H64	She loves a Fiddle, better then a Drum,
HUMOUR22:1	H70	Then here's our sad black Sister, worse then you,
HUMOUR23:35	H145	Then a dead Lyon? by beasts triumpht ore.
HUMOUR24:15	H164	Your patience more then mine, I must confesse.
HUMOUR25:1	H190	But know, I love the blade, more then the hilt. {Hill;}
HUMOUR25:7	H196	Ile go no further then thy nose for test.
HUMOUR26:14	H244	More useful then the rest, don't reason erre;
HUMOUR30:8	H400	Then all the huge beasts of the fertile field.
HUMOUR30:14	H406	If I have not more part, then al ye three:
HUMOUR30:40	H432	Then is thy torrid nose, or brasen brow.
HUMOUR32:36	H510	Nay, I could tel you (what's more true then meet)
HUMOUR34:25	H580	Phrensie's worse, then folly, one would more glad,
HUMOUR34:26	H581	With a tame foole converse, then with a mad.
AGES40:19	H200	For sure my suit more then my vertues shine;
AGES42:17	H275	{again,} mine age (in all) {mine Age} been worse then hell.
AGES42:40	H296	Greater, then was the great'st, was my desire,
AGES43:7	H302	My thirst was higher, then Nobility.
SEASONS48:18	H71	Whose praise deserves a page, from more then me.
SEASONS48:34	H85	Let some describe thee better then can I.
SEASONS52:2	H219	With minds more dark, then is the darkned sky;
SEASONS52:28	H243	The day much longer then it was before,
MASSYR57:8	H155	But much it is, in more then forty years,
MASSYR62:3	H348	He *Israelites,* more then his Father vext;
MASSYR62:27	H372	Hath bred more wonder, then beleefe in hearts;
MASSYR62:33	H378	His Wars none better then himself can boast,
MASSYR63:28	H415	Then being Father to so great a Son.
MASSYR65:31	H496	*Iudah* {They} lost more {now} (then e're they lost) by him;
MASSYR68:16	H602	Was held in more request, {account} then now he was,
MPERS71:2	H714	Innobled more by birth, then by their mind;
MPERS71:39	H753	Is more prophane, then grosse Idolaters;
MPERS73:38	H823	But {That} better one, then many Tyrants reigne.
MPERS75:7	H868	For they beleev'd his nose, more then his tongue;
MPERS75:21	H880	Thy falshood, not thy {craft more then} valour did prevaile;
MPERS75:22	H880	Thy wit was more then was thine honesty,
MPERS75:23	H880	Thou lov'dst thy Master more then verity.
MPERS76:22	H920	His enemies scarce seen, then much lesse, slaine;
MPERS79:3	H1025	Nay, more then monstrous barb'rous cruelty!
MPERS81:29	H1137	No lesse then Grand-sire to great *Alexander.*
MPERS84:4	H1232	To drink more then he list, none bidden was:
MPERS85:33	H1309	More by {To which} his pride, {more} then {his} lust, thereunto
MPERS86:1	H1317	And takes more on him, then was judged fit.
MPERS86:16	H1332	More deare to's mother, then his brother far.

MPERS88:11	H1404	That, more then multitudes, their hearts did awe:
MPERS91:8	H1516	To defend, more then offend, he had {there was} need.
MGREC94:2	H1636	Which makes each moment seem, more then a day:
MGREC96:22	H1742	Would aske more time, then were {was} their bodys worth.
MGREC97:21	H1782	Then that the *Persian* King he over-came;
MGREC97:28	H1789	*Darius* now, more humble {less lofty} then before,
MGREC98:6	H1808	Least he intend more fraud, then sacrifice;
MGREC98:29	H1831	He scorns to have one worse then had the other,
MGREC106:13	H2147	On *Artabasus* more then all bestow'd,
MGREC108:3	H2219	And in this sort, they rather drag, then bring,
MGREC109:39	H2298	Did more his valour then his Crown envie;
MGREC114:19	H2489	Who lov'd his Master more then did the rest,
MGREC~~116:10~~	H2572	She laid it more to heart, then any other,
MGREC116:31	~~H2597~~	More boundles in ambition then the skie;
MGREC118:8	H2655	More then to th' rest, his favour testified:
MGREC121:25	H2807	Then by more trouble to grow eminent.
MGREC122:32	H2851	Who vext the Queen more then the other farre;
MGREC124:26	H2933	More then he bidden was, could act no thing;
MGREC130:24	H3179	Then vengeance just, against the same {them} t' expresse;
MGREC132:1	H3234	(Rather then *Philips* child must {race should} longer live
MGREC~~132:20~~	H3265	His story seems a Fable more then true.
MGREC135:16	H3388	The *Grecian* longer then the *Persian* stood,
MGREC135:30	H3402	The last more strong, and dreadfull, then the rest,
DIALOG144:18	H128	Of more then thou canst heare, or I relate,
SIDNEY149:18	H17	More worth was thine, {his} then *Clio* could set down.
DUBART153:5	H9	Where Art, and more then Art in Nature shines;
DUBART154:3	H48	More sencelesse then the Stones to *Amphions* Lute,
DUBART154:12	H57	Then in thy *Pippin, Martell, Charlemain.*
DUBART154:13	H58	Then in Saint *Lewis,* or thy last *Henry* great,
QELIZ156:5	H32	Nor say I more then duly is her due,
QELIZ156:19	H46	Was ever people better rul'd then hers?
QELIZ156:23	H50	Ships more invincible then *Spaines,* her foe
DAVID159:11	H26	Swifter then swiftest Eagles, so were they,
DAVID159:12	H27	Stronger then Lions, ramping for their prey.
VANITY160:5	H15	More vain then all, that's but to grasp the wind.
TDUDLEY165:11	H13	For who more cause to boast his worth then I?
TDUDLEY165:13	H15	Or who alive then I, a greater debtor?
CONTEM168:5	H15	More Heaven then Earth was here, no winter & no night.
CONTEM171:26	H128	By birth more noble then those creatures all,
CONTEM173:15	H182	I judg'd my hearing better then my sight,
FLESH177:2	H83	More glorious then the glistring Sun;
AUTHOR177:32	H4	Till snatcht from thence by friends, less wise then true
AUTHOR178:7	H17	Yet still thou run'st more hobling then is meet;
1HUSB180:23	H2	If ever two were one, then surely we.
1HUSB180:24	H3	If ever man were lov'd by wife, then thee;
1HUSB180:27	H6	I prize thy love more then whole Mines of gold,
2LETTER182:3	H9	Commend me to the man more lov'd then life,
2LETTER182:8	H14	My Interest's more then all the world beside.
2LETTER182:26	H32	Behold a Chaos blacker then the first.
2LETTER182:27	H33	Tell him here's worse then a confused matter,
3LETTER183:4	H6	A dearer Dear (far dearer Heart) then this.

CHILDRN185:7	H33	Striving for more then to do well,
CHILDRN185:35	H61	My cares are more, and fears then ever,
ANNEB187:28	H18	More fool then I to look on that was lent,
MERCY188:35	H21	Who lov'd thee more (it seem'd) then her own life.
2SIMON195:4	Hp271	Children do natureally, rather follow the failings then the
2SIMON195:8	Hp271	you nor of more ease to my self then these short meditations
MEDDM195:30	Hp272	Theory, then the practique part, but he is a true Christian that
MEDDM197:5	Hp274	bruise, then polish
MEDDM197:8	Hp274	they haue more sence then faith they se what they inioy,
MEDDM197:16	Hp274	more patiently then he that excells him, both in gifts & graces
MEDDM197:23	Hp275	will abase them more, then this What hast thou, but what thou
MEDDM198:7	Hp276	then they
MEDDM198:34	Hp277	rather choose to be buried vnder rocks and mountains then to
MEDDM199:3	Hp277	inheritance, is better, then an inheritance wthout wisedome
MEDDM200:26	Hp279	their former vigor and beavty in a more ample manner then
MEDDM200:29	Hp279	arise in far more glory, then that wch they lost at their creation,
MEDDM202:2	Hp282	There is nothing admits of more admiration, then gods various
MEDDM202:7	Hp282	then ye earth some so wise and learned, that they seeme like
MEDDM202:9	Hp282	like beasts then men, some pious saints, some incarnate
MEDDM203:6	Hp283	them then they are lesse then vanity & more then vexation, so
MEDDM203:32	Hp284	are more ready to receiue mercys then we are to acknowledg
MEDDM204:27	Hp285	vpon one that is in a far better estate then himself, but let him
MEDDM204:28	Hp285	vpon him that is lower then he is and if he se, that such a one
MEDDM204:31	Hp285	Jacob, I am lesse then the least of thy mercys.
MEDDM204:34	Hp285	land askes much more paines, then some other doth to be
MEDDM205:18	Hp286	who is greater then our Conscience will do it much more, but
MEDDM206:21	Hp287	their wayes rather, then to beg forgiuenes for their sinnes,
MEDDM206:22	Hp287	more at a Compensation then at a pardon, but he that will not
MEDDM206:28	Hp288	then his great worke of election and Reprobation, when we
MEDDM207:5	Hp288	Commonly imployed for a Clean Contrary end, then that w^{ch}
MEDDM208:32	Hp290	become firme footing, for peter to walk on, nay more then all
MEDDM209:24	Hp291	hath (perhaps meaner then himself) wch shews us perfection is
MYCHILD217:7	Hp242	child, that no longer then the rod has been on my back
SOREFIT222:4	H23	Longer then still thy Name to praise,
FAINTING222:27	H17	Then I may frvitfull bee.
30SEPT227:23	Hp257	then without food. Lord wth y^y correction giue Instrvction and
30SEPT227:26	Hp257	p^rserved wth sugar then brine, yet will he p^rserve me to his
30SEPT227:33	Hp257	closely with him then before, This is the desire of y^r Loving
HOURS234:19	H33	In Thee Alone is more then All;
HOURS234:31	H45	And serve thee better then before

THEN (212) [then]

FATHER5:28	H29	My first do shew, their good, and then their rage,
FATHER6:13	H47	Then waters, {water} in the boundlesse Ocean flowes.
ELEMEN10:6	H81	The Horse that kill'd *Bellerophon,* then flew.
ELEMEN11:16	H136	Not before then, shal cease my raging ire,
ELEMEN11:17	H137	And then, because no matter more for fire:
ELEMEN13:30	H231	Then dearth prevailes, that Nature to suffice,
ELEMEN15:12	H294	Then seeks me out, in River and in Well;
ELEMEN16:4	H327	Then I have Fountaines, Rivers, Lakes and Ponds:
ELEMEN16:12	H335	Then Seas are deep, Mountains are never high.
ELEMEN17:28	H392	Then wholly perish'd, earths ignoble race;

942

ELEMEN19:14	H459	Then Feavours, Purples, Pox, and Pestilence;
ELEMEN19:22	H467	Then of my tempests, felt at Sea and Land,
ELEMEN19:27	H472	Then in his long hot wars, {war} which *Millain* gain'd.
ELEMEN19:38	H479	Then what prodigious sights, sometimes I show:
HUMOUR22:1	H70	Then here's our sad black Sister, worse then you,
HUMOUR22:8	H77	Then by a quick encounter, to be slaine;
HUMOUR22:20	H89	Then yeeld to me, preheminence in War.
HUMOUR22:37	H106	My absence proves, it plain, her wit then flyes
HUMOUR24:21	H170	Then let my sisters, right their injury.
HUMOUR24:27	H176	So walke thee til thou'rt cold, then let thee go.
HUMOUR25:18	H207	But let her leave the rest, and {then} I presume,
HUMOUR26:29	H259	Then never boast of what thou do'st receive,
HUMOUR27:30	H301	As thus, if hot, then dry; if moist, then cold;
HUMOUR27:30	H301	As thus, if hot, then dry; if moist, then cold;
HUMOUR27:31	H302	If this {you} can't be disprov'd {disprove}, then all I hold:
HUMOUR29:27	H378	I then command, proud Choler stand thy place,
HUMOUR29:33	H384	Then by assault to gain one, not our own.
HUMOUR30:2	H394	Then he whose brain a touch my humour gives.
HUMOUR30:13	H405	Reduce the man to's principles, then see
HUMOUR30:18	H410	When you poor bankrupts prove, then have I most.
HUMOUR30:20	H412	You high born (from that lump) then take your flight
HUMOUR30:21	H413	Then who's mans friend, when life and all forsakes?
HUMOUR31:41	H474	Then cause her blush, while I dilate {relate} the same.
HUMOUR33:5	H519	Rather then loose, one beateous *Hellena;*
HUMOUR34:27	H582	Then, my head {brain} for learning is not the fittest,
HUMOUR34:34	H589	Then I, and thou, must make a mixture here:
AGES35:36	H22	And when tis broke, then ends his life and all.
AGES35:38	H24	Then may he live, til {out} threescore years or past.
AGES36:11	H35	Then prauncing on the Stage, about he wheels;
AGES36:24	H48	This {Thus} writ about: *This out, then I am done.*
AGES37:23	H85	My then ambitious thoughts, were low enough.
AGES38:26	H129	Then nought can please, and yet I know not why.
AGES39:7	H150	And then the worst, in a more ugly hue;
AGES39:9	H152	Then let not him, which {that} hath most craft dissemble;
AGES41:22	H239	And then a world of drosse among my gold.
AGES41:24	H241	I then receiv'd a {an} harvest of mine owne.
AGES41:25	H242	My reason, then bad judge, how little hope,
AGES41:27	H244	I then with both hands, graspt the world together,
AGES41:31	H248	Be my condition mean, I then take paines;
AGES41:33	H249	If rich, I'm urged then to gather more.
AGES41:35	H250	If a father {I}, then for children must provide:
AGES41:36	H251	But if none, then for kindred near ally'd.
AGES41:36	H252	If rich, I'm urged then to gather more,
AGES41:37	H254	If Noble, then mine honour to {o} maintaine.
AGES42:21	H279	Then basenesse was companion unto me.
AGES43:8	H304	Then Kings must be depos'd or put to flight,
AGES43:15	H307	Then heapt up gold, and riches as the clay;
AGES43:16	H308	Then thought my state firm founded sure to last,
AGES44:21	H354	Provides a staffe for {then} to support his age.
AGES44:27	H360	Sometime an abject, then again in place,
AGES44:34	H367	Then saw I *France,* and *Holland* sav'd, *Cales* won,

AGES44:38	H371	And then, me thought, the world {day} at noon grew dark,
AGES44:41	H374	(For 'twas our hopes then kept our hearts alive)
AGES46:2	H433	I then shal go, whence I shal come no more,
SEASONS47:12	H28	Now digs, then sows, his hearbs, his flowers, and roots,
SEASONS48:38	H89	When Spring had done, then {the} Summer must {did} begin,
SEASONS49:7	H98	And {Then} retrograde, now is {must be} my burning Sun.
SEASONS49:33	H126	Of him that was Shepherd, then King go vaunt.
SEASONS50:34	H168	Yet then appears the worthy deeds he 'ath done:
SEASONS50:36	H170	Then drops his Fruits into the Eaters lap.
SEASONS51:14	H188	For then in *Eden* was not only seen
MASSYR54:39	H66	Then drown himself, did *Menon,* for her sake;
MASSYR55:2	H68	The world then was two thousand nineteen old.
MASSYR56:40	H146	Forty two years she reign'd, and then she dy'd,
MASSYR57:12	H159	What then he did, of worth, can no man tel,
MASSYR57:24	H171	And that *Semiramis* then flourished,
MASSYR57:27	H172	Did then incite, them to regain their own.
MASSYR58:11	H196	Unto *Belosus,* then he brake his minde,
MASSYR59:20	H244	Which through much rain, then swelling up so high,
MASSYR59:31	H255	Then on himself, and them, a fire he sets;
MASSYR59:36	H260	His Father was then King (as we suppose)
MASSYR60:8	H273	And then to {unto} *Media* transfer'd his seat.
MASSYR60:22	H287	Then did rebuild destroyed *Ninivie,*
MASSYR61:6	H311	Forty eight years he reign'd, his race then run,
MASSYR61:18	H323	To *Tiglath* then doth *Ahaz* send for ease.
MASSYR61:27	H332	Unto *Damascus* then, comes *Iudah's* King,
MASSYR61:40	H345	Then by his death, releas'd, was *Israels* fears.
MASSYR62:19	H364	Then sent his Colonies, theirs to invest;
MASSYR62:39	H384	With shame then turn'd to *Ninivie* again,
MASSYR64:23	H447	Then into *Ægypt, Necho* did retire,
MASSYR65:22	H487	Thus {Then} cast him out, like to a naked Asse,
MASSYR65:25	H490	Then from his throne, he pull'd {pluck'd} him down again:
MASSYR65:27	H492	And more then {seven and} thirty years in prison fed;
MASSYR66:21	H527	Then *Put,* and *Lud,* doe at his mercy stand,
MPERS69:20	H642	Against great *Cressus,* then of *Lidia* head;
MPERS69:35	H657	Then on a Pike being {wood-pile} set, where all might eye,
MPERS69:38	H661	Then to the King he makes this true report,
MPERS70:41	H712	Then at his Herse great honours to expresse;
MPERS71:4	H716	Unto *Cambyses* then, all did remain.
MPERS71:4	H720	To shew how little Land he then should take.
MPERS71:9	H725	Then sends to finde a Law for these his sins;
MPERS71:17	H731	He seized first of life, and then of Land;
MPERS71:34	H748	The *Ægyptian Apis* then he likewise slew,
MPERS72:7	H756	*Praxaspes* into *Persia* then is sent,
MPERS72:21	H769	Over his Seat, then plac'd his Son therein;
MPERS73:21	H808	Their {Then} Forces instantly they raise, and rout,
MPERS74:9	H834	Then mounting on their snorting coursers proud,
MPERS74:17	H840	They then {all} attend him, to his royall roome,
MPERS74:22	H845	He two of *Cyrus* Daughters now {then} doth wed,
MPERS74:38	H859	Then brave *Zopirus,* for his Masters good,
MPERS75:14	H875	Then thy disgrace, thine honour's manifold,
MPERS76:6	H904	Which two then to assaile, his {royal} Camp was bold:

MPERS76:37	H935	Pursues his flying-foes, and {then} on the strand;
MPERS77:13	H952	Unto {Then to} his eldest {second} Son, all did remain.
MPERS78:15	H996	These {Such} his Land Forces were, then next, a Fleet
MPERS78:34	H1015	Then gives the King, a King-like gift, most {full} large;
MPERS78:37	H1018	He humbly to the King then makes request,
MPERS79:2	H1024	Then laid his parts on both sides of the way,
MPERS79:13	H1036	Then whips the sea, and with a mind most vain
MPERS79:18	H1044	And {Then} in *Abidus* Plaines, mustring his Forces,
MPERS79:34	H1060	Then marching {on} to the streight *Thermopyle,*
MPERS79:40	H1066	And all that Army, then dismay'd, had fled,
MPERS80:23	H1090	Yet {Then} in the Streights of *Salamis* he try'd,
MPERS80:28	H1095	But {the} *Phocians* Land, {Country} he then wasted sore:
MPERS82:2	H1148	Then for one battel shortly all provide,
MPERS83:14	H1202	The {Then} *Artabanus* hirer of this deed,
MPERS83:23	H1211	Such Justice then, in *Persia* {Persian court} did remain, {reign.}
MPERS83:34	H1222	Then when the world, they after over-run:
MPERS84:29	H1265	Provisions, {then} and season now being fit,
MPERS85:8	H1284	Then the surviver is by *Nothus* slaine;
MPERS85:29	H1305	Re-gaines his own, and then {doth} the Rebell breaks: {break,}
MPERS85:34	H1310	*Persian* Kings, did deem {then deem'd} themselves so good,
MPERS86:33	H1349	Then next, the *Lacedemons* {Spartans} he takes to {into} pay;
MPERS87:27	H1379	The mazed King, was now {then} about to fly;
MPERS87:31	H1383	Up then with speed, a mighty trench he throwes,
MPERS89:17	H1451	Forth-with {Then} he sends {that} to's Tent, they straight
MPERS89:27	H1461	Such terrour on the *Persians* then did fall,
MPERS90:26	H1493	They then *Dercilladas,* send with an Hoast,
MPERS90:36	H1503	*Tythraustes* now {then} is placed in his stead,
MPERS90:40	H1507	*Tythraustes* trusts more to his wit then Arms,
MPERS91:23	H1537	Then in voluptuousnesse he leads his life,
MPERS91:29	H1543	Forty three years he rules, then turns to dust,
MPERS91:31	H1545	Forty three years he rul'd, then turn'd to dust,
MPERS91:40	H1554	Then raises forces, conquers *Egypt* land,
MPERS92:13	H1571	reign'd, as Chronicles expresse, {then drank of's fathers cup}
MPERS92:14	H1572	Then Natures debt he paid, quite Issue-lesse.
MGREC93:36	H1633	Restlesse both day and night, his heart now {then} was,
MGREC94:18	H1652	Then with alacrity he after goes:
MGREC94:21	H1659	Then on he march'd, in's way he veiw'd old *Troy;*
MGREC94:31	H1669	Then to his Lieutenant, {he} in *Asia* sends,
MGREC94:33	H1671	To whip him well with rods, and then {so} to bring,
MGREC95:6	H1685	*Sardis,* then he, and *Ephesus,* did gaine,
MGREC95:21	H1700	Then in *Darius* multitudes {multitude} beside:
MGREC95:26	H1705	Now {Then} *Alexander* all *Cilicia* takes:
MGREC95:30	H1709	And on {Then o're} he goes *Darius* {now} so to meet;
MGREC96:24	H1744	Then such a world of Wagons did appear,
MGREC98:8	H1810	In the old town (which now {then} lay like a wood)
MGREC98:18	H1820	Whose glory, now {then} a second time's brought down;
MGREC98:38	H1840	And then at *Tigris,* and *Araxis* side:
MGREC99:19	H1862	Then in the *Persian* Monarchy beside;
MGREC100:5	H1889	Then to the Phane of *Jupiter,* he went,
MGREC100:13	H1897	Then setling all things in lesse *Asia,*
MGREC102:5	H1975	This Conquerour now {then} goes to *Babylon,*

MGREC102:27	H1997	He then to *Sushan* goes, with his fresh {new} bands,
MGREC104:4	H2056	Then still with infamy, to draw his breath.
MGREC104:10	H2062	Then with so few, how likely to be crost.
MGREC104:17	H2069	Bidding his {Then bids} servant *Artabassus* true;
MGREC104:25	H2077	Then draws the Cart along, with chaines of gold;
MGREC105:1	H2094	Then slew his servants, that were faithfull found;
MGREC105:18	H2111	To them he goes, and {repairs then} looking in the Cart,
MGREC106:19	H2153	Then tell her errand, we had better spare
MGREC107:6	H2181	Then {And} hearing, *Bessus* makes himselfe a King,
MGREC107:27	H2202	Then did {all} their wars, against the *Persian* King.
MGREC107:34	H2209	So {Then} from his carriages the Hides he takes,
MGREC109:1	H2258	He enters now {then} the *Indian* Kings among;
MGREC109:23	H2282	And {Then} eighty Tallents to his Captaines down.
MGREC110:12	H2312	Then {When} covertly, the rest gets {get} o're else-where;
MGREC110:33	H2337	Twelve Altars, he for Monuments then rears,
MGREC111:1	H2346	Then down t' *Hidaspis* with his Fleet he went;
MGREC111:12	H2357	Then sayling South, and comming to the {that} shore,
MGREC111:16	H2361	Hence {Then} sayling down by th' mouth of *Indus* floud,
MGREC111:29	H2374	From hence he to {then unto} *Gedrosia* went,
MGREC111:34	H2379	Then visits *Cyrus* Sepulcher in's way,
MGREC111:40	H2385	A Wedding Feast to's Nobles then he makes,
MGREC114:16	H2486	Then all the wrong to brave *Parmenio* done.
MGREC115:39	H2558	His age, and journey long, he now {then} pretends;
MGREC116:19	H2585	The principles of what he then had learn'd
MGREC119:18	H2708	To brave *Craterus,* then, he sends with speed,
MGREC120:4	H2739	Then fall into the hands of mortal foes.
MGREC120:31	H2768	Brave *Ptolomy,* to make a fourth now {then} sent,
MGREC121:17	H2799	Knocks out his braines, to *Ptolomy* then went,
MGREC123:15	H2879	To *Polisperchon,* then his place he gave, {did bequeath}
MGREC123:22	H2886	Now {Then} *Polisperchon* 'gins to act in's place,
MGREC125:12	H2960	Then by intreaties, promises, and coyne,
MGREC125:20	H2968	Then {The} King, and Queen, to *Amphipolis* doe fly, {seeing
MGREC125:38	H2988	In *Pelloponesus* then *Cassander* lay,
MGREC127:10	H3040	Old *Thebes* he then re-built (so much of fame)
MGREC127:22	H3052	*Antigonus,* then takes {who took} his life unjust,
MGREC127:30	H3060	Then with *Seleuchus* straight at ods doth fall,
MGREC128:15	H3088	Now {Then} *Ptolomy* would gaine the *Greeks* likewise,
MGREC129:1	H3115	Who then shall {should} be installed in the throne:
MGREC129:28	H3142	Call'd *Hercules,* and elder then his brother,
MGREC130:5	H3160	She now {then} in *Lydia* at *Sardis* lay,
MGREC130:35	H3181	His wife and sons then slain by this *Cassander,*
MGREC131:2	H3192	To *Athens* then he {*Demetrius* thether} goes, is entertain'd,
MGREC131:10	H3202	*Antigonus* and *Seleuchus,* now {then his} fight
MGREC131:24	H3216	His peace he then with old *Seleuchus* makes,
MGREC134:2	H3333	And then *Antiochus* surnam'd the great,
MGREC134:4	H3337	And then {next} *Epiphanes,* whose wicked deeds,
MGREC134:13	H3344	That {Then} *Tygranes* the great *Armenian* King,
MGREC134:29	H3360	*Philometer:* then *Evergetes* again.
MGREC134:31	H3362	*Alexander,* then *Lathurus* in's stead,
MGREC134:38	H3367	For *Pompey's* life, then plac'd her in his stead,
MGREC135:2	H3374	Then poysonous {His brave *Virago*} Aspes she sets unto {to}

MGREC135:10	H3382	Now up, now down, now chief, and then brought under;
MGREC135:17	H3389	Then came the *Romane,* like a raging flood,
MGREC135:24	H3396	The Stone out of the Mountaine then did rise,
MGREC135:26	H3398	Then gold, silver, brasse, iron, and all that {the} store,
MROMAN136:28	H3442	The double injury, he then did doe:
MROMAN137:5	H3456	Great priviledges then, to all he grants,
MROMAN137:10	H3461	But all disdaine alliance then to make,
MROMAN137:14	H3465	Their Daughters by the *Romans* then were caught,
MROMAN~~137:15~~	H3466	For {Then} to recover them, a Feild was fought;
MROMAN137:20	H3471	But *Romulus* then comes unto his end,
MROMAN138:11	H3501	Thirty two years doth *Tullus* reigne, then dye,
MROMAN138:23	H3513	Then unto death unwillingly gives place.
MROMAN138:33	H3523	To such rude triumphs, as young *Rome* then had,
MROMAN139:7	H3535	To eighty thousand soules then did amount:
MROMAN139:9	H3537	And then by *Tarquin, Priscus* Son, was slaine.
DIALOG141:27	H26	Then weigh our case, if't be not justly sad,
DIALOG~~144:25~~	H134	I then believ'd not, now I feel and see,
DIALOG145:14	H163	Then let's join heads, and hands {& hearts} for your relief.
DIALOG145:16	H165	Well, to the matter then, there's grown of late,
DIALOG147:27	H251	When they are gone, then drown your self in teares.
DIALOG147:28	H252	If now you weep so much, that then no more,
DIALOG147:38	H262	Then Justice shall in all thy Courts take place,
DIALOG147:40	H264	Then bribes shall cease, and suits shall not stick long,
DIALOG148:1	H266	Then High Commissions shall fall to decay,
DIALOG148:18	H283	(For then what is't, but English blades dare do)
DIALOG148:25	H290	Then fulness of the Nations in shall flow,
DIALOG148:27	H292	Then follows dayes of happinesse and rest,
DIALOG148:29	H294	No Canaanite shall then be found ith' land,
DIALOG148:31	H296	If this make way thereto, then sigh no more,
SIDNEY149:10	H9	Then {As} she that sway'd the Scepter with her hand:
SIDNEY149:28	~~H23~~	What doe thy vertues then? Oh, honours crown!
SIDNEY149:33	~~H23~~	Let then, none dis-allow of these my straines,
SIDNEY~~150:12~~	H42	Then let none disallow of these my straines
SIDNEY150:17	~~H49~~	Then let such Crowes as I, thy praises sing,
SIDNEY151:16	~~H69~~	Then wonder lesse, if warlike *Philip* yield,
SIDNEY152:1	~~H75~~	Better my hap, then was his darlings fate,
SIDNEY~~152:13~~	H82	For {Then} to revenge his {this} wrong, themselves ingage,
SIDNEY~~152:14~~	H84	Then wonder not if I no better sped,
SIDNEY152:17	H86	I pensive for my fault, sat down, and then,
DUBART154:7	H52	Vollies of praises could I eccho then,
QELIZ157:31	H99	To read what others write, and then {so} admire.
QELIZ157:41	H109	Then wonder not, *Eliza* moves not here.
QELIZ158:5	H114	If then new things, their old form must {forms shall} retain,
VANITY160:4	H14	What then? content in pleasures canst thou find?
VANITY160:12	H22	Where is it then? in wisdome, learning, arts?
VANITY160:18	H28	What is it then? to do as Stoicks tell,
DDUDLEY167:23	H20	*Then dying, left a blessed memory.*
CONTEM168:7	H16	Then on a stately Oak I cast mine Eye,
CONTEM168:15	H23	Then higher on the glistering Sun I gaz'd,
CONTEM169:6	H48	How full of glory then must thy Creator be?
CONTEM169:18	H58	I heard the merry grashopper then sing,

CONTEM169:31	H70	Then was *Methuselah,* or's grand-sire great:
CONTEM170:23	H94	His brother comes, then acts his fratricide,
CONTEM170:28	H99	Though none on Earth but kindred near then could he find.
CONTEM171:19	H122	And then the earth (though old) stil clad in green,
CONTEM171:22	H125	If winter come, and greeness then do fade,
CONTEM171:34	H135	Shall I then praise the heavens, the trees, the earth
CONTEM173:3	H171	Then to the colder bottome streight they dive,
CONTEM173:31	H196	Then follow thee into a better Region,
FLESH175:33	H33	Then eyes can see, or hands can hold.
FLESH175:36	H36	Then let not goe, what thou maist find,
FLESH176:15	H55	Then when I did what thou bad'st doe.
FLESH176:31	H71	Then can thy hours in pleasure spent.
SICKNES178:33	H16	and then we go to th' Tomb.
SICKNES179:3	H23	Then deaths arrest I shall count best,
DISTEMP179:19	H7	Then eyes lay dry, disabled to weep more;
1HUSB180:33	H12	Then while we live, in love lets so persever,
1LETTER181:16	H14	Then view those fruits which through thy heat I bore?
VERSES184:1	H5	Then may your worthy self from whom it came.
CHILDRN184:20	H9	Chief of the Brood then took his flight,
CHILDRN185:14	H40	Untill they'r grown, then as the rest,
CHILDRN185:17	H43	If birds could weep, then would my tears
ELIZB186:37	H9	Then ta'en away unto Eternity.
MERCY188:28	H14	Thou then on Seas sailing to forreign Coast;
MERCY189:4	H25	And then her sorrows all at once did go;
MEDDM197:33	Hp275	and pain till they turn to dust, and then are they fine manchet
MEDDM198:4	Hp275	then makes them lye down in green pastures and leades them
MEDDM198:6	Hp276	ouer their heads he then leads them to the Rock wch is higher
MEDDM199:12	Hp277	some men into the furnace of affliction and then beats them
MEDDM202:27	Hp282	quite gone out of sight then must we needs walk in darknesse
MEDDM202:28	Hp282	se no light, yet then must we trust in the lord and stay vpon our
MEDDM203:6	Hp283	loose them then they are lesse then vanity & more then
PILGRIM210:39	H39	Then soule and body shall vnite
PILGRIM211:3	H44	then Come deare bridgrome Come away
MYCHILD216:31	Hp242	Then haue I gone to searching, and haue said wth David Lord
MYCHILD218:31	Hp244	vpon ye Earth? & I haue not known what to think, But then
FEVER220:25	H5	Then didst thou rid me out.
SOREFIT221:19	H5	Then Lord thou said'st vnto me Liue.
SOREFIT222:10	H29	And then wth thee which is the Best
MED223:16	Hp250	what he hath done for me, and then shall I bee able to praise
MYSOUL225:13	H17	Then shall I know what thov hast done
30SEPT227:24	Hp257	and then thy stroakes shall bee welcome, I haue not been
SAMUEL228:6	H7	Thou heardst me then and gav'st him me
SAMUEL228:16	H17	Then shall I celebrate thy praise
RESTOR229:22	H5	Then did'st thou rid me out,
2HUSB232:13	H14	Then let thy promis joy his heart
HOURS234:34	H48	Then better shall I bee,
HOUSE236:23	H15	Then coming out beheld a space
HOUSE237:11	H41	Then streight I 'gin my heart to chide,

THEN'S (3) [than is]

AGES36:36	H60	Both good and bad, but yet no more then's true.

THEN'S (2) [than his]

MGREC114:4	H2472	Then's Masters god-head, to defie, and wrong;
MGREC~~132:6~~	H3240	But he a Kingdome more then's friend did eye,

THENCE (19)

ELEMEN12:33	H193	Ye *Galenists,* my Drugs that come from thence
HUMOUR22:27	H96	What comes from thence, my heat refines the same,
HUMOUR~~31:17~~	H450	And so {thence} with jaundise, Safferns al the skin.
AGES38:20	H123	From thence I 'gan to sin, as soon as act.
AGES41:10	H230	Clapt in that prison, never thence to start.
SEASONS47:31	~~H46~~	In *Taurus* Signe, yet hasteth straight from thence;
SEASONS~~47:32~~	H47	And with his warmer beams glanceth from thence
SEASONS52:21	H236	From thence he 'gins to length the shortned morn,
MASSYR53:26	H16	From thence he went *Assyria* to command;
MPERS80:38	H1105	Part of his Hoast to *Delphos* sent from thence,
MPERS88:7	H1400	Was gather'd by the dust that rose from thence:
MGREC100:1	H1885	From thence, to fruitfull *Ægypt* marcht with speed,
MGREC~~100:11~~	H1895	Now {Thence} back to *Ægypt* goes, and in few dayes,
MGREC111:30	H2375	And thence he marcht into *Carmania,*
MGREC113:1	H2428	The King would give no eare, but went from thence;
MGREC123:24	H2888	*Antipater* had banisht her from thence,
AUTHOR177:32	H4	Till snatcht from thence by friends, less wise then true
1LETTER181:25	H23	Where ever, ever stay, and go not thence,
BYNIGHT220:15	H14	And banisht thence my Doubts + feares.

THENCE-FORTH (1)

MPERS81:11	H1119	That all Hostility might {from} thence-forth cease;

THEORY (1)

MEDDM195:30	Hp272	Theory, then the practique part, but he is a true Christian that

THEOS (2)

MGREC133:36	H3326	*Antiochus Theos* was *Soters* son,
MGREC133:40	H3330	This *Theos* he was murthered by his {lewd} wife,

THER (1) [there]

MEDDM205:37	Hp287	and ther are some (and they sincere ones too) who haue not

THERE (169) See also **THERE'S, THER'S**

ELEMEN12:2	H162	But chiefly, 'cause the Muses there did dwell;
ELEMEN12:24	H184	But here, or there, I list now none to name;
ELEMEN15:24	H306	Fishes so numberlesse I there do hold;
ELEMEN15:26	H308	There lives the oyly Whale, whom all men know,
ELEMEN16:32	H355	I now must shew what force {ill} there in me lyes.
ELEMEN19:4	H449	Next, of my Fowles such multitudes there are;
HUMOUR21:35	H63	And there she wil out-bid us all, I think;
HUMOUR24:28	H177	There is no Souldier, but thy selfe thou say'st,
HUMOUR26:12	H242	For there are {is} none, thou say'st, if some, not best.
HUMOUR26:13	H243	That there are some, and best, I dare averre;
HUMOUR26:15	H245	What is there living, which cannot derive
HUMOUR26:33	H263	The spirits through thy heat, are made perfect there,
HUMOUR26:40	H270	Thou know'st I've there to do, as wel as thou;
HUMOUR27:1	H272	There lives the irascible faculty:
HUMOUR27:3	H274	Besides the vehement heat, only there known,
HUMOUR~~29:29~~	H380	For {There} to defend my self, thy better part;
HUMOUR30:35	H427	Of al the rest, thou'st nothing there to do;
HUMOUR31:16	H449	If there thou'rt stopt, to th' Liver thou turn'st in,

HUMOUR31:26	H459	Here, there, her restlesse thoughts do ever flye;
HUMOUR34:5	H560	He was no foole, who thought the Soul lay here {there},
HUMOUR34:8	H563	What wonderments, within your bals there lyes?
HUMOUR34:17	H572	Some other parts there issue from the Brain,
AGES43:13	H306	There set, I rid my selfe straight out of hand.
AGES46:19	H450	There, {Where} I shal rest, til heavens shal be no more;
SEASONS46:36	H14	Three months {(quoth she)} there are allotted to my share,
SEASONS51:29	H205	There rests, untill the Sun give it a birth:
MASSYR53:27	H17	And mighty *Ninivie*, he there begun,
MASSYR54:23	H50	So broad, three Chariots run abrest there might,
MASSYR57:24	H171	Again, the Country was left bare (there is no doubt)
MASSYR59:16	H240	There with all store he was so wel provided,
MASSYR59:18	H242	Who there incamp'd two years, for little end,
MASSYR59:23	H247	For few, or none, did there {it seems} resistance make;
MASSYR60:6	H271	Yet would not {granting} let them {now} to inhabite there;
MASSYR62:18	H363	{He} Plac'd *Israel* in's Land {there}, where he thought best,
MASSYR65:21	H486	minde, and slew him by the way; {& caus'd his life there end,}
MASSYR66:12	H518	There {And} sit bewailing *Zion* seventy years,
MASSYR67:8	H554	Among the Conquered Kings, that there did lye,
MASSYR67:18	H564	His Army routed, and himselfe there slain,
MASSYR68:24	H610	There hears his *Mene,* and his *Tekel* read;
MPERS70:30	H701	There routs his Hoast, himself she prisoner takes,
MPERS71:15	H729	'Gainst *Ægypts* King, who there by him was slain,
MPERS71:31	H745	A second Army there {he} had almost grav'd;
MPERS78:24	H1005	In person {present} there, now for his help {aid} was seen;
MPERS78:38	H1019	One of his five Sons there, might be releast;
MPERS79:11	H1033	Of Boats, together coupled, and there laid;
MPERS79:38	H1064	Two dayes and nights a fight they there maintain,
MPERS80:12	H1079	Amongst the rest, two brothers he lost there;
MPERS80:26	H1093	Received there, a shameful over-throw.
MPERS81:5	H1113	{Fearing} his best {bridge}, no longer for to {there would} stay;
MPERS82:17	H1164	And there so utterly they wrack'd the same,
MPERS83:7	H1195	Which {With} him, and his, most barbarously there slew,
MPERS86:4	H1320	But in his slow approach, ere he came there;
MPERS87:1	H1357	But fame more quick, arrives ere he came {comes} there,
MPERS87:25	H1377	*Cyrus* dispair'd, a passage there to gain;
MPERS87:28	H1380	To th' utmost parts of *Bactr'a,* and {for a time} there lye.
MPERS87:37	H1389	*Cyrus* finding his campe, and no man there;
MPERS87:40	H1392	And here, and there, in carts their Armes they throw,
MPERS88:39	H1432	And for a while unkingly there he lyes;
MPERS89:18	H1452	And there all wait his mercy, weaponlesse;
MPERS89:29	H1463	The King's {King} perplext, there dares not let them stay,
MPERS89:38	H1472	And Villaine-like, there puts them {all} to the sword.
MPERS90:10	H1483	There was of *Greeks,* setled a Colony,
MPERS90:12	H1484	There for some time they were, but whilst they staid,
MPERS91:8	H1516	To defend, more then offend, he had {there was} need.
MGREC95:5	H1684	With losse of thirty four, of his there slaine:
MGREC95:16	H1695	There {where} the Prophetick knot, he cuts in twain;
MGREC95:22	H1701	There {In's stead} *Arsemes* {*Arses*} was plac'd, yet {but} durst
MGREC95:32	H1711	Though some there be, and that {(perhaps)} more likely, write;
MGREC95:35	H1714	(Both sexes there) was almost numberlesse.

MGREC96:3	H1723	Oh {Sure} 'twas a goodly sight, there to behold;
MGREC99:14	H1857	He now to *Gaza* goes, and there doth meet
MGREC~~100:16~~	H1900	For no man to resist {man's there} his valour showes {Army to
MGREC100:17	H1901	Had *Betis* now been there, but with his Band,
MGREC103:38	H2049	(And there with sorrows, fears, and cares surrounded)
MGREC106:18	H2152	Such country there, nor yet such people finde.
MGREC107:39	~~H2214~~	He easily might have made them stay there stil;
MGREC~~107:39~~	H2214	With little pain there might have kept them still:
MGREC108:22	H2238	And there most fiercely set upon the same;
MGREC109:22	H2281	Presents himself, {first} there with a golden Crowne,
MGREC109:35	H2294	That to attend him there, was his intent;
MGREC109:41	H2300	And there {by force} his Soveraignty for to make good;
MGREC110:8	H2308	Did here, and there, Isles full of trees abide;
MGREC110:11	H2311	*Porus* encounters them, thinking {and thinks} all's there,
MGREC110:31	H2335	Huge Bridles made, which here, and there, he left,
MGREC110:38	H2342	Two Cities built, his fame {name} might there abide;
MGREC111:38	H2383	From hence to *Babylon,* some time there spent,
MGREC115:5	H2516	Findes there the want of wise *Parmenio,*
MGREC115:17	H2536	To meet him there, t' *Antipater* had {he'd} sent,
MGREC115:19	H2538	And in a Tragedy there end his age.
MGREC116:12	H2578	And Conquests be talkt of, whilst there is Land;
MGREC116:36	H2602	There was {were} no worlds, more, to be conquered:
MGREC~~116:39~~	H2605	He would have found enough for {there} to be done,
MGREC118:12	H2659	For second offers {offer} there were {was} never made;
MGREC119:30	H2720	For fighting still, whilst there did hope remain,
MGREC120:23	H2760	And by his presence there, to nullifie
MGREC122:40	H2861	All to be order'd there as he thought best:
MGREC126:9	H3000	There by *Cassander* she's block'd up, so long,
MGREC126:13	H3004	*Cassander* is resolv'd, there to remaine,
MGREC126:21	~~H3012~~	But he unwilling longer there to stay,
MGREC127:8	H3038	Among their Ancestors by him there {they're} laid,
MGREC131:16	H3208	Nor to his son did there {e're} one foot remain,
MGREC132:21	H3266	There was he {At last he's} taken and imprisoned
MGREC133:39	H3329	And calls them there, the Kings of South, and North;
MROMAN136:33	H3447	His Brother *Remus* there, by him was slaine,
MROMAN137:8	H3459	Of Wives there was so great a scarsity,
DIALOG144:41	H149	Thousands of starved Christian there also.
DIALOG146:25	H211	my relief now use thy utmost skill {do what there lyes in thee}
DIALOG148:7	H272	There let thy name, thy fame, thy valour {glory} shine,
QELIZ155:17	H8	And so has {hath} vow'd, whilst there is world, or time;
QELIZ~~156:26~~	H53	*Don Anthony* in's right for {there} to install;
DAVID159:3	H18	There had his dignity so sore a soyle,
VANITY160:26	H36	There is a path, no vultures eye hath seen.
CONTEM169:35	H73	Sees glorious *Adam* there made Lord of all,
CONTEM170:22	H93	There *Abel* keeps his sheep, no ill he thinks,
CONTEM171:36	H137	Shall I wish there, or never to had birth,
CONTEM172:12	H148	And if the sun would ever shine, there would I dwell.
CONTEM172:16	H151	I markt, nor crooks, nor rubs that there did lye
CONTEM173:5	H173	To see what trade they great ones there do drive,
FLESH175:17	H17	And dost thou hope to dwell there soon?
FLESH175:18	H18	Hast treasures there laid up in store

FLESH177:10	H91	And Angels are for Porters there;
FLESH177:13	H94	A Chrystal River there doth run,
FLESH177:15	H96	Of Life, there are the waters sure,
FLESH177:19	H100	No Candle there, nor yet Torch light,
FLESH177:20	H101	For there shall be no darksome night.
FLESH177:23	H104	Nor withering age shall e're come there,
FLESH177:26	H107	For things unclean there shall not be:
1LETTER181:6	H4	How stayest thou there, whilst I at *Ipswich* lye?
1LETTER181:28	H26	I here, thou there, yet both but one.
2LETTER182:7	H13	And if he love, how can he there abide?
3LETTER183:17	H19	But lanches on that shore, there for to dye,
3LETTER183:22	H24	I here, he there, alas, both kept by force:
CHILDRN184:15	H4	Four Cocks there were, and Hens the rest,
CHILDRN184:29	H18	And Seasons twain they there did spend:
CHILDRN185:15	H41	Or here or there, they'l take their flight,
CHILDRN185:30	H56	And knew what thoughts there sadly rest,
CHILDRN186:13	H80	And there with Seraphims set song:
MEDDM195:24	Hp272	There is no obiect that we see. no action that we doe, no good
MEDDM198:16	Hp276	skillfull fisher hath his severall baits, for severall fish, but there
MEDDM198:21	Hp276	There is no new thing vnder ye Sun there is nothing that can
MEDDM202:2	Hp281	There is nothing admits of more admiration, then gods various
MEDDM205:16	Hp286	is this Court of Judicature, that there is no appeale from it, no
MEDDM205:19	Hp286	boldnes to go to the throne of grace to be accepted there,
MEDDM205:21	Hp286	stands right there.
MEDDM205:35	Hp286	there are some eminent Christians, that are soe frequent in
MEDDM206:2	Hp287	there are others that haue nothing to commend them, but only
MEDDM206:6	Hp287	We se in the firmament there is but one Sun, among a
MEDDM206:9	Hp287	Sun, so is it in the Church both militant and triumphant, there
MEDDM207:15	Hp288	shadow very comfortable, yet there is some worm or other,
MEDDM208:8	Hp290	wth length of time (if there be no inter course) will coole the
MEDDM208:9	Hp290	friends, though there should be no displeasence betweene
MEDDM209:3	Hp291	but it is so necessary, that wthout faith there is no salvation
MEDDM209:20	Hp291	so there may be a mutuall commerce through ye world As it is
MEDDM209:21	Hp291	so it is with men, there was neuer yet any one man that had
PILGRIM210:31	H31	What tho my flesh shall there consume
PILGRIM210:41	H41	Such lasting ioyes, shall there behold
MYCHILD217:28	Hp243	were it hell it self and could there find ye Love of God toward
MYCHILD217:33	Hp243	times by Atheisme how I could know whether there was a
MYCHILD217:35	Hp243	know but they were feigned. That there is a God my Reason
MYCHILD218:4	Hp243	resolve me that there is an Eternall Being. But how should I
MYCHILD218:7	Hp244	me over. I haue argved thvs wth my self, That there is a God I
MYCHILD218:13	Hp244	it? Is there any story but that wch showes the beginnings of
MYCHILD218:31	Hp244	there Faith vpon ye Earth? & I haue not known what to think,
SAMUEL228:13	H14	Protect him there & bring him back.
HOURS234:20	H34	And there content I'll take
HOUSE236:35	H27	And here and there ye places spye
HOUSE236:37	H29	Here stood that Trunk, and there y^t chest
HOUSE236:38	H30	There lay that store I covnted best

THEREAT (1)

HUMOUR29:25	H376	The blow that's aim'd thereat is latch'd by th'arm,

THEREFORE (7) See also THERFORE

SEASONS53:6	H262	*Accept therefore of what is penn'd,*
MASSYR59:38	H262	He did repent, therefore it {the threatning} was not done,
MGREC97:41	H1802	Therefore a Crown, and great provisions {Provision} send;
MGREC98:30	H1832	And therefore {So} gives this {his little} Lord-ship to another.
MGREC128:13	H3086	Requires them therefore to take up their Armes,
MGREC128:21	H3094	So therefore craves {requests} their help to take him down,
DIALOG146:2	H190	Shews all was done, I'll therefore let it go.

THEREIN (7)

ELEMEN11:15	H135	And all therein at that great day of doome;
MASSYR60:2	H267	With over-plus of all treasures {the wealth} therein,
MPERS72:21	H769	Over his Seat, then plac'd his Son therein;
MPERS~~79:13~~	H1037	He fetters cast therein the same to chain.
MPERS85:15	H1291	Drives out his garison that therein {'mongst them} dwels.
DIALOG148:28	H293	Whose lot doth fall to live therein is blest:
SIDNEY150:1	H26	But some infatuate fooles soone caught therein,

THEREOF (7)

FATHER5:11	H12	Yet view thereof, did cause my thoughts to soare,
HUMOUR27:35	H306	One touch thereof so beautifies the skin;
SEASONS49:21	H112	With robes thereof, Kings have been dignifi'd.
QELIZ155:19	H10	The sound thereof raps every humane sence;
VANITY160:29	H39	Who drinks thereof, the world doth naught account.
FLESH177:11	H92	The Streets thereof transparent gold,
MEDDM205:36	Hp287	many times, the waight thereof impares both their bodys and

THEREON (2)

AGES~~45:22~~	H406	And an Usurper subt'ly mount thereon.
MGREC106:9	H2143	(For scarce the world, or any bounds thereon,

THERE'S (9) [there is]

ELEMEN~~10:3~~	H78	With {There's} *Orion* arm'd, attended by his dog,
ELEMEN10:28	H103	There's none more strange then *Ætna's* sulphery mount
HUMOUR32:24	H498	Nor wonder 'twas, for hatred there's not smal,
MGREC130:40	H3185	For to their Crowns, there's none can title make.
DIALOG145:8	H157	Your fearfull sinnes, great cause there's to lament,
DIALOG145:16	H165	Well, to the matter then, there's grown of late,
DUBART154:36	H81	And whilst there's aire, or fire, or sea or land.
FLESH177:6	H87	There's none on Earth can parallel;
SICKNES179:5	H25	Bestow much cost there's nothing lost,

THERETO (3)

MPERS80:34	H1101	For his retreat, to have an eye thereto:
MROMAN139:28	H3554	My thoughts and my endeavours thereto bent;
DIALOG148:31	H296	If this make way thereto, then sigh no more,

THEREUNTO (1)

MPERS85:33	H1309	by {To which} his pride, {more} then {his} lust, thereunto led.

THEREUPON (2)

HUMOUR23:16	H126	If once thou'rt great, what followes thereupon?
MPERS70:13	H684	Not finding a defendant thereupon;

THEREWITH (1)

ELEMEN17:17	H381	That *Israels* enemies, therewith was {were} brain'd.

THERFORE (4) [therefore]

MEDDM200:21	Hp279	Christian, therfore god cuts their garments short, to keep them
MEDDM203:17	Hp283	sees land we must therfore be heer as strangers and pilgrims,

MEDDM204:10	Hp284	the larger his accounts stands vpon gods score it therfore
MEDDM209:4	Hp291	therfore wth all our seekings and gettings, let vs aboue all seek

THERMOPYLE (1)

MPERS79:34	H1060	Then marching {on} to the streight *Thermopyle,*

THERMUS (1)

MASSYR54:33	H60	*Pharmus, {Thermus}* their King, he caused to be slain;

THER'S (1) [there is]

HOUSE237:25	H55	Ther's wealth enovgh I need no more,

THESE (158)

FATHER5:2	H2-3	*Thomas Dudley* Esq; *these humbly presented.*
FATHER5:19	H20	These same are they, of {from} whom we being have,
FATHER5:20	H21	These are of all, the life, the nurse, the grave,
FATHER5:21	H22	These are, the hot, the cold, the moist, the dry,
FATHER5:23	H24	Of these consists, our bodyes, cloathes, and food,
FATHER5:26	H27	Their discord may {doth} appear, by these harsh rimes.
FATHER6:9	H43	These ragged lines, will do't, when they appear.
PROLOG6:22	H7	Let Poets, and Historians set these forth,
PROLOG7:37	H47	If e're you daigne these lowly lines, your eyes
ELEMEN9:26	H60	But let me leave these things, my flame aspires
ELEMEN10:13	H88	Nay more then these, Rivers 'mongst stars are found,
ELEMEN10:17	H92	Out of a multitude, these few I touch,
ELEMEN11:34	H154	Of these so common things, can make report:
ELEMEN12:15	H175	But ile skip {leap} o're these Hills, not touch a Dale,
ELEMEN14:6	H250	What she hath lost by these my dreadfull {remed'less} woes.
ELEMEN16:31	H354	These be my benefits which may suffice:
ELEMEN17:27	H391	But these are trifles to the Flood of *Noe.*
ELEMEN18:2	H406	Yet Aire, beyond all these ye know t'excell.
HUMOUR22:31	H100	The Animal I claime, as wel as these,
HUMOUR23:5	H115	But a good head from these are disonant;
HUMOUR26:9	H239	For acting these, I have nor wil, nor art,
HUMOUR30:32	H424	These two in one cannot have residence.
HUMOUR31:37	H470	But these with you, are seldome resident.
HUMOUR34:19	H574	Some worthy {curious} learned *Crooke* may these reveal,
AGES35:31	H17	Such cold mean flowers (as these) blossome {the spring puts
AGES36:27	H51	These being met, each in his equipage,
AGES45:23	H413	These are no old wives tales, but this is truth;
AGES46:22	H453	And I shal see, with these same very eyes,
SEASONS46:31	H7	In season all these Seasons I shal bring;
SEASONS48:2	H55	These might as Lace, set out her Garments fine;
MASSYR53:25	H15	These were his first, all stood in *Shinar* land,
MASSYR58:13	H198	These two rul'd *Media* and *Babylon,*
MASSYR58:21	H206	These all agree, and forty thousand make,
MASSYR58:25	H208	These Forces mustered, and in array,
MASSYR58:35	H218	These with celerity, *Arbaces* meets {meet},
MASSYR60:28	H293	From rubbish these, with diligence he rakes,
MASSYR66:13	H519	With all these Conquests, *Babels* King rests not,
MPERS71:9	H725	Then sends to finde a Law for these his sins;
MPERS73:19	H806	And first these noble *Magi* 'gree upon,
MPERS73:26	H811	And two of these great Peers, in place {Field} lay dead:
MPERS76:7	H905	By these alone his Hoast was pinch'd so sore,
MPERS78:6	H987	Eight hundred thousand Horse to them {these} belong;

MPERS78:11	H992	But the command of these Commanders all,
MPERS78:15	H996	These {Such} his Land Forces were, then next, a Fleet
MPERS78:31	H1012	At *Sardis,* in *Lidia,* these all doe meet,
MPERS79:12	H1034	But winds, and waves, these couples soon dissever'd,
MPERS79:23	H1049	That none of these should {those could} live a {an} hundred
MPERS81:1	H1109	And many thousands of these {those} men did kil;
MPERS82:3	H1150	Ten dayes these Armies did each other face,
MPERS83:40	H1228	To be partakers in {of} these festivalls.
MPERS85:10	H1286	These two lewd {first} sons, are by hystorians thought,
MPERS85:25	H1301	So that he might, these tumults {those troubles} soon appease.
MPERS85:28	H1304	The King much profit reapeth, by these leagues {this league},
MPERS86:19	H1335	These and like motives, hurry him amain,
MPERS87:4	H1360	The one {last} accus'd the other, {first} for these {sad} wars:
MPERS87:15	H1370	And yet with these, had neither heart, nor grace;
MPERS90:11	H1484	These {Who} after all, receiv'd them joyfully:
MPERS90:17	H1484	For these incursions he durst not abide;
MPERS91:3	H1511	To these {them} he thirty thousand Tallents sent,
MPERS91:14	H1522	'Mongst these *Epimanondas* wants no fame;
MPERS91:17	H1525	But let us leave these *Greeks,* to discord bent,
MPERS92:19	H1577	By one of these, he must obtain the place.
MPERS92:30	H1588	Yet in these {such} differences, we may behold; {be bold,}
MGREC93:17	H1614	His Education, much to these {those} did adde.
MGREC94:20	H1658	To these {which} were joyn'd, five thousand goodly horse.
MGREC98:39	H1841	These he may scape, and if he so desire,
MGREC99:6	H1849	Tels him, these proffers great (in truth were none)
MGREC99:20	H1863	And by these walls, so many men were slaine,
MGREC103:41	H2052	Was straight in *Bactria* these {soon} to augment,
MGREC104:24	H2076	Who wanting means t' resist, these wrongs abides.
MGREC105:16	H2109	So chanc'd these bloudy Horses to espy,
MGREC107:25	H2200	Where most {so} immoderatly these thirsty drink;
MGREC107:36	H2211	On these, together ty'd, in six dayes space,
MGREC108:9	H2225	These not a little joy'd, this day to see,
MGREC108:23	H2239	Repelling these two marks of honour got,
MGREC110:35	H2339	But doubting, wearing Time would {might} these decay,
MGREC111:6	H2351	These, all he feasts in state, on beds of gold,
MGREC111:13	H2358	These {Those} obscure Nations yeelded as before;
MGREC111:32	H2377	Now through these goodly countries as he past,
MGREC112:8	H2394	To shadow forth these short felicities:
MGREC113:14	H2441	But how these Captaines should, or yet their Master,
MGREC113:22	H2449	Wherefore at once all these to satisfie,
MGREC114:17	H2487	The next of worth, that suffered after these,
MGREC117:33	H2640	By Natures right, these had enough to claime,
MGREC118:13	H2660	'Mongst these contentions, tumults, jealousies,
MGREC118:16	H2663	So much these Princes their owne ends respected.
MGREC118:41	H2690	These now to govern for the King pretends,
MGREC119:12	H2702	In these tumultuous dayes, the thralled *Greeks*
MGREC120:26	H2763	And summons him, to answer these {his} complaints;
MGREC120:33	H2770	In midst of these, *Garboyles,* with wondrous state,
MGREC123:13	H2876	But while these Chieftains doe in Asia fight,
MGREC123:38	H2902	Unto these helps, in *Greece,* {at home} he seeks out more,
MGREC124:1	H2906	By these, and all, to grant him some supply,

MGREC124:4	H2909	Hoping still {yet} more to gaine by these new stirs;
MGREC124:10	H2917	That no supply by these here might be lent,
MGREC124:17	H2924	Whilst hot in wars these two in *Greece* remaine,
MGREC124:37	H2944	These, with his love, unto the amorous Queen
MGREC125:7	H2955	The better to accomplish these her ends;
MGREC125:23	H2973	And to the Queen, these presents she doth {did} send;
MGREC128:14	H3087	And to requite this Traytor for those {these} harmes:
MGREC128:23	H3096	*Antigonus* {These princes} at {the} Sea soone had a fight,
MGREC128:37	H3110	At last these Princes tired out with warres,
MGREC130:6	H3161	Where, by Embassage, all these Princes pray,
MGREC130:39	H3184	These Captains now, the stile of Kings do take,
MGREC131:6	H3196	These Kings fall now afresh to {their} warres again,
MGREC131:14	H3206	This day twixt these two foes {Kings} ends all the strife,
MGREC132:19	H3256	These to recover, musters all his might,
MGREC132:20	H3259	With these he hopes to turn the world about:
MGREC132:34	H3281	*Seleuchus,* and *Lysimachus;* those {these} twaine
MGREC132:41	H3288	Whilst with these hopes, in *Greece* he did remaine,
MGREC133:6	H3294	Thus with these Kingly Captaines have we done,
MGREC134:33	H3364	To all these names we *Ptolomy* must adde,
MGREC135:36	H3408	With these three Monarchies, now have I done,
MROMAN137:6	H3457	That wil within these strong built walls reside,
MROMAN137:13	H3464	To see these sports, the *Sabins* all are bent;
DIALOG141:9	H8	And sit i'th dust, to sigh these sad alarms?
DIALOG141:15	H14	Art ignorant indeed, of these my woes?
DIALOG141:16	H15	Or must my forced tongue these griefes disclose?
DIALOG142:22	H51	If none of these, deare Mother, what's your woe?
DIALOG144:15	H125	These be the *Hydra's* of my stout transgression;
DIALOG144:16	H126	These be the bitter fountains, heads, and roots,
DIALOG144:20	H130	For these, were threatned the wofull day,
DIALOG144:24	H133	These Prophets mouthes (alas the while) was stopt,
DIALOG146:11	H199	But these may be beginnings of more woe,
DIALOG146:34	H220	To see these {those} latter dayes of hop'd for good,
DIALOG147:10	H236	These are the dayes, the Churches foes to crush,
DIALOG147:30	H254	These, these, are they (I trust) with *Charles* our King,
SIDNEY149:33	H23	Let then, none dis-allow of these my straines,
SIDNEY150:12	H42	Then let none disallow of these my straines
SIDNEY151:2	H69	If such Stars as these, sad presages be,
QELIZ157:23	H91	And of all these without compare the best;
VANITY160:14	H24	Yet these, the wisest man of men did find,
TDUDLEY165:22	H24	These to the world his merits could make known,
CONTEM168:13	H22	If so, all these as nought, Eternity doth scorn.
CONTEM174:1	H202	From some of these he never finds cessation,
CONTEM174:36	H233	Shall last and shine when all of these are gone.
FLESH176:16	H56	Ile stop mine ears at these thy charms,
BIRTH180:2	H12	These farewell lines to recommend to thee,
BIRTH180:16	H26	These O protect from step Dames injury.
2LETTER182:30	H36	Hath power to dry the torrent of these streams.
3LETTER183:26	H28	The substance gone, O me, these are but dreams.
2SIMON195:8	Hp271	you nor of more ease to my self then these short meditations
MEDDM200:11	Hp279	these empty brests, that god is forced to hedg vp their way w^th
MEDDM201:22	Hp281	some black Clouds that impends them, wch produces these

THICK (3)

SEASONS49:17	H108	To wash their {the} thick cloath'd flocks, with pipes ful glad.
MGREC108:32	H2248	They flew so thick they seem'd to dark the aire:
MEDDM201:20	Hp280	from a thick ayre about them so may we sometime se, marble

THICKER (1)

SEASONS48:13	H66	Our Winter {thicker} rayment, makes us lay aside,

THIEF See THEIFE

THIGH (1)

MPERS72:41	H787	And with a mortall thrust, wounds him ith' thigh,

THIGHS (2) [pl.]

MGREC135:22	H3394	The third, belly and thighs of brasse in sight,
MGREC135:25	H3397	And smote those feet, those legs, those arms and thighs;

THIN See THINNE

THING (37)

FATHER6:2	H36	Some thing {something} of all (though mean) I did intend,
ELEMEN14:19	H261	Ile say no more, yet {but} this thing adde I must,
HUMOUR23:31	H141	Like our sixt *Henry,* that same worthy {virtuous} thing.
HUMOUR24:5	H154	And one thing more to close with {up} my narration.
AGES45:3	H381	I've seen from *Rome,* an execrable thing,
MASSYR63:19	H404	Of whom is little said in any thing; [22 years.
MASSYR68:8	H594	To him that could interpret clear this thing:
MASSYR68:18	H604	Who doth not flatter, nor once cloake the thing.
MASSYR68:25	H611	And did one thing worthy a King (though late)
MPERS72:30	H774	'T would be no pleasant {pleasure}, but a tedious thing,
MPERS74:21	H844	His title to make strong omits no thing;
MPERS75:32	H889	Shall let the work, or keep back any thing,
MPERS79:8	H1030	First thing, *Xerxes* {he} did worthy {of} recount,
MPERS92:32	H1590	And this 'mongst all's no controverted thing.
MGREC100:40	H1924	Had used her, and hers, in every thing,
MGREC106:27	H2161	His temperance, is but a sordid thing,
MGREC111:8	H2353	The meat, and drink, attendants, every thing,
MGREC112:28	H2414	His Royall pardon gave, for this same thing;
MGREC112:32	H2418	Who to the height doth aggravate each thing;
MGREC115:25	H2544	Though to his Mother he disprov'd the thing;
MGREC118:28	H2677	Under his name begins {began} to rule each thing.
MGREC118:34	H2683	To authorize his Acts in every thing.
MGREC119:41	H2731	Act any thing of worth, as heretofore,
MGREC124:26	H2933	More then he bidden was, could act no thing;
MROMAN137:26	H3477	Held for his Piety, some sacred thing;
DIALOG142:15	H44	And call in Forreign ayde, to help the thing?
DIALOG145:19	H168	One saith its he, the other no such thing.
DAVID158:28	H8	In *Gath,* let not this thing {things} be spoken on,
DAVID158:35	H15	Nor any pleasant thing e're may you show;
BIRTH179:32	H8	A common thing, yet oh inevitable;
2SIMON195:6	Hp271	once desired me to leaue some thing for you in writeing that
MEDDM198:21	Hp276	There is no new thing vnder ye Sun there is nothing that can
MEDDM198:32	Hp277	It is a pleasant thing to behold the light, but sore eyes are not
MEDDM199:16	Hp278	haue any thing to stay vpon, but take away their props and
MEDDM206:20	Hp287	themselues of turning to god, the first thing wch they eye, is
MYCHILD217:11	Hp242	Answers to me, either in granting ye Thing I prayed for, or else
28AUG226:10	Hp254	Thing. O let me ever see Thee that Art invisible, and I shall not

THINGS (50) [pl.]		
PROLOG6:20	H5	For my mean Pen, are too superiour things,
ELEMEN8:30	H28	What is my worth (both ye) and all things {men} know,
ELEMEN9:26	H60	But let me leave these things, my flame aspires
ELEMEN11:34	H154	Of these so common things, can make report:
ELEMEN19:12	H457	As my fresh Aire preserves, all things in life;
HUMOUR23:24	H134	Thus {But} arms, and arts I claim, and higher things;
HUMOUR25:19	H208	Both them and all things else, she will {would} consume.
HUMOUR32:12	H486	And things that never were, nor shal I see.
AGES38:12	H115	Nor yet on future things did place {set} my hope.
AGES42:36	H292	To greater things, I never did aspire,
MPERS73:29	H814	All things in peace, and Rebells throughly quel'd,
MPERS81:21	H1129	Their infamy would last till all things ends:
MPERS85:23	H1299	Before to quietnesse things could be brought,
MPERS92:1	H1555	In after wars were burnt, 'mongst other things?
MGREC100:13	H1897	Then setling all things in lesse *Asia,*
MGREC103:8	H2019	Here lay the bulk, of all those precious things;
MGREC105:40	H2133	Of all good things (quoth he) once in my power,
MGREC109:15	H2274	Had to his mind, made all things now {to} accord:
MGREC111:5	H2350	Bringing their Presents, rare, and precious things:
MGREC118:18	H2665	That he, who late, possest all earthly things,
MGREC122:37	H2858	When to his pleasure all things they had done,
MROMAN140:4	H3567	And thus my pains (with better things) I lost,
QELIZ158:5	H114	If then new things, their old form must {forms shall} retain,
DAVID158:28	H8	In *Gath,* let not this thing {things} be spoken on,
VANITY159:29	H1	*Of the vanity of all worldly creatures {things}.*
VANITY160:19	H29	Nor laugh, nor weep, let things go ill or well:
TDUDLEY166:12	H54	Nor wonder 'twas, low things ne'r much did move
CONTEM169:28	H67	It makes things gone perpetually to last,
CONTEM174:29	H226	O Time the fatal wrack of mortal things,
FLESH175:5	H5	Things that are past, and things to come;
FLESH175:5	H5	Things that are past, and things to come;
FLESH175:16	H16	Dost dream of things beyond the Moon
FLESH175:37	H37	For things unknown, only in mind.
FLESH176:34	H74	But reach at things that are so high,
FLESH177:26	H107	For things unclean there shall not be:
BIRTH179:27	H3	All things within this fading world hath end,
CHILDRN186:5	H72	And things that past, to mind I'le bring.
ANNEB187:19	H9	When I on fading things my hopes have set?
ANNEB187:21	H11	To value things according to their price:
2SIMON195:5	Hp271	their predecessors, but I am perswaded better things of yᵒ you
MEDDM203:4	Hp283	for what do we obtaine of all these things, but it is wᵗʰ labour
MEDDM208:3	Hp289	these things must be what manner of persons ought we to be,
MEDDM208:28	Hp290	is admirable to Consider the power of faith, by wᶜʰ all things
MYCHILD217:37	Hp243	+ yᵉ Earth, the order of all things night and day, Summer
MYCHILD218:3	Hp243	End, The consideration of these things would wᵗʰ amazement
MYCHILD218:26	Hp244	The consideration of these things and many yᵉ like would soon
SOREFIT221:18	H4	And when my Soul these things abhor'd
11MAYB228:32	Hp259	to doe. Lord Thou yᵗ knowest All things know'st that I desire to
HOUSE237:1	H31	My pleasant things in ashes lye
HOUSE237:6	H36	Nor things recovnted done of old.

THINK (14)

ELEMEN14:7	~~H250~~	And *Rome,* her *Curtius,* can't forget I think;
HUMOUR21:35	H63	And there she wil out-bid us all, I think;
MASSYR55:30	H96	Some think the *Greeks,* this slander on her cast,
MASSYR57:7	H154	Which made the people think they serv'd her Son;
MGREC94:40	H1678	And think {strive} to keep his men from off the land,
MGREC96:18	H1738	Would think {Suppos'd} he neither thought {meant} to fight nor
DIALOG141:25	H24	If I decease, dost think thou shalt survive?
DIALOG141:26	H25	Or by my wasting state, dost think to thrive?
CONTEM170:10	H83	His Mother sighs, to think of Paradise,
CONTEM172:32	H165	Now salt, now fresh where you think best to glide
2SIMON195:7	Hp271	you should see me no more, I could think of nothing more
PILGRIM210:5	H5	Blesses himself, to think vpon
MYCHILD218:31	Hp244	there Faith vpon ye Earth? & I haue not known what to think,
MED223:13	Hp250	in me at ye consideration y^rof, and I am confovnded to think

THINKE (2) [think]

ELEMEN11:39	H159	I have not time to thinke of every part,
HUMOUR30:33	H425	But thou most grosly do'st mistake, to thinke

THINKES (1) [thinks]

MEDDM197:28	Hp275	thinkes to mount to heaven clog'd wth the Cares and riches of

THINKING (4)

MPERS80:17	H1084	Yet thinking to out-match his foes at Sea,
MPERS84:20	H1256	Thinking his *Grecian* wars now to advance.
MGREC110:11	H2311	*Porus* encounters them, thinking {and thinks} all's there,
MGREC113:27	H2454	Thinking {Fearing} no harme, because he none did owe {doe},

THINKS (12) See also **THINKES**

HUMOUR22:34	H103	She thinks I never shot so farre amisse;
MASSYR65:12	H477	Thinks this the fittest time to break his bands,
MPERS77:37	H978	Vaine *Xerxes* thinks his counsell hath most wit,
MGREC~~110:11~~	H2311	*Porus* encounters them, thinking {and thinks} all's there,
MGREC115:12	H2521	This act (me thinks) his god-head should ashame;
MGREC123:27	H2891	Thinks by her Majesty much help to finde;
MGREC124:28	H2935	Thinks to enthrone the Prince when riper grown;
MGREC130:19	H3174	And now he thinks {hopes}, he's ordered all so well,
MGREC132:39	H3286	Possession he of *Europe* thinks to take,
CONTEM170:22	H93	There *Abel* keeps his sheep, no ill he thinks,
CONTEM170:27	H98	Thinks each he sees will serve him in his kind,
CONTEM171:2	H107	Who thinks not oft upon the Fathers ages.

THINK'ST (1)

HUMOUR~~31:6~~	H439	Thou witless think'st that I am thy excretion,

THINNE (2) [thin]

ELEMEN18:31	H435	My moist hot nature, is so purely thinne,
SEASONS48:39	H90	With melted tauny face, and garments thinne.

THIRD (14)

HUMOUR20:28	H20	The second, third, or last could not digest;
AGES35:23	H9	The third, of fire, and choler is compos'd,
MASSYR59:19	H243	But in the third, the River prov'd his friend,
MPERS84:22	H1258	Fair *Attica,* a third time to invade.
MPERS~~92:2~~	H1556	And in the twenty third of's cruel raign
MGREC93:6	H1603	The third Monarchy was
MGREC108:39	H2255	His {A} third supply, *Antipater* now sent,

MGREC116:9   H2569   The thirty third of's age doe all agree,
MGREC134:1   H3332   A third *Seleuchus* next sits on the seat,
MGREC135:22   H3394   The third, belly and thighs of brasse in sight,
MGREC135:29   H3401   The third a Leopard, which four wings did rear;
MROMAN137:38 H3489   *Tullus Hostilius,* was third *Roman* King,
DIALOG143:13   H82   By *Edward* third, and *Henry* fifth of fame,
CHILDRN184:34 H23   I have a third of colour white,

THIRDLY (1)
HUMOUR30:9   H401   Thirdly, {Again} thou dost confine me to the spleen,

THIRST (6)
ELEMEN14:36   H278   Thy extream thirst is moistened by my love,
AGES42:41   H297   And greater stil, did {and thirst for honour,} set my heart on
AGES43:7   H302   My thirst was higher, then Nobility.
MPERS79:31   H1057   His Hoast, who {all} *Lissus* drinks to quench their thirst,
MGREC105:39   H2132   To quench his thirst, and to allay his heat;
PILGRIM210:14 H14   for thirst no more shall parch his tongue

THIRSTING (1)
MGREC116:32   H2598   Vain thirsting after immortality:

THIRSTY (2)
ELEMEN18:9   H413   The famisht, thirsty man, that craves supply:
MGREC107:25   H2200   Where most {so} immoderatly these thirsty drink;

THIRTEEN (2)
MASSYR65:6   H471   Full thirteen yeares in this strange work he spent,
MGREC98:21   H1823   And thirteen thousand Gally slaves he made,

THIRTIETH See **THIRTYETH**

THIRTY (14)
ELEMEN10:24   H99   And man from thirty unto fifty frame.
MASSYR65:27   H492   And more then {seven and} thirty years in prison fed;
MASSYR67:7   H553   In seven and thirty years, had seen no jot,
MPERS71:3   ~~H715~~   Some thirty years this potent Prince did reign,
MPERS~~71:3~~   H715   Thirty two years in all this Prince
MPERS77:12   H951   Thirty six years this royall {noble} Prince did reign,
MPERS91:3   H1511   To these {them} he thirty thousand Tallents sent,
MGREC94:19   H1657   Thirty two thousand made up his foot force,
MGREC95:5   H1684   With losse of thirty four, of his there slaine:
MGREC95:28   H1707   To *Greece* he thirty thousand talents sends;
MGREC101:12   H1937   With thirty thousand Tallents, to be paid
MGREC102:21   H1991   Where four and thirty dayes he now doth stay,
MGREC116:9   H2569   The thirty third of's age doe all agree,
MROMAN138:11 H3501   Thirty two years doth *Tullus* reigne, then dye,
MROMAN138:35 H3525   Thirty eight yeares (this Stranger borne) did reigne,

THIRTYETH (1) [thirtieth]
MROMAN137:22 H3473   Others, the seven and thirtyeth of his reigne

THIS (552)
PROLOG7:4   H19   And this to mend, alas, no Art is able,
PROLOG7:11   H25   Art can doe much, but this maxime's most sure,
PROLOG7:25   H37   But this weake knot they will full soone untye,
PROLOG8:1   H49   This meane and unrefined stuffe {ure} of mine,
ELEMEN8:10   H8   But enmity, this amity did breake:
ELEMEN11:27   H147   Among my praises this I count not least,
ELEMEN14:3   H245   O dreadfull Sepulcher! that this is true,

ELEMEN14:19	H261	Ile say no more, yet {but} this thing adde I must,
ELEMEN14:28	H270	This your neglect, shewes your ingratitude;
ELEMEN15:9	H291	Do cease to flourish in this misery.
ELEMEN15:16	H298	That this is true, earth thou canst not deny;
ELEMEN15:17	H299	I call thine *Egypt,* this to verifie;
ELEMEN16:11	H334	But note this maxime in Philosophy:
ELEMEN17:29	H393	And to this day, impaires her beautious face.
ELEMEN18:39	H443	Some for this cause (of late) have been so bold,
HUMOUR22:18	H87	Nor hath she wit, or heat, to blush at this.
HUMOUR22:33	H102	But Flegme her self, is now provok'd at this,
HUMOUR22:39	H108	Oh, who would misse this influence of thine,
HUMOUR23:6	H116	But Melancholy, wouldst have this glory thine?
HUMOUR23:38	H148	Its not your muscles, nerves, nor this nor that:
HUMOUR24:19	H168	Is't ignorance, {arrogance} or folly causeth this?
HUMOUR24:24	H173	I will annalise, {this} thy so proud relation;
HUMOUR25:10	H199	Of thy black calumnies, this is but part:
HUMOUR25:34	H223	Wilt thou this valour, manhood, courage cal:
HUMOUR27:6	H277	That this is true, I easily can assent,
HUMOUR27:22	H293	This hot, moist, nurtritive humour of mine,
HUMOUR27:31	H302	If this {you} can't be disprov'd {disprove}, then all I hold:
HUMOUR27:34	H305	This scarlet die's a badge of what's within,
HUMOUR28:11	H323	All to prevent, this curious care I take;
HUMOUR29:20	H371	Thy fiery spirit shal bear away this prize,
HUMOUR29:30	H381	This warinesse count not for cowardise,
HUMOUR31:6	H439	This transmutation is, but not excretion,
HUMOUR31:14	H445	If any doubt this {the} truth, whence this should come;
HUMOUR31:24	H457	Choler's too rash, this golden gift to hold.
HUMOUR32:1	H475	Nor are ye free, from this inormity,
HUMOUR33:6	H520	But 'twere as vain, to prove the {this} truth of mine,
HUMOUR33:28	H542	Within this stately place of eminence,
HUMOUR33:34	H548	Within this high built Cittadel doth lye,
HUMOUR33:40	H554	This point for {now} to discusse longs not to me,
HUMOUR35:1	H597	Lest we too late, this rashnesse do repent,
HUMOUR35:14	H610	This loving counsel pleas'd them all so wel,
AGES36:19	H43	And last of al, to act upon this Stage;
AGES36:24	H48	This {Thus} writ about: *This out, then I am done.*
AGES37:10	H72	With tears into this {the} world I did arrive;
AGES37:26	H88	This little house of flesh, did spacious count:
AGES37:28	H90	Yet this advantage, had mine ignorance,
AGES37:36	H98	No malice bare, to this, or that great Peer,
AGES38:13	H116	This was mine innocence, but oh {ah!} the seeds,
AGES39:8	H151	For thus to do, we on this Stage assemble,
AGES39:32	H175	This is my best, but youth (is known) alas,
AGES40:29	H210	I want a {have no} heart {at} all this for to deplore.
AGES44:7	H340	And on this Stage am come to act my last:
AGES44:23	H356	In this short Pilgrimage I oft have had;
AGES45:22	H411	What are my thoughts, this is no time to say.
AGES45:23	H413	These are no old wives tales, but this is truth;
AGES46:20	H451	And when this flesh shal rot, and be consum'd,
AGES46:21	H452	This body, by this soul, shal be assum'd;
SEASONS47:36	H48	This is the month whose fruitfull showers produces

SEASONS48:34	H85	In this harsh strain, I find no melody,
SEASONS48:35	H86	Yet above all, this priviledge is thine,
SEASONS49:34	H127	This Month the Roses are distill'd in Glasses,
SEASONS49:37	H130	And for all sorts of Pease this is the time.
SEASONS50:1	H135	This month from *Julius Cæsar* took the {its} name,
SEASONS50:9	H143	The groaning Carts to bear away this prise,
SEASONS50:13	H147	This month he keeps with *Virgo* for a space,
SEASONS50:40	H174	The tenth {twelfth} of this, *Sol* riseth in the Line,
SEASONS51:1	H175	And doth in poyzing *Libra* this month shine.
SEASONS51:12	H186	Sure at this time, Time first of all began,
SEASONS51:13	H187	And in this month was made apostate man;
SEASONS51:20	H196	*October* is my next, we heare in this,
SEASONS51:36	H212	This month's {moneth} the Sun {Sun's} in *Sagitarius,*
SEASONS52:3	H219	This month is timber for all uses fell'd,
SEASONS52:7	H222	This time warm cloaths, ful diet, and good fires,
SEASONS52:20	H235	This month he's hous'd in horned *Capricorn,*
MASSYR53:19	H9	This was the Golden Age, but after came
MASSYR54:3	H30	But yet this blot for ever on him lyes,
MASSYR54:7	H34	This is that *Bell,* the *Chaldees* worshipped,
MASSYR54:9	H36	This is that *Bell,{Baal}* to whom the *Israelites*
MASSYR54:11	H38	This is *Belzebub,* god of *Ekronites,*
MASSYR54:25	H52	This stately seat of warlike *Ninus* stood.
MASSYR54:26	H53	This *Ninus* for a god, his father canoniz'd,
MASSYR54:28	H55	This Tyrant did his neighbours all oppresse,
MASSYR55:4	H70	This great oppressing *Ninus* dead, and gone,
MASSYR55:14	H80	Sure from this fiction, *Dagon* first began,
MASSYR55:17	H83	This great renowned Empresse, issued.
MASSYR55:20	H86	This gallant dame, unto the *Bactrian* war;
MASSYR55:30	H96	Some think the *Greeks,* this slander on her cast,
MASSYR56:14	H120	Which is the midst, of this brave Town was plac'd,
MASSYR56:18	H124	This to discribe, {deseribe} in each particular,
MASSYR56:23	H129	This wonder of the world, this *Babell* stood.
MASSYR56:30	H136	But this is marvelous, of all those men,
MASSYR56:34	H140	This was last progresse of this mighty Queen,
MASSYR57:9	H156	This fraud, in war, nor peace, at all appears;
MASSYR57:16	H163	But this is farre unlike, he being Son
MASSYR57:18	H165	This answer may suffice, whom it wil please,
MASSYR58:10	H195	Longer to serve this Metamorphos'd beast;
MASSYR58:34	H217	Prest for this service, by the Kings command;
MASSYR59:8	H232	But all {And now} surpris'd, by this unlookt for fright,
MASSYR59:27	H251	By this accomplishment, their hearts were shaken:
MASSYR59:29	H253	This his inevitable destiny;
MASSYR59:32	H256	This the last Monarch was, of {great} *Ninus* race,
MASSYR60:14	H279	Who did this Monarchy begin anew.
MASSYR60:30	H295	He thus inricht, by this new tryed gold,
MASSYR60:32	H297	And from this heap did after Ages see,
MASSYR60:34	H299	When this was built, and all matters in peace,
MASSYR61:15	H320	*Iuda's* bad King occasioned this War,
MASSYR61:23	H328	Gladly doth *Tiglath* this advantage take,
MASSYR61:38	H343	(This was that *Ahaz,* which so much {high} transgrest.)
MASSYR62:14	H359	This was that strange degenerated brood,

MASSYR62:28	H373	But what, or where they are, yet know we this;
MASSYR63:5	H390	In *Babylon,* Leiutenant to this man,
MASSYR63:18	H403	*Ben. Merodach,* Successor to this King,
MASSYR63:20	H405	But by conjecture this, and none but he,
MASSYR63:23	H408	Brave *Nebulassar* to this King was Sonne,
MASSYR63:28	H414	This King's less fam'd for all the acts he's done,
MASSYR63:30	H417	The famous Wars {acts}, of this Heroyick King,
MASSYR63:37	H424	This Prince in's magnitude doth ever shine;
MASSYR64:1	H425	This was of Monarchies that head of gold,
MASSYR64:3	H427	This was that tree, whose brances fill'd the earth,
MASSYR64:5	H429	This was that King of Kings, did what he pleas'd,
MASSYR64:7	H431	And this is {was} he, who when he fear'd the least,
MASSYR64:9	H433	This Prince, the last year of his Fathers reign,
MASSYR64:27	H451	Such was the scituation of this place,
MASSYR64:35	H459	Within an Island had this City seat,
MASSYR65:6	H471	Full thirteen yeares in this strange work he spent,
MASSYR65:10	H475	When in the *Tyrian* wars, the {this} King was hot,
MASSYR65:12	H477	Thinks this the fittest time to break his bands,
MASSYR65:16	H481	For this great King, with-drawes part of his force,
MASSYR65:23	H488	For this was {is} he, for whom none said, Alas!
MASSYR66:38	H544	This King among the righteous had a part:
MASSYR67:36	H582	Protectors of his {this} Crown, and *Babylon,*
MASSYR68:5	H591	This language strange, to read, and to unfold;
MASSYR68:8	H594	To him that could interpret clear this thing:
MPERS69:13	H635	This is of *Cyrus* the true pedigree,
MPERS69:38	H661	Then to the King he makes this true report,
MPERS70:8	H679	To drain this ditch, he many sluces cut,
MPERS70:17	H688	Forty five mile {miles} this City scarce could round;
MPERS70:18	H689	This head of Kingdoms, *Caldes* excellence,
MPERS70:20	H691	Yet wondrous Monuments this stately Queen,
MPERS70:26	H697	Long after this, he 'gainst the *Sythians* goes,
MPERS70:38	H709	But in this {his} Tombe was only to be found
MPERS71:3	H714	Some thirty years this potent Prince did reign,
MPERS71:3	H715	Thirty two years in all this Prince
MPERS71:36	H750	If all his {this} heat, had been for a good {pious} end,
MPERS72:2	H754	He after this, saw in a Vision {upon suspition vain},
MPERS72:7	H756	*Praraspes* now must act this tragedy;
MPERS72:9	H757	Accomplished this wicked Kings intent;
MPERS72:9	H757	To act in secret, this his lewd intent:
MPERS72:18	H766	This strange severity, one time {sometimes} he us'd,
MPERS72:22	H770	To whom he gave this in rememberance,
MPERS72:31	H775	To tell the facts, of this most bloody King.
MPERS72:38	H784	Toucht with this newes, to *Persia* he makes,
MPERS73:22	H809	This King, with {his} conspirators so stout,
MPERS73:25	H810	But yet, 'fore this was done, much blood was shed,
MPERS74:3	H828	All envie to avoyd, this was thought on,
MPERS74:18	H841	Thanks for all this to's crafty Stable-groome.
MPERS75:5	H866	This violence was done him by his Leige;
MPERS75:6	H867	This told, for enterance he stood not long,
MPERS75:20	H879	Yet o're thy glory we must cast this vaile,
MPERS76:20	H918	His {This} fruitlesse war, began late to repent;

MPERS76:23	H921	He after this, intends *Greece* to invade,
MPERS76:33	H931	At *Marathon* this bloudy field was fought,
MPERS77:6	H945	His Queen *Attossa,* caused all {author of} this stir,
MPERS~~77:11~~	H950	('Tis thought) through grief and his {this} succeslesse strife.
MPERS77:12	H951	Thirty six years this royall {noble} Prince did reign,
MPERS~~77:16~~	H957	Because this was, first born of *Cyrus* race.)
MPERS77:39	H980	And by this choyce, unwarily posts on,
MPERS78:2	H983	In great provisions, for this great intent;
MPERS78:21	H1002	Besides, the Vessels for this transportation,
MPERS78:33	H1014	Feasts all this multitude, of his own charge,
MPERS79:4	H1026	For his great love, is this thy recompence?
MPERS79:5	H1027	Is this to doe like *Xerxes,* or a Prince?
MPERS79:17	H1043	Was marching o're this interrupting Bay; {new devised way.}
MPERS79:22	H1048	But yet this goodly sight {from him} produced teares,
MPERS79:27	H1053	How of this enterprise his thoughts now stands;
MPERS79:36	H1062	This 'twixt the Mountains lyes (half Acre wide)
MPERS80:11	H1078	This shamefull Victory cost *Xerxes* deare,
MPERS80:20	H1087	In this Streight, as the other, firmly stand.
MPERS80:30	H1097	That brave *Thymistocles* takes this wise course,
MPERS80:35	H1102	He hearing this, his thoughts, and course home bended,
MPERS81:9	H1117	(Chief instigater of this hopelesse {hapless} War;)
MPERS~~81:16~~	H1124	And leave them out, the {this} shock {now} for to sustaine,
MPERS81:22	H1130	But the *Athenians,* this peace detest,
MPERS81:28	~~H1136~~	Though of this Nation borne a great Commander,
MPERS81:30	H1138	*Mardonius* proud, hearing this answer stout,
MPERS82:14	H1161	To certifie this finall over-throw.
MPERS82:25	H1172	Some years by him in this vain suit was spent,
MPERS82:29	H1176	When jealous Queen *Amestris,* of this knew,
MPERS83:14	H1202	The {Then} *Artabanus* hirer of this deed,
MPERS83:20	H1208	But in short time, this wickednesse was knowne,
MPERS83:27	H1215	Amongst the Monarchs next, this Prince had place
MPERS84:8	H1236	By *Memucan's* advice, this {so} was the doome.
MPERS84:13	H1249	Unto this King *Thymistocles* did flye.
MPERS84:16	H1252	This valiant Knight, whom they so much did owe;
MPERS84:17	H1253	entertainment {royal bounty} with this {his} Prince he found,
MPERS84:19	H1255	The King not little joyfull of this chance,
MPERS~~84:26~~	H1262	The {This} noble *Greek,* now fit for generall.
MPERS~~84:30~~	H1266	T'*Thymistocles* he doth his {this} war commit,
MPERS84:37	H1273	In this sad conflict, marching on his ways,
MPERS84:39	H1275	The King this noble Captaine having lost,
MPERS85:14	H1290	Disquiet {Revolting} Egypt, 'gainst this King rebells,
MPERS85:18	H1294	A second trouble, after this succeeds.
MPERS~~85:28~~	H1304	The King much profit reapeth, by these leagues {this league},
MPERS~~85:32~~	H1308	The {This} King, his sister, like *Cambyses,* wed;
MPERS~~86:6~~	H1322	{this} *Nothus* reign'd {'bout} nineteen years, which run,
MPERS87:11	H1367	And others to be warm'd by this new sun,
MPERS87:21	~~H1374~~	*Abrocomes,* was this base cowards name,
MPERS87:23	H1375	This place was {so} made, by nature, and by art;
MPERS87:39	H1391	On this, he and his Souldiers carelesse grow,
MPERS88:2	H1395	In this confusion, each man as he might,
MPERS~~88:28~~	H1421	His Host in chase, knowes not of his {this} disaster,

MPERS88:31	H1424	Who knowes the sudden change made by this chance;
MPERS88:33	H1426	Nor *Gorgons* {head} like to this, transform'd to stones.
MPERS88:34	H1427	After this trance, revenge, new spirits blew,
MPERS89:10	H1444	Of this dayes cowardize, he feares the effects;
MPERS90:1	H1476	To {Did} stop the way in this their enterprise;
MPERS90:30	H1497	The *Greeks* by this successe, incourag'd so,
MPERS90:38	H1505	Of that false perjur'd wretch, this was the last {fate},
MPERS91:31	H1545	But this of him is worth the memory,
MPERS92:16	~~H1574~~	How this *Darius* did attain the Crown,
MPERS~~92:16~~	H1574	*Darius* by this *Bogoas* set in throne,
MPERS~~92:22~~	H1580	And so this wretch (a punishment too small)
MPERS~~92:24~~	H1582	This *Codomanus* now upon the stage
MPERS~~92:27~~	H1585	But from some daughter this new king was sprung
MPERS92:32	H1590	And this 'mongst all's no controverted thing,
MPERS92:33	H1591	That this *Darius* was last *Persian* King,
MGREC93:14	H1611	This Prince (his father by *Pausanias* slain)
MGREC6:23	H1620	Whose glory to the Earth, this Prince {king} did throw,
MGREC6:26	H1623	This is the hee-goat, which from *Grecia* came,
MGREC6:30	H1627	*Phillip,* on this great conquest had an eye;
MGREC94:5	H1639	This done, against all {both} right, and natures laws,
MGREC95:4	H1683	This Victory did *Alexander* gain;
MGREC95:36	H1715	For this wise King, had brought to see the sport;
MGREC96:17	H1737	But they that saw him in this state to lye;
MGREC96:27	H1747	This brave Virago, to the King was mother;
MGREC96:29	H1749	Now least this Gold, and all this goodly stuffe,
MGREC96:29	H1749	Now least this Gold, and all this goodly stuffe,
MGREC96:41	H1761	The cowards feeling this sharp stinging charge,
MGREC97:12	H1773	Yet all this grief, this losse, this over-throw,
MGREC97:12	H1773	Yet all this grief, this losse, this over-throw,
MGREC97:12	H1773	Yet all this grief, this losse, this over-throw,
MGREC97:20	H1781	And this to *Alexander* is more a fame,
MGREC97:24	H1785	No sooner had this Captaine {Victor} won the field,
MGREC~~97:34~~	H1795	His {This} Letter *Alexander* doth disdaine,
MGREC97:35	H1796	And in short termes, sends this reply againe;
MGREC98:5	H1807	But they accept not this, in any wise,
MGREC98:9	H1811	With this reply, he was so sore {deep} enrag'd,
MGREC98:17	H1819	space {time} he takes this lofty {took that wealthy} town,
MGREC98:23	H1825	The rule of this he to *Philotas* gave,
MGREC98:30	H1832	And therefore {So} gives this {his little} Lord-ship to another.
MGREC99:22	H1865	But yet, this well defended town is {was} taken,
MGREC99:39	H1882	How he should over-throw this Monarchy;
MGREC100:26	H1910	Of Horse, and Foot, this {his} Army did amount;
MGREC100:31	H1915	About this time, *Darius* beauteous Queen,
MGREC100:36	~~H1920~~	For this lost Queen (though in captivity).
MGREC100:37	H1921	When this sad newes (at first) *Darius* heares,
MGREC101:1	H1926	Great *Alexander,* for this good regard;
MGREC~~101:3~~	H1928	Let them on him, that {this} dignity bestow:
MGREC101:14	H1939	And till all this be wel perform'd, and sure,
MGREC101:16	H1941	To this, stout *Alexander,* gives no eare,
MGREC101:40	H1969	At *Arbela,* this victory gain'd,
MGREC102:5	H1975	This Conquerour now {then} goes to *Babylon,*

MGREC102:11	H1981	In this a masse {world} of gold, and treasure lay,
MGREC102:13	H1983	With greedy eyes, he views this City round,
MGREC102:20	H1990	This City did abundantly abound;
MGREC103:5	H2016	None like to this in riches did abound.
MGREC103:7	H2018	Yet to compare with this, they might not do.
MGREC103:22	H2033	The pleasures and the riches of this town,
MGREC103:23	H2034	Now makes this King, his vertues all to drown.
MGREC103:29	H2040	Commands to set this goodly town on fire.
MGREC104:2	H2054	Thought now this once, to try his fortunes here,
MGREC104:11	H2063	This counsell, for his safety, he pretended,
MGREC104:13	H2065	Next day this treason, to *Darius* known,
MGREC104:29	H2081	But some detesting, this his wicked fact,
MGREC104:30	H2082	To *Alexander* fly, {flyes} and told {tells} this act;
MGREC104:39	H2091	This {The} wofull King, his courtesie refuses,
MGREC105:4	H2097	*(Bessus,* his Partner in this Tragedy,
MGREC105:6	H2099	This done, they with their Hoast, soon speed away,
MGREC105:11	H2104	But this unheard of injury {treachery} much more;
MGREC~~105:21~~	H2114	The witnesse of his dying misery: {this horrid Tragedy;}
MGREC105:23	H2116	The just revenge of this his wofull end;
MGREC105:38	H2131	This said, the *Greek* for water doth intreat,
MGREC105:41	H2134	I've nothing left, at this my dying hour;
MGREC~~106:2~~	H2136	But *Alexander* will, for this regard
MGREC106:3	H2137	This said, his fainting breath did fleet away,
MGREC106:38	H2172	Griev'd at this change of manners, and of minde:
MGREC107:17	H2192	The Souldiers should let passe this injury;
MGREC107:26	H2201	This {Which} more mortality to them did bring,
MGREC108:3	H2219	And in this sort, they rather drag, then bring,
MGREC108:4	H2220	This Malefactor vild, {vile} before the King,
MGREC108:9	H2225	These not a little joy'd, this day to see,
MGREC108:17	H2233	Nor could he reason give, for this great wrong,
MGREC108:35	H2251	Upon this River banck in seventeen dayes,
MGREC109:7	H2266	Whose feasts are celebrated by this Prince;
MGREC109:34	H2293	But Kingly *Porus* this brave answer sent,
MGREC109:38	H2297	Great *Alexander* vext at this reply,
MGREC110:7	H2307	Within this spacious river, deep, and wide,
MGREC112:2	H2388	That by this match he might be yet more neare.
MGREC~~112:4~~	H2390	At the {this} same time, unto his Captains brave;
MGREC112:5	H2391	Six thousand Guests he to {unto} this feast invites,
MGREC112:10	H2396	They were so wrapt with this externall glory.
MGREC112:12	H2398	He might this feast imagine by the same.
MGREC112:14	H2400	So after many dayes this {the} Banquet ends.
MGREC112:26	H2412	He death deserv'd, for this so high offence;
MGREC112:28	H2414	His Royall pardon gave, for this same thing;
MGREC113:4	H2431	*Philotas* after him sends out this cry,
MGREC113:15	H2442	Look on *Parmenio,* after this disaster,
MGREC113:18	H2445	This sound advice, at heart, pleas'd *Alexander,*
MGREC113:19	H2446	Who was so much engag'd, to this Commander,
MGREC113:25	H2452	To doe this deed, they into *Media* send;
MGREC113:30	H2457	This is *Parmenio,* which {who} so much had done,
MGREC113:34	H2461	This that *Parmenio,* who still over-came,
MGREC114:6	H2474	Like this, against his deity to kick:

MGREC114:8	H2476	Upon this dangerous theam fond *Clitus* fell;
MGREC~~114:12~~	H2480	Nought but his life for this could satisfie;
MGREC114:15	H2485	This pot companion he did more bemoan,
MGREC114:23	H2493	For this alone, and for no other cause,
MGREC114:27	H2497	Of this unkingly deed, {act} doth *Seneca*
MGREC114:28	H2498	This censure passe, and not unwisely, say,
MGREC114:29	H2499	Of *Alexander,* this th' eternall crime,
MGREC114:39	H2509	All this he did, who knows not to be true,
MGREC115:2	H2513	All this he did, yea, and much more, 'tis true,
MGREC115:12	H2521	This act (me thinks) his god-head should ashame;
MGREC~~115:15~~	H2528	A rueful face in this so general woe;
MGREC115:23	H2542	This great indignity for to {he should} requite.
MGREC116:10	H2570	This Conquerour did yeeld to destiny;
MGREC~~116:10~~	H2571	When this sad news came to *Darius* Mother,
MGREC~~116:11~~	H2577	Whose famous Acts {This Monarchs fame} must last, whilst
MGREC116:35	H2601	This conquerour did oft lament ('tis sed)
MGREC116:37	H2603	This folly great *Augustus* did deride,
MGREC117:27	H2634	Each Captain wisht this prize to beare away,
MGREC118:3	H2650	This choyse *Perdicas,* vehemently disclaim'd,
MGREC118:11	H2658	He hold of {on} this occasion should have laid,
MGREC118:23	H2670	After this {some} time, when stirs began to calme,
MGREC119:8	H2698	But *Cleopatra,* this suitour did deny,
MGREC119:21	H2711	(Which at this time well suited his desires)
MGREC119:33	H2723	For personage, none was like {to} this Commander:
MGREC119:40	H2730	After this {which} time, the *Greeks* did never more
MGREC120:19	H2754	But this again dislikes, and {he} would remain,
MGREC120:27	H2764	This he avoyds, and ships himself, and's Son,
MGREC120:39	H2776	Great love did *Ptolomy* by this act gain.
MGREC~~121:16~~	H2797	Who vow to make this captain recompence,
MGREC122:1	H2824	For this great {sad} strife, he pours out his complaints,
MGREC122:9	H2834	For all that should be said, let this suffice,
MGREC122:34	H2855	And this no man durst question, or resist;
MGREC122:36	H2857	Acknowledged for chief, this old Commander:
MGREC123:10	H2872	In this Epitomy, too long to tell
MGREC123:26	H2890	This new Protector's of another minde,
MGREC123:29	H2893	This *Polisperchons* great ability,
MGREC124:3	H2908	For this *Antigonus* needed {did need} no spurs,
MGREC124:16	~~H2923~~	Firme to *Cassander* at this time abides:
MGREC124:22	H2929	Put trust in any, but in this Commander;
MGREC124:29	H2936	*Euridice* this injury disdaines,
MGREC124:30	H2937	And to *Cassander* of this wrong complaines;
MGREC124:32	H2939	Was to this proud, vindicative *Cassander,*
MGREC125:11	H2959	and succour {To save the King} her, in this great {their} need;
MGREC125:30	H2980	This done, the cruell Queen rests not content,
MGREC125:39	H2989	Where hearing of this newes he speeds away,
MGREC125:41	H2991	So goes to finde this {cruel} Queen in *Macedon;*
MGREC~~126:15~~	H3006	Faine would she come now to {this wretched Queen}
MGREC126:17	H3008	The Souldiers pinched with this scarcity,
MGREC126:29	H3020	This was the end of this most cruell Queen,
MGREC~~127:41~~	H3071	{clear} what cause they {he} had to take up {make this} warre.
MGREC128:14	H3087	And to requite this Traytor for those {these} harmes:

MGREC129:2	H3116	This touch'd *Cassander* sore, for what he'd done,
MGREC129:10	H3124	This *Roxane* for her beautie all commend,
MGREC129:15	H3129	*Perdicas* was her partner in this plot:
MGREC129:21	H3135	But from {by} their hands, who thought not once of this.
MGREC129:26	H3140	When this foul tragedy was past, and done,
MGREC129:31	H3145	This {Orphan} Prince began for to compassionate.
MGREC129:34	H3148	*Cassander* fear'd what might of this insue,
MGREC129:39	H3153	Extinct, by this inhumane wretch *Cassander;*
MGREC129:40	H3154	*Antigonus* for all this doth not mourn,
MGREC~~129:41~~	H3155	He knows to's profit, all i'th end {this at last} will turn,
MGREC130:15	H3170	Her women are appointed to this deed,
MGREC130:35	~~H3181~~	His wife and sons then slain by this *Cassander,*
MGREC131:4	H3194	Most grossely base, was this {their} great adulation,
MGREC131:14	H3206	This day twixt these two foes {Kings} ends all the strife,
MGREC131:22	H3214	He sorely griev'd at this his desperate state,
MGREC131:27	H3219	Is for this fresh young Lady half {quite} undone,
MGREC132:3	H3236	This by *Lysimachus* soon {was} after slain,
MGREC132:27	H3272	For his posterity unto this day,
MGREC133:5	H3293	Yet by him had this most unworthy end.
MGREC133:26	H3316	This of *Antigonus,* his seed's the fate,
MGREC133:34	H3324	But this is perished with many more,
MGREC133:40	H3330	This *Theos* he was murthered by his {lewd} wife,
MGREC135:34	H3406	But yet this Lion, Bear, this Leopard, Ram,
MGREC135:41	H3413	This taske befits not women, like to men:
MGREC136:7	H3420	This my presumption (some now) to requite,
MGREC136:12	H3426	*This fourth to th' other three, now might be brought.*
MGREC136:15	H3429	*Yet in this Chaos, one shall easily spy,*
MROMAN136:37	H3451	This City built, and Sacrifices done,
MROMAN137:7	H3458	And this new gentle Government abide:
MROMAN137:11	H3462	So *Romulus* was forc'd this course to take.
MROMAN137:33	H3484	Goddesse *Ægeria* this to him told,
MROMAN138:9	H3499	Of *Latine* Kings this was long since the Seat,
MROMAN138:20	H3510	Faire *Ostia* he built, this Town, it stood,
MROMAN138:34	H3524	Much {Some} state, and glory, {splendor} did this *Priscus* adde:
MROMAN138:35	H3525	Thirty eight yeares (this Stranger borne) did reigne,
MROMAN139:18	H3546	Her Husband sore incens'd, to quit this wrong,
MROMAN140:8	H3571	Nor matter is't this last, the world now sees,
DIALOG141:12	H11	What meanes this wailing tone, this mourning guise?
DIALOG141:21	H20	This Phisick-purging-potion I have taken,
DIALOG141:24	H23	Which present help may ease this {my} malady.
DIALOG142:2	H31	What Medicine shall I seek to cure this woe,
DIALOG142:27	H56	Whence is this {the} storme, from Earth, or Heaven above?
DIALOG142:36	H65	My beauteous Body at this present maime;
DIALOG142:40	H69	Whose proud contention cause this slaughter;
DIALOG144:33	H141	This is fore-runner of my after clap,
DIALOG145:11	H160	But all you say, amounts to this effect,
DIALOG145:32	H181	This done, an Act they would have passed fain,
DIALOG145:35	H184	This must be done by Gospel, not by law.
DIALOG145:37	H186	This was deny'd, I need not say wherefore.
DIALOG146:9	H197	But could the field alone this cause {strife} decide,
DIALOG~~146:12~~	H200	Who knows, the worst, the best {this} may {be my} overthrow;

DIALOG146:15	H201	Oh pity me, in this sad perturbation,
DIALOG147:25	H249	And to this blessed {hopeful} Cause closely adhere
DIALOG148:17	H282	This done, with brandish'd swords, to *Turky* go,
DIALOG148:31	H296	If this make way thereto, then sigh no more,
SIDNEY149:24	H23	That this one Volumne should exhaust your store.
SIDNEY149:25	H23	I praise thee not for this, it is unfit,
SIDNEY149:26	H23	This was thy shame, O miracle of wit:
SIDNEY150:22	H47	Of which, {at} this day, faire *Belgia* doth {may} boast.
SIDNEY150:25	H52	Ah, in his blooming prime, death pluckt this Rose,
SIDNEY150:31	H58	But yet impartiall Death {Fates} this Boone did give,
SIDNEY150:36	H63	Of this our noble *Scipio* some good word?
SIDNEY150:37	H64	Noble {Great} *Bartas,* this to thy praise adds more,
SIDNEY151:18	H69	Yet this preheminence thou hast above,
SIDNEY152:9	H79	That this contempt it did the more perplex,
SIDNEY152:13	H82	For {Then} to revenge his {this} wrong, themselves ingage,
SIDNEY152:24	H93	*Here lies intomb'd in fame, under this stone,*
SIDNEY152:28	H97	*His praise is much, this shall suffice my pen,*
DUBART152:33	H2	Amongst the happy wits this Age hath showne,
DUBART153:11	H15	A homely flower in this my latter spring:
DUBART154:25	H70	If e'r this golden gift was showr'd on any,
QELIZ156:6	H33	Millions will testifie that this is true;
QELIZ156:13	H40	But can you Doctors now this point dispute,
QELIZ158:8	H117	*Here sleeps THE Queen, this is the royall bed.*
QELIZ158:11	H120	*This Rose is withered, once so lovely faire,*
DAVID158:28	H8	In *Gath,* let not this thing {things} be spoken on,
VANITY161:1	H52	This pearl of price, this tree of life, this spring,
VANITY161:5	H56	This satiates the soul, this stayes the mind,
TDUDLEY165:30	H32	True Patriot of this little Commonweal,
TDUDLEY166:35	H77	*Within this Tomb a Patriot lyes*
CONTEM167:31	H8	Rapt were my sences at this delectable view.
CONTEM168:4	H14	That hath this under world so richly dight:
CONTEM168:19	H27	Soul of this world, this Universes Eye,
CONTEM169:7	H49	Who gave this bright light luster unto thee:
CONTEM172:30	H163	Ye Fish which in this liquid Region 'bide,
CONTEM174:5	H205	And yet this sinfull creature, frail and vain,
CONTEM174:6	H206	This lump of wretchedness, of sin and sorrow,
CONTEM174:7	H207	This weather-beaten vessel wrackt with pain,
CONTEM174:21	H219	So he that saileth in this world of pleasure,
CONTEM174:24	H222	Fond fool, he takes this earth ev'n for heav'ns bower.
FLESH177:25	H106	This City pure is not for thee,
AUTHOR178:10	H20	In this array, 'mongst Vulgars mayst thou roam,
SICKNES178:23	H6	this cannot be revok'd.
SICKNES178:24	H7	For Adams sake, this word God spake
SICKNES178:26	H9	Yet live I shall, this life's but small,
SICKNES178:29	H12	no life is like to this.
SICKNES178:30	H13	For what's this life, but care and strife?
SICKNES179:1	H21	O whil'st I live, this grace me give,
BIRTH179:27	H3	All things within this fading world hath end,
BIRTH180:17	H27	And if chance to thine eyes shall bring this verse,
BIRTH180:19	H29	And kiss this paper for thy loves dear sake,
BIRTH180:20	H30	Who with salt tears this last Farewel did take.

1LETTER181:9	H7	I like the earth this season, mourn in black,
1LETTER181:15	H13	In this dead time, alas, what can I more
2LETTER181:33	H3	But stay this once, unto my suit give ear,
2LETTER182:2	H8	I crave this boon, this Errand by the way,
3LETTER183:4	H6	A dearer Dear (far dearer Heart) then this.
VERSES184:3	H7	Yet handled ill, amounts but to this crum;
VERSES184:5	H9	My Bond remains in force unto this day;
VERSES184:6	H10	Yet for part payment take this simple mite,
CHILDRN184:25	H14	Fly back and sing amidst this Quire.
CHILDRN185:19	H45	Lest this my brood some harm should catch,
ANNEB187:20	H10	Experience might 'fore this have made me wise,
ANNEB187:32	H22	Mean time my throbbing heart's chear'd up with this
MERCY188:21	H7	And yet survive to sound this wailing tone;
MERCY189:14	H35	In him alone, that caused all this smart;
2SIMON195:12	Hp271	though in value they fall short of all in this kinde yet I presume
MEDDM197:7	Hp274	reason why christians are so loth to exchang this world for a
MEDDM197:23	Hp275	nothing will abase them more, then this What hast thou, but
MEDDM197:28	Hp275	to mount to heaven clog'd wth the Cares and riches of this Life,
MEDDM198:10	Hp276	his foot And he that passes through the wildernes of this world,
MEDDM200:9	Hp279	sweets of this life, that so they might feed vpon more
MEDDM200:30	Hp279	and in this transcends the spring, that their leafe shall neuer
MEDDM202:13	Hp282	among the dead, and no other reason can be giuen of all this
MEDDM202:16	Hp282	The treasures of this world may well be compared to huskes,
MEDDM203:2	Hp283	Had not the wisest of men, taught vs this lesson, that all is
MEDDM203:13	Hp283	bussines lyes, a christian is sailing through this world vnto his
MEDDM203:15	Hp283	must beware of desireing to make this the place of his abode,
MEDDM204:4	Hp284	the paw of the Beare will deliuer mee from this vncircumscised
MEDDM205:16	Hp286	is this Court of Judicature, that there is no appeale from it, no
MEDDM206:12	Hp287	euen in this life, some are Stars of the first magnitude,
MEDDM207:13	Hp288	All the Comforts of this Life, may be compared to the gourd of
MEDDM208:21	Hp290	so is it wth the wealth honours and pleasures of this world
MEDDM209:5	Hp291	this pearle of prise
PILGRIM210:25	H25	This body shall in silence sleep,
PILGRIM210:34	H34	this mortall shall be cloth'd vpon
TOCHILD215:2	H2	This Book by Any yet vnread,
MYCHILD215:18	Hp240	haue not studyed in this yov read to shew my skill, but to
MYCHILD215:22	Hp240	I will observe shall bee this—I will begin wth Gods dealing
MYCHILD215:23	Hp240	wth me fr my childhood to this Day.
MYCHILD216:8	Hp241	into this Covntry, where I fovnd a new World and new manners
MYCHILD216:18	Hp241	+ feares brovght yov to this, I now travail in birth again of yov
MYCHILD216:21	Hp241	constantly observed this y^t he hath never suffered me long to
MYCHILD218:1	Hp243	Winter, Spring and Autvmne, the dayly providing for this great
MYCHILD218:6	Hp243	this hath thovsands of Times been svggested to me, yet
MYCHILD218:8	Hp244	If ever this God hath revealed himself it mvst bee in his word,
MYCHILD218:9	Hp244	this mvst bee it or none. Haue I not fovnd y^t operation by it
MYCHILD218:17	Hp244	When I haue gott over this Block y^n have I another pvtt in my
MYCHILD218:18	Hp244	that admitt this bee ye true God whom wee worship, and y^t bee
MYCHILD218:22	Hp244	This hath somt. stuck with me, and more it would, by ye vain
MYCHILD218:35	Hp244	o my Soul to thy Rest, vpon this Rock Xt Jesus will I build
MYCHILD219:6	Hp245	This was written in mvch sicknesse and weaknes, and is very
BYNIGHT220:18	H16	Who freely hath done this for me,

SOREFIT222:9	H28	O gravnt I doe it in this state,
MED223:8	Hp250	vnto my God and your God—But least this should not bee
MED223:15	Hp250	But this is my comfort, When I come into Heaven, I shall
MED223:17	Hp250	I ovght. Lord haueing this hope let me purefye my self as thou
JULY223:27	Hp251	to read this hereafter, and to others that shall read it when I
28AUG225:28	Hp254	heart, and to manifest his Loue to me, and this is that w^{ch}
28AUG225:29	Hp254	stayes my Soul that this condition y^t I am in is ye best for me,
28AUG226:6	Hp254	gravnt y^t while I live I may doe y^t service I am able in this frail
11MAYA226:14	Hp255	lasted all this spring till this 11. May, yet hath my God given
11MAYA226:17	Hp255	Many refreshments haue I fovnd in this my weary pilgrimage,
11MAYA226:18	Hp255	this valley of Baca many pools of water, That wch now I cheifly
11MAYA226:22	Hp255	while my body decayes, and ye weaknes of this outward
30SEPT227:33	Hp257	him then before, This is the desire of y^r Loving mother. A. B.
11MAYB228:24	Hp259	I haue had no great fitt of sicknes, but this year from ye middle
11MAYB228:26	Hp259	this month I had a feaver seatd vpon me wch indeed was the
SON231:27	H39	Lord gravnt that I may never forgett thy Loving kindness in this
HOURS234:11	H25	I in this world no comfort haue,
HOURS234:21	H35	O hear me Lord in this Reqvest
ACK235:16	H16	In this his Buisnes and Addresse.
REMB236:4	H19	I hu͞bly this Require.
HOUSE237:20	H50	Stands permanent tho: this bee fled.

THISTLES (1) [pl.]

ELEMEN13:25	H226	Thistles and thornes, where he expected graine;

THITHER (2) See also THETHER

MASSYR67:33	H579	The holy vessells, thither brought long since,
MGREC109:14	H2273	Who comming thither, long before his Lord;

TH'KING (1) [the king]

MPERS73:18	H805	And kinsmen in account, to th'King they stood,

TH'KINGDOMS (1) [the kingdoms]

MGREC99:11	H1854	But th'Kingdoms, and the Ladies, {Lady} soone accept;

TH'LIKE (1) [the like]

ELEMEN17:9	H373	*Cicily* from *Italy,* by th'like chance.

THO: (12) [though]

PILGRIM210:31	H31	What tho my flesh shall there consume
MYCHILD215:28	Hp241	I was also troubled at ye neglect of private Dutyes tho:
MYCHILD218:5	Hp243	a God as I worship in Trinity, + such a Sav^r as I rely upon, tho:
FEVER221:4	H19	Tho: flesh consume to novght,
FEVER221:5	H20	What tho: in dust it shall bee lay'd
FAINTING222:22	H12	And tho: as dead mad'st me aliue
MYSOUL225:1	H5	What tho: thy outward Man decay,
28AUG226:11	Hp254	vnwilling to come tho: by so rovgh a Messenger.
HOURS233:26	H9	Tho: losse and sicknes me assail'd,
HOURS234:1	H15	Tho: husband dear bee from me gone
HOURS234:13	H27	Tho: children thou hast given me
HOUSE237:20	H50	Stands permanent tho: this bee fled.

THOMAS (2)

FATHER5:2	H2-3	*Thomas Dudley* Esq; *these humbly presented.*
TDUDLEY165:2	H3	*Thomas Dudley* Esq;

THORNES (4) [thorns]

ELEMEN13:25	H226	Thistles and thornes, where he expected graine;
MEDDM200:11	Hp279	brests, that god is forced to hedg vp their way wth thornes

MEDDM209:11	Hp291	eyes and thornes in their sides, and at last ouercame them,
PILGRIM210:9	H9	The bryars and thornes no more shall scrat

THORNS (1) [pl.]

MEDDM198:9	Hp276	He that walks among briars and thorns will be very carefull,

THOROUGHLY See THROUGHLY

THOSE (108)

FATHER5:7	H8	Their worth so shines, in those rich lines you show.
FATHER5:12	H13	My lowly pen, might wait upon those four,
PROLOG7:22	H34	Else of our Sex, why feigned they those nine,
ELEMEN9:9	H43	Set ope those gates, that 'fore so strong was {were} barr'd.
ELEMEN10:20	H95	And influence if divers of those starres,
ELEMEN11:11	H131	But to leave those to'th' wise, I judge is {it} best,
ELEMEN13:2	H203	Was {Were} those compiled heapes of massy stones?
ELEMEN13:37	H238	To ope those veines of Mine, audacious bold:
ELEMEN19:2	H447	And what those Sages, did, or {either} spake, or writ,
HUMOUR30:7	H399	Those {Whose} cold dry heads, {head} more subtilly doth yeild,
AGES44:37	H370	But ah, I saw at last those eyes to close:
SEASONS47:2	H17	And now makes glad those blinded Northern wights,
SEASONS49:16	H107	Now go those frolick swaines, the shepheard lad,
MASSYR56:30	H136	But this is marvelous, of all those men,
MASSYR57:20	H167	Nor can those Reasons which wise *Raleigh* finds,
MASSYR59:37	H261	When *Jonah* for their sins denounc'd such {those} woes;
MASSYR60:25	H290	And those which {that} seem'd with *Sardanapal's* gone;
MASSYR60:27	H292	The fire, those Mettals could not damnifie;
MASSYR61:3	H308	That those two made but one, we need not doubt:
MASSYR61:10	H315	Next treads the {those} steps, by which his Father won.
MASSYR62:12	H357	Those that from *Ioshua's* time had been Estate {a state},
MASSYR62:22	H367	Where now those ten Tribes are, can no man tel,
MASSYR62:26	H371	Or else those *Chinoes* rare, whose wealth, and Arts,
MASSYR66:36	H542	Contemplating those times he lost his wits;
MPERS69:37	H659	The Reason of those words *Cyrus* demands,
MPERS70:11	H682	He cuts those banks, and let the river out;
MPERS71:28	H742	But as they marched o're those desart sands,
MPERS73:30	H815	A Consultation by the {those} States was held.
MPERS74:35	H858	But strength {men} against those walls was {were} of no use;
MPERS75:35	H892	That shall, but {once} dare {to} raze those firme foundations;
MPERS79:12	H1034	But winds, and waves those iron bands did break;
MPERS79:23	H1049	That none of these should {those could} live a {an} hundred
MPERS80:2	H1069	And wound the backs of those bold {brave} Warriours stout.
MPERS81:1	H1109	And many thousands of these {those} men did kil;
MPERS81:32	H1140	And of those *Greeks,* which by his skil he'd won,
MPERS82:13	H1160	For pitty, let those few to *Xerxes* go,
MPERS82:39	H1186	To see those breasts, where chastity did dwel,
MPERS84:12	H1247	Rebuilt those walls which long in rubbish lay,
MPERS85:25	H1301	So that he might, these tumults {those troubles} soon appease.
MPERS86:35	H1351	Great care was his pretence, those Souldiers stout,
MPERS87:18	H1372	To keep those streights, to hinder his intent.
MPERS91:38	H1552	And being king commands those that remain,
MGREC93:17	H1614	His Education, much to these {those} did adde.
MGREC6:31	H1628	But death did terminate, those thoughts so high.
MGREC94:41	H1679	Those banks so steep, the *Greeks,* now {yet} scramble up

MGREC97:30	H1791	Those mournfull Ladies, from captivity,
MGREC99:2	H1845	All those rich Kingdoms large, which {that} doe abide
MGREC101:8	H1933	And all those Countries, which (betwixt) did lye,
MGREC101:11	H1936	And all those Kingdoms in lesse *Asia;*
MGREC102:35	H2005	Those purple hangings, mixt with green, and white,
MGREC102:36	H2006	Those beds of gold, and couches of delight,
MGREC103:8	H2019	Here lay the bulk, of all those precious things;
MGREC103:35	H2046	Those stately streets with raging flames doth {flame did} fil.
MGREC104:32	H2084	*Darius* from those Traitors hands to gain;
MGREC107:2	H2177	With those of worth, he still desires esteem,
MGREC107:12	H2187	Which done, sets fire upon those costly {goodly} spoyls
MGREC109:2	H2259	Those that submit, he doth restore {give them rule} again.
MGREC109:3	H2260	Those that {Such as} doe not, both they, {them} and theirs, are
MGREC~~111:13~~	H2358	These {Those} obscure Nations yeelded as before;
MGREC111:21	H2366	Upon those Flats they did not long abide;
MGREC112:19	H2405	'Mongst those, that of his cruelty did taste,
MGREC116:28	H2594	For those that {such as} pleas'd him: had both wealth and
MGREC117:4	H2611	Of all those kingdomes large which he had got,
MGREC117:35	H2642	Alleadg'd by those, which {who} by their subtill plea
MGREC120:14	H2749	For's Souldiers 'gainst those Captains would not goe;
MGREC124:8	~~H2913~~	Upon those friends, his father rais'd on high,
MGREC124:9	~~H2914~~	Those absent, banished, or else he slew
MGREC128:8	H3081	Which none e're did but those of royall fame;
MGREC128:14	H3087	And to requite this Traytor for those {these} harmes:
MGREC131:17	H3209	Of those dominions {vast Kindgomes} he did sometimes gain,
MGREC132:18	H3255	Those Countries large, his father got before,
MGREC132:34	H3281	*Seleuchus,* and *Lysimachus;* those {these} twaine
MGREC133:18	H3306	I must let passe those many battels fought,
MGREC133:19	H3307	Between those Kings, and noble *Pyrrus* stout,
MGREC134:16	H3347	Vanquish'd in fight, and took those kingdomes all,
MGREC135:25	H3397	And smote those feet, those legs, those arms and thighs;
MROMAN137:3	H3454	And with the stile of *Patres* honour'd those;
DIALOG142:35	H64	I must confesse, some of those Sores you name,
DIALOG~~146:34~~	H220	To see these {those} latter dayes of hop'd for good,
DIALOG147:6	H232	And shall I not on those {them} with *Mero's* curse,
DIALOG147:20	H246	But those that hurt his people and his Crown,
SIDNEY152:4	~~H76~~	That those that name his fame, he needs must ~~spare,~~
DUBART153:19	H23	To comprehend the worth of all those knacks;
DUBART154:39	H84	Ile leave thy praise, to those shall doe thee right,
QELIZ157:39	H107	O {Yea} happy, happy, had those dayes still been,
VANITY160:13	H23	Sure if on earth, it must be in those parts;
TDUDLEY165:40	H42	Those titles loath'd, which some too much do love
CONTEM169:27	H66	And men in being fancy those are dead,
CONTEM171:4	H109	The starry observations of those Sages,
CONTEM171:26	H128	By birth more noble then those creatures all,
DISTEMP179:21	H9	Who sendeth help to those in misery;
DISTEMP179:22	H10	He chac'd away those clouds, and let me see
1LETTER181:16	H14	Then view those fruits which through thy heat I bore?
2LETTER182:20	H26	Like those far scituate under the pole,
MERCY188:30	H16	But ah too soon those heavy tydings fly,
MEDDM196:30	Hp274	are best preserued wth sugar, those parents are wise that can

MEDDM199:24	Hp278	those that are eyes of a Republique, foretels a declineing
MEDDM200:28	Hp279	when the Sun of righteoussnes shall appear those dry bones
MEDDM206:7	Hp287	starres and those starres also, to differ much one from the
MEDDM206:11	Hp287	Company of Saints, and Angels those Saintes haue their
MEDDM208:20	Hp290	nothing, and so leaue those in the lurch that most relyed
MEDDM208:25	Hp290	wells in the time of drought, that those that go to finde water in
MEDDM209:12	Hp291	slauery, so it is most certain that those that are disobedient
MYCHILD215:11	Hp240	leaue to speak, and those espec. sink deepest wch are spoke
MYCHILD215:30	Hp241	espec: those places I thought most concerned my Condition,
MYCHILD217:34	Hp243	I never saw any miracles to confirm me, and those wch I read

THO'ST (2) [thou hast] See also THOU'ST, THOV'ST

SON231:22	H34	Tho'st done for him, + so for me.
HOURS233:28	H11	And thy Abode tho'st made wth me

THOU'RT (5) [thou art]

HUMOUR23:16	H126	If once thou'rt great, what followes thereupon?
HUMOUR24:27	H176	So walke thee til thou'rt cold, then let thee go.
HUMOUR25:33	H222	So spils {shed'st} that life {blood}, thou'rt bounden to preserve.
HUMOUR26:28	H258	If thou'rt the taker, I must be the giver:
HUMOUR31:16	H449	If there thou'rt stopt, to th' Liver thou turn'st in,

THOU'ST (7) [thou hast] See also THO'ST, THOV'ST

HUMOUR24:20	H169	Ile only shew the wrongs, thou'st done to me.
HUMOUR25:12	H201	And though thou'st us'd me, with opprobrious spight, {right:}
HUMOUR25:24	H213	Witnesse the execrable deeds thou'st done:
HUMOUR25:29	H218	How often for the lye, thou'st giv'n the stab.
HUMOUR30:35	H427	Of al the rest, thou'st nothing there to do;
HUMOUR31:4	H437	When by thy heat, thou'st bak'd thy selfe to crust,
WHAT224:8	H8	For what thou'st done for me.

THOUGH (73) See also THO:

FATHER5:6	H7	(though made a pedestall for *Adams* Race) /world
FATHER6:2	H36	Some thing {something} of all (though mean) I did intend,
FATHER6:5	H39	My goods are true (though poor) I love no stealth,
ELEMEN9:14	H48	Though strong limb'd *Vulcan* forg'd it by his skill,
ELEMEN9:38	H72	And though nought but *Sal'manders* live in fire;
ELEMEN10:33	H108	And though I be a servant to each man;
ELEMEN12:25	H185	No, though the fawning dog did urge me sore
ELEMEN17:36	H400	Though {Yet am} not through ignorance, {ignorant} first was my
ELEMEN18:1	H405	And though you love Fire, Earth, and Water wel;
ELEMEN18:11	H415	So loath he is to go, though nature's spent,
HUMOUR21:12	H40	Though under fire, we comprehend all heat,
HUMOUR25:12	H201	And though thou'st us'd me, with opprobrious spight, {right:}
HUMOUR27:19	H290	Though cast upon my guiltlesse blushing face;
HUMOUR28:9	H321	Her languishing diseases, though not quick,
HUMOUR28:37	H349	Such venome lyes in words, though but a blast,
HUMOUR29:6	H359	Though Choler rage, and raile, i'le not do so,
HUMOUR30:27	H419	Likewise the useful spleen, though not the best,
HUMOUR30:31	H423	Laughter (though thou sayst malice) flowes from hence,
HUMOUR32:20	H494	Though wit I want, and anger I have lesse,
HUMOUR32:34	H508	And {But} though the pitched field i've ever fled,
HUMOUR33:16	H530	And though I grant, thou art my helper here,
HUMOUR33:27	H541	Though it in all, and every part be whole:
AGES38:29	H132	And though I misse, the tossings of the mind:

AGES39:24	H167	Though thus in field, at home, to all most kind,
AGES40:34	H213	Though dangers do attend me every houre,
AGES43:16	H310	Though cemented with more the noble bloud,
AGES43:36	H331	Though some more incident to age, or youth:
AGES46:12	H443	Though reading other Works, doth much refresh,
SEASONS47:24	H40	For though the Frost hath lost his binding power,
SEASONS47:32	H47	For though in's running progresse he doth take
SEASONS49:10	H101	The reason why {Though he decline}, because his flames so
SEASONS49:25	H114	Though you repose on grasse under the skye.
SEASONS53:5	H261	*The last, though bad, I could not mend,*
MASSYR58:27	H210	And though of wars, he did abhor the sight;
MASSYR60:26	H291	But {For} though his Palace, did in ashes lye,
MASSYR65:8	H473	And though a Victor home his Army leads,
MASSYR68:25	H611	And did one thing worthy a King (though late)
MPERS71:4	H717	And though his conquests made the earth to groan,
MPERS71:12	H727	Which Law includes all Lawes, though lawlesse stil,
MPERS71:40	H753	And though no gods, if he esteem them some,
MPERS75:39	H896	Set up a Temple (though, a lesse) again.
MPERS81:28	H1136	Though of this Nation borne a great Commander,
MGREC95:32	H1711	Though some there be, and that {(perhaps)} more likely, write;
MGREC97:16	H1777	For though their beauties were unparalled
MGREC99:31	H1874	Though in an enemy it should be found;
MGREC100:36	H1920	For this lost Queen (though in captivity).
MGREC101:17	H1942	No, though *Parmenio* plead, he {yet} will not heare;
MGREC102:17	H1987	Though worn by time, and raz'd {rac'd} by foes full sore,
MGREC103:6	H2017	Though *Babylon* was rich, and *Sushan* too;
MGREC106:4	H2138	And though a Monarch once {late}, now lyes like clay;
MGREC106:6	H2140	Though gods on earth, like Sons of men shall {they} dye.
MGREC106:17	H2151	Though some {most} of reading best, and soundest minde,
MGREC115:25	H2544	Though to his Mother he disprov'd the thing;
MGREC115:27	H2546	He might well dye, though he had done no wrong;
MGREC132:9	H3244	Yea {And} though *Cassander* died in his bed,
MGREC132:16	H3252	Though men and mony both he hath at will,
MROMAN139:34	H3560	Though oft perswaded, I as oft deny'd,
MROMAN140:1	H3564	And weary lines (though lanke) I many pen'd:
DIALOG142:31	H60	Though Armes, nor Purse she hath, for your releif:
DIALOG143:16	H85	Though she hath bin injurious heretofore.
DIALOG146:34	H221	Though now beclouded all with tears and blood:
SIDNEY150:32	H59	Though *Sidney* dy'd, his valiant name should live;
QELIZ155:22	H13	Thousands bring off'rings, (though out of date)
QELIZ155:31	H22	Though I resound thy greatnesse {praises} 'mongst the throng.
QELIZ157:35	H103	But she though dead, will vindicate our wrong.
QELIZ158:18	H127	Whose living vertues speak (though dead long since)
CONTEM170:28	H99	Though none on Earth but kindred near then could he find.
CONTEM171:12	H116	And though thus short, we shorten many wayes,
CONTEM171:19	H122	And then the earth (though old) stil clad in green,
SICKNES179:7	H27	O great's the gain, though got with pain,
MERCY189:15	H36	What though, thy strokes full sad & grievous be,
2SIMON195:12	Hp271	though in value they fall short of all in this kinde yet I presume
MEDDM208:9	Hp290	friends, though there should be no displeasence betweene

THOUGH'T (1) [though it]

DIALOG146:35	H221	That Right may have its right, though't be with blood;

THOUGHT (52) See also THOVGHT

ELEMEN8:8	H6	For to declare, themselves they all ingage;
ELEMEN15:39	H321	For it, to search my waves, they thought no scorne.
ELEMEN17:8	H372	Thus *Albion* {*Britain* fair} (tis thought) was cut from *France,*
HUMOUR20:30	H22	Her wisedome spake not much, but thought the more.
HUMOUR30:5	H397	If I be partial judg'd, or thought to erre,
HUMOUR34:5	H560	He was no foole, who thought the Soul lay here {there},
AGES43:16	H308	Then thought my state firm founded sure to last,
AGES44:38	H371	And then, me thought, the world {day} at noon grew dark,
MASSYR53:17	H7	But each one thought his petty rule was high,
MASSYR55:24	H90	And thought her fit, to make a Monarch's wife,
MASSYR62:18	H363	{He} Plac'd *Israel* in's Land {there}, where he thought best,
MPERS70:4	H675	Next war, the restlesse *Cyrus* thought upon,
MPERS70:33	H704	Using such taunting words as she thought good.
MPERS72:33	H777	All thought {wisht} his short reign long, till {past before} it was
MPERS72:37	H781	Ruling as they thought good, {best} under his head.
MPERS73:35	H820	And thought the people, would more happy be,
MPERS73:37	H822	But others thought (none of the dullest braine,)
MPERS74:3	H828	All envie to avoyd, this was thought on,
MPERS77:11	H950	('Tis thought) through grief and his {this} succeslesse strife.
MPERS78:28	H1009	For to command alone, she thought {judg'd} was best.
MPERS79:20	H1046	Long viewing them, thought it great happinesse,
MPERS81:5	H1113	Thought it {Fearing} his best {bridge}, no longer for to {there
MPERS85:10	H1286	These two lewd {first} sons, are by hystorians thought,
MPERS86:21	H1337	And thought it best, now in his mothers time,
MPERS92:7	H1565	It may be thought, surely he had no Son,
MPERS92:10	H1568	But as 'tis thought, {most suppose} in him had {did} *Cyrus* end:
MGREC96:18	H1738	think {Suppos'd} he neither thought {meant} to fight nor fly,
MGREC96:33	H1753	For sure *Darius* thought, at the first sight,
MGREC104:2	H2054	Thought now this once, to try his fortunes here,
MGREC106:16	H2150	Her traine to *Alexander* (as 'tis thought)
MGREC112:30	H2416	Must suffer, not for what he did, but thought:
MGREC115:15	H2531	What e're he did, or thought not so content,
MGREC116:3	H2563	Poyson had put an end to's dayes 'twas thought,
MGREC116:7	H2567	By others thought, and that more generally,
MGREC118:36	H2685	Thought timely for themselves, now to provide.
MGREC120:17	H2752	With *Antipater* t' joyn, sometimes he thought,
MGREC122:40	H2861	All to be order'd there as he thought best:
MGREC123:37	H2901	On whom ('twas thought) she set her chief delight;
MGREC124:35	H2942	Nor counts {thought} he that indignity but {was} small,
MGREC124:41	H2948	She gave him poyson formerly ('tis thought)
MGREC126:35	H3024	To Husbands death ('twas {'tis} thought) she gave consent,
MGREC129:21	H3135	But from {by} their hands, who thought not once of this.
MGREC129:29	H3143	(But, *Olympias,* thought to {would} preferre th' other:)
MGREC130:23	H3178	And by their means, who thought of nothing lesse
CONTEM167:33	H9	I wist not what to wish, yet sure thought I,
CONTEM169:13	H54	To sing some Song, my mazed Muse thought meet.
CONTEM172:11	H147	Now thought the rivers did the trees excel,
MEDDM209:9	Hp291	that they could do (as they thought) wth lesse hazard and more

MYCHILD215:30	Hp241	espec: those places I thought most concerned my Condition,
MYCHILD217:25	Hp243	Lord, and when I haue been in sicknes + pain, I haue thought if
SOREFIT222:2	H21	To praise in thought, in Deed, in Word.
MED223:12	Hp250	pʳsumed to haue thought it? So wonderfull are these thoughts

THOUGHTS (32) [pl.] See also THOVGHTS

FATHER5:11	H12	Yet view thereof, did cause my thoughts to soare,
ELEMEN18:41	H445	Let such suspend their thoughts, and silent be;
HUMOUR31:26	H459	Here, there, her restlesse thoughts do ever flye;
AGES37:23	H85	My then ambitious thoughts, were low enough.
AGES39:29	H172	elevates {elevate} my {high} thoughts above {beyond} the
AGES42:27	H285	My wakefull thoughts, up to my painefull gaine.
AGES42:37	H293	My dunghil thoughts, or hopes, could reach no higher.
AGES45:22	H411	What are my thoughts, this is no time to say.
MASSYR57:29	H174	We may suggest our thoughts, but cannot tel;
MPERS79:25	H1051	Of so long time, his thoughts had never been.
MPERS79:27	H1053	How of this enterprise his thoughts now stands;
MPERS80:35	H1102	He hearing this, his thoughts, and course home bended,
MPERS89:9	H1443	After a while his {hurri'd} thoughts he re-collects,
MGREC93:31	H1628	But death did terminate, those thoughts so high.
MGREC104:28	H2080	Great recompence, in's thoughts, he did propose;
MGREC116:41	H2607	His thoughts are perish'd he aspires no more,
MGREC136:10	H3424	*To finish what {what's} begun, new thoughts impart*
MROMAN139:28	H3554	My thoughts and my endeavours thereto bent;
MROMAN139:33	H3559	All thoughts of further progress laid aside,
TDUDLEY165:38	H40	High thoughts he gave no harbour in his heart,
TDUDLEY166:10	H52	His thoughts were more sublime, his actions wise,
CONTEM170:19	H91	Hath thousand thoughts to end his brothers dayes,
CONTEM173:20	H186	Feels no sad thoughts, nor cruciating cares
FLESH175:9	H9	Her thoughts unto a higher sphere:
FLESH176:30	H70	My thoughts do yield me more content
2LETTER182:5	H11	My dumpish thoughts, my groans, my brakish tears
CHILDRN185:30	H56	And knew what thoughts there sadly rest,
MEDDM196:9	Hp273	Corruptions, and yᵗ will damp his high thoughts
MEDDM199:19	Hp278	wearys the body, and many thoughts oppresse the minde
MEDDM205:10	Hp286	his more fixed and resolued thoughts, are like to
MEDDM205:11	Hp286	inhabitants his slight and flitting thoughts are like passengers,
MED223:12	Hp250	to haue thought it? So wonderfull are these thoughts that my

THOUSAND (63)

HUMOUR28:33	H345	Thousand examples, you may daily see
AGES45:19	H401	Three hundred thousand slaughtered innocents,
MASSYR55:2	H68	The world then was two thousand nineteen old.
MASSYR56:2	H108	Each Square, was fifteen thousand paces long,
MASSYR56:10	H116	Three hundred thousand men, here day, by day;
MASSYR58:21	H206	These all agree, and forty thousand make,
MASSYR60:36	H301	A thousand tallents of *Menahem* had,
MPERS70:21	H692	Had after {A} thousand yeares faire to be seen.
MPERS74:15	H838	A thousand times, God save {long live} the King, they cry,
MPERS76:30	H928	Arm'd all they could, which elev'n thousand make;
MPERS78:5	H986	His Foot was seventeen hundred thousand strong,
MPERS78:6	H987	Eight hundred thousand Horse to them {these} belong;
MPERS78:16	H997	Of two and twenty thousand Gallies meet,

MPERS78:22	H1003	{Which to} Three thousand (or more) {came} by best relation,
MPERS78:35	H1016	Three thousand Tallents of the purest gold;
MPERS79:14	H1040	Seven thousand Gallies chain'd, by *Tyrians* skil,
MPERS79:39	H1065	Till twenty thousand *Persians* falls down slain;
MPERS80:9	H1076	When as one thousand, could some Millions {a million} daunt;
MPERS81:6	H1114	Three hundred thousand yet he left behind,
MPERS81:33	H1141	He fifty thousand joynes unto his own;
MPERS81:35	H1143	{In all} One hundred thousand, and ten thousand make.
MPERS81:40	H1144	The *Athenians* could but forty thousand arme,
MPERS82:11	H1158	All's lost, and of three hundred thousand men,
MPERS82:12	H1159	Three thousand scapes, for to {only can} run home agen;
MPERS87:14	H1370	And counts nine hundred thousand foot and horses:
MPERS87:17	H1371	Three hundred thousand, yet {he} to *Syria* sent;
MPERS88:21	H1414	Of six thousand, wherein the King was yet;
MPERS90:23	H1490	The many thousand *Persians* they had slain;
MPERS91:3	H1511	To these {them} he thirty thousand Tallents sent,
MGREC94:19	H1657	Thirty two thousand made up his foot force,
MGREC94:20	H1658	To these {which} were joyn'd, five thousand goodly horse.
MGREC95:2	H1681	And twenty thousand, of their lives bereave,
MGREC95:28	H1707	To *Greece* he thirty thousand talents sends;
MGREC95:31	H1710	Who came with thousand thousands at his feet,
MGREC95:33	H1712	He but four hundred thousand had to fight,
MGREC96:31	H1751	A thousand Mules, and Camells ready wait.
MGREC97:6	H1767	Two hundred thousand men that day were slaine,
MGREC97:7	H1768	And forty thousand Prisoners also tane;
MGREC98:19	H1821	Two thousand of the cheif he crucifi'd,
MGREC98:20	H1822	Eight thousand by the sword now also dy'd,
MGREC98:21	H1823	And thirteen thousand Gally slaves he made,
MGREC100:25	H1909	Two hundred fifty thousand by account,
MGREC101:12	H1937	With thirty thousand Tallents, to be paid
MGREC101:36	H1965	Forty five thousand *Alexander* had,
MGREC103:15	H2026	To a {an} hundred thousand Tallents by account.
MGREC103:40	H2051	Which forty thousand made; but his intent,
MGREC108:21	H2237	Down from the mountains twenty thousand came,
MGREC108:41	H2257	And being an {one} hundred twenty thousand strong,
MGREC109:27	H2286	And of his own, a thousand Tallents more.
MGREC112:5	H2391	Six thousand Guests he to {unto} this feast invites,
MGREC114:33	H2503	When e're 'tis said, he thousand thousands slew,
MGREC115:9	H2518	Twelve thousand Tallents on it franckly spent;
MGREC115:15	H2529	Twelve thousand Tallents also did intend,
MGREC134:22	H3353	{And} With seven hundred thousand volumes fill'd,
MROMAN139:7	H3535	To eighty thousand soules then did amount:
DUBART153:22	H26	And thousand times his mazed minde doth wish
DUBART154:1	H46	A thousand thousand times my senslesse Sences,
CONTEM168:12	H21	Or thousand since thou brakest thy shell of horn,
CONTEM170:19	H91	Hath thousand thoughts to end his brothers dayes,
CONTEM173:11	H178	And thousand fancies buzzing in my brain,
3LETTER183:14	H16	With thousand doleful sighs & mournfull Cooes.

THOUSANDS (10) [pl.] See also THOVSANDS

ELEMEN12:23	H183	Thousands in woods, and planes, both wild, and tame,
ELEMEN15:30	H312	With thousands moe, which now I list not name,

ELEMEN19:10   H455   With thousands moe, which now I may omit;
MPERS81:1   H1109   And many thousands of these {those} men did kil;
MGREC95:31   H1710   Who came with thousand thousands at his feet,
MGREC114:33   H2503   When e're 'tis said, he thousand thousands slew,
DIALOG144:41   H149   Thousands of starved Christian there also.
DIALOG146:6   H194   That thousands lay on heaps, here bleeds my woes.
QELIZ155:22   H13   Thousands bring off'rings, (though out of date)
MEDDM196:33   Hp274   That town wch thousands of enemys w^thout hath not been able

THOV'ST (2) [thou hast] See also THO'ST, THOU'ST
HANNA230:15   H8   Gravnt shee rember w^t thov'st done
ACK235:15   H15   And hope thov'st given of good successe,

THOVGHT (2) [thought]
MYCHILD215:13   Hp240   speak to any of yov much lesse to All, thovght it ye best whilst
MYCHILD217:28   Hp243   thovght were it hell it self and could there find ye Love of God

THOVGHTS (1) [thoughts]
HOUSE237:15   H45   Raise vp thy thovghts above the skye

THOVSANDS (1) [thousands]
MYCHILD218:6   Hp243-4   this hath thovsands of Times been svggested to me, yet

THRACE (1)
MPERS79:30   H1056   But *Xerxes* resolute, to *Thrace* goes first,

THRAL (1) [thrall] See also THRALE
CONTEM170:1   H75   That turn'd his Sovereign to a naked thral.

THRALDOME (1)
MASSYR62:11   H356   Into perpetual thraldome that time bring;

THRALE (1) [thrall] See also THRALE
MGREC133:23   H3312   *Philip* had *Perseus,* who was made a Thrale

THRALLED (1)
MGREC119:12   H2702   In these tumultuous dayes, the thralled *Greeks*

THRAWLED (1) [thralled]
MGREC104:26   H2078   In more dispight, the thrawled Prince to hold.

THREAD (2) See also THRED
MGREC116:2   H2562   The thread of *Alexanders* life was spun;
SICKNES178:20   H3   My race is run, my thread is spun,

THREAT (4)
ELEMEN8:15   H13   The sea did threat the heavens, the heavens the earth,
ELEMEN8:22   H20   The worlds confusion it did seeme to threat;
HUMOUR20:12   H4   Ceasing to vaunt, their good, or threat their force.
DIALOG143:6   H77   Whose tearing tusks did wound, and kill, and threat:

THREAT'NING (1)
MEDDM199:6   Hp277   do not often fall till after threat'ning.

THREATEN (1)
HUMOUR22:13   H82   If any threaten her, she'l in a trice,

THREATENING See THREAT'NING

THREATENS (2)
MEDDM203:23   Hp283   malady that threatens him wth death, he will gladly entertaine
MEDDM208:23   Hp290   them, but when death threatens and distresse lays hold vpon

THREATNED (2) [threatened]
DIALOG144:20   H130   For these, were threatned the wofull day,
DIALOG148:12   H277   Execute toth' full {And on her pour} the vengeance threatned.

THREATNING (1) [threatening] See also THREAT'NING
MASSYR59:38   H262   He did repent, therefore it {the threatning} was not done,

three

THREATS (3) n.

MASSYR62:15	H360	On whom, nor threats, nor mercies could do good;
MGREC127:17	H3047	Such as nor {no} threats, nor favour could acquire;
MEDDM201:13	Hp280	alayed, by cold words and not by blustering threats.

THREATS (2) v.

AGES40:35	H214	And gastly death oft threats me with her {his} power,
MPERS75:31	H888	Threats punishment to him, that through default

THRED (1) [thread]

SIDNEY150:26	H53	E're he was ripe; his thred cut *Atropos.*

THREE (49)

ELEMEN10:8	H83	The maid with ballance, wayn with horses three;
ELEMEN12:31	H191	After three years, when men and meat is spent,
ELEMEN14:31	H273	Ever in craving, from the other three:
ELEMEN17:40	H404	Aboundantly more then my sisters three?
ELEMEN20:5	H487	I have said lesse, then did my sisters three;
HUMOUR22:19	H88	Here's three of you, all sees {see} now what you are,
HUMOUR23:12	H122	The sinke of all us three, the hatefull spleen;
HUMOUR30:14	H406	If I have not more part, then al ye three:
HUMOUR30:34	H426	The Spleen for al you three, was made a sinke,
HUMOUR31:9	H442	What officer thou art to al us three.
HUMOUR32:19	H493	To bear {with} the injurious taunts of three;
HUMOUR33:18	H532	With all your flourishes, now Sisters three,
HUMOUR33:39	H553	Of three, its hard to say, which doth excel;
HUMOUR33:41	H555	I'le touch the Sight, great'st wonder of the three;
AGES36:37	H61	With heed now stood, three ages of fraile man;
AGES45:19	H401	Three hundred thousand slaughtered innocents,
SEASONS46:36	H14	Three months {(quoth she)} there are allotted to my share,
MASSYR54:23	H50	So broad, three Chariots run abrest there might,
MASSYR54:34	H61	An army of three Millions he led out,
MASSYR56:4	H110	Three hundred sixty foot, the walls in heighth:
MASSYR56:10	H116	Three hundred thousand men, here day, by day;
MASSYR65:24	H489	His Son three months he suffered to reign,
MPERS71:1	H713	Three Daughters, and two Sons, he left behind,
MPERS74:27	H850	Three strings to's bow, the least of which is good;
MPERS78:22	H1003	{Which to} Three thousand (or more) {came} by best relation,
MPERS78:35	H1016	Three thousand Tallents of the purest gold;
MPERS81:6	H1114	Three hundred thousand yet he left behind,
MPERS82:11	H1158	All's lost, and of three hundred thousand men,
MPERS82:12	H1159	Three thousand scapes, for to {only can} run home agen;
MPERS85:4	H1280	Three sons great *Artaxerxes* left behind;
MPERS87:17	H1371	Three hundred thousand, yet {he} to *Syria* sent;
MPERS91:31	H1545	Forty three years he rul'd, then turn'd to dust,
MPERS92:2	H1556	That three and twenty years he reign'd, I finde,
MPERS92:13	H1571	Three years he reign'd, as Chronicles expresse, {then drank
MGREC121:5	H2783	From the invasions of the other three;
MGREC121:27	H2809	That *Eumenes* got of the other three,
MGREC132:25	H3270	After three years he dyed, left what he'd won
MGREC133:11	H3299	So three Successors only did remaine;
MGREC135:36	H3408	With these three Monarchies, now have I done,
MGREC136:12	H3426	*This fourth to th' other three, now might be brought.*
MROMAN137:35	H3486	Forty three yeares he rul'd with generall praise;

MROMAN138:3	H3493	Three call'd *Horatii,* on *Romans* side,
MROMAN138:4	H3494	And *Curiatii,* three *Albans* provide;
DIALOG146:10	H198	One battell, two or three I might abide,
CHILDRN185:13	H39	My other three, still with me nest,
ANNEB187:14	H3-4	*Who deceased* June 20. 1669. *being three years and*
1SIMON188:6	H7	Three flours, two scarcely blown, the last i'th' bud,
MEDDM199:26	Hp278	We read in Scripture of three sorts of Arrows the arrow of an

THREESCORE (1)

AGES35:38	H24	Then may he live, til {out} threescore years or past.

THRESHING-FLOOR (1)

MGREC135:27	H3399	Became like chaffe upon the threshing-floor;

THREW (4)

MASSYR65:1	H466	And in the channell throw {threw} each burden down;
MGREC93:28	H1625	That broke {brake} his hornes, that threw him on the ground,
MGREC125:35	H2985	And throwes {threw} his bones about, to shew her spight.
SIDNEY152:18	H87	*Errata,* through their leave threw me my pen,

THRICE (1)

MPERS69:36	H658	He *Solon, Solon, Solon,* thrice did cry.

THRIVE (2)

AGES37:11	H73	My mother stil did waste, as I did thrive:
DIALOG141:26	H25	Or by my wasting state, dost think to thrive?

THRIVING (1)

AGES42:34	H290	My fatted Oxe {thriving Cattle}, and my exuberous {new-milch-

THRO (7) [through]

SEASONS49:39	H132	The Sun in {thro} Leo now hath {takes} his carrear,
MYCHILD216:28	Hp242	by losses in estate, and these Times (thro: his great mercy)
MYCHILD218:11	Hp244	who haue scornd + contemd it, hath it not been p^{r}served thro:
30SEPT227:29	Hp257	that I haue passed thro: to ye End y^t if you meet wth the like
SON231:16	H28	Thro: want and Dangers manifold,
HOURS233:27	H10	Thro: the I've kept my Grovnd.
HOURS234:15	H29	Yet if I see Thee not thro: them

THROATS (1) [pl.]

MEDDM202:18	Hp282	their throats, but cannot fill their bellys, they may be choaked

THROBBING (1)

ANNEB187:32	H22	Mean time my throbbing heart's chear'd up with this

THROBS (1) [pl.]

CHILDRN185:36	H62	My throbs such now, as 'fore were never:

THRONE (26)

HUMOUR21:14	H42	I in his heart erect my regal throne,
AGES43:8	H305	I might possess that throne which was their right;
AGES45:22	H405	I've seen a King by force thrust from his throne,
MASSYR55:5	H71	His wife, *Semiramis,* usurp'd the throne,
MASSYR65:25	H490	Then from his throne, he pull'd {pluck'd} him down again:
MPERS72:3	H755	His brother *Smerdis* sit upon his throne;
MPERS73:20	H807	To thrust th' Imposter *Smerdis* out of throne,
MPERS77:16	H955	Grand-childe to *Cyrus,* now sits on the throne;
MPERS86:9	H1325	*Mnemon* now sits {set} upon his fathers Throne,
MPERS89:13	H1447	may come, and {in short time might} place one in his Throne,
MPERS91:35	H1549	Succeeds in th' throne his father being gone.
MPERS92:16	H1574	*Darius* by this *Bogoas* set in throne,
MGREC113:33	H2460	By him was set upon the *Persian* Throne:

MGREC120:22	H2759	Which of his Ancestors was once the throne,
MGREC122:18	H2843	Grandchild to him, who once sat on that throne,
MGREC129:1	H3115	Who then shall {should} be installed in the throne:
MGREC134:20	H3351	Cal'd *Philadelphus,* next sat on {did possess} the throne,
MGREC134:28	H3359	After *Epiphanes,* sat on the Throne
MROMAN138:14	H3504	Next, *Ancus Martius* sits upon the Throne,
MROMAN138:38	H3528	Next, *Servius Tullius* sits upon {gets into} the Throne,
MROMAN139:13	H3541	Sate on the Throne, when he had slaine his foe;
CONTEM169:4	H46	And is thy splendid Throne erect so high?
FLESH177:14	H95	Which doth proceed from the Lambs Throne:
DISTEMP179:20	H8	And looking up unto his Throne on high,
MEDDM205:19	Hp286	haue boldnes to go to the throne of grace to be accepted
13MAY227:7	H16	I haue accesse vnto his Throne,

THRONG (2)

MPERS69:27	H649	Disguised *Cressus,* hop'd to scape i'th throng,
QELIZ155:31	H22	Though I resound thy greatnesse {praises} 'mongst the throng.

THROUGH (44) See also THRO

ELEMEN9:23	H57	A transmutation, it was through mine aide.
ELEMEN11:1	H117	The Army through my helpe victorious rose;
ELEMEN17:36	H400	Though {Yet am} not through ignorance, {ignorant} first was my
HUMOUR22:28	H97	And through the arteries sends {it} o're the frame,
HUMOUR26:26	H256	Through th' warme, blew conduits of my veinal rils;
HUMOUR26:33	H263	The spirits through thy heat, are made perfect there,
HUMOUR27:20	H291	Now through your leaves, some little time i'le spend;
HUMOUR34:12	H567	Which runs through all the spondles of the rack,
AGES37:27	H89	Through ignorance, all troubles did surmount.
AGES45:14	H396	fly their Country, through their {struck both with gilt and} dread.
SEASONS52:22	H237	Through Christendome, with great festivity
MASSYR59:20	H244	Which through much rain, then swelling up so high,
MASSYR61:35	H340	Through *Syria* now he marcht, none stopt his way,
MPERS72:27	H773	Shot through the heart of his beloved son:
MPERS75:31	H888	Threats punishment to him, that through default
MPERS77:11	H950	('Tis thought) through grief and his {this} succeslesse strife.
MPERS88:37	H1430	grew weake, through {by their} slaughters that they made.
MPERS90:2	H1477	But when through difficulties still {all} they brake,
MPERS90:6	H1479	But on they march, through hunger, and through cold,
MPERS90:6	H1479	But on they march, through hunger, and through cold,
MGREC94:16	H1650	And through the *Hellispont,* his ships make {made} way.
MGREC99:24	H1867	Captaine {Thus *Betis*} tane, had holes bor'd through his feet,
MGREC99:25	H1868	And by command was drawn through every street,
MGREC100:7	H1891	The Pagan Priest through hire, or else mistake,
MGREC109:18	H2277	Through his perswasion *Alexander* meets;
MGREC111:32	H2377	Now through these goodly countries as he past,
MGREC114:12	H2482	And in a rage him through the body ran,
MGREC116:8	H2568	That through excessive drinking he did dye.
MGREC119:36	H2726	Long marches through *Cilicia* he makes,
MGREC131:41	H3233	his Sword did pierce his mothers {run her through the} heart,
SIDNEY150:33	H60	And live it doth, in spight of death, through fame,
SIDNEY152:18	H87	*Errata,* through their leave threw me my pen,
DUBART154:6	H51	Through grief it wants a faculty to speak,
QELIZ156:39	H66	Her Sea-men through all straights the world did round,

1LETTER181:16 H14		Then view those fruits which through thy heat I bore?
3LETTER182:37 H2		Scuds through the woods and Fern with harkning ear,
MEDDM197:31	Hp275	Corne till it haue past through the Mill and been ground to
MEDDM198:10	Hp276	his foot And he that passes through the wildernes of this world,
MEDDM201:15	Hp280	A sharp appetite and a through Concoction, is a signe of an
MEDDM202:32	Hp282	and the eares are the inlets or doores of the soule, through wch
MEDDM203:13	Hp283	his bussines lyes, a christian is sailing through this world vnto
MEDDM206:34	Hp288	trembling, lest they through vnbeleif fall short of a promise, it
MEDDM209:20	Hp291	so there may be a mutuall commerce through ye world As it is
MYCHILD217:13	Hp242	becavse I have fovnd my heart through his goodnes enlarged

THROUGHLY (6) [thoroughly]

ELEMEN18:34	H438	And when I'm throughly rarifi'd, turn fire.
AGES35:32	H18	Before the Sun hath throughly warm'd {heat} the clime.
SEASONS49:11	H102	Have throughly dry'd the earth, and heat the air.
MPERS73:29	H814	All things in peace, and Rebells throughly quel'd,
ELIZB187:6	H14	And Plumbs and Apples throughly ripe do fall,
MEDDM199:11	Hp277	Iron till it be throughly heat is vncapable to be wrought, so god

THROUGHOUT (2)

MGREC102:14	H1984	Whose fame throughout the world, was so renown'd;
MGREC116:30	H2596	As oft his Acts throughout his reigne did {doth} shew:

THROW (6)

MASSYR65:1	H466	And in the channell throw {threw} each burden down;
MPERS87:40	H1392	And here, and there, in carts their Armes they throw,
MGREC93:23	H1620	Whose glory to the Earth, this Prince {king} did throw,
MGREC101:2	H1927	And if they down, his Monarchy wil throw,
MEDDM198:30	Hp277	wthin ouer throw it
MEDDM200:20	Hp279	wealth, or a helthfull body, would quite ouer throw, some weak

THROWES (4) [throws]

MPERS87:31	H1383	Up then with speed, a mighty trench he throwes,
MGREC94:17	H1651	Comming to land, his dart on shoar he throwes,
MGREC104:23	H2075	Into a cart him throwes, covered with hides;
MGREC125:35	H2985	And throwes {threw} his bones about, to shew her spight.

THROWING (1)

MGREC104:41	H2093	By throwing Darts, gives {gave} him his mortall wound,

THROWN (1)

MGREC129:14	H3128	Both thrown into a well to hide her blot,

THROWS See THROWES

THRUSH (2)

ELEMEN19:9	H454	The Pye {Thrush}, the Jay {wren}, the Larke, a prey to th'
SEASONS47:18	H34	The Nitingale, the Black-bird, and the Thrush,

THRUST (3)

AGES45:22	H405	I've seen a King by force thrust from his throne,
MPERS72:41	H787	And with a mortall thrust, wounds him ith' thigh,
MPERS73:20	H807	To thrust th' Imposter *Smerdis* out of throne,

THRUSTS (1)

HUMOUR27:38	H309	But here's {here} one thrusts her heat, where'ts not requir'd

THUCIDIDES (1) [poss.]

MASSYR63:33	H420	From some *Thucidides* grave History;

THUNDER (3)

ELEMEN8:12	H10	Whence issu'd raines, and winds, lightning and thunder;
ELEMEN11:6	H126	What shal I say of Lightning, and of Thunder,

MEDDM199:5	Hp277	Lightening doth vsually preceed thunder, and stormes raine,

THUNDERING (1)

HUMOUR32:32	H506	I love no thundering Drums {guns}, nor bloody Wars,

THUNDRING (2) [thundering]

MASSYR62:37	H382	Until the thundring hand of heaven he felt,
HOUSE236:15	H7	I waken'd was wth thundring nois

THUS (122)

FATHER5:17	H18	But by my humble hand thus rudely pen'd
PROLOG7:16	H29	A Poets Pen, all scorne, I should thus wrong;
ELEMEN13:38	H239	While they thus in my {mine} intralls seem {love} to dive;
ELEMEN14:13	H255	Thus I occasion death to man and beast,
ELEMEN17:8	H372	Thus *Albion* {*Britain* fair} (tis thought) was cut from *France,*
ELEMEN18:37	H441	Thus I another body can assume,
HUMOUR20:33	H25	Wel, thus they parle, and chide, but to be briefe,
HUMOUR23:21	H131	Nor is't my pleasure, thus to blur thy name:
HUMOUR23:24	H134	Thus {But} arms, and arts I claim, and higher things;
HUMOUR27:18	H289	Your slanders thus refuted, takes no place,
HUMOUR27:30	H301	As thus, if hot, then dry; if moist, then cold;
HUMOUR28:32	H344	But why, alas, thus tedious should I be?
HUMOUR29:18	H369	What mov'd thee thus to villifie my name?
HUMOUR29:41	H392	But's not thy {thine} ignorance shal thus deceive me.
HUMOUR30:23	H415	Thus he is ours, his portion is the grave.
AGES~~36:24~~	H48	This {Thus} writ about: *This out, then I am done.*
AGES36:38	H62	To hear the child, who crying, thus began.
AGES39:8	H151	For thus to do, we on this Stage assemble,
AGES39:24	H167	Though man in field, at home, to all most kind,
AGES40:30	~~H210~~	Thus, thus alas! I have mispent my time,
AGES41:12	H231	Thus I have said, and what i've said {been,} you see,
AGES41:28	H245	Thus out of one extreame, into another.
AGES42:16	H274	Thus hath mine age (in all) sometimes done wel.
AGES43:25	H320	Thus good, and bad, and what I am, you see,
SEASONS46:35	~~H11~~	She gently thus began, like some fair Queen;
SEASONS49:3	H94	With haire all wet, she puffing thus began.
SEASONS~~52:39~~	H255	And thus the year in circle runneth round:
MASSYR53:33	H23	When thus with rule he had been dignified,
MASSYR57:5	H152	To sit, thus long (obscure) wrong'd {rob'd} of his seat;
MASSYR57:17	~~H164~~	How he thus suddenly should be thus small?
MASSYR57:19	~~H166~~	He thus voluptuous, and given to ease;
MASSYR59:40	H264	*Arbaces* thus, of all becomming Lord,
MASSYR60:9	H274	Thus {Such} was the {his} promise bound, since first {which} he
MASSYR60:30	H295	He thus inricht, by this new tryed gold,
MASSYR61:39	H344	Thus *Tiglath* reign'd, and warr'd, twenty seven years,
MASSYR62:20	H365	Thus *Iacobs* Sons, in exile must remain,
MASSYR65:13	H478	While *Babels* King thus deep ingaged stands;
MASSYR~~65:19~~	H484	Whom he chastised {thus} for his proud offence;
MASSYR65:22	H487	Thus {Then} cast him out, like to a naked Asse,
MASSYR68:13	H599	As thus amort {dead, alive} he sits, as all {one} undone:
MPERS69:33	H655	*Cressus* thus known, it was great *Cyrus* doome,
MPERS71:30	H744	But scorning thus by *Jove* to be out-brav'd,
MPERS72:11	H759	Hearing her harmlesse brother thus was dead,
MPERS75:36	H893	They thus backt of {by} the King, in spight of foes,

MPERS80:3	H1070	They thus behemm'd with multitude of foes,
MPERS80:27	H1094	Twice beaten thus by {at} Sea, he warr'd no more:
MPERS81:4	H1112	He seeing {finding} all thus tend unto {to his} decay,
MPERS81:17	H1125	By their Ambassador they thus complain;
MPERS81:20	H1128	now in {their} need, they should thus fail {forsake} their friends,
MPERS81:23	H1131	And thus reply'd unto *Mardon's* request;
MPERS82:19	H1166	Thus did the *Greeks* destroy, consume, disperce,
MPERS82:32	H1179	And leaves her thus, besmear'd with {in} blood, and tears.
MPERS82:33	H1180	Straight comes her Lord, and finds his wife thus lie,
MPERS82:40	H1187	Thus cut, and mangled by a hag of hell.
MPERS83:24	H1212	The eldest son, thus immaturely dead,
MPERS90:18	H1485	So after all {Thus finishing} their travell, danger, pain,
MPERS92:26	H1584	Thus learned *Pemble,* whom we may not slight,
MGREC94:13	H1647	Thus eased now, of troubles, and of fears;
MGREC98:22	H1824	And thus the *Tyrians* for mistrust were paid,
MGREC99:24	H1867	The Captaine {Thus *Betis*} tane, had holes bor'd through his
MGREC99:29	H1872	Can *Alexander* deale thus cruelly?
MGREC101:22	H1947	Thus to *Darius* he writes back again,
MGREC104:27	H2079	And thus to {t'ward} *Alexander,* on he goes,
MGREC104:40	H2092	Whom thus the execrable wretch abuses:
MGREC105:3	H2096	And leaves him thus, to gaspe out his last breath.
MGREC105:14	H2107	And thus he lay, *Polistratus* a *Greeke*
MGREC105:26	H2119	If not, because *Darius* thus did pray,
MGREC106:5	H2139	Yea, {And} thus must every Son of *Adam* lye,
MGREC107:14	H2189	And thus unwisely, in one raging {mading} fume,
MGREC108:19	H2235	Whilst thus he spent some time in *Bactria,*
MGREC109:10	H2269	When thus, ten dayes, his brain with wine he'd soak'd,
MGREC109:28	H2287	Thus all the *Indian* Kings, to him submit;
MGREC109:30	H2289	To him doth *Alexander* thus declare,
MGREC111:28	H2373	Thus Winter, Souldiers, and provision {provisions} spent,
MGREC112:39	H2425	*Philotas* thus o're-charg'd, with wrong, and greif,
MGREC114:26	H2496	Thus was he tortur'd, till his life was spent.
MGREC115:26	H2545	But now, *Antipater* had liv'd thus {so} long,
MGREC120:9	H2744	Whilst they in *Macedon* doe thus agree,
MGREC121:30	H2812	Thus *Ptolomy* rich *Ægypt* did retaine,
MGREC121:32	H2814	Whilst *Perdicas* thus staid {encamp'd} in *Africa,*
MGREC123:2	H2864	And thus *Antipater* the ground-work layes,
MGREC124:6	H2911	And so he quick returns thus well appaid,
MGREC127:24	H3054	Thus lost he all for his fidelity,
MGREC128:39	H3112	The terms of their agreement thus expresse,
MGREC129:38	H3152	Thus was the race, and house of *Alexander*
MGREC130:12	H3167	*Antigonus* thus had a wolf by th' ears,
MGREC130:21	H3176	Thus *Philips* house was quite extinguished,
MGREC130:37	H3182	Thus may we hear, and fear, and ever say,
MGREC132:7	H3242	Thus *Philips,* and *Cassander's* race is {both} gone,
MGREC132:15	H3250	*Demetrius,* {thus} *Cassanders* Kingdomes gains,
MGREC133:6	H3294	Thus with these Kingly Captaines have we done,
MGREC134:17	H3348	Of *Greece,* and *Syria* thus the rule did end,
MGREC135:8	H3380	Thus Kings, and Kingdoms, have their times, and dates,
MGREC135:11	H3383	The Heavens thus rule, to fill the earth {world} with wonder.
MROMAN136:27	H3441	Thus he deceiv'd his Neece, she might not know

MROMAN140:4	H3567	And thus my pains (with better things) I lost,
DIALOG141:10	H9	What deluge of new woes thus over-whelme
DIALOG141:30	H29	And thus, alas, your state you much deplore,
DIALOG142:12	H41	Or is't intestine Wars that thus offend?
DIALOG148:4	H269	When truth and righteousnesse they thus shall nourish.
DIALOG148:5	H270	When thus in Peace: thine Armies brave send out,
SIDNEY150:27	H54	Thus man is borne to dye, and dead is he,
SIDNEY150:34	H61	Thus being over-come, he over-came.
SIDNEY~~152:15~~	H85	Since I the Muses thus have injured.
DUBART153:32	H36	Thus weake brain'd I, reading the lofty stile,
DUBART154:35	H80	Thus *Bartas* fame shall last while starres do stand,
QELIZ157:34	H102	Nay Masculines, you have thus tax'd us long,
CONTEM169:15	H56	That nature had, thus decked liberally:
CONTEM169:22	H62	Shall Creatures abject, thus their voices raise?
CONTEM171:12	H116	And though thus short, we shorten many wayes,
CONTEM173:10	H177	While musing thus with contemplation fed,
CONTEM173:30	H195	And thus they pass their youth in summer season,
AUTHOR178:15	H25	Which caus'd her thus to send thee out of door.
2LETTER182:23	H29	O *Phoebus,* hadst thou but thus long from thine
3LETTER183:11	H13	Ev'n thus doe I, with many a deep sad groan
CHILDRN186:26	H93	Thus gone, amongst you I may live,
ANNEB187:29	H19	As if mine own, when thus impermanent.
MEDDM209:3	Hp291	thus potent but it is so necessary, that wthout faith there is no
11MAYA226:20	Hp255	ye will of God it should bee thus. Who am I y^t I should repine
30SEPT227:28	Hp257	Thus (dear children) haue yee seen ye many sicknesses and

THVS (6) [thus]

MYCHILD216:23	Hp242	So vsually thvs it hath been wth me that I haue no sooner
MYCHILD218:7	Hp244	me over. I haue argved thvs wth my self, That there is a God I
FAINTING222:17	H7	Thvs fainting haue I said
13MAY227:10	H19	Thvs pleasant fair and good,
SON231:17	H29	And thvs hath granvnted my Reqvest
HOURS234:32	H46	Whose Blessings thvs surmovnt.

THYME (1)

PROLOG~~7:38~~	H48	Give wholsome {Thyme or} Parsley wreath, I aske no Bayes:

THYMISTOCLES (3)

MPERS80:30	H1097	That brave *Thymistocles* takes this wise course,
MPERS84:13	H1249	Unto this King *Thymistocles* did flye.
MPERS84:30	H1266	T'*Thymistocles* he doth his {this} war commit,

TIDE (3)

MGREC111:20	H2365	But well observing th' nature of the tide,
CONTEM167:25	H2	Sometime now past in the Autumnal Tide,
CONTEM174:15	H214	As if he had command of wind and tide,

TIDINGS See TYDINGS

TIE See TYE

TIED See TY'D, TYED

TIES (1) [pl.] See also TYES

HUMOUR24:17	H166	Or honestie such ties, unfriendly break?

TIGER See TYGER

TIGLATH (7)

MASSYR61:8	H313	*Tiglath Palasser.*
MASSYR61:9	H314	*Belosus* dead, *Tiglath* his warlike Son

MASSYR61:18	H323	To *Tiglath* then doth *Ahaz* send for ease.
MASSYR61:23	H328	Gladly doth *Tiglath* this advantage take,
MASSYR61:31	H336	But *Tiglath,* having gain'd his wished end,
MASSYR61:39	H344	Thus *Tiglath* reign'd, and warr'd, twenty seven years,
MASSYR62:2	H347	*Tiglath* deceas'd, *Salmanasser* is next,

TIGLATH'S (1) [poss.]

MASSYR61:24	H329	And succours *Ahaz,* yet for *Tiglath's* sake,

TIGRIS (2)

MASSYR54:24	H51	Upon the pleasant banks of *Tigris* flood,
MGREC98:38	H1840	And then at *Tigris,* and *Araxis* side:

TIL (12) [until] See also TIL, UNTILL

HUMOUR24:27	H176	So walke thee til thou'rt cold, then let thee go.
HUMOUR31:13	Til	filth and thee, nature exhonorates.
AGES35:37	H23	But if he hold, til it have run its last,
AGES35:38	H24	Then may he live, til {out} threescore years or past.
AGES39:21	H164	Nor wait til good advice {success} our hopes do crown;
AGES46:19	H450	There, {Where} I shal rest, til heavens shal be no more;
SEASONS47:5	H19	Stil adds to th' last, til after pleasant *May;*
MASSYR53:28	H18	Not finished, til he his race had run;
MASSYR57:11	H158	He sought no rule, til she was gone, and dead;
MASSYR60:19	H284	Til *Mesopotamia* he got in's hands,
MASSYR66:5	H511	In mid'st of *Babel* now, til death he lyes,
MPERS91:12	H1520	Til many a Captain fel, both wise, and strong,

TILBERRY (1)

QELIZ157:10	H78	Our *Amazon* i'th' Campe at {of} *Tilberry:*

TILL (54) [until] See also TIL, UNTILL

ELEMEN8:23	H21	But {Till gentle} Aire at length, contention so abated,
ELEMEN17:21	H385	Till Sun release, their ships can saile no more.
HUMOUR31:15	H448	Till filth and thee nature exonerates:
AGES38:40	H143	That wonder tis, my glasse till now doth hold.
SEASONS49:19	H110	Rubbing their dirty coates, till they look white.
MASSYR55:27	H93	Till her ambition, caus'd him to be slaine:
MASSYR56:15	H121	(Continuing, till *Xerxes* it defac'd)
MPERS70:9	H680	But till convenient time their heads kept shut;
MPERS72:33	H777	{wisht} his short reign long, till {past before} it was done.
MPERS75:37	H894	Built on, and prosper'd, till their walls did {house they} close;
MPERS79:39	H1065	Till twenty thousand *Persians* falls down slain;
MPERS81:21	H1129	Their infamy would last till all things ends:
MPERS82:7	H1154	Till in the entrails of their Sacrifice,
MPERS85:7	H1283	That nought appeas'd him, but his brothers life.
MGREC98:12	H1814	He leaves not, till he makes {made} the sea firme shoar;
MGREC101:14	H1939	And till all this be wel perform'd, and sure,
MGREC113:9	H2436	Or flesh, or {and} life, could bear, till both were spent
MGREC114:26	H2496	Thus was he tortur'd, till his life was spent.
MGREC116:10	H2574	But pin d in grief till life did her forsake:
MGREC116:10	H2576	Till death inwrapt her in perpetual night.
MGREC120:38	H2775	And yet till now, at quiet was not laid.
MGREC125:31	H2981	Till {'Gainst} all that lov'd *Cassander* was nigh spent; {she was
MGREC128:41	H3114	Till *Alexander* unto age was grown,
MGREC134:41	H3370	Till great *Augustus* had with him a fight,
DIALOG147:23	H247	And sturdy *Tyburn* loaded till it crack,

SIDNEY151:11	~~H69~~	To wait till she, her influence distill,
SIDNEY151:34	~~H75~~	Till taught to's cost, for his too hasty hand,
SIDNEY151:38	~~H75~~	Till terrour-struck for my too weighty charge.
DDUDLEY167:21	H18	*Preparing still for death, till end of dayes:*
CONTEM172:19	H154	Till thou arrive at thy beloved place,
AUTHOR177:32	H4	Till snatcht from thence by friends, less wise then true
DISTEMP179:18	H6	Till nature had exhausted all her store,
1LETTER181:26	H24	Till natures sad decree shall call thee hence;
3LETTER183:30	H32	Let's still remain but one, till death divide.
CHILDRN184:18	H7	Till at the last they felt their wing.
CHILDRN184:23	H12	Till he return, or I do end,
CHILDRN184:30	H19	Till after blown by *Southern* gales,
CHILDRN186:3	H70	Till my weak layes with me shall end,
CHILDRN186:21	H88	And nurst you up till you were strong,
MEDDM197:31	Hp275	Corne till it haue past through the Mill and been ground to
MEDDM197:33	Hp275	greif and pain till they turn to dust, and then are they fine
MEDDM198:19	Hp276	the hook till it be to late.
MEDDM199:6	Hp277	do not often fall till after threat'ning.
MEDDM199:11	Hp277	Iron till it be throughly heat is vncapable to be wrought, so god
MEDDM202:23	Hp282	darknes till he arise againe, so god doth somtime vaile his face
MEDDM203:19	Hp283	dayes of our appointed time till our chang shall come,
MEDDM207:24	Hp289	cannot passe, and till the expiratnon of that time, no dangers
MEDDM209:2	Hp291	not let thee go replys Jacob till thou blesse me, faith is not only
MYCHILD215:27	Hp240	Trouble, & I could not be at rest 'till by prayer I had confest
MYCHILD216:18	Hp241	feares brovght yov to this, I now travail in birth again of yov till
JULY223:34	Hp251	my faith in Thee, 'till I shall attain ye End of my hopes, Even
MYSOUL225:24	H28	'Till I dissolved bee.
11MAYA226:14	Hp255	lasted all this spring till this 11. May, yet hath my God given
11MAYB228:25	Hp259	of January 'till May I haue been by fitts very ill & weak. The

TILT (2)

MGREC96:6	H1726	As if they were, {if addrest} now all to run at {a} tilt:
MROMAN137:12	H3463	Great shewes he makes at Tilt, and Turnament,

TILTH (1)

MEDDM204:35	Hp285	brought into tilth yet all must be ploughed and harrowed Some

TIMBER (1)

SEASONS52:3	~~H219~~	This month is timber for all uses fell'd,

TIME (122)

ELEMEN~~8:31~~	H29	Where {In} little is, {time} I can but little show,
ELEMEN9:13	H47	That so in time it might requite your paine;
ELEMEN11:32	H152	Would so passe time, I could say nothing else;
ELEMEN11:39	H159	I have not time to thinke of every part,
ELEMEN16:37	H360	As I with showers oft time {times} refresh the earth;
HUMOUR25:38	H227	But if in fitting time, and place, on foes; {'gainst foe}
HUMOUR27:20	H291	Now through your leaves, some little time i'le spend;
HUMOUR27:37	H308	Mans life to boundlesse time might stil endure;
HUMOUR28:34	H346	If time I have transgrest, and been too long,
HUMOUR29:11	H364	I'le flatter for a time, as thou did'st me,
HUMOUR30:16	H408	Yet time and age, shal soon declare it mine.
HUMOUR31:18	H451	No further time ile spend, in confutations, {confutation}
HUMOUR34:41	H596	Let's now be freinds, 'tis {its} time our spight was {were} spent,
AGES40:20	H201	If any time from company {leud Companions} I {can} spare,

AGES40:30	H210	Thus, thus alas! I have mispent my time,
AGES41:39	H256	For time, for place, likewise for each relation,
AGES43:14	H307	my son, {Competitors} or his {as might in time} withstand.
AGES45:22	H411	What are my thoughts, this is no time to say.
SEASONS48:20	H73	Her shelves, and Firkins fill'd for winter time.
SEASONS48:27	H80	More solid fruits, require a longer time.
SEASONS49:12	H103	Like as an oven, that long time hath been heat.
SEASONS49:15	H106	She's {Tis} for a time as fervent as before.
SEASONS49:37	H130	And for all sorts of Pease this is the time.
SEASONS51:12	H186	Sure at this time, Time first of all began,
SEASONS51:12	H186	Sure at this time, Time first of all began,
SEASONS51:27	H203	Decrepit age must also have its time;
SEASONS51:31	H207	Where also he, his Winter time must have;
SEASONS51:34	H210	*November* is my last, for time doth haste,
SEASONS52:7	H222	This time warm cloaths, ful diet, and good fires,
SEASONS52:33	H248	I care not how the Winter time doth haste;
MASSYR53:15	H5	When Time was young, and World in infancy,
MASSYR59:34	H258	Twenty he reign'd, same time, as Stories tel,
MASSYR62:11	H356	Into perpetual thraldome that time bring;
MASSYR62:12	H357	Those that from *Ioshua's* time had been Estate {a state},
MASSYR65:12	H477	Thinks this the fittest time to break his bands,
MASSYR66:33	H539	The time expir'd, remains a Beast no more,
MPERS69:8	H630	And from that time, had held it as his own;
MPERS70:9	H680	But till convenient time their heads kept shut;
MPERS72:18	H766	This strange severity, one time {sometimes} he us'd,
MPERS73:9	H796	Eight years he reign'd, a short, yet too long time,
MPERS75:27	H884	Since *Cyrus* time, *Cambyses* did molest;
MPERS79:25	H1051	Of so long time, his thoughts had never been.
MPERS83:20	H1208	But in short time, this wickednesse was knowne,
MPERS84:22	H1258	Fair *Attica,* a third time to invade.
MPERS85:1	H1277	'Rest of his time in peace he did remain;
MPERS86:21	H1337	And thought it best, now in his mothers time,
MPERS87:28	H1380	To th' utmost parts of *Bactr'a,* and {for a time} there lye.
MPERS89:13	H1447	They soone may come, and {in short time might} place one in
MPERS90:12	H1484	There for some time they were, but whilst they staid,
MPERS92:9	H1567	What Acts he did, time hath not now left pend,
MPERS92:11	H1569	Whose race long time had worn the Diadem,
MGREC94:10	H1644	Now taste of death, (least they deserv't {deserv'd} in time)
MGREC95:40	H1719	Sure its {much} beyond my time, and little Art;
MGREC96:22	H1742	Would aske more time, then were {was} their bodys worth.
MGREC98:13	H1815	But far lesse cost, and time, he doth {did} expend,
MGREC98:17	H1819	In seven months space {time} he takes this lofty {took that
MGREC98:26	H1828	For now's the time, Captains like Kings may live;
MGREC100:31	H1915	About this time, *Darius* beauteous Queen,
MGREC100:33	H1917	Now bids the world adieu, her time {with pain} being spent,
MGREC102:17	H1987	Though worn by time, and raz'd {rac'd} by foes full sore,
MGREC108:19	H2235	Whilst thus he spent some time in *Bactria,*
MGREC108:26	H2242	But he their stubbornnesse full soone {in time} doth quel;
MGREC110:35	H2339	But doubting, wearing Time would {might} these decay,
MGREC111:2	H2347	Some time he after spent upon that shore,
MGREC111:33	H2378	Much time in feasts, and ryoting doth {did} wast;

MYCHILD216:14 Hp241 pleased God to keep me a long time wthout a child wch was a
MYCHILD217:1 Hp242 If at any time yov are chastened of God take it as Thankfully
11MAYB228:23 Hp259 It hath pleased God to giue me a long Time of respite for these
THEART229:5   H7   And in due time thou succour'st me
THEART229:7   H9   Lord whilst my fleeting time shall last
SON231:9   H21   When royall ones y^t Time did dye,

TIME'S (3) [time is]
ELEMEN12:28   H188 But time's too short, and precious so to spend.
MGREC98:18   H1820 Whose glory, now {then} a second time's brought down;
DIALOG146:19 H205 The seed time's come, but Ploughman hath no hope,

TIMELY (3)
MPERS~~92:21~~ H1579 But that his treason timely was found out.
MGREC118:36   ~~H2685~~ Thought timely for themselves, now to provide.
TDUDLEY166:19 H61   Death as a Sickle hath him timely mown,

TIMERARIOUS (1) [timorous]
HUMOUR25:2   H191 Yet do abhorre, such timerarious deeds,

TIMEROUS (1) [timorous]
HUMOUR21:27   H55   Then timerous Hares, whom Castles doe immure?

TIMES (36)
FATHER5:13   H14   I bring my four times {and} four, now meanly clad,
FATHER5:25   H26   Sweet harmony they keep, yet jar oft times,
PROLOG7:8   H22   lisp'd at first, speake afterwards more {in future times} plaine
ELEMEN~~16:37~~ H360 As I with showers oft time {times} refresh the earth;
ELEMEN17:4   H368 Nay many times, my Ocean breaks his bounds:
ELEMEN17:30   H394 That after times, shall never feel like woe:
HUMOUR21:16   H44   Yet many times, unto my great disgrace,
AGES38:37   H140 Some times in fire, sometimes in waters {water} fall:
AGES44:29   H362 In various times of state i've also been.
SEASONS46:29 H5   Of four times four, the last quaternian;
MASSYR53:32   H22   Whom succeeding times a god did call:
MASSYR61:2   H307 And times of both computed, so fall out,
MASSYR66:26   H532 Although the Furnace be seven times more hot;
MASSYR66:36   H542 Contemplating those times he lost his wits;
MPERS74:15   H838 A thousand times, God save {long live} the King, they cry,
MPERS74:24   H847 By which he cuts their hopes (for future times)
MGREC135:8   H3380 Thus Kings, and Kingdoms, have their times, and dates,
DUBART153:22 H26   And thousand times his mazed minde doth wish
DUBART154:1   H46   A thousand thousand times my senslesse Sences,
CONTEM169:26 H65   When present times look back to Ages past,
CONTEM174:34 H231 Nor wit nor gold, nor buildings scape times rust;
CHILDRN185:39 H65   Oft times in grass, on trees, in flight,
MEDDM197:12   Hp274 some times tast of adversity, prosperity would not be so
MEDDM201:3   Hp280 and many times he imposes waighty burdens on their
MEDDM204:17   Hp285 god doth many times, both reward and punish for one and y^e
MEDDM205:36   Hp287 that many times, the waight thereof impares both their bodys
MYCHILD216:28 Hp242 by losses in estate, and these Times (thro: his great mercy)
MYCHILD216:29 Hp242 haue been the times of my greatest Getting and Advantage,
MYCHILD216:30 Hp242 fovnd them ye Times w^n ye Lord hath manifested ye most
MYCHILD217:3 Hp242 by it: It hath been no small support to me in times of Darknes
MYCHILD217:22 Hp243 never p^rvail: yet haue I many Times sinkings & droopings,
MYCHILD217:32 Hp243 Many times hath Satan troubled me concerning ye verity of y^e

MYCHILD217:33 Hp243 Scriptures, many times by Atheisme how I could know whether
MYCHILD218:6 Hp243 this hath thovsands of Times been svggested to me, yet
MYCHILD218:14 Hp244 Times, + how yᵉ world came to bee as wee see, Do wee not
28AUG225:27 Hp254 many times my faith weak likewise, the Lord was pleased to

TIMOROUS See TIMERARIOUS, TIMEROUS

TIMPANY (1)
HUMOUR23:1 H111 Wil feed a Dropsie, or a Timpany,

T'INFRANCHISE (1) [to enfranchise]
MASSYR58:39 H222 T'infranchise them, to grant what they could crave,

TIPPLED (1)
MGREC~~114:7~~ H2475 Both at a Feast when they had tippled well

TIRE (1) [attire]
DIALOG147:13 H239 Their Myters, Surplices, and all their tire,

TIRED (3) [fatigued]
MASSYR64:34 H458 Can *Babels* tired Souldiers tell with pain;
MGREC128:37 H3110 At last these Princes tired out with warres,
MGREC135:40 H3412 My tired braine, leaves to a {some} better pen,

TIRES (1) [attire, pl.]
DUBART153:21 H25 The Hats, and Fans, the Plumes, and Ladies tires,

TIRIAN (1) See also TYRIAN
ELEMEN15:37 H319 The *Roman* Purple, double *Tirian* dye.

TIRON (1)
QELIZ156:34 H61 And {the proud} *Tiron* bound, before her picture fell.

'TIS (33) [it is]
ELEMEN11:40 H160 Yet let me name my *Grecia*, 'tis my heart
ELEMEN17:12 H376 Some say I swallowed up (sure 'tis a notion)
HUMOUR25:16 H205 As with thy mother Fire, so 'tis with thee,
HUMOUR25:35 H224 Nay; {No,} know 'tis pride, most diabolical.
HUMOUR26:18 H248 Thine without mine, is not, 'tis evident:
HUMOUR27:23 H294 When 'tis untaint, pure, and most genuine
HUMOUR32:4 H478 But wisdome 'tis, my wisdom to conceale.
HUMOUR32:30 H504 Valour {Valours} I want, no Souldier am, 'tis true,
HUMOUR33:17 H531 No debtor I, because 'tis {it's} paid else where;
HUMOUR34:24 H579 But a mad one, say I, where 'tis too great,
HUMOUR34:41 H596 Let's now be freinds, 'tis {its} time our spight was {were} spent,
AGES39:2 H145 For 'tis but little, that a childe can say.
AGES40:18 H199 If any care I take, 'tis to be fine,
AGES40:21 H202 'Tis spent in curling {to curle}, frisling up {and pounce my
AGES41:6 H226 That wonder 'tis I yet behold the light,
AGES~~43:16~~ H309 But in a trice 'tis ruin'd by a blast,
AGES45:15 H397 I've seen, and so have ye, for 'tis but late,
MPERS77:7 H946 For *Grecian* Maids ('tis said) to wait on her;
MPERS77:11 H950 ('Tis thought) through grief and his {this} succeslesse strife.
MPERS92:10 H1568 But as 'tis thought, {most suppose} in him had {did} *Cyrus* end:
MGREC101:37 H1966 But 'tis not known what slaughters here they {was} made.
MGREC102:28 H1998 But needs no force, 'tis rendred to his hands;
MGREC106:16 H2150 Her traine to *Alexander* (as 'tis thought)
MGREC107:16 H2191 But marvell 'tis, that without muteny,
MGREC114:33 H2503 When e're 'tis said, he thousand thousands slew,
MGREC115:2 H2513 All this he did, yea, and much more, 'tis true,
MGREC116:35 H2601 This conquerour did oft lament ('tis sed)

MGREC124:41	H2948	She gave him poyson formerly ('tis thought)
MGREC~~126:35~~	H3024	To Husbands death ('twas {'tis} thought) she gave consent,
DIALOG~~145:20~~	H169	{'Tis said,} My better part in Court of Parliament,
QELIZ157:37	H105	Know 'tis a slander now, but once was treason.
MEDDM197:29	Hp275	'tis no wonder if he faint by the way.
PILGRIM210:38	H38	in power 'tis rais'd by Christ alone

TIS (15) [it is]

ELEMEN17:8	H372	Thus *Albion* {*Britain* fair} (tis thought) was cut from *France,*
ELEMEN18:23	H427	Ye Mariners, tis I that fill your Sailes,
HUMOUR~~22:24~~	H93	{But tis} Not from our dul slow Sisters motions:
HUMOUR23:8	H118	Tis true, when I am midwife to thy birth;
HUMOUR24:40	H189	Thou sayst I love my sword, because tis {it's} guilt. {gilt,}
HUMOUR25:14	H203	Thy Choler is but rage, when tis most pure.
HUMOUR25:36	H225	If murthers be thy glory, tis no lesse.
HUMOUR30:38	H430	That black is black, and I am black, tis true;
AGES35:36	H22	And when tis broke, then ends his life and all.
AGES38:40	H143	That wonder tis, my glasse till now doth hold.
SEASONS~~49:15~~	H106	She's {Tis} for a time as fervent as before.
MPERS73:28	H813	But so or no, sure tis, they won the day.
MPERS73:40	H825	Too politicke (tis {its} like) for me to tell,
MPERS84:5	H1233	Queen *Vashty* also feasts, but 'fore tis ended,
MPERS~~92:7~~	H1565	His brother, as tis said, long since was slain,

TISSAPHERNES (1)

MPERS90:32	H1499	By th' Kings Lieutenant {*Tissaphernes*} is encountered,

TITAN (1)

QELIZ158:2	H111	She set, she set, like *Titan* in his rayes,

TITLE (9)

AGES~~45:11~~	H393	But neither favour, riches, title, State,
MPERS74:21	H844	His title to make strong omits no thing;
MGREC94:8	H1642	In seeking after {Nor making Title unto} Soveraignity:
MGREC106:20	H2154	To th' ignorant, her title may {will} declare.
MGREC128:4	H3077	And that some title he might seeme to bring,
MGREC130:1	H3156	But that some title he might now pretend,
MGREC130:40	H3185	For to their Crowns, there's none can title make.
MGREC134:34	H3365	For since the first, that title still they had,
DIALOG144:7	H117	For nought, but title to a fading Crown?

TITLES (4) [pl.]

MASSYR54:5	H32	Titles divine, he to himself did take,
MGREC103:18	H2029	On their old Governours, titles he laid;
MGREC135:19	H3391	Their Crownes, their Titles, riches beares by force.
TDUDLEY165:40	H42	Those titles loath'd, which some too much do love

TITUS (1)

MGREC~~133:22~~	H3311	(Part of whose Kingdomes *Titus Quintius* won)

TO'VE (1) [to have]

MPERS~~79:13~~	H1039	Because they wanted skill the same to've staid.

TOES (1) [pl.]

SEASONS52:30	H245	Now toes, and eares, and fingers often freeze,

TOGETHER (16)

ELEMEN16:15	H338	My wholesome Bathes, together with their cures.
AGES41:27	H244	I then with both hands, graspt the world together,
MASSYR59:30	H254	But all his wealth, and friends, together gets,

MPERS79:11	H1033	Of Boats, together coupled, and there laid;
MGREC~~101:41~~	H1970	And now {Together} with it, the town also obtain'd.
MGREC107:36	H2211	On these, together ty'd, in six dayes space,
MGREC119:25	H2715	With speed his forces {Army} doth together call,
1LETTER181:8	H6	If but a neck, soon should we be together:
3LETTER183:27	H29	Together at one Tree, oh let us brouze,
MEDDM200:8	Hp279	bitter together so is it wth some Christians, let god imbitter all
MEDDM204:14	Hp284	Sin and shame euer goe together He that would be freed from
MEDDM207:26	Hp289	that time will come, together, wth the vncertainty, how where,
MEDDM208:7	Hp290	other meanes to extinguish them so distance of place together
MYCHILD216:12	Hp241	together wth a lamenesse w[ch] correction I saw the Lord sent to
MYCHILD218:23	Hp244	are in their Relign: together wth their lying miracles, and cruell
2HUSB233:13	H46	That wee together may sing praise

TOILE (2) [toil] See also TOYL, TOYLE

AGES42:19	H277	Did toile, did broile, oppress'd, did steal and lye.
AGES42:30	H286	My weary beast, rest from his toile can find;

TOILING See TOYLING

TOILS See TOYLES, TOYLS

TOKENS (1) [pl.]

2HUSB233:7	H40	But Tokens of thy favour Give,

TOLD (17)

ELEMEN9:29	H63	Our Sages new, another tale have told:
ELEMEN10:40	H115	*Carthage,* and hundred moe, in stories told,
AGES36:31	H55	And to the rest, his reason mildly told;
aGES37:9	H71	To tel that paine, which cann't be told by tongue;
MASSYR55:1	H67	Fifty two years he reign'd (as we are told)
MASSYR66:6	H512	Yet as was told, ne're saw it with his eyes;
MASSYR68:26	H612	Perform'd his word, to him, that told his fate;
MPERS69:38	~~H660~~	And told, how *Solon* in his hight had spoke.
MPERS75:6	H867	This told, for enterance he stood not long,
MGREC104:30	H2082	To *Alexander* fly, {flyes} and told {tells} this act;
MGREC113:13	H2440	And told the world, that for desert {his guilt} he dyed.
MGREC114:10	H2478	That of *Parmenio's* death him plainly told.
MROMAN137:33	H3484	Goddesse *Ægeria* this to him told,
SICKNES178:18	H1	Twice ten years old, not fully told
PILGRIM211:1	H42	as eare ner' heard nor tongue ere told
MYCHILD218:34	Hp244	Sav[r]. I have told yov before. That hath stayed my heart, and I
HOUSE237:5	H35	No pleasant tale shall 'ere be told

TOMB (4)

MGREC120:35	H2772	At *Alexandria,* in *Ægypt* Land, {his tomb he plac'd}
SIDNEY151:29	~~H75~~	To fix my faltring lines upon his tomb:
TDUDLEY166:35	H77	*Within this Tomb a Patriot lyes*
SICKNES178:33	H16	and then we go to th' Tomb.

TOMBE (2) [tomb]

MPERS70:38	H709	But in this {his} Tombe was only to be found
MGREC94:22	H1660	And on *Achillis* Tombe, with wondrous joy,

TOMORROW (1)

MGREC101:27	H1952	Prepares against tomorrow for the war;

TOMRIS (2)

MPERS70:27	H698	And *Tomris* Son, an Army over-throwes;
QELIZ157:8	H76	Feirce *Tomris* (*Cirus* Heads-man, *Sythians* Queen)

TONE (2)

DIALOG141:12	H11	What meanes this wailing tone, this mourning guise?
MERCY188:21	H7	And yet survive to sound this wailing tone;

TONGU'D (2) [tongued]

PROLOG7:7	H21	Nor can I, like that fluent sweet tongu'd *Greek*
MGREC120:4	H2735	*Demosthenes,* that sweet tongu'd oratour.

TONGUE (18) See also TONGUE'S, TONGVE

PROLOG6:32	H15	From School-boyes tongue, no Rhethorick we expect,
PROLOG7:14	H27	I am obnoxious to each carping tongue,
HUMOUR24:16	H165	Did ever sober tongue, such language speak?
AGES37:9	H71	To tel that paine, which cann't be told by tongue;
AGES38:23	H126	A lying tongue as soon as it could speak,
AGES40:8	H189	Trusteth my loving looks, and glozing tongue,
MPERS75:7	H868	For they beleev'd his nose, more then his tongue;
MGREC114:3	H2471	Nothing more pleasing to mad *Clitus* tongue,
DIALOG141:16	H15	Or must my forced tongue these griefes disclose?
SIDNEY150:8	H33	(O brave Refiner of our *Brittish* Tongue;)
SIDNEY150:35	H62	Where is that envious tongue, but can afford,
DUBART152:35	H4	My ravisht eyes, and heart, with faltering tongue,
DUBART154:4	H49	Mine eyes are sightlesse, and my tongue is mute;
QELIZ157:2	H70	But time would faile me, so my wit {tongue} would to,
MEDDM199:27	Hp278	of pestilence, and the arrow of a slanderous tongue, the two
PILGRIM210:14	H14	for thirst no more shall parch his tongue
PILGRIM211:1	H42	as eare ner' heard nor tongue ere told
WHAT224:6	H6	My Tongue shall talk of Thee

TONGUED See TONGU'D

TONGUE'S (1) [tongue is]

HUMOUR29:7	H360	The tongue's no weapon to assault a foe,

TONGUES (3) [pl.]

AGES39:13	H156	Of Science, Arts, and Tongues, I know the rules,
DIALOG144:30	H138	Their silent tongues to heaven did vengeance cry,
DUBART154:22	H67	Leadst millions chained by eyes, by eares, by tongues,

TONGVE (1) [tongue]

THEART228:35	H1	My thankfull heart wth glorying Tongve

TOO (63)

PROLOG6:20	H5	For my mean Pen, are too superiour things,
ELEMEN9:4	H38	Your Cannon's bootlesse, and your powder too
ELEMEN9:20	H54	Ye Paracelsians too, in vaine's your skil
ELEMEN10:22	H97	Augment his heat, which was too hot before:
ELEMEN12:13	H173	Sweet *Parnassus,* I dote too much on thee,
ELEMEN12:28	H188	But time's too short, and precious so to spend.
ELEMEN12:39	H199	Your Tackling, Anchor, Compasse too, is mine;
ELEMEN19:7	H452	The Phoenix too (if any be) are mine;
HUMOUR28:34	H346	If time I have transgrest, and been too long,
HUMOUR29:3	H356	Had need be armed wel, and active too,
HUMOUR29:21	H372	To play such furious pranks I am too wise;
HUMOUR30:3	H395	What is too hot, my coldnesse doth abate;
HUMOUR31:24	H457	Choler's too rash, this golden gift to hold.
HUMOUR34:24	H579	But a mad one, say I, where 'tis too great,
HUMOUR34:39	H594	And too much talk; both which, I do {here} confesse,
HUMOUR35:1	H597	Lest we too late, this rashnesse do repent,

AGES38:27	H130	As many was {are} my sins, so dangers too:
AGES41:5	H225	Too many's {many} my Diseases to recite,
AGES44:9	H342	But now, *Bis pueri senes,* is too true;
SEASONS47:8	H24	The Seeds-man now {too} doth lavish out his Grain,
MASSYR54:29	H56	Where e're he warr'd he had too good successe,
MASSYR59:14	H238	But he once in, pursuers came too late,
MASSYR66:15	H521	*Kedar,* {and} *Hazer,* the *Arabians* too,
MPERS70:2	H673	Gave him at once, his life, and Kingdom too,
MPERS73:9	H796	Eight years he reign'd, a short, yet too long time,
MPERS73:40	H825	Too politicke (tis {its} like) for me to tell,
MPERS77:33	H974	Against the *Sythians,* and *Grecians* too,
MPERS79:13	H1035	To cross the sea such strength he found too weak,
MPERS88:19	H1412	Had not his too much valour put him by.
MPERS89:3	H1437	But they too faint, still to pursue their game,
MPERS89:24	H1458	They were too hungry to capitulate;
MPERS92:22	H1580	And so this wretch (a punishment too small)
MGREC95:25	H1704	Goes {Runs} after too {two}, and leaves all to disaster.
MGREC97:23	H1784	By too much heat, not wounds (as Authors write.)
MGREC103:6	H2017	Though *Babylon* was rich, and *Sushan* too;
MGREC111:15	H2360	Which could not sound too oft, with too much fame;
MGREC111:15	H2360	Which could not sound too oft, with too much fame;
MGREC113:26	H2453	He walking in his Garden, too and fro,
MGREC115:34	H2553	So to be caught, *Antipater's* too wise,
MGREC115:35	H2554	*Parmenio's* death's too fresh before his eyes;
MGREC115:36	H2555	He was too subtile for his crafty foe,
MGREC116:29	H2595	Cruell by nature, and by custome too,
MGREC123:10	H2872	In this Epitomy, too long to tell
MGREC123:17	H2881	Too young {rash} to beare that charge, if on him lay'd;
MGREC126:39	H3028	Her out-rages too tedious to relate,
MGREC130:4	H3159	And vile {lewd} *Cassander* too, sticks not for shame;
MGREC133:25	H3315	Such riches too As Rome did never see:
MGREC136:4	H3417	The Subject was too high, beyond my straine;
SIDNEY151:28	H75	Too late my errour see, that durst presume
SIDNEY151:34	H75	Till taught to's cost, for his too hasty hand,
SIDNEY151:38	H75	Till terrour-struck for my too weighty charge.
DUBART153:28	H32	But findes too soone his want of Eloquence,
TDUDLEY165:8	H10	Who was my Father, Guide, Instructor too,
TDUDLEY165:40	H42	Those titles loath'd, which some too much do love
2LETTER181:31	H1	*Phoebus* make haste, the day's too long, be gone,
ELIZB186:34	H6	Farewel dear babe, my hearts too much content,
MERCY188:30	H16	But ah too soon those heavy tydings fly,
MEDDM196:25	Hp273	words are like hony, a little may refresh, but too much gluts the
MEDDM205:37	Hp287	and ther are some (and they sincere ones too) who haue not
MYCHILD215:29	Hp241	too often tardy y^t way. I also fovnd much comfort in reading y^e
MYCHILD217:9	Hp242	too. Before I was afflicted I went astray, but now I keep thy
30SEPT227:21	Hp257	to my straying Soul wch in prosperity is too much in Love wth
HOUSE237:21	H51	'Its purchasèd + paid for too

TOOK (29)

AGES42:15	H273	As chearfully as ere I took my pay.
SEASONS50:1	H135	This month from *Julius Cæsar* took the {its} name,
SEASONS50:15	H149	*August,* of great *Augustus* took its name,

MASSYR63:35	H422	Nor his restoring from old legends took;
MASSYR65:4	H469	And took the wealthy town, but all the gain
MASSYR65:36	H501	And after eighteen months he took them all,
MASSYR66:30	H536	Which for seven years his reason took away;
MASSYR68:27	H613	That night victorious *Cyrus* took the town,
MPERS69:9	H631	*Cyrus, Darius* Daughter took to wife,
MPERS~~70:2~~	H673	Gave him his life, and took him for a friend,
MPERS84:38	H1274	Strong poyson took, and {so} put an end to's dayes.
MGREC~~98:17~~	H1819	space {time} he takes this lofty {took that wealthy} town,
MGREC117:8	H2615	And {But} as he took delight, much bloud to spill,
MGREC118:32	H2681	And {So} took his life unworthily that houre:
MGREC119:2	H2692	*Perdicas* took no Province, like the rest,
MGREC~~127:22~~	H3052	*Antigonus,* then takes {who took} his life unjust,
MGREC130:18	H3173	As vile conspiratours that took {stopt} her breath,
MGREC132:6	~~H3239~~	Who took away his now pretended right:
MGREC134:16	H3347	Vanquish'd in fight, and took those kingdomes all,
DIALOG144:34	H142	Nor took I warning by my neighbours falls,
DIALOG145:29	H178	They took high *Strafford* lower by the head,
SIDNEY152:11	H80	They took from me, the scribling pen I had,
QELIZ157:1	H69	Her *Essex* took *Cades,* their *Herculean* hold:
CHILDRN184:20	H9	Chief of the Brood then took his flight,
MYCHILD215:31	Hp241	to haue more vnderstanding, so ye more solace I took in them.
JULY223:22	Hp251	wch at first it took me, and so mvch the sorer it was to me
11MAYA226:13	Hp255	I had a sore sicknes and weaknes took hold of me wch hath by
HOUSE236:13	H5	In silent night when rest I took
HOUSE236:26	H18	I blest his Name y^t gave + took,

TOOLE (1) [tool]

ELEMEN8:36	H34	What toole was ever fram'd, but by my might;

TOP (6)

MASSYR56:16	H122	Whose stately top, beyond {above} the clouds did rise;
MPERS86:22	H1338	By lesser {lower} steps, towards the top to climbe;
MPERS92:36	H1594	How from the top of the worlds felicity;
MGREC95:1	H1680	And beat the coward *Persians* from the top,
CONTEM168:8	H17	Whose ruffling top the Clouds seem'd to aspire;
CHILDRN186:10	H77	And from the top bough take my flight,

TOPAS (1)

VANITY160:32	H42	For *Saphyre, Onix, Topas,* who will {would} change,

TOPS (2) [pl.]

SEASONS47:22	H38	The tender tops of budding Grasse they crop,
DAVID158:33	H13	Nor fruitfull showers your barren tops bestrew,

TORCH (1)

FLESH177:19	H100	No Candle there, nor yet Torch light,

TORE (1)

MGREC114:13	H2483	Next day, he tore his face, for what he'd done,

TORMENTS (2) [pl.]

MGREC113:8	H2435	Such torments great, as wit could first {worst} invent,
MGREC125:22	H2972	The King by extreame torments had his end,

TORMENTS (1) v.

AGES43:28	H323	{The Strangury} Torments me with intollerable {sore} paines;

TORNE (1) [torn]

MGREC~~115:15~~	H2526	The battlements from off the walls are torne.

TORRENT (4)
ELEMEN17:2 H366 And with my wasting floods, and roaring torrent;
MPERS82:38 H1185 O're-flown with torrent of her ruby {guiltless} blood.
MGREC135:18 H3390 And with the torrent of his rapid course,
2LETTER182:30 H36 Hath power to dry the torrent of these streams.

TORRID (1)
HUMOUR30:40 H432 Then is thy torrid nose, or brasen brow.

TORTUR'D (1) [tortured]
MGREC114:26 H2496 Thus was he tortur'd, till his life was spent.

TORTURE (1)
AGES43:31 H326 The knotty {Cramp and} Gout doth sadly torture me,

TORTURED See TORTUR'D

TORTURES (2) [pl.]
AGES38:32 H135 What tortures I, in breeding teeth sustain?
MGREC108:6 H2222 With wracks, and tortures, every limbe to stretch.

TOSS'D (1) [tossed]
DIALOG144:39 H147 Wives forc'd, babes toss'd, her houses calcined,

TOSSING (1)
DISTEMP179:16 H4 In tossing slumbers on my wakeful bed,

TOSSINGS (2) [pl.]
AGES38:29 H132 And though I misse, the tossings of the mind:
MEDDM203:16 Hp283 lest he meet wth such tossings that may cause him to long for

TOTAL (1)
SEASONS52:1 H218 Poor wretches, that in total darknesse lye,

TOTALL (1) [total]
MASSYR66:17 H523 A totall Conquest of rich Ægypt makes,

TOUCH (7)
ELEMEN10:17 H92 Out of a multitude, these few I touch,
ELEMEN12:15 H175 But ile skip {leap} o're these Hills, not touch a Dale,
HUMOUR27:35 H306 One touch thereof so beautifies the skin;
HUMOUR30:2 H394 Then he whose brain a touch my humour gives.
HUMOUR30:37 H429 Again, you often touch my swarthy hew,
HUMOUR33:41 H555 I'le touch the Sight, great'st wonder of the three;
MGREC95:15 H1694 Whose touch turn'd all to gold, yea even his meat:

TOUCH'D (2) [touched]
MGREC129:2 H3116 This touch'd *Cassander* sore, for what he'd done,
MGREC129:30 H3144 The *Greeks* touch'd with the murther done so {of} late,

TOUCHT (2)
MPERS72:38 H784 Toucht with this newes, to *Persia* he makes,
MGREC114:5 H2473 Nothing toucht *Alexander* to the quick

TOUGH (1)
MEDDM205:1 Hp285 (like sowre land) are of so tough and morose a dispotion that

TOURNAMENT See TURNAMENT

TOWARD (1) See also T'WARD
MYCHILD217:28 Hp243 were it hell it self and could there find ye Love of God toward

TOWARDS (5) See also T'WARDS
SEASONS51:28 H204 The sap doth slily creep towards the earth,
MPERS86:22 H1338 By lesser {lower} steps, towards the top to climbe;
MPERS86:40 H1356 With posting speed {on} towards the King he goes;
MEDDM207:7 Hp288 draw men to god in consideration of his bounty towards them,
MYCHILD216:27 Hp242 Sincerity towards him. Somt. he hath smott a child wth

TOWER (3)

MASSYR65:35	H500	Besieg'd his City, Temple, *Zions* Tower;
DIALOG142:17	H46	That second *Richard* must be clapt i'th' Tower?
DIALOG145:30	H179	And to their *Laud* be't spoke, they held i'th' Tower,

TOWERS (4) [pl.]

MASSYR54:21	H48	On which stood fifteen hundred towers stout:
MASSYR55:40	H106	With Towers, and Bulwarks made of costly stone
MASSYR66:8	H514	The Towers, and Palaces, brought to decay;
MGREC102:16	H1986	The Towers, and Bowers, of proud *Semiramis:*

TOWN (32) See also TOWN'S

ELEMEN10:39	H114	Where's *Ninus* great wal'd Town, and *Troy* of old?
HUMOUR29:32	H383	It's no lesse glory to defend a town,
AGES39:20	H163	I cannot lye in trench, {intrench'd} before a Town,
MASSYR56:14	H120	Which is the midst, of this brave Town was plac'd,
MASSYR59:22	H246	*Arbaces* marches in, the town did {he} take {takes},
MASSYR59:26	H250	Their strong wall'd town should suddenly be taken;
MASSYR60:33	H298	As fair a Town, as the first *Ninivie.*
MASSYR62:9	H354	Besieg'd his regal town, and spoyl'd his Coast,
MASSYR64:41	H465	Fetch {Fetcht} rubbish from the opposite old town,
MASSYR65:4	H469	And took the wealthy town, but all the gain
MASSYR68:27	H613	That night victorious *Cyrus* took the town,
MPERS69:25	H647	Who him pursues to *Sardis,* takes the town,
MPERS70:14	H685	Enters the town, the sottish King he slayes,
MPERS70:36	H707	And in his Town of *Pasargada* {Pasargades} lyes,
MPERS74:36	H858	For twice ten months before the town he lay,
MPERS75:1	H862	And with a faithfull fraud to' th' town he goes,
MPERS75:11	H872	Delivers up the town, and all in it.
MPERS90:28	H1495	Town after town, with small resistance take,
MPERS90:28	H1495	Town after town, with small resistance take,
MGREC98:3	H1805	Protector of their Town; by whom defended,
MGREC98:8	H1810	In the old town (which now {then} lay like a wood)
MGREC98:10	H1812	To win their {the} town, his honour he engag'd;
MGREC98:17	H1819	space {time} he takes this lofty {took that wealthy} town,
MGREC99:16	H1859	Where valiant *Betis,* doth defend {stoutly keeps} the town,
MGREC99:22	H1865	But yet, this well defended town is {was} taken,
MGREC101:41	H1970	And now {Together} with it, the town also obtain'd.
MGREC103:2	H2013	With open Gates, the wealthy town did stand,
MGREC103:22	H2033	The pleasures and the riches of this town,
MGREC103:29	H2040	Commands to set this goodly town on fire.
MGREC108:7	H2223	Here was of *Greeks,* a town in *Bactria,*
MROMAN138:20	H3510	Faire *Ostia* he built, this Town, it stood,
MEDDM196:33	Hp274	That town wch thousands of enemys w^thout hath not been able

TOWNE (1) [town] See also TOWN'S

MASSYR55:22	H88	Taking a towne, such valour she did show,

TOWNES (7) [towns]

ELEMEN10:35	H110	What famous Townes to cinders have I turn'd?
ELEMEN11:5	H125	With neighbouring Townes I did consume to dust,
MPERS85:27	H1303	All Townes, held by his Ancestors before.
MPERS86:28	H1344	Some Townes commodious in lesse *Asia,*
MGREC124:15	H2922	*Athens,* with many Townes in *Greece* besides, {beside}
MGREC127:4	H3034	Now many Townes in *Macedon* supprest,

DIALOG146:16 H202 My plundered Townes, my houses devastation,
TOWN'S (1) [town is]
MPERS75:12 H873 To loose a nose, to win a Town's no shame,
TOWNS (1) [pl.]
MPERS91:1 H1509 He knows that many towns in *Greece* envies
TOYES (1) [toys]
CHILDRN186:7 H74 But former toyes (no joyes) adieu.
TOYISH (1)
AGES37:22 H84 In Rattles, Bables, and such toyish stuffe.
TOYL (4) [toil] See also TOYLE
HUMOUR28:19 H331 But yet for all my toyl, my care, my skil,
SEASONS47:6 H22 Now goes the Plow-man to his merry toyl,
SEASONS50:3 H137 Now go the Mowers to their slashing toyl,
SEASONS50:25 H159 His sweat, his toyl, his careful, wakeful nights,
TOYLE (4) [toil] See also TOYL
ELEMEN16:29 H352 Unlesse I ease his toyle, and doe transport,
MASSYR65:5 H470 Requited not the cost {loss}, the toyle, and pain.
TDUDLEY166:25 H67 Who after all his toyle, is now at rest:
FEVER220:28 H8 From side to side for ease I toyle,
TOYLES (1) [toils] See also TOYLS
CONTEM173:19 H185 That neither toyles nor hoards up in thy barn,
TOYLING (1) [toiling]
ELEMEN13:24 H225 He sometimes findes, maugre his toyling paine,
TOYLS (2) [toils] See also TOYLES
MASSYR53:21 H11 That mighty Hunter, who in his strong toyls,
MGREC107:13 H2188 The recompence of travels, wars, and toyls;
TOYS See TOYES
TRABEZOND (1)
MPERS90:9 H1482 But on to *Trabezond* they kept their way;
TRACE (1)
2LETTER182:15 H21 Tell him, the countless steps that thou dost trace,
TRADE (2)
HUMOUR24:8 H157 I love no boasting, that's but childrens trade:
CONTEM173:5 H173 To see what trade they great ones there do drive,
TRADES (1) [pl.]
ELEMEN13:8 H209 And ye Artificers, all trades and sorts;
TRADING (1)
DIALOG146:18 H204 My wealthy trading faln, my dearth of grain,
TRAGEDY (5)
MPERS72:7 ~~H756~~ *Praraspes* now must act this tragedy;
MGREC105:4 H2097 *(Bessus,* his Partner in this Tragedy,
MGREC105:21 H2114 The witnesse of his dying misery: {this horrid Tragedy;}
MGREC115:19 H2538 And in a Tragedy there end his age.
MGREC129:26 H3140 When this foul tragedy was past, and done,
TRAGICK (1)
SIDNEY149:21 H20 Are not his Tragick Comedies so acted,
TRAIN (2) See also TRAINE
MASSYR64:10 H434 Against *Iehoiakim* marcht with his train;
MGREC102:6 H1976 Is entertain'd with joy, and pompous train {showes},
TRAIN'D (1) [trained]
AGES42:10 H268 A Captain I, with skil I train'd my band;

1001

TRAINE (1) [train]
MGREC106:16   H2150   Her traine to *Alexander* (as 'tis thought)
TRAINED (2) See also TRAIN'D
AGES39:12   H155   With nurture trained up in vertues Schools,
MASSYR57:15   H162   'Gainst whom his trained Bands *Abram* did bring.
TRAITEROUS (2) [traitorous] See also TRAYTEROUS
HUMOUR34:7   H562   O! good, O bad, O true, O traiterous eyes!
MGREC104:21   H2073   Straight *Bessus* comes, and with his traiterous hands,
TRAITOR (1) See also TRAYTOR
MGREC107:7   H2182   Intends with speed, that Traitor down {to his end} to bring;
TRAITOROUS See TRAITEROUS, TRAYTEROUS
TRAITOROUSLY See TRAITROUSLY
TRAITORS (2) [pl.; poss.]
MGREC104:32   H2084   *Darius* from those Traitors hands to gain;
MGREC105:29   H2122   And not by Traitors hands untimely dye.
TRAITROUSLY (1) [traitorously]
MGREC~~132:6~~   H3241   Seaz'd upon that, and slew him traitrously.
TRAMPLE (1)
MYSOUL225:17 H21   Base World I trample on thy face,
TRANCE (1)
MPERS88:34   H1427   After this trance, revenge, new spirits blew,
TRANSCENDENTLY (1)
MEDDM206:16   Hp287   bright while they moue on earth, how transcendently splendid
TRANSCENDS (1)
MEDDM200:30   Hp279   and in this transcends the spring, that their leafe shall neuer
TRANSFER'D (1) [transferred]
MASSYR60:8   H273   And then to {unto} *Media* transfer'd his seat.
TRANSFERS (2)
ELEMEN16:28   H351   Transfers his goods, from North and South and East;
MASSYR54:17   H44   Transfers his Seat, to the *Assyrian* plain,
TRANSFORM'D (2) [transformed]
MASSYR55:12   H78   Transform'd into a fish, by *Venus* will,
MPERS88:33   H1426   Nor *Gorgons* {head} like to this, transform'd to stones.
TRANSGRESSION (1)
DIALOG144:15 H125   These be the *Hydra's* of my stout transgression;
TRANSGREST (2)
HUMOUR28:34   H346   If time I have transgrest, and been too long,
MASSYR61:38   H343   (This was that *Ahaz,* which so much {high} transgrest.)
TRANSLATE (1)
MGREC134:24   H3355   They might translate the Bible into *Greek,*
TRANSLATION (1)
CONTEM174:11 H211   Can make him deeply groan for that divine Translation.
TRANSMUTATION (2)
ELEMEN9:23   H57   A transmutation, it was through mine aide.
HUMOUR31:6   ~~H439~~   This transmutation is, but not excretion,
TRANSPARENT (1)
FLESH177:11   H92   The Streets thereof transparent gold,
TRANSPORT (2)
ELEMEN16:29   H352   Unlesse I ease his toyle, and doe transport,
MPERS90:16   ~~H1484~~   Straight to transport them to the other side,

TRANSPORTATION (2)

MPERS78:21   H1002   Besides, the Vessels for this transportation,

MGREC107:33   H2208   Would by {without} some means a transportation finde;

TRANSPORTED (2)

HUMOUR31:33   H466   Now up, now down, transported like the Aire.

MGREC104:14   H2066   Transported sore, with griefe and passion;

TRAPS (1) [pl.]

MGREC123:12   H2874   That {And} by the selfe-same traps the other laid,

TRAPT (1)

MGREC96:5   H1725   The stately Horses trapt, the launces guilt;

TRASH (3)

ELEMEN18:7   H411   No world {earth}, thy witching trash, were all but vain.

DIALOG147:14   H240   Copes, Rochets, Crossiers, and such {empty} trash,

FLESH176:41   H81   Nor such like trash which Earth doth hold,

TRAUELL (1) [travel] See also TRAVELL

MEDDM205:11   Hp286   his slight and flitting thoughts are like passengers, that trauell

TRAVAIL (1)

MYCHILD216:18   Hp241   feares brovght yov to this, I now travail in birth again of yov till

TRAVAILE (1) [travail]

MGREC100:32   H1916   Who had long {sore} travaile, and much sorrow seen,

TRAVAILES (2) [travails]

MGREC110:23   H2327   Long with excessive travailes wearied,

PILGRIM210:6   H6   his dangers past, and travailes done

TRAVELL (1) [travel]

MPERS90:18   H1485   So after all {Thus finishing} their travell, danger, pain,

TRAVELLERS (1) [pl.]

SEASONS52:31   H246   And Travellers sometimes their noses leese.

TRAVELLS (1) [travels]

MGREC112:16   H2402   And his long travells past, and over-gone;

TRAVELS (3)

MGREC107:4   H2179   And for the rest new wars, and travels findes,

MGREC107:13   H2188   The recompence of travels, wars, and toyls;

MGREC110:34   H2338   Whereon his acts, and travels, long appears;

TRAYTEROUS (1) [traitorous] See also TRAITEROUS

MGREC134:37   ~~H3367~~   Her brother by him, lost his trayterous head

TRAYTOR (3) [traitor]

MPERS93:4   H1601   Him, to the grave, did Traytor *Bessus* send.

MGREC128:14   H3087   And to requite this Traytor for those {these} harmes:

MEDDM196:34   Hp274   hath been deliuered vp by one traytor w^{th}in, and that man w^{ch}

TREACHERY (2)

MGREC~~105:11~~   H2104   But this unheard of injury {treachery} much more;

MGREC107:41   H2216   Hated of all, for's former treachery,

TREAD (3)

DIALOG147:21   H247   By force {As Duty binds,} expell, destroy, and tread them

SIDNEY151:20   H70   I shew, how thou {he} fame's path didst {paths did} tread,

PILGRIM210:11   H11   He erring pathes no more shall tread

TREADS (2)

MASSYR61:10   H315   Next treads the {those} steps, by which his Father won.

MPERS88:29   H1422   But treads down all, for to advance their Master;

TREASON (6)

MPERS~~92:21~~   H1579   But that his treason timely was found out.

MGREC104:13 H2065 Next day this treason, to *Darius* known,
MGREC105:25 H2118 Of Treason, murther, and base cruelty,
MGREC112:22 H2408 The King of treason, and conspiracy;
MGREC120:25 H2762 *Antigonus* of Treason first attaints,
QELIZ157:37 H105 Know 'tis a slander now, but once was treason.

TREASONS (1) [pl.]
MPERS92:23 H1581 Lost but his life for horrid treasons all.

TREASURE (13)
AGES40:9 H190 Until her freinds, treasure, and honour's gone.
MPERS85:21 H1297 Revolts, having treasure, and people gain'd:
MGREC97:10 H1771 The Regall ornaments now {were} lost, the treasure
MGREC102:3 H1973 At *Arbela* left, his ornaments, and treasure,
MGREC102:11 H1981 In this a masse {world} of gold, and treasure lay,
MGREC102:29 H1999 He likewise here a world of treasure found,
MGREC103:11 H2022 And taken mony, plate, and golden treasure;
MGREC127:16 H3046 Having Command o'th treasure he can hire,
MGREC127:29 H3059 And Master of the treasure he remains; {sole remain:}
SIDNEY150:6 H31 A world of treasure, in {wealth within} that rubbish lye;
VANITY160:22 H32 If not in honour, beauty, age, nor treasure,
CONTEM174:23 H221 That's full of friends, of honour and of treasure,
HOUSE237:28 H58 My hope, and Treasure lyes Above.

TREASURES (8) [pl.]
ELEMEN13:5 H206 For gemmes, for silver, treasures which I hold:
MASSYR60:2 H267 With over-plus of all treasures {the wealth} therein,
MASSYR60:24 H289 Who own'd the treasures of proud *Babylon,*
MPERS69:38 H663 His Treasures, pleasures, pomp and power dfd see,
MPERS92:38 H1596 Whose honours, treasures, pleasures, had short stay;
VANITY159:38 H10 What is't in wealth, great treasures for to gain {obtain}?
FLESH175:18 H18 Hast treasures there laid up in store
MEDDM202:16 Hp282 The treasures of this world may well be compared to huskes,

TREAT (3)
MPERS89:36 H1470 Gets them to treat with him in privacy,
CONTEM169:32 H71 While of their persons & their acts his mind doth treat.
2LETTER182:17 H23 And when thou canst not treat by loving mouth,

TREBBLE (1)
MPERS70:6 H677 Now trebble wall'd, and moated so about,

TREBLE (1)
CONTEM170:34 H104 Branded with guilt, and crusht with treble woes,

TREE (12)
ELEMEN14:35 H277 Thou bear'st no {nor} grasse, nor {or} plant, nor tree, nor
ELEMEN15:8 H290 The Pine, the Cedars, yea and *Daph'nes* tree;
AGES44:30 H363 I've seen a Kingdom flourish like a tree,
SEASONS51:7 H181 The Orange, Lemon, Dangle on the tree;
MASSYR64:3 H427 This was that tree, whose brances fill'd the earth,
QELIZ158:12 H121 *On neither tree did grow such Rose before,*
VANITY161:1 H52 This pearl of price, this tree of life, this spring,
CONTEM168:16 H24 Whose beams was shaded by the leavie Tree,
CONTEM169:36 H74 Fancyes the Apple, dangle on the Tree,
3LETTER183:27 H29 Together at one Tree, oh let us brouze,
MERCY188:24 H10 I saw the branches lopt the Tree now fall,
MERCY188:27 H13 That thou dear Son has lost both Tree and fruit:

TREEN (1)
CHILDRN184:33 H22   Along the Beach among the treen,

TREES (20) [pl.]
ELEMEN13:26	H227	My sap, to plants and trees, I must not grant,
ELEMEN13:29	H230	And buds from fruitfull trees, before they'r {as soon as} blowne:
ELEMEN19:34	H475	Where neither houses, trees, nor plants, I spare;
HUMOUR26:20	H250	As plants, trees, and small Embryon know'th,
SEASONS47:13	H29	And carefully manures his trees of fruits.
SEASONS48:4	H57	In trees, and wals, in cities, and in fields;
SEASONS51:17	H191	But trees with goodly fruits replenished;
SEASONS51:24	H200	The fruitful trees, all withered now do stand,
MGREC110:8	H2308	Did here, and there, Isles full of trees abide;
CONTEM167:27	H4	The trees all richly clad, yet void of pride,
CONTEM171:20	H123	The stones and trees, insensible of time,
CONTEM171:34	H135	Shall I then praise the heavens, the trees, the earth
CONTEM172:11	H147	Now thought the rivers did the trees excel,
CHILDRN184:19	H8	Mounted the Trees, and learn'd to sing;
CHILDRN185:23	H49	Or whilst on trees they sit and sing,
CHILDRN185:39	H65	Oft times in grass, on trees, in flight,
ELIZB187:5	H13	By nature Trees do rot when they are grown.
MEDDM200:25	Hp279	we se the leavlesse trees and dry stocks (at the approach of
MEDDM205:31	Hp286	We see in orchards, some trees soe fruitfull, that the waight of
13MAY226:27	H3	And leaues the naked Trees doe dresse

TREMBLING (6)
AGES45:40	H430	Now trembling, and {is all} fearful, sad, and cold;
MGREC135:35	H3407	All trembling stand, before that powerfull Lambe.
TDUDLEY165:6	H8	My mournfull mind, sore prest, in trembling verse
CONTEM173:7	H175	And take the trembling prey before it yield,
ANNEB187:16	H6	With troubled heart & trembling hand I write,
MEDDM206:34	Hp288	and trembling, lest they through vnbeleif fall short of a

TRENCH (2)
AGES39:20	H163	I cannot lye in trench, {intrench'd} before a Town,
MPERS87:31	H1383	Up then with speed, a mighty trench he throwes,

TRESSE (1) [tress]
SEASONS50:18 H152   The russling tresse of *terra* for {down} to moe,

TRIBES (1) [pl.]
MASSYR62:22 H367   Where now those ten Tribes are, can no man tel,

TRIBUNES (1) [pl.]
ELEMEN15:38 H320   Which *Cæsars, Consuls, Tribunes* all adorne;

TRIBUTARY (2)
MASSYR54:31	H58	By force, {and fraud} his tributary, he did {under Tribute} bring.
MASSYR62:5	H350	And him six years his tributary made;

TRIBUTE (4)
MASSYR54:31	H58	By force, {and fraud} his tributary, he did {under Tribute} bring.
MPERS84:12	H1240	The might o'th' Prince, the tribute on {of} the Isles.
QELIZ155:27	H18	T' accept the tribute of a loyall Braine;
MEDDM209:8	Hp291	Canaanites, not destroy them, but put them vnder tribute, for

TRICE (3)
ELEMEN18:38	H442	And in a trice, my own nature resume.
HUMOUR22:13	H82	If any threaten her, she'l in a trice,
AGES43:16	H309	But in a trice 'tis ruin'd by a blast,

TRIED See TRY'D, TRYED
TRIES (1)
MGREC131:23　H3215　Tries foes, since friends will not compassionate,
TRIFLES (1) [pl.]
ELEMEN17:27　H391　But these are trifles to the Flood of *Noe*.
TRIM (3)
ELEMEN9:35　H70　And trim thee gay {brave}, in green, after thy blacks?
AUTHOR178:8　H18　In better dress to trim thee was my mind,
MEDDM200:22　Hp279　a trim that they might run the wayes of his Commandment
TRIM'D (1) [trimmed]
SEASONS46:35　H11　She trim'd her locks, which late had frosted been,
TRINITY (1)
MYCHILD218:5　Hp243　such a God as I worship in Trinity, + such a Sav^r as I rely
TRIUMPH (4)
AGES46:24　H455　Triumph I shal, o're Sin, o're Death, o're Hel,
MGREC133:24　H3314　Him with his Sons in Triumph lead did he,
MGREC135:5　H3377　But some disgrace, in triumph to be led.
FLESH176:24　H64　And triumph shall, with laurel head,
TRIUMPHANT (2)
MASSYR62:17　H362　Returns triumphant Victor to his soyl;
MEDDM206:9　Hp287　so is it in the Church both militant and triumphant, there is
TRIUMPHS (2) [pl.] See also TRYUMPHS
MPERS77:30　H971　And *Greece* such wondrous triumphs ne're had made.
MROMAN138:33 H3523　To such rude triumphs, as young *Rome* then had,
TRIUMPHT (1)
HUMOUR23:35　H145　Then a dead Lyon? by beasts triumpht ore.
TROD (2)
DIALOG142:7　H36　And {Or} by tempestuous Wars thy fields trod down?
DIALOG143:32　H101　The Gospel is trod {troden} down, and hath no right;
TRODEN (2)
DIALOG143:32　H101　The Gospel is trod {troden} down, and hath no right;
PILGRIM210:4　H4　That myrie steps, haue troden oft
TROOPS (2) [pl.]
MGREC131:18　H3210　*Demetrius* with his troops to *Athens* flies,
QELIZ156:25　H52　Her stately Troops advanc'd to *Lisbons* wall,
TROPHE (1) [trophy]
MPERS77:3　H942　As the best trophe that {which} ye won in *Greece*.
TROPHIES (1) [pl.] See also TROPHYES
DUBART154:17　H62　Their trophies were but heaps of wounded slain,
TROPHY See TROPHE
TROPHYES (1) [trophies]
FLESH175:28　H28　And trophyes to thy name erect
TROPICK (2) [tropic]
SEASONS49:8　H99　Who to his Southward tropick still is bent,
SEASONS52:19 H234　To th' Southward tropick his swift race hath {doth} run;
TROUBLE (5)
MPERS85:18　H1294　A second trouble, after this succeeds.
MPERS85:22　H1298　{Plunders} the Country, and much trouble {mischief} wrought,
MGREC121:25　H2807　Then by more trouble to grow eminent.
MEDDM203:36　Hp284　trouble
MYCHILD215:27 Hp240　a great Trouble, & I could not be at rest 'till by prayer I had

TROUBLED (7)

MPERS89:21	H1455	The troubled King, his Herauld sends again,
MGREC121:1	H2779	('Gainst which to goe, is troubled in his minde;)
DIALOG143:26	H95	To shew the grievance of my troubled Land;
DISTEMP179:25	H13	And brought me to the shore from troubled Main.
ANNEB187:16	H6	With troubled heart & trembling hand I write,
MYCHILD215:28	Hp241	vnto God. I was also troubled at yᵉ neglect of private Dutyes
MYCHILD217:32	Hp243	Many times hath Satan troubled me concerning yᵉ verity of yᵉ

TROUBLES (18) [pl.]

AGES37:27	H89	Through ignorance, all troubles did surmount.
AGES45:22	H404	But out of troubles, ye may see much good,
SEASONS49:27	H116	Whilst they're imbroyl'd in Wars, and troubles ripe; {rife:}
MPERS76:24	H922	But troubles in lesse *Asia* him stay'd;
MPERS85:25	H1301	So that he might, these tumults {those troubles} soon appease.
MPERS91:20	H1528	His home-bred troubles seeketh {sought how} to appease;
MPERS91:28	H1542	What troubles in his house he did sustain,
MGREC94:13	H1647	Thus eased now, of troubles, and of fears;
MGREC98:33	H1835	*Darius* finding troubles still increase,
MGREC117:14	H2621	What troubles, and contentions did ensue,
MGREC132:20	H3262	*Demetrius* with so many troubles met,
DIALOG141:3	H3	their present troubles.
DIALOG146:32	H219	Out of your troubles much good fruit to be;
CONTEM174:3	H204	Troubles from foes, from friends, from dearest, near'st
MEDDM207:25	Hp289	no paines nor troubles, shall put a period to our dayes, the
MYCHILD218:28	Hp244	But some new Troubles I haue had since yᵉ world has been
SON231:11	H23	From troubles and Incuⁿbers Thov
HOURS233:22	H5	My Troubles All are Thee before

TROUBLESOME (1)

MPERS82:10	H1157	And troublesome *Mardonius* now must dye:

TROY (4)

ELEMEN10:39	H114	Where's *Ninus* great wal'd Town, and *Troy* of old?
MASSYR57:25	H172	When famous *Troy* was so beleaguered:
MGREC94:21	H1659	Then on he march'd, in's way he veiw'd old *Troy;*
SIDNEY150:28	H55	Brave *Hector* by the walls of *Troy,* we see:

TROYS (1) [poss.]

HUMOUR33:4	H518	Under *Troys* wals, ten years wil wast {wear} away,

TRUDGE (1)

AUTHOR177:34	H6	Made thee in raggs, halting to th' press to trudge,

TRUE (40)

FATHER6:5	H39	My goods are true (though poor) I love no stealth,
ELEMEN13:20	H221	I should here make a short, yet true narration,
ELEMEN14:3	H245	O dreadfull Sepulcher! that this is true,
ELEMEN15:16	H298	That this is true, earth thou canst not deny;
HUMOUR23:8	H118	Tis true, when I am midwife to thy birth;
HUMOUR27:6	H277	That this is true, I easily can assent,
HUMOUR30:38	H430	That black is black, and I am black, tis true;
HUMOUR32:30	H504	Valour {Valours} I want, no Souldier am, 'tis true,
HUMOUR32:36	H510	Nay, I could tel you (what's more true then meet)
HUMOUR34:7	H562	O! good, O bad, O true, O traiterous eyes!
AGES36:36	H60	Both good and bad, but yet no more then's true.
AGES44:9	H342	But now, *Bis pueri senes,* is too true;

1007

MASSYR57:36	H181	It is enough {may suffice}, if all be true that's past,
MASSYR64:32	H456	None but the true *Ezekiel* need to tell:
MPERS69:13	H635	This is of *Cyrus* the true pedigree,
MPERS~~69:38~~	H661	Then to the King he makes this true report,
MGREC97:9	H1770	If *Curtius* be true, in his report.
MGREC104:17	H2069	Bidding his {Then bids} servant *Artabassus* true;
MGREC114:39	H2509	All this he did, who knows not to be true,
MGREC115:2	H2513	All this he did, yea, and much more, 'tis true,
MGREC121:37	H2819	But he was true to's masters family,
MGREC124:10	~~H2915~~	All such as he suspected to him true.
MGREC127:14	H3044	True *Eumenes* endeavours by all skill,
MGREC~~132:20~~	H3265	His story seems a Fable more then true.
SIDNEY151:19	~~H69~~	That thine was true, but theirs adul'rate love.
QELIZ156:6	H33	Millions will testifie that this is true;
TDUDLEY165:30	H32	True Patriot of this little Commonweal,
TDUDLEY165:34	H36	Thy love to true Religion e're shall shine,
DDUDLEY167:16	H13	*A true Instructer of her Family,*
CONTEM167:29	H6	Their leaves & fruits seem'd painted, but was true
CONTEM172:26	H160	Thou Emblem true, of what I count the best,
FLESH175:25	H25	True substance in variety?
AUTHOR177:32	H4	Till snatcht from thence by friends, less wise then true
1LETTER181:18	H16	True living Pictures of their Fathers face.
3LETTER183:12	H14	Bewail my turtle true, who now is gone,
3LETTER183:15	H17	Or as the loving Mullet, that true Fish,
CHILDRN184:36	H25	Coupled with mate loving and true,
2SIMON195:10	Hp271	true friends much more by duty full children, I haue avoyded
MEDDM195:30	Hp272	then the practique part, but he is a true Christian that is a
MYCHILD218:18	Hp244	that admitt this bee ye true God whom wee worship, and y^t bee

TRUELY (1) [truly]

MEDDM208:18	Hp290	the Apostle call riches deceitfull riches, and they may truely

TRULY (10)

HUMOUR29:31	H382	He is not truly valiant that's not wise;
HUMOUR33:14	~~H528~~	But yet thou art as much, I truly say,
VANITY160:39	H49	And truly beautifies without deceit.
TDUDLEY166:1	H43	For truly his ambition lay above.
VERSES183:35	H2	Most truly honoured, and as truly dear,
MEDDM201:9	Hp280	by many, but what he did not say, cannot (truly) be vttered
MEDDM207:21	Hp289	All men are truly sayd to be tenants at will, and it may as truly
MEDDM207:21	Hp289	men are truly sayd to be tenants at will, and it may as truly be
WHAT224:4	H4	For truly I am thine.

TRUMPERIE (1) [trumpery]

DIALOG147:17	H243	We hate *Romes* Whore, with all her trumperie.

TRUMPET (1)

AGES39:18	H161	The snorting Horse, the Trumpet, Drum I like,

TRUMPETERS (1) [pl.]

TDUDLEY165:17	H19	That pitty might some Trumpeters procure.

TRUMPETS (1) [pl.]

ELEMEN18:15	H419	Your Drums, your Trumpets, and your Organs sound,

TRUNK (1)

HOUSE236:37	H29	Here stood that Trunk, and there y^t chest

TRUNKE (1) [trunk]
ELEMEN15:34   H316   Was ever gem so rich found in thy trunke?

TRUST (17) See also TRVST
ELEMEN12:27   H187   Whose trust, and valour I might here commend:
HUMOUR31:19   H452   I trust I've clear'd your slandrous imputations {inputation}.
AGES45:21   H403   Oh may you live, and so you will I trust
MPERS69:23   H645   And the ambiguous Oracle did trust,
MGREC100:27   H1911   For in his multitudes his trust still lay,
MGREC103:21   H2032   For such revolters false, what Prince will {King can} trust:
MGREC113:36   H2463   Who for his prudence, valour, care, and trust,
MGREC124:22   H2929   Put trust in any, but in this Commander;
MGREC127:23   H3053   Because he never would let go {forgoe} his trust:
DIALOG143:18   H87   But trust not much unto his Excellence;
DIALOG147:30   H254   These, these, are they (I trust) with *Charles* our King,
DIALOG147:36   H260   And discipline erected, so I trust,
FLESH176:11   H51   Thy flatt'ring shews Ile trust no more.
MERCY189:10   H31   All freed from grief (I trust) among the blest;
MEDDM202:28   Hp282   se no light, yet then must we trust in the lord and stay vpon our
JULY223:28   Hp251   that I now hope for, y^t so they may bee encourag^d to trust in
SAMUEL228:10   H11   No freind I haue like Thee to trust

TRUSTED See TRVSTED
TRUSTETH (1)
AGES40:8   H189   Trusteth my loving looks, and glozing tongue,
TRUSTS (1)
MPERS90:40   H1507   *Tythraustes* trusts more to his wit then Arms,
TRUTH (20)
HUMOUR24:23   H172   But to evince the truth, by argument.
HUMOUR29:19   H370   Not past all reason, but in truth all shame:
HUMOUR31:14   H445   If any doubt this {the} truth, whence this should come;
HUMOUR32:26   H500   To what is truth, I freely wil assent,
HUMOUR33:6   H520   But 'twere as vain, to prove the {this} truth of mine,
HUMOUR33:12   H526   Thou speakest truth, and I can speak {say} no lesse,
AGES43:35   H330   Subject to all Diseases, {distempers} that's the truth,
AGES45:23   H413   These are no old wives tales, but this is truth;
MASSYR64:13   H437   His Vassal is, gives pledges for his truth,
MGREC99:6   H1849   Tels him, these proffers great (in truth were none)
MGREC116:18   H2584   Had so instructed him in morall truth.
DIALOG144:1   H111   Thy flying for the Truth I made a jeast;
DIALOG148:4   H269   When truth and righteousnesse they thus shall nourish.
SIDNEY149:19   H18   *Thalia,* and *Melpomene,* say th' truth,
SIDNEY150:13   H48   But to {The more I} say truth, {the more} thy worth I shall but
SIDNEY152:26   H95   *Heire to the Muses, the Son of* Mars *in truth,*
TDUDLEY166:37   H79   *To Truth a shield, to right a Wall,*
MYCHILD215:19   Hp240   Truth, not to sett forth my self, but ye Glory of God. If I had
MYCHILD217:30   Hp243   of God, it would haue been a Hell to me for in Truth it is the
MED223:10   Hp250   he my head. Such priviledges had not ye word of Truth made
TRUTH'S (1) [truth is]
MPERS78:8   H989   For truth's asham'd how many to expresse;
TRUTHS (2) [poss.]
DIALOG146:39   H225   With (ventur'd lives) for truths defence that stand,
TDUDLEY165:32   H34   Truths friend thou wert, to errors still a foe,

TRVST (3) [trust]
  30SEPT227:20 Hp257 thankfully to submitt to him for I trvst it is out of his abvndant
  30SEPT227:31 Hp257 will doe yᵉ like for yov if you trvst in him; And when he shall
  HOUSE237:14   H44   The arm of flesh didst make thy trvst?
TRVSTED (1) [trusted]
  MYCHILD219:1 Hp244-5 neuer prevail against it, I know whom I haue trvsted, and
TRY (6)
  ELEMEN9:2   H36   To try your valour by, but it must feele
  MGREC104:2   H2054 Thought now this once, to try his fortunes here,
  MGREC123:9   H2871 'Gainst him, that all deceits could scan, and try:
  MGREC132:35 H3282 Must needs goe try their fortune, and their might,
  MYCHILD216:13 Hp241 and try me & doe me Good: and it was not altogether
  MYCHILD216:32 Hp242 me and try me, see what wayes of wickednes are in me, and
TRY'D (3) [tried] See also TRYED
  AGES36:9   H33   No wooden horse, but one of mettal try'd:
  MPERS80:23   H1090 Yet {Then} in the Streights of *Salamis* he try'd,
  FEVER221:1   H16   Thov knowst my heart, and hast me try'd
TRYED (2) [tried] See also TRY'D
  MASSYR60:30   H295   He thus inricht, by this new tryed gold,
  MEDDM208:15 Hp290 Judgment we must be tryed and as he passes the sentence, so
TRYUMPHS (1) [triumphs]
  DUBART154:21 H66   Who in thy tryumphs (never won by wrongs)
TUDOR (1)
  DIALOG143:9   H78   No need of *Tudor,* Roses to unite,
TUGG'D (1) [tugged]
  DIALOG145:34 H183   Here tugg'd they hard indeed, for all men saw,
TULLIUS (3)
  MROMAN138:37 H3527 *Servius Tullius.*
  MROMAN138:38 H3528 Next, *Servius Tullius* sits upon {gets into} the Throne,
  MROMAN139:8 H3536 Forty foure yeares did *Servius Tullius* reigne,
TULLUS (3)
  MROMAN137:37 H3488 *Tullus Hostilius.*
  MROMAN137:38 H3489 *Tullus Hostilius,* was third *Roman* King,
  MROMAN138:11 H3501 Thirty two years doth *Tullus* reigne, then dye,
TUMBLING (1)
  ELEMEN14:16 H258   Which rise like mighty {tumbling} billowes on the lands: {Land}
TUMOURS (1) [pl.]
  ELEMEN16:34 H357   All humours, Tumours, that {which} are bred of cold.
TUMULT (5)
  MPERS69:31   H653   Amidst {Among} the tumult, bloud-shed, and the strife,
  MPERS87:2   H1358 And fills the Court with tumult, and with fear.
  MPERS88:12   H1405 For tumult and confusion they expected,
  MGREC101:30 H1955 For tumult in the dark {night} doth cause most dread,
  MGREC117:39 H2646 After much tumult, they at last proclaim'd
TUMULTS (2) [pl.]
  MPERS85:25   H1301 So that he might, these tumults {those troubles} soon appease.
  MGREC118:13 H2660 'Mongst these contentions, tumults, jealousies,
TUMULTUOUS (1)
  MGREC119:12 H2702 In these tumultuous dayes, the thralled *Greeks*
TUNE (2)
  SEASONS47:19 H35   Now tune their layes, on sprays of every bush;

CONTEM169:20 H60 They kept one tune, and plaid on the same string,

TUNES (2) [pl.]
ELEMEN18:19 H423 Your songs and pleasant tunes, they are the same,
CHILDRN186:2 H69 Mean while my dayes in tunes Ile spend,

TUNES (1) v.
CONTEM173:28 H193 So each one tunes his pretty instrument,

T'UPHOLD (1) [to uphold]
MGREC127:25 H3055 Striving t'uphold his Masters family,

TURBLENCE (1) [turbulence]
MGREC123:25 H2889 Into *Epire,* for her great turblence;

TURKY (1) [turkey]
DIALOG148:17 H282 This done, with brandish'd swords, to *Turky* go,

TURN (11) See also TURNE
ELEMEN18:34 H438 And when I'm throughly rarifi'd, turn fire.
HUMOUR28:8 H320 As if she'd leave no flesh to turn to clay,
HUMOUR28:15 H327 I turn into his cel, close by my side,
HUMOUR28:22 H334 That mortal man, might turn to his corruption.
MGREC~~123:13~~ H2877 To *Greece* and *Macedon* lets turn our sight.
MGREC127:13 H3043 And {now} for a while, let's into *Asia* turn,
MGREC129:41 H3155 He knows to's profit, all i'th end {this at last} will turn,
MGREC~~132:20~~ H3259 With these he hopes to turn the world about:
VANITY159:36 H8 And whilst they live, how oft doth turn their State? {fate,}
MEDDM197:33 Hp275 greif and pain till they turn to dust, and then are they fine
MYCHILD218:26 Hp244 consideration of these things and many ye like would soon turn

TURNAMENT (2)
HUMOUR24:39 H188 And scorn'st all Knightly sports, at turnament.
MROMAN137:12 H3463 Great shewes he makes at Tilt, and Turnament,

TURN'D (10) [turned] See also TURND
ELEMEN10:35 H110 What famous Townes to cinders have I turn'd?
MASSYR56:36 H142 The Poets feign her turn'd into a Dove,
MASSYR62:39 H384 With shame then turn'd to *Ninivie* again,
MPERS~~91:31~~ H1545 Forty three years he rul'd, then turn'd to dust,
MGREC95:15 H1694 Whose touch turn'd all to gold, yea even his meat:
MGREC121:31 H2813 And *Pithon* turn'd to *Asia* againe.
DAVID159:6 H21 The bow of *Jonathan* ne're turn'd in vaine,
CONTEM170:1 H75 That turn'd his Sovereign to a naked thral.
FLESH175:20 H20 Art fancy sick, or turn'd a Sot
SON230:20 H3 All praise to him who hath now turn'd

TURND (1) [turned] See also TURN'D
RESTOR230:7 H22 Nor turnd his ear away from me

TURNE (6) [turn]
ELEMEN8:9 H7 And {That} in due order each her turne should speake,
ELEMEN18:27 H431 I {help to} ripe the corne, I turne the grinding mill;
ELEMEN18:35 H439 So when I am condens'd, I turne to water;
AGES37:35 H97 Make strong my selfe, and turne aside weak right.
MPERS91:18 H1526 And turne to *Persia,* as is pertinent;
DAVID159:8 H23 Did *Saul* with bloodlesse Sword turne back agen:

TURNED (1) See also TURN'D, TURND
MASSYR64:8 H432 Was turned {changed} from a King, unto {into} a Beast;

TURNES (1) [turns; pl.]
SIDNEY151:22 H72 With endlesse turnes, the way I find not out,

1011

TURNES (3) v. [turns]

HUMOUR22:30	H99	For when they faile, man turnes unto his clay:
MPERS69:40	H670	Now up, now {and} down, as fortune turnes her hand,
DUBART153:25	H29	At night turnes to his Mothers cot againe,

TURNING (2)

ANNEB187:27	H17	Or like a shadow turning as it was.
MEDDM206:20	Hp287	themselues of turning to god, the first thing wch they eye, is

TURNS (2) v. See also TURNES

HUMOUR28:4	H316	And turns him to the wombe of's earthy mother,
MPERS91:29	~~H1543~~	Forty three years he rules, then turns to dust,

TURN'ST (1) [turnest]

HUMOUR31:16	H449	If there thou'rt stopt, to th' Liver thou turn'st in,

TURTLE (1)

3LETTER183:12	H14	Bewail my turtle true, who now is gone,

TURTLES (1) [pl.]

3LETTER183:28	H30	And like two Turtles roost within one house,

TUSCANY (1)

MROMAN138:32	H3522	And Nations twelve, of *Tuscany* subdues:

TUSH (1)

MEDDM200:3	Hp278	not a little one? will ere long say of a greater Tush god regards

TUSHES (1) [pl.]

DIALOG142:21	H50	To come, and break the tushes of the Boar?

TUSKS (1) [pl.]

DIALOG143:6	H77	Whose tearing tusks did wound, and kill, and threat:

TUTOUR (1) [tutor]

MGREC116:17	H2583	Wise *Aristotle,* tutour to his youth,

TWAIN (7)

HUMOUR25:6	H195	For drink, which of us twain, like it the best,
HUMOUR33:8	H522	Next difference {that} betwixt us twain doth lye,
AGES45:22	H407	I've seen a state unmoulded, rent in twain,
MPERS79:1	H1023	Cuts him in twain, for whom his Sire besought.
MGREC95:16	H1695	There {where} the Prophetick knot, he cuts in twain;
CHILDRN184:29	H18	And Seasons twain they there did spend:
1SIMON188:14	H15	Go pretty babe, go rest with Sisters twain

TWAINE (2) [twain]

ELEMEN17:11	H375	Untill straight {proud} *Gibralter,* did make them twaine,
MGREC132:34	H3281	*Seleuchus,* and *Lysimachus;* those {these} twaine

T'WARD (2) [toward]

MGREC97:15	H1776	T'ward them, demean'd himself like a Commander;
MGREC~~104:27~~	H2079	And thus to {t'ward} *Alexander,* on he goes,

T'WARDS (1) [towards]

MGREC95:12	H1691	Next *Alexander* marcht, t'wards the black sea;

TWAS (18) [it was]

ELEMEN14:18	H260	But windy sister, 'twas when you have blown.
HUMOUR32:24	H498	Nor wonder 'twas, for hatred there's not smal,
AGES42:33	H289	'Twas in the crop of my manured ground:
AGES44:41	H374	(For 'twas our hopes then kept our hearts alive)
MPERS77:22	H963	None write by whom, nor how, 'twas over-past;
MPERS78:30	H1011	But pitty 'twas, thine ayde that {thou} here did'st lend,
MGREC96:3	H1723	Oh {Sure} 'twas a goodly sight, there to behold;
MGREC99:23	H1866	(For 'twas decreed, that Empire should be shaken)

MGREC102:30 H2000 For 'twas the seat of *Persian* Kings renown'd;
MGREC115:30 H2549 The King doth intimate 'twas his intent,
MGREC116:3 H2563 Poyson had put an end to's dayes 'twas thought,
MGREC123:37 H2901 On whom ('twas thought) she set her chief delight;
MGREC126:35 H3024 To Husbands death ('twas {'tis} thought) she gave consent,
MGREC129:23 H3137 But 'twas in shew, in heart it pleas'd them best.
MGREC132:37 H3284 'Twas no small joy, unto *Seleuchus* breast,
MGREC135:4 H3376 For 'twas not death, nor danger, she did dread,
TDUDLEY166:12 H54 Nor wonder 'twas, low things ne'r much did move
HOUSE236:28 H20 Yea so it was, and so 'twas jvst.

TWELFTH (1)
SEASONS~~50:40~~ H174 The tenth {twelfth} of this, *Sol* riseth in the Line,

TWELVE (7)
SEASONS47:33 ~~H47~~ Twelve houses of the oblique Zodiack,
MASSYR59:33 H257 Which {That} for twelve hundred years had held that place;
MASSYR63:10 H395 After twelve years did *Essarhadon* dye,
MGREC110:33 H2337 Twelve Altars, he for Monuments then rears,
MGREC115:9 ~~H2518~~ Twelve thousand Tallents on it franckly spent;
MGREC~~115:15~~ H2529 Twelve thousand Talents also did intend,
MROMAN138:32 H3522 And Nations twelve, of *Tuscany* subdues:

TWENTIETH (1)
MPERS~~84:12~~ H1245 And *Nehemiah* in his twentieth year,

TWENTY (14)
MASSYR54:14 H41 At twenty five, ended his regal date.
MASSYR56:31 H137 (They say) but twenty, ere came back agen.
MASSYR59:34 H258 Twenty he reign'd, same time, as Stories tel,
MASSYR61:39 H344 Thus *Tiglath* reign'd, and warr'd, twenty seven years,
MPERS70:16 H687 Here twenty yeares provision {good} he found,
MPERS78:16 H997 Of two and twenty thousand Gallies meet,
MPERS79:39 H1065 Till twenty thousand *Persians* falls down slain;
MPERS92:2 ~~H1556~~ That three and twenty years he reign'd, I finde,
MPERS~~92:2~~ H1556 And in the twenty third of's cruel raign
MGREC93:15 H1612 The twenty first of's age, began to reign.
MGREC95:2 H1681 And twenty thousand, of their lives bereave,
MGREC108:21 H2237 Down from the mountains twenty thousand came,
MGREC108:41 H2257 And being an {one} hundred twenty thousand strong,
MROMAN138:22 H3512 Twenty foure yeare, {years} th' time of his royall race,

TWERE (3)
ELEMEN13:35 H236 But to such auditours 'twere of no use.
HUMOUR29:37 H388 'Twere but a mad, irregular distemper;
HUMOUR33:6 H520 But 'twere as vain, to prove the {this} truth of mine,

TWICE (6)
MPERS74:36 ~~H858~~ For twice ten months before the town he lay,
MPERS80:27 H1094 Twice beaten thus by {at} Sea, he warr'd no more:
MGREC~~101:34~~ H1960 By Captains twice is call'd before hee'l rise,
QELIZ156:16 H43 And earth had twice {once} a yeare, a new old face:
SICKNES178:18 H1 Twice ten years old, not fully told
MEDDM200:34 Hp280 he knows is enough for one of twice his strength, much lesse

TWINS (1) [pl.]
FLESH176:4 H44 Sisters we are, yea twins we be,

'TWIXT (13) [betwixt]

PROLOG6:28	H12	'Twixt him and me, that over-fluent store;
HUMOUR21:29	H57	'Twixt them and others, what ist makes the odds
AGES37:39	H101	I'd nought to do, 'twixt Prince, {King} and peoples strife.
MASSYR62:36	H381	'Twixt them and *Israels* he knew no odds. [7 *years.*
MPERS~~79:3~~	H1025	'Twixt which his souldiers marcht in good array.
MPERS79:36	H1062	This 'twixt the Mountains lyes (half Acre wide)
MGREC94:38	H1676	Which twixt *Phrigia,* and *Propontis* lyes.
MGREC123:40	H2904	By all the Bonds 'twixt him and's father past,
MGREC131:14	H3206	This day twixt these two foes {Kings} ends all the strife,
DIALOG145:17	H166	'Twixt King and Peeres a question of state,
DIALOG146:4	H192	Contention's {Contention} grown 'twixt Subjects and their
FLESH176:5	H45	Yet deadly feud 'twixt thee and me;
RESTOR230:3	H18	And 'twixt ye good and evill way

TWO (66)

ELEMEN17:25	H389	That in two hundred year, it ne'r prov'd good.
HUMOUR21:32	H60	Here's Sister Ruddy, worth the other two,
HUMOUR29:2	H355	He that with two assaylents hath to do,
HUMOUR30:32	H424	These two in one cannot have residence.
HUMOUR35:8	H604	Two hot, two moist, two cold, two dry here be,
AGES~~41:1~~	H221	Sometimes the loathsome {two fold} Pox, my face {me sore}
MASSYR55:1	H67	Fifty two years he reign'd (as we are told)
MASSYR55:2	H68	The world then was two thousand nineteen old.
MASSYR56:40	H146	Forty two years she reign'd, and then she dy'd,
MASSYR58:13	H198	These two rul'd *Media* and *Babylon,*
MASSYR59:18	H242	Who there incamp'd two years, for little end,
MASSYR61:3	H308	That those two made but one, we need not doubt:
MPERS68:36	H622	with him about two years.
MPERS69:10	H632	And so unites two Kingdoms, without strife;
MPERS70:39	H710	Two *Sythian* bowes, a sword, and target round;
MPERS71:1	H713	Three Daughters, and two Sons, he left behind,
MPERS~~71:3~~	H715	Thirty two years in all this Prince
MPERS72:34	H778	At last, two of his Officers he hears,
MPERS73:26	H811	And two of these great Peers, in place {Field} lay dead:
MPERS74:22	H845	He two of *Cyrus* Daughters now {then} doth wed,
MPERS74:23	H846	Two of his Neeces takes to nuptiall bed;
MPERS76:6	H904	Which two then to assaile, his {royal} Camp was bold:
MPERS78:16	H997	Of two and twenty thousand Gallies meet,
MPERS79:38	H1064	Two dayes and nights a fight they there maintain,
MPERS80:12	H1079	Amongst the rest, two brothers he lost there;
MPERS80:41	H1108	Two mighty Rocks, brake from *Parnassus* Hil,
MPERS85:2	H1278	And dy'd the two and fortieth of his reign.
MPERS85:10	H1286	These two lewd {first} sons, are by hystorians thought,
MPERS85:36	H1312	Two sons she bore, the youngest *Cyrus* nam'd,
MPERS91:21	H1529	The two Queens, by his means, 'gin {seem} to abate
MPERS~~91:36~~	H1550	Two of his brothers in his Fathers dayes
MGREC94:19	H1657	Thirty two thousand made up his foot force,
MGREC~~95:25~~	H1704	Goes {Runs} after too {two}, and leaves all to disaster.
MGREC97:6	H1767	Two hundred thousand men that day were slaine,
MGREC97:22	H1783	Two hundred eighty *Greeks* he lost in fight,
MGREC98:19	H1821	Two thousand of the cheif he crucifi'd,

MGREC100:25	H1909	Two hundred fifty thousand by account,
MGREC101:23	H1948	The Firmament two Suns cannot contain;
MGREC101:24	H1949	Two Monarchies on Earth cannot abide,
MGREC101:25	H1950	Nor yet two Monarchs in one World reside;
MGREC108:23	H2239	Repelling these two marks of honour got,
MGREC110:38	H2342	Two Cities built, his fame {name} might there abide;
MGREC120:37	H2774	Two years and more since, Natures debt he paid,
MGREC121:40	H2822	Two battells now he fought, and had {of both} the best,
MGREC122:39	H2860	Two Sons of *Alexander,* and the rest,
MGREC124:17	H2924	Whilst hot in wars these two in *Greece* remaine,
MGREC128:9	H3082	And in despight of their two famous Kings,
MGREC130:31	H3181	Two other children by *Olympias* kill'd,
MGREC131:14	H3206	This day twixt these two foes {Kings} ends all the strife,
MGREC131:36	H3228	Two sons he left, born of King *Philips* daughter,
MGREC132:33	H3280	Of the old Heroes, now but two remaine,
MGREC134:23	H3354	The seventy two interpreters did seek,
MROMAN138:11	H3501	Thirty two years doth *Tullus* reigne, then dye,
DIALOG143:21	H90	Famine, and Plague, two sisters of the Sword,
DIALOG146:10	H198	One battell, two or three I might abide,
SIDNEY152:19	H88	For to conclude my poem two lines they daigne,
FLESH175:4	H4	I heard two sisters reason on
1HUSB180:23	H2	If ever two were one, then surely we.
1LETTER181:5	H3	If two be one, as surely thou and I,
3LETTER183:28	H30	And like two Turtles roost within one house,
1SIMON188:6	H7	Three flours, two scarcely blown, the last i'th' bud,
MEDDM199:27	Hp278	of pestilence, and the arrow of a slanderous tongue, the two
MEDDM199:28	Hp278	the body, the last the good name the two former leaue a man

'TWOULD (1) [it would]

MGREC131:8	H3198	'Twould be an endlesse story to relate

TY'D (1) [tied] See also TYED

MGREC107:36	H2211	On these, together ty'd, in six dayes space,

TYBER (2)

MROMAN138:18	H3508	A stately Bridge he over *Tyber* made,
MROMAN138:21	H3511	Close by the mouth of famous *Tyber* flood:

TYBURN (1)

DIALOG147:23	H247	And sturdy *Tyburn* loaded till it crack,

TYDINGS (1) [tidings]

MERCY188:30	H16	But ah too soon those heavy tydings fly,

TYE (1) [tie]

TDUDLEY165:10	H12	Nor is't Relation near my hand shall tye;

TYED (1) [tied] See also TY'D

MEDDM206:31	Hp288	Souerainty of god, who will not be tyed to time nor place, nor

TYES (1) [ties, pl.]

BIRTH179:29	H5	No tyes so strong, no friends so clear and sweet,

TYES (1) v. [ties]

HUMOUR34:16	H571	With {Which} joynt to joynt, the entire body tyes;

TYGER (1) [tiger]

ELEMEN14:40	H282	Thy Bear, thy Tyger, and thy Lyon stout,

TYGRANES (1)

MGREC134:13	H3344	That {Then} *Tygranes* the great *Armenian* King,

TYGRIS (1) n.
MASSYR~~59:20~~ H244 For by the rain, was *Tygris* so o'reflown,
TYGRIS (1) [poss.]
MGREC110:6 H2306 On *Tygris* side, here now he had not been;
TYRANNIZE (1) See also TYTANNIZE
MGREC~~117:13~~ H2620 The great Horn broke, the lesse did tytannize; {tyrannize}
TYRANNY (2)
MPERS73:34 H819 So late crusht by their Princes Tyranny;
MPERS74:16 H839 Let tyranny now with {dead} *Cambyses* dye.
TYRANT (3)
MASSYR54:28 H55 This Tyrant did his neighbours all oppresse,
DIALOG143:5 ~~H73~~ No Crook-backt Tyrant, now usurps the Seat,
DIALOG~~143:8~~ H76 No crafty Tyrant now usurps the Seat,
TYRANTS (3) [pl.]
HUMOUR34:32 H587 If Tyrants be the best, i'le it allow;
MPERS73:38 H823 But {That} better one, then many Tyrants reigne.
MYCHILD218:12 Hp244 All Ages maugre all yᵉ heathen Tyrants + all of the Enemyes
TYRE (2)
MASSYR64:26 H450 And unto wealthy *Tyre* with {in} hast repaire.
MGREC97:38 H1799 Now {Next} *Alexander* unto *Tyre* doth goe,
TYRIAN (1)
MASSYR65:10 H475 When in the *Tyrian* wars, the {this} King was hot,
TYRIANS (2) [pl.]
MGREC97:40 H1801 To gain his love, the *Tyrians* do intend,
MGREC98:22 H1824 And thus the *Tyrians* for mistrust were paid,
TYRIANS (1) [pl.; poss.]
MPERS79:14 H1040 Seven thousand Gallies chain'd, by *Tyrians* skil,
TYSSAPHERN (2)
MPERS89:33 H1467 As *Tyssaphern,* knowing his Masters minde,
MPERS89:41 H1475 But *Tyssaphern* did what he could devise,
TYSSAPHERNE (1)
MPERS90:35 H1502 That *Tyssapherne* must be Vice-roy no more;
TYSSAPHERNES (1)
MPERS90:33 ~~H1500~~ But *Tyssaphernes* with his Army fled;
TYTANNIZE (1) [tyrannize]
MGREC117:13 H2620 The great Horn broke, the lesse did tytannize;
TYTHRAUSTES (2)
MPERS90:36 H1503 *Tythraustes* now {then} is placed in his stead,
MPERS90:40 H1507 *Tythraustes* trusts more to his wit then Arms,

U

UGLY (2)
AGES39:7   H150   And then the worst, in a more ugly hue;
AGES41:2   H222   With ugly {outward} marks of his eternal {inward loathsome}
ULCER See VLCER
ULTRA (1)
MGREC136:8   H3421   *Ne sutor ultra crepidum,* may write.
ULYSSES (1)
MGREC117:21   H2628   But by *Ulysses,* having lost his sight,
UNAWARES (2) See also UN'WARES
MGREC128:30   H3103   And comming unawares put him to flight;
CONTEM171:15   H119   So unawares comes on perpetual night,
UNBELIEF See VNBELEIF
UNBLEMISH'D (1) [unblemished]
MASSYR64:14   H438   Children of Royal bloud, unblemish'd youth;
UNBORN (1)
MGREC118:4   H2651   And th' unborn babe of *Roxan* be proclaim'd;
UNBRIDLED (1)
HUMOUR25:3   H192   As thy unbridled, barb'rous Choler yeelds. {breeds:}
UNCAPABLE See VNCAPABLE
UNCERTAIN (1)
ELEMEN16:17   H340   Th' uncertain cause, of certain ebbs and flowes;
UNCERTAINTY See VNCERTAINTY
UNCHAST (1)
MASSYR55:31   H97   As of {on} her life, licentious, and unchast.
UNCHEERFUL (1)
HUMOUR28:2   H314   With her uncheerful visage, swarth and wan;
UNCIRCUMCIS'D (1) [uncircumcised] See also VNCIRCUMSCISED
DAVID158:31   H11   Lest the uncircumcis'd lift up their voyce:
UNCKLE (1) [uncle] See also VNCLE
MASSYR65:28   H493   His Unckle, he established in's place,
UNCLE (1) See also UNCKLE, VNCLE
MPERS83:10   H1198   At last his Uncle, did his death conspire,
UNCLEAN (1)
FLESH177:26   H107   For things unclean there shall not be:
UNCLES (1) [poss.]
MASSYR67:27   H573   Who with his own, and Uncles power anon;
UNCONSTANCY (1) [inconstancy]
HUMOUR~~31:27~~   H460   Constant in nothing, but inconstancy {unconstancy},
UNCOUTHLY (1)
3LETTER183:8   H10   (On withered bough) most uncouthly bemoan

UNCOVERED (1)
MGREC118:15　H2662　Untoucht, uncovered, slighted, and neglected,

UNDAUNTED (1)
MGREC~~110:18~~　H2321　But him a Prince of an undaunted mind

UNDERGO See VNDERGO

UNDERSTAND (1) See also VNDERSTAND
MGREC131:32　H3224　Who did no sooner understand the same,

UNDERSTANDING (1) See also VNDERSTANDING
DUBART153:18　H22　　He feeds his eyes, but understanding lacks,

UNDERTAKE See VNTERTAKE

UNDESERV'D (1) [undeserved]
MASSYR~~55:32~~　H98　　That undeserv'd, they blur'd her name and fame

UNDONE (5)
AGES44:35　　H368　And *Philip,* and *Albertus,* half undone;
MASSYR68:13　H599　As thus amort {dead, alive} he sits, as all {one} undone:
MPERS72:14　　H762　She with her fruit was {were} both at once undone,
MGREC120:16　H2751　Was to give way, himself might be undone;
MGREC131:27　H3219　Is for this fresh young Lady half {quite} undone,

UNEQUALLY (1)
HUMOUR26:41　H271　But thou wilt say, I deale unequally,

UNEXHAUSTED See VNEXHAUSTED

UNEXPECTED (1)
MASSYR65:18　H483　And unexpected findes the feeble Prince,

UNEXPRESSED (1)
MPERS83:1　　H1189　Tels as he could, his unexpressed woes,

UNFEIGNEDLY See VNFEIGNEDLY

UNFIT (2)
SIDNEY149:25　~~H23~~　I praise thee not for this, it is unfit,
AUTHOR177:38　H10　I cast thee by as one unfit for light,

UNFIXT (1)
ELEMEN14:10　~~H252~~　As *Stibium* and unfixt *Mercury:*

UNFOLD (1)
MASSYR68:5　　H591　This language strange, to read, and to unfold;

UNFORTUNATE (1)
3LETTER183:10 H12　Whose loss hath made her so unfortunate:

UNFRIENDLY (1)
HUMOUR24:17　H166　Or honestie such ties, unfriendly break?

UNGRATE (1) [ingrate]
AGES37:17　　H79　When wretched I (ungrate) {ingrate} had done the wrong.

UNHAPPILY (1)
MASSYR67:16　H562　Wars with the *Medes,* unhappily he wag'd,

UNHAPPY (1)
MASSYR66:28　H534　And his unhappy change with grief fore-tel;

UNHEARD (1)
MGREC105:11　H2104　But this unheard of injury {treachery} much more;

UNICORNE (1) [unicorn]
ELEMEN12:19　H179　The Behemoth, and rare found Unicorne,

UNITE (2) See also VNITE
MASSYR59:4　　H228　Both sides their hearts, their hands, their {&} bands unite,
DIALOG143:9　　H78　No need of *Tudor,* Roses to unite,

UNITED (1)
QELIZ156:28   H55   The States united now her fame doe sing;
UNITES (1)
MPERS69:10   H632   And so unites two Kingdoms, without strife;
UNITY (2)
FATHER6:1   H35   How divers natures, make one unity.
HUMOUR35:9   H605   A golden Ring, the Posey, *Unity:*
UNIVERSALL (3) [universal]
MPERS90:25   H1492 Might win {gain} the universall Monarchy;
MGREC123:5   H2867 For universall Monarchy he hopes;
MGREC128:22 H3095 Before he weare the universall Crown;
UNIVERSE (2)
MPERS82:20   H1167 That Army, which did fright the Universe;
MGREC93:25   H1622 The universe, scarce bounds {bound} his large {proud} vast
UNIVERSES (1) [poss.]
CONTEM168:19 H27   Soul of this world, this Universes Eye,
UNJUST (2)
MGREC113:37 H2464 Had his reward most cruel, and unjust.
MGREC127:22 H3052 *Antigonus,* then takes {who took} his life unjust,
UNJUSTLY (6)
PROLOG7:30   H41   It is but vaine, unjustly to wage war,
HUMOUR27:13 H̶2̶8̶4̶   Thou do'st unjustly claime, her property,
MPERS7̶2̶:̶3̶   H755   Unjustly caus'd his brother to be slain.
MGREC128:19 H3092 Had {The} valiant *Eumenes* unjustly slaine,
DIALOG143:2   H71   French *Lewis* {Jews} unjustly to the Crown to bring;
DIALOG148:10 H275   Of what unjustly once she poll'd from thee,
UNKIND (1)
AGES40:6   H187   Sometimes I cheat (unkind) a female Heir,
UNKINGLY (2)
MPERS88:39   H1432 And for a while unkingly there he lyes;
MGREC114:27 H2497 Of this unkingly deed, {act} doth *Seneca*
UNKNOWN (5) See also VNKNOWN
ELEMEN19:30 H̶4̶7̶2̶   Some have I forc'd, to gaine an unknown shoare;
MPERS76:17   H915   Or fly like birds, in unknown wayes full quick;
CONTEM170:9   H82   Bewails his unknown hap, and fate forlorn;
CONTEM172:33 H166   To unknown coasts to give a visitation,
FLESH175:37   H37   For things unknown, only in mind.
UNLESS (1) See also UNLESSE, VNLESS
HUMOUR2̶7̶:̶1̶2̶ H283   Unless as heat, it be thy faculty,
UNLESSE (8) [unless] See also VNLESS
ELEMEN9:21   H55   In chymestry, unlesse I help you Stil,
ELEMEN12:14 H174   Unlesse thou prove a better friend to me;
ELEMEN16:29 H352   Unlesse I ease his toyle, and doe transport,
HUMOUR21:34 H62   Unlesse to court, and claw, and {to} dice, and drink,
HUMOUR35:3   H599   Unlesse we 'gree all fals into confusion.
MGREC118:19 H2666 And yet not so content, unlesse that he
DIALOG141:23 H22   Unlesse some Cordial thou fetch from high,
DIALOG143:24 H93   Unlesse thy {our} teares prevent it speedily.
UNLIKE (2)
MASSYR5̶7̶:̶1̶6̶ H163   But this is farre unlike, he being Son
MASSYR67:12 H558   Unlike his father, *Evilmerodach,*

UNLIMITED (1)
MGREC101:20 H1945 For his unlimited prosperity,
UNLOOKT (1)
MASSYR59:8 H232 But all {And now} surpris'd, by this unlookt for fright,
UNLOOSE (1)
SEASONS47:7 H23 For to {He might} unloose his Winter-locked soyl;
UNMADE (1)
CONTEM172:3 H140 And when unmade, so ever shall they lye,
UNMANLY (1)
QELIZ156:17 H44 Since time was time, and man unmanly man,
UNMOULDED (2)
AGES45:19 ~~H401~~ I've seen a land unmoulded with great paine.
AGES~~45:22~~ H407 I've seen a state unmoulded, rent in twain,
UNMOV'D (1) [unmoved]
DIALOG144:38 H146 I saw (unmov'd) her Armies foil'd and fled,
UNPARALEL'D (1) [unparalleled] See also UNPARALLED, UNPARALLELD, UNPARRALELL'D
MGREC116:14 H2580 Unparalel'd, for ever had remain'd;
UNPARALLED (1) [unparalleled] See also UNPARALEL'D, UNPARALLELD, UNPARRALELL'D
MGREC97:16 H1777 For though their beauties were unparalled
UNPARALLELD (1) [unparalleled] See also UNPARALEL'D, UNPARALLED, UNPARRALELL'D
MGREC126:30 H3021 Whose fury yet unparalleld {scarcely parallel'd} hath been;
UNPARDONABLE (1)
MGREC112:35 H2421 But *Philotas,* his unpardonable crime,
UNPARRALELL'D (1) [unparalleled] See also UNPARALEL'D, UNPARALLED, UNPARALLELD
QELIZ158:17 H126 Here lies the envy'd, yet unparralell'd Prince,
UNPITIED (1)
DIALOG146:22 H208 Their wofull mother's tears unpitied.
UNPROFITABLE (1)
SIDNEY149:36 ~~H23~~ But leaves the rest, as most unprofitable:
UNREAD See VNREAD
UNREFINED (1)
PROLOG8:1 H49 This meane and unrefined stuffe {ure} of mine,
UNREGENERATE (1)
FLESH175:38 H38 *Spir.* Be still thou unregenerate part,
UNRESISTED (1)
MASSYR64:19 H443 The next year he, with unresisted hand,
UNRIPE (1)
SEASONS~~51:15~~ H189 Boughs full of leaves, or fruits, but raw, and {unripe or} green,
UNSAFE (1)
HUMOUR34:29 H584 Thy judgement is unsafe, thy fancy little,
UNSAY See VNSAY
UNSEARHABLE See VNSEARCHABLE
UNSEEN See VNSEEN
UNSHEATHES (1)
MPERS72:40 H786 Unsheathes, as he his horse mounted on high,
UNSPOTTED (1)
DDUDLEY167:10H7 *A worthy Matron of unspotted life,*
UNSTABLE (2)
HUMOUR31:29 H462 Unstable is the one, so is {and} the other.
AGES35:20 H6 Unstable, supple, moist, and cold's his Naure.

UNSTAY'D (1) [unstayed]
MGREC123:16   H2880   Fearing his Son *Cassander* was unstay'd,
UNTAINT (1)
HUMOUR27:23   H294   When 'tis untaint, pure, and most genuine
UNTAMED (1)
QELIZ156:33   H60   The rude untamed *Irish* she did quell,
UNTHANKFULNESS See VNTHANKFULNESS
UNTHRONE (1)
MASSYR63:8   H393   And {As} *Belosus,* first, his {Soveraign} did unthrone,
UNTIE See UNTYE
UNTIED See UNTY'D
UNTIL (8) See also TIL, TILL, UNTILL
AGES40:9   H190   Until her freinds, treasure, and honour's gone.
AGES40:11   H192   Until mine own be gone, my wit, and wealth;
SEASONS50:33   H167   Until his head be gray, and strength be gone,
SEASONS52:39   H254   Until by's heat he drives {drive} all cold away.
MASSYR57:23   ~~H170~~   Until that potent Empire did decay.
MASSYR62:37   H382   Until the thundring hand of heaven he felt,
MASSYR63:14   H399   Until his Grand-childe made her bow the knee;
VERSES184:11   H15   Yet paying is not payd until I dye.
UNTILL (8) [until] See also TIL, TILL
ELEMEN17:11   H375   Untill straight {proud} *Gibralter,* did make them twaine,
AGES~~45:22~~   H404   To see them swill in blood untill they burst.
SEASONS51:29   H205   There rests, untill the Sun give it a birth:
MGREC126:10   H3001   Untill the Famine growes exceeding strong.
MGREC130:10   H3165   Untill he further know his Masters will;
QELIZ158:4   H113   Untill the heavens great revolution:
FLESH176:3   H43   Untill I see thee laid in th' dust.
CHILDRN185:14   H40   Untill they'r grown, then as the rest,
UNTIMELY (3)
MGREC105:29   H2122   And not by Traitors hands untimely dye.
MGREC113:38   H2465   The next that {who} in untimely death had part,
SIDNEY149:3   H3   Sir *Philip Sidney,* who was untimely
UNTOUCHT (1)
MGREC118:15   H2662   Untoucht, uncovered, slighted, and neglected,
UNTOWARD (1) See also VNTOWARD
CHILDRN185:24   H50   Some untoward boy at them do fling.
UNTY'D (1) [untied]
BIRTH180:3   H13   That when that knot's unty'd that made us one,
UNTYE (1) [untie]
PROLOG7:25   H37   But this weake knot they will full soone untye,
UN'WARES (1) [unawares]
CHILDRN185:22   H48   They fall un'wares in Fowlers snare:
UNWARILY (2)
MASSYR58:7   H192   At last {It chanc'd} *Arbaces* brave, unwarily,
MPERS77:39   H980   And by this choyce, unwarily posts on,
UNWEARIED (1)
SEASONS52:27   H242   And North-ward his unwearied race {Course} doth run;
UNWILLING (2) See also VNWILLING
MGREC115:40   H2559   And pardon craves, for his unwilling stay,
MGREC126:21   ~~H3012~~   But he unwilling longer there to stay,

UNWILLINGLY (1)
MROMAN138:23 H3513   Then unto death unwillingly gives place.
UNWISE (1)
SIDNEY151:33   H75   Like unwise *Phaeton* his ill guided sonne,
UNWISELY (2)
MGREC107:14   H2189   And thus unwisely, in one raging {mading} fume,
MGREC114:28   H2498   This censure passe, and not unwisely, say,
UNWORTHILY (3)
MGREC118:32   H2681   And {So} took his life unworthily that houre:
MROMAN139:14 H3542   *Sextus* his Son, doth {did} (most unworthily)
DIALOG144:25   H134   Unworthily, some backs whipt, and eares cropt;
UNWORTHINESS See VNWORTHYNES
UNWORTHY (4) See also VNWORTHY
AGES45:9   H391   I've seen base {unworthy} men, advanc'd to great degree
MASSYR58:22   H207   The rule from their unworthy Prince to take.
MASSYR67:21   H567   Unworthy *Belshazzar* next weares the Crown,
MGREC133:5   H3293   Yet by him had this most unworthy end.
UN-YOAK (1) [un-yoke]
MASSYR58:37   H220   Makes {With} promises, their necks for {now} to un-yoak,
UPHOLD (2) See also T'UPHOLD
ELEMEN16:33   H356   The flegmy constitution I uphold;
AGES44:13   H346   My ruin'd house, now falling can uphold;
UPPER (3)
MGREC124:14   H2921   his opponent still got {*Cassanders* forces had the} upper hand;
MGREC131:9   H3201   How some when down, straight got the upper hand
MGREC135:13   H3385   But yet the *Persian* got the upper hand;
UPRIGHT (2) See also VPRIGHT
SEASONS48:22 H75   One hangs his head, the other stands upright:
MASSYR54:22   H49   The walls one hundred sixty foot upright,
UPWARDS (1) See also VPWARDS
FATHER5:22   H23   That sinke, that swim, that fill, that upwards flye,
UPSHOT See VPSHOT
URE (2) [ore]
PROLOG8:1   H49   This meane and unrefined stuffe {ure} of mine,
ELEMEN9:24   H58   Ye Silver-smiths, your ure I do refine,
URG'D (1) [urged]
MPERS69:38   H665   That *Cressus* angry, urg'd him to express,
URGE (1)
ELEMEN12:25   H185   No, though the fawning dog did urge me sore
URGED (3) See also URG'D
AGES41:33   H249   If rich, I'm urged then to gather more.
AGES41:36   H252   If rich, I'm urged then to gather more,
DIALOG145:36   H185   Next the *Militia* they urged sore,
URN (1)
MGREC127:12   H3042   But leave him building, other in their urn,
US'D (7) [used] See also VSED
HUMOUR25:12   H201   And though thou'st us'd me, with opprobrious spight, {right:}
HUMOUR28:38   H350   No braggs i've us'd, t' your selves {to you} I dare appeale,
HUMOUR28:40   H352   I've us'd no bitternesse, nor taxt your name,
AGES36:16   H40   But neither us'd (as yet) for he was wise.
MPERS72:18   H766   This strange severity, one time {sometimes} he us'd,

MPERS73:39   H824   What arguments they us'd, I know not well,
MGREC97:18   H1779 Preserv'd their honour, us'd them courteously {bounteously},

USE (16) See also VSE
ELEMEN8:7   H5   Who was of greatest use and might'est force;
ELEMEN11:23 H143   In wealth and use I doe surpasse you all,
ELEMEN12:35 H195   Besides the use you have {of roots}, of Hearbs and Plants,
ELEMEN13:10 H211   If ought you have to use, to wear, to eate?
ELEMEN13:35 H236   But to such auditours 'twere of no use.
HUMOUR26:14 H244   Of greatest use, if reason do not erre:
HUMOUR28:17 H329   Likewise the Whey, some use I in the veines,
HUMOUR29:28 H379   To use thy sword, thy courage, and thy Art,
HUMOUR34:18 H573   Whose use and worth to tel, I must refrain;
MASSYR58:18 H203   Against their monstrous King to bring {use} their might,
MPERS74:35   H858   But strength {men} against those walls was {were} of no use;
MPERS81:25   H1133   Against the *Persians* they would use {bend} their force.
MGREC111:19 H2364 Depriv'd at once, the use of Saile, and Oare;
MGREC123:8   H2870 But vaine it was to use his policy,
MROMAN137:39 H3490 Who Martiall Discipline in use did bring;
DIALOG146:25 H211   For my relief now use thy utmost skill {do what there lyes in

USED (2) See also US'D, VSED
SEASONS51:5 H179   But its a precious juyce, when wel it's used.
MGREC100:40 H1924 Had used her, and hers, in every thing,

USEFUL (3)
HUMOUR25:15 H204   But useful, when a mixture can indure.
HUMOUR26:14 H244   More useful then the rest, don't reason erre;
HUMOUR30:27 H419   Likewise the useful spleen, though not the best,

USEFULL (1) [useful]
FATHER5:24   H25   The world, the usefull, hurtfull, and the good:

USEFULNESSE (1) [usefulness]
ELEMEN11:19 H139   As I: impart your usefulnesse, and force.

USES (2) [pl.]
SEASONS47:37 H49   Plants, and Flowers, {set and sown} for all delights, and uses;
SEASONS52:3   H219   This month is timber for all uses fell'd,

USHER (1) See also VSHER
CONTEM168:25 H32   The morn doth usher thee, with smiles & blushes,

USING (2)
MPERS70:33   H704   Using such taunting words as she thought good.
MGREC118:33 H2682 Using the name, and the command o'th' King

USUALLY See VSUALLY

USURP'D (2) [usurped]
MASSYR55:5   H71   His wife, *Semiramis,* usurp'd the throne,
DIALOG142:6   H35   By fraud, and {or} force, usurp'd thy flowring crown,

USURPER (1)
AGES45:22   H406   And an Usurper subt'ly mount thereon.

USURPS (2)
DIALOG143:5   H73   No Crook-backt Tyrant, now usurps the Seat,
DIALOG143:8   H76   No crafty Tyrant now usurps the Seat,

USURPT (1)
HUMOUR26:31 H261   But why the heart, should be usurpt by thee,

USURY (1)
DIALOG144:14 H124   With Usury, Extortion, and Oppression,

UTMOST (5) See also VTMOST
  MPERS87:28   H1380 To th' utmost parts of *Bactr'a,* and {for a time} there lye.
  MPERS89:26   H1460 And courtesie to th' utmost he pretends;
  MGREC111:9   H2354 To th' utmost shew'd, the glory of a King;
  MGREC121:7   H2785 Brave *Ptolomy* to th' utmost to oppose.
  DIALOG146:25 H211 For my relief now use thy utmost skill {do what there lyes in
UTTERANCE (1)
  DUBART153:30 H34 And {But} seeing utterance fayle his great desires,
UTTERED See VTTERED
UTTERLY (2)
  MPERS82:17   H1164 And there so utterly they wrack'd the same,
  MGREC135:14 H3386 The *Grecian,* them did utterly subdue,

V

VACANT (1)
  HUMOUR20:32 H24 Only she crav'd, to have a vacant space.
VACATION (1)
  MEDDM200:28 Hp279 vacation, when the Sun of righteoussnes shall appear those
VACUUM (1)
  ELEMEN18:28 H432 And with my selfe, I every vacuum fill.
VAGABOND (1)
  CONTEM170:35 H105 A Vagabond to Land of *Nod* he goes,
VAIL'D (1) [veiled]
  MGREC~~122:36~~ H2857 Their bonnets vail'd to him as chief Commander.
VAILE (1) n. [veil]
  MPERS75:20   H879 Yet o're thy glory we must cast this vaile,
VAILE (2) v. [veil]
  HUMOUR31:40 H473 But I rather with silence, vaile her shame;
  MEDDM202:23 Hp282 till he arise againe, so god doth somtime vaile his face but for
VAIN (24) See also VAINE'S
  ELEMEN18:7   H411 No world {earth}, thy witching trash, were all but vain.
  HUMOUR21:3   H31 Your selves would judge, but vain prolixity.
  HUMOUR33:6   H520 But 'twere as vain, to prove the {this} truth of mine,
  AGES39:34   H177 As vain as froth, as {or} vanity can be,
  AGES39:35   H178 That who would see vain man, may look on me:
  MPERS~~70:37~~ H708 Where some long after fought in vain for prize
  MPERS71:32   H746 But vain he found, to fight with Elements,
  MPERS72:2   H754 He after this, saw in a Vision {upon suspition vain},
  MPERS~~79:13~~ H1036 Then whips the sea, and with a mind most vain
  MPERS82:25   H1172 Some years by him in this vain suit was spent,
  MGRÉC116:32 H2598 Vain thirsting after immortality:
  MGREC124:20 H2927 But to the last {all in vain} he faithfull did abide;
  VANITY159:30 H2 As he said vanity, so vain say I,

VANITY159:31	H3	O vanity, O vain all under skie,
VANITY160:5	H15	More vain then all, that's but to grasp the wind.
VANITY160:20	H30	Such stoicks are but stocks, such teaching vain:
VANITY161:6	H57	{And all} The rest's {rest} but vanity, and vain we find.
CONTEM171:14	H118	In eating, drinking, sleeping, vain delight
CONTEM171:16	H120	And puts all pleasures vain unto eternal flight.
CONTEM173:34	H198	Man at the best a creature frail and vain,
CONTEM174:5	H205	And yet this sinfull creature, frail and vain,
FLESH176:33	H73	Nor fancies vain at which I snatch,
MYCHILD218:22	Hp244	somt. stuck with me, and more it would, by ye vain fooleries
BYNIGHT220:10	H10	In vain I did not seek or cry.

VAINE (10) [vain] See also VAINE'S

PROLOG7:30	H41	It is but vaine, unjustly to wage war,
AGES41:13	H232	Child-hood and youth is {are} vaine, yea {ye} vanity.
AGES42:26	H284	The early Cock, did summon but in vaine,
MPERS77:37	H978	Vaine *Xerxes* thinks his counsell hath most wit,
MPERS79:29	H1055	Which was not vaine, as it {after} soon appeared:
MGREC94:35	H1673	Ah! fond vaine man, whose pen was taught ere while,
MGREC123:8	H2870	But vaine it was to use his policy,
MGREC126:14	H3005	So succours, and endeavours proves but vaine:
MGREC136:3	H3416	Pardon to crave, for errours, is but vaine,
DAVID159:6	H21	The bow of *Jonathan* ne're turn'd in vaine,

VAINE-GLORY (1)

AGES43:17	H312	Sometimes vaine-glory is the only bait,

VAINE'S (1) [vaine is]

ELEMEN9:20	H54	Ye Paracelsians too, in vaine's your skil

VALE (3)

ELEMEN12:16	~~H176~~	Nor yet expatiate, in Temple vale;
ELEMEN~~12:16~~	H176	Nor will I stay, no not in *Tempe* Vale,
DISTEMP179:23	H11	My Anchor cast i'th' vale with safety.

VALES (1) [pl.]

ELEMEN16:3	H326	Earth, thou hast not more Countrys, Vales and Mounds,

VALIANT (16)

ELEMEN10:5	H80	The Valiant *Perseus* who *Medusa* slew,
HUMOUR29:31	H382	He is not truly valiant that's not wise;
AGES39:16	H159	The brave attempts of valiant Knights I prize,
MASSYR61:13	H318	*Resin* their valiant King, he also slew,
MPERS76:36	H934	Where an *Athenian* shew'd a valiant deed,
MPERS80:19	H1086	But they as valiant by {fortunate at} Sea, as Land,
MPERS84:16	H1252	This valiant Knight, whom they so much did owe;
MPERS89:39	H1473	The *Greeks,* having {seeing} their valiant Captaines slaine,
MPERS~~91:32~~	H1546	A King nor good, nor valiant, wise nor just
MGREC99:16	H1859	Where valiant *Betis,* doth defend {stoutly keeps} the town,
MGREC119:31	H2721	The valiant Chief, amidst his foes was slain,
MGREC122:10	H2835	He was both valiant, faithfull, patient, wise.
MGREC128:19	H3092	Had {The} valiant *Eumenes* unjustly slaine,
DIALOG142:8	H37	Or hath *Canutus,* that brave valiant *Dane,*
SIDNEY150:32	H59	Though *Sidney* dy'd, his valiant name should live;
DAVID159:14	H29	For valiant *Saul,* who on Mount *Gilbo* lyes;

VALIANTLY (1)

MGREC110:13	H2313	But {And} whilst the first he valiantly assayl'd,

VALIDITY (1)
  HUMOUR25:9   H198   Shal vanish as of no validity.
VALLEY (1)
  11MAYA226:18 Hp255 this valley of Baca many pools of water, That wch now I cheifly
VALLOUR (1) [valour]
  MPERS76:4   H902   Sharp wants, not swords, his vallour did oppose;
VALOUR (37)
  ELEMEN9:2   H36   To try your valour by, but it must feele
  ELEMEN12:27   H187   Whose trust, and valour I might here commend:
  HUMOUR21:30   H58   But valour, when comes that? from none of you;
  HUMOUR24:29   H178   No valour upon earth, but what thou hast.
  HUMOUR24:31   H180   And leave't to all, to judge where valour lyes.
  HUMOUR25:34   H223   Wilt thou this valour, manhood, courage cal:
  HUMOUR25:41   H230   Ile praise that fury, {prowess} valour, choler, heat.
  HUMOUR29:16   H368   Thy boasted valour stoutly's been repell'd,
  HUMOUR32:30   H504   Valour {Valours} I want, no Souldier am, 'tis true,
  AGES39:39   H182   My valour, in some beastly quarrel's spent;
  AGES44:12   H345   It's not my valour, honour, nor my gold,
  MASSYR55:22   H88   Taking a towne, such valour she did show,
  MASSYR58:29   H212   And either by his valour, or his fate,
  MPERS75:21   H880   Thy falshood, not thy {craft more then} valour did prevaile;
  MPERS78:29   H1010   O noble Queen, thy valour I commend,
  MPERS80:8   H1075   Where is the valour, of your antient State?
  MPERS88:19   H1412   Had not his too much valour put him by.
  MGREC94:4   H1638   But he their mutinies, {by valour} full soon doth {he} quell.
  MGREC95:20   H1699   For in that Peer, more valour did abide;
  MGREC96:36   H1756   That valour was more worth than Pearls, or gold,
  MGREC97:39   H1800   (His valour, and his victories they know)
  MGREC99:30   H1873   Sith valour, with Heroyicks is renown'd,
  MGREC100:16   H1900   to resist {man's there} his valour showes {Army to oppose};
  MGREC100:20   H1904   And now of valour both were {are} destitute;
  MGREC100:23   H1907   Men in shape, and name, of valour none,
  MGREC101:33   H1958   The Sun should witnesse of his valour be:
  MGREC107:38   H2213   Had *Bessus* had but valour to his wil,
  MGREC108:28   H2244   Where *Scithians* rude, his valour {army} doth oppose,
  MGREC109:39   H2298   Did more his valour then his Crown envie;
  MGREC113:36   H2463   Who for his prudence, valour, care, and trust,
  MGREC132:30   H3277   Renown'd for bounty, valour, clemency,
  MGREC134:26   H3357   That valour shew'd, vertue or excellence.
  DIALOG148:7   H272   There let thy name, thy fame, thy valour {glory} shine,
  SIDNEY150:9   H34   That sees not learning, valour, and morality,
  SIDNEY152:27 H96   *Learning, valour, beauty {Wisdome}, all in vertuous youth:*
  DUBART153:39 H43   Valour in War, in Peace good Husbandry.
  QELIZ157:11   H79   (Judging all valour, and all Majesty)
VALOURS (1)
  HUMOUR32:30   H504   Valour {Valours} I want, no Souldier am, 'tis true,
VALUE (2)
  ANNEB187:21   H11   To value things according to their price:
  2SIMON195:12 Hp271 though in value they fall short of all in this kinde yet I presume
VALUED (1)
  VANITY160:31 H41   With pearl and gold it shall not valued be:

VANISH (1)
HUMOUR25:9   H198   Shal vanish as of no validity.
VANISHETH (1)
QELIZ157:17   H85   How vanisheth her glory, wealth, and powers;
VANITIE (1) [vanity]
AGES44:10   H343   In every Age i've found much vanitie,
VANITIES (1) See also VANITYES
WHAT224:9   H9   Goe Worldlings to your Vanities
VANITY (22) See also VANITIE
HUMOUR25:4   H193   Thy rudenesse counts, good manners vanity,
AGES39:34   H177   As vain as froth, as {or} vanity can be,
AGES41:13   H232   Child-hood and youth is {are} vaine, yea {ye} vanity.
AGES43:38   H333   Man at his best estate is vanity.
AGES46:9   H440   But vanity, vexation of the minde;
VANITY159:29   H1   *Of the vanity of all worldly creatures {things}.*
VANITY159:30   H2   As he said vanity, so vain say I,
VANITY159:31   H3   O vanity, O vain all under skie,
VANITY160:15   H25   But vanity, vexation of the mind,
VANITY161:6   H57   {And all} The rest's {rest} but vanity, and vain we find.
FLESH175:7   H7   On worldly wealth and vanity;
MEDDM195:36   Hp272   vanity and lyes must needs lye down in the Bed of sorrow.
MEDDM199:21   Hp278   of both, and findes nothing but vanity and vexation of spirit
MEDDM203:2   Hp283   not the wisest of men, taught vs this lesson, that all is vanity
MEDDM203:5   Hp283   When we inioy them it is wth vanity and vexation, and if we
MEDDM203:6   Hp283   them then they are lesse then vanity & more then vexation, so
MEDDM203:7   Hp283   good cause often to repeat that sentence, vanity of vanityes
MEDDM203:8   Hp283   vanity of vanityes, all is vanity
MEDDM203:8   Hp283   vanity of vanityes, all is vanity
MYCHILD216:2   Hp241   loose from God, vanity & ye follyes of Youth take hold of me.
MYCHILD216:5   Hp241   my pride and Vanity and he was entreated of me, and again
HOUSE237:10   H40   Adeiu, Adeiu, All's Vanity.
VANITYES (3) [vanities]
TDUDLEY166:11 H53   Such vanityes he justly did despise.
MEDDM203:7   Hp283   good cause often to repeat that sentence, vanity of vanityes
MEDDM203:8   Hp283   vanity of vanityes, all is vanity
VANQUISH (1)
MGREC~~101:29~~   H1954   To force his Camp, so put {vanquish} them all to {by} flight;
VANQUISH'D (3) [vanquished]
MASSYR64:20   H444   Quite vanquish'd *Pharaoh Necho,* and {with} his Band;
MGREC134:16   H3347   Vanquish'd in fight, and took those kingdomes all,
DUBART155:8   H93   *But Nature vanquish'd Art, so* Bartas *dy'd,*
VAPOUR (1)
ELEMEN18:36   H440   Which may be done, by holding down my vapour.
VARIANCE (2)
HUMOUR20:21   H13   But 'mongst themselves they were at variance,
MGREC131:38   H3230   Which should succeed, at variance they fell,
VARIETY (2)
DAVID159:16   H31   And choyse delights, full of variety.
FLESH175:25   H25   True substance in variety?
VARIOUS (2)
AGES44:29   H362   In various times of state i've also been.

MEDDM202:2   Hp281   There is nothing admits of more admiration, then gods various
VARLET (1)
HUMOUR23:32   H142   That when a Varlet, struck him o're the side,
VASHTY (1)
MPERS84:5   H1233   Queen *Vashty* also feasts, but 'fore tis ended,
VASSAL (1)
MASSYR64:13   H437   His Vassal is, gives pledges for his truth,
VASSAL'S (1) [vassal is]
MASSYR64:18   H442   And in his Idols house the Vassal's {vessels} plac'd.
VASSALLS (1) [vassals]
DIALOG148:6   H271   To sack proud *Rome,* and all her vassalls rout:
VASSALS (1) [pl.]
MASSYR66:16   H522   All Vassals, at his hands, for grace must sue;
VAST (10)
ELEMEN16:6   H329   *Ionian, Balticke,* and the vast *Atlantique;*
MPERS78:4   H985   That the large {vast} *Persian* government surrounded;
MGREC93:25   H1622   universe, scarce bounds {bound} his large {proud} vast minde;
MGREC131:17   H3209   Of those dominions {vast Kindgomes} he did sometimes gain,
MGREC136:16   H3430   *The vast limbs of a mighty Monarchy.*
DUBART154:30 H75   Oh pregnant brain, Oh comprehension vast:
CONTEM172:28 H162   So may we press to that vast mansion, ever blest.
MEDDM202:4   Hp281   vast a disproportion that they scarcly seem made of the same
MYCHILD217:36 Hp243   soon tell me by the wondrovs workes that I see, the vast frame
HOUSE237:23   H53   A prise so vast as is vnknown
VAUNT (3)
HUMOUR20:12   H4   Ceasing to vaunt, their good, or threat their force.
HUMOUR23:4   H114   Of greasie paunch, and palled {bloated} cheeks, go vaunt,
SEASONS49:33 H126   Of him that was Shepherd, then King go vaunt.
VEANGENCE (1) [vengeance]
MEDDM204:19   Hp285   generation for takeing veangence on the house of Ahab and
VEGATIVE (2)
HUMOUR26:16   H246   His life now animal, from vegative?
CONTEM168:27 H34   Birds, insects, Animals with Vegative,
VEHEMENCY (1)
SEASONS49:13 H104   Whose vehemency, at length doth grow so great,
VEHEMENT (1)
HUMOUR27:3   H274   Besides the vehement heat, only there known,
VEHEMENTLY (1)
MGREC118:3   H2650   This choyse *Perdicas,* vehemently disclaim'd,
VEIL See VAILE
VEILED See VAIL'D
VEINAL (1)
HUMOUR26:26   H256   Through th' warme, blew conduits of my veinal rils;
VEINES (5) [veins]
ELEMEN13:37   H238   To ope those veines of Mine, audacious bold:
ELEMEN14:9   H251   Again, what veines of poyson in me lye;
ELEMEN15:14   H296   If I supply, his heart and veines rejoyce;
HUMOUR28:17   H329   Likewise the Whey, some use I in the veines,
SIDNEY149:34 H23   Which have the self-same blood yet in my veines;
VEINS (1) [pl.]
SIDNEY150:12 H43   Whilst English blood yet runs within my veins.

VEIW'D (1) [viewed]
MGREC94:21   H1659   Then on he march'd, in's way he veiw'd old *Troy;*

VENGEANCE (5) See also VEAGENCE
MPERS72:39   H785   But in the way, his sword just vengeance takes.
MGREC129:17   H3131   But yet at {the} last the hand of vengeance came,
MGREC130:24   H3179   Then vengeance just, against the same {them} t' expresse;
DIALOG144:30   H138   Their silent tongues to heaven did vengeance cry,
DIALOG148:12   H277   Execute toth' full {And on her pour} the vengeance threatned.

VENOME (1) [venom]
HUMOUR28:37   H349   Such venome lyes in words, though but a blast,

VENT (1)
HUMOUR24:13   H162   To vent my griefe, and wipe off my disgrace.

VENTER (1)
HUMOUR29:14   H367   But Choler, be thou cool'd, or chaf'd, i'le venter,

VENTRICLES (1) [pl.]
HUMOUR33:24   H538   Its ventricles, membranes, and wond'rous net,

VENTUR'D (1) [ventured]
DIALOG146:39   H225   With (ventur'd lives) for truths defence that stand,

VENTURE (2)
MPERS75:13   H874   But who dare venture such a stake for th' game;
MPERS81:8   H1116   Who for his sake, he knew, would venture far,

VENTURED (1) See also VENTUR'D
MPERS71:26   H740   Yea, in his pride, he ventured so farre,

VENUS (1) n.
MASSYR56:37   H143   Leaving the world, to *Venus,* soar'd above,

VENUS (3) [poss.]
MASSYR55:12   H78   Transform'd into a fish, by *Venus* will,
SIDNEY151:15   H69   And *Mars* himself was ta'n by *Venus* gin;
SIDNEY151:31   H75   As *Vulcan* is, of *Venus* native hue.

VERDUOUS (1) [verdurous]
SEASONS47:41   H53   Among the verduous Grasse hath Nature set,

VERIFIE (1) [verify]
ELEMEN15:17   H299   I call thine *Egypt,* this to verifie;

VERITY (5)
HUMOUR27:33   H304   My sweet complexion, proves the verity,
AGES42:7   H265   The lyars curb'd but nourisht verity.
MASSYR61:1   H306   But circumstance, doth prove the verity;
MPERS75:23   H880   Thou lov'dst thy Master more then verity.
MYCHILD217:32   Hp243   Many times hath Satan troubled me concerning ye verity of ye

VERSE (7)
PROLOG6:23   H8   My obscure Verse, {Lines} shal not so dim their worth.
MGREC122:3   H2826   I should but snip a story into verse, {bits}
SIDNEY150:38   H65   In sad, sweet verse, thou didst his death deplore;
DUBART153:14   H18   They shall be consecrated in my Verse,
QELIZ155:24   H15   'Mongst hundred Hecatombs of roaring Verse,
TDUDLEY165:6   H8   My mournfull mind, sore prest, in trembling verse
BIRTH180:17   H27   And if chance to thine eyes shall bring this verse,

VERSES (1) [pl.]
VERSES183:34   H1   *To her Father with some verses.*

VERTUE (3) [virtue]
HUMOUR31:35   H468   But I by vertue, do acquire the same.

AGES41:29	H246	But yet laid hold, on vertue seemingly,
MGREC134:26	H3357	That valour shew'd, vertue or excellence.

VERTUES (12) [virtues]

HUMOUR27:32	H303	My vertues hid, i've let you dimly see;
HUMOUR31:22	H455	My vertues yours surpasse, without compare:
AGES40:19	H200	For sure my suit more then my vertues shine;
MASSYR55:34	H100	But were her vertues, more, or lesse, or none;
MPERS91:16	H1524	All the peculiar vertues of a Prince:
MGREC103:23	H2034	Now makes this King, his vertues all to drown.
MGREC106:22	H2156	So daily of his vertues doth he lose;
MGREC112:17	H2403	His vertues dead, buried, and all {quite} forgot,
MGREC116:15	H2581	But with the world his vertues overcame,
SIDNEY149:28	H23	What doe thy vertues then? Oh, honours crown!
QELIZ158:18	H127	Whose living vertues speak (though dead long since)
2SIMON195:5	Hp271	vertues of their predecessors, but I am perswaded better

VERTUES (2) [virtue's]

AGES39:12	H155	With nurture trained up in vertues Schools,
MGREC114:31	H2501	Which vertues fame can ne're redeem by farre,

VERTUOUS (3) [virtuous]

AGES39:40	H182	Martial deeds I love not, 'cause they're vertuous,
MGREC114:18	H2488	Was vertuous, learned wise *Calisthines,*
SIDNEY152:27	H96	*Learning, valour, beauty {Wisdome}, all in vertuous youth:*

VERTUOUSLY (1) [virtuously]

MGREC106:37	H2171	His Captains, that were vertuously enclin'd,

VERY (11)

AGES46:22	H453	And I shal see, with these same very eyes,
MASSYR57:4	H151	Or else was his obedience very great,
MPERS91:22	H1536	(A Lady very wicked, but yet wise)
MGREC93:20	H1617	The very day of his nativity,
MEDDM198:9	Hp276	He that walks among briars and thorns will be very carefull,
MEDDM206:19	Hp287	Men that haue walked very extrauagantly, and at last bethink
MEDDM207:15	Hp288	find their shadow very comfortable, yet there is some worm or
MYCHILD218:33	Hp244	it were possible ye very elect should bee deceived. Behold
MYCHILD219:6	Hp245	written in mvch sicknesse and weaknes, and is very weakly
11MAYB228:25	Hp259	of January 'till May I haue been by fitts very ill & weak. The
11MAYB228:27	Hp259	y^t ever I had lasting 4 dayes, and ye weather being very hott

VESSEL (1) See also VESSELL, VESSELS

CONTEM174:7	H207	This weather-beaten vessel wrackt with pain,

VESSELL (1) [vessel]

28AUG226:1	Hp254	to make me a vessell fitt for his vse why should I not bare it

VESSELLS (3) [vessels]

ELEMEN19:28	H472	How many rich fraught vessells, have I split?
MASSYR67:33	H579	The holy vessells, thither brought long since,
MGREC109:16	H2275	The Vessells ready were, at his command;

VESSELS (3) [pl.]

MASSYR66:7	H513	The Temple's burnt, the Vessels had away,
MPERS78:21	H1002	Besides, the Vessels for this transportation,
MPERS80:15	H1082	Of Vessels small almost innumerable,

VESSELS (1) [vessel is]

MASSYR64:18	H442	And in his Idols house the Vassal's {vessels} plac'd.

VESTAL (1)
MASSYR55:10   H76   Others report, she was a vestal Nun,
VESTALL (2) [vestal]
MROMAN136:24 H3438   Whom vestall *Rhea,* into {to} th' world did bring
MROMAN137:32 H3483   And vestall Maids to keep the holy fire.
VESTMENTS (1) [pl.]
DIALOG147:12   H238   Let's bring *Baals* vestments out, {forth} to make a fire,
VESUVIUS (1)
ELEMEN10:29   H104   The choaking flames, that from *Vesuvius* flew
VEX (2)
AGES38:7   H110   I had no Suits at law, neighbours to vex.
MPERS84:23   H1259   His Grand-sires old disgrace, did vex him sore,
VEXATION (9)
AGES46:9   H440   But vanity, vexation of the minde;
VANITY160:15   H25   But vanity, vexation of the mind,
CONTEM174:2   H203   But day or night, within, without, vexation,
CONTEM174:9   H209   Nor all his losses, crosses and vexation,
MEDDM199:21   Hp278   of both, and findes nothing but vanity and vexation of spirit
MEDDM203:3   Hp283   vexation of spirit, yet our owne experience would soon haue
MEDDM203:5   Hp283   vexation? When we inioy them it is wth vanity and vexation,
MEDDM203:6   Hp283   then they are lesse then vanity & more then vexation, so that
VEXING (1)
AGES43:27   H322   The vexing Stone, in bladder and in reines,
VEXT (6)
MASSYR62:3   H348   He *Israelites,* more then his Father vext;
MPERS91:26   H1540   His sons soer vext him by disloyalty.
MGREC109:38   H2297   Great *Alexander* vext at this reply,
MGREC122:32   H2851   Who vext the Queen more then the other farre;
MGREC134:10   H3341   By Rebells and imposters daily vext;
PILGRIM210:20 H20   W^th sinns wth cares and sorrows vext
VICE (3)
MGREC101:21   H1946   Him boundlesse made, in vice, and cruelty;
MGREC112:18   H2404   But vice remaines, to his eternall blot.
VANITY160:11   H21   The first is prone to vice, the last to rage.
VICE-ROY (5) [viceroy]
MASSYR63:27   H412   A Vice-roy from her foe, she's glad t' accept,
MPERS85:20   H1296   *Amerges,* whom their {for} Vice-roy he ordain'd
MPERS90:35   H1502   That *Tyssapherne* must be Vice-roy no more;
MGREC95:18   H1697   Now newes, of *Memnons* death (the Kings Vice-roy)
MGREC120:24   H2761   The Acts of his Vice-royes, {Vice-Roy} now grown so high:
VICE-ROYES (1) [viceroys]
MGREC120:24   H2761   The Acts of his Vice-royes, {Vice-Roy} now grown so high:
VICTOR (5) See also VICTOR'S
MASSYR62:17   H362   Returns triumphant Victor to his soyl;
MASSYR65:8   H473   And though a Victor home his Army leads,
MGREC97:24   H1785   No sooner had this Captaine {Victor} won the field,
MGREC127:20   H3050   When victor oft had {he'd} been, and so might still,
FLESH176:23   H63   When I am victor over thee,
VICTORIE (2) [victory]
MGREC101:32   H1957   But he disdain'd to steale a victorie,
MGREC128:36   H3109   His lost repute with victorie had won;

VICTORIES (4) See also VICTORYES
MPERS90:22   H1489   The many victories themselves did gain,
MGREC97:39   H1800   (His valour, and his victories they know)
MGREC~~131:9~~   H3200   Their fights by Sea, their victories by land,
QELIZ156:22   H49   Her Victories in forraigne Coasts resound?

VICTORIOUS (4)
ELEMEN11:1   H117   The Army through my helpe victorious rose;
MASSYR64:16   H440   By the victorious King to *Babel's* prest;
MASSYR68:27   H613   That night victorious *Cyrus* took the town,
DIALOG142:10   H39   Or is't a *Norman,* whose victorious hand

VICTOR'S (1) [victor is]
MGREC~~110:18~~   H2319   The kingly Captive 'fore the Victor's brought,

VICTORS (1) [pl.]
MPERS89:4   H1438   Being Victors oft, now to their Camp they came;

VICTORY (9) See also VICTORIE
MASSYR59:7   H231   For victory obtain'd the other day;
MPERS80:11   H1078   This shamefull Victory cost *Xerxes* deare,
MPERS82:2   H1147   Was Victory, by Oracle fore-told:
MPERS82:8   H1155   The signall of their victory doth {did} rise;
MPERS88:18   H1411   So had he been, and got the victory,
MGREC95:4   H1683   This Victory did *Alexander* gain;
MGREC100:30   H1914   His numbers might the victory obtaine.
MGREC101:40   H1969   At *Arbela,* this victory gain'd,
MGREC121:26   H2808   Now comes the newes of a great victory,

VICTORY'S (1) [victory is]
SICKNES179:10   H30   the victory's mine I see,

VICTORYES (1) [victories]
MPERS~~90:21~~   H1488   The *Asiatiques,* cowardize detects; {victoryes}

VICTUALL (1) [victual]
MPERS76:19   H917   The King, seeing his men, and victuall spent;

VICTUALS (1) [victuals]
MPERS82:4   H1151   *Mardonius* finding victuals wast apace,

VIEW (6)
FATHER5:11   H12   Yet view thereof, did cause my thoughts to soare,
AGES39:6   H149   But what is best i'le first present to view,
TDUDLEY166:8   H50   Which all they have, and more still set to view,
CONTEM167:31   H8   Rapt were my sences at this delectable view.
AUTHOR177:33   H5   Who thee abroad, expos'd to publick view,
1LETTER181:16   H14   Then view those fruits which through thy heat I bore?

VIEW'D (1) [viewed] See also VEIW'D
MASSYR56:17   H123   From whence, Astrologers, oft view'd the skies.

VIEWING (4)
SEASONS49:32   H121   Viewing the Sun by day, the Moon by night,
MPERS~~69:38~~   H664   And viewing all, at all nought mov'd was he:
MPERS79:20   H1046   Long viewing them, thought it great happinesse,
DUBART153:33   H37   Thy profound Learning; viewing other while

VIEWS (1)
MGREC102:13   H1983   With greedy eyes, he views this City round,

VIGOR (2)
MEDDM199:9   Hp277   and sapless performances are simptoms of little spiritull vigor
MEDDM200:26   Hp279   to resume their former vigor and beavty in a more ample

VILD (1) [viled]
MGREC108:4　　H2220　This Malefactor vild, {vile} before the King,
VILE (4)
MGREC~~108:4~~　　H2220　This Malefactor vild, {vile} before the King,
MGREC130:4　　H3159　And vile {lewd} *Cassander* too, sticks not for shame;
MGREC130:18　H3173　As vile conspiratours that took {stopt} her breath,
MYSOUL225:3　H7　　　Thy body vile it shall bee chang'd,
VILED See **VIL'D**
VILELY (1)
DAVID159:2　　H17　　　The Shield of *Saul* was vilely cast away;
VILER (1)
MEDDM202:6　　Hp281　is capable of, and some again so base that they are Viler
VILLAGE (1)
MPERS88:38　　H1431　The King unto a country Village flyes,
VILLAINE-LIKE (1) [villain-like]
MPERS89:38　　H1472　And Villaine-like, there puts them {all} to the sword.
VILLANY (1)
MPERS82:22　　H1169　Yet ceases not to act his villany:
VILLIFIE (1) [villify]
HUMOUR29:18　H369　　What mov'd thee thus to villifie my name?
VINDICATE (1)
QELIZ157:35　　H103　　But she though dead, will vindicate our wrong.
VINDICATIVE (2)
AGES35:24　　　H10　　　Vindicative, and quarelsome dispos'd.
MGREC124:32　H2939　Was to this proud, vindicative *Cassander,*
VINE (2)
ELEMEN13:27　H228　　The Vine, the Olive, and the Figtree want:
MEDDM196:16　Hp273　that hath wrought hard in gods vine yard and hath born the
VINE-YARDS (1) [vineyards]
ELEMEN11:30　H150　　In vine-yards, orchards, gardens, and corne fields,
VINTAGE (1)
SEASONS51:2　　H176　　The Vintage now is ripe, the Grapes are prest,
VIOLATES (1)
MPERS89:37　　H1471　But violates his honour, and his word,
VIOLENCE (2)
MPERS75:5　　　H866　　This violence was done him by his Leige;
MEDDM208:31　Hp290　reversed the order of nature, quenched the violence of the fire,
VIOLET (2)
AGES35:30　　　H16　　　Of Dazy, Primrose, and {or} the Violet.
SEASONS47:40　H52　　　The Primrose pale, and azure Violet,
VIPERS (1) [poss.]
MGREC131:40　H3232　The eld'st enrag'd did play the vipers part,
VIRAGO (4)
MASSYR55:6　　H72　　　She like a brave Virago, play'd the rex,
MGREC96:27　　H1747　This brave Virago, to the King was mother;
MGREC135:2　　H3374　Then poysonous {His brave *Virago*} Aspes she sets unto {to}
QELIZ156:30　　H57　　　Unto our dread Virago, what they owe:
VIRGIL (1)
MASSYR63:31　H418　　Did neither *Homer, Hesiode, Virgil* sing;
VIRGIN (1)
CONTEM170:24 H95　　The Virgin Earth, of blood her first draught drinks

VIRGINS (1) [pl.]
DIALOG146:17   H203   My ravisht {weeping} virgins, and my young men slain,
VIRGO (1)
SEASONS50:13   H147   This month he keeps with *Virgo* for a space,
VIRTUE (1) See also VERTUE, VERTUES
BIRTH180:9   H19   If any worth or virtue were in me,
VIRTUES See VERTUES
VIRTUOUS (1) See also VERTUOUS
HUMOUR23:31   H141   Like our sixt *Henry,* that same worthy {virtuous} thing.
VIRTUOUSLY See VERTUOUSLY
VISAGE (2)
HUMOUR28:2   H314   With her uncheerful visage, swarth and wan;
AUTHOR178:1   H11   Thy Visage was so irksome in my sight;
VISET (1) [visit]
30SEPT227:18   Hp257   It pleased god to viset me wth my old Distemper of weaknes
VISION (1)
MPERS72:2   H754   He after this, saw in a Vision {upon suspition vain},
VISIT See VISET
VISITATION (1)
CONTEM172:33 H166   To unknown coasts to give a visitation,
VISITS (1)
MGREC111:34   H2379   Then visits *Cyrus* Sepulcher in's way,
VITAL (2)
HUMOUR26:6   H236   Which natural, vital, animal we name.
HUMOUR26:21   H251   And if vital spirits do flow from thee,
VITALL (1) [vital]
HUMOUR22:29   H98   The vitall spirits they're call'd, and wel they may,
VLCER (1) [ulcer]
MEDDM198:28   Hp277   finger may disquiet the whole body, but an vlcer w^thin destroys
VNBELEIF (2) [unbelief]
MEDDM206:34   Hp288   trembling, lest they through vnbeleif fall short of a promise, it
MEDDM206:36   Hp288   they abide not in vnbeleif, god is able to grafte them in, the
VNCAPABLE (1) [uncapable]
MEDDM199:11   Hp277   Iron till it be throughly heat is vncapable to be wrought, so god
VNCERTAINTY (1) [uncertainty]
MEDDM207:26   Hp289   that time will come, together, wth the vncertainty, how where,
VNCIRCUMSCISED (1) [uncircumcised]
MEDDM204:4   Hp284   the paw of the Beare will deliuer mee from this vncircumscised
VNCKLE (4) [uncle]
MPERS68:34   H620   *Cyrus, Darius* (being his Vnckle,
MPERS70:1   H672   (His Mothers Vnckle, stories doe evince:)
MPERS70:24   H695   He with his Vnckle *Daniel* sets on high,
MPERS72:16   H764   O hellish Husband, Brother, Vnckle, Sire,
VNDER (11) [under]
MEDDM197:14   Hp274   A low man, can goe vpright, vnder that door, wher a taller is
MEDDM198:17   Hp276   a hooke vnder all, Satan that great Angler hath his sundry
MEDDM198:21   Hp276   There is no new thing vnder ye Sun there is nothing that can
MEDDM198:34   Hp277   shall rather choose to be buried vnder rocks and mountains
MEDDM201:4   Hp280   they go vpright vnder them, but it matters not whether the load
MEDDM209:8   Hp291   the Canaanites, not destroy them, but put them vnder tribute,
MEDDM209:12   Hp291   them vnder slauery, so it is most certain that those that are

MEDDM209:15　Hp291　to perpetuall bondage vnder them vnlesse the great deliuerer,
MYCHILD216:34　Hp242　some sin I lay vnder wch God would haue reformed, or some
11MAYA226:19　Hp255　for is a contented thankfull h^t vnder my affliction & weaknes
HOUSE237:3　　H33　　Vnder thy roof no gvest shall sitt,

VNDERGO (1) [undergo]
MEDDM197:15　Hp274　a man of weak faith and mean abilities, may vndergo a Crosse

VNDERSTAND (1) [understand]
MED223:15　　Hp250　is my comfort, When I come into Heaven, I shall vnderstand

VNDERSTANDING (1) [understanding]
MYCHILD215:31　Hp241　as I grew to haue more vnderstanding, so ye more solace I

VNEXHAUSTED (1) [unexhausted]
MYSOUL225:7　　H11　　And drink at vnexhausted fovnt

VNFEIGNEDLY (1) [unfeignedly]
MEDDM203:27　Hp284　he must needs perish if he haue no remedy, will vnfeignedly

VNITE (1) [unite]
PILGRIM210:39　H39　　Then soule and body shall vnite

VNKNOWN (1) [unknown]
HOUSE237:23　　H53　　A prise so vast as is vnknown

VNLESSE (2) [unless]
MEDDM209:15　Hp291　to perpetuall bondage vnder them vnlesse the great deliuerer,
HOURS234:37　　H51　　Vnlesse thou help w^t can I doe

VNREAD (1) [unread]
TOCHILD215:2　H2　　This Book by Any yet vnread,

VNSAY (1) [unsay]
WHAT224:18　　H18　　Nor son of man to 'vnsay

VNSEARCHABLE (1) [unsearchable]
MEDDM207:1　　Hp288　god and say how vnsearchable are his wayes and his footsteps

VNSEEN (1) [unseen]
MYSOUL225:6　　H10　　To Blisse vnseen by Eye,

VNTERTAKE (1) [undertake]
MEDDM197:26　Hp275　He that will vntertake to climb vp a steep mountain wth a great

VNTHANKFULLNES (1) [unthankfulness]
2HUSB232:23　　H24　　Vnthankfullnes for mercyes past

VNTOWARD (1) [untoward]
MYCHILD217:7　Hp242　an vntoward child, that no longer then the rod has been on my

VNWILLING (1) [unwilling]
28AUG226:11　Hp254　vnwilling to come tho: by so rovgh a Messenger.

VNWORTHY (1) [unworthy]
MYSOUL225:14　H18　　For me, vnworthy me

VNWORTHYNES (1) [unworthiness]
MEDDM204:30　Hp285　let him look on his owne vnworthynes and that will make him

VOICE (5) See also VOYCE
DUBART154:8　　H53　　Had I an Angels voice, or *Barta's* pen,
3LETTER183:6　　H8　　His voice to hear, or person to discry.
13MAY226:33　　H9　　To him that heard my wailing Voice.
HOUSE236:16　　H8　　And piteovs shreiks of dreadfull voice.
HOUSE237:8　　H38　　Nor bridegroom's voice ere heard shall bee.

VOICES (1) [pl.]
CONTEM169:22　H62　　Shall Creatures abject, thus their voices raise?

VOID (4)
MGREC103:27　H2038　(Filled with madnesse, and quite void of reason)

QELIZ157:36	H104	Let such, as say our sex is void of reason,
CONTEM167:27	H4	The trees all richly clad, yet void of pride,
CHILDRN185:21	H47	Whilst pecking corn, and void of care

VOLLIES (1) [pl.]

| DUBART154:7 | H52 | Vollies of praises could I eccho then, |

VOLUME (1) See also VOLUMNE

| ELEMEN10:16 | H91 | My story to a Volume would amount: |

VOLUMES (2) [pl.]

| MGREC134:22 | H3353 | {And} With seven hundred thousand volumes fill'd, |
| QELIZ156:1 | H28 | No memories, nor volumes can containe, |

VOLUMNE (1) [volume]

| SIDNEY149:24 | H23 | That this one Volumne should exhaust your store. |

VOLUMNIOUS (1) [voluminous]

| HUMOUR28:30 | H342 | A most volumnious large memory, |

VOLUPTUOUS (1)

| MASSYR57:19 | H166 | He thus voluptuous, and given to ease; |

VOLUPTUOUSNESSE (2) [voluptuousness]

| MASSYR57:40 | H185 | Who wallowed in all voluptuousnesse, |
| MPERS91:23 | H1537 | Then in voluptuousnesse he leads his life, |

VOMITS (1) [pl.]

| AGES38:34 | H137 | Whence vomits, wormes, and flux have issued? |

VOTE (1)

| AGES37:38 | H100 | I gave no hand, nor vote, for death, or life: |

VOUCHSAFE (2)

| FATHER6:11 | H45 | Accept my best, my worst vouchsafe a grave. |
| MERCY189:12 | H33 | The Heavens vouchsafe she may so ever be. |

VOW (2)

| MGREC121:16 | H2797 | Who vow to make this captain recompence, |
| MGREC124:38 | H2945 | Did make him vow her servant to be seen. |

VOW'D (3) [vowed]

DUBART153:1	H5	In humble wise have vow'd their service long;
QELIZ155:17	H8	And so has {hath} vow'd, whilst there is world, or time;
FLESH175:40	H40	For I have vow'd (and so will doe)

VOWES (5) [vows]

MYCHILD216:35	Hp242	he would haue performed, and by his help I haue layd vowes
SAMUEL228:4	H5	The Son of prayers, of vowes, of teares
11MAYB228:34	Hp259	Conversation may speak that thy vowes are vpon me.
SON231:19	H31	O help me pay my Vowes O Lord
HOURS234:35	H49	To pay the vowes wch I doe owe

VOYCE (6) [voice]

ELEMEN12:21	H181	And my *Hyæna* (imitates mans voyce)
ELEMEN15:15	H297	If not, soon ends his life, as did his voyce.
AGES45:32	H422	{waking glad to hear} at the cocks clanging {shrill} voyce.
SEASONS50:23	H157	The Carter leads all home, with whistling voyce,
MASSYR66:10	H516	*Zim,* and *lim, {Jim}* lift up their shriking {scrieching} voyce;
DAVID158:31	H11	Lest the uncircumcis'd lift up their voyce:

VPHOLD (3) [uphold]

28AUG225:27	Hp254	times my faith weak likewise, the Lord was pleased to vphold
2HUSB232:15	H16	Vphold my heart in Thee O God
HOURS234:6	H20	Vphold my fainting soul

VPRIGHT (4) [upright]
MEDDM197:14   Hp274   A low man, can goe vpright, vnder that door, wher a taller is
MEDDM201:4   Hp280   they go vpright vnder them, but it matters not whether the load
SON231:26   H38   Ouʳ vpright walking may expresse.
REMB236:12   H27   In strict + vpright wayes.
VPSHOT (1) [upshot]
MEDDM206:36   Hp288   not in vnbeleif, god is able to grafte them in, the vpshot of
VPWARDS (1) [upwards]
MEDDM207:10   Hp288   as wings to help vs mount vpwards, they will Certainly proue
VSE (4) [use]
MEDDM203:33   Hp284   men can vse great importunity when they are in distresses and
MEDDM208:7   Hp289   you vse no other meanes to extinguish them so distance of
TOCHILD215:6   H6   Make vse of what I leaue in Loue
28AUG226:1   Hp254   me a vessell fitt for his vse why should I not bare it not only
VSED (1) [used] See also US'D
MEDDM201:26   Hp281   vsed for Contrary ends, the one holds fast, the other puts
VSHER (1) [usher]
MASSYR~~57:22~~   H169   We may with learned *Vsher* better say,
VSUALLY (3) [usually]
MEDDM195:34   Hp272   a negligent youth is vsually attended by an ignorant middle
MEDDM199:5   Hp277   Lightening doth vsually preceed thunder, and stormes raine,
MYCHILD216:23 Hp242   So vsually thvs it hath been wᵗʰ me that I haue no sooner
VTMOST (1) [utmost]
MEDDM209:13   Hp291   of god, and endeavour not to the vtmost to driue out
VTTERED (1) [uttered]
MEDDM201:9   Hp280   by many, but what he did not say, cannot (truly) be vttered
VULCAN (2)
ELEMEN9:14   H48   Though strong limb'd *Vulcan* forg'd it by his skill,
SIDNEY151:31   ~~H75~~   As *Vulcan* is, of *Venus* native hue.
VULGARS (1) [pl.]
AUTHOR178:10 H20   In this array, 'mongst Vulgars mayst thou roam,
VULTURES (1) [pl.]
VANITY160:26   H36   There is a path, no vultures eye hath seen.

W

WADE (1)
ELEMEN17:23   H387   Wherein not men, but mountaines seem'd to wade
WAFT (2)
MPERS87:26   H1378   So hir'd a fleet, to waft him ore the Maine,
MGREC107:31   H2206   To make them rafts, to waft them or'e the floud;
WAG'D (1) [waged]
MASSYR67:16   H562   Wars with the *Medes,* unhappily he wag'd,

WAGE (2)

PROLOG7:30   H41   It is but vaine, unjustly to wage war,

MROMAN138:1   H3491   War with the antient *Albans* he doth {did} wage,

WAGED See WAG'D

WAGES (1)

MPERS71:14   H728   He wages warre, the fifth year of his reign,

WAGONS (1) [pl.]

MGREC96:24   H1744   Then such a world of Wagons did appear,

WAIGHT (2) [weight]

MEDDM205:31   Hp286   in orchards, some trees soe fruitfull, that the waight of their

MEDDM205:36   Hp287   many times, the waight thereof impares both their bodys and

WAIGHTS (1) [weights]

MEDDM207:11   Hp288   and waights that will pull us lower downward

WAIGHTY (1) [weighty]

MEDDM201:3   Hp280   many times he imposes waighty burdens on their shoulders,

WAIL (1)

MROMAN140:5   H3568   Which none had cause to wail, nor I to boast.

WAILING (4)

AGES45:2   H380   Wailing his fate. & our own destinies.

DIALOG141:12   H11   What meanes this wailing tone, this mourning guise?

MERCY188:21   H7   And yet survive to sound this wailing tone;

13MAY226:33   H9   To him that heard my wailing Voice.

WAIN See WAYN

WAIT (11)

FATHER5:12   H13   My lowly pen, might wait upon those four,

AGES39:21   H164   Nor wait til good advice {success} our hopes do crown;

AGES40:4   H185   Sometimes lay wait to take a wealthy purse,

MPERS77:7   H946   For *Grecian* Maids ('tis said) to wait on her;

MPERS89:18   H1452   And there all wait his mercy, weaponlesse;

MGREC96:31   H1751   A thousand Mules, and Camells ready wait.

SIDNEY151:11   H69   To wait till she, her influence distill,

2LETTER182:21   H27   Which day by day long wait for thy arise,

3LETTER183:5   H7   Still wait with doubts, & hopes, and failing eye,

MEDDM203:18   Hp283   may plainly declare that we seek a citty aboue and wait all the

28AUG226:5   Hp254   Now I can wait, looking every day when my Sav^r shall call for

WAITED (2)

AGES36:12   H36   But as he went, death waited at his heeles.

SON230:23   H6   He's come for whom I waited long.

WAK'D (1) [waked]

MGREC101:19   H1944   Nor infamy had wak'd, when he had slept;

WAKEFUL (2)

SEASONS50:25   H159   His sweat, his toyl, his careful, wakeful nights,

DISTEMP179:16   H4   In tossing slumbers on my wakeful bed,

WAKEFULL (1) [wakeful]

AGES42:27   H285   My wakefull thoughts, up to my painefull gaine.

WAKEN'D (1) [wakened]

HOUSE236:15   H7   I waken'd was wth thundring nois

WAKING (2)

AGES45:32   H422   But do awake, {waking glad to hear} at the cocks clanging

BYNIGHT220:4   H5   My waking eyes were open kept

WAL (2) [wall]
HUMOUR21:25	H53	To storme a Breach, or scale a City wal?
MASSYR59:21	H245	Part of the {that stately} wal it level caus'd to lye; {was

WAL'D (1) [walled]
ELEMEN10:39	H114	Where's *Ninus* great wal'd Town, and *Troy* of old?

WALK (9)
MEDDM202:22	Hp282	although we may walk by his light, but when he is set, we
MEDDM202:27	Hp282	quite gone out of sight then must we needs walk in darknesse
MEDDM206:33	Hp288	alsoe teach the children of godly parents to walk wth feare
MEDDM208:32	Hp290	the water become firme footing, for peter to walk on, nay more
MYSOUL224:27	H3	Walk in his Law, and kisse his Rod
30SEPT227:32	Hp257	of distresse forget not to giue him thankes, but to walk more
THEART229:12	H14	For ever let me walk
HOURS233:31	H14	Where I doe kneel or walk.
REMB236:11	H26	And walk before thee as they ought,

WALKE (1) [walk]
HUMOUR24:27	H176	So walke thee til thou'rt cold, then let thee go.

WALKED (1)
MEDDM206:19	Hp287	Men that haue walked very extrauagantly, and at last bethink

WALKING (3)
MGREC113:26	H2453	He walking in his Garden, too and fro,
MYCHILD217:6	Hp242	circu¯spection in my walking after I haue been afflicted. I haue
SON231:26	H38	Ou^r vpright walking may expresse.

WALKS (1)
MEDDM198:9	Hp276	He that walks among briars and thorns will be very carefull,

WALL (7) See also WAL, WAL'S, WALL'S
MASSYR56:8	H114	About the wall, a ditch so deep and wide,
MASSYR67:39	H585	The King, upon the wall casting his eye,
MGREC124:36	H2943	When *Alexander* knockt his head to th' wall:
MROMAN~~136:34~~	H3448	For leaping o're the Walls {wall} with some disdaine;
MROMAN138:16	H3506	*Rome* he inlarg'd, new built againe the wall,
QELIZ156:25	H52	Her stately Troops advanc'd to *Lisbons* wall,
TDUDLEY166:37	H79	*To Truth a shield, to right a Wall,*

WALL'D (3) [walled]
MASSYR54:20	H47	Four hundred forty Furlongs, wall'd about,
MASSYR59:26	H250	Their strong wall'd town should suddenly be taken;
MPERS70:6	H677	Now trebble wall'd, and moated so about,

WALLOWED (1)
MASSYR57:40	H185	Who wallowed in all voluptuousnesse,

WALLOWETH (1)
MGREC103:24	H2035	He walloweth now, {That wallowing} in all licenciousnesse,

WALLOWING (1)
MGREC~~103:24~~	H2035	He walloweth now, {That wallowing} in all licenciousnesse,

WALL'S (1) [wall is]
ELEMEN9:6	H40	The adverse wall's not shak'd, the Mine's not blowne,

WALLS (18) [pl.] See also WALS
AGES39:17	H160	climbe Battlements, {scale walls and forts} rear'd to the skies;
MASSYR54:22	H49	The walls one hundred sixty foot upright,
MASSYR55:38	H104	The walls so strong, and curiously were {was} wrought;
MASSYR56:4	H110	Three hundred sixty foot, the walls in heighth:
MASSYR67:29	H575	The coward King, whose strength lay in his walls,

MPERS70:12	H683	And to the walls securely marches on,
MPERS74:35	H858	But strength {men} against those walls was {were} of no use;
MPERS75:37	H894	Built on, and prosper'd, till their walls did {house they} close;
MPERS~~84:12~~	H1247	Rebuilt those walls which long in rubbish lay,
MGREC99:20	H1863	And by these walls, so many men were slaine,
MGREC~~115:15~~	H2526	The battlements from off the walls are torne.
MROMAN136:34	H3448	For leaping o're the Walls {wall} with some disdaine;
MROMAN137:6	H3457	That wil within these strong built walls reside,
DIALOG144:35	H143	I saw sad *Germanie's* dismantled walls.
SIDNEY150:28	H55	Brave *Hector* by the walls of *Troy,* we see:
QELIZ157:6	H74	She plac'd {built} her glory but on *Babels* walls,
QELIZ157:14	H82	*Dido* first Foundresse of proud *Carthage* walls,
FLESH177:7	H88	The stately Walls both high and strong,

WAL'S (1) [wal is]

HUMOUR25:30	H219	To take the wal's a sin, of such {so} high rate,

WALS (6) [walls]

HUMOUR33:4	H518	Under *Troys* wals, ten years wil wast {wear} away,
SEASONS48:4	H57	In trees, and wals, in cities, and in fields;
MASSYR59:13	H237	The King pursu'd unto the City wals;
MASSYR59:15	H239	The wals, and gates, their course {hast} did terminate;
MASSYR65:37	H502	The wals so strong, that stood so long, now fall;
CONTEM170:36	H106	A City builds, that wals might him secure from foes.

WAN (1) See also wan's

HUMOUR28:2	H314	With her uncheerful visage, swarth and wan;

WAN (1) [won]

MGREC~~114:37~~	H2507	All Kingdoms, Countries, Provinces, he won, {wan}

WAN'S (1) [wan is]

HUMOUR22:15	H84	Her teeth wil chatter, dead and wan's her face,

WANDRING (1) [wandering]

CONTEM169:11	H52	In pathless paths I lead my wandring feet,

WANT (20)

ELEMEN13:27	H228	The Vine, the Olive, and the Figtree want:
ELEMEN15:21	H303	To meet with want, each woefull man bethinks.
ELEMEN16:26	H349	Did they but want my Ocean, and my Flood.
HUMOUR32:20	H494	Though wit I want, and anger I have lesse,
HUMOUR32:30	H504	Valour {Valours} I want, no Souldier am, 'tis true,
AGES40:29	H210	I want a {have no} heart {at} all this for to deplore.
MASSYR58:40	H223	To want no priviledge, Subjects should have,
MPERS79:7	H1029	I Rhethorick want, to poure out execration:
MPERS80:10	H1077	Alas, it is *Leonades* you want!
MPERS89:31	H1465	But Kings ne're want such as can serve their will,
MGREC115:5	H2516	Findes there the want of wise *Parmenio,*
DIALOG146:21	H207	The poore they want their pay, their children bread,
DIALOG148:2	H267	And Pursevants and Catchpoles want their pay,
DUBART153:28	H32	But findes too soone his want of Eloquence,
CHILDRN185:20	H46	And be surpriz'd for want of watch,
CHILDRN185:37	H63	Alas my birds, you wisdome want,
MEDDM198:13	Hp276	Want of prudence as well as piety hath brought men into great
MEDDM199:8	Hp277	Yellow leaues argue want of sap and gray haires want of
SON231:16	H28	Thro: want and Dangers manifold,

WANTED (3)

AGES41:40	H257	I wanted not my ready allegation.
MPERS~~79:13~~	H1039	Because they wanted skill the same to've staid.
CONTEM167:26	H3	When *Phœbus* wanted but one hour to bed,

WANTETH (2)

HUMOUR22:36	H105	But know'ts a foolish brain, that wanteth heat;
AGES40:13	H194	For he that loveth Wine, wanteth no woes;

WANTING (3)

HUMOUR28:31	H343	And nothing wanting but solidity.
HUMOUR34:23	H578	A foolish Brain (saith {quoth} Choler) wanting heat,
MGREC104:24	H2076	Who wanting means t' resist, these wrongs abides.

WANTON (2)

ELEMEN15:35	H317	As *Ægypts* wanton *Cleopatra* drunke.
SEASONS47:20	H36	The wanton frisking Kids, and soft fleec'd Lambs,

WANTONS (1) [pl.]

CONTEM173:2	H170	Look how the wantons frisk to tast the air,

WANTS (3) [pl.]

ELEMEN12:36	H196	with lesse cost, neare home, supplyes {supply} your wants.
MPERS76:4	H902	Sharp wants, not swords, his vallour did oppose;
DIALOG143:19	H88	For wants, sure some I feele, but more I feare,

WANTS (7) v.

ELEMEN15:10	H292	Man wants his bread, and wine, and pleasant fruits;
HUMOUR31:7	~~H440~~	Thou wants Philosophy, and yet discretion.
MPERS91:14	H1522	'Mongst these *Epimanondas* wants no fame;
MROMAN137:4	H3455	His City to replenish, men he wants,
DUBART154:6	H51	Through grief it wants a faculty to speak,
3LETTER182:36	H1	As loving Hind that (Hartless) wants her Deer,
MEDDM209:19	Hp291	Commoditys w^th^in it self, but what it wants, another shall

WAR (20) See also WARR, WARRE

PROLOG7:30	H41	It is but vaine, unjustly to wage war,
ELEMEN~~19:27~~	H472	Then in his long hot wars, {war} which *Millain* gain'd.
HUMOUR22:20	H89	Then yeeld to me, preheminence in War.
MASSYR55:20	H86	This gallant dame, unto the *Bactrian* war;
MASSYR57:9	H156	This fraud, in war, nor peace, at all appears;
MASSYR61:15	H320	*Iuda's* bad King occasioned this War,
MPERS70:4	H675	Next war, the restlesse *Cyrus* thought upon,
MPERS75:40	H897	*Darius* on the *Sythians* made a war,
MPERS76:20	H918	His {This} fruitlesse war, began late to repent;
MPERS81:9	H1117	(Chief instigater of this hopelesse {hapless} War;)
MPERS81:36	~~H1143~~	The *Beotian* Fields, of war, the seats,
MPERS83:29	H1217	He first, war with revolting *Ægypt* made.
MPERS84:30	H1266	T'*Thymistocles* he doth his {this} war commit,
MPERS~~85:7~~	H1283	Stil making war, till first had lost his life:
MPERS91:36	~~H1550~~	Was it because the *Grecians* now at war,
MGREC101:27	H1952	Prepares against tomorrow for the war;
MGREC110:4	H2304	And ninety Elephants for war did bring;
MGREC114:32	H2502	Nor all felicity, of his in war;
MROMAN138:1	H3491	War with the antient *Albans* he doth {did} wage,
DUBART153:39	H43	Valour in War, in Peace good Husbandry.

WARBLE (1)

CONTEM169:24	H64	Whilst I as mute, can warble forth no higher layes.

WARBLING (1)

CONTEM173:29 H194   And warbling out the old, begin anew,

WARDEN (1)

SEASONS51:10 H184   Of Medlar, Quince, of Warden, {Almonds, Quinces, Wardens}

WARDENS (1) [pl.]

SEASONS51:10 H184   of Warden, {Almonds, Quinces, Wardens} and of Peach,

WARFARE (1)

AGES44:15   H348   Now hath the power, Deaths Warfare, to discharge;

WARINESSE (1) [wariness]

HUMOUR29:30 H381   This warinesse count not for cowardise,

WAR-LIKE (1) [warlike]

DAVID159:28   H43   And war-like weapons perished away.

WARLIKE (5)

MASSYR54:25   H52   This stately seat of warlike *Ninus* stood.

MASSYR61:9   H314   *Belosus* dead, *Tiglath* his warlike Son

MGREC93:13   H1610   Shee to the rich *Molossians* {*Epirus* warlike} King, was

MGREC119:15   H2705   {Sometimes} By warlike *Philip,* and his conquering son.

SIDNEY151:16   H69   Then wonder lesse, if warlike *Philip* yield,

WARM (6) See also WARME

HUMOUR22:32 H101   The nerves should I not warm, soon would they freeze.

SEASONS51:37 H213   So farre remote, his glances warm not us;

SEASONS52:7   H222   This time warm cloaths, ful diet, and good fires,

SEASONS52:37 H252   And some warm glances from the Sun {his face} are felt,

MGREC122:16 H2841   To warm the {his} seat, was never her intent,

CHILDRN185:33 H59   Long did I keep you soft and warm,

WARM'D (2) [warmed]

AGES35:32   H18   Before the Sun hath throughly warm'd {heat} the clime.

MPERS87:11   H1367   And others to be warm'd by this new sun,

WARME (3) [warm]

ELEMEN9:18   H52   Your dainty {dayly} food, I wholsome make, I warme

HUMOUR26:26 H256   Through th' warme, blew conduits of my veinal rils;

SEASONS48:5   H58   The outside strong, the inside warme and neat.

WARMED See WARM'D

WARMER (1)

SEASONS47:32 H47   And with his warmer beams glanceth from thence

WARMTH (2)

ELEMEN9:34   H68   How doth his warmth refresh thy frozen backs, {back}

1LETTER181:12 H10   His warmth such frigid colds did cause to melt.

WARN (1)

MEDDM204:22   Hp285   wch should warn him, that doth any speciall seruice for god, to

WARNING (2)

HUMOUR34:40 H595   A warning good, hereafter i'le say lesse.

DIALOG144:34 H142   Nor took I warning by my neighbours falls,

WARNS (1)

MPERS80:33   H1100   And as a friend, warns him, what e're he doe,

WARR (1) [war]

CONTEM170:32 H102   Nor Male-factor ever felt like warr,

WARR'D (5) [warred]

MASSYR54:29   H56   Where e're he warr'd he had too good success,

MASSYR57:14   H161   Who warr'd with *Sodoms,* and *Gomorahs* King,

MASSYR61:39   H344   Thus *Tiglath* reign'd, and warr'd, twenty seven years,

MPERS76:8	H906	He warr'd defensive, not offensive, more;
MPERS80:27	H1094	Twice beaten thus by {at} Sea, he warr'd no more:

WARRE (6) [war]

MPERS71:14	H728	He wages warre, the fifth year of his reign,
MPERS73:1	H788	Which ends before begun, the *Persian* {his home-bred} Warre,
MPERS77:19	H960	He with his Crown, receive a double warre,
MGREC120:3	H2734	Now dy'd (about the end of th' *Lamian* warre)
MGREC127:41	~~H3072~~	{clear} what cause they {he} had to take up {make this} warre.
MGREC133:37	H3327	Who a long warre with *Egypts* King begun.

WARRED See WARR'D

WARRES (8) [wars] See also WARRS

ELEMEN10:19	H94	Ile here let passe, my Choler cause of warres,
MPERS92:34	H1592	Whose warres and losses we may better tell;
MGREC128:37	H3110	At last these Princes tired out with warres,
MGREC131:6	H3196	These Kings fall now afresh to {their} warres again,
MGREC133:33	H3323	Tells of their warres, their names, their riches, fates;
MGREC133:38	H3328	The affinities and warres *Daniel* set forth,
MROMAN138:31	H3521	Warres with the *Latins* he againe renewes,
DIALOG146:7	H195	I that no warres, so many yeares have known,

WARRIOURS (1) [pl.]

MPERS80:2	H1069	And wound the backs of those bold {brave} Warriours stout.

WARRS (3) [wars]

MPERS~~91:27~~	H1541	Such as would know at large his warrs and reign,
MGREC~~109:4~~	H2261	His warrs with sundry nations I'le omit,
DUBART~~154:14~~	H59	Who tam'd his foes, in bloud, in skarres {warrs,} and sweat,

WARS (23) [pl.]

PROLOG6:18	H3	To sing of Wars, of Captaines, and of Kings,
ELEMEN19:27	H472	Then in his long hot wars, {war} which *Millain* gain'd.
ELEMEN20:2	H484	Portentious signes, of Famines, Plagues and Wars.
HUMOUR32:32	H506	I love no thundering Drums {guns}, nor bloody Wars,
AGES38:4	H107	My little wrath did cease {end} soon as my wars.
SEASONS49:27	H116	Whilst they're imbroyl'd in Wars, and troubles ripe; {rife:}
MASSYR58:27	H210	And though of wars, he did abhor the sight;
MASSYR62:33	H378	His Wars none better then himself can boast,
MASSYR63:30	H417	The famous Wars {acts}, of this Heroyick King,
MASSYR~~63:32~~	H419	Nor of his acts {Wars} have we the certainty,
MASSYR65:10	H475	When in the *Tyrian* wars, the {this} King was hot,
MASSYR67:16	H562	Wars with the *Medes,* unhappily he wag'd,
MPERS84:20	H1256	Thinking his *Grecian* wars now to advance.
MPERS87:4	H1360	The one {last} accus'd the other, {first} for these {sad} wars:
MPERS92:1	~~H1555~~	In after wars were burnt, 'mongst other things?
MGREC100:2	H1886	Where happily in's wars he did succeed;
MGREC107:4	H2179	And for the rest new wars, and travels findes,
MGREC107:13	H2188	The recompence of travels, wars, and toyls;
MGREC107:27	H2202	Then did {all} their wars, against the *Persian* King.
MGREC124:17	H2924	Whilst hot in wars these two in *Greece* remaine,
DIALOG142:7	H36	And {Or} by tempestuous Wars thy fields trod down?
DIALOG142:12	H41	Or is't intestine Wars that thus offend?
QELIZ155:35	H26	*Eliza's* works, wars, praise, can e're compact,

WARS (1) [poss.]

MPERS69:21	H643	Who over-curious of wars event,

WARY (1)

ELEMEN16:27	H350	The wary Merchant, on his weary beast

WAS (510) See also TWAS, WAS'T

FATHER6:3	H37	But fear'd you'ld judge, one *Bartas* was my friend,
PROLOG7:19	H32	They'l say its stolne, or else, it was by chance.
ELEMEN8:6	H4	Which was the strongest, noblest, & the best,
ELEMEN8:7	H5	Who was of greatest use and might'est force;
ELEMEN8:21	H19	The rumbling, hissing, puffing was so great,
ELEMEN8:36	H34	What toole was ever fram'd, but by my might;
ELEMEN9:9	H43	Set ope those gates, that 'fore so strong was {were} barr'd.
ELEMEN9:23	H57	A transmutation, it was through mine aide.
ELEMEN9:28	H62	The Sun, an Orbe of Fire was held of old,
ELEMEN10:14	H89	*Eridanus,* where *Phaeton* was drown'd,
ELEMEN10:22	H97	Augment his heat, which was too hot before:
ELEMEN10:26	H101	I of acceptance was the holy signe.
ELEMEN11:3	H123	So great *Diana's* Temple was by me.
ELEMEN11:25	H145	Such was {is} my fruitfulnesse; and Epithite
ELEMEN12:12	H172	That heaven it selfe was oft call'd by that name;
ELEMEN13:2	H203	Was {Were} those compiled heapes of massy stones?
ELEMEN14:17	H259	whole Armies {*Cambyses* Armie} I have {was} overthrown;
ELEMEN15:34	H316	Was ever gem so rich found in thy trunke?
ELEMEN17:7	H371	And that an Island makes, which once was maine.
ELEMEN17:8	H372	Thus *Albion* {*Britain* fair} (tis thought) was cut from *France,*
ELEMEN17:10	H374	And but one land was *Affrica* and *Spayne,*
ELEMEN17:17	H381	That *Israels* enemies, therewith was {were} brain'd.
ELEMEN17:36	H400	{Yet am} not through ignorance, {ignorant} first was my due,
ELEMEN19:25	H470	If nought was {were} known, but that before *Algire.*
ELEMEN20:7	H489	To adde to all I've said, was my intent,
HUMOUR20:17	H9	Choler was own'd by Fire, and Blood by Aire,
HUMOUR20:26	H18	Pleading her selfe, was most of all desir'd;
HUMOUR20:29	H21	She was the silencest {silentest} of all the foure,
HUMOUR30:10	H402	As of that only part I was {were} the Queen:
HUMOUR30:34	H426	The Spleen for al you three, was made a sinke,
HUMOUR32:33	H507	My polish'd skin was not ordain'd for skars,
HUMOUR33:10	H524	Shame forc'd thee say, the matter that was mine,
HUMOUR34:5	H560	He was no foole, who thought the Soul lay here {there},
HUMOUR34:28	H583	Ne're did {Nor will} I heare {yield} that Choler was the witt'est;
HUMOUR34:38	H593	The worst she said, was, instability,
HUMOUR34:41	H596	Let's now be freinds, 'tis {its} time our spight was {were} spent,
HUMOUR35:15	H611	That Flegme was judg'd, for kindnesse to excel.
AGES35:27	H13	Childhood was cloath'd in white, and given {green} to show,
AGES35:28	H14	His spring was intermixed with some snow.
AGES36:4	H28	In's countenance, his pride quickly was seen.
AGES36:16	H40	But neither us'd (as yet) for he was wise.
AGES36:18	H42	His golden god in's purse, which was his charm.
AGES36:32	H56	That he was young, before he grew so old.
AGES36:34	H58	Their method was, that of the Elements,
AGES37:13	H75	Spending was willing, to be spent for me;
AGES37:18	H80	When Infancy was past, my Childishnesse,
AGES37:24	H86	My high-borne soule, so straitly was confin'd:
AGES37:32	H94	Nor studious was, Kings favours how to buy,

AGES37:41	H103	Where e're I went, mine innocence was shield.
AGES38:5	H108	My duel was no challenge, nor did seek.
AGES38:13	H116	This was mine innocence, but oh {ah!} the seeds,
AGES38:27	H130	As many was {are} my sins, so dangers too:
AGES41:17	H236	What they have done, the same was done by me,
AGES41:18	H237	As was their praise, or shame, so mine must be.
AGES42:4	H262	Yea justice I have done, was I in place;
AGES42:8	H266	Was I a pastor, I my flock did feed:
AGES42:14	H272	Was I a laborer, I wrought all day,
AGES42:20	H278	Was I as poor, as poverty could be,
AGES42:21	H279	Then basenesse was companion unto me.
AGES42:24	H282	If to Agricolture, I was ordain'd:
AGES42:38	H294	If to be rich, or great, it was my fate;
AGES42:39	H295	How was I broy'd with envy, and with hate?
AGES42:40	H296	Greater, then was the great'st, was my desire,
AGES42:40	H296	Greater, then was the great'st, was my desire,
AGES43:1	H297	If honour was the point, to which I steer'd;
AGES43:3	H298	But {And} by ambitious sailes, I was so carryed;
AGES43:7	H302	My thirst was higher, then Nobility.
AGES43:8	H305	I might possess that throne which was their right;
AGES44:31	H364	When it was rul'd by that Celestial she;
AGES45:1	H374	I saw hopes dasht, our forwardnesse was shent,
SEASONS47:34	H47	Yet never minute stil was known to stand,
SEASONS49:23	H114	Was like that noble, brave *Archadian.*
SEASONS49:33	H126	Of him that was Shepherd, then King go vaunt.
SEASONS51:13	H187	And in this month was made apostate man;
SEASONS51:14	H188	For then in *Eden* was not only seen
SEASONS51:19	H193	Great *Adam* {Our Grand-Sire} was of Paradice made King.
SEASONS52:28	H243	The day much longer then it was before,
MASSYR53:15	H5	When Time was young, and World in infancy,
MASSYR53:17	H7	But each one thought his petty rule was high,
MASSYR53:19	H9	This was the Golden Age, but after came
MASSYR53:31	H21	Of *Saturn,* he was the original,
MASSYR54:13	H40	His reign was short, for as I calculate,
MASSYR54:19	H46	Whose foundation was by his Grand-sire laid;
MASSYR55:2	H68	The world then was two thousand nineteen old.
MASSYR55:7	H73	And was both shame, and glory of her sex;
MASSYR55:8	H74	Her birth-place was *Philistrius Ascalon,*
MASSYR55:10	H76	Others report, she was a vestal Nun,
MASSYR55:18	H84	For which, she was obscurely nourished.
MASSYR55:19	H85	Whence rose that fable, she by birds was fed.
MASSYR55:25	H91	Which was the cause, poor *Menon* lost his life,
MASSYR55:38	H104	The walls so strong, and curiously were {was} wrought;
MASSYR55:39	H105	That after ages, skil, by them were {was} taught.
MASSYR56:1	H107	Quadrangle was the forme, it stood upon:
MASSYR56:2	H108	Each Square, was fifteen thousand paces long,
MASSYR56:13	H119	The wondrous Temple was, she rear'd to *Bell;*
MASSYR56:14	H120	Which is the midst, of this brave Town was plac'd,
MASSYR56:34	H140	This was last progresse of this mighty Queen,
MASSYR56:35	H141	Who in her Country never more was seen.
MASSYR57:4	H151	Or else was his obedience very great,

MASSYR57:11	H158	He sought no rule, til she was gone, and dead;
MASSYR57:24	H171	Again, the Country was left bare (there is no doubt)
MASSYR57:25	H172	When famous *Troy* was so beleaguered:
MASSYR57:26	H172	Which to her neighbours, when it was made known,
MASSYR57:28	H173	What e're he was, they {or} did, or how it fel,
MASSYR58:33	H216	From *Bactaria* an Army was at hand,
MASSYR59:1	H225	And win the Crown, which was the way to blisse,
MASSYR59:16	H240	There with all store he was so wel provided,
MASSYR59:17	H241	That what *Arbaces* did, was but derided;
MASSYR59:20	H244	For by the rain, was *Tygris* so o'reflown,
MASSYR59:21	H245	of the {that stately} wal it level caus'd to lye; {was overthrown.}
MASSYR59:32	H256	This the last Monarch was, of {great} *Ninus* race,
MASSYR59:35	H259	That *Amazia* was King of *Israel;*
MASSYR59:36	H260	His Father was then King (as we suppose)
MASSYR59:38	H262	He did repent, therefore it {the threatning} was not done,
MASSYR59:39	H263	But was accomplished now, in his {wicked} Son.
MASSYR60:9	H274	Thus {Such} was the {his} promise bound, since first {which} he
MASSYR60:34	H299	When this was built, and all matters in peace,
MASSYR60:37	H302	Who to be rid of such a guest, was glad;
MASSYR61:37	H342	Who stil implor'd his love, but was distress'd,
MASSYR61:38	H343	(This was that *Ahaz,* which so much {high} transgrest.)
MASSYR61:40	H345	Then by his death, releas'd, was *Israels* fears.
MASSYR62:14	H359	This was that strange degenerated brood,
MASSYR62:40	H385	And by his Sons in's Idols house was slain.
MASSYR63:23	H408	Brave *Nebulassar* to this King was Sonne,
MASSYR63:24	H409	The ancient {famous} *Niniveh* by him was won;
MASSYR64:1	H425	This was of Monarchies that head of gold,
MASSYR64:3	H427	This was that tree, whose brances fill'd the earth,
MASSYR64:5	H429	This was that King of Kings, did what he pleas'd,
MASSYR64:7	H431	And this is {was} he, who when he fear'd the least,
MASSYR64:8	H432	Was turned {changed} from a King, unto {into} a Beast;
MASSYR64:22	H446	Which was the losse of *Syria* withall;
MASSYR64:27	H451	Such was the scituation of this place,
MASSYR64:30	H454	Whether her wealth, or yet her strength was most;
MASSYR64:33	H457	And for her strength, how hard she was to gain,
MASSYR65:10	H475	When in the *Tyrian* wars, the {this} King was hot,
MASSYR65:23	H488	For this was {is} he, for whom none said, Alas!
MASSYR65:29	H494	Who was last King of holy *Davids* race;
MASSYR66:1	H507	Where to the sword, all but himself was {were} put,
MASSYR66:4	H510	Was nothing, but such gastly meditation;
MASSYR66:6	H512	Yet as was told, ne're saw it with his eyes;
MASSYR66:9	H515	Where late, of Harp, and Lute, was {were} heard the noyse,
MASSYR66:32	H538	For by the Heavens above it was decreed:
MASSYR67:17	H563	(Within which broiles, rich *Crœsus* was engaged,)
MASSYR68:16	H602	Was held in more request, {account} then now he was,
MASSYR68:16	H602	Was held in more request, {account} then now he was,
MPERS69:5	H627	*Cambyses* was of *Achemenes* race,
MPERS69:7	H629	When *Sardanapalus* was over-thrown,
MPERS69:11	H633	*Darius* was unto *Mandana* brother,
MPERS69:24	H646	So over-thrown of *Cyrus,* as was just;
MPERS69:29	H651	But as he past, his Son, who was born dumbe,

MPERS69:33	H655	*Cressus* thus known, it was great *Cyrus* doome,
MPERS69:38	H660	Who *Solon* was? to whom he lifts his hands;
MPERS69:38	H664	And viewing all, at all nought mov'd was he:
MPERS70:5	H676	Was conquest of the stately *Babylon,*
MPERS70:38	H709	But in this {his} Tombe was only to be found
MPERS71:15	H729	'Gainst *Ægypts* King, who there by him was slain,
MPERS72:11	H759	Hearing her harmlesse brother thus was dead,
MPERS72:14	H762	She with her fruit was {were} both at once undone,
MPERS72:24	H772	His cruelty was come unto that height,
MPERS72:33	H777	{wisht} his short reign long, till {past before} it was done.
MPERS72:37	H782	The people ignorant of what was done,
MPERS73:15	H802	Of which the cheife were {was} seven, call'd *Satrapes,*
MPERS73:25	H810	But yet, 'fore this was done, much blood was shed,
MPERS73:25	H810	But yet, 'fore this was done, much blood was shed,
MPERS73:30	H815	A Consultation by the {those} States was held.
MPERS74:3	H828	All envie to avoyd, this was thought on,
MPERS74:35	H858	But strength {men} against those walls was {were} of no use;
MPERS75:5	H866	This violence was done him by his Leige;
MPERS75:10	H871	When opportunity he saw was fit,
MPERS75:22	H880	Thy wit was more then was thine honesty,
MPERS76:6	H904	Which two then to assaile, his {royal} Camp was bold:
MPERS76:7	H905	By these alone his Hoast was pinch'd so sore,
MPERS76:33	H931	At *Marathon* this bloudy field was fought,
MPERS77:16	H957	Because this was, first born of *Cyrus* race.)
MPERS77:18	H959	As is {was} the Son, of pride, and cruelty;
MPERS78:1	H982	Although he hasted, yet foure yeares was spent,
MPERS78:3	H984	His Army of all Nations, was compounded,
MPERS78:5	H986	His Foot was seventeen hundred thousand strong,
MPERS78:13	H994	He was the Son of the fore-nam'd *Gobrias,*
MPERS78:24	H1005	In person {present} there, now for his help {aid} was seen;
MPERS78:26	H1007	Save the *Zidonians,* where *Xerxes* was.
MPERS78:28	H1009	For to command alone, she thought {judg'd} was best.
MPERS79:17	H1043	Was marching o're this interrupting Bay; {new devised way.}
MPERS79:28	H1054	His answer was, both Land and Sea he feared,
MPERS79:29	H1055	Which was not vaine, as it {after} soon appeared:
MPERS79:33	H1059	Was scarce enough, for each a draught to take.
MPERS80:13	H1080	And as at Land, so he at Sea was crost,
MPERS80:14	H1081	Four hundred stately Ships by stormes was lost,
MPERS80:16	H1083	{The Harbours} to receive, {contain} the Harbour was not able;
MPERS80:36	H1103	Much, {fearing} that which never was intended!
MPERS81:18	H1126	That *Xerxes* quarrel was 'gainst *Athens* State,
MPERS82:2	H1147	Was Victory, by Oracle fore-told:
MPERS82:18	H1165	Scarce one was left, to carry home the fame;
MPERS82:25	H1172	Some years by him in this vain suit was spent,
MPERS82:28	H1175	But she was stil, as when it {he} first begun.
MPERS83:3	H1191	His brothers recompence was naught but jears:
MPERS83:13	H1201	But yet by search, he was found murthered,
MPERS83:17	H1205	To be the Authour of the deed {crime} was done,
MPERS83:20	H1208	But in short time, this wickednesse was knowne,
MPERS83:22	H1210	But all his family was likewise slain,
MPERS83:25	H1213	The second was inthron'd, in's fathers stead.

MPERS84:4	H1232	To drink more then he list, none bidden was:
MPERS84:8	H1236	By *Memucan's* advice, this {so} was the doome.
MPERS84:9	H1237	What *Hester* {*Esther*} was, and did, her story reed,
MPERS84:18	H1254	That in all {his} Loyalty his heart was bound;
MPERS85:5	H1281	The eldest to succeed, that was his mind.
MPERS85:12	H1288	If {so} they were hers, the greater was her moan;
MPERS85:24	H1300	The King was glad, with *Sparta* to make peace,
MPERS85:30	H1306	{strength} by their {*Grecians*} helpe were {was} overthrown,
MPERS85:35	H1311	No match was high enough, but their own blood,)
MPERS86:1	H1317	And takes more on him, then was judged fit.
MPERS86:32	H1348	For what was done, seemed no whit offended.
MPERS86:35	H1351	Great care was his pretence, those Souldiers stout,
MPERS87:21	H1374	*Abrocomes,* was this base cowards name,
MPERS87:23	H1375	This place was {so} made, by nature, and by art;
MPERS87:27	H1379	The mazed King, was now {then} about to fly;
MPERS87:36	H1388	He surest {safest} was, when furthest {farthest} out o'th' way.
MPERS87:38	H1390	Rejoyced {Was} not a little {jocund} at his feare.
MPERS88:7	H1400	Was gather'd by the dust that rose from thence:
MPERS88:21	H1414	Of six thousand, wherein the King was yet;
MPERS89:1	H1435	But was deceiv'd; to it they make amain,
MPERS89:15	H1449	That their return be stopt, he judg'd was best,
MPERS90:10	H1483	There was of *Greeks,* setled a Colony,
MPERS90:38	H1505	Of that false perjur'd wretch, this was the last {fate},
MPERS91:8	H1516	To defend, more then offend, he had {there was} need.
MPERS91:25	H1539	His Mothers wicked counsell was the cause,
MPERS91:32	H1546	He was the Master of good *Nehemie*
MPERS91:36	H1550	Was it because the *Grecians* now at war,
MPERS92:3	H1557	Was by his *Eunuch* the proud *Bagoas* slain.
MPERS92:5	H1561	Some write that *Arsames* was *Ochus* brother,
MPERS92:7	H1565	His brother, as tis said, long since was slain,
MPERS92:18	H1576	And was no sooner setled in his reign,
MPERS92:20	H1578	Some writers say, that he was *Arses* son,
MPERS92:21	H1579	And that great *Cyrus* line, yet was not run,
MPERS92:21	H1579	But that his treason timely was found out.
MPERS92:22	H1580	That *Ochus* unto *Arsames* was father,
MPERS92:25	H1583	Was to his Predecessors Chamber page.
MPERS92:26	H1584	Some write great *Cyrus* line was not yet run,
MPERS92:27	H1585	But from some daughter this new king was sprung
MPERS92:33	H1591	That this *Darius* was last *Persian* King,
MGREC93:6	H1603	The third Monarchy was
MGREC6:10	H1607	Great *Alexander,* was wise *Phillips* son,
MGREC6:12	H1609	The cruell, proud, *Olimpias,* was his mother,
MGREC6:13	H1610	to the rich *Molossians* {*Epirus* warlike} King, was daughter.
MGREC6:18	H1615	By Art, and Nature both, he was made fit,
MGREC6:19	H1616	T'accomplish that, which long before was writ.
MGREC6:21	H1618	To th' ground was burnt, *Diana's* Temple high,
MGREC6:29	H1626	To save him from his might, no man was found.
MGREC6:36	H1633	Restlesse both day and night, his heart now {then} was,
MGREC94:12	H1646	For cruelty now, was his parentall sin.
MGREC94:18	H1655	And being ask'd what for himself was left,
MGREC94:35	H1673	Ah! fond vaine man, whose pen was taught ere while,

MGREC94:36	H1674	In lower termes to write {was taught} a higher stile,
MGREC95:22	H1701	There {In's stead} *Arsemes* {*Arses*} was plac'd, yet {but} durst
MGREC95:35	H1714	(Both sexes there) was almost numberlesse.
MGREC96:2	H1722	For since the world, was no such Pageant seen.
MGREC96:7	H1727	The Holy fire, was borne before the Host:
MGREC96:20	H1740	For so to fright the *Greekes* he judg'd was best,
MGREC96:22	H1742	Would aske more time, then were {was} their bodys worth.
MGREC96:27	H1747	This brave Virago, to the King was mother;
MGREC96:36	H1756	That valour was more worth than Pearls, or gold,
MGREC97:13	H1774	Was but beginning of his future woe;
MGREC97:36	H1797	A King he was, and that not only so,
MGREC98:9	H1811	With this reply, he was so sore {deep} enrag'd,
MGREC98:24	H1826	Who was the son of that *Parmenio* brave;
MGREC99:7	H1850	For all he offered {offers} now, was but his owne:
MGREC99:9	H1852	Was I as great, as is great *Alexander,*
MGREC99:21	H1864	That *Greece* must {was forc'd to} yeeld a fresh supply againe;
MGREC99:22	H1865	But yet, this well defended town is {was} taken,
MGREC99:25	H1868	And by command was drawn through every street,
MGREC99:40	H1883	By which he was so much incouraged,
MGREC100:3	H1887	To see how fast he gain'd, is {was} no small wonder,
MGREC100:6	H1890	For to be call'd {install'd} a god, was his intent;
MGREC100:38	H1922	Some injury was offered, he feares;
MGREC101:7	H1932	(Nor was such match, in all the world beside)
MGREC101:37	H1966	But 'tis not known what slaughters here they {was} made.
MGREC101:39	H1968	But *Quintus Curtius,* as was said before.
MGREC102:12	H1982	Which in few hours was carried all away;
MGREC102:14	H1984	Whose fame throughout the world, was so renown'd;
MGREC102:19	H1989	With all pleasures that on earth was {are} found,
MGREC103:3	H2014	And all in it was at his high command;
MGREC103:4	H2015	Of all the Cities, that on Earth was found;
MGREC103:6	H2017	Though *Babylon* was rich, and *Sushan* too;
MGREC103:20	H2031	Their charge, {place} gave to his Captains (as most {was} just)
MGREC103:37	H2048	Who was retir'd, and gone to {as far as} *Media.*
MGREC103:41	H2052	Was straight in *Bactria* these {soon} to augment,
MGREC104:1	H2053	But hearing, *Alexander* was so near;
MGREC104:5	H2057	But *Bessus* false, who was his cheife Commander;
MGREC104:19	H2071	Who was of hopes, and comfort quite bereft;
MGREC104:35	H2087	Whose Army now, was almost within sight,
MGREC105:5	H2098	Was the false Governour of *Media)*
MGREC107:32	H2207	But he that was resolved in his minde,
MGREC108:7	H2223	Here was of *Greeks,* a town in *Bactria,*
MGREC109:35	H2294	That to attend him there, was his intent;
MGREC110:41	H2345	His fourth, and last supply, was hither sent,
MGREC112:20	H2406	*Philotas* was not least, nor yet the last;
MGREC112:24	H2410	Nothing was found {prov'd}, wherein he had offended;
MGREC112:25	H2411	His silence, guilt was, of such consequence,
MGREC112:38	H2424	By which his Majesty was deifi'd.
MGREC113:17	H2444	Was to dispatch the Father, as the Son.
MGREC113:19	H2446	Who was so much engag'd, to this Commander,
MGREC113:23	H2450	It was decreed *Parmenio* should dye:
MGREC113:28	H2455	Most wickedly was slaine, without least crime,

MGREC113:33	H2460	By him was set upon the *Persian* Throne:
MGREC113:39	H2466	Was one of more esteem, but lesse desart;
MGREC114:1	H2469	When both were drunk, *Clitus* was wont to jeere;
MGREC114:18	H2488	Was vertuous, learned wise *Calisthines,*
MGREC114:26	H2496	Thus was he tortur'd, till his life was spent.
MGREC115:15	H2524	The other was the greatest Deity.
MGREC115:36	H2555	He was too subtile for his crafty foe,
MGREC116:2	H2562	The thread of *Alexanders* life was spun;
MGREC116:36	H2602	There was {were} no worlds, more, to be conquered:
MGREC117:19	H2626	When of his monstrous bulk it was the guide,
MGREC117:32	H2639	Was neare her time to be delivered;
MGREC~~118:12~~	H2659	For second offers {offer} there were {was} never made;
MGREC118:30	H2679	Was stiffe *Meleager,* whom he would take down {away},
MGREC119:3	H2693	But held command o'th' Armies {Army} which was best;
MGREC119:5	H2695	Which was his Masters sister for {secretly} to wed:
MGREC119:28	H2718	The *Athenian* Army was the greater far,
MGREC119:31	H2721	The valiant Chief, amidst his foes was slain,
MGREC119:33	H2723	For personage, none was like {to} this Commander:
MGREC120:16	H2751	Was to give way, himself might be undone;
MGREC120:22	H2759	Which of his Ancestors was once the throne,
MGREC120:38	H2775	And yet till now, at quiet was not laid.
MGREC121:2	~~H2780~~	With *Ptolomy* for to begin was best,
MGREC~~121:2~~	H2780	But first 'gainst *Ptolomy* he judg'd was
MGREC121:24	H2806	With what he held, he now was well {more} content,
MGREC121:37	H2819	But he was true to's masters family,
MGREC122:10	H2835	He was both valiant, faithfull, patient, wise.
MGREC122:16	H2841	To warm the {his} seat, was never her intent,
MGREC122:19	H2844	Who was *Perdicas, Philips* elder {eldest} brother,
MGREC123:8	H2870	But vaine it was to use his policy,
MGREC123:13	H2875	He to his cost was righteously repaid.
MGREC123:16	H2880	Fearing his Son *Cassander* was unstay'd,
MGREC123:36	H2900	Besides, he was the young Queens favourite,
MGREC~~124:13~~	H2920	But had the worst {beaten was} at Sea, as well as {and foil'd
MGREC124:26	H2933	More then he bidden was, could act no thing;
MGREC124:32	H2939	Was to this proud, vindicative *Cassander,*
MGREC~~124:35~~	H2942	Nor counts {thought} he that indignity but {was} small,
MGREC125:31	H2981	Till {'Gainst} all that lov'd *Cassander* was nigh spent; {she was
MGREC125:31	H2981	all that lov'd *Cassander* was nigh spent; {she was bent}
MGREC126:27	H3018	And so was he acquitted of his word,
MGREC126:29	H3020	This was the end of this most cruell Queen,
MGREC126:33	~~H3023~~	So boundlesse was her pride, and cruelty,
MGREC~~128:24~~	H3097	{great Antigonus} *Ptolomy,* and the rest {was} put him to flight;
MGREC128:41	H3114	Till *Alexander* unto age was grown,
MGREC129:11	H3125	But for one act she did, just was her end,
MGREC129:12	H3126	No sooner was great *Alexander* dead,
MGREC129:15	H3129	*Perdicas* was her partner in this plot:
MGREC129:24	H3138	That he was {is} odious to the world, they'r glad,
MGREC129:26	H3140	When this foul tragedy was past, and done,
MGREC129:38	H3152	Thus was the race, and house of *Alexander*
MGREC130:21	H3176	Thus *Philips* house was quite extinguished,
MGREC130:25	H3180	Now blood was paid with blood, for what was done

MGREC130:33	~~H3181~~	If *Alexander* was not poysoned,
MGREC131:4	H3194	Most grossely base, was this {their} great adulation,
MGREC~~132:3~~	H3236	This by *Lysimachus* soon {was} after slain,
MGREC132:10	H3245	His seed to be extirpt, was destined,
MGREC132:11	H3246	For blood which was decreed, that he should spill,
MGREC132:21	H3266	There was he {At last he's} taken and imprisoned
MGREC132:22	H3267	Within an Isle that was with pleasures fed,
MGREC~~132:28~~	H3275	Whose obsequies with wondrous pomp was done.
MGREC132:36	H3283	And so *Lysimachus* was slaine in fight.
MGREC133:1	H3289	He was by *Ptolomy Cerannus* slaine.
MGREC133:4	H3292	*Seleuchus* was as {a} Father, and a friend,
MGREC133:16	H3304	*Demetrius* Son was call'd *Antigonus,*
MGREC~~133:17~~	H3305	And his againe, also {was nam'd} *Demetrius.*
MGREC~~133:23~~	H3312	*Philip* had *Perseus,* who was made a Thrale
MGREC~~133:27~~	H3317	Whose kingdomes {Empire was} were subdu'd by {to} th'
MGREC133:30	H3320	*Antiochus Soter* his son was nam'd,
MGREC~~133:35~~	H3325	Which we oft wish were {was} extant as before.
MGREC133:36	H3326	*Antiochus Theos* was *Soters* son,
MGREC133:40	H3330	This *Theos* he was murthered by his {lewd} wife,
MGREC~~134:2~~	H3334	Whose large Dominions after was made small,
MGREC134:7	~~H3339~~	By him was set up the abomination
MGREC134:9	H3340	*Antiochus Eupator* was the next,
MGREC134:12	H3343	The Royall blood was quite {nigh} extinguished.
MGREC134:14	H3345	To take the government was called in,
MGREC134:25	H3356	His son was *Evergetes* the last Prince
MGREC134:27	H3358	*Philopater* was *Evergete's* son,
MGREC135:20	H3392	The first, was likened to a head of gold,
MGREC135:23	H3395	And last was Iron, which breaketh all with might.
MGREC135:28	H3400	The first a Lion, second was a Beare,
MGREC136:4	H3417	The Subject was too high, beyond my straine;
MROMAN136:25	H3439	His Father was not *Mars,* as some devis'd,
MROMAN136:33	H3447	His Brother *Remus* there, by him was slaine,
MROMAN136:35	H3449	The Stones at first was cimented with bloud,
MROMAN137:8	H3459	Of Wives there was so great a scarsity,
MROMAN137:11	H3462	So *Romulus* was forc'd this course to take.
MROMAN137:15	H3466	For {Then} to recover them, a Feild was fought;
MROMAN137:23	H3474	Affirme, that by the Senate he was slaine.
MROMAN137:28	H3479	Kept shut in peace, but {set} ope when bloud was spilt;
MROMAN137:34	H3485	So to delude the people he was bold:
MROMAN137:38	H3489	*Tullus Hostilius,* was third *Roman* King,
MROMAN138:9	H3499	Of *Latine* Kings this was long since the Seat,
MROMAN138:36	H3526	And after all, by *Ancus* Sons was slaine.
MROMAN139:9	H3537	And then by *Tarquin, Priscus* Son, was slaine.
MROMAN139:27	H3553	To finish what's begun, was my intent,
MROMAN139:30	H3556	The more I mus'd, the more I was in doubt:
DIALOG144:11	H121	Because of Royall Stem, that was thy crime;
DIALOG144:24	~~H133~~	These Prophets mouthes (alas the while) was stopt,
DIALOG145:37	H186	This was deny'd, I need not say wherefore.
DIALOG146:2	H190	Shews all was done, I'll therefore let it go.
SIDNEY149:3	H3	Sir *Philip Sidney,* who was untimely
SIDNEY~~149:14~~	H13	Of Poesie, and of Musick thou wert {he was} King;

SIDNEY149:18	H17	More worth was thine, {his} then *Clio* could set down.
SIDNEY149:26	H23	This was thy shame, O miracle of wit:
SIDNEY149:31	H23	Which shewes, thy worth was great, thine honour such,
SIDNEY149:32	H23	The love thy Country ought thee, was as much.
SIDNEY149:35	H23	Who honours thee for what was honourable,
SIDNEY150:12	H40	Which shews his worth was great, his honour such,
SIDNEY150:12	H41	The love his Country ought him, was as much.
SIDNEY150:15	H49	Yet great *Augustus* was content (we know)
SIDNEY150:26	H53	E're he was ripe; his thred cut *Atropos.*
SIDNEY150:29	H56	Oh, who was neare thee, but did sore repine;
SIDNEY150:40	H68	If thine aspect was milde to *Astrophell;*
SIDNEY151:7	H69	That such an omen once was in our land,
SIDNEY151:15	H69	And *Mars* himself was ta'n by *Venus* gin;
SIDNEY151:19	H69	That thine was true, but theirs adul'rate love.
SIDNEY152:1	H75	Better my hap, then was his darlings fate,
SIDNEY152:12	H81	I to be eas'd of such a task was glad.
SIDNEY152:15	H85	Not because, sweet *Sydney's* fame was not dear,
DUBART153:23	H27	Some part, at least, of that brave wealth was his;
DUBART154:25	H70	If e'r this golden gift was showr'd on any,
DUBART155:3	H88	*The world rejoyc'd at's birth, at's death was sorry;*
QELIZ156:3	H30	Who was so good, so just, so learn'd, so wise,
QELIZ156:17	H44	Since time was time, and man unmanly man,
QELIZ156:19	H46	Was ever people better rul'd then hers?
QELIZ156:20	H47	Was ever Land more happy, freed from stirs?
QELIZ156:29	H56	She their Protectrix was, they well doe know,
QELIZ157:21	H89	But that she was a rich *Ægyptian* Queen;
QELIZ157:26	H94	She was a Phoenix Queen, so shall she be,
QELIZ157:37	H105	Know 'tis a slander now, but once was treason.
QELIZ158:13	H122	*The greater was our gain, our losse the more.*
DAVID159:2	H17	The Shield of *Saul* was vilely cast away;
DAVID159:10	H25	And in their deaths {death} was found no parting strife;
DAVID159:24	H39	Thy love was wonderfull, passing {surpassing} a man;
VANITY159:37	H9	He's now a slave {captive}, that was a Prince {King} of late.
VANITY160:9	H19	They'r foul enough to day, that once was {were} fair,
TDUDLEY165:8	H10	Who was my Father, Guide, Instructor too,
TDUDLEY165:15	H17	He was my Father, and Ile praise him still.
TDUDLEY165:16	H18	Nor was his name, or life lead so obscure
TDUDLEY166:17	H59	He did exult his end was drawing near,
TDUDLEY166:26	H68	His hoary head in righteousness was found:
TDUDLEY166:36	H78	*That was both pious, just and wise,*
TDUDLEY167:3	H85	*And when his time with years was spent*
CONTEM167:29	H6	Their leaves & fruits seem'd painted, but was true
CONTEM168:5	H15	More Heaven then Earth was here, no winter & no night.
CONTEM168:16	H24	Whose beams was shaded by the leavie Tree,
CONTEM169:31	H70	Then was *Methuselah,* or's grand-sire great:
CONTEM170:12	H85	Believing him that was, and is, Father of lyes.
CONTEM172:4	H141	But man was made for endless immortality.
FLESH175:6	H6	One flesh was call'd, who had her eye
AUTHOR177:36	H8	At thy return my blushing was not small,
AUTHOR178:1	H11	Thy Visage was so irksome in my sight;
AUTHOR178:8	H18	In better dress to trim thee was my mind,

1HUSB180:25	H4		If ever wife was happy in a man,
CHILDRN184:32	H21		A prettier bird was no where seen,
CHILDRN185:31	H57		Great was my pain when I you bred,
CHILDRN185:32	H58		Great was my care, when I you fed,
CHILDRN186:24	H91		Taught what was good, and what was ill,
ELIZB186:36	H8		Farewel fair flower that for a space was lent,
ANNEB187:22	H12		Was ever stable joy yet found below?
ANNEB187:24	H14		I knew she was but as a withering flour,
ANNEB187:27	H17		Or like a shadow turning as it was.
ANNEB187:28	H18		More fool then I to look on that was lent,
1SIMON188:9	H10		Such was his will, but why, let's not dispute,
MERCY188:29	H15		Was ignorant what riches thou hadst lost.
MEDDM203:21	Hp283		He that neuer felt, what it was to be sick or wounded, doth not
MEDDM204:21	Hp285		of Jehu, he was rewarded for the matter, and yet punished for
MEDDM209:10	Hp291		but what was y^c Issue, they became a snare vnto them,
MEDDM209:21	Hp291		so it is with men, there was neuer yet any one man that had
TOCHILD215:5	H5		What was yr liueing mothers mind.
MYCHILD215:14	Hp240		I was able to compose some short matters, (for w^t else to call
MYCHILD215:25	Hp240		my wayes, & what I knew was sinfull as lying, disobed^c. to
MYCHILD215:26	Hp240		I avoided it. If at any time I was overtaken wth ye evills, it was
MYCHILD215:28	Hp241		God. I was also troubled at ye neglect of private Dutyes tho:
MYCHILD216:4	Hp241		When I was in my afflict^n. I besovght the Lord, and confessed
MYCHILD216:5	Hp241		my pride and Vanity and he was entreated of me, and again
MYCHILD216:7	Hp241		After a short time I changed my Condition & was marryed, and
MYCHILD216:9	Hp241		heart rose, But after I was convinced it was ye way of God, I
MYCHILD216:13	Hp241		me & doe me Good: and it was not altogether ineffectuall. It
MYCHILD216:14	Hp241		God to keep me a long time wthout a child wch was a great
MYCHILD216:23	Hp242		w^t was amisse. So vsually thvs it hath been wth me that I haue
MYCHILD217:9	Hp242		Before I was afflicted I went astray, but now I keep thy
MYCHILD217:33	Hp243		times by Atheisme how I could know whether there was a
MYCHILD219:6	Hp245		This was written in mvch sicknesse and weaknes, and is very
FEVER220:24	H4		When in my flesh no part was fovnd
FEVER220:30	H10		Beclouded was my Soul wth fear
SOREFIT221:26	H12		Yea when I was most low and poor,
JULY223:22	Hp251		it took me, and so mvch the sorer it was to me because my
JULY223:23	Hp251		dear husband was from home (who is my cheifest comforter on
JULY223:24	Hp251		God who never failed me, was not absent but helped me, and
28AUG225:27	Hp254		times my faith weak likewise, the Lord was pleased to vphold
13MAY227:4	H13		I'le rvn where I was succoured.
11MAYB228:26	Hp259		I had a feaver seatd vpon me wch indeed was the longest
HANNA230:14	H7		And life was ended near.
2HUSB232:21	H22		It was my Duty so to doe
2HUSB232:26	H27		Was to sing praise to Thee.
ACK235:14	H14		And rais'd him vp when he was sick.
HOUSE236:15	H7		I waken'd was wth thundring nois
HOUSE236:28	H20		Yea so it was, and so 'twas jvst.
HOUSE236:29	H21		It was his own it was not mine

WASH (1)

SEASONS49:17	H108		To wash their {the} thick cloath'd flocks, with pipes ful glad.

WASH'D (1) [washed]

AUTHOR178:4	H14		I wash'd thy face, but more defects I saw,

WASHT (1)

BYNIGHT220:14 H13   My smarting wounds washt in his blood,

WAS'T (1) [was it]

MGREC110:17   H2317   Nor was't dishonour, at the length to yeeld;

WAST (14)

HUMOUR23:3   H113   Thou wast not made for Souldier, or for Schollar;

HUMOUR33:4   H518   Under *Troys* wals, ten years wil wast {wear} away,

AGES43:34   ~~H329~~   And the Consumption, to the bones doth wast me;

MPERS82:4   H1151   *Mardonius* finding victuals wast apace,

MGREC111:33   H2378   Much time in feasts, and ryoting doth {did} wast;

DIALOG143:41   H110   And thou, poore soule, wast {wert} jeer'd among the rest,

DIALOG148:19   H284   And lay her wast, for so's the sacred doom,

SIDNEY151:5   ~~H69~~   And as thy beauty, so thy name would wast,

DAVID~~159:21~~   H36   O! lovely *Jonathan,* how wert {wast} thou slaine,

TDUDLEY165:27 H29   Who staid thy feeble sides when thou wast low,

CONTEM168:9   H18   How long since thou wast in thine Infancy?

CONTEM168:11 H20   Hath hundred winters past since thou wast born?

FLESH176:7   H47   Thou by old Adam wast begot,

ACK235:13   H13   Thou wast the pilott to the ship

WASTE (2)

AGES37:11   H73   My mother stil did waste, as I did thrive:

SICKNES178:32 H15   Our strength doth waste, our time doth hast,

WASTED (3)

MPERS80:28   H1095   But {the} *Phocians* Land, {Country} he then wasted sore:

PILGRIM210:3   H3   His wasted limbes, now lye full soft

SOREFIT221:24 H10   My wasted flesh thou didst restore

WASTING (4)

ELEMEN17:2   H366   And with my wasting floods, and roaring torrent;

HUMOUR23:17   H127   But bodies wasting, and destruction.

DIALOG141:26   H25   Or by my wasting state, dost think to thrive?

DISTEMP179:15 H3   And wasting pains, which best my body knows,

WATCH (1)

CHILDRN185:20 H46   And be surpriz'd for want of watch,

WATER (28)

FATHER~~6:13~~   H47   Then waters, {water} in the boundlesse Ocean flowes.

ELEMEN8:5   H3   Fire, Aire, Earth, and Water, did all contest

ELEMEN8:18   H16   Both by their darings; Water so provoked,

ELEMEN~~10:12~~   H87   The Hidra, Dolphin, Boys, that waters {water} bear.

ELEMEN14:23   H265   *Water.*

ELEMEN~~14:24~~   H266   Scarce Earth had done, but th' angry waters {water} mov'd;

ELEMEN16:16   H339   My water *Syrens,* with their guilefull lures:

ELEMEN16:24   H347   Both when we list, to water we convert.

ELEMEN17:24   H388   As when *Achaia,* all under water stood,

ELEMEN18:1   H405   And though you love Fire, Earth, and Water wel;

ELEMEN18:35   H439   So when I am condens'd, I turne to water;

HUMOUR20:18   H10   Earth knew her black swarth childe, Water her faire;

HUMOUR22:14   H83   Convert from water, to conjealed Ice;

HUMOUR35:12   H608   Nor be discern'd, here's water, earth, aire, fire,

AGES35:19   H5   The first: son unto Flegme, grand-child to water,

AGES~~38:37~~   H140   Some times in fire, sometimes in waters {water} fall:

SEASONS48:24 H77   More at her showers, which water them a space.

MPERS76:13	H911	Possession of water, earth, and aire,
MPERS76:15	H913	Quoth he, like Frogs, in water we must dive;
MGREC105:15	H2108	Wearied with his long march, did water seek,
MGREC105:38	H2131	This said, the *Greek* for water doth intreat,
MGREC107:22	H2197	But sore {much} distrest for water, in their march,
CONTEM173:23	H189	Thy bed a bough, thy drink the water cleer,
2LETTER182:28	H34	His little world's a fathom under water,
MEDDM201:12	Hp280	Fire hath its force abated by water not by wind, and anger
MEDDM208:25	Hp290	wells in the time of drought, that those that go to finde water in
MEDDM208:32	Hp290	the water become firme footing, for peter to walk on, nay more
11MAYA226:18	Hp255	this valley of Baca many pools of water, That wch now I cheifly

WATERS (9) [pl.]

FATHER6:13	H47	Then waters, {water} in the boundlesse Ocean flowes.
ELEMEN10:12	H87	The Hidra, Dolphin, Boys, that waters {water} bear.
ELEMEN14:24	H266	Scarce Earth had done, but th' angry waters {water} mov'd;
ELEMEN16:13	H336	To speake of kinds of Waters I'le {I} neglect,
ELEMEN16:19	H342	Nor will I speake of waters made by Art,
AGES38:37	H140	Some times in fire, sometimes in waters {water} fall:
FLESH177:15	H96	Of Life, there are the waters sure,
MEDDM198:5	Hp276	the still waters, if they stick in deepe mire and clay, and all his
PILGRIM210:13	H13	for waters cold he doth not long

WATERS (1) [poss.]

ELEMEN19:5	H450	Earths Beasts, and Waters Fish, scarce can compare.

WATRY (2)

HUMOUR34:2	H557	Both {The} watry, glassie, and the christaline.
CONTEM172:36	H169	You watry folk that know not your felicity.

WAUES (1) [waves]

MEDDM198:5	Hp276	if they stick in deepe mire and clay, and all his waues and

WAVE (1)

MPERS82:6	H1153	The other not a hand, nor sword will {would} wave,

WAVES (6) [pl.] See also WAUES

ELEMEN15:39	H321	For it, to search my waves, they thought no scorne.
ELEMEN19:31	H472	Some overwelm'd with waves, and seen no more.
MPERS79:12	H1034	But winds, and waves, these couples soon dissever'd,
MPERS79:12	H1034	But winds, and waves those iron bands did break;
CONTEM172:23	H157	But hundred brooks in thy cleer waves do meet,
CONTEM174:13	H212	The Mariner that on smooth waves doth glide,

WAX (1) n.

MEDDM196:11	Hp273	bread hath the least bran the purest hony the least wax and

WAX (2) v.

MGREC102:23	H1993	He, and his Souldiers, wax effeminate,
SIDNEY149:16	H15	Thine {His} Eloquence made *Mercury* wax red;

WAXE (1) v. [wax]

MYSOUL225:2	H6	Thy inward shall waxe strong,

WAY (45)

HUMOUR33:15	H529	Beholding unto me another way.
HUMOUR33:15	H529	I do as much for thee another way:
AGES36:25	H49	His hoary haires, and grave aspect made way;
AGES39:1	H144	I've done unto my elders I give way.
AGES43:5	H300	Opprest, and sunke, and sact, {stav'd} all in my way;
AGES43:12	H305	When to a Monarchy, my way they barr'd.

SEASONS50:5	H139	With weary stroaks, they take all in their way,
MASSYR59:1	H225	And win the Crown, which was the way to blisse,
MASSYR61:35	H340	Through *Syria* now he marcht, none stopt his way,
MASSYR65:21	H486	But chang'd his minde, and slew him by the way; {& caus'd his
MPERS72:39	H785	But in the way, his sword just vengeance takes.
MPERS79:2	H1024	Then laid his parts on both sides of the way,
MPERS79:17	H1043	Was marching o're this interrupting Bay; {new devised way.}
MPERS80:29	H1096	They no way able to withstand his force,
MPERS87:36	H1388	He surest {safest} was, when furthest {farthest} out o'th' way.
MPERS90:1	H1476	To {Did} stop the way in this their enterprise;
MPERS90:9	H1482	But on to *Trabezond* they kept their way;
MGREC93:37	H1634	His high resolves which way to bring to passe:
MGREC94:16	H1650	And through the *Hellispont,* his ships make {made} way.
MGREC94:21	H1659	Then on he march'd, in's way he veiw'd old *Troy;*
MGREC95:13	H1692	And easily takes old *Gordium* in his way;
MGREC99:5	H1848	And the distressed King no way {whit} respects;
MGREC99:35	H1878	But in no hostile way (as I suppose)
MGREC103:36	H2047	Now {The} to *Darius,* he directs his way,
MGREC111:34	H2379	Then visits *Cyrus* Sepulcher in's way,
MGREC119:23	H2713	His Lady take i'th' way, and no man know.
MGREC120:16	H2751	Was to give way, himself might be undone;
MGREC123:33	H2897	Or by his favour {favours} any way did grace, {had grac'd}
MGREC130:17	H3172	For straight way by command they'r put to death,
DIALOG145:24	H173	So many obstacles comes {came} in their way,
DIALOG148:31	H296	If this make way thereto, then sigh no more,
SIDNEY151:22	H72	With endlesse turnes, the way I find not out,
AUTHOR178:12	H22	And take thy way where yet thou art not known,
1HUSB180:31	H10	Thy love is such I can no way repay,
2LETTER182:2	H8	I crave this boon, this Errand by the way,
MEDDM197:29	Hp275	'tis no wonder if he faint by the way.
MEDDM200:11	Hp279	brests, that god is forced to hedg vp their way wth thornes
MEDDM202:25	Hp282	time, yet he affords so much light as may direct our way, that
MYCHILD215:29	Hp241	too often tardy y^t way. I also fovnd much comfort in reading y^e
MYCHILD216:9	Hp241	heart rose, But after I was convinced it was ye way of God, I
MYCHILD216:33	Hp242	in ye way everlasting: and seldome or never but I haue fovnd
MYCHILD218:17	Hp244	I haue gott over this Block y^n have I another pvtt in my way, &
MYCHILD218:21	Hp244	way wee another.
RESTOR230:3	H18	And 'twixt ye good and evill way
REMB236:8	H23	Or any way expresse.

WAYES (12) [ways]

MPERS71:6	H722	*Cambyses,* no wayes like, his noble Sire,
MPERS76:17	H915	Or fly like birds, in unknown wayes full quick;
TDUDLEY166:6	H48	No ostentation seen in all his wayes,
DDUDLEY167:20	H17	*Religious in all her words and wayes,*
CONTEM170:18	H90	With sullen hateful looks he goes his wayes.
CONTEM171:12	H116	And though thus short, we shorten many wayes,
MEDDM200:22	Hp279	a trim that they might run the wayes of his Commandment
MEDDM206:21	Hp287	their wayes rather, then to beg forgiuenes for their sinnes,
MEDDM207:1	Hp288	say how vnsearchable are his wayes and his footsteps past
MYCHILD215:25	Hp240	my wayes, & what I knew was sinfull as lying, disobed^c. to
MYCHILD216:32	Hp242	me and try me, see what wayes of wickednes are in me, and

REMB236:12   H27   In strict + vpright wayes.

WAYN (1) [wain]
  ELEMEN10:8   H83   The maid with ballance, wayn with horses three;

WAYS (2) [pl.] See also WAYES
  MPERS84:37   H1273 In this sad conflict, marching on his ways,
  MGREC106:28 H2162 No ways becomming such a mighty King;

WAYWARD (1)
  AGES37:14   H76   With wayward cryes, I did disturbe her rest;

WE'L (1) [we will]
  MGREC134:18 H3349 In *Egypt* now {next,} a little time we'l spend.

WEAK (16)
  AGES37:35   H97   Make strong my selfe, and turne aside weak right.
  MASSYR63:2   H387   His Son, weak *Essarhadon* reign'd in's place,
  MPERS~~79:13~~   H1035 To cross the sea such strength he found too weak,
  MROMAN139:31 H3557 The subject large my mind and body weak,
  CONTEM173:35 H199 In knowledg ignorant, in strength but weak,
  CHILDRN186:3 H70   Till my weak layes with me shall end,
  MEDDM197:15 Hp274 stoop, so a man of weak faith and mean abilities, may vndergo
  MEDDM200:20 Hp279 wealth, or a helthfull body, would quite ouer throw, some weak
  MEDDM200:36 Hp280 weak children as would crush them to the dust, but according
  MEDDM202:12 Hp281 and some againe so weak and feeble, that while they liue, they
  MEDDM207:31 Hp289 All weak and diseased bodys, haue hourly mementos of their
  28AUG225:27 Hp254 many times my faith weak likewise, the Lord was pleased to
  11MAYB228:25 Hp259 of January 'till May I haue been by fitts very ill & weak. The
  2HUSB232:17 H18   Thou see'st how weak + frail I am,
  2HUSB232:25 H26   O Lord thov know'st my weak desires
  REMB235:26   H7   O Lord thov know'st I'm weak.

WEAKE (4) [weak]
  PROLOG7:12   H26   A weake or wounded braine admits no cure.
  PROLOG7:25   H37   But this weake knot they will full soone untye,
  MPERS88:37   H1430 Their armes grew weake, through {by their} slaughters that
  DUBART153:32 H36   Thus weake brain'd I, reading the lofty stile,

WEAKENED See WEAKNED

WEAKLY (1)
  MYCHILD219:6 Hp245 written in mvch sicknesse and weaknes, and is very weakly

WEAKNED (1) [weakened]
  DIALOG141:20 H19   My weakned fainting body now to reele?

WEAKNES (11) [weakness]
  PILGRIM210:37 H37 In weaknes and dishonour sowne
  MYCHILD216:17 Hp241 yov into ye world, and wth great paines, weaknes, cares
  MYCHILD216:25 Hp242 hath been vpon my own person, in sicknesse weaknes, paines,
  MYCHILD219:6 Hp245 This was written in mvch sicknesse and weaknes, and is very
  28AUG225:26 Hp254 After mvch weaknes & sicknes when my spirits were worn out,
  28AUG225:33 Hp254 by it— And if he knowes that weaknes, & a frail body is ye best
  11MAYA226:13 Hp255 I had a sore sicknes and weaknes took hold of me wch hath by
  11MAYA226:19 Hp255 contented thankfull h^t vnder my affliction & weaknes seing it is
  11MAYA226:22 Hp255 while my body decayes, and ye weaknes of this outward
  30SEPT227:18 Hp257 It pleased god to viset me wth my old Distemper of weaknes
  HOURS234:9   H23   My weaknes thou do'st know full well,

WEAKNESSE (2) [weakness]
  HUMOUR24:10 H159 And to your weaknesse, gently condescend.

MGREC101:31	H1956	And weakenesse of a foe is covered;

WEAKNESSES (1) [pl.]

30SEPT227:28	Hp257	children) haue yee seen ye many sicknesses and weaknesses

WEAL (2)

MPERS71:25	H739	But {For} he would be profest god of their Weal;
DIALOG147:34	H258	Thy Church and Weal, establish'd in such manner,

WEALTH (46)

FATHER5:27	H28	Yours did contest, for Wealth, for Arts, for Age,
FATHER6:4	H38	I honour him, but dare not wear his wealth,
ELEMEN11:23	H143	In wealth and use I doe surpasse you all,
ELEMEN15:23	H305	But what's the wealth that my rich Ocean brings?
ELEMEN15:27	H309	Such wealth, but not such like, Earth thou mayst show.
ELEMEN18:5	H409	And all the wealth, that ever earth did give,
AGES40:11	H192	Until mine own be gone, my wit, and wealth;
AGES41:38	H255	If not, yet wealth, {riches} Nobility can gain.
AGES43:24	H319	I glory in my wealth, I have within.
SEASONS49:26	H115	Carelesse of worldly wealth, you sit {sing} and pipe,
MASSYR55:36	H102	Her wealth she shew'd, in building *Babylon;*
MASSYR57:25	~~H172~~	Of men, and wealth, his mother carried out;
MASSYR59:30	H254	But all his wealth, and friends, together gets,
MASSYR~~60:2~~	H267	With over-plus of all treasures {the wealth} therein,
MASSYR60:35	H300	Molests poor *Israel,* his wealth t' encrease.
MASSYR62:26	H371	Or else those *Chinoes* rare, whose wealth, and Arts,
MASSYR64:30	H454	Whether her wealth, or yet her strength was most;
MASSYR66:24	H530	Which wealth, and strong ambition made so great;
MASSYR66:40	H546	He left his Wealth, and Conquest, to his Son.
MASSYR67:3	H549	His son possesses wealth, and rule, as just;
MPERS70:35	H706	In honour, peace, and wealth, with a grey head,
MPERS77:29	H970	His Souldiers, credit, wealth, at home had stay'd,
MGREC~~94:18~~	H1654	His little wealth among his Souldiers gave.
MGREC96:37	H1757	And how {that} his wealth serv'd but for baits t'allure,
MGREC102:32	H2002	Where Kings have shown their glory, wealth, and might;
MGREC107:15	H2190	The wealth of many Cities doth {Kindomes did} consume:
MGREC116:28	H2594	For those that {such as} pleas'd him: had both wealth and
MROMAN138:8	H3498	And from old *Alba* fetch the wealth away;
MROMAN138:12	H3502	Leaves {Left} *Rome,* in wealth and power, still growing high.
MROMAN138:28	H3518	By wealth, and favour, doth to honour climbe;
MROMAN139:5	H3533	As wealth had made them of abilitie;
DIALOG141:7	H6	With honour, wealth, and peace, happy and blest;
DIALOG147:33	H257	At that thy setled Peace, thy wealth and splendour,
SIDNEY~~150:6~~	H31	A world of treasure, in {wealth within} that rubbish lye;
DUBART153:23	H27	Some part, at least, of that brave wealth was his;
QELIZ156:21	H48	Did ever wealth in *England* so {more} abound?
QELIZ157:17	H85	How vanisheth her glory, wealth, and powers;
VANITY159:38	H10	What is't in wealth, great treasures for to gain {obtain}?
VANITY160:37	H47	It steeres {stores} with wealth, which time cann't wear away.
CONTEM174:26	H224	Here's neither honour, wealth, or safety;
FLESH175:7	H7	On worldly wealth and vanity;
MEDDM200:20	Hp279	honour, wealth, or a helthfull body, would quite ouer throw,
MEDDM207:6	Hp288	they were giuen for, as health wealth and honour, wch might be
MEDDM208:21	Hp290	on them, so is it wth the wealth honours and pleasures of this

HOUSE237:12	H42	And did thy wealth on earth abide,
HOUSE237:25	H55	Ther's wealth enovgh I need no more,

WEALTHY (8)

ELEMEN16:30	H353	The wealthy fraught, unto his wished Port.
AGES40:4	H185	Sometimes lay wait to take a wealthy purse,
MASSYR64:26	H450	And unto wealthy *Tyre* with {in} hast repaire.
MASSYR65:4	H469	And took the wealthy town, but all the gain
MPERS80:39	H1106	To rob the wealthy Temple of *Apollo,*
MGREC98:17	H1819	space {time} he takes this lofty {took that wealthy} town,
MGREC103:2	H2013	With open Gates, the wealthy town did stand,
DIALOG146:18	H204	My wealthy trading faln, my dearth of grain,

WEANED (1)

MEDDM200:6	Hp279	Some children are hardly weaned although the teat be rub'd

WEAPON (2)

ELEMEN9:1	H35	O {Ye} Martialist! what weapon {weapons} for your fight?
HUMOUR29:7	H360	The tongue's no weapon to assault a foe,

WEAPONLESSE (1) [weaponless]

MPERS89:18	H1452	And there all wait his mercy, weaponlesse;

WEAPONS (3) [pl.]

ELEMEN9:1	H35	O {Ye} Martialist! what weapon {weapons} for your fight?
MPERS81:41	H1145	For other {The rest had} Weapons, they had none would {do
DAVID159:28	H43	And war-like weapons perished away.

WEAR (7)

FATHER6:4	H38	I honour him, but dare not wear his wealth,
ELEMEN13:10	H211	If ought you have to use, to wear, to eate?
HUMOUR33:4	H518	Under *Troys* wals, ten years wil wast {wear} away,
MASSYR58:3	H188	Did wear their garb, their gestures imitate,
VANITY160:37	H47	It steeres {stores} with wealth, which time cann't wear away.
VANITY161:4	H55	But wear his Crown unto eternitie,
CONTEM173:22	H188	Thy cloaths ne're wear, thy meat is every where,

WEARE (1) [wear]

MGREC128:22	H3095	Before he weare the universall Crown;

WEARES (2)

HUMOUR28:7	H319	The Lungs, she rots, the body weares away,
MASSYR67:21	H567	Unworthy *Belshazzar* next weares the Crown,

WEARIED (3)

MGREC105:15	H2108	Wearied with his long march, did water seek,
MGREC110:23	H2327	Long with excessive travailes wearied,
MGREC122:29	H2848	He wearied out, at last, would needs be gone,

WEARIES See WEARYS

WEARINESSE (1) [weariness]

AGES46:13	H444	Yet studying much, brings wearinesse to th' flesh;

WEARING (2)

MGREC110:35	H2339	But doubting, wearing Time would {might} these decay,
FLESH175:29	H29	Which wearing time shall ne're deject.

WEARISOME See WEARYSOME

WEARS See WEARES

WEARY (11)

ELEMEN16:27	H350	The wary Merchant, on his weary beast
HUMOUR23:20	H130	But I am weary to dilate thy shame;
AGES37:7	H69	Her nine months weary burden not declare.

AGES37:16	H78	With weary armes, she danc'd, and *By, By,* sung,
AGES42:30	H286	My weary beast, rest from his toile can find;
SEASONS50:5	H139	With weary stroaks, they take all in their way,
MASSYR62:6	H351	But weary of his servitude, he sought,
MROMAN140:1	H3564	And weary lines (though lanke) I many pen'd:
1LETTER181:20	H18	I weary grow, the tedious day so long;
PILGRIM210:1	H1	As weary pilgrim, now at rest
11MAYA226:17	Hp255	Many refreshments haue I fovnd in this my weary pilgrimage,

WEARYS (1) [wearies]

MEDDM199:19	Hp278	Much Labour wearys the body, and many thoughts oppresse

WEARYSOME (1) [wearisome]

MEDDM197:27	Hp275	will finde it a wearysome if not an impossible task so he that

WEATHER (1)

11MAYB228:27	Hp259	y^t ever I had lasting 4 dayes, and ye weather being very hott

WEATHER-BEATEN (1)

CONTEM174:7	H207	This weather-beaten vessel wrackt with pain,

WEB (1)

MASSYR65:15	H480	Had all his hopes like to a Spiders web;

WEBB'S (1) [web is]

FAINTING222:16	H6	My life as Spiders webb's cutt off

WED (6)

MPERS72:10	H758	His sister, whom incestuously he wed,
MPERS74:22	H845	He two of *Cyrus* Daughters now {then} doth wed,
MPERS85:32	H1308	The {This} King, his sister, like *Cambyses,* wed;
MGREC119:5	H2695	Which was his Masters sister for {secretly} to wed:
MGREC120:7	H2742	*Craterus* doth his daughter *Phisa* {*Phila*} wed,
MGREC128:5	H3078	*Thessalonica* he had newly wed,

WEDDED (1)

MASSYR57:3	H150	A Prince wedded to ease, and to delight,

WEDDING (1)

MGREC111:40	H2385	A Wedding Feast to's Nobles then he makes,

WEDS (1)

MPERS91:24	H1538	And weds his Daughter for a second wife;

WEEDS (1) [pl.]

AGES38:14	H117	Lay raked up; of all the cursed weeds,

WEEK (1)

MERCY189:3	H24	One week she only past in pain and woe,

WEEP (8)

DIALOG146:33	~~H219~~	To weep for that we both have pray'd for long,
DIALOG147:26	H250	O mother, can you weep, and have such Peeres.
DIALOG147:28	H252	If now you weep so much, that then no more,
VANITY160:19	H29	Nor laugh, nor weep, let things go ill or well:
DISTEMP179:19	H7	Then eyes lay dry, disabled to weep more;
CHILDRN185:17	H43	If birds could weep, then would my tears
1SIMON188:5	H6	Acquaintance short, yet parting caus'd us weep,
PILGRIM210:26	H26	Mine eyes no more shall ever weep

WEEPING (3)

ELEMEN16:21	H344	Nor fruitfull dewes, nor drops {distil'd} from weeping eyes;
DIALOG~~146:17~~	H203	My ravisht {weeping} virgins, and my young men slain,
CONTEM170:8	H81	The weeping Imp oft looks her in the face,

WEIGH (1)
DIALOG141:27 H26 Then weigh our case, if't be not justly sad,
WEIGHED (1)
MEDDM208:14 Hp290 Commends vs to god, for by his ballance we must be weighed,
WEIGHING (1)
MPERS69:41 H671 Weighing the age, and greatnesse of the Prince,
WEIGHS (1)
MPERS86:13 H1329 *Cyrus* o'th' other side, weighs in his mind,
WEIGHT (1) See also WAIGHT
CONTEM174:10 H210 In weight, in frequency and long duration
WEIGHTS See WAIGHTS
WEIGHTY (2) See also WAIGHTY
SEASONS50:19 H153 And bundles up in sheaves the weighty Wheat,
SIDNEY151:38 ~~H75~~ Till terrour-struck for my too weighty charge.
WEL (24) [well]
ELEMEN18:1 H405 And though you love Fire, Earth, and Water wel;
ELEMEN19:24 H469 What woeful wracks I've made, may wel appear,
HUMOUR20:33 H25 Wel, thus they parle, and chide, but to be briefe,
HUMOUR21:37 H65 A Chamber wel, in field she dares not come;
HUMOUR22:29 H98 The vitall spirits they're call'd, and wel they may,
HUMOUR22:31 H100 The Animal I claime, as wel as these,
HUMOUR24:35 H184 A rosie cheek'd {cheek} musitian, thou know'st wel.
HUMOUR24:37 H186 And how to strike ful sweet, as wel as sharpe.
HUMOUR26:40 H270 Thou know'st I've there to do, as wel as thou;
HUMOUR29:3 H356 Had need be armed wel, and active too,
HUMOUR30:11 H403 Let me wel make thy precincts, the gal;
HUMOUR30:28 H420 Yet is a bowel cal'd wel as the rest.
HUMOUR31:5 ~~H438~~ Thou do'st assume my name, wel be it just;
HUMOUR34:35 H590 Wel, to be breif, Choler I hope now's laid,
HUMOUR35:14 H610 This loving counsel pleas'd them all so wel,
AGES39:19 H162 glistring {glitt'ring} Sword, {the Pistol} and wel advanced Pike;
AGES42:16 H274 Thus hath mine age (in all) sometimes done wel.
AGES44:19 H352 But what I have done wel, that is my prop;
SEASONS51:5 H179 But its a precious juyce, when wel it's used.
MASSYR59:16 H240 There with all store he was so wel provided,
MASSYR62:23 H368 Or how they fare, rich, poor, or ill, or wel;
MASSYR65:39 H504 His wel deserv'd, and fore-told misery;
MASSYR66:27 H533 His Dreams, wise *Daniel* doth expound ful wel,
MGREC101:14 H1939 And till all this be wel perform'd, and sure,
WELCOM (1) [welcome]
MEDDM201:32 Hp281 all seasons the most welcom so a faithfull friend in time of
WELCOME (6)
MGREC~~110:2~~ H2302 For to receive {To give} him, {welcome} when he comes to
MGREC119:11 H2701 That if he came, good welcome he should find:
1LETTER181:24 H22 The welcome house of him my dearest guest.
MEDDM197:12 Hp274 times tast of adversity, prosperity would not be so welcome
MEDDM203:28 Hp284 bid him welcome, that brings a plaister for his sore, or a
30SEPT227:24 Hp257 and then thy stroakes shall bee welcome, I haue not been
WELL (62) adv. See also WEL
PROLOG7:18 H31 If what I doe prove well, it wo'nt advance,
PROLOG7:31 H42 Men can doe best, and Women know it well;

ELEMEN8:33	H31	What I can doe, well skill'd Mechanicks may,
ELEMEN12:1	H161	For Learning, Armes, and Arts, I love it well:
ELEMEN12:30	H190	Send forth your well man'd ships, where sun doth rise.
ELEMEN13:13	H214	Well knowest, my fuell must maintain thy fire.
ELEMEN14:4	H246	*Korah {Dathan}* and all his Company well knew.
ELEMEN14:25	H267	Sister (quoth she) it had full well behov'd
HUMOUR24:18	H167	Do'st know thy selfe so well, us so amisse?
HUMOUR24:36	H185	He knew {well} how, for to handle, Sword and Harpe,
MASSYR57:21	H168	Well satisfie the most considerate minds:
MASSYR58:6	H191	Kept ever close, fearing some dismal {his well deserved} fate;
MPERS73:39	H824	What arguments they us'd, I know not well,
MPERS74:32	H855	Yet notwithstanding he did all so well,
MPERS91:19	H1527	The King from forraign foes, and all {parts now well} at ease,
MPERS92:27	H1585	But as before doth (well read) *Raleigh* write,
MGREC94:33	H1671	To whip him well with rods, and then {so} to bring,
MGREC99:22	H1865	But yet, this well defended town is {was} taken,
MGREC100:35	H1919	Great *Alexander* mourns, as well as he,
MGREC101:35	H1964	So make {made} an end, before they {as soon as} well begun;
MGREC109:36	H2295	And come as well provided as he could,
MGREC111:20	H2365	But well observing th' nature of the tide,
MGREC114:7	H2475	Upon a time, when both had drunken well,
MGREC114:7	H2475	Both at a Feast when they had tippled well
MGREC115:27	H2546	He might well dye, though he had done no wrong;
MGREC118:26	H2675	But all his bowels, coloured well, and sound.
MGREC119:21	H2711	(Which at this time well suited his desires)
MGREC121:24	H2806	With what he held, he now was well {more} content,
MGREC124:6	H2911	And so he quick returns thus well appaid,
MGREC124:13	H2920	the worst {beaten was} at Sea, as well as {and foil'd at} Land,
MGREC125:21	H2971	And needs will have their lives as well as State:
MGREC126:8	H2999	Well fortified, and on the Sea it lies;
MGREC127:41	H3073	Shews his ambitious practises as well.
MGREC130:19	H3174	And now he thinks {hopes}, he's ordered all so well,
MGREC131:1	H3190	With Arms and with provision stores them well,
MGREC132:13	H3248	*Jehu* in killing *Ahabs* house did well,
DIALOG145:16	H165	Well, to the matter then, there's grown of late,
SIDNEY149:9	H8	No lesse {As well} an Honour to our *British* Land,
SIDNEY150:39	H67	Illustrious *Stella,* thou didst thine full well,
QELIZ156:29	H56	She their Protectrix was, they well doe know,
VANITY160:19	H29	Nor laugh, nor weep, let things go ill or well:
TDUDLEY165:20	H22	Well known and lov'd, where ere he liv'd, by most
CONTEM172:10	H146	I once that lov'd the shady woods so well,
BIRTH180:7	H17	The many faults that well you know I have,
2LETTER182:31	H37	Tell him I would say more, but cannot well,
CHILDRN185:7	H33	Striving for more then to do well,
CHILDRN186:19	H86	You had a Dam that lov'd you well,
CHILDRN186:29	H96	I happy am, if well with you.
1SIMON188:11	H12	Let's say he's merciful, as well as just,
MEDDM195:26	Hp272	of all and he that makes such improvment is wise as well as
MEDDM195:29	Hp272	Many can speak well, but few can do well. We are better
MEDDM198:13	Hp276	Want of prudence as well as piety hath brought men into great
MEDDM198:14	Hp276	but he that is well stored wth both, seldom is so insnared

MEDDM202:16	Hp282	The treasures of this world may well be compared to huskes,
MEDDM204:7	Hp284	in need of him, to day as well as yesterday, and so shall for
MEDDM204:33	Hp285	produced wth much labour (as the husbandman well knowes)

MEDDM202:16	Hp282	The treasures of this world may well be compared to huskes,
MEDDM204:7	Hp284	in need of him, to day as well as yesterday, and so shall for
MEDDM204:33	Hp285	produced wth much labour (as the husbandman well knowes)
MEDDM207:17	Hp289	the pleasure wch else we should take in them, and well it is
MEDDM208:18	Hp290	Well doth the Apostle call riches deceitfull riches, and they
MYCHILD217:19	Hp243	shall bee well with me. I haue somt. tasted of y^t hidden Manna
HOURS234:2	H16	Whom I doe loue so well
HOURS234:9	H23	My weaknes thou do'st know full well,

WELL (3) n.

ELEMEN15:12	H294	Then seeks me out, in River and in Well;
MGREC129:14	H3128	Both thrown into a well to hide her blot,
QELIZ157:29	H97	Must dip his Pen i'th' Heliconian Well;

WELLS (1) [pl.]

MEDDM208:25	Hp290	empty wells in the time of drought, that those that go to finde

WELTERING (1)

AGES38:6	H109	My foe should weltering, with {in} his bowels reek.

WENT (19)

AGES36:12	H36	But as he went, death waited at his heeles.
AGES37:41	H103	Where e're I went, mine innocence was shield.
MASSYR53:26	H16	From thence he went *Assyria* to command;
MPERS69:22	H644	For information to *Apollo* went:
MPERS80:37	H1104	Yet 'fore he went, to help out his expence,
MPERS84:12	H1246	Went to *Jerusalem* his city dear,
MPERS90:4	H1478	Before them burnt the country as they went,
MGREC100:5	H1889	Then to the Phane of *Jupiter,* he went,
MGREC111:1	H2346	Then down t' *Hidaspis* with his Fleet he went;
MGREC111:29	H2374	From hence he to {then unto} *Gedrosia* went,
MGREC111:39	H2384	He at the last to royall *Sushan* went;
MGREC113:1	H2428	The King would give no eare, but went from thence;
MGREC115:16	H2535	From *Media* to *Babylon* he went,
MGREC119:38	H2728	With them and his, he into *Grecia* went,
MGREC121:17	H2799	Knocks out his braines, to *Ptolomy* then went,
DIALOG144:29	H137	Some grossely fin'd, from {house &} friends to exile went:
MYCHILD217:9	Hp242	too. Before I was afflicted I went astray, but now I keep thy
SON230:24	H7	Thou di'st p^{r}serve him as he went,
2HUSB232:11	H12	At thy comand O Lord he went

WEPT (1)

SIDNEY151:12	H69	I rather judg'd thee of his mind that wept,

WERE (106)

PROLOG7:21	H33	But sure the antick *Greeks* were far more milde,
ELEMEN9:9	H43	Set ope those gates, that 'fore so strong was {were} barr'd.
ELEMEN10:25	H100	Of old, when Sacrifices were divine,
ELEMEN10:32	H107	*Apulia's* jacent parts were covered;
ELEMEN13:2	H203	Was {Were} those compiled heapes of massy stones?
ELEMEN17:17	H381	That *Israels* enemies, therewith was {were} brain'd.
ELEMEN18:7	H411	No world {earth}, thy witching trash, were all but vain.
ELEMEN18:21	H425	Ye forging Smiths, if Bellowes once were gone;
ELEMEN19:25	H470	If nought was {were} known, but that before *Algire.*
HUMOUR20:21	H13	But 'mongst themselves they were at variance,
HUMOUR30:10	H402	As of that only part I was {were} the Queen:
HUMOUR32:12	H486	And things that never were, nor shal I see.

HUMOUR34:41	H596	Let's now be freinds, 'tis {its} time our spight was {were} spent,
AGES37:23	H85	My then ambitious thoughts, were low enough.
AGES41:23	H240	When my Wilde Oates, were sown, and ripe, & mown,
SEASONS49:23	H114	Hath envy bred in Kings that were at strife,
SEASONS51:16	H190	Or withered stocks, {which were} all dry, and dead,
MASSYR53:25	H15	These were his first, all stood in *Shinar* land,
MASSYR55:34	H100	But were her vertues, more, or lesse, or none;
MASSYR55:38	H104	The walls so strong, and curiously were {was} wrought;
MASSYR55:39	H105	That after ages, skil, by them were {was} taught.
MASSYR56:5	H111	Almost incredible, they were in breadth.
MASSYR59:9	H233	Bereft of wits, were slaughtered down right.
MASSYR59:27	H251	By this accomplishment, their hearts were shaken:
MASSYR65:14	H479	But he (alas) whose fortunes {all were} now i'th ebbe,
MASSYR66:1	H507	Where to the sword, all but himself was {were} put,
MASSYR66:9	H515	Where late, of Harp, and Lute, was {were} heard the noyse,
MPERS69:14	H636	Whose Ancestors, were royal in degree;
MPERS72:14	H762	She with her fruit was {were} both at once undone,
MPERS73:15	H802	Of which the cheife were {was} seven, call'd *Satrapes,*
MPERS74:35	H858	But strength {men} against those walls was {were} of no use;
MPERS78:15	H996	These {Such} his Land Forces were, then next, a Fleet
MPERS81:34	H1142	The other *Greeks,* which were confederate,
MPERS85:12	H1288	If {so} they were hers, the greater was her moan;
MPERS85:30	H1306	{strength} by their {*Grecians*} helpe were {was} overthrown,
MPERS88:23	H1416	They {ready} were about to leave their King and fly,
MPERS89:24	H1458	They were too hungry to capitulate;
MPERS90:12	H1484	There for some time they were, but whilst they staid,
MPERS91:9	H1517	{Their winnings} lost all, and were a peace {their glad} to
MPERS92:1	H1555	In after wars were burnt, 'mongst other things?
MPERS92:24	H1582	That son, and father, both were murthered
MGREC93:16	H1613	Great were the guifts of nature, which he had;
MGREC94:20	H1658	To these {which} were joyn'd, five thousand goodly horse.
MGREC96:6	H1726	As if they were, {if addrest} now all to run at {a} tilt:
MGREC96:15	H1735	A number of spare horses next were led,
MGREC96:22	H1742	Would aske more time, then were {was} their bodys worth.
MGREC97:6	H1767	Two hundred thousand men that day were slaine,
MGREC97:10	H1771	The Regall ornaments now {were} lost, the treasure
MGREC97:16	H1777	For though their beauties were unparalled
MGREC98:22	H1824	And thus the *Tyrians* for mistrust were paid,
MGREC99:6	H1849	Tels him, these proffers great (in truth were none)
MGREC99:13	H1856	And so if I *Parmenio* were, would I.
MGREC99:20	H1863	And by these walls, so many men were slaine,
MGREC100:20	H1904	And now of valour both were {are} destitute;
MGREC105:1	H2094	Then slew his servants, that were faithfull found;
MGREC106:37	H2171	His Captains, that were vertuously enclin'd,
MGREC109:16	H2275	The Vessells ready were, at his command;
MGREC112:6	H2392	Whose Sences all, were glutted with delights:
MGREC112:10	H2396	They were so wrapt with this externall glory.
MGREC113:9	H2436	Or flesh, or {and} life, could bear, till both were spent
MGREC113:10	H2437	Are {Were} now inflicted on *Parmenio's* Son,
MGREC113:12	H2439	At last he did: So they were justified,
MGREC114:1	H2469	When both were drunk, *Clitus* was wont to jeere;

MGREC~~116:36~~	H2602	There was {were} no worlds, more, to be conquered:
MGREC118:12	H2659	For second offers {offer} there were {was} never made;
MGREC125:33	H2983	That were {fell} within her reach, came to their ends;
MGREC~~129:25~~	H3139	And now they are, {were} free Lords, of what they had,
MGREC130:29	~~H3181~~	*Philip* and *Olympias* both were slain,
MGREC133:10	H3298	*Cassanders* Sons, soone after's death were slaine,
MGREC133:27	H3317	kingdomes {Empire was} were subdu'd by {to} th' *Roman* state.
MGREC133:35	H3325	Which we oft wish were {was} extant as before.
MGREC134:11	H3342	So many Princes still were murthered,
MGREC135:15	H3387	And Millions were subjected unto few:
MROMAN137:14	H3465	Their Daughters by the *Romans* then were caught,
DIALOG~~143:33~~	H102	Church Offices are {were} sold, and bought, for gaine,
DIALOG144:20	H130	For these, were threatned the wofull day,
SIDNEY150:12	H37	Such were prejudicate, and did not look:
DUBART154:17	H62	Their trophies were but heaps of wounded slain,
QELIZ156:38	H65	As were the subjects of our *(Pallas)* Queen:
DAVID159:9	H24	Pleasant and lovely were they both in life,
DAVID159:11	H26	Swifter then swiftest Eagles, so were they,
VANITY~~160:9~~	H19	They'r foul enough to day, that once was {were} fair,
TDUDLEY166:10	H52	His thoughts were more sublime, his actions wise,
CONTEM167:28	H5	Were gilded o're by his rich golden head.
CONTEM167:31	H8	Rapt were my sences at this delectable view.
CONTEM171:5	H110	And how their precepts to their sons were law,
AUTHOR177:35	H7	Where errors were not lessened (all may judg).
BIRTH180:9	H19	If any worth or virtue were in me,
1HUSB180:23	H2	If ever two were one, then surely we.
1HUSB180:24	H3	If ever man were lov'd by wife, then thee;
CHILDRN184:15	H4	Four Cocks there were, and Hens the rest,
CHILDRN185:36	H62	My throbs such now, as 'fore were never:
CHILDRN186:21	H88	And nurst you up till you were strong,
ELIZB187:2	H11	Or sigh thy dayes so soon were terminate;
MEDDM203:31	Hp284	We read of ten lepers that were Cleansed, but of one that
MEDDM207:6	Hp288	they were giuen for, as health wealth and honour, wch might be
MEDDM207:18	Hp289	perceiue a decay, in their greennes for were earthly comforts
MEDDM208:29	Hp290	possible to be done, it can remoue mountaines (if need were)
MYCHILD217:28	Hp243	thovght were it hell it self and could there find ye Love of God
MYCHILD217:35	Hp243	how did know but they were feigned. That there is a God my
MYCHILD218:24	Hp244	p^{r}secutions of the Saints, wch admitt were y^y as they terme y^m
MYCHILD218:33	Hp244	it were possible ye very elect should bee deceived. Behold
BYNIGHT220:4	H5	My waking eyes were open kept
SOREFIT221:21	H7	My plaints & Groanes were heard of Thee
28AUG225:26	Hp254	After mvch weaknes & sicknes when my spirits were worn out,
SON230:29	H12	Of pyrates who were neer at hand

WER'T (1) [wert]

SON231:8	H20	His help & his physitian wer't

WERT (7)

DIALOG~~143:41~~	H110	And thou, poore soule, wast {wert} jeer'd among the rest,
SIDNEY149:14	H13	Of Poesie, and of Musick thou wert {he was} King;
SIDNEY150:41	~~H69~~	I feare thou wert a Commet, did portend
SIDNEY151:9	~~H69~~	Who wert of honours band, the chief Commander.
QELIZ155:21	H12	To say, thou wert a fleshly Deity:

DAVID159:21	H36	O! lovely *Jonathan,* how wert {wast} thou slaine,
TDUDLEY165:32	H34	Truths friend thou wert, to errors still a foe,

WEST (1)

MASSYR62:24	H369	Whether the *Indians* of the East, or West,

WESTERN (1)

ELEMEN19:33	H474	Knowes {Know} Western Isles, *Christophers, Barbadoes;*

WET (3)

ELEMEN16:39	H362	And with aboundant wet, so coole the ground,
AGES38:11	H114	I fear'd no drought, nor wet, I had no crop,
SEASONS49:3	H94	With haire all wet, she puffing thus began.

WHALE (2)

ELEMEN10:11	H86	The Crown, the Whale, the Archer, Bernice Hare,
ELEMEN15:26	H308	There lives the oyly Whale, whom all men know,

W^T (5) [what] See also WHAT'S, WHATS

MYCHILD215:14	Hp240	to compose some short matters, (for w^t else to call y^m I know
MYCHILD215:16	Hp240	dayly in y^r rembrance, (Altho: y^t is the least in my aim in w^t I
MYCHILD216:23	Hp242	w^t was amisse. So vsually thvs it hath been wth me that I haue
HANNA230:15	H8	Gravnt shee rember w^t thov'st done
HOURS234:37	H51	Vnlesse thou help w^t can I doe

WHAT (250) See also W^T, WHAT'S, WHATS

FATHER6:10	H44	On what they are, your mild aspect I crave,
PROLOG6:29	H13	A *Bartas* can, doe what a *Bartas* wil,
PROLOG7:9	H23	By Art, he gladly found what he did seeke,
PROLOG7:18	H31	If what I doe prove well, it wo'nt advance,
PROLOG7:28	H39	Let *Greeks* be *Greeks,* and Women what they are,
ELEMEN8:30	H28	What is my worth (both ye) and all things {men} know,
ELEMEN8:32	H30	But what I am, let learned *Grecians* say;
ELEMEN8:33	H31	What I can doe, well skill'd Mechanicks may,
ELEMEN8:36	H34	What toole was ever fram'd, but by my might;
ELEMEN9:1	H35	O {Ye} Martialist! what weapon {weapons} for your fight?
ELEMEN9:5	H39	Without mine ayd, alas, what can they doe?
ELEMEN9:11	H45	Your shares, {Hooes} your mattocks, and what e're you see,
ELEMEN9:17	H51	Your spits, pots, jacks, what else I need not name,
ELEMEN9:25	H59	What mingled lay with earth, I cause to shine.
ELEMEN9:30	H64	But be he what they list {will}, yet his aspect,
ELEMEN10:35	H110	What famous Townes to cinders have I turn'd?
ELEMEN10:36	H111	What lasting Forts my kindled wrath hath burn'd?
ELEMEN11:6	H126	What shal I say of Lightning, and of Thunder,
ELEMEN11:29	H149	To tell what sundry fruits my fat soyle yeelds,
ELEMEN13:7	H208	But you will see what in my bowels lyes?
ELEMEN13:11	H212	But what I freely yeeld upon your sweat?
ELEMEN14:6	H250	What she hath lost by these my dreadfull {remed'less} woes.
ELEMEN14:9	H251	Again, what veines of poyson in me lye;
ELEMEN14:34	H276	If I withhold, what art thou, dead, dry lump
ELEMEN16:32	H355	I now must shew what force {ill} there in me lyes.
ELEMEN17:22	H386	All know, what {that} innundations I have made;
ELEMEN17:39	H403	Mortalls, what one of you, that loves not me,
ELEMEN18:13	H417	Nay, what are words, which doe reveale the mind?
ELEMEN18:14	H418	Speak, who, or what they will, they are but wind.
ELEMEN18:16	H420	What is't? but forced Aire which must {doth} rebound,
ELEMEN19:2	H447	And what those Sages, did, or {either} spake, or writ,

ELEMEN19:24	H469	What woeful wracks I've made, may wel appear,
ELEMEN19:32	H473	Again, what tempests,{furious storms} and what hericanoes
ELEMEN19:32	H473	Again, what tempests,{furious storms} and what hericanoes
ELEMEN19:38	H479	Then what prodigious sights, sometimes I show:
HUMOUR20:25	H17	But Sanguine did disdaine, what she requir'd,
HUMOUR21:5	H33	It shal suffice, to tel {shew} you what I am:
HUMOUR21:24	H52	What makes him face his foe, without appal?
HUMOUR21:29	H57	'Twixt them and others, what ist makes the odds
HUMOUR22:19	H88	Here's three of you, all sees {see} now what you are,
HUMOUR22:27	H96	What comes from thence, my heat refines the same,
HUMOUR23:16	H126	If once thou'rt great, what followes thereupon?
HUMOUR23:34	H144	Take choler from a Prince, what is he more,
HUMOUR24:4	H153	What differences the Sex, but only heat?
HUMOUR24:7	H156	I have been sparing, what I might have said,
HUMOUR24:9	H158	To what you now shal say, I wil attend,
HUMOUR24:29	H178	No valour upon earth, but what thou hast.
HUMOUR25:11	H200	But now Ile shew, what Souldier thou art.
HUMOUR26:15	H245	What is there living, which cannot derive
HUMOUR26:27	H257	What hath the heart, but what's sent from the liver?
HUMOUR26:29	H259	Then never boast of what thou do'st receive,
HUMOUR27:11	H282	But by what right, nor do'st, nor canst thou name;
HUMOUR27:19	H290	Nor what you've said, doth argue my disgrace,
HUMOUR27:27	H298	And what you singly {single} are, the whole I make.
HUMOUR27:29	H300	I moderately am all, what need I more:
HUMOUR29:18	H369	What mov'd thee thus to villifie my name?
HUMOUR30:1	H393	What greater Clerke, or polititian lives?
HUMOUR30:3	H395	What is too hot, my coldnesse doth abate;
HUMOUR30:15	H407	What is without, within, of theirs, or thine.
HUMOUR30:24	H416	But whilst he lives, Ile shew what part I have.
HUMOUR31:9	H442	What officer thou art to al us three.
HUMOUR31:28	H461	And what Flegme is, we know, likewise {like to} her mother,
HUMOUR31:32	H465	What Sanguine is, she doth not heed, nor care.
HUMOUR32:10	H484	What I imagine, that's my malady.
HUMOUR32:26	H500	To what is truth, I freely wil assent,
HUMOUR34:8	H563	What wonderments, within your bals there Iyes?
HUMOUR34:36	H591	And I passe by what sister Sanguine said;
AGES36:22	H46	A {An} Harvest of the best, what needs he more.
AGES36:26	H50	And al gave eare, to what he had to say.
AGES36:35	H59	That each should tel, what of himselfe he knew;
AGES38:31	H134	What gripes of wind, mine infancy did pain?
AGES38:32	H135	What tortures I, in breeding teeth sustain?
AGES38:33	H136	What crudities my cold stomach hath bred?
AGES38:35	H138	What breaches, knocks, and falls I daily have?
AGES39:6	H149	But what is best i'le first present to view,
AGES39:15	H158	Nor ignorant {And so likewise} what they in Country do;
AGES40:26	H207	And in a word, if what I am you'd heare,
AGES41:12	H231	Thus I have said, and what i've said {been,} you see,
AGES41:17	H236	What they have done, the same was done by me,
AGES43:25	H320	Thus good, and bad, and what I am, you see,
AGES43:26	H321	Now in a word, what my diseases be.
AGES44:2	H335	What you have been, ev'n such have I before,

AGES44:19	H352	But what I have done wel, that is my prop;
AGES45:22	H411	What are my thoughts, this is no time to say.
AGES45:34	H424	Nor sapors find, in what I drink or eat.
SEASONS47:23	H39	They joy in what they have, but more in hope,
SEASONS52:12	H227	What Winter hath to tel, now let him say.
SEASONS53:6	H262	*Accept therefore of what is penn'd,*
MASSYR55:11	H77	Adjudged to be drown'd, for what {th' crime} she'd done;
MASSYR56:41	H147	But by what means, we are not certifi'd.
MASSYR57:12	H159	What then he did, of worth, can no man tel,
MASSYR57:28	H173	What e're he was, they {or} did, or how it fel,
MASSYR57:34	H179	And such as care not, what befals their fames,
MASSYR58:39	H222	T'infranchise them, to grant what they could crave,
MASSYR59:3	H227	T' accept of what they could, they him {all} beseech.
MASSYR59:17	H241	That what *Arbaces* did, was but derided;
MASSYR60:12	H277	Not pertinent to what we have in hand;
MASSYR61:4	H309	What else he did, his Empire to advance,
MASSYR62:28	H373	But what, or where they are, yet know we this;
MASSYR64:5	H429	This was that King of Kings, did what he pleas'd,
MPERS72:29	H773	Who said but what, the King bad him expresse.
MPERS72:37	H782	The people ignorant of what was done,
MPERS73:31	H816	What forme of Government now to erect,
MPERS73:32	H817	The old, or new, which best, in what respect,
MPERS73:39	H824	What arguments they us'd, I know not well,
MPERS75:33	H890	Of what is freely granted by the King;
MPERS77:34	H975	What infamy to's honour did accrue.
MPERS79:24	H1050	What after did ensue, had he fore-seen,
MPERS80:33	H1100	And as a friend, warns him, what e're he doe,
MPERS84:9	H1237	What *Hester* {*Esther*} was, and did, her story reed,
MPERS84:12	H1243	With gold and silver, and what ere they need:
MPERS86:14	H1330	What helps, {help} in's enterprize he's like to find,
MPERS86:20	H1336	To win by force, what right could not obtain.
MPERS86:32	H1348	For what was done, seemed no whit offended.
MPERS89:12	H1446	What dastards in the field the *Persians* are;
MPERS89:32	H1466	Fit instruments t' accomplish what is ill;
MPERS89:41	H1475	But *Tyssaphern* did what he could devise,
MPERS90:14	H1484	The King afraid what further they might doe,
MPERS91:28	H1542	What troubles in his house he did sustain,
MPERS92:9	H1567	What Acts he did, time hath not now left pend,
MGREC94:18	H1655	And being ask'd what for himself was left,
MGREC95:29	H1708	To raise more force, for what he yet {to further his} intends.
MGREC98:37	H1839	First, at *Euphrates,* what he's like to abide,
MGREC99:28	H1871	What, hast thou lost thy late magnanimity?
MGREC101:37	H1966	But 'tis not known what slaughters here they {was} made.
MGREC103:21	H2032	For such revolters false, what Prince will {King can} trust:
MGREC107:1	H2176	But yet no notice takes, of what he hears;
MGREC109:5	H2262	And also of the *Mallians* what is writ.
MGREC112:30	H2416	Must suffer, not for what he did, but thought:
MGREC114:13	H2483	Next day, he tore his face, for what he'd done,
MGREC115:15	H2531	What e're he did, or thought not so content,
MGREC116:19	H2585	The principles of what he then had learn'd
MGREC117:14	H2621	What troubles, and contentions did ensue,

MGREC121:24	H2806	With what he held, he now was well {more} content,
MGREC122:28	H2847	What he appoints, She purposely withstands.
MGREC123:35	H2899	Prest to accomplish what he would have done;
MGREC125:8	H2956	*Euridice* hearing what she intends,
MGREC125:17	H2965	Remembring {Calling to mind} what sometime she had been,
MGREC126:11	H3002	Her Cousen of *Epire* did what he might,
MGREC127:34	H3064	Fearing their state {his force}, and what might hap ere long
MGREC127:41	H3071	And shews {clear} what cause they {he} had to take up {make
MGREC128:40	H3113	That each shall {should} hold what he doth {did} now possesse,
MGREC129:2	H3116	This touch'd *Cassander* sore, for what he'd done,
MGREC129:25	H3139	And now they are, {were} free Lords, of what they had,
MGREC129:34	H3148	*Cassander* fear'd what might of this insue,
MGREC130:20	H3175	The world must needs believe what he doth tell:
MGREC130:25	H3180	Now blood was paid with blood, for what was done
MGREC132:23	H3268	Injoy'd what so {ere} beseem'd his Royalty,
MGREC132:25	H3270	After three years he dyed, left what he'd won
MGREC132:31	H3278	Rich *Ægypt* left, and what else he had won
MGREC136:1	H3414	For what is past I blush, excuse to make,
MGREC136:10	H3424	*To finish what {what's} begun, new thoughts impart*
MGREC136:17	H3431	*What e're is found amisse, take in best {good} part,*
DIALOG141:8	H7	What ayles thee hang thy head, and crosse thine armes?
DIALOG141:10	H9	What deluge of new woes thus over-whelme
DIALOG141:12	H11	What meanes this wailing tone, this mourning guise?
DIALOG142:2	H31	What Medicine shall I seek to cure this woe,
DIALOG142:5	H34	What, hath some *Hengist,* like that *Saxon* stout,
DIALOG143:17	H86	What *Holland* is, I am in some suspence,
DIALOG143:25	H94	But yet, I answer not what you demand,
DIALOG143:37	H106	What scorning of the Saints of the most high,
DIALOG143:38	H107	What injuries did daily on them lye;
DIALOG143:39	H108	What false reports, which nick-names did they take,
DIALOG145:12	H161	Not what you feel, but what you do expect.
DIALOG145:13	H162	Pray in plain termes, what is your present grief,
DIALOG146:25	H211	my relief now use thy utmost skill {do what there lyes in thee}
DIALOG148:10	H275	Of what unjustly once she poll'd from thee,
DIALOG148:18	H283	(For then what is't, but English blades dare do)
SIDNEY149:28	H23	What doe thy vertues then? Oh, honours crown!
SIDNEY149:35	H23	Who honours thee for what was honourable,
SIDNEY150:21	H46	What famous feats thou didst, on *Flanders* coast,
DUBART154:24	H69	In giving one, what would have served seven.
DUBART155:5	H90	*Now shew'd what once they ought, Humanity,*
QELIZ156:30	H57	Unto our dread Virago, what they owe:
QELIZ157:20	H88	Of her what worth in Story's to be seen,
QELIZ157:31	H99	To read what others write, and then {so} admire.
VANITY159:34	H6	What is't in honour, to be set on high?
VANITY159:38	H10	What is't in wealth, great treasures for to gain {obtain}?
VANITY160:4	H14	What then? content in pleasures canst thou find?
VANITY160:8	H18	What is't in beauty? no, that's but a snare,
VANITY160:10	H20	What, Is't in flowring youth, or manly age?
VANITY160:18	H28	What is it then? to do as Stoicks tell,
VANITY160:35	H45	But where, and what it is, from heaven's declar'd,
TDUDLEY165:37	H39	But as a Pilgrim what he had, possest.

TDUDLEY166:9	H51	Their greatness may be judg'd by what they shew.
CONTEM167:33	H9	I wist not what to wish, yet sure thought I,
CONTEM168:18	H26	And softly said, what glory's like to thee?
CONTEM172:26	H160	Thou Emblem true, of what I count the best,
CONTEM173:5	H173	To see what trade they great ones there do drive,
CONTEM173:21	H187	To gain more good, or shun what might thee harm
CONTEM173:24	H190	Reminds not what is past, nor whats to come dost fear.
FLESH175:10	H10	Sister, quoth Flesh, what liv'st thou on
FLESH175:24	H24	What canst desire, but thou maist see
FLESH175:35	H35	Earth hath enough of what you will.
FLESH175:36	H36	Then let not goe, what thou maist find,
FLESH176:13	H53	When I believ'd, what thou hast said,
FLESH176:15	H55	Then when I did what thou bad'st doe.
FLESH176:39	H79	What is Invisible to thee.
BIRTH180:6	H16	What nature would, God grant to yours and you;
1LETTER181:15	H13	In this dead time, alas, what can I more
2LETTER182:33	H39	Now post with double speed, mark what I say,
CHILDRN185:18	H44	Let others know what are my fears
CHILDRN185:30	H56	And knew what thoughts there sadly rest,
CHILDRN186:20	H87	That did what could be done for young,
CHILDRN186:24	H91	Taught what was good, and what was ill,
CHILDRN186:25	H92	What would save life, and what would kill.
ELIZB187:8	H16	And time brings down what is both strong and tall.
MERCY188:29	H15	Was ignorant what riches thou hadst lost.
MERCY189:15	H36	What though, thy strokes full sad & grievous be,
MEDDM197:8	Hp274	they haue more sence then faith they se what they inioy,
MEDDM197:23	Hp275	abase them more, then this What hast thou, but what thou hast
MEDDM199:13	Hp277	on his anuile into what frame he pleases
MEDDM200:16	Hp279	garment, she easily foresees what euents it is like to produce,
MEDDM200:27	Hp279	what they lost in the Autumn so shall it be at that great day
MEDDM201:8	Hp280	I haue seen an end of all Sinning, what he did say, may be
MEDDM201:9	Hp280	sayd by many, but what he did not say, cannot (truly) be
MEDDM203:4	Hp283	for what do we obtaine of all these things, but it is wth labour
MEDDM203:21	Hp283	He that neuer felt, what it was to be sick or wounded, doth not
MEDDM208:3	Hp289	these things must be what manner of persons ought we to be,
MEDDM209:10	Hp291	but what was y^c Issue, they became a snare vnto them,
MEDDM209:19	Hp291	Commoditys wthin it self, but what it wants, another shall
PILGRIM210:31	H31	What tho my flesh shall there consume
TOCHILD215:5	H5	What was yr liueing mothers mind.
TOCHILD215:6	H6	Make vse of what I leaue in Loue
MYCHILD215:25	Hp240	wayes, & what I knew was sinfull as lying, disobed^c. to parents.
MYCHILD216:32	Hp242	try me, see what wayes of wickednes are in me, and lead me
MYCHILD218:31	Hp244	Faith vpon ye Earth? & I haue not known what to think, But
BYNIGHT220:17	H15	What to my Sav^r. shall I giue?
FEVER221:5	H20	What tho: in dust it shall bee lay'd
SOREFIT221:28	H14	What shall I render to my God
MED223:16	Hp250	p^{r}fectly what he hath done for me, and then shall I bee able to
WHAT224:1	H1	What God is like to him I serve
WHAT224:2	H2	What Sav^r. like to mine?
WHAT224:8	H8	For what thou'st done for me.
MYSOUL225:1	H5	What tho: thy outward Man decay,

MYSOUL225:13	H17	Then shall I know what thov hast done
13MAY227:13	H22	I studiovs am what I shall doe
THEART229:17	H19	What thou bestow'st I shall restore
SON231:21	H33	And may putt him in mind of what
HOURS234:7	H21	And when I know not what to doe
HOURS234:12	H26	But what from Thee I find.
HOURS235:2	H54	Return Thee what I owe.
REMB235:23	H4	What shall I render to thy Name
REMB236:1	H16	What did I ask but thov gav'st?
REMB236:2	H17	What could I more desire?

WHATEVER (1)

TDUDLEY165:9	H11	To whom I ought whatever I could doe:

WHAT'S (17) [what is]

ELEMEN15:23	H305	But what's the wealth that my rich Ocean brings?
ELEMEN20:6	H488	But what's their worth, {wrath} or force, but more's {same's} in
HUMOUR26:27	H257	What hath the heart, but what's sent from the liver?
HUMOUR27:34	H305	This scarlet die's a badge of what's within,
HUMOUR30:4	H396	What's diffluent, I do consolidate.
HUMOUR32:28	H502	What's slanderous, repel; doubtful, dispute;
HUMOUR32:36	H510	Nay, I could tel you (what's more true then meet)
HUMOUR34:22	H577	For what's the Brains, is mine, by consequence;
AGES38:21	H124	A perverse will, a love to what's forbid:
AGES41:21	H230	But what's of worth, your eyes shal first behold,
AGES45:24	H414	We old men love to tell, what's done in youth.
MGREC120:28	H2765	Goes to *Antipater,* and tels what's done;
MGREC136:10	H3424	*To finish what {what's} begun, new thoughts impart*
MROMAN139:27	H3553	To finish what's begun, was my intent,
DIALOG142:22	H51	If none of these, deare Mother, what's your woe?
SIDNEY151:40	H75	*Apollo* laught to patch up what's begun,
SICKNES178:30	H13	For what's this life, but care and strife?

WHATS (1) [what is]

CONTEM173:24	H190	Reminds not what is past, nor whats to come dost fear.

WHEAT (4)

AGES36:21	H45	Under his arme a Sheafe of wheat he bore,
SEASONS50:19	H153	And bundles up in sheaves the weighty Wheat,
MPERS75:30	H887	Gives sacrifices, wheat, wine, oyle, and salt,
TDUDLEY166:18	H60	Now fully ripe, as shock of wheat that's grown,

WHEELES (1) [wheels]

MGREC96:25	H1745	Like severall houses moving upon wheeles:

WHEELS (2) [pl.]

AGES36:11	H35	Then praancing on the Stage, about he wheels;
2LETTER181:35	H5	(And if the whirling of thy wheels don't drown'd)

WHELPS (1) [pl.]

VANITY160:27	H37	Where lions fierce, nor lions whelps hath {have} been,

W^N (2) [when]

MYCHILD216:30	Hp242	fovnd them ye Times w^n ye Lord hath manifested ye most
MED223:3	Hp250	should I doubt any more w^n thov hast given me such assured

WN (1) [when]

MYCHILD215:10	Hp240	by exper^c. y^t ye exhortat^s. of parents take most effect wn y^e

WHEN (208) See also WHEN'TS

FATHER6:9	H43	These ragged lines, will do't, when they appear.

PROLOG6:25	H9	But when my wondring eyes, and envious heart,
ELEMEN10:21	H96	When in conjunction with the sun, yet {do} more,
ELEMEN10:25	H100	Of old, when Sacrifices were divine,
ELEMEN10:41	H116	Which when they could not be o're come by foes
ELEMEN11:13	H133	Not sparing life when I can take the same;
ELEMEN12:31	H191	After three years, when men and meat is spent,
ELEMEN12:38	H198	And Oares to row, when both my sisters failes?
ELEMEN12:40	H200	Which guides, when Sun, nor Moon, nor Stars do shine.
ELEMEN13:36	H237	Again, when Delvers dare in hope of gold,
ELEMEN~~13:41~~	H242	If {When} once you feele me, your foundation, quake,
ELEMEN14:14	H256	When they seek food, and harme mistrust the least.
ELEMEN14:18	H260	But windy sister, 'twas when you have blown.
ELEMEN14:39	H281	Complaines to th'heaven, when {if} I withhold my drops:
ELEMEN15:1	H283	When I am gone, their fiercenesse none need {needs} doubt;
ELEMEN15:19	H301	That she can spare, when Nations round are poore.
ELEMEN15:20	H302	When I run low, and not o'reflow her brinks;
ELEMEN16:24	H347	Both when we list, to water we convert.
ELEMEN17:24	H388	As when *Achaia,* all under water stood,
ELEMEN18:25	H429	When burning heat, doth cause you faint, I coole,
ELEMEN18:26	H430	And when I smile, your Ocean's like a Poole.
ELEMEN18:34	H438	And when I'm throughly rarifi'd, turn fire.
ELEMEN18:35	H439	So when I am condens'd, I turne to water;
HUMOUR21:30	H58	But valour, when comes that? from none of you;
HUMOUR22:30	H99	For when they faile, man turnes unto his clay:
HUMOUR23:8	H118	Tis true, when I am midwife to thy birth;
HUMOUR23:32	H142	That when a Varlet, struck him o're the side,
HUMOUR25:14	H203	Thy Choler is but rage, when tis most pure.
HUMOUR25:15	H204	But useful, when a mixture can indure.
HUMOUR25:17	H206	The best of al the four, when they agree.
HUMOUR25:22	H211	But when thou scorn'st to take the helpe we lend,
HUMOUR26:1	H231	But such thou never art, when al alone;
HUMOUR26:2	H232	Yet such, when we al four are joyn'd in one.
HUMOUR26:3	H233	And when such thou art, even such are we.
HUMOUR27:23	H294	When 'tis untaint, pure, and most genuine
HUMOUR29:4	H357	Especially when freindship is pretended:
HUMOUR29:12	H365	But when the first offenders {offender} I have laid,
HUMOUR29:26	H377	When in Battalia my foes I face,
HUMOUR30:17	H409	When death doth seize the man, your stock is lost,
HUMOUR30:18	H410	When you poor bankrupts prove, then have I most.
HUMOUR30:21	H413	Then who's mans friend, when life and all forsakes?
HUMOUR31:4	H437	When by thy heat, thou'st bak'd thy selfe to crust,
HUMOUR32:29	H503	And when i've nothing left to say, be mute;
HUMOUR32:38	H512	When sister Sanguine paints my Ivory face,
HUMOUR32:40	H514	My Lilly white, when joyned with her red,
AGES35:36	H22	And when tis broke, then ends his life and all.
AGES36:8	H32	When blushing first, she 'gins to red {light} the Aire.
AGES37:17	H79	When wretched I (ungrate) {ingrate} had done the wrong.
AGES37:18	H80	When Infancy was past, my Childishnesse,
AGES41:23	H240	When my Wilde Oates, were sown, and ripe, & mown,
AGES43:12	~~H305~~	When to a Monarchy, my way they barr'd.
AGES44:31	H364	When it was rul'd by that Celestial she;

AGES44:39	H372	When it had lost that radiant Sun-like spark,
AGES46:20	H451	And when this flesh shal rot, and be consum'd,
SEASONS48:1	H54	That when the Sun (on's love) the earth doth shine,
SEASONS48:38	H89	When Spring had done, then {the} Summer must {did} begin,
SEASONS49:20	H111	Whose fleece when purely {finely} spun, and deeply dy'd,
SEASONS51:5	H179	But its a precious juyce, when wel it's used.
SEASONS51:26	H202	Which notes, when youth, and strength, have past their prime,
SEASONS51:32	H208	But when the Son of Righteousnesse drawes nigh,
SEASONS52:4	H219	When cold, the sap to th' roots hath low'st repell'd;
MASSYR53:15	H5	When Time was young, and World in infancy,
MASSYR53:33	H23	When thus with rule he had been dignified,
MASSYR57:25	H172	When famous *Troy* was so beleaguered:
MASSYR57:26	H172	Which to her neighbours, when it was made known,
MASSYR59:25	H249	That when the River prov'd their enemy,
MASSYR59:37	H261	When *Jonah* for their sins denounc'd such {those} woes;
MASSYR60:10	H275	{To} *Medes,* and *Persians,* {when he crav'd} their assisting
MASSYR60:34	H299	When this was built, and all matters in peace,
MASSYR61:16	H321	When *Resins* force his borders sore did mar.
MASSYR61:25	H330	When *Rezin's* slain, his Army over-thrown,
MASSYR64:7	H431	And this is {was} he, who when he fear'd the least,
MASSYR65:10	H475	When in the *Tyrian* wars, the {this} King was hot,
MASSYR66:14	H520	No, nor {not} when *Moab, Edom* he had got.
MPERS69:7	H629	When *Sardanapalus* was over-thrown,
MPERS75:10	H871	When opportunity he saw was fit,
MPERS76:40	H938	Renews his hold; but {and} when of that bereft,
MPERS80:9	H1076	When as one thousand, could some Millions {a million} daunt;
MPERS82:28	H1175	But she was stil, as when it {he} first begun.
MPERS82:29	H1176	When jealous Queen *Amestris,* of this knew,
MPERS83:34	H1222	Then when the world, they after over-run:
MPERS84:14	H1250	When under Ostracisme he did lye.
MPERS87:36	H1388	He surest {safest} was, when furthest {farthest} out o'th' way.
MPERS87:41	H1393	When suddenly their Scouts come in and cry,
MPERS88:10	H1403	But when their order, and {their} silence they saw;
MPERS88:30	H1423	At {But when} last his head they spy upon a Launce,
MPERS90:2	H1477	But when through difficulties still {all} they brake,
MGREC94:25	H1663	When newes of *Alexander,* came to th' Court,
MGREC96:35	H1755	But when both Armies met, he might behold,
MGREC100:37	H1921	When this sad newes (at first) *Darius* heares,
MGREC100:39	H1923	But when inform'd, how royally the King
MGREC101:19	H1944	Nor infamy had wak'd, when he had slept;
MGREC103:10	H2021	For when the Souldiers, had rifled their pleasure,
MGREC104:9	H2061	If when he'd multitudes, the day he lost;
MGREC109:10	H2269	When thus, ten dayes, his brain with wine he'd soak'd,
MGREC110:2	H2302	For to receive {To give} him, {welcome} when he comes to
MGREC110:12	H2312	Then {When} covertly, the rest gets {get} o're else-where;
MGREC110:18	H2318	When *Alexander* strives to win the field,
MGREC114:1	H2469	When both were drunk, *Clitus* was wont to jeere;
MGREC114:7	H2475	Upon a time, when both had drunken well,
MGREC114:7	H2475	Both at a Feast when they had tippled well
MGREC114:33	H2503	When e're 'tis said, he thousand thousands slew,
MGREC116:10	H2571	When this sad news came to *Darius* Mother,

MGREC116:20	H2586	Might to the last (when sober) be discern'd.
MGREC116:24	H2590	And under's pillow laid them when he slept.
MGREC117:19	H2626	When of his monstrous bulk it was the guide,
MGREC118:23	H2670	After this {some} time, when stirs began to calme,
MGREC~~122:37~~	H2858	When to his pleasure all things they had done,
MGREC~~123:14~~	H2878	Now {When} great *Antipater,* the world doth {must} leave
MGREC124:28	H2935	Thinks to enthrone the Prince when riper grown;
MGREC124:36	H2943	When *Alexander* knockt his head to th' wall:
MGREC125:16	H2964	But when her Souldiers saw their ancient Queen,
MGREC127:20	H3050	When victor oft had {he'd} been, and so might still,
MGREC129:26	H3140	When this foul tragedy was past, and done,
MGREC~~131:9~~	H3201	How some when down, straight got the upper hand
MGREC131:30	H3222	When his disease the skilfull Physician found,
MGREC133:41	H3331	*Seleuchus* reign'd, when he had lost his life,
MGREC135:32	H3404	And when he had no appetite to eate,
MROMAN137:28	H3479	Kept shut in peace, but {set} ope when bloud was spilt;
MROMAN139:13	H3541	Sate on the Throne, when he had slaine his foe;
MROMAN139:35	H3561	At length resolv'd, when many years had past,
DIALOG147:27	H251	When they are gone, then drown your self in teares.
DIALOG148:4	H269	When truth and righteousnesse they thus shall nourish.
DIALOG148:5	H270	When thus in Peace: thine Armies brave send out,
SIDNEY149:7	H6	When *England* did injoy her Halsion dayes,
SIDNEY151:17	~~H69~~	When such a *Hero* shoots him out o'th' field,
DUBART154:10	H55	Pardon, if I adore, when I admire.
TDUDLEY165:27	H29	Who staid thy feeble sides when thou wast low,
TDUDLEY165:39	H41	Nor honours pufft him up, when he had part:
TDUDLEY167:3	H85	*And when his time with years was spent*
CONTEM167:26	H3	When *Phœbus* wanted but one hour to bed,
CONTEM169:26	H65	When present times look back to Ages past,
CONTEM170:33	H103	When deep dispair, with wish of life hath fought,
CONTEM171:18	H121	When I behold the heavens as in their prime,
CONTEM172:3	H140	And when unmade, so ever shall they lye,
CONTEM174:36	H233	Shall last and shine when all of these are gone.
FLESH176:13	H53	When I believ'd, what thou hast said,
FLESH176:15	H55	Then when I did what thou bad'st doe.
FLESH176:23	H63	When I am victor over thee,
FLESH176:25	H65	When thou my Captive shalt be led,
SICKNES178:25	H8	when he so high provok'd.
BIRTH180:3	H13	That when that knot's unty'd that made us one,
BIRTH180:11	H21	And when thou feel'st no grief, as I no harms,
BIRTH180:13	H23	And when thy loss shall be repaid with gains
1HUSB180:34	H13	That when we live no more, we may live ever.
1LETTER181:21	H19	But when thou *Northward* to me shalt return,
2LETTER182:17	H23	And when thou canst not treat by loving mouth,
2LETTER182:22	H28	O how they joy when thou dost light the skyes.
CHILDRN185:31	H57	Great was my pain when I you bred,
CHILDRN185:32	H58	Great was my care, when I you fed,
CHILDRN186:16	H83	When each of you shall in your nest
ELIZB187:5	H13	By nature Trees do rot when they are grown.
ANNEB187:19	H9	When I on fading things my hopes have set?
ANNEB187:29	H19	As if mine own, when thus impermanent.

2SIMON195:7	Hp271	look vpon when you should see me no more, I could think of
MEDDM196:14	Hp273	that labours all the day comforts himself, that when night
MEDDM196:17	Hp273	drought of the day, when he perceiues his sun apace to decline
MEDDM199:29	Hp278	when he is once dead, but the last mangles him in his graue
MEDDM200:28	Hp279	when the Sun of righteoussnes shall appear those dry bones
MEDDM202:22	Hp282	although we may walk by his light, but when he is set, we are
MEDDM202:26	Hp282	go forwards to the Citty of habitation, but when he seemes to
MEDDM202:29	Hp282	god, and when ye morning (wch is the appointed time) is come
MEDDM203:5	Hp283	vexation? When we inioy them it is wth vanity and vexation,
MEDDM203:26	Hp283	skill to cure it, but when he findes his diseases to disrest him,
MEDDM203:33	Hp284	men can vse great importunity when they are in distresses and
MEDDM204:11	Hp284	man so to improue his talents, that when his great master
MEDDM205:4	Hp285	of morality, much lesse of grace in them But when by prudent
MEDDM206:17	Hp287	shall they be, when they are fixt in their heauenly spheres
MEDDM206:28	Hp288	his great worke of election and Reprobation, when we consider
MEDDM206:32	Hp288	but takes and chuses, when and where and whom he pleases,
MEDDM207:27	Hp289	when, should make vs so to number our dayes as to apply our
MEDDM207:28	Hp289	that when wee are put out of these houses of Clay, we
MEDDM208:23	Hp290	but when death threatens and distresse lays hold vpon them
MEDDM208:33	Hp290	it hath ouer come the omnipotent himself, as when Moses
MEDDM208:36	Hp291	armes of the mighty god of Jacob yea Jacob himself when he
PILGRIM210:33	H33	And when a few yeares shall be gone
TOCHILD215:3	H3	I leaue for yov when I am dead,
MYCHILD215:15	Hp240	not) and bequeath to yov, that when I am no more wth yov, yet
MYCHILD216:4	Hp241	small pox, When I was in my afflict^n. I besovght the Lord, and
MYCHILD217:4	Hp242	when ye Almighty hath hid his face from me, that yet I haue
MYCHILD217:23	Hp243	that felicity that somt. I haue done, But when I haue been
MYCHILD217:25	Hp243	ye Lord, and when I haue been in sicknes + pain, I haue
MYCHILD218:17	Hp244	When I haue gott over this Block y^n have I another pvtt in my
BYNIGHT220:2	H3	By night when others soundly slept,
FEVER220:22	H2	When Sorrowes had begyrt me rovnd,
FEVER220:24	H4	When in my flesh no part was fovnd
SOREFIT221:17	H3	When novght on Earth could comfort giue
SOREFIT221:18	H4	And when my Soul these things abhor'd
SOREFIT221:26	H12	Yea when I was most low and poor,
MED223:1	Hp250	Meditations when my Soul hath been refreshed wth the
MED223:15	Hp250	But this is my comfort, When I come into Heaven, I shall
JULY223:26	Hp251	y^t it may bee a support to me when I shall haue occasion
JULY223:27	Hp251	read this hereafter, and to others that shall read it when I shall
MYSOUL225:22	H26	Thy face when shall I see
28AUG225:26	Hp254	After mvch weaknes & sicknes when my spirits were worn out,
28AUG226:5	Hp254	I can wait, looking every day when my Sav^r shall call for me.
28AUG226:8	Hp254	thy great Love to my soul so lately expressed, when I could
30SEPT227:31	Hp257	ye like for yov if you trvst in him; And when he shall deliuer
RESTOR229:21	H4	When feares and sorrowes me besett
RESTOR229:23	H6	When heart did faint & Spirits quail
HANNA230:13	H6	When death did seem ev'n to approach
SON231:7	H19	In sicknes when he lay full sore
SON231:9	H21	When royall ones y^t Time did dye,
HOURS234:7	H21	And when I know not what to doe
ACK235:14	H14	And rais'd him vp when he was sick.

HOUSE236:13	H5	In silent night when rest I took
HOUSE236:25	H17	And when I could no longer look
HOUSE236:33	H25	When by the Ruines oft I past

WHENCE (15)

ELEMEN8:12	H10	Whence issu'd raines, and winds, lightning and thunder;
HUMOUR21:4	H32	It is acknowledged, from whence I came,
HUMOUR22:23	H92	{From} Whence flow fine spirits, and witty notions?
HUMOUR31:14	H445	If any doubt this {the} truth, whence this should come;
HUMOUR33:37	H551	The spirits animal, from whence doth {hence do} slide,
HUMOUR34:6	H561	Whence her affections, passions, speak so clear;
AGES38:34	H137	Whence vomits, wormes, and flux have issued?
AGES43:9	H305	Whence poyson, Pistols, and dread instruments,
AGES45:25	H415	But I returne, from whence I stept awry,
AGES46:2	H433	I then shal go, whence I shal come no more,
MASSYR55:19	H85	Whence rose that fable, she by birds was fed.
MASSYR56:17	H123	From whence, Astrologers, oft view'd the skies.
DIALOG142:27	H56	Whence is this {the} storme, from Earth, or Heaven above?
DIALOG144:17	H127	Whence flow'd the source, the sprigs, the boughs, and fruits;
FLESH176:9	H49	Whence my dear father I do love.

WHEN'TS (1) [when it is]

ELEMEN19:13	H458	So when'ts corrupt, mortality is rife.

WHER (2) [where]

MEDDM197:14	Hp274	man, can goe vpright, vnder that door, wher a taller is glad to
MEDDM203:13	Hp283	wher his bussines lyes, a christian is sailing through this world

WHERE (106) See also WHERE'S, WHERE'TS

FATHER5:30	H31	Each others faults, and where themselves excell:
ELEMEN8:31	H29	Where {In} little is, {time} I can but little show,
ELEMEN10:14	H89	*Eridanus,* where *Phaeton* was drown'd,
ELEMEN12:30	H190	Send forth your well man'd ships, where sun doth rise.
ELEMEN12:37	H197	But Marriners, where got you ships and sailes?
ELEMEN13:25	H226	Thistles and thornes, where he expected graine;
ELEMEN16:8	H331	*Asphaltis* Lake, where nought remains alive.
ELEMEN19:26	H471	Where famous *Charles* the fift, more losse sustain'd,
ELEMEN19:34	H475	Where neither houses, trees, nor plants, I spare;
HUMOUR21:15	H43	Where Monarch-like I play, and sway alone.
HUMOUR21:18	H46	Where if your rule once grow {prove} predominant,
HUMOUR23:14	H124	Where paine and sore obstructions, {obstruction} thou dost
HUMOUR23:15	H125	Where envy, malice, thy companions lurke.
HUMOUR24:31	H180	And leave't to all, to judge where valour lyes.
HUMOUR29:5	H358	That blow's most deadly, where it is intended;
HUMOUR32:25	H499	Where opposition is diametrical:
HUMOUR33:17	H531	No debtor I, because 'tis {it's} paid else where;
HUMOUR34:24	H579	But a mad one, say I, where 'tis too great,
AGES37:41	H103	Where e're I went, mine innocence was shield.
AGES43:30	H325	To break the darksome prison, where it's pend;
AGES46:19	H450	There, {Where} I shal rest, til heavens shal be no more;
SEASONS50:10	H144	To Barns, and Stacks, where it for Fodder lyes.
SEASONS51:31	H207	Where also he, his Winter time must have;
SEASONS52:39	H256	Where first it did begin, in th' end its found.
MASSYR54:29	H56	Where e're he warr'd he had too good successe,
MASSYR62:18	H363	{He} Plac'd *Israel* in's Land {there}, where he thought best,

MASSYR62:22	H367	Where now those ten Tribes are, can no man tel,
MASSYR62:28	H373	But what, or where they are, yet know we this;
MASSYR65:2	H467	Where after many assayes, they make {made} at last,
MASSYR66:1	H507	Where to the sword, all but himself was {were} put,
MASSYR66:9	H515	Where late, of Harp, and Lute, was {were} heard the noyse,
MASSYR66:22	H528	Where e're he goes, he Conquers every Land;
MPERS69:26	H648	Where all that doe {dare} resist, are slaughter'd down;
MPERS69:35	H657	Then on a Pike being {wood-pile} set, where all might eye,
MPERS70:37	H708	Where *Alexander* fought, in hope of prize,
MPERS70:37	H708	Where some long after fought in vain for prize
MPERS70:40	H711	Where that proud Conquerour could doe no lesse,
MPERS76:34	H932	Where *Grecians* prov'd themselves right Souldiers, stout;
MPERS76:36	H934	Where an *Athenian* shew'd a valiant deed,
MPERS78:26	H1007	Save the *Zidonians,* where *Xerxes* was.
MPERS80:8	H1075	Where is the valour, of your antient State?
MPERS81:37	H1143	Where both sides exercis'd their manly feats;
MPERS82:2	H1149	Where both their Controversies they'l decide;
MPERS82:36	H1183	Where he had sometime gaz'd with great delight.
MPERS82:37	H1184	To see that face, where Rose and Lilly stood,
MPERS82:39	H1186	To see those breasts, where chastity did dwel,
MPERS83:38	H1226	Where ninescore days, are spent in banquetting,
MPERS89:20	H1454	Asking no favour, where they fear'd no bands.
MGREC95:7	H1686	Where stood of late *Diana's,* wondrous Phane,
MGREC95:16	H1695	There {where} the Prophetick knot, he cuts in twain;
MGREC99:16	H1859	Where valiant *Betis,* doth defend {stoutly keeps} the town,
MGREC100:2	H1886	Where happily in's wars he did succeed;
MGREC102:21	H1991	Where four and thirty dayes he now doth stay,
MGREC102:32	H2002	Where Kings have shown their glory, wealth, and might;
MGREC107:25	H2200	Where most {so} immoderatly these thirsty drink;
MGREC108:28	H2244	Where *Scithians* rude, his valour {army} doth oppose,
MGREC110:40	H2344	Where he entomb'd his stately stallion.
MGREC111:3	H2348	Where one hundred {Whether} Embassadours, {ninety} or
MGREC115:13	H2522	To punish, where himself deserved blame:
MGREC119:17	H2707	To *Lamia,* where he shut up doth ly:
MGREC125:39	H2989	Where hearing of this newes he speeds away,
MGREC128:24	H3097	Where {great Antigonus} *Ptolomy,* and the rest {was} put him
MGREC130:6	H3161	Where, by Embassage, all these Princes pray,
MGREC135:1	H3371	At *Actium* slain, {where} his Navy {Navy's} put to flight.
MROMAN136:29	H3443	Where Shepheards once had Coats, and Sheep their Folds,
MROMAN136:30	H3444	Where Swaines, and rustick Peasants made {kept} their Holds.
DIALOG144:13	H123	Where is the Nation, I cann't paralize;
SIDNEY150:35	H62	Where is that envious tongue, but can afford,
DUBART153:5	H9	Where Art, and more then Art in Nature shines;
QELIZ155:36	H27	The World's the Theater where she did act;
VANITY159:32	H4	Where is the man can say, lo, I have found
VANITY160:12	H22	Where is it then? in wisdome, learning, arts?
VANITY160:24	H34	Where shall I climbe, sound, seek, search or find,
VANITY160:27	H37	Where lions fierce, nor lions whelps hath {have} been,
VANITY160:35	H45	But where, and what it is, from heaven's declar'd,
TDUDLEY165:20	H22	Well known and lov'd, where ere he liv'd, by most
TDUDLEY166:21	H63	Where storms, nor showrs, nor ought can damnifie.

TDUDLEY166:32	H74	Where we with joy each others face shall see,
CONTEM169:10	H51	Silent alone, where none or saw, or heard,
CONTEM171:24	H127	But Man grows old, lies down, remains where once he's laid.
CONTEM172:8	H144	Where gliding streams the Rocks did overwhelm;
CONTEM172:25	H159	To *Thetis* house, where all imbrace and greet:
CONTEM172:32	H165	Now salt, now fresh where you think best to glide
CONTEM173:22	H188	Thy cloaths ne're wear, thy meat is every where,
CONTEM173:32	H197	Where winter's never felt by that sweet airy legion.
FLESH175:2	H2	In secret place where once I stood
FLESH177:5	H86	The City where I hope to dwell,
AUTHOR177:35	H7	Where errors were not lessened (all may judg).
AUTHOR178:12	H22	And take thy way where yet thou art not known,
SICKNES178:28	H11	Where I shall have all I can crave,
1LETTER181:25	H23	Where ever, ever stay, and go not thence,
3LETTER183:18	H20	Where she her captive husband doth espy.
3LETTER183:32	H34	*At home, abroad, and every where.*
VERSES184:7	H11	Where nothing's to be had Kings loose their right
CHILDRN184:32	H21	A prettier bird was no where seen,
CHILDRN185:1	H27	And where *Aurora* first appears,
CHILDRN186:12	H79	Where old ones, instantly grow young,
MEDDM198:9	Hp276	walks among briars and thorns will be very carefull, where he
MEDDM206:32	Hp288	but takes and chuses, when and where and whom he pleases,
MEDDM207:26	Hp289	that time will come, together, wth the vncertainty, how where,
MYCHILD216:8	Hp241	into this Covntry, where I fovnd a new World and new manners
SOREFIT221:31	H17	Where pitty most of all I see.
MED223:11	Hp250	them known who or where is the man that durst in his heart
13MAY227:4	H13	I'le rvn where I was succoured.
HOURS233:31	H14	Where I doe kneel or walk.
HOUSE236:36	H28	Where oft I sate and long did lye,

WHEREBY (2)

AGES43:18	H313	Whereby my empty soule, is lur'd and caught.
MGREC133:21	H3309	Whereby immortall honour they acquire.

WHEREFORE (5)

MGREC106:2	~~H2136~~	Wherefore the gods requite thy kinde regard.
MGREC113:16	H2443	They knew not; wherefore, best now to be done,
MGREC113:22	H2449	Wherefore at once all these to satisfie,
DIALOG142:1	H30	In generall terms, but will not say wherefore:
DIALOG145:37	H186	This was deny'd, I need not say wherefore.

WHEREIN (8)

ELEMEN14:17	H259	Wherein whole Armies {*Cambyses* Armie} I have {was} over
ELEMEN17:23	H387	Wherein not men, but mountaines seem'd to wade
AGES37:34	H96	No office coveted, wherein I might
SEASONS48:10	H63	Wherein the earth, is clad in rich aray:
MPERS88:21	H1414	Of six thousand, wherein the King was yet;
MGREC108:10	H2226	Wherein their own had {got the} soveraignity.
MGREC112:24	H2410	Nothing was found {prov'd}, wherein he had offended;
MGREC122:6	H2829	His stratagems, wherein he did excel,

WHEREOF (2)

ELEMEN17:16	H380	Whereof the first, so ominous I rain'd,
ELEMEN19:16	H461	Whereof such multitudes have dy'd and fled,

WHEREON (2)

MASSYR65:3 H468 The Sea firm Land, whereon the Army past,

MGREC110:34 H2338 Whereon his acts, and travels, long appears;

WHERE'S (2) [where is]

PROLOG7:2 H17 Nor perfect beauty, where's a maine defect,

ELEMEN10:39 H114 Where's *Ninus* great wal'd Town, and *Troy* of old?

WHERE'TS (1) [where it is]

HUMOUR27:38 H309 But here's {here} one thrusts her heat, where'ts not requir'd

WHETHER (8)

ELEMEN12:4 H164 Whether Pyrenian, or the Alpes; both lyes

ELEMEN14:21 H263 And after death, whether inter'd, or burn'd;

MASSYR62:24 H369 Whether the *Indians* of the East, or West,

MASSYR64:30 H454 Whether her wealth, or yet her strength was most;

MGREC~~111:3~~ H2348 Where one hundred {Whether} Embassadours, {ninety} or

MEDDM201:4 Hp280 go vpright vnder them, but it matters not whether the load be

MYCHILD215:12 Hp240 latest, + being ignorant whether on my death bed I shall haue

MYCHILD217:33 Hp243 many times by Atheisme how I could know whether there was

WHETTED (1)

MPERS76:41 H939 His whetted teeth he sticks {claps} in the firm wood,

WHEY (1)

HUMOUR28:17 H329 Likewise the Whey, some use I in the veines,

W^{CH} (53)

2SIMON195:15 Hp271 reioyceing at that great day of appearing, wch is the continuall

MEDDM196:28 Hp273 children, haue their different natures, some are like flesh w^{ch}

MEDDM196:33 Hp274 That town wch thousands of enemys wthout hath not been able

MEDDM196:34 Hp274 been deliuered vp by one traytor wthin, and that man wch all

MEDDM197:9 Hp274 they do but hope for that wch is to Come

MEDDM197:18 Hp275 That house wch is not often swept makes the cleanly inhabitant

MEDDM197:19 Hp275 loath it, and that heart wch is not continually purifieing it self is

MEDDM198:6 Hp276 ouer their heads he then leads them to the Rock wch is higher

MEDDM198:18 Hp276 of men, wch they all catch gre͞dily at but few perceiues

MEDDM200:29 Hp279 arise in far more glory, then that wch they lost at their creation,

MEDDM200:33 Hp280 father will not lay a burden on a child of seven yeares old, w^{ch}

MEDDM201:22 Hp281 some black Clouds that impends them, wch produces these

MEDDM202:29 Hp282 when ye morning (wch is the appointed time) is come the Sun

MEDDM202:32 Hp282 and the eares are the inlets or doores of the soule, through w^{ch}

MEDDM202:35 Hp282 giue, & wch is most strang, the more it receius the more empty

MEDDM204:22 Hp285 manner, wch should warn him, that doth any speciall seruice

MEDDM204:24 Hp285 wth Jehu's reward, wch will end in punishment

MEDDM205:13 Hp286 wch is alway kept by Conscience, who is both accuser excuser

MEDDM205:34 Hp286 them are dry stocks so is it in the church wch is gods orchard,

MEDDM206:3 Hp287 and these are but leauie Christians, wch are in as much

MEDDM206:20 Hp287 of turning to god, the first thing wch they eye, is how to reform

MEDDM207:5 Hp288 Commonly imployed for a Clean Contrary end, then that w^{ch}

MEDDM207:6 Hp288 giuen for, as health wealth and honour, wch might be so many

MEDDM207:16 Hp288 or feare, or greife that lyes at the root wch in great part

MEDDM207:17 Hp288 withers the pleasure wch else we should take in them, and well

MEDDM207:23 Hp289 great landlord to let: All haue their bounds set ouer wch they

MEDDM207:33 Hp289 of death, wch is their sleep (for so is death often calld) and

MEDDM208:13 Hp290 to haue a good repute among good men, yet it is not that, w^{ch}

MEDDM208:22 Hp290 wch miserably delude men and make them put great

MEDDM208:28	Hp290	admirable to Consider the power of faith, by wch all things are
MEDDM209:23	Hp291	so large, yet he stands in need of something wch another man
MEDDM209:24	Hp291	(perhaps meaner then himself) wch shews us perfection is not
MYCHILD215:32	Hp241	a long fitt of sicknes wch I had on my bed I often comvned wth
MYCHILD216:9	Hp241	wch my heart rose, But after I was convinced it was ye way of
MYCHILD216:12	Hp241	together wth a lamenesse wch correction I saw the Lord sent to
MYCHILD216:14	Hp241	God to keep me a long time wthout a child wch was a great
MYCHILD216:24	Hp242	heart out of order, but I haue expected correctn for it, wch most
MYCHILD216:34	Hp242	some sin I lay vnder wch God would haue reformed, or some
MYCHILD216:35	Hp242	neglected wch he would haue performed, and by his help I
MYCHILD217:16	Hp243	and refreshing wch I supposed most of the servants of God
MYCHILD217:34	Hp243	I never saw any miracles to confirm me, and those wch I read
MYCHILD218:13	Hp244	it? Is there any story but that wch showes the beginnings of
FEVER220:33	H13	wch oft I read before.
MED223:2	Hp250	Consolations wch the world knowes not.
MED223:19	Hp250	bee dissolved and bee wth thee wch is best of All.
JULY223:21	Hp251	I had a sore fitt of fainting wch lasted 2 or 3 dayes, but not in yt
JULY223:22	Hp251	wch at first it took me, and so mvch the sorer it was to me
JULY223:25	Hp251	manifested his Love to me, wch I dare not passe by without
28AUG225:28	Hp254	heart, and to manifest his Loue to me, and this is that wch
11MAYA226:13	Hp255	a sore sickness and weaknes took hold of me wch hath by fitts
11MAYA226:18	Hp255	of Baca many pools of water, That wch now I cheifly labour
30SEPT227:21	Hp257	Love to my straying Soul wch in prosperity is too much in Love
11MAYB228:26	Hp259	I had a feaver seatd vpon me wch indeed was the longest

WCH (5)

MYCHILD215:11	Hp240	leaue to speak, and those espec. sink deepest wch are spoke
MYCHILD218:15	Hp244	prophecyes in it fullfilled wch could not haue been so long
MYCHILD218:24	Hp244	of the Saints, wch admitt were yy as they terme ym yet not
MYCHILD219:8	Hp245	the mark wch I aimed at.
HOURS234:35	H49	To pay the vowes wch I doe owe

WHICH (271)

ELEMEN8:6	H4	Which was the strongest, noblest, & the best,
ELEMEN9:19	H53	Your shrinking limbs, which winters cold doth harme;
ELEMEN10:22	H97	Augment his heat, which was too hot before:
ELEMEN10:27	H102	'Mong all my wonders which I might recount;
ELEMEN10:41	H116	Which when they could not be o're come by foes
ELEMEN11:7	H127	Which Kings, and mighty ones; amaz'd with wonder,
ELEMEN11:8	H128	Which made a *Cæsar*, (Romes) the worlds proud head,
ELEMEN11:26	H146	Which none ere gave, nor {or} you could claime of right,
ELEMEN12:40	H200	Which guides, when Sun, nor Moon, nor Stars do shine.
ELEMEN13:5	H206	For gemmes, for silver, treasures which I hold:
ELEMEN14:16	H258	Which rise like mighty {tumbling} billowes on the lands: {Land}
ELEMEN14:33	H275	Which {Who} am thy drink, thy blood, thy sap, and best.
ELEMEN15:18	H300	Which by my fatting Nile, doth yeeld such store;
ELEMEN15:30	H312	With thousands moe, which now I list not name,
ELEMEN15:38	H320	Which *Cæsars, Consuls, Tribunes* all adorne;
ELEMEN16:2	H325	Which *Spaines Americans,* do gladly hold.
ELEMEN16:18	H341	Which wondring *Aristotles* wit, ne'r knowes.
ELEMEN16:20	H343	Which can to life, restore a fainting heart:
ELEMEN16:22	H345	Which pitty moves, and oft deceives the wise.
ELEMEN16:31	H354	These be my benefits which may suffice:

ELEMEN16:34	H357	All humours, Tumours, that {which} are bred of cold.
ELEMEN17:7	H371	And that an Island makes, which once was maine.
ELEMEN17:15	H379	My Ice and extream cold, which all men know.
ELEMEN18:13	H417	Nay, what are words, which doe reveale the mind?
ELEMEN18:16	H420	What is't? but forced Aire which must {doth} rebound,
ELEMEN18:18	H422	Which {That} tells afar, th' exployt which he {it} hath done.
ELEMEN18:20	H424	And so's the notes which Nightingales do frame.
ELEMEN18:36	H440	Which may be done, by holding down my vapour.
ELEMEN19:10	H455	With thousands moe, which now I may omit;
ELEMEN19:23	H468	Which neither ships nor houses could withstand.
ELEMEN19:27	H472	Then in his long hot wars, {war} which *Millain* gain'd.
ELEMEN20:3	H485	Which makes {make} the mighty Monarchs fear their Fates,
HUMOUR20:22	H14	Which of the foure should have predominance;
HUMOUR21:10	H38	Unto your Sister-hood, which makes us tender {render}
HUMOUR22:26	H95	Poor spirits the Liver breeds, which is thy seat,
HUMOUR25:6	H195	For drink, which of us twain, like it the best,
HUMOUR26:6	H236	Which natural, vital, animal we name.
HUMOUR26:15	H245	What is there living, which cannot derive
HUMOUR26:23	H253	But thine the nobler, which I grant, yet mine
HUMOUR26:25	H255	I am the Fountaine which thy Cisterns fils,
HUMOUR27:2	H273	Which without all dispute, is Cholers owne;
HUMOUR27:5	H276	Which is thy self, thy Mother, and thy Sire;
HUMOUR27:8	H279	And let me by thy Partner, which is due.
HUMOUR27:41	H312	Which makes the mansion, by the soul soon left;
HUMOUR29:39	H390	I'le come to that which wounds me somewhat more:
HUMOUR30:41	H433	But that which shewes how high thy spight is bent,
HUMOUR33:11	H525	But the spirits, by which it acts are thine;
HUMOUR33:31	H545	Which life and motion to each Creature gives,
HUMOUR33:33	H547	shew, hence flowes {flow} the power {pow'rs} which they retain;
HUMOUR33:39	H553	Of three, its hard to say, which doth excel;
HUMOUR34:12	H567	Which runs through all the spondles of the rack,
HUMOUR34:16	H571	With {Which} joynt to joynt, the entire body tyes;
HUMOUR34:39	H594	And too much talk; both which, I do {here} confesse,
AGES36:18	H42	His golden god in's purse, which was his charm.
AGES37:9	H71	To tel that paine, which cann't be told by tongue;
AGES37:21	H83	In that which riper age did scorn, and slight:
AGES38:15	H118	Which sprouted forth, in my {mine} insuing age,
AGES39:9	H152	Then let not him, which {that} hath most craft dissemble;
AGES40:16	H197	All counsel hate, which tends to make me wise,
AGES43:1	H297	If honour was the point, to which I steer'd;
AGES43:8	H305	I might possess that throne which was their right;
AGES43:16	H308	Which others scatter, like the dew in *May*.
AGES45:2	H379	Which fil'd our hearts with fears, with tears our eyes,
SEASONS46:35	H11	She trim'd her locks, which late had frosted been,
SEASONS48:24	H77	More at her showers, which water them a space.
SEASONS49:28	H117	Which made great *Bajazet* cry out in's woes,
SEASONS49:29	H118	Oh! happy Shepheard, which had not to lose,
SEASONS50:8	H142	Which makes the aged fields look young again,
SEASONS50:20	H154	Which after Manchet's made, {makes} for Kings to eat;
SEASONS51:16	H190	Or withered stocks, {which were} all dry, and dead,
SEASONS51:18	H192	Which shewes, nor Summer, Winter, nor the Spring,

SEASONS51:26	H202	Which notes, when youth, and strength, have past their prime,
SEASONS52:10	H225	And melancholy, which most of all dissembles.
SEASONS52:38	H253	Which is increased by the lengthened day,
SEASONS53:7	H263	*And all the faults which {that} you shall spy,*
MASSYR54:21	H48	On which stood fifteen hundred towers stout:
MASSYR55:18	H84	For which, she was obscurely nourished.
MASSYR55:25	H91	Which was the cause, poor *Menon* lost his life,
MASSYR56:12	H118	But {And} that which did, all cost, and art excell,
MASSYR56:14	H120	Which is the midst, of this brave Town was plac'd,
MASSYR56:38	H144	Which made the *Assyrians* many a day,
MASSYR57:7	H154	Which made the people think they serv'd her Son;
MASSYR57:20	H167	Nor can those Reasons which wise *Raleigh* finds,
MASSYR57:26	H172	Which to her neighbours, when it was made known,
MASSYR59:1	H225	And win the Crown, which was the way to blisse,
MASSYR59:20	H244	Which through much rain, then swelling up so high,
MASSYR59:33	H257	Which {That} for twelve hundred years had held that place;
MASSYR60:9	H274	promise bound, since first {which} he crav'd {firmly made},
MASSYR60:23	H288	A costly work, which none could doe but he,
MASSYR60:25	H290	And those which {that} seem'd with *Sardanapal's* gone;
MASSYR60:39	H304	Which makes the world of differences {difference} so ful,
MASSYR61:10	H315	Next treads the {those} steps, by which his Father won.
MASSYR61:38	H343	(This was that *Ahaz,* which so much {high} transgrest.)
MASSYR62:7	H352	To *Ægypts* King, which did avail him nought;
MASSYR62:38	H383	Which made his Army into nothing melt;
MASSYR64:22	H446	Which was the losse of *Syria* withall;
MASSYR64:24	H448	Which in few years proves the *Assyrians* hire;
MASSYR64:29	H453	That in her pride, she knew not which to boast,
MASSYR66:24	H530	Which wealth, and strong ambition made so great;
MASSYR66:30	H536	Which for seven years his reason took away;
MASSYR66:31	H537	Which from no natural causes did proceed,
MASSYR66:39	H545	Forty four years he reign'd, which being run,
MASSYR67:17	H563	(Within which broiles, rich *Crœsus* was engaged,)
MASSYR68:1	H587	Which horrid sight, he fears, must needs portend,
MPERS70:28	H699	Which to revenge, she hires a mighty power,
MPERS70:32	H703	The which she bak'd {bath'd} within a But of bloud,
MPERS71:12	H727	Which Law includes all Lawes, though lawlesse stil,
MPERS73:1	H788	Which ends before begun, the *Persian* {his home-bred} Warre,
MPERS73:15	H802	Of which the cheife were {was} seven, call'd *Satrapes,*
MPERS73:32	H817	The old, or new, which best, in what respect,
MPERS74:24	H847	By which he cuts their hopes (for future times)
MPERS74:27	H850	Three strings to's bow, the least of which is good;
MPERS74:29	H852	Made wholsome gentle Laws, which pleas'd each mind.
MPERS76:1	H899	A bridge he made, which serv'd for boat, and barge,
MPERS76:6	H904	Which two then to assaile, his {royal} Camp was bold:
MPERS76:25	H923	Which husht, he straight so orders his affaires;
MPERS76:30	H928	Arm'd all they could, which elev'n thousand make;
MPERS76:39	H937	Which soon cut off, {inrag'd,} he with the {his} left
MPERS77:3	H942	As the best trophe that {which} ye won in *Greece.*
MPERS78:22	H1003	{Which to} Three thousand (or more) {came} by best relation,
MPERS78:36	H1017	Which mighty sum, all wondred to behold.
MPERS79:3	H1025	'Twixt which his souldiers marcht in good array.

MPERS79:29	H1055	Which was not vaine, as it {after} soon appeared:
MPERS80:36	H1103	Much, {fearing} that which never was intended!
MPERS81:2	H1110	Which accident, the rest affrighted so,
MPERS81:32	H1140	And of those *Greeks,* which by his skil he'd won,
MPERS81:34	H1142	The other *Greeks,* which were confederate,
MPERS82:1	H1146	But that which helpt defects, and made them bold,
MPERS82:9	H1156	Which found, like *Greeks* they fight, the *Persians* fly,
MPERS82:20	H1167	That Army, which did fright the Universe;
MPERS83:7	H1195	Which {With} him, and his, most barbarously there slew,
MPERS83:12	H1200	Which wretch, {Who} him privately smother'd in's bed,
MPERS83:21	H1209	For which he dyed, and not he alone.
MPERS83:33	H1221	Which had they kept, *Greece* had more nobly done,
MPERS83:37	H1225	Which done, a sumptuous feast; makes like a King
MPERS~~84:12~~	H1247	Rebuilt those walls which long in rubbish lay,
MPERS85:19	H1295	Which from remissenesse, in *{Less} Asia* proceeds {breeds.}
MPERS~~85:33~~	H1309	More by {To which} his pride, {more} then {his} lust, thereunto
MPERS86:6	H1322	{this} *Nothus* reign'd {'bout} nineteen years, which run,
MPERS87:8	H1364	Which *Cyrus* heares, and so fore-slowes his pace:
MPERS88:8	H1401	Which like a mighty cloud darkned the skye;
MPERS88:16	H1409	Which did such courage to the *Grecians* bring,
MPERS90:29	H1496	Which rumor makes great *Artaxerxes* quake;
MPERS90:34	H1501	Which over-throw incens'd the King so sore,
MPERS91:2	H1510	height, *{Spartan* State} which now apace doth {so fast did} rise;
MPERS~~92:1~~	H1555	Which in rebellion sixty years did stand:
MPERS92:8	~~H1566~~	So fell to him, which else it had not done:
MPERS92:23	~~H1581~~	Which by some probabilities (seems rather;)
MGREC93:16	H1613	Great were the guifts of nature, which he had;
MGREC6:19	H1616	T'accomplish that, which long before was writ.
MGREC6:26	H1623	This is the hee-goat, which from *Grecia* came,
MGREC6:33	H1630	Which honour to his son, now did befall.
MGREC6:37	H1634	His high resolves which way to bring to passe:
MGREC94:2	H1636	Which makes each moment seem, more then a day:
MGREC~~94:20~~	H1658	To these {which} were joyn'd, five thousand goodly horse.
MGREC94:38	H1676	Which twixt *Phrigia,* and *Propontis* lyes.
MGREC95:17	H1696	Which who so did {doth}, must Lord of all remain,
MGREC95:34	H1713	The rest attendants, which made up no lesse;
MGREC96:38	H1758	Which made {To make} his over-throw more fierce, and sure.
MGREC97:26	H1787	Of which, the Government he doth commit
MGREC98:8	H1810	In the old town (which now {then} lay like a wood)
MGREC98:27	H1829	For that which easily comes, as freely goes;
MGREC99:2	H1845	All those rich Kingdoms large, which {that} doe abide
MGREC99:12	H1855	To which, brave {proud} *Alexander* did {made} reply,
MGREC99:40	H1883	By which he was so much incouraged,
MGREC101:8	H1933	And all those Countries, which (betwixt) did lye,
MGREC101:18	H1943	Which had he done (perhaps) his fame had {he'd} kept,
MGREC102:4	H1974	Which *Alexander* deals, as suits his pleasure.
MGREC102:12	H1982	Which in few hours was carried all away;
MGREC102:40	H2010	Which newes doth still augment *Darius* woes;
MGREC103:9	H2020	Which {That} did pertain unto the *Persian* Kings.
MGREC103:40	H2051	Which forty thousand made; but his intent,
MGREC105:33	H2126	Which made their long restraint, seeme to be none;

MGREC107:12	H2187	Which done, sets fire upon those costly {goodly} spoyls
MGREC107:26	H2201	This {Which} more mortality to them did bring,
MGREC108:37	H2253	Which *Alexandria* he doth also {likewise} name,
MGREC108:40	H2256	Which did his former Army {forces} much augment,
MGREC110:31	H2335	Huge Bridles made, which here, and there, he left,
MGREC110:32	H2336	Which might be found, and so for {great} wonders kept:
MGREC111:15	H2360	Which could not sound too oft, with too much fame;
MGREC111:18	H2363	Which the stout *Macedonians* mazed sore
MGREC111:23	H2368	To th' coast which by *Euphrates* mouth appear'd;
MGREC112:36	H2422	Which no merit could obliterate, or time:
MGREC112:38	H2424	By which his Majesty was deifi'd.
MGREC113:30	H2457	This is *Parmenio,* which {who} so much had done,
MGREC114:11	H2479	Which *Alexanders* wrath incens'd so high,
MGREC114:30	H2500	Which shall not be obliterate by time,
MGREC114:31	H2501	Which vertues fame can ne're redeem by farre,
MGREC117:4	H2611	Of all those kingdomes large which he had got,
MGREC117:6	H2613	For by that hand, which still revengeth bloud,
MGREC117:35	H2642	Alleadg'd by those, which {who} by their subtill plea
MGREC118:25	H2674	On which, no signe of poyson could be {in his intrails} found,
MGREC119:3	H2693	But held command o'th' Armies {Army} which was best;
MGREC119:5	H2695	Which was his Masters sister for {secretly} to wed:
MGREC119:21	H2711	(Which at this time well suited his desires)
MGREC119:29	H2719	(Which did his match with *Cleopatra* mar)
MGREC119:40	H2730	After this {which} time, the *Greeks* did never more
MGREC120:22	H2759	Which of his Ancestors was once the throne,
MGREC120:36	H2773	Which eating time hath scarcely yet defac'd.
MGREC121:1	H2779	('Gainst which to goe, is troubled in his minde;)
MGREC122:26	H2845	Which made her now begin to play her part;
MGREC123:3	H2865	On which *Antigonus* his height doth raise:
MGREC123:41	H2905	And for that great gift, which he gave him last;
MGREC125:1	H2949	Which damage both to minde and body brought:
MGREC125:29	H2979	On which *Olimpias* of the like might taste.
MGREC127:3	H3033	Which she had often made others to sup:
MGREC128:8	H3081	Which none e're did but those of royall fame;
MGREC128:12	H3085	Which their late King in dust had damnified;
MGREC129:18	H3132	And for that double fact which she had done,
MGREC130:38	H3183	That hand is righteous still which doth repay:
MGREC131:38	H3230	Which should succeed, at variance they fell,
MGREC132:11	H3246	For blood which was decreed, that he should spill,
MGREC133:35	H3325	Which we oft wish were {was} extant as before.
MGREC134:8	H3339	I'th' holy place, which caused desolation;
MGREC135:7	H3379	Which by the *Romans* had its destiny.
MGREC135:23	H3395	And last was Iron, which breaketh all with might.
MGREC135:29	H3401	The third a Leopard, which four wings did rear;
MROMAN139:6	H3534	A generall Muster takes, which by account,
MROMAN140:5	H3568	Which none had cause to wail, nor I to boast.
DIALOG141:18	H17	Which 'mazed Christendome stands wondring at?
DIALOG141:24	H23	Which present help may ease this {my} malady.
DIALOG143:10	H79	None knowes which is the Red, or which the White:
DIALOG143:28	H97	Which are my Sins, the breach of sacred Lawes;
DIALOG143:39	H108	What false reports, which nick-names did they take,

DIALOG144:8	H118	'Mongst all the cruelties which I have {by great ones} done,
DIALOG145:18	H167	Which is the chief, the law, or else the King,
DIALOG145:28	H177	Which by their prudence stood them in such stead,
DIALOG147:2	H228	Blest be thy Counties which do {who did} aid thee still
SIDNEY149:31	~~H23~~	Which shewes, thy worth was great, thine honour such,
SIDNEY149:34	~~H23~~	Which have the self-same blood yet in my veines;
SIDNEY150:3	H28	Which makes severer eyes but scorn thy {slight that} Story,
SIDNEY~~150:12~~	H40	Which shews his worth was great, his honour such,
SIDNEY150:22	H47	Of which, {at} this day, faire *Belgia* doth {may} boast.
SIDNEY~~151:26~~	H74	And {Which} makes me now with *Sylvester* confesse,
SIDNEY151:30	~~H75~~	Which are in worth, as far short of his due,
SIDNEY152:20	H89	Which writ, she bad return't to them again.
DUBART153:8	H12	Which Rayes, darting upon some richer ground,
QELIZ155:30	H21	Which makes me deeme, my rudenesse is no wrong,
QELIZ157:30	H98	Which I may not, my pride doth but aspire,
QELIZ157:38	H106	But happy *England,* which had such a Queen,
DAVID159:18	H33	Which made you yet more beauteous to behold.
VANITY160:25	H35	That *summum Bonum* which may stay my mind?
VANITY160:28	H38	Which leads unto that living Christall fount,
VANITY160:36	H46	It brings to honour, which shall not {ne're} decay,
VANITY160:37	H47	It steeres {stores} with wealth, which time cann't wear away.
TDUDLEY165:33	H35	Which caus'd Apostates to maligne so.
TDUDLEY165:40	H42	Those titles loath'd, which some too much do love
TDUDLEY166:8	H50	Which all they have, and more still set to view,
TDUDLEY166:14	H56	For which he sigh'd and pray'd & long'd full sore
DDUDLEY167:17	H14	*The which she ordered with dexterity.*
CONTEM172:15	H150	Which to the long'd for Ocean held its course,
CONTEM172:30	H163	Ye Fish which in this liquid Region 'bide,
CONTEM173:14	H181	Which rapt me so with wonder and delight,
CONTEM174:19	H218	Which 'gainst all adverse winds may serve for fort.
FLESH175:21	H21	To catch at shadowes which are not?
FLESH175:29	H29	Which wearing time shall ne're deject.
FLESH176:32	H72	Nor are they shadows which I catch,
FLESH176:33	H73	Nor fancies vain at which I snatch,
FLESH176:37	H77	With which inriched I would be:
FLESH176:41	H81	Nor such like trash which Earth doth hold,
FLESH177:14	H95	Which doth proceed from the Lambs Throne:
FLESH177:16	H97	Which shall remain for ever pure,
AUTHOR178:15	H25	Which caus'd her thus to send thee out of door.
DISTEMP179:15	H3	And wasting pains, which best my body knows,
1LETTER181:16	H14	Then view those fruits which through thy heat I bore?
1LETTER181:17	H15	Which sweet contentment yield me for a space,
2LETTER182:21	H27	Which day by day long wait for thy arise,
3LETTER183:3	H5	So doth my anxious soul, which now doth miss,
SOREFIT222:10	H29	And then wth thee which is the Best

WHILE (41)

ELEMEN13:38	H239	While they thus in my {mine} intralls seem {love} to dive;
HUMOUR21:9	H37	Now Feminines (a while) for love we owe
HUMOUR31:41	H474	Then cause her blush, while I dilate {relate} the same.
MASSYR60:11	H276	A while he, and his race, aside must stand,
MASSYR65:13	H478	While *Babels* King thus deep ingaged stands;

MPERS88:39	H1432	And for a while unkingly there he lyes;
MPERS89:9	H1443	After a while his {hurri'd} thoughts he re-collects,
MGREC94:1	H1635	Yet for a while, in *Greece* is forc'd to stay,
MGREC94:35	H1673	Ah! fond vaine man, whose pen was taught ere while,
MGREC~~101:34~~	H1961	The Armyes joyn'd a while, the Persians fight,
MGREC~~118:24~~	H2673	That for a while they durst not come so near:
MGREC122:37	~~H2858~~	After a while, to *Macedon* he makes;
MGREC~~123:13~~	H2876	But while these Chieftains doe in Asia fight,
MGREC126:4	H2995	*Polisperchon* to hold a while in play,
MGREC127:13	H3043	And {now} for a while, let's into *Asia* turn,
DIALOG141:28	H27	Let me lament alone, while thou art glad.
DIALOG144:24	~~H133~~	These Prophets mouthes (alas the while) was stopt,
DIALOG148:34	H299	And in a while you'l tell another tale.
DUBART153:33	H37	Thy profound Learning; viewing other while
DUBART154:35	H80	Thus *Bartas* fame shall last while starres do stand,
QELIZ~~157:7~~	H75	Worlds wonder for a time {while}, but yet it falls;
VANITY160:7	H17	Mean while the conscience rage, who shall appease?
VANITY160:21	H31	While man is man, he shall have ease or pain.
TDUDLEY165:25	H27	While others tell his worth, I'le not be dumb:
CONTEM169:32	H71	While of their persons & their acts his mind doth treat.
CONTEM171:13	H117	Living so little while we are alive;
CONTEM172:14	H149	While on the stealing stream I fixt mine eye,
CONTEM173:10	H177	While musing thus with contemplation fed,
CONTEM173:16	H183	And wisht me wings with her a while to take my flight.
1HUSB180:33	H12	Then while we live, in love lets so persever,
VERSES184:9	H13	But as I can, I'le pay it while I live:
CHILDRN186:2	H69	Mean while my dayes in tunes Ile spend,
ANNEB187:31	H21	But yet a while, and I shall go to thee;
MEDDM202:12	Hp281	some againe so weak and feeble, that while they liue, they are
MEDDM204:20	Hp285	while (sath god) and I will avenge the blood of Jezerel vpon
MEDDM206:16	Hp287	shine so bright while they moue on earth, how transcendently
FAINTING222:23	H13	I here a while might 'bide.
28AUG226:6	Hp254	Lord gravnt y^t while I live I may doe y^t service I am able in this
11MAYA226:22	Hp255	shall flourish while my body decayes, and ye weaknes of this
11MAYA226:24	Hp255	Yet a little while and he that shall come will come and will not
HOURS234:26	H40	Ev'n while my Dayes shall last

WHIL'ST (2)

HUMOUR25:20	H209	Whil'st us, for thine associates thou takest,
SICKNES179:1	H21	O whil'st I live, this grace me give,

WHILST (29)

HUMOUR30:24	H416	But whilst he lives, Ile shew what part I have.
SEASONS49:27	H116	Whilst they're imbroyl'd in Wars, and troubles ripe; {rife:}
MPERS~~71:4~~	H716	But eight whilst *Babylon*, he did retain:
MPERS75:19	~~H878~~	In that thy fame shall sound whilst men have sence;
MPERS81:24	H1132	That whilst the Sun did run his endlesse course,
MPERS90:12	~~H1484~~	There for some time they were, but whilst they staid,
MGREC102:25	H1995	Whilst revelling at *Babylon,* he lyes,
MGREC108:19	H2235	Whilst thus he spent some time in *Bactria,*
MGREC110:13	H2313	But {And} whilst the first he valiantly assayl'd,
MGREC116:11	H2577	Monarchs fame} must last, whilst world shall {doth} stand,
MGREC116:12	H2578	And Conquests be talkt of, whilst there is Land;

MGREC119:30	H2720	For fighting still, whilst there did hope remain,
MGREC120:9	H2744	Whilst they in *Macedon* doe thus agree,
MGREC121:32	H2814	Whilst *Perdicas* thus staid {encamp'd} in *Africa,*
MGREC124:17	H2924	Whilst hot in wars these two in *Greece* remaine,
MGREC132:41	H3288	Whilst with these hopes, in *Greece* he did remaine,
SIDNEY~~150:12~~	H43	Whilst English blood yet runs within my veins.
DUBART154:36	H81	And whilst there's aire, or fire, or sea or land.
QELIZ155:17	H8	And so has {hath} vow'd, whilst there is world, or time;
VANITY159:36	H8	And whilst they live, how oft doth turn their State? {fate,}
CONTEM169:24	H64	Whilst I as mute, can warble forth no higher layes.
1LETTER181:6	H4	How stayest thou there, whilst I at *Ipswich* lye?
1LETTER181:11	H9	Whom whilst I 'joy'd, nor storms, nor frosts I felt,
CHILDRN185:21	H47	Whilst pecking corn, and void of care
CHILDRN185:23	H49	Or whilst on trees they sit and sing,
CHILDRN185:25	H51	Or whilst allur'd with bell and glass,
MYCHILD215:13	Hp240	speak to any of yov much lesse to All, thovght it ye best whilst
BYNIGHT220:19	H17	I'le serve him here whilst I shall liue
THEART229:7	H9	Lord whilst my fleeting time shall last

WHIP (2)

MGREC94:33	H1671	To whip him well with rods, and then {so} to bring,
TDUDLEY166:38	H80	*To Sectaryes a whip and Maul,*

WHIPS (1)

MPERS~~79:13~~	H1036	Then whips the sea, and with a mind most vain

WHIPT (1)

DIALOG144:25	~~H134~~	Unworthily, some backs whipt, and eares cropt;

WHIRLING (1)

2LETTER181:35	H5	(And if the whirling of thy wheels don't drown'd)

WHISPERORS (1) [pl.]

AGES37:37	H99	Nor unto buzzing whisperors, gave ear.

WHIST'LETH (1)

SEASONS49:31	H120	But whist'leth to thy Flock in cold, and heat,

WHISTLING (2)

HUMOUR29:9	H362	To spare our selves, and beat the whistling winde.
SEASONS50:23	H157	The Carter leads all home, with whistling voyce,

WHIT (4)

HUMOUR24:14	H163	Your selves may plead, your wrongs are no whit lesse,
MPERS86:32	H1348	For what was done, seemed no whit offended.
MGREC~~99:5~~	H1848	And the distressed King no way {whit} respects;
MGREC115:24	H2543	His doing so, no whit displeas'd the King,

WHITE (14)

FATHER5:4	H5	Of your four sisters, deckt {cloth'd} in black & white /four parts
ELEMEN16:5	H328	My sundry Seas, Black, White, and Adriatique
HUMOUR22:11	H80	But {Now} let's give, cold, white, Sister Flegme her right.
HUMOUR32:40	H514	My Lilly white, when joyned with her red,
AGES35:27	H13	Childhood was cloath'd in white, and given {green} to show,
SEASONS49:19	H110	Rubbing their dirty coates, till they look white.
SEASONS50:22	H156	Although their Bread have not so white a face.
MPERS84:1	H1229	His hangings, white, and green, and purple dye;
MGREC102:35	H2005	Those purple hangings, mixt with green, and white,
DIALOG142:19	H48	That from the red, white pricking Roses sprung?
DIALOG143:10	H79	None knowes which is the Red, or which the White:

QELIZ158:9	H118	*O'th' Damask Rose, sprung from the white and red,*
CONTEM174:35	H232	But he whose name is grav'd in the white stone
CHILDRN184:34	H23	I have a third of colour white,

WHITHER (1)

MPERS78:32	H1013	Whither rich *Pithyus* comes, *Xerxes* to greet;

WHO'S (2) [who is]

HUMOUR30:21	H413	Then who's mans friend, when life and all forsakes?
VANITY160:3	H13	Its his to day, but who's his heire to morrow?

WHOLE (10)

ELEMEN14:17	H259	Wherein whole Armies {*Cambyses* Armie} I have {was}
HUMOUR27:15	H286	Who th' benefit o'th' whole ever intends:
HUMOUR27:27	H298	And what you singly {single} are, the whole I make.
HUMOUR33:27	H541	Though it in all, and every part be whole:
HUMOUR35:13	H609	But here's a {so} compact body, whole, entire:
AGES40:14	H195	Dayes, {Whole} nights, with Ruffins, Roarers, Fidlers spend,
MGREC96:26	H1746	As if she'd drawne, whole *Sushan* at her heeles.
1HUSB180:27	H6	I prize thy love more then whole Mines of gold,
MEDDM198:28	Hp277	A sore finger may disquiet the whole body, but an vlcer w^{th}in
MEDDM205:27	Hp286	vs, or else we should not so often faile in our whole Course of

WHOLESOME (2) [wholesome]

ELEMEN16:15	H338	My wholesome Bathes, together with their cures.
SEASONS48:26	H79	The hasty Pease, and wholesome red {cool} Strawberry,

WHOLLY (4)

ELEMEN17:28	H392	Then wholly perish'd, earths ignoble race;
HUMOUR26:5	H235	Nextly, the spirits thou do'st wholly claime,
MROMAN137:19	H3470	And *Fedinates* they wholly over-throw:
SOREFIT221:32	H18	My heart I wholly giue to Thee

WHOLSOME (3) [wholesome]

PROLOG7:38	H48	Give wholsome {Thyme or} Parsley wreath, I aske no Bayes:
ELEMEN9:18	H52	Your dainty {dayly} food, I wholsome make, I warme
MPERS74:29	H852	Made wholsome gentle Laws, which pleas'd each mind.

WHORE (1)

DIALOG147:17	H243	We hate *Romes* Whore, with all her trumperie.

WHORES (1) [pl.]

MASSYR58:2	H187	Ne're shew'd his face, but revell'd with his Whores,

WHY (18)

PROLOG7:22	H34	Else of our Sex, why feigned they those nine,
HUMOUR26:31	H261	But why the heart, should be usurpt by thee,
HUMOUR28:32	H344	But why, alas, thus tedious should I be?
AGES38:26	H129	Then nought can please, and yet I know not why.
SEASONS49:10	H101	The reason why {Though he decline}, because his flames so
MPERS92:5	~~H1559~~	Why *Arsames* his brother should succeed,
MPERS~~92:5~~	H1563	But why brother 'fore his son succeeds
MGREC99:33	H1876	Why didst not heap up honour, and reward?
MGREC115:10	H2519	Hangs his Phisitian, the reason why,
DIALOG144:10	H120	O *Jane,* why didst thou dye in flowring prime,
CONTEM172:35	H168	So nature taught, and yet you know not why,
ELIZB187:1	H10	Blest babe why should I once bewail thy fate,
1SIMON188:9	H10	Such was his will, but why, let's not dispute,
MEDDM197:7	Hp274	The reason why christians are so loth to exchang this world for
MYCHILD218:19	Hp244	word, yet why may not ye popish Relign. bee ye right, They

DDUDLEY167:11	H8	*A loving Mother and obedient wife,*
1HUSB180:24	H3	If ever man were lov'd by wife, then thee;
1HUSB180:25	H4	If ever wife was happy in a man,
2LETTER182:4	H10	Shew him the sorrows of his widdowed wife;
3LETTER183:20	H22	I have a loving phere, yet seem no wife:
MERCY188:34	H20	I lost a daughter dear, but thou a wife,

WIGGIN (1)

HANNA230:9	H1-2	Vpon my Daughter Hannah Wiggin her recouery from a

WIGHTS (3) [pl.]

ELEMEN13:40	H241	Ye affrighted wights, appall'd how do you shake
SEASONS47:2	H17	And now makes glad those blinded Northern wights,
SEASONS47:5	H20	And now makes glad the darkned northern wights

WILL (6) n. [will]

HUMOUR25:32	H221	To crosse thy wil, a challenge doth deserve.
HUMOUR26:9	H239	For acting these, I have nor wil, nor art,
HUMOUR28:20	H332	It's doom'd by an irrevocable wil:
AGES40:3	H184	I know no Law, nor reason, but my wil;
MPERS79:15	H1041	Firmly at length, {last} accomplished his wil;
MGREC107:38	H2213	Had *Bessus* had but valour to his wil,

WIL (28) v. [will] See also HEE'L, HE'L, SHE'L, THEY'L, WE'L

PROLOG6:29	H13	A *Bartas* can, doe what a *Bartas* wil,
HUMOUR20:34	H26	Or wil they nil they, Choler wil be cheife;
HUMOUR20:34	H26	Or wil they nil they, Choler wil be cheife;
HUMOUR21:33	H61	That much wil talk, but little dares she do,
HUMOUR21:35	H63	And there she wil out-bid us all, I think;
HUMOUR22:2	H71	She'l neither say, she wil, nor wil she doe:
HUMOUR22:2	H71	She'l neither say, she wil, nor wil she doe:
HUMOUR22:15	H84	Her teeth wil chatter, dead and wan's her face,
HUMOUR23:1	H111	Wil feed a Dropsie, or a Timpany,
HUMOUR24:9	H158	To what you now shal say, I wil attend,
HUMOUR27:9	H280	So wil {shall} I give the dignity to you.
HUMOUR32:26	H500	To what is truth, I freely wil assent,
HUMOUR33:4	H518	Under *Troys* wals, ten years wil wast {wear} away,
HUMOUR33:23	H537	The scituation, and {Its} form wil it avow,
HUMOUR35:2	H598	Such premises wil force a sad conclusion,
HUMOUR35:5	H601	To take her moyst, my moistnesse {moisture} wil be bold;
MASSYR57:18	H165	This answer may suffice, whom it wil please,
MASSYR57:37	H182	T' *Sardanapalus* next we wil make haste.
MPERS71:13	H727	And makes it lawful Law, if he but wil;
MGREC101:2	H1927	And if they down, his Monarchy wil throw,
MROMAN137:6	H3457	That wil within these strong built walls reside,
MEDDM200:7	Hp279	wormwood or mustard, they wil either wipe it off, or else suck

WILD (3)

ELEMEN12:23	H183	Thousands in woods, and planes, both wild, and tame,
MASSYR62:25	H370	Or wild *Tartarians,* as yet ne're blest,
PILGRIM210:12	H12	Nor wild fruits eate, in stead of bread

WILDE (2) [wild]

AGES39:33	H176	To be as wilde as is the snuffing Asse,
AGES41:23	H240	When my Wilde Oates, were sown, and ripe, & mown,

WILDERNES (1) [wilderness]

MEDDM198:10	Hp276	his foot And he that passes through the wildernes of this world,

WILDERNESSE (1) [wilderness]
2HUSB233:4   H37   To Wildernesse ha'st brovght
WILDNES (1) [wildness]
AGES44:4   H337   Babes innocence, Youths wildnes I have seen,
WILE (2)
MGREC118:31   H2680   Him {And} by a wile he got within his power,
MGREC127:21   H3051   *Pencestas* did betray him by a wile,
WILL (20) n. See also WIL
ELEMEN9:15   H49   I made it flexible unto his will.
AGES38:21   H124   A perverse will, a love to what's forbid:
MASSYR55:12   H78   Transform'd into a fish, by *Venus* will,
MPERS82:23   H1170   His brothers wife, sollicites to his will;
MPERS87:29   H1381   Had not a Captain; {his Captains} sore against his will;
MPERS89:31   H1465   But Kings ne're want such as can serve their will,
MGREC103:34   H2045   But deafe to reason, (bent to have his will;)
MGREC110:22   H2326   But so to doe, his Souldiers had no will;
MGREC130:10   H3165   Untill he further know his Masters will;
MGREC~~132:16~~   H3252   Though men and mony both he hath at will,
DIALOG147:3   H229   With hearts, and states, to testifie their will.
SIDNEY151:10   ~~H69~~   How could that *Stella,* so confine thy will?
SIDNEY~~152:4~~   H76   The Muses aid I crav'd, they had no will
SIDNEY152:5   He   promis'd much, but th' muses had no will,
DUBART154:40   H85   Good will, not skill, did cause me bring my mite.
1SIMON188:9   H10   Such was his will, but why, let's not dispute,
MEDDM202:14   Hp282   it pleased him, whose will is the perfect rule of righteousnesse,
MEDDM207:21   Hp289   All men are truly sayd to be tenants at will, and it may as truly
11MAYA226:20   Hp255   ye will of God it should bee thus. Who am I y^t I should repine
2HUSB232:19   H20   I in obed^c to thy Will
WILL (96) v. See also HEE'L, HE'L, SHE'L, THEY'L, WE'L, WIL
FATHER6:9   H43   These ragged lines, will do't, when they appear.
PROLOG7:25   H37   But this weake knot they will full soone untye,
PROLOG8:2   H50   Will make your glistering gold but more to shine.
ELEMEN~~9:30~~   H64   But be he what they list {will}, yet his aspect,
ELEMEN~~12:16~~   H176   Nor will I stay, no not in *Tempe* Vale,
ELEMEN13:6   H207   Will not my goodly face, your rage suffice?
ELEMEN13:7   H208   But you will see what in my bowels lyes?
ELEMEN16:19   H342   Nor will I speake of waters made by Art,
ELEMEN18:14   H418   Speak, who, or what they will, they are but wind.
HUMOUR24:24   H173   I will annalise, {this} thy so proud relation;
HUMOUR24:32   H181   No pattern, nor no Patron will I bring,
HUMOUR25:19   H208   Both them and all things else, she will {would} consume.
HUMOUR~~34:28~~   H583   Ne're did {Nor will} I heare {yield} that Choler was the witt'est;
AGES37:6   H68   My mothers breeding sicknes, I will spare;
AGES~~45:21~~   H403   Oh may you live, and so you will I trust
MPERS72:17   H765   Thy cruelty will {all} Ages still admire.
MPERS76:12   H910   The King will needs interpret their intent;
MPERS82:6   H1153   The other not a hand, nor sword will {would} wave,
MPERS91:10   H1518   {on such} conditions they are forc't to take; {as King will make}
MPERS92:29   H1587   That severall men, will have their severall mind;
MGREC94:9   H1643   And many more, {all} whom he suspects {or fears} will climbe,
MGREC100:10   H1894   That his humanity will not retaine;

MGREC101:17	H1942	No, though *Parmenio* plead, he {yet} will not heare;
MGREC103:21	H2032	For such revolters false, what Prince will {King can} trust:
MGREC~~106:2~~	H2136	But *Alexander* will, for this regard
MGREC~~106:20~~	H2154	To th' ignorant, her title may {will} declare.
MGREC109:29	H2288	But *Porus* stout, who will not yeeld as yet;
MGREC~~125:21~~	H2971	And needs will have their lives as well as State:
MGREC126:16	H3007	Cassander will not heare {Her foe would give no Ear}, such is
MGREC129:41	H3155	He knows to's profit, all i'th end {this at last} will turn,
MGREC131:23	H3215	Tries foes, since friends will not compassionate,
MGREC132:20	H3257	And with his son in law, will needs go fight:
MGREC136:14	H3428	*Will force me to a confus'd brevity;*
DIALOG141:22	H21	Will bring Consumption, or an Ague quaking,
DIALOG142:1	H30	In generall terms, but will not say wherefore:
DIALOG144:32	H140	And will repay it sevenfold in my lap,
DIALOG147:29	H253	The briny Ocean will o'rflow your shore,
DIALOG147:31	H255	Out of all mists, such glorious dayes will {shall} bring,
QELIZ156:6	H33	Millions will testifie that this is true;
QELIZ157:35	H103	But she though dead, will vindicate our wrong.
VANITY160:32	H42	For *Saphyre, Onix, Topas,* who will {would} change,
TDUDLEY166:31	H73	At last will bring us to that happy place
CONTEM170:27	H98	Thinks each he sees will serve him in his kind,
FLESH175:35	H35	Earth hath enough of what you will.
FLESH175:40	H40	For I have vow'd (and so will doe)
FLESH176:2	H42	And combate with thee will and must,
FLESH176:20	H60	Thine honours doe, nor will I love;
FLESH177:28	H109	Take thou the world, and all that will.
CHILDRN186:8	H75	My age I will not once lament,
1SIMON188:12	H13	He will return, and make up all our losses,
2SIMON195:13	Hp271	they will be better pris'd by you, for the Authors sake. the lord
MEDDM196:9	Hp273	Corruptions, and yᵗ will damp his high thoughts
MEDDM196:29	Hp273	nothing but salt will keep from putrefaction, some again like
MEDDM197:23	Hp275	nothing will abase them more, then this What hast thou, but
MEDDM197:26	Hp275	He that will vntertake to climb vp a steep mountain wᵗʰ a great
MEDDM197:27	Hp275	on his back, will finde it a wearysome if not an impossible task
MEDDM198:3	Hp275	conditions, if he will make his face to shine vpon them,
MEDDM198:9	Hp276	He that walks among briars and thorns will be very carefull,
MEDDM200:3	Hp278	not a little one? will ere long say of a greater Tush god regards
MEDDM200:15	Hp279	A prudent mother will not cloth her little childe wᵗʰ a long and
MEDDM200:18	Hp279	will the alwise god proportion his dispensations according to
MEDDM200:33	Hp280	A wise father will not lay a burden on a child of seven yeares
MEDDM200:34	Hp280	is enough for one of twice his strength, much lesse will our
MEDDM201:1	Hp280	strength he will proportion the load, as god hath his little
MEDDM202:30	Hp282	of righteousnes will arise wᵗʰ healing in his wings.
MEDDM203:23	Hp283	that threatens him wᵗʰ death, he will gladly entertaine him,
MEDDM203:27	Hp284	he must needs perish if he haue no remedy, will vnfeignedly
MEDDM203:35	Hp284	conuersation aright will glorifie him that heard him in the day of
MEDDM204:4	Hp284	the paw of the Beare will deliuer mee from this vncircumscised
MEDDM204:5	Hp284	and he that hath deliuered mee saith paul, will deliuer me, god
MEDDM204:20	Hp285	god) and I will avenge the blood of Jezerel vpon the house
MEDDM204:24	Hp285	wᵗʰ Jehu's reward, wᶜʰ will end in punishment
MEDDM204:29	Hp285	pouerty comfortably it will help to quiet him, but if that will not

MEDDM204:30	Hp285	look on his owne vnworthynes and that will make him say wth
MEDDM205:18	Hp286	who is greater then our Conscience will do it much more, but
MEDDM205:25	Hp286	allseeing eye will be a bridle to restrain from evill, and a spur,
MEDDM205:29	Hp286	will not sinne against him.
MEDDM206:22	Hp287	at a Compensation then at a pardon, but he that will not Come
MEDDM206:31	Hp288	Souerainty of god, who will not be tyed to time nor place, nor
MEDDM207:9	Hp288	we are lords we will come no more at thee If outward
MEDDM207:10	Hp288	to help vs mount vpwards, they will Certainly proue Clogs
MEDDM207:11	Hp288	and waights that will pull us lower downward
MEDDM207:26	Hp289	that time will come, together, wth the vncertainty, how where,
MEDDM208:6	Hp289	of a fire, if once severed, will of themselues goe out altho
MEDDM208:8	Hp290	of time (if there be no inter course) will coole the affectiones
MEDDM209:2	Hp291	will not let thee go replys Jacob till thou blesse me, faith is not
MEDDM209:25	Hp291	below, as also that god will haue vs beholden one to another
MYCHILD215:22	Hp240	The method I will observe shall bee this—I will begin wth Gods
MYCHILD215:22	Hp240	I will observe shall bee this—I will begin wth Gods dealing
MYCHILD218:35	Hp244	o my Soul to thy Rest, vpon this Rock Xt Jesus will I build
11MAYA226:24	Hp255	a little while and he that shall come will come and will not tarry.
30SEPT227:26	Hp257	wth sugar then brine, yet will he p^rserve me to his heavenly
30SEPT227:31	Hp257	will doe ye like for yov if you trvst in him; And when he shall
SAMUEL228:19	H20	Thy Will bee done, for that is best

WILLING (1)

AGES37:13	H75	Spending was willing, to be spent for me;

WILLINGLY (4)

MGREC131:33	H3225	But willingly resign'd the beauteous dame:
28AUG225:30	Hp254	doth not afflict willingly, nor take delight in greiving ye children
28AUG226:2	Hp254	willingly but joyfully? The Lord knowes I dare not desire that
30SEPT227:19	Hp257	not in y^t sore manner somt. he hath. I desire not only willingly

WILLS (1)

MGREC126:19	H3010	*Olimpias* wills to keep it, {means to hold out} to the last,

WILT (3)

HUMOUR25:34	H223	Wilt thou this valour, manhood, courage cal:
HUMOUR26:41	H271	But thou wilt say, I deale unequally,
ACK235:17	H17	And y^t thov wilt return him back

WIN (8)

MASSYR59:1	H225	And win the Crown, which was the way to blisse,
MPERS74:31	~~H854~~	Did win him loyalty, and all respect;
MPERS75:12	H873	To loose a nose, to win a Town's no shame,
MPERS82:26	H1173	Yet words {Nor prayers}, nor guifts, could win him least
MPERS86:20	H1336	To win by force, what right could not obtain.
MPERS90:25	H1492	Might win {gain} the universall Monarchy;
MGREC98:10	H1812	To win their {the} town, his honour he engag'd;
MGREC110:18	H2318	When *Alexander* strives to win the field,

WIND (7)

ELEMEN18:14	H418	Speak, who, or what they will, they are but wind.
AGES38:31	H134	What gripes of wind, mine infancy did pain?
SEASONS~~47:27~~	H43	Nor-west {North-west} cold, {wind} of fierce *December*.
VANITY160:5	H15	More vain then all, that's but to grasp the wind.
CONTEM174:15	H214	As if he had command of wind and tide,
MEDDM201:12	Hp280	Fire hath its force abated by water not by wind, and anger
SON231:1	H13	And order'st so the adverse wind

WINDE (1) [wind]

HUMOUR29:9   H362   To spare our selves, and beat the whistling winde.

WINDES (1) [winds]

AGES38:9   H112   I fear'd no stormes, nor al the windes that blows,

WINDING (1)

MPERS93:2   H1599   Of all, did scarce his winding sheet retaine.

WINDS (5) See also WINDES

ELEMEN8:12   H10   Whence issu'd raines, and winds, lightning and thunder;

SEASONS51:25 H201   Whose yellow saplesse leaves by winds are fann'd:

MPERS79:12   H1034   But winds, and waves, these couples soon dissever'd,

MPERS~~79:12~~   H1034   But winds, and waves those iron bands did break;

CONTEM174:19 H218   Which 'gainst all adverse winds may serve for fort.

WINDY (2)

ELEMEN14:18   H260   But windy sister, 'twas when you have blown.

AGES43:29   H324   The windy Cholick oft my bowels rend,

WINE (6)

ELEMEN15:10   H292   Man wants his bread, and wine, and pleasant fruits;

AGES40:13   H194   For he that loveth Wine, wanteth no woes;

MPERS75:30   H887   Gives sacrifices, wheat, wine, oyle, and salt,

MPERS84:3   H1231   The royall wine, in golden cups doth {did} passe,

MGREC103:26 H2037   Being inflam'd with wine upon a season,

MGREC109:10 H2269   When thus, ten dayes, his brain with wine he'd soak'd,

WING (1)

CHILDRN184:18 H7   Till at the last they felt their wing.

WINGS (11) [pl.]

SEASONS48:8   H61   With wings, and beak, defends them from the gleads.

MGREC117:12 H2619   The Leopard down, his {the} four wings 'gan to rise,

MGREC135:29 H3401   The third a Leopard, which four wings did rear;

QELIZ158:16   H125   So blaze it fame, here's feathers for thy wings,

CONTEM173:16 H183   And wisht me wings with her a while to take my flight.

CHILDRN185:11 H37   And as his wings increase in strength,

CHILDRN185:34 H60   And with my wings kept off all harm,

MEDDM202:30 Hp282   of righteousnes will arise wth healing in his wings.

MEDDM207:10 Hp288   as wings to help vs mount vpwards, they will Certainly proue

13MAY226:30 H6   My Svns return'd wth healing wings

SON231:15   H27   On Eagles wings him hether brovght

WINNINGS (1) [pl.]

MPERS~~91:9~~   H1517   They now {Their winnings} lost all, and were a peace {their

WINS (2)

MGREC123:21 H2885   All *Syria,* and, *Phenicia* he wins;

MGREC126:22 H3013   Gives promise for her life, and {so} wins the day:

WINTER (20) See also WINTER'S, WINTERS

ELEMEN16:35   H358   O're childehood, and {ore} Winter, I bear the sway;

SEASONS46:30 H6   The Winter, Summer, Autumne, and the Spring,

SEASONS47:16 H32   The croaking Frogs, whom nipping Winter kild,

SEASONS48:13 H66   Our Winter {thicker} rayment, makes us lay aside,

SEASONS48:20 H73   Her shelves, and Firkins fill'd for winter time.

SEASONS51:18 H192   Which shewes, nor Summer, Winter, nor the Spring,

SEASONS51:21 H197   The Northern Winter blasts begin to hisse;

SEASONS51:31 H207   Where also he, his Winter time must have;

SEASONS52:12 H227   What Winter hath to tel, now let him say.

SEASONS52:13 H228   *Winter.*
SEASONS52:14 H229   Cold, moist, young, flegmy Winter now doth lye
SEASONS52:33 H248   I care not how the Winter time doth haste;
MGREC111:24 H2369   Whose inlets neare unto, he winter spent,
MGREC111:28 H2373   Thus Winter, Souldiers, and provision {provisions} spent,
CONTEM168:5 H15   More Heaven then Earth was here, no winter & no night.
CONTEM171:22 H125   If winter come, and greeness then do fade,
MEDDM197:11 Hp274   If we had no winter the spring would not be so pleasant, if we
MEDDM200:24 Hp279   is a liuely emblem of the resurrection, after a long winter
MYCHILD218:1 Hp243   & Winter, Spring and Autvmne, the dayly providing for this
13MAY226:26 H2   As spring the winter doth succeed

WINTER-LOCKED (1)
SEASONS47:7 H23   For to {He might} unloose his Winter-locked soyl;

WINTER'S (1) [winter is]
CONTEM173:32 H197   Where winter's never felt by that sweet airy legion.

WINTERS (1) [winter is]
13MAY227:1 H10   My winters past my stormes are gone

WINTERS (2) [pl.]
SEASONS47:1 H17   And bids defiance to all tedious Winters:
SEASONS51:35 H211   We now of Winters sharpness 'gin to taste;

WINTERS (2) [poss.]
ELEMEN9:19 H53   Your shrinking limbs, which winters cold doth harme;
CONTEM168:11 H20   Hath hundred winters past since thou wast born?

WIP'D (2) [wiped]
HUMOUR28:36 H348   I've scarce wip'd off the spots, proud Choler cast,
QELIZ156:7 H34   She hath wip'd off th' aspersion of her Sex,

WIPE (3)
HUMOUR24:13 H162   To vent my griefe, and wipe off my disgrace.
DIALOG146:28 H214   Dear mother cease complaints, and wipe your eyes,
MEDDM200:7 Hp279   wormwood or mustard, they wil either wipe it off, or else suck

WIPING (1)
SEASONS49:2 H93   Wiping her {the} sweat from off {of} her brow, that ran,

WISDOM (3) See also WISDOME, WISEDOM, WISEDOME
ELEMEN10:18 H93   Your wisdom out of little gathers {gather} much,
HUMOUR32:4 H478   But wisdome 'tis, my wisdom to conceale.
CONTEM171:30 H132   Nor youth, nor strength, nor wisdom spring again

WISDOME (9) [wisdom] See also WISEDOM, WISEDOME
HUMOUR32:4 H478   But wisdome 'tis, my wisdom to conceale.
MGREC116:38 H2604   For had he had but wisdome to his pride,
SIDNEY~~152:27~~ H96   *Learning, valour, beauty {Wisdome}, all in vertuous youth:*
QELIZ156:8 H35   That women wisdome lack to play the Rex;
VANITY160:12 H22   Where is it then? in wisdome, learning, arts?
VANITY160:23 H33   Nor yet in learning, wisdome, youth nor pleasure,
VANITY160:40 H50   Nor strength nor wisdome, nor fresh youth shall fade,
CONTEM168:3 H13   Sure he is goodness, wisdome, glory, light,
CHILDRN185:37 H63   Alas my birds, you wisdome want,

WISE (1) [manner]
MASSYR65:38 H503   The cursed King, by flight could no wise flee {fly}

WISE (48) [judicians]
ELEMEN11:11 H131   But to leave those to'th' wise, I judge is {it} best,
ELEMEN11:33 H153   The rich and {the} poore, wise, foole, and every sort,

ELEMEN14:4	H247	So did that Roman, far more stout then wise,
ELEMEN16:22	H345	Which pitty moves, and oft deceives the wise.
HUMOUR23:27	H137	They're held for Oracles, they are so wise.
HUMOUR29:21	H372	To play such furious pranks I am too wise;
HUMOUR29:31	H382	He is not truly valiant that's not wise;
HUMOUR29:35	H386	Wise *Fabius* is her buckler: all accord.
AGES36:16	H40	But neither us'd (as yet) for he was wise.
AGES36:29	H53	But wise Old-age, did with all gravity,
AGES40:7	H188	Of all at once, who not so wise, as fair,
AGES40:16	H197	All counsel hate, which tends to make me wise,
AGES44:8	H341	I have bin young, and strong, and wise as you,
AGES44:20	H353	He that in youth is godly, wise, and sage,
MASSYR57:20	H167	Nor can those Reasons which wise *Raleigh* finds,
MASSYR64:15	H439	Wise *Daniel,* and his fellows 'mongst the rest,
MASSYR66:27	H533	His Dreams, wise *Daniel* doth expound ful wel,
MASSYR68:4	H590	For the Soothsayers, and Magicians wise;
MPERS76:14	H912	But wise *Gobrias* reads not half so farre:
MPERS80:30	H1097	That brave *Thymistocles* takes this wise course,
MPERS91:12	H1520	Til many a Captain fel, both wise, and strong,
MPERS91:22	H1536	(A Lady very wicked, but yet wise)
MPERS91:32	H1546	A King nor good, nor valiant, wise nor just
MGREC93:10	H1607	Great *Alexander,* was wise *Phillips* son,
MGREC95:36	H1715	For this wise King, had brought to see the sport;
MGREC98:5	H1807	But they accept not this, in any wise,
MGREC103:30	H2041	*Parmenio* wise, intreats him to desist,
MGREC114:18	H2488	Was vertuous, learned wise *Calisthines,*
MGREC115:5	H2516	Findes there the want of wise *Parmenio,*
MGREC115:34	H2553	So to be caught, *Antipater's* too wise,
MGREC116:17	H2583	Wise *Aristotle,* tutour to his youth,
MGREC122:10	H2835	He was both valiant, faithfull, patient, wise.
DUBART153:1	H5	In humble wise have vow'd their service long;
QELIZ156:3	H30	Who was so good, so just, so learn'd, so wise,
TDUDLEY166:4	H46	And oft and oft, with speeches mild and wise,
TDUDLEY166:10	H52	His thoughts were more sublime, his actions wise,
TDUDLEY166:36	H78	*That was both pious, just and wise,*
CONTEM170:11	H84	And how she lost her bliss, to be more wise,
AUTHOR177:32	H4	Till snatcht from thence by friends, less wise then true
ANNEB187:20	H10	Experience might 'fore this have made me wise,
MEDDM195:26	Hp272	of all and he that makes such improvment is wise as well as
MEDDM196:30	Hp274	are best preserued wth sugar, those parents are wise that can
MEDDM200:33	Hp280	A wise father will not lay a burden on a child of seven yeares
MEDDM201:25	Hp281	The words of the wise (sath Solom) are as nailes, and as
MEDDM201:27	Hp281	should be the precepts of the wise masters of assemblys to
MEDDM202:7	Hp281	then ye earth some so wise and learned, that they seeme like
MYCHILD219:3	Hp245	Now to ye King Imortall, Eternall invisible, the only wise God,
MYSOUL225:20	H24	For God hath made me wise.

WISEDOM (1) [wisdom] See also WISDOME, WISEDOME

MEDDM199:2	Hp277	Wisedom with an inheritance is good, but wisedome without an

WISEDOME (5) [wisdom] See also WISDOME, WISEDOM

HUMOUR20:30	H22	Her wisedome spake not much, but thought the more.
MEDDM197:4	Hp274	Authority wthout wisedome is like a heavy axe, wthout an edg

MEDDM199:2	Hp277	Wisedom with an inheritance is good, but wisedome without an
MEDDM199:3	Hp277	inheritance, is better, then an inheritance wthout wisedome
MEDDM207:28	Hp289	to wisedome, that when wee are put out of these houses of

WISELY (2)

HUMOUR20:15	H7	But first they wisely shew'd their high descent,
DDUDLEY167:14	H11	*To Servants wisely aweful, but yet kind,*

WISER (1)

SIDNEY149:37	H24	Thy {His} wiser dayes, condemn'd thy {his} witty works,

WISEST (3)

MPERS89:16	H1450	He judg'd his wisest and his safest Course.
VANITY160:14	H24	Yet these, the wisest man of men did find,
MEDDM203:2	Hp283	Had not the wisest of men, taught vs this lesson, that all is

WISH (10)

HUMOUR34:10	H565	Yet some may wish, oh, {O} had mine eyes ne're seene.
MGREC133:35	H3325	Which we oft wish were {was} extant as before.
SIDNEY150:19	H44	O brave *Achilles,* I wish some *Homer* would
SIDNEY151:3	H69	I wish no more such Blazers we may see;
DUBART153:22	H26	And thousand times his mazed minde doth wish
CONTEM167:33	H9	I wist not what to wish, yet sure thought I,
CONTEM170:33	H103	When deep dispair, with wish of life hath fought,
CONTEM171:36	H137	Shall I wish there, or never to had birth,
1LETTER181:22	H20	I wish my Sun may never set, but burn
3LETTER183:16	H18	Her fellow lost, nor joy nor life do wish,

WISHED (4)

ELEMEN16:30	H353	The wealthy fraught, unto his wished Port.
ELEMEN18:24	H428	And speed you to your Port, with wished gales.
MASSYR61:31	H336	But *Tiglath,* having gain'd his wished end,
MGREC118:5	H2652	Some wished him, to take the stile of King,

WISHES (3) [pl.]

MPERS74:13	H836	His happy wishes now doth no man spare,
DUBART153:24	H28	But seeing empty wishes nought obtaine,
DUBART154:9	H54	But wishes cann't accomplish my desire,

WISHT (6)

SEASONS52:26	H241	In *Aquarias,* now keeps the loved {long wisht} Sun,
MPERS72:33	H777	All thought {wisht} his short reign long, till {past before} it was
MGREC101:28	H1953	*Parmenio, Alexander* wisht, that night,
MGREC117:27	H2634	Each Captain wisht this prize to beare away,
MGREC125:37	H2987	Wisht in *Epire* she still had been confin'd;
CONTEM173:16	H183	And wisht me wings with her a while to take my flight.

WIST (1)

CONTEM167:33	H9	I wist not what to wish, yet sure thought I,

WIT (23)

ELEMEN15:29	H311	The crafty {witty} Barbell, whose wit {craft} doth her commend;
ELEMEN16:18	H341	Which wondring *Aristotles* wit, ne'r knowes.
ELEMEN19:3	H448	Is more authentick then their {our} moderne wit.
ELEMEN19:11	H456	Without impeachment, to my tale or wit.
HUMOUR22:18	H87	Nor hath she wit, or heat, to blush at this.
HUMOUR22:37	H106	My absence proves, it plain, her wit then flyes
HUMOUR32:20	H494	Though wit I want, and anger I have lesse,
AGES39:30	H173	My wit, my bounty, and my courtesie,
AGES39:38	H181	My wit, evaporates in meriment:

AGES40:11	H192	Until mine own be gone, my wit, and wealth;
AGES43:~~19~~	H314	Be I of worth {wit}, of learning, or {and} of parts;
AGES44:14	H347	It's not my Learning, Rhetorick, wit so large,
MPERS75:22	~~H880~~	Thy wit was more then was thine honesty,
MPERS77:37	H978	Vaine *Xerxes* thinks his counsell hath most wit,
MPERS85:40	H1316	But *Cyrus* scornes, his brothers feeble wit;
MPERS90:40	H1507	*Tythraustes* trusts more to his wit then Arms,
MGREC113:8	H2435	Such torments great, as wit could first {worst} invent,
MGREC118:1	H2648	That so under his feeble wit, and reign,
SIDNEY149:22	H21	As if your nine-fold wit had been compacted;
SIDNEY149:26	~~H23~~	This was thy shame, O miracle of wit:
DUBART154:31	H76	Thy haughty stile, and rapted wit sublime,
QELIZ157:2	H70	But time would faile me, so my wit {tongue} would to,
CONTEM174:34	H231	Nor wit nor gold, nor buildings scape times rust;

WITCHING (1)

ELEMEN18:7	H411	No world {earth}, thy witching trash, were all but vain.

W^(TH)ALL (1) [withall]

MEDDM204:10	Hp284	w^(th)all, the larger his accounts stands vpon gods score it

WITHAL (1)

MERCY188:25	H11	I stood so nigh, it crusht me down withal;

WITHALL (7) [withall]

MASSYR64:22	H446	Which was the losse of *Syria* withall;
MASSYR68:20	H606	And of his own notorious sins, withall;
MGREC114:40	H2510	But yet withall, *Calisthines* he slew;
MGREC115:3	H2514	But yet withall, *Calisthines* he slew.
MROMAN138:17	H3507	Much stronger, and more beautifull withall;
DUBART153:3	H7	Gave o're the work, before begun withall:
MYCHILD218:25	Hp244	so to bee dealt withall.

WITHDTAW (1) [withdraw]

SEASONS~~49:14~~	H105	That if you do, remove {withdtaw} her burning store,

WITH-DRAWES (1) [withdraws]

MASSYR65:16	H481	For this great King, with-drawes part of his force,

WITHERED (4)

SEASONS51:16	H190	Or withered stocks, {which were} all dry, and dead,
SEASONS51:24	H200	The fruitful trees, all withered now do stand,
QELIZ158:11	H120	*This Rose is withered, once so lovely faire,*
3LETTER183:8	H10	(On withered bough) most uncouthly bemoan

WITHERING (2)

FLESH177:23	H104	Nor withering age shall e're come there,
ANNEB187:24	H14	I knew she was but as a withering flour,

WITHERS (1)

MEDDM207:17	Hp288	withers the pleasure w^(ch) else we should take in them, and well

WITHHOLD (2)

ELEMEN14:34	H276	If I withhold, what art thou, dead, dry lump
ELEMEN14:39	H281	Complaines to th'heaven, when {if} I withhold my drops:

WITHSTAND (5)

ELEMEN19:23	H468	Which neither ships nor houses could withstand.
AGES43:14	H307	my son, {Competitors} or his {as might in time} withstand.
MPERS80:29	H1096	They no way able to withstand his force,
MGREC122:23	~~H2845~~	*Ceria* the *Phrigian* Queen for to withstand,
MGREC~~124:8~~	H2913	His proud opponent hopes soon to withstand.

WITHSTANDS (1)
MGREC122:28 H2847 What he appoints, She purposely withstands.
WITLESS (1)
HUMOUR~~31:6~~ H439 Thou witless think'st that I am thy excretion,
WITNES (1) [witness] See also WITNESSE, WITTNES
MEDDM205:13 Hp286 alway kept by Conscience, who is both accuser excuser witnes
WITNESS'D (1) [witnessed]
MPERS80:22 H1089 That their split sides, witness'd his overthrow;
WITNESSE (5) [witness] See also WITNES, WITTNES
ELEMEN9:33 H67 Good {Cold} sister Earth, no witnesse needs but thine;
HUMOUR25:24 H213 Witnesse the execrable deeds thou'st done:
MGREC101:33 H1958 The Sun should witnesse of his valour be:
MGREC105:21 H2114 The witnesse of his dying misery: {this horrid Tragedy;}
SIDNEY149:20 H19 (Witnesse *Arcadia,* penn'd in his youth)
WITS (6) [pl.]
PROLOG7:17 H30 For such despight they cast on female wits:
HUMOUR22:4 H73 And by misprisions, like to loose her wits;
HUMOUR23:7 H117 Thou sayst, thy wits are stai'd, subtle and fine:
MASSYR59:9 H233 Bereft of wits, were slaughtered down right.
MASSYR66:36 H542 Contemplating those times he lost his wits;
DUBART152:33 H2 Amongst the happy wits this Age hath showne,
WITT'EST (1)
HUMOUR34:28 H583 Ne're did {Nor will} I heare {yield} that Choler was the witt'est;
WITTEST (1)
HUMOUR28:28 H340 And maugre (Choler) stil they are the wittest,
WITTILY (1)
MGREC131:31 H3223 He wittily his fathers mind did sound,
WITTNES (1) [witness] See also WITNES, WITNESSE
MYCHILD217:17 Hp243 although he hath not left me altogether wthout the wittnes of
WITTY (4)
ELEMEN~~15:29~~ H311 The crafty {witty} Barbell, whose wit {craft} doth her commend;
HUMOUR22:23 H92 {From} Whence flow fine spirits, and witty notions?
SEASONS~~48:17~~ H70 Now swarmes the busie buzzing {witty,} hony Bee.
SIDNEY149:37 H24 Thy {His} wiser dayes, condemn'd thy {his} witty works,
WIVES (5) [pl.]
MASSYR65:41 H506 With Children, Wives, and Nobles, all they bring,
MGREC~~126:41~~ H3030 Her Husbands Wife, {wives} and Children, after's death
MROMAN137:8 H3459 Of Wives there was so great a scarsity,
DIALOG144:39 H147 Wives forc'd, babes toss'd, her houses calcined,
SIDNEY150:4 H~~29~~ And modest Maids, and Wives, blush at thy glory;
WIVES (1) [pl.; poss.]
AGES45:23 H413 These are no old wives tales, but this is truth;
WOE (17)
ELEMEN15:7 H289 The Peacock, and the Ostrich, share in woe:
ELEMEN17:30 H394 That after times, shall never feel like woe:
AGES38:28 H131 For sin brings sorrow, sicknesse, death, and woe.
AGES~~41:9~~ H229 Marrow {aches} ful my bones, of Milk {woe} my breasts {heart},
MGREC93:22 H1619 An Omen, to their near approaching woe;
MGREC97:13 H1774 Was but beginning of his future woe;
MGREC~~115:15~~ H2528 A rueful face in this so general woe;
MGREC135:39 H3411 To fill the world with terrour, and with woe:

DIALOG142:2	H31	What Medicine shall I seek to cure this woe,
DIALOG142:22	H51	If none of these, deare Mother, what's your woe?
DIALOG146:11	H199	But these may be beginnings of more woe,
FLESH176:14	H54	And never had more cause of woe
DISTEMP179:24	H12	He eas'd my Soul of woe, my flesh of pain,
ANNEB187:23	H13	Or perfect bliss without mixture of woe.
MERCY188:22	H8	Ah, woe is me, to write thy Funeral Song,
MERCY189:3	H24	One week she only past in pain and woe,
HOURS234:16	H30	They are no Joy, but woe.

WOEFUL (1) See also WOEFULL, WOFUL, WOFULL

ELEMEN19:24	H469	What woeful wracks I've made, may wel appear,

WOEFULL (1) [woeful] See also WOFUL, WOFULL

ELEMEN15:21	H303	To meet with want, each woefull man bethinks.

WOES (12) [pl.]

ELEMEN14:6	H250	What she hath lost by these my dreadfull {remed'less} woes.
AGES40:13	H194	For he that loveth Wine, wanteth no woes;
SEASONS49:28	H117	Which made great *Bajazet* cry out in's woes,
MASSYR59:37	H261	When *Jonah* for their sins denounc'd such {those} woes;
MPERS83:1	H1189	Tels as he could, his unexpressed woes,
MGREC102:40	H2010	Which newes doth still augment *Darius* woes;
DIALOG141:10	H9	What deluge of new woes thus over-whelme
DIALOG141:15	H14	Art ignorant indeed, of these my woes?
DIALOG146:6	H194	That thousands lay on heaps, here bleeds my woes.
DIALOG148:11	H276	Of all the woes thou canst let her be sped,
CONTEM170:34	H104	Branded with guilt, and crusht with treble woes,
DISTEMP179:14	H2	In anguish of my heart repleat with woes,

WOFUL (6) [woeful] See also WOEFULL, WOFULL

AGES39:37	H180	My woful Parents longing hopes all {are} crost,
MASSYR61:34	H339	In *Galilee,* he woful havock makes;
MASSYR66:2	H508	And with that woful sight his eyes close shut.
MPERS72:1	H753	And contemn them, woful is his doome.
MPERS72:12	H760	His woful fate with tears did so bemoane,
2LETTER181:36	H6	The woful accents of my doleful sound,

WOFULL (5) [woeful] See also WOEFULL, WOFUL

MGREC100:34	H1918	{Whose death} her wofull Lord for to {full sadly did} lament.
MGREC104:39	H2091	This {The} wofull King, his courtesie refuses,
MGREC105:23	H2116	The just revenge of this his wofull end;
DIALOG144:20	H130	For these, were threatned the wofull day,
DIALOG146:22	H208	Their wofull mother's tears unpitied.

WOLF (1)

MGREC130:12	H3167	*Antigonus* thus had a wolf by th' ears,

WOLUES (1) [wolves] See also WOOLVES

PILGRIM210:10	H10	nor hungry wolues at him shall catch

WOMANS (1) [poss.]

MASSYR55:15	H81	Changing his {the} womans face, into a man.

WOMB (2)

CONTEM168:29	H36	And in the darksome womb of fruitful nature dive.
SICKNES178:31	H14	since first we came from womb,

WOMBE (3) [womb]

ELEMEN14:1	H243	Because in the abysse of my darke wombe:
HUMOUR28:4	H316	And turns him to the wombe of's earthy mother,

HUMOUR30:22	H414	His mother (mine) him to her wombe retakes,

WOMEN (8)

PROLOG7:28	H39	Let *Greeks* be *Greeks,* and Women what they are,
PROLOG7:31	H42	Men can doe best, and Women know it well;
MGREC96:19	H1739	He fifteen hundred had like women drest,
MGREC130:15	H3170	Her women are appointed to this deed,
MGREC135:41	H3413	This taske befits not women, like to men:
QELIZ156:8	H35	That women wisdome lack to play the Rex;
QELIZ157:32	H100	Now say, have women worth, or have they none?
1HUSB180:26	H5	Compare with me ye women if you can.

WON (23)

AGES44:34	H367	Then saw I *France,* and *Holland* sav'd, *Cales* won,
MASSYR~~57:17~~	H164	Unto a Father that all Countryes won
MASSYR59:2	H226	Won by his loving looks, more loving {by his} speech,
MASSYR61:10	H315	Next treads the {those} steps, by which his Father won.
MASSYR63:24	H409	The ancient {famous} *Niniveh* by him was won;
MPERS73:28	H813	But so or no, sure tis, they won the day.
MPERS77:3	H942	As the best trophe that {which} ye won in *Greece.*
MPERS81:32	H1140	And of those *Greeks,* which by his skil he'd won,
MGREC97:24	H1785	No sooner had this Captaine {Victor} won the field,
MGREC114:37	H2507	All Kingdoms, Countries, Provinces, he won, {wan}
MGREC116:40	H2606	To govern that he had already won:
MGREC128:36	H3109	His lost repute with victorie had won;
MGREC131:35	H3227	And leaves the ill got kingdomes he had won,
MGREC~~132:6~~	H3239	Against *Lysimachus* who from him won.
MGREC132:25	H3270	After three years he dyed, left what he'd won
MGREC132:31	H3278	Rich *Ægypt* left, and what else he had won
MGREC~~133:22~~	H3311	(Part of whose Kingdomes *Titus Quintius* won)
MGREC133:23	H3312	He *Perseus,* from him the kingdom's won,
MGREC135:37	H3409	But how the fourth, their Kingdoms from them won;
SIDNEY149:17	H16	Thy {His} Logick from *Euterpe* won the Crown,
DUBART154:21	H66	Who in thy tryumphs (never won by wrongs)
QELIZ156:4	H31	From all the Kings on earth she won the prize;
SICKNES179:9	H29	The race is run, the field is won,

WONDER (22)

ELEMEN11:7	H127	Which Kings, and mighty ones; amaz'd with wonder,
ELEMEN19:41	H482	That earth appeares in heaven, oh wonder great!
HUMOUR32:24	H498	Nor wonder 'twas, for hatred there's not smal,
HUMOUR33:41	H555	I'le touch the Sight, great'st wonder of the three;
AGES38:40	H143	That wonder tis, my glasse till now doth hold.
AGES41:6	H226	That wonder 'tis I yet behold the light,
MASSYR56:23	H129	This wonder of the world, this *Babell* stood.
MASSYR62:27	H372	Hath bred more wonder, then beleefe in hearts;
MGREC94:11	H1645	Nor wonder is't, if he in blood begin,
MGREC100:3	H1887	To see how fast he gain'd, is {was} no small wonder,
MGREC107:18	H2193	Nor wonder lesse, to Readers may it bring,
MGREC135:11	H3383	The Heavens thus rule, to fill the earth {world} with wonder.
DIALOG147:32	H256	That dazzled eyes beholding much shall wonder
SIDNEY151:16	~~H69~~	Then wonder lesse, if warlike *Philip* yield,
SIDNEY~~152:14~~	H84	Then wonder not if I no better sped,
QELIZ157:7	H75	Worlds wonder for a time {while}, but yet it falls;

QELIZ157:41	H109	Then wonder not, *Eliza* moves not here.
TDUDLEY166:12	H54	Nor wonder 'twas, low things ne'r much did move
CONTEM168:20	H28	No wonder, some made thee a Deity:
CONTEM173:14	H181	Which rapt me so with wonder and delight,
MERCY189:8	H29	No wonder it no longer did survive.
MEDDM197:29	Hp275	'tis no wonder if he faint by the way.

WONDERED See WONDRED

WONDERFULL (3) [wonderful]

DAVID159:24	H39	Thy love was wonderfull, passing {surpassing} a man;
MEDDM206:27	Hp288	All the works and doings of god are wonderfull, but none more
MED223:12	Hp250	to haue thought it? So wonderfull are these thoughts that my

WONDERING (1)

MGREC125:36	H2986	The Courtiers wondering at her furious minde,

WONDERMENTS (1) [pl.]

HUMOUR34:8	H563	What wonderments, within your bals there lyes?

WONDEROUS (1) [wondrous] See also WOND'ROUS, WONDROVS

ELEMEN12:11	H171	And wonderous high *Olimpus,* of such fame,

WONDERS (3) [pl.]

ELEMEN10:27	H102	'Mong all my wonders which I might recount;
MGREC110:32	H2336	Which might be found, and so for {great} wonders kept:
MYSOUL225:16	H20	For wonders that I see.

WONDRED (2) [wondered]

MPERS78:36	H1017	Which mighty sum, all wondred to behold.
DUBART154:23	H68	Oft have I wondred at the hand of heaven,

WONDRING (4) [wondering]

PROLOG6:25	H9	But when my wondring eyes, and envious heart,
ELEMEN16:18	H341	Which wondring *Aristotles* wit, ne'r knowes.
DIALOG141:18	H17	Which 'mazed Christendome stands wondring at?
DUBART154:32	H77	All ages wondring at, shall never clime.

WOND'ROUS (1) [wondrous] See also WONDEROUS, WONDROVS

HUMOUR33:24	H538	Its ventricles, membranes, and wond'rous net,

WONDROUS (11) See also WONDEROUS, WOND'ROUS, WONDROVS

HUMOUR26:35	H265	Their wondrous mixture, is of blood, and ayre,
MASSYR56:13	H119	The wondrous Temple was, she rear'd to *Bell;*
MPERS70:20	H691	Yet wondrous Monuments this stately Queen,
MPERS76:28	H926	Return'd with wondrous losse, and honour lesse:
MPERS77:30	H971	And *Greece* such wondrous triumphs ne're had made.
MGREC94:22	H1660	And on *Achillis* Tombe, with wondrous joy,
MGREC95:7	H1686	Where stood of late *Diana's,* wondrous Phane,
MGREC120:33	H2770	In midst of these, *Garboyles,* with wondrous state,
MGREC~~132:28~~	H3275	Whose obsequies with wondrous pomp was done.
QELIZ155:16	H7	Thy wondrous worth proclaime, in every clime,
13MAY227:8	H17	Who is a God so wondrous great.

WONDROVS (1) [wondrous] See also WONDEROUS, WOND'ROUS

MYCHILD217:36	Hp243	would soon tell me by the wondrovs workes that I see, the vast

WO'NT (1) [won't]

PROLOG7:18	H31	If what I doe prove well, it wo'nt advance,

WONT (1) [won't]

MGREC114:1	H2469	When both were drunk, *Clitus* was wont to jeere;

WOOD (4)

MASSYR67:35	H581	Did praise his gods of mettall, wood, and stone,

MPERS76:41	H939	His whetted teeth he sticks {claps} in the firm wood,
MGREC98:8	H1810	In the old town (which now {then} lay like a wood)
MGREC107:30	H2205	For Boats here's none, nor neare it any wood,

WOODEN (1)

AGES36:9	H33	No wooden horse, but one of mettal try'd:

WOOD-PILE (1)

MPERS69:35	H657	Then on a Pike being {wood-pile} set, where all might eye,

WOODS (5) [pl.]

ELEMEN12:23	H183	Thousands in woods, and planes, both wild, and tame,
CONTEM172:10	H146	I once that lov'd the shady woods so well,
2LETTER182:11	H17	The leaves in th' woods, the hail or drops of rain,
3LETTER182:37	H2	Scuds through the woods and Fern with harkning ear,
CHILDRN186:4	H71	In shady woods I'le sit and sing,

WOOES (1) [woos]

3LETTER183:13	H15	His presence and his safe return, still wooes,

WOOLVES (1) [wolves] See also WOLUES

ELEMEN15:5	H287	The Woolves and savage Beasts, forsake their Dens.

WOOS See WOOES

WORD (27)

ELEMEN11:14	H134	And in a word, the World I shal consume,
ELEMEN12:26	H186	In his behalfe to speak a word the more;
AGES40:26	H207	And in a word, if what I am you'd heare,
AGES43:26	H321	Now in a word, what my diseases be.
MASSYR59:41	H265	Ingeniously with each {all} did keep his word;
MASSYR68:26	H612	Perform'd his word, to him, that told his fate;
MPERS80:31	H1098	In secret manner word to *Xerxes* sends,
MPERS89:37	H1471	But violates his honour, and his word,
MGREC98:7	H1809	Sent word, that *Hercules* his Temple stood,
MGREC102:41	H2011	In his approach, the Governour sends word,
MGREC108:14	H2230	Without {least} cause, given by {from} them, in deed, or word:
MGREC113:7	H2434	Thy Kingly word can easily terminate;
MGREC120:20	H2755	If not in word {stile}, in deed a Soveraigne.
MGREC126:27	H3018	And so was he acquitted of his word,
SIDNEY150:36	H63	Of this our noble *Scipio* some good word?
DUBART153:29	H33	The silly Pratler speakes no word of sence;
FLESH176:29	H69	The word of life it is my meat.
SICKNES178:24	H7	For Adams sake, this word God spake
SICKNES178:37	H20	ev'n as a word that's speaking.
MYCHILD217:18	Hp243	spirit who hath oft given me his word & sett to his Seal that it
MYCHILD218:8	Hp244	If ever this God hath revealed himself it mvst bee in his word,
MYCHILD218:19	Hp244	word, yet why may not ye popish Relign. bee ye right, They
MYCHILD218:20	Hp244	same God, the same Christ, ye same word, They only
SOREFIT222:2	H21	To praise in thought, in Deed, in Word.
MED223:10	Hp250	he my head. Such priviledges had not ye word of Truth made
WHAT224:19	H19	His word he plighted hath on high
11MAYB228:33	Hp259	testefye my thankfullnes not only in word, but in Deed, that my

WORDED (1)

DIALOG146:5	H193	They worded it so long, they fell to blows,

WORDS (15) [pl.]

ELEMEN18:13	H417	Nay, what are words, which doe reveale the mind?
HUMOUR23:28	H138	Their wrathfull looks are death, their words are laws;

HUMOUR28:37	H349	Such venome lyes in words, though but a blast,
HUMOUR29:8	H361	But sith we fight with words, we might be kind,
HUMOUR32:14	H488	Nor multitude of words, argues our strength;
AGES40:12	H193	From pipe to pot, from pot to words, and blows,
MASSYR66:37	H543	And if by words, we may guesse at the heart,
MPERS69:37	H659	The Reason of those words *Cyrus* demands,
MPERS70:33	H704	Using such taunting words as she thought good.
MPERS82:26	H1173	Yet words {Nor prayers}, nor guifts, could win him least
DDUDLEY167:20	H17	*Religious in all her words and wayes,*
MEDDM196:25	Hp273	Sweet words are like hony, a little may refresh, but too much
MEDDM201:13	Hp280	alayed, by cold words and not by blustering threats.
MEDDM201:25	Hp281	The words of the wise (sath Solom) are as nailes, and as
MYCHILD218:32	Hp244	I haue reme̅bred the words of Christ that so it must bee, and

WORE (1)

SIDNEY149:8	H7	Her noble *Sidney* wore the Crown of Bayes;

WORK (13)

ELEMEN13:23	H224	And how I oft work mans mortality.
ELEMEN18:22	H426	Your red hot work, more coldly would go on.
HUMOUR23:14	H124	paine and sore obstructions, {obstruction} thou dost work;
MASSYR60:23	H288	A costly work, which none could doe but he,
MASSYR65:6	H471	Full thirteen yeares in this strange work he spent,
MPERS75:32	H889	Shall let the work, or keep back any thing,
MPERS91:37	H1551	Made Writers work at home, they sought not far?
MGREC110:15	H2315	Yet work enough, here *Alexander* found,
DIALOG142:38	H67	For they have work enough (thou knowst) elsewhere;
DUBART153:3	H7	Gave o're the work, before begun withall:
MYCHILD218:10	Hp244	humane Invention can work vpon yᵉ Soul, hath no Judgments
11MAYA226:15	Hp255	& some ability to pʳform yᵉ Dutyes I owe to him, and the work
2HUSB232:31	H32	Vnto thy Work he hath in hand

WORKE (3) [work]

ELEMEN19:15	H460	With divers moe, worke deadly consequence.
SIDNEY150:7	H32	And doth thy {his} selfe, thy {his} worke, and {his} honour
MEDDM206:28	Hp288	then his great worke of election and Reprobation, when we

WORKES (1) [works]

MYCHILD217:36	Hp243	would soon tell me by the wondrovs workes that I see, the vast

WORKING (1)

HUMOUR28:29	H341	{With} An ingenius working phantasie,

WORK-MEN (1)

MPERS79:13	H1038	The work-men put to death the bridge that made,

WORKS (7) [pl.]

AGES46:12	H443	Though reading other Works, doth much refresh,
MASSYR62:32	H377	Whose haughty heart is shewn in works, and deeds;
SIDNEY149:37	H24	Thy {His} wiser dayes, condemn'd thy {his} witty works,
DUBART154:33	H78	Thy sacred works are not for imitation,
QELIZ155:35	H26	*Eliza's* works, wars, praise, can e're compact,
CONTEM168:2	H12	Whose power and beauty by his works we know.
MEDDM206:27	Hp288	All the works and doings of god are wonderfull, but none more

WORKS (1) v.

ELEMEN13:16	H217	But how my cold, dry temper, works upon

WORLD (80) See also WORLD'S

FATHER5:6	H7	(though made a pedestall for *Adams* Race) /world

FATHER5:24	H25	The world, the usefull, hurtfull, and the good:
ELEMEN11:14	H134	And in a word, the World I shal consume,
ELEMEN17:5	H369	And with astonishment, the world confounds.
ELEMEN18:7	H411	No world {earth}, thy witching trash, were all but vain.
HUMOUR21:8	H36	We both once Masculines, the world doth know,
HUMOUR24:34	H183	Whose glorious deeds in armes, the world can tel,
AGES37:10	H72	With tears into this {the} world I did arrive;
AGES41:22	H239	And then a world of drosse among my gold.
AGES41:27	H244	I then with both hands, graspt the world together,
AGES41:34	H249	To bear me out i'th' world, and feed the poor,
AGES41:36	H253	To bear a port i'th' world, and feed the poor.
AGES44:38	H371	And then, me thought, the world {day} at noon grew dark,
MASSYR53:15	H5	When Time was young, and World in infancy,
MASSYR54:2	H29	Left to the world, by any History;
MASSYR55:2	H68	The world then was two thousand nineteen old.
MASSYR56:23	H129	This wonder of the world, this *Babell* stood.
MASSYR56:37	H143	Leaving the world, to *Venus,* soar'd above,
MASSYR60:39	H304	Which makes the world of differences {difference} so ful,
MASSYR64:28	H452	As might not him, but all the world out-face;
MPERS70:7	H678	That all the world they neither {need not} feare, nor doubt;
MPERS83:34	H1222	Then when the world, they after over-run:
MGREC96:2	H1722	For since the world, was no such Pageant seen.
MGREC96:24	H1744	Then such a world of Wagons did appear,
MGREC100:33	H1917	Now bids the world adieu, her time {with pain} being spent,
MGREC101:7	H1932	(Nor was such match, in all the world beside)
MGREC101:25	H1950	Nor yet two Monarchs in one World reside;
MGREC102:11	H1981	In this a masse {world} of gold, and treasure lay,
MGREC102:14	H1984	Whose fame throughout the world, was so renown'd;
MGREC102:29	H1999	He likewise here a world of treasure found,
MGREC106:9	H2143	(For scarce the world, or any bounds thereon,
MGREC113:13	H2440	And told the world, that for desert {his guilt} he dyed.
MGREC116:11	H2577	{This Monarchs fame} must last, whilst world shall {doth}
MGREC116:15	H2581	But with the world his vertues overcame,
MGREC123:14	H2878	Now {When} great *Antipater,* the world doth {must} leave
MGREC129:24	H3138	That he was {is} odious to the world, they'r glad,
MGREC130:20	H3175	The world must needs believe what he doth tell:
MGREC132:20	H3259	With these he hopes to turn the world about:
MGREC135:11	H3383	The Heavens thus rule, to fill the earth {world} with wonder.
MGREC135:39	H3411	To fill the world with terrour, and with woe:
MROMAN136:24	H3438	Whom vestall *Rhea,* into {to} th' world did bring
MROMAN136:32	H3446	The Mistris of the World, in each respect.
MROMAN140:8	H3571	Nor matter is't this last, the world now sees,
DIALOG147:16	H242	Light Christendome, and all the world to see,
DIALOG148:13	H278	Bring forth the beast that rul'd the world with's beck,
SIDNEY149:23	H22	To shew the world, they never saw before,
SIDNEY150:6	H31	A world of treasure, in {wealth within} that rubbish lye;
SIDNEY151:13	H69	To be within the bounds of one world kept,
DUBART155:3	H88	*The world rejoyc'd at's birth, at's death was sorry;*
QELIZ155:17	H8	And so has {hath} vow'd, whilst there is world, or time;
QELIZ155:23	H14	Thy world of honours to accumulate,
QELIZ156:39	H66	Her Sea-men through all straights the world did round,

VANITY160:29   H39   Who drinks thereof, the world doth naught account.
TDUDLEY165:22 H24   These to the world his merits could make known,
CONTEM168:4   H14   That hath this under world so richly dight:
CONTEM168:19 H27   Soul of this world, this Universes Eye,
CONTEM174:21 H219   So he that saileth in this world of pleasure,
FLESH175:19   H19   That all in th' world thou count'st but poor?
FLESH177:28   H109   Take thou the world, and all that will.
BIRTH179:27   H3   All things within this fading world hath end,
2LETTER182:8   H14   My Interest's more then all the world beside.
MEDDM197:7   Hp274   reason why christians are so loth to exchang this world for a
MEDDM198:10   Hp276   his foot And he that passes through the wildernes of this world,
MEDDM200:13   Hp279   world before it bid them farwell
MEDDM202:16   Hp282   The treasures of this world may well be compared to huskes,
MEDDM203:13   Hp283   bussines lyes, a christian is sailing through this world vnto his
MEDDM205:9   Hp286   As man is called the little world so his heart may be cal'd the
MEDDM208:21   Hp290   so is it wth the wealth honours and pleasures of this world
MEDDM209:20   Hp291   so there may be a mutuall commerce through ye world As it is
MYCHILD216:8   Hp241   this Covntry, where I fovnd a new World and new manners at
MYCHILD216:17 Hp241   I have brovght yov into ye world, and wth great paines,
weaknes,
MYCHILD217:20 Hp243   world knowes not, & haue sett vp my Ebenez^r. and haue
MYCHILD218:14 Hp244   Times, + how ye world came to bee as wee see, Do wee not
MYCHILD218:28 Hp244   new Troubles I haue had since ye world has been filled wth
MED223:2   Hp250   Consolations wch the world knowes not.
MYSOUL225:17   H21   Base World I trample on thy face,
28AUG226:4   Hp254   sett vpon the world.
30SEPT227:22 Hp257   world. I haue fovnd by Exper^c. I can no more liue wthout
HOURS234:11   H25   I in this world no comfort haue,
HOUSE237:27   H57   The world no longer let me Love

WORLDLINGS (1)
WHAT224:9   H9   Goe Worldlings to your Vanities

WORLDLY (3)
SEASONS49:26 H115   Carelesse of worldly wealth, you sit {sing} and pipe,
VANITY159:29   H1   *Of the vanity of all worldly creatures {things}.*
FLESH175:7   H7   On worldly wealth and vanity;

WORLD'S (2) [world is]
QELIZ155:36   H27   The World's the Theater where she did act;
2LETTER182:28 H34   His little world's a fathom under water,

WORLDS (2) [pl.]
MGREC116:36   H2602   There was {were} no worlds, more, to be conquered:
QELIZ158:19   H128   If many worlds, as that fantastick framed,

WORLDS (6) [poss.]
ELEMEN8:22   H20   The worlds confusion it did seeme to threat;
ELEMEN11:8   H128   Which made a *Cæsar,* (Romes) the worlds proud head,
MPERS70:31   H702   And at one blow, worlds head, she headlesse makes;
MPERS92:36   H1594   How from the top of the worlds felicity;
MGREC93:34   H1631   (For as worlds Monarch, now we speak not on,
MGREC116:36   H2602   There was {were} no worlds, more, to be conquered:
QELIZ157:7   H75   Worlds wonder for a time {while}, but yet it falls;

WORM (1)
MEDDM207:15   Hp288   their shadow very comfortable, yet there is some worm or

WORMES (1) [worms]

AGES38:34	H137	Whence vomits, wormes, and flux have issued?

WORMS (1)

AGES46:17	H448	Mother, and sisters both; the worms, that crawl,

WORMWOOD (1)

MEDDM200:7	Hp279	wormwood or mustard, they wil either wipe it off, or else suck

WORN (3)

MPERS92:11	H1569	Whose race long time had worn the Diadem,
MGREC102:17	H1987	Though worn by time, and raz'd {rac'd} by foes full sore,
28AUG225:26	Hp254	After mvch weaknes & sicknes when my spirits were worn out,

WORSE (7)

HUMOUR22:1	H70	Then here's our sad black Sister, worse then you,
HUMOUR34:25	H580	Phrensie's worse, then folly, one would more glad,
AGES40:5	H186	Or stab the man, in's own defence, that's worse.
AGES42:17	H275	{again,} mine age (in all) {mine Age} been worse then hell.
MGREC98:29	H1831	He scorns to have one worse then had the other,
2LETTER182:27	H33	Tell him here's worse then a confused matter,
MEDDM200:17	Hp279	but falls and bruises, or perhaps somewhat worse, much more

WORSER (1)

MPERS86:37	H1353	But least {lest} some worser newes should fly to Court,

WORSHIP (5)

MASSYR66:25	H531	His Image, *Iudahs* Captives worship not,
MGREC96:8	H1728	(For Sun and Fire the *Persians* worship most)
DIALOG148:26	H291	And Jew and Gentile, to one worship go,
MYCHILD218:5	Hp243	such a God as I worship in Trinity, + such a Sav^r as I rely
MYCHILD218:18	Hp244	that admitt this bee ye true God whom wee worship, and y^t bee

WORSHIPPED (1)

MASSYR54:7	H34	This is that *Bell,* the *Chaldees* worshipped,

WORST (7)

FATHER6:11	H45	Accept my best, my worst vouchsafe a grave.
HUMOUR34:38	H593	The worst she said, was, instability,
AGES39:7	H150	And then the worst, in a more ugly hue;
MGREC~~113:8~~	H2435	Such torments great, as wit could first {worst} invent,
MGREC124:13	H2920	But had the worst {beaten was} at Sea, as well as {and foil'd
DIALOG146:12	H200	Who knows, the worst, the best {this} may {be my} overthrow;
3LETTER183:21	H23	But worst of all, to him can't steer my course,

WORTH (36)

FATHER5:7	H8	Their worth so shines, in those rich lines you show.
FATHER5:15	H16	Who for their age, their worth, and quality,
PROLOG6:23	H8	My obscure Verse, {Lines} shal not so dim their worth.
ELEMEN8:30	H28	What is my worth (both ye) and all things {men} know,
ELEMEN11:22	H142	Sister, in worth {quoth shee} I come not short of you;
ELEMEN20:6	H488	But what's their worth, {wrath} or force, but more's {same's} in
HUMOUR21:32	H60	Here's Sister Ruddy, worth the other two,
HUMOUR27:21	H292	My worth in humble manner, to commend.
HUMOUR28:39	H351	If modesty my worth do not conceale.
HUMOUR34:18	H573	Whose use and worth to tel, I must refrain;
AGES37:25	H87	That its own worth, it did not know, nor mind.
AGES41:21	~~H230~~	But what's of worth, your eyes shal first behold,
AGES43:19	H314	Be I of worth {wit}, of learning, or {and} of parts;
MASSYR55:32	~~H98~~	And that her worth, deserved no such blame,

MASSYR57:12	H159	What then he did, of worth, can no man tel,
MASSYR66:11	H517	All now of worth, are captive led with tears,
MPERS85:37	H1313	A hopefull Prince, whose worth {by *Xenophon*} is ever fam'd.
MPERS91:31	H1545	But this of him is worth the memory,
MGREC96:22	H1742	Would aske more time, then were {was} their bodys worth.
MGREC96:36	H1756	That valour was more worth than Pearls, or gold,
MGREC107:2	H2177	With those of worth, he still desires esteem,
MGREC114:17	H2487	The next of worth, that suffered after these,
MGREC119:41	H2731	Act any thing of worth, as heretofore,
SIDNEY149:18	H17	More worth was thine, {his} then *Clio* could set down.
SIDNEY149:31	H23	Which shewes, thy worth was great, thine honour such,
SIDNEY150:12	H40	Which shews his worth was great, his honour such,
SIDNEY150:13	H48	{The more I} say truth, {the more} thy worth I shall but staine,
SIDNEY151:30	H75	Which are in worth, as far short of his due,
DUBART153:19	H23	To comprehend the worth of all those knacks;
QELIZ155:16	H7	Thy wondrous worth proclaime, in every clime,
QELIZ157:20	H88	Of her what worth in Story's to be seen,
QELIZ157:32	H100	Now say, have more women worth, or have they none?
TDUDLEY165:11	H13	For who more cause to boast his worth then I?
TDUDLEY165:25	H27	While others tell his worth, I'le not be dumb:
BIRTH180:9	H19	If any worth or virtue were in me,
VERSES183:36	H3	If worth in me, or ought I do appear,

WORTHIES (1) [pl.]

HUMOUR21:28	H56	Have ye not heard of Worthies, Demi-gods?

WORTHINESSE (1) [worthiness]

SIDNEY151:27	H75	But *Sydney's* Muse, can sing his worthinesse.

WORTHY (17)

ELEMEN10:2	H77	Poor Heathen judg'd worthy a Diety:
ELEMEN12:29	H189	But hark, ye worthy Merchants who for prize
HUMOUR23:30	H140	But one of you would make a worthy King:
HUMOUR23:31	H141	Like our sixt *Henry,* that same worthy {virtuous} thing.
HUMOUR25:8	H197	Thy other scoffes not worthy of reply:
HUMOUR34:19	H574	Some worthy {curious} learned *Crooke* may these reveal,
AGES45:10	H392	And worthy {better} ones, put to {suffer} extremity:
SEASONS50:34	H168	Yet then appears the worthy deeds he 'ath done:
MASSYR68:25	H611	And did one thing worthy a King (though late)
MPERS79:8	H1030	First thing, *Xerxes* {he} did worthy {of} recount,
MPERS84:7	H1235	And a {one} more worthy, placed in her roome,
MPERS87:22	H1374	Not worthy to be known, but for his shame:
MGREC132:32	H3279	To *Philadelphus,* his more worthy Son.
DDUDLEY167:10	H7	*A worthy Matron of unspotted life,*
VERSES184:1	H5	Then may your worthy self from whom it came.
SOREFIT222:5	H24	Nor ovght on Earth worthy Desire,
FAINTING222:12	H2	Worthy art Thou o Ld of praise,

WOULD (120) See also HE'D, SHE'D, 'TWOULD

ELEMEN8:11	H9	All would be cheife, and all scorn'd to be under,
ELEMEN10:16	H91	My story to a Volume would amount:
ELEMEN11:32	H152	Would so passe time, I could say nothing else;
ELEMEN11:36	H156	Soone would they passe, not hundreds, but legions,
ELEMEN14:29	H271	And how your subtilty would men delude.
ELEMEN15:25	H307	Shouldst thou but buy, it would exhaust thy gold.

ELEMEN18:22	H426	Your red hot work, more coldly would go on.
HUMOUR21:3	H31	Your selves would judge, but vain prolixity.
HUMOUR22:32	H101	The nerves should I not warm, soon would they freeze.
HUMOUR22:39	H108	Oh, who would misse this influence of thine,
HUMOUR23:30	H140	But one of you would make a worthy King:
HUMOUR25:19	H208	Both them and all things else, she will {would} consume.
HUMOUR34:25	H580	Phrensie's worse, then folly, one would more glad,
AGES39:35	H178	That who would see vain man, may look on me:
MASSYR57:21	H168	Would now advantage take, their own to gain;
MASSYR60:6	H271	Yet would not {granting} let them {now} to inhabite there;
MPERS71:25	H739	But {For} he would be profest god of their Weal;
MPERS72:15	H763	Who would have born a Nephew, and a Son.
MPERS72:30	H774	'T would be no pleasant {pleasure}, but a tedious thing,
MPERS73:35	H820	And thought the people, would more happy be,
MPERS81:5	H1113	{Fearing} his best {bridge}, no longer for to {there would} stay;
MPERS81:8	H1116	Who for his sake, he knew, would venture far,
MPERS81:12	H1120	And that with *Xerxes* they would be at one,
MPERS81:14	H1122	The *Spartans,* fearing *Athens* would agree,
MPERS81:21	H1129	Their infamy would last till all things ends:
MPERS81:25	H1133	Against the *Persians* they would use {bend} their force.
MPERS81:41	H1145	rest had} Weapons, they had none would {do little} harme;
MPERS82:6	H1153	The other not a hand, nor sword will {would} wave,
MPERS84:28	H1264	His Country, nor his Kindred {Friends} would {much} esteem,
MPERS84:33	H1269	Nor yet disloyall to his Prince would prove,
MPERS85:38	H1314	His father would no notice of that take;
MPERS86:24	H1340	She to the King, would make a fair report:
MPERS86:25	H1341	He hop'd, if fraud, nor force the Crown could {would} gaine;
MPERS91:27	H1541	Such as would know at large his warrs and reign,
MGREC96:18	H1738	Would think {Suppos'd} he neither thought {meant} to fight nor
MGREC96:22	H1742	Would aske more time, then were {was} their bodys worth.
MGREC96:34	H1754	The *Greekes* would all adore, and {but} would none fight.
MGREC97:29	H1790	Writes unto {To} *Alexander,* to {he would} restore
MGREC99:10	H1853	*Darius* offers I would not reject,
MGREC99:13	H1856	And so if I *Parmenio* were, would I.
MGREC100:44	H1925	He prayes the immortall gods, for to {they would} reward
MGREC107:33	H2208	Would by {without} some means a transportation finde;
MGREC109:8	H2267	Nor had that drunken god, one that {who} would take
MGREC110:21	H2325	East-ward, now *Alexander* would goe still,
MGREC110:35	H2339	But doubting, wearing Time would {might} these decay,
MGREC110:36	H2340	And so his memory might {would} fade away,
MGREC112:11	H2397	If an Ideall Paradise, a man should {would} frame,
MGREC112:41	H2427	Faine would have spoke, and made his owne defence,
MGREC113:1	H2428	The King would give no eare, but went from thence;
MGREC113:20	H2447	As he would ne're confesse, nor could {yet} reward,
MGREC114:14	H2484	And would have slaine himself, for *Clitus* gone,
MGREC114:22	H2492	Nor would adore him for a Deity:
MGREC116:10	H2573	Nor meat, nor drink, nor comfort would she take,
MGREC116:39	H2605	He would have found enough for {there} to be done,
MGREC118:30	H2679	Was stiffe *Meleager,* whom he would take down {away},
MGREC119:14	H2704	{And gladly would} Shakes {shake} off the yoke, sometimes
MGREC120:4	H2736	Who fear'd *Antipater* would take his life

1109

MGREC120:14	H2749	For's Souldiers 'gainst those Captains would not goe;
MGREC120:19	H2754	But this again dislikes, and {he} would remain,
MGREC121:19	H2801	With stile of the Protector, would him {to} grace;
MGREC121:29	H2811	With greater joy it would have been receiv'd;
MGREC121:34	H2816	And fain would draw *Eumenes* to their side,
MGREC~~122:8~~	H2832	He that at large would satisfie his mind,
MGREC122:29	H2848	He wearied out, at last, would needs be gone,
MGREC123:35	H2899	Prest to accomplish what he would have done;
MGREC~~124:19~~	H2926	Still labours *Eumenes* might {would} with him side,
MGREC126:15	H3006	Faine would she come now to {this wretched Queen}
MGREC126:16	H3007	Cassander will not heare {Her foe would give no Ear}, such is
MGREC127:23	H3053	Because he never would let go {forgoe} his trust:
MGREC128:15	H3088	Now {Then} *Ptolomy* would gaine the *Greeks* likewise,
MGREC~~129:29~~	H3143	(But, *Olympias,* thought to {would} preferre th' other:)
MGREC131:39	H3231	The mother would the youngest should {might} excell,
DIALOG142:4	H33	But you perhaps would have me guesse it out,
DIALOG145:32	H181	This done, an Act they would have passed fain,
DIALOG146:31	H217	Your sunken bowels gladly would refresh:
SIDNEY150:19	H44	O brave *Achilles,* I wish some *Homer* would
SIDNEY151:5	~~H69~~	And as thy beauty, so thy name would wast,
SIDNEY151:20	H70	Fain would I shew, how thou {he} fame's path didst {paths did}
SIDNEY151:41	~~H75~~	He bad me drive, and he would hold the Sun;
DUBART154:24	H69	In giving one, what would have served seven.
DUBART154:26	H71	Thy double portion would have served many.
QELIZ157:2	H70	But time would faile me, so my wit {tongue} would to,
QELIZ157:28	H96	Her personall perfections, who would tell,
VANITY~~160:32~~	H42	For *Saphyre, Onix, Topas,* who will {would} change,
CONTEM169:14	H55	My great Creator I would magnifie,
CONTEM172:12	H148	And if the sun would ever shine, there would I dwell.
FLESH176:37	H77	With which inriched I would be:
AUTHOR178:2	H12	Yet being mine own, at length affection would
BIRTH180:6	H16	What nature would, God grant to yours and you;
2LETTER182:31	H37	Tell him I would say more, but cannot well,
CHILDRN185:17	H43	If birds could weep, then would my tears
CHILDRN185:29	H55	O would my young, ye saw my breast,
CHILDRN186:22	H89	And 'fore she once would let you fly,
CHILDRN186:25	H92	What would save life, and what would kill.
MERCY189:7	H28	E're nature would, it hither did arrive,
2SIMON195:11	Hp271	conceptions because I would leaue you nothing but myne
MEDDM197:11	Hp274	If we had no winter the spring would not be so pleasant, if we
MEDDM197:12	Hp274	times tast of adversity, prosperity would not be so welcome
MEDDM200:20	Hp279	honour, wealth, or a helthfull body, would quite ouer throw,
MEDDM200:36	Hp280	weak children as would crush them to the dust, but according
MEDDM203:3	Hp283	of spirit, yet our owne experience would soon haue speld it out,
MEDDM204:14	Hp284	shame euer goe together He that would be freed from the last,
MEDDM204:26	Hp285	He that would be content, wth a mean condition, must not cast
MEDDM205:19	Hp286	would haue boldnes to go to the throne of grace to be
MEDDM205:23	Hp286	He that would keep a pure heart and lead a blamlesse life,
MEDDM207:19	Hp289	permanent who would look for heauenly?
MYCHILD216:34	Hp242	some sin I lay vnder wch God would haue reformed, or some
MYCHILD216:35	Hp242	neglected wch he would haue performed, and by his help I

MYCHILD217:26 Hp243 ye Lord would but lift vp ye light of his Covnten^c vpon me,
MYCHILD217:27 Hp243 grovnd me to powder it would bee but Light to me, yea oft
MYCHILD217:29 Hp243 me, it would bee a Heaven And could I haue been in Heaven
MYCHILD217:30 Hp243 ye Love of God, it would haue been a Hell to me for in Truth it
MYCHILD217:36 Hp243 would soon tell me by the wondrovs workes that I see, the vast
MYCHILD218:3 Hp243 consideration of these things would wth amazement certainly
MYCHILD218:22 Hp244 This hath somt. stuck with me, and more it would, by ye vain
MYCHILD218:26 Hp244 consideration of these things and many ye like would soon turn

WOULD'ST (1)
HUMOUR29:40 H391 Of Learning, and of Policie, thou would'st bereave me,

WOULDST (2)
HUMOUR23:6 H116 But Melancholy, wouldst have this glory thine?
HUMOUR25:28 H217 Nay should I tel, thou wouldst count me no blab,

WOUND (8) See also WOUND'S
MPERS80:2 H1069 And wound the backs of those bold {brave} Warriours stout.
MPERS84:35 H1271 Either to wrong, did wound his heart so sore,
MPERS89:6 H1440 Nor wound receiv'd, but one among them all:
MGREC104:41 H2093 By throwing Darts, gives {gave} him his mortall wound,
DIALOG142:3 H32 If th' wound's {wound} so dangerous I may not know?
DIALOG143:6 H77 Whose tearing tusks did wound, and kill, and threat:

WOUNDED (3)
PROLOG7:12 H26 A weake or wounded braine admits no cure.
DUBART154:17 H62 Their trophies were but heaps of wounded slain,
MEDDM203:21 Hp283 He that neuer felt, what it was to be sick or wounded, doth not

WOUNDING (1)
MPERS82:35 H1182 He dying to behold, that wounding sight;

WOUND'S (1) [wound is]
DIALOG142:3 H32 If th' wound's {wound} so dangerous I may not know?

WOUNDS (8) [pl.]
HUMOUR21:40 H68 But shuns to look on wounds, and bloud that's spilt,
AGES38:3 H106 stroks did cause no death {blood}, nor wounds, nor {or} skars.
AGES40:36 H215 Sometimes by wounds in idle combates taken,
MGREC95:3 H1682 Who in their backs did all their wounds receive.
MGREC97:23 H1784 By too much heat, not wounds (as Authors write.)
MGREC105:17 H2110 Whose wounds had made their skins of purple dye;
MEDDM203:25 Hp283 the wounds of a guilty Conscience, cares not how far he keeps
BYNIGHT220:14 H13 My smartIng wounds washt in his blood,

WOUNDS (3) v.
HUMOUR29:39 H390 I'le come to that which wounds me somewhat more:
MPERS72:41 H787 And with a mortall thrust, wounds him ith' thigh,
MGREC105:2 H2095 Yea, wounds the beasts (that drew him) unto death,

WRACK (5)
MGREC114:25 H2495 He on the wrack, his limbs in peeces rent,
MROMAN140:6 H3569 No more I'le do, sith I have suffer'd wrack,
DIALOG142:24 H53 Doth your Allye, faire *France,* conspire your wrack?
CONTEM174:29 H226 O Time the fatal wrack of mortal things,
SAMUEL228:12 H13 P^rserve O Lord from stormes & wrack

WRACK'D (1) [wracked] See also RACT
MPERS82:17 H1164 And there so utterly they wrack'd the same,

WRACKING (1)
AGES46:1 H432 Shal both be broke, by wracking death so strong;

WRACKS (3) [pl.]

ELEMEN17:32	H396	Much might I say of wracks, but that Ile spare,
ELEMEN19:24	H469	What woeful wracks I've made, may wel appear,
MGREC108:6	H2222	With wracks, and tortures, every limbe to stretch.

WRACKT (1) See also RACT

CONTEM174:7	H207	This weather-beaten vessel wrackt with pain,

WRAPT (1)

MGREC112:10	H2396	They were so wrapt with this externall glory.

WRATH (5)

ELEMEN10:36	H111	What lasting Forts my kindled wrath hath burn'd?
ELEMEN20:6	H488	But what's their worth, {wrath} or force, but more's {same's} in
AGES38:4	H107	My little wrath did cease {end} soon as my wars.
MGREC104:34	H2086	Had *Alexanders* wrath incensed high;
MGREC114:11	H2479	Which *Alexanders* wrath incens'd so high,

WRATHFUL (1)

MASSYR65:40	H505	But being caught, to *Babels* wrathful King,

WRATHFULL (1) [wrathful]

HUMOUR23:28	H138	Their wrathfull looks are death, their words are laws;

WREAK (1)

MGREC113:3	H2430	To wreak their spight, and hate, on every limbe.

WREATH (1)

PROLOG7:38	H48	Give wholsome {Thyme or} Parsley wreath, I aske no Bayes:

WREN (1)

ELEMEN19:9	H454	The Pye {Thrush}, the Jay {wren}, the Larke, a prey to th'

WRESTLED (1)

MEDDM209:1	Hp291	wrestled wth god face to face in penvel Let me go, sath that

WRETCH (8)

AGES40:28	H209	Such wretch, such monster am I; but yet more,
MPERS83:12	H1200	Which wretch, {Who} him privately smother'd in's bed,
MPERS90:38	H1505	Of that false perjur'd wretch, this was the last {fate},
MPERS92:22	H1580	And so this wretch (a punishment too small)
MGREC104:40	H2092	Whom thus the execrable wretch abuses:
MGREC108:5	H2221	Who to *Darius* Brother gives the wretch,
MGREC129:39	H3153	Extinct, by this inhumane wretch *Cassander;*
CONTEM170:26	H97	The wretch with gastly face and dreadful mind,

WRETCHED (3)

AGES37:17	H79	When wretched I (ungrate) {ingrate} had done the wrong.
MGREC126:15	H3006	Faine would she come now to {this wretched Queen}
SOREFIT222:6	H25	In drawing out these wretched Dayes.

WRETCHEDNESS (1)

CONTEM174:6	H206	This lump of wretchedness, of sin and sorrow,

WRETCHEDNESSE (1) [wretchedness]

MGREC118:22	H2669	The wretchednesse of mans mortality.

WRETCHES (2) [pl.]

SEASONS52:1	H218	Poor wretches, that in total darknesse lye,
MPERS85:13	H1289	That for such gracelesse wretches she did groan,

WRINKLE (1)

CONTEM171:21	H124	Nor age nor wrinkle on their front are seen;

WRINKLED (1)

AGES45:30	H420	My skin is wrinkled, and my cheeks are pale.

WRIT (7)

ELEMEN19:2	H447	And what those Sages, did, or {either} spake, or writ,
AGES36:24	H48	This {Thus} writ about: *This out, then I am done.*
MASSYR57:33	H178	Save a few names anew, *Berosus* writ.
MASSYR60:38	H303	In sacred Writ, he's known by name of *Pul,*
MGREC93:19	H1616	T'accomplish that, which long before was writ.
MGREC~~109:5~~	H2262	And also of the *Mallians* what is writ.
SIDNEY152:20	H89	Which writ, she bad return't to them again.

WRITE (14)

MASSYR57:6	H153	Some write, his Mother put his habite on,
MPERS73:27	H812	Some write that sorely hurt, they 'scap'd away;
MPERS77:22	H963	None write by whom, nor how, 'twas over-past;
MPERS~~92:5~~	H1561	Some write that *Arsames* was *Ochus* brother,
MPERS~~92:26~~	H1584	Some write great *Cyrus* line was not yet run,
MPERS92:27	~~H1585~~	But as before doth (well read) *Raleigh* write,
MGREC94:36	H1674	In lower termes to write {was taught} a higher stile,
MGREC95:32	H1711	Though some there be, and that {(perhaps)} more likely, write;
MGREC97:23	H1784	By too much heat, not wounds (as Authors write.)
MGREC101:38	H1967	Some write, th' other had a million, some more,
MGREC136:8	H3421	*Ne sutor ultra crepidum,* may write.
QELIZ157:31	H99	To read what others write, and then {so} admire.
ANNEB187:16	H6	With troubled heart & trembling hand I write,
MERCY188:22	H8	Ah, woe is me, to write thy Funeral Song,

WRITEING (1) [writing]

2SIMON195:6	Hp271	me to leaue some thing for you in writeing that you might

WRITERS (3) [pl.]

MASSYR56:6	H112	Most {Some} writers say, six chariots might a front,
MPERS91:37	~~H1551~~	Made Writers work at home, they sought not far?
MPERS92:20	~~H1578~~	Some writers say, that he was *Arses* son,

WRITES (2)

MGREC97:29	H1790	Writes unto {To} *Alexander,* to {he would} restore
MGREC101:22	H1947	Thus to *Darius* he writes back again,

WRITING (2) See also WRITEING

MASSYR68:10	H596	Amazed at the writing, and the hand.
DIALOG146:1	H189	The writing, printing, posting to and fro,

WRITTEN (1)

MYCHILD219:6	Hp245	This was written in mvch sicknesse and weaknes, and is very

WRONG (25)

PROLOG7:16	H29	A Poets Pen, all scorne, I should thus wrong;
HUMOUR26:37	H267	But i'le not force retorts, nor do thee wrong,
HUMOUR28:35	H347	Yet could not be more breif, without much wrong.
AGES37:8	H70	To shew her bearing pangs {pains}, I should do wrong,
AGES37:17	H79	When wretched I (ungrate) {ingrate} had done the wrong.
MPERS69:28	H650	Who had no might to save himself from wrong;
MPERS72:6	~~H755~~	Who for no wrong, poore innocent must dye,
MPERS84:27	H1263	Who for his wrong, he could not chuse but deem,
MPERS84:35	H1271	Either to wrong, did wound his heart so sore,
MPERS84:36	H1272	To wrong himselfe by death, he chose before:
MGREC108:17	H2233	Nor could he reason give, for this great wrong,
MGREC112:39	H2425	*Philotas* thus o're-charg'd, with wrong, and greif,
MGREC114:4	H2472	Then's Masters god-head, to defie, and wrong;

MGREC114:16   H2486   Then all the wrong to brave *Parmenio* done.
MGREC115:27   H2546   He might well dye, though he had done no wrong;
MGREC124:30   H2937   And to *Cassander* of this wrong complaines;
MROMAN139:18 H3546   Her Husband sore incens'd, to quit this wrong,
DIALOG146:32   H218   Your griefs I pity much, but should do wrong {hope to see},
DIALOG147:41   H265   Patience, and purse of Clients for {oft} to wrong:
SIDNEY150:7   H32   doth thy {his} selfe, thy {his} worke, and {his} honour wrong,
SIDNEY152:13   H82   For {Then} to revenge his {this} wrong, themselves ingage,
DUBART154:37   H82   But lest my {mine} ignorance should doe thee wrong,
QELIZ155:30   H21   Which makes me deeme, my rudenesse is no wrong,
QELIZ157:18   H86   Proud profuse *Cleopatra,* whose wrong name,
QELIZ157:35   H103   But she though dead, will vindicate our wrong.

WRONG'D (1) [wronged]
MASSYR57:5   H152   To sit, thus long (obscure) wrong'd {rob'd} of his seat;

WRONGED (1)
MASSYR57:20   ~~H167~~   Each wronged Prince, or childe that did remain,

WRONGING (1)
MGREC130:28   ~~H3181~~   And wronging innocents whose blood they spilt,

WRONGS (7) [pl.]
HUMOUR24:14   H163   Your selves may plead, your wrongs are no whit lesse,
HUMOUR24:20   H169   Ile only shew the wrongs, thou'st done to me.
HUMOUR32:21   H495   Enough of both, my wrongs for {now} to expresse;
MGREC104:24   H2076   Who wanting means t' resist, these wrongs abides.
MGREC~~121:16~~   H2795   But of his wrongs his friends doth certifie;
DIALOG144:31   H139   Who heard {saw} their cause, and wrongs {hath} judg'd
DUBART154:21   H66   Who in thy tryumphs (never won by wrongs)

WROUGHT (6)
AGES42:14   H272   Was I a laborer, I wrought all day,
MASSYR55:38   H104   The walls so strong, and curiously were {was} wrought;
MPERS85:22   H1298   {Plunders} the Country, and much trouble {mischief} wrought,
MGREC136:11   H3425   *And maugre all resolves, my fancy wrought*
MEDDM196:16   Hp273   christian that hath wrought hard in gods vine yard and hath
MEDDM199:11   Hp277   Iron till it be throughly heat is vncapable to be wrought, so god

X

XENOPHON (2)
MPERS~~85:37~~   H1313   A hopefull Prince, whose worth {by *Xenophon*} is ever fam'd.
MPERS89:40   H1474   Chose *Xenophon,* to lead them home again;

XERXES (18)
MASSYR56:15   H121   (Continuing, till *Xerxes* it defac'd)
MPERS77:14   H953   *Xerxes.*
MPERS77:15   H954   *Xerxes, Darius,* and *Attossa's* Son,

MPERS77:37	H978	Vaine *Xerxes* thinks his counsell hath most wit,
MPERS78:26	H1007	Save the *Zidonians,* where *Xerxes* was.
MPERS78:32	H1013	Whither rich *Pithyus* comes, *Xerxes* to greet;
MPERS79:5	H1027	Is this to doe like *Xerxes,* or a Prince?
MPERS79:8	H1030	First thing, *Xerxes* {he} did worthy {of} recount,
MPERS79:13	~~H1035~~	Yet *Xerxes* in his enterprise persever'd;
MPERS79:30	H1056	But *Xerxes* resolute, to *Thrace* goes first,
MPERS80:11	H1078	This shamefull Victory cost *Xerxes* deare,
MPERS80:21	H1088	And *Xerxes* mighty Gallies batter'd so,
MPERS80:31	H1098	In secret manner word to *Xerxes* sends,
MPERS81:12	H1120	And that with *Xerxes* they would be at one,
MPERS82:13	H1160	For pitty, let those few to *Xerxes* go,
MPERS82:21	H1168	Scorn'd *Xerxes,* hated for his cruelty,
MPERS83:31	H1219	Although to *Xerxes,* they not long before,
MGREC108:8	H2224	Whom *Xerxes* from their country led away;

XERXES (3) [poss.]

MPERS81:18	H1126	That *Xerxes* quarrel was 'gainst *Athens* State,
MPERS83:16	H1204	Accus'd *Darius, Xerxes* eldest son,
MPERS84:24	H1260	His father *Xerxes* losse, and shame, much more,

XPECTAT (1) [expectation]

28AUG226:7	Hp254	Body, and bee in continuall xpectat ^{n} of my change, and let me

XPER^C (1) [experience]

MYCHILD217:10	Hp242	I haue had great xper ^{c} of Gods hearing my prayers, and

XT (1) [christ]

MYCHILD218:35	Hp244	o my Soul to thy Rest, vpon this Rock Xt Jesus will I build

XTIANS (1) [christians]

MYCHILD218:30	Hp244	Xtians haue been carryed away wth them, that somt: I haue

XTREMITY (1) [extremity]

JULY223:21	Hp251	fitt of fainting wch lasted 2 or 3 dayes, but not in y^t xtremity

Y

YARD (1)

MEDDM196:16	Hp273	christian that hath wrought hard in gods vine yard and hath

YARDS (1) [pl.]

MPERS87:33	H1385	Six yards the {in} depth, and forty miles the length,

YAWNING (1)

ELEMEN14:8	~~H250~~	Who bravely rode into my yawning chinke.

YEA (24)

ELEMEN15:8	H290	The Pine, the Cedars, yea and *Daph'nes* tree;
ELEMEN19:18	H463	Yea so contagious, Countries have me {we} known;
AGES41:13	H232	Child-hood and youth is {are} vaine, yea {ye} vanity.
AGES42:4	H262	Yea justice I have done, was I in place;
AGES46:10	H441	Yea knowing much, the pleasant'st {pleasants} life of all,

MPERS71:26	H740	Yea, in his pride, he ventured so farre,
MGREC95:15	H1694	Whose touch turn'd all to gold, yea even his meat:
MGREC105:2	H2095	Yea, wounds the beasts (that drew him) unto death,
MGREC105:12	H2105	Yea, {But} above all, that neither eare, nor eye,
MGREC106:5	H2139	Yea, {And} thus must every Son of *Adam* lye,
MGREC114:34	H2504	Yea, and *Calisthines* to death he drew,
MGREC114:36	H2506	Yea, and he kild *Calisthines* by name; {of fame.}
MGREC115:2	H2513	All this he did, yea, and much more, 'tis true,
MGREC~~116:10~~	H2575	All friends she shuns, yea, banished the light,
MGREC132:9	H3244	Yea {And} though *Cassander* died in his bed,
SIDNEY150:11	H36	Yea, and Divinity within thy {his} Book,
QELIZ~~157:39~~	H107	O {Yea} happy, happy, had those dayes still been,
FLESH176:4	H44	Sisters we are, yea twins we be,
MEDDM205:15	Hp286	the evidence, so he absolues or condemnes, yea so Absolute
MEDDM208:36	Hp291	armes of the mighty god of Jacob yea Jacob himself when he
MYCHILD216:29	Hp242	the times of my greatest Getting and Advantage, yea I haue
MYCHILD217:27	Hp243	me to powder it would bee but Light to me, yea oft haue I
SOREFIT221:26	H12	Yea when I was most low and poor,
HOUSE236:28	H20	Yea so it was, and so 'twas jvst.

YEAR (13)

ELEMEN17:25	H389	That in two hundred year, it ne'r prov'd good.
SEASONS49:38	H131	*July* my next, the hot'st in all the year,
SEASONS~~52:39~~	H255	And thus the year in circle runneth round:
MASSYR64:9	H433	This Prince, the last year of his Fathers reign,
MASSYR64:19	H443	The next year he, with unresisted hand,
MASSYR67:4	H550	And in the first year of his royalty,
MPERS71:14	H728	He wages warre, the fifth year of his reign,
MPERS~~84:12~~	H1241	Good *Ezra* in the seventh year of his reign,
MPERS~~84:12~~	H1245	And *Nehemiah* in his twentieth year,
MPERS93:1	H1598	And in the sixt year of his haplesse reigne,
ELIZB186:33	H4-5	*being a year and half old.*
MERCY188:19	H4-5	1669. *in the 28. year of her Age.*
11MAYB228:24	Hp259	I haue had no great fitt of sicknes, but this year from ye middle

YEARE (6) [year]

SEASONS46:26	H1-2	The four Seasons of the Yeare.
MPERS75:38	H895	And in the sixth yeare of his friendly reign
MPERS77:10	H949	And the ensuing yeare ended his life,
MROMAN138:22	H3512	Twenty foure yeare, {years} th' time of his royall race,
SIDNEY149:6	~~H5~~	By *A. B.* in the yeare, 1638.
QELIZ156:16	H43	And earth had twice {once} a yeare, a new old face:

YEARES (13) [years]

MASSYR53:13	H3	beginning under *Nimrod,* 131. yeares
MASSYR65:6	H471	Full thirteen yeares in this strange work he spent,
MPERS70:21	H692	Had after {A} thousand yeares faire to be seen.
MPERS78:1	H982	Although he hasted, yet foure yeares was spent,
MPERS79:23	H1049	none of these should {those could} live a {an} hundred yeares:
MROMAN137:35	H3486	Forty three yeares he rul'd with generall praise;
MROMAN138:35	H3525	Thirty eight yeares (this Stranger borne) did reigne,
MROMAN139:8	H3536	Forty foure yeares did *Servius Tullius* reigne,
DIALOG146:7	H195	I that no warres, so many yeares have known,
MEDDM200:33	Hp280	father will not lay a burden on a child of seven yeares old, w^ch

MEDDM205:7	Hp285	plentifull crop may be expected in the haruest of their yeares.
PILGRIM210:33	H33	And when a few yeares shall be gone
SAMUEL228:5	H6	The child I stay'd for many yeares.

YEARES (1) [years']

MPERS70:16	H687	Here twenty yeares provision {good} he found,

YEARLY (1)

CONTEM168:32	H38	Thy daily streight, and yearly oblique path,

YEARS (58) [pl.] See also YEARES

ELEMEN12:31	H191	After three years, when men and meat is spent,
HUMOUR33:4	H518	Under *Troys* wals, ten years wil wast {wear} away,
AGES35:38	H24	Then may he live, til {out} threescore years or past.
MASSYR53:34	H24	One hundred fourteen years, he after dyed.
MASSYR55:1	H67	Fifty two years he reign'd (as we are told)
MASSYR56:40	H146	Forty two years she reign'd, and then she dy'd,
MASSYR57:8	H155	But much it is, in more then forty years,
MASSYR57:32	H177	And eleav'n {many} hundred of years in silence sit,
MASSYR59:18	H242	Who there incamp'd two years, for little end,
MASSYR59:33	H257	Which {That} for twelve hundred years had held that place;
MASSYR61:6	H311	Forty eight years he reign'd, his race then run,
MASSYR61:39	H344	Thus *Tiglath* reign'd, and warr'd, twenty seven years,
MASSYR62:5	H350	And him six years his tributary made;
MASSYR62:13	H358	Did Justice now, by him, eradicate: [10 *years.*
MASSYR62:36	H381	'Twixt them and *Israels* he knew no odds. [7 *years.*
MASSYR63:10	H395	After twelve years did *Essarhadon* dye,
MASSYR63:15	H400	Embassadours to *Hezekiah* sent, [21 *years.*
MASSYR63:19	H404	Of whom is little said in any thing; [22 years.
MASSYR63:25	H410	For fifty years, or more, it had been free,
MASSYR63:26	H411	Now yeelds her neck unto captivity: [12 *years.*
MASSYR64:24	H448	Which in few years proves the *Assyrians* hire;
MASSYR65:27	H492	And more then {seven and} thirty years in prison fed;
MASSYR65:32	H497	Seven years he keeps his faith, and safe he dwels,
MASSYR66:12	H518	There {And} sit bewailing *Zion* seventy years,
MASSYR66:19	H525	Who had for sixteen hundred years born sway,
MASSYR66:30	H536	Which for seven years his reason took away;
MASSYR66:39	H545	Forty four years he reign'd, which being run,
MASSYR67:7	H553	In seven and thirty years, had seen no jot,
MPERS68:36	H622	with him about two years.
MPERS71:3	H715	Some thirty years this potent Prince did reign,
MPERS71:3	H715	Thirty two years in all this Prince
MPERS72:5	H755	Complots the Princes death, in his green years,
MPERS72:35	H779	Had set a *Smerdis* up, of the same years;
MPERS73:9	H796	Eight years he reign'd, a short, yet too long time,
MPERS77:12	H951	Thirty six years this royall {noble} Prince did reign,
MPERS82:25	H1172	Some years by him in this vain suit was spent,
MPERS85:17	H1293	For sixty years maugre the *Persians* might.
MPERS86:6	H1322	{this} *Nothus* reign'd {'bout} nineteen years, which run,
MPERS91:29	H1545	Forty three years he rules, then turns to dust,
MPERS92:1	H1555	Which in rebellion sixty years did stand:
MPERS92:2	H1556	That three and twenty years he reign'd, I finde,
MPERS92:13	H1571	Three years he reign'd, as Chronicles expresse, {then drank
MGREC120:37	H2774	Two years and more since, Natures debt he paid,

MGREC123:4	H2866	Who in few years the rest so over-tops,
MGREC129:6	H3120	That in few years he must be forc'd or glad
MGREC132:25	H3270	After three years he dyed, left what he'd won
MROMAN138:11	H3501	Thirty two years doth *Tullus* reigne, then dye,
MROMAN138:22	H3512	Twenty foure yeare, {years} th' time of his royall race,
MROMAN139:35	H3561	At length resolv'd, when many years had past,
TDUDLEY165:28	H30	Who spent his state, his strength, & years with care
TDUDLEY167:3	H85	*And when his time with years was spent*
CONTEM168:10	H19	Thy strength, and stature, more thy years admire,
CONTEM169:29	H68	And calls back moneths and years that long since fled
SICKNES178:18	H1	Twice ten years old, not fully told
CHILDRN185:2	H28	She now hath percht, to spend her years;
ANNEB187:14	H3-4	*Who deceased* June 20. 1669. *being three years and*
MYCHILD215:24	Hp240	In my yovng years about 6. or 7. as I take it I began to make
11MAYB228:23	Hp259	God to giue me a long Time of respite for these 4 years

YEELD (16) [yield] See also YEILD

ELEMEN13:11	H212	But what I freely yeeld upon your sweat?
ELEMEN15:18	H300	Which by my fatting Nile, doth yeeld such store;
ELEMEN17:37	H401	I doe suppose, you'l yeeld without controle;
HUMOUR21:20	H48	But if ye yeeld sub-servient unto me,
HUMOUR22:20	H89	Then yeeld to me, preheminence in War.
AGES41:26	H243	Such {My} empty seed should yeeld a better crop.
AGES42:22	H280	Such scum, as Hedges, and High-wayes do yeeld,
MGREC97:25	H1786	But all *Phenicia* to his pleasures {pleasure} yeeld;
MGREC99:21	H1864	That *Greece* must {was forc'd to} yeeld a fresh supply againe;
MGREC109:29	H2288	But *Porus* stout, who will not yeeld as yet;
MGREC110:17	H2317	Nor was't dishonour, at the length to yeeld;
MGREC116:10	H2570	This Conquerour did yeeld to destiny;
MGREC127:5	H3035	And *Pellas* faine to yeeld amongst the rest;
MGREC128:26	H3099	So *Syria* to *Ptolomy* did yeeld;
MROMAN138:5	H3495	The *Romans* Conquereth, others {other} yeeld the day,
DUBART153:12	H16	If Summer, or my Autumne age, doe yeeld

YEELDED (3) [yielded]

HUMOUR20:36	H28	At present yeelded, to necessity.
MGREC111:13	H2358	These {Those} obscure Nations yeelded as before;
QELIZ157:13	H81	And prostrate yeelded to her Excellence:

YEELDETH (1) [yieldeth]

VANITY160:38	H48	It yeeldeth pleasures, farre beyond conceit,

YEELDING (2) [yielding]

MPERS73:2	H789	Yeelding {So yields} to death, that dreadfull Conquerer.
DIALOG144:40	H148	I saw strong *Rochel* yeelding to her foe,

YEELDS (11) [yields]

ELEMEN11:29	H149	To tell what sundry fruits my fat soyle yeelds,
ELEMEN15:33	H315	Not thou, but shell-fish yeelds, as *Pliny* clears.
HUMOUR25:3	H192	As thy unbridled, barb'rous Choler yeelds. {breeds:}
SEASONS48:25	H78	For fruits, my season yeelds, the early Cherry,
SEASONS48:31	H83	Some subject, shallow braines, much matter yeelds,
MASSYR63:13	H398	All yeelds to him, but *Ninivie* kept free,
MASSYR63:26	H411	Now yeelds her neck unto captivity: [12 *years.*
MASSYR64:12	H436	Yeelds to his mercy, and the present stresse;
MASSYR66:20	H526	To *Babylons* proud King, now yeelds the day.

MPERS88:27	H1420	Down *Cyrus* fals, and yeelds to destiny;
MGREC125:27	H2977	At length yeelds to the Halter, her faire neck;

YEILD (1) [yield] See also YEELD

HUMOUR30:7	H399	Those {Whose} cold dry heads, {head} more subtilly doth yeild,

YELLOW (5)

HUMOUR26:38	H268	Thy fiery yellow froth, is mixt among.
SEASONS51:9	H183	And Apples now their yellow sides do show;
SEASONS51:25	H201	Whose yellow saplesse leaves by winds are fann'd:
CONTEM167:30	H7	Of green, of red, of yellow, mixed hew,
MEDDM199:8	Hp277	Yellow leaues argue want of sap and gray haires want of

YERST (1) [erst]

QELIZ155:28	H19	Thy clemency did yerst esteeme as much

YESTERDAY (2)

MEDDM204:6	Hp284	is the same yesterday, to day and for euer, we are the same
MEDDM204:7	Hp284	in need of him, to day as well as yesterday, and so shall for

YET (236)

FATHER5:11	H12	Yet view thereof, did cause my thoughts to soare,
FATHER5:25	H26	Sweet harmony they keep, yet jar oft times,
FATHER5:33	H34	And yet in equall tempers, how they gree,
PROLOG7:1	H16	Nor yet a sweet Consort, from broken strings,
PROLOG7:33	H44	Yet grant some small acknowledgement of ours.
ELEMEN9:30	H64	But be he what they list {will}, yet his aspect,
ELEMEN9:40	H74	Yet men and beasts, {beast} Astronomers can tell,
ELEMEN10:21	H96	When in conjunction with the sun, yet {do} more,
ELEMEN10:34	H109	Yet by my force, master my master can.
ELEMEN11:40	H160	Yet let me name my *Grecia,* 'tis my heart
ELEMEN12:16	H176	Nor yet expatiate, in Temple vale;
ELEMEN13:20	H221	I should here make a short, yet true narration,
ELEMEN14:19	H261	Ile say no more, yet {but} this thing adde I must,
ELEMEN16:23	H346	Nor yet of Salt, and Sugar, sweet and smart,
ELEMEN16:36	H359	Yet {And} *Luna* for my Regent I obey.
ELEMEN17:36	H400	Though {Yet am} not through ignorance, {ignorant} first was my
ELEMEN18:2	H406	Yet Aire, beyond all these ye know t'excell.
HUMOUR21:13	H41	Yet man for Choler, is the proper seat.
HUMOUR21:16	H44	Yet many times, unto my great disgrace,
HUMOUR23:11	H121	Yet hast thy {the} seat assign'd, a goodly part,
HUMOUR24:3	H152	And yet to make, my greatnesse far {still} more great:
HUMOUR25:2	H191	Yet do abhorre, such timerarious deeds,
HUMOUR26:2	H232	Yet such, when we al four are joyn'd in one.
HUMOUR26:8	H238	Nor yet Phisitian, nor Anatomist.
HUMOUR26:10	H240	Yet shal with equity give thee thy part,
HUMOUR26:23	H253	But thine the nobler, which I grant, yet mine
HUMOUR28:19	H331	But yet for all my toyl, my care, my skil,
HUMOUR28:35	H347	Yet could not be more breif, without much wrong.
HUMOUR29:17	H368	If not as yet, by me, thou shalt be quell'd:
HUMOUR30:16	H408	Yet time and age, shal soon declare it mine.
HUMOUR30:28	H420	Yet is a bowel cal'd wel as the rest.
HUMOUR30:39	H431	But yet more comely far, I dare avow,
HUMOUR31:7	H440	Thou wants Philosophy, and yet discretion. x
HUMOUR33:14	H528	But yet thou art as much, I truly say,
HUMOUR33:14	H528	Yet without ostentation I may say,

HUMOUR34:10	H565	Yet some may wish, oh, {O} had mine eyes ne're seene.
AGES36:16	H40	But neither us'd (as yet) for he was wise.
AGES36:36	H60	Both good and bad, but yet no more then's true.
AGES37:12	H74	Who yet with love, and all alacrity,
AGES37:28	H90	Yet this advantage, had mine ignorance,
AGES38:12	H115	Nor yet on future things did place {set} my hope.
AGES38:17	H120	But yet let me relate, before I go,
AGES38:26	H129	Then nought can please, and yet I know not why.
AGES38:30	H133	Yet griefs, in my fraile flesh, I still do find.
AGES38:38	H141	Strangely preserv'd, yet mind it not at all.
AGES40:28	H209	Such wretch, such monster am I; but yet more,
AGES40:33	H212	Nor yet that heavy reckoning for {soon} to come;
AGES41:6	H226	That wonder 'tis I yet behold the light,
AGES41:7	H227	That yet my bed in darknesse is not made,
AGES41:29	H246	But yet laid hold, on vertue seemingly,
AGES41:38	H255	If not, yet wealth, {riches} Nobility can gain.
AGES41:41	H258	Yet all my powers, for self-ends are not spent,
AGES45:20	H402	But yet may live, to see't made up again:
AGES46:11	H442	Hath yet amongst that sweet, some bitter gall.
AGES46:13	H444	Yet studying much, brings wearinesse to th' flesh;
SEASONS46:28	H4	Another Four i've {left} yet for to bring on,
SEASONS47:25	H41	Yet many a fleece of Snow, and stormy showre,
SEASONS47:31	H46	In *Taurus* Signe, yet hasteth straight from thence;
SEASONS47:34	H47	Yet never minute stil was known to stand,
SEASONS48:35	H86	Yet above all, this priviledge is thine,
SEASONS49:9	H100	Yet doth his parching heat the {but} more augment,
SEASONS49:24	H114	Yet hath your life, made Kings the same envy,
SEASONS49:30	H119	*Orthobulus,* nor yet *Sebastia* great,
SEASONS50:12	H146	For yet {For much,} the South-ward Sun abateth not;
SEASONS50:34	H168	Yet then appears the worthy deeds he 'ath done:
MASSYR54:3	H30	But yet this blot for ever on him lyes,
MASSYR60:6	H271	Yet would not {granting} let them {now} to inhabite there;
MASSYR61:24	H329	And succours *Ahaz,* yet for *Tiglath's* sake,
MASSYR62:25	H370	Or wild *Tartarians,* as yet ne're blest,
MASSYR62:28	H373	But what, or where they are, yet know we this;
MASSYR64:30	H454	Whether her wealth, or yet her strength was most;
MASSYR66:6	H512	Yet as was told, ne're saw it with his eyes;
MASSYR67:10	H556	But yet in *Babell,* he must still remain:
MPERS70:20	H691	Yet wondrous Monuments this stately Queen,
MPERS71:7	H723	But {Yet} to enlarge his state, had some desire;
MPERS73:9	H796	Eight years he reign'd, a short, yet too long time,
MPERS73:25	H810	But yet, 'fore this was done, much blood was shed,
MPERS74:28	H851	Yet more the peoples hearts firmly to binde,
MPERS74:32	H855	Yet notwithstanding he did all so well,
MPERS75:18	H878	But yet thou has sufficient recompence,
MPERS75:20	H879	Yet o're thy glory we must cast this vaile,
MPERS77:4	H943	*Darius* light, he {yet} heavie, home returnes,
MPERS77:25	H966	Yet all his men, and instruments of slaughter,
MPERS78:1	H982	Although he hasted, yet foure yeares was spent,
MPERS79:13	H1035	Yet *Xerxes* in his enterprise persever'd;
MPERS79:22	H1048	But yet this goodly sight {from him} produced teares,

MPERS80:5	H1072	None cryes for quarter, nor yet seeks to run,
MPERS80:17	H1084	Yet thinking to out-match his foes at Sea,
MPERS80:23	H1090	Yet {Then} in the Streights of *Salamis* he try'd,
MPERS80:37	H1104	Yet 'fore he went, to help out his expence,
MPERS81:6	H1114	Three hundred thousand yet he left behind,
MPERS82:22	H1169	Yet ceases not to act his villany:
MPERS82:26	H1173	Yet words {Nor prayers}, nor guifts, could win him least
MPERS83:13	H1201	But yet by search, he was found murthered,
MPERS84:33	H1269	Nor yet disloyall to his Prince would prove,
MPERS86:10	H1326	Yet doubts, {fears} all he injoyes, is not his own.
MPERS87:15	H1370	And yet with these, had neither heart, nor grace;
MPERS87:17	H1371	Three hundred thousand, yet {he} to *Syria* sent;
MPERS87:35	H1387	Yet for his brothers comming, durst not stay,
MPERS88:21	H1414	Of six thousand, wherein the King was yet;
MPERS88:32	H1425	Sencelesse and mute they stand, yet breath out groans,
MPERS89:34	H1468	as most {Commanders feasts and yet more} kinde;
MPERS91:22	H1536	(A Lady very wicked, but yet wise)
MPERS91:27	H1541	But yet for all his greatnesse, and long reign,
MPERS92:21	H1579	And that great *Cyrus* line, yet was not run,
MPERS92:26	H1584	Some write great *Cyrus* line was not yet run,
MPERS92:30	H1588	Yet in these {such} differences, we may behold; {be bold,}
MGREC94:1	H1635	Yet for a while, in *Greece* is forc'd to stay,
MGREC94:41	H1679	Those banks so steep, the *Greeks,* now {yet} scramble up
MGREC95:22	H1701	stead} *Arsemes {Arses}* was plac'd, yet {but} durst not stay;
MGREC95:23	H1702	But sets {Yet set} one in his roome, and ran away.
MGREC95:29	H1708	To raise more force, for what he yet {to further his} intends.
MGREC97:12	H1773	Yet all this grief, this losse, this over-throw,
MGREC99:22	H1865	But yet, this well defended town is {was} taken,
MGREC100:21	H1905	Yet he (poore Prince) another Hoast doth muster,
MGREC100:29	H1913	Yet had some hope, that on that even {the spacious} plain,
MGREC101:17	H1942	No, though *Parmenio* plead, he {yet} will not heare;
MGREC101:25	H1950	Nor yet two Monarchs in one World reside;
MGREC102:18	H1988	Yet old foundations shew'd, and somewhat more;
MGREC103:7	H2018	Yet to compare with this, they might not do.
MGREC103:13	H2024	Yet after all, as stories do expresse,
MGREC105:27	H2120	Yet that succeeding Kings in safety may
MGREC106:18	H2152	Such country there, nor yet such people finde.
MGREC107:1	H2176	But yet no notice takes, of what he hears;
MGREC109:25	H2284	He glory sought, no silver, nor yet {no} gold;
MGREC109:29	H2288	But *Porus* stout, who will not yeeld as yet;
MGREC110:15	H2315	Yet work enough, here *Alexander* found,
MGREC110:25	H2329	Yet that his fame might to posterity,
MGREC112:2	H2388	That by this match he might be yet more neare.
MGREC112:20	H2406	*Philotas* was not least, nor yet the last;
MGREC112:29	H2415	Yet is *Philotas* unto Judgement brought,
MGREC113:14	H2441	But how these Captaines should, or yet their Master,
MGREC113:20	H2447	As he would ne're confesse, nor could {yet} reward,
MGREC113:35	H2462	Yet gave his Master the immortall fame;
MGREC114:40	H2510	But yet withall, *Calisthines* he slew;
MGREC115:3	H2514	But yet withall, *Calisthines* he slew.
MGREC115:29	H2548	Or if remembred, yet regarded not;

MGREC117:28	H2635	Yet {But} none so hardy found as so durst say.
MGREC118:19	H2666	And yet not so content, unlesse that he
MGREC120:13	H2748	Yet to regain them, how he did not know,
MGREC120:36	H2773	Which eating time hath scarcely yet defac'd.
MGREC120:38	H2775	And yet till now, at quiet was not laid.
MGREC124:4	H2909	Hoping still {yet} more to gaine by these new stirs;
MGREC126:30	H3021	Whose fury yet unparalleld {scarcely parallel'd} hath been;
MGREC129:17	H3131	But yet at {the} last the hand of vengeance came,
MGREC130:22	H3177	Except *Cassanders* wife, who yet not dead,
MGREC130:34	H3181	Yet in the flower of's age, he must lie dead,
MGREC131:29	H3221	Yet dares {durst} not say, he loves {lov'd} his fathers wife;
MGREC132:12	H3247	Yet must his children pay for fathers ill.
MGREC132:14	H3249	Yet be aveng'd, must th' blood of *Jesreel.*
MGREC133:5	H3293	Yet by him had this most unworthy end.
MGREC135:13	H3385	But yet the *Persian* got the upper hand;
MGREC135:34	H3406	But yet this Lion, Bear, this Leopard, Ram,
MGREC136:15	H3429	*Yet in this Chaos, one shall easily spy,*
MROMAN138:6	H3496	Yet for {in} their compact, after false they play:
DIALOG142:32	H61	Such is her poverty, yet shall be found
DIALOG143:25	H94	But yet, I answer not what you demand,
DIALOG144:4	H114	From crying bloods, yet cleansed am not I,
DIALOG144:22	H132	The Sermons yet upon record doe stand,
DIALOG145:3	H152	My {Mine} heart obdurate, stood not yet agast.
SIDNEY149:27	H23	Yet doth thy shame (with all) purchase renown,
SIDNEY149:34	H23	Which have the self-same blood yet in my veines;
SIDNEY150:5	H30	Yet, {But} he's a beetle head, that cann't discry
SIDNEY150:12	H43	Whilst English blood yet runs within my veins.
SIDNEY150:15	H49	Yet great *Augustus* was content (we know)
SIDNEY150:31	H58	But yet impartiall Death {Fates} this Boone did give,
SIDNEY151:18	H69	Yet this preheminence thou hast above,
QELIZ155:15	H6	Yet thy loud Herauld Fame, doth to the sky
QELIZ156:9	H36	*Spaines* Monarch sa's not so; nor yet his Hoast,
QELIZ157:7	H75	Worlds wonder for a time {while}, but yet it falls;
QELIZ157:25	H93	Yet for our Queen is no fit parallel:
QELIZ158:17	H126	Here lies the envy'd, yet unparralell'd Prince,
DAVID159:18	H33	Which made you yet more beauteous to behold.
VANITY160:14	H24	Yet these, the wisest man of men did find,
VANITY160:23	H33	Nor yet in learning, wisdome, youth nor pleasure,
DDUDLEY167:14	H11	*To Servants wisely aweful, but yet kind,*
CONTEM167:27	H4	The trees all richly clad, yet void of pride,
CONTEM167:33	H9	I wist not what to wish, yet sure thought I,
CONTEM171:8	H113	Who neither guilt, nor yet the punishment could fly.
CONTEM171:27	H129	Yet seems by nature and by custome curs'd,
CONTEM172:35	H168	So nature taught, and yet you know not why,
CONTEM174:5	H205	And yet this sinfull creature, frail and vain,
FLESH176:5	H45	Yet deadly feud 'twixt thee and me;
FLESH177:19	H100	No Candle there, nor yet Torch light,
AUTHOR178:2	H12	Yet being mine own, at length affection would
AUTHOR178:7	H17	Yet still thou run'st more hobling then is meet;
AUTHOR178:12	H22	And take thy way where yet thou art not known,
SICKNES178:26	H9	Yet live I shall, this life's but small,

BIRTH179:32	H8	A common thing, yet oh inevitable;
BIRTH180:1	H11	We both are ignorant, yet love bids me
BIRTH180:12	H22	Yet love thy dead, who long lay in thine arms:
1LETTER181:28	H26	I here, thou there, yet both but one.
3LETTER183:20	H22	I have a loving phere, yet seem no wife:
VERSES184:3	H7	Yet handled ill, amounts but to this crum;
VERSES184:6	H10	Yet for part payment take this simple mite,
VERSES184:11	H15	Yet paying is not payd until I dye.
CHILDRN185:9	H35	My fifth, whose down is yet scarce gone
CHILDRN186:27	H94	And dead, yet speak, and counsel give:
ANNEB187:22	H12	Was ever stable joy yet found below?
ANNEB187:31	H21	But yet a while, and I shall go to thee;
1SIMON188:5	H6	Acquaintance short, yet parting caus'd us weep,
1SIMON188:7	H8	Cropt by th' Almighties hand; yet is he good,
MERCY188:21	H7	And yet survive to sound this wailing tone;
MERCY188:23	H9	Who might in reason yet have lived long,
2SIMON195:12	Hp271	though in value they fall short of all in this kinde yet I presume
MEDDM200:10	Hp279	yet they are so childishly sottish that they are still huging and
MEDDM201:3	Hp280	times he imposes waighty burdens on their shoulders, and yet
MEDDM202:25	Hp282	time, yet he affords so much light as may direct our way, that
MEDDM202:28	Hp282	se no light, yet then must we trust in the lord and stay vpon our
MEDDM202:33	Hp282	obiects enter, yet is not that spacious roome filled neither
MEDDM203:3	Hp283	of spirit, yet our owne experience would soon haue speld it out,
MEDDM203:11	Hp283	be all convenient and comfortable for him yet he hath no
MEDDM204:19	Hp285	for takeing veangence on the house of Ahab and yet a little
MEDDM204:21	Hp285	he was rewarded for the matter, and yet punished for the
MEDDM204:35	Hp285	brought into tilth yet all must be ploughed and harrowed Some
MEDDM206:8	Hp287	of bignes and brightnes, yet all receiue their light from that
MEDDM206:14	Hp287	and obscure, yet all receiue their luster (be it more or lesse)
MEDDM206:31	Hp288	of god, who will not be tyed to time nor place, nor yet to
MEDDM207:15	Hp288	shadow very comfortable, yet there is some worm or other,
MEDDM208:13	Hp290	to haue a good repute among good men, yet it is not that, w^{ch}
MEDDM209:21	Hp291	Covntrys so it is with men, there was neuer yet any one man
MEDDM209:23	Hp291	so large, yet he stands in need of something wch another man
TOCHILD215:2	H2	This Book by Any yet vnread,
MYCHILD215:15	Hp240	bequeath to yov, that when I am no more wth yov, yet I may
MYCHILD217:4	Hp242	ye Almighty hath hid his face from me, that yet I haue had
MYCHILD217:22	Hp243	never p^{r}vail: yet haue I many Times sinkings & droopings,
MYCHILD217:24	Hp243	and seen no light, yet haue I desired to stay my self upon
MYCHILD218:6	Hp244	thovsands of Times been svggested to me, yet God hath
MYCHILD218:19	Hp244	word, yet why may not ye popish Relign. bee ye right, They
MYCHILD218:24	Hp244	of the Saints, wch admitt were y^y as they terme y^m yet not
11MAYA226:14	Hp255	all this spring till this 11. May, yet hath my God given me many
11MAYA226:24	Hp255	Yet a little while and he that shall come will come and will not
30SEPT227:26	Hp257	wth sugar then brine, yet will he p^{r}serve me to his heavenly
HOURS234:15	H29	Yet if I see Thee not thro: them
HOUSE236:32	H24	But yet sufficient for us left.
HOUSE237:24	H54	Yet by his Gift is made thine own.

YIELD (6) See also YEELD, YEILD

HUMOUR~~34:28~~	H583	Ne're did {Nor will} I heare {yield} that Choler was the witt'est;
SIDNEY151:16	~~H69~~	Then wonder lesse, if warlike *Philip* yield,

CONTEM173:7	H175	And take the trembling prey before it yield,
FLESH176:30	H70	My thoughts do yield me more content
1LETTER181:17	H15	Which sweet contentment yield me for a space,
VERSES184:2	H6	The principle might yield a greater sum,

YIELDED (1) See also YEELDED

MPERS~~72:37~~	H783	Obedience yielded as to *Cyrus* son.

YIELDETH See YEELDETH

YIELDING See YEELDING

YIELDS (2) See also YEELDS

MPERS~~73:2~~	H789	Yeelding {So yields} to death, that dreadfull Conquerer.
MGREC~~121:23~~	H2805	Confers {Yields} them {to} *Pithon* on, for's courtesie;

YOKE (1)

MGREC119:14	H2704	{And gladly would} Shakes {shake} off the yoke, sometimes

YORK (2)

DIALOG143:7	H74	No Duke of *York,* nor Earle of *March,* to soyle
DIALOG145:38	H187	The King displeas'd, at *York* himself absents,

YOU'D (1) See also YOU'LD

AGES40:26	H207	And in a word, if what I am you'd heare,

YOU'L (3) [you'll]

ELEMEN17:37	H401	I doe suppose, you'l yeeld without controle;
HUMOUR30:19	H411	You'l say, here none shal ere disturbe my right;
DIALOG148:34	H299	And in a while you'l tell another tale.

YOU'LD (1) [you'd]

FATHER6:3	H37	But fear'd you'ld judge, one *Bartas* was my friend,

YOU'VE (2)

HUMOUR~~27:19~~	H290	Nor what you've said, doth argue my disgrace,
DIALOG145:7	H156	To all you've said, sad mother, I assent

YOUNG (24) See also YOVNG

AGES36:32	H56	That he was young, before he grew so old.
AGES40:22	H203	Some young {new} *Adonis* I do strive to be,
AGES44:8	H341	I have bin young, and strong, and wise as you,
AGES46:6	H437	To great, to rich, to poore, to young, or old,
SEASONS~~47:11~~	H27	And Poles erects, for his green {young} clambering Hops;
SEASONS50:8	H142	Which makes the aged fields look young again,
SEASONS52:14	H229	Cold, moist, young, flegmy Winter now doth lye
MASSYR53:15	H5	When Time was young, and World in infancy,
MPERS77:28	H969	And's cousen, young *Mardonius* forsaken,
MPERS87:3	H1359	The young Queen, and old, at bitter jars:
MPERS~~91:22~~	H1532	By poyson caus'd, the young one to lose her life.
MGREC122:14	H2839	If once young *Alexander* grow more strong,
MGREC123:17	H2881	Too young {rash} to beare that charge, if on him lay'd;
MGREC123:36	H2900	Besides, he was the young Queens favourite,
MGREC125:4	H2952	And her young Nephew {grand-child} in his stead {State} t'
MGREC129:4	H3118	He sees the *Greeks* now favour their young Prince,
MGREC131:27	H3219	Is for this fresh young Lady half {quite} undone,
MROMAN138:33	H3523	To such rude triumphs, as young *Rome* then had,
DIALOG146:17	H203	My ravisht {weeping} virgins, and my young men slain,
CHILDRN185:29	H55	O would my young, ye saw my breast,
CHILDRN186:6	H73	Once young and pleasant, as are you,
CHILDRN186:12	H79	Where old ones, instantly grow young,
CHILDRN186:17	H84	Among your young ones take your rest,

CHILDRN186:20	H87	That did what could be done for young,

YOUNGER (2)

SEASONS50:31	H165	Like good Old Age, whose younger juycie roots,
MPERS69:19	H641	He in his younger dayes an Army led,

YOUNGEST (4)

MPERS85:36	H1312	Two sons she bore, the youngest *Cyrus* nam'd,
MGREC131:39	H3231	The mother would the youngest should {might} excell,
MGREC132:5	H3238	The youngest by *Demetrius* kill'd in fight,
MGREC132:5	H3238	*Demetrius* is call'd in by th' youngest Son,

YOUTH (29)

ELEMEN18:30	H434	And youth, and spring, sages to me compare.
AGES35:18	H4	Childhood, and Youth, the Manly, and Old-age.
AGES36:1	H25	Next, youth came up, in gorgeous attire;
AGES39:3	H146	*Youth.*
AGES39:32	H175	This is my best, but youth (is known) alas,
AGES40:31	H210	My youth, my best, my strength, my bud, and prime:
AGES41:13	H232	Child-hood and youth is {are} vaine, yea {ye} vanity.
AGES41:15	H234	Childehood and youth, forgot, sometimes I've seen,
AGES43:36	H331	Though some more incident to age, or youth:
AGES44:20	H353	He that in youth is godly, wise, and sage,
AGES45:2	H378	In prime of youth seiz'd by heavens angry hand,
AGES45:24	H414	We old men love to tell, what's done in youth.
SEASONS49:1	H92	As Spring did aire, blood, youth in's equipage.
SEASONS51:26	H202	Which notes, when youth, and strength, have past their prime,
MASSYR64:14	H438	Children of Royal bloud, unblemish'd youth;
MPERS78:41	H1022	The Kings cals for the Youth, who being brought,
MGREC116:17	H2583	Wise *Aristotle*, tutour to his youth,
SIDNEY149:20	H19	(Witnesse *Arcadia*, penn'd in his youth)
SIDNEY152:27	H96	*Learning, valour, beauty {Wisdome}, all in vertuous youth:*
VANITY160:10	H20	What, Is't in flowring youth, or manly age?
VANITY160:23	H33	Nor yet in learning, wisdome, youth nor pleasure,
VANITY160:40	H50	Nor strength nor wisdome, nor fresh youth shall fade,
CONTEM171:30	H132	Nor youth, nor strength, nor wisdom spring again
CONTEM173:30	H195	And thus they pass their youth in summer season,
MEDDM195:33	Hp272	Youth is the time of getting middle age of improuing, and old
MEDDM195:34	Hp272	a negligent youth is vsually attended by an ignorant middle
MEDDM205:6	Hp285	and exhortation be sown, in the spring of their youth, and a
MYCHILD216:2	Hp241	loose from God, vanity & yᵉ follyes of Youth take hold of me.
13MAY227:11	H20	Blessd me in Youth, and elder Age

YOUTHFULL (1) [youthful]

CONTEM171:23	H126	A Spring returns, and they more youthfull made;

YOUTHS (1) [pl.]

DIALOG144:9	H119	Oh, *Edwards* Babes {youths}, and *Clarence* haplesse Son,

YOUTHS (1) [poss.]

AGES44:4	H337	Babes innocence, Youths wildnes I have seen,

YOVNG (1) [young]

MYCHILD215:24	Hp240	In my yovng years about 6. or 7. as I take it I began to make

Z

ZAMIES (1)
MASSYR57:1　　H148　*Ninias* or *Zamies.*

ZEAL (2)
MPERS71:24　　H738　The Temples {Their Temple} he destroyes not, for his zeal,
TDUDLEY165:31 H33　Who is't can tax thee ought, but for thy zeal?

ZENOBIA (1)
QELIZ157:22　　H90　*Zenobia,* potent Empresse of the East,

ZENOPHON (1)
MPERS70:34　　H705　But *Zenophon* reports, he dy'd in's bed,

ZIDON (1)
MGREC98:28　　H1830　*Zidon* he on *Ephestion* bestowes:

ZIDONIANS (1) [pl.]
MPERS78:26　　H1007　Save the *Zidonians,* where *Xerxes* was.

ZIM (1)
MASSYR66:10　　H516　Now *Zim,* and *Iim, {Jim}* lift up their shriking {scrieching}

ZION (3)
ELEMEN11:2　　H122　Old sacred *Zion,* I demolish'd thee;
MASSYR62:29　　H374　They shal return, and *Zion* see, with blisse.
MASSYR66:12　　H518　There {And} sit bewailing *Zion* seventy years,

ZION'S (1) [poss.]
DIALOG146:14　~~H200~~　Pray now dear child, for sacred *Zion's* sake,

ZIONS (1) [poss.]
MASSYR65:35　　H500　Besieg'd his City, Temple, *Zions* Tower;

ZODIACK (2)
SEASONS47:33　~~H47~~　Twelve houses of the oblique Zodiack,
1LETTER181:10 H8　My sun is gone so far in's Zodiack,

ZONES (1)
DUBART154:16　H61　In all the Zones, the temp'rate, hot and cold,

ZOPIRUS (1)
MPERS74:38　　H859　Then brave *Zopirus,* for his Masters good,

ZOROASTER (1)
MASSYR54:36　　H63　*Zoroaster,* their King, he likewise slew,

ZUTPHON (3)
SIDNEY149:4　　H4　slaine at the Seige of *Zutphon,*
SIDNEY150:23　　H50　O *Zutphon, Zutphon,* that most fatall City,

Appendix

Word List, Word Index, and Numeral Index
of Items Omitted from Main Concordance

List of Words Omitted from Main Concordance

The following articles, conjunctions, prepositions, and pronouns are omitted
from the main concordance. These words appear in the verbal index,
with frequency numbers, context codes, and cross references.

&	in	o^r	thy	with's
a	in's	ou^r	o	within
an	into	our	to	without
and	it	ours	to's	wth
and's	ith	out	to'th	wth
at	me	ovt	toth'	wthin
at's	mee	over	under	wthout
but	mine	's	under's	wthout
by	my	she	unto	y^e
by's	myne	shee	up	ye
for	o'	't	upon	yee
for's	of	t'	upon't	y^m
for't	of's	th'	us	y^o
fr	on	that	vnto	you
from	on's	the	vp	your
from's	o're	thee	vpon	yours
he	o'th	their	vs	yov
her	o^r	theirs	we	yr
hers	or	them	wee	y^{r}of
him	or'e	they	who	|*y^{rs}
his	or's	thine	whom	yt
i	ore	thou	whose	y^y
i'	ouer	thov	with	

Index of Words Omitted from Main Concordance

HUMOUR25:32	H221	AGES42:8	H266	MASSYR~~57:17~~	H164
HUMOUR26:19	H249	AGES42:10	H268	MASSYR~~57:18~~	H165
HUMOUR27:34	H305	AGES42:12	H270	MASSYR57:33	H178
HUMOUR28:1	H313	AGES42:14	H272	MASSYR58:8	H193
HUMOUR28:30	H342	AGES43:12	H305	MASSYR59:24	H248
HUMOUR28:37	H349	AGES~~43:16~~	H309	MASSYR59:31	H255
HUMOUR29:7	H360	AGES~~43:16~~	H309	MASSYR60:11	H276
HUMOUR29:11	H364	AGES43:26	H321	MASSYR60:23	H288
HUMOUR29:22	H373	AGES44:21	H354	MASSYR60:31	H296
HUMOUR29:23	H374	AGES44:30	H363	MASSYR60:33	H298
HUMOUR29:32	H383	AGES44:32	H365	MASSYR60:36	H301
HUMOUR29:37	H388	AGES~~45:2~~	H377	MASSYR60:37	H302
HUMOUR30:2	H394	AGES45:4	H382	MASSYR61:20	H325
HUMOUR30:28	H420	AGES~~45:4~~	H385	MASSYR61:26	H331
HUMOUR30:34	H426	AGES45:7	H390	MASSYR61:32	H337
HUMOUR31:3	H436	AGES45:8	~~H390~~	MASSYR62:8	H353
HUMOUR33:25	H539	AGES45:16	H398	MASSYR62:12	H357
HUMOUR34:23	H578	AGES45:19	~~H401~~	MASSYR63:27	H412
HUMOUR34:24	H579	AGES~~45:22~~	H407	MASSYR~~63:28~~	H415
HUMOUR34:26	H581	SEASONS~~46:35~~	H12	MASSYR64:8	H432
HUMOUR34:34	H589	SEASONS47:25	H41	MASSYR64:25	H449
HUMOUR34:40	H595	SEASONS47:29	H45	MASSYR65:8	H473
HUMOUR35:2	H598	SEASONS48:6	H59	MASSYR65:15	H480
HUMOUR35:9	H605	SEASONS48:18	H71	MASSYR65:17	H482
HUMOUR35:13	H609	SEASONS48:24	H77	MASSYR65:22	H487
AGES35:29	H15	SEASONS48:27	H80	MASSYR66:3	H509
AGES35:35	H21	SEASONS48:32	~~H83~~	MASSYR66:17	H523
AGES36:13	H37	SEASONS49:15	H106	MASSYR66:33	H539
AGES36:14	H38	SEASONS50:13	H147	MASSYR66:38	H544
AGES36:17	H41	SEASONS50:22	H156	MASSYR67:22	H568
AGES36:21	H45	SEASONS51:5	H179	MASSYR67:24	H570
AGES36:22	H46	SEASONS51:29	H205	MASSYR67:38	H584
AGES36:23	H47	SEASONS52:23	H238	MASSYR67:40	H586
AGES37:3	H65	MASSYR53:32	H22	MASSYR68:25	H611
AGES37:31	H93	MASSYR54:6	H33	MPERS69:17	H639
AGES38:21	H124	MASSYR54:26	H53	MPERS69:34	H656
AGES38:22	H125	MASSYR55:6	H72	MPERS69:35	H657
AGES38:23	H126	MASSYR55:9	H75	MPERS~~70:2~~	H673
AGES39:2	H145	MASSYR55:10	H76	MPERS70:13	H684
AGES39:7	H150	MASSYR55:12	H78	MPERS70:19	H690
AGES39:20	H163	MASSYR55:15	H81	MPERS70:21	H692
AGES40:4	H185	MASSYR55:22	H88	MPERS70:28	H699
AGES40:6	H187	MASSYR55:24	H90	MPERS70:29	H700
AGES40:26	H207	MASSYR56:6	H112	MPERS70:32	H703
AGES40:27	H208	MASSYR56:8	H114	MPERS70:35	H706
AGES40:29	H210	MASSYR56:9	H115	MPERS70:39	H710
AGES41:22	~~H239~~	MASSYR56:19	H125	MPERS71:9	H725
AGES41:24	H241	MASSYR56:36	H142	MPERS71:19	H733
AGES41:26	H243	MASSYR56:38	H144	MPERS71:31	H745
AGES41:35	H250	MASSYR56:39	H145	MPERS71:36	H750
AGES~~41:36~~	H253	MASSYR57:3	H150	MPERS72:2	H754

MPERS72:15	H763	MPERS85:18	H1294	MGREC97:36	H1797
MPERS72:19	H767	MPERS85:37	H1313	MGREC97:41	H1802
MPERS72:30	H774	MPERS86:11	H1327	MGREC98:8	H1810
MPERS72:35	H779	MPERS86:24	H1340	MGREC98:15	H1817
MPERS72:41	H787	MPERS86:26	H1342	MGREC98:18	H1820
MPERS73:7	H794	MPERS87:7	H1363	MGREC98:40	H1842
MPERS73:9	H796	MPERS87:24	H1376	MGREC99:1	H1844
MPERS73:30	H815	MPERS87:25	H1377	MGREC99:17	H1860
MPERS73:33	H818	MPERS87:26	H1378	MGREC99:21	H1864
MPERS74:2	H827	MPERS87:28	H1380	MGREC100:6	H1890
MPERS74:4	H829	MPERS87:29	H1381	MGREC100:22	H1906
MPERS74:8	H833	MPERS87:31	H1383	MGREC101:15	H1940
MPERS74:15	H838	MPERS87:38	H1390	MGREC101:31	H1956
MPERS74:20	H843	MPERS88:8	H1401	MGREC101:32	H1957
MPERS74:26	H849	MPERS88:20	H1413	MGREC~~101:34~~	H1961
MPERS75:1	H862	MPERS88:25	H1418	MGREC101:38	H1967
MPERS75:12	H873	MPERS88:26	H1419	MGREC102:11	H1981
MPERS75:13	H874	MPERS88:30	H1423	MGREC102:29	H1999
MPERS75:15	H876	MPERS88:38	H1431	MGREC103:15	H2026
MPERS75:28	H885	MPERS88:39	H1432	MGREC103:16	H2027
MPERS75:39	H896	MPERS88:40	H1433	MGREC103:26	H2037
MPERS75:40	H897	MPERS89:9	H1443	MGREC103:28	H2039
MPERS76:1	H899	MPERS90:10	H1483	MGREC104:23	H2075
MPERS76:2	H900	MPERS~~90:39~~	H1506	MGREC104:37	H2089
MPERS76:11	H909	MPERS91:9	H1517	MGREC105:14	H2107
MPERS76:36	H934	MPERS91:12	H1520	MGREC105:20	H2113
MPERS76:38	H936	MPERS91:16	H1524	MGREC106:4	H2138
MPERS77:19	H960	MPERS~~91:22~~	H1536	MGREC106:24	H2158
MPERS78:15	H996	MPERS91:24	H1538	MGREC106:27	H2161
MPERS78:34	H1015	MPERS~~91:32~~	H1546	MGREC106:28	H2162
MPERS78:39	H1020	MPERS~~91:34~~	H1548	MGREC107:6	H2181
MPERS79:5	H1027	MPERS~~92:8~~	H1566	MGREC107:28	H2203
MPERS79:9	H1031	MPERS~~92:22~~	H1580	MGREC107:33	H2208
MPERS79:10	H1032	MPERS93:3	H1600	MGREC108:2	H2218
MPERS~~79:13~~	H1036	MGREC94:1	H1635	MGREC108:7	H2223
MPERS79:23	H1049	MGREC94:2	H1636	MGREC108:9	H2225
MPERS79:33	H1059	MGREC~~94:18~~	H1653	MGREC108:29	H2245
MPERS79:38	H1064	MGREC94:27	H1665	MGREC108:33	H2249
MPERS79:41	H1067	MGREC94:30	H1668	MGREC108:36	H2252
MPERS80:9	H1076	MGREC94:36	H1674	MGREC108:39	H2255
MPERS80:26	H1093	MGREC96:3	H1723	MGREC109:22	H2281
MPERS80:33	H1100	MGREC96:6	H1726	MGREC109:27	H2286
MPERS81:28	~~H1136~~	MGREC96:11	H1731	MGREC110:3	H2303
MPERS~~81:28~~	H1136	MGREC96:14	H1734	MGREC110:3	H2303
MPERS82:6	H1153	MGREC96:15	H1735	MGREC~~110:18~~	H2321
MPERS82:40	H1187	MGREC96:24	H1744	MGREC110:27	H2331
MPERS83:6	H1194	MGREC96:31	H1751	MGREC111:9	H2354
MPERS83:32	H1220	MGREC96:39	H1759	MGREC111:14	H2359
MPERS83:37	H1225	MGREC97:15	H1776	MGREC111:40	H2385
MPERS84:7	H1235	MGREC97:20	H1781	MGREC112:11	H2397
MPERS84:22	H1258	MGREC97:31	H1792	MGREC112:13	H2399

CONTEM170:36	H106	MERCY188:34	H20	MEDDM204:28	HP285
CONTEM171:23	H126	MERCY189:5	H26	MEDDM205:1	HP285
CONTEM172:6	H142	MERCY189:11	H32	MEDDM205:5	HP285
CONTEM172:7	H143	MEDDM195:30	HP272	MEDDM205:6	HP285
CONTEM172:9	H145	MEDDM195:34	HP272	MEDDM205:20	HP286
CONTEM172:33	H166	MEDDM196:2	HP272	MEDDM205:23	HP286
CONTEM173:13	H180	MEDDM196:22	HP273	MEDDM205:25	HP286
CONTEM173:16	H183	MEDDM196:25	HP273	MEDDM206:2	HP287
CONTEM173:23	H189	MEDDM197:4	HP274	MEDDM206:6	HP287
CONTEM173:31	H196	MEDDM197:7	HP274	MEDDM206:13	HP287
CONTEM173:34	H198	MEDDM197:14	HP274	MEDDM206:22	HP287
CONTEM174:17	H216	MEDDM197:15	HP274	MEDDM206:34	HP288
CONTEM174:18	H217	MEDDM197:26	HP275	MEDDM206:35	HP288
CONTEM174:32	H229	MEDDM197:27	HP275	MEDDM207:5	HP288
FLESH175:9	H9	MEDDM198:17	HP276	MEDDM207:14	HP288
FLESH175:20	H20	MEDDM198:25	HP276	MEDDM207:18	HP289
FLESH176:1	H41	MEDDM198:28	HP276	MEDDM207:22	HP289
FLESH177:13	H94	MEDDM198:29	HP277	MEDDM207:25	HP289
AUTHOR178:5	H15	MEDDM198:32	HP277	MEDDM208:6	HP289
AUTHOR178:5	H15	MEDDM199:24	HP278	MEDDM208:12	HP290
SICKNES178:16	H0	MEDDM199:27	HP278	MEDDM208:13	HP290
SICKNES178:35	H18	MEDDM199:28	HP278	MEDDM209:10	HP291
SICKNES178:37	H20	MEDDM200:2	HP278	MEDDM209:14	HP291
BIRTH179:32	H8	MEDDM200:3	HP278	MEDDM209:20	HP291
1HUSB180:25	H4	MEDDM200:15	HP279	PILGRIM210:19	H19
1LETTER181:1	H0	MEDDM200:20	HP279	PILGRIM210:33	H33
1LETTER181:8	H6	MEDDM200:22	HP279	PILGRIM210:35	H35
1LETTER181:17	H15	MEDDM200:24	HP279	PILGRIM210:36	H36
2LETTER182:12	H18	MEDDM200:26	HP279	TOCHILD215:8	H8
2LETTER182:16	H22	MEDDM200:27	HP279	MYCHILD215:27	HP240
2LETTER182:26	H32	MEDDM200:33	HP280	MYCHILD215:32	HP241
2LETTER182:27	H33	MEDDM201:2	HP280	MYCHILD216:7	HP241
2LETTER182:28	H34	MEDDM201:15	HP280	MYCHILD216:8	HP241
3LETTER183:4	H6	MEDDM201:16	HP280	MYCHILD216:11	HP241
3LETTER183:11	H13	MEDDM201:20	HP280	MYCHILD216:12	HP241
3LETTER183:19	H21	MEDDM201:31	HP281	MYCHILD216:14	HP241
3LETTER183:20	H22	MEDDM201:32	HP281	MYCHILD216:27	HP242
VERSES184:2	H6	MEDDM202:4	HP281	MYCHILD217:21	HP243
CHILDRN184:32	H21	MEDDM202:21	HP282	MYCHILD217:29	HP243
CHILDRN184:34	H23	MEDDM202:24	HP282	MYCHILD217:30	HP243
CHILDRN186:11	H78	MEDDM203:10	HP283	MYCHILD217:33	HP243
CHILDRN186:19	H86	MEDDM203:13	HP283	MYCHILD217:35	HP243
ELIZB186:33	H4-5	MEDDM203:18	HP283	MYCHILD218:5	HP243
ELIZB186:36	H8	MEDDM203:22	HP283	MYCHILD218:7	HP244
ELIZB187:10	H18	MEDDM203:25	HP283	FEVER220:21	H1
ANNEB187:24	H14	MEDDM203:28	HP284	FAINTING222:11	H1
ANNEB187:26	H16	MEDDM204:2	HP284	FAINTING222:23	H13
ANNEB187:27	H17	MEDDM204:18	HP285	MED223:9	HP250
ANNEB187:31	H21	MEDDM204:19	HP285	JULY223:21	HP251
1SIMON188:3	H4	MEDDM204:26	HP285	JULY223:26	HP251
MERCY188:33	H19	MEDDM204:27	HP285	JULY223:32	HP251

ELEMEN8:19	H17	ELEMEN12:19	H179	ELEMEN16:23	H346
ELEMEN8:24	H22	ELEMEN12:21	H181	ELEMEN16:25	H348
ELEMEN8:26	H24	ELEMEN12:23	H183	ELEMEN16:26	H349
ELEMEN8:28	H26	ELEMEN12:27	H187	ELEMEN16:28	H351
ELEMEN8:30	H28	ELEMEN12:28	H188	ELEMEN16:29	H352
ELEMEN8:35	H33	ELEMEN12:31	H191	ELEMEN16:35	H358
ELEMEN9:3	H37	ELEMEN12:35	H195	ELEMEN16:36	H359
ELEMEN9:4	H38	ELEMEN12:37	H197	ELEMEN16:39	H362
ELEMEN9:7	H41	ELEMEN12:38	H198	ELEMEN16:41	H364
ELEMEN9:11	H45	ELEMEN13:8	H209	ELEMEN17:1	H365
ELEMEN9:12	H46	ELEMEN13:12	H213	ELEMEN17:2	H366
ELEMEN9:22	H56	ELEMEN13:19	H220	ELEMEN17:3	H367
ELEMEN9:32	H66	ELEMEN13:23	H224	ELEMEN17:5	H369
ELEMEN9:35	H70	ELEMEN13:25	H226	ELEMEN17:6	H370
ELEMEN9:36	H70	ELEMEN13:26	H227	ELEMEN17:7	H371
ELEMEN9:37	H71	ELEMEN13:27	H228	ELEMEN17:10	H374
ELEMEN9:38	H72	ELEMEN13:28	H229	ELEMEN17:14	H378
ELEMEN9:40	H74	ELEMEN13:29	H230	ELEMEN17:15	H379
ELEMEN10:9	H84	ELEMEN14:2	H244	ELEMEN17:18	H382
ELEMEN10:10	H85	ELEMEN14:4	H246	ELEMEN17:29	H393
ELEMEN10:15	H90	ELEMEN14:5	H249	ELEMEN17:33	H397
ELEMEN10:20	H95	ELEMEN14:7	H250	ELEMEN18:1	H405
ELEMEN10:24	H99	ELEMEN14:10	H252	ELEMEN18:5	H409
ELEMEN10:31	H106	ELEMEN14:10	H252	ELEMEN18:15	H419
ELEMEN10:33	H108	ELEMEN14:11	H253	ELEMEN18:17	H421
ELEMEN10:39	H114	ELEMEN14:12	H254	ELEMEN18:19	H423
ELEMEN10:40	H115	ELEMEN14:13	H255	ELEMEN18:20	H424
ELEMEN11:1	H118	ELEMEN14:14	H256	ELEMEN18:24	H428
ELEMEN11:4	H124	ELEMEN14:21	H263	ELEMEN18:26	H430
ELEMEN11:6	H126	ELEMEN14:29	H271	ELEMEN18:28	H432
ELEMEN11:7	H127	ELEMEN14:33	H275	ELEMEN18:30	H434
ELEMEN11:10	H130	ELEMEN14:37	H279	ELEMEN18:33	H437
ELEMEN11:14	H134	ELEMEN14:38	H280	ELEMEN18:34	H438
ELEMEN11:15	H135	ELEMEN14:40	H282	ELEMEN18:38	H442
ELEMEN11:17	H137	ELEMEN15:5	H287	ELEMEN18:41	H445
ELEMEN11:19	H139	ELEMEN15:6	H288	ELEMEN19:2	H447
ELEMEN11:23	H143	ELEMEN15:7	H289	ELEMEN19:5	H450
ELEMEN11:24	H144	ELEMEN15:8	H290	ELEMEN19:8	H453
ELEMEN11:25	H145	ELEMEN15:10	H292	ELEMEN19:14	H459
ELEMEN11:28	H148	ELEMEN15:12	H294	ELEMEN19:16	H461
ELEMEN11:30	H150	ELEMEN15:14	H296	ELEMEN19:22	H467
ELEMEN11:31	H151	ELEMEN15:20	H302	ELEMEN19:31	H472
ELEMEN11:33	H153	ELEMEN15:22	H304	ELEMEN19:32	H473
ELEMEN11:35	H155	ELEMEN16:3	H326	ELEMEN19:35	H476
ELEMEN11:37	H157	ELEMEN16:4	H327	ELEMEN19:36	H477
ELEMEN12:1	H161	ELEMEN16:5	H328	ELEMEN19:40	H481
ELEMEN12:6	H166	ELEMEN16:6	H329	ELEMEN20:1	H483
ELEMEN12:7	H167	ELEMEN16:11	H334	ELEMEN20:2	H484
ELEMEN12:9	H169	ELEMEN16:14	H337	HUMOUR20:17	H9
ELEMEN12:11	H171	ELEMEN16:17	H340	HUMOUR20:33	H25
ELEMEN12:18	H178	ELEMEN16:22	H345	HUMOUR21:2	H30

HUMOUR21:6	H34	HUMOUR28:26	H338	AGES35:24	H10
HUMOUR21:15	H43	HUMOUR28:27	H339	AGES35:25	H11
HUMOUR21:29	H57	HUMOUR28:28	H340	AGES35:26	H12
HUMOUR21:34	H62	HUMOUR28:31	H343	AGES35:27	H13
HUMOUR21:35	H63	HUMOUR28:34	H346	AGES35:30	H16
HUMOUR21:39	H67	HUMOUR29:3	H356	AGES35:34	H20
HUMOUR21:40	H68	HUMOUR29:6	H359	AGES35:36	H22
HUMOUR22:4	H73	HUMOUR29:9	H362	AGES36:3	H27
HUMOUR22:15	H84	HUMOUR29:15	H368	AGES36:5	H29
HUMOUR22:16	H85	HUMOUR29:28	H379	AGES36:10	H34
HUMOUR22:23	H92	HUMOUR29:34	H385	AGES36:15	H39
HUMOUR22:28	H97	HUMOUR29:36	H387	AGES36:19	H43
HUMOUR22:29	H98	HUMOUR29:40	H391	AGES36:25	H49
HUMOUR23:4	H114	HUMOUR30:16	H408	AGES36:26	H50
HUMOUR23:7	H117	HUMOUR30:21	H413	AGES36:31	H55
HUMOUR23:14	H124	HUMOUR30:25	H417	AGES36:36	H60
HUMOUR23:17	H127	HUMOUR30:38	H430	AGES37:2	H64
HUMOUR23:24	H134	HUMOUR31:5	H438	AGES37:3	H65
HUMOUR23:29	H139	HUMOUR31:7	H440	AGES37:5	H67
HUMOUR23:41	H149	HUMOUR31:13	H444	AGES37:12	H74
HUMOUR24:3	H152	HUMOUR31:15	H448	AGES37:16	H78
HUMOUR24:5	H154	HUMOUR31:17	H450	AGES37:21	H83
HUMOUR24:10	H159	HUMOUR31:21	H454	AGES37:22	H84
HUMOUR24:13	H162	HUMOUR31:25	H458	AGES37:29	H91
HUMOUR24:25	H174	HUMOUR31:28	H461	AGES37:35	H97
HUMOUR24:31	H180	HUMOUR31:29	H462	AGES37:39	H101
HUMOUR24:36	H185	HUMOUR32:12	H486	AGES38:18	H121
HUMOUR24:37	H186	HUMOUR32:20	H494	AGES38:24	H127
HUMOUR24:39	H188	HUMOUR32:29	H503	AGES38:25	H128
HUMOUR25:5	H194	HUMOUR32:34	H508	AGES38:26	H129
HUMOUR25:12	H201	HUMOUR32:39	H513	AGES38:28	H131
HUMOUR25:18	H207	HUMOUR33:1	H515	AGES38:29	H132
HUMOUR25:19	H208	HUMOUR33:12	H526	AGES38:34	H137
HUMOUR25:26	H215	HUMOUR33:16	H530	AGES38:35	H138
HUMOUR25:38	H227	HUMOUR33:23	H537	AGES38:36	H139
HUMOUR25:40	H229	HUMOUR33:24	H538	AGES39:4	H147
HUMOUR26:3	H233	HUMOUR33:27	H541	AGES39:7	H150
HUMOUR26:13	H243	HUMOUR33:30	H544	AGES39:10	H153
HUMOUR26:20	H250	HUMOUR33:31	H545	AGES39:11	H154
HUMOUR26:21	H251	HUMOUR33:35	H549	AGES39:13	H156
HUMOUR26:35	H265	HUMOUR34:2	H557	AGES39:15	H158
HUMOUR27:5	H276	HUMOUR34:15	H570	AGES39:17	H160
HUMOUR27:8	H279	HUMOUR34:18	H573	AGES39:19	H162
HUMOUR27:13	H284	HUMOUR34:34	H589	AGES39:27	H170
HUMOUR27:23	H294	HUMOUR34:36	H591	AGES39:29	H172
HUMOUR27:27	H298	HUMOUR34:39	H594	AGES39:30	H173
HUMOUR27:40	H311	AGES35:18	H4	AGES40:8	H189
HUMOUR28:2	H314	AGES35:18	H4	AGES40:9	H190
HUMOUR28:4	H316	AGES35:20	H6	AGES40:11	H192
HUMOUR28:5	H317	AGES35:22	H8	AGES40:12	H193
HUMOUR28:25	H337	AGES35:23	H9	AGES40:17	H198

AGES40:21	H202	AGES44:32	H365	SEASONS47:38	H50
AGES40:24	H205	AGES44:34	H367	SEASONS47:39	H51
AGES40:26	H207	AGES44:35	H368	SEASONS47:40	H52
AGES40:31	H̶2̶1̶0̶	AGES44:38	H371	SEASONS48:4	H57
AGES40:35	H214	AGES45:2	H̶3̶7̶5̶	SEASONS48:5	H58
AGES40:39	H218	AGES45̶:̶2̶	H376	SEASONS48:8	H61
AGES41:8	H228	AGES45:4	H382	SEASONS48:9	H62
AGES41:12	H231	AGES45̶:̶4̶	H384	SEASONS48:12	H65
AGES41:13	H232	AGES45:5	H389	SEASONS48:16	H69
AGES41:15	H234	AGES45:6	H390	SEASONS48:20	H73
AGES41:16	H235	AGES45:10	H392	SEASONS48:26	H79
AGES41:22	H̶2̶3̶9̶	AGES45:13	H395	SEASONS48:39	H90
AGES41:23	H240	AGES45:14	H396	SEASONS48:40	H91
AGES41:34	H̶2̶4̶9̶	AGES45:15	H397	SEASONS49:4	H95
AGES41̶:̶3̶6̶	H253	AGES45:17	H399	SEASONS49:7	H98
AGES42:2	H260	AGES45:21	H̶4̶0̶3̶	SEASONS49:11	H̶1̶0̶2̶
AGES42:3	H261	AGES45̶:̶2̶1̶	H403	SEASONS49̶:̶1̶1̶	H102
AGES42:5	H263	AGES45̶:̶2̶2̶	H409	SEASONS49:20	H111
AGES42:9	H267	AGES45:26	H416	SEASONS49:26	H115
AGES42:11	H269	AGES45:28	H418	SEASONS49:27	H116
AGES42:19	H277	AGES45:30	H420	SEASONS49:31	H120
AGES42:22	H280	AGES45:35	H425	SEASONS49:37	H130
AGES42:28	H̶2̶8̶5̶	AGES45:38	H428	SEASONS50:7	H141
AGES42:34	H290	AGES45:40	H430	SEASONS50:10	H144
AGES42:35	H291	AGES45:41	H431	SEASONS50:11	H145
AGES42:39	H295	AGES46:4	H435	SEASONS50:19	H153
AGES42:41	H297	AGES46:15	H446	SEASONS50:21	H155
AGES43:3	H298	AGES46:17	H448	SEASONS50:27	H161
AGES43:4	H299	AGES46:20	H451	SEASONS50:33	H167
AGES43:5	H300	AGES46:22	H453	SEASONS50:39	H173
AGES43:8	H303	AGES46:25	H456	SEASONS51:1	H175
AGES43:9	H̶3̶0̶5̶	SEASONS46:30	H6	SEASONS51:3	H177
AGES43:15	H̶3̶0̶7̶	SEASONS46:33	H9	SEASONS51:9	H183
AGES43̶:̶1̶6̶	H311	SEASONS46:34	H10	SEASONS51:10	H184
AGES43:18	H313	SEASONS47:1	H17	SEASONS51:11	H185
AGES43:19	H314	SEASONS47:2	H̶1̶7̶	SEASONS51:13	H187
AGES43:21	H316	SEASONS47:4	H18	SEASONS51:15	H189
AGES43:25	H320	SEASONS47̶:̶5̶	H20	SEASONS51:16	H190
AGES43:27	H322	SEASONS47:11	H27	SEASONS51:23	H199
AGES43:31	H326	SEASONS47:12	H28	SEASONS51:26	H202
AGES43:32	H327	SEASONS47:13	H29	SEASONS52:5	H220
AGES43:33	H̶3̶2̶8̶	SEASONS47:15	H31	SEASONS52:6	H221
AGES43:34	H̶3̶2̶9̶	SEASONS47:17	H33	SEASONS52:7	H222
AGES43:37	H332	SEASONS47:18	H34	SEASONS52:8	H223
AGES44:3	H336	SEASONS47:20	H36	SEASONS52:9	H224
AGES44:5	H338	SEASONS47:21	H37	SEASONS52:10	H225
AGES44:6	H339	SEASONS47:25	H41	SEASONS52:11	H226
AGES44:7	H340	SEASONS47:28	H44	SEASONS52:16	H231
AGES44:8	H341	SEASONS47:29	H45	SEASONS52:17	H232
AGES44:20	H353	SEASONS47̶:̶3̶2̶	H47	SEASONS52:18	H233
AGES44:22	H355	SEASONS47:37	H49	SEASONS52:25	H240

SEASONS52:27	H242	MASSYR58:38	H221	MASSYR64:20	H444
SEASONS52:30	H245	MASSYR59:1	H225	MASSYR64:26	H450
SEASONS52:31	H246	MASSYR59:5	H229	MASSYR64:33	H457
SEASONS52:35	H250	MASSYR59:8	H232	MASSYR64:37	H461
SEASONS52:36	H251	MASSYR59:11	H235	MASSYR64:38	H462
SEASONS52:37	H252	MASSYR59:15	H239	MASSYR65:1	H466
SEASONS52:39	H255	MASSYR59:24	H248	MASSYR65:4	H469
SEASONS53:7	H263	MASSYR59:30	H254	MASSYR65:5	H470
MASSYR53:15	H5	MASSYR59:31	H255	MASSYR65:8	H473
MASSYR53:22	H12	MASSYR60:8	H273	MASSYR65:9	H474
MASSYR53:24	H14	MASSYR60:10	H275	MASSYR65:18	H483
MASSYR53:27	H17	MASSYR60:11	H276	MASSYR65:21	H486
MASSYR53:29	H19	MASSYR60:20	H285	MASSYR65:27	H492
MASSYR54:1	H28	MASSYR60:25	H290	MASSYR65:32	H497
MASSYR54:6	H33	MASSYR60:29	H294	MASSYR65:36	H501
MASSYR54:18	H45	MASSYR60:32	H297	MASSYR65:39	H504
MASSYR54:31	H58	MASSYR60:34	H299	MASSYR65:41	H506
MASSYR54:37	H64	MASSYR60:40	H305	MASSYR66:2	H508
MASSYR55:4	H70	MASSYR61:2	H307	MASSYR66:8	H514
MASSYR55:7	H73	MASSYR61:14	H319	MASSYR66:9	H515
MASSYR55:24	H90	MASSYR61:17	H322	MASSYR66:10	H516
MASSYR55:31	H97	MASSYR61:20	H325	MASSYR66:12	H518
MASSYR55:32	H98	MASSYR61:21	H326	MASSYR66:15	H521
MASSYR55:32	H98	MASSYR61:22	H327	MASSYR66:21	H527
MASSYR55:38	H104	MASSYR61:24	H329	MASSYR66:24	H530
MASSYR55:40	H106	MASSYR61:36	H341	MASSYR66:28	H534
MASSYR56:8	H114	MASSYR61:39	H344	MASSYR66:35	H541
MASSYR56:11	H117	MASSYR62:5	H350	MASSYR66:37	H543
MASSYR56:12	H118	MASSYR62:9	H354	MASSYR66:40	H546
MASSYR56:20	H126	MASSYR62:10	H355	MASSYR67:3	H549
MASSYR56:40	H146	MASSYR62:16	H361	MASSYR67:4	H550
MASSYR57:3	H150	MASSYR62:21	H366	MASSYR67:7	H553
MASSYR57:11	H158	MASSYR62:26	H371	MASSYR67:11	H557
MASSYR57:14	H161	MASSYR62:29	H374	MASSYR67:13	H559
MASSYR57:19	H166	MASSYR62:32	H377	MASSYR67:15	H561
MASSYR57:24	H171	MASSYR62:34	H379	MASSYR67:18	H564
MASSYR57:25	H172	MASSYR62:35	H380	MASSYR67:23	H569
MASSYR57:30	H175	MASSYR62:36	H381	MASSYR67:25	H571
MASSYR57:32	H177	MASSYR62:40	H385	MASSYR67:27	H573
MASSYR57:34	H179	MASSYR63:3	H388	MASSYR67:30	H576
MASSYR58:4	H189	MASSYR63:7	H392	MASSYR67:32	H578
MASSYR58:5	H190	MASSYR63:8	H393	MASSYR67:34	H580
MASSYR58:13	H198	MASSYR63:11	H396	MASSYR67:35	H581
MASSYR58:17	H202	MASSYR63:20	H405	MASSYR67:36	H582
MASSYR58:20	H205	MASSYR64:2	H426	MASSYR67:38	H584
MASSYR58:21	H206	MASSYR64:4	H428	MASSYR68:3	H589
MASSYR58:25	H208	MASSYR64:7	H431	MASSYR68:4	H590
MASSYR58:27	H210	MASSYR64:11	H435	MASSYR68:5	H591
MASSYR58:29	H212	MASSYR64:12	H436	MASSYR68:6	H592
MASSYR58:31	H214	MASSYR64:15	H439	MASSYR68:7	H593
MASSYR58:36	H219	MASSYR64:18	H442	MASSYR68:10	H596

MPERS84:9	H1237	MPERS89:13	H1447	MGREC94:13	H1647
MPERS84:10	H1238	MPERS89:14	H1448	MGREC94:16	H1650
MPERS84:11	H1239	MPERS89:16	H1450	MGREC94:18	H1655
MPERS84:12	H1243	MPERS89:18	H1452	MGREC94:22	H1660
MPERS84:21	H1257	MPERS89:22	H1456	MGREC94:23	H1661
MPERS84:24	H1260	MPERS89:26	H1460	MGREC94:27	H1665
MPERS84:29	H1265	MPERS89:30	H1464	MGREC94:28	H1666
MPERS84:32	H1268	MPERS89:34	H1468	MGREC94:33	H1671
MPERS84:34	H1270	MPERS89:35	H1469	MGREC94:38	H1676
MPERS84:38	H1274	MPERS89:37	H1471	MGREC94:40	H1678
MPERS85:2	H1278	MPERS89:38	H1472	MGREC95:1	H1680
MPERS85:16	H1292	MPERS90:6	H1479	MGREC95:2	H1681
MPERS85:21	H1297	MPERS90:7	H1480	MGREC95:6	H1685
MPERS85:22	H1298	MPERS90:24	H1491	MGREC95:8	H1687
MPERS85:29	H1305	MPERS90:37	H1504	MGREC95:9	H1688
MPERS85:31	H1307	MPERS90:41	H1508	MGREC95:10	H1689
MPERS86:1	H1317	MPERS91:6	H1514	MGREC95:13	H1692
MPERS86:19	H1335	MPERS91:9	H1517	MGREC95:23	H1702
MPERS86:21	H1337	MPERS91:12	H1520	MGREC95:25	H1704
MPERS86:30	H1346	MPERS91:18	H1526	MGREC95:30	H1709
MPERS86:39	H1355	MPERS91:19	H1527	MGREC95:32	H1711
MPERS87:2	H1358	MPERS91:22	H1530	MGREC95:38	H1717
MPERS87:3	H1359	MPERS91:24	H1538	MGREC95:40	H1719
MPERS87:8	H1364	MPERS91:25	H1539	MGREC96:1	H1721
MPERS87:11	H1367	MPERS91:27	H1541	MGREC96:4	H1724
MPERS87:14	H1370	MPERS91:27	H1541	MGREC96:8	H1728
MPERS87:15	H1370	MPERS91:28	H1542	MGREC96:12	H1732
MPERS87:20	H1374	MPERS91:30	H1544	MGREC96:13	H1733
MPERS87:23	H1375	MPERS91:34	H1548	MGREC96:28	H1748
MPERS87:28	H1380	MPERS91:38	H1552	MGREC96:29	H1749
MPERS87:30	H1382	MPERS91:39	H1553	MGREC96:30	H1750
MPERS87:33	H1385	MPERS92:2	H1556	MGREC96:31	H1751
MPERS87:37	H1389	MPERS92:2	H1556	MGREC96:32	H1752
MPERS87:39	H1391	MPERS92:8	H1566	MGREC96:34	H1754
MPERS87:40	H1392	MPERS92:18	H1576	MGREC96:37	H1757
MPERS87:41	H1393	MPERS92:20	H1578	MGREC96:38	H1758
MPERS88:4	H1397	MPERS92:21	H1579	MGREC96:39	H1759
MPERS88:9	H1402	MPERS92:22	H1580	MGREC97:1	H1762
MPERS88:10	H1403	MPERS92:24	H1582	MGREC97:3	H1764
MPERS88:12	H1405	MPERS92:28	H1586	MGREC97:5	H1766
MPERS88:13	H1406	MPERS92:31	H1589	MGREC97:7	H1768
MPERS88:18	H1411	MPERS92:32	H1590	MGREC97:8	H1769
MPERS88:22	H1415	MPERS92:34	H1592	MGREC97:20	H1781
MPERS88:23	H1416	MPERS92:39	H1597	MGREC97:35	H1796
MPERS88:25	H1418	MPERS93:1	H1598	MGREC97:36	H1797
MPERS88:26	H1419	MPERS93:3	H1600	MGREC97:39	H1800
MPERS88:27	H1420	MGREC6:18	H1615	MGREC97:41	H1802
MPERS88:32	H1425	MGREC6:36	H1633	MGREC98:4	H1806
MPERS88:35	H1428	MGREC94:3	H1637	MGREC98:11	H1813
MPERS88:36	H1429	MGREC94:5	H1639	MGREC98:13	H1815
MPERS88:39	H1432	MGREC94:9	H1643	MGREC98:21	H1823

MGREC98:22	H1824	MGREC102:24	H1994	MGREC106:36	H2170
MGREC98:30	H1832	MGREC102:32	H2002	MGREC106:38	H2172
MGREC98:32	H1834	MGREC102:34	H2004	MGREC106:40	H2174
MGREC98:35	H1837	MGREC102:35	H2005	MGREC107:4	H2179
MGREC98:38	H1840	MGREC102:36	H2006	MGREC107:6	H2181
MGREC98:39	H1841	MGREC102:37	H2007	MGREC107:9	H2184
MGREC98:40	H1842	MGREC103:3	H2014	MGREC107:13	H2188
MGREC99:1	H1844	MGREC103:6	H2017	MGREC107:14	H2189
MGREC99:3	H1846	MGREC103:11	H2022	MGREC107:23	H2198
MGREC99:5	H1848	MGREC103:12	H2023	MGREC107:29	H2204
MGREC99:11	H1854	MGREC103:17	H2028	MGREC107:35	H2210
MGREC99:13	H1856	MGREC103:22	H2033	MGREC108:3	H2219
MGREC99:14	H1857	MGREC103:25	H2036	MGREC108:6	H2222
MGREC99:20	H1863	MGREC103:27	H2038	MGREC108:11	H2227
MGREC99:25	H1868	MGREC103:31	H2042	MGREC108:20	H2236
MGREC99:33	H1876	MGREC103:33	H2044	MGREC108:22	H2238
MGREC100:11	H1895	MGREC103:37	H2048	MGREC108:25	H2241
MGREC100:14	H1898	MGREC103:38	H2049	MGREC108:29	H2245
MGREC100:15	H1899	MGREC103:39	H2050	MGREC108:31	H2247
MGREC100:20	H1904	MGREC104:3	H2055	MGREC108:38	H2254
MGREC100:23	H1907	MGREC104:14	H2066	MGREC108:41	H2257
MGREC100:26	H1910	MGREC104:15	H2067	MGREC109:3	H2260
MGREC100:32	H1916	MGREC104:16	H2068	MGREC109:5	H2262
MGREC100:34	H1918	MGREC104:18	H2070	MGREC109:5	H2263
MGREC100:40	H1924	MGREC104:19	H2071	MGREC109:11	H2270
MGREC101:2	H1927	MGREC104:20	H2072	MGREC109:17	H2276
MGREC101:4	H1929	MGREC104:21	H2073	MGREC109:19	H2278
MGREC101:5	H1930	MGREC104:22	H2074	MGREC109:21	H2280
MGREC101:8	H1933	MGREC104:27	H2079	MGREC109:23	H2282
MGREC101:9	H1934	MGREC104:30	H2082	MGREC109:27	H2286
MGREC101:10	H1935	MGREC104:38	H2090	MGREC109:32	H2291
MGREC101:11	H1936	MGREC105:3	H2096	MGREC109:36	H2295
MGREC101:13	H1938	MGREC105:9	H2102	MGREC109:41	H2300
MGREC101:14	H1939	MGREC105:13	H2106	MGREC110:4	H2304
MGREC101:21	H1946	MGREC105:14	H2107	MGREC110:7	H2307
MGREC101:31	H1956	MGREC105:18	H2111	MGREC110:8	H2308
MGREC101:34	H1962	MGREC105:24	H2117	MGREC110:11	H2311
MGREC101:41	H1970	MGREC105:25	H2118	MGREC110:13	H2313
MGREC102:2	H1972	MGREC105:28	H2121	MGREC110:14	H2314
MGREC102:3	H1973	MGREC105:29	H2122	MGREC110:20	H2324
MGREC102:6	H1976	MGREC105:32	H2125	MGREC110:28	H2332
MGREC102:8	H1978	MGREC105:34	H2127	MGREC110:31	H2335
MGREC102:10	H1980	MGREC105:36	H2129	MGREC110:32	H2336
MGREC102:11	H1981	MGREC105:39	H2132	MGREC110:34	H2338
MGREC102:15	H1985	MGREC106:1	H2135	MGREC110:36	H2340
MGREC102:16	H1986	MGREC106:4	H2138	MGREC110:41	H2345
MGREC102:17	H1987	MGREC106:5	H2139	MGREC111:5	H2350
MGREC102:18	H1988	MGREC106:12	H2146	MGREC111:8	H2353
MGREC102:21	H1991	MGREC106:17	H2151	MGREC111:12	H2357
MGREC102:22	H1992	MGREC106:24	H2158	MGREC111:17	H2362
MGREC102:23	H1993	MGREC106:31	H2165	MGREC111:19	H2364

MGREC111:26	H2371	MGREC117:14	H2621	MGREC122:34	H2855
MGREC111:28	H2373	MGREC117:25	H2632	MGREC122:38	H2859
MGREC111:30	H2375	MGREC117:31	H2638	MGREC122:39	H2860
MGREC111:31	H2376	MGREC118:1	H2648	MGREC123:1	H2863
MGREC111:33	H2378	MGREC118:4	H2651	MGREC123:2	H2864
MGREC111:37	H2382	MGREC118:7	H2654	MGREC123:7	H2869
MGREC111:41	H2386	MGREC118:15	H2662	MGREC123:9	H2871
MGREC112:16	H2402	MGREC118:19	H2666	MGREC123:12	H2874
MGREC112:17	H2403	MGREC118:26	H2675	MGREC~~123:13~~	H2877
MGREC112:22	H2408	MGREC118:31	H2680	MGREC123:20	H2884
MGREC112:31	H2417	MGREC118:32	H2681	MGREC123:21	H2885
MGREC112:39	H2425	MGREC118:33	H2682	MGREC123:31	H2895
MGREC112:41	H2427	MGREC118:35	H2684	MGREC123:39	H2903
MGREC113:3	H2430	MGREC118:38	H2687	MGREC123:41	H2905
MGREC113:6	H2433	MGREC119:4	H2694	MGREC124:1	H2906
MGREC113:9	H2436	MGREC119:14	H2704	MGREC~~124:6~~	H2911
MGREC113:13	H2440	MGREC119:15	H2705	MGREC124:13	H2920
MGREC113:26	H2453	MGREC119:19	H2709	MGREC124:14	H2921
MGREC113:31	H2458	MGREC119:23	H2713	MGREC124:24	H2931
MGREC113:36	H2463	MGREC119:26	H2716	MGREC124:25	H2932
MGREC113:37	H2464	MGREC119:37	H2727	MGREC124:30	H2937
MGREC113:41	H2468	MGREC119:38	H2728	MGREC124:31	H2938
MGREC114:2	H2470	MGREC120:5	H2740	MGREC125:1	H2949
MGREC114:4	H2472	MGREC120:6	H2741	MGREC125:4	H2952
MGREC114:9	H2477	MGREC120:19	H2754	MGREC125:10	H2958
MGREC~~114:12~~	H2482	MGREC120:23	H2760	MGREC125:11	H2959
MGREC114:14	H2484	MGREC120:26	H2763	MGREC125:12	H2960
MGREC114:23	H2493	MGREC120:27	H2764	MGREC125:18	H2966
MGREC114:28	H2498	MGREC120:28	H2765	MGREC125:20	H2968
MGREC114:34	H2504	MGREC120:29	H2766	MGREC~~125:21~~	H2971
MGREC114:36	H2506	MGREC120:30	H2767	MGREC125:23	H2973
MGREC115:2	H2513	MGREC120:37	H2774	MGREC125:24	H2974
MGREC~~115:15~~	H2525	MGREC120:38	H2775	MGREC125:26	H2976
MGREC115:19	H2538	MGREC120:40	H2777	MGREC125:32	H2982
MGREC115:22	H2541	MGREC121:3	H2781	MGREC125:35	H2985
MGREC115:31	H2550	MGREC121:6	H2784	MGREC125:40	H2990
MGREC115:33	H2552	MGREC121:8	H2786	MGREC126:2	H2993
MGREC115:39	H2558	MGREC121:11	H2789	MGREC126:5	H2996
MGREC115:40	H2559	MGREC121:13	H2791	MGREC126:8	H2999
MGREC116:4	H2564	MGREC~~121:15~~	H2793	MGREC126:12	H3003
MGREC116:5	H2565	MGREC~~121:16~~	H2798	MGREC126:14	H3005
MGREC116:7	H2567	MGREC121:18	H2800	MGREC126:22	H3013
MGREC116:12	H2578	MGREC121:21	H2803	MGREC126:25	H3016
MGREC116:16	H2582	MGREC121:31	H2813	MGREC126:25	H3016
MGREC116:21	H2587	MGREC121:34	H2816	MGREC126:27	H3018
MGREC116:22	H2588	MGREC121:40	H2822	MGREC126:33	H~~3023~~
MGREC116:24	H2590	MGREC121:41	H2823	MGREC126:41	H3030
MGREC116:28	H2594	MGREC122:2	H2825	MGREC127:5	H3035
MGREC116:29	H2595	MGREC122:4	H2827	MGREC127:7	H3037
MGREC116:34	H2600	MGREC122:24	H~~2845~~	MGREC127:9	H3039
MGREC117:8	H2615	MGREC122:30	H2849	MGREC127:11	H3041

MGREC127:13	H3043	MGREC131:41	H3233	MROMAN136:29	H3443
MGREC127:20	H3050	MGREC~~132:6~~	H3241	MROMAN136:30	H3444
MGREC127:29	H3059	MGREC132:7	H3242	MROMAN136:36	H3450
MGREC127:31	H3061	MGREC132:8	H3243	MROMAN136:37	H3451
MGREC127:34	H3064	MGREC132:9	H3244	MROMAN137:3	H3454
MGREC127:40	H3070	MGREC132:16	H3251	MROMAN137:7	H3458
MGREC127:41	H3071	MGREC~~132:16~~	H3252	MROMAN137:12	H3463
MGREC128:2	H3075	MGREC132:20	H3257	MROMAN137:17	H3468
MGREC128:3	H3076	MGREC~~132:20~~	H3263	MROMAN137:19	H3470
MGREC128:4	H3077	MGREC132:21	H3266	MROMAN137:22	H3473
MGREC128:7	H3080	MGREC132:29	H3276	MROMAN137:29	H3480
MGREC128:9	H3082	MGREC132:31	H3278	MROMAN137:30	H3481
MGREC128:14	H3087	MGREC132:34	H3281	MROMAN137:31	H3482
MGREC128:16	H3089	MGREC132:35	H3282	MROMAN137:32	H3483
MGREC128:18	H3091	MGREC132:36	H3283	MROMAN138:4	H3494
MGREC128:20	H3093	MGREC132:40	H3287	MROMAN138:8	H3498
MGREC128:24	H3097	MGREC133:4	H3292	MROMAN138:12	H3502
MGREC128:27	H3100	MGREC133:8	H3296	MROMAN138:15	H3505
MGREC128:30	H3103	MGREC133:15	H3303	MROMAN138:17	H3507
MGREC128:32	H3105	MGREC133:17	H3305	MROMAN138:19	H3509
MGREC128:32	H3105	MGREC133:19	H3307	MROMAN138:25	H3515
MGREC128:38	H3111	MGREC133:20	H3308	MROMAN138:27	H3517
MGREC129:3	H3117	MGREC133:25	~~H3315~~	MROMAN138:28	H3518
MGREC129:5	H3119	MGREC133:38	H3328	MROMAN138:32	H3522
MGREC129:9	H3123	MGREC133:39	H3329	MROMAN138:34	H3524
MGREC129:9	H3123	MGREC134:2	H3333	MROMAN138:36	H3526
MGREC129:18	H3132	MGREC134:4	H3337	MROMAN139:2	H3530
MGREC129:19	H3133	MGREC134:10	H3341	MROMAN139:9	H3537
MGREC129:25	H3139	MGREC134:16	H3347	MROMAN139:17	H3545
MGREC129:26	H3140	MGREC134:17	H3348	MROMAN139:19	H3547
MGREC129:28	H3142	MGREC134:22	H3353	MROMAN139:23	H3551
MGREC129:33	H3147	MGREC134:30	H3361	MROMAN139:25	~~H3551~~
MGREC129:36	H3150	MGREC135:3	H3375	MROMAN139:28	H3554
MGREC129:38	H3152	MGREC135:8	H3380	MROMAN139:31	H3557
MGREC130:3	H3158	MGREC135:9	H3381	MROMAN139:37	H3563
MGREC130:4	H3159	MGREC135:10	H3382	MROMAN140:1	H3564
MGREC130:19	H3174	MGREC135:15	H3387	MROMAN140:4	H3567
MGREC130:23	H3178	MGREC135:18	H3390	DIALOG141:2	H2
MGREC130:28	~~H3181~~	MGREC135:21	H3393	DIALOG141:6	H5
MGREC130:29	~~H3181~~	MGREC135:22	H3394	DIALOG141:7	H6
MGREC130:30	~~H3181~~	MGREC135:23	H3395	DIALOG141:8	H7
MGREC130:32	~~H3181~~	MGREC135:25	H3397	DIALOG141:9	H8
MGREC130:35	~~H3181~~	MGREC135:26	H3398	DIALOG141:17	H16
MGREC130:37	H3182	MGREC135:30	H3402	DIALOG141:19	H18
MGREC~~131:1~~	H3190	MGREC135:32	H3404	DIALOG141:30	H29
MGREC131:5	H3195	MGREC135:38	H3410	DIALOG142:6	H35
MGREC131:9	H3199	MGREC135:39	H3411	DIALOG142:7	H36
MGREC131:10	H3202	MGREC136:11	H3425	DIALOG142:13	H42
MGREC131:12	H3204	MGREC136:13	H3427	DIALOG142:14	H43
MGREC131:15	H3207	MROMAN136:20	H3434	DIALOG142:15	H44
MGREC131:35	H3227	MROMAN136:23	H3437	DIALOG142:21	H50

CHILDRN184:29	H18	MERCY189:16	H37	MEDDM200:30	HP279
CHILDRN184:36	H25	2SIMON195:3	HP271	MEDDM201:3	HP280
CHILDRN185:1	H27	2SIMON195:14	HP271	MEDDM201:12	HP280
CHILDRN185:10	H36	MEDDM195:22	HP272	MEDDM201:13	HP280
CHILDRN185:11	H37	MEDDM195:26	HP272	MEDDM201:15	HP280
CHILDRN185:20	H46	MEDDM195:33	HP272	MEDDM201:16	HP280
CHILDRN185:21	H47	MEDDM195:35	HP272	MEDDM201:25	HP281
CHILDRN185:23	H49	MEDDM195:36	HP272	MEDDM202:6	HP281
CHILDRN185:25	H51	MEDDM196:2	HP274	MEDDM202:7	HP281
CHILDRN185:26	H52	MEDDM196:3	HP274	MEDDM202:8	HP281
CHILDRN185:30	H56	MEDDM196:8	HP273	MEDDM202:10	HP281
CHILDRN185:33	H59	MEDDM196:9	HP273	MEDDM202:11	HP281
CHILDRN185:34	H60	MEDDM196:11	HP273	MEDDM202:12	HP281
CHILDRN185:35	H61	MEDDM196:15	HP273	MEDDM202:13	HP282
CHILDRN186:1	H68	MEDDM196:16	HP273	MEDDM202:17	HP282
CHILDRN186:4	H71	MEDDM196:17	HP273	MEDDM202:27	HP282
CHILDRN186:5	H72	MEDDM196:18	HP273	MEDDM202:28	HP282
CHILDRN186:6	H73	MEDDM196:34	HP273	MEDDM202:29	HP282
CHILDRN186:10	H77	MEDDM197:15	HP274	MEDDM202:32	HP282
CHILDRN186:13	H80	MEDDM197:19	HP275	MEDDM202:36	HP282
CHILDRN186:21	H88	MEDDM197:22	HP275	MEDDM203:2	HP283
CHILDRN186:22	H89	MEDDM197:28	HP275	MEDDM203:4	HP283
CHILDRN186:23	H90	MEDDM197:31	HP275	MEDDM203:5	HP283
CHILDRN186:24	H91	MEDDM197:33	HP275	MEDDM203:10	HP283
CHILDRN186:25	H92	MEDDM197:33	GREIF	MEDDM203:11	HP283
CHILDRN186:27	H94	MEDDM198:2	HP275	MEDDM203:14	HP283
CHILDRN186:27	H94	MEDDM198:4	HP276	MEDDM203:17	HP283
ELIZB186:33	H4-5	MEDDM198:5	HP276	MEDDM203:18	HP283
ELIZB187:6	H14	MEDDM198:9	HP276	MEDDM203:27	HP284
ELIZB187:6	H14	MEDDM198:10	HP276	MEDDM203:33	HP284
ELIZB187:7	H15	MEDDM198:22	HP276	MEDDM204:4	HP284
ELIZB187:7	H15	MEDDM198:25	HP276	MEDDM204:5	HP284
ELIZB187:8	H16	MEDDM198:34	HP277	MEDDM204:6	HP284
ELIZB187:8	H16	MEDDM199:5	HP277	MEDDM204:7	HP284
ELIZB187:10	H18	MEDDM199:5	HP277	MEDDM204:14	HP284
ELIZB187:11	H19	MEDDM199:8	HP277	MEDDM204:17	HP285
ANNEB187:14	H3-4	MEDDM199:9	HP277	MEDDM204:19	HP285
ANNEB187:31	H21	MEDDM199:12	HP277	MEDDM204:20	HP285
1SIMON188:3	H4	MEDDM199:16	HP278	MEDDM204:21	HP285
1SIMON188:4	H5	MEDDM199:19	HP278	MEDDM204:23	HP285
1SIMON188:10	H11	MEDDM199:21	HP278	MEDDM204:28	HP285
1SIMON188:12	H13	MEDDM199:23	HP278	MEDDM204:30	HP285
1SIMON188:13	H14	MEDDM199:27	HP278	MEDDM204:34	HP285
MERCY188:20	H6	MEDDM199:31	HP278	MEDDM204:35	HP285
MERCY188:21	H7	MEDDM200:7	HP279	MEDDM205:1	HP285
MERCY188:27	H13	MEDDM200:10	HP279	MEDDM205:2	HP285
MERCY188:33	H19	MEDDM200:15	HP279	MEDDM205:6	HP285
MERCY189:3	H24	MEDDM200:17	HP279	MEDDM205:10	HP286
MERCY189:4	H25	MEDDM200:19	HP279	MEDDM205:11	HP286
MERCY189:6	H27	MEDDM200:25	HP279	MEDDM205:12	HP286
MERCY189:11	H32	MEDDM200:26	HP279	MEDDM205:14	HP286

MEDDM207:9	HP288	ELEMEN8:36	H34	HUMOUR20:30	H22
MEDDM207:16	HP288	ELEMEN9:2	H36	HUMOUR20:33	H25
MEDDM207:21	HP289	ELEMEN9:8	H42	HUMOUR21:3	H31
MEDDM208:1	HP289	ELEMEN9:26	H60	HUMOUR21:7	H35
MEDDM209:11	HP291	ELEMEN9:30	H64	HUMOUR21:20	H48
MEDDM209:14	HP291	ELEMEN9:33	H67	HUMOUR21:30	H58
PILGRIM210:1	H1	ELEMEN9:38	H72	HUMOUR21:31	H59
PILGRIM210:10	H10	ELEMEN11:1	H120	HUMOUR21:33	H61
PILGRIM210:23	H23	ELEMEN11:11	H131	HUMOUR21:40	H68
MYCHILD215:26	HP240	ELEMEN11:36	H156	HUMOUR22:3	H72
MYCHILD215:27	HP240	ELEMEN12:2	H162	HUMOUR22:9	H78
MYCHILD215:28	HP241	ELEMEN12:10	H170	HUMOUR22:11	H80
MYCHILD216:8	HP241	ELEMEN12:15	H175	HUMOUR22:24	H93
MYCHILD216:10	HP241	ELEMEN12:24	H184	HUMOUR22:33	H102
MYCHILD217:1	HP242	ELEMEN12:28	H188	HUMOUR22:36	H105
MYCHILD217:8	HP242	ELEMEN12:29	H189	HUMOUR23:5	H115
MYCHILD219:8	HP245	ELEMEN12:37	H197	HUMOUR23:6	H116
BYNIGHT220:3	H4	ELEMEN13:3	H204	HUMOUR23:17	H127
SOREFIT221:27	H13	ELEMEN13:7	H208	HUMOUR23:20	H130
MED223:13	HP250	ELEMEN13:11	H212	HUMOUR23:24	H134
JULY223:22	HP251	ELEMEN13:16	H217	HUMOUR23:30	H140
MYSOUL225:7	H11	ELEMEN13:21	H222	HUMOUR24:4	H153
11MAYA226:20	HP255	ELEMEN13:33	H234	HUMOUR24:8	H157
13MAY226:29	H5	ELEMEN13:35	H236	HUMOUR24:23	H172
13MAY227:16	H25	ELEMEN14:18	H260	HUMOUR24:28	H177
RESTOR230:4	H19	ELEMEN14:19	H261	HUMOUR24:29	H178
SON230:29	H12	ELEMEN14:24	H266	HUMOUR24:33	H182
2HUSB232:11	H12	ELEMEN14:32	H274	HUMOUR25:1	H190
HOUSE237:4	H34	ELEMEN15:22	H304	HUMOUR25:10	H199
AT'S (2) [at his]		ELEMEN15:23	H305	HUMOUR25:11	H200
DUBART155:3	H88	ELEMEN15:25	H307	HUMOUR25:14	H203
DUBART155:3	H88	ELEMEN15:27	H309	HUMOUR25:15	H204
BUT (817)		ELEMEN15:33	H315	HUMOUR25:18	H207
FATHER5:17	H18	ELEMEN16:9	H332	HUMOUR25:22	H211
FATHER6:3	H37	ELEMEN16:11	H334	HUMOUR25:31	H220
FATHER6:4	H38	ELEMEN16:26	H349	HUMOUR25:38	H227
FATHER6:6	H40	ELEMEN17:10	H374	HUMOUR26:1	H231
FATHER6:7	H41	ELEMEN17:23	H387	HUMOUR26:19	H249
PROLOG6:25	H9	ELEMEN17:27	H391	HUMOUR26:23	H253
PROLOG6:26	H10	ELEMEN17:32	H396	HUMOUR26:27	H257
PROLOG6:30	H14	ELEMEN18:7	H411	HUMOUR26:31	H261
PROLOG7:11	H25	ELEMEN18:14	H418	HUMOUR26:34	H264
PROLOG7:21	H33	ELEMEN18:16	H420	HUMOUR26:37	H267
PROLOG7:25	H37	ELEMEN18:32	H436	HUMOUR26:41	H271
PROLOG7:26	H38	ELEMEN19:25	H470	HUMOUR27:4	H275
PROLOG7:30	H41	ELEMEN19:35	H476	HUMOUR27:11	H282
PROLOG8:2	H50	ELEMEN20:6	H488	HUMOUR27:16	H287
ELEMEN8:10	H8	ELEMEN20:8	H490	HUMOUR27:28	H299
ELEMEN8:23	H21	HUMOUR20:15	H7	HUMOUR27:36	H307
ELEMEN8:31	H29	HUMOUR20:21	H13	HUMOUR27:38	H309
ELEMEN8:32	H30	HUMOUR20:25	H17	HUMOUR28:19	H331

MPERS69:29	H651	MPERS81:40	H1144	MPERS~~92:19~~	H1577
MPERS70:9	H680	MPERS82:1	H1146	MPERS~~92:21~~	H1579
MPERS70:32	H703	MPERS82:5	H1152	MPERS~~92:23~~	H1581
MPERS70:34	H705	MPERS82:28	H1175	MPERS92:27	~~H1585~~
MPERS70:38	H709	MPERS83:2	H1190	MPERS~~92:27~~	H1585
MPERS~~71:4~~	H716	MPERS83:3	H1191	MPERS~~92:28~~	H1586
MPERS71:7	H723	MPERS83:13	H1201	MGREC6:31	H1628
MPERS71:11	H727	MPERS83:20	H1208	MGREC6:35	H1632
MPERS71:13	~~H727~~	MPERS83:22	H1210	MGREC94:4	H1638
MPERS71:18	H732	MPERS84:5	H1233	MGREC95:22	H1701
MPERS71:25	H739	MPERS84:27	H1263	MGREC95:23	H1702
MPERS71:28	H742	MPERS84:31	H1267	MGREC95:33	H1712
MPERS71:30	H744	MPERS85:6	H1282	MGREC96:17	H1737
MPERS71:32	H746	MPERS85:7	~~H1283~~	MGREC96:34	H1754
MPERS71:38	H752	MPERS85:26	H1302	MGREC96:35	H1755
MPERS72:29	~~H773~~	MPERS85:35	H1311	MGREC96:37	H1757
MPERS72:30	H774	MPERS85:40	H1316	MGREC97:13	H1774
MPERS72:32	H776	MPERS86:4	H1320	MGREC97:25	H1786
MPERS72:39	H785	MPERS86:37	H1353	MGREC97:32	H1793
MPERS73:25	H810	MPERS87:1	H1357	MGREC97:37	H1798
MPERS73:28	H813	MPERS87:9	H1365	MGREC98:5	H1807
MPERS73:37	H822	MPERS87:19	H1373	MGREC98:13	H1815
MPERS73:38	H823	MPERS87:22	~~H1374~~	MGREC99:4	H1847
MPERS74:1	H826	MPERS87:24	H1376	MGREC99:7	H1850
MPERS74:14	H837	MPERS88:10	H1403	MGREC99:8	H1851
MPERS74:35	H858	MPERS88:14	H1407	MGREC99:11	H1854
MPERS75:13	H874	MPERS88:26	H1419	MGREC99:22	H1865
MPERS75:18	~~H878~~	MPERS88:29	H1422	MGREC99:35	H1878
MPERS75:35	H892	MPERS88:30	H1423	MGREC100:17	H1901
MPERS76:3	H901	MPERS89:1	H1435	MGREC100:19	H1903
MPERS76:14	H912	MPERS89:3	H1437	MGREC100:23	H1907
MPERS76:24	H922	MPERS89:6	H1440	MGREC100:28	H1912
MPERS76:27	H925	MPERS89:31	H1465	MGREC100:39	H1923
MPERS76:40	H938	MPERS89:37	H1471	MGREC101:32	H1957
MPERS77:23	H964	MPERS89:41	H1475	MGREC~~101:34~~	H1963
MPERS77:26	H967	MPERS90:2	H1477	MGREC101:37	H1966
MPERS78:11	H992	MPERS90:6	H1479	MGREC101:39	H1968
MPERS78:27	H1008	MPERS90:9	H1482	MGREC102:28	H1998
MPERS78:30	H1011	MPERS90:12	~~H1484~~	MGREC103:19	H2030
MPERS79:12	~~H1034~~	MPERS90:33	~~H1500~~	MGREC103:34	H2045
MPERS~~79:12~~	H1034	MPERS~~90:33~~	H1500	MGREC103:40	H2051
MPERS79:22	H1048	MPERS91:13	H1521	MGREC104:1	H2053
MPERS79:30	H1056	MPERS91:17	H1525	MGREC104:5	H2057
MPERS79:41	H1067	MPERS~~91:22~~	H1531	MGREC104:12	H2064
MPERS80:6	H1073	MPERS~~91:25~~	H1539	MGREC104:29	H2081
MPERS80:19	H1086	MPERS91:27	~~H1541~~	MGREC105:11	H2104
MPERS80:25	H1092	MPERS91:31	~~H1545~~	MGREC105:12	H2105
MPERS80:28	H1095	MPERS92:3	~~H1557~~	MGREC~~106:2~~	H2136
MPERS80:40	H1107	MPERS~~92:5~~	H1563	MGREC106:27	H2161
MPERS81:22	H1130	MPERS92:10	H1568	MGREC106:31	H2165
MPERS81:38	~~H1143~~	MPERS92:12	H1570	MGREC107:1	H2176

MGREC107:16	H2191	MGREC120:19	H2754	MROMAN136:26	H3440
MGREC107:22	H2197	MGREC~~121:2~~	H2780	MROMAN137:10	H3461
MGREC107:32	H2207	MGREC121:10	H2788	MROMAN137:16	H3467
MGREC107:38	H2213	MGREC~~121:16~~	H2795	MROMAN137:20	H3471
MGREC107:40	H2215	MGREC121:28	H2810	MROMAN137:28	H3479
MGREC108:13	H2229	MGREC121:35	H2817	MROMAN138:10	H3500
MGREC108:16	H2232	MGREC121:37	H2819	MROMAN139:2	H3530
MGREC108:18	H2234	MGREC122:3	H2826	MROMAN139:29	H3555
MGREC108:26	H2242	MGREC122:15	H2840	MROMAN140:2	H3565
MGREC108:33	H2249	MGREC123:8	H2870	DIALOG142:1	H30
MGREC108:38	H2254	MGREC~~123:13~~	H2876	DIALOG142:4	H33
MGREC109:5	~~H2262~~	MGREC~~124:9~~	H2914	DIALOG142:37	H66
MGREC109:24	H2283	MGREC124:13	H2920	DIALOG143:18	H87
MGREC109:29	H2288	MGREC124:20	H2927	DIALOG143:19	H88
MGREC109:34	H2293	MGREC124:22	H2929	DIALOG143:25	H94
MGREC109:37	H2296	MGREC124:35	H2942	DIALOG143:40	H109
MGREC110:1	H2301	MGREC125:16	H2964	DIALOG144:7	H117
MGREC110:13	H2313	MGREC125:21	~~H2969~~	DIALOG145:11	H160
MGREC~~110:18~~	H2321	MGREC~~125:21~~	H2970	DIALOG145:12	H161
MGREC110:22	H2326	MGREC126:1	H2992	DIALOG146:3	H191
MGREC110:35	H2339	MGREC126:14	H3005	DIALOG146:9	H197
MGREC111:20	H2365	MGREC126:20	H3011	DIALOG146:11	H199
MGREC112:18	H2404	MGREC126:21	~~H3012~~	DIALOG146:19	H205
MGREC112:27	H2413	MGREC~~126:21~~	H3012	DIALOG146:32	H218
MGREC112:30	H2416	MGREC126:24	H3015	DIALOG146:37	H223
MGREC112:35	H2421	MGREC126:32	H3023	DIALOG147:15	H241
MGREC113:1	H2428	MGREC126:40	H3029	DIALOG147:20	H246
MGREC113:14	H2441	MGREC127:12	H3042	DIALOG148:18	H283
MGREC113:39	H2466	MGREC127:26	H3056	DIALOG148:32	H297
MGREC114:12	~~H2480~~	MGREC127:31	H3061	SIDNEY149:36	~~H23~~
MGREC~~114:12~~	H2480	MGREC128:8	H3081	SIDNEY150:1	H26
MGREC114:40	H2510	MGREC128:31	H3104	SIDNEY150:3	H28
MGREC115:3	H2514	MGREC129:11	H3125	SIDNEY150:5	H30
MGREC115:26	H2545	MGREC129:13	H3127	SIDNEY150:13	H48
MGREC115:38	H2557	MGREC129:17	H3131	SIDNEY150:13	H48
MGREC~~116:10~~	H2574	MGREC129:21	H3135	SIDNEY150:29	H56
MGREC116:15	H2581	MGREC129:23	H3137	SIDNEY150:31	H58
MGREC116:38	H2604	MGREC129:29	H3143	SIDNEY150:35	H62
MGREC117:8	H2615	MGREC130:1	H3156	SIDNEY151:4	~~H69~~
MGREC117:21	H2628	MGREC131:3	H3193	SIDNEY151:6	~~H69~~
MGREC117:24	H2631	MGREC131:20	H3212	SIDNEY151:14	~~H69~~
MGREC117:26	H2633	MGREC131:33	H3225	SIDNEY151:19	~~H69~~
MGREC117:28	H2635	MGREC~~132:6~~	H3240	SIDNEY151:21	H71
MGREC117:34	H2641	MGREC132:33	H3280	SIDNEY151:27	H75
MGREC117:37	H2644	MGREC133:34	H3324	SIDNEY152:5	~~H79~~
MGREC118:9	H2656	MGREC135:5	H3377	SIDNEY152:16	~~H85~~
MGREC118:26	H2675	MGREC135:13	H3385	DUBART153:2	H6
MGREC119:1	H2691	MGREC135:34	H3406	DUBART153:2	H6
MGREC119:3	H2693	MGREC135:37	H3409	DUBART153:10	H14
MGREC119:8	H2698	MGREC136:2	H3415	DUBART153:18	H22
MGREC120:1	H2732	MGREC136:3	H3416	DUBART153:24	H28

DUBART153:28 H32	CONTEM174:2 H203	MEDDM195:30 HP272
DUBART153:30 H34	CONTEM174:17 H216	MEDDM195:35 HP272
DUBART154:9 H54	CONTEM174:25 H223	MEDDM196:7 HP272
DUBART154:17 H62	CONTEM174:35 H232	MEDDM196:21 HP273
DUBART154:29 H74	FLESH175:11 H11	MEDDM196:22 HP273
DUBART154:34 H79	FLESH175:19 H19	MEDDM196:25 HP273
DUBART154:37 H82	FLESH175:24 H24	MEDDM196:29 HP273
DUBART155:8 H93	FLESH176:8 H48	MEDDM197:9 HP274
DUBART155:9 H94	FLESH176:10 H50	MEDDM197:23 HP275
QELIZ156:13 H40	FLESH176:34 H74	MEDDM198:14 HP276
QELIZ157:2 H70	FLESH177:1 H82	MEDDM198:16 HP276
QELIZ157:4 H72	FLESH177:4 H85	MEDDM198:18 HP276
QELIZ157:6 H74	FLESH177:24 H105	MEDDM198:22 HP276
QELIZ157:7 H75	AUTHOR178:4 H14	MEDDM198:28 HP277
QELIZ157:9 H77	AUTHOR178:9 H19	MEDDM198:29 HP277
QELIZ157:16 H84	SICKNES178:26 H9	MEDDM198:32 HP277
QELIZ157:21 H89	SICKNES178:30 H13	MEDDM198:33 HP277
QELIZ157:24 H92	SICKNES178:36 H19	MEDDM199:2 HP277
QELIZ157:30 H98	BIRTH179:30 H6	MEDDM199:16 HP278
QELIZ157:33 H101	1HUSB180:30 H9	MEDDM199:20 HP278
QELIZ157:35 H103	1LETTER181:8 H6	MEDDM199:21 HP278
QELIZ157:37 H105	1LETTER181:21 H19	MEDDM199:29 HP278
QELIZ157:38 H106	1LETTER181:22 H20	MEDDM200:17 HP279
QELIZ157:40 H108	1LETTER181:28 H26	MEDDM200:36 HP280
VANITY160:1 H11	1LETTER181:33 H3	MEDDM201:4 HP280
VANITY160:3 H13	2LETTER182:19 H25	MEDDM201:7 HP280
VANITY160:5 H15	2LETTER182:23 H29	MEDDM201:9 HP280
VANITY160:8 H18	2LETTER182:29 H35	MEDDM201:19 HP280
VANITY160:15 H25	2LETTER182:31 H37	MEDDM201:21 HP281
VANITY160:20 H30	3LETTER183:17 H19	MEDDM201:22 HP281
VANITY160:35 H45	3LETTER183:21 H23	MEDDM201:28 HP281
VANITY160:41 H51	3LETTER183:26 H28	MEDDM202:14 HP282
VANITY161:4 H55	3LETTER183:30 H32	MEDDM202:18 HP282
VANITY161:6 H57	VERSES184:3 H7	MEDDM202:19 HP282
TDUDLEY165:24 H26	VERSES184:9 H13	MEDDM202:22 HP282
TDUDLEY165:31 H33	VERSES184:10 H14	MEDDM202:23 HP282
TDUDLEY165:37 H39	CHILDRN186:7 H74	MEDDM202:26 HP282
DDUDLEY167:14 H11	CHILDRN186:9 H76	MEDDM202:34 HP282
CONTEM167:26 H3	CHILDRN186:15 H82	MEDDM202:36 HP282
CONTEM167:29 H6	ELIZB187:9 H17	MEDDM203:4 HP283
CONTEM169:16 H57	ANNEB187:24 H14	MEDDM203:12 HP283
CONTEM170:17 H89	ANNEB187:31 H21	MEDDM203:15 HP283
CONTEM170:25 H96	1SIMON188:2 H2-3	MEDDM203:22 HP283
CONTEM170:28 H99	1SIMON188:4 H5	MEDDM203:26 HP283
CONTEM171:24 H127	1SIMON188:9 H10	MEDDM203:31 HP284
CONTEM171:28 H130	MERCY188:30 H16	MEDDM203:34 HP284
CONTEM171:32 H134	MERCY188:34 H20	MEDDM204:27 HP285
CONTEM172:4 H141	2SIMON195:5 HP271	MEDDM204:29 HP285
CONTEM172:17 H152	2SIMON195:11 HP271	MEDDM205:4 HP285
CONTEM172:23 H157	MEDDM195:25 HP272	MEDDM205:14 HP286
CONTEM173:35 H199	MEDDM195:29 HP272	MEDDM205:18 HP286

AGES44:33	H366	MASSYR59:37	H261	MPERS77:5	H944
AGES44:41	H374	MASSYR60:7	H272	MPERS77:7	H946
AGES~~45:2~~	H375	MASSYR60:26	H291	MPERS77:23	H964
AGES~~45:4~~	H387	MASSYR61:18	H323	MPERS78:2	H983
AGES45:5	H389	MASSYR61:24	H329	MPERS78:7	H988
AGES45:6	H390	MASSYR62:8	H353	MPERS78:8	H989
AGES45:15	H397	MASSYR63:25	H410	MPERS78:21	H1002
AGES46:3	H434	MASSYR~~63:28~~	H414	MPERS78:24	H1005
SEASONS46:28	H4	MASSYR64:13	H437	MPERS78:28	H1009
SEASONS47:3	~~H17~~	MASSYR64:33	H457	MPERS78:41	H1022
SEASONS~~47:5~~	H21	MASSYR65:16	H481	MPERS79:1	H1023
SEASONS47:7	H23	MASSYR65:19	H484	MPERS79:4	H1026
SEASONS47:11	H27	MASSYR65:23	H488	MPERS79:32	H1058
SEASONS47:24	H40	MASSYR66:16	H522	MPERS79:33	H1059
SEASONS47:32	~~H47~~	MASSYR66:19	H525	MPERS80:5	H1072
SEASONS47:37	H49	MASSYR66:30	H536	MPERS80:34	H1101
SEASONS48:20	H73	MASSYR66:32	~~H538~~	MPERS81:5	H1113
SEASONS48:25	H78	MASSYR~~66:32~~	H538	MPERS81:8	H1116
SEASONS49:15	H106	MASSYR68:4	H590	MPERS81:10	H1118
SEASONS49:37	H130	MPERS69:12	H634	MPERS81:16	H1124
SEASONS50:10	H144	MPERS69:18	H640	MPERS81:39	~~H1143~~
SEASONS50:12	H146	MPERS69:22	H644	MPERS81:41	H1145
SEASONS50:13	H147	MPERS~~69:38~~	H667	MPERS~~82:2~~	H1148
SEASONS50:18	H152	MPERS~~70:2~~	H673	MPERS82:12	H1159
SEASONS50:20	H154	MPERS70:19	H690	MPERS82:13	H1160
SEASONS51:4	H178	MPERS~~70:37~~	H708	MPERS82:21	H1168
SEASONS51:14	H188	MPERS71:9	H725	MPERS83:2	H1190
SEASONS51:34	H210	MPERS71:24	H738	MPERS83:11	H1199
SEASONS52:3	~~H219~~	MPERS71:25	H739	MPERS83:21	H1209
SEASONS53:8	H264	MPERS71:36	H750	MPERS~~84:12~~	H1242
MASSYR53:16	H6	MPERS72:6	~~H755~~	MPERS84:15	H1251
MASSYR54:1	H28	MPERS72:19	H767	MPERS84:21	H1257
MASSYR54:3	H30	MPERS72:23	H771	MPERS84:25	H1261
MASSYR54:13	H40	MPERS72:26	~~H773~~	MPERS84:26	H1262
MASSYR54:26	H53	MPERS72:28	~~H773~~	MPERS84:27	H1263
MASSYR54:39	H66	MPERS73:3	H790	MPERS85:13	H1289
MASSYR55:11	H77	MPERS73:8	H795	MPERS85:17	H1293
MASSYR55:18	H84	MPERS73:40	H825	MPERS85:20	H1296
MASSYR55:29	H95	MPERS74:8	H833	MPERS85:34	H1310
MASSYR55:35	H101	MPERS74:18	H841	MPERS85:39	H1315
MASSYR56:25	H131	MPERS74:24	H847	MPERS86:2	H1318
MASSYR57:30	H175	MPERS74:36	~~H858~~	MPERS86:32	H1348
MASSYR58:14	H199	MPERS74:38	H859	MPERS86:39	H1355
MASSYR58:34	H217	MPERS75:3	H864	MPERS87:4	H1360
MASSYR58:37	H220	MPERS75:6	H867	MPERS87:10	H1366
MASSYR59:7	H231	MPERS75:13	H868	MPERS87:22	~~H1374~~
MASSYR59:8	H232	MPERS75:25	H874	MPERS87:28	H1380
MASSYR59:18	H242	MPERS75:26	H882	MPERS87:32	H1384
MASSYR~~59:20~~	H244	MPERS76:1	H883	MPERS87:35	H1387
MASSYR59:23	H247	MPERS76:26	H899	MPERS88:3	H1396
MASSYR59:33	H257	MPERS76:26	H924	MPERS88:12	H1405

MPERS88:15	H1408	MGREC101:27	H1952	MGREC116:39	H2605		
MPERS88:17	H1410	MGREC101:30	H1955	MGREC117:6	H2613		
MPERS88:29	H1422	MGREC102:30	H2000	MGREC117:22	H2629		
MPERS88:39	H1432	MGREC103:1	H2012	MGREC117:23	H2630		
MPERS89:22	H1456	MGREC103:10	H2021	MGREC118:12	H2659		
MPERS90:12	~~H1484~~	MGREC103:21	H2032	MGREC118:20	H2667		
MPERS90:17	~~H1484~~	MGREC104:11	H2063	MGREC~~118:24~~	H2673		
MPERS91:24	H1538	MGREC104:36	H2088	MGREC118:36	~~H2685~~		
MPERS91:27	~~H1541~~	MGREC105:31	H2124	MGREC~~118:36~~	H2685		
MPERS~~92:23~~	H1581	MGREC105:38	H2131	MGREC118:37	H2686		
MGREC6:34	H1631	MGREC~~106:2~~	H2136	MGREC118:41	H2690		
MGREC94:1	H1635	MGREC106:9	H2143	MGREC119:5	H2695		
MGREC94:12	H1646	MGREC106:14	H2148	MGREC119:9	H2699		
MGREC~~94:18~~	H1655	MGREC107:4	H2179	MGREC119:19	H2709		
MGREC94:23	H1661	MGREC107:19	H2194	MGREC119:22	H2712		
MGREC94:29	H1667	MGREC107:22	H2197	MGREC119:30	H2720		
MGREC94:32	H1670	MGREC107:30	H2205	MGREC119:33	H2723		
MGREC94:39	H1677	MGREC108:17	H2233	MGREC~~120:4~~	H2737		
MGREC95:11	H1690	MGREC109:37	H2296	MGREC~~120:20~~	H2757		
MGREC95:20	H1699	MGREC109:41	H2300	MGREC121:2	~~H2780~~		
MGREC95:27	H1706	MGREC110:2	H2302	MGREC122:1	H2824		
MGREC95:29	H1708	MGREC110:4	H2304	MGREC122:9	H2834		
MGREC95:36	H1715	MGREC110:16	H2316	MGREC122:15	H2840		
MGREC96:2	H1722	MGREC110:27	H2331	MGREC122:23	~~H2845~~		
MGREC96:8	H1728	MGREC110:28	H2332	MGREC122:35	H2856		
MGREC96:20	H1740	MGREC110:32	H2336	MGREC122:36	~~H2857~~		
MGREC96:33	H1753	MGREC110:33	H2337	MGREC123:5	H2867		
MGREC96:37	H1757	MGREC111:11	H2356	MGREC123:25	H2889		
MGREC97:3	H1764	MGREC112:26	H2412	MGREC123:41	H2905		
MGREC97:16	H1777	MGREC112:27	H2413	MGREC124:3	H2908		
MGREC97:31	H1792	MGREC112:28	H2414	MGREC124:6	~~H2911~~		
MGREC98:22	H1824	MGREC112:30	H2416	MGREC~~124:7~~	H2912		
MGREC98:26	H1828	MGREC112:34	H2420	MGREC~~124:10~~	H2915		
MGREC98:27	H1829	MGREC113:11	H2438	MGREC~~124:16~~	H2923		
MGREC98:34	H1836	MGREC113:13	H2440	MGREC125:6	H2954		
MGREC99:7	H1850	MGREC113:31	H2458	MGREC126:6	H2997		
MGREC99:18	H1861	MGREC113:36	H2463	MGREC126:22	H3013		
MGREC99:23	H1866	MGREC~~114:12~~	H2480	MGREC126:26	H3017		
MGREC100:4	H1888	MGREC114:13	H2483	MGREC126:28	H3019		
MGREC100:6	H1890	MGREC114:14	H2484	MGREC126:40	H3029		
MGREC100:16	H1900	MGREC114:22	H2492	MGREC127:9	H3039		
MGREC100:24	H1908	MGREC114:23	H2493	MGREC127:13	H3043		
MGREC100:27	H1911	MGREC115:8	~~H2518~~	MGREC127:24	H3054		
MGREC100:34	H1918	MGREC~~115:15~~	H2525	MGREC127:31	H3061		
MGREC100:36	~~H1920~~	MGREC115:23	H2542	MGREC128:14	H3087		
MGREC100:41	H1925	MGREC115:33	H2552	MGREC128:16	H3089		
MGREC101:1	H1926	MGREC115:36	H2555	MGREC128:38	H3111		
MGREC101:4	H1929	MGREC115:40	H2559	MGREC129:2	H3116		
MGREC101:6	H1931	MGREC116:14	H2580	MGREC129:10	H3124		
MGREC101:13	H1938	MGREC116:28	H2594	MGREC129:11	H3125		
MGREC101:20	H1945	MGREC116:38	H2604	MGREC129:18	H3132		

MGREC129:20	H3134	DIALOG146:14	~~H200~~	CONTEM174:11	H211
MGREC129:31	H3145	DIALOG146:25	H211	CONTEM174:18	H217
MGREC129:36	H3150	DIALOG146:26	H212	CONTEM174:19	H218
MGREC129:40	H3154	DIALOG146:33	~~H219~~	CONTEM174:24	H222
MGREC130:2	H3157	DIALOG146:34	H220	FLESH175:30	H30
MGREC130:4	H3159	DIALOG146:39	H225	FLESH175:37	H37
MGREC130:16	H3171	DIALOG146:40	H226	FLESH175:40	H40
MGREC130:17	H3172	DIALOG147:8	H234	FLESH176:6	H46
MGREC130:25	H3180	DIALOG147:41	H265	FLESH176:17	H57
MGREC130:40	H3185	DIALOG148:18	H283	FLESH176:21	H61
MGREC131:15	H3207	DIALOG148:19	H284	FLESH176:27	H67
MGREC131:27	H3219	DIALOG148:22	H287	FLESH177:10	H91
MGREC132:11	H3246	SIDNEY149:25	~~H23~~	FLESH177:16	H97
MGREC132:12	H3247	SIDNEY149:35	~~H23~~	FLESH177:18	H99
MGREC132:27	H3272	SIDNEY~~150:41~~	H69	FLESH177:20	H101
MGREC132:30	H3277	SIDNEY151:23	H73	FLESH177:22	H103
MGREC133:3	H3291	SIDNEY151:25	~~H73~~	FLESH177:25	H106
MGREC134:34	H3365	SIDNEY151:34	~~H75~~	FLESH177:26	H107
MGREC134:38	~~H3367~~	SIDNEY151:37	~~H75~~	AUTHOR177:38	H10
MGREC134:40	H3369	SIDNEY151:38	~~H75~~	AUTHOR178:13	H23
MGREC135:4	H3376	SIDNEY152:2	~~H75~~	AUTHOR178:14	H24
MGREC136:1	H3414	SIDNEY152:13	H82	SICKNES178:24	H7
MGREC136:3	H3416	SIDNEY152:17	H86	SICKNES178:30	H13
MGREC136:5	H3418	SIDNEY152:19	H88	SICKNES179:11	H31
MROMAN136:34	H3448	DUBART154:33	H78	BIRTH180:19	H29
MROMAN137:9	H3460	DUBART154:34	H79	1LETTER181:17	H15
MROMAN137:15	H3466	QELIZ156:12	H39	2LETTER181:32	H2
MROMAN137:26	H3477	QELIZ156:26	H53	2LETTER182:19	H25
MROMAN137:36	H3487	QELIZ157:7	H75	2LETTER182:21	H27
MROMAN138:6	H3496	QELIZ157:25	H93	3LETTER183:17	H19
MROMAN138:26	H3516	QELIZ158:16	H125	VERSES184:6	H10
MROMAN139:37	H3563	DAVID158:22	H1-2	CHILDRN185:7	H33
DIALOG142:13	H42	DAVID159:1	H16	CHILDRN186:20	H87
DIALOG142:26	H55	DAVID159:12	H27	ELIZB186:36	H8
DIALOG142:31	H60	DAVID159:14	H29	MERCY189:16	H37
DIALOG142:33	H62	DAVID159:23	H38	2SIMON195:1	HP271
DIALOG142:38	H67	VANITY159:38	H10	2SIMON195:6	HP271
DIALOG143:19	H88	VANITY160:6	H16	2SIMON195:8	HP271
DIALOG143:20	H89	VANITY160:32	H42	2SIMON195:13	HP271
DIALOG143:23	H92	TDUDLEY165:11	H13	MEDDM197:7	HP274
DIALOG143:33	H102	TDUDLEY165:31	H33	MEDDM197:9	HP274
DIALOG143:35	H104	TDUDLEY166:1	H43	MEDDM197:20	HP275
DIALOG143:40	H109	TDUDLEY166:3	H45	MEDDM197:32	HP275
DIALOG144:1	H111	TDUDLEY166:13	H55	MEDDM197:33	HP275
DIALOG144:2	H112	TDUDLEY166:14	H56	MEDDM198:2	HP275
DIALOG144:7	H117	TDUDLEY166:15	H57	MEDDM198:16	HP276
DIALOG144:12	H122	DDUDLEY167:21	H18	MEDDM198:17	HP276
DIALOG144:20	H130	CONTEM169:8	H50	MEDDM200:34	HP280
DIALOG145:5	H154	CONTEM172:4	H141	MEDDM201:26	HP281
DIALOG145:14	H163	CONTEM172:15	H150	MEDDM202:16	HP282
DIALOG145:34	H183	CONTEM172:31	H164	MEDDM202:23	HP282

from

AGES40:12	H193	MPERS83:15	H1203	MGREC~~122:32~~	H2852	
AGES40:20	H201	MPERS84:6	H1234	MGREC123:24	H2888	
AGES42:30	H286	MPERS84:10	H1238	MGREC127:15	H3045	
AGES44:18	H351	MPERS85:19	H1295	MGREC127:40	H3070	
AGES45:3	H381	MPERS86:27	H1343	MGREC128:18	H3091	
AGES~~45:4~~	H386	MPERS87:12	H1368	MGREC129:21	H3135	
AGES45:8	~~H390~~	MPERS88:7	H1400	MGREC~~132:6~~	H3239	
AGES~~45:22~~	H405	MPERS90:3	~~H1477~~	MGREC133:23	~~H3312~~	
AGES45:25	H415	MPERS91:19	H1527	MGREC135:3	H3375	
AGES46:8	H439	MPERS~~91:22~~	H1534	MGREC135:37	H3409	
SEASONS~~46:35~~	H13	MPERS~~92:27~~	H1585	MGREC135:38	H3410	
SEASONS47:31	~~H46~~	MPERS92:36	H1594	MGREC136:18	H3432	
SEASONS~~47:32~~	H47	MGREC6:26	H1623	MROMAN138:8	H3498	
SEASONS48:8	H61	MGREC6:29	H1626	MROMAN138:26	H3516	
SEASONS48:18	H71	MGREC94:40	H1678	MROMAN139:12	H3540	
SEASONS49:2	H93	MGREC95:1	H1680	MROMAN139:20	H3548	
SEASONS49:40	H133	MGREC97:2	H1763	DIALOG141:23	H22	
SEASONS50:1	H135	MGREC97:30	H1791	DIALOG142:9	H38	
SEASONS52:21	H236	MGREC98:4	H1806	DIALOG142:19	H48	
SEASONS52:37	H252	MGREC99:34	H1877	DIALOG142:27	H56	
MASSYR53:26	H16	MGREC100:1	H1885	DIALOG143:36	H105	
MASSYR54:38	H65	MGREC100:12	H1896	DIALOG144:4	H114	
MASSYR55:14	H80	MGREC100:18	H1902	DIALOG144:29	H137	
MASSYR55:16	H82	MGREC102:26	H1996	DIALOG148:10	H275	
MASSYR56:17	H123	MGREC102:39	H2009	DIALOG148:23	H288	
MASSYR58:22	H207	MGREC104:32	H2084	SIDNEY149:17	H16	
MASSYR58:33	H216	MGREC107:8	H2183	SIDNEY~~150:40~~	H68	
MASSYR60:28	H293	MGREC107:34	H2209	SIDNEY152:11	H80	
MASSYR60:31	H296	MGREC108:8	H2224	SIDNEY152:14	H83	
MASSYR60:32	H297	MGREC108:12	H2228	DUBART153:6	H10	
MASSYR61:22	H327	MGREC108:14	H2230	DUBART155:7	H92	
MASSYR62:12	H357	MGREC108:21	H2237	QELIZ156:4	H31	
MASSYR63:27	H412	MGREC108:27	H2243	QELIZ156:20	H47	
MASSYR63:33	H420	MGREC111:4	H2349	QELIZ158:9	H118	
MASSYR63:34	H421	MGREC111:29	H2374	DAVID159:5	H20	
MASSYR63:35	H422	MGREC111:38	H2383	DAVID159:7	H22	
MASSYR64:8	H432	MGREC113:1	H2428	VANITY160:33	H43	
MASSYR64:36	H460	MGREC113:32	H2459	VANITY160:35	H45	
MASSYR64:41	H465	MGREC114:9	H2477	TDUDLEY165:23	H25	
MASSYR65:25	H490	MGREC~~114:12~~	H2481	CONTEM168:23	H30	
MASSYR66:18	H524	MGREC114:38	H2508	CONTEM168:28	H35	
MASSYR66:31	H537	MGREC114:41	H2511	CONTEM170:2	H76	
MPERS69:4	H626	MGREC~~115:15~~	H2526	CONTEM170:16	H88	
MPERS69:8	H630	MGREC115:16	H2535	CONTEM170:36	H106	
MPERS69:28	H650	MGREC120:32	H2769	CONTEM174:1	H202	
MPERS78:27	H1008	MGREC121:3	H2781	CONTEM174:3	H204	
MPERS79:22	H1048	MGREC121:5	H2783	FLESH176:6	H46	
MPERS79:37	H1063	MGREC121:9	H2787	FLESH176:8	H48	
MPERS80:38	H1105	MGREC121:13	H2791	FLESH177:14	H95	
MPERS80:41	H1108	MGREC121:39	H2821	FLESH177:18	H99	
MPERS81:11	H1119	MGREC122:8	H2831	FLESH177:21	H102	

MPERS81:10	H1118	MPERS89:17	H1451	MGREC96:19	H1739
MPERS81:26	H1134	MPERS89:26	H1460	MGREC96:20	H1740
MPERS81:33	H1141	MPERS89:41	H1475	MGREC96:35	H1755
MPERS82:28	H1175	MPERS90:3	H1477	MGREC97:4	H1765
MPERS82:35	H1182	MPERS90:17	H1484	MGREC97:17	H1778
MPERS82:36	H1183	MPERS90:33	H1500	MGREC97:21	H1782
MPERS82:41	H1188	MPERS91:1	H1509	MGREC97:22	H1783
MPERS83:1	H1189	MPERS91:3	H1511	MGREC97:26	H1787
MPERS83:11	H1199	MPERS91:8	H1516	MGREC97:29	H1790
MPERS83:13	H1201	MPERS91:23	H1537	MGREC97:31	H1792
MPERS83:15	H1203	MPERS91:28	H1542	MGREC97:36	H1797
MPERS83:21	H1209	MPERS91:28	H1542	MGREC97:37	H1798
MPERS83:29	H1217	MPERS91:29	H1543	MGREC98:1	H1803
MPERS83:35	H1223	MPERS91:31	H1545	MGREC98:4	H1806
MPERS83:36	H1224	MPERS91:32	H1546	MGREC98:6	H1808
MPERS84:4	H1232	MPERS91:37	H1551	MGREC98:9	H1811
MPERS84:14	H1250	MPERS92:2	H1556	MGREC98:10	H1812
MPERS84:17	H1253	MPERS92:7	H1565	MGREC98:12	H1814
MPERS84:27	H1263	MPERS92:9	H1567	MGREC98:13	H1815
MPERS84:30	H1266	MPERS92:13	H1571	MGREC98:15	H1817
MPERS84:31	H1267	MPERS92:14	H1572	MGREC98:17	H1819
MPERS84:36	H1272	MPERS92:19	H1577	MGREC98:19	H1821
MPERS85:1	H1277	MPERS92:20	H1578	MGREC98:21	H1823
MPERS85:6	H1282	MPERS92:28	H1586	MGREC98:23	H1825
MPERS85:20	H1296	MPERS92:37	H1595	MGREC98:25	H1827
MPERS85:25	H1301	MGREC6:11	H1608	MGREC98:28	H1830
MPERS86:4	H1320	MGREC6:16	H1613	MGREC98:29	H1831
MPERS86:10	H1326	MGREC6:18	H1615	MGREC98:39	H1841
MPERS86:23	H1339	MGREC6:24	H1621	MGREC98:41	H1843
MPERS86:25	H1341	MGREC94:4	H1638	MGREC99:4	H1847
MPERS86:27	H1343	MGREC94:9	H1643	MGREC99:7	H1850
MPERS86:30	H1346	MGREC94:11	H1645	MGREC99:14	H1857
MPERS86:33	H1349	MGREC94:14	H1648	MGREC99:34	H1877
MPERS86:38	H1354	MGREC94:17	H1651	MGREC99:39	H1882
MPERS86:39	H1355	MGREC94:18	H1652	MGREC99:40	H1883
MPERS86:40	H1356	MGREC94:18	H1656	MGREC99:41	H1884
MPERS87:1	H1357	MGREC94:21	H1659	MGREC100:2	H1886
MPERS87:9	H1365	MGREC94:23	H1661	MGREC100:3	H1887
MPERS87:17	H1371	MGREC94:31	H1669	MGREC100:4	H1888
MPERS87:31	H1383	MGREC94:32	H1670	MGREC100:5	H1889
MPERS87:36	H1388	MGREC95:6	H1685	MGREC100:9	H1893
MPERS87:39	H1391	MGREC95:11	H1690	MGREC100:21	H1905
MPERS88:2	H1395	MGREC95:16	H1695	MGREC100:28	H1912
MPERS88:18	H1411	MGREC95:27	H1706	MGREC100:35	H1919
MPERS88:20	H1413	MGREC95:28	H1707	MGREC100:38	H1922
MPERS88:25	H1418	MGREC95:29	H1708	MGREC100:41	H1925
MPERS88:39	H1432	MGREC95:30	H1709	MGREC101:4	H1929
MPERS89:9	H1443	MGREC95:33	H1712	MGREC101:5	H1930
MPERS89:10	H1444	MGREC96:1	H1721	MGREC101:17	H1942
MPERS89:15	H1449	MGREC96:16	H1736	MGREC101:18	H1943
MPERS89:16	H1450	MGREC96:18	H1738	MGREC101:19	H1944

MGREC101:22	H1947	MGREC109:6	H2265	MGREC114:26	H2496
MGREC101:32	H1957	MGREC109:12	H2271	MGREC114:33	H2503
MGREC101:34	H1959	MGREC109:13	H2272	MGREC114:34	H2504
MGREC102:9	H1979	MGREC109:20	H2279	MGREC114:35	H2505
MGREC102:13	H1983	MGREC109:25	H2284	MGREC114:36	H2506
MGREC102:15	H1985	MGREC109:26	H2285	MGREC114:37	H2507
MGREC102:21	H1991	MGREC109:31	H2290	MGREC114:39	H2509
MGREC102:23	H1993	MGREC109:36	H2295	MGREC114:40	H2510
MGREC102:25	H1995	MGREC110:2	H2302	MGREC115:2	H2513
MGREC102:27	H1997	MGREC110:6	H2306	MGREC115:3	H2514
MGREC102:29	H1999	MGREC110:13	H2313	MGREC115:7	H2518
MGREC102:39	H2009	MGREC110:29	H2333	MGREC115:11	H2520
MGREC103:16	H2027	MGREC110:31	H2335	MGREC115:14	H2523
MGREC103:18	H2029	MGREC110:33	H2337	MGREC115:15	H2531
MGREC103:19	H2030	MGREC110:37	H2341	MGREC115:16	H2535
MGREC103:24	H2035	MGREC110:40	H2344	MGREC115:18	H2537
MGREC103:28	H2039	MGREC111:1	H2346	MGREC115:23	H2542
MGREC103:31	H2042	MGREC111:2	H2347	MGREC115:25	H2544
MGREC103:36	H2047	MGREC111:6	H2351	MGREC115:27	H2546
MGREC104:7	H2059	MGREC111:10	H2355	MGREC115:36	H2555
MGREC104:9	H2061	MGREC111:14	H2359	MGREC115:38	H2557
MGREC104:11	H2063	MGREC111:22	H2367	MGREC115:39	H2558
MGREC104:27	H2079	MGREC111:24	H2369	MGREC115:41	H2560
MGREC104:28	H2080	MGREC111:29	H2374	MGREC116:8	H2568
MGREC104:37	H2089	MGREC111:30	H2375	MGREC116:13	H2579
MGREC105:14	H2107	MGREC111:31	H2376	MGREC116:19	H2585
MGREC105:18	H2111	MGREC111:32	H2377	MGREC116:21	H2587
MGREC105:30	H2123	MGREC111:36	H2381	MGREC116:23	H2589
MGREC105:31	H2124	MGREC111:39	H2384	MGREC116:24	H2590
MGREC105:40	H2133	MGREC111:40	H2385	MGREC116:25	H2591
MGREC106:11	H2145	MGREC112:2	H2388	MGREC116:38	H2604
MGREC106:12	H2146	MGREC112:3	H2389	MGREC116:39	H2605
MGREC106:22	H2156	MGREC112:5	H2391	MGREC116:40	H2606
MGREC106:23	H2157	MGREC112:12	H2398	MGREC116:41	H2607
MGREC106:29	H2163	MGREC112:13	H2399	MGREC117:1	H2608
MGREC107:1	H2176	MGREC112:21	H2407	MGREC117:3	H2610
MGREC107:2	H2177	MGREC112:24	H2410	MGREC117:4	H2611
MGREC107:20	H2195	MGREC112:26	H2412	MGREC117:8	H2615
MGREC107:32	H2207	MGREC112:30	H2416	MGREC117:31	H2638
MGREC107:34	H2209	MGREC112:37	H2423	MGREC118:9	H2656
MGREC107:35	H2210	MGREC113:11	H2438	MGREC118:11	H2658
MGREC107:39	H2214	MGREC113:12	H2439	MGREC118:18	H2665
MGREC107:40	H2215	MGREC113:13	H2440	MGREC118:19	H2666
MGREC108:17	H2233	MGREC113:20	H2447	MGREC118:30	H2679
MGREC108:19	H2235	MGREC113:26	H2453	MGREC118:31	H2680
MGREC108:26	H2242	MGREC113:27	H2454	MGREC119:6	H2696
MGREC108:27	H2243	MGREC114:12	H2481	MGREC119:11	H2701
MGREC108:37	H2253	MGREC114:13	H2483	MGREC119:11	H2701
MGREC109:1	H2258	MGREC114:15	H2485	MGREC119:17	H2707
MGREC109:2	H2259	MGREC114:21	H2491	MGREC119:18	H2708
MGREC109:5	H2263	MGREC114:25	H2495	MGREC119:20	H2710

DUBART153:20	H24	MEDDM196:7	HP273	MEDDM204:23	HP285
DUBART153:31	H35	MEDDM196:8	HP273	MEDDM204:26	HP285
DUBART155:9	H94	MEDDM196:15	HP273	MEDDM204:28	HP285
VANITY159:30	H2	MEDDM196:17	HP273	MEDDM205:15	HP286
VANITY160:2	H12	MEDDM197:16	HP275	MEDDM205:17	HP286
VANITY160:16	H26	MEDDM197:26	HP275	MEDDM205:18	HP286
VANITY160:17	H27	MEDDM197:27	HP275	MEDDM205:20	HP286
VANITY160:21	H31	MEDDM197:29	HP275	MEDDM205:23	HP286
TDUDLEY165:15	H17	MEDDM197:32	HP275	MEDDM205:28	HP286
TDUDLEY165:20	H22	MEDDM198:3	HP275	MEDDM206:22	HP287
TDUDLEY165:36	H38	MEDDM198:6	HP276	MEDDM206:32	HP288
TDUDLEY165:37	H39	MEDDM198:9	HP276	MEDDM208:15	HP290
TDUDLEY165:38	H40	MEDDM198:10	HP276	MEDDM208:36	HP291
TDUDLEY165:39	H41	MEDDM198:14	HP276	MEDDM209:23	HP291
TDUDLEY166:3	H45	MEDDM199:13	HP277	PILGRIM210:11	H11
TDUDLEY166:11	H53	MEDDM199:29	HP278	PILGRIM210:13	H13
TDUDLEY166:13	H55	MEDDM200:2	HP278	PILGRIM210:17	H17
TDUDLEY166:14	H56	MEDDM200:19	HP279	MYCHILD216:5	HP241
TDUDLEY166:15	H57	MEDDM200:34	HP280	MYCHILD216:21	HP241
TDUDLEY166:17	H59	MEDDM201:1	HP280	MYCHILD216:27	HP242
CONTEM168:1	H11	MEDDM201:2	HP280	MYCHILD216:35	HP242
CONTEM168:3	H13	MEDDM201:3	HP280	MYCHILD217:17	HP243
CONTEM169:34	H72	MEDDM201:7	HP280	MYCHILD217:26	HP243
CONTEM170:18	H90	MEDDM201:8	HP280	MYCHILD218:4	HP243
CONTEM170:20	H92	MEDDM201:9	HP280	MYCHILD219:2	HP245
CONTEM170:22	H93	MEDDM202:3	HP281	BYNIGHT220:9	H9
CONTEM170:27	H98	MEDDM202:22	HP282	BYNIGHT220:13	H12
CONTEM170:28	H99	MEDDM202:23	HP282	MED223:10	HP250
CONTEM170:35	H105	MEDDM202:25	HP282	MED223:16	HP250
CONTEM171:29	H131	MEDDM202:26	HP282	WHAT224:13	H13
CONTEM174:1	H202	MEDDM203:7	HP283	WHAT224:17	H17
CONTEM174:15	H214	MEDDM203:10	HP283	WHAT224:19	H19
CONTEM174:21	H219	MEDDM203:11	HP283	28AUG225:31	HP254
CONTEM174:24	H222	MEDDM203:14	HP283	28AUG225:32	HP254
CONTEM174:35	H232	MEDDM203:15	HP283	28AUG225:33	HP254
SICKNES178:25	H8	MEDDM203:16	HP283	11MAYA226:24	HP255
DISTEMP179:22	H10	MEDDM203:17	HP283	30SEPT227:19	HP257
DISTEMP179:24	H12	MEDDM203:21	HP283	30SEPT227:26	HP257
2LETTER182:7	H13	MEDDM203:22	HP283	30SEPT227:31	HP257
2LETTER182:7	H13	MEDDM203:23	HP283	RESTOR229:32	H15
2LETTER182:9	H15	MEDDM203:24	HP283	SON230:24	H7
3LETTER183:22	H24	MEDDM203:25	HP283	SON231:2	H14
CHILDRN184:23	H12	MEDDM203:26	HP283	SON231:7	H19
CHILDRN185:6	H32	MEDDM203:27	HP284	SON231:13	H25
CHILDRN185:8	H34	MEDDM203:34	HP284	2HUSB232:11	H12
1SIMON188:7	H8	MEDDM204:3	HP284	2HUSB232:31	H32
1SIMON188:12	H13	MEDDM204:5	HP284	2HUSB233:2	H35
MERCY189:16	H37	MEDDM204:12	HP284	ACK235:14	H14
MEDDM195:26	HP272	MEDDM204:14	HP284	HOUSE236:31	H23
MEDDM195:30	HP272	MEDDM204:18	HP285	**HER (309)**	
MEDDM195:35	HP272	MEDDM204:21	HP285	FATHER5:1	H1

FATHER6:12	H46	HUMOUR35:5	H601	MPERS72:14	H762
ELEMEN8:9	H7	HUMOUR35:7	H603	MPERS77:7	H946
ELEMEN9:7	H41	AGES37:7	H69	MPERS77:8	H947
ELEMEN11:1	H121	AGES37:8	H70	MPERS82:27	H1174
ELEMEN11:4	H124	AGES37:14	H76	MPERS82:31	H1178
ELEMEN11:18	H138	AGES37:15	H77	MPERS82:32	H1179
ELEMEN11:21	H141	AGES40:9	H190	MPERS82:33	H1180
ELEMEN13:31	H232	AGES40:35	H214	MPERS82:38	H1185
ELEMEN14:7	H250	SEASONS46:35	H11	MPERS84:6	H1234
ELEMEN15:20	H302	SEASONS48:2	H55	MPERS84:7	H1235
ELEMEN17:29	H393	SEASONS48:7	H60	MPERS84:9	H1237
ELEMEN17:31	H395	SEASONS48:20	H73	MPERS84:10	H1238
ELEMEN19:6	H451	SEASONS48:24	H77	MPERS85:11	H1287
HUMOUR20:18	H10	SEASONS49:2	H93	MPERS85:12	H1288
HUMOUR20:23	H15	SEASONS49:2	H93	MPERS86:26	H1342
HUMOUR20:26	H18	SEASONS49:14	H105	MPERS91:22	H1532
HUMOUR20:30	H22	MASSYR54:39	H66	MGREC96:26	H1746
HUMOUR20:35	H27	MASSYR55:7	H73	MGREC99:1	H1844
HUMOUR21:41	H69	MASSYR55:8	H74	MGREC100:33	H1917
HUMOUR22:4	H73	MASSYR55:9	H75	MGREC100:34	H1918
HUMOUR22:5	H74	MASSYR55:13	H79	MGREC100:40	H1924
HUMOUR22:6	H75	MASSYR55:21	H87	MGREC102:34	H2004
HUMOUR22:7	H76	MASSYR55:23	H89	MGREC106:16	H2150
HUMOUR22:11	H80	MASSYR55:24	H90	MGREC106:19	H2153
HUMOUR22:13	H82	MASSYR55:27	H93	MGREC106:20	H2154
HUMOUR22:15	H84	MASSYR55:30	H96	MGREC112:1	H2387
HUMOUR22:33	H102	MASSYR55:31	H97	MGREC115:21	H2540
HUMOUR22:35	H104	MASSYR55:32	H98	MGREC115:22	H2541
HUMOUR22:37	H106	MASSYR55:32	H98	MGREC116:10	H2576
HUMOUR22:38	H107	MASSYR55:34	H100	MGREC117:32	H2639
HUMOUR25:18	H207	MASSYR55:35	H101	MGREC117:38	H2645
HUMOUR27:12	H283	MASSYR55:36	H102	MGREC119:9	H2699
HUMOUR27:13	H284	MASSYR56:20	H126	MGREC119:10	H2700
HUMOUR27:13	H284	MASSYR56:26	H132	MGREC122:15	H2840
HUMOUR27:24	H295	MASSYR56:28	H134	MGREC122:16	H2841
HUMOUR27:38	H309	MASSYR56:35	H141	MGREC122:17	H2842
HUMOUR28:2	H314	MASSYR56:36	H142	MGREC122:21	H2845
HUMOUR28:5	H317	MASSYR57:7	H154	MGREC122:24	H2845
HUMOUR28:9	H321	MASSYR57:26	H172	MGREC122:25	H2845
HUMOUR29:35	H386	MASSYR63:14	H399	MGREC122:26	H2845
HUMOUR30:22	H414	MASSYR63:26	H411	MGREC123:24	H2888
HUMOUR31:26	H459	MASSYR63:27	H412	MGREC123:25	H2889
HUMOUR31:28	H461	MASSYR64:29	H453	MGREC123:27	H2891
HUMOUR31:34	H467	MASSYR64:30	H454	MGREC123:37	H2901
HUMOUR31:39	H472	MASSYR64:33	H457	MGREC124:38	H2945
HUMOUR31:40	H473	MASSYR68:14	H600	MGREC124:40	H2947
HUMOUR31:41	H474	MPERS69:12	H634	MGREC125:4	H2952
HUMOUR32:23	H497	MPERS69:40	H670	MGREC125:6	H2954
HUMOUR32:40	H514	MPERS72:11	H759	MGREC125:7	H2955
HUMOUR34:6	H561	MPERS72:13	H761	MGREC125:9	H2957
HUMOUR35:4	H600	MPERS72:13	H761	MGREC125:11	H2959

MGREC125:13	H2961	DIALOG144:40	H148	CONTEM173:16	H183
MGREC125:15	H2963	DIALOG145:1	H150	FLESH175:6	H6
MGREC125:16	H2964	DIALOG147:17	H243	FLESH175:9	H9
MGREC125:21	H2970	DIALOG148:6	H271	AUTHOR177:29	H1
MGREC125:25	H2975	DIALOG148:9	H274	AUTHOR178:15	H25
MGREC125:27	H2977	DIALOG148:11	H276	DISTEMP179:18	H6
MGREC125:33	H2983	DIALOG148:12	H277	BIRTH179:26	H1-2
MGREC125:35	H2985	DIALOG148:19	H284	1LETTER181:1	H0
MGREC125:36	H2986	SIDNEY149:7	H6	2LETTER182:18	H24
MGREC126:6	H2997	SIDNEY149:8	H7	3LETTER182:36	H1
MGREC126:11	H3002	SIDNEY149:10	H9	3LETTER183:2	H4
MGREC126:12	H3003	SIDNEY150:41	H69	3LETTER183:9	H11
MGREC126:16	H3007	SIDNEY151:11	H69	3LETTER183:10	H12
MGREC126:22	H3013	DUBART153:26	H30	3LETTER183:16	H18
MGREC126:23	H3014	QELIZ156:2	H29	3LETTER183:18	H20
MGREC126:24	H3015	QELIZ156:5	H32	VERSES183:34	H1
MGREC126:33	H3023	QELIZ156:7	H34	CHILDRN184:13	H1-2
MGREC126:39	H3028	QELIZ156:22	H49	CHILDRN184:26	H15
MGREC126:40	H3029	QELIZ156:23	H50	CHILDRN184:27	H16
MGREC126:41	H3030	QELIZ156:25	H52	CHILDRN184:37	H26
MGREC127:2	H3032	QELIZ156:28	H55	CHILDRN185:2	H28
MGREC129:3	H3117	QELIZ156:31	H58	MERCY188:19	H4-5
MGREC129:9	H3123	QELIZ156:34	H61	MERCY188:35	H21
MGREC129:10	H3124	QELIZ156:36	H63	MERCY189:2	H23
MGREC129:11	H3125	QELIZ156:39	H66	MERCY189:4	H25
MGREC129:14	H3128	QELIZ156:40	H67	MERCY189:6	H27
MGREC129:15	H3129	QELIZ156:41	H68	MERCY189:9	H30
MGREC129:16	H3130	QELIZ157:1	H69	MEDDM200:15	Hp279
MGREC129:19	H3133	QELIZ157:4	H72	HANNA230:9	H1-2
MGREC130:8	H3163	QELIZ157:6	H74	HANNA230:17	H10
MGREC130:9	H3164	QELIZ157:9	H77	**HERS (4)**	
MGREC130:11	H3166	QELIZ157:13	H81	MPERS78:27	H1008
MGREC130:14	H3169	QELIZ157:15	H83	MPERS85:12	H1288
MGREC130:15	H3170	QELIZ157:17	H85	MGREC100:40	H1924
MGREC130:18	H3173	QELIZ157:19	H87	QELIZ156:19	H46
MGREC131:41	H3233	QELIZ157:20	H88	**HIM (306)**	
MGREC132:2	H3235	QELIZ157:27	H95	FATHER6:4	H38
MGREC134:37	H3367	QELIZ157:28	H96	PROLOG6:28	H12
MGREC134:38	H3367	QELIZ158:7	H116	HUMOUR21:24	H52
MGREC134:39	H3368	QELIZ158:20	H129	HUMOUR23:32	H142
MGREC135:2	H3374	DDUDLEY167:8	H4-5	HUMOUR28:4	H316
MGREC135:3	H3375	DDUDLEY167:13	H10	HUMOUR30:22	H414
MROMAN139:16	H3544	DDUDLEY167:16	H13	AGES39:9	H152
MROMAN139:17	H3545	DDUDLEY167:19	H16	SEASONS49:33	H126
MROMAN139:18	H3546	DDUDLEY167:20	H17	SEASONS52:12	H227
DIALOG142:32	H61	DDUDLEY167:22	H19	MASSYR53:30	H20
DIALOG143:14	H83	CONTEM168:26	H33	MASSYR54:3	H30
DIALOG144:36	H144	CONTEM170:7	H80	MASSYR54:6	H33
DIALOG144:37	H145	CONTEM170:8	H81	MASSYR55:27	H93
DIALOG144:38	H146	CONTEM170:11	H84	MASSYR58:16	H201
DIALOG144:39	H147	CONTEM170:24	H95	MASSYR58:28	H211

MASSYR59:3	H227	MPERS88:19	H1412	MGREC109:19	H2278
MASSYR62:5	H350	MPERS88:25	H1418	MGREC109:21	H2280
MASSYR62:7	H352	MPERS88:26	H1419	MGREC109:24	H2283
MASSYR63:13	H398	MPERS89:14	H1448	MGREC109:28	H2287
MASSYR63:24	H409	MPERS89:36	H1470	MGREC109:30	H2289
MASSYR64:28	H452	MPERS91:26	H1540	MGREC109:33	H2292
MASSYR65:20	H485	MPERS91:26	H1540	MGREC109:35	H2294
MASSYR65:21	H486	MPERS91:31	H1545	MGREC109:37	H2296
MASSYR65:22	H487	MPERS92:5	H1560	MGREC110:2	H2302
MASSYR65:25	H490	MPERS92:8	H1566	MGREC110:3	H2303
MASSYR65:31	H496	MPERS92:10	H1568	MGREC110:18	H2321
MASSYR66:29	H535	MPERS92:14	H1572	MGREC110:20	H2324
MASSYR68:8	H594	MPERS92:17	H1575	MGREC112:34	H2420
MASSYR68:19	H605	MPERS92:20	H1578	MGREC113:2	H2429
MASSYR68:26	H612	MPERS92:35	H1593	MGREC113:4	H2431
MASSYR68:29	H615	MPERS93:4	H1601	MGREC113:33	H2460
MPERS68:36	H622	MGREC6:28	H1625	MGREC114:10	H2478
MPERS69:2	H624	MGREC6:29	H1626	MGREC114:12	H2480
MPERS69:25	H647	MGREC6:32	H1629	MGREC114:12	H2482
MPERS69:38	H665	MGREC94:3	H1637	MGREC114:20	H2490
MPERS70:2	H673	MGREC94:24	H1662	MGREC114:22	H2492
MPERS70:2	H673	MGREC94:26	H1664	MGREC115:8	H2518
MPERS70:3	H674	MGREC94:27	H1665	MGREC115:17	H2536
MPERS71:15	H729	MGREC94:28	H1666	MGREC115:20	H2539
MPERS72:20	H768	MGREC94:29	H1667	MGREC116:4	H2564
MPERS72:29	H773	MGREC94:33	H1671	MGREC116:18	H2584
MPERS72:41	H787	MGREC95:37	H1716	MGREC116:28	H2594
MPERS74:17	H840	MGREC96:17	H1737	MGREC117:2	H2609
MPERS74:31	H854	MGREC97:31	H1792	MGREC118:5	H2652
MPERS75:5	H866	MGREC98:14	H1816	MGREC118:6	H2653
MPERS75:8	H869	MGREC98:41	H1843	MGREC118:7	H2654
MPERS75:31	H888	MGREC99:6	H1849	MGREC118:31	H2680
MPERS76:24	H922	MGREC99:36	H1879	MGREC119:19	H2709
MPERS79:1	H1023	MGREC99:38	H1881	MGREC120:26	H2763
MPERS79:22	H1048	MGREC100:8	H1892	MGREC120:29	H2766
MPERS79:35	H1061	MGREC101:3	H1928	MGREC121:3	H2781
MPERS80:33	H1100	MGREC101:21	H1946	MGREC121:15	H2793
MPERS82:25	H1172	MGREC101:26	H1951	MGREC121:18	H2800
MPERS82:26	H1173	MGREC103:30	H2041	MGREC121:19	H2801
MPERS83:6	H1194	MGREC104:6	H2058	MGREC121:39	H2821
MPERS83:7	H1195	MGREC104:12	H2064	MGREC122:18	H2843
MPERS83:12	H1200	MGREC104:18	H2070	MGREC122:36	H2857
MPERS84:23	H1259	MGREC104:22	H2074	MGREC122:38	H2859
MPERS85:6	H1282	MGREC104:23	H2075	MGREC123:1	H2863
MPERS85:7	H1283	MGREC104:38	H2090	MGREC123:7	H2869
MPERS86:1	H1317	MGREC104:41	H2093	MGREC123:9	H2871
MPERS86:2	H1318	MGREC105:2	H2095	MGREC123:17	H2881
MPERS86:3	H1319	MGREC105:3	H2096	MGREC123:40	H2904
MPERS86:19	H1335	MGREC105:10	H2103	MGREC123:41	H2905
MPERS87:26	H1378	MGREC105:22	H2115	MGREC124:1	H2906
MPERS87:30	H1382	MGREC108:25	H2241	MGREC124:5	H2910

MGREC124:10	H2915	2LETTER182:27	H33	30SEPT227:20	HP257
MGREC124:16	H2923	2LETTER182:31	H37	30SEPT227:31	HP257
MGREC124:19	H2926	2LETTER182:34	H40	30SEPT227:32	HP257
MGREC124:38	H2945	3LETTER183:21	H23	30SEPT227:33	HP257
MGREC124:41	H2948	1SIMON188:8	H9	SAMUEL228:6	H7
MGREC125:5	H2953	MERCY189:14	H35	SAMUEL228:7	H8
MGREC126:21	H3012	MEDDM196:23	HP273	SAMUEL228:9	H10
MGREC127:8	H3038	MEDDM197:16	HP275	SAMUEL228:13	H14
MGREC127:12	H3042	MEDDM199:29	HP278	SAMUEL228:20	H21
MGREC128:21	H3094	MEDDM202:14	HP282	RESTOR229:25	H8
MGREC128:24	H3097	MEDDM202:36	HP282	RESTOR229:26	H9
MGREC128:30	H3103	MEDDM203:11	HP283	RESTOR229:28	H11
MGREC128:34	H3107	MEDDM203:16	HP283	RESTOR230:5	H20
MGREC129:36	H3150	MEDDM203:23	HP283	SON230:20	H3
MGREC130:14	H3169	MEDDM203:25	HP283	SON230:24	H7
MGREC132:6	H3239	MEDDM203:26	HP283	SON230:28	H11
MGREC132:17	H3254	MEDDM203:28	HP284	SON231:4	H16
MGREC132:20	H3264	MEDDM203:35	HP284	SON231:12	H24
MGREC133:3	H3291	MEDDM204:7	HP284	SON231:15	H27
MGREC133:5	H3293	MEDDM204:12	HP284	SON231:21	H33
MGREC133:23	H3312	MEDDM204:22	HP285	SON231:22	H34
MGREC133:24	H3314	MEDDM204:27	HP285	2HUSB233:12	H45
MGREC134:7	H3339	MEDDM204:28	HP285	ACK235:11	H11
MGREC134:15	H3346	MEDDM204:29	HP285	ACK235:14	H14
MGREC134:30	H3361	MEDDM204:30	HP285	ACK235:17	H17
MGREC134:37	H3367	MEDDM205:29	HP286	HOUSE237:22	H52
MGREC134:41	H3370	MEDDM207:8	HP288	**HIS** (1396) See also AFTER'S,
MROMAN136:33	H3447	MEDDM208:34	HP290	NOR'S, THEN'S
MROMAN137:33	H3484	PILGRIM210:8	H8	FATHER6:4	H38
DIALOG148:24	H289	PILGRIM210:10	H10	FATHER6:7	H41
SIDNEY150:12	H41	PILGRIM210:16	H16	PROLOG7:10	H24
SIDNEY151:17	H69	MYCHILD216:6	HP241	ELEMEN9:14	H48
DUBART154:11	H56	MYCHILD216:16	HP241	ELEMEN9:15	H49
DUBART155:7	H92	MYCHILD216:22	HP241-2	ELEMEN9:30	H64
TDUDLEY165:12	H14	MYCHILD216:27	HP242	ELEMEN9:34	H68
TDUDLEY165:15	H17	MYCHILD217:8	HP242	ELEMEN9:36	H70
TDUDLEY165:18	H20	MYCHILD217:13	HP242	ELEMEN9:37	H71
TDUDLEY165:26	H28	MYCHILD217:14	HP242	ELEMEN10:3	H78
TDUDLEY165:39	H41	BYNIGHT220:7	H7	ELEMEN10:4	H79
TDUDLEY166:19	H61	BYNIGHT220:8	H8	ELEMEN10:22	H97
TDUDLEY166:20	H62	BYNIGHT220:19	H17	ELEMEN12:20	H180
TDUDLEY167:2	H84	BYNIGHT220:20	H18	ELEMEN12:26	H186
CONTEM170:12	H85	FEVER221:14	H29	ELEMEN13:24	H225
CONTEM170:27	H98	MED223:17	HP250	ELEMEN14:4	H246
CONTEM170:36	H106	JULY223:29	HP251	ELEMEN15:10	H292
CONTEM174:11	H211	WHAT224:1	H1	ELEMEN15:13	H295
CONTEM174:18	H217	MYSOUL224:26	H2	ELEMEN15:14	H296
CONTEM174:25	H223	MYSOUL224:28	H4	ELEMEN15:15	H297
1LETTER181:24	H22	28AUG226:3	HP254	ELEMEN16:27	H350
2LETTER182:4	H10	11MAYA226:15	HP255	ELEMEN16:28	H351
2LETTER182:15	H21	13MAY226:33	H9	ELEMEN16:29	H352

ELEMEN16:30	H353	SEASONS47:12	H28	MASSYR55:5	H71
ELEMEN17:4	H368	SEASONS47:13	H29	MASSYR55:15	H81
ELEMEN18:3	H407	SEASONS47:24	H40	MASSYR56:25	H131
ELEMEN18:4	H408	SEASONS47:30	H45	MASSYR56:27	H133
ELEMEN18:10	H414	SEASONS47:31	H46	MASSYR57:2	H149
ELEMEN18:12	H416	SEASONS47:32	H47	MASSYR57:4	H151
ELEMEN19:27	H472	SEASONS48:3	H56	MASSYR57:5	H152
HUMOUR21:14	H42	SEASONS48:12	H65	MASSYR57:6	H153
HUMOUR21:22	H50	SEASONS48:14	H67	MASSYR57:10	H157
HUMOUR21:24	H52	SEASONS48:15	H68	MASSYR57:15	H162
HUMOUR22:30	H99	SEASONS48:22	H75	MASSYR57:16	H163
HUMOUR26:16	H246	SEASONS48:28	H81	MASSYR57:25	H172
HUMOUR28:15	H327	SEASONS48:29	H82	MASSYR57:30	H175
HUMOUR28:22	H334	SEASONS49:6	H97	MASSYR58:2	H187
HUMOUR30:22	H414	SEASONS49:8	H99	MASSYR58:5	H190
HUMOUR30:23	H415	SEASONS49:9	H100	MASSYR58:6	H191
HUMOUR32:8	H482	SEASONS49:10	H101	MASSYR58:8	H193
AGES35:20	H6	SEASONS49:39	H132	MASSYR58:9	H194
AGES35:21	H7	SEASONS50:2	H136	MASSYR58:11	H196
AGES35:28	H14	SEASONS50:14	H148	MASSYR58:12	H197
AGES35:29	H15	SEASONS50:25	H159	MASSYR58:20	H205
AGES35:33	H19	SEASONS50:25	H159	MASSYR58:26	H209
AGES35:34	H20	SEASONS50:26	H160	MASSYR58:28	H211
AGES35:36	H22	SEASONS50:30	H164	MASSYR58:29	H212
AGES36:3	H27	SEASONS50:33	H167	MASSYR58:41	H224
AGES36:4	H28	SEASONS50:35	H169	MASSYR59:2	H226
AGES36:7	H31	SEASONS50:36	H170	MASSYR59:2	H226
AGES36:12	H36	SEASONS51:23	H199	MASSYR59:10	H234
AGES36:15	H39	SEASONS51:30	H206	MASSYR59:12	H236
AGES36:17	H41	SEASONS51:31	H207	MASSYR59:19	H243
AGES36:18	H42	SEASONS51:33	H209	MASSYR59:29	H253
AGES36:20	H44	SEASONS51:37	H213	MASSYR59:30	H254
AGES36:21	H45	SEASONS52:19	H234	MASSYR59:36	H260
AGES36:25	H49	SEASONS52:27	H242	MASSYR59:39	H263
AGES36:27	H51	SEASONS52:37	H252	MASSYR59:41	H265
AGES36:31	H55	MASSYR53:17	H7	MASSYR60:8	H273
AGES38:6	H109	MASSYR53:18	H8	MASSYR60:9	H274
AGES40:35	H214	MASSYR53:21	H11	MASSYR60:11	H276
AGES41:2	H222	MASSYR53:22	H12	MASSYR60:16	H281
AGES42:30	H286	MASSYR53:25	H15	MASSYR60:26	H291
AGES43:14	H307	MASSYR53:28	H18	MASSYR60:35	H300
AGES43:38	H333	MASSYR53:36	H26	MASSYR61:4	H309
AGES44:21	H354	MASSYR53:37	H27	MASSYR61:6	H311
AGES45:2	H380	MASSYR54:13	H40	MASSYR61:7	H312
AGES45:13	H395	MASSYR54:14	H41	MASSYR61:9	H314
AGES45:22	H405	MASSYR54:16	H43	MASSYR61:10	H315
SEASONS46:32	H8	MASSYR54:17	H44	MASSYR61:12	H317
SEASONS47:6	H22	MASSYR54:19	H46	MASSYR61:16	H321
SEASONS47:7	H23	MASSYR54:26	H53	MASSYR61:19	H324
SEASONS47:8	H24	MASSYR54:28	H55	MASSYR61:25	H330
SEASONS47:11	H27	MASSYR54:31	H58	MASSYR61:26	H331

MASSYR61:28	H333	MASSYR66:25	H531	MPERS70:2	~~H673~~
MASSYR61:31	H336	MASSYR66:27	H533	MPERS~~70:2~~	H673
MASSYR61:35	H340	MASSYR66:28	H534	MPERS~~70:3~~	H674
MASSYR61:36	H341	MASSYR66:30	H536	MPERS70:10	H681
MASSYR61:37	H342	MASSYR~~66:32~~	H538	MPERS70:15	H686
MASSYR61:40	H345	MASSYR66:34	H540	MPERS70:24	H695
MASSYR62:3	H348	MASSYR66:36	H542	MPERS70:25	H696
MASSYR62:5	H350	MASSYR66:40	H546	MPERS70:30	H701
MASSYR62:6	H351	MASSYR67:3	H549	MPERS70:36	H707
MASSYR62:9	H354	MASSYR67:4	H550	MPERS70:38	H709
MASSYR62:17	H362	MASSYR67:12	H558	MPERS70:41	~~H712~~
MASSYR62:19	H364	MASSYR67:14	H560	MPERS~~70:41~~	H712
MASSYR62:33	H378	MASSYR67:18	H564	MPERS~~71:4~~	H717
MASSYR62:38	H383	MASSYR67:19	H565	MPERS71:6	H722
MASSYR62:40	H385	MASSYR67:23	H569	MPERS71:7	H723
MASSYR63:2	H387	MASSYR67:25	H571	MPERS71:8	H724
MASSYR63:7	H392	MASSYR67:26	H572	MPERS71:9	H725
MASSYR63:8	H393	MASSYR67:27	H573	MPERS71:11	H727
MASSYR63:14	H399	MASSYR67:29	H575	MPERS71:14	H728
MASSYR63:16	H401	MASSYR67:31	H577	MPERS71:19	H733
MASSYR63:32	H419	MASSYR67:32	H578	MPERS71:20	H734
MASSYR63:35	H422	MASSYR67:35	H581	MPERS71:23	H737
MASSYR64:9	H433	MASSYR67:36	H582	MPERS71:24	H738
MASSYR64:10	H434	MASSYR67:37	H583	MPERS71:26	H740
MASSYR64:12	H436	MASSYR67:38	H584	MPERS71:29	H743
MASSYR64:13	H437	MASSYR67:39	H585	MPERS71:33	H747
MASSYR64:15	H439	MASSYR67:40	H586	MPERS71:36	H750
MASSYR64:18	H442	MASSYR68:2	H588	MPERS72:1	~~H753~~
MASSYR64:20	H444	MASSYR68:15	H601	MPERS72:3	~~H755~~
MASSYR64:21	H445	MASSYR68:19	H605	MPERS~~72:3~~	H755
MASSYR65:7	H472	MASSYR68:20	H606	MPERS72:5	~~H755~~
MASSYR65:8	H473	MASSYR68:21	H607	MPERS~~72:9~~	H757
MASSYR65:11	H476	MASSYR68:22	H608	MPERS72:10	H758
MASSYR65:12	H477	MASSYR68:24	H610	MPERS72:12	H760
MASSYR65:15	H480	MASSYR68:26	H612	MPERS72:20	H768
MASSYR65:16	H481	MASSYR68:26	H612	MPERS72:21	H769
MASSYR65:19	H484	MASSYR68:28	H614	MPERS~~72:24~~	H772
MASSYR65:21	H486	MPERS68:34	H620	MPERS72:26	~~H773~~
MASSYR65:24	H489	MPERS68:35	H621	MPERS72:27	~~H773~~
MASSYR65:25	H490	MPERS69:8	H630	MPERS72:28	~~H773~~
MASSYR65:26	H491	MPERS69:12	H634	MPERS72:33	H777
MASSYR65:28	H493	MPERS69:15	H637	MPERS72:34	H778
MASSYR65:32	H497	MPERS69:16	H638	MPERS72:37	H781
MASSYR65:33	H498	MPERS69:17	H639	MPERS72:39	H785
MASSYR65:35	H500	MPERS69:19	H641	MPERS72:40	H786
MASSYR65:39	H504	MPERS69:29	H651	MPERS73:1	H788
MASSYR66:2	H508	MPERS69:32	H654	MPERS73:3	H790
MASSYR66:6	H512	MPERS69:37	~~H659~~	MPERS73:8	H795
MASSYR66:16	H522	MPERS69:38	~~H660~~	MPERS73:14	H801
MASSYR66:21	H527	MPERS~~69:38~~	H660	MPERS73:22	H809
MASSYR66:23	H529	MPERS70:1	H672	MPERS73:23	~~H809~~

MPERS73:24	~~H809~~	MPERS78:3	H984	MPERS83:7	H1195
MPERS74:12	~~H836~~	MPERS78:5	H986	MPERS83:8	H1196
MPERS74:13	~~H836~~	MPERS78:7	H988	MPERS83:10	H1198
MPERS74:17	H840	MPERS78:15	H996	MPERS83:11	H1199
MPERS74:21	H844	MPERS78:24	H1005	MPERS83:18	H1206
MPERS74:23	H846	MPERS78:33	H1014	MPERS83:22	H1210
MPERS74:30	H853	MPERS78:38	H1019	MPERS83:39	H1227
MPERS~~74:31~~	H854	MPERS79:1	H1023	MPERS84:1	H1229
MPERS74:38	H859	MPERS~~79:2~~	H1024	MPERS~~84:12~~	H1241
MPERS74:39	H860	MPERS~~79:3~~	H1025	MPERS84:17	H1253
MPERS74:40	H861	MPERS79:4	H1026	MPERS84:18	H1254
MPERS75:3	H864	MPERS79:13	~~H1035~~	MPERS84:18	H1254
MPERS75:5	H866	MPERS79:15	H1041	MPERS84:20	H1256
MPERS75:7	H868	MPERS79:16	H1042	MPERS84:23	H1259
MPERS75:16	H877	MPERS79:18	H1044	MPERS84:24	H1260
MPERS75:24	H881	MPERS79:19	H1045	MPERS84:27	H1263
MPERS75:29	H886	MPERS79:25	H1051	MPERS84:28	H1264
MPERS75:38	H895	MPERS79:27	H1053	MPERS84:30	H1266
MPERS76:3	H901	MPERS79:28	H1054	MPERS84:32	H1268
MPERS76:4	H902	MPERS79:31	H1057	MPERS84:33	H1269
MPERS76:5	H903	MPERS79:32	H1058	MPERS84:35	H1271
MPERS76:6	H904	MPERS80:17	H1084	MPERS84:37	H1273
MPERS76:7	H905	MPERS80:22	H1089	MPERS84:40	H1276
MPERS76:9	H907	MPERS80:24	H1091	MPERS85:1	H1277
MPERS76:19	H917	MPERS80:25	H1092	MPERS85:2	H1278
MPERS76:20	H918	MPERS80:29	H1096	MPERS85:5	H1281
MPERS76:22	H920	MPERS80:32	H1099	MPERS85:6	H1282
MPERS76:25	H923	MPERS80:34	H1101	MPERS85:7	~~H1283~~
MPERS76:37	H935	MPERS80:35	H1102	MPERS~~85:7~~	H1283
MPERS76:38	H936	MPERS80:37	H1104	MPERS85:15	H1291
MPERS76:39	H937	MPERS80:38	H1105	MPERS85:27	H1303
MPERS76:40	H938	MPERS81:4	H1112	MPERS85:29	H1305
MPERS76:41	H939	MPERS81:5	H1113	MPERS85:31	H1307
MPERS77:1	H940	MPERS81:7	H1115	MPERS85:32	H1308
MPERS77:1	H940	MPERS81:8	H1116	MPERS85:33	H1309
MPERS77:5	H944	MPERS81:24	H1132	MPERS85:38	H1314
MPERS77:6	H945	MPERS81:31	H1139	MPERS85:39	H1315
MPERS77:9	H948	MPERS81:32	H1140	MPERS85:40	H1316
MPERS77:10	H949	MPERS81:33	H1141	MPERS86:4	H1320
MPERS77:11	H950	MPERS82:15	H1162	MPERS86:5	H1321
MPERS77:13	H952	MPERS82:21	H1168	MPERS86:7	H1323
MPERS~~77:16~~	H956	MPERS82:22	H1169	MPERS86:9	H1325
MPERS77:17	H958	MPERS82:23	H1170	MPERS86:10	H1326
MPERS77:19	H960	MPERS82:27	H1174	MPERS86:11	H1327
MPERS77:25	H966	MPERS82:33	H1180	MPERS86:12	H1328
MPERS77:29	H970	MPERS82:34	H1181	MPERS86:13	H1329
MPERS77:31	H972	MPERS83:1	H1189	MPERS86:15	H1331
MPERS77:32	H973	MPERS83:2	H1190	MPERS86:16	H1332
MPERS77:36	H977	MPERS83:3	H1191	MPERS86:17	H1333
MPERS77:37	H978	MPERS83:5	H1193	MPERS86:18	H1334
MPERS77:38	H979	MPERS83:6	H1194	MPERS86:21	H1337

MPERS86:23	H1339	MPERS91:28	H1542	MGREC96:13	H1733
MPERS86:35	H1351	MPERS91:29	H1543	MGREC96:13	H1733
MPERS87:8	H1364	MPERS91:30	H1544	MGREC96:16	H1736
MPERS87:9	H1365	MPERS91:35	H1549	MGREC96:37	H1757
MPERS87:10	H1366	MPERS91:35	H1549	MGREC96:38	H1758
MPERS87:12	H1368	MPERS91:36	H1550	MGREC97:2	H1763
MPERS87:13	H1369	MPERS91:37	H1551	MGREC97:3	H1764
MPERS87:16	H1370	MPERS92:3	H1557	MGREC97:9	H1770
MPERS87:18	H1372	MPERS92:5	H1557	MGREC97:13	H1774
MPERS87:20	H1374	MPERS92:5	H1563	MGREC97:25	H1786
MPERS87:22	H1374	MPERS92:7	H1565	MGREC97:32	H1793
MPERS87:29	H1381	MPERS92:18	H1576	MGREC97:33	H1794
MPERS87:32	H1384	MPERS92:21	H1579	MGREC97:34	H1795
MPERS87:35	H1387	MPERS92:23	H1581	MGREC97:39	H1800
MPERS87:37	H1389	MPERS92:25	H1583	MGREC97:40	H1801
MPERS87:38	H1390	MPERS93:1	H1598	MGREC98:7	H1809
MPERS87:39	H1391	MPERS93:2	H1599	MGREC98:10	H1812
MPERS88:1	H1394	MGREC6:12	H1609	MGREC98:14	H1816
MPERS88:3	H1396	MGREC6:14	H1611	MGREC98:16	H1818
MPERS88:19	H1412	MGREC6:17	H1614	MGREC98:30	H1832
MPERS88:22	H1415	MGREC6:20	H1617	MGREC98:34	H1836
MPERS88:26	H1419	MGREC6:24	H1621	MGREC98:41	H1843
MPERS88:28	H1421	MGREC6:25	H1622	MGREC99:4	H1847
MPERS88:30	H1423	MGREC6:28	H1625	MGREC99:7	H1850
MPERS88:40	H1433	MGREC6:29	H1626	MGREC99:15	H1858
MPERS89:7	H1441	MGREC6:33	H1630	MGREC99:24	H1867
MPERS89:9	H1443	MGREC6:36	H1633	MGREC99:26	H1869
MPERS89:13	H1447	MGREC6:37	H1634	MGREC99:36	H1879
MPERS89:16	H1450	MGREC94:6	H1640	MGREC100:6	H1890
MPERS89:18	H1452	MGREC94:7	H1641	MGREC100:10	H1894
MPERS89:19	H1453	MGREC94:12	H1646	MGREC100:16	H1900
MPERS89:21	H1455	MGREC94:14	H1648	MGREC100:17	H1901
MPERS89:22	H1456	MGREC94:16	H1650	MGREC100:26	H1910
MPERS89:33	H1467	MGREC94:17	H1651	MGREC100:27	H1911
MPERS89:37	H1471	MGREC94:18	H1654	MGREC100:30	H1914
MPERS90:27	H1494	MGREC94:19	H1657	MGREC101:2	H1927
MPERS90:33	H1500	MGREC94:24	H1662	MGREC101:6	H1931
MPERS90:36	H1503	MGREC94:29	H1667	MGREC101:13	H1938
MPERS90:39	H1506	MGREC94:30	H1668	MGREC101:15	H1940
MPERS90:40	H1507	MGREC94:31	H1669	MGREC101:18	H1943
MPERS90:41	H1508	MGREC94:40	H1678	MGREC101:20	H1945
MPERS91:4	H1512	MGREC95:5	H1684	MGREC101:29	H1954
MPERS91:20	H1528	MGREC95:11	H1690	MGREC101:33	H1958
MPERS91:21	H1529	MGREC95:13	H1692	MGREC101:34	H1959
MPERS91:23	H1537	MGREC95:15	H1694	MGREC102:3	H1973
MPERS91:24	H1538	MGREC95:23	H1702	MGREC102:4	H1974
MPERS91:25	H1539	MGREC95:24	H1703	MGREC102:23	H1993
MPERS91:26	H1540	MGREC95:29	H1708	MGREC102:27	H1997
MPERS91:26	H1540	MGREC95:31	H1710	MGREC102:28	H1998
MPERS91:27	H1541	MGREC95:38	H1717	MGREC102:41	H2011
MPERS91:27	H1541	MGREC95:41	H1720	MGREC103:1	H2012

MGREC103:3	H2014	MGREC106:34	H2168	MGREC110:19	H2323
MGREC103:16	H2027	MGREC106:35	H2169	MGREC110:20	H2324
MGREC103:20	H2031	MGREC106:37	H2171	MGREC110:22	H2326
MGREC103:23	H2034	MGREC106:40	H2174	MGREC110:25	H2329
MGREC103:31	H2042	MGREC106:41	H2175	MGREC110:27	H2331
MGREC103:32	H2043	MGREC107:3	H2178	MGREC110:28	H2332
MGREC103:34	H2045	MGREC107:7	H2182	MGREC110:29	H2333
MGREC103:36	H2047	MGREC107:8	H2183	MGREC110:30	H2334
MGREC103:39	H2050	MGREC107:9	H2184	MGREC110:34	H2338
MGREC103:40	H2051	MGREC107:10	H2185	MGREC110:36	H2340
MGREC104:2	H2054	MGREC107:20	H2195	MGREC110:38	H2342
MGREC104:4	H2056	MGREC107:32	H2207	MGREC110:40	H2344
MGREC104:5	H2057	MGREC107:34	H2209	MGREC110:41	H2345
MGREC104:7	H2059	MGREC107:38	H2213	MGREC111:1	H2346
MGREC104:11	H2063	MGREC108:1	H2217	MGREC111:7	H2352
MGREC104:15	H2067	MGREC108:2	H2218	MGREC111:14	H2359
MGREC104:17	H2069	MGREC108:16	H2232	MGREC111:17	H2362
MGREC104:20	H2072	MGREC108:20	H2236	MGREC111:22	H2367
MGREC104:21	H2073	MGREC108:28	H2244	MGREC111:25	H2370
MGREC104:29	H2081	MGREC108:30	H2246	MGREC111:36	H2381
MGREC104:31	H2083	MGREC108:33	H2249	MGREC111:37	H2382
MGREC104:33	H2085	MGREC108:39	H2255	MGREC112:1	H2387
MGREC104:36	H2088	MGREC108:40	H2256	MGREC112:4	H2390
MGREC104:39	H2091	MGREC~~109:4~~	H2261	MGREC112:16	H2402
MGREC104:41	H2093	MGREC109:5	~~H2262~~	MGREC112:17	H2403
MGREC105:1	H2094	MGREC~~109:5~~	H2263	MGREC112:18	H2404
MGREC105:3	H2096	MGREC~~109:5~~	H2263	MGREC112:19	H2405
MGREC105:4	H2097	MGREC109:9	H2268	MGREC112:25	H2411
MGREC105:8	H2101	MGREC109:10	H2269	MGREC112:27	H2413
MGREC105:9	H2102	MGREC109:11	H2270	MGREC112:28	H2414
MGREC105:10	H2103	MGREC109:12	H2271	MGREC112:31	H2417
MGREC105:13	H2106	MGREC109:14	H2273	MGREC112:33	H2419
MGREC105:15	H2108	MGREC109:15	H2274	MGREC112:35	H2421
MGREC105:21	H2114	MGREC109:16	H2275	MGREC112:38	H2424
MGREC105:23	H2116	MGREC109:18	H2277	MGREC112:41	H2427
MGREC105:30	H2123	MGREC109:19	H2278	MGREC113:2	H2429
MGREC105:35	H2128	MGREC109:21	H2280	MGREC113:13	H2440
MGREC105:36	H2129	MGREC109:23	H2282	MGREC113:21	H2448
MGREC105:39	H2132	MGREC109:26	H2285	MGREC113:26	H2453
MGREC106:3	H2137	MGREC109:27	H2286	MGREC113:29	H2456
MGREC106:8	H2142	MGREC109:31	H2290	MGREC113:31	H2458
MGREC106:10	H2144	MGREC109:32	H2291	MGREC113:35	H2462
MGREC106:14	H2148	MGREC109:33	H2292	MGREC113:36	H2463
MGREC106:21	H2155	MGREC109:35	H2294	MGREC113:37	H2464
MGREC106:22	H2156	MGREC109:37	H2296	MGREC113:41	H2468
MGREC106:23	H2157	MGREC109:39	H2298	MGREC114:6	H2474
MGREC106:25	H2159	MGREC109:41	H2300	MGREC~~114:12~~	H2480
MGREC106:26	H2160	MGREC110:9	H2309	MGREC114:13	H2483
MGREC106:27	H2161	MGREC110:14	H2314	MGREC114:19	H2489
MGREC106:29	H2163	MGREC110:16	H2316	MGREC114:21	H2491
MGREC106:30	H2164	MGREC~~110:18~~	H2322	MGREC114:24	H2494

MGREC114:24	H2494	MGREC118:6	H2653	MGREC122:7	H2830
MGREC114:25	H2495	MGREC118:8	H2655	MGREC~~122:8~~	H2832
MGREC114:26	H2496	MGREC118:24	H2671	MGREC~~122:8~~	H2833
MGREC114:32	H2502	MGREC~~118:24~~	H2672	MGREC122:12	H2837
MGREC114:41	H2511	MGREC118:25	H2674	MGREC122:16	H2841
MGREC115:6	H2517	MGREC118:26	H2675	MGREC122:20	H2845
MGREC115:7	H2518	MGREC118:28	H2677	MGREC122:30	H2849
MGREC115:10	H2519	MGREC118:29	H2678	MGREC~~122:37~~	H2858
MGREC115:11	H2520	MGREC118:31	H2680	MGREC123:3	H2865
MGREC115:12	H2521	MGREC118:32	H2681	MGREC123:7	H2869
MGREC~~115:15~~	H2532	MGREC118:34	H2683	MGREC123:8	H2870
MGREC115:19	H2538	MGREC118:37	H2686	MGREC123:13	H2875
MGREC115:24	H2543	MGREC119:4	H2694	MGREC123:15	H2879
MGREC115:25	H2544	MGREC119:5	H2695	MGREC123:16	H2880
MGREC115:28	H2547	MGREC119:7	H2697	MGREC123:18	H2882
MGREC115:30	H2549	MGREC119:15	H2705	MGREC123:28	H2892
MGREC115:31	H2550	MGREC119:19	H2709	MGREC123:30	H2894
MGREC115:33	H2552	MGREC119:21	H2711	MGREC123:31	H2895
MGREC115:35	H2554	MGREC119:23	H2713	MGREC123:32	H2896
MGREC115:36	H2555	MGREC119:25	H2715	MGREC123:33	H2897
MGREC115:37	H2556	MGREC119:29	H2719	MGREC124:8	~~H2913~~
MGREC115:38	H2557	MGREC119:31	H2721	MGREC~~124:8~~	H2913
MGREC115:39	H2558	MGREC119:35	H2725	MGREC~~124:9~~	H2914
MGREC115:40	H2559	MGREC119:38	H2728	MGREC~~124:10~~	H2915
MGREC115:41	H2560	MGREC~~120:4~~	H2738	MGREC124:11	H2918
MGREC116:1	H2561	MGREC120:7	H2742	MGREC124:14	H2921
MGREC116:5	H2565	MGREC120:18	H2753	MGREC~~124:16~~	H2923
MGREC116:13	H2579	MGREC120:22	H2759	MGREC124:33	H2940
MGREC116:15	H2581	MGREC120:23	H2760	MGREC124:34	H2941
MGREC116:16	H2582	MGREC120:24	H2761	MGREC124:36	H2943
MGREC116:17	H2583	MGREC120:26	H2763	MGREC124:37	H2944
MGREC116:26	H2592	MGREC120:34	H2771	MGREC124:40	H2947
MGREC116:30	H2596	MGREC120:35	H2772	MGREC125:3	H2951
MGREC116:33	H2599	MGREC120:36	~~H2773~~	MGREC125:4	H2952
MGREC116:38	H2604	MGREC120:40	H2777	MGREC125:10	H2958
MGREC116:41	H2607	MGREC120:41	H2778	MGREC125:22	H2972
MGREC117:5	H2612	MGREC121:1	H2779	MGREC125:32	H2982
MGREC117:7	H2614	MGREC121:6	H2784	MGREC125:34	H2984
MGREC117:9	H2616	MGREC121:8	H2786	MGREC125:35	H2985
MGREC117:10	H2617	MGREC121:9	H2787	MGREC126:3	H2994
MGREC117:12	H2619	MGREC121:11	H2789	MGREC126:16	H3007
MGREC117:17	H2624	MGREC121:12	H2790	MGREC~~126:21~~	H3012
MGREC117:18	H2625	MGREC~~121:14~~	H2792	MGREC126:23	H3014
MGREC117:19	H2626	MGREC~~121:16~~	H2798	MGREC126:27	H3018
MGREC117:20	H2627	MGREC121:17	H2799	MGREC126:37	H3026
MGREC117:21	H2628	MGREC121:18	H2800	MGREC126:38	H3027
MGREC117:22	H2629	MGREC121:39	H2821	MGREC127:7	H3037
MGREC117:23	H2630	MGREC122:1	H2824	MGREC127:11	H3041
MGREC117:24	H2631	MGREC122:2	H2825	MGREC127:22	H3052
MGREC117:40	H2647	MGREC122:4	H2827	MGREC127:23	H3053
MGREC118:1	H2648	MGREC122:6	H2829	MGREC127:24	H3054

MGREC127:25	H3055	MGREC~~132:28~~	H3274	SIDNEY149:37	H24
MGREC127:33	H3063	MGREC132:32	H3279	SIDNEY149:38	H25
MGREC127:34	H3064	MGREC133:12	H3300	SIDNEY~~150:3~~	H29
MGREC127:40	H3070	MGREC133:14	H3302	SIDNEY150:7	H32
MGREC~~127:41~~	H3073	MGREC133:15	H3303	SIDNEY150:11	H36
MGREC128:2	H3075	MGREC133:17	H3305	SIDNEY~~150:12~~	H38
MGREC128:7	H3080	MGREC133:20	H3308	SIDNEY150:25	H52
MGREC128:16	H3089	MGREC133:22	H3310	SIDNEY150:26	H53
MGREC128:17	H3090	MGREC~~133:24~~	H3314	SIDNEY150:32	H59
MGREC128:25	H3098	MGREC133:25	~~H3315~~	SIDNEY150:38	H65
MGREC128:35	H3108	MGREC133:26	H3316	SIDNEY~~150:38~~	H66
MGREC128:36	H3109	MGREC133:29	H3319	SIDNEY~~150:39~~	H67
MGREC129:8	H3122	MGREC133:30	H3320	SIDNEY151:1	~~H69~~
MGREC129:20	H3134	MGREC133:32	H3322	SIDNEY151:12	~~H69~~
MGREC129:28	H3142	MGREC133:40	H3330	SIDNEY151:27	H75
MGREC129:35	H3149	MGREC133:41	H3331	SIDNEY151:29	~~H75~~
MGREC129:36	H3150	MGREC134:19	H3350	SIDNEY151:30	~~H75~~
MGREC130:8	H3163	MGREC134:25	H3356	SIDNEY151:33	~~H75~~
MGREC130:10	H3165	MGREC134:37	~~H3367~~	SIDNEY151:34	~~H75~~
MGREC130:30	~~H3181~~	MGREC134:38	~~H3367~~	SIDNEY152:1	~~H75~~
MGREC130:35	~~H3181~~	MGREC135:1	H3371	SIDNEY152:3	~~H75~~
MGREC131:1	H3187	MGREC~~135:1~~	H3372	SIDNEY152:4	~~H76~~
MGREC131:10	H3202	MGREC~~135:1~~	H3373	SIDNEY152:13	H82
MGREC131:11	H3203	MGREC135:2	H3374	SIDNEY152:22	H91
MGREC131:16	H3208	MGREC135:18	H3390	SIDNEY152:23	H92
MGREC131:18	H3210	MROMAN136:25	H3439	SIDNEY152:28	H97
MGREC131:19	H3211	MROMAN136:27	H3441	DUBART153:18	H22
MGREC131:21	H3213	MROMAN136:33	H3447	DUBART153:22	H26
MGREC131:22	H3214	MROMAN137:4	H3455	DUBART153:23	H27
MGREC131:24	H3216	MROMAN137:20	H3471	DUBART153:25	H29
MGREC131:25	H3217	MROMAN137:22	H3473	DUBART153:26	H30
MGREC131:28	H3220	MROMAN137:26	H3477	DUBART153:27	H31
MGREC131:29	H3221	MROMAN138:22	H3512	DUBART153:28	H32
MGREC131:30	H3222	MROMAN138:26	H3516	DUBART153:30	H34
MGREC131:31	H3223	MROMAN139:1	H3529	DUBART154:14	H59
MGREC131:34	H3226	MROMAN139:13	H3541	DUBART154:27	H72
MGREC131:41	H3233	MROMAN139:14	H3542	DUBART155:1	H86
MGREC132:2	H3235	MROMAN140:9	H3572	QELIZ156:9	H36
MGREC132:6	~~H3239~~	DIALOG143:18	H87	QELIZ156:15	H42
MGREC132:9	H3244	DIALOG145:33	H182	QELIZ156:24	H51
MGREC132:10	H3245	DIALOG147:20	H245	QELIZ157:29	H97
MGREC132:12	H3247	DIALOG148:14	H279	QELIZ158:2	H111
MGREC132:18	H3255	DIALOG148:15	H280	DAVID159:3	H18
MGREC132:19	H3256	DIALOG148:16	H281	DAVID159:4	H19
MGREC132:20	H3257	SIDNEY149:15	H14	VANITY160:3	H13
MGREC~~132:20~~	H3260	SIDNEY149:16	H15	VANITY161:4	H55
MGREC132:23	H3268	SIDNEY149:17	H16	TDUDLEY165:3	H4-5
MGREC132:24	H3269	SIDNEY149:18	H17	TDUDLEY165:7	H9
MGREC132:26	H3271	SIDNEY149:20	H19	TDUDLEY165:11	H13
MGREC132:27	H3272	SIDNEY149:21	H20	TDUDLEY165:16	H18
MGREC~~132:28~~	H3274	SIDNEY149:37	H24	TDUDLEY165:21	H23

MYCHILD215:26	HP240	MYCHILD218:17	HP244	JULY223:21	HP251
MYCHILD215:27	HP240	MYCHILD218:28	HP244	JULY223:25	HP251
MYCHILD215:28	HP241	MYCHILD218:30	HP244	JULY223:26	HP251
MYCHILD215:29	HP241	MYCHILD218:31	HP244	JULY223:27	HP251
MYCHILD215:30	HP241	MYCHILD218:32	HP244	JULY223:28	HP251
MYCHILD215:31	HP241	MYCHILD218:34	HP244	JULY223:31	HP251
MYCHILD215:32	HP241	MYCHILD218:35	HP244	JULY223:34	HP251
MYCHILD216:1	HP241	MYCHILD218:36	HP244	WHAT224:1	H1
MYCHILD216:4	HP241	MYCHILD219:1	HP244-5	WHAT224:4	H4
MYCHILD216:6	HP241	MYCHILD219:2	HP245	WHAT224:15	H15
MYCHILD216:7	HP241	MYCHILD219:8	HP245	WHAT224:20	H20
MYCHILD216:8	HP241	BYNIGHT220:5	H6	MYSOUL225:13	H17
MYCHILD216:9	HP241	BYNIGHT220:7	H7	MYSOUL225:15	H19
MYCHILD216:11	HP241	BYNIGHT220:8	H8	MYSOUL225:16	H20
MYCHILD216:12	HP241	BYNIGHT220:10	H10	MYSOUL225:17	H21
MYCHILD216:15	HP241	BYNIGHT220:17	H15	MYSOUL225:18	H22
MYCHILD216:16	HP241	BYNIGHT220:19	H17	MYSOUL225:19	H23
MYCHILD216:17	HP241	FEVER220:28	H8	MYSOUL225:22	H26
MYCHILD216:18	HP241	FEVER220:29	H9	MYSOUL225:24	H28
MYCHILD216:20	HP241	FEVER220:32	H12	28AUG225:29	HP254
MYCHILD216:23	HP242	FEVER220:33	H13	28AUG225:32	HP254
MYCHILD216:24	HP242	FEVER220:34	H14	28AUG226:1	HP254
MYCHILD216:29	HP242	FEVER221:2	H17	28AUG226:2	HP254
MYCHILD216:31	HP242	FEVER221:3	H18	28AUG226:3	HP254
MYCHILD216:33	HP242	FEVER221:12	H27	28AUG226:5	HP254
MYCHILD216:34	HP242	SOREFIT221:16	H2	28AUG226:6	HP254
MYCHILD216:35	HP242	SOREFIT221:20	H6	28AUG226:8	HP254
MYCHILD217:4	HP242	SOREFIT221:22	H8	28AUG226:10	HP254
MYCHILD217:6	HP242	SOREFIT221:26	H12	11MAYA226:13	HP255
MYCHILD217:8	HP242	SOREFIT221:27	H13	11MAYA226:15	HP255
MYCHILD217:9	HP242	SOREFIT221:28	H14	11MAYA226:17	HP255
MYCHILD217:10	HP242	SOREFIT221:31	H17	11MAYA226:18	HP255
MYCHILD217:11	HP242	SOREFIT221:32	H18	11MAYA226:20	HP255
MYCHILD217:12	HP242	SOREFIT222:3	H22	11MAYA226:21	HP255
MYCHILD217:13	HP242	SOREFIT222:9	H28	13MAY227:4	H13
MYCHILD217:15	HP243	FAINTING222:14	H4	13MAY227:5	H14
MYCHILD217:16	HP243	FAINTING222:15	H5	13MAY227:7	H16
MYCHILD217:19	HP243	FAINTING222:17	H7	13MAY227:13	H22
MYCHILD217:22	HP243	FAINTING222:23	H13	13MAY227:15	H24
MYCHILD217:23	HP243	FAINTING222:24	H14	30SEPT227:19	HP257
MYCHILD217:24	HP243	FAINTING222:27	H17	30SEPT227:20	HP257
MYCHILD217:25	HP243	MED223:3	HP250	30SEPT227:22	HP257
MYCHILD217:27	HP243	MED223:4	HP250	30SEPT227:24	HP257
MYCHILD217:29	HP243	MED223:5	HP250	30SEPT227:29	HP257
MYCHILD217:33	HP243	MED223:6	HP250	SAMUEL228:3	H4
MYCHILD217:34	HP243	MED223:7	HP250	SAMUEL228:5	H6
MYCHILD217:36	HP243	MED223:9	HP250	SAMUEL228:7	H8
MYCHILD218:4	HP243	MED223:13	HP250	SAMUEL228:10	H11
MYCHILD218:5	HP243	MED223:15	HP250	SAMUEL228:15	H16
MYCHILD218:7	HP244	MED223:16	HP250	SAMUEL228:16	H17
MYCHILD218:9	HP244	MED223:17	HP250	SAMUEL228:18	H19

HUMOUR31:27	H460	AGES43:26	H321	SEASONS51:36	H212
HUMOUR32:9	H483	AGES43:27	H322	SEASONS52:1	H218
HUMOUR32:11	H485	AGES44:5	H338	SEASONS52:5	H220
HUMOUR32:13	H487	AGES44:10	H343	SEASONS52:15	H230
HUMOUR32:15	H489	AGES44:20	H353	SEASONS52:20	H235
HUMOUR33:27	H541	AGES44:23	H356	SEASONS52:24	H239
AGES35:27	H13	AGES44:26	H359	SEASONS52:26	H241
AGES35:34	H20	AGES44:27	H360	SEASONS52:34	H249
AGES35:35	H21	AGES44:29	H362	SEASONS~~52:39~~	H256
AGES36:1	H25	AGES44:40	H373	SEASONS53:3	H259
AGES36:13	H37	AGES~~45:2~~	H376	MASSYR53:15	H5
AGES36:15	H39	AGES45:21	~~H403~~	MASSYR53:21	H11
AGES36:27	H51	AGES~~45:22~~	H404	MASSYR53:25	H15
AGES37:2	H64	AGES45:24	H414	MASSYR54:8	H35
AGES37:21	H83	AGES45:34	H424	MASSYR55:36	H102
AGES37:22	H84	AGES46:4	H435	MASSYR56:4	H110
AGES38:6	H109	AGES46:4	H435	MASSYR56:5	H111
AGES38:15	H118	AGES46:18	H449	MASSYR56:18	H124
AGES38:22	H125	AGES46:23	H454	MASSYR56:22	H128
AGES38:30	H133	AGES46:25	H456	MASSYR56:28	H134
AGES38:32	H135	SEASONS46:31	H7	MASSYR56:33	H139
AGES38:37	H140	SEASONS46:32	H8	MASSYR56:35	H141
AGES39:7	H150	SEASONS47:9	H25	MASSYR57:8	H155
AGES39:12	H155	SEASONS47:23	H39	MASSYR57:9	H156
AGES39:15	H158	SEASONS47:31	~~H46~~	MASSYR57:31	H176
AGES39:20	H163	SEASONS~~47:31~~	H46	MASSYR57:32	H177
AGES39:24	H167	SEASONS48:4	H57	MASSYR57:40	H185
AGES39:38	H181	SEASONS48:4	H57	MASSYR58:4	H189
AGES39:39	H182	SEASONS48:4	H57	MASSYR58:9	H194
AGES40:21	H202	SEASONS48:10	H63	MASSYR58:25	H208
AGES40:23	H204	SEASONS48:30	H83	MASSYR58:31	H214
AGES40:26	H207	SEASONS48:34	~~H85~~	MASSYR59:6	H230
AGES40:36	H215	SEASONS49:5	H96	MASSYR59:14	H238
AGES41:4	H224	SEASONS49:18	H109	MASSYR59:19	H243
AGES41:7	H227	SEASONS~~49:23~~	H114	MASSYR59:22	H246
AGES41:8	H228	SEASONS49:27	H116	MASSYR59:39	H263
AGES41:10	H230	SEASONS49:31	H120	MASSYR60:12	H277
AGES42:4	H262	SEASONS49:34	H127	MASSYR60:16	H281
AGES42:11	H269	SEASONS49:38	H131	MASSYR60:26	H291
AGES42:16	H274	SEASONS49:39	H132	MASSYR60:34	H299
AGES42:17	H275	SEASONS50:5	H139	MASSYR60:38	H303
AGES42:18	H276	SEASONS50:19	H153	MASSYR61:5	H310
AGES42:26	H284	SEASONS50:32	H166	MASSYR61:28	H333
AGES42:33	H289	SEASONS50:39	H173	MASSYR61:34	H339
AGES43:5	H300	SEASONS50:40	H174	MASSYR62:20	H365
AGES43:14	H307	SEASONS51:1	H175	MASSYR62:27	H372
AGES43:16	~~H308~~	SEASONS51:6	H180	MASSYR62:32	H377
AGES~~43:16~~	H309	SEASONS51:13	H187	MASSYR63:5	H390
AGES43:20	H315	SEASONS51:14	H188	MASSYR63:19	H404
AGES43:22	H317	SEASONS51:20	H196	MASSYR63:28	H413
AGES43:24	H319	SEASONS51:22	H198	MASSYR64:18	H442

MASSYR64:24	H448	MPERS73:32	H817	MPERS86:15	H1331
MASSYR64:26	H450	MPERS74:1	H826	MPERS86:21	H1337
MASSYR64:29	H453	MPERS74:14	H837	MPERS86:23	H1339
MASSYR64:31	H455	MPERS75:11	H872	MPERS86:28	H1344
MASSYR65:1	H466	MPERS75:16	H877	MPERS86:30	H1346
MASSYR65:6	H471	MPERS75:19	~~H878~~	MPERS86:36	H1352
MASSYR65:10	H475	MPERS75:24	H881	MPERS87:12	H1368
MASSYR65:27	H492	MPERS75:36	H893	MPERS87:16	~~H1370~~
MASSYR65:33	H498	MPERS75:38	H895	MPERS87:33	H1385
MASSYR66:5	H511	MPERS76:3	H901	MPERS87:34	H1386
MASSYR66:35	H541	MPERS76:15	H913	MPERS87:40	H1392
MASSYR67:2	H548	MPERS76:17	H915	MPERS87:41	H1393
MASSYR67:4	H550	MPERS76:18	H916	MPERS88:2	H1395
MASSYR67:7	H553	MPERS76:24	H922	MPERS88:26	H1419
MASSYR67:10	H556	MPERS76:41	H939	MPERS88:28	H1421
MASSYR67:23	H569	MPERS77:3	H942	MPERS89:12	H1446
MASSYR67:29	H575	MPERS77:21	H962	MPERS89:13	H1447
MASSYR67:34	H580	MPERS78:2	H983	MPERS89:36	H1470
MASSYR68:14	H600	MPERS78:24	H1005	MPERS90:1	H1476
MASSYR68:15	H601	MPERS78:25	H1006	MPERS90:19	H1486
MASSYR68:16	H602	MPERS78:31	H1012	MPERS90:36	H1503
MASSYR68:17	H603	MPERS79:1	H1023	MPERS91:1	H1509
MPERS68:35	H621	~~MPERS79:3~~	H1025	MPERS91:11	H1519
MPERS69:4	H626	MPERS79:13	~~H1035~~	~~MPERS91:22~~	H1531
MPERS69:6	H628	MPERS79:18	H1044	MPERS91:23	H1537
MPERS69:14	H636	MPERS79:19	H1045	~~MPERS91:25~~	H1539
MPERS69:16	H638	MPERS80:20	H1087	MPERS91:28	~~H1542~~
MPERS69:19	H641	MPERS80:23	H1090	MPERS91:28	H1542
MPERS69:38	~~H660~~	MPERS80:25	H1092	~~MPERS91:30~~	H1544
MPERS70:25	H696	MPERS80:31	H1098	~~MPERS91:35~~	H1549
MPERS70:29	H700	MPERS81:20	H1128	~~MPERS91:36~~	H1550
MPERS70:35	H706	MPERS81:35	H1143	MPERS92:1	~~H1555~~
MPERS70:36	H707	MPERS82:7	H1154	~~MPERS92:1~~	H1555
MPERS70:37	~~H708~~	MPERS82:16	H1163	~~MPERS92:2~~	H1556
~~MPERS70:37~~	H708	MPERS82:25	H1172	~~MPERS92:5~~	H1562
MPERS70:38	H709	MPERS82:32	H1179	MPERS92:10	H1568
~~MPERS71:3~~	H715	MPERS83:20	H1208	~~MPERS92:16~~	H1574
MPERS71:26	H740	MPERS83:23	H1211	~~MPERS92:17~~	H1575
MPERS72:2	H754	MPERS83:38	H1226	~~MPERS92:18~~	H1576
MPERS72:5	~~H755~~	MPERS83:40	H1228	MPERS92:30	H1588
~~MPERS72:9~~	H757	MPERS84:3	H1231	MPERS92:35	H1593
MPERS72:22	H770	MPERS84:7	H1235	MPERS93:1	H1598
MPERS72:25	~~H773~~	~~MPERS84:12~~	H1241	MGREC6:9	H1606
MPERS72:36	H780	MPERS84:18	H1254	MGREC6:27	H1624
MPERS72:39	H785	MPERS84:37	H1273	MGREC94:1	H1635
MPERS73:7	H794	MPERS85:1	H1277	MGREC94:7	H1641
MPERS73:14	H801	MPERS85:19	H1295	MGREC94:8	H1642
MPERS73:18	H805	MPERS85:26	H1302	MGREC94:10	H1644
MPERS73:23	~~H809~~	MPERS86:3	H1319	MGREC94:11	H1645
MPERS73:26	H811	MPERS86:4	H1320	MGREC94:31	H1669
MPERS73:29	H814	MPERS86:13	H1329	MGREC94:36	H1674

AGES42:38	H294	MGREC107:30	H2205	FLESH176:29	H69
AGES44:31	H364	MGREC112:7	H2393	VERSES184:1	H5
AGES44:39	H372	MGREC113:23	H2450	VERSES184:9	H13
AGES45:21	~~H403~~	MGREC115:9	~~H2518~~	ANNEB187:27	H17
AGES~~45:22~~	H409	MGREC~~116:10~~	H2572	MERCY188:25	H11
SEASONS50:10	H144	MGREC117:19	H2626	MERCY188:35	H21
SEASONS51:4	H178	MGREC121:28	H2810	MERCY189:7	H28
SEASONS51:29	H205	MGREC121:29	H2811	MERCY189:8	H29
SEASONS52:17	H232	MGREC122:13	H2838	MERCY189:16	H37
SEASONS52:28	H243	MGREC123:8	H2870	MEDDM196:6	HP272
SEASONS~~52:39~~	H256	MGREC126:8	H2999	MEDDM197:19	HP275
MASSYR56:1	H107	MGREC126:19	H3010	MEDDM197:27	HP275
MASSYR56:3	H109	MGREC129:23	H3137	MEDDM197:31	HP275
MASSYR56:9	H115	MGREC135:38	H3410	MEDDM198:19	HP276
MASSYR56:15	H121	MROMAN136:36	H3450	MEDDM198:22	HP276
MASSYR56:27	H133	MROMAN138:20	H3510	MEDDM198:29	HP277
MASSYR57:8	H155	DIALOG142:4	H33	MEDDM198:30	HP277
MASSYR57:10	H157	DIALOG142:39	H68	MEDDM198:32	HP277
MASSYR57:18	~~H165~~	DIALOG143:24	H93	MEDDM198:33	HP277
MASSYR57:26	~~H172~~	DIALOG144:21	H131	MEDDM199:11	HP277
MASSYR57:28	H173	DIALOG144:32	H140	MEDDM200:3	HP278
MASSYR57:36	H181	DIALOG146:2	H190	MEDDM200:4	HP278
MASSYR58:7	H192	DIALOG146:5	H193	MEDDM200:7	HP279
MASSYR59:21	H245	DIALOG147:23	~~H247~~	MEDDM200:8	HP279
MASSYR59:23	H247	SIDNEY149:15	H14	MEDDM200:13	HP279
MASSYR59:38	H262	SIDNEY149:25	~~H23~~	MEDDM200:16	HP279
MASSYR63:25	H410	SIDNEY150:33	H60	MEDDM200:27	HP279
MASSYR66:6	H512	SIDNEY151:6	~~H69~~	MEDDM201:4	HP280
MASSYR66:32	~~H538~~	SIDNEY152:9	~~H79~~	MEDDM201:21	HP281
MPERS69:8	H630	DUBART154:6	H51	MEDDM202:14	HP282
MPERS69:33	H655	DUBART155:6	H91	MEDDM202:34	HP282
MPERS71:13	~~H727~~	QELIZ155:20	H11	MEDDM202:35	HP282
MPERS72:33	H777	QELIZ157:7	H75	MEDDM202:36	HP282
MPERS75:11	H872	QELIZ158:16	H125	MEDDM203:3	HP283
MPERS79:20	H1046	VANITY160:12	H22	MEDDM203:4	HP283
MPERS79:29	H1055	VANITY160:13	H23	MEDDM203:5	HP283
MPERS80:10	H1077	VANITY160:18	H28	MEDDM203:21	HP283
MPERS81:5	H1113	VANITY160:31	H41	MEDDM203:26	HP283
MPERS82:28	H1175	VANITY160:33	H43	MEDDM204:10	HP284
MPERS86:21	H1337	VANITY160:35	H45	MEDDM204:29	HP285
MPERS87:24	H1376	VANITY160:36	H46	MEDDM205:16	HP286
MPERS89:1	H1435	VANITY160:37	H47	MEDDM205:18	HP286
MPERS91:36	~~H1550~~	VANITY160:38	H48	MEDDM205:34	HP286
MPERS92:7	~~H1565~~	TDUDLEY166:3	H45	MEDDM206:9	HP287
MPERS92:8	~~H1566~~	CONTEM168:35	H41	MEDDM206:14	HP287
MGREC95:27	H1706	CONTEM169:5	H47	MEDDM206:24	HP287
MGREC95:39	H1718	CONTEM169:28	H67	MEDDM206:30	HP288
MGREC99:31	H1874	CONTEM169:30	H69	MEDDM206:33	HP288
MGREC101:41	H1970	CONTEM172:20	H155	MEDDM206:34	HP288
MGREC103:3	H2014	CONTEM173:7	H175	MEDDM207:17	HP289
MGREC107:18	H2193	FLESH176:22	H62	MEDDM207:21	HP289

ELEMEN13:21	H222	HUMOUR23:21	H131	HUMOUR33:20	H534
ELEMEN13:22	H223	HUMOUR23:22	H132	HUMOUR34:21	H576
ELEMEN13:26	H227	HUMOUR23:39	H149	HUMOUR34:27	H582
ELEMEN13:38	H239	HUMOUR23:41	H149	HUMOUR35:5	H601
ELEMEN14:1	H243	HUMOUR24:2	H151	HUMOUR35:6	H602
ELEMEN14:6	H250	HUMOUR24:3	H152	AGES37:6	H68
ELEMEN14:8	H250	HUMOUR24:5	H154	AGES37:11	H73
ELEMEN14:20	H262	HUMOUR24:12	H161	AGES37:18	H80
ELEMEN14:36	H278	HUMOUR24:13	H162	AGES37:20	H82
ELEMEN14:39	H281	HUMOUR24:21	H170	AGES37:23	H85
ELEMEN15:18	H300	HUMOUR24:40	H189	AGES37:24	H86
ELEMEN15:23	H305	HUMOUR25:13	H202	AGES37:31	H93
ELEMEN15:32	H314	HUMOUR26:26	H256	AGES37:35	H97
ELEMEN15:39	H321	HUMOUR26:36	H266	AGES38:1	H104
ELEMEN16:5	H328	HUMOUR27:7	H278	AGES38:3	H106
ELEMEN16:9	H332	HUMOUR27:19	H290	AGES38:4	H107
ELEMEN16:12	H335	HUMOUR27:19	H290	AGES38:5	H108
ELEMEN16:14	H337	HUMOUR27:21	H292	AGES38:6	H109
ELEMEN16:15	H338	HUMOUR27:24	H295	AGES38:12	H115
ELEMEN16:16	H339	HUMOUR27:32	H303	AGES38:15	H118
ELEMEN16:26	H349	HUMOUR27:33	H304	AGES38:27	H130
ELEMEN16:31	H354	HUMOUR28:15	H327	AGES38:30	H133
ELEMEN16:36	H359	HUMOUR28:19	H331	AGES38:33	H136
ELEMEN16:38	H361	HUMOUR28:21	H333	AGES38:36	H139
ELEMEN17:2	H366	HUMOUR28:39	H351	AGES38:39	H142
ELEMEN17:4	H368	HUMOUR29:18	H369	AGES38:40	H143
ELEMEN17:14	H378	HUMOUR29:26	H377	AGES39:1	H144
ELEMEN17:15	H379	HUMOUR29:29	H380	AGES39:4	H147
ELEMEN17:18	H382	HUMOUR29:36	H387	AGES39:10	H153
ELEMEN17:31	H395	HUMOUR30:2	H394	AGES39:11	H154
ELEMEN17:36	H400	HUMOUR30:3	H395	AGES39:27	H170
ELEMEN17:40	H404	HUMOUR30:19	H411	AGES39:28	H171
ELEMEN18:8	H412	HUMOUR30:37	H429	AGES39:29	H172
ELEMEN18:28	H432	HUMOUR31:5	H438	AGES39:30	H173
ELEMEN18:31	H435	HUMOUR31:22	H455	AGES39:32	H175
ELEMEN18:36	H440	HUMOUR31:23	H456	AGES39:36	H179
ELEMEN18:38	H442	HUMOUR31:36	H469	AGES39:36	H179
ELEMEN19:4	H449	HUMOUR31:38	H471	AGES39:37	H180
ELEMEN19:11	H456	HUMOUR32:3	H477	AGES39:38	H181
ELEMEN19:12	H457	HUMOUR32:4	H478	AGES39:39	H182
ELEMEN19:22	H467	HUMOUR32:9	H483	AGES40:2	H183
ELEMEN20:5	H487	HUMOUR32:10	H484	AGES40:3	H184
ELEMEN20:7	H489	HUMOUR32:11	H485	AGES40:8	H189
ELEMEN20:8	H490	HUMOUR32:21	H495	AGES40:11	H192
HUMOUR21:2	H30	HUMOUR32:27	H501	AGES40:15	H196
HUMOUR21:6	H34	HUMOUR32:33	H507	AGES40:19	H200
HUMOUR21:14	H42	HUMOUR32:37	H511	AGES40:21	H202
HUMOUR21:16	H44	HUMOUR32:38	H512	AGES40:30	H210
HUMOUR21:17	H45	HUMOUR32:39	H513	AGES40:31	H210
HUMOUR22:27	H96	HUMOUR32:40	H514	AGES40:37	H216
HUMOUR22:37	H106	HUMOUR33:16	H530	AGES40:38	H217

AGES40:39	H218	AGES44:19	H352	DIALOG141:20	H19
AGES41:1	H221	AGES45:22	H411	DIALOG141:24	H23
AGES41:3	H223	AGES45:26	H416	DIALOG141:26	H25
AGES41:5	H225	AGES45:27	H417	DIALOG142:36	H65
AGES41:7	H227	AGES45:29	H419	DIALOG143:12	H81
AGES41:9	H229	AGES45:30	H420	DIALOG143:15	H84
AGES41:20	H239	AGES45:35	H425	DIALOG143:23	H92
AGES41:22	H239	AGES45:37	H427	DIALOG143:26	H95
AGES41:23	H240	AGES45:39	H429	DIALOG143:28	H97
AGES41:25	H242	AGES45:41	H431	DIALOG144:15	H125
AGES41:26	H243	AGES46:3	H434	DIALOG144:23	H133
AGES41:31	H248	AGES46:14	H445	DIALOG144:32	H140
AGES41:32	H249	AGES46:15	H446	DIALOG144:33	H141
AGES41:40	H257	AGES46:16	H447	DIALOG144:34	H142
AGES41:41	H258	AGES46:18	H449	DIALOG145:3	H152
AGES42:1	H259	AGES46:23	H454	DIALOG145:9	H158
AGES42:3	H261	SEASONS46:36	H14	DIALOG145:10	H159
AGES42:8	H266	SEASONS47:28	H44	DIALOG145:20	H169
AGES42:10	H268	SEASONS48:9	H62	DIALOG145:21	H170
AGES42:13	H271	SEASONS48:25	H78	DIALOG146:3	H191
AGES42:15	H273	SEASONS49:7	H98	DIALOG146:6	H194
AGES42:27	H285	SEASONS49:38	H131	DIALOG146:12	H200
AGES42:30	H286	SEASONS50:11	H145	DIALOG146:16	H202
AGES42:31	H287	SEASONS51:20	H196	DIALOG146:17	H203
AGES42:32	H288	SEASONS51:34	H210	DIALOG146:18	H204
AGES42:33	H289	SEASONS52:18	H233	DIALOG146:25	H211
AGES42:34	H290	SEASONS52:32	H247	DIALOG146:26	H212
AGES42:35	H291	SEASONS53:1	H257	DIALOG146:30	H216
AGES42:37	H293	MPERS92:3	H1557	DIALOG147:8	H234
AGES42:38	H294	MGREC95:40	H1719	SIDNEY149:33	H23
AGES42:40	H296	MGREC105:40	H2133	SIDNEY149:34	H23
AGES42:41	H297	MGREC105:41	H2134	SIDNEY150:12	H43
AGES43:2	H297	MGREC112:7	H2393	SIDNEY150:14	H49
AGES43:5	H300	MGREC113:6	H2433	SIDNEY151:23	H73
AGES43:6	H301	MGREC135:40	H3412	SIDNEY151:28	H75
AGES43:7	H302	MGREC136:4	H3417	SIDNEY151:29	H75
AGES43:12	H305	MGREC136:7	H3420	SIDNEY151:32	H75
AGES43:13	H306	MGREC136:9	H3423	SIDNEY151:38	H75
AGES43:14	H307	MGREC136:11	H3425	SIDNEY152:1	H75
AGES43:16	H308	MGREC136:18	H3432	SIDNEY152:17	H86
AGES43:18	H313	MROMAN139:27	H3553	SIDNEY152:18	H87
AGES43:23	H318	MROMAN139:28	H3554	SIDNEY152:19	H88
AGES43:24	H319	MROMAN139:31	H3557	SIDNEY152:28	H97
AGES43:26	H321	MROMAN139:36	H3562	DUBART152:35	H4
AGES43:29	H324	MROMAN140:2	H3565	DUBART153:4	H8
AGES44:7	H340	MROMAN140:3	H3566	DUBART153:7	H11
AGES44:12	H345	MROMAN140:4	H3567	DUBART153:10	H14
AGES44:12	H345	MROMAN140:7	H3570	DUBART153:11	H15
AGES44:13	H346	DIALOG141:15	H14	DUBART153:12	H16
AGES44:14	H347	DIALOG141:16	H15	DUBART153:14	H18
AGES44:16	H349	DIALOG141:17	H16	DUBART153:16	H20

1199

MYCHILD218:7	HP244	MED223:17	HP250	THEART229:15	H17
MYCHILD218:17	HP244	JULY223:22	HP251	RESTOR229:19	H1-2
MYCHILD218:27	HP244	JULY223:23	HP251	RESTOR229:29	H12
MYCHILD218:34	HP244	JULY223:24	HP251	RESTOR230:6	H21
MYCHILD218:35	HP244	JULY223:31	HP251	RESTOR230:8	H23
MYCHILD218:36	HP244	JULY223:34	HP251	HANNA230:9	H1-2
BYNIGHT220:4	H5	JULY223:35	HP251	HANNA230:12	H5
BYNIGHT220:7	H7	WHAT224:5	H5	SON230:19	H1-2
BYNIGHT220:12	H11	WHAT224:6	H6	SON230:21	H4
BYNIGHT220:13	H12	WHAT224:7	H7	SON230:22	H5
BYNIGHT220:14	H13	WHAT224:13	H13	SON231:17	H29
BYNIGHT220:15	H14	MYSOUL224:25	H1	SON231:19	H31
BYNIGHT220:17	H15	28AUG225:26	HP254	SON231:28	H39
FEVER220:24	H4	28AUG225:27	HP254	2HUSB232:1	H1-2
FEVER220:26	H6	28AUG225:28	HP254	2HUSB232:5	H6
FEVER220:27	H7	28AUG225:29	HP254	2HUSB232:6	H7
FEVER220:30	H10	28AUG225:31	HP254	2HUSB232:10	H11
FEVER220:32	H12	28AUG225:32	HP254	2HUSB232:15	H16
FEVER220:35	H15	28AUG226:3	HP254	2HUSB232:16	H17
FEVER221:1	H16	28AUG226:5	HP254	2HUSB232:21	H22
FEVER221:3	H18	28AUG226:7	HP254	2HUSB232:25	H26
FEVER221:10	H25	28AUG226:8	HP254	2HUSB233:8	H41
FEVER221:11	H26	28AUG226:9	HP254	2HUSB233:11	H44
FEVER221:12	H27	11MAYA226:14	HP255	HOURS233:19	H1-2
FEVER221:13	H28	11MAYA226:16	HP255	HOURS233:20	H3
SOREFIT221:16	H2	11MAYA226:17	HP255	HOURS233:21	H4
SOREFIT221:18	H4	11MAYA226:19	HP255	HOURS233:22	H5
SOREFIT221:21	H7	11MAYA226:21	HP255	HOURS233:23	H6
SOREFIT221:24	H10	11MAYA226:22	HP255	HOURS233:24	H7
SOREFIT221:25	H11	11MAYA226:23	HP255	HOURS233:25	H8
SOREFIT221:28	H14	13MAY226:30	H6	HOURS233:27	H10
SOREFIT221:32	H18	13MAY226:31	H7	HOURS233:29	H12
SOREFIT222:1	H20	13MAY226:32	H8	HOURS234:5	H19
SOREFIT222:8	H27	13MAY226:33	H9	HOURS234:6	H20
FAINTING222:14	H4	13MAY227:1	H10	HOURS234:9	H23
FAINTING222:16	H6	13MAY227:9	H18	HOURS234:18	H32
FAINTING222:20	H10	13MAY227:12	H21	HOURS234:23	H37
FAINTING222:21	H11	13MAY227:14	H23	HOURS234:24	H38
FAINTING222:25	H15	30SEPT227:18	HP257	HOURS234:26	H40
FAINTING222:26	H16	30SEPT227:21	HP257	HOURS234:27	H41
MED223:1	HP250	SAMUEL228:1	H1-2	HOURS234:38	H52
MED223:4	HP250	SAMUEL228:17	H18	ACK235:3	H1-3
MED223:4	HP250	SAMUEL228:20	H21	ACK235:7	H7
MED223:5	HP250	11MAYB228:28	HP259	ACK235:8	H8
MED223:5	HP250	11MAYB228:29	HP259	ACK235:9	H9
MED223:6	HP250	11MAYB228:33	HP259	ACK235:10	H10
MED223:7	HP250	THEART228:35	H1	ACK235:20	H20
MED223:8	HP250	THEART229:7	H9	REMB235:21	H1-3
MED223:10	HP250	THEART229:10	H12	REMB235:25	H6
MED223:12	HP250	THEART229:13	H15	REMB235:29	H10
MED223:15	HP250	THEART229:14	H16	REMB235:34	H15

REMB236:3	H18	ELEMEN11:26	H146	HUMOUR22:19	H88
HOUSE236:18	H10	ELEMEN11:28	H148	HUMOUR22:39	H108
HOUSE236:20	H12	ELEMEN11:34	H154	HUMOUR23:4	H114
HOUSE236:21	H13	ELEMEN11:35	H155	HUMOUR23:12	H122
HOUSE236:24	H16	ELEMEN11:39	H159	HUMOUR23:13	H123
HOUSE236:27	H19	ELEMEN12:5	H165	HUMOUR23:19	H129
HOUSE236:34	H26	ELEMEN12:11	H171	HUMOUR23:30	H140
HOUSE237:1	H31	ELEMEN12:17	H177	HUMOUR24:6	H155
HOUSE237:11	H41	ELEMEN12:18	H178	HUMOUR24:25	H174
HOUSE237:26	H56	ELEMEN12:22	H182	HUMOUR25:6	H195
HOUSE237:28	H58	ELEMEN12:35	H195	HUMOUR25:8	H197
MYNE (1) [mine]		ELEMEN13:2	H203	HUMOUR25:9	H198
2SIMON195:11	HP271	ELEMEN13:35	H236	HUMOUR25:10	H199
O' (2) [of]		ELEMEN13:36	H237	HUMOUR25:17	H206
MGREC98:31	H1833	ELEMEN13:37	H238	HUMOUR25:27	H216
MGREC110:10	H2310	ELEMEN14:1	H243	HUMOUR25:30	H219
OF (1290)		ELEMEN14:9	H251	HUMOUR26:4	H234
FATHER5:3	H4	ELEMEN14:15	H257	HUMOUR26:14	H244
FATHER5:4	H5	ELEMEN14:20	H262	HUMOUR26:24	H254
FATHER5:5	H6	ELEMEN14:27	H269	HUMOUR26:26	H256
FATHER5:16	H17	ELEMEN14:30	H272	HUMOUR26:29	H259
FATHER5:19	H20	ELEMEN15:31	H313	HUMOUR26:30	H260
FATHER5:20	H21	ELEMEN16:1	H324	HUMOUR26:34	H264
FATHER5:23	H24	ELEMEN16:13	H336	HUMOUR26:35	H265
FATHER6:2	H36	ELEMEN16:17	H340	HUMOUR27:22	H293
PROLOG6:18	H3	ELEMEN16:19	H342	HUMOUR27:26	H297
PROLOG6:19	H4	ELEMEN16:23	H346	HUMOUR27:34	H305
PROLOG7:10	H24	ELEMEN16:34	H357	HUMOUR27:40	H311
PROLOG7:22	H34	ELEMEN17:1	H365	HUMOUR28:13	H325
PROLOG7:33	H44	ELEMEN17:14	H378	HUMOUR28:23	H335
PROLOG8:1	H49	ELEMEN17:18	H382	HUMOUR28:24	H336
ELEMEN8:7	H5	ELEMEN17:27	H391	HUMOUR29:38	H389
ELEMEN8:35	H33	ELEMEN17:32	H396	HUMOUR29:40	H391
ELEMEN9:3	H37	ELEMEN17:35	H399	HUMOUR30:8	H400
ELEMEN9:28	H62	ELEMEN17:38	H402	HUMOUR30:10	H402
ELEMEN9:32	H66	ELEMEN18:39	H443	HUMOUR30:15	H407
ELEMEN10:1	H76	ELEMEN19:1	H446	HUMOUR30:26	H418
ELEMEN10:17	H92	ELEMEN19:4	H449	HUMOUR30:29	H421
ELEMEN10:18	H93	ELEMEN19:20	H465	HUMOUR30:35	H427
ELEMEN10:19	H94	ELEMEN19:22	H467	HUMOUR31:10	H443
ELEMEN10:20	H95	ELEMEN19:36	H477	HUMOUR32:14	H488
ELEMEN10:25	H100	ELEMEN20:2	H484	HUMOUR32:19	H493
ELEMEN10:26	H101	ELEMEN20:4	H486	HUMOUR32:21	H495
ELEMEN10:37	H112	HUMOUR20:9	H1	HUMOUR33:6	H520
ELEMEN10:38	H113	HUMOUR20:22	H14	HUMOUR33:21	H535
ELEMEN10:39	H114	HUMOUR20:24	H16	HUMOUR33:28	H542
ELEMEN11:6	H126	HUMOUR20:26	H18	HUMOUR33:32	H546
ELEMEN11:10	H130	HUMOUR20:29	H21	HUMOUR33:36	H550
ELEMEN11:15	H135	HUMOUR21:17	H45	HUMOUR33:39	H553
ELEMEN11:22	H142	HUMOUR21:28	H56	HUMOUR33:41	H555
ELEMEN11:24	H144	HUMOUR21:30	H58	HUMOUR34:9	H564

MASSYR64:17	H441	MPERS73:26	H811	MPERS80:38	H1105
MASSYR64:22	H446	MPERS73:31	H816	MPERS80:39	H1106
MASSYR64:27	H451	MPERS73:37	H822	MPERS81:1	H1109
MASSYR64:37	H461	MPERS74:2	H827	MPERS81:7	H1115
MASSYR65:16	H481	MPERS74:6	H831	MPERS81:9	H1117
MASSYR65:29	H494	MPERS74:22	H845	MPERS81:28	H1136
MASSYR66:5	H511	MPERS74:23	H846	MPERS81:32	H1140
MASSYR66:9	H515	MPERS74:27	H850	MPERS81:36	H1143
MASSYR66:11	H517	MPERS74:31	H854	MPERS82:7	H1154
MASSYR66:17	H523	MPERS74:35	H858	MPERS82:8	H1155
MASSYR67:4	H550	MPERS75:4	H865	MPERS82:11	H1158
MASSYR67:35	H581	MPERS75:15	H876	MPERS82:15	H1162
MASSYR67:36	H582	MPERS75:24	H881	MPERS82:27	H1174
MASSYR67:40	H586	MPERS75:29	H886	MPERS82:29	H1176
MASSYR68:6	H592	MPERS75:33	H890	MPERS82:34	H1181
MASSYR68:15	H601	MPERS75:36	H893	MPERS82:38	H1185
MASSYR68:19	H605	MPERS75:38	H895	MPERS82:40	H1187
MASSYR68:20	H606	MPERS76:13	H911	MPERS83:2	H1190
MASSYR68:29	H615	MPERS76:40	H938	MPERS83:9	H1197
MASSYR68:31	H617	MPERS77:6	H945	MPERS83:14	H1202
MPERS69:1	H623	MPERS77:16	H957	MPERS83:17	H1205
MPERS69:5	H627	MPERS77:17	H958	MPERS83:28	H1216
MPERS69:13	H635	MPERS77:18	H959	MPERS83:32	H1220
MPERS69:20	H642	MPERS77:25	H966	MPERS83:40	H1228
MPERS69:21	H643	MPERS77:36	H977	MPERS84:11	H1239
MPERS69:24	H646	MPERS78:3	H984	MPERS84:12	H1240
MPERS69:37	H659	MPERS78:9	H990	MPERS84:12	H1241
MPERS69:41	H671	MPERS78:10	H991	MPERS84:19	H1255
MPERS70:5	H676	MPERS78:11	H992	MPERS84:25	H1261
MPERS70:18	H689	MPERS78:13	H994	MPERS85:1	H1277
MPERS70:32	H703	MPERS78:14	H995	MPERS85:2	H1278
MPERS70:36	H707	MPERS78:16	H997	MPERS85:9	H1285
MPERS70:37	H708	MPERS78:33	H1014	MPERS85:38	H1314
MPERS71:14	H728	MPERS78:35	H1016	MPERS86:29	H1345
MPERS71:16	H730	MPERS78:38	H1019	MPERS87:6	H1362
MPERS71:17	H731	MPERS79:2	H1024	MPERS87:19	H1373
MPERS71:23	H737	MPERS79:6	H1028	MPERS87:28	H1380
MPERS71:25	H739	MPERS79:6	H1028	MPERS88:5	H1398
MPERS71:27	H741	MPERS79:8	H1030	MPERS88:6	H1399
MPERS72:4	H755	MPERS79:11	H1033	MPERS88:21	H1414
MPERS72:19	H767	MPERS79:23	H1049	MPERS88:28	H1421
MPERS72:27	H773	MPERS79:25	H1051	MPERS89:5	H1439
MPERS72:31	H775	MPERS79:26	H1052	MPERS89:10	H1444
MPERS72:32	H776	MPERS79:27	H1053	MPERS89:14	H1448
MPERS72:34	H778	MPERS80:2	H1069	MPERS89:25	H1459
MPERS72:35	H779	MPERS80:3	H1070	MPERS90:5	H1478
MPERS72:37	H782	MPERS80:8	H1075	MPERS90:10	H1483
MPERS73:5	H792	MPERS80:15	H1082	MPERS90:38	H1505
MPERS73:15	H802	MPERS80:18	H1085	MPERS90:39	H1506
MPERS73:17	H804	MPERS80:23	H1090	MPERS91:16	H1524
MPERS73:20	H807	MPERS80:25	H1092	MPERS91:29	H1543

MPERS91:31	H1545	MGREC100:22	H1906	MGREC108:2	H2218
MPERS91:32	H1546	MGREC100:23	H1907	MGREC108:7	H2223
MPERS91:35	H1549	MGREC100:24	H1908	MGREC108:23	H2239
MPERS91:36	H1550	MGREC100:26	H1910	MGREC108:31	H2247
MPERS91:39	H1553	MGREC101:31	H1956	MGREC109:5	H2262
MPERS91:40	H1554	MGREC101:33	H1958	MGREC109:17	H2276
MPERS92:3	H1557	MGREC102:1	H1971	MGREC109:21	H2280
MPERS92:5	H1562	MGREC102:7	H1977	MGREC109:27	H2286
MPERS92:18	H1576	MGREC102:9	H1979	MGREC110:8	H2308
MPERS92:19	H1577	MGREC102:11	H1981	MGREC110:18	H2321
MPERS92:36	H1594	MGREC102:16	H1986	MGREC111:6	H2351
MPERS92:37	H1595	MGREC102:29	H1999	MGREC111:9	H2354
MPERS93:1	H1598	MGREC102:30	H2000	MGREC111:16	H2361
MPERS93:2	H1599	MGREC102:31	H2001	MGREC111:19	H2364
MPERS93:5	H1602	MGREC102:33	H2003	MGREC111:20	H2365
MGREC6:11	H1608	MGREC102:34	H2004	MGREC111:27	H2372
MGREC6:16	H1613	MGREC102:36	H2006	MGREC112:13	H2399
MGREC6:20	H1617	MGREC102:37	H2007	MGREC112:19	H2405
MGREC6:35	H1632	MGREC103:4	H2015	MGREC112:22	H2408
MGREC94:10	H1644	MGREC103:8	H2019	MGREC112:25	H2411
MGREC94:13	H1647	MGREC103:12	H2023	MGREC112:37	H2423
MGREC94:25	H1663	MGREC103:14	H2025	MGREC112:40	H2426
MGREC95:2	H1681	MGREC103:16	H2027	MGREC113:29	H2456
MGREC95:5	H1684	MGREC103:22	H2033	MGREC113:32	H2459
MGREC95:7	H1686	MGREC103:27	H2038	MGREC113:39	H2466
MGREC95:8	H1687	MGREC103:33	H2044	MGREC114:10	H2478
MGREC95:14	H1693	MGREC104:8	H2060	MGREC114:17	H2487
MGREC95:17	H1696	MGREC104:19	H2071	MGREC114:27	H2497
MGREC95:18	H1697	MGREC104:20	H2072	MGREC114:29	H2499
MGREC95:37	H1716	MGREC104:25	H2077	MGREC114:32	H2502
MGREC96:10	H1730	MGREC104:31	H2083	MGREC114:36	H2506
MGREC96:11	H1731	MGREC105:5	H2098	MGREC115:1	H2512
MGREC96:15	H1735	MGREC105:11	H2104	MGREC115:5	H2516
MGREC96:24	H1744	MGREC105:17	H2110	MGREC115:14	H2523
MGREC97:4	H1765	MGREC105:21	H2114	MGREC115:15	H2527
MGREC97:8	H1769	MGREC105:23	H2116	MGREC115:32	H2551
MGREC97:13	H1774	MGREC105:25	H2118	MGREC116:2	H2562
MGREC97:26	H1787	MGREC105:40	H2133	MGREC116:5	H2565
MGREC97:27	H1788	MGREC106:5	H2139	MGREC116:6	H2566
MGREC97:33	H1794	MGREC106:6	H2140	MGREC116:12	H2578
MGREC97:37	H1798	MGREC106:15	H2149	MGREC116:19	H2585
MGREC98:3	H1805	MGREC106:17	H2151	MGREC116:23	H2589
MGREC98:19	H1821	MGREC106:22	H2156	MGREC117:4	H2611
MGREC98:23	H1825	MGREC106:38	H2172	MGREC117:7	H2614
MGREC98:24	H1826	MGREC106:41	H2175	MGREC117:10	H2617
MGREC98:40	H1842	MGREC107:1	H2176	MGREC117:18	H2625
MGREC99:27	H1870	MGREC107:2	H2177	MGREC117:19	H2626
MGREC99:32	H1875	MGREC107:13	H2188	MGREC117:34	H2641
MGREC100:5	H1889	MGREC107:15	H2190	MGREC118:4	H2651
MGREC100:8	H1892	MGREC107:19	H2194	MGREC118:5	H2652
MGREC100:20	H1904	MGREC107:41	H2216	MGREC118:11	H2658

MGREC118:14	H2661	MGREC127:27	H3057	MROMAN138:9	H3499
MGREC118:22	H2669	MGREC127:29	H3059	MROMAN138:19	H3509
MGREC118:25	H2674	MGREC127:38	H3068	MROMAN138:21	H3511
MGREC118:38	H2687	MGREC128:1	H3074	MROMAN138:22	H3512
MGREC119:10	H2700	MGREC128:8	H3081	MROMAN138:32	H3522
MGREC119:20	H2710	MGREC128:9	H3082	MROMAN139:1	H3529
MGREC119:32	H2722	MGREC128:39	H3112	MROMAN139:3	H3531
MGREC119:37	H2727	MGREC129:17	H3131	MROMAN139:5	H3533
MGREC119:41	H2731	MGREC129:19	H3133	MROMAN139:11	H3539
MGREC120:3	H2734	MGREC129:21	H3135	MROMAN139:15	H3543
MGREC~~120:4~~	H2739	MGREC129:25	H3139	MROMAN139:23	H3551
MGREC~~120:20~~	H2756	MGREC129:30	H3144	MROMAN139:24	~~H3551~~
MGREC120:22	H2759	MGREC129:33	H3147	MROMAN139:33	H3559
MGREC120:24	H2761	MGREC129:34	H3148	DIALOG141:10	H9
MGREC120:25	H2762	MGREC129:38	H3152	DIALOG141:11	H10
MGREC120:33	H2770	MGREC130:7	H3162	DIALOG141:15	H14
MGREC121:5	H2783	MGREC130:14	H3169	DIALOG142:21	H50
MGREC~~121:15~~	H2793	MGREC130:23	H3178	DIALOG142:22	H51
MGREC121:16	~~H2795~~	MGREC130:39	H3184	DIALOG142:35	H64
MGREC~~121:16~~	H2795	MGREC131:7	H3197	DIALOG143:7	H74
MGREC121:19	H2801	MGREC131:13	H3205	DIALOG143:7	H74
MGREC121:21	H2803	MGREC131:17	H3209	DIALOG143:9	H78
MGREC121:26	H2808	MGREC131:36	H3228	DIALOG143:12	H81
MGREC121:27	H2809	MGREC132:14	H3249	DIALOG143:13	H82
MGREC121:40	H2822	MGREC132:24	H3269	DIALOG143:21	H90
MGREC122:8	H2831	MGREC132:33	H3280	DIALOG143:26	H95
MGREC122:11	H2836	MGREC132:39	H3286	DIALOG143:28	H97
MGREC122:35	H2856	MGREC133:2	H3290	DIALOG143:29	H98
MGREC122:39	H2860	MGREC133:13	H3301	DIALOG143:31	H100
MGREC123:1	H2863	MGREC133:20	H3308	DIALOG143:37	H106
MGREC123:18	H2882	MGREC~~133:22~~	H3311	DIALOG144:11	H121
MGREC123:19	H2883	MGREC133:26	H3316	DIALOG144:15	H125
MGREC123:26	H2890	MGREC133:32	H3322	DIALOG144:18	H128
MGREC123:34	H2898	MGREC133:33	H3323	DIALOG~~144:26~~	H135
MGREC124:21	H2928	MGREC133:39	H3329	DIALOG144:27	~~H135~~
MGREC124:30	H2937	MGREC134:17	H3348	DIALOG144:33	H141
MGREC124:31	H2938	MGREC134:35	H3366	DIALOG144:41	H149
MGREC125:18	H2966	MGREC135:18	H3390	DIALOG145:4	H153
MGREC125:24	H2974	MGREC135:20	H3392	DIALOG145:16	H165
MGREC125:29	H2979	MGREC135:21	H3393	DIALOG145:17	H166
MGREC125:39	H2989	MGREC135:22	H3394	DIALOG145:20	H169
MGREC126:11	H3002	MGREC135:24	H3396	DIALOG146:3	H191
MGREC126:20	H3011	MGREC~~136:8~~	H3422	DIALOG146:11	H199
MGREC126:25	H3016	MGREC136:9	H3423	DIALOG146:18	H204
MGREC126:27	H3018	MGREC136:13	H3427	DIALOG~~146:32~~	H219
MGREC126:29	H3020	MGREC136:16	H3430	DIALOG146:34	H220
MGREC126:34	~~H3023~~	MROMAN136:32	H3446	DIALOG146:38	H224
MGREC127:1	H3031	MROMAN137:1	H3452	DIALOG147:5	H231
MGREC127:7	H3037	MROMAN137:3	H3454	DIALOG147:9	H235
MGREC127:9	H3039	MROMAN137:8	H3459	DIALOG147:22	~~H247~~
MGREC127:10	H3040	MROMAN137:22	H3473	DIALOG147:31	H255

AUTHOR177:30	H2	MEDDM196:18	HP273	MEDDM202:24	HP282
AUTHOR178:15	H25	MEDDM196:33	HP274	MEDDM202:26	HP282
SICKNES178:16	H0	MEDDM197:1	HP274	MEDDM202:27	HP282
SICKNES178:27	H10	MEDDM197:12	HP274	MEDDM202:30	HP282
DISTEMP179:13	H1	MEDDM197:15	HP274	MEDDM202:32	HP282
DISTEMP179:14	H2	MEDDM197:20	HP275	MEDDM202:34	HP282
DISTEMP179:24	H12	MEDDM197:22	HP275	MEDDM203:2	HP283
BIRTH179:26	H1-2	MEDDM197:24	HP275	MEDDM203:3	HP283
BIRTH179:26	H1-2	MEDDM197:28	HP275	MEDDM203:4	HP283
1HUSB180:27	H6	MEDDM198:10	HP276	MEDDM203:7	HP283
1LETTER181:4	H2	MEDDM198:13	HP276	MEDDM203:8	HP283
1LETTER181:18	H16	MEDDM198:18	HP276	MEDDM203:12	HP283
1LETTER181:23	H21	MEDDM198:35	HP277	MEDDM203:15	HP283
1LETTER181:24	H22	MEDDM199:8	HP277	MEDDM203:19	HP283
1LETTER181:27	H25	MEDDM199:9	HP277	MEDDM203:22	HP283
2LETTER181:35	H5	MEDDM199:12	HP277	MEDDM203:24	HP283
2LETTER181:36	H6	MEDDM199:16	HP278	MEDDM203:25	HP283
2LETTER182:4	H10	MEDDM199:21	HP278	MEDDM203:31	HP284
2LETTER182:11	H17	MEDDM199:23	HP278	MEDDM203:35	HP284
2LETTER182:24	H30	MEDDM199:24	HP278	MEDDM204:2	HP284
2LETTER182:29	H35	MEDDM199:26	HP278	MEDDM204:3	HP284
2LETTER182:30	H36	MEDDM199:27	HP278	MEDDM204:4	HP284
3LETTER183:9	H11	MEDDM200:2	HP278	MEDDM204:7	HP284
3LETTER183:21	H23	MEDDM200:3	HP278	MEDDM204:15	HP284
VERSES183:37	H4	MEDDM200:9	HP279	MEDDM204:19	HP285
CHILDRN184:20	H9	MEDDM200:19	HP279	MEDDM204:20	HP285
CHILDRN184:27	H16	MEDDM200:22	HP279	MEDDM204:21	HP285
CHILDRN184:34	H23	MEDDM200:24	HP279	MEDDM204:31	HP285
CHILDRN185:20	H46	MEDDM200:25	HP279	MEDDM205:1	HP285
CHILDRN185:21	H47	MEDDM200:28	HP279	MEDDM205:2	HP285
CHILDRN185:38	H64	MEDDM200:33	HP280	MEDDM205:3	HP285
CHILDRN186:16	H83	MEDDM200:34	HP280	MEDDM205:4	HP285
ELIZB186:31	H1-2	MEDDM201:7	HP280	MEDDM205:5	HP285
ELIZB186:35	H7	MEDDM201:8	HP280	MEDDM205:6	HP285
ANNEB187:12	H1-2	MEDDM201:15	HP280	MEDDM205:7	HP285
ANNEB187:23	H13	MEDDM201:21	HP281	MEDDM205:12	HP286
MERCY188:17	H1-2	MEDDM201:25	HP281	MEDDM205:16	HP286
MERCY188:19	H4-5	MEDDM201:27	HP281	MEDDM205:17	HP286
MERCY189:6	H27	MEDDM201:28	HP281	MEDDM205:19	HP286
2SIMON195:5	HP271	MEDDM201:31	HP281	MEDDM205:20	HP286
2SIMON195:7	HP271	MEDDM201:32	HP281	MEDDM205:24	HP286
2SIMON195:8	HP271	MEDDM201:33	HP281	MEDDM205:26	HP286
2SIMON195:12	HP271	MEDDM202:2	HP281	MEDDM205:27	HP286
2SIMON195:15	HP271	MEDDM202:3	HP281	MEDDM205:31	HP286
2SIMON195:16	HP271	MEDDM202:4	HP281	MEDDM205:32	HP286
MEDDM195:26	HP272	MEDDM202:5	HP281	MEDDM206:4	HP287
MEDDM195:33	HP272	MEDDM202:6	HP281	MEDDM206:6	HP287
MEDDM195:36	HP272	MEDDM202:11	HP281	MEDDM206:8	HP287
MEDDM196:4	HP272	MEDDM202:13	HP282	MEDDM206:10	HP287
MEDDM196:6	HP272	MEDDM202:14	HP282	MEDDM206:11	HP287
MEDDM196:17	HP273	MEDDM202:16	HP282	MEDDM206:12	HP287

MEDDM206:13	HP287	MYCHILD216:2	HP241	WHAT224:6	H6
MEDDM206:15	HP287	MYCHILD216:5	HP241	WHAT224:16	H16
MEDDM206:20	HP287	MYCHILD216:9	HP241	WHAT224:18	H18
MEDDM206:25	HP287	MYCHILD216:16	HP241	MYSOUL224:26	H2
MEDDM206:27	HP288	MYCHILD216:18	HP241	MYSOUL225:8	H12
MEDDM206:28	HP288	MYCHILD216:20	HP241	28AUG225:30	HP254
MEDDM206:31	HP288	MYCHILD216:24	HP242	28AUG226:7	HP254
MEDDM206:33	HP288	MYCHILD216:26	HP242	11MAYA226:13	HP255
MEDDM206:34	HP288	MYCHILD216:29	HP242	11MAYA226:16	HP255
MEDDM206:36	HP288	MYCHILD216:32	HP242	11MAYA226:18	HP255
MEDDM206:37	HP288	MYCHILD217:1	HP242	11MAYA226:20	HP255
MEDDM207:4	HP288	MYCHILD217:3	HP242	11MAYA226:22	HP255
MEDDM207:7	HP288	MYCHILD217:5	HP242	30SEPT227:18	HP257
MEDDM207:13	HP288	MYCHILD217:10	HP242	30SEPT227:20	HP257
MEDDM207:16	HP288	MYCHILD217:16	HP243	30SEPT227:25	HP257
MEDDM207:22	HP289	MYCHILD217:17	HP243	30SEPT227:32	HP257
MEDDM207:24	HP289	MYCHILD217:19	HP243	30SEPT227:33	HP257
MEDDM207:28	HP289	MYCHILD217:21	HP243	SAMUEL228:2	H3
MEDDM207:29	HP289	MYCHILD217:26	HP243	SAMUEL228:4	H5
MEDDM207:31	HP289	MYCHILD217:28	HP243	11MAYB228:23	HP259
MEDDM207:32	HP289	MYCHILD217:30	HP243	11MAYB228:24	HP259
MEDDM207:33	HP289	MYCHILD217:31	HP243	11MAYB228:25	HP259
MEDDM207:35	HP289	MYCHILD217:32	HP243	11MAYB228:29	HP259
MEDDM207:36	HP289	MYCHILD217:34	HP243	11MAYB228:31	HP259
MEDDM208:1	HP289	MYCHILD217:37	HP243	THEART229:18	H20
MEDDM208:2	HP289	MYCHILD218:2	HP243	RESTOR229:19	H1-2
MEDDM208:3	HP289	MYCHILD218:3	HP243	RESTOR229:30	H13
MEDDM208:6	HP289	MYCHILD218:6	HP243-4	SON230:19	H1-2
MEDDM208:7	HP290	MYCHILD218:12	HP244	SON230:29	H12
MEDDM208:8	HP290	MYCHILD218:13	HP244	SON231:5	H17
MEDDM208:9	HP290	MYCHILD218:24	HP244	SON231:14	H26
MEDDM208:21	HP290	MYCHILD218:26	HP244	SON231:21	H33
MEDDM208:24	HP290	MYCHILD218:32	HP244	SON231:24	H36
MEDDM208:25	HP290	MYCHILD218:36	HP244	2HUSB232:4	H5
MEDDM208:28	HP290	MYCHILD219:7	HP245	2HUSB232:8	H9
MEDDM208:30	HP290	FEVER220:31	H11	2HUSB232:22	H23
MEDDM208:31	HP290	SOREFIT221:21	H7	2HUSB233:7	H40
MEDDM208:35	HP290	SOREFIT221:31	H17	2HUSB233:15	H48
MEDDM208:36	HP291	FAINTING222:11	H1	HOURS234:10	H24
MEDDM209:5	HP291	FAINTING222:12	H2	HOURS234:28	H42
MEDDM209:13	HP291	MED223:4	HP250	HOURS234:29	H43
MEDDM209:23	HP291	MED223:9	HP250	ACK235:4	H3-4
PILGRIM210:12	H12	MED223:10	HP250	ACK235:5	H5
PILGRIM210:40	H40	MED223:13	HP250	ACK235:15	H15
TOCHILD215:6	H6	MED223:18	HP250	HOUSE236:16	H8
MYCHILD215:10	HP240	MED223:19	HP250	HOUSE236:17	H9
MYCHILD215:13	HP240	JULY223:21	HP251	HOUSE236:31	H23
MYCHILD215:19	HP240	JULY223:29	HP251	HOUSE237:6	H36
MYCHILD215:24	HP240	JULY223:32	HP251	HOUSE237:14	H44
MYCHILD215:28	HP241	JULY223:34	HP251	**OF'S (6) [of his]**	
MYCHILD215:32	HP241	JULY223:35	HP251	HUMOUR28:4	H316

MPERS~~92:2~~	H1556	
MPERS92:13	H1571	
MGREC6:15	H1612	
MGREC116:9	H2569	
MGREC130:34	~~H3181~~	
ON (248)		
FATHER5:3	H4	
FATHER6:10	H44	
PROLOG7:17	H30	
ELEMEN9:27	H61	
ELEMEN12:5	H165	
ELEMEN12:13	H173	
ELEMEN13:31	H232	
ELEMEN14:16	H258	
ELEMEN16:27	H350	
ELEMEN18:22	H426	
HUMOUR21:40	H68	
HUMOUR22:40	H109	
HUMOUR25:38	H227	
HUMOUR28:1	H313	
HUMOUR32:23	H497	
AGES36:11	H35	
AGES36:17	H41	
AGES38:12	H115	
AGES38:16	H119	
AGES39:8	H151	
AGES39:31	H174	
AGES39:35	H178	
AGES41:29	H246	
AGES42:41	H297	
AGES43:8	H303	
AGES44:7	H340	
AGES44:24	H357	
AGES~~45:4~~	H385	
AGES45:7	~~H390~~	
SEASONS46:28	H4	
SEASONS47:19	H35	
SEASONS49:25	~~H114~~	
SEASONS51:7	H181	
SEASONS51:33	H209	
MASSYR54:3	H30	
MASSYR54:21	H48	
MASSYR55:30	H96	
MASSYR55:31	H97	
MASSYR56:22	H128	
MASSYR57:6	H153	
MASSYR59:31	H255	
MASSYR62:15	H360	
MASSYR62:34	H379	
MASSYR62:34	H379	
MASSYR62:35	H380	
MASSYR62:35	H380	
MASSYR63:7	H392	
MASSYR66:29	H535	
MASSYR67:9	H555	
MPERS69:35	H657	
MPERS70:12	H683	
MPERS70:24	H695	
MPERS70:29	H700	
MPERS72:40	H786	
MPERS73:13	H800	
MPERS74:3	H828	
MPERS74:7	H832	
MPERS74:9	H834	
MPERS75:34	H891	
MPERS75:37	H894	
MPERS75:40	H897	
MPERS76:37	H935	
MPERS77:7	H946	
MPERS77:16	H955	
MPERS77:35	H976	
MPERS77:39	H980	
MPERS~~79:2~~	H1024	
MPERS79:34	H1060	
MPERS80:4	H1071	
MPERS80:6	H1073	
MPERS84:12	H1240	
MPERS84:37	H1273	
MPERS86:1	H1317	
MPERS86:11	H1327	
MPERS86:40	H1356	
MPERS87:39	H1391	
MPERS88:3	H1396	
MPERS88:20	H1413	
MPERS88:22	H1415	
MPERS88:36	H1429	
MPERS88:40	H1433	
MPERS89:27	H1461	
MPERS90:6	H1479	
MPERS90:9	H1482	
MPERS90:27	H1494	
MPERS91:6	H1514	
MPERS91:10	H1518	
MGREC6:27	H1624	
MGREC6:28	H1625	
MGREC6:30	H1627	
MGREC6:34	H1631	
MGREC94:17	H1651	
MGREC94:21	H1659	
MGREC94:22	H1660	
MGREC95:30	H1709	
MGREC96:13	H1733	
MGREC96:39	H1759	
MGREC98:28	H1830	
MGREC100:28	H1912	
MGREC100:29	H1913	
MGREC101:3	H1928	
MGREC101:24	H1949	
MGREC102:8	H1978	
MGREC102:19	H1989	
MGREC103:4	H2015	
MGREC103:18	H2029	
MGREC103:19	H2030	
MGREC103:29	H2040	
MGREC104:27	H2079	
MGREC104:31	H2083	
MGREC106:6	H2140	
MGREC106:13	H2147	
MGREC106:34	H2168	
MGREC107:36	H2211	
MGREC110:1	H2301	
MGREC110:6	H2306	
MGREC110:14	H2314	
MGREC110:37	H2341	
MGREC111:6	H2351	
MGREC111:37	H2382	
MGREC113:3	H2430	
MGREC113:10	H2437	
MGREC113:15	H2442	
MGREC114:25	H2495	
MGREC115:9	~~H2518~~	
MGREC118:11	H2658	
MGREC118:25	H2674	
MGREC119:14	H2704	
MGREC120:15	H2750	
MGREC120:40	H2777	
MGREC121:23	H2805	
MGREC122:18	H2843	
MGREC123:3	H2865	
MGREC123:17	H2881	
MGREC123:19	H2883	
MGREC123:37	H2901	
MGREC124:8	~~H2913~~	
MGREC125:15	H2963	
MGREC125:29	H2979	
MGREC125:40	H2990	
MGREC126:8	H2999	
MGREC128:28	H3101	
MGREC~~132:20~~	H3264	
MGREC134:1	H3332	
MGREC134:20	H3351	
MGREC134:28	H3359	
MROMAN138:3	H3493	

CONTEM171:10 H114	MPERS79:7 H1029	MYCHILD216:24 HP242
SICKNES178:32 H15	MPERS80:37 H1104	MYCHILD217:12 HP242
BIRTH179:28 H4	MPERS81:16 H1124	MYCHILD219:7 HP245
2LETTER182:34 H40	MPERS85:15 H1291	FEVER220:23 H3
1SIMON188:12 H13	MPERS86:36 H1352	FEVER220:25 H5
1SIMON188:13 H14	MPERS88:24 H1417	SOREFIT222:6 H25
MEDDM200:34 HP280	MPERS88:32 H1425	28AUG225:26 HP254
MEDDM200:35 HP280	MPERS92:21 H1579	30SEPT227:20 HP257
MEDDM202:25 HP282	MGREC105:3 H2096	30SEPT227:22 HP257
MEDDM202:28 HP282	MGREC105:8 H2101	30SEPT227:32 HP257
MEDDM203:3 HP283	MGREC107:21 H2196	11MAYB228:29 HP259
MEDDM203:19 HP283	MGREC113:4 H2431	RESTOR229:22 H5
MEDDM205:17 HP286	MGREC121:17 H2799	SON230:19 H1-2
MEDDM205:18 HP286	MGREC122:1 H2824	SON231:13 H25
MEDDM205:27 HP286	MGREC122:8 H2831	HOUSE236:23 H15
MEDDM207:23 HP289	MGREC122:29 H2848	**OVT (1) [out]**
MEDDM207:25 HP289	MGREC123:38 H2902	ACK235:4 H3-4
MEDDM207:27 HP289	MGREC126:19 H3010	**OVER (12)**
MEDDM209:4 HP291	MGREC128:37 H3110	HUMOUR28:18 H330
OURS (3)	MGREC132:8 H3243	AGES43:4 H299
PROLOG7:33 H44	MGREC135:24 H3396	MPERS72:21 H769
HUMOUR30:23 H415	MROMAN139:29 H3555	MPERS76:2 H900
QELIZ157:16 H84	DIALOG142:4 H33	MGREC100:15 H1899
OUT (96)	DIALOG145:1 H150	MGREC107:29 H2204
ELEMEN10:17 H92	DIALOG146:32 H219	MGREC107:37 H2212
ELEMEN10:18 H93	DIALOG147:11 H237	MROMAN138:18 H3508
ELEMEN12:22 H182	DIALOG147:12 H238	CONTEM174:30 H227
ELEMEN15:12 H294	DIALOG147:31 H255	FLESH176:23 H63
HUMOUR22:38 H107	DIALOG148:5 H270	MYCHILD218:7 HP244
HUMOUR31:11 H444	SIDNEY151:17 H69	MYCHILD218:17 HP244
AGES35:38 H24	SIDNEY151:22 H72	**'S (1) [his]**
AGES36:24 H48	QELIZ155:22 H13	MGREC106:14 H2148
AGES40:27 H208	CONTEM173:29 H194	**SHE (167)**
AGES41:28 H245	AUTHOR178:15 H25	ELEMEN8:24 H22
AGES41:34 H249	CHILDRN184:27 H16	ELEMEN14:6 H250
AGES43:13 H306	MEDDM196:18 HP273	ELEMEN14:25 H267
AGES45:22 H404	MEDDM196:33 HP274	ELEMEN15:19 H301
AGES45:22 H410	MEDDM197:4 HP274	HUMOUR20:25 H17
SEASONS47:8 H24	MEDDM198:29 HP277	HUMOUR20:29 H21
SEASONS48:2 H55	MEDDM199:3 HP277	HUMOUR20:32 H24
SEASONS49:28 H117	MEDDM202:5 HP281	HUMOUR21:7 H35
MASSYR54:34 H61	MEDDM202:27 HP282	HUMOUR21:33 H61
MASSYR57:25 H172	MEDDM203:3 HP283	HUMOUR21:35 H63
MASSYR58:1 H186	MEDDM206:23 HP287	HUMOUR21:36 H64
MASSYR61:2 H307	MEDDM207:2 HP288	HUMOUR21:37 H65
MASSYR65:22 H487	MEDDM207:28 HP289	HUMOUR21:41 H69
MPERS70:11 H682	MEDDM208:1 HP289	HUMOUR22:2 H71
MPERS73:20 H807	MEDDM208:6 HP289	HUMOUR22:3 H72
MPERS74:2 H827	MEDDM208:30 HP290	HUMOUR22:9 H78
MPERS75:29 H886	MEDDM209:3 HP291	HUMOUR22:12 H81
MPERS75:34 H891	MEDDM209:13 HP291	HUMOUR22:16 H85

FLESH177:28	H109	MEDDM197:27	HP275	MEDDM204:14	HP284
SICKNES178:35	H18	MEDDM198:9	HP276	MEDDM204:22	HP285
DISTEMP179:17	H5	MEDDM198:10	HP276	MEDDM204:26	HP285
BIRTH180:3	H13	MEDDM198:14	HP276	MEDDM204:27	HP285
BIRTH180:7	H17	MEDDM198:17	HP276	MEDDM204:28	HP285
BIRTH180:10	H20	MEDDM198:21	HP276	MEDDM204:29	HP285
1HUSB180:28	H7	MEDDM198:22	HP276	MEDDM204:30	HP285
1HUSB180:29	H8	MEDDM199:15	HP278	MEDDM205:1	HP285
1HUSB180:34	H13	MEDDM199:24	HP278	MEDDM205:11	HP286
2LETTER182:9	H15	MEDDM200:2	HP278	MEDDM205:16	HP286
2LETTER182:10	H16	MEDDM200:9	HP279	MEDDM205:18	HP286
2LETTER182:13	H19	MEDDM200:10	HP279	MEDDM205:20	HP286
2LETTER182:15	H21	MEDDM200:11	HP279	MEDDM205:23	HP286
2LETTER182:16	H22	MEDDM200:12	HP279	MEDDM205:28	HP286
3LETTER182:36	H1	MEDDM200:22	HP279	MEDDM205:31	HP286
3LETTER183:15	H17	MEDDM200:27	HP279	MEDDM205:35	HP287
3LETTER183:17	H19	MEDDM200:29	HP279	MEDDM205:36	HP287
CHILDRN185:4	H30	MEDDM200:30	HP279	MEDDM206:1	HP287
CHILDRN185:6	H32	MEDDM201:22	HP281	MEDDM206:2	HP287
CHILDRN185:8	H34	MEDDM201:29	HP281	MEDDM206:8	HP287
CHILDRN186:5	H72	MEDDM202:4	HP281	MEDDM206:15	HP287
CHILDRN186:19	H86	MEDDM202:6	HP281	MEDDM206:19	HP287
CHILDRN186:20	H87	MEDDM202:7	HP281	MEDDM206:22	HP287
ELIZB186:36	H8	MEDDM202:8	HP281	MEDDM206:35	HP288
ELIZB187:11	H19	MEDDM202:12	HP281	MEDDM207:4	HP288
ANNEB187:28	H18	MEDDM202:17	HP282	MEDDM207:5	HP288
MERCY188:27	H13	MEDDM202:21	HP282	MEDDM207:8	HP288
MERCY189:14	H35	MEDDM202:24	HP282	MEDDM207:11	HP288
2SIMON195:6	HP271	MEDDM202:25	HP282	MEDDM207:14	HP288
2SIMON195:14	HP271	MEDDM202:33	HP282	MEDDM207:16	HP288
2SIMON195:15	HP271	MEDDM203:2	HP283	MEDDM207:18	HP289
MEDDM195:24	HP272	MEDDM203:6	HP283	MEDDM207:22	HP289
MEDDM195:25	HP272	MEDDM203:7	HP283	MEDDM207:24	HP289
MEDDM195:26	HP272	MEDDM203:10	HP283	MEDDM207:25	HP289
MEDDM195:30	HP272	MEDDM203:12	HP283	MEDDM207:26	HP289
MEDDM195:35	HP272	MEDDM203:16	HP283	MEDDM207:28	HP289
MEDDM196:2	HP272	MEDDM203:18	HP283	MEDDM207:29	HP289
MEDDM196:3	HP272	MEDDM203:21	HP283	MEDDM208:13	HP290
MEDDM196:6	HP272	MEDDM203:23	HP283	MEDDM208:20	HP290
MEDDM196:8	HP273	MEDDM203:24	HP283	MEDDM208:24	HP290
MEDDM196:14	HP273	MEDDM203:26	HP283	MEDDM208:25	HP290
MEDDM196:16	HP273	MEDDM203:27	HP284	MEDDM208:34	HP290
MEDDM196:30	HP274	MEDDM203:28	HP284	MEDDM209:1	HP291
MEDDM196:33	HP274	MEDDM203:31	HP284	MEDDM209:3	HP291
MEDDM196:34	HP274	MEDDM203:34	HP284	MEDDM209:9	HP291
MEDDM197:9	HP274	MEDDM203:35	HP284	MEDDM209:12	HP291
MEDDM197:14	HP274	MEDDM204:3	HP284	MEDDM209:18	HP291
MEDDM197:16	HP275	MEDDM204:5	HP284	MEDDM209:19	HP291
MEDDM197:18	HP275	MEDDM204:6	HP284	MEDDM209:21	HP291
MEDDM197:19	HP275	MEDDM204:9	HP284	MEDDM209:25	HP291
MEDDM197:26	HP275	MEDDM204:11	HP284	PILGRIM210:4	H4

SEASONS47:39	H51	SEASONS50:21	H155	MASSYR53:31	H21
SEASONS47:40	H52	SEASONS50:23	H157	MASSYR53:36	H26
SEASONS47:41	H53	SEASONS50:27	H161	MASSYR53:37	H27
SEASONS48:1	H54	SEASONS50:28	H162	MASSYR54:2	H29
SEASONS48:3	H56	SEASONS50:29	H163	MASSYR54:4	H31
SEASONS48:5	H58	SEASONS50:34	H168	MASSYR54:7	H34
SEASONS48:7	H60	SEASONS50:36	H170	MASSYR54:9	H36
SEASONS48:8	H61	SEASONS50:38	H172	MASSYR54:12	H39
SEASONS48:10	H63	SEASONS50:40	H174	MASSYR54:17	H44
SEASONS48:11	H64	SEASONS51:2	H176	MASSYR54:22	H49
SEASONS48:12	H65	SEASONS51:6	H180	MASSYR54:24	H51
SEASONS48:15	H68	SEASONS51:7	H181	MASSYR54:27	H54
SEASONS48:16	H69	SEASONS51:8	H182	MASSYR54:30	H57
SEASONS48:17	H70	SEASONS51:11	H185	MASSYR54:32	H59
SEASONS48:19	H72	SEASONS51:18	H192	MASSYR54:35	H62
SEASONS48:21	H74	SEASONS51:19	H195	MASSYR54:37	H64
SEASONS48:22	H75	SEASONS51:21	H197	MASSYR55:2	H68
SEASONS48:25	H78	SEASONS51:22	H198	MASSYR55:5	H71
SEASONS48:26	H79	SEASONS51:24	H200	MASSYR55:6	H72
SEASONS48:38	H89	SEASONS51:28	H204	MASSYR55:15	H81
SEASONS49:2	H93	SEASONS51:29	H205	MASSYR55:20	H86
SEASONS49:6	H97	SEASONS51:32	H208	MASSYR55:25	H91
SEASONS49:9	H100	SEASONS51:36	H212	MASSYR55:30	H96
SEASONS49:10	H101	SEASONS51:38	H214	MASSYR55:33	H99
SEASONS49:11	H102	SEASONS51:39	H215	MASSYR55:38	H104
SEASONS49:11	H102	SEASONS52:2	H219	MASSYR56:1	H107
SEASONS49:16	H107	SEASONS52:4	H219	MASSYR56:4	H110
SEASONS49:17	H108	SEASONS52:11	H226	MASSYR56:8	H114
SEASONS49:18	H109	SEASONS52:18	H233	MASSYR56:13	H119
SEASONS49:24	H114	SEASONS52:21	H236	MASSYR56:14	H120
SEASONS49:25	H114	SEASONS52:25	H240	MASSYR56:16	H122
SEASONS49:32	H121	SEASONS52:26	H241	MASSYR56:17	H123
SEASONS49:33	H123	SEASONS52:28	H243	MASSYR56:22	H128
SEASONS49:34	H127	SEASONS52:29	H244	MASSYR56:23	H129
SEASONS49:36	H129	SEASONS52:33	H248	MASSYR56:24	H130
SEASONS49:37	H130	SEASONS52:34	H249	MASSYR56:32	H138
SEASONS49:38	H131	SEASONS52:35	H250	MASSYR56:33	H139
SEASONS49:39	H132	SEASONS52:36	H251	MASSYR56:36	H142
SEASONS49:41	H134	SEASONS52:37	H252	MASSYR56:37	H143
SEASONS50:1	H135	SEASONS52:38	H253	MASSYR56:38	H144
SEASONS50:3	H137	SEASONS52:39	H255	MASSYR57:7	H154
SEASONS50:4	H138	SEASONS53:3	H259	MASSYR57:21	H168
SEASONS50:6	H140	SEASONS53:5	H261	MASSYR57:24	H171
SEASONS50:7	H141	SEASONS53:7	H263	MASSYR58:5	H190
SEASONS50:8	H142	MASSYR53:11	H1	MASSYR58:9	H194
SEASONS50:9	H143	MASSYR53:12	H2	MASSYR58:17	H202
SEASONS50:12	H146	MASSYR53:14	H4	MASSYR58:19	H204
SEASONS50:14	H148	MASSYR53:18	H8	MASSYR58:20	H205
SEASONS50:17	H151	MASSYR53:19	H9	MASSYR58:22	H207
SEASONS50:18	H152	MASSYR53:20	H10	MASSYR58:27	H210
SEASONS50:19	H153	MASSYR53:23	H13	MASSYR58:31	H214

MPERS73:28	H813	MPERS78:4	H985	MPERS82:19	H1166
MPERS73:30	H815	MPERS78:9	H990	MPERS82:20	H1167
MPERS73:32	H817	MPERS78:10	H991	MPERS82:24	H1171
MPERS73:33	H818	MPERS78:11	H992	MPERS82:30	H1177
MPERS73:35	H820	MPERS78:13	H994	MPERS82:34	H1181
MPERS73:37	H822	MPERS78:14	H995	MPERS82:41	H1188
MPERS74:2	H827	MPERS78:20	H1001	MPERS83:4	H1192
MPERS74:5	H830	MPERS78:21	H1002	MPERS83:14	H1202
MPERS74:6	H831	MPERS78:25	H1006	MPERS83:17	H1205
MPERS74:7	H832	MPERS78:26	H1007	MPERS83:18	H1206
MPERS74:11	H836	MPERS78:27	H1008	MPERS83:19	H1207
MPERS74:14	H837	MPERS78:34	H1015	MPERS83:24	H1212
MPERS74:15	H838	MPERS78:35	H1016	MPERS83:25	H1213
MPERS74:27	H850	MPERS78:37	H1018	MPERS83:27	H1215
MPERS74:28	H851	MPERS78:40	H1021	MPERS83:28	H1216
MPERS~~74:31~~	H854	MPERS78:41	H1022	MPERS83:30	H1218
MPERS74:33	H856	MPERS~~79:2~~	H1024	MPERS83:34	H1222
MPERS74:34	H857	MPERS79:6	H1028	MPERS84:3	H1231
MPERS74:36	~~H858~~	MPERS79:10	H1032	MPERS84:8	H1236
MPERS75:2	H863	MPERS~~79:13~~	H1035	MPERS84:12	H1240
MPERS75:4	H865	MPERS79:34	H1060	MPERS~~84:12~~	H1248
MPERS75:8	H869	MPERS79:35	H1061	MPERS84:19	H1255
MPERS75:9	H870	MPERS79:36	H1062	MPERS84:26	H1262
MPERS75:11	H872	MPERS80:1	H1068	MPERS84:39	H1275
MPERS75:24	H881	MPERS80:2	H1069	MPERS85:2	H1278
MPERS75:25	H882	MPERS80:8	H1075	MPERS85:5	H1281
MPERS75:26	H883	MPERS80:12	H1079	MPERS85:8	H1284
MPERS75:29	H886	MPERS80:16	H1083	MPERS85:12	H1288
MPERS75:32	H889	MPERS80:20	H1087	MPERS85:16	H1292
MPERS75:33	H890	MPERS80:23	H1090	MPERS85:17	H1293
MPERS75:36	H893	MPERS80:28	H1095	MPERS85:22	H1298
MPERS75:38	H895	MPERS80:39	H1106	MPERS85:24	H1300
MPERS75:40	H897	MPERS81:2	H1110	MPERS85:28	H1304
MPERS76:9	H907	MPERS81:14	H1122	MPERS85:29	H1305
MPERS76:12	H910	MPERS81:16	H1124	MPERS85:32	H1308
MPERS76:16	H914	MPERS81:22	H1130	MPERS85:36	H1312
MPERS76:19	H917	MPERS81:24	H1132	MPERS86:2	H1318
MPERS76:35	H933	MPERS81:25	H1133	MPERS86:15	H1331
MPERS76:37	H935	MPERS81:26	H1134	MPERS86:22	H1338
MPERS76:39	H937	MPERS81:34	H1142	MPERS86:24	H1340
MPERS76:41	H939	MPERS81:36	~~H1143~~	MPERS86:25	H1341
MPERS77:3	H942	MPERS81:40	H1144	MPERS86:27	H1343
MPERS77:10	H949	MPERS81:41	H1145	MPERS86:29	H1345
MPERS77:16	H955	MPERS82:6	H1153	MPERS86:31	H1347
MPERS~~77:16~~	H956	MPERS82:7	H1154	MPERS86:33	H1349
MPERS77:17	H958	MPERS82:8	H1155	MPERS86:36	H1352
MPERS77:18	H959	MPERS82:9	H1156	MPERS86:38	H1354
MPERS77:21	H962	MPERS82:15	H1162	MPERS86:40	H1356
MPERS77:23	H964	MPERS82:16	H1163	MPERS87:2	H1358
MPERS77:31	H972	MPERS82:17	H1164	MPERS87:3	H1359
MPERS77:33	H974	MPERS82:18	H1165	MPERS87:4	H1360

MPERS87:4	H1360	MPERS90:38	H1505	MGREC94:41	H1679
MPERS87:5	H1361	MPERS~~90:39~~	H1506	MGREC95:1	H1680
MPERS87:6	H1362	MPERS91:2	H1510	MGREC95:12	H1691
MPERS87:7	H1363	MPERS91:10	H1518	MGREC95:14	H1693
MPERS87:13	H1369	MPERS91:16	H1524	MGREC95:16	H1695
MPERS87:16	~~H1370~~	MPERS91:19	H1527	MGREC95:18	H1697
MPERS87:20	~~H1374~~	MPERS91:21	H1529	MGREC95:34	H1713
MPERS87:26	H1378	MPERS~~91:22~~	H1533	MGREC95:36	H1715
MPERS87:27	H1379	MPERS91:25	~~H1539~~	MGREC95:37	H1716
MPERS87:33	H1385	MPERS91:28	~~H1542~~	MGREC95:39	H1718
MPERS88:1	H1394	MPERS91:30	~~H1544~~	MGREC96:1	H1721
MPERS88:5	H1398	MPERS91:31	~~H1545~~	MGREC96:2	H1722
MPERS88:7	H1400	MPERS91:32	~~H1546~~	MGREC96:4	H1724
MPERS88:8	H1401	MPERS91:36	~~H1550~~	MGREC96:5	H1725
MPERS88:15	H1408	MPERS91:38	~~H1552~~	MGREC96:7	H1727
MPERS88:16	H1409	MPERS91:40	~~H1554~~	MGREC96:8	H1728
MPERS88:18	H1411	MPERS~~92:2~~	H1556	MGREC96:9	H1729
MPERS88:21	H1414	MPERS92:3	~~H1557~~	MGREC96:11	H1731
MPERS88:24	H1417	MPERS~~92:3~~	H1557	MGREC96:20	H1740
MPERS88:31	H1424	MPERS~~92:5~~	H1562	MGREC96:23	H1743
MPERS88:38	H1431	MPERS92:11	H1569	MGREC96:27	H1747
MPERS88:41	H1434	MPERS~~92:14~~	H1572	MGREC96:33	H1753
MPERS89:2	H1436	MPERS92:16	~~H1574~~	MGREC96:34	H1754
MPERS89:7	H1441	MPERS~~92:17~~	H1575	MGREC96:39	H1759
MPERS89:10	H1444	MPERS92:19	~~H1577~~	MGREC96:40	H1760
MPERS89:12	H1446	MPERS~~92:20~~	H1578	MGREC96:41	H1761
MPERS89:19	H1453	MPERS~~92:24~~	H1582	MGREC97:8	H1769
MPERS89:21	H1455	MPERS92:36	H1594	MGREC97:10	H1771
MPERS89:23	H1457	MPERS93:1	H1598	MGREC97:11	H1772
MPERS89:25	H1459	MPERS93:4	H1601	MGREC97:14	H1775
MPERS89:27	H1461	MPERS93:5	H1602	MGREC97:21	H1782
MPERS89:29	H1463	MGREC93:6	H1603	MGREC97:24	H1785
MPERS89:35	H1469	MGREC6:7	H1604	MGREC97:26	H1787
MPERS89:38	H1472	MGREC6:8	H1605	MGREC97:33	H1794
MPERS89:39	H1473	MGREC6:9	H1606	MGREC97:40	H1801
MPERS90:1	H1476	MGREC6:12	H1609	MGREC98:8	H1810
MPERS90:4	~~H1478~~	MGREC6:13	H1610	MGREC98:10	H1812
MPERS~~90:4~~	H1478	MGREC6:15	H1612	MGREC98:12	H1814
MPERS90:14	~~H1484~~	MGREC6:16	H1613	MGREC98:14	H1816
MPERS90:15	~~H1484~~	MGREC6:20	H1617	MGREC98:16	H1818
MPERS90:16	~~H1484~~	MGREC6:23	H1620	MGREC98:19	H1821
MPERS90:20	H1487	MGREC6:25	H1622	MGREC98:20	H1822
MPERS90:21	H1488	MGREC6:26	H1623	MGREC98:22	H1824
MPERS90:22	H1489	MGREC6:27	H1624	MGREC98:23	H1825
MPERS90:23	H1490	MGREC6:28	H1625	MGREC98:24	H1826
MPERS90:25	H1492	MGREC6:32	H1629	MGREC98:26	H1828
MPERS90:27	H1494	MGREC6:35	H1632	MGREC98:29	H1831
MPERS90:30	H1497	MGREC94:16	H1650	MGREC98:31	H1833
MPERS~~90:33~~	H1500	MGREC94:34	H1672	MGREC98:36	H1838
MPERS90:34	H1501	MGREC94:39	H1677	MGREC99:3	H1846
MPERS90:37	H1504	MGREC94:40	H1678	MGREC99:5	H1848

MGREC99:11	H1854	MGREC104:9	H2061	MGREC109:17	H2276
MGREC99:16	H1859	MGREC104:25	H2077	MGREC109:21	H2280
MGREC99:18	H1861	MGREC104:26	H2078	MGREC109:28	H2287
MGREC99:19	H1862	MGREC104:39	H2091	MGREC109:37	H2296
MGREC99:24	H1867	MGREC104:40	H2092	MGREC110:1	H2301
MGREC99:27	H1870	MGREC105:2	H2095	MGREC110:12	H2312
MGREC99:38	H1881	MGREC105:5	H2098	MGREC110:13	H2313
MGREC100:5	H1889	MGREC105:9	H2102	MGREC110:14	H2314
MGREC100:7	H1891	MGREC105:18	H2111	MGREC110:16	H2316
MGREC100:8	H1892	MGREC105:19	H2112	MGREC110:17	H2317
MGREC100:12	H1896	MGREC105:21	H2114	MGREC110:18	H2318
MGREC100:19	H1903	MGREC105:23	H2116	MGREC~~110:18~~	H2319
MGREC100:24	H1908	MGREC105:31	H2124	MGREC110:37	H2341
MGREC100:29	H1913	MGREC105:34	H2127	MGREC110:39	H2343
MGREC100:30	H1914	MGREC105:37	H2130	MGREC111:4	H2349
MGREC100:33	H1917	MGREC105:38	H2131	MGREC111:8	H2353
MGREC~~100:36~~	H1920	MGREC106:2	~~H2136~~	MGREC111:9	H2354
MGREC100:39	H1923	MGREC106:7	H2141	MGREC111:12	H2357
MGREC100:41	H1925	MGREC106:9	H2143	MGREC111:17	H2362
MGREC101:7	H1932	MGREC106:30	H2164	MGREC111:18	H2363
MGREC101:13	H1938	MGREC106:34	H2168	MGREC111:19	H2364
MGREC101:23	H1948	MGREC106:39	H2173	MGREC111:20	H2365
MGREC101:26	H1951	MGREC106:41	H2175	MGREC111:27	H2372
MGREC101:27	H1952	MGREC107:4	H2179	MGREC111:39	H2384
MGREC101:30	H1955	MGREC107:11	H2186	MGREC112:4	H2390
MGREC101:33	H1958	MGREC107:13	H2188	MGREC112:9	H2395
MGREC101:34	~~H1959~~	MGREC107:15	H2190	MGREC112:12	H2398
MGREC~~101:34~~	H1962	MGREC107:17	H2192	MGREC112:14	H2400
MGREC101:41	H1970	MGREC107:19	H2194	MGREC112:20	H2406
MGREC102:7	H1977	MGREC107:23	H2198	MGREC112:22	H2408
MGREC102:8	H1978	MGREC107:27	H2202	MGREC112:27	H2413
MGREC102:9	H1979	MGREC107:29	H2204	MGREC112:32	H2418
MGREC102:10	H1980	MGREC107:29	H2204	MGREC112:37	H2423
MGREC102:14	H1984	MGREC107:31	H2206	MGREC113:1	H2428
MGREC102:16	H1986	MGREC107:34	H2209	MGREC113:13	H2440
MGREC102:30	H2000	MGREC107:37	H2212	MGREC113:17	H2444
MGREC102:31	H2001	MGREC108:2	H2218	MGREC113:29	H2456
MGREC102:33	H2003	MGREC108:4	H2220	MGREC113:33	H2460
MGREC102:37	H2007	MGREC108:5	H2221	MGREC113:35	H2462
MGREC102:38	H2008	MGREC108:10	H2226	MGREC113:38	H2465
MGREC102:41	H2011	MGREC108:13	H2229	MGREC114:5	H2473
MGREC103:2	H2013	MGREC108:21	H2237	MGREC~~114:12~~	H2482
MGREC103:4	H2015	MGREC108:22	H2238	MGREC114:16	H2486
MGREC103:8	H2019	MGREC108:25	H2241	MGREC114:17	H2487
MGREC103:9	H2020	MGREC108:32	H2248	MGREC114:19	H2489
MGREC103:10	H2021	MGREC108:33	H2249	MGREC114:20	H2490
MGREC103:14	H2025	MGREC108:38	H2254	MGREC114:25	H2495
MGREC103:22	H2033	MGREC109:1	H2258	MGREC114:35	H2505
MGREC103:33	H2044	MGREC~~109:5~~	H2262	MGREC115:1	H2512
MGREC103:36	H2047	MGREC~~109:5~~	H2263	MGREC115:5	H2516
MGREC104:8	H2060	MGREC109:16	H2275	MGREC115:10	H2519

MGREC115:15	H2524	MGREC120:18	H2753	MGREC125:11	H2959
MGREC~~115:15~~	H2525	MGREC~~120:20~~	H2756	MGREC125:15	H2963
MGREC115:18	H2537	MGREC120:21	H2758	MGREC125:18	H2966
MGREC115:20	H2539	MGREC120:22	H2759	MGREC125:20	H2968
MGREC115:21	H2540	MGREC120:24	H2761	MGREC~~125:21~~	H2970
MGREC115:24	H2543	MGREC120:40	H2777	MGREC125:22	H2972
MGREC115:25	H2544	MGREC121:3	H2781	MGREC125:23	H2973
MGREC115:30	H2549	MGREC121:4	H2782	MGREC125:26	H2976
MGREC115:32	H2551	MGREC121:5	H2783	MGREC125:27	H2977
MGREC115:33	H2552	MGREC121:9	H2787	MGREC125:29	H2979
MGREC116:2	H2562	MGREC121:13	H2791	MGREC125:30	H2980
MGREC116:9	H2569	MGREC121:16	~~H2795~~	MGREC125:36	H2986
MGREC~~116:10~~	H2575	MGREC~~121:16~~	H2796	MGREC126:5	H2996
MGREC116:15	H2581	MGREC121:19	H2801	MGREC126:7	H2998
MGREC116:19	H2585	MGREC121:20	H2802	MGREC126:8	H2999
MGREC116:20	H2586	MGREC121:26	H2808	MGREC126:10	H3001
MGREC116:23	H2589	MGREC121:27	H2809	MGREC126:12	H3003
MGREC116:31	~~H2597~~	MGREC121:36	H2818	MGREC126:17	H3008
MGREC117:9	H2616	MGREC121:40	H2822	MGREC126:19	H3010
MGREC117:12	H2619	MGREC121:41	H2823	MGREC126:22	H3013
MGREC117:13	H2620	MGREC122:5	H2828	MGREC126:25	H3016
MGREC117:19	H2626	MGREC122:11	H2836	MGREC126:29	H3020
MGREC117:34	H2641	MGREC122:16	H2841	MGREC126:31	H3022
MGREC117:36	H2643	MGREC122:23	~~H2845~~	MGREC126:36	H3025
MGREC118:2	H2649	MGREC122:31	H2850	MGREC127:1	H3031
MGREC118:5	H2652	MGREC122:32	H2851	MGREC127:5	H3035
MGREC118:14	H2661	MGREC~~122:32,~~	H2853	MGREC127:6	H3036
MGREC118:22	H2669	MGREC122:35	H2856	MGREC127:27	H3057
MGREC118:24	H2671	MGREC122:38	H2859	MGREC127:29	H3059
MGREC118:29	H2678	MGREC122:39	H2860	MGREC127:32	H3062
MGREC118:33	H2682	MGREC122:41	H2862	MGREC127:38	H3068
MGREC118:35	H2684	MGREC123:2	H2864	MGREC128:1	H3074
MGREC118:41	H2690	MGREC123:4	H2866	MGREC128:15	H3088
MGREC119:2	H2692	MGREC123:12	H2874	MGREC128:16	H3089
MGREC119:6	H2696	MGREC123:14	H2878	MGREC128:17	H3090
MGREC119:12	H2702	MGREC123:23	H2887	MGREC128:19	H3092
MGREC119:14	H2704	MGREC123:34	H2898	MGREC128:22	H3095
MGREC119:16	H2706	MGREC123:34	H2898	MGREC128:23	H3096
MGREC119:20	H2710	MGREC123:36	H2900	MGREC128:24	H3097
MGREC119:24	H2714	MGREC123:40	H2904	MGREC128:25	H3098
MGREC119:28	H2718	MGREC~~124:7~~	H2912	MGREC128:31	H3104
MGREC119:28	H2718	MGREC124:13	H2920	MGREC128:32	H3105
MGREC119:31	H2721	MGREC124:14	H2921	MGREC128:39	H3112
MGREC119:32	H2722	MGREC124:20	H2927	MGREC129:1	H3115
MGREC119:37	H2727	MGREC124:23	H2930	MGREC129:3	H3117
MGREC119:40	H2730	MGREC124:25	H2932	MGREC129:3	H3117
MGREC120:3	H2734	MGREC124:28	H2935	MGREC129:4	H3118
MGREC~~120:4~~	H2737	MGREC124:31	H2938	MGREC129:9	H3123
MGREC~~120:4~~	H2739	MGREC124:37	H2944	MGREC129:16	H3130
MGREC120:8	H2743	MGREC125:3	H2951	MGREC129:17	H3131
MGREC120:11	H2746	MGREC125:7	H2955	MGREC129:19	H3133

MEDDM196:34	HP274	MEDDM202:13	HP282	MEDDM205:36	HP287
MEDDM197:7	HP274	MEDDM202:14	HP282	MEDDM206:4	HP287
MEDDM197:11	HP274	MEDDM202:16	HP282	MEDDM206:6	HP287
MEDDM197:18	HP275	MEDDM202:21	HP282	MEDDM206:7	HP287
MEDDM197:20	HP275	MEDDM202:24	HP282	MEDDM206:9	HP287
MEDDM197:28	HP275	MEDDM202:26	HP282	MEDDM206:10	HP287
MEDDM197:29	HP275	MEDDM202:28	HP282	MEDDM206:12	HP287
MEDDM197:31	HP275	MEDDM202:29	HP282	MEDDM206:13	HP287
MEDDM198:5	HP276	MEDDM202:32	HP282	MEDDM206:20	HP287
MEDDM198:6	HP276	MEDDM202:34	HP282	MEDDM206:25	HP287
MEDDM198:10	HP276	MEDDM202:35	HP282	MEDDM206:27	HP288
MEDDM198:16	HP276	MEDDM203:2	HP283	MEDDM206:30	HP288
MEDDM198:19	HP276	MEDDM203:10	HP283	MEDDM206:33	HP288
MEDDM198:28	HP277	MEDDM203:15	HP283	MEDDM206:36	HP288
MEDDM198:32	HP277	MEDDM203:18	HP283	MEDDM206:37	HP288
MEDDM198:33	HP277	MEDDM203:22	HP283	MEDDM207:4	HP288
MEDDM198:35	HP277	MEDDM203:24	HP283	MEDDM207:8	HP288
MEDDM199:12	HP277	MEDDM203:25	HP283	MEDDM207:13	HP288
MEDDM199:17	HP278	MEDDM203:35	HP284	MEDDM207:13	HP288
MEDDM199:19	HP278	MEDDM204:2	HP284	MEDDM207:16	HP288
MEDDM199:20	HP278	MEDDM204:3	HP284	MEDDM207:17	HP288
MEDDM199:23	HP278	MEDDM204:4	HP284	MEDDM207:24	HP289
MEDDM199:26	HP278	MEDDM204:6	HP284	MEDDM207:25	HP289
MEDDM199:27	HP278	MEDDM204:9	HP284	MEDDM207:26	HP289
MEDDM199:28	HP278	MEDDM204:10	HP284	MEDDM207:32	HP289
MEDDM199:29	HP278	MEDDM204:14	HP284	MEDDM207:35	HP289
MEDDM200:6	HP279	MEDDM204:15	HP284	MEDDM207:36	HP289
MEDDM200:8	HP279	MEDDM204:18	HP285	MEDDM208:1	HP289
MEDDM200:12	HP279	MEDDM204:19	HP285	MEDDM208:2	HP289
MEDDM200:17	HP279	MEDDM204:20	HP285	MEDDM208:6	HP289
MEDDM200:18	HP279	MEDDM204:21	HP285	MEDDM208:8	HP290
MEDDM200:19	HP279	MEDDM204:23	HP285	MEDDM208:15	HP290
MEDDM200:22	HP279	MEDDM204:31	HP285	MEDDM208:18	HP290
MEDDM200:24	HP279	MEDDM204:33	HP285	MEDDM208:20	HP290
MEDDM200:25	HP279	MEDDM205:1	HP285	MEDDM208:21	HP290
MEDDM200:27	HP279	MEDDM205:2	HP285	MEDDM208:24	HP290
MEDDM200:28	HP279	MEDDM205:3	HP285	MEDDM208:25	HP290
MEDDM200:30	HP279	MEDDM205:5	HP285	MEDDM208:28	HP290
MEDDM200:36	HP280	MEDDM205:6	HP285	MEDDM208:30	HP290
MEDDM201:1	HP280	MEDDM205:7	HP285	MEDDM208:31	HP290
MEDDM201:4	HP280	MEDDM205:9	HP286	MEDDM208:32	HP290
MEDDM201:7	HP280	MEDDM205:12	HP286	MEDDM208:33	HP290
MEDDM201:25	HP281	MEDDM205:15	HP286	MEDDM208:34	HP290
MEDDM201:26	HP281	MEDDM205:17	HP286	MEDDM208:35	HP290
MEDDM201:27	HP281	MEDDM205:19	HP286	MEDDM208:35	HP291
MEDDM201:28	HP281	MEDDM205:20	HP286	MEDDM208:36	HP291
MEDDM201:31	HP281	MEDDM205:24	HP286	MEDDM209:7	HP291
MEDDM201:32	HP281	MEDDM205:28	HP286	MEDDM209:8	HP291
MEDDM202:3	HP281	MEDDM205:31	HP286	MEDDM209:13	HP291
MEDDM202:4	HP281	MEDDM205:32	HP286	MEDDM209:15	HP291
MEDDM202:5	HP281	MEDDM205:34	HP286	PILGRIM210:7	H7

PILGRIM210:9	H9	11MAYB228:26	HP259	SIDNEY149:35	~~H23~~
PILGRIM210:24	H24	RESTOR229:19	H1-2	SIDNEY150:29	H56
PILGRIM210:32	H32	RESTOR229:30	H13	SIDNEY151:12	~~H69~~
PILGRIM210:40	H40	SON230:27	H10	DUBART153:41	H45
MYCHILD215:16	HP240	SON231:1	H13	DUBART154:20	H65
MYCHILD215:21	HP240	2HUSB232:4	H5	DUBART154:37	H82
MYCHILD215:22	HP240	2HUSB233:15	H48	DUBART154:39	H84
MYCHILD215:33	HP241	HOURS233:27	H10	DAVID159:23	H38
MYCHILD216:3	HP241	HOURS234:35	H49	TDUDLEY165:31	H33
MYCHILD216:4	HP241	ACK235:13	H13	CONTEM168:18	H26
MYCHILD216:12	HP241	ACK235:13	H13	CONTEM168:20	H28
MYCHILD216:29	HP242	HOUSE236:24	H16	CONTEM168:25	H32
MYCHILD217:2	HP242	HOUSE236:33	H25	CONTEM169:7	H49
MYCHILD217:7	HP242	HOUSE237:14	H44	CONTEM172:24	H158
MYCHILD217:16	HP243	HOUSE237:15	H45	CONTEM173:21	H187
MYCHILD217:17	HP243	HOUSE237:27	H57	CONTEM173:31	H196
MYCHILD217:30	HP243	**THEE (118)**		FLESH175:12	H12
MYCHILD217:36	HP243	ELEMEN9:35	H70	FLESH176:1	H41
MYCHILD217:37	HP243	ELEMEN11:2	H122	FLESH176:2	H42
MYCHILD218:1	HP243	ELEMEN12:13	H173	FLESH176:3	H43
MYCHILD218:3	HP243	ELEMEN14:30	H272	FLESH176:5	H45
MYCHILD218:12	HP244	ELEMEN16:9	H332	FLESH176:23	H63
MYCHILD218:13	HP244	HUMOUR23:13	H123	FLESH176:39	H79
MYCHILD218:19	HP244	HUMOUR24:27	H176	FLESH177:25	H106
MYCHILD218:20	HP244	HUMOUR24:27	H176	AUTHOR177:33	H5
MYCHILD218:24	HP244	HUMOUR25:13	H202	AUTHOR177:34	H6
MYCHILD218:26	HP244	HUMOUR25:16	H205	AUTHOR177:38	H10
MYCHILD218:32	HP244	HUMOUR26:4	H234	AUTHOR178:6	H16
MYCHILD219:3	HP245	HUMOUR26:10	H240	AUTHOR178:8	H18
MYCHILD219:8	HP245	HUMOUR26:17	H247	AUTHOR178:15	H25
SOREFIT221:20	H6	HUMOUR26:21	H251	SICKNES179:12	H32
SOREFIT222:10	H29	HUMOUR26:30	H260	BIRTH180:2	H12
MED223:1	HP250	HUMOUR26:31	H261	1HUSB180:24	H3
MED223:2	HP250	HUMOUR26:37	H267	1HUSB180:30	H9
MED223:11	HP250	HUMOUR29:18	H369	1HUSB180:32	H11
JULY223:22	HP251	HUMOUR30:12	H404	1LETTER181:26	H24
JULY223:29	HP251	HUMOUR31:13	~~H444~~	ANNEB187:31	H21
WHAT224:23	H23	HUMOUR~~31:15~~	H448	MERCY188:31	H17
28AUG225:27	HP254	HUMOUR33:10	H524	MERCY188:35	H21
28AUG226:2	HP254	HUMOUR~~33:15~~	H529	MERCY189:2	H23
28AUG226:4	HP254	SEASONS~~48:34~~	H85	MERCY189:11	H32
11MAYA226:15	HP255	DIALOG141:8	H7	MERCY189:16	H37
13MAY226:26	H2	DIALOG142:9	H38	MEDDM207:9	HP288
13MAY226:27	H3	DIALOG146:25	H211	MEDDM209:2	HP291
13MAY226:28	H4	DIALOG146:26	H212	SOREFIT221:21	H7
30SEPT227:29	HP257	DIALOG147:2	H228	SOREFIT221:27	H13
30SEPT227:33	HP257	DIALOG147:4	H230	SOREFIT221:32	H18
SAMUEL228:4	H5	DIALOG147:7	H233	SOREFIT222:10	H29
SAMUEL228:5	H6	DIALOG148:10	H275	FAINTING222:14	H4
SAMUEL228:17	H18	SIDNEY149:25	~~H23~~	FAINTING222:15	H5
11MAYB228:25	HP259	SIDNEY149:32	~~H23~~	FAINTING222:25	H15

MED223:19	HP250	ELEMEN16:14	H337	MASSYR57:21	H168
JULY223:34	HP251	ELEMEN16:15	H338	MASSYR57:27	H172
WHAT224:3	H3	ELEMEN16:16	H339	MASSYR57:34	H179
WHAT224:6	H6	ELEMEN17:3	H367	MASSYR58:3	H188
MYSOUL225:15	H19	ELEMEN17:21	H385	MASSYR58:4	H189
28AUG226:9	HP254	ELEMEN18:41	H445	MASSYR58:14	H199
28AUG226:10	HP254	ELEMEN19:3	H448	MASSYR58:18	H203
SAMUEL228:7	H8	ELEMEN19:40	H481	MASSYR58:22	H207
SAMUEL228:10	H11	ELEMEN20:3	H485	MASSYR58:23	H207
SAMUEL228:21	H22	ELEMEN20:4	H486	MASSYR58:24	H207
RESTOR229:32	H15	ELEMEN20:6	H488	MASSYR58:37	H220
RESTOR230:1	H16	HUMOUR20:11	H3	MASSYR58:38	H221
HANNA230:18	H11	HUMOUR20:12	H4	MASSYR58:41	H224
2HUSB232:15	H16	HUMOUR20:15	H7	MASSYR59:4	H228
2HUSB232:26	H27	HUMOUR23:28	H138	MASSYR59:5	H229
2HUSB233:14	H47	HUMOUR23:29	H139	MASSYR59:15	H239
2HUSB233:18	H51	HUMOUR24:21	H170	MASSYR59:25	H249
HOURS233:22	H5	HUMOUR26:35	H265	MASSYR59:26	H250
HOURS233:29	H12	HUMOUR30:29	H421	MASSYR59:37	H261
HOURS233:30	H13	HUMOUR32:37	H511	MASSYR60:3	H268
HOURS234:5	H19	AGES36:28	H52	MASSYR60:5	H270
HOURS234:12	H26	AGES36:34	H58	MASSYR60:10	H275
HOURS234:15	H29	AGES39:31	H174	MASSYR61:13	H318
HOURS234:19	H33	AGES41:18	H237	MASSYR62:4	H349
HOURS234:31	H45	AGES43:8	H305	MASSYR62:10	H355
HOURS234:36	H50	AGES45:4	H382	MASSYR64:40	H464
HOURS235:2	H54	AGES45:4	H387	MASSYR66:10	H516
ACK235:12	H12	AGES45:11	H393	MPERS70:9	H680
ACK235:19	H19	AGES45:12	H394	MPERS71:2	H714
REMB235:32	H13	AGES45:12	H394	MPERS71:22	H736
REMB236:10	H25	AGES45:13	H395	MPERS71:24	H738
REMB236:11	H26	AGES45:14	H396	MPERS71:25	H739
HOUSE237:7	H37	AGES45:35	H425	MPERS73:21	H808
THEIR (451)		SEASONS47:14	H30	MPERS73:34	H819
FATHER5:7	H8	SEASONS47:19	H35	MPERS74:9	H834
FATHER5:8	H9	SEASONS47:21	H37	MPERS74:11	H836
FATHER5:9	H10	SEASONS49:17	H108	MPERS74:24	H847
FATHER5:14	H15	SEASONS49:19	H110	MPERS74:33	H856
FATHER5:15	H16	SEASONS50:3	H137	MPERS75:3	H864
FATHER5:26	H27	SEASONS50:4	H138	MPERS75:37	H894
FATHER5:28	H29	SEASONS50:5	H139	MPERS76:10	H908
PROLOG6:21	H6	SEASONS50:22	H156	MPERS76:12	H910
PROLOG6:23	H8	SEASONS51:9	H183	MPERS76:29	H927
ELEMEN8:18	H16	SEASONS51:26	H202	MPERS76:31	H929
ELEMEN8:20	H18	SEASONS51:41	H217	MPERS76:35	H933
ELEMEN10:15	H90	SEASONS52:31	H246	MPERS78:12	H993
ELEMEN11:31	H151	MASSYR54:33	H60	MPERS79:31	H1057
ELEMEN13:33	H234	MASSYR54:36	H63	MPERS80:4	H1071
ELEMEN15:1	H283	MASSYR55:33	H99	MPERS80:6	H1073
ELEMEN15:4	H286	MASSYR56:11	H117	MPERS80:18	H1085
ELEMEN15:5	H287	MASSYR56:39	H145	MPERS80:22	H1089

MROMAN137:9	H3460	CONTEM171:10	H114	MEDDM207:15	HP288
MROMAN137:14	H3465	CONTEM171:18	H121	MEDDM207:18	HP289
MROMAN137:31	H3482	CONTEM171:21	H124	MEDDM207:22	HP289
MROMAN138:6	H3496	CONTEM171:31	H133	MEDDM207:23	HP289
MROMAN138:7	H3497	CONTEM171:35	H136	MEDDM207:31	HP289
MROMAN140:7	H3570	CONTEM172:1	H138	MEDDM207:32	HP289
DIALOG141:3	H3	CONTEM173:8	H176	MEDDM207:33	HP289
DIALOG142:14	H43	CONTEM173:30	H195	MEDDM207:34	HP289
DIALOG143:8	H75	CONTEM174:31	H228	MEDDM207:35	HP289
DIALOG143:40	H109	CONTEM174:32	H229	MEDDM208:1	HP289
DIALOG144:26	H135	CONTEM174:33	H230	MEDDM208:26	HP290
DIALOG144:28	H136	FLESH175:27	H27	MEDDM209:7	HP291
DIALOG144:30	H138	1LETTER181:18	H16	MEDDM209:10	HP291
DIALOG144:31	H139	VERSES184:7	H11	MEDDM209:11	HP291
DIALOG145:21	H170	CHILDRN184:18	H7	MEDDM209:14	HP291
DIALOG145:24	H173	CHILDRN184:28	H17	MEDDM209:16	HP291
DIALOG145:28	H177	CHILDRN185:15	H41	PILGRIM210:40	H40
DIALOG145:30	H179	ELIZB187:7	H15	MYCHILD218:23	HP244
DIALOG145:39	H188	ANNEB187:21	H11	WHAT224:12	H12
DIALOG146:4	H192	2SIMON195:3	HP271	13MAY226:29	H5
DIALOG146:21	H207	2SIMON195:4	HP271	2HUSB233:1	H34
DIALOG146:22	H208	2SIMON195:5	HP271	**THEIRS** (6)	
DIALOG147:3	H229	MEDDM196:28	HP273	HUMOUR30:15	H407
DIALOG147:13	H239	MEDDM196:31	HP274	MASSYR62:19	H364
DIALOG147:15	H241	MEDDM197:22	HP275	MGREC109:3	H2260
DIALOG148:2	H267	MEDDM198:3	HP275	SIDNEY151:19	H69
SIDNEY152:6	H77	MEDDM198:6	HP276	SIDNEY152:16	H85
SIDNEY152:8	H79	MEDDM199:16	HP278	CONTEM171:11	H115
SIDNEY152:10	H79	MEDDM200:11	HP279	**THEM** (159) See also Y^M	
SIDNEY152:18	H87	MEDDM200:12	HP279	FATHER6:6	H40
DUBART153:1	H5	MEDDM200:21	HP279	ELEMEN16:12	H335
DUBART153:6	H10	MEDDM200:26	HP279	ELEMEN17:11	H375
DUBART154:17	H62	MEDDM200:29	HP279	HUMOUR20:14	H6
DUBART154:19	H64	MEDDM200:30	HP279	HUMOUR21:29	H57
QELIZ156:10	H37	MEDDM200:31	HP279	HUMOUR25:19	H208
QELIZ156:29	H56	MEDDM201:3	HP280	HUMOUR31:15	H446
QELIZ156:31	H58	MEDDM201:27	HP281	HUMOUR35:14	H610
QELIZ157:1	H69	MEDDM202:11	HP281	AGES42:11	H269
QELIZ158:5	H114	MEDDM202:18	HP282	AGES45:22	H404
DAVID158:31	H11	MEDDM203:34	HP284	SEASONS48:8	H61
DAVID159:10	H25	MEDDM205:2	HP285	SEASONS48:24	H77
DAVID159:12	H27	MEDDM205:6	HP285	SEASONS50:7	H141
VANITY159:36	H8	MEDDM205:7	HP285	MASSYR55:39	H105
TDUDLEY166:9	H51	MEDDM205:31	HP286	MASSYR56:32	H138
CONTEM167:29	H6	MEDDM205:32	HP286	MASSYR57:27	H172
CONTEM169:21	H61	MEDDM205:36	HP287	MASSYR58:36	H219
CONTEM169:22	H62	MEDDM206:8	HP287	MASSYR58:39	H222
CONTEM169:23	H63	MEDDM206:11	HP287	MASSYR58:41	H224
CONTEM169:32	H71	MEDDM206:14	HP287	MASSYR59:31	H255
CONTEM171:3	H108	MEDDM206:17	HP287	MASSYR60:6	H271
CONTEM171:5	H110	MEDDM206:21	HP287	MASSYR62:36	H381

MASSYR65:36	H501	MGREC121:23	H2805	MEDDM206:2	HP287
MPERS71:40	H753	MGREC125:21	H2970	MEDDM206:15	HP287
MPERS72:1	H753	MGREC127:9	H3039	MEDDM206:36	HP288
MPERS75:2	H863	MGREC127:39	H3069	MEDDM207:7	HP288
MPERS76:32	H930	MGREC128:13	H3086	MEDDM207:8	HP288
MPERS78:6	H987	MGREC129:23	H3137	MEDDM207:14	HP288
MPERS79:20	H1046	MGREC130:24	H3179	MEDDM207:17	HP289
MPERS80:16	H1083	MGREC131:1	H3190	MEDDM207:35	HP289
MPERS81:16	H1124	MGREC133:39	H3329	MEDDM208:7	HP289
MPERS81:19	H1127	MGREC135:14	H3386	MEDDM208:10	HP290
MPERS82:1	H1146	MGREC135:37	H3409	MEDDM208:21	HP290
MPERS83:36	H1224	MROMAN137:15	H3466	MEDDM208:22	HP290
MPERS85:15	H1291	MROMAN139:5	H3533	MEDDM208:23	HP290
MPERS89:6	H1440	DIALOG143:38	H107	MEDDM208:26	HP290
MPERS89:28	H1462	DIALOG145:28	H177	MEDDM208:35	HP290
MPERS89:29	H1463	DIALOG147:6	H232	MEDDM209:8	HP291
MPERS89:30	H1464	DIALOG147:21	H247	MEDDM209:10	HP291
MPERS89:36	H1470	SIDNEY152:20	H89	MEDDM209:11	HP291
MPERS89:38	H1472	QELIZ156:10	H37	MEDDM209:12	HP291
MPERS89:40	H1474	QELIZ156:32	H59	MEDDM209:14	HP291
MPERS90:3	H1477	QELIZ156:36	H63	MEDDM209:15	HP291
MPERS90:4	H1478	TDUDLEY165:29	H31	MYCHILD215:31	HP241
MPERS90:5	H1478	CONTEM174:31	H228	MYCHILD218:30	HP244
MPERS90:11	H1484	FLESH176:17	H57	MED223:11	HP250
MPERS90:16	H1484	CHILDRN184:16	H5	WHAT224:11	H11
MPERS91:3	H1511	CHILDRN185:24	H50	SON231:2	H14
MPERS92:39	H1597	CHILDRN186:18	H85	2HUSB232:28	H29
MGREC96:16	H1736	MEDDM196:7	HP272	HOURS234:15	H29
MGREC97:15	H1776	MEDDM197:23	HP275	HOUSE237:2	H32
MGREC97:18	H1779	MEDDM197:32	HP275	**THEY (342)**	
MGREC97:19	H1780	MEDDM198:3	HP275	FATHER5:18	H19
MGREC101:3	H1928	MEDDM198:4	HP276	FATHER5:19	H20
MGREC101:29	H1954	MEDDM198:6	HP276	FATHER5:26	H26
MGREC105:18	H2111	MEDDM199:12	HP277	FATHER5:33	H34
MGREC107:26	H2201	MEDDM200:13	HP279	FATHER6:9	H43
MGREC107:31	H2206	MEDDM200:19	HP279	FATHER6:10	H44
MGREC107:35	H2210	MEDDM200:21	HP279	PROLOG6:21	H6
MGREC107:39	H2214	MEDDM200:36	HP280	PROLOG7:17	H30
MGREC107:39	H2214	MEDDM201:4	HP280	PROLOG7:22	H34
MGREC108:13	H2229	MEDDM201:20	HP280	PROLOG7:24	H36
MGREC108:14	H2230	MEDDM201:22	HP281	PROLOG7:25	H37
MGREC108:33	H2249	MEDDM201:28	HP281	PROLOG7:28	H39
MGREC109:2	H2259	MEDDM202:17	HP282	ELEMENT8:8	H6
MGREC109:3	H2260	MEDDM202:18	HP282	ELEMEN8:8	H6
MGREC110:11	H2311	MEDDM202:19	HP282	ELEMEN8:26	H24
MGREC111:10	H2355	MEDDM203:5	HP283	ELEMEN9:5	H39
MGREC111:27	H2372	MEDDM203:6	HP283	ELEMEN9:30	H64
MGREC116:24	H2590	MEDDM203:33	HP284	ELEMEN10:41	H116
MGREC119:38	H2728	MEDDM205:3	HP285	ELEMEN11:36	H156
MGREC120:13	H2748	MEDDM205:4	HP285	ELEMEN13:38	H239
MGREC120:15	H2750	MEDDM205:34	HP286	ELEMEN13:39	H240

ELEMEN13:39	H240	MPERS71:28	H742	MPERS88:36	H1429
ELEMEN14:14	H256	MPERS72:37	H781	MPERS88:37	H1430
ELEMEN15:39	H321	MPERS73:16	H803	MPERS89:1	H1435
ELEMEN16:26	H349	MPERS73:18	H805	MPERS89:3	H1437
ELEMEN18:14	H418	MPERS73:21	H808	MPERS89:4	H1438
ELEMEN19:19	H464	MPERS73:27	H812	MPERS89:5	H1439
HUMOUR20:15	H7	MPERS73:28	H813	MPERS89:13	H1447
HUMOUR20:21	H13	MPERS73:39	H824	MPERS89:17	H1451
HUMOUR20:33	H25	MPERS74:1	H826	MPERS89:20	H1454
HUMOUR20:34	H26	MPERS74:7	H832	MPERS89:22	H1456
HUMOUR20:35	H27	MPERS74:14	H837	MPERS89:23	H1457
HUMOUR22:29	H98	MPERS74:15	H838	MPERS89:24	H1458
HUMOUR22:30	H99	MPERS74:17	H840	MPERS89:28	H1462
HUMOUR22:32	H101	MPERS75:7	H868	MPERS90:2	H1477
HUMOUR23:27	H137	MPERS75:8	H869	MPERS90:4	~~H1478~~
HUMOUR23:41	~~H149~~	MPERS75:36	H893	MPERS~~90:4~~	H1478
HUMOUR25:17	H206	MPERS75:37	H894	MPERS90:6	H1479
HUMOUR28:27	H339	MPERS76:10	H908	MPERS90:9	H1482
HUMOUR28:28	H340	MPERS76:30	H928	MPERS90:12	~~H1484~~
HUMOUR33:33	H547	MPERS~~79:13~~	H1039	MPERS90:14	~~H1484~~
AGES39:15	H158	MPERS79:38	H1064	MPERS90:19	H1486
AGES41:17	H236	MPERS80:3	H1070	MPERS90:23	H1490
AGES42:9	H267	MPERS80:6	H1073	MPERS90:26	H1493
AGES43:12	~~H305~~	MPERS80:19	H1086	MPERS91:5	H1513
AGES44:33	H366	MPERS80:29	H1096	MPERS91:9	H1517
AGES~~45:22~~	H404	MPERS81:3	H1111	MPERS91:10	H1518
SEASONS47:22	H38	MPERS81:12	H1120	MPERS91:37	~~H1551~~
SEASONS47:23	H39	MPERS81:17	H1125	MGREC94:10	H1644
SEASONS49:18	H109	MPERS81:19	H1127	MGREC96:6	H1726
SEASONS49:19	H110	MPERS81:20	H1128	MGREC96:17	H1737
SEASONS50:5	H139	MPERS81:25	H1133	MGREC97:39	H1800
MASSYR54:6	H33	MPERS81:41	H1145	MGREC98:5	H1807
MASSYR55:13	H79	MPERS82:9	H1156	MGREC100:41	H1925
MASSYR~~55:32~~	H98	MPERS82:17	H1164	MGREC101:2	H1927
MASSYR56:5	H111	MPERS83:31	H1219	MGREC~~101:34~~	H1963
MASSYR56:31	H137	MPERS83:33	H1221	MGREC101:35	H1964
MASSYR57:7	H154	MPERS83:34	H1222	MGREC101:37	H1966
MASSYR57:28	H173	MPERS~~84:12~~	H1243	MGREC103:1	H2012
MASSYR58:39	H222	MPERS84:16	H1252	MGREC103:7	H2018
MASSYR59:3	H227	MPERS85:12	H1288	MGREC105:6	H2099
MASSYR59:3	H227	MPERS85:26	H1302	MGREC106:6	H2140
MASSYR59:24	H248	MPERS87:24	H1376	MGREC107:24	H2199
MASSYR62:23	H368	MPERS87:40	H1392	MGREC107:37	H2212
MASSYR62:28	H373	MPERS88:9	H1402	MGREC108:3	H2219
MASSYR62:29	H374	MPERS88:10	H1403	MGREC108:16	H2232
MASSYR65:2	H467	MPERS88:12	H1405	MGREC108:18	H2234
MASSYR65:31	H496	MPERS88:14	H1407	MGREC108:32	H2248
MASSYR65:41	H506	MPERS88:17	H1410	MGREC109:3	H2260
MASSYR67:34	H580	MPERS88:23	H1416	MGREC111:21	H2366
MPERS70:7	H678	MPERS88:30	H1423	MGREC112:10	H2396
MPERS71:10	H726	MPERS88:32	H1425	MGREC113:11	H2438

MGREC113:12	H2439	SIDNEY152:7	H78	MEDDM199:16	HP278
MGREC113:16	H2443	SIDNEY152:11	H80	MEDDM200:7	HP279
MGREC113:25	H2452	SIDNEY152:19	H88	MEDDM200:9	HP279
MGREC114:7	H2475	DUBART153:14	H18	MEDDM200:10	HP279
MGREC115:15	H2534	DUBART155:5	H90	MEDDM200:12	HP279
MGREC117:39	H2646	QELIZ156:29	H56	MEDDM200:22	HP279
MGREC118:2	H2649	QELIZ156:30	H57	MEDDM200:27	HP279
MGREC118:24	H2673	QELIZ157:32	H100	MEDDM200:29	HP279
MGREC120:9	H2744	QELIZ157:33	H101	MEDDM201:4	HP280
MGREC120:10	H2745	DAVID159:9	H24	MEDDM201:29	HP281
MGREC120:15	H2750	DAVID159:11	H26	MEDDM202:4	HP281
MGREC121:16	H2798	VANITY159:35	H7	MEDDM202:6	HP281
MGREC122:37	H2858	VANITY159:36	H8	MEDDM202:7	HP281
MGREC124:24	H2931	VANITY160:6	H16	MEDDM202:8	HP281
MGREC127:41	H3071	VANITY160:33	H43	MEDDM202:12	HP281
MGREC128:32	H3105	TDUDLEY166:8	H50	MEDDM202:16	HP282
MGREC129:25	H3139	TDUDLEY166:9	H51	MEDDM202:17	HP282
MGREC130:16	H3171	DDUDLEY167:15	H12	MEDDM202:18	HP282
MGREC130:28	H3181	CONTEM169:20	H60	MEDDM203:6	HP283
MGREC131:3	H3193	CONTEM171:3	H108	MEDDM203:33	HP284
MGREC131:20	H3212	CONTEM171:23	H126	MEDDM205:3	HP285
MGREC131:38	H3230	CONTEM172:2	H139	MEDDM205:5	HP285
MGREC133:21	H3309	CONTEM172:3	H140	MEDDM205:37	HP287
MGREC134:24	H3355	CONTEM172:24	H158	MEDDM206:1	HP287
MGREC134:34	H3365	CONTEM173:3	H171	MEDDM206:13	HP287
MROMAN137:9	H3460	CONTEM173:5	H173	MEDDM206:16	HP287
MROMAN137:16	H3467	CONTEM173:30	H195	MEDDM206:17	HP287
MROMAN137:19	H3470	FLESH176:32	H72	MEDDM206:20	HP287
MROMAN137:25	H3476	FLESH177:17	H98	MEDDM206:34	HP288
MROMAN138:6	H3496	FLESH177:22	H103	MEDDM206:36	HP288
MROMAN138:19	H3509	2LETTER182:22	H28	MEDDM207:6	HP288
MROMAN139:20	H3548	CHILDRN184:18	H7	MEDDM207:8	HP288
MROMAN139:22	H3550	CHILDRN184:28	H17	MEDDM207:10	HP288
DIALOG142:38	H67	CHILDRN184:29	H18	MEDDM207:23	HP289
DIALOG143:8	H75	CHILDRN184:31	H20	MEDDM208:1	HP289
DIALOG143:39	H108	CHILDRN185:16	H42	MEDDM208:18	HP290
DIALOG145:27	H176	CHILDRN185:22	H48	MEDDM208:23	HP290
DIALOG145:29	H178	CHILDRN185:23	H49	MEDDM209:9	HP291
DIALOG145:30	H179	CHILDRN185:27	H53	MEDDM209:10	HP291
DIALOG145:32	H181	CHILDRN186:14	H81	MEDDM209:14	HP291
DIALOG145:34	H183	ELIZB187:5	H13	MYCHILD217:35	HP243
DIALOG145:36	H185	2SIMON195:9	HP271	MYCHILD218:19	HP244
DIALOG145:39	H188	2SIMON195:12	HP271	MYCHILD218:20	HP244
DIALOG146:5	H193	2SIMON195:13	HP271	MYCHILD218:24	HP244
DIALOG146:21	H207	MEDDM197:8	HP274	JULY223:28	HP251
DIALOG147:27	H251	MEDDM197:9	HP274	13MAY227:3	H12
DIALOG147:30	H254	MEDDM197:33	HP274	HOURS234:16	H30
DIALOG148:4	H269	MEDDM198:5	HP276	REMB236:11	H26
SIDNEY149:23	H22	MEDDM198:7	HP276	**THINE** (44)	
SIDNEY152:4	H76	MEDDM198:18	HP276	ELEMEN9:33	H67
SIDNEY152:7	H78	MEDDM199:15	HP278	ELEMEN13:12	H213

1240

ELEMEN15:17	H299	ELEMEN15:33	H315	HUMOUR31:16	H449
HUMOUR22:39	H108	ELEMEN15:36	H318	HUMOUR33:9	H523
HUMOUR23:6	H116	ELEMEN16:3	H326	HUMOUR33:12	H526
HUMOUR25:20	H209	ELEMEN16:10	H333	HUMOUR33:14	H528
HUMOUR26:18	H248	HUMOUR22:41	H110	HUMOUR33:16	H530
HUMOUR26:23	H253	HUMOUR23:3	H113	HUMOUR34:31	H586
HUMOUR26:24	H254	HUMOUR23:7	H117	HUMOUR34:34	H589
HUMOUR26:34	H264	HUMOUR23:10	H120	MPERS75:18	H878
HUMOUR29:41	H392	HUMOUR23:14	H124	MPERS75:23	H880
HUMOUR30:15	H407	HUMOUR23:18	H128	MPERS78:30	H1011
HUMOUR33:11	H525	HUMOUR24:28	H177	MPERS79:6	H1028
SEASONS48:35	H86	HUMOUR24:29	H178	MGREC99:28	H1871
MPERS75:14	H875	HUMOUR24:35	H184	MGREC99:32	H1875
MPERS75:22	H880	HUMOUR24:38	H187	DIALOG141:19	H18
MPERS78:30	H1011	HUMOUR24:40	H189	DIALOG141:23	H22
DIALOG141:8	H7	HUMOUR25:11	H200	DIALOG141:25	H24
DIALOG147:1	H227	HUMOUR25:20	H209	DIALOG141:28	H27
DIALOG148:5	H270	HUMOUR25:22	H211	DIALOG142:38	H67
DIALOG148:8	H273	HUMOUR25:23	H212	DIALOG143:41	H110
SIDNEY149:16	H15	HUMOUR25:27	H216	DIALOG144:10	H120
SIDNEY149:18	H17	HUMOUR25:28	H217	DIALOG144:18	H128
SIDNEY149:31	H23	HUMOUR25:34	H223	DIALOG146:24	H210
SIDNEY150:30	H57	HUMOUR25:39	H228	DIALOG147:18	H244
SIDNEY150:39	H67	HUMOUR26:1	H231	DIALOG147:35	H259
SIDNEY150:40	H68	HUMOUR26:3	H233	DIALOG148:11	H276
SIDNEY151:19	H69	HUMOUR26:5	H235	DIALOG148:20	H285
DUBART154:18	H63	HUMOUR26:11	H241	DIALOG148:32	H297
QELIZ155:18	H9	HUMOUR26:12	H242	SIDNEY149:12	H11
CONTEM168:9	H18	HUMOUR26:17	H247	SIDNEY149:14	H13
FLESH176:20	H60	HUMOUR26:29	H259	SIDNEY150:21	H46
BIRTH180:4	H14	HUMOUR26:40	H270	SIDNEY150:38	H65
BIRTH180:12	H22	HUMOUR26:41	H271	SIDNEY150:39	H67
BIRTH180:17	H27	HUMOUR27:7	H278	SIDNEY150:41	H69
2LETTER182:23	H29	HUMOUR27:10	H281	SIDNEY151:4	H69
WHAT224:4	H4	HUMOUR27:11	H282	SIDNEY151:18	H69
13MAY227:15	H24	HUMOUR27:13	H284	SIDNEY151:20	H70
SAMUEL228:8	H9	HUMOUR27:13	H284	DUBART152:34	H3
THEART229:18	H20	HUMOUR29:10	H363	DUBART154:11	H56
2HUSB232:4	H5	HUMOUR29:11	H364	DUBART154:29	H74
2HUSB233:5	H38	HUMOUR29:14	H367	QELIZ155:14	H5
ACK235:5	H5	HUMOUR29:17	H368	QELIZ155:21	H12
HOUSE237:24	H54	HUMOUR29:40	H391	QELIZ155:26	H17
THOU (221)		HUMOUR30:9	H401	DAVID159:21	H36
ELEMEN12:14	H174	HUMOUR30:31	H423	DAVID159:22	H37
ELEMEN13:12	H213	HUMOUR30:33	H425	DAVID159:26	H41
ELEMEN14:32	H274	HUMOUR30:36	H428	VANITY160:4	H14
ELEMEN14:34	H276	HUMOUR31:5	H438	TDUDLEY165:27	H29
ELEMEN14:35	H277	HUMOUR31:6	H439	TDUDLEY165:32	H34
ELEMEN15:16	H298	HUMOUR31:7	H440	CONTEM168:9	H18
ELEMEN15:25	H307	HUMOUR31:7	H440	CONTEM168:11	H20
ELEMEN15:27	H309	HUMOUR31:9	H442	CONTEM168:12	H21

CONTEM168:23	H30	MERCY189:1	H22	ACK235:11	H11
CONTEM169:2	H44	MEDDM197:23	HP275	ACK235:13	H13
CONTEM172:19	H154	MEDDM209:2	HP291	REMB235:31	H12
CONTEM172:22	H156	FEVER220:25	H5	REMB235:33	H14
CONTEM172:26	H160	FEVER221:7	H22	HOUSE237:9	H39
CONTEM173:26	H191	FEVER221:7	H22	HOUSE237:17	H47
FLESH175:10	H10	FEVER221:9	H24	**THOV (22)**	
FLESH175:17	H17	SOREFIT221:19	H5	FEVER221:1	H16
FLESH175:19	H19	SOREFIT221:20	H6	FEVER221:3	H18
FLESH175:24	H24	SOREFIT221:24	H10	SOREFIT221:23	H9
FLESH175:30	H30	SOREFIT222:3	H22	SOREFIT221:23	H9
FLESH175:34	H34	FAINTING222:12	H2	MED223:3	HP250
FLESH175:36	H36	FAINTING222:20	H10	MED223:4	HP250
FLESH175:38	H38	FAINTING222:21	H11	JULY223:31	HP251
FLESH176:7	H47	MED223:5	HP250	MYSOUL225:13	H17
FLESH176:10	H50	MED223:17	HP250	THEART229:3	H5
FLESH176:12	H52	JULY223:31	HP251	SON231:11	H23
FLESH176:13	H53	JULY223:32	HP251	SON231:28	H39
FLESH176:15	H55	JULY223:32	HP251	2HUSB232:3	H4
FLESH176:25	H65	WHAT224:7	H7	2HUSB232:20	H21
FLESH176:26	H66	MYSOUL224:25	H1	2HUSB232:24	H25
FLESH176:27	H67	13MAY227:9	H18	2HUSB232:25	H26
FLESH177:28	H109	SAMUEL228:2	H3	2HUSB232:27	H28
AUTHOR177:30	H2	SAMUEL228:6	H7	2HUSB232:32	H33
AUTHOR178:7	H17	SAMUEL228:14	H15	2HUSB233:12	H45
AUTHOR178:10	H20	11MAYB228:32	HP259	ACK235:17	H17
AUTHOR178:11	H21	THEART229:5	H7	REMB235:26	H7
AUTHOR178:12	H22	THEART229:17	H19	REMB236:1	H16
AUTHOR178:13	H23	RESTOR229:22	H5	**THY (350)**	
SICKNES179:11	H31	RESTOR229:24	H7	ELEMEN9:34	H68
BIRTH180:11	H21	RESTOR229:25	H8	ELEMEN9:35	H70
BIRTH180:15	H25	RESTOR229:27	H10	ELEMEN13:13	H214
1LETTER181:5	H3	RESTOR230:2	H17	ELEMEN13:15	H216
1LETTER181:6	H4	RESTOR230:4	H19	ELEMEN13:21	H222
1LETTER181:19	H17	SON230:24	H7	ELEMEN14:33	H275
1LETTER181:21	H19	SON230:28	H11	ELEMEN14:36	H278
1LETTER181:28	H26	SON231:3	H15	ELEMEN14:38	H280
2LETTER182:1	H7	SON231:10	H22	ELEMEN14:40	H282
2LETTER182:15	H21	2HUSB232:16	H17	ELEMEN15:2	H284
2LETTER182:16	H22	2HUSB232:17	H18	ELEMEN15:25	H307
2LETTER182:17	H23	2HUSB233:3	H36	ELEMEN15:31	H313
2LETTER182:22	H28	HOURS233:20	H3	ELEMEN15:32	H314
2LETTER182:23	H29	HOURS233:24	H7	ELEMEN15:34	H316
2LETTER182:25	H31	HOURS234:9	H23	ELEMEN15:40	H322
ELIZB187:3	H12	HOURS234:13	H27	ELEMEN16:9	H332
ANNEB187:30	H20	HOURS234:22	H36	ELEMEN16:11	H334
ANNEB187:33	H23	HOURS234:24	H38	ELEMEN16:25	H348
MERCY188:27	H13	HOURS234:37	H51	ELEMEN18:7	H411
MERCY188:28	H14	HOURS235:1	H53	ELEMEN18:8	H412
MERCY188:29	H15	ACK235:5	H5	HUMOUR22:25	H94
MERCY188:34	H20	ACK235:9	H9	HUMOUR22:26	H95

1242

HUMOUR22:41	H110	HUMOUR~~31:15~~	H447	SIDNEY149:26	~~H23~~
HUMOUR23:7	H117	HUMOUR33:13	H527	SIDNEY149:27	~~H23~~
HUMOUR23:8	H118	HUMOUR34:4	H559	SIDNEY149:28	~~H23~~
HUMOUR23:9	H119	HUMOUR34:29	H584	SIDNEY149:29	~~H23~~
HUMOUR23:11	H121	SEASONS48:33	H84	SIDNEY149:31	~~H23~~
HUMOUR23:15	H125	SEASONS48:36	H87	SIDNEY149:32	~~H23~~
HUMOUR23:20	H130	SEASONS49:31	H120	SIDNEY149:37	H24
HUMOUR23:21	H131	MASSYR61:21	H326	SIDNEY149:38	H25
HUMOUR24:18	H167	MPERS72:17	H765	SIDNEY150:3	H28
HUMOUR24:24	H173	MPERS75:14	H875	SIDNEY150:4	~~H29~~
HUMOUR24:26	H175	MPERS75:17	H878	SIDNEY150:7	H32
HUMOUR24:28	H177	MPERS75:19	~~H878~~	SIDNEY150:11	H36
HUMOUR24:30	H179	MPERS75:20	H879	SIDNEY150:13	H48
HUMOUR25:3	H192	MPERS75:21	H880	SIDNEY150:14	H49
HUMOUR25:4	H193	MPERS75:22	~~H880~~	SIDNEY150:17	~~H49~~
HUMOUR25:7	H196	MPERS75:23	~~H880~~	SIDNEY150:24	H51
HUMOUR25:8	H197	MPERS78:29	H1010	SIDNEY150:37	H64
HUMOUR25:10	H199	MPERS79:4	H1026	SIDNEY151:5	~~H69~~
HUMOUR25:14	H203	MGREC99:28	H1871	SIDNEY151:10	~~H69~~
HUMOUR25:16	H205	MGREC99:32	H1875	DUBART153:4	H8
HUMOUR25:26	H215	MGREC106:1	H2135	DUBART153:33	H37
HUMOUR25:32	H221	MGREC106:2	~~H2136~~	DUBART153:34	H38
HUMOUR25:36	H225	MGREC113:5	H2432	DUBART153:35	H39
HUMOUR25:37	H226	MGREC113:7	H2434	DUBART153:36	H40
HUMOUR25:39	H228	DIALOG141:8	H7	DUBART153:38	H42
HUMOUR26:10	H240	DIALOG141:11	H10	DUBART154:2	H47
HUMOUR26:19	H249	DIALOG141:13	H12	DUBART154:12	H57
HUMOUR26:25	H255	DIALOG142:6	H35	DUBART154:13	H58
HUMOUR26:33	H263	DIALOG142:7	H36	DUBART154:15	H60
HUMOUR26:38	H268	DIALOG142:11	H40	DUBART154:21	H66
HUMOUR27:5	H276	DIALOG143:24	H93	DUBART154:26	H71
HUMOUR27:8	H279	DIALOG144:1	H111	DUBART154:29	H74
HUMOUR27:12	~~H283~~	DIALOG144:11	H121	DUBART154:31	H76
HUMOUR~~27:12~~	H283	DIALOG146:23	H209	DUBART154:33	H78
HUMOUR29:13	H366	DIALOG146:25	H211	DUBART154:38	H83
HUMOUR29:16	~~H368~~	DIALOG146:38	H224	DUBART154:39	H84
HUMOUR29:20	H371	DIALOG146:40	H226	QELIZ155:15	H6
HUMOUR29:27	H378	DIALOG147:1	H227	QELIZ155:16	H7
HUMOUR29:28	H379	DIALOG147:2	H228	QELIZ155:18	H9
HUMOUR29:29	H380	DIALOG147:4	H230	QELIZ155:23	H14
HUMOUR29:36	H387	DIALOG147:9	H235	QELIZ155:25	H16
HUMOUR29:41	H392	DIALOG147:19	H245	QELIZ155:28	H19
HUMOUR30:11	H403	DIALOG147:33	H257	QELIZ155:31	H22
HUMOUR30:40	H432	DIALOG147:34	H258	QELIZ158:16	H125
HUMOUR30:41	H433	DIALOG147:35	H259	DAVID158:26	H6
HUMOUR31:1	H434	DIALOG147:37	H261	DAVID159:24	H39
HUMOUR31:2	H435	DIALOG147:38	H262	TDUDLEY165:26	H28
HUMOUR31:4	H437	DIALOG148:3	H268	TDUDLEY165:27	H29
HUMOUR~~31:6~~	H439	DIALOG148:7	H272	TDUDLEY165:31	H33
HUMOUR31:12	~~H444~~	SIDNEY149:15	H14	TDUDLEY165:34	H36
HUMOUR31:15	H446	SIDNEY149:17	H16	CONTEM168:10	H19

SEASONS52:19	H234	MASSYR60:3	H268	MASSYR67:32	H578
SEASONS52:21	H236	MASSYR60:4	H269	MASSYR68:2	H588
SEASONS52:35	H250	MASSYR60:5	H270	MASSYR68:5	H591
SEASONS52:36	H251	MASSYR60:6	H271	MASSYR68:7	H593
SEASONS52:36	H251	MASSYR60:8	H273	MASSYR68:8	H594
SEASONS53:4	H260	MASSYR60:10	H275	MASSYR68:14	H600
MASSYR53:20	H10	MASSYR60:12	H277	MASSYR68:26	H612
MASSYR53:22	H12	MASSYR60:17	H282	MPERS69:2	H624
MASSYR53:26	H16	MASSYR60:37	H302	MPERS69:9	H631
MASSYR53:30	H20	MASSYR61:4	H309	MPERS69:22	H644
MASSYR54:2	H29	MASSYR61:5	H310	MPERS69:25	H647
MASSYR54:4	H31	MASSYR61:7	H312	MPERS69:27	H649
MASSYR54:5	H32	MASSYR61:18	H323	MPERS69:28	H650
MASSYR54:9	H36	MASSYR61:19	H324	MPERS69:34	H656
MASSYR54:17	H44	MASSYR61:20	H325	MPERS69:37	~~H659~~
MASSYR54:27	H54	MASSYR61:28	H333	~~MPERS69:38~~	H660
MASSYR54:33	H60	MASSYR61:30	H335	~~MPERS70:3~~	~~H674~~
MASSYR55:11	H77	MASSYR62:7	H352	~~MPERS70:3~~	H674
MASSYR55:24	H90	MASSYR62:17	H362	MPERS70:8	H679
MASSYR55:27	H93	MASSYR62:19	H364	MPERS70:12	H683
MASSYR56:13	H119	MASSYR62:39	H384	MPERS70:21	H692
MASSYR56:18	H124	MASSYR63:5	H390	MPERS70:25	H696
MASSYR56:24	H130	MASSYR63:13	H398	MPERS70:28	H699
MASSYR56:25	H131	MASSYR63:15	H400	MPERS70:38	H709
MASSYR56:29	H135	MASSYR63:18	H403	~~MPERS70:40~~	H711
MASSYR56:37	H143	MASSYR63:21	H406	MPERS70:41	~~H712~~
MASSYR56:39	H145	MASSYR63:23	H408	~~MPERS71:4~~	H720
MASSYR57:3	H150	~~MASSYR63:28~~	H415	MPERS71:7	H723
MASSYR57:5	H152	MASSYR64:2	H426	MPERS71:9	H725
MASSYR57:13	H160	MASSYR64:12	H436	MPERS71:16	H730
MASSYR57:19	~~H166~~	MASSYR64:16	H440	MPERS71:20	H734
~~MASSYR57:19~~	H166	MASSYR64:29	H453	MPERS71:23	H737
MASSYR57:21	~~H168~~	MASSYR64:32	H456	MPERS71:27	H741
MASSYR57:26	~~H172~~	MASSYR64:33	H457	MPERS71:30	H744
MASSYR57:27	~~H172~~	MASSYR64:38	H462	MPERS71:32	H746
MASSYR58:8	H193	MASSYR65:12	H477	MPERS71:35	H749
MASSYR58:10	H195	MASSYR65:15	H480	MPERS71:37	H751
MASSYR58:16	H201	MASSYR65:17	H482	~~MPERS72:3~~	H755
MASSYR58:18	H203	MASSYR65:20	H485	MPERS72:4	~~H755~~
MASSYR58:20	H205	MASSYR65:22	H487	~~MPERS72:9~~	H757
MASSYR58:22	H207	MASSYR65:24	H489	MPERS72:22	H770
MASSYR58:37	H220	MASSYR65:26	H491	MPERS72:24	~~H772~~
MASSYR58:38	H221	MASSYR65:40	H505	MPERS72:31	H775
MASSYR58:39	H222	MASSYR66:1	H507	MPERS72:36	H780
MASSYR58:40	H223	MASSYR66:8	H514	~~MPERS72:37~~	H783
MASSYR58:41	H224	MASSYR66:20	H526	MPERS72:38	H784
MASSYR59:1	H225	MASSYR66:40	H546	MPERS73:2	H789
MASSYR59:10	H234	MASSYR67:19	H565	MPERS73:6	H793
MASSYR59:11	H235	MASSYR67:26	H572	MPERS73:14	H801
MASSYR59:21	H245	MASSYR67:30	H576	MPERS73:16	H803
MASSYR59:28	H252	MASSYR67:31	H577	MPERS73:18	H805

MPERS73:20	H807	MPERS80:29	H1096	MPERS86:22	H1338
MPERS73:31	H816	MPERS80:31	H1098	MPERS86:24	H1340
MPERS73:40	H825	MPERS80:32	H1099	MPERS86:33	H1349
MPERS74:3	H828	MPERS80:34	H1101	MPERS86:37	H1353
MPERS74:4	H829	MPERS80:37	H1104	MPERS86:38	H1354
MPERS74:8	H833	MPERS80:38	H1105	MPERS87:6	H1362
MPERS74:11	H836	MPERS80:39	H1106	MPERS87:11	H1367
MPERS74:17	H840	MPERS81:3	H1111	MPERS87:16	H1370
MPERS74:21	H844	MPERS81:4	H1112	MPERS87:17	H1371
MPERS74:23	H846	MPERS81:5	H1113	MPERS87:18	H1372
MPERS74:25	H848	MPERS81:10	H1118	MPERS87:20	H1374
MPERS74:28	H851	MPERS81:13	H1121	MPERS87:22	H1374
MPERS74:34	H857	MPERS81:16	H1124	MPERS87:25	H1377
MPERS75:1	H862	MPERS81:29	H1137	MPERS87:26	H1378
MPERS75:4	H865	MPERS81:31	H1139	MPERS87:27	H1379
MPERS75:12	H873	MPERS81:38	H1143	MPERS87:28	H1380
MPERS75:17	H878	MPERS82:12	H1159	MPERS88:5	H1398
MPERS75:26	H883	MPERS82:13	H1160	MPERS88:13	H1406
MPERS75:31	H888	MPERS82:14	H1161	MPERS88:16	H1409
MPERS75:35	H892	MPERS82:18	H1165	MPERS88:23	H1416
MPERS76:6	H904	MPERS82:22	H1169	MPERS88:27	H1420
MPERS76:16	H914	MPERS82:23	H1170	MPERS88:29	H1422
MPERS76:20	H918	MPERS82:27	H1174	MPERS88:33	H1426
MPERS76:23	H921	MPERS82:35	H1182	MPERS88:33	H1426
MPERS76:35	H933	MPERS82:37	H1184	MPERS88:41	H1434
MPERS77:7	H946	MPERS82:39	H1186	MPERS89:1	H1435
MPERS77:13	H952	MPERS83:5	H1193	MPERS89:3	H1437
MPERS77:16	H955	MPERS83:17	H1205	MPERS89:4	H1438
MPERS77:20	H961	MPERS83:19	H1207	MPERS89:15	H1449
MPERS77:24	H965	MPERS83:30	H1218	MPERS89:24	H1458
MPERS77:40	H981	MPERS83:31	H1219	MPERS89:26	H1460
MPERS78:6	H987	MPERS83:40	H1228	MPERS89:28	H1462
MPERS78:8	H989	MPERS84:4	H1232	MPERS89:30	H1464
MPERS78:10	H991	MPERS84:12	H1246	MPERS89:36	H1470
MPERS78:12	H993	MPERS84:20	H1256	MPERS89:38	H1472
MPERS78:22	H1003	MPERS84:22	H1258	MPERS89:40	H1474
MPERS78:28	H1009	MPERS84:32	H1268	MPERS90:1	H1476
MPERS78:32	H1013	MPERS84:33	H1269	MPERS90:3	H1477
MPERS78:36	H1017	MPERS84:34	H1270	MPERS90:5	H1478
MPERS78:37	H1018	MPERS84:35	H1271	MPERS90:9	H1482
MPERS78:39	H1020	MPERS84:36	H1272	MPERS90:16	H1484
MPERS79:5	H1027	MPERS85:5	H1281	MPERS90:33	H1500
MPERS79:7	H1029	MPERS85:11	H1287	MPERS90:37	H1504
MPERS79:13	H1035	MPERS85:23	H1299	MPERS90:40	H1507
MPERS79:30	H1056	MPERS85:24	H1300	MPERS90:41	H1508
MPERS79:31	H1057	MPERS85:33	H1309	MPERS91:3	H1511
MPERS79:33	H1059	MPERS86:2	H1318	MPERS91:5	H1513
MPERS79:34	H1060	MPERS86:3	H1319	MPERS91:8	H1516
MPERS80:5	H1072	MPERS86:14	H1330	MPERS91:9	H1517
MPERS80:16	H1083	MPERS86:17	H1333	MPERS91:10	H1518
MPERS80:17	H1084	MPERS86:20	H1336	MPERS91:17	H1525

MGREC106:32	H2166	MGREC112:13	H2399	MGREC117:5	H2612
MGREC106:41	H2175	MGREC112:18	H2404	MGREC117:8	H2615
MGREC107:3	H2178	MGREC112:32	H2418	MGREC117:9	H2616
MGREC107:7	H2182	MGREC113:2	H2429	MGREC117:12	H2619
MGREC107:18	H2193	MGREC113:3	H2430	MGREC117:18	H2625
MGREC107:19	H2194	MGREC113:11	H2438	MGREC117:22	H2629
MGREC107:21	H2196	MGREC113:16	H2443	MGREC117:27	H2634
MGREC107:24	H2199	MGREC113:17	H2444	MGREC117:32	H2639
MGREC107:26	H2201	MGREC113:19	H2446	MGREC117:33	H2640
MGREC107:29	H2204	MGREC113:22	H2449	MGREC117:36	H2643
MGREC107:31	H2206	MGREC113:25	H2452	MGREC118:5	H2652
MGREC107:37	H2212	MGREC113:40	H2467	MGREC118:6	H2653
MGREC107:38	H2213	MGREC114:1	H2469	MGREC118:7	H2654
MGREC108:5	H2221	MGREC114:2	H2470	MGREC118:8	H2655
MGREC108:6	H2222	MGREC114:3	H2471	MGREC118:10	H2657
MGREC108:9	H2225	MGREC114:4	H2472	MGREC118:17	H2664
MGREC108:12	H2228	MGREC114:5	H2473	MGREC118:21	H2668
MGREC108:13	H2229	MGREC114:6	H2474	MGREC118:23	H2670
MGREC108:27	H2243	MGREC114:9	H2477	MGREC118:28	H2677
MGREC108:32	H2248	MGREC114:12	~~H2480~~	MGREC118:34	H2683
MGREC108:33	H2249	MGREC114:16	H2486	MGREC118:36	~~H2685~~
MGREC109:4	~~H2261~~	MGREC114:34	H2504	MGREC118:41	H2690
~~MGREC109:5~~	H2264	MGREC114:38	H2508	MGREC119:5	H2695
MGREC109:12	H2271	MGREC114:39	H2509	MGREC119:6	H2696
MGREC109:13	H2272	MGREC115:4	H2515	MGREC119:7	H2697
MGREC109:15	H2274	MGREC115:11	H2520	MGREC119:10	H2700
MGREC109:23	H2282	MGREC115:13	H2522	MGREC119:16	H2706
MGREC109:24	H2283	MGREC~~115:15~~	H2532	MGREC119:17	H2707
MGREC109:28	H2287	MGREC115:16	H2535	MGREC119:18	H2708
MGREC109:30	H2289	MGREC115:17	H2536	MGREC119:19	H2709
MGREC109:33	H2292	MGREC115:21	H2540	MGREC119:22	H2712
MGREC109:35	H2294	MGREC115:23	H2542	MGREC119:26	H2716
MGREC109:40	H2299	MGREC115:25	H2544	MGREC119:33	H2723
MGREC109:41	H2300	MGREC115:31	H2550	MGREC119:34	H2724
MGREC110:2	H2302	MGREC115:32	H2551	MGREC~~120:4~~	H2738
MGREC110:16	H2316	MGREC115:33	H2552	MGREC120:11	H2746
MGREC110:17	H2317	MGREC115:34	H2553	MGREC120:12	H2747
MGREC110:18	H2318	MGREC115:41	H2560	MGREC120:13	H2748
MGREC110:22	H2326	MGREC116:1	H2561	MGREC120:15	H2750
MGREC110:25	H2329	MGREC116:4	H2564	MGREC120:16	H2751
MGREC111:7	H2352	MGREC116:6	H2566	MGREC120:21	H2758
MGREC111:9	H2354	MGREC116:10	H2570	MGREC120:23	H2760
MGREC111:12	H2357	MGREC~~116:10~~	H2572	MGREC120:26	H2763
MGREC111:23	H2368	MGREC116:17	H2583	MGREC120:28	H2765
MGREC111:29	H2374	MGREC116:20	H2586	MGREC120:31	H2768
MGREC111:31	H2376	MGREC116:26	H2592	MGREC120:32	H2769
MGREC111:38	H2383	MGREC116:33	H2599	MGREC121:1	H2779
MGREC111:39	H2384	MGREC116:36	H2602	MGREC121:2	~~H2780~~
MGREC112:1	H2387	MGREC116:38	H2604	MGREC121:4	H2782
MGREC112:5	H2391	MGREC116:39	H2605	MGREC121:7	H2785
MGREC112:8	H2394	MGREC116:40	H2606	MGREC121:12	H2790

MGREC~~121:16~~	H2797	MGREC124:30	H2937	MGREC128:24	H3097
MGREC121:17	H2799	MGREC124:32	H2939	MGREC128:26	H3099
MGREC121:19	H2801	MGREC124:36	H2943	MGREC128:30	H3103
MGREC121:23	H2805	MGREC124:38	H2945	MGREC128:34	H3107
MGREC121:25	H2807	MGREC125:1	H2949	MGREC129:7	H3121
MGREC121:31	H2813	MGREC125:3	H2951	MGREC129:8	H3122
MGREC121:34	H2816	MGREC125:6	H2954	MGREC129:9	H3123
MGREC122:4	H2827	MGREC125:7	H2955	MGREC129:14	H3128
MGREC122:5	H2828	MGREC125:10	H2958	MGREC129:24	H3138
MGREC122:12	H2837	MGREC125:11	H2959	MGREC129:29	H3143
MGREC122:16	H2841	MGREC125:13	H2961	MGREC129:31	H3145
MGREC122:18	H2843	MGREC125:15	H2963	MGREC129:32	H3146
MGREC122:20	H2845	MGREC125:17	H2965	MGREC129:35	H3149
MGREC122:21	~~H2845~~	MGREC125:20	H2968	MGREC129:37	H3151
MGREC122:23	~~H2845~~	MGREC~~125:21~~	H2969	MGREC130:2	H3157
MGREC122:24	~~H2845~~	MGREC125:23	H2973	MGREC130:11	H3166
MGREC122:26	~~H2845~~	MGREC125:27	H2977	MGREC130:15	H3170
MGREC~~122:32~~	H2852	MGREC125:33	H2983	MGREC130:17	H3172
MGREC~~122:36~~	H2857	MGREC125:35	H2985	MGREC130:40	H3185
MGREC122:37	~~H2858~~	MGREC125:41	H2991	MGREC131:1	H3187
MGREC~~122:37~~	H2858	MGREC126:4	H2995	MGREC~~131:1~~	H3188
MGREC122:38	H2859	MGREC126:6	H2997	MGREC131:2	H3192
MGREC122:40	H2861	MGREC126:7	H2998	MGREC131:6	H3196
MGREC123:1	H2863	MGREC126:12	H3003	MGREC131:8	H3198
MGREC123:7	H2869	MGREC126:13	H3004	MGREC131:16	H3208
MGREC123:8	H2870	MGREC126:15	H3006	MGREC131:18	H3210
MGREC123:10	H2872	MGREC126:19	H3010	MGREC131:19	H3211
MGREC123:13	H2875	MGREC126:20	H3011	MGREC131:37	H3229
MGREC~~123:13~~	H2877	MGREC126:21	~~H3012~~	MGREC132:8	H3243
MGREC123:15	H2879	MGREC126:28	H3019	MGREC132:10	H3245
MGREC123:17	H2881	MGREC126:31	H3022	MGREC132:19	H3256
MGREC123:20	H2884	MGREC126:35	H3024	MGREC~~132:20~~	H3261
MGREC123:22	H2886	MGREC126:39	H3028	MGREC~~132:28~~	H3274
MGREC123:23	H2887	MGREC127:2	H3032	MGREC132:32	H3279
MGREC123:27	H2891	MGREC127:3	H3033	MGREC132:39	H3286
MGREC123:31	H2895	MGREC127:5	H3035	MGREC133:22	H3310
MGREC123:32	H2896	MGREC127:15	H3045	MGREC133:27	H3317
MGREC123:35	H2899	MGREC127:26	H3056	MGREC133:31	H3321
MGREC123:39	H2903	MGREC127:31	H3061	MGREC134:14	H3345
MGREC124:1	H2906	MGREC127:32	H3062	MGREC134:30	H3361
MGREC124:2	H2907	MGREC127:37	H3067	MGREC134:33	H3364
MGREC124:4	H2909	MGREC127:39	H3069	MGREC135:1	H3371
MGREC~~124:8~~	H2913	MGREC127:41	H3071	MGREC135:2	H3374
MGREC124:10	~~H2915~~	MGREC128:1	H3074	MGREC135:3	H3375
MGREC124:11	H2918	MGREC128:3	H3076	MGREC135:5	H3377
MGREC124:12	H2919	MGREC128:4	H3077	MGREC135:11	H3383
MGREC124:16	~~H2923~~	MGREC128:6	H3079	MGREC135:20	H3392
MGREC~~124:16~~	H2923	MGREC128:10	H3083	MGREC135:21	H3393
MGREC124:20	H2927	MGREC128:13	H3086	MGREC135:32	H3404
MGREC124:23	H2930	MGREC128:14	H3087	MGREC135:39	H3411
MGREC124:28	H2935	MGREC128:21	H3094	MGREC135:40	H3412

MEDDM198:32	Hp277	MEDDM206:31	Hp288	MYCHILD216:6	Hp241
MEDDM198:34	Hp277	MEDDM206:33	Hp288	MYCHILD216:6	Hp241
MEDDM199:11	Hp277	MEDDM206:35	Hp288	MYCHILD216:10	Hp241
MEDDM199:12	Hp277	MEDDM206:36	Hp288	MYCHILD216:12	Hp241
MEDDM199:16	Hp278	MEDDM206:37	Hp288	MYCHILD216:14	Hp241
MEDDM200:2	Hp278	MEDDM207:7	Hp288	MYCHILD216:15	Hp241
MEDDM200:11	Hp279	MEDDM207:8	Hp288	MYCHILD216:18	Hp241
MEDDM200:16	Hp279	MEDDM207:10	Hp288	MYCHILD216:21	Hp241
MEDDM200:18	Hp279	MEDDM207:13	Hp288	MYCHILD216:30	Hp242
MEDDM200:21	Hp279	MEDDM207:21	Hp289	MYCHILD216:31	Hp242
MEDDM200:26	Hp279	MEDDM207:23	Hp289	MYCHILD216:36	Hp242
MEDDM200:36	Hp280	MEDDM207:25	Hp289	MYCHILD217:3	Hp242
MEDDM201:2	Hp280	MEDDM207:27	Hp289	MYCHILD217:8	Hp242
MEDDM201:27	Hp281	MEDDM207:28	Hp289	MYCHILD217:11	Hp242
MEDDM201:28	Hp281	MEDDM208:3	Hp289	MYCHILD217:14	Hp242
MEDDM202:16	Hp282	MEDDM208:7	Hp289	MYCHILD217:18	Hp243
MEDDM202:26	Hp282	MEDDM208:13	Hp290	MYCHILD217:24	Hp243
MEDDM202:36	Hp282	MEDDM208:14	Hp290	MYCHILD217:27	Hp243
MEDDM203:7	Hp283	MEDDM208:19	Hp290	MYCHILD217:30	Hp243
MEDDM203:10	Hp283	MEDDM208:25	Hp290	MYCHILD217:34	Hp243
MEDDM203:12	Hp283	MEDDM208:28	Hp290	MYCHILD218:2	Hp243
MEDDM203:15	Hp283	MEDDM208:29	Hp290	MYCHILD218:6	Hp243-4
MEDDM203:16	Hp283	MEDDM208:32	Hp290	MYCHILD218:14	Hp244
MEDDM203:21	Hp283	MEDDM208:34	Hp290	MYCHILD218:25	Hp244
MEDDM203:26	Hp283	MEDDM208:35	Hp291	MYCHILD218:27	Hp244
MEDDM203:32	Hp284	MEDDM209:1	Hp291	MYCHILD218:31	Hp244
MEDDM204:6	Hp284	MEDDM209:4	Hp291	MYCHILD218:35	Hp244
MEDDM204:7	Hp284	MEDDM209:13	Hp291	MYCHILD219:2	Hp245
MEDDM204:11	Hp284	MEDDM209:15	Hp291	MYCHILD219:3	Hp245
MEDDM204:12	Hp284	MEDDM209:16	Hp291	BYNIGHT220:5	H6
MEDDM204:15	Hp284	MEDDM209:25	Hp291	BYNIGHT220:17	H15
MEDDM204:18	Hp285	PILGRIM210:5	H5	BYNIGHT220:20	H18
MEDDM204:22	Hp285	PILGRIM210:16	H16	FEVER220:28	H8
MEDDM204:29	Hp285	PILGRIM210:18	H18	FEVER221:4	H19
MEDDM204:34	Hp285	PILGRIM210:21	H21	FEVER221:6	H21
MEDDM205:3	Hp285	PILGRIM210:23	H23	FEVER221:9	H24
MEDDM205:10	Hp286	TOCHILD215:1	H1	FEVER221:11	H26
MEDDM205:12	Hp286	MYCHILD215:11	Hp240	FEVER221:12	H27
MEDDM205:14	Hp286	MYCHILD215:13	Hp240	FEVER221:14	H29
MEDDM205:16	Hp286	MYCHILD215:14	Hp240	SOREFIT221:22	H8
MEDDM205:19	Hp286	MYCHILD215:15	Hp240	SOREFIT221:28	H14
MEDDM205:20	Hp286	MYCHILD215:18	Hp240	SOREFIT221:29	H15
MEDDM205:25	Hp286	MYCHILD215:19	Hp240	SOREFIT221:32	H18
MEDDM205:26	Hp286	MYCHILD215:20	Hp240	SOREFIT222:2	H21
MEDDM205:33	Hp286	MYCHILD215:21	Hp240	SOREFIT222:4	H23
MEDDM206:1	Hp287	MYCHILD215:23	Hp240	SOREFIT222:7	H26
MEDDM206:2	Hp287	MYCHILD215:24	Hp240	FAINTING222:24	H14
MEDDM206:7	Hp287	MYCHILD215:25	Hp240	MED223:12	Hp250
MEDDM206:20	Hp287	MYCHILD215:31	Hp241	MED223:13	Hp250
MEDDM206:21	Hp287	MYCHILD215:33	Hp241	MED223:16	Hp250
MEDDM206:23	Hp287	MYCHILD216:1	Hp241	MED223:18	Hp250

JULY223:22	HP251	2HUSB232:21	H22	HUMOUR21:12	H40
JULY223:25	HP251	2HUSB232:24	H25	HUMOUR33:4	H518
JULY223:26	HP251	2HUSB232:26	H27	AGES36:21	H45
JULY223:27	HP251	2HUSB232:27	H28	AGES45:2	H375
JULY223:28	HP251	2HUSB233:1	H34	SEASONS49:25	H114
JULY223:31	HP251	2HUSB233:4	H37	MASSYR53:13	H3
JULY223:32	HP251	2HUSB233:17	H50	MASSYR54:31	H58
WHAT224:1	H1	HOURS234:7	H21	MASSYR61:12	H317
WHAT224:2	H2	HOURS234:27	H41	MASSYR64:4	H428
WHAT224:9	H9	HOURS234:35	H49	MPERS68:33	H619
WHAT224:10	H10	ACK235:11	H11	MPERS71:4	H718
WHAT224:13	H13	ACK235:13	H13	MPERS72:37	H781
WHAT224:18	H18	REMB235:23	H4	MPERS76:16	H914
MYSOUL224:28	H4	REMB235:32	H13	MPERS84:14	H1250
MYSOUL225:6	H10	REMB236:7	H22	MPERS88:14	H1407
28AUG225:27	HP254	HOUSE236:20	H12	MGREC93:8	H1605
28AUG225:28	HP254	HOUSE236:21	H13	MGREC100:4	H1888
28AUG226:1	HP254	HOUSE236:22	H14	MGREC118:1	H2648
28AUG226:8	HP254	HOUSE237:11	H41	MGREC118:28	H2677
28AUG226:9	HP254	HOUSE237:22	H52	MGREC120:1	H2732
28AUG226:11	HP254	**TO'S (22)** [to his]		MGREC125:5	H2953
11MAYA226:15	HP255	HUMOUR30:13	H405	MGREC135:10	H3382
11MAYA226:23	HP255	MASSYR67:28	H574	SIDNEY152:24	H93
13MAY226:33	H9	MASSYR68:2	H588	VANITY159:31	H3
13MAY227:14	H23	MPERS74:16	H841	CONTEM168:4	H14
30SEPT227:18	HP257	MPERS74:27	H850	CONTEM172:6	H142
30SEPT227:20	HP257	MPERS77:34	H975	2LETTER182:20	H26
30SEPT227:21	HP257	MPERS78:39	H1020	2LETTER182:28	H34
30SEPT227:26	HP257	MPERS84:38	H1274	**UNDER'S (3)** [under his]	
30SEPT227:29	HP257	MPERS86:5	H1321	ELEMEN11:9	H129
30SEPT227:30	HP257	MPERS86:7	H1323	MGREC116:24	H2590
30SEPT227:32	HP257	MPERS86:12	H1328	MGREC135:33	H3405
SAMUEL228:10	H11	MPERS86:16	H1332	**UNTO (105)**	
SAMUEL228:18	H19	MPERS89:17	H1451	FATHER5:14	H15
11MAYB228:23	HP259	MPERS92:19	H1577	ELEMEN9:15	H49
11MAYB228:28	HP259	MGREC104:12	H2064	ELEMEN10:24	H99
11MAYB228:29	HP259	MGREC105:32	H2125	ELEMEN16:30	H353
11MAYB228:30	HP259	MGREC109:20	H2279	ELEMEN17:33	H397
11MAYB228:32	HP259	MGREC111:40	H2385	HUMOUR21:10	H38
THEART229:3	H5	MGREC116:3	H2563	HUMOUR21:16	H44
RESTOR229:25	H8	MGREC121:37	H2819	HUMOUR21:20	H48
RESTOR230:5	H20	MGREC129:41	H3155	HUMOUR22:12	H81
HANNA230:12	H5	SIDNEY151:34	H75	HUMOUR22:30	H99
HANNA230:13	H6	**TO'TH (1)** [to the]		HUMOUR27:4	H275
SON230:20	H3	ELEMEN11:11	H131	HUMOUR28:18	H330
SON230:21	H4	**TOTH' (2)** [to the]		HUMOUR31:20	H453
SON230:22	H5	HUMOUR33:32	H546	HUMOUR32:5	H479
SON230:26	H9	DIALOG148:12	H277	HUMOUR33:15	H529
SON231:2	H14	**UNDER (30)**		AGES35:19	H5
SON231:14	H26	ELEMEN8:11	H9	AGES37:37	H99
2HUSB232:19	H20	ELEMEN17:24	H388	AGES39:1	H144

AGES42:21	H279	MGREC121:6	H2784	AGES45:4	H382
AGES43:23	H318	MGREC123:38	H2902	AGES45:20	H402
SEASONS51:30	H206	MGREC124:37	H2944	AGES45:22	H408
MASSYR55:20	H86	MGREC125:9	H2957	SEASONS50:19	H153
MASSYR57:17	H164	MGREC126:18	H3009	SEASONS50:32	H166
MASSYR58:11	H196	MGREC126:38	H3027	SEASONS52:16	H231
MASSYR59:13	H237	MGREC128:41	H3114	SEASONS52:25	H240
MASSYR60:8	H273	MGREC129:36	H3150	MASSYR59:20	H244
MASSYR61:27	H332	MGREC132:4	H3237	MASSYR64:6	H430
MASSYR61:32	H337	MGREC132:26	H3271	MASSYR66:10	H516
MASSYR63:26	H411	MGREC132:27	H3272	MASSYR67:9	H555
MASSYR64:8	H432	MGREC132:37	H3284	MPERS69:40	H670
MASSYR64:26	H450	MGREC133:3	H3291	MPERS72:20	H768
MPERS69:3	H625	MGREC133:13	H3301	MPERS72:35	H779
MPERS69:11	H633	MGREC135:2	H3374	MPERS75:11	H872
MPERS71:4	H716	MGREC135:15	H3387	MPERS75:39	H896
MPERS72:24	H772	MROMAN137:20	H3471	MPERS87:31	H1383
MPERS77:13	H952	MROMAN138:15	H3505	MPERS91:26	H1540
MPERS81:4	H1112	MROMAN138:23	H3513	MPERS92:14	H1572
MPERS81:23	H1131	DIALOG143:18	H87	MGREC94:19	H1657
MPERS81:31	H1139	SIDNEY150:38	H66	MGREC94:41	H1679
MPERS81:33	H1141	DUBART153:16	H20	MGREC95:34	H1713
MPERS82:41	H1188	DUBART154:27	H72	MGREC96:23	H1743
MPERS83:8	H1196	QELIZ156:30	H57	MGREC99:33	H1876
MPERS84:13	H1249	VANITY160:28	H38	MGREC107:3	H2178
MPERS88:38	H1431	VANITY161:4	H55	MGREC107:5	H2180
MPERS89:11	H1445	CONTEM169:7	H49	MGREC108:11	H2227
MPERS90:15	H1484	CONTEM171:16	H120	MGREC110:29	H2333
MPERS91:22	H1534	CONTEM173:27	H192	MGREC119:17	H2707
MPERS92:22	H1580	FLESH175:9	H9	MGREC119:35	H2725
MGREC94:8	H1642	FLESH175:22	H22	MGREC125:34	H2984
MGREC97:27	H1788	DISTEMP179:20	H8	MGREC126:9	H3000
MGREC97:29	H1790	2LETTER181:33	H3	MGREC127:33	H3063
MGREC97:38	H1799	3LETTER183:24	H26	MGREC127:41	H3071
MGREC98:2	H1804	VERSES184:5	H9	MGREC128:13	H3086
MGREC100:15	H1899	ELIZB186:37	H9	MGREC129:7	H3121
MGREC103:9	H2020	**UP (70)**		MGREC129:27	H3141
MGREC103:32	H2043	ELEMEN17:6	H370	MGREC134:7	H3339
MGREC104:37	H2089	ELEMEN17:12	H376	MGREC135:10	H3382
MGREC105:2	H2095	ELEMEN19:35	H476	MROMAN139:1	H3529
MGREC109:32	H2291	HUMOUR20:13	H5	DIALOG145:9	H158
MGREC109:33	H2292	HUMOUR24:5	H154	DIALOG146:29	H215
MGREC111:24	H2369	HUMOUR31:33	H466	DIALOG148:21	H286
MGREC111:25	H2370	AGES36:1	H25	SIDNEY151:40	H75
MGREC111:29	H2374	AGES36:13	H37	DAVID158:31	H11
MGREC112:4	H2390	AGES36:20	H44	VANITY160:2	H12
MGREC112:5	H2391	AGES38:14	H117	VANITY160:2	H12
MGREC112:29	H2415	AGES39:12	H155	TDUDLEY165:39	H41
MGREC115:1	H2512	AGES40:21	H202	CONTEM173:19	H185
MGREC116:34	H2600	AGES42:27	H285	FLESH175:18	H18
MGREC121:3	H2781	AGES43:15	H307	DISTEMP179:20	H8

MEDDM204:20	HP285	HUMOUR35:3	H599	SICKNES178:31	H14
MEDDM204:27	HP285	AGES39:8	H151	SICKNES178:33	H16
MEDDM204:28	HP285	AGES45:2	~~H375~~	BIRTH180:1	H11
MEDDM208:23	HP290	AGES~~45:2~~	H376	1HUSB180:23	H2
PILGRIM210:5	H5	AGES45:24	H414	1HUSB180:33	H12
PILGRIM210:34	H34	SEASONS48:14	H67	1HUSB180:34	H13
MYCHILD216:3	HP241	SEASONS51:20	H196	1LETTER181:8	H6
MYCHILD216:25	HP242	SEASONS51:35	H211	MEDDM195:24	HP272
MYCHILD216:36	HP242	MASSYR55:1	H67	MEDDM195:25	HP272
MYCHILD217:26	HP243	MASSYR56:41	H147	MEDDM195:29	HP272
MYCHILD218:2	HP243	MASSYR~~57:22~~	H169	MEDDM197:11	HP274
MYCHILD218:10	HP244	MASSYR57:29	H174	MEDDM199:26	HP278
MYCHILD218:31	HP244	MASSYR57:37	H182	MEDDM200:25	HP279
MYCHILD218:35	HP244	MASSYR59:36	H260	MEDDM201:19	HP280
28AUG226:4	HP254	MASSYR60:12	H277	MEDDM201:20	HP280
SAMUEL228:1	H1-2	MASSYR61:3	H308	MEDDM202:22	HP282
11MAYB228:26	HP259	MASSYR61:5	H310	MEDDM202:24	HP282
11MAYB228:34	HP259	MASSYR62:28	H373	MEDDM202:26	HP282
HANNA230:9	H1-2	MASSYR63:32	H419	MEDDM202:27	HP282
2HUSB232:1	H1-2	MASSYR66:37	H543	MEDDM202:28	HP282
HOURS234:17	H31	MASSYR67:23	H569	MEDDM203:4	HP283
VS (11) [us]		MPERS~~69:38~~	H667	MEDDM203:5	HP283
MEDDM203:2	HP283	MPERS71:37	H751	MEDDM203:17	HP283
MEDDM205:17	HP286	MPERS75:20	H879	MEDDM203:18	HP283
MEDDM205:27	HP286	MPERS76:15	H913	MEDDM203:31	HP284
MEDDM206:30	HP288	MPERS92:26	~~H1584~~	MEDDM203:32	HP284
MEDDM206:37	HP288	MPERS~~92:28~~	H1586	MEDDM204:6	HP284
MEDDM207:10	HP288	MPERS92:30	H1588	MEDDM204:18	HP285
MEDDM207:27	HP289	MPERS92:34	H1592	MEDDM205:26	HP286
MEDDM208:14	HP290	MGREC93:34	H1631	MEDDM205:27	HP286
MEDDM209:4	HP291	MGREC106:19	H2153	MEDDM205:28	HP286
MEDDM209:25	HP291	MGREC117:15	H2622	MEDDM205:31	HP286
HOURS234:29	H43	MGREC130:37	H3182	MEDDM206:6	HP287
WE (125)		MGREC133:6	H3294	MEDDM206:28	HP288
FATHER5:19	H20	MGREC133:35	H3325	MEDDM207:9	HP288
PROLOG6:32	H15	MGREC134:6	H3339	MEDDM207:14	HP288
ELEMEN9:31	H65	MGREC134:33	H3364	MEDDM207:17	HP289
ELEMEN16:24	H347	DIALOG146:33	~~H219~~	MEDDM207:18	HP289
ELEMEN19:18	H463	DIALOG147:17	H243	MEDDM207:28	HP289
HUMOUR21:8	H36	SIDNEY150:15	~~H49~~	MEDDM208:3	HP289
HUMOUR21:9	H37	SIDNEY150:28	H55	MEDDM208:14	HP290
HUMOUR21:12	H40	SIDNEY151:3	~~H69~~	MEDDM208:15	HP290
HUMOUR25:22	H211	VANITY161:6	H57	**WEE (7) [we]**	
HUMOUR26:2	H232	TDUDLEY166:32	H74	MEDDM202:21	HP282
HUMOUR26:3	H233	CONTEM168:2	H12	MEDDM207:28	HP289
HUMOUR26:6	H236	CONTEM171:10	H114	MYCHILD218:14	HP244
HUMOUR26:39	H269	CONTEM171:12	H116	MYCHILD218:18	HP244
HUMOUR29:8	H361	CONTEM171:13	H117	MYCHILD218:21	HP244
HUMOUR31:28	H461	CONTEM172:28	H162	2HUSB233:13	H46
HUMOUR32:16	H490	FLESH176:4	H44	**WHO (245)**	
HUMOUR35:1	H597	FLESH176:6	H46	FATHER5:15	H16

FATHER6:7	H41	MASSYR68:12	H598	MGREC108:5	H2221
PROLOG7:8	H22	MASSYR68:15	H601	MGREC109:8	H2267
PROLOG7:15	H28	MASSYR68:18	H604	MGREC109:14	H2273
ELEMENT	H5	MASSYR68:28	H614	MGREC109:29	H2288
ELEMEN8:7	H5	MPERS69:6	H628	MGREC111:35	H2380
ELEMEN10:5	H80	MPERS69:21	H643	MGREC112:32	H2418
ELEMEN12:29	H189	MPERS69:25	H647	MGREC112:34	H2420
ELEMEN12:41	H201	MPERS69:28	H650	MGREC113:19	H2446
ELEMEN13:4	H205	MPERS69:29	H651	MGREC113:24	H2451
ELEMEN14:8	H250	MPERS69:38	H660	MGREC113:30	H2457
ELEMEN14:33	H275	MPERS71:15	H729	MGREC113:32	H2459
ELEMEN18:14	H418	MPERS71:19	H733	MGREC113:34	H2461
HUMOUR20:24	H16	MPERS71:21	H735	MGREC113:36	H2463
HUMOUR22:21	H90	MPERS72:6	H755	MGREC113:38	H2465
HUMOUR22:22	H91	MPERS72:8	H756	MGREC114:19	H2489
HUMOUR22:39	H108	MPERS72:15	H763	MGREC114:39	H2509
HUMOUR27:15	H286	MPERS72:29	H773	MGREC115:15	H2527
HUMOUR33:9	H523	MPERS73:16	H803	MGREC117:26	H2633
HUMOUR33:19	H533	MPERS73:23	H809	MGREC117:35	H2642
HUMOUR34:4	H559	MPERS75:13	H874	MGREC118:18	H2665
HUMOUR34:5	H560	MPERS75:15	H876	MGREC118:29	H2678
AGES36:38	H62	MPERS78:14	H995	MGREC120:4	H2736
AGES37:12	H74	MPERS78:41	H1022	MGREC121:15	H2794
AGES37:15	H77	MPERS79:31	H1057	MGREC121:16	H2797
AGES39:35	H178	MPERS81:8	H1116	MGREC122:18	H2843
AGES40:7	H188	MPERS83:12	H1200	MGREC122:19	H2844
AGES41:16	H235	MPERS84:27	H1263	MGREC122:20	H2845
AGES41:30	H247	MPERS85:9	H1285	MGREC122:22	H2845
AGES42:29	H285	MPERS88:31	H1424	MGREC122:32	H2851
AGES45:4	H388	MPERS90:11	H1484	MGREC123:4	H2866
AGES45:18	H400	MPERS90:27	H1494	MGREC127:22	H3052
SEASONS47:3	H17	MPERS90:39	H1506	MGREC128:34	H3107
SEASONS47:5	H21	MPERS91:15	H1523	MGREC129:1	H3115
SEASONS49:8	H99	MPERS91:26	H1540	MGREC129:21	H3135
MASSYR53:21	H11	MPERS92:14	H1572	MGREC129:37	H3151
MASSYR56:35	H141	MPERS92:35	H1593	MGREC130:22	H3177
MASSYR57:14	H161	MGREC93:27	H1624	MGREC130:23	H3178
MASSYR57:40	H185	MGREC94:6	H1640	MGREC130:27	H3181
MASSYR58:12	H197	MGREC95:3	H1682	MGREC131:5	H3195
MASSYR59:6	H230	MGREC95:17	H1696	MGREC131:25	H3217
MASSYR59:18	H242	MGREC95:31	H1710	MGREC131:32	H3224
MASSYR60:14	H279	MGREC97:2	H1763	MGREC131:37	H3229
MASSYR60:24	H289	MGREC98:24	H1826	MGREC132:6	H3239
MASSYR60:37	H302	MGREC99:27	H1870	MGREC132:6	H3239
MASSYR61:37	H342	MGREC100:32	H1916	MGREC133:3	H3291
MASSYR64:7	H431	MGREC103:37	H2048	MGREC133:23	H3312
MASSYR64:11	H435	MGREC104:5	H2057	MGREC133:37	H3327
MASSYR65:29	H494	MGREC104:19	H2071	MGREC134:32	H3363
MASSYR66:19	H525	MGREC104:24	H2076	MROMAN137:39	H3490
MASSYR67:6	H552	MGREC104:31	H2083	MROMAN138:26	H3516
MASSYR67:27	H573	MGREC105:20	H2113	DIALOG143:20	H89

MYCHILD216:16	HP241	MPERS78:25	H1006	MEDDM202:14 HP282
MYCHILD218:18	HP244	MPERS85:30	H1306	MEDDM208:1 HP289
MYCHILD219:1	HP244-5	MPERS85:37	H1313	HOURS234:4 H18
MYCHILD219:1	HP244-5	MPERS86:30	H1346	HOURS234:32 H46
BYNIGHT220:7	H7	MPERS88:6	H1399	ACK235:18 H18
SON230:23	H6	MPERS91:13	H1521	**WITH (534)**
2HUSB233:1	H34	MPERS92:11	H1569	FATHER5:3 H4
2HUSB233:3	H36	MPERS92:34	H1592	FATHER5:31 H32
2HUSB233:12	H45	MPERS92:38	H1596	FATHER6:7 H41
HOURS234:2	H16	MGREC93:23	H1620	PROLOG7:36 H46
ACK235:12	H12	MGREC94:35	H1673	ELEMEN8:19 H17
WHOSE (95)		MGREC95:15	H1694	ELEMEN9:8 H42
ELEMEN10:1	H76	MGREC98:18	H1820	ELEMEN9:25 H59
ELEMEN11:38	H158	MGREC100:34	H1918	ELEMEN9:27 H61
ELEMEN12:9	H169	MGREC102:14	H1984	ELEMEN9:32 H66
ELEMEN12:27	H187	MGREC104:35	H2087	ELEMEN10:3 H78
ELEMEN15:29	H311	MGREC105:17	H2110	ELEMEN10:4 H79
HUMOUR23:26	H136	MGREC108:34	H2250	ELEMEN10:8 H83
HUMOUR24:34	H183	MGREC109:7	H2266	ELEMEN10:8 H83
HUMOUR30:2	H394	MGREC111:24	H2369	ELEMEN10:21 H96
HUMOUR30:7	H399	MGREC112:6	H2392	ELEMEN10:31 H106
HUMOUR34:18	H573	MGREC116:11	H2577	ELEMEN11:5 H125
AGES37:4	H66	MGREC126:30	H3021	ELEMEN11:7 H127
AGES42:2	H260	MGREC130:28	~~H3181~~	ELEMEN12:34 H194
AGES~~45:2~~	H375	MGREC132:4	H3237	ELEMEN12:36 H196
SEASONS47:36	H48	MGREC~~132:28~~	H3275	ELEMEN13:14 H215
SEASONS48:18	H71	MGREC~~133:22~~	H3310	ELEMEN14:11 ~~H253~~
SEASONS49:13	H104	MGREC133:27	H3317	ELEMEN14:12 ~~H254~~
SEASONS49:20	H111	MGREC~~134:2~~	H3333	ELEMEN14:37 H279
SEASONS49:35	H128	MGREC134:4	H3337	ELEMEN15:21 H303
SEASONS49:40	H133	MGREC135:31	H3403	ELEMEN15:30 H312
SEASONS50:28	H162	DIALOG142:10	H39	ELEMEN16:1 H324
SEASONS50:31	H165	DIALOG142:40	H69	ELEMEN~~16:12~~ H335
SEASONS51:3	H177	DIALOG143:6	~~H73~~	ELEMEN16:15 H338
SEASONS51:25	H201	DIALOG~~143:8~~	H77	ELEMEN16:16 H339
MASSYR54:1	H28	DIALOG147:18	H244	ELEMEN16:37 H360
MASSYR54:8	H35	DIALOG148:28	H293	ELEMEN16:39 H362
MASSYR54:19	H46	SIDNEY~~150:40~~	H68	ELEMEN17:2 H366
MASSYR56:16	H122	QELIZ157:18	H86	ELEMEN17:5 H369
MASSYR62:26	H371	QELIZ158:10	H119	ELEMEN17:26 H390
MASSYR62:32	H377	QELIZ158:18	H127	ELEMEN18:24 H428
MASSYR64:3	H427	DAVID158:25	H5	ELEMEN18:28 H432
MASSYR64:4	H428	CONTEM168:2	H12	ELEMEN19:6 H451
MASSYR65:14	H479	CONTEM168:8	H17	ELEMEN19:6 H451
MASSYR66:3	H509	CONTEM168:16	H24	ELEMEN19:10 H455
MASSYR67:22	H568	CONTEM170:20	H92	ELEMEN19:15 H460
MASSYR67:29	H575	CONTEM173:8	H176	ELEMEN19:31 ~~H472~~
MPERS69:14	H636	CONTEM174:35	H232	ELEMEN19:35 H476
MPERS69:18	H640	3LETTER183:10	H12	HUMOUR23:26 H136
MPERS~~69:38~~	H668	CHILDRN185:9	H35	HUMOUR23:40 ~~H149~~
MPERS74:5	H830	MEDDM196:3	HP272	HUMOUR24:5 H154

with

HUMOUR24:22	H171	AGES43:28	H323	MASSYR62:8	H353
HUMOUR25:12	H201	AGES44:24	H357	MASSYR62:16	H361
HUMOUR25:16	H205	AGES45:2	H379	MASSYR62:29	H374
HUMOUR26:10	H240	AGES45:4	H384	MASSYR62:39	H384
HUMOUR28:2	H314	AGES45:14	H396	MASSYR63:16	H401
HUMOUR28:6	H318	AGES45:19	H401	MASSYR64:10	H434
HUMOUR28:21	H333	AGES46:22	H453	MASSYR64:19	H443
HUMOUR28:29	H341	SEASONS46:34	H10	MASSYR64:20	H444
HUMOUR29:2	H355	SEASONS46:35	H12	MASSYR64:26	H450
HUMOUR29:8	H361	SEASONS47:32	H47	MASSYR64:34	H458
HUMOUR31:17	H450	SEASONS48:8	H61	MASSYR65:9	H474
HUMOUR31:30	H463	SEASONS48:12	H65	MASSYR65:9	H474
HUMOUR31:37	H470	SEASONS48:15	H68	MASSYR65:17	H482
HUMOUR31:39	H472	SEASONS48:21	H74	MASSYR65:26	H491
HUMOUR31:40	H473	SEASONS48:33	H84	MASSYR65:34	H499
HUMOUR32:19	H493	SEASONS48:39	H90	MASSYR65:41	H506
HUMOUR32:40	H514	SEASONS49:3	H94	MASSYR66:2	H508
HUMOUR33:2	H516	SEASONS49:17	H108	MASSYR66:6	H512
HUMOUR33:2	H516	SEASONS49:18	H109	MASSYR66:11	H517
HUMOUR33:18	H532	SEASONS49:21	H112	MASSYR66:13	H519
HUMOUR33:19	H533	SEASONS50:5	H139	MASSYR66:28	H534
HUMOUR34:16	H571	SEASONS50:13	H147	MASSYR67:16	H562
HUMOUR34:26	H581	SEASONS50:14	H148	MASSYR67:27	H573
HUMOUR34:26	H581	SEASONS50:17	H151	MASSYR67:38	H584
HUMOUR35:4	H600	SEASONS50:23	H157	MASSYR68:3	H589
AGES35:28	H14	SEASONS50:24	H158	MASSYR68:6	H592
AGES36:6	H30	SEASONS51:17	H191	MASSYR68:23	H609
AGES36:29	H53	SEASONS52:2	H219	MASSYR68:29	H615
AGES36:37	H61	SEASONS52:16	H231	MPERS68:36	H622
AGES37:2	H64	SEASONS52:22	H237	MPERS69:30	H652
AGES37:5	H67	MASSYR53:33	H23	MPERS69:39	H669
AGES37:10	H72	MASSYR55:26	H92	MPERS70:3	H674
AGES37:12	H74	MASSYR55:40	H106	MPERS70:24	H695
AGES37:14	H76	MASSYR56:7	H113	MPERS70:35	H706
AGES37:15	H77	MASSYR57:10	H157	MPERS70:41	H712
AGES37:16	H78	MASSYR57:14	H161	MPERS71:4	H719
AGES37:33	H95	MASSYR57:19	H166	MPERS71:8	H724
AGES38:6	H109	MASSYR57:22	H169	MPERS71:10	H726
AGES38:19	H122	MASSYR58:2	H187	MPERS71:22	H736
AGES39:12	H155	MASSYR58:32	H215	MPERS71:32	H746
AGES40:14	H195	MASSYR58:35	H218	MPERS72:8	H756
AGES40:35	H214	MASSYR58:36	H219	MPERS72:12	H760
AGES40:37	H216	MASSYR58:37	H220	MPERS72:14	H762
AGES40:41	H220	MASSYR58:41	H224	MPERS72:38	H784
AGES41:2	H222	MASSYR59:16	H240	MPERS72:41	H787
AGES41:27	H244	MASSYR59:41	H265	MPERS73:22	H809
AGES42:3	H261	MASSYR60:2	H267	MPERS73:24	H809
AGES42:10	H268	MASSYR60:5	H270	MPERS74:16	H839
AGES42:12	H270	MASSYR60:25	H290	MPERS74:37	H858
AGES42:39	H295	MASSYR60:28	H293	MPERS74:40	H861
AGES43:16	H310	MASSYR61:28	H333	MPERS75:1	H862

MPERS75:8	H869	MPERS91:6	H1514	MGREC104:23	H2075
MPERS76:2	H900	MPERS91:7	H1515	MGREC104:25	H2077
MPERS76:5	H903	MPERS91:38	H1552	MGREC105:6	H2099
MPERS76:5	H903	MPERS92:17	H1575	MGREC105:15	H2108
MPERS76:21	H919	MPERS92:31	H1589	MGREC106:33	H2167
MPERS76:27	H925	MGREC94:18	H1652	MGREC107:2	H2177
MPERS76:28	H926	MGREC94:18	H1653	MGREC107:7	H2182
MPERS76:35	H933	MGREC94:22	H1660	MGREC107:9	H2184
MPERS76:38	H936	MGREC94:33	H1671	MGREC107:20	H2195
MPERS76:39	H937	MGREC95:5	H1684	MGREC107:35	H2210
MPERS77:19	H960	MGREC95:11	H1690	MGREC107:39	H2214
MPERS77:36	H977	MGREC95:31	H1710	MGREC108:6	H2222
MPERS78:17	H998	MGREC95:37	H1716	MGREC108:11	H2227
MPERS79:13	H1036	MGREC96:12	H1732	MGREC108:29	H2245
MPERS80:3	H1070	MGREC96:32	H1752	MGREC109:4	H2261
MPERS81:3	H1111	MGREC96:39	H1759	MGREC109:10	H2269
MPERS81:7	H1115	MGREC98:1	H1803	MGREC109:11	H2270
MPERS81:12	H1120	MGREC98:9	H1811	MGREC109:22	H2281
MPERS81:27	H1135	MGREC99:1	H1844	MGREC109:26	H2285
MPERS82:32	H1179	MGREC99:4	H1847	MGREC110:3	H2303
MPERS82:36	H1183	MGREC99:15	H1858	MGREC110:10	H2310
MPERS82:38	H1185	MGREC99:30	H1873	MGREC110:23	H2327
MPERS82:41	H1188	MGREC99:37	H1880	MGREC111:1	H2346
MPERS83:7	H1195	MGREC100:1	H1885	MGREC111:4	H2349
MPERS83:29	H1217	MGREC100:17	H1901	MGREC111:10	H2355
MPERS84:2	H1230	MGREC100:33	H1917	MGREC111:15	H2360
MPERS84:12	H1243	MGREC101:10	H1935	MGREC112:6	H2392
MPERS84:17	H1253	MGREC101:12	H1937	MGREC112:10	H2396
MPERS85:6	H1282	MGREC101:41	H1970	MGREC112:39	H2425
MPERS85:16	H1292	MGREC102:2	H1972	MGREC115:21	H2540
MPERS85:24	H1300	MGREC102:6	H1976	MGREC115:38	H2557
MPERS86:40	H1356	MGREC102:7	H1977	MGREC116:15	H2581
MPERS87:2	H1358	MGREC102:13	H1983	MGREC116:16	H2582
MPERS87:2	H1358	MGREC102:19	H1989	MGREC118:9	H2656
MPERS87:15	H1370	MGREC102:27	H1997	MGREC119:18	H2708
MPERS87:31	H1383	MGREC102:35	H2005	MGREC119:25	H2715
MPERS88:1	H1394	MGREC103:1	H2012	MGREC119:27	H2717
MPERS88:20	H1413	MGREC103:2	H2013	MGREC119:29	H2719
MPERS88:25	H1418	MGREC103:7	H2018	MGREC119:38	H2728
MPERS88:41	H1434	MGREC103:26	H2037	MGREC120:17	H2752
MPERS89:7	H1441	MGREC103:27	H2038	MGREC120:29	H2766
MPERS89:8	H1442	MGREC103:35	H2046	MGREC120:33	H2770
MPERS89:19	H1453	MGREC103:38	H2049	MGREC121:2	H2780
MPERS89:35	H1469	MGREC104:4	H2056	MGREC121:6	H2784
MPERS89:36	H1470	MGREC104:6	H2058	MGREC121:19	H2801
MPERS90:24	H1491	MGREC104:7	H2059	MGREC121:22	H2804
MPERS90:26	H1493	MGREC104:10	H2062	MGREC121:24	H2806
MPERS90:27	H1494	MGREC104:14	H2066	MGREC121:29	H2811
MPERS90:28	H1495	MGREC104:16	H2068	MGREC122:38	H2859
MPERS90:33	H1500	MGREC104:21	H2073	MGREC122:41	H2862
MPERS91:4	H1512	MGREC104:22	H2074	MGREC123:6	H2868

FAINTING222:25	H15	MEDDM198:21	HP276	MED223:10	HP250
MED223:1	HP250	MEDDM202:5	HP281	MED223:13	HP250
MED223:19	HP250	MEDDM202:7	HP281	JULY223:34	HP251
MYSOUL225:5	H9	MEDDM202:29	HP282	MYSOUL224:26	H2
13MAY226:30	H6	MEDDM204:17	HP285	28AUG225:29	HP254
13MAY227:14	H23	MEDDM209:20	HP291	28AUG225:30	HP254
30SEPT227:18	HP257	MYCHILD215:10	HP240	28AUG225:31	HP254
30SEPT227:21	HP257	MYCHILD215:13	HP240	28AUG225:33	HP254
30SEPT227:23	HP257	MYCHILD215:18	HP240	11MAYA226:15	HP255
30SEPT227:26	HP257	MYCHILD215:19	HP240	11MAYA226:20	HP255
30SEPT227:29	HP257	MYCHILD215:20	HP240	11MAYA226:22	HP255
SAMUEL228:21	H22	MYCHILD215:26	HP240	13MAY227:5	H14
11MAYB228:31	HP259	MYCHILD215:28	HP241	13MAY227:6	H15
THEART228:35	H1	MYCHILD215:29	HP241	13MAY227:16	H25
RESTOR229:28	H11	MYCHILD215:31	HP241	30SEPT227:21	HP257
RESTOR229:29	H12	MYCHILD216:2	HP241	30SEPT227:25	HP257
RESTOR230:1	H16	MYCHILD216:3	HP241	30SEPT227:28	HP257
2HUSB233:8	H41	MYCHILD216:6	HP241	30SEPT227:29	HP257
2HUSB233:10	H43	MYCHILD216:9	HP241	30SEPT227:30	HP257
2HUSB233:17	H50	MYCHILD216:10	HP241	30SEPT227:31	HP257
HOURS233:28	H11	MYCHILD216:16	HP241	11MAYB228:24	HP259
HOURS233:29	H12	MYCHILD216:17	HP241	11MAYB228:27	HP259
HOURS234:30	H44	MYCHILD216:30	HP242	11MAYB228:28	HP259
REMB235:30	H11	MYCHILD216:33	HP242	11MAYB228:30	HP259
HOUSE236:15	H7	MYCHILD217:4	HP242	11MAYB228:31	HP259
HOUSE237:19	H49	MYCHILD217:11	HP242	RESTOR230:3	H18
WTH (2) [with]		MYCHILD217:19	HP243	2HUSB232:27	H28
MYCHILD215:22	HP240	MYCHILD217:21	HP243	ACK235:3	H1-3
MYCHILD215:23	HP240	MYCHILD217:25	HP243	ACK235:5	H5
WTHIN (4) [within]		MYCHILD217:26	HP243	HOUSE236:19	H11
MEDDM196:34	HP274	MYCHILD217:28	HP243	HOUSE236:27	H19
MEDDM201:21	HP281	MYCHILD217:30	HP243	HOUSE236:35	H27
MEDDM197:2	HP274	MYCHILD217:32	HP243	**YE** (35)	
MEDDM198:28	HP277	MYCHILD217:37	HP243	PROLOG7:35	H45
MEDDM198:30	HP277	MYCHILD218:2	HP243	ELEMEN8:30	H28
MEDDM209:19	HP291	MYCHILD218:2	HP243	ELEMEN8:35	~~H33~~
WTH**OUT** (11) [without]		MYCHILD218:10	HP244	ELEMEN9:1	H35
MEDDM196:33	HP274	MYCHILD218:12	HP244	ELEMEN9:10	H44
MEDDM197:4	HP274	MYCHILD218:14	HP244	ELEMEN9:16	H50
MEDDM197:4	HP274	MYCHILD218:18	HP244	ELEMEN9:20	H54
MEDDM198:29	HP277	MYCHILD218:19	HP244	ELEMEN9:24	H58
MEDDM199:3	HP277	MYCHILD218:20	HP244	ELEMEN10:38	H113
MEDDM206:23	HP287	MYCHILD218:22	HP244	ELEMEN12:29	H189
MEDDM209:3	HP291	MYCHILD218:26	HP244	ELEMEN12:33	H193
MYCHILD217:12	HP242	MYCHILD218:28	HP244	ELEMEN12:41	H201
30SEPT227:22	HP257	MYCHILD218:31	HP244	ELEMEN13:4	H205
SON231:13	H25	MYCHILD218:33	HP244	ELEMEN13:8	H209
WTHOUT (2) [without]		MYCHILD218:36	HP244	ELEMEN13:40	H241
MYCHILD216:14	HP241	MYCHILD219:3	HP245	ELEMEN18:2	H406
MYCHILD217:17	HP243	SOREFIT221:16	H2	ELEMEN18:21	H425
Y^E (94) [the]		MED223:6	HP250	ELEMEN18:23	H427

HUMOUR21:20	H48	ELEMEN17:35	H399	DIALOG143:25	H94
HUMOUR21:28	H56	ELEMEN17:39	H403	DIALOG145:9	H158
HUMOUR23:36	H146	ELEMEN18:1	H405	DIALOG145:11	H160
HUMOUR28:41	H353	ELEMEN18:24	H428	DIALOG145:12	H161
HUMOUR30:14	H406	ELEMEN18:25	H429	DIALOG146:30	H216
HUMOUR32:1	H475	HUMOUR21:5	H33	DIALOG147:26	H250
HUMOUR32:5	H479	HUMOUR21:6	H34	DIALOG147:28	H252
AGES41:13	H232	HUMOUR21:30	H58	DIALOG148:24	H289
AGES41:19	H238	HUMOUR21:31	H59	QELIZ156:13	H40
AGES45:15	H397	HUMOUR22:1	H70	QELIZ156:14	H41
AGES45:22	H404	HUMOUR22:19	H88	QELIZ156:18	H45
AGES45:22	H408	HUMOUR23:30	H140	QELIZ157:34	H102
SEASON49:112	H113	HUMOUR23:33	H143	DAVID158:34	H14
MPERS77:3	H942	HUMOUR24:9	H158	DAVID158:35	H15
CONTEM172:30	H163	HUMOUR27:9	H280	DAVID159:15	H30
1HUSB180:26	H5	HUMOUR27:25	H296	DAVID159:18	H33
CHILDRN185:29	H55	HUMOUR27:27	H298	CONTEM172:32	H165
YEE (5)		HUMOUR27:31	H302	CONTEM172:34	H167
DIALOG147:24	H248	HUMOUR27:32	H303	CONTEM172:35	H168
MYCHILD217:2	Hᴘ242	HUMOUR28:33	H345	CONTEM172:36	H169
MED223:6	Hᴘ250	HUMOUR28:38	H350	FLESH175:35	H35
30SEPT227:28	Hᴘ257	HUMOUR28:41	H353	BIRTH180:6	H16
Yᴹ (3) [them]		HUMOUR30:18	H410	BIRTH180:7	H17
MYCHILD215:14	Hᴘ240	HUMOUR30:20	H412	1HUSB180:26	H5
MYCHILD218:24	Hᴘ244	HUMOUR30:34	H426	CHILDRN185:31	H57
ACK235:6	H6	HUMOUR30:36	H428	CHILDRN185:32	H58
Yᴼ (1) [you]		HUMOUR30:37	H429	CHILDRN185:33	H59
2SIMON195:5	Hᴘ271	HUMOUR31:37	H470	CHILDRN185:37	H63
YOU (131) See also ʏᴏᴠ		HUMOUR31:39	H472	CHILDRN185:38	H64
FATHER5:7	H8	HUMOUR32:31	H505	CHILDRN185:40	H66
FATHER6:6	H40	HUMOUR32:36	H510	CHILDRN186:1	H68
PROLOG7:37	H47	AGES41:12	H231	CHILDRN186:6	H73
ELEMEN9:11	H45	AGES43:25	H320	CHILDRN186:16	H83
ELEMEN9:21	H55	AGES44:2	H335	CHILDRN186:19	H86
ELEMEN9:22	H56	AGES44:3	H336	CHILDRN186:19	H86
ELEMEN9:22	H56	AGES44:8	H341	CHILDRN186:21	H88
ELEMEN10:7	H82	AGES45:21	H403	CHILDRN186:22	H89
ELEMEN11:22	H142	AGES45:22	H410	CHILDRN186:23	H90
ELEMEN11:23	H143	AGES46:25	H456	CHILDRN186:26	H93
ELEMEN11:26	H146	SEASONS49:14	H105	CHILDRN186:29	H96
ELEMEN11:35	H155	SEASONS49:25	H114	2SIMON195:5	Hᴘ271
ELEMEN12:35	H195	SEASONS49:26	H115	2SIMON195:6	Hᴘ271
ELEMEN12:37	H197	SEASONS53:2	H258	2SIMON195:7	Hᴘ271
ELEMEN13:3	H204	SEASONS53:7	H263	2SIMON195:8	Hᴘ271
ELEMEN13:7	H208	MPERS80:10	H1077	2SIMON195:9	Hᴘ271
ELEMEN13:9	H210	DIALOG141:30	H29	2SIMON195:11	Hᴘ271
ELEMEN13:10	H211	DIALOG142:4	H33	2SIMON195:13	Hᴘ271
ELEMEN13:40	H241	DIALOG142:23	H52	2SIMON195:14	Hᴘ271
ELEMEN13:41	H242	DIALOG142:26	H55	MEDDM208:7	Hᴘ289
ELEMEN14:18	H260	DIALOG142:30	H59	30SEPT227:29	Hᴘ257
ELEMEN14:27	H269	DIALOG142:35	H64	30SEPT227:31	Hᴘ257

YOUR (135) See also Y^R

FATHER5:4	H5
FATHER5:18	H19
FATHER6:10	H44
FATHER6:12	H46
PROLOG7:36	H46
PROLOG7:37	H47
PROLOG8:2	H50
ELEMENT	~~H33~~
ELEMEN~~8:35~~	H33
ELEMEN9:1	H35
ELEMEN9:2	H36
ELEMEN9:3	~~H37~~
ELEMEN~~9:3~~	H37
ELEMEN9:4	H38
ELEMEN9:10	H44
ELEMEN9:11	H45
ELEMEN9:12	H46
ELEMEN9:13	H47
ELEMEN9:16	H50
ELEMEN9:17	H51
ELEMEN9:18	H52
ELEMEN9:19	H53
ELEMEN9:20	H54
ELEMEN9:24	H58
ELEMEN10:18	H93
ELEMEN11:18	H138
ELEMEN11:19	H139
ELEMEN12:30	H190
ELEMEN12:34	H194
ELEMEN12:36	H196
ELEMEN12:39	H199
ELEMEN12:41	H201
ELEMEN13:1	H202
ELEMEN13:6	H207
ELEMEN13:11	H212
ELEMEN13:41	H242
ELEMEN14:2	H244
ELEMEN14:20	H262
ELEMEN14:26	H268
ELEMEN14:27	H269
ELEMEN14:28	H270
ELEMEN14:29	H271
ELEMEN18:15	H419
ELEMEN18:19	H423
ELEMEN18:22	H426
ELEMEN18:23	H427
ELEMEN18:24	H428
ELEMEN18:26	H430
HUMOUR21:3	H31
HUMOUR21:10	H38
HUMOUR21:17	H45
HUMOUR21:18	H46
HUMOUR23:38	H148
HUMOUR24:10	H159
HUMOUR24:14	H163
HUMOUR24:15	H164
HUMOUR27:18	H289
HUMOUR27:20	H291
HUMOUR27:26	H297
HUMOUR27:28	H299
HUMOUR27:36	H307
HUMOUR28:38	H350
HUMOUR28:40	H352
HUMOUR30:17	H409
HUMOUR30:20	H412
HUMOUR31:8	H441
HUMOUR31:19	H452
HUMOUR33:18	H532
HUMOUR34:8	H563
AGES41:21	~~H239~~
SEASONS~~49:22~~	H113
SEASONS49:24	~~H114~~
SEASONS~~49:33~~	H123
SEASONS~~49:33~~	H125
SEASONS53:8	H264
SEASONS53:9	~~H264~~
MPERS80:8	H1075
DIALOG141:30	H29
DIALOG142:22	H51
DIALOG142:24	H53
DIALOG142:25	H54
DIALOG142:26	H55
DIALOG142:30	H59
DIALOG142:31	H60
DIALOG142:33	H62
DIALOG145:8	H157
DIALOG145:10	H159
DIALOG145:13	H162
DIALOG145:14	H163
DIALOG146:28	H214
DIALOG146:29	H215
DIALOG146:30	H216
DIALOG146:31	H217
DIALOG146:32	H218
DIALOG~~146:32~~	H219
DIALOG147:27	H251
DIALOG147:29	H253
DIALOG148:14	H279
DIALOG148:21	H286
DIALOG148:22	H287
DIALOG148:23	H288
SIDNEY149:22	H21
SIDNEY149:24	H23
DAVID158:33	H13
DAVID159:13	H28
DAVID159:17	H32
CONTEM172:31	H164
CONTEM172:34	H167
CONTEM172:36	H169
VERSES184:1	H5
CHILDRN185:41	H67
CHILDRN186:16	H83
CHILDRN186:17	H84
2SIMON195:17	HP271
MED223:7	HP250
MED223:8	HP250
WHAT224:9	H9
WHAT224:10	H10
WHAT224:14	H14

YOURS (6)

FATHER5:14	H15
FATHER5:16	H17
FATHER5:27	H28
PROLOG7:32	H43
HUMOUR31:22	H455
BIRTH180:6	H16

YOV (20) [you] See also Y^O

TOCHILD215:3	H3
TOCHILD215:4	H4
TOCHILD215:7	H7
MYCHILD215:13	HP240
MYCHILD215:15	HP240
MYCHILD215:17	HP240
MYCHILD215:18	HP240
MYCHILD215:20	HP240
MYCHILD215:21	HP240
MYCHILD216:17	HP241
MYCHILD216:18	HP241
MYCHILD216:19	HP241
MYCHILD217:1	HP242
MYCHILD218:34	HP244
MYCHILD219:7	HP245
30SEPT227:29	HP257
30SEPT227:31	HP257
30SEPT227:32	HP257

YR (2) [your]

TOCHILD215:5	H5
30SEPT227:33	HP257

Y^{R}OF (1) [thereof]

MED223:13	HP250

Y^{RS} (1) [yours]

WHAT224:13	H13

YT (39) [that]		MYCHILD218:18	HP244	30SEPT227:19	HP257
MEDDM196:9	HP273	MYCHILD219:2	HP245	30SEPT227:29	HP257
MEDDM202:11	HP281	SOREFIT221:20	H6	11MAYB228:27	HP259
MEDDM203:12	HP283	JULY223:21	HP251	11MAYB228:32	HP259
MYCHILD215:10	HP240	JULY223:26	HP251	SON231:9	H21
MYCHILD215:16	HP240	JULY223:28	HP251	ACK235:17	H17
MYCHILD215:17	HP240	JULY223:32	HP251	REMB235:31	H12
MYCHILD215:29	HP241	WHAT224:17	H17	REMB236:9	H24
MYCHILD216:16	HP241	WHAT224:21	H21	HOUSE236:26	H18
MYCHILD216:21	HP241	WHAT224:23	H23	HOUSE236:30	H22
MYCHILD217:15	HP243	28AUG225:32	HP254	HOUSE236:37	H29
MYCHILD217:19	HP243	28AUG226:3	HP254	Y^Y (1) [they]	
MYCHILD217:31	HP243	28AUG226:6	HP254	30SEPT227:23	HP257
MYCHILD218:9	HP244	11MAYA226:20	HP255		

Index of Numerals Omitted from Main Concordance

2 (2)		13 (1)		23 (1)	
DAVID158:23	H2-3	13MAY226:25	H1	CHILDRN184:13	H1-2
JULY223:21	HP251	14 (1)		27 (1)	
3 (2)		MYCHILD216:1	HP241	DDUDLEY167:8	H4-5
JULY223:21	HP251	15 (1)		28 (2)	
REMB235:22	H3	MYCHILD216:1	HP241	MERCY188:19	H4-5
4 (2)		112 (1)		28AUG225:25	HP254
11MAYB228:23	HP259	MGREC6:9	H1606	30 (1)	
11MAYB228:27	HP259	131 (1)		30SEPT227:17	HP257
6 (3)		MASSYR53:13	H3	31 (2)	
MERCY188:18	H2-4	16 (3)		TDUDLEY165:3	H4-5
MYCHILD215:24	HP240	1SIMON188:2	H2-3	PILGRIM211:4	H45
SAMUEL228:1	H1-2	MYCHILD216:3	HP241	61 (1)	
7 (2)		2HUSB232:2	H3	DDUDLEY167:8	H4-5
MASSYR62:36	H381	17 (1)		69 (1)	
MYCHILD215:24	HP240	SON230:19	H1-2	PILGRIM211:4	H45
8 (1)		19 (2)		77 (1)	
JULY223:20	HP251	DAVID158:23	H2-3	TDUDLEY165:3	H4-5
10 (1)		SICKNES178:17	H0	1586 (1)	
MASSYR62:13	H358	20 (2)		SIDNEY149:5	H5
11 (3)		ANNEB187:14	H3-4	1632 (1)	
11MAYA226:12	HP255	2SIMON195:19	HP271	SICKNES178:16	H0
11MAYA226:14	HP255	21 (1)		1638 (1)	
11MAYB228:22	HP259	MASSYR63:15	H400	SIDNEY149:6	H5
12 (3)		22 (3)		1641 (1)	
MASSYR63:26	H411	MASSYR63:19	H404	DUBART152:31	H1